JIM MURRAY'S
WHISKEY
BIBLE
2 0 1 8

This edition first published 2017 by Dram Good Books Ltd
Distributed in North America exclusively by Whitman Publishing, LLC

10 9 8 7 6 5 4 3 2 1

The "Jim Murray's" logo and the "Whisk(e)y Bible" logo are trade marks of Jim Murray.

Text, tasting notes & rankings, artwork, Jim Murray's logo and the Whisky Bible logo copyright
© Jim Murray 2017

Design copyright © Dram Good Books Ltd 2017

For information regarding using tasting notes from Jim Murray's Whisky Bible contact:
Dram Good Books Ltd, Unit 2, Barnstones Business Park, Litchborough, UK, NN12 8JJ
Tel: 44 (0)117 317 9777. Or contact us via www.whiskybible.com

A CIP catalogue record for this book is available from the British Library

ISBN: 978-0-9932986-2-2

Printed in China

Written by: Jim Murray
Edited by: Peter Mayne and David Rankin
Design: Rob-indesign, Jim Murray and Vincent Flint-Hill
Maps: James Murray, Rob-indesign and Vincent Flint-Hill
Production: Rob-indesign, Vincent Flint-Hill, Billy Jeffrey and Jane Garnett
Chief Researcher: Vincent Flint-Hill
Sample Research: Vincent Flint-Hill, Ally Telfer, Julia Nourney, Mick Secor
Other Research: Emma Thomson
Sales: Billy Jeffrey
European Dictionary: Julie Nourney, Tom Wyss, Mariette Duhr-Merges, Stefan Baumgart,
Erik Molenaar, Jürgen Vromans, Henric Molin and Kalle Valkonen.

Author's Note
I have used the spelling "whiskey" or "whisky" depending on how the individual distillers
prefer. All Scotch is "whisky". So is Canadian. All Irish, these days, is "whiskey", though
that was not always the case. In Kentucky, bourbon and rye are spelt "whiskey", with the
exception of the produce of the early Times/Old Forester Distillery and Maker's Mark which
they bottle as "whisky". In Tennessee, it is a 50-50 split: Dickel is "whisky", while Daniel's
is "whiskey".

JIM MURRAY'S
WHISKEY
BIBLE
2018

Whitman

Contents

Introduction

I can't quite work it out: is the whisky world getting smaller or larger?

Sounds like a daft thing to muse over. After all, it must be getting larger as the number of distilleries, regions and countries producing grain spirit of one sort or another is expanding year on year as are the number of people falling under its spell. But then, as things change, as communications expand, as choices increase, we tend to agree that the world is getting smaller.

When in 2003 I was tasting for the first-ever Jim Murry's Whisky Bible, for me to have driven from my tasting lab in England to my nearest distillery to seek inspiration from the sight of gleaming stills and breathing in the rich, dank air of the warehouse, I would have had to spend something like eight hours on the road driving the 340 miles to the Lowland Scotch outpost of Bladnoch, Scotland's southern-most point of distilling. Within a year or two the travelling time was halved as it was a mere 175 miles to the newly built Penderyn Distillery in Wales.

This year, when I had tasted the last of the 1,201 new whiskies for this 2018 edition and spent a further ten days tasting and re-tasting the finer entries as I worked out for certain all the category award winners, I decided to celebrate in a way I had dared not think possible even a decade earlier.

It was just a matter of minutes as I drove the 21 miles as the parrot flies to the Hook Norton Brewery in Oxfordshire, a stunning turn of the 20th century pile made of local ironstone created in the imposing yet elegant tower style and seemingly preserved in aspic. Then, after fortifying myself with a faultless half pint of their bitter (a beer I have cherished for the last 40 years of my life and used to savour with my late father), I set out on the country path which bisects the plant and walked – on the hottest June day in Britain for over 40 years - the four miles or so to the Cotswold Distillery.

This is a glorious walk, through and beside fields of barley and wheat, along meadows and up hills yielding soul-soothingly panoramic views of the undulating Cotswolds beyond, all the while to the accompaniment of serenading larks and chiff chaffs, and with buzzards, red kites and, miraculously and quite magically, even a polecat and a hen harrier keeping an eye on my sun-drenched progress.

Finally, to the distillery where it would have been rude not to have accepted the high quality new make malt offered to me and which I downed and enjoyed like a cowboy might in a saloon after drifting over the western plains for several days. And as the spirit filled my palate, as my taste buds soaked up the malt and uncovered and then pinpointed the clues to its excellence, I marvelled that such a thing was possible at all. Indeed, being the longest day of the year, had I put my mind to it I could have set off before sun up and taken the country path that passes through my lovely village and walked first to the brewery and then on to the distillery, a journey by foot achievable within a day. How long would it have taken me to walk to Bladnoch in 2003? Two weeks maybe, barring injury and fatigue. But Hook Norton now also had a whisky connection. For the brewery had made the special mash from which the Cotswold Distillery had distilled their soon-to-be rye whisky. Around the world I had previously visited breweries that worked to this arrangement, from the Sierra Nevada in California to the Cascade in Tasmania and many throughout mainland Europe, breweries that had linked up with distilleries so their respective skills and resources were maximized. Now, having travelled, quite literally, the world to see this in action here it was on my very own doorstep.

There was only one point I stopped for a beer on my walk between brewery and distillery. It was on a back of beyond road along which the Oxfordshire and Warwickshire county border runs. It connected, less than a mile away, to the byway to Temple Mills where the second generation member of the family who began the brewery died after crashing off his pushbike. It was almost exactly 100 years to the week that Alban Clark, who had to battle sometimes against the odds to keep his brewery profitable, had met his untimely end and as I raised my Hooky Bitter to him I did wonder if he would in his wildest dreams have imagined that people now visited his brewery because of their links to a neighbouring whisky distillery, for which they made rye mash.

And when I eventually returned to the twilit brewery, having come the long way round to take in the 4,000 year old Rollright Stone circle – how can you not on Midsummer's Day? – I happened, purely by chance, to bump into the man who was responsible for the production of the rye mash: one of the newest members of the international whisky-making fraternity.

Perhaps I shouldn't have been surprised. It is, after all, a very small world...

Jim Murray
Willow Cottage
Somewhere in rural Northamptonshire
July 2017

How to Read
The Bible

The whole point of this book is for the whisky lover – be he or she an experienced connoisseur or, better fun still, simply starting out on the long and joyous path of discovery – to have ready access to easy-to-understand information about as many whiskies as possible. And I mean a lot. Thousands.

This book does not quite include every whisky on the market... just by far and away the vast majority. And those that have been missed this time round – either through accident, logistics or design – will appear in later editions once we can source a sample.

WHISKY SCORING

The marking for this book is tailored to the consumer and scores run out just a little higher than I use for my own personal references. But such is the way it has been devised that it has not affected my order of preference.

Each whisky is given a rating out of 100. Twenty-five marks are given to each of four factors: nose (n), taste (t), finish (f), balance and overall complexity (b). That means that 50% of the marks are given for flavour alone and 25% for the nose, often an overlooked part of the whisky equation. The area of balance and complexity covers all three previous factors and a usually hidden one besides:

Nose: this is simply the aroma. Often requires more than one inspection as hidden aromas can sometimes reveal themselves after time in the glass, increased contact with air and changes in temperature. The nose very often tells much about a whisky, but – as we shall see – equally can be quite misleading.

Taste: this is the immediate arrival on the palate and involves the flavour profile up to, and including, the time it reaches maximum intensity and complexity.

Finish: often the least understood part of a tasting. This is the tail and flourish of the whisky's signature, often revealing the effects of ageing. The better whiskies tend to finish well and linger without too much oak excess. It is on the finish, also, that certain notes which are detrimental to the whisky may be observed. For instance, a sulphur-tarnished cask may be fully revealed for what it is by a dry, bitter residue on the palate which is hard to shake off. It is often worth waiting a few minutes to get the full picture of the finish before having a second taste of a whisky.

Balance: This is the part it takes a little experience to appreciate but it can be mastered by anyone. For a whisky to work well on the nose and palate, it should not be too one-sided in its character. If you are looking for an older whisky, it should have evidence of oak, but not so much that all other flavours and aromas are drowned out. Likewise, a whisky matured or finished in a sherry butt must offer a lot more than just wine alone and the greatest Islay malts, for instance, revel in depth and complexity beyond the smoky effects of peat.

Each whisky has been analysed by me without adding water or ice. I have taken each whisky as it was poured from the bottle and used no more than warming in an identical glass to extract and discover the character of the whisky. To have added water would have been pointless: it would have been an inconsistent factor as people, when pouring water, add different amounts at varying temperatures. The only constant with the whisky you and I taste will be when it has been poured directly from the bottle.

Even if you and I taste the same whiskies at the same temperature and from identical glasses – and even share the same values in whisky – our scores may still be different. Because a factor that is built into my evaluation is drawn from expectation and experience. When I sample a whisky from a certain distillery at such-and-such an age or from this type of barrel or that, I would expect it to offer me certain qualities. It has taken me 30 years to acquire this knowledge (which I try to add to day by day!) and an enthusiast cannot be expected to learn it overnight. But, hopefully, Jim Murray's Whisky Bible will help...!

SCORE CHART

Within the parentheses () is the overall score out of 100.

0–50.5 Nothing short of absolutely diabolical.

51–64.5 Nasty and well worth avoiding.

65–69.5 Very unimpressive indeed.

70–74.5 Usually drinkable but don't expect the earth to move.

75–79.5 Average and usually pleasant though sometimes flawed.

80–84.5 Good whisky worth trying.

85–89.5 Very good to excellent whiskies definitely worth buying.

90–93.5 Brilliant.

94–97.5 Superstar whiskies that give us all a reason to live.

98–100 Better than anything I've ever tasted!

KEY TO ABBREVIATIONS & SYMBOLS

% Percentage strength of whisky measured as alcohol by volume. **b** Overall balance and complexity. **bott** Date of bottling. **db** Distillery bottling. In other words, an expression brought out by the owners of the distillery. **dist** Date of distillation or spirit first put into cask. **f** Finish. **n** Nose. **nc** Non-coloured. **ncf** Non-chill-filtered. **sc** Single cask. **t** Taste. ❊ New entry for 2018. ⊙ Retasted – no change. ⊙⊙ Retasted and re-evaluated. **v** Variant WB18-001 Code for Whisky Club bottling.

Finding Your Whisky

Worldwide Malts: Whiskies are listed alphabetically throughout the book. In the case of single malts, the distilleries run A–Z style with distillery bottlings appearing at the top of the list in order of age, starting with youngest first. After age comes vintage. After all the "official" distillery bottlings are listed, next come other bottlings, again in alphabetical order. Single malts without a distillery named (or perhaps named after a dead one) are given their own section, as are vatted malts.

Worldwide Blends: These are simply listed alphabetically, irrespective of which company produce them. So "Black Bottle" appears ahead of "White Horse" and Japanese blends begin with "Ajiwai Kakubin" and end with "Za". In the case of brands being named after companies or individuals the first letter of the brand will dictate where it is listed. So William Grant, for instance, will be found under "W" for William rather "G" for Grant.

Bourbon/Rye: One of the most confusing types of whiskey to list because often the name of the brand bears no relation to the name of the distillery that made it. Also, brands may be sold from one company to another, or shortfalls in stock may see companies buying bourbons from another. For that reason all the brands have been listed alphabetically with the name of the bottling distiller being added at the end.

Irish Whiskey: There are four types of Irish whiskey: (i) pure pot still; (ii) single malt; (iii) single grain and (iv) blended. Some whiskies may have "pure pot still" on the label, but are actually single malts. So check both sections.

Bottle Information

As no labels are included in this book I have tried to include all the relevant information you will find on the label to make identification of the brand straightforward. Where known I have included date of distillation and bottling. Also the cask number for further recognition. At the end of the tasting notes I have included the strength and, if known, number of bottles (sometimes abbreviated to btls) released and in which markets.

PRICE OF WHISKY

You will notice that Jim Murray's Whisky Bible very rarely refers to the cost of a whisky. This is because the book is a guide to quality and character rather than the price tag attached. Also, the same whiskies are sold in different countries at varying prices due to market forces and variations of tax, so there is a relevance factor to be considered. Equally, much depends on the size of an individual's pocket. What may appear a cheap whisky to one could be an expensive outlay to another. With this in mind prices are rarely given in the Whisky Bible.

How to Taste Whisky

I t is of little use buying a great whisky, spending a comparative fortune in doing so, if you don't get the most out of it.

So when giving whisky tastings, no matter how knowledgeable the audience may be I take them through a brief training schedule in how to nose and taste as I do for each sample included in the Whisky Bible.

I am aware that many aspects are contrary to what is being taught by distilleries' whisky ambassadors. And for that we should be truly thankful. However, at the end of the day we all find our own way of doing things. If your old tried and trusted technique suits you best, that's fine by me. But I do ask you try out the instructions below at least once to see if you find your whisky is talking to you with a far broader vocabulary and clearer voice than it once did. I strongly suspect you will be pleasantly surprised – amazed, even - by the results.

Amusingly, someone tried to teach me my own tasting technique some years back in an hotel bar. He was not aware who I was and I didn't let on. It transpired that a friend of his had been to one of my tastings a few years earlier and had passed on my words of "wisdom". I'd be lying if I said I didn't smile when he informed me it was called "The Murray Method." It was the first time I had heard the phrase... though certainly not the last!

"THE MURRAY METHOD"

1. Drink a black, unsweetened, coffee or chew on 90% minimum cocoa chocolate to cleanse the palate, especially of sugars.

2. Find a room free from distracting noises as well as the aromas of cooking, polish, flowers and other things which will affect your understanding and appreciation of the whisky.

3. Make sure you have not recently washed your hands using heavily scented soap or are wearing a strong aftershave or perfume.

4. Use a tulip shaped glass with a stem. This helps contain the alcohols at the bottom yet allows the more delicate whisky aromas you are searching for to escape.

5. Never add ice. This tightens the molecules and prevents flavours and aromas from being released. It also makes your whisky taste bitter. There is no better way to get the least from your whisky than by freezing it.

6. Likewise, ignore any advice given to put the bottle in the fridge before drinking.

7. Don't add water! Whatever anyone tells you. It releases aromas but can mean the whisky falls below 40%...so it is no longer whisky. Also, its ability to release flavours and aromas diminish quite quickly. Never add ridiculous "whisky rocks" or other supposed tasting aids.

8. Warm the undiluted whisky in the glass to body temperature before nosing or tasting. Hence the stem, so you can cradle in your hand the curve of the thin base. This excites the molecules and unravels the whisky in your glass, maximising its sweetness and complexity.

9. Keep an un-perfumed hand over the glass to keep the aromas in while you warm. Only a minute or two after condensation appears at the top of your glass should you extend your arms, lift your covering hand and slowly bring the glass to your nose, so the alcoholic vapours have been released before the glass reaches your face.

10. Never stick your nose in the glass. Or breathe in deeply. Allow glass to gently touch your top lip, leaving a small space below the nose. Move from nostril to nostril, breathing normally. This allows the aromas to break up in the air, helping you find the more complex notes.

11. Take no notice of your first mouthful. This is a marker for your palate.

12. On second, bigger mouthful, close your eyes to concentrate on the flavour and chew the whisky - moving it continuously around the palate. Keep your mouth slightly open to let air in and alcohol out. It helps if your head is tilted back very slightly.

13. Occasionally spit – if you have the willpower! This helps your senses to remain sharp for the longest period of time.

14. Look for the balance of the whisky. That is, which flavours counter others so none is too dominant. Also, watch carefully how the flavours and aromas change in the glass over time.

15. Assess the "shape" and mouth feel of the whisky, its weight and how long its finish. And don't forget to concentrate on the first flavours as intensely as you do the last. Look out for the way the sugars, spices and other characteristics form.

16. Never make your final assessment until you have tasted it a third or fourth time.

17. Be honest with your assessment: don't like a whisky because someone (yes, even me!), or the label, has tried to convince you how good it is.

18. When you cannot discriminate between one whisky and another, stop immediately.

Immortal Drams:
The Whisky Bible
Winners 2004-2017

	World Whisky of the Year	Second Finest Whisky of the Year	Third Finest Whisky of the Year
2004	George T Stagg	N/A	N/A
2005	George T Stagg	N/A	N/A
2006	George T Stagg	Glen Moray 1986 Cask 4696 distillery bottling	N/A
2007	Old Parr Superior 18 Years Old	Buffalo Trace Experimental Collection Twice Barreled	N/A
2008	Ardbeg 10 Years Old	The Ileach Single Islay Malt Cask Strength	N/A
2009	Ardbeg Uigedail	Nikka Whisky Single Coffey Malt 12 Years	N/A
2010	Sazerac Rye 18 Years Old (bottled Fall 2008)	Ardbeg Supernova	Amrut Fusion
2011	Ballantine's 17 Years Old	Thomas H Handy Sazerac Rye (129 proof)	Wiliam Larue Weller (134.8 proof)
2012	Old Pulteney Aged 21 Years	George T Stagg	Parker's Heritage Collection Wheated Mash Bill Bourbon Aged 10 Years
2013	Thomas H Handy Sazerac Rye (128.6 proof)	William Larue Weller (133.5 proof)	Ballantine's 17 Years Old
2014	Glenmorangie Ealanta 1993	William Larue Weller (123.4 proof)	Thomas Handy Sazerac Rye (132.4 proof)
2015	Yamazaki Single Malt Sherry 2013	William Larue Weller (68.1 abv)	Sazerac Rye 18 Years Old (bottled Fall 2013)
2016	Crown Royal Northern Harvest Rye	Pikesville 110 Proof Straight Rye	Midleton Dair Ghaelach
2017	Booker's Rye 13 Years, 1 Month, 12 Days	Glen Grant 18 Year Old	William Larue Weller (134.6 proof)

Who has won this year? Find out on page 14

Bible Thumping
They Are Hid From
Thy Taste Buds

A few weeks ago my eldest son and his wife did what all people with good taste do: divest themselves of 1970s tat.

It might have been 1960s tat; even 1950s. Whichever, what they had in their new – old - home was evidence of the complete lack of sound design judgement which inexplicably infected much of the world for the first 30 years after the Second World War.

In this case, it was ugly, soul-less linoleum that had been laid down by culprits unknown in the hallway of their late Victorian Scottish home, which itself lay under a no less dreadful carpet of indeterminable years. To their utter amazement – and joy – what the young couple discovered beneath this amalgam of rotting thread and festering plastic was a late Victorian/early Edwardian tiled floor, a staggeringly beautiful mosaic of triangles and squares which is now the centerpiece of their home: a long dead craftsman's work of art now gracing the dwelling, most fittingly, of an artist.

I am sure a healthy percentage of readers of the Whisky Bible will have similar tales to tell. Grim 1950s fudge-coloured fireplaces and surrounds, some converted to gas or electric, removed to reveal masterpieces of 19th or even 18th century craftsmanship behind; or charmless flowery wallpaper of a box or even dining room stripped off to expose the tasteful pastel shades of the original paintwork beneath.

Why we, as a race, seem so determined to bury beauty under a layer, sometimes a pile, of unsightly dross is beyond me. But from documented evidence of the last few hundred years, hidden aesthetic gems found in old castles, churches, historic houses and public buildings reveals that this is a problem not confined to a more recent generation alone, nor just in the UK. It appears to be a mysterious and unfortunate element of human nature, though when the Second World War ended the outbreak appeared to be of Spanish flu proportions.

What, then, has this to do with whisky? Well, quite a lot as it happens.

Because it has increasingly occurred to me in recent years that much of my time when evaluating whisky appears to be spent stripping away the tasteless junk that is obscuring the real, original whisky beneath. This is not a new problem by any means. Indeed, it goes back to the very first days of commercialized whisky selling, that period after a malt spirit was made solely by farmers to make the most of their threshed grains and warm them through inhospitable, even vicious winters. Drunk new, it was the colour of water – rather, it had no colour at all. The spirit from the still which was placed into barrel might, depending on size, type of barrel and what it had previously held, pick up colour. And extra taste.

Likewise, in Maryland and then the frontier lands of Virginia, Pennsylvania and, of course, Kentucky and Tennessee, whiskey would be drunk by the distillers who also made it clear in colour, other than the haze of their own ineptitude. But when some was sold and sent down river to the specified buyer, or speculatively to seek new markets, the whiskey placed in barrel would miraculously redden in hue. And, as in Scotland, the flavour would change and in a way most thought was for the better. So coloured whiskey, signifying age and natural mellowing, was sought and fetched a higher market price.

What, though, if you were not a farmer, but a businessman recognizing the potential commercial value of matured malt spirit and starting up a whisky company in Scotland where the summers were short and sometimes cool and the winters bitter? In other words, where maturation was very slow. You needed to buy the raw spirit, which was not cheap. And you required barrels, which was equally expensive. Only so much colour could be drawn from the oak, so it needed a little helping along. And so the adding of caramel was not only begun, but it quickly became standard practice in Scotland and Ireland, following the long established practice of the rum makers. It was found by this new breed of blenders that, also, as with rum, the adding of caramel could alter the texture of the whisky they were selling and even calm some of the less desirable characteristics of the lesser quality whiskies which were being added to their blend.

In effect, blenders were obscuring the true sight of what they were selling: they were creating an illusion. If there was complexity between the light marriage of oak with grain you had to battle hard through the toffee to find it.

During the 19th century these men – for there is scant evidence of a woman's hand then in this trade – were still the honest ones, even though they were creating this illusion as regards the whisky's age and personality. For they are not to be remotely confused with those responsible for an altogether different branch of so-called whisky blending at work during this period. On both sides of the Atlantic the darker arts were performed...and not just in the colour of the spirit. An entire cannon of books was published to show how to make "whisky" of differing styles with barely an atom of malted spirit being used in the process. These faux-whiskies were a blight on the genuine but still fledgling industry and too often people bought a Scotch or Irish in good faith, or a bourbon or rye were they in an American city, though the spirits, full of adjuncts, additives and neutral alcohol had never been within 200 miles of where they are supposed to have originated. It was not unknown for the duped customer to pay for this spirit in much more than money alone....for this was an injurious liquid: often to those who drank it, always to the legitimate industry itself.

We have, thankfully, come a long way from the work of these charlatans, though that such individuals and their appalling liquors still exist today in some of the world's backwaters is a sad and unedifying fact of life.

No, this Bible Thumping is to do with the decent branch of the industry: the distillers and blenders who produce their products with honesty and integrity. Yet still, after all this time, after all this experience, sometimes through cosmetic reasons or maybe carelessness, manage to obscure the very whisky they have gone at pains to produce or create.

When I work with the new breed of blenders around the world, be it to train or help them maximize the stocks they have at their disposal, one of the things I try to get them to do is imagine clearly in their mind's eye and palate how they wish their whisk(e)y to be. In aroma, flavour development on the palate and also in colour. First they have to completely understand the range and depth of stocks of the whisky they have maturing. That's pretty tricky in itself. Then I have to ask them: is the colour they have in mind compatible, indeed possible in any way, with the type of whisky they wish to produce, or even have in their warehouses. You would be surprised how often the answer to that is "no".... unless they added colouring.

But then, often, they have overlooked a vital point. Whatever you add to a whisky, be it colour and fruit (though hopefully not sulphur) from a sherry butt, a darkening agent in caramel, a smokiness to give extra depth or tannin from older stock, something within the character of the original whisky has to make way for it. The first thing to suffer are the lighter, more delicate tones, both on aroma and taste. When you blend, when you add in a whisky or artificial colouring, something else is taken away: occasionally it is what you don't want to be there in the first place, so it serves its purpose as a mask. But very often a character you desire and wish to preserve falls victim. And if it is not taken away completely, then it is certainly altered so now that note is still there but maybe muffled and doing slightly different things.

This problem is by no means new. Indeed, from the very first days of whisky becoming a commercial product, its appearance was something that was taken seriously and worked upon. The more determined blenders set about creating the illusion of greatness from increasingly elaborate label designs to not only catch the eye but give the impression of provenance and permanence. They, in turn, would be contacting distillers whose letter heads often included impressive line drawings of their distilleries which without fail erred on the side of overstating the size and dramatic qualities of the buildings rather than understating it.

And, so it was a natural progression to make the whiskies look that little bit older than they actually were. The use of caramel became standard practice ostensibly so each batch looked very much the same as the last but the reality was, of course, to create that illusion.

Today most blenders get it. After well over a century of denial within the industry that artificial colouring has any effect on the taste or smell of whisky whatsoever, the majority now privately, if not publicly, admit that the exact opposite is true. Maybe it is because far fewer are smokers now than was once the case so better able now to detect the more delicate nuances of the whiskies in their care, or that they are not only listening but carrying out experiments which prove without doubt that what was long preached was false. Sadly, a few still stick their fingers in their ears refusing to hear and churn out one teak-coloured whisky after another – each tasting remarkably similar to the next – but, thankfully, the dinosaurs are dying out.

However, despite this new-found awareness the blender too often is under strict order to work to the instructions of marketing types. And what they usually want, especially for the ever-expanding Asian markets, are dark whiskies. They don't care how the blender gets there, whether it is via sherry butt, freshly charred oak or caramel or a mixture of any or all of them. But, unless it is a brand designated for the specialist connoisseur end of the market, the last thing they wish to see is the whisky in its natural state. For that could be a lot lighter than you might think a whisky of a good age might be.

There is another way of impressing customers: big age. Which often means bottling the whisky at a greater age than is good for it. This takes us back to blenders learning how to understand their maturing whiskies and maximizing the qualities they possess. It could be that to show the distillery in its most beautiful, complex and mouthwatering light you need x percent of first fill cask at one age, y percent of second fill at another and z percent of third fill at another entirely. The result is a whisky whose beauty might make you weep. However, because the youngest age has to be mentioned if they are looking for age statements, that may not fit in with the plans of the marketeers, so the blender might be asked to make the youngest that little bit older. This will shift the balance towards oak, and that fragile equilibrium which set the whisky apart is upset. Or they may opt for the whisky without an age statement but because it is so pale, they will request that the colour is nudged towards something darker. Caramel is added and the magic disappears. Or sherry, and the fruit cancels out the crisper barley. Is this just theory? Alas, no: I have been told these sad tales by frustrated blenders in very recent years: with greater expectation from the public, their lot is not getting any easier.

And the overall result? It is the linoleum over the stunningly beautiful floor. The suspended ceiling over the 18th century frieze. The false wall before the 19th century fireplace. The hiding away of something special due, and there is no way of getting around this, a criminal lack of taste. Because if someone covers over the finest details in a blender's work of art for the sake of cold commercialism alone, something in whisky has died.

That is why when I taste the whiskies before me for each edition of the Whisky Bible it takes me so long to work out each dram. If it is a single cask, no colouring added, then straightforward enough. But if it from a distillery, be it a blend, a single malt or an Irish, I look more carefully again. Both on nose and palate I strip down the outer layers, trying to figure out if they were there by accident, design or order. Take away the excess, the false walls and ceilings and grotty lino – in effect, the tat - and what, if anything, is left?

Is the core of the whisk(e)y a mosaic? Do we have a true work of art lost but revealed once more?

Sometimes I am accused of giving a whisky a higher score than some people think it deserves (and, of course, lower if I spot sulphur and they can't). Could it be because I didn't add water so breaking up the structure completely and beyond hope and form, because I warmed the glass allowing the silenced notes to sing, because I refused to taste it alongside some supposedly matching French cuisine which would have blotted out every last chance of spotting a whisky's potential brilliance.

Could it be because I gave the dram time enough for me to uncover the true whisky within? Start pulling away at the old oaky carpet in your malt or blend, the boring, toffeed lino which smothers all. See what is beneath. You might just be in for a surprise...

Jim Murray's Whisky Bible Awards 2018

It is a strange and wonderful thing just how often the choice of World Whisky of the Year comes down to a battle of the classic whisky styles.

This year, again, is no exception. The top three is represented by bourbon at its most complex, demanding and improbably subtle, Irish in its truest and most traditional form, and single malt Scotch extracting every atom of possible individualism and charm from barley and barrel. For once Rye, probably the least spoiled of all true whisky styles on the planet, and certainly one of the most successful over the last decade in Jim Murray's Whisky Bible with the major Award going to both Kentucky and Canada in the last two years, missed out. Though very narrowly.

It is also odd how often a whisk(e)y stands out against the rest during the course of writing this book; it having that indefinable something, that x-factor which cannot simply be ignored or very easily created. The 1,200 new whiskies tasted for this edition once more underlined that there are more genuinely excellent whiskies than had even recently been the case. But the moment that truly exceptional whisky or whiskey is poured into the glass, it is though time in the tasting room stands still: you just know...

That happened twice this year. It was going to be a dog fight between two glorious whiskeys. But one was disqualified from any 2018 Award as it had been bottled just a little bit too long ago and should have been sent to us on release for last year's edition. Oooops! Which left just the Colonel Taylor 4 Grain and though all the other high scorers were measured against it, it proved an unequal battle: nothing could match the astonishing beauty of its surprisingly delicate weight and comlexity combined.

But it was still wonderful to see that Irish Pot Still whiskey, when bottled from outstanding casks, was able to eclipse all but the Colonel Taylor and underline that, surely, this style is a World Whisky of the Year waiting to happen. Indeed, Pot Still - a mixture of malted and unmalted barley offering a firm texture and massive flavour profile - is again no longer just confined to Ireland (it was once commonly made in the Lowlands of Scotland in order to circumvent the paying of high malt taxes) and European Whisky of the Year went to The English Whisky Company with their own version, Norfolk Parched, which through its youth and use of bourbon barrel (as opposed to a high sherry content from Ireland) was able to display the grain in its freshest and most invigorating style.

Once more Scotland owes a debt of honour to the celebrated Glen Grant distillery which again displayed Speyside whisky in its most sparkling light and landed third place in the World Awards. Indeed, it pulled off a truly remarkable achievement by not only winning Scotch Whisky of the Year, but also saw its 10-year-old version pick up top gong for its category.... and the 41 Years and Over Award thanks to Gordon and MacPhail's stunning 1957 Glen Grant bottling. The gauntlet has been flung down. Who in Scotland is up to the challenge?

2018 World Whisky of the Year

Colonel E.H. Taylor 4 Grain Bottled in Bond Aged 12 Years

Second Finest Whisky in the World
Redbreast Aged 21 Years

Third Finest Whisky in the World
Glen Grant Aged 18 Years

SCOTCH

Scotch Whisky of the Year
Glen Grant Aged 18 Years Rare Edition
Single Malt of the Year (Multiple Casks)
Glen Grant Aged 18 Years Rare Edition
Single Malt of the Year (Single Cask)
Cadenhead's Glendullan 20 Year Old
Scotch Blend of the Year
Compass Box The Double Single
Scotch Grain of the Year
Cambus Aged 40 Years
Scotch Vatted Malt of the Year
Compass Box 3 Year Old Deluxe

Single Malt Scotch

No Age Statement (Multiple Casks)
Ardbeg Corryvreckan
10 Years & Under (Multiple Casks)
Glen Grant Aged 10 Years
10 Years & Under (Single Cask)
Scotch Malt Whisky Society Tomatin
Cask 11.32 8 Year Old
11-15 Years (Multiple Casks)
Gordon & MacPhail Ardmore 2002
11-15 Years (Single Cask)
That Boutique-y Co. Clynelish 15 Year Old
16-21 Years (Multiple Casks)
Glen Grant Aged 18 Years Rare Edition
16-21 Years (Single Cask)
The First Editions Ardmore Aged 20 Years
22-27 Years (Multiple Casks)
Sansibar Whisky Glen Moray 25 Years Old
22-27 Years (Single Cask)
Hunter Laing's Old & Rare Auchentoshan 24 Year Old
28-34 Years (Multiple Casks)
Glen Castle Aged 28 Years
28-34 Years (Single Cask)
Old Particular Glenturret 28 Year Old
35-40 Years (Multiple Casks)
Brora Aged 38 Years
35-40 Years (Single Cask)
Xtra Old Particular Caol Ila 36 Year Old
41 Years & Over (Multiple Casks)
Gordon & MacPhail Glen Grant 1957

BLENDED SCOTCH

No Age Statement (Standard)
Ballantine's Finest
No Age Statement (Premium)
Compass Box The Double Single
5-12 Years
Grant's Aged 12 Years
13-18 Years
Ballantine's Aged 17 Years
19 - 25 Years
Royal Salute 21 Years Old
26 - 50 Years
The Antiquary Aged 35 Years

IRISH WHISKEY

Irish Whiskey of the Year
Redbreast Aged 21 Years
Irish Pot Still Whiskey of the Year
Redbreast Aged 21 Years
Irish Single Malt of the Year
Bushmills 16 Year Old
Irish Blend of the Year
Bushmills Black Bush
Irish Single Cask of the Year
Dunville's VR First Edition Aged 15 Years

AMERICAN WHISKEY

Bourbon of the Year
Colonel E.H. Taylor Four Grain
Rye of the Year
Thomas H. Handy Sazerac 126.2 Proof
US Micro Whisky of the Year
Balcone's Texas Blue Corn Batch BCB 16-1
US Micro Whisky of the Year (Runner Up)
291 E Colorado Aged 333 Days

BOURBON

No Age Statement (Multiple Barrels)
George T. Stagg 144.1 Proof
9 Years & Under
Buffalo Trace Experimental Collection Organic 6 Grain Whisky
10 Years & Over (Multiple Barrels)
Colonel E.H. Taylor Four Grain

RYE

No Age Statement
Thomas H. Handy Sazerac 126.2 Proof
Up to 10 Years
Pikesville 110 Proof
11 Years & Over
Sazerac 18 Years Old

WHEAT

Wheat Whiskey of the Year
Bernheim Original

CANADIAN WHISKY

Canadian Whisky of the Year
Crown Royal Northern Harvest Rye

JAPANESE WHISKY

Japanese Whisky of the Year
Nikka Coffey Malt Whisky
Single Malt of the Year (Multiple Barrels)
Nikka Coffey Malt Whisky

EUROPEAN WHISKY

European Whisky of the Year (Multiple)
Penderyn Bryn Terfel (Wales)
European Whisky of the Year (Single)
The Norfolk Parched (England)

WORLD WHISKIES

Asian Whisky of the Year
Paul John Kanya (India)
Southern Hemisphere Whisky of the Year
Limeburner's Dark Winter (Australia)

*Overall age category and/or section winners are presented in **bold**.*

The Whisky Bible Liquid Gold Awards (97.5-94)

Jim Murray's Whisky Bible is delighted to again make a point of celebrating the very finest whiskies you can find in the world. So we salute the distillers who have maintained or even furthered the finest traditions of whisky making and taken their craft to the very highest levels. And the bottlers who have brought some of them to us.

After all, there are over 4,600 different brands and expressions listed in this guide and from every corner of the planet. Those which score 94 and upwards represents only a very small fraction of them. These whiskies are, in my view, the élite: the finest you can currently find on the whisky shelves of the world. Rare and precious, they are Liquid Gold.

So it is our pleasure to announce that all those scoring 94 and upwards automatically qualify for the Jim Murray's Whisky Bible Liquid Gold Award. Congratulations!

97.5
Scottish Single Malt
Glenmorangie Ealanta 1993 Vintage
Old Pulteney Aged 21 Years
Scottish Blends
Ballantine's 17 Years Old
Irish Pure Pot Still
Midleton Dair Ghaelach Grinsell's Wood Ballaghtobin Estate
Bourbon
Colonel E.H. Taylor Four Grain Bottled in Bond
George T Stagg
William Larue Weller
William Larue Weller bott Spring 2001
American Straight Rye
Booker's Rye 13 Years, 1 Month, 12 Days
Pikesville Straight Rye Whiskey aged at least 6 years
Thomas H. Handy Sazerac Straight Rye Whiskey
Canadian Blended Malt
Crown Royal Northern Harvest Rye
Japanese Single Malt
Yamazaki Single Malt Whisky Sherry Cask

97
Scottish Single Malt
Ardbeg 10 Years Old
Ardbeg Day Bottling
Cadenhead's Small Batch Caol Ila 31 Year Old
Glen Grant Aged 18 Years Rare Edition
Gordon & MacPhail Rare Vintage Glen Grant 1957
Glenfiddich 50 Years Old
That Boutique-y Whisky Company Macallan 25 Year Old
Port Ellen 32 Year Old
Scottish Grain
Cambus Aged 40 Years
Xtra Old Particular Cambus 40 Years Old
Scottish Blends
Compass Box The Double Single
Johnnie Walker Blue Label The Casks Edition
The Last Drop 50 Year Old
The Last Drop 1971 Blended Scotch Whisky
Old Parr Superior 18 Years Old
Irish Blend
Midleton Dair Ghaelach
Irish Pure Pot Still
Redbreast Aged 21 Years
Bourbon
George T. Stagg

Parker's Heritage Collection Wheated Mash Bill Bourbon Aged 10 Years
William Larue Weller
American Straight Rye
Colonel E.H. Taylor Straight Rye
Sazerac Rye 18 Year Old
Sazerac 18 Years Old
Japanese Single Malt
Nikka Whisky Single Coffey Malt 12 Years
The Yamazaki Single Malt Whisky Mizunara
Czech Rebublic Single Malt
Gold Cock Single Malt Whisky 1992 Limited Release Whisky Festival.cz
French Single Malt
Kornog Taouarc'h Chwec'hved 14
German Single Malt
Spinnaker Single Cask Malt Whisky Fassstärke
Indian Single Malt
Amrut Fusion
Taiwanese Single Malt
Kavalan Solist Fino Sherry Cask
Kavalan Single Malt Amontillado Sherry

96.5
Scottish Single Malt
Ardbeg 21 Years Old
Ardbeg Corryvreckan
Ardbeg Supernova
The First Editions Ardmore Aged 20 Years 1996
Gordon & MacPhail Cask Strength Ardmore 2002
Balblair 1965
Balblair 1983 Vintage 1st Release
Bowmore Black 50 Year Old
Octomore Edition 7.1 Aged 5 years
Brora Aged 38 Years
Caol Ila 30 Year Old
Acla Selection Clynelish 21 Years Old
That Boutique-y Whisky Company Clynelish 15 Year Old
Kingsbury Silver Craigellachie 18 Year Old 1995
Dalwhinnie 25 Year Old
Glencadam Aged 18 Years
The Glendronach Aged 10 Years PX Casks
Cadenhead's Small Batch International Glendullan 20 Year Old
Gordon & MacPhail Rare Vintage Glen Grant 1952
Gordon & MacPhail Rare Vintage Glen Grant 1960
The Glenlivet Cipher

Glenmorangie Sonnalta PX
Svenska Eldvatten Glen Moray 1991
The Single Cask Glentauchers 14 Year Old
Highland Park 50 Years Old
WoodWinters Northern Star 21 Year Old
Simon Brown Arran Distillery 1997
AnCnoc Cutter 20.5 ppm
AnCnoc Rutter 11 ppm
That Boutique-y Whisky Company
Lagavulin 10 Year Old
  Signatory Cask Strength Collection
Laphroaig Aged 15 Years
  Berry's Own Selection Linkwood 1987
Aged 26 Years
  The Cooper's Choice Lochside 1967
Aged 44 Years
  Hidden Spirits Longmorn LNG.315 11
Years Old
  Scyfion Mortlach 1996
  Tomatin 36 Year Old
  Tullibardine 1970
  Alos Sansibar Whisky Speyside Region 1975
  Glen Castle Aged 28 Years
  Port Askaig 100 Proof
  Saar Whisky Gruwehewwel
Scottish Grain
  Clan Denny Cambus Vintage Aged 25
Years Old
  Xtra Old Particular Cameronbridge 32
Years Old
  The Whisky Barrel Dumbarton 30 Year Old
Scottish Vatted Malt
  Compass Box Flaming Heart Fifteenth
Anniversary
  The Last Vatted Malt
Scottish Blends
  The Antiquary Aged 35 Years
  Ballantine's Limited Release no. L40055
  The Last Drop 1965
  Royal Salute 32 Years Old Union of the
Crowns
  Teacher's Aged 25 Years
Irish Pure Pot Still
  Powers John's Lane Release
Aged 12 Years
Irish Single Malt
  Dunville's VR First Edition Aged 15 Years
Single Malt
  Teeling Whiskey Single Cask 2004
Bourbon
  Blanton's Gold Original Single Barrel
  Blanton's Uncut/Unfiltered
  Elmer T. Lee Bourbon 1919 - 2013
  Four Roses 125th Anniversary Small Batch
Bourbon
  George T. Stagg Limited Edition
  George T Stagg
  Virgin Bourbon 7 Years Old
American Straight Rye
  Sazerac Rye 18 Year Old
  Thomas H. Handy Sazerac
American Microdistilleries
  Balcones Texas Blue Corn Straight Bourbon
Whisky Aged At Least 24 Months
  Garrison Brothers Cowboy Bourbon
Aged Four Years
  The Notch Aged 12 Years
Canadian Blended
  Crown Royal Northern Harvest Rye
  Masterson's 10 Year Old Straight Rye
Japanese Single Malt
  Chichibu 'The Peated' 2013

The Hakushu Single Malt Whisky
Sherry Cask
  Yamazaki Single Malt Sherry Cask 2016
English Single Malt
  The Norfolk Single Grain Parched
Swiss Single Malt
  Langatun Single Malt Whisky 6 Year Old
  Langatun 10 Years
Welsh Single Malt
  Penderyn Icons of Wales No 5/50 Bryn
Terfel
  Penderyn Portwood
Indian Single Malt
  Amrut Greedy Angels 10 Years Old
  Paul John Edited

96

Scottish Single Malt
  Aberlour A'Bunadh Batch No. 54
  Ardbeg 1977
  Ardbeg Provenance 1974
  Old Malt Cask Ardmore Aged 20 Years
  Kingsbury Gold Bowmore 18 Year Old
  Bruichladdich Ocotomore 7.1 5 Years Old
  Octomore 5 Years Old
  Gordon & MacPhail Cask Strength
Bruichladdich 1994
  Eiling Lim Bunnahabhain
34 Years Old 1980
  The Golden Cask Caol Ila 13 Year Old
  Old Particular Caol Ila 19 Years Old
  Gordon & MacPhail Connoisseurs Choice
Clynelish 2004
  The Dalmore Candela Aged 50 Years
  Gordon & MacPhail Rare Vintage Glen
Albyn 1976
  Gordon & MacPhail Cask Strength
Glenburgie 1995
  Maltbarn Glen Elgin 1995
  Glenfarclas 1966 Fino Cask
  Kirsch Import Glenfarclas 2008
  The Last Drop Glen Garioch 47 Year Old
  Glen Grant Aged 10 Years
  Gordon & MacPhail Rare Vintage
Glen Grant 1948
  Gordon & MacPhail Connoisseurs
Choice Glenlossie
  Sansibar Whisky Glen Moray 25 Year Old
  The Glenturret Fly's 16 Masters Edition
  That Boutique-y Whisky Company
Glenturret 35 Year Old
  Highland Park Sigurd
  Highland Park Loki Aged 15 Years
  Highland Park Aged 25 Years
  Old Particular Arran 20 Years Old
  Lagavulin 12 Years Old
  Laphroaig PX Cask
  Laphroaig Quarter Cask
  Single Cask Collection Longmorn
Aged 23 Years
  Scotch Malt Whisky Society Cask 29.191 16
Year Old
  Rosebank 25 Years Old
  Gordon & MacPhail Rare Vintage Strathisla
1960
  Ledaig Dùsgadh 42 Aged 42 Years
  The Cooper's Choice Tormore Sweet &
Smoky
  Ben Bracken Islay Single Malt 22 Years Old
  Lotus Lord 28 Year Old 1988
  SaarWhisky Gruwehewwel Edition 3
  Whisky-Fässle Speyside Region 1975

Scottish Vatted Malt
Compass Box 3 Year Old Deluxe

Scottish Grain
That Boutique-y Whisky Company Caledonian 29 Year Old
The Last Drop Dumbarton 54 Year Old
The Cooper's Choice Garnheath 48 Year Old
Cadenhead's Small Batch Port Dundas Aged 25 Years
Whiskyjace Invergordon 24 Years Old 1991
The Sovereign Blended Grain 28 Years Old

Scottish Blends
Ballantine's Aged 30 Years
Ballantine's Finest
Ballantine's Limited
Grant's Aged 12 Years
Islay Mist Aged 17 Years
Oishii Wisukii Aged 36 Years
Royal Salute 21 Years Old
That Boutique-y Whisky Company Blended Whisky No. 1 50 Year Old

Irish Pure Pot Still
Powers Aged 12 Years John's Lane Release
Redbreast Aged 12 Years Cask Strength
Redbreast Aged 21 Years

Irish Single Malt
Glendalough 13 Year Old Irish Single Malt Mizunara Finish
Teeling Whiskey Single Malt Aged 26 Years

Irish Blends
Powers Gold label

Bourbon
1792 Full Proof Kentucky Straight Bourbon
1792 High Rye Kentucky Straight Bourbon
Ancient Ancient Age 10 Years Old
Buffalo Trace Experimental Collection Organic 6 Grain Whiskey 7 Years, 1 Month
Buffalo Trace Single Oak Project Barrel #101
Mayor Pingree Aged 9 Years Straight Bourbon Whiskey batch no. 16-314
Old Weller Antique 107
Pappy Van Winkle's Family Reserve 15 YO
Parker's Heritage Collection 24 Year Old Bottled in Bond Bourbon dist Spring 91
William Larue Weller

American Straight Rye
Bulleit 95 Rye
John David Albert's Taos Lightning
Very Rare 21 YO Barrel 28
Rittenhouse Rye Single Barrel Aged 25 Years Barrel 19

American Microdistilleries
291 E Colorado Bourbon Whiskey Aged 333 Days
Garrison Brothers Cowboy Bourbon Barrel Proof Aged Four Years
Koval Single Barrel Four Grain Whiskey

Canadian Blended
Crown Royal Special Reserve
Lot No. 40 Rye Whisky
J. P. Wiser's 35 Year Old

Japanese Single Malt
ePower Komagatake
The Yamazaki Single Malt Aged 18 Years

Japanese Single Grain
Nikka Coffey Malt Whisky

Austrian Single Malt
J.H. 13 Years Old Single Malt

Belgian Single Malt
Belgian Owl Single Malt Whisky The

Private Angels Aged 36 Months
Gouldys 12 Years Old Distillers Range

Czech Republic Single Malt
Gold Cock Single Malt Whisky 2008 Virgin Oak

English Single Malt
Hicks & Healey Cornish Whiskey 2004
The English Whisky Co. Chapter 6 English Single Malt Not Peated
The English Whisky Co. Chapter 14

German Single Malt
Eifel Whisky Einzelfass Single Rye 2015

Swedish Single Malt
Mackmyra Moment "Malström"

Welsh Single Malt
Penderyn Madeira Finish
Penderyn Single Cask PT9 LMDW Vintage

Australian Single Malt
The Good Convict Port Cask
Heartwood @#$% · &*
Heartwood Any Port in a Storm
Heartwood Calm Before The Storm 2009
Limeburners Single Malt Whisky Darkest Winter
Timboon Single Malt Whisky
Timboon Single Malt Whisky Port Expression

Indian Single Malt
Amrut Greedy Angels 10 Years Old
Amrut Greedy Angels
Paul John Kanya
Paul John Single Malt Single Cask No 164
Paul John Single Malt Cask No 780
Paul John Single Malt Cask No 1846

95.5

Scottish Single Malt
Aberlour A'bunadh Batch No. 50
Ardbeg An Oa
Kingsbury Gold Ardmore 6 Year Old 2008
Old Particular Ardmore 16 Years Old
Hunter Laing's Old & Rare Auchentoshan Aged 24 Years
Gordon & MacPhail Rare Old Banff 1966
The BenRiach Aged 12 Years Matured In Sherry Wood
The BenRiach Aged 18 Years Dunder
Benromach 30 Years Old
Benromach Organic 2010
Scotch Malt Whisky Society Cask 50.75 Aged 25 Years
Cadenhead's Authentic Collection Bowmore 15 Year Old
Gleann Mór Bowmore 30 Year Old
Port Charlotte The Peat Project
Caol Ila Aged 15 Years
Xtra Old Particular Islay Caol Ila 36 Years Old
The Dalmore Visitor Centre Exclusive
Old Malt Cask Glencadam Aged 19 Years
Gordon & MacPhail Connoisseurs Choice Glendullan 2004
Glenfarclas 105
Glenfarclas 1994
Glenfiddich Project XX
Glen Grant Distillery Edition Cask Strength Aged 20 Years
Gordon & MacPhail Rare Vintage Glen Grant 1956
Eiling Lim Glen Keith 21 Years Old
Glengoyne 25 Year Old
The Glenlivet Archive 21 Years of Age
The Glenlivet Nàdurra First Fill Selection

The Glenlivet Nàdurra Peated Whisky Cask Finish Batch No. PW0715

Glenmorangie 25 Years Old

Glenmorangie Private Edition 9 Spios

Cadenhead's Authentic Collection Glen Ord 11 Year Old

Cadenhead's Authentic Collection Glentauchers 38 Year Old

Scotch Malt Whisky Society Cask 35.185 22 Year Old

Old Particular Glentauchers 20 Years Old

Old Particular Glenturret 28 Years Old

Old Particular Highland Glenturret 28 Years Old

Scotch Malt Whisky Society Cask 30.92 24 Year Old

Gordon & MacPhail Rare Old Glenury Royal 1984

Highland Park Aged 18 Years

Kilchoman 2007 Vintage

Kilchoman 100% Islay The 5th Edition

Kilchoman Single Cask Release

AnCnoc 1999

Lagavulin 12 Year Old

Dramfool Avian Gull 8 Year Old

That Boutique-y Whisky Company Linkwood 26 Year Old

The First Editions Laphroaig Aged 19 Years 1996

Scotch Malt Whisky Society Cask 7.129 Aged 30 Years

The Macallan Fine Oak 12 Years Old

The Macallan Oscuro

The Warehouse Collection Macduff Aged 18 Years

Cadenhead Single Cask Mannochmore 37 Year Old

Gordon & MacPhail Connoisseurs Choice Mannochmore 1994

Rosebank 21 Year Old

Le Gus't Selection V Ledaig 2008

Old Particular Highland Leidag Aged 21 Yrs

Hunter Laing's Old & Rare Longmorn Aged 30 Years

Scotch Malt Whisky Society Cask 11.32 8 Year Old

Cù Bòcan Highland Single Malt 1989 Vintage

The Whisky Agency Speyside Region Single Malt 1973

Scottish Vatted Malt

Wemyss Malts Spice King Batch Strength

Scottish Grain

MacAlabur Cambus 25 Years Old

That Boutique-y Whisky Company Girvan 52 Year Old

The Pearls of Scotland North of Scotland 1971

The Sovereign Port Dundas 27 Years Old

Scottish Vatted Malt

Compass Box The Lost Blend

Compass Box The Spice Tree

Scottish Blends

Ballantine's Aged 30 Years

The Chivas 18 Ultimate Cask Collection First Fill American Oak

Chivas Regal Aged 25 Years

Glenalba Aged 34 Years Sherry Cask Finish

Johnnie Walker Black Label 12 Years Old

John Walker & Sons Private Collection 2015 Edition

Royal Salute "62 Gun Salute"

Irish Single Malt

Eiling Lim Irish Single Malt

22 Years Old 1991

Teeling Whiskey Single Malt Aged 24 Years

The Tyrconnell Single Cask 11 Year Old

Bushmills Aged 21 Years

Whisky-Fässle Irish Single Malt 1989

Bourbon

Blade and Bow 22 Year Old

Buffalo Trace Single Oak Project Barrel #27

Buffalo Trace Single Oak Project Barrel #30

Buffalo Trace Single Oak Project Barrel #63

Buffalo Trace Single Oak Project Barrel #183

Buffalo Trace Experimental Collection 12 Year Old Bourbon From Floor #9

Charter 101

Elijah Craig Barrel Proof Bourbon 12 Years

Knob Creek Aged 9 Years

Parker's Heritage Collection 24 Year Old Bottled in Bond Bourbon dist Fall 90

American Straight Rye

George Dickel Rye

Michter's No. 1 Straight Rye

Sazerac 18 Years Old bott Spring 2016

Sazerac Kentucky Straight Rye 18 Years Old

Thomas H. Handy Sazerac

Thomas H. Handy Sazerac Straight Rye

American Straight Wheat

Parker's Heritage Collection Original Batch Kentucky Straight Wheat Whiskey Aged 13 Years

American Microdistilleries

291 E Colorado 100% Rye Malt Whiskey Aged 291 Days

291 M Colorado Whiskey Rye Malt

Hillrock Single Malt Whiskey

Iron Smoke Apple Wood Smoked Whiskey batch no. 10

Reservoir Distillery Rye Whiskey

Rock Town Arkansas Rye Whiskey

Stranahan's Snowflake Cab Franc

Other American Whiskey

Buffalo Trace Experimental Collection French Oak Barrel Head Aged

Canadian Blended

Alberta Premium

Forty Creek Port Wood Reserve

Gibson's Finest Rare Aged 18 Years

Masterson's 10 Year Old Straight Rye Whiskey

Japanese Single Malt

Ichiro's Malt Aged 20 Years

Japanese Single Grain

Kawasaki Single Grain

Austrian Single Malt

Peter Affenzeller Single Malt Whisky 7 Years Old

Czech Republic Single Malt

Gold Cock Single Malt Whisky Aged 24 Years 1992

English Single Malt

Bimber Single Malt New-Make Test Batch Sample

The English Whisky Co. Chapter 6 English Single Malt Not Peated

The English Whisky Co. Chapter 15 Heavily Peated

German Single Malt

Valerie Amarone Single Malt Whisky 4 Years Old

Valerie Single Malt Amarone Cask Strength

Derrina Purpur Ur-Weizen Schwarzwälder

Swiss Single Malt
Langatun Old Deer Cask Strength
Langatun Old Mustang Bourbon 4 Year Old recipe
The Swiss Malt
Swedish Single Malt
Gute Single Malt Whisky
Australian Single Malt
Heartwood 2 of /3 Tasmanian Malt Whisky
Heartwood The Beagle 3 Tasmania Vatted Malt Whisky
Heartwood Devil in the Detail
Sullivan's Cove American Oak Single Cask
Indian Single Malt
Paul John Indian Single Malt Bold
Paul John Single Cask No 1833
Paul John Single Malt Cask No 692
Paul John Single Malt Cask No 784
Paul John Single Malt Cask No 1444
Indian Blends
Rendezvous
Taiwanese Single malt
Kavalan Single Malt Manzanilla Sherry Cask

95 (New Entries Only)

Scottish Single Malt
Ardbeg Kelpie
The BenRiach Peated Cask Strength
Old Malt Cask Braeval Aged 25 Years
Hunter Laing's Old & Rare Clynelish Aged 20 Years
The Whisky Agency Cragganmore 12 Years Old
World of Orchids Glen Elgin 21 Year Old
Gordon & MacPhail Rare Old Glenesk 1980
Glenfarclas 40 Years Old
The First Editions Glengoyne Aged 21 Years 1995
Gordon & MacPhail Rare Vintage Glen Grant 1961
Glenkinchie Aged 24 Years
Demijohn Glen Moray 9 Year Old
Old Malt Cask Glen Spey Aged 25 Years
Hunter Laing's Old & Rare Highland Park Aged 18 Years
Kingsbarns Spirit Drink
Gleann Mor Lagavulin
Glen Fahrn Airline Nr. 16 Littlemill 23 Year Old
Hunter Laing's Old & Rare Littlemill Aged 27 Years
WoodWinters Fiadhaich 27 Year Old
Tomatin Five Virtues Series Metal Bourbon Barrels
Kingsbury Gold Tomintoul 16 Year Old
Lotus Lord 24 Year Old 1992
That Boutique-y Whisky Company Secret Distillery 2 21 Year Old
Scotch Universe Mercury I 106° U.1.1' 1897.2"
Scottish Vatted Malt
Glenbrynth Ruby 40 Year Old
Scottish Grain
The Sovereign Cambus 25 Years Old
Old Particular Cameronbridge 24 Years Old
Dramfool Carsebridge 52 Year Old
That Boutique-y Whisky Company Carsebridge 52 Year Old
Sansibar Whisky Invergordon 1973
That Boutique-y Whisky Company Port Dundas 25 Year Old
Scottish Blends
Clan Gold 18 Years of Age

Royal Salute 21 Years Old The Polo Collection
Irish Pure Pot Still
Green Spot
Midleton Barry Crockett Legacy
Irish Single Malt
Teeling Whiskey Single Malt Vol IV Revival Aged 14 Years
Irish Blends
Bushmills Black Bush
Bourbon
Eagle Rare 17 Years Old bott Spring 2016
American Microdistilleries
Balcones True Blue Cask Strength Straight Corn Whisky Aged At Least 24 Months
Copperworks American Single Malt Whiskey Release No. 002 Aged 30 Months
291 Barrel Proof Colorado Whiskey Aged Less Than 2 Years
Sonoma County West of Kentucky Bourbon Whiskey No.1
Woodinville Straight 100% Rye Whiskey
Austrian Single Malt
Bodding Lokn Single Malt Lagerung Double Cask Sherry Finish
English Single Malt
Cotswolds Distillery New Make Spirit Plumage Archer
The English Whisky Co. Chapter 16
Finnish Single Malt
Teerenpeli Suomi 100 Single Malt Whisky
Swedish Single Malt
Box Single Malt The 2nd Step Collection 03
Welsh Single Malt
Penderyn Celt
Penderyn Portwood
Australian Single Malt
Belgrove Distillery Oat Whisky
Belgrove Distillery Peated Rye Whisky
Limeburners Single Malt Whisky Directors Cut
Overeem Single Malt Whisky Sherry Cask Matured
Indian Single Malt
Paul John Exceptional

94.5 (New Entries Only)

Scottish Single Malt
The Whisky Chamber Aberlour 10 Year Old
That Boutique-y Whisky Company Ardmore 10 Year Old
Port Charlotte 2007 CC:01 Aged 8 Years
Xtra Old Particular Islay Bruichladdich 25 Years Old
Old Particular Caol Ila 20 Years Old
Whisky Castle Glenburgie 18 Year Old
The GlenDronach Aged 18 Years Tawny Port Wood Finish
Old Particular Glen Elgin 21 Years Old
Glenfarclas 17 Years Old
Whisky Krüger Glentauchers 10 Years Old AnCnoc Rùdhan
Gleann Mor Macallan 1985
Cadenhead's Authentic Collection Ledaig 11 Year Old
Tullibardine The Murray
Master of Malt Single Cask Williamson 6 Year Old
Scottish Vatted Malt
Compass Box Spice Tree Extravaganza
That Boutique-y Whisky Company Islay Blended Malt 23 Year Old No. 1
Wemyss Malts Kiln Embers

Scottish Grain
Old Particular Carsebridge 33 Years Old
The Cooper's Choice Garnheath 28 Year Ol
Saar Whisky Invergordon 1972
The Sovereign Port Dundas 28 Years Old
Scottish Blends
Black Bottle
Catto's Aged 25 Years
Grand Macnish Black Edition
Irish Single Malt
Glendalough 24 Year Old Irish Single Malt
Sherry Finish
Irish Blends
Dunville's Three Crowns Peated
Jameson The Cooper's Croze
Bourbon
Elijah Craig Barrel Proof Kentucky Straight
Bourbon batch no. A117
American Microdistilleries
10th Mountain Rye Whiskey Aged 6
Months
Copper Fox Rye Whisky Aged 21 Months
That Boutique-y Whisky Company FEW 2
Year Old
Garrison Brothers Single Barrel Texas
Straight Bourbon Whiskey Aged Three Years
Cadenhead's Garrison Brothers 4 Years Old
Journeyman Buggy Whip Wheat Whiskey
batch 38
A.D. Law Straight Corn Whiskey Bottled in
Bond Aged No Less Than 4 Years
Canadian Blends
Masterson's 10 Year Old Straight Rye
Whiskey
Japanese Single Grain
Nikka Coffey Grain Whisky
German Single Malt
That Boutique-y Whisky Company Slyrs 3
Year Old
St. Kilian Distillers White Dog Cask Strength
Swedish Single Malt
Spirit of Hven Seven Stars No. 5 Alioth
Single Malt
Swiss Single Malt
Langantun 400 Years Kornhaus Single
Malt
Welsh Single Malt
Penderyn Legend
Australian Single Malt
Heartwood The Beagle 4
Heartwood Dare To Be Different
Limeburners Single Malt Whisky Heavy Peat

94 (New Entries Only)
Scottish Single Malt
Ardbeg Kelpie Committee Edition
Whisky Castle Auchroisk 7 Year Old
The First Editions Ben Nevis Aged 20
Years 1996
The Whisky Barrel Burns Malt Bowmore
15 Year Old 2001
Bruichladdich Bere Barley 2009 7 Years
Old
That Boutique-y Whisky Company
Bruichladdich 12 Year Old
The Whisky Agency Bunnahabhain 1989
World of Orchids Bunnahabhain 25 Year
Old
Kirsch Import Caol Ila 1997
Glencadam Aged 13 Years
Cadenhead's Authentic Collection Glen
Grant 31 Year Old

Gordon & MacPhail Rare Vintage Glen
Grant 1949
Old Particular Glen Grant 21 Years Old
Glenmorangie 19 Year Old
Glenmorangie Grand Vintage Malt 1989
Glen Moray Aged 25 Years Port Cask Finish
Alos Sansibar Whisky Glen Moray 1988
Glenturret 30 Year Old
Cadenhead's Authentic Collection
Highland Park 28 Year Old
That Boutique-y Whisky Company Arran
19 Year Old
Xtra Old Particular Speyside Macallan 25
Years Old
Best Dram Ledaig 8 Year Old
The Single Cask Tobermory Aged 22 Years
Tomatin Five Virtues Series Fire Heavily
Charred Oak
Glen Castle Aged 20 Years Sherry Cask
Finish
Scottish Vatted Malt
Master of Malt Single Cask Wardhead 19
Year Old
Whisky-Fässle Blended Malt Whisky
Scottish Grain
The Cooper's Choice Cambus 25 Year Old
Old Particular Cameronbridge 25 Years Old
Old Particular Invergordon 21 Years Old
Scottish Blends
Gleann Mor 40 Year Old Blend
Highland Queen 1561
Lauder's Ruby Cask
Irish Single Malt
The Irishman Single Malt 17 Year Old
Liquid Sun Irish Single Malt XO
Teeling Whiskey Single Cask Port
Tennessee Whiskey
George Dickel Aged 17 Years
American Microdistilleries
Kings County Bottled-in-Bond Straight
Bourbon Whiskey Four Years Old batch no. 3
A.D. Law Four Grain Straight Bourbon
Whiskey Aged No Less Than 3 Years Cask
Strength
Abomination The Sayers of the Law
Heavily Peated Malt
Canadian Single Malt
Glen Saanich Single Malt
Two Brewers Yukon Single Malt Release
05 Innovative
Canadian Blends
Gooderham & Worts Little Trinity Three
Grain Blend
J.P. Wiser's 18 Years Old
Austrian Single Malt
J.H. Rare Selection Original Rye Whisky
Danish Single Malt
Trolden Nimbus The Kolding Single Malt
No 3
English Single Malt
Bimber Single Malt Test Batch Sample
The English Whisky Co. Founders Private
Cellar 2010
Swedish Single Malt
Swedish Whisky Federation Box Distillery
Welsh Single Malt
Penderyn Single Cask Portwood
Australian Single Malt
Heartwood 3of/3
Heartwood Mediocrity Be Damned

Scottish Malts

For those of you deciding to take the plunge and head off into the labyrinthine world of Scotch malt whisky, a piece of advice. And that is, be careful who you take your advice from. Because, too often, I hear that you should leave the Islays until you have tackled the featherlight Speysiders and the bolder, weightier Highlanders. This is just complete, patronising nonsense. The only time that rings true is if you are tasting a number of whiskies in one day. Then leave the smoky ones till last, so the lighter chaps get a fair hearing.

I know many people who didn't like whisky until they got a Talisker from Skye inside them, or a Lagavulin to swamp their tastebuds with oily iodine. The fact is, you can take your map of malt whisky, start at any point and head in whichever direction you feel. There are no hard and fast rules. Certainly with nearly 3,000 tasting notes for Scottish malts here you should have some help in picking where this journey of a lifetime begins.

It is also worth remembering not always to be seduced by age. It is true that many of the highest scores are given to big-aged whiskies. The truth is that the majority of malts, once they have lived beyond 25 years or so, suffer from oak influence rather than benefit. Part of the fun of discovering whiskies is to see how malts from different distilleries perform to age and type of cask. Happy discovering.

Islay

**ORKNEY
ISLANDS**

Highland Park
Scapa

Wolfburn

Pultney

Clynelish
†Brora

Balblair
Dalmore
Teaninich
Glen Ord

Inverness
Glen Albyn †
Glen Mhor †
Millburn †

Glenmorangie
Invergordon

Speyside see page 24
Glenglassaugh

Royal Brackla

Tomatin

The Speyside Distillery
Royal Lochnagar

Banff †
Macduff

Knockdhu

Glendronach
Ardmore

Glenugie

Glen Garioch

Aberdeen

Dalwhinnie

† Glenury Royal
Fettercairn

Blair Athol
Edradour
Aberfeldy

Glencadam
† North Port
† Lochside
Arbikie

Glenesk †

Fort William
Ben Nevis †
Glenlochy †

Strathearn
Glenturret

Dundee

Perth

Tullibardine
Deanston

Daftmill
Eden Mill
Cameronbridge

Kingsbarns

Glengoyne
† Rosebank
† St. Magdelene

Loch Lomond
Dumbarton
† Interleven
† Littlemill
Auchentoshan

Glasgow
*Strathclyde
Port Dundas*
Kinclaith †

Starlaw

Glenkinchie

Edinburgh
North British

Girvan
Ailsa Bay
Ladyburn †

Annandale

Bladnoch

Key

● **Major Town or City**
▲ Single Malt Distillery
▲ (*Italics*) Grain Distillery
✝ Dead Distillery

Speyside

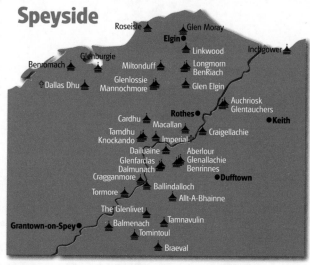

Distilleries by Town

Dufftown	Mortlach	Glenrothes
Glenfiddich	Dufftown	Glenspey
Convalmore	Pittyvaich	**Keith**
Balvenie	**Rothes**	Aultmore
Kininvie	Speyburn	Strathmill
Glendullan	Glen Grant	Glen Keith
	Caperdonich	Strathisla

SINGLE MALTS
ABERFELDY

Highlands (Perthshire), 1898. John Dewar & Sons. Working.

Aberfeldy 12 Year Old db **(81)** n21 t21 f19 b20. A puzzling malt. Aberfeldy makes and matures some of the greatest whisky on this planet, make no mistake. So why this conservative, ultra safe toffee-sultana-fudge offering when their warehouses are crammed with casks which could blow the world away? Pleasant. But so relentlessly dull and disappointing. And 40% abv...? Really...? *40% WB16/031*

Aberfeldy 16 Year Old db **(89.5)** n22.5 Light, leathery and with a citrus freshness; t23.5 succulent, with a ripe melon sweetness meeting an earthier, almost semi-phenolic, substrata; a beautiful match; f21.5 should recede in layers. Yet, despite some lingering sugars, fades with a surprising flatness; b22 finishes far too fast and tamely. But the thrust of the malt is wonderful. *40%*

Aberfeldy 21 Year Old db **(88)** n22 t22.5 f21.5 b22 The kind of malt I wish I could be let loose on...this really could be world class. But... *40% WB16/032*

Aberfeldy Aged 25 Years db **(85)** n24 t21 f19 b21. Just doesn't live up to the nose. When Tommy Dewar wrote, "We have a great regard for old age when it is bottled," as quoted on the label, I'm not sure he had as many as 25 years in mind. *40%.*

Gordon & MacPhail Connoisseurs Choice Aberfeldy 1999 (95) n23.5 t24 f23.5 b24 This is a great distillery: I am always a little disappointed when bottlings of it aren't up to this standard. Gordon and MacPhail set the benchmark. One of the most old-fashioned styles of malt still found in the Highlands and almost perfectly weighted. *46%*

ABERLOUR

Speyside, 1826. Chivas Brothers. Working.

Aberlour 10 Years Old db **(87.5)** n22.5 t22 f21 b22. Remains a lusty fellow though here nothing like as sherry-cask faultless as before, nor displaying its usual honeyed twinkle. *43%*

Aberlour 10 Years Old Sherry Cask Finish db **(85)** n21 t21 f21 b22. Bipolar and bitter-sweet with the firmness of the grain in vivid contrast to the gentle grape. *43%*

Aberlour 12 Years Old Double Cask Matured db (88.5) n22 t22.5 f22 b22. Voluptuous and mouth-watering in some areas, firmer and less expansive in others. Pretty tasty in all of them. 43%

Aberlour 12 Years Old Non Chill-Filtered db (87) n22.5 t22 f21 b21.5. There are many excellent facets to this malt, not least the balance between barley and grape and the politeness of the gristy sugars. But a sulphured butt has crept into this one, taking the edge off the excellence and bringing down the score like a cold front drags down the thermometer. 48%. ncf.

Aberlour 12 Years Old Sherry Cask Matured db (88) n23 t22 f21 b22. Could do with some delicate extra sweetness to take it to the next level. Sophisticated nonetheless. 40%

Aberlour 15 Years Cuvee Marie d'Ecosse db (91) n22 t24 f22 b23. This always was a deceptive lightweight, and it's got lighter still. It is sold primarily in France, and one can assume only that this is God's way of making amends for that pretentious, over-rated, caramel-ridden rubbish called Cognac they've had to endure. 43%

Aberlour 15 Year Old Double Cask Matured db (84) n23 t22 f19 b20. Brilliant nose full of vibrant apples and spiced sultana, but then, after a complex, chewy, malt-enriched kick-off, falls surprisingly flat on its face. 40%

Aberlour 15 Year Old Sherry Finish db (91) n24 exceptionally clever use of oak to add a drier element to the sharper boiled cooking apple. And a whiff of the fermenting vessel, too; t22 the sharp fruit of the nose is magnified here ten times; f23 wave upon wave of malt concentrate; b22 quite unique: freaky, even. Really a whisky to be discovered and ridden. Once you acclimatize, you'll adore it. 43%

Aberlour 18 Years Old db (91) n22 thick milkshake with various fruits and vanilla; t22 immediate fresh juice which curdles beautifully as the vanilla is added; f24 wonderful fruit-chocolate fudge development: long, and guided by a gentle oiliness; b23 another high performance distillery dram-stated bottling. 43%

Aberlour 100 Proof db (91) n23 t23 f22 b23. Stunning, sensational whisky, the most extraordinary Speysider of them all...which it was when I wrote those official notes for the bottling back in '97, I think. Other malts have superseded it now, but on re-tasting I stand by those original notes, though I disassociate myself entirely with the rubbish: "In order to savour Aberlour 100 at its best add 1/3 to 1/2 pure water." 57⅓%

Aberlour A'Bunadh Batch No. 50 db (95.5) n23.5 t24.5 f24 b23.5 It seems a long time ago now. But I can remember sitting with the good people of Aberlour when they showed me what they had planned for batch 1 of a new brand called a'bunadh. I was thrilled that they were going for it with a no-holds barred malt...but nervous they were using sherry butts. That was some time ago...and now they have reached 50 not out. Miraculously, they have managed, usually, to avoid the worst excesses of present day sherry butts. And they have done so again here to bring their half century up in style. Ladies and gentlemen of Aberlour: I raise a glass to you in celebration. 59.6% WB16/027

Aberlour A'Bunadh Batch No. 53 db (95) n23 t24 f24 b24 A truly beautiful whisky. But, oh! had only Batch 54 been this sulphur free we would have entered a new experience of whisky perfection. 59.7%

Aberlour A'Bunadh Batch No. 54 db (96) n23.5 t25 f23 b24.5 Had the nose and finish been quite up there with the delivery, we would have had a record score. Just a slight sulphur trace, but probably enough to dash the World Whisky of the Year (indeed, this is the closest to a Yamazaki 17 I have yet unearthed) this might have otherwise so fully deserved. For just the delivery alone – and for the ensuing two minutes with its perfect weight, oils, distribution of flavours and pace of evolvement – no whisky will be better this year, or probably next. It had even crossed my mind to give it 25.5...! A privilege to experience... 60.7%

◈ **Aberlour A'Bunadh Batch No. 57** Spanish Oloroso sherry butts db (81) n20.5 t22.5 f18 b20 Read my notes to batch 47, and we have a similar malt, though here there is not quite so much sparkle on delivery and there may be two rather than one butt at fault. 60.7%. ncf.

Distilleries Collection Aberlour Aged 19 Years 1994 bott 2014 (89.5) n22.5 t22 f22.5 b22.5 A steady, confident bottling with massive accent on the honey. 56.8%. Bottled for Scotch Malt Sales Ltd.

Hunter Laing's Old & Rare Aberlour Aged 25 Years refill hogshead, cask no. 15133, dist Oct 90, bott Mar 16 (94.5) n24 t23.5 b23.5 A seriously classy dram from the first magnificent sniff onwards. 50.3%. nc ncf sc. 150 bottles.

◈ **MacAlabur Aberlour 10 Years Old** bourbon barrel, cask no. 110, dist 27 Apr 06, recasked 2010, bott 10 Oct 16 (86.5) n21.5 t22.5 f20.5 b22 By no means your standard, common or garden Aberlour. This has the thin body of an Aberlour of the 1960s – a real journey back through time. A tad on the fiery side but the Demerara sugars are truly lovely, as is the vanilla which punctuates throughout. Bitters out awkwardly towards the finish. *56.1%. nc ncf sc. 221 bottles.*

Old Particular Speyside Aberlour 20 Years Old refill hogshead, cask no. 10779, dist Feb 95, bott Feb 15 (86.5) n21.5 t22 f21.5 b21.5. A steady old dram concentrating on the high propane barley which, early on, is juicy, thick and intense. The oak element is a touch tangy. *51.5%. nc ncf sc. 300 bottles.*

Old Particular Speyside Aberlour 21 Years Old refill hogshead, dist Feb 95, bott Feb 16 (94.5) n23.5 t23.5; f23.5 b24 Well, an Aberlour with a dab of smoke. Some smoked malt accidentally got into the mix? Or matured in an old Laphroaig or Ardbeg cask? Who knows? Really doesn't matter as the result is truly wonderful. *51.5%. nc ncf sc. 278 bottles.*

Simon Brown Aberlour 1991 bourbon casks, dist Sept 91, bott Jun 05 (95) n24 t23.5 f23.5 b24 A stunner of a bottling which rewards time spent with it handsomely. *46%. nc ncf.*

That Boutique-y Whisky Company Aberlour 23 Year Old batch 4 (92) n22 t23.5 f23 b23.5 Not a malt interested much in complexity. But the malt and muscovado show it puts on is pretty dazzling! *51%. 432 bottles.*

◈ **The Whisky Chamber Aberlour 10 Year Old** bourbon cask, dist 2006 (94.5) n23 outwardly a lazy aroma, until you start homing in on the subtleties of the fragile marzipan, dessicated coconut and rogue spice notes. At once warming, astringent...and compelling...; t24 the aggression hinted at on the nose is confirmed on the blistering delivery. But there is a gorgeous citrus lilt to the barley as it gristilly fights back; f23.5 so splendidly nutty, complete with oils! b24 think of a boxer painting in finest detail a primrose...while he is still wearing his gloves. *54.1%.*

Xtra Old Particular Speyside Aberlour 25 Years Old sherry butt, dist Nov 90, bott Nov 15 (90) n24 t24 f20 b22 A near Puss Mitchell Special. The then distillery manager at Aberlour set great store by the quality of his sherry-matured stock. And was deeply offended – to the point of near anger – if he was delivered one of the new breed of sulphur-treated butts which had just begun creeping into the system and which he so roundly detested. As an affront to all he was trying to achieve, he would reject them on sight and send them back to whence they came. Or, mischievously, tell the driver to take them to nearby Macallan, where they were welcome to them... This one does have a trace of sulphur that can be detected on the finish, but is initially so well hidden it would have evaded even the sensitive and censorial nose of old Puss. *51.7%. nc ncf sc. 289 bottles.*

ABHAINN DEARG
Highlands (Outer Hebrides), 2008. Marko Tayburn. Working.

Abhainn Dearg New Make db (92.5) n23 t23 f23.5 b23. Exceptionally well made with no feints and no waste, either. Oddly salty – possibly the saltiest new make I have encountered, and can think of no reason why it should be – with excellent weight as some extra copper from the new still takes hold. Given a good cask, no reason this impressive new born son of the Outer Hebrides won't go on to become something significant. *67%*

AILSA BAY
Lowland, 2007. William Grant & Sons. Working.

Ailsa Bay db (92.5) n23.5 t23.5 f22.5 b23 I remember years back being told they wanted to make an occasional peaty malt at this new distillery different in style to Islay's. They have been only marginally successful: only the finish gives the game away. But they have certainly matched the island when it comes to the average high quality. A resounding success of a first effort, though I'd like to see the finish offer a little more than it currently does. Early days, though. *48.9%.*

ALLT-Á-BHAINNE
Speyside, 1975. Chivas Brothers. Working.

Big Market Sonderabfüllung Nr. 14 Allt-a-Bhainne 1995 bott 2015 (88) n22 t22 f22 b22 Puts me in mind of an unsugared gooseberry tart. *54.8%. 50th Anniversary bottling.*

◈ **The Cooper's Choice Allt-Á-Bhainne 22 Year Old** port finish, dist 1993 (92.5) n23 clean as a nut: fruity and nutty as a fruitcake; as spicy as a What the Butler Saw peepshow...; t23 soft, salivating, simplistic but sensuous; f23.5 ah, some complexity at last. The fruit dries towards a dried date and spices roll in later than expected. Some amazing chocolate and cherry cake moments very late on; b23 takes some time to show its true credentials. But stick with it because...wow...!!! *46%. nc ncf sc. The Vintage Malt Whisky Co.*

The First Editions Allt-A-Bhainne Aged 22 Years 1993 refill hogshead, cask no. 12123, bott 2015 **(89.5)** n22.5 t22.5 f22 b22.5 A good all-rounder flexing its malt and oak muscles in equal measure. *51.4%. nc ncf sc. 177 bottles.*

Hepburn's Choice Allt-A-Bhainne 7 Years Old refill hogshead, dist 2008, bott 2016 **(80)** n19 t21 f20 b20. A boiled sugar candy sweetness to this. But wrapped in an unkind cask. *46%. nc ncf sc. 300 bottles.*

⬧ Hepburn's Choice Allt-A-Bhainne 7 Years Old sherry butt, dist 2008, bott 2016 **(85)** n21.5 t21 f21 b21.5 A slightly dull cove with the youth of the malt entirely and, surprisingly, blunted by a gentle cream sherry theme. Some late spices do no harm at all. *46%. nc ncf sc. 615 bottles.*

⬧ Liquid Sun Allt-A-Bhainne 22 Years Old dist 1993 **(92.5)** n23.5 walnut cake with light acacia honey topping; some slight peppering; t23 It is the acacia honey which pops up first, again with that playful pepper. But a now mixed nut late middle really is delightful; f22.5 walnuts...; b23.5 a malt to go nuts about. *50.2%.*

⬧ Old Malt Cask Allt-A-Bhainne Aged 18 Years refill hogshead, cask no. 10198, dist Nov 95, bott Oct 14 **(91)** n22.5 freshly baked lemon drizzle cake; t23 the concentrated barley sugar still boasts a degree of grist. Light oils do nothing to obscure the prevailing citrus; f22.5 what a beautifully level barley fade; the vanillas are friendly and discreet, the spices genteel; b23 how charming is that...??? *50%. nc ncf sc. 138 bottles.*

Old Particular Speyside Allt-A-Bhainne 22 Years Old refill hogshead, dist Mar 93, bott Dec 15 **(87)** n21 t23 f22 b21. Clean, well made and refreshing, the oak has kept a distance, giving this a much younger, rather immature feel. But if you like concentrated, juicy barley this might just be your bag. *51.5%. nc ncf sc. 295 bottles.*

ARDBEG
Islay, 1815. Glenmorangie Plc. Working.

Ardbeg 10 Years Old db **(97)** n24 more complex, citrus-led and sophisticated than recent bottlings, though the peat is no less but now simply displayed in an even greater elegance; a beautiful sea salt strain to this; t24 gentle oils carry on them a lemon-lime edge, sweetened by barley and a weak solution of golden syrup; the peat is omnipotent, turning up in every crevice and wave, yet never one once overstepping its boundary; f24 stunningly clean, the oak offers not a bitter trace but rather a vanilla and butterscotch edge to the barley. Again the smoke wafts around in a manner unique in the world of whisky when it comes to sheer élan and adroitness; b25 like when you usually come across something that goes down so beautifully and with such a nimble touch and disarming allure, just close your eyes and enjoy... *46%*

Ardbeg 10 bottling mark L10 152 db **(95)** n24.5 t23.5 f23.5 b23.5 A bigger than normal version, but still wonderfully delicate. Fabulous and faultless. *46%. Canadian market bottling in English and French dual language label.*

Ardbeg 17 Years Old earlier bottlings db **(92)** n23 t22 f23 b24. OK, I admit I had a big hand in this, creating it with the help of Glenmorangie Plc's John Smith. It was designed to take the weight off the better vintages of Ardbeg whilst ensuring a constant supply around the world. Certainly one of the more subtle expressions you are likely to find, though criticised by some for not being peaty enough. As the whisky's creator, all I can say is they are missing the point. *40%*

Ardbeg 17 Years Old later bottlings db **(90)** n22 t23 f22 b23. The peat has all but vanished and cannot really be compared to the original 17-year-old: it's a bit like tasting a Macallan without the sherry: fascinating to see the naked body underneath, and certainly more of a turn on. Peat or no peat, great whisky by any standards. *40%*

Ardbeg 21 Years Old db **(96.5)** n24 it is as though there are three levels of smokiness working in tandem: the layering is ridiculously well-structured. The deepest notes are earthy, rich with even a hint of unpicked tomato; the middle layer is flightier and spiced, seemingly in league with the gristier notes. And a third layer of phenols are sooty and wispy, like thin clouds scudding across on a windy day...amazing....; t24 the delivery by contrast is only two-toned. The malt, sans smoke, is gristy, lemon tinged and juices up with intense barley as the sugars strike home. But it is kept in check by the phenols which hit first with a combined weight, but then scatters about the palate until it reforms later on in liquorice and chocolate vogue; f24 much more ethereal now, though we have moved more towards crystalline sugars only too willing to melt and discreet spices which occasionally nip. To say the finish is long is a little bit of an understatement...; b24.5 tap into Ardbeg with great care, like someone has done here, and there is no describing what beauty can be unleashed. For much of the time, the smoke performs in brilliant fashion somewhere between the ethereal and profound. *46%*

◇ **Ardbeg 23 Year Old** db (93) n22.5 takes time for the strongarm oak to get anything less than too firm a grip of proceedings: if there is smoke in there, it has taken cover...; vague citrus pops its head up for a quick look – then quickly down again as it hides with the phenols...; t24 yep, full on tannin....at first. The fragile citrus and and more ample barley begins the job of restoring balance, which it does with typical Ardbegian elegance. There is a delicate smokiness which can be found lightly brushed over the milky, vaguely minty mocha which has gathered up enough dark sugars to form the nucleus of the resistance movement; just enough gristy barley lurks about to ensure a degree of defiant salivation, too; f23 those big tannins return to mount a guard, but some lovely chocolate malt and spice manage to get through without being spotted...; b23.5 a malt forever treading on eggshells, trying not to disturb the tannins. As a dram, makes a nervous wreck of you, as you spend the entire time waiting for the shallow truce to be broken and the oak to declare war and come pouring in. Thankfully, it never quite happens. As all whiskies, not be taken with water. But, in this instance, a tranquiliser might not go amiss... 46.3%.

Ardbeg 1977 db (96) n25 t24 f23 b24. When working through the Ardbeg stocks, I earmarked '77 a special vintage, the sweetest of them all. So it has proved. Only the '74 absorbed that extra oak that gave better all-round complexity. Either way, the quality of the distillate is beyond measure: simply one of the greatest experiences – whisky or otherwise – of your life. 46%

Ardbeg 1978 db (91) n23 t24 f22 b22. An Ardbeg on the edge of losing it because of encroaching oak, hence the decision made by John Smith and I to bottle this vintage early alongside the 17-year-old. Nearly ten years on, still looks a pretty decent bottling, though slightly under strength! 43%

◇ **Ardbeg An Oa** db (95.5) n24 Ardbeg at its driest and most sooty: a real acidic bite to the huge phenol...; t24 sublimely textured with an immediate roll call of sugars, which had been absent on the nose. Being called "Oa", a dramatic part of Islay with the sheerest of cliffs falling vertically into the sea, you might expect a bit of a cliff hanger here. But instead the transformation from the delicate, molassed sugars into a softer vanilla is carried out on in the least demanding way and even the smoke makes no attempt to recreate the fog I have been caught in there myself. It is effortless and easy, like gear changes on an automatic car. It is also beautifully delicious...; f23.5 more softly texture caramel, but with punchier spices; b24 I'd never say "whoa" if someone poured me an Oa... 46%.

Ardbeg Aurivedes American oak casks with specially toasted cask lids. db (91.5) n22 t22.5 f24 b23 I have spoken to nobody at Ardbeg about this one but from the slight bourbon character of the nose and the heavy vanilla, this version appears to be about the casks, possibly the char of the barrels. Fascinating, enjoyable...but whatever this is, the usual complexity of the peat feels compromised in the same way a wine cask might. Except here I detect no telling fruit. A real curiosity, whatever it is... 49.9%. Moet Hennessy.

Ardbeg Blasda db (90.5) n23.5 t22.5 f22 b22.5 A beautiful, if slightly underpowered malt, which shows Ardbeg's naked self to glowing effect. Overshadowed by some degree in its class by the SMWS bottling, but still something to genuinely make the heart flutter. 40%

Ardbeg Corryvreckan db (96.5) n23 t24.5 f24 b25 As famous writers – including the occasional genius film director (stand up wherever you are my heroes Powell and Pressburger) – appear to be attracted to Corryvreckan, the third most violent whirlpool found in the world and just off Islay, to boot, - I selected this as my 1,500th whisky tasted for the historic Jim Murray Whisky Bible 2009. I'm so glad I did because many have told me they thought Blasda ahead of this. To me, it's not even a contest. Currently I have only a sample. Soon I shall have a bottle. I doubt if even the feared whirlpool is this deep and perplexing. 57.1%. 5000 bottles.

Ardbeg Dark Cove db (86) n22.5 t22.5 f19.5 b21.5. For whatever reason, this is a much duller version than the Committee Edition. And strength alone can't explain it, or solely the loss of the essential oils from reduction. There is a slight nagging to this one so perhaps any weakness to the sherry butts has been accentuated by the reduction of oil, if it has been bottled from the same vatting – which I doubt. Otherwise, the tasting notes are along the lines of below, except with just a little less accent on the sugars. 46.5%

Ardbeg Dark Cove Committee Edition db (90.5) n23.5 oh, sherry! And some! Gives the wrong signal about the depth of the peat involvement, as the grape is sticky enough to hide some of the phenols, though not the more sooty types. Liquorice and dates at play. Sticky, indeed...; t23 an immediate blast of dark molassed sugars point towards Melton Hunt Cake at first, but the smoke arrives in droves to drive you off that particular scent. Spices begin to compensate; chewy until your jaw hurts...; f21.5 just leans towards a slight burnt bitterness and a cloying of the fruit; b22.5 big sherry and bigger peat always struggle somewhere along the line. This one does pretty well until we reach the finale when it unravels slightly. But sulphur-free. And challenging. 55%

Ardbeg Day Bottling db **(97)** n24.5 t24.5 f23.5 b24.5 I left this to be one of the last whiskies I tasted this year. I had an inkling that they might come up with something a little special, especially with the comparative disappointment of the fundamentally flawed Galileo. On first sweep I thought it was pretty ordinary. but I know this distillery a little too well. So I left the glass for some 20 minutes to breathe and compose itself and returned. To find a potential world whisky of the year... 56.8%. *Available at distillery and Ardbeg embassies.*

Ardbeg Guaranteed 30 Years Old db **(91)** n24 t23 f21 b23. An unsual beast, one of the last ever bottled by Allied. The charm and complexity early on is enormous, but the fade rate is surprising. That said, still a dram of considerable magnificence. 40%

◇ **Ardbeg Kelpie** db **(95)** n24 that drier style of peat, a kind of mix of chalk and soot, though here the shyest of citrus tones speak out, barely above a whisper, for balance. Complex and demanding of time and patience for maximum results...; t23.5 soft icing sugars melt in the mouth as the grist makes for the juiciest of Ardbeg deliveries: the smoke is on the lighter side though spices build up impressively through the middle as a fruit-toffee notes embeds on the palate; f23.5 remains steadfastly on that sweet smoked caramel path...; b24 beautifully crafted and cleverly – and intriguingly - structured. An understated Ardbeg for true Ardbeg lovers... 46%.

◇ **Ardbeg Kelpie Committee Edition** db **(94)** n24 as Kelpie (above) but extra oils disperse a slightly broader span of sugars...; t24 as above (again!). Except, once more a different, richer texture does nothing to detract from the juiciness, but certainly makes the toffee a little more chewy; f22.5 different from the 46% version in that here some bitterness is extracted from the oak to lay alongside the big caramels; b23.5 as Burns might have said: I'se no speer nae to anither helpie o' Kelpie... 51.7%.

Ardbeg Mor db **(95)** n24 t24 f23 b24 Quite simply... more the merrier... 57.5%

Ardbeg Perpetuum db **(94.5)** n23.5 t23.5 f23.5 b24 what a beautifully structured malt. There is no escaping the youth of some of the phrases. But you can't help enjoying what it says. 47.4%. ncf.

Ardbeg Provenance 1974 bott 1999 db **(96)** n24 t25 f23 b24. This is an exercise in subtlety and charisma, the beauty and the beast drawn into one. Until I came across the 25-year-old OMC verson during a thunderstorm in Denmark, this was arguably the finest whisky I had ever tasted: I opened this and drank from it to see in the year 2000. When I went through the Ardbeg warehouse stocks in 1997 I earmarked the '74 and '77 vintages as something special. This bottling has done me proud. 55.6%

Ardbeg Renaissance db **(92)** n22.5 t22.5 f23.5 b23.5. How fitting that the 1,200th (and almost last) new-to-market whisky I sampled for the 2009 Bible was Renaissance... because that's what I need after tasting that lot...!! This is an Ardbeg that comes on strong, is not afraid to wield a few hefty blows and yet, paradoxically, the heavier it gets the more delicate, sophisticated and better-balanced it becomes. Enigmatically Ardbegian. 55.9%

Ardbeg Uigeadail db **(89)** n25 t22 f20 b22. A curious Ardbeg with a nose to die for. Some tinkering - please guys, as the re-taste is not better - regarding the finish may lift this to being a true classic 54.1%

Cadenhead's Authentic Collection Ardbeg 21 Year Old bourbon hogshead, dist 1993 **(95)** n24 t24 f23 b24 simply Ardbeg. 53.2%. sc.

That Boutique-y Whisky Company Ardbeg 12 Year Old batch 7 **(92.5)** n23 t23 f23 b23.5 essential, effortless Ardbeg. 52%. 203 bottles.

ARDMORE

Speyside, 1899. Beam Inc. Working.

Ardmore 12 Year Old Port Wood Finish db **(90)** n21.5 t23.5 f22 b23 not sure how many years it took me to get the owners of this great distillery to get the malt out there in to the public domain (it certainly runs to well into double figures), but I will never forget the day when the executive at the time met up with me and told me they had listened to my arguments and were going for it. Since then the personnel have changed, more the pity. Because I genuinely understand this distillery better than most and just wish they'd come to me before unleashing a bottling such as this. Yes, this is in part a beautiful whisky. But forget all this hand-crafted stuff on the label: this is a blending whisky criminally overlooked for a century. Here we have a lovely fruit-rich malt, but one which has compromised on the very essence of the complexity which sets this distillery apart. Lovely whisky I am delighted to say...but, dammit, by playing to its unique nuances it could have been so much better...I mean absolutely sensational...! 46%. ncf.

Ardmore 25 Years Old db (89.5) n21 t23.5 f22.5 b22.5 A 25-y-o box of chocolates: coffee creams, fudge, orange cream...they are all in there. The nose maybe ordinary: what follows is anything but. 51.4%. ncf.

Ardmore 30 Years Old Cask Strength db (94) n23.5 t23.5 f23 b24 I remember when the present owners of Ardmore launched their first ever distillery bottling. Over a lunch with the hierarchy there I told them, with a passion, to ease off with the caramel so the world can see just how complex this whisky can be. This brilliant, technically faultless, bottling is far more eloquent and persuasive than I was that or any other day... 53.7%. nc ncf. 1428 bottles.

Ardmore 1996 db (87) n22 t22 f21 b22. Very curious Ardmore, showing little of its usual dexterity. Perhaps slightly more heavily peated than the norm, but there is also much more intense heavy caramel extracted from the wood. Soft, very pleasant and easy drinking it is almost obsequious. 43%.

Ardmore Fully Peated Quarter Casks db (89) n21 t23 f23 b22. This is an astonishingly brave attempt by the new owners of Ardmore who, joy of all joys, are committed to putting this distillery in the public domain. Anyone with a 2004 copy of the Whisky Bible will see that my prayers have at last been answered. However, this bottling is for Duty Free and, due to the enormous learning curve associated with this technique, a work in progress. They have used the Quarter Cask process which has been such a spectacular success at its sister distillery Laphroaig. Here I think they have had the odd slight teething problem. Firstly, Ardmore has rarely been filled in ex-bourbon and that oak type is having an effect on the balance and smoke weight; also they have unwisely added caramel, which has flattened things further. I don't expect the caramel to be in later bottlings and, likewise, I think the bourbon edge might be purposely blunted a little. But for a first attempt this is seriously big whisky that shows enormous promise. When they get this right, it could – and should – be a superstar. Now I await the more traditional vintage bottlings... 46%. ncf.

Ardmore Legacy db (71.5) n17 t19 f17.5 b18. Must win an award as the most disappointing whisky of the year. Not least because this is one of the world's great distilleries. The nose is dirty and off-key. After a too brief fight back on delivery, it soon descends on the palate to the same mess found on the nose. As this distillery's first and oldest advocate, frankly, for me, a massive shock and disappointment. 40%

Ardmore Traditional Cask db (88.5) n21.5 t22 f23 b22. Not quite what I expected. "Jim. Any ideas on improving the flavour profile?" asked the nice man from Ardmore distillery when they were originally launching the thing. "Yes. Cut out the caramel." "Ah, right..." So what do I find when the next bottling comes along? More caramel. It's good to have influence... Actually, I can't quite tell if this is a result of natural caramelization from the quarter casking or just an extra dollop of the stuff in the bottling hall. The result is pretty similar: some of the finer complexity is lost. My guess, due to an extra fraction of sweetness and spice, is that it is the former. All that said, the overall experience remains quite beautiful. And this remains one of my top ten distilleries in the world. 46%. ncf.

Acla Selection Ardmore 14 Years Old hogshead, dist 2000, bott 2014 (94) n23.5 t23.5 f23 b24 Nutshells the distillery quite beautifully. And the best blends always have a little bite: here you can see exactly why this malt is a blender's dream. 51.6%. nc ncf.

◈ **Best Dram Ardmore 8 Year Old** ex-Laphroaig barrel, dist 2008, bott 2016 (88.5) n21.5 bruising smoke: usually the phenols are dovetailing with the oak, with the tannins having control of the steering wheel Not this time as the peat surges on. Slightly ungainly, but; t22.5 hold tight chaps and chapesses! This is one thumping delivery, devoid of charm of dexterity and full of slightly metallic phenols. Slowly some semblance of sanity can be detected with a sublime oil-fuelled arrival of molasses and butterscotch. A slight saltiness adds a degree of piquancy and balance before the heftier cocoa tones begin to weigh in; f22.5 smoked spiced cocoa; b22 what a fascinating if random dram. Ardmore is that peaty malt which makes a little phenol go a long way. Here, just by altering the type of cask in favour of smoke, you can see just how fragile the ecosystem of this malt really is. 59.2%.

C & S Dram Collection Ardmore Aged 4 Years hogshead, cask no. 804208, dist 28 Jun 11, bott 18 Jan 16 (85.5) n22 t21.5 f21 b21. Wow, this is young! Has something of the pre-pubescent Bowmore about it, as there appears to be an upped peating level. This sugar-laden fledgling whisky still hasn't found its legs as the smoke and oak clash. But you have to be a right miserable git not to enjoy the fun on offer! 60.8%. sc.

◈ **C & S Dram Collection Ardmore 8 Years Old** bourbon barrel, cask no. 702425, dist 19 Jun 08, bott 20 Feb 17 (89) n22 not sure if this a well-smoked version, or if the oak influence is so meagre that the phenols appear heftier than they actually are; t22.5 attractive, creamy grist up to the nines in barley sugar. The phenols offer both a gentle cloud of smoke and initially busy spices which eventually settle; quite nutty, too; f22 lightly smoked praline; b22.5 a fragile, well-used cask adds only a limited degree of depth. *58.3%. sc. 261 bottles.*

⬧ **The Cooper's Choice Ardmore 15 Year Old** dist 2001, bott 2016 (88.5) n22.5 much more prominent smoke than is the norm for an Ardmore, but there is little resistance from the vague oak; t22 sweet and gristy, the sugars all appear to spring from the barley well; f22 trace vanilla and a little banana while trace chocolate accompanies the smoke; b22 this is 15 years going on 15 months by the look of it. A third fill bourbon barrel at work which fully maximises the smoky value of the malt. *51.5%. ncf ncf sc. The Vintage Malt Whisky Co.*

⬧ **The First Editions Ardmore Aged 20 Years 1996** refill hogshead, cask no. 12930, bott 2016 (96.5) n24 the perfect intertwangling of the thin clove and phenols is a thing of rare sophistication and beauty...; t24 brilliant glint and sparkle to the muscovado sugars as they hit the plate. The smoke builds slowly to gain quiet control; f24 just look at those spices...! b24.5 .It may be 20 years old but there is not a single blemish from ageing, nor a discordant note to be heard. A thing of genuine beauty. *50.1%. nc ncf sc. 124 bottles.*

The Golden Cask Ardmore 14 Years Old cask no. CM 217, dist 2000, bott 2015 (91) n23 t22.5 f22.5 b23 a fierce, yet brutally and sometimes deliciously honest, account of the distillery in its more fiery mode. No frills, but plenty of thrills. *57.3%. sc. 178 bottles.*

Gordon & MacPhail Distillery Label Ardmore 1998 (92.5) n22.5 t23 f23 b24 from one of its lesser peating days. But the overall weight and structure is superb! *43%*

⬧ **Gordon & MacPhail Cask Strength Ardmore 2002** bott 27 Oct 16 (96.5) n24 an essay in complexity: a gentle smoky bacon meets Arbroath Smokies, but all lightened by a beautiful marmalade on toast sub plot and rolling spices which threaten but never attack; the tannins also grow, and as they do so the marmalade note increases; t24 citrus appears to have sweetened up slightly as the grist tumbles around, sugary and increasingly smoky. The weight becomes heavier by the moment as more flavour appear to be drawn into the growing oils; f24 long, with the most pathetic spice and the creamiest smoked mocha on whisky record; b24.5 Ardmore revelling in all its understated genius. *57.5%.*

⬧ **Hidden Spirits Ardmore 6 Year Old** cask no. AM016, dist 2010, bott 2016 (85.5) n21.5 t22 f21 b21 A youngster very much at an awkward age. The peat, sugars and early tannin tang all seems to be out of sync. Brusque. *50%. sc*

Kingsbury Gold Ardmore 6 Year Old 2008 hogshead, cask no. 800006 (95.5) n24 t23.5 f24 b24 young, adorable and fabulous example of why this is one of the great blending malts in the world at this age. Truly faultless. *59.5%. sc. 187 bottles.*

⬧ **Old Malt Cask Ardmore Aged 20 Years** refill hogshead, cask no. 12929, dist Oct 96, bott Nov 16 (96) n24 orange blossom honey on a very smoky field; a very light hint of clove confirms the antiquity; t24 a slightly drier delivery than its twin First Editions cask accentuating the vanilla rather than the smoke; barley sugar peaks here and there; f24 the gentlest of finishes: this is relatively spice free, allowing any warming aspects to be met by those lurking sugars. The smoke, though vital, appears little more than background noise; b24 if you really want to learn something about great whisky, worth investing in First editions cask 12930 and this bottling...and then spending a good week comparing the subtle differences of the two. It will be one of the best weeks of your life... *50%. nc ncf sc. 148 bottles.*

⬧ **Old Particular Ardmore 16 Years Old** refill barrel, cask no. 11168, dist May 00, bott Jun 16 (95.5) n24 sublimely complex: the smoke goes through all kinds of hoops as it links up with a gorgeously adroit citrus thread while at the same time dovetailing with subtle licorice...; t24 deft and delicate on delivery, the molassed sugars melt slowly, leaving the smoke room to make a significant statement...; f23.5 the complexity lessens little on the long fade. Some lovely mocha is in delightful accord with the peat...; b24 a blinding example of the distillery at this healthy age: truly magnificent malt. *44.5%. nc ncf sc. 283 bottles.*

⬧ **Provenance Ardmore Aged 8 Years** refill barrel, cask no. 11329, dist Jul 08, bott Aug 16 (88.5) n22 youthfully green, firm and making no bones about its phenolic countenance; t22.5 salivating, with all the emphasis on a metallic smokiness. The oak is nowhere to be seen...; f22 dry and sooty; b22 at these younger ages the smoke is more happily and emphatically pronounced. *46%. nc ncf sc. 301 bottles.*

⬧ **Provenance Ardmore Aged 8 Years** refill barrel, cask no. 11536, dist Jul 08, bott Nov 16 (89.5) n22.5 just enough oak to ensure a bit of complexity enters the smoky fray; t22 the sugars are hiding as the drier phenols and vanillas make for a delicious battle; f22.5 still dry with a little smoked cocoa powder in evidence; b22.5 a better balanced offering than the starker cask 11329. *46%. nc ncf sc. 317 bottles.*

⬧ **Scotch Malt Whisky Society Cask 66.101 9 Year Old** refill ex-bourbon barrel, dist 15 May 07 (89.5) n22.5 a hint of a hint of smoke: vaguely minty – vaguely everything...; t22.5

salivating delivery showing the grist is still active and the sugars lively. The smoke offers a touch more oomph, but not a lot; **f22** charming though non-spectacular butterscotch with a little peat spice on the sign off; **b22.5** at the low end of Ardmore's phenol spectrum. 60.1%.

Teacher's Highland Single Malt quarter cask finish db **(89)** n22.5 t23 f21.5 b22. This is Ardmore at its very peatiest. And had not the colouring levels been heavily tweaked to meet the flawed perceptions of what some markets believe makes a good whisky, this malt would have been better still. As it is: superb. With the potential of achieving greatness if only they have the confidence and courage... 40%. India/Far East Travel Retail exclusive.

⬦ **That Boutique-y Whisky Company Ardmore 10 Year Old** batch 1 **(94.5)** n23.5 crisp and youthful, with the phenols getting a good cleansing from the citrus; lovely prickly spice; **t24** oily delivery, then a big gristy surge first flexing the barley sugar then the rampant smoke; **f23.5** long with a spice glow bursting through the billowing smoke; **b23.5** a beautiful age for Ardmore to show off its smoky dexterity. And this bottling shows the distillery at the higher end of its phenol spectrum. 55.5%. 350 bottles.

The Whisky Agency Acla Selection Ardlair Aged 5 Years sherry cask, dist 2009, bott 2015 **(72)** n17 t19 f17 b19. Memo to the guys at Ardlair. You have one of the great distilleries of the world here: great selection, so well done – especially at an age it rarely appears in the market place. But always (and I mean, like, 100% of the time) go for ex-bourbon. Don't fuck about with sulphur-screwed sherry. Whatever the guys flogging you the cask say. Capiche? 47.6%. nc ncf. 391 bottles.

⬦ **Whisky Krüger Ardmore 2010 6 Years Old** bott 2016 **(88.5)** n22 a raw nose with the phenols showing unusual aggression. Sugary porridge backdrop; **t21.5** again, the bite and indent on the palate has a slight attitude which means the phenols and fudge take a while to link happily; **f23** much more like Ardmore as we know and love it as the smoke finds its natural place amid the spices and light vanillas **b22** not a bad cask. But one that has a minor problem in maximising and brodcasting its positive points. 60.8%.

AUCHENTOSHAN

Lowlands, 1800. Morrison Bowmore. Working.

Auchentoshan 10 Years Old db **(81)** n22 t21 f19 b19. Much better, maltier, cleaner nose than before. But after the initial barley surge on the palate it shows a much thinner character. 40%

Auchentoshan 12 Years Old db **(91.5)** n22.5 sexy fruit element – citrus and apples in particular – perfectly lightens the rich, oily barley; **t23.5** oily and buttery; intense barley carrying delicate marzipan and vanilla; **f22.5** simplistic, but the oils keep matters lush and the delicate sugars do the rest; **b23** a delicious malt very much happier with itself than it has been for a while. 40%

Auchentoshan 14 Years Old Cooper's Reserve db **(83.5)** n20 t21.5 f21 b21. Malty, a little nutty and juicy in part. 46%. ncf.

Auchentoshan 18 Years Old db **(78)** n21 t21.5 f17 b19. Although matured for 18 years in ex-bourbon casks, as according to the label, this is a surprisingly tight and closed malt in far too many respects. Some heart-warming sugars early on, but the finish is bitter and severely limited in scope. 43%

Auchentoshan 21 Years Old db **(93)** n23.5 a sprig of mint buried in barely warmed peat, all with an undercoat of the most delicate honeys; **t23** velvety and waif-like, the barley-honey theme is played out in hushed tones and unspoiled elegance; **f23** the smoke deftly returns as the vanillas and citrus slowly rise but the gentle honey-barley plays to the end, despite the shy introduction of cocoa; **b23.5** one of the finest Lowland distillery bottlings of our time. A near faultless masterpiece of astonishing complexity to be cherished and discussed with deserved reverence. So delicate, you fear that sniffing too hard will break the poor thing...! 43%.

Auchentoshan 1975 db **(88)** n22.5 t22.5 f21 b22 Goes heavy on the natural caramels. Does not even remotely show its enormous age for this distillery. I detest the word "smooth". But for those who prefer that kind of malt...well, your dreams have come true...; 45.6%

Auchentoshan 1979 db **(94)** n23.5 t24 f23 b23.5 It's amazing what a near faultless sherry butt can do. 50.1%

Auchentoshan 1988 25 Year Old Wine Cask Finish db **(94.5)** n23 t24 f23.5 b24 The thing about a triple distilled malt is that a confident influence can have a very loud say. And the clean wine here certainly calls the shots, though some pretty high quality oak ensures the speech is balanced. A delightful malt which makes a very respectful nod to the combined skills of distiller, wood manager and blender. 47%

Auchentoshan 1998 Sherry Cask Matured fino sherry cask db **(81.5)** n21 t22 f18.5 b20. A genuine shame. Before these casks were treated in Jerez, I imagine they were spectacular.

Even with the obvious faults apparent, the nuttiness is profound and milks every last atom of the oils at work to maximum effect. The sugars, also, are delicate and gorgeously weighted. There is still much which is excellent to concentrate on here. *54.6%. ncf. 6000 bottles.*

Auchentoshan American Oak db **(85.5) n21.5 t22 f20.5 b21.5.** Very curious: reminds me very much of Penderyn Welsh whisky before it hits the Madeira casks. Quite creamy with some toasted honeycomb making a brief cameo appearance. *40%*

Auchentoshan Blood Oak French red wine & American bourbon casks db **(76.5) n20.5 t19 f18 b19.** That's funny: always thought blood tasted a little sweet. This is unremittingly bitter. *48%. ncf.*

Auchentoshan Classic db **(80) n19 t20 f21 b20.** Classic what exactly...? Some really decent barley, but goes little further. *40%*

Auchentoshan Noble Oak Aged 24 Years Oloroso sherry casks & American bourbon hogsheads db **(87.5) n22 t23 f21 b21.5.** Normally a skinny soul on account of its triple distillation, unusual to find a 'Toshan with so much muscle. The fruit from the sherry is piled on high, yet it is a massive toffee effect which takes the firmest grip, presumably tannins from the oak. So the finish is a little flat. But the good news is that this is one fruit cake that is happily sulphur-free. *50.3%. ncf. 2015 Limited Release.*

Auchentoshan Select db **(85) n20 t21.5 f22 b21.5.** Has changed shape of late, if not quality. Much more emphasis on the enjoyable juicy barley sharpness these days. *40%*

Auchentoshan Silveroak 1990 Limited Release db **(94.5) n23.5 t23 f24 b24.** Okay... tasting pretty blind on this: have only the sample bottle, showing the name of the brand and the strength, but no accompanying production notes. Appears to have good age, probably above 17, and the sherry butts used here (and I don't think it is exclusively wine oak at work) are of rare high quality for these days. Appears to have the imprint of outstanding blender Rachael Barry. *50.9%. Exclusive for Global Travel Retail.*

Auchentoshan Solera db **(88) n23 t22 f22 b21.** Enormous grape input and enjoyable for all its single mindedness. Will benefit when a better balance with the malt is struck. *48%. ncf.*

Auchentoshan Three Wood db **(76) n20 t18 f20 b18.** Takes you directly into the rough. Refuses to harmonise, except maybe for some late molassed sugar. *43%*

Auchentoshan Virgin Oak db **(92) n23.5** like a busy bourbon with the accent on the buzzing small grains: all the regulation manuka honey and liquorice there in respectful amounts; **t23** big, sugary delivery, but a cushion of hickory and vanilla keeps the sweetness under control; **f22.5** pretty dry, with a bit of a coppery sheen, as though some work had recently been done to a still; **b23** not quite how I've seen 'Toshan perform before: but would love to see it again! *46%*

◈ **Cadenhead's Small Batch Cask Strength Auchentoshan 17 Year Old** bourbon casks, dist 1999 **(92.5) n22.5** pushes out the envelope age-wise with the tannins creaking a little. But there is enough apple blossom and barley sugar to match the spices...just...; **t23.5** ah, so those sweeter notes on the nose weren't an illusion! Superb early delivery: thickened barley grist and over-ripe pear moves slowly towards a creamy custard and mocha note. Everything in slow motion: brilliant! **f23** allows the heavier tannins so far before it thickens into virtually unknown territory for a 'Toshan. Crème brule of the highest order...; **b23.5** the kind of dram that makes you emit a little groan of pleasure... *55.5%.*

Eiling Lim Auchentoshan 23 Years Old 1992 bott 2015 **(93) n23.5 t23 f23 b23.5** A quite beautiful and well percussioned rendition of a usually light song. *45.7%. nc ncf sc. 132 bottles. 9th Release.*

Hepburn's Choice Auchentoshan 12 Years Old refill hogshead, dist 2003, bott 2015 **(83) n21 t21 f20 b21.** Zesty, malty, salivating. But never far from the feel of a new make, despite its age. *46%. nc ncf sc. 152 bottles.*

Hunter Laing's Distiller's Art Auchentoshan Aged 12 Years refill hogshead, dist 2003, bott 2015 **(85) n21.5 t21.5 f21 b21.** A degree of oaky chunkiness and some extra spice fizz help eek out the most of an otherwise light, borderline austere, offering. *48%. nc ncf sc. 257 bottles.*

◈ **Hunter Laing's Old & Rare Auchentoshan Aged 24 Years** refill hogshead, dist Oct 91, bott Apr 16 **(95.5) n24.5** not quite what it says on the tin! This is massive... a beguiling marriage of maple syrup, muscovado sugars, Manuka honey and light bourbon. In short, this is much more like a virgin oak cask than the OP 18...!!! **t24** lush delivery with a fragile fruitiness in keeping with boiled sweets. Caramelised chestnut along with intense barley and vanilla; **f24** much drier and some fizzing spice; **b24** there are refill hogshead and then there are refill hogsheads... And this is some refill hogshead...!!As it happens, this was my 69th whisky for the 2018 Bible...and, my word, this one went down beautifully... *58.4%. nc ncf sc. 216 bottles.*

Old Malt Cask Auchentoshan Aged 18 Years refill hogshead, cask no. 11294, dist Sept 97, bott Apr 16 (89) n22.5 t22.5 f22 b22 proving that clean simplicity can be quietly beautiful... 50%. nc ncf sc. 150 bottles.

Old Malt Cask Auchentoshan Aged 18 Years refill hogshead, cask no. 12128, dist Oct 97, bott Nov 15 (87.5) n21.5 t22 f22 b22. A very enjoyable, though only gently challenging dram which makes the most of its triple distillation to allow the oak to offer an almost bourbon sweetness. Perhaps lacks complexity, though the spices more than make amends. What it does, it does especially well indeed. 46.9%. nc ncf sc. 258 bottles.

⬦ **Old Malt Cask Auchentoshan Aged 19 Years** refill hogshead, cask no. 13300, dist May 97, bott Feb 17 (89) n22.5 a little bourbonesque but a hint of coriander and nutmeg; t22 after the initial sweet barley burst almost a gin-like botanical feel to this: dry gin at that...; f22 continues along its herbal way...; b22.5 for serious malt lovers you'll just have to gin and bear it... 50%. nc ncf sc. 285 bottles.

Old Malt Cask Auchentoshan Aged 21 Years refill hogshead, cask no. 11782, dist Oct 93, bott Aug 15 (94) n23.5 t23.5 f23 b24 a classic must find 'Toshan. As rich as it gets with what appears to be a coppery depth to this integrating sublimely with the liquorice-bourbon lustre of the oak. Must have put in a new still, or done some coppery repair work just prior to this being distilled 50%. nc ncf sc. 156 bottles.

⬦ **Old Particular Auchentoshan 18 Years Old** virgin oak hogshead, cask no. 11203, dist Dec 97, bott Jun 16 (89.5) n22.5 brittle but some real bite to the spice; t23 superb delivery of barley concentrate, natural caramels and intense vanilla; spices fizz quietly in the background; f22 a little butterscotch and lot of tart; bitters out a tad; b22 slightly confused here: doesn't give the impression of having spent 18 years in virgin oak. 48.4%. nc ncf sc. 278 bottles.

⬦ **Provenance Auchentoshan Aged 14 Years** refill hogshead, cask no. 11484, dist Oct 02, bott Nov 16 (84) n22 t21 f20 b21 Plenty of sherbet lemon on the nose and thrusting barley on the palate. But just a little extra bitterness from the oak. 46%. nc ncf sc. 284 bottles.

⬦ **Scotch Malt Whisky Society Cask 5.52 5 Year Old** refill ex-bourbon hogshead, dist 11 Oct 00 (86.5) n21.5 t23 f21 b21 Perfectly enjoyable, lively, citrusy maltfest. Outrageously young for a triple distillation, which means that the harmonisation between the malt and grouchy tannin is far from ideal. The delivery, though, is a wonder to experience. 54.5%.

AUCHROISK

Speyside, 1974. Diageo. Working.

Auchroisk Aged 10 Years db (84) n20 t22 f21 b21. Tangy orange on the nose, the malt amplified by a curious saltiness on the palate. 43%. Flora and Fauna.

⬦ **Auchroisk Aged 25 Years** dist 1990 db (89) n22 a lovely intertwangling of healthy though by no means dominant bourbon-oaky notes and softer sweet malt; limited in scope but effective; t22.5 satisfying mouthfeel as the oils allow the barley to maximise intensity; a little hot in part but the malt is unambiguous; f22 thins, allowing the cocoa full say; b22.5 one of the most rampant Auchroisks I've encountered since the distillery issued its first-ever bottling. The full strength helps galvanise the malt and accentuate the barley sugar. A little rough, but very satisfying. 51.2%. 3,954 bottles. Diageo Special Releases 2016.

Distilleries Collection Auchroisk Aged 17 Years 1997 bott 2015 (84.5) n21 t20.5 f22 b21. At times a thin but firebrand dram, branding the barley on to your taste buds. But as it settles, the malt offers a more sensible, sober and enjoyable presence. 55%. Bottled for Scotch Malt Sales Ltd.

The Golden Cask Auchroisk 17 Years Old cask no. CM 209, dist 1997, bott 2014 (78.5) n19 t19.5 f21 b19. Salivating, almost concentrated malt. But the oak's contribution is very limited, leaving a Speyside malt much closer to seven years in style (if that!) than 17... 53%. sc. 280 bottles.

⬦ **Hepburn's Choice Auchroisk 7 Years Old** refill hogshead, dist 2009, bott 2017 (86.5) n21.5 t22.5 f21 b21.5 Malt dominates the story. However, a little sharpness on the nose and finish where the copper and oak don't se e eye to eye interrupts the flow. 46%. nc ncf sc. 405 bottles.

⬦ **Hepburn's Choice Auchroisk 7 Years Old** refill hogshead, dist 2009, bott 2017 (88) n22 grassy barley swaying on a salty breeze; citrusy grist; t22.5 for a malt so young, this is genuinely gorgeous: gristy but with some extra muscovado sugars for backup; f21.5 the vaguest hint of vanilla; b22 forget the age: gentle and deliciously moreish. 46%. nc ncf sc. 406 bottles.

Hepburn's Choice Auchroisk 12 Years Old refill hogshead, dist 2003, bott 2016 (85) n21.5 t21 f21.5 b21.5. Untaxing, simplistic malt. Excellent oak has sparked off a bit of a bourbony trait, though displayed on a thin malty body. Quite pleasant, though. 46%. nc ncf sc. 375 bottles.

   ◈ **Limburg Dramclub Auchroisk 10 Year Old** Oloroso sherry cask, dist 2007, bott 2017 (69) n17 t20 f15 b17 Yep, can see this celebration of all things citrus and sulphur going down a storm in Europe... 53.5%.

Old Malt Cask Auchroisk Aged 15 Years refill hogshead, cask no. 11944, dist Oct 00, bott Oct 15 (82) n20 t21.5 f20 b20.5. Pleasant, intensely malty, sweet in part and very clean. But rather bereft of character. 50%. nc ncf sc. 645 bottles.

   ◈ **Old Malt Cask Auchroisk Aged 22 Years** refill hogshead, cask no. 13302, dist Feb 94, bott Feb 17 (90) n22 custard cream biscuit – with a lemon cream nearby...; t23.5 unusually dense body on arrival, the barley ganging up to deliver a symphony of gristiness; f22 this significantly in the distillery's time-honoured tradition..; b22.5 rare that an Auchroisk keeps its integrity quite so well. The early moments of the delivery are sublime. 50%. nc ncf sc. 287 bottles.

   ◈ **Provenance Auchroisk Aged 8 Years** refill hogshead, cask no. 11190, dist Apr 08, bott May 16 (85) n21 t22 f21 b21 Faultlessly clean and mouth-watering. But a little too clean and lightweight, perhaps, allowing the lingering new-makey aspect a little too much rope. Attractive late cocoa. 46%. nc ncf sc.

   ◈ **Provenance Auchroisk Aged 8 Years** refill hogshead, cask no. 11489, dist Apr 08, bott Nov 16 (84) n21 t21.5 f20.5 b21 Very similar to cask 11190, though perhaps lacking a little of the sparkle on the maltiness. 46%. nc ncf sc. 249 bottles.

   ◈ **Whisky Castle Auchroisk 7 Year Old** bourbon hogshead, dist 2009, bott 2017 (94) n23 so rare to find this distillery offering a nose which takes a good while to master: still a citrusy youthfulness to the barley but it intertwangles with the oak-laden liquorice and ulmo honey elegantly; t23.5 one of the richest deliveries from this distillery I have encountered in 33 years. Excellent weight to the body captures the caramel revealing serious depth, while the spices begin to bombard the palate; f23.5 almost unique for the distillery, it retains its weight, the vanillas now benefitting; the spices now have a sublime intensity b24 In this kind of cask Auchroisk is probably at its optimum age as the marriage between its vibrancy and still measured elements of the oak is at its happiest. Well worth a trip to Tomintoul to grab this one, as this, for me, is numbered among the best ever bottlings from the distillery. 46%. Bottled by Morrison and Mackay Ltd.

AULTMORE
Speyside, 1896. John Dewar & Sons. Working.

Aultmore 12 Year Old db (85.5) n22 t22 f20 b21.5. Not quite firing on all cylinders due to the uncomfortably tangy oak. But relish the creamy malt for the barley is the theme of choice and for its sheer intensity alone, it doesn't disappoint; a little ulmo honey and marzipan doff their cap to the kinder vanillas. 46% WB16/028

Aultmore 18 Year Old db (88.5) n22.5 soft, though with a vague spice nip. Otherwise, a mix of ulmo honey, treacle and cream toffee combine; t22.5 the barley makes the first play on delivery, a grassy volley which slowly vanishes into a mist of caramel; f22 that caramel persists – again of Toffo variety - but at least the spices can be heard; b21.5 charming, but could do with having the toffee blended out... 46%

Aultmore 25 Year Old db (92.5) n23 t23.5; f23 b23 Now here's a curiosity: this is the first brand I have ever encountered which on the label lists the seasons the distillery was silent (1917-19, 1943-45, 1970-71) like a football club would once list on the front page of their official programme the years they won the FA Cup! Strange, but rather charming. And as for the whisky: succulent stuff!! 46% WB16/029

Endangered Drams Aultmore 7 Year Old bourbon hogshead, cask no. 100149, dist 03 Apr 08, bott 02 Sept 15 (86) n21 t22.5 f21 b21.5. Rather puts the tart in tartan. A light smokiness offers a minor degree of weight, but it is the vaguely salty, juicy barley which dominates. Sadly, a jaded old cask subtracts from the balance slightly. 62.3%. sc

   ◈ **Liquid Treasures Aultmore 10 Year Old** bourbon cask, dist 2006, bott 2017 (83) n20 t21 f21 b21 Not quite the greatest cask at work here makes for a jerky and uncomfortable ride. Some tangy salt and thick malt does offer compensation. 58.7%. Artist Edition.

Provenance Aultmore Aged 7 Years sherry cask, bott Mar 16 (94) n23 t24 f23 b24 Clean and beautifully subtle: now, that's the kind of sherry influence I want to see...! 46%. nc ncf sc.

   ◈ **Scotch Malt Whisky Society Cask 73.82 14 Year Old** virgin char, heavy toasted heads American barrel, dist 23 Sept 02 (91.5) n21.5 the tannins come screeching at you from on high like swifts on a feeding frenzy: with the tannins comes spice, of course. The malt, alas, has been sacrificed...; t23.5 from the nose you expect a sugary avalanche on delivery, and that is precisely what you get. The sweetness meets the big orange and fudge second wave eye-to-eye. At last the malt gets a chance to make itself heard, and does so with char and almost perfect weight; **f23** the tannins still offer a warming pulse but the citrus holds tight; **b23.5** about as subtle as a punch in the kisser. Very different and no shortage of magnificent moments. *55.3%*.

◇ **Simon Brown Aultmore** sherry cask, dist Mar 07, bott Jan 14 (89.5) **n23.5** nosed blind I'd mistake this for a delicate small grain bourbon, with a busy liquorice and leather theme. A few spikes of citrus enlivens the vanilla and chocolate wafer; **t23** briefly mouth-watering as the malt really makes an early impact. But a succession of muscovado sugar notes merge into a more oak-infused burnt fudge, with no less burnt raisin; **f21** a little give-away off key sherry tang at last but not before the essential oils really give the malt a good polish; **b22** Sherry cask it may be but certain aspects of this whisky have more in common with Kentucky than Spain.... except, of course, the weaker spots. *43%. nc ncf sc.*

That Boutique-y Whisky Company Aultmore batch 6 (84) **n21 t22 f21 b20**. Not a particularly bad barrel. But this is smothered in fruit in the same way a child would be swamped in his parents' clothes: the malt, indeed the whisky, makes no impact whatsoever. Juicy, with a pleasant degree of herbal notes. But just too much of a good thing, I'm afraid. *52.5%. 98 bottles.*

The Whisky Barrel Aultmore 1990 Burns Malt 25 Years Old cask no. 2341 (76) **n19 t20 f18 b19**. One of those heart-breakers. What a whisky this would have been except for that nagging sulphur. *57.8%. sc.*

◇ **Whisky Broker Aultmore 23 Year Old** (89) **n22** an intense, scurrying nose. The big barley flits about as though a storm is pending. A salty bite and a brief shaft of sweetness is quickly doused; **t22.5** a more relaxed delivery, but there is no let-up in the malty intensity. This time a gristy sweetness flickers uncertainly; **f22** a little spice buzz plus an attractive malt-vanilla fade; **b22.5** a novel Aultmore displaying in a way unusual even by its own non-conformist standards. Both on nose and finish there is a tang I cannot place for certain. *51.1%.*

◇ **World of Orchids Aultmore 10 Year Old** bourbon cask, dist 2006 (86) **n21.5 t22 f21.5 b21** Magnificent colour for a bourbon cask of this vintage. However, the tannins and malt are at times happily as one, then at odds with each other. It is like picking a fruit ripe on one side, over-ripe on another and then under-ripe in the middle. Some attractive orange-citrus thrust, intense barley and chocolate, but all are quite divorced from each other. *55.7%.*

Xtra Old Particular Speyside Aultmore 25 Years Old sherry butt, cask no. 11066, dist Feb 90, bott Feb 16 (83) **n19 t22 f20 b22**. Is this a perfect cask? No. Has it been ruined by the sulphur? No. Is there still plenty to find for the sherry lover? Yes. Because the sherry is also beautifully supported by the malt which weighs in to give extra depth. *44.2%. nc ncf sc. 302 bottles.*

BALBLAIR

Highlands (Northern), 1872. Inver House Distillers. Working.

Balblair 10 Years Old db (86) **n21 t22 f22 b21**. Such an improved dram away from the clutches of caramel. *40%*

Balblair Aged 16 Years db (84) **n22 t22 f20 b20**. Definitely gone up a notch in the last year. The lime on the nose has been replaced by dim Seville oranges; the once boring finish reveals elements of fruit and spice. It's the barley- rich middle that shines, though, and some more work will belt this up into the high 90s where this great distillery belongs. *40%*

Balblair 1965 db (96.5) **n23 t24.5 f24.5 b24.5** Many malts of this age have the spirit hanging on in there for grim life. This is an exception: the malt is in joint control and never for a moment allows the oak to dominate. It is almost too beautiful for words. *52.3%*

Balblair 1969 db (94.5) **n22.5 t23.5 f24 b24.5**. A charmer. Don't even think about touching this until it has stood in the glass for ten minutes. And if you are not prepared to give each glass a minimum half hour of your time (and absolutely no water), then don't bother getting it for, to be honest, you don't deserve it... *41.4%*

Balblair 1975 db (94.5) **n24.5 t23.5 f23 b23.5**. Essential Balblair. *46%*

Balblair 1978 db (94) **n24 t24 f23 b23**. Just one of those drams that exudes greatness and charm in equal measures. Some malts fall apart when hitting thirty: this one is totally intact and in command. A glorious malt underlining the greatness of this mostly under-appreciated distillery. *46%*

Balblair 1983 Vintage 1st Release dist 1983 bott 2013. db (96.5) **n24.5 t24 f23.5 b24.5** Very few malts are this comfortable, or vibrant, by the time they reach their third decade in the cask. A Highland gathering of sensational casks resulting in a celebration of what great Scotch whisky is really all about. Magnificent. *46%. nc ncf. Inverhouse Distilleries.*

Balblair 1983 Vintage 1st Release dist 1983, bott 2014 db **(95) n23.5 t23 f24.5 b24** the last Balblair 83 I tasted fair won my heart and undying devotion with its beauty and complexity. This may also be a beautiful and shapely morsel, but the over exuberance of the oak means this is more of a spicy, pleasure-indulging, hedonistic one night-stand than lasting, tender love. Mind you... 46%. nc ncf.

Balblair 1989 db **(91) n23 t23 f22.5 b22.5.** Don't expect gymnastics on the palate or the pyrotechnics of the Cadenhead 18: in many ways a simple malt, but one beautifully told. Almost Cardhu-esque in the barley department. 43%

Balblair 1989 db **(88) n21.5 t22 f22.5 b22.** A clean, pleasing malt, though hardly one that will induce anyone to plan a night raid on any shop stocking it... 46%

Balblair 1990 db **(92.5) n24 t23.5 f22 b23.** Tangy in the great Balblair tradition. Except here this is warts and all with the complexity and greatness of the distillery left in no doubt. 46%

Balblair 1990 Vintage 2nd Release dist 1990, bott 2014 db **(93) n23.5 t23 f23.5 b23** This is major malt. It does not try to take a polite course but hurls the tannins in all directions with abandon. Luckily, the overall lushness absorbs the greatest impacts. 46%. nc ncf.

Balblair 1997 2nd Release db **(94) n23.5 t23.5 f23 b24** a very relaxed well-made and matured malt, comfortable in its own skin, bursting with complexity and showing an exemplary barley-oak ratio. A minor classic. 46%. nc ncf.

Balblair 1999 Vintage 2nd Release dist 1999, bott 2015 db **(91.5) n23.5 t22.5 f23 b22.5** Always subtle and sensual. 46%. nc ncf.

Balblair 2000 db **(87.5) n21.5 t22.5 f21.5 b22.** No toffee yet still a clever degree of chewy weight for all the apparent lightness. 43%

Balblair 2001 db **(90.5) n23.5 t23.5 f21.5 b22.5** A typically high quality whisky from this outrageously underestimated distillery. 46%

Balblair 2002 1st release bott 2012 db **(90.5) n22 t23 f22.5 b23.** A malt which reminds you how cold it is during Scottish winters...there is a lot of fresh-faced youth to this. But just so beautiful thanks to its understated complexity and honesty. 46%. nc ncf.

Balblair 2003 Vintage 1st Release dist 2003 bott 2013. db **(88.5) n20 t23.5 f22 b23** the nose maybe a bit odd, even unattractively flawed. But this a tale with a happy ending. 46%. nc ncf. Inverhouse distilleries.

Balblair 2003 Vintage 1st Release dist 2003, bott 2015 db **(89) n21 t23 f22.5 b22.5** just like their 2013 bottling, gets off to an uncertain start on the nose but makes its mark on delivery. 46%. nc ncf.

Balblair 2005 Vintage 1st Release dist 2005, bott 2015 db **(86.5) n20 t23 f21.5 b22.** The nose is tight and has problems expanding, while the finish is short and quickly out of puff. But the delivery and follow through are superb with the malt really on maximum volume, and not without a little saline sharpness. Some good citrus, too. 46%. nc ncf.

Gordon & MacPhail MacPhail's Collection Balblair 10 Year Old **(87) n21.5 t22 f22 b21.5.** Enjoyable and very true to the distillery at this age and from cross-sectional bourbon cask: tart with a malty abrasiveness. A distillery where the complexity levels take off further down the line. 43%

Gordon & MacPhail MacPhail's Collection Balblair 21 Year Old **(90.5) n23 t23 f22 b22.5** Oh, if only they had kept this at a bigger strength: the reduction breaks up the oils somewhat so we don't get the full story told. Even so, still a delight. 43%

BALMENACH

Speyside, 1824. Inver House Distillers. Working.

Balmenach Aged 25 Years Golden Jubilee db **(89) n21 t23 f22 b23.** What a glorious old charmer this is! An essay in balance despite the bludgeoning nature of the beast early on. Takes a little time to get to know and appreciate: persevere with this belter because it is classic stuff for its age. 58%. Around 800 decanters.

◇ **Cadenhead's Small Batch International Balmenach 11 Year Old** sherry cask, dist 2005 **(92.5) n22.5** intriguing and unusual mix of malt from the new mown hay school interacting with a spiced but light grape blanket; **t24** salivating and fresh in the extreme: a mix of muscovado sugars and maple syrup work to good effect though pulses of rich barley are easily distinguishable; the slow development of the spice is a treat; **f22.5** the load lightens as the sugars retreat leaving uncomplicated vanilla and pulsing spices amid the grapey residue; **b23.5** a malt which doesn't sit still on the palate for a second. 46%.

Old Malt Cask Balmenach Aged 14 Years refill hogshead, cask no. 12129, dist Nov 01, bott Nov 15 **(86.5) n20.5 t23 f21.5 b21.5.** A very curious cask, this. A tad feinty on the nose, with the ultra oily, thickset finish confirming the problem. But a massive delivery of concentrated malt and even a little ulmo honey ensuring some quite wonderful moments in mid stream. A chewing whisky with excellent late caramel and cocoa, too. *50%. nc ncf sc. 348 bottles.*

⟡ **Provenance Balmenach Aged 10 Years** refill hogshead, cask no. 11247, dist Nov 05, bott May 16 **(85.5) n21.5 t22.5 f21 b21** Intensely malty but perhaps a little one-dimensional. Dries with a slightly bitter twist. *46%. nc ncf sc.*

⟡ **Provenance Balmenach Aged 10 Years** refill hogshead, cask no. 11636, dist Mar 07, bott Mar 17 **(83.5) n21 t21.5 f20 b21** A little new makey and wide cut from top to bottom, so never sits quite right. *46%. nc ncf sc. 408 bottles.*

⟡ **Scotch Malt Whisky Society Cask 48.89 11 Year Old** first fill ex-bourbon barrel, dist 29 Mar 05 **(93) n23** classic lemon drops and chocolate limes; **t23.5** the lime has melted: didn't take long to get through to the chocolate...; the barley is ridiculously thick; **f23** excellent tannin follow through. Inevitable spice; no surprise about the mocha, either; **b23.5** beautiful, high-grade malt that fills the mouth with all kinds of goodies. *57.9%.*

THE BALVENIE
Speyside, 1892. William Grant & Sons. Working.

The Balvenie Aged 10 Years Founders Reserve db **(90) n23** astonishing complexity: the fruit is relaxed, crushed sultanas and malty suet. A sliver of smoke and no more: everything is hinted and nudged at rather than stated. Superb; **t24** here we go again: threads of malt binding together barely detectable nuances. Thin liquorice here, grape there, smoke and vanilla somewhere else; **f20** Light muscovado-toffee flattens out the earlier complexity. The bitter-sweet balance remains brilliant to the end; **b23** just one of those all-time-great standard 10-year-olds from a great distillery – pity they've decided to kill it off. *40%*

The Balvenie Double Wood Aged 12 Years db **(80.5) n22 t20.5 f19 b19.** OK. So here's the score: Balvenie is one of my favourite distilleries in the world, I confess. I admit it. The original Balvenie 10 is a whisky I would go to war for. It is what Scotch malt whisky is all about. It invented complexity; or at least properly introduced me to it. But I knew that it was going to die, sacrificed on the altar of ageism. So I have tried to get to love Double Wood. And I have tasted and/or drunk it every month for the last couple of years to get to know it and, hopefully fall in love. But still I find it rather boring company. We may have kissed and canoodled. But still there is no spark. No romance whatsoever. *40%*

The Balvenie 14 Years Old Cuban Selection db **(86) n20 t22 f22.5 b21.5.** Unusual malt. No great fan of the nose but the roughness of the delivery grows on you; there is a jarring, tongue-drying quality which actually works quite well and the development of the inherent sweetness is almost in slow motion. Some sophistication here, but also the odd note which, on the nose especially, is a little out of tune. *43%*

The Balvenie 14 Years Old Golden Cask db **(91) n23.5 t23 f22 b22.5** A confident, elegant malt which doesn't stint one iota on complexity. Worth raiding the Duty Free shops for this little gem alone. *47.5%*

The Balvenie 16 Year Old Triple Cask db **(84.5) n22 t22.5 f19 b21.** Well, after their single cask and then double wood, who saw this coming...? There is nothing about this whisky you can possibly dislike: no diminishing off notes (OK, well maybe at the very death) and a decent injection of sugar, especially early on. The trouble is, when you mix together sherry butts (even mainly good ones, like here) and first fill bourbon ̇casks, the intense toffee produced tends to make for a monosyllabic, toffeed, dullish experience. And so it proves here. *40% WB16/030*

The Balvenie Double Wood Aged 17 Years db **(84) n22 t21 f20 b21.** Balvenie does like 17 years as an age to show off its malt at its most complex, & understandably so as it is an important stage in its development before its usual premature over maturity: the last years or two when it remains full of zest and vigour. Here, though, the oak from the bourbon cask has offered a little too much of its milkier, older side while the sherry is a fraction overzealous and a shade too tangy. Enjoyable, but like a top of the range Mercedes engine which refuses to run evenly. *43%.*

The Balvenie Double Wood Aged 17 Years bott 2012 db **(91) n22.5 t23.5 f22 b23** A far friskier date than the 12-year-old. Here, maturity equals sophistication. Still not as outrageously sexy as a straightforward high grade bourbon cask offering from the distillery. But easily enough to get you hot under the collar. Lip smacking, high quality entertainment. *43%*

The Balvenie Roasted Malt Aged 14 Years db **(90) n21 t23 f22 b24.** Balvenie very much as you've never seen it before. An absolute, mouth-filling cracker! *47.1%*

The Balvenie Rum Wood Aged 14 Years db **(88) n22 t23 f21 b22.** Tasted blind I would never have recognized the distillery: I'm not sure if that's a good thing. *47.1%*

Balvenie 17 Years Old Rum Cask db (88.5) n22 t22.5 f22 b22. For all the best attentions of the rum cask at times this feels all its 17 years, and perhaps a few Summers more. Impossible not to love, however. 43%

Balvenie New Wood Aged 17 Years db (85) n23 t22 f19 b21. A naturally good age for Balvenie; the nose is lucid and exciting, the early delivery is thick with rich malt. This, though, has sucked out lots of caramel from the wood to leave an annoyingly flat finish. 40%

The Balvenie 17 Year Old Sherry Oak db (88) n23 t22.5 f21 b21.5. Clean as a nut. High-class sherry it may be but the price to pay is a flattening out of the astonishing complexity one normally finds from this distillery. Bitter-sweet in every respect. 43%

The Balvenie Aged 21 Years Port Wood db (94.5) n24 t24 f23 b23.5 What a magnificently improved malt. Last time out I struggled to detect the fruit. Here, there's no escaping. 40%

The Balvenie Thirty Aged 30 Years db (92) n24 t23 f22 b23 Rarely have I come across a bottling of a whisky of these advanced years which is so true to previous ones. Amazing. 47.3%

The Balvenie Tun 1509 Batch 1 db (89) n23 t22.5 f21.5 b22 Balvenie is a distillery which struggles with age. And this is hanging on for life by its bloodied claws... 47.1%

The Balvenie TUN 1509 batch 2 db (94) n23.5 t24 f23 b23.5 A far happier and all round better balanced bottling than Batch 1. A big whisky, though you won't at first realise it... 50.3%

BANFF

Speyside, 1863–1983. Diageo. Demolished.

Gordon & MacPhail Rare Old Banff 1966 (95.5) n24 t24 f23.5 b24 A rare whisky on at least two major counts: one because casks of this are harder to come by than Millwall wins under Ian Holloway. And, secondly, because few casks get to this kind of age with its honey and sugars still intact. What a loss this distillery was. But what a gain it is for anyone who finds this bottle: it is a true classic. 45.2%

⬧ **Gordon & MacPhail Rare Old Banff 1966** (90) n22.5 if there is harmony to this, it is being played by a splinter group... The scars of passing years are getting deeper and darker as the tannins become progressively aggressive. But enough orange blossom honey and caramel hangs around to protect; t23 soft, toffee-laden delivery and follow through; a little mocha towards the middle; f22 late spiced marmalade and caramel again fight off the warming tannins; b22.5 quite a remarkable tail off in quality from their last bottling – but the age is going now into unknown territory for this lost distillery. Still excellent, though, and so much to enjoy... 46%

BEN NEVIS

Highlands (Western), 1825. Nikka. Working.

Ben Nevis 10 Years Old db (88) n21 t22 f23 b22. A massive malt that has steadied itself in recent bottlings, but keep those knives and forks to hand! 46%

Ben Nevis Synergy 13 Years Old db (88) n22 t22 f21.5 b22.5 One of the sweetest Ben Nevises for a long time, but as chewy as ever! A bit of a lady's dram to be honest. 46%

Best Dram Ben Nevis 18 Years Old (86.5) n21 t22.5 f21.5 b21.5. The huge oak takes absolutely no prisoners here. There is an imbalance of tannin over barley from the word go and the malt seems at least double its 18 years. Still, the chunky sugars do their best to take the sting from the oak, though it proves an unequal battle. 51.2%

⬧ **Best Dram Ben Nevis 20 Year Old** refill sherry butt, dist 1996, bott 2017 (81.5) n21 t23.5 f17 b20 There are those who will not feel the sulphur in this, like those who cannot tell the shudder of a minor earthquake rippling through their apartment. But it is there, sadly. A shame, as the early signals of plum pudding and Melton Hunt cake, all topped off with fabulous spiced sultana, were very promising. 57.1%

Big Market Sonderabfüllung Nr. 16 Ben Nevis 1997 bott 2015 (90.5) n21.5 t23.5 f23 b23 Tart....in every sense. A great, enlivening whisky to come home from work to. 56.5%.

Chapter 7 Ben Nevis 1996 18 Years Old (90.5) n22.5 t22.5 f22.5 b23 An usually singular and understated whisky in that it barely departs from the track it first starts out upon. Highly attractive. 51.8%. sc. 273 bottles.

⬧ **The Cooper's Choice Ben Nevis 19 Year Old** port finish, dist 1996, bott 2016 (73) n18 t19 f18 b18 Seems more like a sherry wood to me, alas... 46%. nc ncf sc. The Vintage Malt Whisky Co.

⬧ **The Cooper's Choice Ben Nevis 19 Year Old** sherry wood, dist 1996, bott 2016 (87) n20.5 t23 f22 b22.5 Somewhat on the tight side, especially on the nose, but really wraps out a lush, grapey malt of good weight with a big toffee undertone. 50%. nc ncf sc. The Vintage Malt Whisky Co.

⬧ **Deerstalker Ben Nevis 18 Years** 3 Months dist Jan 99 (90) n23 what a curious nose; all hints and whispers, though loud ones! A peculiarly phenolic weightiness envelopes the tangier blood orange and warm butterscotch...; **t22.5** firm, salivating delivery with a very quick blast of mocha and praline – a very unusual combination to find so early in the narrative. Needless to say, the spices strike like a thunderbolt...and hang around...; **f22** just a little tangy, spicy and vaguely bitter. Some chocolate raisin fudge cling on to the oily end...; **b22.5** by no means your usual Ben Nevis at work; and not the usual ultra-delicate Deerstalker, either. A surprise package, and a delicious one at that...! *52%. sc.*

Eiling Lim Ben Nevis 43 Years Old 1970 bott 2014 (81) **n22 t19 f20 b20.** The nose is as puzzling as it is intriguing. A real mish-mash of suet and stewed fruit, and porridge, too..!! A kind of spotted dog pudding breakfast. Less joy on delivery, though. An unhappy cask makes for a tangy, bitter unstructured free for all. *44.8%. nc ncf sc. 60 bottles. 2nd Release.*

The First Editions Ben Nevis Aged 18 Years 1996 refill hogshead, cask no. 11790, bott 2015 (90.5) **n23 t23 f22 b22.5** Though delightful as a single malt in its own right, just love to think what I could do with this in a blend...!! *46.5%. nc ncf sc. 339 bottles.*

⬩ **The First Editions Ben Nevis Aged 19 Years 1996** refill hogshead, cask no. 12214, bott 2016 (83.5) **n21 t21.5 f20 b21** This, to the taste buds, is similar to you and me having a bucket of ice cold water thrown over us. The malt arrives with the most startling, eye-watering tang which drenches the palate to eye-watering effect. The sugars are soon waving a white flag... *53.1%. nc ncf sc. 150 bottles.*

⬩ **The First Editions Ben Nevis Aged 20 Years 1996** refill hogshead, cask no. 13188, bott 2017 (94) **n23.5** oh, just adore the marriage of orange-blossom honey and salty barley...; **t24** brilliant!! This is as mouth-watering as Nevis ever gets: a stunning mix of intense grassy barley and gristy malt concentrate; vague citrus and the oaky vanilla adds a little weight but only as an afterthought; **f23** long, though the malt is more sombre and thoughtful now with a light digestive biscuit dryness; **b23.5** top of the range Ben Nevis... *56.9%. nc ncf sc. 66 bottles.*

Grindlay's Selection Ben Nevis 1997 (91) **n22.5 t23 f22.5 b23** The sugars sparkle quite beautifully. *52.6%. nc ncf. 228 bottles.*

⬩ **Hepburn's Choice Ben Nevis 6 Years Old** refill barrel, dist 2011, bott 2017 (86) **n21.5 t22 f21.5 b21** A fresh citrus theme combines with the light oils and sugars to loosen some of the tighter notes. *46%. nc ncf sc. 353 bottles.*

⬩ **Hepburn's Choice Ben Nevis 6 Years Old** refill barrel, dist 2011, bott 2017 (87.5) **n21 t22.5 f22.5 b21.5** This is the slightly paler version of two Hepburn Choice Ben Nevis of the same vintage. That lighter shade is reflected by the more distinct new make nose, though the clean, unfettered gristiness throughout is a joy. *46%. nc ncf sc. 359 bottles.*

⬩ **Hidden Spirits Ben Nevis 13 Year Old** cask no. BN417, dist 2004, bott 2017 (90.5) **n22.5** from that lovely mint chocolate ice cream school of smoky noses...; **t23.5** beautifully soft landing on the palate with a lovely buttercream glaze carrying the phenol: like a smoked a smoky coffee Swiss Roll; **f22** wouldn't be a Ben Nevis without a bit of tang in there somewhere...; **b22.5** all the usual Nevis idiosyncrasies plus a delicious smoked storyline. *57.5%. sc.*

⬩ **Hidden Spirits Ben Nevis 16 Year Old** cask no. BN9916, dist 1999, bott 2016 (88) **n22** a blistering aroma full of caramel, grass and, believe it or not, buttercups..!! **t22.5** big and chewy as the vanillas take root. But also a bit of bite from both the cask and spirit...; **f21.5** warms up even more, ignoring the continuing vanilla – rough and ready at the end; **b22.5** Nevis at its most wonderfully pugnacious. *57.4%. sc.*

Hunter Laing's Distiller's Art Ben Nevis Aged 19 Years refill hogshead, dist May 96, bott 2016 (90) **n22 t23 f22.5 b22.5** Exemplary, high class Nevis. *48%. nc ncf sc. 111 bottles.*

Kingsbury Gold Ben Nevis 17 Year Old 1998 sherry butt, cask no. 11336 (73) **n18 t23 f15 b17.** Loads of chocolate spiced fruit cake, if such a thing exists. Well, it does in liquid form, make no mistake! But if you are into sulphur, here's your lad! If you are one of those genetically unable to pick up sulphur, this might well be your whisky of the year! *57.9%. sc. 460 bottles.*

⬩ **Kintra Whisky Ben Nevis Aged 15 Years** sherry butt, cask no. 152, dist 23 Apr 01, bott 17 Nov 16 (91) **n23** the nose is like a bar-room brawl with chairs, tables and people flying through the air, sometimes landing on the piano to create a bum note. But so lively, salty, earthy and like the language, fruity...; **t23.5** and there is immediate punch on delivery: the malt is ridiculously muscular and brawny, offers little sophistication and biffs the taste buds at every opportunity. The oak crashes home its vanilla credentials; **f21.5** tangy and awkward; **b23** a near faultless sherry butt and an outrageously flavoursome whisky! About as sophisticated as a punch in the kisser... *53.7%. nc ncf sc. Bottled by Whiskybroker Ltd.*

⬩ **Le Gus't Selection VI Ben Nevis 2006** sherry butt, cask no. 3, bott 2016 (84) **n22 t22.5 f19 b20.5** Stupendously rich oloroso at play here – and from a faultless butt, also. The grape lends the malt a glossiness of texture which is hardly matched by the whisky's eccentric personality. Never quite sits still or allows the tannins and fruit to happily fuse, it is a dram always on the march. At times delicious, sometimes fascinating, always frustrating! 51.3%. 762 bottles.

⬧ **Liquid Treasures Ben Nevis 19 Year Old** bourbon cask, dist 1997, bott 2016 (86.5) n21 t22.5 f22 b21 A massive mouth-puckering, eye-watering dram where balance and elegance step back from taking part very early on. But for sheer mouth-watering juicy barley bludgeoning, this wins hands down. 51.9%. Fairy Tales Edition.

Maltbarn Ben Nevis 1996 ex-bourbon cask, bott 2015 (81.5) n20 t21 f20 b20.5. The odd malty sharpness entertains. But just a little too rough and ready for its own good. 50.9%. sc. 121 bottles.

Old Malt Cask Ben Nevis 14 Years Old (81) n21 t20 f20 b20. Thick and glutinous. Little layering to the intense barley or tangy, tired oak. A tad hot, too. 48.4%. sc.

⬧ **Old Malt Cask Ben Nevis Aged 15 Years** refill hogshead, cask no. 13297, dist Nov 01, bott Feb 17 (81.5) n19 t22.5 f20 b20 The nose warns with a strident voice that all is not well. And once the first malty rays are extinguished, the off-key oak begins to take its toll. 50%. nc ncf sc. 77 bottles.

Old Malt Cask Ben Nevis Aged 19 Years sherry butt, cask no. 12148, dist Jun 96, bott Nov 15 (93.5) n23.5 t23.5 f23 b23.5 good grief! A sulphur-free sherry butt from 1996! Not the most common of happenings. The grape pings around the palate like a whisky possessed. But still cannot get the better of the spice. Delightful and intriguing. 50%. nc ncf sc. 572 bottles.

⬧ **Old Particular Ben Nevis 20 Years Old** refill hogshead, cask no. 11354, dist Nov 96, bott Nov 16 (87) n20 t22.5 f22.5 b22 A beautifully bright whisky which celebrates the crystalline clarity of the crisp, sugary barley. Yet somehow fails to offer up the trimmings you might expect from a malt of this age. Still, well balanced and charming with none of the usual Ben Nevis weightiness. 49.8%. nc ncf sc. 260 bottles.

⬧ **Sansibar Whisky Ben Nevis 1996** bott 2016 (82) n20 t22 f19 b21 Has all the directional skills of a North Korean missile. Both the nose and finish veer wildly off course but the sugars on delivery are explosive. 51.9%.

That Boutique-y Whisky Company Ben Nevis batch 2 (91.5) n22 busy sugars, plus Brazilian biscuit and vanilla; t23.5 you could drown in your own saliva – this is so ridiculously juicy. Profoundly light, gristy sugars; f23 a beautiful malt fade...but those spices...my word!! b23 if anyone remembers Batch 1 – more of the same but much more spice! 48.7%. 52 bottles.

That Boutique-y Whisky Company Ben Nevis 19 Year Old batch 4 (84.5) n21.5 t21.5 f19.5 b21. A distinctly bitter-sweet experience. 49.5%. 166 bottles.

Whic Ben Nevis 18 Years Old bourbon hogshead, dist Jun 96, bott Apr 15 (88) n21.5 some chewing gum sticking to the nose; t22.5 good, crisp barley. A very lazy hint of citrus and ulmo honey, but really it is the lightly spiced vanilla which makes the running; f22 dries with almost indecent haste. But the malt battles on gamely; b22 very simplistic bending malt, but pleasant. 53.7%. 126 bottles.

⬧ **The Whisky Agency Ben Nevis 1988** (85) n20.5 t21.5 f22 b21 Malty, fat and initially well short of the sugars required for balance. But, slowly the big juices arrive and with it some residual grist to do battle with the spiced oak. 50.9%.

⬧ **The Whisky Agency Ben Nevis 17 Years Old** dist 1999 (85.5) n21 t22 f21.5 b21 No prizes for its gait, wit or elegance: this is a hobbling, lumpy old scruff of a thing. But there is something very appealing about the sharpness of the barley and its rough texture, like an old piece of tweed. 50.9%. Bottled for Casa de Vinos, Australia.

⬧ **The Whisky Agency Ben Nevis 18 Years Old** dist 1996 (89) n21.5 untidy and thin with a sharp, pith note; t22 a searing delivery with a much thinner body than a normal Ben Nevis. Out of nowhere a salty maltiness starts to shrill; f23.5 simply massive malt now with astonishing barley intensity; b22 a blending malt this would do a very useful job stirring up the lowish m knuckle-dragger, ungainly and looking for a fight at any moment. There is something almost endearing about its roughhouse style and the intensity of its maltiness deserves a standing ovation. 50.5%.

⬧ **The Whisky Agency Ben Nevis 18 Years Old** dist 1996 (92.5) n23.5 now that is some nose! Superb distillate in a happy home for the last 18 years means we have an array of aromas to be celebrated. The freshness to the barley is almost eclipsed by the salty, ozone coastal feel which, in itself, frames the gentle liquorice and lightly molassed tannins quite beautifully; t23.5 the malt arrives confidently and cleanly early on; soon after a brief, shuddering jolt of oak a more refreshing, soft Jaffa cake moment is reached; f22.5 time for the busy spices to play out the last moments...; b23 wonderfully coastal and alive! 51.2%.

Whiskybroker Ben Nevis 18 Year Old hogshead, cask no. 596, dist 22 May 97, bott 24 Sept 15 (87) n21.5 t22.5 f21.5 b22. Very malty. But the sugars star too briefly. Just a tad too warm, thin and austere. 53.4%. sc.

Whisky-Fässle Ben Nevis 1996 sherry butt, bott 2015 (91.5) n23 t23 f22.5 b23 A beautiful sherry butt has done a good job here. 52.7%

Whiskyjace Ben Nevis 16 Years Old 1998 bourbon hogshead, bott 2015 (88) n22 t22.5 f21.5 b22 For a simplistically malty dram, this is pretty big stuff...! 52.6%

BENRIACH
Speyside, 1898. The BenRiach Distillery Co. Working.

BenRiach 10 Year Old db (87.5) n20 t23 f22.5 b22. A much fatter spirit than from any time when I worked those stills. The dry nose never quite decides where it is going. But there's no doubting the creamy yet juicy credentials on the palate. Malty, with graceful fruit sugars chipping in delightfully. 43%

The BenRiach Aged 12 Years db (82.5) n21 t20 f21 b20.5. More enjoyable than the 43% I last tasted. But still an entirely inoffensive malt determined to offer minimal complexity. 40%

The BenRiach Aged 12 Years Matured In Sherry Wood db (95.5) n23.5 t24 f24 b24 Since I last tasted this the number of instances of sampling a sherry wood whisky and not finding my taste buds caked in sulphur has nosedived dramatically. Therefore, to start my tasting day at 7am with something as honest as this propels one with myriad reasons to continue the day. A celebration of a malt whisky in more ways than you could believe. 46%. nc ncf.

The BenRiach Aged 16 Years db (83.5) n21.5 t21 f20 b21. Although maltily enjoyable, if over dependent on caramel flavours, you get the feeling that a full works 46% version would offer something more gripping and true to this great distillery. 40%

The BenRiach Aged 16 Years db (83.5) n21.5 t21 f20 b21. Pleasant malt but now without the dab of peat which gave it weight; also a marked reduction of the complexity that once gave this such a commanding presence. 43%. nc ncf.

◈ **The BenRiach Aged 17 Years Pedro Ximénez Sherry Wood Finish** db (81) n21 t22.5 f17.5 b20 A prevailing problem with PX casks is that the influence of the hyper-sweet grape can have an overwhelming effect on a whisky. So while a number of eye-watering, succulent tones might arrive thanks to the grape influence, the overall picture of the malt may be obscured. That has happened to an extent here, and the bitter blood-orange finale doesn't help, either. 46%.

The BenRiach Aged 17 Years "Septendecim" Peated Malt db (93.5) n24 t24.5 f23 b24 proof, not that it is now needed, that Islay is not alone in producing phenomenal phenols... 46%. nc ncf.

◈ **The BenRiach Aged 18 Years Albariza** db (92.5) n23 bit of a clunking, grizzled heavyweight, this. The peat and grape are like two old champions facing each other in the eye for one last match, one last knockout blow...; t23.5 as it happens, neither has the power to overcome the other. This is soft fat, rather than muscular, and the phenols and toasted raisin hang on to each other for dear life; f23 some deft spices attached to the peat liven things up while the vanillas and treacle parry the attack; b23.5 always preferable to see a fruit influence that is floored rather than flawed... 46%.

◈ **The BenRiach Aged 18 Years Dunder** db (95.5) n24 a colossal and complex smoke signature, veering from smouldering anthracite to peat, all the more remarkable for the softness and dexterity of its approach, its fruity clarity and magnificent layering: what a treat! t24 as on the nose, the smoke has a gentleness rare among such phenolic malts, as though an anvil is drifting downwards and landing with all the impact of a feather. Setting this even further apart from the norm is the way in which the sugars, varying from lights fruits such as lychee through to thumping molasses, appear happy to give way to each other and then the spices; f23 gentle vanillas and butterscotch link nimbly with the drifting smoke; b24.5 it may be Dunder, but it certainly ain't the pits...! 46%.

◈ **The BenRiach Aged 18 Years Latada** db (92) n24 a half hour nose: ultra-complex with spectacular sugar and honey layering with the most gentle smoke forming the sandwich. As polite a peaty nose as you could ever wish for...; t23 the delivery is no more than a caress: silky heather honey underlines the malt while the smoke arrives fractionally later, eventually ensuring a spiced dryness; f22 just a little honey residue, almost of the cough sweet variety; b23 the nose and delivery are the best I have encountered so far today...and I began tasting some nine hours ago.... 46%.

The BenRiach Aged 20 Years db (85.5) n21.5 t23 f19 b22. A much more attractive version than the American Release 46%. The barley offers a disarming intensity and sweetness which makes the most of the light oils. Only a bittering finish shuts the gate on excellence. 43%. nc ncf.

The BenRiach Aged 20 Years db (78) n19 t20 f19 b20. This is big, but not necessarily for the right reasons or in the right places. A big cut of oiliness combines with some surging sugars for a most un-BenRiachy ride. 46%. US Market.

⚜ **The BenRiach Aged 21 Years Tawny Port Wood Finish** db (87.5) n22 t21 f22 b21.5 I'm not sure if the cask finish was designed to impart a specific fruitiness profile or simply repair some tired old oak. In either case, it has been a partial success only. The intemperance of the tannin makes its mark in no small measure both on nose and delivery and it is only in the finish that the sugars bond strongly enough together to form a balance with the woody input. 46%.

⚜ **The BenRiach Aged 22 years Moscatel Wood Finish** db (81) n21 t23 f17 b20 Not sure any wine finish I have tasted this year has thrown up so many huge, one might even say challenging, perfumed notes which score so highly for sheer lip-smacking effect. Had this cask not given the impression of being sulphur treated what an enormous score it would have amassed...! 46%.

The BenRiach 25 Years Old db (87.5) n21.5 t23 f21 b22. The tranquillity and excellent balance of the middle is the highlight by far. 50%

⚜ **The BenRiach Aged 25 Years Authenticus** db (91) n23 grey bearded, wizened yet elegant, the tannins creak at every sniff. The peat works hard to fill in the crumbling holes but it is an unequal battle; t23 a cool, sweet, soothing delivery. Even the big sugars have a feel of age about them; chocolate chip mint with the smoke thin and unable to contain the building tannins and spices towards the late middle; f22 feels some authentic time catching up with it...; b23 every moment feels as old as a Roman senator...who is eventually stabbed in the back by Oakicus. 46%.

BenRiach 35 Year Old db (90) n23 juicy dates and plums are tipped into a weighty fruitcake; t24 sit right back in your armchair (no..? Then go and find one...!!) having dimmed the lights and silenced the room and just let your taste buds run amok: those plums and toasted raisins really do get you salivating, with the spices also whipping up a mid-life storm; f21.5 angular oak dries and bitters at a rate of knots; b22 sexy fruit, but has late oaky bite. 42.5%

BenRiach Cask Strength batch 1 db (93) n22.5 very green and grassy malt; t24 masterful: how many layers of maltiness can you count? I have made five – before it moves into a delightful and very milky Malteser middle; f23 those of you into vaguely fruity fudge will adore this...; b23.5 if you don't fall in love with this one, you should just stick to vodka... 57.2%

The BenRiach Curiositas Aged 10 Years Single Peated Malt db (90.5) n23 t23 f22 b22.5 "Hmmmm. Why have my research team marked this down as a 'new' whisky" I wondered to myself. Then immediately on nosing and tasting I discovered the reason without having to ask: the pulse was weaker, the smoke more apologetic...it had been watered down from the original 46% to 40%. This is excellent malt. But can we have our truly great whisky back, please? As lovely as it is, this is a bit of an imposter. As Emperor Hadrian might once have said: "ifus itus aintus brokus..." 40%

The BenRiach "Heart of Speyside" db (85.5) n21.5 t22 f21 b21. A decent, non-fussy malt where the emphasis is on biscuity barley. At times juicy and sharp. Just a tease of very distant smoke here and there adds weight. 40%

⚜ **The BenRiach Peated Cask Strength** batch 1 db (95) n24 the gentle, zesty lemon offers a clinically precise degree of lightness to the rolling smoke. A hint of acrid burnt toast in the air but of no greater intensity than the subtle dark sugars which perform a textbook balancing act; t23 youthful gristiness shows those Demerara sugars up to the max; the smoke is layered though each next one is deeper and with spices mounting...; f24 as a buttery dimension develops it just gets better and better...; b24 stunning whisky magnificently distilled and, though relatively young, almost perfectly matured. 56%.

BenRiach Peated Quarter Casks db (93) n23.5 there's a lot of peat in them barrels. The citrus is vital...; t24 a plethora of sugars and caramel leached from the casks make for a safe landing when the smoke and malt – with a slightly new make feel - arrive in intensive form; f22.5 the caramel continues, now with spice; b23 though seemingly youthful in some phases, works a treat! 46%

The BenRiach "Solstice" db (94) n23.5 t24 f23 b23.5. On midsummer's day 2011, the summer solstice, I took a rare day off from writing this book. With the maximum light available in my part of the world for the day I set off at daybreak to see how many miles I could walk along remote country paths stopping, naturally, only at a few remote pubs on the way. It was a fraction under 28 miles. Had this spellbinding whisky been waiting for me just a little further down the road, I am sure, despite my troubled left knee and blistered right foot, I would have made it 30... 50%. nc ncf.

Birnie Moss Intensely Peated db (90) n22 youthful, full of fresh barley and lively, clean smoke; t23.5 juicy, fabulously smoked, wet-behind the ears gristy sugars; f22 some vanillas try to enter a degree of complexity; **b22.5** before Birnie Moss started shaving... or even possibly toddling. Young and stunning. *48%. nc ncf.*

The First Editions Ben Riach Aged 26 Years 1989 refill puncheon, cask no. 12002, bott 2015 **(90) n22 t23.5 f21.5 b22.5** So brittle and clipped. you feel like it could chip your teeth. But doesn't stint on the big flavours. *56.1%. nc ncf sc. 258 bottles.*

That Boutique-y Whisky Company BenRiach batch 3 **(88) n22** malt; **t22** malt; **f22** malt; **b22** this is not far off the most basic and simplistic of styles I encountered at this distillery when I first worked there so many years ago... *48.9%. 103 bottles.*

BENRINNES
Speyside, 1826. Diageo. Working.

Benrinnes Aged 15 Years db **(70) n16 t19 f17 b18.** What a shame that in the year the independent bottlers at last get it right for Benrinnes, the actual owners of the distillery make such a pig's ear of it. Sulphured and sicklysweet, this bottling has little to do with the very good whisky made there day in day out by its talented team. Depressing. *43%. Flora and Fauna.*

Benrinnes 21 Year Old ex-sherry European oak casks, dist 1992 db **(83.5) n21 t22 f19 b21.5.** Salty and tangy. Some superb cocoa moments mixing with the muscovado sugars as it peaks. But just a little too furry and bitter at the finish. *56.9%. 2,892 bottles. Diageo Special Releases 2014.*

Chapter 7 Benrinnes 1997 18 Years Old bourbon hogshead, cask no. 898 **(89) n22 t23.5 f21 b22.5** The high intensity of the barley has just enough clout to fend off the strong-arm oak. A big Benrinnes. *61.5%. sc.*

The First Editions Benrinnes Aged 18 Years 1997 refill hogshead, cask no. 12124, bott 2015 **(85.5) n21 t22.5 f21 b21.** Plenty of old oak tang to get you puckering. Very good texture and even a degree of saltiness creeps in. Enough barley to keep the balance honest. *52.8%. nc ncf sc. 285 bottles.*

Hepburn's Choice Benrinnes 6 Years Old European oak quarter cask, dist 2009, bott 2015 **(92.5) n22.5 t23.5 f23 b23.5** Now there's a fascinating proposition: take Speyside's lightest malt and place it in a quarter cask. Well, the outcome is obvious. The oak will dominate throughout. The questions are: how and will the barley make any telling mark at all? The answer given here might surprise you, for this is a very fine malt from many angles. Satisfying and, as expected, big for its age. *46%. nc ncf sc. 86 bottles.*

Hepburn's Choice Benrinnes 6 Years Old European oak quarter cask, dist 2009, bott 2015 **(73.5) n17.5 t19 f18 b19.** An honest whisky: the less than pleasant, discordant nose tells you that you are in for an unhappy time of it on the palate. And it doesn't lie... *46%. nc ncf sc. 84 bottles.*

Hepburn's Choice Benrinnes 6 Years Old European oak quarter cask, dist 2009, bott 2015 **(87) n20 t22.5 f22 b22.5.** There's some gristle on the meaty nose, and a little hoarseness to the finish. But between the odd unhappy moment, there is plenty to get on with and enjoy, especially on the chunky, malty delivery which moves into barley-sugary country within no time. *46%. nc ncf sc. 82 bottles.*

◇ **Hepburn's Choice Benrinnes 8 Years Old** rosé wine finished refill hogshead, dist 2007, bott 2016 **(72) n14 t20 f19 b19** A thorn among roses: plenty of prickle. *46%. nc ncf sc. 373 botts.*

Hepburn's Choice Benrinnes 11 Years Old sherry butt, dist 2002, bott 2014 **(84) n20.5 t22 f20 b21.5.** A crisp, juicy edge to this one. Fruit doesn't for a moment enter the fray, though spice certainly does. *46%. nc ncf sc. 761 bottles.*

Old Malt Cask Benrinnes Aged 15 Years sherry butt, cask no. 10891, dist Jul 99, bott Oct 14 **(85.5) n21 t22.5 f20.5 b21.5.** Steams in from the word go with no shortage of malty muscle. A better Benrinnes. The barley impacts beautifully on both nose and delivery and its positive all the way. *50%. nc ncf sc. 567 bottles.*

◇ **Old Malt Cask Benrinnes Aged 19 Years** refill hogshead, cask no. 13272, dist Oct 97, bott Feb 17 **(86) n22 t22.5 f20.5 b21** An attractively lively Benrinnes, making the very best of the fresh grist and citrus start. Afterwards the oak gains a niggardly foothold. Even so, a better example of the distillery's work. *50%. nc ncf sc. 316 bottles.*

Old Masters Benrinnes 15 Year Old cask no. 306771, bott 2016 **(92.5) n22.5 t23 f23 b24** this is Benrinnes? My flabber is fully gasted... *57.5%*

Provenance Benrinnes Aged 8 Years bott Mar 16 **(79) n19 t21 f19.5 b19.5.** The barley-rich sugars try to keep this malt buoyant for as long as possible. But an unfriendly cask takes its toll. Unusually oily and fat for this triple-distilled malt. *46%. nc ncf sc.*

◇ **Provenance Benrinnes Aged 8 Years** refill hogshead, cask no. 11326, dist Feb 08, bott Aug 16 **(83.5) n20 t21.5 f21 b21** Youthful, malty and attractively fat. You can see why this is so useful in a blend. *46%. nc ncf sc. 435 bottles.*

Scotch Malt Whisky Society Cask 36.99 Aged 9 Years 1st fill barrel, dist 08 Nov 06, bott 22 Feb 16 (84.5) n21 t21.5 f20.5 b21.5. Typically torch-like, the intense yet strangely thin malts are blasted seeringly onto the palate. As a blender, I would not be too happy to see this wasted as a single malt. Rather, it should be used to impact on a low-ish malt content blend, and one using the softer grains. 57.8%. nc ncf sc. 234 bottles.

◇ Scotch Malt Whisky Society Cask 36.121 9 Year Old first fill ex-bourbon barrel, dist 8 Nov 06 (90) n22.5 a few red liquorice bourbon notes drift among the salty maple syrup; t23 the delivery is typically brutal, but calms down for the malt to gain a foothold before a slow introduction, delightful of ulmo honey; a little spice matches the salt; f22 a little hint of off-balance weirdness, but the ulmo honey persists beautifully, coaxing the malt into play in the process; b22.5 an outstanding cask influence results in the distillery at the top of its game for this age. All the usual bite and haphazardness. But some top drawer honey tones, too. 57.8%.

Stronachie 18 Years Old (83.5) n21.5 t21 f20 b21. This is so much like the older brother of the Stronachie 12: shows the same hot temper on the palate and even sharper teeth. Also, the same slim-line body. Have to say, though, something strangely irresistible about the intensity of the crisp malt. 46%

Whiskybroker Benrinnes 17 Year Old bourbon barrel, cask no. 893, dist 15 Oct 97, bott 28 Aug 15 (86) n22 t21 f21.5 b21.5. A tad fierce on the palate – and we ain't talking spice. But rather enjoy the vanilla ice cream theme, especially on the nose 57%. sc.

Whiskybroker Benrinnes 18 Year Old refill bourbon barrel, cask no. 906, dist 15 Aug 97, bott 01 Feb 16 (87) n22 t21.5 f22 b21.5. Carries many similar traits to their 17-year-old version, especially with the thin burn. But here the vanilla-rich oak and barley travel more hand in hand. 50%. sc.

The Whisky Chamber Benrinnes 18 Years Old ex-bourbon hogshead, cask no. 890/1997, dist 12 Oct 95, bott 08 Mar 16 (84.5) n20.5 t21.5 f21 b21.5. A warming malt, with the barley forming some attractive layering – often sandwiched between molten light refined sugars. Decent caramelised biscuit. But just a tad too hot for comfort. 56.6%. nc sc.

◇ Whisky-Fässle Benrinnes 18 Year Old hogshead, dist 1997, bott 2016 (89) n22.5 mocks its 18 years by upping the grassy gristiness: refreshing and sleek; t22.5 every bit as salivating as the nose demands. Some slightly aggressive oak tries to display a bitter character. But the light maple syrup intensifies the barley as required; f22 a little bitterness creeps in but a buttery toastiness counters with style; b22 as fettles go, this is Benrinnes in its finest... 52.2%.

BENROMACH

Speyside, 1898. Gordon & MacPhail. Working.

Benromach 10 Years Old matured in hand selected oak casks db (87.5) n22 t22 f21.5 b22. For a relatively small still using peat, the experience is an unexpected and delicately light one. 43%

Benromach 15 Year Old db (78) n20 t22 f17 b19. Some charming early moments, especially when the grape escapes its marker and reveals itself in its full juicy and sweet splendour. But it is too short lived as the sulphur, inevitably takes over. 43%

Benromach 21 Years Old db (91.5) n22 t23.5 f23 b23 An entirely different, indeed lost, style of malt from the old, now gone, big stills. The result is an airier whisky which has embraced such good age with a touch of panache and grace. 43%

Benromach 22 Years Old Finished in Port Pipes db (86) n22 t23 f20 b21. Slightly Jekyll and Hyde. 45%. 3500 bottles.

Benromach 25 Years Old db (92) n24 t22 f23 b23 A classic old-age Speysider, showing all the quality you'd hope for. 43%

Benromach 30 Years Old db (95.5) n23.5 t24 f24 b24 You will struggle to find a 30-year-old with less wrinkles than this.. Magnificent: one of the outstanding malts of the year. 43%

Benromach 100° Proof db (94) n23 proof positive that toasty oak, a dash of fruit and several puffs of peat can go a long, long way...; t23.5 beautiful mouth-feel, as thick as anything I have seen from the new Benromach before. The fabulous spice really does make a name for itself, but all those notes recognised on the nose are present and correct here; f23.5 more of the same, but a layer of Jaffa Cake towards the finish, though it is short-lived as it dries...; b24 for any confused US readers, the strength is based on the old British proof strength, not American! What is not confusing is the undisputed complexity and overall excellence of this malt. 57%

Benromach 2005 Sassicaia Finish db (92.5) n22.5 t24 f23 b23. A sassy dram in every way... 45%

Benromach Cask Strength 1981 db (91) n21.5 t23 f23.5 b23. Really unusual with that seaweedy aroma awash with salt: stunningly delicious stuff. 54.2%

Benromach Cask Strength 2001 db (89) n21.5 t23 f22 b22.5. Just fun whisky which has been very well made and matured with total sympathy to the style. Go get. 59.9%

Benromach Cask Strength 2003 db (92) n22.5 t23.5 f23 b23.5 Hats off to the most subtle and sophisticated Benromach I have tasted in a while. 59.4%

Benromach Heritage 35 Year Old db (87) n22 t21.5 f22 b21.5. A busy exchange of complex tannin notes, some backed by the most faded spice and caramel. All charming and attractive, but the feeling of decay is never far away. 43%

Benromach Heritage 1974 db (93) n23.5 t23 f23 b23.5 Made in the year I left school to become a writer, this appears to have survived the years in better nick than I... 49.1%

⬩ **Benromach Heritage 1975** db (89) n22 a few splinters on the loose, with associated spice prickle. But both barley and vanilla make a bit input, too...; t22.5 a sound delivery: mainly yielding but with a backbone, also. As on the nose, the vanilla has much to say, but a little salted ulmo honey makes the speech sweeter; f22 long a big Worther's Original signature, as well as major old age spice; the saltiness persists, keeping matters lively; b22.5 a bottling where the malt is hanging on for grim death against the passing of time. But the discreet light honey notes do just the trick. 49.9%

⬩ **Benromach Heritage 1976** db (86.5) n21.5 t21 f22.5 b21.5 There are times when you can have a little too much tannin and this has crossed the Rubicon. That said, look closely on the nose for some staggering lime and redcurrant notes which escape the onslaught as well as the gorgeous butterscotch on the finish as the sugars fight back in the death in style. Some moments of genius in the oakiest of frames. 53.5%.

Benromach Madeira Wood db (92) n22 t24 f23 b23. If you want a boring, safe, timid malt, stay well away from this one. Fabulous: you are getting the feeling that the real Benromach is now beginning to stand up. 45%

Benromach Marsala Wood db (86.5) n21.5 t22 f22 b21. Solid, well made, enjoyable malt, which in some ways is too solid: the imperviousness of both the peat and grape appears not to allow much else get through. Not a dram to say no to, however, and the spices in particular are a delight. 45%

Benromach Organic db (91) n23 t23 f22 b23. Young and matured in possibly first fill bourbon or, more likely, European (even Scottish) oak; you cannot do other than sit up and take notice of this guns-blazing big 'un. An absolute treat! 43%. nc ncf.

Benromach Organic Special Edition db (85.5) n22 t21 f21.5 b21. The smoky bacon crisp aroma underscores the obvious youth. Also, one of the driest malts of the year. Overall, pretty. But pretty pre-pubescent, too... 43%

Benromach Organic 2008 bott 2014 db (93) n23 t23.5 f23 b23.5 For a whisky at a meagre 43%, the most astonishing explosion of intense barley and oak. More orgasmic than organic... 43%

⬩ **Benromach Organic 2010** db (95.5) n24 a charming, understated essay in which malt, salted spice and barley sugar are described to perfection; the most delicate lavender and mint sub strata does no harm, either; t24 the melting of the gristy sugars on the palate is truly a work of art: one of the great moments of the 2017 whisky year and possible the most awe inspiring few moments since the distillery returned to production: barley simply doesn't come better defined or weighted than this. The delicate spice which follows is also straight off the blueprint; f23 the malt recaptures its intensity to dominate over the developing vanilla and butterscotch. The spices stay on course, also; b24.5 gentle, refined and exquisitely elegant. 43%.

Benromach Peat Smoke Batch 3 db (90.5) n22 t23 f22.5 b23 An excellent malt that has been beautifully made. Had it been bottled at 46 we would have seen it offer an extra degree of richness. 40%

Benromach Peat Smoke 2005 67ppm db (88.5) n22 t22.5 f21.5 b22.5 This may be 67 parts per million phenols when it started. But size, so I have been told, is not important. Stamina and finesse both are. And while this may enjoy a degree of the latter, it has little of the former. 46%.

Benromach Peat Smoke 2006 db (90.5) n22.5 t23.5 f22 b22.5 A more measured malt than the previous vintage. 46%

⬩ **Benromach Peat Smoke 2008** db (85.5) n22 t22 f20.5 b21 Well, that was certainly different! The nose has the oily hallmark of a Caol Ila, though without the phenol intensity. The palate, those oils apart, is a very different tale. A unique flavour profile for sure: a kind of smoked toffee fudge which actually makes your tongue ache while tasting! And there is a bitterness, also. Normally I can spot exactly from where it originates...this one leaves me baffled...though I'd go from the distillation if pushed. *46%.*

Benromach Traditional db **(86)** n22 t21 f21.5 b21.5. Deliciously clean and smoky. But very raw and simplistic, too. *40%*

Benromach Vintage 1976 db **(89.5)** n23 t23.5 f21 b22 hardly complex and shows all the old age attributes to be expected. That said...a very comfortable and satisfying ride. *46%*

Benromach Wood Finish 2007 Sassicaia db **(86.5)** n22 t22 f21 b21.5. Now back to the new distillery. Problem with this wood finish is that even when free from any taint, as this is, it is a harsh taskmaster and keeps a firm grip of any malty development – even on a dram so young. A brave cask choice. *45%*

BLADNOCH
Lowlands, 1817. David Prior. Working.

Bladnoch Aged 6 Years Bourbon Matured db **(91)** n21.5 t22.5 f24 b23 The fun starts with the late middle, where those extra oils congregate and the taste buds are sent rocking. Great to see a Lowlander bottled at an age nearer its natural best and even the smaller cut, in a roundabout way, ensures a mind-blowing dram. *57.3%*

Bladnoch Aged 6 Years Lightly Peated db **(93)** n23 t23 f23.5 b23.5 The peat has nothing to do with the overall score here: this is a much better-made whisky with not a single off-note and the cut is spot on. And although it claims to be lightly peated, that is not exactly true: such is the gentle nature of the distillate, the smoke comes through imperiously and on several levels. "Spirit of the Lowlands" drones the label. Since when has outstanding peated malt been associated with that part of the whisky world...?? *58.5%*

Bladnoch Aged 6 Years Sherry Matured db **(73.5)** n18 t19 f18.5 b18. A sticky, lop-sided malt where something, or a group of somethings, conjures up a very unattractive overture. Feints on the palate but no excellent bourbon cask to the rescue here. *56.9%*

Bladnoch Aged 10 Years db **(94)** n23 t24 f23 b24 This is probably the ultimate Bladnoch, certainly the best I have tasted in over 25 years. This Flora and Fauna bottling by then owners United Distillers should be regarded as the must-get-at-all-costs Bladnoch. If the new owner can create something even to hang on to this one's coat-tails then he has excelled himself. For those few of us lucky enough to experience this, this dram is nothing short of a piece of Lowland legend and folklore. *43%.*

Bladnoch Aged 15 Years db **(91)** n22.5 remnants of zest and barley sit comfortably with the gentle oaks; t22.5 excellent delivery and soon gets into classic Bladnoch citric stride; f23 wonderfully clean barley belies the age and lowers the curtain so delicately you hardly notice; b23 quite outstanding Lowland whisky which, I must admit, is far better than I would have thought possible at this age. *55%*

Bladnoch 18 Years Old db **(88.5)** n21 t23.5 f22 b22. The juiciness and clarity to the barley, and especially the big gooseberry kick, early on makes this a dram well worth finding. *55%*

Acla Selection Bladnoch 25 Years Old barrel, dist 1990, bott 2015 **(95)** n24 t24 f23 b24 The distillery in top gear. *52.2%. nc ncf.*

⟐ **Kirsch Import Bladnoch 1989** refill bourbon barrel, cask no. 1297, bott 2016 **(93)** n23 an unusual fruit note for a bourbon cask: warm raison fudge; lime topping on vanilla ice cream...; t23.5 thick and chewy delivery: truly substantial. The malt is there in plenty, but the oak appears to have a rich coffee-stained friendly arm round it; elsewhere an oily, molassed sweetness forms a comfortable bed; f23 some of the more enthusiastic toasty notes have more to say as the sugars die down; b23.5 a malt which carried it great age with pride and honour. Delicious! *48.7%. 156 bottles.*

Scotch Malt Whisky Society Cask 50.71 Aged 25 Years refill barrel, dist 26 Jan 90, bott 21 Sept 15 **(86.5)** n21.5 t23.5 f20 b21.5. Ostensibly, a gloriously honeyed dram full of dark, brooding corners and spices willing to kill without asking questions. But deeper down there are questions about the cask which are not satisfactorily answered. Even so, the better moments are sheer, unadulterated bliss. *58.2%. nc ncf sc. 165 bottles.*

Scotch Malt Whisky Society Cask 50.75 Aged 25 Years refill barrel, dist 26 Jan 90, bott 30 Nov 15 **(95.5)** n23.5 t24 f24 b24 A much sturdier cask than 50.71 pays handsome dividends. A little honeyed nugget.. *54.1%. nc ncf sc. 108 bottles.*

⟐ **Scotch Malt Whisky Society Cask 50.84 25 Year Old** refill ex-bourbon barrel, dist 15 May 90 **(89.5)** n22.5 the oak has made the biggest investment by far. Despite the obvious over cooking, some major caramel notes have also escaped; tangy with a hint of boiled tomato and French toast, too; t23 great recover on the palate. Where the nose isn't quite sure of its ground, the delivery roars and lets rip with a major salted maple syrup and tannin ensemble, all this cushioned by ever thickening malt; **f22** after the crash, bang, wallop of the oak earlier, this is a plain malty sailing; **b22** a malt which takes on you on a long, convoluted journey spending most of its time trying not to crash into oak. *55.1%.*

⬩⬩⬩ **Spirits Shop Selection Bladnoch 1990** sherry cask, bott 2016 (86.5) **n22 t22.5 f20.5 b21.5** you know when you go into a sweet shop on a hot summer's day...oh, actually if you are from Scotland, you probably don't. Anyway, the fruity sweetness on the nose is just so evocative of that. And the sweetness continues onto the plate in full fruity form. Shame about the tired, bitter cask, though. Ironically, nothing to do with sulphur this time. *47.2%. 117 bottles. A joint bottling with Sansibar Whisky.*

⬩⬩⬩ **The Whisky Agency Bladnoch 25 Years Old** dist 1990 (88) **n22** the distillery always used to have a citrusy element and here it is found in soft lemon drizzle form; **t22.5** initially sumptuous, but those oils soon take a back seat as the chalky tannins change the mouth feel completely; good spice to the mid-ground; **f21.5** just a little too much bitterness; **b22** I suspect five or six years ago this malt was at its zenith. *52.2%.*

BLAIR ATHOL
Highlands (Perthshire), 1798. Diageo. Working.

Blair Athol Aged 12 Years db (77) **n18 t19 f21 b19**. Thick, fruity, syrupy and a little sulphury and heavy. The finish has some attractive complexity among the chunkiness. *43%. Flora and Fauna.*

⬩⬩⬩ **Alos Sansibar Whisky Blair Athol 1988** bott 2016 (89) **n22.5** the slight hint of putty is anything but a pane... Instead it holds the butterscotch and barley together beautifully; **t22.5** dense malt on the palate, then a slow burn of spice and a spreading glow of red liquorice and ulmo honey; **f22** long with the oils continuing to intensify and lengthen the ever richer barley; **b22** hardly textbook, but enjoyable. *50.4%.*

Best Dram Blair Athol 26 Years Old wine treated butt (66.5) **n17 t18.5 f15 b16**. I think they meant "sulphur ruined butt". *57.8%*

C & S Dram Collection Blair Athol Aged 5 Years sherry butt, cask no. 301878, dist 05 Mar 10, bott 18 Jan 16 (76) **n18 t20 f19 b19**. Chugging away pleasantly, I was, with a bunch of ex-bourbon malts. Then picked this up by mistake: my nose alerted me to the error. Harsh, off-key and irritatingly unyielding. *58.5%. sc.*

Cadenhead's Sherry Cask Blair Athol 26 Year Old dist 1989 (91.5) **n24.5 t23 f22 b22** A rather lovely, predominantly clean wine cask at work here. However, not quite enough body in the malt to do it full justice *48.9%. sc.*

⬩⬩⬩ **Cadenhead's Small Batch International Blair Athol 28 Year Old** bourbon casks, dist 1988 (87) **n22.5 t22 f21 b21.5** Everything from the nose to the finish tells you that this bottling peaked a few years earlier as the sugars you'd expect to find have now turned to dry tannin. But there remain green shoots still where there is a late flowering, highlighting the richer, remaining elements of the barley itself. A fascinating display of contrary indicators. *53.6%.*

⬩⬩⬩ **The First Editions Blair Athol Aged 19 Years** 1997 refill sherry butt, cask no. 12823, bott 2016 (83) **n22 t21 f20 b20** Tight and sugary. A malt performing as though in a straitjacket, seemingly unable to relax. Good spices, though. *50.7%. nc ncf sc. 241 bottles.*

Gordon & MacPhail Connoisseurs Choice Blair Athol 2006 (88.5) **n22.5 t22.5 f21.5 b22** Attractive, though quite a few splinters for its age. *46%*

⬩⬩⬩ **Hepburn's Choice Blair Athol 7 Years Old** wine cask, dist 2009, bott 2016 (86.5) **n21 t23 f22 b20.5** A real sweetie. Sugars abound, some of a gristy nature, others of a more fruity origin. Enjoyable, especially on delivery, but don't expect too much in the way of balance. *46%. nc ncf sc. 413 bottles.*

⬩⬩⬩ **Hepburn's Choice Blair Athol 7 Years Old** refill butt, dist 2009, bott 2017 (87) **n21 t23 f21 b22** A chocolaty affair where, thankfully, the butt (though not quite perfect) does little damage. Instead the barley makes an early impact, complete with sugary oils and spices before making its sumptuous praline-laden crescendo. *46%. nc ncf sc. 714 bottles.*

Hidden Spirits Blair Athol BLA.214 11 Years Old cask no. 10614, dist 2002, bott 2014 (91) **n22 t23.5 f22.5 b23** For those of you looking for a juicy malt. This is deceptively delicious. *48%. sc.*

Kingsbury Silver Blair Athol 18 Year Old 1995 sherry butt, cask no. 10459 (68) **n16 t19 f16 b17.** Malty and sugary. But can't escape the confines of the sulphur. This is a lovely company who work hard to bottle great whisky. But 20 years ago I warned them to avoid sherry butts unless they were 100% certain of their quality. With the greatest respect and fondness, I warn them again...! *46%. sc. 762 bottles.*

Old Malt Cask Blair Athol Aged 20 Years sherry butt, cask no. 12149, dist Jun 95, bott Nov 15 **(95) n23.5 t24 f23.5 b24** As close to a chocolate liqueur as you are likely to find in a bottle! *50%. nc ncf sc. 597 bottles.*

Old Masters Blair Athol 28 Year Old cask no. 4865, bott 2016 **(88.5) n22.5 t22.5 f21.5 b22** This one falls into the category of pretty unimpressive spirit when first distilled but over the best part of three decades has mellowed into something charming and almost elegant. *56.5%*

⬥ **Old Particular Blair Athol 21 Years Old** sherry butt, cask no. 11355, dist Sept 95, bott Sept 16 **(89.5) n23.5** stunning fruitcake which is moist in fat sultanas, toasty raisins and nuts...; **t23** you expect some molasses to be lurking around somewhere and it takes little time to arrive, along with a jaunty spiciness; a touch of suet pudding amid the sultanas; **f21** tightens very slightly on the short finish; **b22** not quite a flawless cask, but in today's terms this one's a bit of a belter! *51.5%. nc ncf sc. 204 bottles.*

Provenance Blair Athol Aged 12 Years bott Mar 16 **(81.5) n20.5 t21 f20 b20.** Even after a dozen years there is far more a new make quality than old matured malt about this. Not at all unpleasant, especially when the pithy dryness gets to work. But for the age... *46%. nc ncf sc.*

⬥ **Provenance Blair Athol Aged 14 Years** refill hogshead, cask no. 11488, dist Oct 02, bott Nov 16 **(89.5) n22.5** the malty simplicity is intoxicating; **t22.5** a beautiful array of barley sugar and grist; **f22** some light vanillas and even spice emerge as the oak finally wakes up; **b22.5** Blair Athol at its most clean, malty and refreshing. Great fun! *46%. nc ncf sc. 379 bottles.*

⬥ **Sansibar Whisky Blair Athol 1998** bott 2016 **(83.5) n21.5 t22 f19 b21** No apparent flight plan for this malt, so it lands haphazardly offering random flavours, some fruity and malt-creamy, some, alas, unattractively bitter. *50.7%.*

The Single Cask Blair Athol Aged 22 Years cask no. 7284, dist 13 Aug 91, bott 23 Sept 13 **(88) n21 t23.5 f21.5 b22** OTT in so many ways. But you have to give the honeyed sugars attached to snarling tannins some credit for bravery here...! *54.8%. nc ncf sc.*

BOWMORE
Islay, 1779. Morrison Bowmore. Working.

⬥ **Bowmore Aged 10 Years** Spanish oak sherry casks & hogsheads, bott code: L172033 db **(92.5) n23.5** wow...!! This is some nose: the peat is as hefty and cinderish as I have come across from a Bowmore in an age. The fruit s clean and actually backs the phenols, rather than hinders them: superb! **t23.5** a silky mouth feel is first enriched by muscovado sugars and molasses and then a gradual but unrelenting build up in peat. Very gratifying, indeed...; **f22.5** the phenols return to the ashes suggested on the nose and a little oak, marmalade and burnt sugar bitterness creeps in, also...; **b23** a very happy marriage between some full on peat and decent sherry butts makes for the intense malt promised on the label. *40%.*

Bowmore Aged 12 Years db **(91) n22.5** light peats, the air of a room with a man sucking cough sweets; sweet pipe smoke; **t23.5** soft, beautiful delivery of multi-layered peats; lots of effervescent spices and molassed sugars; spices abound; **f22.5** much drier with sharper berries and barley; the peat still rumbles onwards, but has no problems with the light, sawdusty oaks; **b23.5** this new bottling still proudly carries the Fisherman's Friend cough sweet character, but the coastal, saline properties here are a notch or three up: far more representative of Islay and the old distillery style. Easily by far the truest Bowmore I have tasted in a long while with myriad complexity. Even going back more than a quarter of a century, the malt at this age rarely showed such relaxed elegance. Most enjoyable. *40%*

Bowmore "Enigma" Aged 12 Years db **(82) n19 t22 f20 b21.** Sweet, molassed and with that tell-tale Fisherman's Friend tang representing the light smoke. This Enigma hasn't quite cracked it, though. *40%. Duty Free.*

Bowmore Gold Reef oak casks db **(79) n19.5 t21 f19 b19.5.** Simple, standard (and rather boring and safe) fare for the masses gagged by toffee. *43% WB15/280*

⬥ **Bowmore Aged 15 Years** 1st fill bourbon casks, bott code: L172034 031 db **(88) n23.5** the most most wonderful mix of peat reek and allotment bonfires; **t22** a surprisingly dull delivery where the peat seems to be doused by toasted fudge. A little smoked mocha in the mid-ground, but the messages aren't coming through too clearly; **f21** where did it go...? The finish vanishes under a welter of toffee. Some faint spices, but very disappointing... **b21.5** this was going swimmingly until the caramel just went nuts. I know first-fill bourbon casks are at work here, but hard to believe that was all natural... *43%.*

⬥ **Bowmore Aged 15 Years** sherry cask finish, bott code: L172073 db **(91) n23** light peat leaves plenty of room for the salty caramels and delicate fruitcake; **t22.5** salivating: malty with a chocolate and raisin and fudge slowly massaged with peat; **f22.5** more smoked caramel now with a hint of black cherry; **b23** a sherry influenced whisky outpointing a bourbon cask one....how often will you find that in this book...? *43%.*

Bowmore Aged 17 Years db **(77) n18 t22 f18 b19.** For all the attractiveness of the sweet fruit on delivery, the combination of butt and cough sweet makes for pretty hard going. *43%*

Bowmore Aged 18 Years db **(79) n20 t21 f19 b19.** Pleasant, drinkable Fisherman's Friend style – like every Bowmore it appears around this age. But why so toffee-dull? *43%*

 Bowmore Aged 18 Years Oloroso & Pedro Ximénez casks, bott code: L172067 060 db **(82) n20.5 t22.5 f19 b20** A dirty old nose – and I don't just mean the peat – pre-warns of the furry finish. But there is no denying the sheer joy of the voluptuous grape grappling with the phenols on delivery and in the wonderful moments just after. *43%.*

Bowmore Aged 23 Years Port Matured db **(86) n22 t22 f21 b21.** Have you ever sucked Fisherman's Friends and fruit pastels at the same time, and thrown in the odd Palma Violet for good measure...? *50.8%*

Bowmore Aged 25 Years db **(86) n21 t22 f21 b22.** Not the big, chunky guy of yore: the age would surprise you if tasted blind. *43%*

Bowmore Aged 25 Years Small Batch Release db **(85.5) n21 t22 f21 b21.5.** Distilled at the very heart of Bowmore's peculiar and uniquely distinctive Fisherman's Friend cough sweet era. You will never find a more vivid example. *43%*

Bowmore Aged 30 Years db **(94) n23 t24 f23 b24** A Bowmore that no Islay scholar should be without. Shows the distillery at its most intense yet delicate; an essay in balance and how great oak, peat and fruit can combine for those special moments in life. Unquestionably one of the best Bowmores bottled this century. *43%*

Bowmore Black 50 Year Old db **(96.5) n25 t24 f23 b24.5** a little known fact: a long time ago, before the days of the internet and a world of whisky experts which outnumbers the stars that puncture the sky on the very darkest of nights, I actually tasted the first Black Bowmore in their very basic blending lab and gave it the required seal of approval before they allowed it to hit the shelves. It wasn't a 50-year-old beast like this one, though. And it proves that though something may have reached half a century, it knows how to give pleasure on at least a par with anything younger ... *41%*

Bowmore 1985 db **(89) n21.5 t24 f22 b21.5.** I may have tasted a sweeter Islay. Just not sure when. This whisky is so wrong..it's fantastically right...! *52.6%*

Bowmore 100 Degrees Proof db **(90.5) n22** low key smoke. Anyone who has been to Arbroath looking for where the Smokies are cured and homed in on the spot by nose alone will recognise this aroma...; **t23** delicate in all departments, including the peat. The barley is sweet but it is the tenderness of the oils which stars; **f22.5** long with a tapering muscovado finale; **b23** proof positive! A real charmer. *57.1%. ncf.*

Bowmore Black Rock oak casks db **(87.5) n22.5 t22 f21 b22.** A friendly, full bodied dram whose bark is worse than its bite. Smoked toasted fudge is the main theme. But that would not work too well without the aid of a vague backdrop cinnamon and marmalade. If you are looking for a gentle giant, they don't come more wimpish than this. *40% WB15/336*

Bowmore Devil's Casks III db **(92.5) n23 t23 f23.5 b23.5** a whisky created by Charles Williams, surely. So, at last....I'm in league with the devil...! Hawwww-hhaaaa-haaaaaa!!!! *56.7%*

Bowmore Laimrig Aged 15 Years db **(90.5) n22.5 t23.5 f22 b22.5** first things first: absolutely spot on sherry butts at work here with not a hint of an off note. But often it is hard to get smoke and sherry to gel. The exercise here is not without success, but you feel it is straining at every sinew to hit the high spots. *53.7%. 18,000 bottles.*

Bowmore Laimrig III db **(92) n23.5 t23.5 f22.5 b23** I must ask my research team: where the hell are Laimrigs I and II....? *53.7%*

Bowmore Legend db **(88) n22 t22.5 f22 b22.5.** Not sure what has happened here, but it has gone through the gears dramatically to offer a substantial dram with both big peat and excellent balancing molasses. Major stuff. *40%*

Bowmore Mizunara Cask Finish db **(90.5) n22.5 t22 f23.5 b22.5** A Bowmore like no other: not always happy in its own skin, but when it relaxes towards the finish, it positively pulses its Islay credentials. *53.9%. 2,000 bottles.*

 Bowmore No.1 first fill bourbon casks, bott code: L172026 db **(91.5) n23** takes a little while for the peat to be unlocked and released: the honey-spangled tannins slowly yield to the blossoming but never more than suggestive smoke; the saltiness gives a lovely coastal outline; **t23** top-rate mouth feel: silky texture and, like the nose, restrained smoke. A little maple syrup adds sweetness and texture; **f22.5** dying embers of peat but the vanillas control the moment; a little spice takes the finish further; **b23** Bowmore was never the most peaty of Islay's malts. But here the phenols are at their shyest. Delicate and all a rather sexy tease... *40%.*

Bowmore Small Batch "Bourbon Cask Matured" db (86) n22 t22 f21 b21. A big improvement on the underwhelming previous Small Batch from this distillery, then called "Reserve", though there appears to be a naievity to the proceeding which both charm and frustrate. The smoke, hanging on the grist, is very low key. 40%.

Bowmore Small Batch Reserve db (80.5) n20 t21 f19 b20.5. With a name like "Small Batch Reserve" I was expecting a marriage between intense Kentucky and Islay. Alas, this falls well short of the mark. 40%

Bowmore White Sands Aged 17 Years db (88) n20 t22 f23 b23 A muzzled malt which shouldn't work – but somehow does. 43%

Acla Selection Bowmore 11 Years Old bourbon barrel, dist 2002, bott 2014 (89.5) n22 t23.5 f21.5 b22.5 A slightly better cask would have furthered the enormous strides made by the honey and spice. 52.4%. nc ncf.

Cadenhead's Authentic Collection Bowmore 15 Year Old bourbon hogshead, dist 2001, bott Apr 16 (95.5) n23.5 t24 f24 b24 You have to take your hat off to Cadenhead: they really do bottle some stunners. This is no exception. 54.8%. sc. 264 bottles.

The First Editions Bowmore Aged 15 Years 2000 refill hogshead, cask no. 11783, bott 2015 (94.5) n23.5 t24 f23 b24 The real deal. Bowmore groaning under the distillery's unique character: like a vatting in a cask...!! Takes me back to the early '80s, that! 58.7%. nc ncf sc. 101 bottles.

The Golden Cask Bowmore 13 Years Old cask no. CM 201, dist 2000, bott 2014 (86) n20.5 t23 f21 b21.5. A surging malt which really thumps out the peat in no uncertain terms, the highlight of the show being the first three or four waves after delivery. But the nose and finish reveal a slight niggardliness to the oak which refuses to play ball. 55.5%. sc. 300 bottles.

The Golden Cask Bowmore 15 Years Old cask no. CM 219, dist 2000, bott 2015 (92) n23 t23 f22.5 b23.5 Complex, satisfying whisky which forever shape-shifts on the palate. 58.5%. sc. 185 bottles.

◇ **Kingsbury Gold Bowmore 18 Year Old** hogshead, cask no. 800336, dist 1997 (96) n24 wonderful smoked chocolate mint! t24 the way the sugars and smoke dissolve together is enough to keep you quiet for a little while: spellbinding. A glowing oil is not very far behind, massaging the palate; kumquats add a citrusy zing; f24 lovely late spice before the drier vanillas; b24.5 a Bowmore with no little poise and very comfortable in its own skin. Above all, though, the complexity and balance shoots of the scale. A must find malt. 53.5%. 243 bottles. sc.

◇ **Old Malt Cask Bowmore Aged 14 Years** refill hogshead, cask no. 12765, dist Sept 02, bott Oct 16 (90) n22.5 fresh, salty barley...but where's the smoke? t22 so clean you feel your teeth will sparkle at the end of the tasting session: barley sugar all the way with a lively salty tang to the butterscotch; f22.5 spices tease and the late lemon curd tart embraces the oak beautifully; b23 the peat buds on my nose must be missing... 50%. nc ncf sc. 341 bottles.

◇ **Old Malt Cask Bowmore Aged 20 Years** refill hogshead, cask no. 13284, dist Sept 96, bott Feb 17 (90.5) n22 a vague hint of the house Fisherman's Friend style. But there is a Banbury cake toastiness amid the modest smoke, too; t23 uplifting delivery of early spice seems to emphasise the work of the dark sugars; f22.5 dries towards a low- level sootiness; b23 superb sugar involvement and balance. 50%. nc ncf sc. 239 bottles.

◇ **Old Malt Cask Bowmore Aged 20 Years** refill hogshead, cask no. 13301, dist Sept 96, bott Feb 17 (87) n22 t22.5 f21 b21.5 Enjoy the milk chocolate mousse middle, smoked of course. And with a good spoonful of Demerara sugar mixed in. Elsewhere there are a few bumps and grinds as the gears are not quite found. 50%. nc ncf sc. 275 bottles.

◇ **Old Particular Islay Bowmore 15 Years Old** sherry butt, dist May 00, bott Jun 15 (68) n17 t19 f15 b17. My first sulphur-hammered bottling of the 2017 edition. Also, my first sherry butt... 48.4%. nc ncf sc. 468 bottles.

◇ **Old Particular Bowmore 20 Years Old** refill hogshead, cask no. 11590, dist Dec 96, bott Mar 17 (90.5) n22.5 lightweight smoke, as though you are just the wrong side of the sea breezes the reek leaves the chimney; t23 so clean and juicy! Even now there is a citrus theme which seriously cuts into the weight. The smoke is on slow and low burn and takes its time to build up enough phenols to make an impression; f22.5 light oils and an almost lighter spice; b22.5 unusually creamy Bowmore with a plethora of delicate, satisfying moments. 51.5%. nc ncf sc. 291 bottles.

Scotch Malt Whisky Society Cask 3.249 Aged 14 Years refill hogshead, dist 08 May 01, bott 17 Aug 15 (89) n22 t22.5 f22 b22.5 If it wore hats, it'd have a punk-style baseball cap... 56.4%. nc ncf sc. 252 bottles.

Scotch Malt Whisky Society Cask 3.250 Aged 20 Years refill hogshead, dist 06 Apr 95, bott 21 Sept 15 (83) n21 t21 f20.5 b20.5. Neither a great cask, nor quite the best distillate at work. Tangy, aggressive and ill-at-ease. Some good demerara sugars at work, though. *54.3%. nc ncf sc. 254 bottles.*

⟡ **Scotch Malt Whisky Society Cask 3.274 20 Year Old** refill ex-bourbon hogshead, dist 6 Apr 95 **(93) n23.5** surely distilled from a rock pool...? You might as well be sitting on a rocky outcrop with the sea splashing about you. A little seaweed adds to the coastal picture; kumquats adds a bitter-sweet citrus acidity to the unlikely mix; **t23** no less fresh on delivery: a kind of sugar and salt mix with the tide this time being supplied by the smoke which laps on the highly intense barley, the spices are almost apologetic, while the Fisherman's Friend enters with a cough...; **f23** the citrus on the nose at last turns up; the light phenols fade while the sugars get darker; **b23.5** huge profile, as though the salt has brought the flavours out to their maximum effect. A beautiful and significant cask. *53.1%.*

Svenska Eldvatten Bowmore 2002 ex-bourbon hogshead, dist Mar 02 **(92) n22 t23.5 f23 b23.5** A gorgeous little bottling. *57.1%. sc.*

⟡ **The Whisky Barrel Burns Malt Bowmore 15 Year Old 2001** bourbon barrel, cask no. 31931 **(94) n23** what a fabulous marriage between salt and highly smoked malt. As clean as it is complex the darker sugars are there but lying low; **t24** mouth-filling, chewy and strangely bereft of oil. This allows both the vanilla and soot to have a big say, though the molasses finally pops up for a counter bid; **f23** dries to let the soot back in control. At last some late oils; **b24** Bowmore not a million miles in style to 35 years ago...and the smoke appears to be at the high end, too. *52.5%. sc.*

⟡ **WoodWinters The Four Isle Solera Aged 16 Years (83.5) n22 t22 f19 b20.5** Yes, I know: some people will sell their grandmother on eBay to raise the money for this. The huge, juicy grape locking horns with the peat; mega burnt fruitcake abounding. Yes, a Bowmore collectors' item and all that. But this is one of those malts where you have too much of a good thing and integration is at a premium. Also, the furry finish doesn't help... *58.1%. sc. 700 bottles.*

BRAEVAL

Speyside, 1974. Chivas Brothers. Working.

Chapter 7 Braes of Glenlivet 1994 20 Years Old bourbon barrel, cask no. 165681 **(88.5) n23 t22 f21.5 b22** Revels gloriously in a distinct Chivas, barley-centric style. *50.4%. sc. 172 bottles.*

⟡ **The First Editions Braes of Glenlivet Aged 27 Years 1989** refill hogshead, cask no. 13310, bott 2017 **(86) n21.5 t22.5 f21 b21** Works tirelessly hard to overcome the age-induced oaky imbalance. A little orange blossom honey infuses with the house-style big malty juiciness. But the thudding oak – though not without a vague mocha softness – has the biggest say. *54.9%. nc ncf sc. 144 bottles.*

Five Lions Braes of Glenlivet Aged 20 Years 1st fill American bourbon barrel, dist Dec 94, bott Nov 15 **(94.5) n23 t24 f23.5 b24** More eye-watering than a Virginia McKenna film....and about as clean and wholesome, too. A top grade cask, for sure. *55.3%. nc ncf.*

⟡ **Gordon & MacPhail Connoisseurs Choice Braeval 1998 (90.5) n23** an array of citrus notes most of them heavy and depicting the passing of years: this is the aroma of a whisky usually a lot older than the given vintage; **t23** for the first time barley appears. The delivery is gentle and the oak remains far enough back at first for the malt to make its entrance alone. A short burst of boiled sweet reveals a crispiness to the muscovado sugar before some hazelnut heralds the arrival of the tannin – which is far less aggressive than on the nose; **f22** the finish, by degree reverts back to the big age profile as it dries significantly; **b22.5** a distillery which, through its delicate nature, wears its heart on its sleeves. And this is a very old heart... *46%.*

Hunter Laing's Distiller's Art Braeval Aged 13 Years sherry butt, dist May 02, bott 2016 **(94) n23.5 t23.5 f23 b24** As close to a chocolate liqueur as you are likely to find in a bottle! *48%. nc ncf sc. 438 bottles.*

⟡ **Hunter Laing's Distiller's Art Braeval Aged 14 Years** refill hogshead, dist Dec 01, bott 2016 **(89) n22.5** complex, delicate and borderline playful: youthful for its age but the mix of new mown grass and crushed green hazelnuts is alluring; **t22** salivating with just enough oil to do justice to the rampant barley; **f22** long, youthful yet with a teasing degree of vanilla and spice; **b22.5** this distillery does that understated Speysidey thing so well.. *48%. nc ncf sc. 480 bottles.*

⟡ **Kingsbury Gold Braes of Glenlivet 21 Year Old** barrel, cask no. 165589, dist 1994 **(88.5) n21.5** a bit of a muddle as the citrus and vanilla become hopelessly entangled around the malt; **t23** that's better! The barley is the first to straighten itself out again and really makes its mark. A salty grapefruit thrust through makes for an unlikely follow through; **f21.5** a vague tang bites from the oak but the gentle spices compensate; **b22.5** a malt full of malty energy but sometimes runs before it can walk. All very entertaining but, for a 21-year-old, surprisingly unkempt. *52.2%. 195 bottles. sc.*

Maltbarn Braes of Glenlivet 1994 ex-bourbon cask, bott 2016 **(87) n20 t23 f21.5 b21.5.** A very mild butyric note does not quite scupper an otherwise delicious dram. The chocolate input is borderline insane. And the expected oils do ensure a well dispersed degree of muscovado sugar. If I wasn't such a miserable git demanding faultless whisky, I'd mark this much more highly. *51.7%. sc. 197 bottles.*

Old Malt Cask Braeval Aged 14 Years sherry butt, cask no. 11999, dist May 01, bott Oct 15 **(94) n23.5 t24 f22.5 b24** Oh, it gives the soul so much joy to spend half an hour in the company of a mainly unspoiled sherry butt... *50%. nc ncf sc. 612 bottles.*

◆ **Old Malt Cask Braeval Aged 15 Years** sherry butt, cask no. 13270, dist Dec 01, bott Feb 17 **(85.5) n22 t21.5 f20.5 b21.5** Not sure whether to be pleased or disappointed with this. Anything marked "sherry butt" is enough to have me twitching in the chair and expecting the worst when raising my glass to the nose. But the aroma is initially clean and sulphur free: instead, a floral, salty tannin tone with a lovely toffee popcorn edge can be found. Slowly, though, the first traces of the S word are apparent...which can be found again on the finish after duller than expected delivery. Even so, a malt not without its salivating and delicious moments. *50%. nc ncf sc. 677 bottles.*

Old Malt Cask Braeval Aged 18 Years sherry butt, cask no. 12292, dist Dec 97, bott Feb 16 **(79) n19 t21 f19 b20.** No doubting its sherry cask credentials! Lightly tainted by you-know-what. But still plenty of blood orange to be getting on with. *50%. nc ncf sc. 369 bottles.*

◆ **Old Malt Cask Braeval Aged 25 Years** refill hogshead, cask no. 12815, dist Aug 91, bott Oct 16 **(95) n24** lightly toasted; vague strands of marmalade; old tobacconist's sweetness; honey-speckled grist; **t24** truly melts on the palate: the grist on the nose dissolves on impact leaving wonderful waves of vanilla and macaroons underscored by maple syrup and light oils; **f23** dries elegantly with a dusting of vanilla and oak; **b24** an elegant gem of a dram. *50%. nc ncf sc. 238 bottles.*

Old Particular Speyside Braeval 14 Years Old sherry butt, dist May 01, bott Dec 15 **(90.5) n23 t22.5 f22.5 b22.5** Plays the delicate sugars to near perfection. *51.5%. nc ncf sc. 383 bottles.*

◆ **Old Particular Braeval 15 Years Old** sherry butt, cask no. 11562, dist May 01, bott Nov 16 **(90) n22** even at 15 it is wonderfully green and fresh: a real barley buzz to this; **t23** every bit as salivating as was expected: excellent light oils add richness to both the barley and the light muscovado sugars; **f22.5** a seriously pleasant spiciness to the clean finish; **b22.5** don't be put off by the colour or, rather, lack of it. Obvious this sherry butt was probably carved by Jesus' dad and now emptied is probably found somewhere in the British Museum. But because it is of such antiquity it pre-dates the Great Scottish Sulphur Cock-up and here we can experience Braeval in its most charming malty form. Really lovely stuff. *48.4%. nc ncf sc. 377 bottles.*

◆ **Old Particular Braeval 18 Years Old** sherry butt, cask no. 11205, dist Dec 97, bott Jun 16 **(92) n23.5** a beautiful blend of Manuka and Ulmo honeys, offset by a playful degree of lemon and vanilla; **t23** near perfect weight and balance on delivery: the barley and oak harmonise instantly. Some light muscovado sugars ramp up the barley presence amid the vaguest fruitiness; **f22** the light butterscotch tart dries as the oak reminds you of the serious age to this malt; **b23.5** effortlessly satisfying with sublime use of the sweeter elements. A Speysider for Speyside affectionados. *48.4%. nc ncf sc. 323 bottles.*

◆ **The Single Cask Braeval Aged 22 Years** cask no. 165641, dist 1994 **(93) n23.5** a charming malt although there is a quiet forcefulness to the salty barley. Fresh despite the obvious gathering of less than youthful vanillas; slowly, almost, imperceptibly, an orange-blossom honey note broadens; **t23** excellent blast of eye-watering barley. The sugars are light and lithe and dance in a muscovado fashion until the spiced mocha advances; **f23** sublime spice: not a hint of malice. Just purposeful throbbing in tune to the rhythm of the growing vanilla; **b23.5** a typical example of a malt from a distillery which, at this age, is very comfortable in its own skin. *55%. nc ncf sc.*

◆ **Wemyss Malts Braeval 1994 Oak For All Seasons** first fill barrel, bott 2016 **(91) n22.5** roasting yam with a slight polished oak floor depth; a little smoke adds weight; **t23** barley sugar candy, then roughed up slightly by vaguely salty tannin surge; soft phenols can be spotted against the citrus; **f22.5** late heather honey placates the drier, chalkier vanilla; **b23** a high quality, surprising dram which offers less colour and more smoke than you might expect from a first fill Speysider. *46%. sc. 255 bottles.*

◆ **Whisky Broker Braes of Glenlivet 22 Year Old** barrel, cask no. 65683, dist 20 Dec 94, bott 16 May 17 **(90) n22.5** no shortage of prickle: some boiled over-ripe gooseberry helps fund the softer sugar reserves while the barley is delightfully deft, almost ethereal; **t23** beautiful laying of sugars, like a bouquet of sweetness attractively displayed but all seeming to have been generated by rich barley and its accompanying grist; **f22** the tannins arrive and nibble around the tongue a bit; **b22.5** until the oak makes some slightly unwelcome late inroads, this is a story of delightful barley. 48.9%.

BRORA
Highlands (Northern), 1819–1983. Diageo. Closed.

Brora 37 Year Old refill American oak hogsheads, dist 1977 db **(94.5) n23 t24 f23.5 b24** As it was I who first discovered the hidden and unloved hoards of Brora casks over 25 years ago, I feel a proprietorial claim to this distillery – especially as the 1977 stocks were among the first I managed to get bottled as a 12-year old. A quarter of a century on, one has to say that the journey continues against the odds, perhaps with a creaking malt on the wane but one still defiantly refusing to concede that its days of outstanding beauty are over.... Make no mistake: it is still a stunner, after all these years.... 50.4%. 2,976 bottles. Diageo Special Releases 2015.

◈ **Brora Aged 38 Years** dist 1977 db **(96.5) n24** minty phenols linking with exotic fruit in almost perfect harmony; **t24** the smoke displays a quiet authority from the moment it first reaches the lips. The exotic fruit on the nose really does show a few rings on the tree here...but the gentle but assertive maple syrup, heather honey and natural caramel quickly sands down any splinters; **f24** drier, saltier finale with the smoke slowly transmogrifying into a the lightest spiced chocolate caramel imaginable...; **b24.5** where the 2015 bottling was a battle to keep the braying tannins in harness, this version has managed to link up both the peat and oak in thoroughbred pose. Soul-kissingly beautiful. 48.6%. 2,984 bottles. Diageo Special Releases 2016.

BRUICHLADDICH
Islay, 1881. Rémy Cointreau. Working.

Bruichladdich 10 Years Old db **(90) n22** beautifully clean and zesty, the malt is almost juvenile; **t23** sweet, fruity then malty charge along the tastebuds that geets the mouth salivating; **f23** the usual soft vanilla and custard but a bigger barley kick in the latter stages; **b22** more oomph than previous bottlings, yet still retaining its fragile personality. Truly great stuff for a standard bottling. 46%

Bruichladdich 12 Years Old 2nd Edition db **(88) n23 t22 f22 b21.** A similar type of wine involvement to "Waves", but this is oilier in the old-fashioned 'Laddie style and lacks a little of the sparkle. The fruit on the finish is outstanding, though, and I don't think you or I would turn down a third glass... 46%

Bruichladdich 15 Years Old 2nd Edition db **(86) n22 t23 f20 b21.** Delicious, as usual, but something, possibly fruity, appears to be holding back the show. 46%

Bruichladdich 16 Years Old bourbon cask db **(89) n22.5 t22.5 f22 b22.** Plucked from the cask in the nick of time. In this state rather charming, but another Summer or two might have seen the oak take a more sinister turn. 46%

Bruichladdich XVII Aged 17 Years bourbon/renegade rum db **(92) n23 t23.5 f22 b23.5.** Always good to see the casks of drier, more complexly structured rums being put to such intelligent use. My sample doesn't tell me which rum casks were used, but I was getting vivid flashbacks here of Ruby-Topaz Hummingbirds flitting from flower to flower in the gardens of the now closed Eigflucht distillery in Guyana in the long gone days when I used to scramble around the warehouses there. That distinctive dryness though is pure Enmore, though some Barbadian rum can offer a similar effect. Something very different and a top quality experience. 46%. nc ncf.

Bruichladdich 18 Years Old bourbon/cognac cask db **(84.5) n23.5 t21 f20 b20.** Big oak-spice buzz but thin. Sublime grapey nose, for sure, but pays a certain price, ultimately, for associating with such an inferior spirit... 46%

Bruichladdich 2004 Islay Barley Valinch fresh sherry butt db **(89.5) n22.5 t24 f21 b22.** Yet another quite fabulous bottling form Bruichladdich, this one really cranking up the flavours to maximum effect. Having said all that, call me mad if you will...but seeing as this is Islay barley, would it not have been a good idea to shove it into a bourbon barrel, so we could see exactly what it tastes like? Hopefully that is on its way... 57.5%

◈ **Bruichladdich Bere Barley 2009 7 Years Old** bourbon barrel, cask no. 16/102 db **(94) n23** no attempt of phenolic power here: just subtle smoke offering both a light peat and a delicate anthracite-style acidity. Gentle, newly-sharpened pencil tannins integrate with the smoke; **t23.5** not a delivery automatically associated with this distillery. Or, rather, it is but that is if you were around 30 years ago. Then the malt had a light, sweet oiliness to accompany the delivery – and here it is again. Then, though, there was no peat – and now there is. The sugars boast a green sharpness – probably from the grain - which contrasts well with the phenols; **f23.5** long, still green and bright but with the salty vanilla working beautifully in tandem with the smoke; **b24** Bruichladdich wearing very different colours. Fabulous. *50%.*

Bruichladdich Infinity Third Edition refill sherry tempranillo db **(94.5)** n24 t24 f23 b23.5. I dare anybody who says they don't like smoky whisky not to be blown away by this. Go on...I dare you... *50%*

Bruichladdich Islay Barley Aged 5 Years db **(86)** n21 t22.5 f21.5 b21. The nose suggests a trainee has been let loose at the stills. But it makes amends with an almost debauched degree of barley on delivery which lasts the entirety of the experience. Heavens! This is different. But I have to say: it's bloody fun, too! *50%. nc ncf.*

◇ **Bruichladdich Classic Laddie** cask no. 16/175 db **(93)** n22.5 some lovely younger notes give a vibrancy to the deft smoke; **t23.5** yes, we really do have the odd pre-pubescent barley note on the loose, ensuring a spectacular degree of juiciness. The smoke falls into place naturally; **f23.5** my word! Some quite brilliant spirit and excellent casks have been brought together here. Even as the butterscotch merges into the light phenols, there is a joyous celebration of malt at its most natural that is almost giddying...; **b23.5** well, call me an ol' stick in the peat. But I'd regard a Classic Laddie as unsmoked....then, I must be of a certain age now, I suppose. This youthful cracker'll more than do, though... *50%.*

◇ **Bruichladdich Islay Barley 2010 7 Years Old** bourbon/French wine cask, cask no. 17/011 db **(87.5)** n21.5 t23.5 f21 b22 There is a rawness to this which brings a tear to the eye. Both the nose and finish are perhaps a little hamstrung, most probably by the French influence. But the delivery is something else! Brilliantly youthful, the peat doesn't even try to integrate, but comes at you full force. The grist still shews a fresh barley side to its nature divorced from the phenols, while a red liquorice and ulmo honey middle reveals a light degree of oak and sticky sweetness. But it is that no-holds-barred delivery which will win your smoky heart. *50%.*

◇ **Bruichladdich The Laddie Eight Years Old** American & European oak, cask no. 16/070 db **(83)** n21.5 t22 f19 b20.5 Doesn't chime anything like so well as the Classic Laddie, for instance. The sugars surge and soar in impressive manner, the mid-range smokiness benefitting. But there is a tightness which does very few favours. *50%.*

Bruichladdich Laddie Classic Edition 1 db **(89.5)** n23 t23 f21 b22.5. You probably have to be a certain vintage yourself to fully appreciate this one. Hard to believe, but I can remember the days when the most popular malt among those actually living on Islay was the Laddie 10. That was a staunchly unpeated dram offering a breezy complexity. Not sure of the age on this Retroladdich, but the similarities almost bring a lump to the throat... *46%*

Bruichladdich Scottish Barley The Classic Laddie db **(78.5)** n20 t21.5 f18 b19. Not often a Laddie fluffs its lines. But despite some obviously complex and promising moves, the unusual infiltration of some sub-standard casks has undone the good of the local barley. If you manage to tune out of the off-notes, some sublime moments can still be had. *50%. nc ncf sc.*

Bruichladdich Sherry Classic Fusion: Fernando de Castilla bourbon/Jerez de la Frontera db **(91)** n23 t23 f22 b23. What a fantastically stylish piece of work! I had an overwhelming urge to sing Noel Coward songs while tasting this: for the Dry Martini drinkers out there who have never thought of moving on to Scotch... *46%*

Bruichladdich X4 db **(82)** n18 t22 f21 b21. Frankly, like no new make I have ever come across in Scotland before. Thankfully, the taste is sweet, malty and compact: far, far better than the grim, cabbage water nose. Doesn't really have the X-Factor yet, though. *50%*

The Laddie Ten American oak db **(94.5)** n24 t23.5 f23 b24 This, I assume, is the 2012 full strength version of an Islay classic which was the preferred choice of the people of Islay throughout the 70s, 80s and early 90s. And I have to say that this is already a classic in its own right.... *46%. nc ncf.*

The Laddie Sixteen American oak db **(88)** n22 huge natural caramels dipped in brine; **t22.5** very even and gentle with a degree of citrus perking it up; **f21.5** reverts to caramels before the tannins strike hard; **b22** oak 'n' salt all the way... *46%*

The Laddie Twenty Two db **(90.5)** n24 a breakfast plate of three pieces of toast: one with salted butter, another with ulmo honey and the last one with marmalade; light spices, too. Busy yet understated; **t23** silky salted butters again on delivery immediately backed by intense barley sugar; **f21.5** the oak cranks up significantly; **b22** fabulous coastal malt, though the oak is a presence always felt. *46%*

Octomore 5 Years Old db **(96)** n23.5 t24.5 f24 b24. Forget about the age. Don't be frightened by the phenol levels. Great whisky is not about numbers. It is about excellent distillation and careful maturation. Here you have a memorable combination of both... *63.5%*

Octomore Edition 5.1 db (**91.5**) n23 t22.5 f23 b23. A slightly less complex version, probably because of the obvious lack of years. Great fun, though. *59.9%*

Octomore Edition 6.1 Aged 5 Years bourbon cask db (**91.5**) n24 t23 f22 b22.5 A slightly different Octomore, a little more tart than usual and wears its youth with pride. *57%*

Octomore Edition 6.2 Aged 5 Years Cognac cask db (**90**) n22.5 t23.5 f22 b22 One of the sweetest bottlings from this distillery of all time. Some warming late spice, too; *58.2%*.

Octomore Edition 7.1 Aged 5 years (208 ppm) db (**96.5**) n24 t24.5 f24 b24 A gargantuan malt which will make short work of the feint hearted... This, also, was the whisky which Islay whisky maker par excellence Jim McEwen decided to bow out on. Farewell, Jim, my dear old friend of some 35 years. You have been to Scotch whisky what Jock Stein was to Scottish football; what Octomore is to Islay malt.... *59.5%*

Bruichladdich Ocotomore 7.1 5 Years Old ex-bourbon casks, cask no. 16/080 db (**96**) n23.5 it's Octomore, ain't it! And it's a nipper! So it's in your face peat and young malt all the way, sweet, unsophisticated and not for the faint hearted...; t24.5 the delivery is just one of those rare treats I am lucky enough to encounter once every now and again in my job: it makes all those dreadful, heart-breaking sulphured sherry disasters bearable (just)...Not a sherry butt in sight, just good ol' dependable bourbon and it plays a vital part here as the light vanillas which fill the background act as a superb stage. The early lead is the juiciest peated malt you'll ever encounter, green and fresh yet with a mix of gristy sugars, dry Lubeck marzipan and pulsing phenols; acacia honey adds another thin layer of extra sweetness; f24 inevitably the spices have to arrive. And they do here – with a much more power and intent than first seemed possible. The sugars have backed off slightly, allowing the peat a sooty, drier finale; b24 fan-bloody-tastic...!! A kid of a whisky which sorts the men from the boys... *57%*.

Bruichladdich Ocotomore 7.2 5 Years Old bourbon & Syrah casks, cask no. 15/058 db (**81.5**) n21 t23 f18 b19.5 I love the fact that the sample bottles I have been sent under "education." An hilarious first. But here, if anything is to be learned by those who for some reason don't already know, is the fact that you don't piss around with perfection. Five-year-old Octomore in bourbon cask is a joy that has just about proved beyond description for me. Pointlessly add wine casks – and the sulphur which so often accompanies them – and you get a whisky very much reduced in quality and stature. Some superb moments on this, especially round the time of the warts-and-all delivery. But as it settles the faults of the Syrah casks slowly become clear. What a shame. And waste of great whisky. An education, indeed! *58.5%*.

Octomore 10 db (**95**) n24 t24 f23 b24 When I am tasting an Octomore, it means I am in the home straight inside the stadium after running (or should I say nosing and tasting) a marathon. After this, there are barely another 20 more Scotch malts to go and I am closing in on completing my 1,200 new whiskies for the year. So how does this fair? It is Octomore. It is what I expect and demand. It gives me the sustenance and willpower to get to that crossing line. To tell you guys about a whisky like this is always worth it...whatever the pain and price. Because honesty and doing the right thing is beyond value. Just ask David Archer... *50%. nc ncf.*

Port Charlotte 2007 CC:01 Aged 8 Years bourbon/Cognac casks, cask no. 16/072 db (**94.5**) n23.5 very strident, acidic phenols, parched soot with a trace sweetness to the peat; a tight, vaguely fruity belt keeps everything in shape; t23.5 clipped delivery: the peat and sugars arrive staccato and, like the nose, struggle to move particularly freely; some sublime oils carry a degree of chocolate; f23.5 quite an attractive smoked butterscotch with a twist of praline; the late spices are stirring; b24 I think today I have tasted no less than seven Cognac/French wine finishes; a record. I had forgotten, but it turns out to be the day the French have elected a new president. Odd that. Here the Cognac can do little to lessen the impact of the huge peat and even offers a comforting, firm sweetness. However, the success of this over the PC 16/002 is the intensity of the phenol rather than the magic of the Cognac cask alone, though it certainly contributes. *57.8%*.

Port Charlotte Heavily Peated db (**94.5**) n23 t24 f23.5 b24 Rearrange the following two words: "giant" and "gentle". *50%*

Port Charlotte The Peat Project db (**95.5**) n24.5 t24 f23 b24 This is not peat for peat's sake. This appears to be crafted and layered, offering a pleasing timbre and unusual gracefulness. *46% WB15/339*

Port Charlotte Scottish Barley cask no. 16/002 db (**93.5**) n23.5 big smoke, but billows out freely and relaxed: sugars are of a slightly angular, vaguely demerara style, the vanillas only half-formed but still present; something of the mash tun still about this; t24 a gripping delivery: soft and velvety, the sugars soon melt leaving behind ever-intensifying degrees of smoke. By the mid-ground we have moved into mocha and praline mode, despite there being no obvious great age; **f23** silky still and seemingly drawing upon the grist for extra smoke and sugars; **b23** sweet, youthful and a deceptively light smokiness: it sometimes appears heavier than it actually is! *50%*.

Dramfool Lochindaal Aged 5 Years refill bloodtub, cask no. 4411, dist Dec 10, bott Feb 16 **(93.5) n24 t23.5 f23 b23** Can you have too much of a good thing? Well, this is staggering whisky, for sure. And Peat Heads the world over can now happily write their wills and curl up and die once they have tasted this. But, for all the fun, the balance has been compromised by the sheer outrageousness of the phenols. But would I have another glass full....? I'd chop yer bloody fingers off for it...! *61.4%. nc ncf sc. 42 bottles.*

Dramfool Lochindaal 9 Years Old sherry cask, dist 1 Jun 10, bott 20 May 16 **(92) n24 t23 f22 b23** Question. What do you get if you cross a massively peated malt with a big, clean, unsulphured sherry cask? Answer. This. *58.2%. nc ncf sc. 187 bottles.*

◇ **Fadandel.dk Bruichladdich 14 Year Old** cask no. 569, dist Nov 01, bott Jul 16 **(92) n22.5** gorgeously raw nose with even the soften caramel notes possessing some attitude; the vaguest, most laid-back, barely visible smoke; **t24** what a delivery! Like the nose, it is the caramel off the cask which celebrates its starring part with a towering performance; the sugars are pure grist, the salt a heady sprinkling to maximise effect; like the nose the phenols are barely discernible and are busier forming the ballast rather than shaping the malt; **f22.5** buttery and a little bitter on the vanilla fade; **b23** has that wonderful feel of a malt taken directly, and that second, from the cask. Excellent. *57.2%. nc ncf sc. 276 bottles.*

Gordon & MacPhail Cask Strength Bruichladdich 1994 (96) n24 t24 f24 b24 Hear that purring noise? That's me tasting this exquisite original style Bruichladdich which just gives an almost imperceptible nod towards the newer persona. *56.2%*

Hidden Spirits Bruichladdich BRC.315 12 Years Old cask no. 0311A, dist 2003, bott 2015 **(92) n23 t24 f22 b23** A rather lovely cask at play here. *48%. sc.*

◇ **Liquid Treasures Bruichladdich 26 Year Old** bourbon cask, dist 1990, bott 2017 **(91.5) n23.5** elegant egg-custard and muscovado sugar: something of an eggnog. Delicate and brittle barley on equal terms with the light vanillas; **t23** how a whisky can spend over quarter of a century in the cask and still have something of a fresh gristiness at play, you tell me. But the palate is covered in all kinds of light citrusy sugars which melt with the gentle barley; **f22** just a little tang of tiredness, but the spices are still working with the sugars; **b23** traditional unpeated style – and doesn't look any the worse for it. *47.3%. Faces of Angkor Edition.*

◇ **That Boutique-y Whisky Company Bruichladdich 12 Year Old** batch 3 **(94) n24** rather than smoke you'll see a massive degree of diced dry, salty coconut amid the vanilla and malt mix; has a lovely morning cereal feel. Any smoke located is little more than ballast. This is seriously classy **t23.5** again, the smoke has gone AWOL, or rather the vast majority of it has. Which gives us a great opportunity to enjoy the structure of the malt itself. Intriguingly it displays both firm and slightly oilier traits on just about equal footing. The malt – again of a breakfast cereal type – still has enough in reserve to juice the palate up. But the vanilla, tinged with a hint of vaguely smoked mocha, has the biggest say; **f23** more of the same, but more softly now; **b23.5** must be a first fill bourbon in there somewhere as this is showing good age. Great to see a Laddie so close to its old-fashioned form: a treat of a dram. *52.4%. 275 bottles.*

◇ **Xtra Old Particular Islay Bruichladdich 25 Years Old** refill hogshead, cask no. 11204, dist May 91, bott Jun 16 **(94.5) n23** a slightly tiring cask with the oak a little noisier than it might be. But the barley is attractively layered, a tad salty and more than a match for the tannins; **t24** Fox's Butter Crinkle biscuits from yesteryear, with a stunning layering of acacia honey which apparently has been lightly salted; **f23** the oak which has much to say on the nose, can be heard again . But the quality of the perky barley is breathtakingly fine; **b23.5** old school Laddie: peat-free and living entirely off its considerable charm. *54.6%. nc ncf sc. 197 bottles.*

BUNNAHABHAIN

Islay, 1881. Burn Stewart Distillers. Working.

Bunnahabhain Aged 12 Years db **(85.5) n20 t23 f21 b21.5**. Lovers of Cadbury's Fruit and Nut will adore this. There is, incongruously, a big bourbony kick alongside some smoke, too. A lusty fellow who is perhaps a bit too much of a bruiser for his own good. Some outstanding moments, though. But, as before, still a long way removed from the magnificent Bunna 12 of old... *46.3%. nc ncf.*

Bunnahabhain Aged 16 Years Manzanilla Sherry Wood Finish db **(87) n20.5 t23 f21.5 b22.** The kind of undisciplined but fun malt which just makes it up as it goes along... *53.2%*

Bunnahabhain Aged 18 Years db (93.5) n24 a sumptuous amalgam of lightly salted roasted hazelnut shimmering within its own oil. Oloroso bulging with toasted, slightly singed currants, a sliver of kumquat and topped by thick vanilla. Irresistible... t24.5 almost impossible to fault: the oloroso grandly, almost pompously, leads the way exuding thick, Christmas pudding depth; a light muscovado sugar top dressing counters the deeper, lightly salted vanillas which begin to emerge; f22 a very slight sulphury note sullies the tone somewhat, but there is still enough rich vanilla and spotted dick for some enjoyable afters; b23 only an odd cask has dropped this from being a potential award winner to something that is merely magnificent... 46.3%. nc ncf.

Bunnahabhain XXV Aged 25 Years db (94) n23 t24 f23 b24 No major blemishes here at all. Carefully selected sherry butts of the highest quality (well, except maybe one) and a malt with enough personality to still gets its character across after 25 years. Who could ask for more...? 46.3%. nc ncf.

⬧ **Bunnahabhain 46 Year Old** db (91) n24 bourbon...Kentucky-by-the-Sea!! Salty big liquorice-shaped tannins with a mix of molasses and fruit which gets greater as the whisky oxidises in the glass. So many bourbon tones, yet as though it has been reduced by water from a rock pool...; t23 big age kick, but the more militant of the tannins are quietened by the sugars; f21.5 the oak shows one creak too many, though salty caramel moves in fill the cracks; b22.5 needs a good half hour in the glass to open up and have justice done to it. Perishes towards the end, but the nose and build up to that are remarkably beautiful for a whisky which normally doesn't do age very well at all.... 42.1%.

Bunnahabhain Ceòbanach db (87.5) n21.5 t22.5 f21.5 b22. An immensely chewable and sweet malt showing little in years but much in character. A charming liquorice and acacia honey lead then a developing, dry smokiness. Great fun. 46.3%

Bunnahabhain Darach Ùr Batch no. 4 db (95) n24 t24.5 f23 b23.5 Because of my deep love for this distillery, with my association with it spanning some 30 years, I have been its harshest critic in recent times. This, though, is a stunner.. 46.3%. nc ncf.

⬧ **Bunnahabhain Moine 7 Year Old Oloroso Finish** db (85) n22 t23.5 f18 b21.5 Some three decades ago Bunna's warehouse manager and I would spend the odd long summer evening, year after year, going through samples of maturing stock, many of which were coming to life in dripping sherry butts. But that was a different whisky to this entirely: there was no peat. And the sulphur craze which was to dent the quality of so much Scotch had not yet arrived on Islay's shores, or even Scotland's. So the 7-year-old would taste nothing like this – instead it was usually maltier, a little creamier and showing the very first hints of a saltiness. It was even and relaxed. Which, sadly, this isn't. The faults are apparent on both nose and finish especially. But the grape intensity of the delivery is, momentarily, something special. 60.1%.

Bunnahabhain Toiteach db (78) n19 t21 f19 b19. Cloying, sweet, oily, disjointedly smoky. Had you put me in a time capsule at the distillery 30 years ago, whizzed me forward to the present day and given me this, it would have needed some serious convincing for me to believe this to be a Bunna. 46%

Bunnahabhain Toiteach Un-Chillfiltered db (75.5) n18 t21 f17.5 b19. A big gristy, peaty confrontation on the palate doesn't hide the technical fault lines of the actual whisky. 46%. ncf.

Acla Selection Bunnahabhain 23 Years Old refill sherry butt, dist 1990, bott 2013 (84) n20 t23 f20 b21. Back in the summer of 1990, in the days when it was owned by Highland Distillers, I was staying at Bunna when a batch of sherry butts turned up. The warehouseman, a friend of mine, was not impressed: "If I had it my way, every bugger would be sent back" he complained. Then adding with weary resignation, "but what's the point? I'd just get another consignment every bit as bad as these..." Well, the good news is that this is not from the awful sherry butts I saw delivered all those years back. But it is no oil painting, either. This is a clumsy dram where the frailties of the sherry diminish from the absolute brilliance of the honeyed, almost Highland Park style, body of the malt. Tarnished gold if ever there was.... 47.2%. nc ncf.

Eiling Lim Bunnahabhain 34 Years Old 1980 bott 2014 (96) n24 t24 f23.5 b24 When this dram was made, the people at the distillery told me that their whisky peaked at about 18 years and anything older than that really needed to be carted off for blending. Oh, if only those lovey folk of those days could taste this now: how can something survive so long yet be so delicate? We would have such a ceilidh to celebrate. 46.2%. nc ncf sc. 50 bottles. 7th Release.

The First Editions Bunnahabhain Aged 25 Years 1989 refill hogshead, cask no. 11783, bott 2015 (93.5) n23.5 t24 f23 b23 An angular, moody dram which never sits still for a moment. Pretty delicious, though! 49.4%. nc ncf sc. 136 bottles.

⟐ **Gordon & MacPhail Cask Strength Bunnahabhain 2007** bott 22 Nov 16 (93.5) n23.5 easily one of the most interesting Bunna noses I have encountered in phenol form: not technically perfect but the Love Heart candy sharpness works in wonderful tandem with the unlikely Blue Mountain coffee; t23.5 lightly oiled but it is the busy attack of pinprick spices which takes the breath away. Juicy with the grist radiating a beautifully weighted sweetness which works perfectly in tandem with the drier vanilla; f23 long with the spices, still bitty and busy, lingering. The smoke, never of great stature, somehow reaches the end without having diminished; b23.5 some magnificent cask selection at play here. Well done G&M!! 55.8%.

Gordon & MacPhail MacPhail's Collection Bunnahabhain 2006 (88.5) n22 t22 f22.5 b22 Having stayed in the distillery's long defunct workmen's cottages as storms lash against the distillery and my windows, offering the perception that both would give way at any moment, it is strange to encounter a Bunna so placid in temperament... 43%

Gordon & MacPhail MacPhail's Collection Peated Bunnahabhain 8 Year Old (87) n22 t22 f21 b22. An exceptionally polite and understated Bunna. The peat is of the unyielding variety: hard and abrupt. Opens very slowly but closes at thrice the speed. 43%

Hepburn's Choice Bunnahabhain 8 Years Old refill hogshead, dist 2007, bott 2015 (71) n17 t19 f17 b18. Very poorly made whisky. From a distillery as great as Bunna, one expects so much better. 46%. nc ncf sc. 364 bottles.

Hidden Spirits Bunnahabhain 7 Years Old cask no. BU815, dist 2008, bott 2015 (79) n19 t20.5 f19 b20.5. Malty, at times intense, a little wisp of salt on the delicate phenols and light powdering of muscovado sugar. But, for all that, not a great spirit and fails to sit comfortably. 48%. sc.

⟐ **Hunter Laing's Old & Rare Bunnahabhain Aged 27 Years** refill hogshead, dist Oct 89, bott Jan 17 (93) n23.5 that point of exquisite pain when we are just passing the point of exotic fruit and moving into the first phases of over-tired oak. The tannins do possess a harshness, but just enough of the fruit hangs around to ensure a degree of beauty is still there to be savoured; t23 following a nano-second of lush sugar those more aggressive tannins arrive in force. It takes several flavours waves of intense caramel, light ulmo honey and some retained fruitiness to flush out the toastier notes; f23.5 settles back for a long, elegant finish, now adding a light saltiness and kumquat note to the butterscotch; b23 the great age of this malt is etched into every sniff and mouthful. More than the temples are grey, but it remains distinguished nonetheless. 50.8%. nc ncf sc. 198 bottles.

⟐ **Kingsbury Gold Bunnahabhain 14 Year Old** butt, cask no. 2890, dist 2002 (72) n18 t20 f17 b17 A seriously bitter dram. 53.8%. 413 bottles. sc.

Kingsbury Gold Bunnahabhain 17 Year Old 1997 hogshead, cask no. 5382 (91.5) n22.5 t23.5 f22.5 b23 Everything is laid back and/or in slow motion...and very much closer to a Highland Park in character than a usual Bunna. 52.5%. sc. 289 bottles.

The Loch Fyne Bunnahabhain 14 Year Old sherry cask, cask no. 1606, dist Dec 01, bott Dec 15 (86) n22 t22 f20.5 b21.5. Curiously lacking in the riveting coastal feel which was once the byword and trademark of this distillery. Instead offers an attractive fudge and raisin malt with a little bit of a tang at the finish. 48%. sc. 960 bottles.

Old Malt Cask Bunnahabhain Aged 26 Years refill hogshead, cask no. 12142, dist Oct 89, bott Nov 15 (87.5) n22 t22 f21 b21.5. Maybe just a little too eye-watering for its own good. Sharp and uncompromising, this has much more to do with the state of the cask than the distillate, which is honest and massively malt-proud. 50%. nc ncf sc. 215 bottles.

⟐ **Old Malt Cask Bunnahabhain Aged 26 Years** refill hogshead, cask no. 12626, dist Oct 89, bott Jun 16 (92.5) n23.5 dispersing peat reek hanging on the salty wind blowing across a Highland coastal village...; t23.5 excellent array of sugar, ranging from lightly smoked brist to Manuka honey. The tannins are confident yet respectful; f22.5 a surprising degree of late juiciness despite the malt's ever-drying nature; b23 the half-hearted smokiness ensures an attractively understated yet complex dram. 49.8%. nc ncf sc. 127 bottles.

⟐ **Old Particular Bunnahabhain 15 Years Old** sherry butt, cask no. 11604, dist Dec 01, bott Mar 17 (87) n22 t23 f20 b22 A clammy malt, moist and sticky on the palate, especially when the fruitcake kicks in. Not at all bad, but there is a slightly jarring bitterness out of keeping with the excellent dates and raisins. 48.4%. nc ncf sc. 611 bottles.

⟐ **Provenance Bunnahabhain Aged 8 Years** refill hogshead, cask no. 11561, dist Jun 08, bott Nov 16 (83.5) n21.5 t22 f20 b20 A malty cove, quite literally. But just a little too new make heavy for any serious balance to be achieved or for the rougher edges to be blunted. 46%. nc ncf sc. 451 bottles.

⟐ **Provenance Bunnahabhain Aged 9 Years** refill hogshead, cask no. 11185, dist Mar 07, bott May 16 (88) n22 youthful, sensual barley; t22.5 beautifully intense malt which positively puckers the taste buds. A lovely biscuit meal middle; **f21.5** just a little spice to the lazy cocoa; **b22** straight as a die and with a malty intensity which works rather well. 46%. nc ncf sc.

◈ **The Single Cask Bunnahabhain Aged 25 Years** cask no. 5429, dist 1991 **(86) n21.5 t22 f21 b21.5** No off notes as such. But curiously herbal and medicinal without the aid of any peat reek. Somehow the fruit and tannin fail to maximise the husky honeyed depth and, weirdly it ends up as a dry experience. I'm sure some will adore this, and yes it does have some lovely individual moments But I'm struggling to find a narrative here and must rank this as a completely new branch of Bunna personality in the 35 years I have been tasting this stuff! 48.8%. nc ncf sc.

◈ **Wemyss Malts Bunnahabhain 1990 Haven Trail** hogshead, bott 2016 **(87) n22.5 t23.5 f20 b21** Sometimes you just have to hold your hands up and say sorry: this cask is too old to go solo. And what you do is that you find another cask or group of them to be added to so the very best use can be made of the big tannins which are knocking the single cask out of kilter. And perhaps this should have happened here: the salt, tannin and honey could each have made a very special contribution within a blend. If you find yourself with this try it out with some other malts you may possess. Or simple forget the tannin overdose at the death and concentrate on the brief magnificence of the acacia and ulmo honeys mingling with the salted barley concentrate. Just for the odd nano second you think you detect perfection....and then, regrettably, the oak moves in... 46%. sc. 236 bottles.

◈ **The Whisky Agency Bunnahabhain 1989 (94) n23.5** the rhythm of the nose has a citrusy beat: both the oak and barley appear to have contributed to the fruitiness, the grapefruit especially, but there is no escaping the age, either. Salty and deep, the vanilla and butterscotch are almost a given...; **t23.5** adore the weight and structure to this. Oilier than most Bunnas, there is a concentrated over-ripe pear juice sweetness offsetting the stark, drier vanilla: both chalky and juicy at the same time; **f23** the oak dominates the structure, but a little salty barley still holds on tight; **b24** rare to see a Bunna handle so many passing years with such aplomb, though hardly with ease. 44%.

◈ **Whisky Broker Bunnahabhain 26 Year Old** hogshead, cask no. 7728, dist 22 Dec 89, bott 18 Nov 16 **(89) n22.5** a mix of spiced almonds and light maple syrup; busy and fascinating; **t23** much fresher, juicier delivery than nose with a telling barley contribution. The mid-ground becomes a little untidy as some tried oak and spice arrive; **f21.5** the finish remains muddled; **b22** lovely in to start with but wilts under the oak influence. 44.6%.

◈ **Wilson & Morgan Barrel Selection Bunnahabhain 15 Year Old 2016** sherry wood, cask no. 1431, dist 2001 **(88) n23** absolutely dripping in oloroso; a distinctive spotted- dog suet pudding feel to this: thick and clammy; **t22.5** begins brightly as a linear continuation of the rich nose. Voluptuous, but soon a little bitterness begins to take a grip; **f21** dry and slightly fluffy; **b21.5** just about gets away with the sulphur treatment: it is in there, lightly, but is out-muscled by the intense grape. 60.2%. sc.

◈ **World of Orchids Bunnahabhain 25 Year Old** bourbon cask, dist 1990 **(94) n24** now that is a bit special: the honey has a slight heather-gathered feel to it but mainly it is coastal with a big saline flourish. Complex and magnificently weighted; **t23** none of the usual big dance. But the richness of the ulmo honey and intense barley absorb them with ease. A gorgeous, measured oiliness fully implements the will of the spice; **f23.5** long, mildly luxuriant and still pulsing the firm vanilla and slightly salty theme: a confident sign off...; **b23.5** Bunna in all its old-fashioned unpeated, old school excellence. And, not only that, unusually for the distillery, it has thrived in its great age 47.7%.

Xtra Old Particular Islay Bunnahabhain 25 Years Old refill hogshead, cask no. 10894, dist Nov 90, bott Nov 15 **(84.5) n23.5 t21 f20 b20**. Disappointing, as the nose carries you to rocky shorelines and throws in a dab of light orange blossom honey for good measure. But on the palate it is hard to escape from the cramped confines of the tangy oak. That said, a brief blast of juicy barley does try to inject something more luxurious. 44.2%. nc ncf sc. 269 bottles.

CAOL ILA

Islay, 1846. Diageo. Working.

Caol Ila Aged 10 Years "Unpeated Style" bott Aug 09 db **(93.5) n24** a beautiful medley of pear and lime with a thin spread of peanut butter for good measure...not exactly what one might expect...!!! **t23.5** the barley is just so juicy from the kickoff: the citrus on the nose reappears, though any hopes of pear vanishes; the barley, so rarely heard in a Caol-Ila grows in confidence and intensity as the delivery develops; **f23** not as oily as you might expect, allowing extra oak to emerge; **b23** always fascinating to see a traditional peaty Islay stripped bare and in full naked form. Shapely and very high class indeed. 65.4%. Only available at the Distillery.

Caol Ila Aged 12 Years db **(89)** n23 t23 f21 b22. A telling improvement on the old 12-y-o with much greater expression and width. 43%

⬦ **Caol Ila Aged 15 Years** dist 2000 db **(95.5)** n24 just trace smoke on this sophisticated chappie. The oak is the star of the show here and make no mistake. There is added piquancy from a salty edge, too, though I doubt if this was matured at the distillery itself. The vaguest heather honey note is dulled by the purity of the vanilla; t24 not sure you could ask for better mouth feel on delivery. The usual oiliness is tempered with crashing waves of barley concentrate, weighed further by the magnitude of the vanilla; f23.5 the finish remains chewy and heaped in vanilla. Just the odd phrase of butterscotch and kumquat can be heard here and there, but it is only a murmur...; b24 any smoke detected here is token and a mere reflection of the distillery rather than substance. Instead we have a naked malt lustfully showing its beauty and proving there can be fire without smoke... 61.5%. Diageo Special Releases 2016.

Caol Ila 17 Year Old American oak ex-bourbon casks, dist 1997 db **(90)** n23 t23.5 f21.5 b22 a charming malt. But not one the serious Peat Heads out there will much appreciate. 55.9%. Diageo Special Releases 2015.

Caol Ila Aged 18 Years db **(80)** n21 t20 f19 b20. Another improvement on the last bottling, especially with the comfortable integration of citrus. But still too much oil spoils the dram, particularly at the death. 43%

Caol Ila 30 Year Old refill American oak & European oak casks, dist 1983 db **(96.5)** n24 wow! Like being back on Islay: the peat mixes quite brilliantly with rock pools with the tide out...you half expect to see crabs running about and starfish trying not to get stranded..; t24.5 one of the deliveries of the year: the silky oil one expects from this distillery, landing at first with a wave of rounded, understated peat plus salt and malt galore, then thickening with rich fruitcake and ulmo honey. The coastal saltiness bolsters the flavour profile, but not to the extent of overcooking it; f24 just more of the same, but with the slowest of fades...; b24 indisputably, one of the most complex, well-rounded and complete Caol Ilas I have tasted since they rebuilt the distillery... 55.1%. 7,638 bottles. Diageo Special Releases 2014.

Caol Ila Moch db **(87)** n22 t22 f21 b22. Easy drinking, but I think they mean "Mocha"... 43%

Caol Ila Stitchell Reserve "Unpeated Style" bott 2013 db **(89)** n23 t24 f20 b22 Not really a patch on the 2012 bottling, mainly due to inferior sherry butts, any smoke which does appear is like a half-imagined movement in the shadows. The delivery, though, is superb! 59.6% WB15/344

Cadenhead's Small Batch Caol Ila 31 Year Old bourbon hogshead, dist 1984, bott 2016 **(97)** n24 t24.5 f24 b24.5 Dream how you'd like your ultimate Caol Ila to be... Well, you've just found it...! This is one of the most complete single casks I have ever encountered. In fact, I had no idea a single cask could be this complex. 52.1%. sc. 432 bottles.

Cadenhead's Small Batch Caol Ila 32 Year Old bourbon hogshead, dist 1984, bott 2016 **(90.5)** n23 t23 f22.5 b22 you can count the rings... 52.9%. sc. 234 bottles.

Eiling Lim Caol Ila 9 Years Old 2006 bott 2015 **(91.5)** n23 t23.5 f22 b23 An enormous degree of depth for something seemingly so delicate.... 51.2%. nc ncf sc. 109 bottles. 11th Release.

The Golden Cask Caol Ila 13 Years Old cask no. CM 207, dist 2001, bott 2014 **(96)** n24 t24 f23.5 b24.5 Caol Ila at its most subtle and sexy. Just so understatedly beautiful...One of the single casks of the year! 55%. sc. 268 bottles.

Hepburn's Choice Caol Ila 5 Years Old European oak quarter cask, dist 2009, bott 2015 **(94.5)** n23.5 t24 f23 b24 Now what we have here is Caol Ila in all its oily mastery and oak at full volume. The result isn't for the faint hearted. Few five year old Scotch whiskies will take up so much of your time as this one... 46%. nc ncf sc. 98 bottles.

⬦ **Hepburn's Choice Caol Ila 5 Years Old** refill hogshead, dist 2011, bott 2017 **(87)** n22 t22 f21.5 b21.5 Anyone with a penchant for heavily peated, freshly ground grist will be kicking the doors down for this. Very limited complexity, but spices do ensure there is never a dull moment. 46%. nc ncf sc. 393 bottles.

⬦ **Hepburn's Choice Caol Ila 5 Years Old** refill hogshead, dist 2011, bott 2017 **(86)** n22 t22 f20.5 b21.5 Pretty modest smoke by Caol Ila standards, and especially at an age when it is normally more forceful. Citrus, but tagged by a bitter tannin note. The palate is soft and salivating with a beautifully deft vanilla and gristy-phenol mix before the bitterness of the nose at last arrives for the finish 46%. nc ncf sc. 392 bottles.

⬦ **Hepburn's Choice Caol Ila 6 Years Old** refill hogshead, dist 2009, bott 2015 **(83.5)** n21 t21.5 f20 b21 Salivating on delivery. But the entire experience appears surprisingly subdued, with the smoke never quite getting a firm foothold in the dusty terrain. 46%. nc ncf sc. 204 bottles.

⬦ **Hepburn's Choice Caol Ila 6 Years Old** Tonnellerie wine finished hogshead, dist 2009, bott 2016 **(84)** n20 t21.5 f21 b21.5 Never quite hits the heights as the fruit and peat lurch around the palate. The peat hits hard but has its wings clipped before it is allowed to take off. 46%. nc ncf sc. 423 bottles.

◆ **Hepburn's Choice Caol Ila 6 Years Old** wine finished barrel, dist 2009, bott 2016 (87.5) n21 t22.5 f22 b22 Juicy and chewy, the smoke plays surprise second fiddle to the sugar-spice mix. Intriguing, attractive and works hard to create a balance. 46%. nc ncf sc. 138 bottles.

◆ **Hepburn's Choice Caol Ila 7 Years Old** wine cask, dist 2009, bott 2016 (83.5) n21 t21 f20.5 b21 Sharp, jarring and not quite the happiest marriage with neither the fruit or peat willing to compromise. 46%. nc ncf sc. 412 bottles.

◆ **Hunter Laing's Old & Rare Caol Ila Aged 25 Years** refill hogshead, dist Mar 91, bott Jan 17 (84.5) n22 t21.5 f20 b21 The nose radiates some meaningful smoke. But there is a bite beyond the spices that hints of mild potential oak problems further down the line...which are realised. 53.3%. nc ncf sc. 276 bottles.

◆ **Hunter Laing's Old & Rare Caol Ila Aged 35 Years** refill hogshead, dist Sept 80, bott Apr 16 (88.5) n22.5 the oak opens up just one or two too many fissures so the age begins to dominate slightly. That said, the herbal/spice mix works well with the fading phenols; t22 again tired oak hits the taste-buds running. Just some clever sugars and spice patch up the damage; f22 excellent spices; b22 they probably needed a Zimmer to help the cask down from the warehouse... 54.6%. nc ncf sc. 46 bottles.

◆ **Kirsch Import Caol Ila 1997** refill American hogshead, cask no. 12522, bott 2016 (94) n24 a light oiliness and vaguest grapefruit note on the nose, but the pungent smoke is dry and at full throttle; t23.5 spot on delivery: the sugars and oils step up to the plate exactly as expected in a good cask, though the spices arrive slightly ahead of schedule. The Manuka honey, though beautifully smoked, has a field day...; f23 attractive strains of mocha; b23.5 a standard well-casked Caol Ila...which means it's bloody good..!! 54.4%. 226 bottles.

◆ **Le Gus't Selection IX Caol Ila 2008** first fill bourbon, dist 16 Jun 08, bott 28 Feb 17 (93) n23.5 the oiliest malt on Islay is at its most viscous: the peat is softened yet still pounding at the nose, armed with a spiced barb; t23.5 wow...! The oils render this into a peaty sludge which you can chew until your tongue aches. Yet a freshness persists: the barley still retains a salivating quality and the peat a distinctive bite that will be lost in later years. The sugars are dark and heavy, matching the mood of the malt; f23 remains at its oily utmost...; b23 just a lovely age for a Caol Ila when its vibrancy can still be captured – and not a single flaw. 59.5%. 235 bottles.

◆ **Old Malt Cask Caol Ila Aged 7 Years** refill hogshead, cask no. 13267, dist Dec 09, bott Feb 17 (90) n22.5 a little sooty, but room enough for a little cocoa and molasses to be found among the phenols; t23 chewy with a slight hint of Fisherman's Friend cough sweet. The sugars are as dark and forboding as the smoke; f22 smoked butterscotch tart; b22.5 even at such tender years this with its wings hardly spread this whisky has travelled a long way. 50%. nc ncf sc. 365 bottles.

◆ **Old Malt Cask Caol Ila Aged 7 Years** refill hogshead, cask no. 13334, dist Dec 09, bott Feb 17 (86) n22 t22 f20.5 b21.5 Much tighter than its sister cask with the sugars muzzled late on especially, resulting in a starker, less enveloping dram altogether. 50%. nc ncf sc. 403 bottles.

◆ **Old Malt Cask Caol Ila Aged 8 Years** refill hogshead, cask no. 13095, dist Nov 08, bott Nov 16 (91.5) n22.5 light, vaguely earthy and floral with the smoke drifting gently and without intent; t23 crisp barley ramps up the juice levels: the barley-sugar dissolves into the burgeoning phenols; f22.5 much drier with some clever peppery notes offering life and depth beyond its eight years; b23.5 initially docile on the smoke front, but swims in its own charm. Lovely stuff. 50%. nc ncf sc. 158 bottles.

Old Malt Cask Caol Ila Aged 19 Years refill hogshead, cask no. 12159, dist Aug 96, bott Nov 15 (93) n22.5 t24 f23 b23.5 Revels in all its oily glory. A real smoke fest! 50%. nc ncf sc. 239 bottles.

Old Particular Islay Caol Ila 19 Years Old refill hogshead, dist Dec 96, bott Dec 15 (94.5) n23 t24 f23.5 b24 A Caol Ila of very rare poise and beauty. Unusually, don't warm too well in the hand for the best results. 51.5%. nc ncf sc. 313 bottles.

◆ **Old Particular Caol Ila 19 Years Old** refill hogshead, cask no. 11208, dist Sept 96, bott Jun 16 (96) n23.5 some genteel herbal, bourbony notes have crept into the smoky mix; t24 beautifully satisfying delivery: tantalisingly peppery with the oak adding a dash of vanilla and bourbon to add a glorious complexity to the phenols; f24 long, with the spices continuing to simmer. A little chocolate and toffee on the smoky finish, but it is the spice which wins the awards for artistry; b24.5 quite simply a magnificent example of this distillery in full song. 50.7%. nc ncf sc. 279 bottles.

Old Particular Islay Caol Ila 20 Years Old refill hogshead, cask no. 10870, dist Jan 95, bott Aug 15 (86.5) n21.5 t22 f21.5 b21.5. A fascinating contrast to their 19-year-old bottling this year: where the other is an exhibition of grace as it moves around the palate like a ballet dancer, this is a duller, flatter malt where the relatively dullard oak and smoke crash head-first and care little for the consequences. *51.5%. nc ncf sc. 282 bottles.*

⟨⟩ **Old Particular Caol Ila 20 Years Old** refill hogshead, cask no. 11498, dist Sept 96, bott Nov 16 **(94.5) n24** pretty classic stuff: big peat, orange peel, defter sub-smoke notes, a vague oiliness: Caol Ila!! **t23.5** the oils grip immediately to the plate and delivery several waves of eat and spice. A subtle ulmo honey note balances the books; **f23.5** impressive spice waves; **b24** sheer class. Helped by some very understanding oak which interferes to a minimal degree. *51.5%. nc ncf sc. 316 bottles.*

Provenance Caol Ila Aged 5 Years bott Mar 16 **(85.5) n22 t21.5 f21 b21**. Very little meaningful oak or unfurled peat: pleasant, malty and refreshing – but barely out of nappies. *46%. nc ncf sc.*

⟨⟩ **Provenance Caol Ila Aged 5 Years** refill hogshead, cask no. 11346, dist Mar 11, bott Nov 16 **(91) n23** intense, clean, powering smoke if offered no opposition by things such as oak..; **t23** the gristy sugars are at full blast on delivery and the oils ensure the plot thickens...; **f22.5** lightens towards a smoky liquorice finale; **b22.5** so young, but oh so beautiful...! *46%. nc ncf sc. 428 bottles.*

⟨⟩ **Spirits Shop Selection Caol Ila 1990** bourbon cask, bott 2016 **(91.5) n23** half-hearted smoke barely makes a scratch on the much more subtle but telling eucalyptus and lavender oak tones...; **t23.5** an intense delivery. So rare to find a Caol Ila of this antiquity making its case thanks to the flawless structure of the oak rather than its oils or phenols. Here both oil and peat are at pretty low levels while the oak offers both a gentle background spice as well as the more confidently structured vanilla, ulmo honey and crunchy Demerara sugars; a lazy gristiness – smoke – drifts across the palate; **f22** dries leaving the spices to go it alone; **b23** so rare a Caol Ila dependent on its honey and oak tones rather than peat for success. A genuine surprise – and delicious - package. *42.9%. 210 bottles. A joint bottling with Sansibar Whisky.*

Spirits Shop Selection & Sansibar Whisky Caol Ila 1997 sherry butt, bott 2015 **(72) n18 t19 f17 b18**. Fails on so many fronts, hard to know where to start... *40.2%. 599 bottles.*

Spirits Shop Selection & Sansibar Whisky Caol Ila 2006 bourbon cask, bott 2015 **(89.5) n22.5 t22.5 f22 b22.5** A beautifully made Islay which makes no great attempt at complexity. *51.3%*

⟨⟩ **The Whisky Agency Caol Ila 2007 (88) n22.5** uncluttered: excellent clarity to the sooty smoke – boasting an anthracite nip. A few citrus notes ensure the weightiness is measured; **t22** soufle light by this distillery's standards, though the early sugars compliment the delicate smoke; **f22** strangely, it is the vanilla which dominates late along beside the puckering spice; **b21.5** a Caol Ila where the usual oils are remarkable by their absence. *53.7%.*

⟨⟩ **Whisky-Fässle Caol Ila 10 Year Old** hogshead, dist 2006, bott 2017 **(87) n22 t22 f21.5 b21.5** The nose suggests a bitter tightness from the barrel may be on the cards further down the line. As it happens, those restrictions arrive sooner than forecast. Luckily, the full-bodied smokiness has sugars in reserve to still make for an attractive malt overall. *53.6%.*

⟨⟩ **Xtra Old Particular Islay Caol Ila 36 Years Old** refill hogshead, cask no. 11491, dist Sept 80, bott Nov 16 **(95.5) n23** all kinds of aged notes, especially drier eucalyptus and tannin, are busy at work here. But just enough Manuka honey is spared to add balance and platform for the surviving smoke; **t24** now that is rather wonderful...! Yes, the big tannins have much to say. But the liquorice and Manuka honey mix do their job until the spices arrive in force and with some extra oil, too; a chalkier vanilla note adds a more sober and humble note, yet there is barley enough for a salivating surge; **f24** such wonderful spiced phenol, with the last of the honey clinging manfully to the oils...; **b24.5** Cal Ila has the propensity to creak quite noisily when it hits a certain age – often one younger than this. But a superb cask - and a ladle full of honey - has ensured that life has gone on not just with dignity but aplomb. *57.4%. nc ncf sc. 172 bottles.*

CAPERDONICH

Speyside, 1898. Chivas Brothers. Closed.

Acla Selection Caperdonich 21 Years Old bourbon hogshead, dist 1992, bott 2013 **(87) n21.5 t22 f22 b21.5**. Some older Caperdonichs have been among the most complex malts ever listed in the history of the Whisky Bible. However, this tends towards the other direction: simplistically malty. Actually, the malt itself is unerringly attractive. The hot bite which accompanies it is perhaps not quite so desired. *52.3%. nc ncf.*

⟨⟩ **Hunter Laing's Old & Rare Caperdonich Aged 21 Years** refill hogshead, dist Jul 94, bott Apr 16 **(86.5) n21 t22 f21.5 b22** Technically, not the most gifted of single malts. But I have to admit I fully enjoyed this, starting with its attractive bonfire nose, the confiding nature of its ever intensifying malt and then its sweeping Tunnock's Teacake finale. Ignore the nip and fury of the delivery and the incisored bite of the finale: there are other things besides. *59.6%. nc ncf sc. 200 bottles.*

CARDHU

Speyside, 1824. Diageo. Working.

Cardhu 12 Years Old db (83) n22 t22 f18 b21. What appears to be a small change in the wood profile has resulted in a big shift in personality. What was once a guaranteed malt love-in is now a drier, oakier, fruitier affair. Sadly, though, with more than a touch of something furry. *40%*

Cardhu 18 Year Old db (88) n22.5 soft, easy going – one might even say "safe". Attractive amalgam of clean fruit, citrus especially, and vanilla-drenched barley. But perhaps not enough subtle peaks and troughs to excite; t23 more of the same: soft, juicy malt but with a darker side as the fruit fills in the gaps; f20.5 way too bitter for its own good; b22 very attractive at first. But when you consider what a great distillery Cardhu is and how rare stocks of 18 year old must be, have to say that I am disappointed. The fruit masks the more intricate moments one usually experiences on a Cardhu to ensure an acceptable blandness and accounts for a poor finish. Why, though, it is bottled at a pathetic 40% abv instead of an unchillfiltered 46% – the least this magnificent distillery deserves – is a complete mystery to me. *40%*

Cardhu Amber Rock db (87.5) n22 t23 f21 b21.5. Amber is the right colour for this: it appears stuck between green and red, not sure whether to go or not. The delivery, in which the tangerine cream is in full flow reflects the better elements of the nose. But the finish is all about being stuck in neutral. Not helped by the useless 40% abv, you get the feeling that a great whisky is trying to get out. The odd tweak and we'll have a winner. That said, very enjoyable indeed. Just even more frustrating! *40%. Diageo.*

CLYNELISH

Highlands (Northern), 1968. Diageo. Working.

Clynelish Aged 15 Years "The Distillers Edition" double matured in oloroso-seco casks Cl-Br: 169-1f, bott code L6264CM000 03847665, dist 1991, bott 2006 db (79) n20 t20 f19 b20. Big in places, distinctly oily in others but the overall feel is of a potentially brilliant whisky matured in unsympathetic barrels. *46%*

Clynelish Select Reserve ex-bourbon, rejuvenated & refilled American oak, and ex-bodega & refill European oak casks db (92) n23 t24 f22 b23 Does anyone do honey as well as Clynelish? The fact they can even pull it off with European oak involvement underlines the distillery's brilliance. *54.9%. 2,964 bottles. Diageo Special Releases 2014.*

tt Select Reserve ex-bourbon first fill American oak barrels, rejuvenated & refilled American oak hogsheads, and ex-bodega & refill European oak butts db (95) n23 t24.5 f23.5 b24 Stunning. *56.1%. 2,946 bottles. Diageo Special Releases 2015.*

Acla Selection Clynelish 17 Years Old refill sherry hogshead, dist 1996, bott 2013 (80.5) n21.5 t23 f17 b19. Only a Clynelish can fend off a painfully tight sherry influence with such an outpouring of astonishing honey and juicy fruit. Any other distillery and this cask would have reduced the score into the 60s... Oh, had only this hoggie been clean, might well have been on course for one of the whiskies of the year... *49.7%. nc ncf.*

Acla Selection Clynelish 21 Years Old ex-bourbon hogshead, dist 1992, bott 2014 (96.5) n24.5 t24 f23.5 b24.5 Dangerous whisky: I could drink this all day every day. Even spitting this seems like sacrilege... *49.8%. nc ncf.*

Cadenhead's Sherry Cask Clynelish 20 Year Old dist 1994 (87) n20 t23.5 f21.5 b22. By no means the worst sherry cask you'll find from this period and the degree of intense spice, coupled with the trademark honey, ensures it has some lovely moments. *55.4%. sc.*

Gordon & MacPhail Cask Strength Clynelish 2001 (84.5) n21.5 t21 f21 b21. A few wisps of honey, but surprisingly muffled. *54%*

◈ **Gordon & MacPhail Connoisseurs Choice Clynelish 2004** bott 29 Nov 16 (96) n24 such is the clarity and precision of the barley and honey – and the lack of pollution from their designated roles - that the most subtle smoke can be detected with relative ease, ensuring not just balance but something an atom away from perfection; t24 fabulous...just fabulous. A sensory illusion, surely, for the landing both has weight and, seemingly, none at all: the grist, maple syrup and heather honey appear to melt in slow motion leaving smoke and spices as an improbably elegant fingerprint on the palate; the oils are almost too soft to notice, but they are there...; the honey tones, varied in weight and sweetness but not their exceptional length stride the mid-ground with ease, the smoke its barely perceptible shadow; **f24** more of the same, ad infinitum....; **b24** technically faultless. If every distillery was Clynelish, every bottler carried the stocks of Gordon and MacPhail...if every single bottle of whisky was like this, what a world we would live in... *46%*.

◈ **Hunter Laing's Old & Rare Clynelish Aged 20 Years** refill hogshead, dist Dec 96, bott Jan 17 **(95) n24** a wonderful mix of ulmo honey, orange blossom honey and bourbon-style tannin nip: leave the glass overnight for staggering results the next morning...; **t23.5** that well known, delicately oiled malty coating allows the orange blossom honey to stick around and take on a virile spiciness which heralds in some moody liquorice; **f23.5** now heather honey...and spice; **b24** some distilleries just have "it" without even trying. Here is such a case... Brilliant – and so relaxed is this you get the feeling it has barely reached second gear! *55.5%. nc ncf sc. 295 bottles.*

Kingsbury Gold Clynelish 19 Year Old 1995 hogshead, cask no. 10195 **(92) n22 t23 f23.5 b23.5** A lovely, characterful malt which improves as it goes along *57.3%. sc. 250 bottles.*

◈ **Kingsbury Gold Clynelish 19 Year Old** hogshead, cask no. 7101, dist 1997 **(90) n22** a tiring cask showing some saturated tannins but still enough honey and toffee apple to do a job; **t23.5** much more relaxed on delivery despite the surge of oak. The citrus-themed sugars have enough gristy back up to ensure the sugars last the pace; **f22.5** a lengthy and satisfying vanilla-malt interplay; **b22.5** unusual to find a Clynelish feel the effects of time after less than 20 years quite the way this does. But its charisma is barely dented. *53.9%. 210 bottles. sc.*

◈ **Old Particular Clynelish 18 Years Old** refill hogshead, dist Jul 97, bott Dec 15 **(88) n22** a hint of Parkin cake as well as heather honey; **t23** the myriad sugars and honeys make a big fuss of the barley; **f21** the oak bitters out a little too enthusiastically. Some lingering spice. **b22** unusually for a Clynelish is there is a little bit of tiredness in the cask taking the edge off the malt's undoubted beauty. *48.4%. nc ncf sc. 298 bottles.*

◈ **That Boutique-y Whisky Company Clynelish 15 Year Old** batch 3 **(96.5) n24** some massive bourbon tannins come calling from the first moment. A plethora of varying sugars, but all of the darker, earthier kind, add further weight as well as balance. Equally, there are a number of over-ripe fruit notes, too, especially fig and dates. But this could be the muscovado sugars at work. Stupendous...; **t24** a silky caress on the palate is swiftly followed by a part exotic, part erotic burning sensation, a kind of light pain mixing with the pleasure overload. Again the sugars tantalise and delight, once more of the darker, toastier style; **f24** along, with a Venezuelan cocoa mix with raw, unrefined sugar. The spices bite, nip and kiss...; **b24.5** if I took a glass of this to bed with me, not sure whether to drink it or screw it into the middle of next week... *49.3%. 134 bottles.*

The Whisky Cask Company Clynelish 18 Years Old sherry hogshead, dist 1997 **(86.5) n21 t23 f21 b21.5**. Somewhat on the tangy and muted side. But enjoys a few moments of honeyed high drama on delivery. *51.6%*

Whiskyjace 10th Anniversary Clynelish 18 Years Old 1996 bourbon cask, bott 2015 **(84.5) n23 t21 f20 b20.5**. Not entirely what I was expecting. The gentle strands of honey teases you into thinking we have another whisky essay of excellence from this stunning distillery. But there is a sharp, greenish catch to the nose, too. And this is realised with a serious sharpness to the delivery, despite the beauty of the early honeycomb. Excellent spirit in a very aggressively interfering old cask. *51%*

CONVALMORE
Speyside, 1894–1985. William Grant & Sons. Closed.

Gordon & MacPhail Rare Old Convalmore 1975 **(94) n23 t24 f23 b24** The rarest of the rare. And in tasting, the flavour map took me back 30 years, to when I used to buy bottles of this from Gordon and MacPhail as a 10-year-old...probably distilled around 1975. The unique personality and DNA is identical on the palate as it was then; except now, of course, there is far more oak to contend with. Like finding an old lover 30 years further on: a little greyer, not quite in the same lithe shape as three decades earlier...but instantly recognisable and still very beautiful... *46%*

CRAGGANMORE
Speyside, 1870. Diageo. Working.

◈ **Cragganmore** db **(81) n23 t24 f16 b18** A whisky which asks some major questions: such as should I just sit here and sob, or bang my head repeatedly on my tasting table? This had begun as such a promising and sturdy addition to the Cragganmore lexicon, with the complexity of the early sugars really upping the expectations. But the dreaded "s" word arrived in abundance from, presumably, a sherry butt involvement and things went downhill rapidly after that. Tragic. *55.7%. 4,932 bottles. Diageo Special Releases 2016.*

Cragganmore Aged 12 Years db **(81.5)** n20 t21 f20 b20.5. I have a dozen bottles of Cragganmore in my personal cellar dating from the early 90s when the distillery was first bottled as a Classic Malt. Their astonishing dexterity and charm, their naked celebration of all things Speyside, casts a sad shadow over this drinkable but drab and instantly forgettable expression. 40%

Cragganmore Aged 14 Years The Distillers Edition finished in port casks, dist 1993, bott 2007 db **(85)** n22 t21 f21 b21. The tightly closed fruit on the palate doesn't quite match the more expansive and complex nose. 40%

Cragganmore 25 Year Old American oak & refill European oak, dist 1988 db **(94)** n23.5 t24 f23 b24 The secret of Cragganmore is the subtle way the malt and spices intertwangle without anyone really noticing, or able to pick which of the two strands is the thickest. Here, the almost secret subtlety of the nose has been compromised for maximum effect on the palate. It was probably a chance worth taking, as the full on display of the tannins is something that lives long on the taste buds...and memory... 51.4%. 3,372 bottles. Diageo Special Releases 2014.

Hunter Laing's Old & Rare Cragganmore Aged 30 Years refill hogshead, dist Apr 95, bott Oct 15 **(91)** n23 t24 f22.5 b22.5 Not really a malt designed for this kind of age. But this has been matured in a high quality cask...and it shows. 50.3%. nc ncf sc. 180 bottles.

⬦ **Hunter Laing's Old & Rare Cragganmore Aged 30 Years** refill hogshead, dist Jun 86, bott Jan 17 **(89)** n23 oak leads the way here, though the barley has just enough puff to inject a vague citrus note; slightly minty and the essence of overcooked crème brule; the light addition of golden syrup ensures both complexity and a pleasing balance; t22.5 the spices are up for it from the off; the tannins are punchy while burnt fudge and treacle tart add to big toasty feel; f21.5 dries and tires significantly; a huge wave of vanilla tries to bathe the age burns; b22 a malt, caked in vanilla and tannin, coming to the end of its natural life span but having one last golden hurrah... 59.7%. nc ncf sc. 167 bottles.

Scotch Malt Whisky Society Cask 37.64 Aged 30 Years refill hogshead, dist 24 Apr 85, bott 22 Jun 15 **(84)** n22 t21 f21 b20. Certainly has a story to tell. And with some deep marmalade notes and a plethora of dark sugars to hand (all this after a bourbon-esque nose), some of them are a delight. But the brooding presence of the big oak makes others harder to hear. 51.3%. nc ncf sc. 188 bottles.

Scotch Malt Whisky Society Cask 37.67 Aged 29 Years refill hogshead, dist 11 Jun 86, bott 17 Aug 15 **(82)** n21.5 t20 f21.5 b19. This cask should either have made its way into a blend or been bottled at least a decade ago. Far too aggressively tannin dominated, though the spices are interesting. 57.6%. nc ncf sc. 127 bottles.

Scotch Malt Whisky Society Cask 37.69 Aged 29 Years refill hogshead, dist 26 May 87, bott 21 Sept 15 **(93)** n23 t23 f23.5 b23.5 One that has withstood the test of time with its head held defiantly high. 58.1%. nc ncf sc. 188 bottles.

Scotch Malt Whisky Society Cask 37.70 Aged 15 Years refill hogshead, dist 22 Aug 00, bott 12 Oct 15 **(95)** n24.5 t23.5 f23 b24 If we head back four or five decades Cragganmore was often on the list of malts for "top dressing" in their blends: the highest grade malts for flavouring. But very few blends were above the 15-year-old mark and I knew one, back in the '60s and '70s, who swore by this at half the age. Here you get a pretty good idea why: the nose is pure quality 56.9%. nc ncf sc. 303 bottles.

⬦ **Scotch Malt Whisky Society Cask 37.71 14 Year Old** refill ex-bourbon hogshead, dist 15 May 01 **(82.5)** n20 t21 f21 b20.5 Poor oak influence. Salty and gristy. Pure blending fodder. 55.2%.

Scotch Malt Whisky Society Cask 37.72 Aged 29 Years refill hogshead, dist 11 Jun 86, bott 22 Feb 15 **(85.5)** n21.5 t21 f22 b21. Another summer, two at most, and this would have been toast. As it is, a volley of milky notes extracted from a failing cask gives it a wobbly start. But there is enough malt, cream and sugar to see it limp through, though a little unconvincingly. 57.1%. nc ncf sc. 102 bottles.

⬦ **The Whisky Agency Cragganmore 1989 (89)** n22 the tannins are taking a stranglehold; spiced molasses holds out...just; a vague hint of something smoky t23 big, puckering and salivating. This is a forceful delivery as though the barley is trying to give an early show of arms to the insurgent oak; f22 bitters slightly, as expected. Good fudgy sugars and spice save the day; b22 plucked from the cask just as the oak began closing in: a narrow escape! 52.1%.

⬦ **The Whisky Agency Cragganmore 12 Years Old** dist 2004 **(95)** n24 one of the cleanest noses of the year so far: no off notes from either the distillate or cask. And there is a pristine crispness to the barley which sadly far too rare in Scotch these days. A near perfect intertwangling of gentle vanilla and unsullied malt; t24 sublime delivery: the malt is almost crystalline and melts into the palate as though entombed in ulmo honey in the way a bee might be in amber; because of the light nature a little bitterness from the oak travels too far unchecked; f23.5 eventually the oak wears away and we are left with lightly spiced butterscotch tart and a reprise of that astonishing barley; b23.5 there are some malts which appear to carry the perfect DNA of the Speyside style: this is one such bottling. *54.6%*.

◇ **Whisky-Fässle Cragganmore 27 Year Old** sherry butt, dist 1989, bott 2016 (88) n23.5 sumptuous, spicy grape: for a Cragganmore; t23 like the nose, the palate is all about the grape. Here it is silky yet spicy and does little to allow the malt to speechify in any way. Also like the nose, some major fruitcake at work, but juicy and not of the old, heavily molassed type; f19.5 a little late tang, but nothing ruinous; b22 for a Cragganmore, the malt is conspicuous by its absence. Not exactly the perfect sherry butt, but it could have been worse. Those who don't pick up sulphur will adore this. *48.7%*.

CRAIGELLACHIE

Speyside, 1891. John Dewar & Sons. Working.

Craigellachie 13 Year Old db (78.5) n20 t22 f18 b18.5. Oily and intense, it shovels on the malt for all it is worth. That said, the sulphur notes are its undoing. *46%*

Craigellachie 17 Year Old db (88.5) n22 chocolate Liquorice Allsort! A tad oily and boiled vegetable. But enough malt to make the difference; t22.5 just love that delivery. Not the cleanest. But a mix of those heavy duty oils and an almost biting vanilla-barley note is attractive in an unkempt kind of way; f22 almost like an oil slick in a sea of oak-splintered barley; b22 technically falls flat on its face. Yet the whole is way better than the sum parts... *46%*

Craigellachie 23 Year Old db (91.5) n23.5 t23 f22 b23.5 Expected a little house smoke on this (the malt made here in the early 1990s always had delicate phenol), but didn't show. The honey is nothing like so shy. *46% WB16/035*

Cadenhead's Authentic Collection Craigellachie 21 Year Old sauternes cask, dist 1994 (88.5) n22 t22 f22 b22.5 Most Sauternes cask malts are a picture of subtlety; an essay in controlled degree. Here we have the exception... *53.1%*

◇ **The First Editions Craigellachie Aged 19 Years 1995** sherry butt, cask no. 11792, bott 2015 (87.5) n21 t23 f21 b22. A lovely near-as-dammit sulphur-free cask which harnesses together the more juicy elements of the barley and deep toffee-rich, fudgy thread. Simplistic, but very charming. *54.6%. nc ncf sc. 543 bottles.*

◇ **The First Editions Craigellachie Aged 19 Years 1995** sherry butt, cask no. 12362, bott 2016 (87) n21 t23 f21 b22 Fruity, and though not a vintage period for sherry butts from this distillery this has enough honest fruit cake character to ensure some rich and enjoyable moments. Not quite technically perfect, the toasted raisin is there to be savoured in full. *54.4%. nc ncf sc. 305 bottles.*

◇ **The First Editions Craigellachie Aged 21 Years 1995** sherry butt, cask no. 13305, bott 2017 (73) n18 t20 f17 b18 Yes, some massive, eye-watering grape. But furs up considerably. *59%. nc ncf sc. 282 bottles.*

Hepburn's Choice Craigellachie 7 Years Old European oak quarter cask, dist 2008, bott 2015 (81.5) n21.5 t21 f19 b20. Has something of a US single malt about this: young, with a big oak punch. Balance at a premium but some exceptionally thrusting malt at play. *46%. nc ncf sc. 89 bottles.*

Hepburn's Choice Craigellachie 7 Years Old European oak quarter cask, dist 2008, bott 2015 (83.5) n20 t21.5 f21 b21. The sugars have been purged early from the oak and nestle comfortably in the malty grist. Attractive biting spice, too. *46%. nc ncf sc. 92 bottles.*

Hepburn's Choice Craigellachie 7 Years Old European oak quater cask, dist 2008, bott 2015 (75.5) n19 t20 f18 b18.5. About as tight and dry as you can imagine. Not to mention furry at the finale. *46%. nc ncf sc. 90 bottles.*

◇ **Hepburn's Choice Craigellachie 8 Years Old** wine cask, dist 2008, bott 2016 (71) n18 t17 f18 b18 A tight, murky malt which appears further constricted by the cask. Not a success on any level. *46%. nc ncf sc. 293 bottles.*

Kingsbury Silver Craigellachie 18 Year Old 1995 sherry butt, cask no. 10389 (96.5) n24.5 t24 f23.5 b24.5 If you think you have died and gone to heaven, here is the good news: you have been tasting this whisky. Unquestionably the best cask bottled by Kingsbury sampled since I moved on as their cask selector over 20 years ago. They have unearthed an absolute liquid gold nugget. Don't just enjoy this dram. Worship at its faultless, grapey altar. *46%. sc. 398 bottles.*

Old Malt Cask Craigellachie Aged 12 Years sherry butt, cask no. 11872, dist Apr 02, bott Aug 15 (78.5) n18 t22 f19 b19.5. The breath-taking intensity of the maltiness does much to release the malt from its straightjacket. *50%. nc ncf sc. 120 bottles.*

Old Malt Cask Craigellachie Aged 14 Years sherry butt, cask no. 10892, dist Feb 00, bott Oct 14 (85) n21 t22 f20.5 b21.5. An honest malt, essentially untroubled by its sherried origins and even offers a puff of smoke as the malt and untaxing sugars unravel. *50%. nc ncf sc. 680 bottles.*

Old Malt Cask Craigellachie Aged 20 Years sherry butt, cask no. 12112, dist Sept 95, bott Nov 15 (88) n21.5 sharp, vague citrus and salty chocolate. A little unusual...; t23 blood orange delivery and then a succession of hefty malt blows to the palate. Spices gang up in the mid ground, but all seems younger than its age; f21 slightly untidy as the sherry butt takes effect, but the spices still work well; b22.5 an attractively indolent dram, seemingly spoiling for a fight but always allowing its barley-fruit good nature to get the better of it. *50%. nc ncf sc. 360 bottles.*

Old Malt Cask Craigellachie Aged 21 Years sherry butt, cask no. 13304, dist Sept 95, bott Feb 17 (73.5) n20.5 t18 f17 b18 Yikes! Blood orange on steroids. A bitter-sweet experience... without the sweetness... *50%. nc ncf sc. 331 bottles.*

Old Particular Speyside Craigellachie 15 Years Old refill butt, cask no. 10465, dist Apr 99, bott Oct 14 (88) n21 sharp, in the distillery – and probably condenser – style. Some serious tang here; t22.5 super-salivating delivery: non-specific fruit aligns with the mega barley kick, all further enriched by some meaningful oil; f22 settles to allow the soothing vanilla an easy ride; b22.5 beautifully rich, rounded and malt-lush. *48.4%. nc ncf sc. 570 bottles.*

Old Particular Speyside Craigellachie 20 Years Old sherry butt, dist Sept 93, bott Dec 15 (74) n18 t20 f17 b19. An enormous bunch of grapes. Had the silly sods in Spain not waved a lit sulphur stick in this cask, we'd have had one of the great whiskies of the Speyside year... *51.5%. nc ncf sc. 314 bottles.*

Old Particular Craigellachie 21 Years Old sherry butt, cask no. 11343, dist Sept 95, bott Sept 16 (89) n22 a light fruit cake mingles with a dustier, chalky oakiness; t23 a superbly silky delivery allows the barley full voice. The vague fruit hangs on to its coat-tails; f22 a light liquorice and cocoa dusting makes for a nonchalant finale; b22 a malt still offering vitality and very much at ease with itself... *51.5%. nc ncf sc. 504 bottles.*

Scotch Malt Whisky Society Cask 44.76 14 Year Old virgin heavy toast medium char oak hogshead, dist 6 Nov 02 (89) n22.5 if anyone gets off on a mix of heady bourbon and pencil shavings, stick your beak in this...; t23 the delivery follows on predictably from the nose with. Massive sugar surge from the fire-blasted oak, leaving a blood orange tartness in its wake; huge vanilla tickled by spice: a genuinely lovely experience; f22 I have (honestly) just started coughing as something has stuck slightly in the back of my throat: presumably a splinter...; b21.5 subtlety plays no part in this malt. *57.5%.*

The Whisky Chamber Craigellachie 14 Years Old ex-bourbon hogshead, cask no. 46/2001, dist 05 Sept 01, bott 11 Jan 16 (87) n21 t22.5 f21.5 b22. Pleasant dram full of malty vim. The sugars are a little too stark and in your face for greatness. But when they have subsided, the barley sings an attractive ditty, eventually giving up centre stage to the late mocha. *62.8%. nc sc.*

Whisky Live Tel Aviv Craigellachie Aged 7 Years butt, cask no. 900771, dist 2007, bott 2015 (80.5) n19 t21.5 f19 b21. Technically, not the best. But despite its obvious sherry butt flaws, how can you not like the nutty intensity of the malt when it engulfs the palate? Probably the least Kosher whisky ever sold in Tel Aviv. *66%. sc. 654 bottles.*

Whiskybroker Craigellachie 9 Year Old refill hogshead, dist 04 Dec 06, bott 18 Feb 16 (86.5) n21.5 t22 f21.5 b21.5. Malty, oily, biscuity. Yet always curiously ill-at-ease with itself. *57.8%. sc.*

DAILUAINE

Speyside, 1854. Diageo. Working.

Dailuaine 1997 The Manager's Choice db (87.5) n21.5 t23 f21 b22. One of the most enjoyable (unpeated!!) Dailuaines I've come across in an age. There is the usual distillery biff to this, but not without a honeyed safety net. Great fun. *58.6%*

Dailuaine Aged 16 Years bott lot no. L4334 db (79) n19 t21 f20 b19. Syrupy, almost grotesquely heavy at times; the lighter notes of previous bottlings have been lost under an avalanche of sugary, over-ripe tomatoes. One for those who want a massive dram. *43%*

C & S Dram Collection Dailuaine Aged 17 Years hogshead, cask no. 12812, dist 07 Oct 97, bott 10 Aug 15 (80) n21 t19 f20 b20. Clean, monosyllabic malt. And hotter than Hades... *56.6%. sc. 235 bottles.*

Cadenhead's Wine Cask Dailuaine 18 Year Old Chateau Lafitte cask, dist 1997 (93.5) n23 t23 f23 b23.5 If proof were required that you can turn a below average spirit into an above average malt thanks to the casks, here it proudly is. Love it – well done Cadenhead's! *54.4%. sc.*

⟨⟩ Douglas Laing's Premier Barrel Selection Dailuaine Aged 7 Years (60) n16 t17 f17 b16 I could go into all the things that's wrong with this. But, frankly, it doesn't deserve my time. *46%. nc ncf sc. 400 bottles.*

Gordon & MacPhail Connoisseurs Choice Dailuaine 2004 (80) n19 t21 f20 b20. A tetchy malt at the best of times, the unkempt nose suggests it just isn't going to play ball. And despite the odd phase of attractively intense barley, this never quite makes itself feel at home. *46%*

⟨⟩ Gordon & MacPhail Connoisseurs Choice Dailuaine 2006 bott 14 Mar 17 **(82.5) n20 t22 f20 b20.5** A very average distillery displaying very ordinary malt. Nothing offensive, but not a single thing to set the heart racing either. Typically clunky and out of tune. *46%*.

Hepburn's Choice Dailuaine 7 Years Old sherry butt, dist 2008, bott 2015 **(84) n20 t22 f21 b21.** So rough and ungainly, it is actually quite enjoyable – a bit like having a dust up when playing rugby. Still, the sherry butt is clean and malt makes itself heard. Have fun, but expect a few bruises! *46%. nc ncf sc. 389 bottles.*

⟨⟩ Hepburn's Choice Dailuaine 7 Years Old wine cask, dist 2009, bott 2016 **(88) n21** peculiarly phenolic, tantalisingly so; **t22.5** a typically feeble delivery, but picks up slowly and transforms into a vague smokey-cocoa-sprinkled teaser; **f22** decent oils lengthen the experience; **b22.5** well done good people of Hepburn's Choice. Your selection of wine cask is impressive. *46%. nc ncf sc. 280 bottles.*

Old Particular Speyside Dailuaine 12 Years Old refill butt, cask no. 11026, dist Sept 03, bott Feb 16 **(79) n19 t19 f21 b20.** Soft and nutty. *48.4%. nc ncf sc. 291 bottles.*

⟨⟩ Provenance Dailuaine Aged 9 Years sherry butt, cask no. 11250, dist Mar 07, bott May 16 **(87.5) n21 t22 f22.5 b22** An entirely clean butt offers up little in the way of fruit but helps herd the more intense malty qualities into an area where is offers maximum effect. Some lovely late spice, too! *46%. nc ncf sc.*

⟨⟩ Provenance Dailuaine Aged 9 Years refill hogshead, cask no. 11504, dist Jan 07, bott Nov 16 **(85) n20 t22 f21.5 b21.5** Some not unattractive cream soda qualities to this. For a Dailuaine, quite juicy and characterful. *46%. nc ncf sc. 347 bottles.*

Provenance Dailuaine Over 11 Years refill sherry butt, dist Autumn 04, bott Autumn 15 **(74) n18.5 t19 f18.5 b18.** Bog standard single malt. Not particularly well made, harsh on delivery and finish and, beyond basic barley, proffers little else. Like a Vauxhall where seats come as extras.... *46%. nc ncf sc.*

Scotch Malt Whisky Society Cask 41.70 Aged 34 Years 2nd fill Sauternes hogshead, dist 13 Dec 80, bott 25 Jan 16 **(86) n22 t21.5 f21.5 b21.** Well done, SMWS. You have located a Dailuaine which actually puts on a show worth listening to. Distinctly nutty, as in the house style, but the sugars and spices combine rhythmically and even set up a charming coffeed finale; *48.6%. nc ncf sc. 102 bottles.*

⟨⟩ Scotch Malt Whisky Society Cask 41.92 13 Year Old first fill ex-bourbon barrel, dist 14 Aug 03 **(80) n21 t20 f19 b20** More bite than a rabid Jack Russell. Eye-watering, tangy, malty... but just not a great experience. *61%.*

⟨⟩ Simon Brown Dailuaine 2008 ex-bourbon cask, cask no. 20, dist Feb 08, bott Jan 16 **(86) n21.5 t22 f21 b21.5** The distillery nutshelled: a typical rawness to the nose where the oak has a slightly discordant say. And this is repeated on the finish. The highlight is the massively oily and intensely malty delivery which really does possess star quality. *43%. nc ncf sc.*

The Warehouse Dram Dailuaine Aged 8 Years sherry finish octave, cask no. 510S23, dist 21 Feb 08, bott 04 Apr 16 **(72.5) n17.5 t18.5 f18 b18.5.** Lots of sugars at play. But not a malt I can get particularly sweet over. *46%. nc ncf sc. 94 bottles.*

⟨⟩ Whisky Castle Dailuaine 12 Year Old sherry butt, cask no. 13454, dist Jan 05, bott Mar 17 **(87.5) n21 t22 f22.5 b22** Dailuaine, over the years one of Scotland's most consistently inept malts – bottled in a sherry butt! A case of two negatives making a positive, right? Well, probably not far off. The sherry offers up no sulphur at all and the distillate does, for a short while, generate some distinctly attractive malt before vanishing under an avalanche of natural caramel and even spice. Pleasantly surprised. *50%. Bottled by Hunter Laing.*

DALLAS DHU
Speyside, 1899–1983. Closed. Now a museum.

Gordon & MacPhail Rare Vintage Dallas Dhu 1979 (94.5) n23 t23.5 f23.5 b24 I can hardly recall the last time a bottling from this distillery popped along – depressing to think I am old enough to remember when they were so relatively common they were being sold on special offer! It was always a class act; its closure an act of whisky vandalism, whether it be preserved as a museum or not. This, even after all these years, shows the extraordinary quality we are missing day in, day out. *43%*

DALMORE

Highlands (Northern), 1839. Whyte and Mackay. Working.

The Dalmore 12 Years Old db (90) n22 mixed dates: both dry and juicy; t23 fat, rich delivery with a wonderful dovetailing of juicy barley and thick, rumbling fruit; f22.5 lots of toffee on the finish, but gets away with it thanks to the sheer depth to the barley and the busy sherry sub-plot; b22.5 has changed character of late yet remains underpowered and with a shade too much toffee. But such is the quality of the malt in its own right it can overcome any hurdles placed before it to ensure a real mouth-filling, rumbustious dram. 40%

The Dalmore 15 Years Old db (83.5) n21 t21 f20.5 b21. Another pleasant Dalmore that coasts along the runway but simply fails to get off the ground. The odd off note here and there, but it's the blood orange which shines brightest. 40%

The Dalmore 18 Years Old db (76.5) n19 t21 f18 b18.5. Heaps of caramel and the cask choice might have been better. 43%

The Dalmore 21 Year Old db (88.5) n22 date and walnut cake...though light on the walnuts...; t23 fat, chewy, mouth-watering and complex...though light on the complexity; f21.5 remains chewy, bitter and sweet...though light on the sweetness; b22 fat, unsubtle, but pretty enjoyable. 42%

The Dalmore 25 db (88) n23.5 hugely attractive with a sherry-trifle signature; t22.5 a glossy delivery with the accent very much on fruit, plums in particular; an attractive degree of sharpness throughout; f20 just a little dry with a tell-tale tang towards the end; b22 the kind of neat and tidy, if imperfect, whisky which, were it in human form, would sport a carefully trimmed and possibly darkened little moustache, a pin-striped suit, matching tie and square and shiny black shoes. 42%. Whyte & Mackay Ltd.

The Dalmore 30 Year Old db (94) n24 the grape drifts across the glass; not quite perfect but enough panache and class to carry an aura of slight wonder...; t24 so thick, so long, so dripping in fruit....; subtle spice and a slow realisation of aged, confident tannin; f22.5 undone very slightly by a very late degree of bitterness; b23.5 a malt, quite literally for the discerning whisky lover. Essays in complexity are rarely so well written in the glass as found here... 45%

The Dalmore 50 Years Old db (88) n21 t19 f25 b23. Takes a while to warm up, but when it does becomes a genuinely classy and memorable dram befitting one of the world's great and undervalued distilleries. 52%

The Dalmore 62 Years Old db (95) n23 t25 f24 b24 If I am just half as beautiful, elegant and fascinating as this by the time I reach 62, I'll be a happy man. Somehow I doubt it. A once-in-a-lifetime whisky – something that comes around every 62 years, in fact. Forget Dalmore Cigar Malt – even I might be tempted to start smoking just to get a full bottle of this. 40.5%

The Dalmore 1263 King Alexander III db (86) n22 t22.5 f20 b21.5. Starts brightly with all kinds of barley sugar, fruit and decent age and oak combinations, plus some excellent spice prickle. So far, so good...and obviously thoughtfully and complexly structured. But then vanishes without trace on finish. 40%

The Dalmore 1980 db (81.5) n19 t21 f20.5 b21. Wonderful barley intensity on delivery does its best to overcome the so-so nose and finale. 40%

The Dalmore 1981 Amoroso Sherry Finesse amoroso sherry wood cask db (85.5) n21 t22 f21.5 b21. A very tight, fruity, dram which gives away its secrets with all the enthusiasm of an agent under torture. Enjoyable to a degree... but bloody hard work. 42%

The Dalmore Astrum Aged 40 Years db (89) n23.5 t21 f22 b22.5. This guy is all about the nose. The oak is too big for the overall framework and the balance hangs by a thread. Yet somehow the overall effect is impressive. Another summer and you suspect the whole thing would have snapped... 42%

The Dalmore Aurora Aged 45 Years db (90.5) n25 t22 f21.5 b22. Sophisticated for sure. But so huge is the oak on the palate, it cannot hope to match the freakish brilliance of the nose. 45%

The Dalmore Candela Aged 50 Years db (96) n25 t24 f23.5 b23.5. Just one of those whiskies which you come across only a handful of times in your life. All because a malt makes it to 50 does not mean it will automatically be great. This, however, is a masterpiece, the end of which seemingly has never been written. 50% (bottled at 45%).

The Dalmore Cabernet Sauvignon db (79) n22 t19 f19 b19. Too intense and soupy for its own good. 45%

The Dalmore Ceti db (91.5) n24 a nose for fruitcake lovers everywhere: ripe cherries and blood orange abound and work most attractively with the slightly suety, muscovado enriched body...; t23.5 the nose demands a silky delivery and that's exactly what you get.

Rich fruit notes form the principle flavour profile but the backing salivating barley and spice is spot on; the mid ground becomes a little saltier and more coastal...; **f21.5** a vague bitterness to the rapidly thinning finale, almost a pithy element, which is slightly out of sync with the joys of before; **b22.5** a Ceti which warbles rather well... 44.7%

The Dalmore Cigar Malt Reserve Limited Edition db (73.5) **n19 t19.5 f17 b18.** One assumes this off key sugarfest is for the cigar that explodes in your face... 44%

The Dalmore Dominium db (89.5) **n22.5** thick, full-on grape; **t23** lush delivery which becomes progressively more chewy. A few spiced sultanas in there; **f22** big on the caramel; **b22** like so many Dalmores, starts brightly but as the caramels gather it just drifts into a soupy lump. Still, no taint to the fruit and though the finish is dull you can say it is never less than very attractive. 43%. *Fortuna Meritas Collection*

The Dalmore Luceo db (87) **n22 t22 f21.5 b21.5.** Pleasantly malty, exceptionally easy going and perfect for those of you with a toffeed tooth. 40%. *Fortuna Meritas Collection*

The Dalmore Valour db (85.5) **n21 t22 f21 b21.5.** Not often you get the words "Valour" and "fudge" in the same sentence. 40%. *Fortuna Meritas Collection*

The Dalmore Regalis db (86.5) **n22.5 t21.5 f21 b21.5.** For a brief moment, grassy and busy. Then dulls, other than the spice. The caramel held in the bottling hall is such a great leveller. 40%. *Fortuna Meritas Collection*

The Dalmore Visitor Centre Exclusive db (95.5) **n25 t24 f22.5 b24** Not exactly the easiest distillery to find but a bottle of this is worth the journey alone. I have tasted some sumptuous Dalmores over the last 30-odd years. But this one stands among the very finest. 46%

⬦ **The Dalmore Quintessence** db (91) **n22** a sharp prod of tannin awakens a soporific, lightly molassed aroma; **t23.5** delightful procession of sugary notes, all seemingly dimmed by a toastiness which keeps everything in neat order. A little hickory mixes well with the dried molasses while a muscovado – and almost rye-like – fruitiness also adds a degree of firmness which works very well; **f22** soft, with lots of raisins in the dark toasted fudge; a tiny degree of furriness creeps in towards the very death; **b23.5** a late night dram after a hard day. Slump into your favourite chair, dim the lights, pour yourself a glass of this, warm in the hand and then study, quietly, for the next half hour. 45%.

Cadenhead's Small Batch Dalmore 25 Year Old sherry butt, dist 1990, bott 2016 (94.5) **n23 t24 f23.5 b24** mon sherry! Not a sulphur atom in sight...!! 56.3%. sc. 474 bottles.

DALWHINNIE

Highlands (Central), 1898. Diageo. Working.

Dalwhinnie 15 Years Old db (95) **n24** sublime stuff: a curious mixture of coke smoke and peat-reek wafts teasingly over the gently honied malt. A hint of melon offers some fruit but the caressing malt stars; **t24** that rarest of combinations: at once silky and malt intense, yet at the same time peppery and tin-hat time for the tastebuds, but the silk wins out and a sheen of barley sugar coats everything, soft peat included; **f23** some cocoa and coffee notes, yet the pervading slightly honied sweetness means that there is no bitterness that cannot be controlled; **b24** a malt it is hard to decide whether to drink or bath in: I suggest you do both. One of the most complete mainland malts of them all. Know anyone who reckons they don't like whisky? Give them a glass of this – that's them cured. Oh, if only the average masterpiece could be this good. 43%

Dalwhinnie 25 Years Old Special Release 2012 Rejuvenated American oak hogshead, dist 1987, bott 2012 db (92) **n23.5 t23.5 f22 b23** More from the mountains of Kentucky than central Scotland. Anyone with a bourbon bent and a sweet tooth will adore this. As will bee keepers. 52.1 %. nc ncf. Diageo.

Dalwhinnie 25 Year Old refill American oak hogsheads, dist 1989 db (96.5) **n24.5** light smoke buzzes and drifts; heather honey sweetens towards a leathery richness – indeed, a sweet saltiness suggests old riding tackle – and a beautiful crushed walnut oiliness. Together, something rather special... **t24** the mouth feel to end all mouth feels: a light oily caress, like an expert massage, with spicy pressure being applied on just the right points...; the heather honey now shifts to ulmo honey as the vanillas take effect; **f23.5** vague phenols and a spicy buzz...; **b24.5** just exemplary. If only all Scotch single malt was this magnificent... 48.8%. 5,916 bottles. Diageo Special Releases 2015.

Dalwhinnie The Distillers Edition Double Matured special release D. SU. 312, dist 1997, bott 2013 db (94) **n24 t23.5 f23 b23.5** more like a blender's edition: I can count the number of genuinely successful double matured malts probably on both hands. There is some serious skill and understanding of this distillery at work here. Wouldn't have hurt to see it at 46%, mind... 43%

Dalwhinnie Winter's Gold db **(95) n23.5** for such a remote and inland distillery, the coastal saltiness to this is remarkable... golden syrup and earthy heather-honey also at work here; **t24** something of the Johnnie Walker Gold about this: there is a clarity to the malt, the citrus and vanilla which reminds one of the air when looking far away into the mountains on a cool winter's morn; **f23.5** earthy to the end with the honey (ulmo, naturally!) still the dominating theme; just a late hint of bitterness; **b24** whichever blender came up with this deserves a pat of the back. 43%

DEANSTON

Highlands (Perthshire), 1966. Burn Stewart Distillers. Working.

Deanston 6 Years Old db **(83) n20 t21 f22 b20.** Great news for those who remember how good Deanston was a decade or two ago: it's on its way back. A delightfully clean dram with its trademark honey character restored. A little beauty slightly undermined by caramel. 40%

◈ **Deanston 10 Year Old PX Finish** db **(83.5) n21 t22.5 f20 b20** Displays the uncompromising sweetness of a whisky liqueur. A must-have malt for those who like their sherry influence to be way over the top. The finish, like the nose, reveals minor a dry, furry element. 57.5%.

Deanston 12 Years Old db **(74) n18 t19 f18.5 b18.5.** It is quite bizarre how you can interchange this with Tobermory in style; or, rather, at least the faults are the same. 46%. ncf.

Deanston Aged 12 Years db **(75) n18 t21.5 f17.5 b18.** The delivery is, for a brief moment, a malty/orangey delight. But the nose is painfully out of sync and finish is full of bitter, undesirable elements. A lot of work still required to get this up to a second grade malt, let alone a top flight one. 46.3%. ncf. Burn Stewart.

Deanston 18 Year Old batch 2 db **(89.5) n23** celebrates a very healthy degree of ulmo honey: soft and sexy; **t22.5** big malt kick early on; soft oils bring on the vanillas; juicy and just a touch of lime to lighten things; **f22** a little spicier and deeper toned as the tannin takes charge; **b22** a soft treat for the palate... 46.3%. nc ncf.

Deanston 20 Year Old db **(61) n15 t16 f15 b15** Riddled with sulphur. 55.4%. nc ncf.

◈ **Deanston 40 Year Old PX Finish** db **(87.5) n22 t23 f21 b21.5** The PX is doubtless in use here to try and give a sugary wrap around the over-aged malt. Some success, though limited. This type of cask has the unfortunate habit of restricting complexity in a whisky by embracing it too tightly with its wealth of syrupy top notes. The aromas and flavours which do escape often seem brittle and clipped, and this is the case here: the whisky has no chance to tell of its 40 years in the cask – the period that counts most now is the time it has spent in PX. Love the spices, though, and the overall mouth feel. Whatever its limitations, this still does offer a lovely dram. 45.6%.

Deanston Virgin Oak db **(90) n22.5 t23 f22.5 b22** Quirky. Don't expect this to taste anything like Scotch... 46.3%

The Golden Cask Deanston 18 Years Old cask no. CM 208, dist 1996, bott 2014 **(83) n21 t21.5 f19.5 b21.** A stark, fiery whisky helped by the kind of molten sugars you find on very hot porridge. The lack of body allows some of the more aggressive oak to say too much. 54%. sc. 278 bottles.

◈ **Old Malt Cask Deanston Aged 21 Years** refill hogshead, cask no. 12816, dist Aug 95, bott Oct 16 **(88) n21.5** thin and limited. But the lemon drizzle cake offers just enough; **t23** excellent delivery: a thumping degree of concentrated barley sugar dissolves as the butterscotch oak begins to gain ground; **f21.5** delicate and elegant; tires and dries at the death; **b22** a clean, sparkling, honest malt. 50%. nc ncf sc. 263 bottles.

The Single Cask Deanston Aged 15 Years cask no. 1958, dist 10 Dec 97, bott 01 Aug 13 **(76) n19 t21 f18 b18.** A white knuckle roller-coaster dram with more downs than ups. Lurches between over-the-top cloying sugar and an eye-watering oak tang. 45.8%. nc ncf sc.

Whiskyjace Deanston 15 Year Old bourbon hogshead, dist 1997, bott 2013 **(83) n21 t21.5 f20 b20.5.** A hot, sugary dram. Malty, simple and thin but with a hint of citrus. 54.4%

DUFFTOWN

Speyside, 1898. Diageo. Working.

Singleton of Dufftown 12 Years Old db **(71) n18 t18 f17 b18.** A roughhouse malt that's finesse-free. For those who like their tastebuds Dufft up a bit... 40%

The Singleton of Dufftown Spey Cascade db **(80) n19 t20 f21 b20.** A dull whisky, stodgy and a little dirty on the nose. Improves the longer it stays on the palate thanks mainly to sympathetic sugars and an ingratiating oiliness. But if you are looking for quality, prepare to be disappointed. 40%

The Singleton of Dufftown "Sunray" db **(77)** n20 t20 f18 b19. One can assume only that the sun has gone in behind a big toffeed cloud. Apparently, according to the label, this is "intense". About as intense as a ham sandwich. Only not as enjoyable. 40%. WB15/121

The Singleton of Dufftown "Tailfire" db **(79)** n20 t20 f19 b20. Tailspin, more like. 40%. WB15/122

◇ **Cadenhead's Authentic Collection Dufftown 38 Year Old** bourbon hogshead, dist 1978 **(89.5)** n22.5 that unique glass-flat orange blossom honey and vanilla mix you get from once poor spirit now spectacularly reformed...; t23 the silkiness on the nose translates immediately on delivery: massive vanilla depth with a muscovado sugar coating; gorgeously concentrated malt and butterscotch; f21.5 just tangs out slightly as it has every right to do at this age...; b22.5 it is curious that during this period Dufftown, like Littlemill and Fettercairn, was making some of the least impressive whisky in Scotland. Yet nearly four decades on, the malt, if matured in the right cask, can have a genuinely attractive – albeit very different – personality. This is one such cask. 44.6%. sc.

Gordon & MacPhail Connoisseurs Choice Dufftown 2006 (84) n20.5 t21.5 f21 b21. About as fat on the palate as you'll find any Speyside, this bottling is bolstered by some highly attractive spice which manages to pierce the oily and sugary gloom. More than somewhat cloying. 46%

◇ **Hepburn's Choice Dufftown 9 Years Old** refill hogshead, dist 2007, bott 2017 **(84)** n21 t22 f21 b20 An interesting bottling as the oak offers very little of any meaning. So it is possible to see that the basic spirit is a lot cleaner than it once was and the gristy barley is very evident. Beyond that it has little to say. 46%. nc ncf sc. 358 bottles.

EDRADOUR
Highlands (Perthshire), 1837. Signatory Vintage. Working.

Edradour Aged 10 Years db **(79)** n18 t20 f22 b19. A dense, fat malt that tries offer something along the sherry front but succeeds mainly in producing a whisky cloyingly sweet and unfathomable. Some complexity to the finish compensates. 43%

◇ **Kirsch Import Ballechin 12 Year Old** burgundy cask, cask no. 15, dist 2004, bott 2016 **(75)** n19 t21 f17 b18 Too many eye-watering tangy notes by far. Will polarise opinion, though I have no doubts on which side of the fence this falls. 52.2%.

◇ **Kirsch Import Ballechin 12 Year Old** Manzanilla cask, cask no. 278, dist 2004, bott 2016 **(86.5)** n22 t22.5 f21 b21 An adventurous malt where smoke and fruit are slammed into each other with the force of a Hadron Collider. You are more likely to find a Higgs-Bosun particle than anything resembling balance. Still, a fun jape. 55.6%.

FETTERCAIRN
Highland (Eastern), 1824. Whyte and Mackay. Working.

Fettercairn 12 Year Old db **(66)** n14 t19 f16 b17. If the nose doesn't get you, what follows probably will...Grim doesn't quite cover it. 40%

Fettercairn 30 Years Old db **(73)** n19 t18 f18 b18. A bitter disappointment. Literally. 46.3%

Fettercairn 40 Years Old db **(92)** n23 technically, not exactly how you want a 40-y-o to be: a bit like your old silver-haired granny knitting in her rocking chair...and sporting tattoos. But I also have to say there is no shortage of charm, too...and like some old tattooed granny, you know it is full of personality and has a tale to tell... t24 I was expecting dates and walnuts... and I have not been let down. A veritable date and walnut pie you can chew on until your jaw is numb; the sharp raisiny notes, too, plus a metallic sheen which reminds you of its provenance...; f22 those burned raisins get just a little more burned...; b23 yes, everyone knows my views on this distillery. But I'll have to call this spade a wonderfully big, old shovel you can't help loving...just like the memory of me tattooed ol' granny... 40%. 463 bottles.

Fettercairn 1824 db **(69)** n17 t19 f16 b17. By Fettercairn standards, not a bad offering. Relatively free from its inherent sulphury and rubbery qualities, this displays a sweet nutty character not altogther unattractive – though caramel plays a calming role here. Need my arm twisting for a second glass, though. 40%

Acla Selection Fettercairn 24 Years Old refill hogshead, dist 1990, bott 2014 **(72.5)** n19 t17.5 f18 b18. Nutty, though some have gone off. Cloyingly sweet in part. Always chimes a little off key. So everything normal for this distillery, then. 50.3%. nc ncf.

◇ **Alos Sansibar Whisky Fettercairn 1988** bott 2016 **(75.5)** n18.5 t20.5 f18 b18.5 You almost feel like applauding this malt's bloody-minded stubbornness, even after nearly three decades in what appears a half decent barrel, to try and lift itself as high as even below average. Grim. 50.6%.

Best Dram Fettercairn 9 Years Old (82) n20 t21.5 f20 b20.5. Having a label like this is about the only way to get the words "Fettercairn" and "best dram" into the same sentence. That said, this cask is above the norm in terms of average quality for this distillery and there is plenty to enjoy from the nutty, sugary, if very hot, maltiness. 55.9%

⬦ **Bdram Fettercairn 7 Year Old** bourbon barrel, cask no. 1119, dist Mar 09, bott Jan 17 (81) n21 t22.5 f18.5 b19 For a Fettercairn of this age, as opposed to an ordinary malt, it is pretty impressive. Yes, it is as hot as Hades — and that has nothing to do with the strength, rather the poor spirit itself. And the finish has its usual zero character, other than the torturous burn. But for a few moments malt and nuts combine to rise above the roaring flames and offer, thanks to a degree of additional heather honey, something to fleetingly cherish. 60.5%.

⬦ **Cadenhead's Small Batch International Fettercairn 28 Year Old** bourbon casks, dist 1988 (84) n22 t21.5 f20 b20.5 Good old Fettercairn! Lovely nose with malt and butterscotch. But the delivery and beyond reminds you that you can polish an object all you like, it ends up exactly what it started as...only with a sheen. 55.4%.

Hepburn's Choice Fettercairn 6 Years Old European oak quarter cask, dist 2008, bott 2015 (67.5) n15 t18 f17 b17.5. Nice try, lads. But typically rubbery Fettercairn like this is a whisky that needs hanging, drawing and quartering – not quarter casking... 46%. nc ncf sc. 93 bottles.

Hepburn's Choice Fettercairn 6 Years Old European oak quarter cask, dist 2008, bott 2015 (76.5) n19 t19.5 f19 b19. Chewy and rubbery but some base sugars offer a kind of synthetic cream you get in cheaper cakes. Some maltiness can be detected. 46%. nc ncf sc. 95 bottles.

Hepburn's Choice Fettercairn 6 Years Old European oak quarter cask, dist 2008, bott 2015 (77.5) n20 t19.5 f19 b19. Enjoys the odd tenable moment when the barley and oak combine comprehensively enough to see off the worst of the usual nutty-rubber tang. Still proudly maintains a stubborn grimness. 46%. nc ncf sc. 94 bottles.

Hepburn's Choice Fettercairn 7 Years Old red wine finished barrel, dist 2008, bott 2016 (69.5) n18 t18 f17 b17.5. Even if you use a top-notch cask, when the spirit starts off as poorly as this, you have no chance. After tasting a shockingly –one might even say suspiciously - good 6-y-o Fettercairn just a few moments ago, it is very much back to normal now... 46%. nc ncf sc. 383 bottles.

⬦ **Hepburn's Choice Fettercairn 7 Years Old** European oak quarter cask, dist 2008, bott 2016 (73) n17 t18 f19 b19 You can dress Cowdenbeath FC's third team in a Real Madrid kit. But they still will be Cowdenbeath's third team... 46%. nc ncf sc. 140 bottles.

⬦ **Hepburn's Choice Fettercairn 7 Years Old** European oak quarter cask, dist 2008, bott 2016 (70.5) n15 t20 f17 b18.5 At times a far better experience than the dreadful nose promises with the oils doing some Stirling Albion work until the finish kicks in begins to rip at your throat with frenzied relish. Would lose against a Cowdenbeath third team in all white... 46%. nc ncf sc. 85 bottles.

⬦ **Hepburn's Choice Fettercairn 8 Years Old** sherry hogshead, dist 2008, bott 2016 (59) n14 t15 f16 b14 I was tempted to shoot the bottle to put it out of its misery... 46%. nc ncf sc. 407 bottles.

⬦ **Hunter Laing's Distiller's Art Fettercairn Aged 14 Years** refill hogshead, dist Jun 02, bott 2016 (79) n19 t21 f19 b19 A sweet but harsh malt enjoyable a few attractive date and walnut moments. 48%. nc ncf sc. 317 bottles.

⬦ **Provenance Fettercairn Aged 8 Years** refill hogshead, cask no. 11512, dist May 08, bott Nov 16 (87) n21.5 t22 f21.5 b22 Fettercairn in finest fettle. The muscovado and thin marzipan link with the grist quite deliciously. Perhaps a little tang towards the end but marginal and certainly none of the usual nonsense surrounding the distillery: an exceptional and very enjoyable bottling. 46%. nc ncf sc. 393 bottles.

⬦ **The Whisky Agency Fettercairn 28 Years Old** dist 1988 (64) n16 t17 f15 b16 Nutty and dirty with a distinct feints kick. Why anyone would want to bottle this nonsense is beyond me. 49.9%. Bottled for La Maison du Whisky.

Whiskybroker Fettercairn 9 Year Old bourbon barrel, cask no. 107666, dist 20 Nov 06, bott 15 Feb 16 (85.5) n21 t21 f22 b21.5. Hot headed and slightly aggressive, it comes into its own when the high intensity malt and milky chocolate combine. Definitely an extra high quality ex-bourbon barrel at work here ensuring a very decent dram. 55.6%. sc.

⬦ **The Whisky Chamber Fettercairn 10 Year Old** bourbon cask, dist 2006 (84.5) n20 t23 f20 b21.5 That rarest of beasts: a thoroughly drinkable and enjoyable Fettercairn. OK, it won't win any beauty prizes and the nose, like the finish, is hardly something to actually savour. But the delivery and middle – a beautiful malt and muscovado romp – really does have the odd moment of true excellence. 55.2%.

GLEN ALBYN
Highlands (Northern) 1846–1983. Diageo. Demolished.
Gordon & MacPhail Rare Vintage Glen Albyn 1976 (96) n22.5 t24.5 f24.5 b24.5 Wow! My eyes nearly popped out of my head when I spotted this in my sample room. Glen Albyns come round as rarely as Scotsman winning Wimbledon. Well, almost. When I used to buy this (from Gordon and MacPhail in their early Connoisseur's Choice range, as it happens) when the distillery was still alive (just) I always found it an interesting if occasionally aggressive dram. This masterpiece, though, is something else entirely. And the delivery really does take us to places where only the truly great whiskies go... 43%

GLENALLACHIE
Speyside, 1968. Chivas Brothers. Working.
Glenallachie 15 Years Old Distillery Edition db (81) n20 t21 f19 b19. Real battle between nature and nurture: an exceptional sherry butt has silk gloves and honied marzipan, while a hot-tempered bruiser lurks beneath. 58%

Endangered Drams Glenallachie 22 Year Old bourbon hogshead, cask no. 5077, dist Sept 93, bott Oct 15 (82) n20 t20 f22 b20. Dear god...! It's not the dram which is endangered, but your taste buds! A fiery frolic from start to finish. One dimensional malt does its best to retain the barley on an even keel and, at the end, almost succeeds. 57.3%. sc.

◇ **The First Editions Glenallachie Aged 21 Years 1995** refill hogshead, cask no. 13309, bott 2017 (86) n21.5 t22.5 f20.5 b21.5 Worther's original nose and very presentable barley on delivery. Simple but attractive. 58.7%. nc ncf sc. 242 bottles.

Hepburn's Choice Glenallachie 7 Years Old refill hogshead, dist 2008, bott 2016 (65) n16 t17 f16 b16. Just no in so many ways... 46%. nc ncf sc. 301 bottles.

◇ **Old Malt Cask Glenallachie Aged 21 Years** refill hogshead, cask no. 13299, dist Mar 95, bott Feb 17 (87.7) n22 t23 f20.5 b22 Cut from almost identical cloth as the First Editions 1995, except this has much more oomph in the barley department. 50%. nc ncf sc. 229 bottles.

Old Malt Cask Glenallachie Aged 24 Years refill hogshead, cask no. 12307, dist Feb 92, bott Feb 16 (85) n21 t22 f20.5 b21.5. Pretty well built and chunky for a Glenallachie. The malt is fully buttressed by oak. Hot in part, though. 50%. nc ncf sc. 180 bottles.

◇ **Provenance Glenallachie Aged 7 Years** refill hogshead, cask no. 11187, dist Apr 09, bott May 16 (69.5) n18 t17 f17 b17.5 Oddly enough, there are no faults with this as such. It is just a very poor quality whisky – though standard for the distillery – matured in a tiring cask. Harsh and thin. 46%. nc ncf sc.

The Warehouse Collection Glenallachie Aged 22 Years bourbon hogshead, cask no. 5077, dist 09 Sept 93, bott 30 Oct 15 (87.5) n21.5 t23 f21.5 b21.5. Malty and juicy and even a few pears at work. Though thin in its typecast way, rather good for this distillery 57.3%. nc ncf. 244 bottles.

GLENBURGIE
Speyside, 1810. Chivas Brothers. Working.
Glenburgie Aged 15 Years bott code L00/129 db (84) n22 t23 f19 b20. Doing so well until the spectacularly flat, bitter finish. Orangey citrus and liquorice had abounded. 46%

◇ **C & S Dram Collection Glenburgie 5 Years Old** bourbon barrel, cask no. 800538, dist 31 Oct 10, bott 23 Jan 17 (89) n22 lively barley and crushed green acorns; t23 the most beautifully clean and intense malt: one dimensional, but what a dimension! f22 a significant degree of concentrated malt stays the course; b22 a youngster for sure, but a beauty for all that. 61.4%. sc. 240 bottles.

Five Lions Glenburgie Aged 20 Years 2nd fill American bourbon hogshead, dist Jun 95, bott Nov 15 (89) n22 t23.5 f21.5 b22 Solid and true throughout. 53.7%. nc ncf.

◇ **Gordon & MacPhail Cask Strength Glenburgie 1995** bott 29 Sept 16 (96) n24 sheer bliss! Sherry of untainted quality is muscular fruit and spice mode. As rare to find on the nose these days as it is stunningly beautiful; heavily laden fruitcake which has spent ten minutes too long at gas mark eight...; t24.5 the palate is engulfed by a stupendous two-toned delivery of fierce fruit and stinging spice....as well as a much softer module, salivating and rich in sultana and overcooked raisin, sweet but with a distinct toastiness; the mid-ground soon starts towards a more roast coffee and fruitcake mix...borderline perfection; f23.5 long, slightly hinting towards spotted dick pudding, then moving back towards those irresistible toasted raisins...; b24 if you want to encounter nigh-on faultless sherry influence at its most positive, grab a bottle of this... quick! For this is how a sherry cask whisky used to taste...and there is now, tragically, an entire generation of whisky drinkers out there today who really have no idea... 57.9%.

⟡ **Hepburn's Choice Glenburgie 8 Years Old** bourbon wine barrel, dist 2007, bott 2016 (91.5) n22.5 not sure the balance has quite been fully achieved here but the interplay between the vanilla and squishy grape has its fair share of succulence and charm; t23.5 that succulence translates directly onto the palate with a sublime landing, the fruit acting as the cushion on which vanilla and spices land without a single bounce...; f22.5 drier and now even spicier; b23 serene and silky. 46%. nc ncf sc. 283 bottles.

⟡ **Hunter Laing's Old & Rare Glenburgie Aged 36 Years** refill hogshead, dist Nov 80, bott Jan 17 (93) n24.5 the weight of the age has been dispersed evenly over the aroma, with no burdensome notes whatsoever. There is a salted butter quality laying an oily foundation for the lemon curd tart, toasted fudge and Plasticine. The sugars play a subtle, behind-the-scene role...as do the equally well disguised spices. One of the most placid and beautifully paced noses of the year; t23 much more lively on delivery: the light barley-rich fruit sets the salivating tone, the muscovado sugars ping rigidly against the starchy vanilla; f22.5 a slight cask bitterness creeps into play but the barley lasts the course; b23 spend as much time with that nose as you possible can... 47.4%. nc ncf sc. 257 bottles.

⟡ **Old Malt Cask Glenburgie Aged 18 Years** refill hogshead, cask no. 12806, dist Feb 98, bott Aug 16 (90.5) n21.5 hmmm... not that convincing. Not unpleasant with its half-hearted fruitiness but doesn't quite take off, either...; t24 ahhhh...that's much more like it!! Amazingly rich and lush with a superb ulmo honey theme, amply backed by juicy malts, busy spices and vanilla-fudge; f22 thins just a little as the oak takes hold but a light praline flourish is undone only by the famous "Allied-cask" bitterness; b23 the nose is flat, but beyond that this is a very sweet and pretty boy with a long tail. Perhaps it should be called Glenbudgie... 50%. nc ncf sc. 139 bottles.

⟡ **Old Malt Cask Glenburgie Aged 21 Years** refill hogshead, cask no. 12358, dist Apr 95, bott Apr 16 (83.5) n21.5 t22 f20 b20.5 A significant degree of cask tang knocks the big barley surge off track. 50%. nc ncf sc. 170 bottles.

Old Particular Speyside Glenburgie 18 Years Old refill butt, cask no. 10873, dist Jun 97, bott Aug 15 (64) n15 t17 f16 b16. Disappointing on so many levels. From the nose onwards, refuses to gel. 48.4%. nc ncf sc. 744 bottles.

⟡ **Provenance Glenburgie Aged 8 Years** refill hogshead, cask no. 11628, dist Jun 08, bott Feb 17 (87) n21.5 t22 f22 b21.5 Makes no great effort to hide its youth; indeed celebrates its limited scope by concentrating on what it can best: project a lovely custard-rich gristy personality with the aid of a pear-drop sharpness. 46%. nc ncf sc. 234 bottles.

That Boutique-y Whisky Company Glenburgie batch 2 (94.5) n23.5 t24 f23 b24 pretty much faultless, top grade blending malt: quite irresistible! 50.1%. 75 bottles.

⟡ **Whisky Castle Glenburgie 18 Year Old** first fill bourbon, dist 22 Jul 98, bott Aug 16 (94.5) n23 not just a rigid backbone but muscle, too: a real firmness to the grain even after all these years and the liquorice-hickory attachment to it is superb; t24 ah, there is some fat! Light oils cushion it thick with rich, biscuity malt. Tannins are gentler but drier here while ulmo honey corners the later sweetness; f23.5 Maltesers without the chocolate and toasty fudge; b24 my kind of Burgie: brilliant! 55.8%. Bottled by Gordon & MacPhail.

GLENCADAM
Highlands (Eastern), 1825. Angus Dundee. Working.

Glencadam Aged 10 Years db (95) n24 crystal clarity to the sharp, ultra fresh barley. Clean, uncluttered by excessive oak, the apparent lightness is deceptive; the intensity of the malt carries its own impressive weight and the citrus note compliments rather than thins. Enticing; t24 immediately zingy and eye-wateringly salivating with a fabulous layering of sweet barley. Equally delicate oak chimes in to ensure a lightly spiced balance and a degree of attitude; f23 longer than the early barley freshness would have you expecting, with soft oils ensuring an extended, tapering, malty edge to the gentle, clean oak; b24 sophisticated, sensual, salivating and seemingly serene, this malt is all about juicy barley and balance. Just bristles with character and about as puckeringly elegant as single malt gets...and even thirst-quenching. My God: the guy who put this one together must be a genius, or something... 46%

⟡ **Glencadam Aged 13 Years** db (94) n23.5 Glencadam in slightly abstract mode: very hard to fathom the driving force of its personality here. There is honey, light and thinned, which takes us only so far; then there is the oak with its gentle vanilla and liquorice breeze which appears directionless; the random lime and vague lemon drop – all very pretty...and eclectic; t24 you find yourself laughing on delivery. As all those confusing elements on the nose appear to have formed a malty soup for the delivery, with every single profile visible in varying weights and shapes on the palate at one time or another; however, it is the barley itself – barely a suggestion on the nose – which dominates; the sugars are demerara-led, at first crisp then melt-in-the-mouth before linking with the tannins to orma non-specific honey; **f23** soft, though a little bitterness off the oak gives the persistent honey something to rail against...; **b23.5** tasting this within 24 hours of Brechin City, the cheek by jowl neighbours of this distillery winning promotion after a penalty shoot out success in their play off final. This malt, every bit as engrossing and with more twists and turns than their seven-goal-thriller yesterday, is the perfect way to toast their success. *46%. nc ncf. 6,000 bottles.*

Glencadam Aged 15 Years db (**90.5**) **n22.5 t23 f22 b23** The spices keep the taste buds on full alert but the richness and depth of the barley defies the years. Another exhibition of Glencadam's understated elegance. Some more genius malt creation... *46%*

Glencadam Aged 17 Years Triple Cask Portwood Finish db (**93.5**) **n23** that is one beguiling and sexy nose: so many layers of fruit and of varying intensity; the background is choc-a-bloc (almost literally) with vanilla and natural caramels in the shape of chocolate fudge; **t24.5** is it the mouth feel which blows you away most? Or the way the lush, fruitcake notes take on an extra dimension – especially when the intense dark chocolate begins to form? One of the flavour profiles of the year...; **f22** some dry, bitter powdery notes emphasise the wine casks, but the fruit-chocolate-alcohol mix really does underline the innate greatness and profound beauty of this whisky; **b24** a 17-year-old whisky truffle. A superb late night or after dinner dram, where even the shadowy sulphur cannot spoil its genius. *46%. nc ncf. 1128 bottles.*

⬙ **Glencadam Aged 18 Years** db (**96.5**) **n24.5** this is exceptional: the balance between the light spreading of orange-blossom honey on the lightly cooked toast has to be sniffed to be believed. Ridiculously elegant and gentle; **t24** initially dry delivery with the oak playing complex patterns which accentuates the crispness of the sugars; the honey operates almost below the radar, but once you pick it up a more heather-honey style is detected; **f23.5** long, thanks to the understated oils which have benefitted from non-filtration. A gentle saltiness also enriches and concentrates the mind; dries but with the most subtle of spicy back-ups; **b24.5** so, here we go again: head down and plough on with the Whisky Bible 2018. This is the first whisky tasted in anger for the new edition and I select Glencadam for the strangest of reasons: it is the closest distillery to a football ground (North British, apart) I can think of, being a drop kick from Brechin City's pretty Glebe Park ground. And why is that relevant? Well today is a Saturday and I should really be at a game but decided to start off a weekend when there are fewest interruptions and I can get back into the swing of things before settling into the rhythm of a six day tasting week. Also, Glencadam, though criminally little known beyond readers of the Whisky Bible, is among the world's greatest distilleries producing one of the most charming whiskies of them all. So, hopefully, it will be a little reward for me. And offering the bourbon cask induced natural, light gold - which perfectly matches the buzzard which has just drifted on the winds into my garden - this enticingly fills the gap between their 17- and 19- years old. Strikes me there is a fraction more first fill cask at play here than usual, ensuring not just a distinctively honeyed, bourbony edge but a drier element also. Distinguished and elegant this is a fabulous, almost unbelievable way to start the new Bible as it has the hallmarks of a malt likely to end up winning some kind of major award. Somehow I think the bar set here, one fashioned from gold, will be far too high for the vast majority that will follow over the next five months... *46%. nc ncf.*

Glencadam Aged 19 Years Oloroso Sherry Cask Finish db (**84**) **n21.5 t22 f19.5 b21.** Mainly, though not quite, free of sulphur so the whisky after 19 years gets a good chance to speak relatively ungagged, though somewhat muffled. *46%. nc ncf. 6,000 bottles.*

Glencadam Aged 21 Years "The Exceptional" bott 2011 db (**94**) **n23.5 t24 f23 b23.5.** This distillery is emerging out of the shadows from its bad old Allied days as one of the great Scottish single malt distilleries. So good is some of their whisky, this "exceptional" bottling is almost becoming the norm. *46%. nc ncf.*

Glencadam Aged 25 Years db (**95**) **n25** some 1,600 of you will get the chance to discover exactly what the perfect nose looks like. Trying to describe it is like attempting to paint a picture of an orgasm. Impossible. But let's just say it carries on for a very long time, kind of peaking but not. And here, do you concentrate on the gooseberries or the lemon curd tart? The ulmo honey or the orange-blossom? The salt or the lightest white peppers...? I think I'm in love....; **t24** more of the same. In fact, near identical on the delivery, except here malt - full of concentrated gristy sugar – really does seriously enter the equation; **f22** this is an old Allied distillery. And for some reason many of their barrels had just a hint of bitterness to their finish. This does, but the sugars are so intact and stunningly presentable, the damage is negligible. Perhaps just enough to steer it off course from World Whisky of the Year...; **b24** imagine the best-balanced team Mourinho ever produced for Chelsea. Well, it was never as good as this nose... *46%. nc ncf. 1,600 bottles.*

⬧ **The First Editions Glencadam Aged 19 Years 1996** refill hogshead, cask no. 12785, bott 2016 (87.5) n22 t22.5 f21 b22 A very light tang to the oak undermines the excellence of the malty intensity. The sugars remain a little shy, though the citrus helps ensure an attractive juiciness. 52%. nc ncf sc. 145 bottles.

⬧ **Old Malt Cask Glencadam Aged 19 Years** refill hogshead, cask no. 12775, dist Nov 96, bott Aug 16 (95.5) n25 seems almost sacrilege to drink this: you could pamper your proboscis for hours on end by allowing your nose buds to absorb and decode the extraordinary complexity of the aroma. I can detect three types of honey in tandem here: orange blossom, heather and ulmo. With liberal sprinklings of butterscotch and vanilla and a further further muscovado fruity flourish, this is a delight. But to make things better still, the barley still retains a slightly green, gristy property...; t23.5 the complex sugars merge, as though uniting to fend off the early spices and gathering drier tones from the tannin. Busy, satisfying with a wonderful barley sub-strata; f23 becomes a little saltier as it moves towards its finish. Big emphasis on the vanilla; b24 the palate, though a thorough delight, still struggles to live up to the perfection of the nose. There again, very few whiskies would... 50%. nc ncf sc. 145 bottles.

⬧ **Old Particular Glencadam 18 Years Old** refill hogshead, cask no. 11474, dist May 98, bott Nov 16 (92.5) n23.5 the effortless balance between the natural caramels and ulmo honey is ridiculously sexy; t23.5 it is though some great wizard of whisky has dropped just enough oak in with the barley to forge a glorious potion: every aspect, including the understated yet mind-bogglingly complex sugars, are in just-so amounts; f22 a little bitterness creeps in late on, but nothing that the sugared vanilla can't easily cope with; b23.5 wallows in charm. 48.4%. nc ncf sc. 310 bottles.

GLENCRAIG
Speyside, 1958. Chivas Brothers. Silent.

Cadenhead's Single Malt Glencraig 31 Years Old (92) n22.5 t23.5 f23 b23 Well done Cadenhead in coming up with one of the last surviving Glencraig casks on the planet. The feintiness shows why it was eventually done away with. But this is a malt with great distinction, too. 50.8%

GLENDRONACH
Highlands, 1826. The BenRiach Distillery Co. Working.

GlenDronach 8 Year Old The Hielan db (82) n20 t22 f20 b20. Intense malt. But doesn't quite feel as happy with the oil on show as it might. 46%

⬧ **Glendronach Aged 10 Years PX Casks** bott code 2016/09/20 LK31312 db (96.5) n24.5 my word...what can you say....? Faultless fruit: we are talking the juiciest dates known to mankind; the most elegant high ester rum; clever, nipping peppers; deliciously over-ripened pear; muscovado sugar emboldened by molasses....all this soft and beyond sensuous...; t24 you expect a viscous delivery...and get one: my, do you get one...! You also, for a while, get a few rounds of rich malt, though this transforms in slow motion into thick caramel; the fruit is less complex here than on the nose – much more about effect. A chewy blend of Fruit Salad and Black Jacks candy seems to perfectly round off the mid-ground; f24 a light, unctuous spiciness....then, amazingly, a burst of something sharp and salivating – so late! An apple boiled sweet freshness brings the curtain down on a very different finish. b24 if you find a more intense, clean, sulphur-free exhibition of PX this year, then I need to see it. As astonishing as it is beautiful! This was the 1,197th new whisky I tasted for the 2018 Bible, and not a single PX cask has come anywhere near as close to this for unbridled excellence. If there was a Whisky Bible award for Sheer Voluptuousness among single malts, this would win hands down... 48%.

The GlenDronach 12 Years Old db (92) n22 t24 f22.5 b23.5 An astonishingly beautiful malt despite the fact that a rogue sherry butt has come in under the radar. But for that, this would have been a mega scorer: potentially an award-winner. Fault or no fault, seriously worth discovering this bottling of this too long undiscovered great distillery 43%

The GlenDronach Aged 12 Years "Original" db (86.5) n21 t22 f22 b21.5. One of the more bizarre moments of the year: thought I'd got this one mixed up with a German malt whisky I had tasted earlier in the day. There is a light drying tobacco feel to this and the exact same corresponding delivery on the palate. That German version is distilled in a different type of still; this is made in probably the most classic stillhouse on mainland Scotland. Good, enjoyable whisky. But I see a long debate with distillery owner Billy Walker on the near horizon, though it was in Allied's hands when this was produced. 43%

GlenDronach 12 Year Old Sauternes db (93.5) n23 t24 f23 b23.5 Despite the magnificently delicate fruit, it is the malt which wins on points. Superb! 46%

The GlenDronach 14 Years Old Virgin Oak db (87) n22.5 t22 f21 b21.5. Charming, pretty, but perhaps lacking in passion... 46%. nc ncf.

The GlenDronach Aged 18 Years "Allardice" db (83.5) n19 t22 f21 b21.5. Huge fruit. But a long-running bitter edge to the toffee and raisin sits awkwardly on the palate. 46%

⬩⬩⬩ **The GlenDronach Aged 18 Years Tawny Port Wood Finish** db (94.5) n23.5 the cleanest grape! Dense fruit with succulent sultanas and greengages ripe enough to explode; t24 ...oh, that mouth feel! Sumptuous without being oily, grapey without losing its malty roots and such clever intertwangling of butterscotch and Dundee cake; f23 long with a spiced marzipan and chocolate fade; b24 a malt with not just an excellent flavour profile but sits on the palate as comfortably as you might snuggle into an old Jag. 46%.

⬩⬩⬩ **The GlenDronach Aged 21 Years Parliament** db (76) n23 t21.5 f15 b16.5 Red-hued, myopically one dimensional, rambles on and on, sulphur-tongued, bitter and does its best to leave a bad taste in the mouth while misrepresenting its magnificent land. Now, who does that remind me of...? 48%.

GlenDronach Cask Strength batch 5 db (89.5) n22 gentle vanillas are straight and unerring; t23 salivating as the malt takes command on delivery; the middle is more intense malt with a Victoria sponge edge; f22 butterscotch tart with a pinch of spice; b22.5 a very safe malt which does everything to keep its shape intact. 55.3%

⬩⬩⬩ **The GlenDronach Cask Strength Batch 6** db (92) n23.5 the lightest of bourbon notes holds court: red liquorice backed by just-so quantities of hickory and honey; on another level citrus notes lighten the experience, though the tannins –first of a caramel nature – begin to slowly mount; t24 that bourbon thread is extended and amplified by the ulmo honey and red liquorice delivery. Malt comes flooding in soon after, then a spiced butterscotch; f22 slightly disappointing bitterness towards the death, but not remotely unknown in ex-Allied distillery casks; b22.5 with the exception of the very last phase, this shows Glendronach in a deliciously shining light. 56.1%.

GlenDronach Peated db (93.5) n23.5 no prisoners taken here: this is one smoky dude...; t23.5 sublime clarity to the ulmo honey which underlines the malt despite the hefty smoke slowly making its presence felt; f23 good spice, confident peat still, but a little late bitterness creeps in; b23.5 I rarely mark the smoky whisky from a distillery which makes peat as an afterthought higher than its standard distillate. But here it is hard not to give massive marks. Only a failing cask at the very death docks a point or so... 46%

Classic Whisky & Lifestyle Glendronach 20 Year Old 1994 sherry cask (86) n22 t22 f20.5 b21.5. Top heavy with tannin, the sugars are in a losing battle with the proudly more bitter elements. 55%. 300 bottles.

GLENDULLAN (see also below)
Speyside, 1972. Diageo. Working.

Glendullan Aged 8 Years db (89) n20 t22 f24 b23. This is just how I like my Speysiders: young fresh and uplifting. A truly charming malt. 40%

Singleton of Glendullan 12 Years Old db (87) n22 t22 f21 b22. Much more age than is comfortable for a 12-y-o. 40%

The Singleton of Glendullan 38 Year Old European oak casks, dist 1975 db (94) n23.5 custard creams with a Garibaldi accompaniment; this nose really does take the biscuit...; t24 lively delivery: gorgeous crushed sultana and golden syrup...; the malt, even half way through, shows some magically rich touches; f22.5 spicy; a little tiredness has crept in to bitter effect; b24 gather round and let me tell you a little story about the excellence of European oak casks before sulphur reared its ugly head. No, better still, take a glass of this and allow it to do it so much more eloquently... 59.8%. 3,756 bottles. Diageo Special Releases 2014.

Singleton of Glendullan Liberty db (73) n17 t19 f18 b19. For showing such a really unforgiving off key bitter furriness, it should be clamped in irons... 40% WB16/036

Singleton of Gendullan Trinity db (92.5) n24 t23 f22.5 b23 Designed for airports, this complex little beauty deserves to fly off the shelves... 40% WB16/037

⬩⬩⬩ **Cadenhead's Small Batch International Glendullan 20 Year Old** Lafitte cask, dist 1996 (96.5) n24.5 one of the most soul-kissingly erotic fruit noses of the year: the secret is the elegant peppery attachment to the grape which gives a buzz to every nuance. Clean yet intense and busy, the sugars are kept under strict and careful control, thus intensifying the grape further; t24 pure silk. The grape, for a moment without those spices, land parachute first on the palate, a concentrated grape balm again all the more telling because of the tight rein kept on the sugars. After the initial high salivation greeting, the fruit goes on Latour of the taste buds, seemingly massaging each one personally. Only slowly do the peppers build;

f24 a little ulmo honey, pepper and that refined, gentlemanly grape keeps extends the magic for a very long time, and the final notes are one of that unique dreggy echo one finds only in a Grand Cru wine; **b24** a malt which is truly Lafitte for purpose... 52.4%. sc.

The Golden Cask Glendullan 18 Years Old cask no. CM 220, dist 1999, bott 2015 **(87.5)** n22 t23 f21 b21.5. Celebrates the spiky oak which, at times, is driven like a stake through the taste buds. Early on, the barley does get the chance to show some honeyed turns during some complex moments. 59.8%. sc. 186 bottles.

Gordon & MacPhail Connoisseurs Choice Glendullan 2004 bott 18 Nov 16 **(95.5)** n24 one of the most sensual praline noses of the year: a creamy sweetness also touches upon lime glace and the most elegant and well-mannered spices on the scene; a little over-ripe banana, too; **t24** you get the feeling the barley is crisp and crunchy. But you can't be too sure as the softness of the oils absorb anything which may be a little too firm. However, it is the mid-ground where it hits superstar status as those praline notes on the nose are reprised to truly captivating awe-inspiring effect; **f23** quieter, though still the barley reverberates; soft spices offer extra life; vanillas trickle to the very end; **b24.5** another GlenStunning... 46%.

GLEN ELGIN
Speyside, 1900. Diageo. Working.

Glen Elgin Aged 12 Years db **(89)** n23 t24 f20 b22. Absolutely murders Cragganmore as Diageo's top dog bottled Speysider. The marks would be several points further north if one didn't get the feeling that some caramel was weaving a derogatory spell. Brilliant stuff nonetheless. States Pot Still on label – not to be confused with Irish Pot Still. This is 100% malt... and it shows! 43%

Maltbarn Glen Elgin 1995 ex-bourbon cask, bott 2015 **(96)** n24.5 t24 f23 b24.5 Such an old-fashioned experience. Some 30 years ago, many of the casks in Speyside boasted what is on offer here. Though seldom actually from the same barrel....This is quite brilliantly made and matured malt; if each one of Scotland's barrels were anything like this, the overall quality would be a good 30% higher than it actually is...Anyway, if you were ever to kiss your partner and swap whisky in mid-kiss, this is the dram to do it. Truly sensual and erotic stuff. 51.7%. sc. 116 bottles.

Old Malt Cask Glen Elgin Aged 25 Years refill hogshead, cask no. 12155, dist Mar 90, bott Nov 15 **(94)** n23 t23.5 f23.5 b24 For a dram with some faults, the utter magnificence of the good bits ensures a gorgeous experience. 50%. nc ncf. 205 bottles.

Old Particular Glen Elgin 21 Years Old refill hogshead, cask no. 11596, dist Dec 95, bott Mar 17 **(94.5)** n23.5 light for its age, but given time you can be only mesmerised by its understated complexity. A sprinkling of lemon sherbet ensures that age has not wearied it while the maple syrup and green banana is likewise lightly distributed. A fresh malty grist is weighted only by the most polite of oak tannin...; **t23.5** has to be salivating....and it is!! So gristy! Melt-in-the-mouth castor sugar with a light squirt of lemon mans the teaming malt is full of life...; **f23.5** some late spices, even a slice of coffee and walnut cake but the salivating continues....; **b24** a distillery which rarely lets you down if in a decent cask. Playfully, almost coquettishly adorable. 51.5%. nc ncf sc. 226 bottles.

World of Orchids Glen Elgin 21 Year Old bourbon cask, dist 1995 **(95)** n23.5 no off note: no tiredness from the cask whatsoever. Just a procession of busy barley showing a degree of brightness still, and just the right amount of oaky wear and tear to give a bow of respect to its age. Neither too sweet or dry with the sugars confined to a healthy gristiness; **t23.5** fabulously salivating and alive with the palate gently massages by the softest but most apposite oils which appear to maximise the light sugar cane and castor sugars; excellent spices form, as well as subtle cocoa tones; **f23.5** the longest fade you might expect with those spices showing just a little more tannin as it progresses but the barley standing quietly firm; **b24.5** one of those rare malts where the mouth feel matches the malt in pure excellence. A blender's malt if ever there was one... 50.3%.

GLENESK
Highlands (Eastern), 1897–1985. Diageo. Demolished.

The Cooper's Choice Glen Esk 31 Year Old dist 1984, bott 2016 **(92)** n22.5 sharp malt still despite the age; a little lemon lightens it further; **t23** lovely delivery of intense malt which is clean, mildly salivating and embraces the growing vanilla gently; **f23** a little cocoa dries the basic gristy, vanilla finale. **b23.5** a very simple, un-taxing but well preserved, unblemished, quietly delicious and poignant malt from the last days of a small and little known distillery. 50%. nc ncf sc. The Vintage Malt Whisky Co.

Gordon & MacPhail Rare Old Glenesk 1980 (95) n23.5 raspberry sauce on vanilla ice cream: you can even sniff the caramel cornet! t24 malt doesn't arrive any softer than this and, for the age, much more intense. A real malt shake richness to the barley and again the oak is offering up a caramel wafer, both in taste and dryness; f23.5 more of a chocolate sundae now, with some extra nuts thrown in; the oak tries to throw up an acidic sharpness late on, but it fails to do any harm and instead a delightful spice sparkles; b24 what a charmer: better dead than when alive, some might argue. But this has weathered the passing three and half decades with ease and really does something of an ice cream feel to it from beginning to the end...well I suppose the distillery was located close to the seaside...One of the most understated but beautiful lost distillery bottlings of the year. 46%.

GLENFARCLAS
Speyside, 1836. J&G Grant. Working.

Glenfarclas 8 Years Old db (86) n21 t22 f22 b21. Less intense sherry allows the youth of this malt to stand out. Mildly quirky as a Glenfarclas and enormous entertainment. 40%

Glenfarclas 10 Years Old db (80) n19 t20 f22 b19. Always an enjoyable malt, but for some reason this version never seems to fire on all cylinders. There is a vague honey sheen which works well with the barley, but struggles for balance and the nose is a bit sweaty. Still has distinctly impressive elements but an odd fish. 40%

Glenfarclas 12 Years Old db (94) n23.5 a wonderfully fresh mix of grape and mint; t24 light, youthful, playful, mouthwatering. Less plodding honey, more vibrant Demerara and juiced-up butterscotch; f23 long, with soft almost ice-cream style vanillas with a grapey topping; b23.5 a superb re-working of an always trustworthy malt. This dramatic change in shape works a treat and suits the malt perfectly. What a sensational success!! 43%

Glenfarclas 15 Years Old db (85.5) n21.5 t23 f20 b21. One thing is for certain: working with sherry butts these days is a bit like working with ACME dynamite.....you are never sure when it is about to blow up in your face. There is only minimal sulphur here, but enough to take the edge off a normally magnificent whisky, at the death. Instead it is now merely, in part, quite lovely. The talent at Glenfarclas is unquestionably among the highest in the industry: I'll be surprised to see the same weaknesses with the next bottling. 46%

Glenfarclas 17 Years Old db (93) n23 t23 f23 b24 an excellent age for this distillery, allowing just enough oak in to stir up the complexity. A stupendous addition to the range. 46%

Glenfarclas 17 Years Old db (94.5) n23.5 a significantly different nose to other 17-y-o from this distillery I have encountered: much more pineapple and custard at play; t24 massively salivating with malt concentrate and a non-specific, acidic fruitiness burrowing into the taste buds; a mix of muscovado sugars and ulmo honey deals with the surprisingly confident oak; f23 wonderful cocoa, lightly but significantly oiled. Malt still has the major say even this late on, but it is brittle and bolstered by a little citrus; b24 when a malt is this delicate, it is surprising the difference that just 3% can make to the oils and keeping the structure together. A dram for those with a patient disposition. 43%.

Glenfarclas 18 Years Old db (84) n21 t22 f20 b21. Tight, nutty and full of crisp muscovado sugar. 43%. Travel Retail Exclusive.

Glenfarclas 21 Years Old db (83) n20 t23 f19 b21. A chorus of sweet, honied malt and mildly spiced, teasing fruit on the fabulous mouth arrival and middle compensates for the few blips. 43%

Glenfarclas 25 Years Old db (84) n20 t22 f20 b22. A curious old bat: by no means free from imperfect sherry but compensating with some staggering age – seemingly way beyond the 25-year statement. Enjoys the deportment of a doddering old classics master from a family of good means and breeding. 43%

Glenfarclas 30 Years Old db (85) n20 t22 f21 b22. Flawed yet juicy. 43%

Glenfarclas 40 Years Old db (95) n24.5 please nose for a good half hour before tasting: pretty closed at first, but opens imperceptibly until the fruit has not only sweetened but taken on a sheen which embraces a mix of heather honey, gooseberry tart and the lightest molasses. There is even now trace smoke which ensures a near perfect weight; t23.5 the tannins are full on no matter what point you taste: salivating grape and malt mixes on the slick delivery to act as a diversion, though the biggest surprise is the slow build of light smoke and mint...; f23 delicate oil on the finale allows the tannins to retreat and those orangey-minty elements to ensure a soft finish; b24 a few moments ago an RAF plane flew low over my usually quiet cottage, violently shaking the windows, silencing my parrot and turning a great spotted woodpecker feeding in my garden to stone: it was too shocked to know whether to stay or fly. And I thought, immediately: Glenfarclas 40! For when, a long time ago now, John Grant paid me the extraordinary compliment of opening his very first bottle of Glenfarclas 40 so we could taste it together, a pair of RAF fighters chose that exact moment to roar feet above his distillery forcing the opened bottle from John's startled hands and onto the lush carpet...into which the initial measures galloopingly poured, rather than our waiting glasses. And it so happened I had a new sample to hand. So, with this whisky I made a fond toast: to John. And to the RAF. 43%.

Glenfarclas 40 Years Old db (94) n23 old Demerara rum laced with well aged oloroso. Spicy, deep though checked by vanilla; t23 toasty fruitcake with just the right degree of burnt raisin; again the spices are central to the plot though now a Jamaican Blue Mountain/Mysore medium roast mix makes an impressive entrance; f24 long, with the oak not just ticking every box, but doing so with a flourish. The Melton Hunt cake finale is divine... b24 couldn't help but laugh: this sample was sent by the guys at Glenfarclas after they spotted that I had last year called their disappointing 40-year-old a "freak". I think we have both proved a point... 46%

Glenfarclas 50 Years Old db (92) n24 Unique. Almost a marriage between 20-y-o bourbon and intense, old-fashioned sherry. Earthy, weighty stuff that repays time in the glass and oxidization because only then does the subtlety become apparent and a soft peat-reek reveal itself; t23 an unexpected sweet – even mouthwatering - arrival, again with a touch of peat to add counter ballast to the intense richness of the sherry. The oak is intense from the middle onwards, but of such high quality that it merely accompanies rather then dominates; f22 warming black peppers ping around the palate; some lovely cocoa oils coat the mouth for a bitter-sweet, warming and very long finish; b23 Most whiskies cannot survive such great age. This one really does bloom in the glass and the earthy, peaty aspect makes it all the more memorable. It has taken 50 years to reach this state. Give a glass of this at least an hour's inquisition, as I have. Your patience will be rewarded many times over. 44.4%

Glenfarclas 50 Years Old lll ex-Oloroso sherry casks db (88.5) n23.5 just about every single note of tiring whisky can be found here, with the exception of eucalyptus...though another summer might have seen that one sprout up, too. Still offers brilliant and delicious complexity and such attractive and unusual combinations, such as Banbury cake and chocolate mousse, for instance...; t21 here the degree of oak takes a tougher line and despite the big caramel incursion, is much less forgiving; f22 settles slightly as the vanilla takes up a softer approach aided by the delicate Demarar sugars; b22 you can actually hear it wheezing as it has run out of puff. But it is easy to recognise the mark of an old champion... 41.1%. ncf. 937 bottles.

Glenfarclas 105 db (95.5) n23.5 the youthful grape comes in clean, juicy bunches; the herbs and spices on a rack on the kitchen wall; t24 any lovers of the old Jennings books will here do a Mr Wilkins explosive snort as the magnificent barley-grape mix is propelled with the force of dynamite into the taste buds; survivors of this experience still able to speak may mention something about cocoa notes forming; f24 long, luxurious, with a pulsing vanilla-grape mix and a build up of spices; light oils intensify and elongate; b24 I doubt if any restorative on the planet works quite as well as this one does. Or if any sherry cask whisky is so clean and full of the joys of Jerez. A classic malt which has upped a gear or two and has become exactly what it is: a whisky of pure brilliance... 60%

Glenfarclas £511.19s.0d Family Reserve db (88) n22.5 t22.5 f21 b22 Not the best, but this still ain't no two bob whisky, mister, and make no mistake... 43%

Glenfarclas 1966 Fino Cask cask nos. 4194, 4195 & 4197 db (96) n24 t24 f23.5 b24.5 As it was exactly 50 years ago today – July 30th 1966 – that England won the World Cup, I thought it entirely fitting that I should taste this 50 year old bottling. No matter how well they fared, or even badly, none of the new whiskies I tasted this year could be any worse than the gutless, leaderless, shameful, embarrassing apology of a display England put up in the European Championships this summer. On my travels a very long time ago I once saw Alf Ramsey, manager of England on that day in 1966, on a railway platform. I had to get off – and wait an hour for another train to complete the journey - just so I could shake the great man by the hand and thank him for what he achieved. Likewise, in the course of my whisky life, I was fortunate enough to share a changing room in a TV studio with the great Kenneth Wolstenholme (who, like me, spent some of his life in Belmont, Surrey). And where, with great grace, and with only me as an audience, he gave the greatest soliloquy in English football history: "There are some people running on to the pitch: they think it's all over. (Beat) It is now...." 50.5%

Glenfarclas 1994 db (95.5) n23.5 t24.5 f23.5 b24 Very close in character and quality with to distillery's latest official 1994 release. Which means it's not far off God's gift to present day sherried malt whisky... 43%. 1200 bottles. The Whisky Shop exclusive.

Glenfarclas The Family Casks 2000 Release W15 refill sherry butt, cask no. 4075 db (94) n23.5 t24 f23 b23.5 One of those malts which releases its manifold secrets at an absurdly slow pace. 58.5%. sc.

Glenfarclas Family Cask 2002 sherry butt, cask no. 3770 db (93) n23.5 huge oloroso: rich date and walnut plus the mandatory molasses... and not even the hint of a hint of an off note. The malt, however, is lost in there somewhere...; t23.5 brilliant spice on the first silky, then quicksandy delivery; the fruit is almost a caricature of itself: fat, enveloping and delicious. A little bitterness creeps in as the oak fight back, but the spices realign with the muscovado sugar to counter...; f23 long spice and fruitcake fade...; b23 like some of the sexiest things in life have... a faultless butt... 53%.

Glenfarclas The Family Casks 2003 cask no. 1450, bott 2013 db (87) n21.5 t22.5 f22 b21. Not sulphured. So, Le Yay! But still just slightly oversaturated with rather course, unrefined grape to get the balance quite where we want it to be. 56.8%. Selected for Le Gus't.

Eiling Lim Glenfarclas 37 Year Old cask no. 88/8, dist 1979, bott 2016 (90) n23 huge oak on this: a malt which has struggled hard to maintain its equilibrium and needs a good half hour breathing in the glass before the delicate exotic fruit notes have conjured up enough sugars for a degree of elegance to be achieved; t23 salivating with an intense barley-exotic fruit mix, yet all the time the tannins are flooding in; f22 the tired oak continues but a wonderful surge of banana milkshake saves the day...; b22 the tannins' attempted take-over sums up this malt: utterly fascinating... 46.9%. 188 bottles.

Kirsch Import Glenfarclas 2008 oloroso sherry hogshead, cask nos. 2132 & 2178, bott 2016 (96) n23.5 superb marriage of relatively young malt with fruit which knows its place: a little sharp here and there and the natural caramels at a loss at which side they should be taking; t25 magnificent, glorious, divine. Possibly the best Scottish delivery of the year so far with the weight, intensity and freshness of the grape truly flawless. Sweet, but never cloyingly so, sharp but never aggressive. And despite the big berry fruit arrival – raspberries and blackberries are among the plums and grape – there is still room enough to take on board the soft tannins and malty hangers on. Amazing...; f23.5 light spices make their mark but the chewy fruit candy hangs on forever; b24 clean as a whistle: this is how sherry matured whisky should always be. A stunner! 60.2%. 611 bottles.

Scotch Malt Whisky Society Cask 1.189 Aged 21 Years refill hogshead, dist 24 Mar 93, bott 22 Jun 15 (87) n22 t23 f21 b21.5. No shortage of natural caramels. Excellent, full-blooded delivery that has plenty of spice in the mix. But a flattish, bitter finale. 54.3%. nc ncf sc. 245 bottles.

Scotch Malt Whisky Society Cask 1.193 Aged 21 Years refill hogshead, dist 23 Sept 93, bott 27 Jul 15 (89.5) n22 t23 f22 b22.5 Similar to 1.189 but with better consistency. 53.4%. nc ncf sc. 196 bottles.

GLENFIDDICH
Speyside, 1887. William Grant & Sons. Working.

Glenfiddich 12 Years Old db (85.5) n21 t22 f21 b21.5. A malt now showing a bit of zap and spark. Even displays a flicker of attractive muscovado sugars. Simple, untaxing and safe. 40%

Glenfiddich 12 Years Old Toasted Oak Reserve db (92.5) n22.5 t23.5 f22.5 b24. Another bottling to confound the critics of Glenfiddich. This is as fine an essay in balance, charm and sophistication as you are likely to find in the whole of Speyside this year. Crack open a bottle... but only when you have a good hour to spend. 40%

Glenfiddich Caoran Reserve Aged 12 Years db (89) n22.5 t22 f21.5 b23. Has fizzed up a little in the last year or so with some salivating charm from the barley and a touch of cocoa from the oak. A complex little number. 40%

Glenfiddich Rich Oak Over 14 Years Old new American & new Spanish oak finish db (90.5) n23 t22 f23.5 b22. From the moment you nose this, there is absolutely no doubting its virgin oak background. It pulls towards bourbon, but never gets there. Apparently European oak is used, too. The result is something curiously hinting at Japanese, but without the crushing intensity. Delicious, thoughtful whisky and one to tick off on your journey of malt whisky discovery. Though a pity we don't see it at 46% and in full voluptuous nudity: you get the feeling that this would have been something really exceptional to conjure with. 40%.

Glenfiddich 15 Years Old db (94.5) n23 t23 f24.5 b24 If an award were to be given for the most consistently beautiful dram in Scotland, this would win more often than not. This under-rated distillery has won more friends with this masterpiece than probably any other brand. 40%

Glenfiddich Aged 15 Years Cask Strength db (85.5) n20 t23 f21 b21.5. Improved upon the surprisingly bland bottlings of old, especially on the fabulously juicy delivery. Still off the pace due to an annoying toffee-ness towards the middle and at the death. 51%

Glenfiddich Distillery Edition 15 Years Old db (93.5) n24.5 t24 f22 b23. Had this exceptional whisky been able to maintain the pace through to the finish, this would have been a single malt of the year contender - at least. *51%. ncf.*

Glenfiddich 18 Years Old db (95) n23.5 the smoke, which for long marked this aroma, appears to have vanished. But the usual suspects of blood orange and various other fruit appear to thrive in the lightly salted complexity; t24.5 how long are you allowed to actually keep the whisky held on the palate before you damage your teeth? One to really close your eyes and study because here we have one of the most complex deliveries Speyside can conjour: the peat may have gone, but there is coal smoke around as the juicy barley embeds with big fat sultanas, plums, dates and grapes. Despite the distinct lack of oil, the mouthfeel is entirely yielding to present one of the softest and most complete essays on the palate you can imagine, especially when you take the bitter-sweet ratio and spice into balance; f23 long, despite the miserly 40% offered, with plenty of banana-custard and a touch of pear; b24 at the moment, the ace in the Glenfiddich pack. If this was bottled at 46%, unchilfiltered etc, I dread to think what the score might be... *40%*

Glenfiddich Age Of Discovery Aged 19 Years Bourbon Cask Reserve db (92) n23.5 t24 f22 b22.5. For my money Glenfiddich turns from something quite workaday to a malt extraordinaire between the ages of 15 and 18. So, depending on the casks chosen, a year the other side of that golden age shouldn't make too much difference. The jury is still out on whether it was helped by being at 40%, which means the natural oils have been broken down somewhat, allowing the intensity and richness only an outside chance of fully forming. *40%*

Glenfiddich Age Of Discovery Aged 19 Years Madeira Cask Finish db (88.5) n22.5 t22.5 f21 b22.5. Oddly enough, almost a breakfast malt: it is uncommonly soft and light yet carries a real jam and marmalade character. *40%*

Glenfiddich 21 Years Old db (86) n21 t23 f21 b21. A much more uninhibited bottling with loads of fun as the mouth-watering barley comes rolling in. But still falls short on taking the hair-raisingly rich delivery forward and simply peters out. *40%*

Glenfiddich 30 Years Old db (93.5) n23 t23.5 f23.5 b23.5 a 'Fiddich which has changed its spots. Much more voluptuous than of old and happy to mine a grapey seam while digging at the sweeter bourbon elements for all it is worth. Just one less than magnificent butt away from near perfection and a certain Bible Award... *40%*

Glenfiddich Rare Collection 40 Years Old db (86.5) n22.5 t23 f20 b21. A quite different version to the last with the smoke having all but vanished, allowing the finish to show the full weight of its considerable age. The nose and delivery are superb, though. The barley sheen on arrival really deserves better support. *43.5%*

Glenfiddich 50 Years Old db (97) n25 t24 f24 b24 For the record, my actual words, after tasting my first significant mouthful, were: "fuck! This is brilliant." It was an ejaculation of genuine surprise, as any fly on the wall of my Tasting Room at 1:17am on Tuesday 4th August would testify. Because I have tasted many 50-year-old whiskies over the years, quite possibly as many as anyone currently drawing breath. For not only have I tasted those which have made it onto the whisky shelves, but, privately, or as a consultant, an untold number which didn't: the heroic but doomed oak-laden failures. This, however, is a quite different animal. We were on the cusp of going to press when this was released, so we hung back. William Grant blender David Stewart, whom I rank above all other blenders on this planet, has known me long and well enough to realise that the surrounding hype, with this being the most expensive whisky ever bottled at £10,000 a go or a sobering £360 a pour, would bounce off me like a pebble from a boulder. "Honestly, David," he told my chief researcher with a timorous insistence, "please tell Jim I really think this isn't too oaky." He offered almost an apology for bringing into the world this 50-year-old babe. Well, as usual David Stewart, doyen of the blending lab and Ayr United season ticket holders, was absolutely spot on. And, as is his wont, he was rather understating his case. For the record, David, next time someone asks you how good this whisky is, just for once do away with the Ayeshire niceness installed by generations of very nice members of the Stewart family and tell them: "Actually, it's bloody brilliant if I say so myself! And I don't give a rat's bollocks what Murray thinks." *46.1%*

Glenfiddich Cask Collection Select Cask db (78.5) n19 t22.5 f18 b19. Bourbon and wine casks may be married together...but they are on course for a messy divorce. The honeymoon on delivery is pretty rich and exotic. But it is all too short-lived as things soon turn pretty bitter. *40% WB16/041*

Glenfiddich Cask Collection Reserve Cask db (83) n20 t22 f20 b21. Soft, chewy, occasionally sparkling but the overdose of toffee and a disappointing degree of late furriness means its speech is distinctly limited in its topic. *40% WB16/040*

⬥ **Glenfiddich IPA Experiment Experimental Series No 1** bott code: L34A4972141211 db (86) n21.5 t22.5 f21 b21 IPA and XX...all very Greene King brewery of the early 1980s... An IPA is, by definition, extra hopped in order to preserve the beer on a long journey (to India, originally). I can't say I am picking out hop here, exactly, unless it is responsible for the off-key bitter finale. Something is interfering with the navigation and after an attractive early malty blast on delivery everything goes a little bland. 43%.

Glenfiddich Malt Master's Edition double matured in oak and sherry butts db (84) n21 t22 f20 b21. I would have preferred to have seen this double matured in bourbon barrels and bourbon barrels... The sherry has done this no great favours. 43%

Glenfiddich Millennium Vintage dist 2000, bott 2012 db (83.5) n21.5 t22 f20 b20. Short and not very sweet. Good juicy delivery though, reminiscent of the much missed original old bottling. 40%

⬥ **Glenfiddich Project XX Experimental Series No 2** bott code: L34B4041170207 db (95.5) n24 complex. Not just complex but crafted, obviously, as there doesn't appear to be a single aroma strand out of place: it is like a malt that has spent the last few years in curlers. It is also the first Glenfiddich that shows signs of the old non-age statement personality, of barley sharpness (lost since the introduction of the 12-years-old) – thus suggesting some younger malts are involved to give bounce and vitality. This is balanced against a vague cough sweet bite, which may well come from age. I very much approve...and love! t24 such a soft delivery you are not quite sure it has landed. Again, there are some contrasting signals, perhaps the quickest to reach the brain are from younger malts stoking up as much barley juiciness as they can; slowly a spice forms alongside a little mocha and against those older hybrid nuances...; f23.5 heftier now, the spices caught up in a much more oak-induced vanilla thread; b24 "20 minds, one unexpected whisky" goes the blurb on the label. And, in fairness, they have a point. It has been a long time since I have encountered a distillery-produced malt this exceptionally well rounded and balanced. All 20 involved should take a bow: this is Glenfiddich as it should be...xxellent, in fact! 47%.

GLEN GARIOCH
Highlands (Eastern), 1798. Morrison Bowmore. Working.

Glen Garioch 8 Years Old db (85.5) n21 t22 f21 b21.5. A soft, gummy, malt – not something one would often write about a dram of this or any age from Geary! However, this may have something to do with the copious toffee which swamps the light fruits which try to emerge. 40%

Glen Garioch 10 Years Old db (80) n19 t22 f19 b20. Chunky and charming, this is a malt that once would have ripped your tonsils out. Much more sedate and even a touch of honey to the rich body. Toffeed at the finish. 40%

Glen Garioch 12 Years Old db (88.5) n22 t23 f21.5 b22. A significant improvement on the complexity front. The return of the smoke after a while away was a surprise and treat. 43%

Glen Garioch 12 Years Old db (88) n22.5 t22.5 f21.5 b22. Sticks, broadly, to the winning course of the original 43% version, though here there is a fraction more toffee at the expense of the smoke. 48%. ncf.

Glen Garioch 15 Years Old db (86.5) n20.5 t22 f22 b22. In the bottling I sampled last year the peat definitely vanished. Now it's back again, though in tiny, if entertaining, amounts. 43%

Glen Garioch 21 Years Old db (91) n21 a few wood shavings interrupt the toasty barley; t23 really good bitter-sweet balance with honeycomb and butterscotch leading the line; pretty juicy, busy stuff; f24 dries as it should with some vague spices adding to the vanilla and hickory; b23 an entirely re-worked, now smokeless, malt that has little in common with its predecessors. Quite lovely, though. 43%

Glen Garioch 1797 Founders Reserve db (87.5) n21 t22 f22.5 b22. Impressively fruity and chewy: some serious flavour profiles in there. 48%

Glen Garioch 1958 db (90) n24 t21 f23 b22. The distillery in its old smoky clothes: and quite splendid it looks! 43%. 328 bottles.

Glen Garioch 1995 db (86) n21 t22 f21.5 b21.5. Typically noisy on the palate, even though the malty core is quite thin. Some big natural caramels, though. 55.3%. ncf.

Glen Garioch 1997 db (89) n22 t22.5 f22 b22.5 had you tasted this malt as a 15-year-old back in 1997, you would have tasted something far removed from this, with a peaty bite ripping into the palate. To say this malt has evolved is an understatement. 56.5%. Whisky Shop Exclusive. 204 bottles.

Glen Garioch 1997 db (89.5) n22 t23 f22 b22.5. I have to say: I have long been a bit of a voice in the wilderness among whisky professionals as regards this distillery. This not so subtly muscled malt does my case no harm whatsoever. 56.7%. ncf.

Glen Garioch 1998 db (89.5) n21 t23.5 f22.5 b23 with dates this good, a chocolate-loving, non-Islamic Tuareg will adore this one...one of the best flawed whiskies I have tasted in a while... 48% WB16/039

◈ **Abbey Whisky The Rare Casks Glen Garioch Aged 21 Years** dist 1994, bott 2016 (88) n23 the most oceanic aroma of all time: not sure: is this the Atlantic? Or North Sea....? t22 malty, but on a saline drip. The saltiness increases the salivation factor significantly; f21 feels a little tired and confused; b22 not sure if this was from a rare cask or sunken treasure chest...a hard one to fathom. 55%.

Acla Selection Glen Garioch 21 Years Old bourbon hogshead, dist 1992, bott 2013 (86.5) n22.5 t20.5 f22 b21.5. Retains a firewater house style which was not so prevalent in 1992 than it had been in previous years. The light muscovado and spiced smoke does give it a certain attractiveness, though it always speaks harshly. 52.8%. nc ncf.

Acla Selection Glen Garioch 23 Years Old bourbon hogshead, dist 1990, bott 2013 (85) n21.5 t21 f21.5 b21. The attractive smoky butterscotch does little to disguise the overly aggressive nature of this malt. 49.2%. nc ncf.

◈ **The First Editions Glen Garioch Aged 25 Years 1991** refill hogshead, cask no. 12828, bott 2016 (88) n21 sharp, aggressive, of the paint-stripping mould.; t22.5 malty and salivating: simple and effective; f22 excellent oils stretch out the intense barley ad sugars; b22.5 a macho malt of limited scope but fully benefitting from its full strength status. 56.2%. nc ncf sc. 129 bottles.

Gleann Mór Glen Garioch 1986 (92.5) n23 t24 f22.5 b23 Easily one of the most complex Geerys I have tasted for a long while. 49.2%. sc.

The Last Drop Glen Garioch 47 Year Old hogshead, cask no. 662 dist 23 Mar 67 (96) n24 t23.5 f24 b24.5 When this distillery produced the whisky in the bottle before me it was making probably the smokiest malt on mainland Scotland. Which is just as well for this grizzled old greybeard. Because things preserve rather well in peat – and this Glen Garioch is no exception. Just a standard low- or non-peated malt would have vanished behind the layers of tannins which have formed a crust around some of the lighter components of the dram. But here the smoke softens the oaky blows until they become only caresses. It is a quite extraordinary - and in many ways lucky – experience. 45.4%.

Maltbarn Glen Garioch 1993 ex-bourbon cask, bott 2015 (85.5) n21 t22.5 f21 b21. So many good aspects to this: not least the crisp barley sugar. But just a little of a stray lactic note from the cask takes the edge off its sparkle. 52.5%. sc. 142 bottles.

◈ **Old Malt Cask Glen Garioch Aged 25 Years** refill hogshead, cask no. 12811, dist Apr 91, bott Aug 16 (87.5) n21.5 t22 f22 b22 Nutty throughout, though the main statement here is lack of peat. This was a smoky malt almost right up to the time this was made and the lack of phenols fully exposes the more fiery nature of the spirit. No shrinking violet, this... 50%. nc ncf sc. 121 bottles.

Old Particular Highland Glen Garioch 20 Years Old refill hogshead, dist Sept 95, bott Feb 16 (76) n19 t20 f18 b19. A huge injection of sugars isn't quite enough to overcome the off-key cask. 51.5%. nc ncf sc. 234 bottles.

◈ **Old Particular Glen Garioch 21 Years Old** refill hogshead, cask no. 11471, dist Sept 95, bott Nov 16 (86.5) n21.5 t22 f21 b22 A little too much pear drop hangs on the aroma even after all these years, though if there are awards for the ability to salivate, this would pick up something. Thin-bodied, but enough bite and oomph to entertain though always a touch too thin for greatness. 51.5%. nc ncf sc. 298 bottles.

◈ **Provenance Glen Garioch Aged 6 Years** refill hogshead, cask no. 11560, dist Jan 10, bott Nov 16 (83.5) n19 t21 f22 b21.5 Unapologetically new-makey with its youth worn on its sleeve. Takes a little time to hit a rhythm, but when it does makes for a vigorously malty dram. 46%. nc ncf sc. 402 bottles.

Sansibar Whisky Glen Garioch Aged 23 Years 1991 bott 2014 (94.5) n23 t24 f23.5 b24 presumably the cask was re-toasted because the sugars of the oak are phenomenal. Superb. 51.7%. sc. 288 bottles.

The Single Cask Glen Garioch Aged 19 Years cask no. 145, dist 19 Sept 95, bott 03 Oct 14 (87) n21.5 t21.5 f22.5 b21.5. Blenders used to look upon this malt with a degree of trepidation: it had the reputation as one of the most fiery malts in Scotland. It has been calmed down in recent decades. But here we get a little insight into how I first found the whisky three decades ago – though then it was smoky. Now it concentrates on an intense maltiness. At times juicy and some attractive vanilla, too. 62.7%. nc ncf sc.

World of Orchids Glen Garioch 1991 22 Year Old bourbon cask, cask no. 7936 (84) n22 t23 f18.5 b20.5. Huge, fat juicy grape, spice....and even the odd phenol or two. But a little furriness on the finish. 53.2%. sc. 204 bottles.

GLENGLASSAUGH

Speyside, 1875. The BenRiach Distillery Co. Working.

Glenglassaugh 30 Year Old db (87) n22.5 t23 f20 b21.5. A gentle perambulation around soft fruitcake. Moist and nutty it still has a major job on its hands overcoming the enormity of the oak. The buzzing spices underline the oak involvement. Meek, charming though a touch furry on the finish. 44.8%.

Glenglassaugh Evolution db (85) n21 t22 f21 b21. Cumbersome, oily and sweet, this youngster is still evolving. 50%.

Glenglassaugh Madeira db (93) n23.5 spices rarely come sexier: busy, pulsing and of varying tone and heat; mainly appear to be oak led, though the sultana concentrate makes its mark, also; t23.5 thick grape dulls the expected spice kick; the sugars, at first beaming, are also quickly subdued, though of a lightly molassed style; supremely chewy, though, with just so sugar impact; f22.5 a gorgeous creamy mocha with a tea spoon of molasses; a slightly muffled, furry finale; b23.5 a deliciously rich but surprising malt in that the spices fanfared on the nose never quite arrive. Love it, warts and all. 44.8% nc ncf sc. 437 bottles.

Glenglassaugh Octaves Classic db (91.5) n23 beautiful: like molten jammy dodger biscuits; t23.5 pristine malt backed up by Demerara sugar and a light touch of ulmo honey; f22 quietens as the vanillas begin to take control; b23 very high quality malt with a clean, intense persona which makes the most of any sweetness going. 44%

Glenglassaugh Octaves Peated db (93) n23.5 the phenols offer only the most subtle of anchors; t23.5 fabulously crisp: Demerara sugars meet with much loftier, more fruity dark muscovado; again, the peat rumbles – though nothing like it might...; f22.5 the oak at last gets a word in with a volley of caramels; b23.5 because of the apparent extra degree of oil, this really is a treat. Quite splendid and scarily seductive malt. 44%

Glenglassaugh Revival new, refill and Oloroso sherry casks db (75) n19 t20 f17 b19. Rule number one: if you are going to spend a lot of money to rebuild a distillery and make great whisky, then ensure you put the spirit into excellent oak. Which is why it is best avoiding present day sherry butts at all costs as the chances of running into sulphur is high. There is some stonkingly good malt included in this bottling, and the fabulous chocolate raisin is there to see. But I look forward to seeing a bottling from 100% ex-bourbon. 46%. nc ncf.

Glenglassaugh Torfa db (90) n23.5 not stinting on the phenols: the peat appears to have been shovelled into the furnace like a fireman feeding coals to the Flying Scotsman; t22.5 crisp, sugary delivery with some meaningful smoke layering. Some Parma Violet candy nuzzles alongside the treacle-cocnut; f22 good phenolic grist fade; b22 appears happy and well suited in its new smoky incarnation. 50%.

GLENGOYNE

Highlands (Southwest), 1833. Ian Macleod Distillers. Working.

Glengoyne 10 Years Old db (90) n22 beautifully clean despite coal-gas bite. The barley is almost in concentrate form with a marmalade sweetness adding richness; t23 crisp, firm arrival with massive barley surge, seriously chewy and textbook bitter-sweet balance; but now some oils have tucked in to intensify and lengthen; f22 incredibly long and refined for such a light malt. The oak, which made soft noises in the middle now intensifies, but harmonises with the intense barley; an added touch of coffee signals some extra oak in recent bottlings; b23 proof that to create balance you do not have to have peat at work. The secret is the intensity of barley intertwangling with oak. Not a single negative note from first to last and now a touch of oil and coffee has upped the intensity further. 40%

Glengoyne 12 Years Old db (91.5) n22.5 salty, sweet, lightly fruity; t23 one of the softest deliveries on the market: the fruit, gristy sugars and malt combine to melt in the mouth: there is not a single hint of firmness; f23 a graduation of spices and vanilla. Delicate and delightful...; b23 the nose has a curiously intimate feel but the tasting experience is a wonderful surprise. 43%

Glengoyne 12 Years Old Cask Strength db (79) n18 t22 f19 b20. Not quite the happiest Glengoyne I've ever come across with the better notes compromised. 57.2%. nc ncf.

Glengoyne 15 Years sherry casks db (81) n19 t20 f21 b21. Brain-numbingly dull and heavily toffeed in style. Just don't get what is trying to be created here. Some late spices remind me I'm awake, but still the perfect dram to have before bed – simply to send you to sleep. Or maybe I just need to see a Doctor... 43%. nc. Ian Macleod Distillers.

Glengoyne 17 Years Old db (86) n21 t23 f21 b21. Some of the guys at Glengoyne think I'm nuts. They couldn't get their head around the 79 I gave it last time. And they will be shaking my neck not my hand when they see the score here...Vastly improved but there is an off sherry tang which points to a naughty butt or two somewhere. Elsewhere mouth-watering and at times fabulously intense. 43%

Glengoyne 18 Years first-fill sherry casks db **(82)** n22 t22 f18 b20. Bunches of lush grape on nose and delivery, where there is no shortage of caramel. But things go downhill once the dreaded "s" word kicks in. 43%. nc. Ian Macleod Distillers.

Glengoyne 21 Years Old db **(90)** n21 t22 f24 b23 A vastly improved dram where the caramel has vanished and the tastebuds are constantly assailed and questioned. A malt which builds in pace and passion to delivery a final, wonderful coup-de-grace. Moments of being quite cerebral stuff. 43%

Glengoyne 21 Years Old Sherry Edition db **(93)** n22 t24 f23 b24. The nose at first is not overly promising, but it settles at it warms and what follows on the palate is at times glorious. Few whiskies will match this for its bitter-sweet depth which is pure textbook. Glengoyne as few will have seen it before. 43%

Glengoyne 25 Year Old db **(95.5)** n24 an old-fashioned, sopping-with-oloroso nose, resplendent in orange peel and molasses; t24.5 voluptuous and curvy in all the right places, hard not to be turned on by a delivery like this. Being pedantic, the sherry is slightly OTT and two decades ago I would have marked this down as being a little too gushing in grape. But such is the rarity of finding un-ruined sherry butts at work, one is easily tempted to turn a blind eye and just enjoy this soaking-moist fruitcake moment; f22.5 slightly bitter as the ancient tannins begin to dig in; b23.5 a beautiful sherry-matured malt from the pre-cock up sulphur days. Not a single off note of note and a reminder of what a sherry cask malt meant to those of us who were involved in whisky a quarter of a century ago... 48% WB16/042

Glengoyne 40 Years Old db **(83)** n23 t21 f19 b20. Thick fruit intermittently pads around the nose and palate but the oak is pretty colossal. Apparent attempts to reinvigorate it appear to have backfired. 45.9%

Cadenhead's Wine Cask Glengoyne 19 Year Old Chateau Lafitte barrel, dist 1996 **(81.5)** n21.5 t21 f19 b20. Exceptionally tight. The fruit is massive and the spices quite brilliant. But never quite comes together. 55%

◇ **The First Editions Glengoyne Aged 20 Years 1995** refill hogshead, cask no. 12825, bott 2016 **(92)** n23 grassy, but a hint of bourbon-style tangerine, also; t24 good grief: pack a handkerchief as the super-intense barley will bring a tear to the eye. This is huge and the delivery never less than beautiful. Uncomplicated, but I think it intends to be; f22.5 a little bit of lemon sherbet fizz on the fade; the barley refuses to be shaken off; b22.5 a seriously malty beast for the herds of Glengoyne collectors out there. 60.4%. nc ncf sc. 83 bottles.

◇ **The First Editions Glengoyne Aged 21 Years 1995** refill barrel, cask no. 13308, bott 2017 **(95)** n23.5 almost where bourbon meets Speyside: massive red liquorice kick with a kumquat and molasses theme; elsewhere lighter vanilla and orange blossom honey ensure a slightly more ethereal note; t24 sublime delivery: a blend of Manuka honey and maple syrup sweetens the intense and sharper barley grassiness while the tannins throb out their intent; f23.5 long, with a varying degree of vanilla and treacle, the toasty aspect becoming more profound; b24 huge: a Glengoyne classic. 55.9%. nc ncf sc. 21 bottles.

Hepburn's Choice Glengoyne 7 Years Old refill hogshead, dist 2007, bott 2014 **(83)** n21 t21 f20 b21. If you are looking for a jolly, juicy bottling, full of youthful fizz and fulsome malt, here you go. If complexity and the meaning of life is what you are after, then move along: there is nothing to see here. 46%. nc ncf sc. 478 bottles.

◇ **Hepburn's Choice Glengoyne 8 Years Old** refill hogshead, dist 2008, bott 2017 **(80.5)** n19 t21.5 f20 b20 Young it may be, but old enough to have a broken nose. Struggles to find any meaningful balance though the barley sugar concentrate does offer some respite. 46%. nc ncf sc. 390 bottles.

Hunter Laing's Distiller's Art Glengoyne Aged 19 Years refill hogshead, dist Nov 96, bott 2016 **(86)** n21 t22.5 f21 b21.5. The green nose is matched by the modest, thin finish. But there is much more to grapple with and enjoy on delivery which is oily, juicy and barley dominant. 48%. nc ncf sc. 82 bottles.

◇ **Old Malt Cask Glengoyne Aged 21 Years** refill hogshead, cask no. 13266, dist Dec 95, bott Feb 17 **(86)** n21 t23.5 f20 b21.5 What can you say? Inoffensive. Unless you are offended by a 21-year-old having relatively so little to tell. There is a sherbet sharpness to this which celebrates the intense effervescence of the maltiness and gristy sugars. But beyond that... 50%. nc ncf sc. 282 bottles.

◇ **Old Particular Glengoyne 20 Years Old** refill hogshead, cask no. 11212, dist Apr 96, bott Jun 16 **(92)** n22.5 forceful barley, but has to give way to a salty bourbon oakiness brimming with red liquorice and dates; t23.5 sensual delivery which intensifies seemingly by the second. The oak has a deceptively telling say in all this, all very much confirmed by the pulsing spices; f23 the very unusual aspect of the honey arriving as late as the middle finale; b23 an eccentric dram which appears to throw the rule book out of the window: all the flavour profiles refuse to follow the accepted course. A wonderfully intriguing journey. *51.5%. nc ncf sc. 245 bottles.*

Old Particular Highland Glengoyne 28 Years Old refill hogshead, dist Dec 96, bott Aug 15 (89.5) n22 t22.5 f22.5 b22.5 Apart from that crushed pip moment, hardly moves away from its malty, spicy path. Austere yet strangely enchanting. *48.4%. nc ncf sc. 306 bottles.*

⬧ **Provenance Glengoyne Aged 9 Years** refill hogshead, cask no. 11339, dist Mar 09, bott Mar 16 (83) n21 t21 f20 b21 Not unpleasant, as there is plenty of decent malt to be going on with. But seriously undercooked. *46%. nc ncf sc.*

GLEN GRANT
Speyside, 1840. Campari. Working.

Glen Grant db (87) n21.5 t23 f21 b21.5. This is a collector's malt for the back label alone: truly one of the most bizarre I have ever seen. "James Grant, 'The Major'" it cheerfully chirrups, "was only 25 when he set about achieving his vision of a single malt with a clear colour. The unique flavour and appearance was due to the purifiers and the tall slender stills he designed and the decision to retain its natural colour..." Then underneath is written: "Farven Justeter Med Karamel/Mit Farbstoff'" Doh! Or, as they say in German: "Doh!" Need any more be said about the nonsense, the pure insanity, of adding colouring to whisky. *40%*

Glen Grant 5 Years Old db (89) n22.5 t22 f21.5 b23. Elegant malt which has noticeably grown in stature and complexity of late. *40%*

Glen Grant Aged 10 Years db (96) n23.5 t24 f23.5 b24 Unquestionably the best official 10-y-o distillery bottling I have tasted from this distillery. Oh, and had they bottled this at 46% abv and without the trimmings...my word! Might well have been a contender for Scotch of the Year. It won't be long before word finally gets around about just how bloody good this distillery is. *40%*

Glen Grant Aged 10 Years db (96) n24.5 t24 f23.5 b24 This is the new bottling purely for the UK market without, alas for a traditionalist like me, the famous, magnificent white label. The bottle design may not be a patch on the beautifully elegant one that had served the distillery with distinction for so long, but the malt effortlessly stands up to all scrutiny. The only difference between this and the original bottling available world-wide is a slight reduction in the work of the sugars, the muscovado ones in particular, and an upping in the green, grassy, sharper barley. Overall, this is a little drier yet slightly tarter, more reserved and stylish. My one and only regret is that it is not yet upped to 46% so the people of Britain could see a whisky, as I have so many times in the private and privileged enclave of my blending lab, as close to perfection as it comes... *40%*.

Glen Grant Aged 12 Years db (95) n23.5 a subtle nose: a little cream toffee, but a wonderful sleight of hand for a citrus slant as well as a totally unexpected hint of weak lavender; t24 sharp malt, as though barley sugar candy has been melted down – with a bunch of grist stirred in for good measure; slightly more oils than expected; f23.5 remains refreshing and determined to show the fresh barley is all its stunning dimensions; some very late mocha gives a nod to the oak; far more spices than the norm for a Gen Grant adding, with those oils, some welcome extra length; b24 beautifully distilled, thoughtfully matured and deeply satisfying malt. *43%*.

Glen Grant Aged 12 Years Non Chill-Filtered db (91.5) n23 some lovely oils give the startling barley much extra; t23 a much weightier cove than your average Glen Grant with the oils maximising the fruity qualities of the muscovado sugars which brood and enrich in equal measure; f22.5 the tannins have much more to say than normal, perhaps also reflected by the above average spice. And there is also that persistent fruity note which even hints at the faintest degree of furriness. This is a rumbler: a very long finish indeed which just refuses to go quietly...or soon...; b23 in so many ways speaks volumes about what non-filtration can do to one of the world's truly great distilleries... *48%. Exclusive to travel retail.*

Glen Grant Aged 16 Years bott Mar 10 db (91.5) n23 t23.5 f21.5 b22 Again the finish doesn't do justice to the earlier jousting on the nose and palate. The label talks about orchard fruits, and they are absolutely spot on. Apples are order of the day, but not sure about the ripe bit: they appear slightly green to me...and that suits the nature of the crisp malt. A gorgeous whisky I fully expect to see improve over coming batches: it's one that has potential to hit superstar status. *43%*

Glen Grant Aged 18 Years Rare Edition db (97) n24.5 the hardest decision to make here: full marks or not. Actually, no: an even harder decision is trying to work out the leading forces behind this extraordinary nose. This is so in tune and well balanced it is impossible to nail exactly what leads and which follows. Instead, one is left mesmerised by the incredible brittleness of the barley, which seems to snap if you sniff slightly too hard; the sugars at once delicate and fruity yet with the crafted sharpness of a newly forged sword. And those tannins, somehow caught up in the overall firmness, the friability of it all. Has to be the essential Speyside nose...; t24.5 oh, wow! When the barley does arrive this beautifully manicured, not a malty molecule out of place? The sugars are as clipped as a 1940's English actor's enunciation, and probably more precise. From somewhere light oils ooze to the surface to ensure some velvet caresses the sword. The oak builds up some steam, but the tannins never once outpoint the sugars and by the mid-ground, when a little cocoa can be detected, honours are even...; so complex it was on about the fifth go I realised just what a vital role those big early spices play; f23.5 the firmness here is so complete, that I have only tasted whisky like this in commercially bottled form in pure Irish Pot still and rye, though here without the same intensity of spice you find in either. That said, the spices teasingly impact all the same....; b24.5 the most crystalline, technically sublime Speysider I have tasted in a very long time... I didn't expect to find a better distillery bottled Glen Grant than their superlative 10-year-old. I was wrong... 43%.

Glen Grant 40 Year Old db (83.5) n22.5 t21 f20 b20. Probably about ten summers too many. The nose threatens an oakfest, though there are enough peripheral sugars for balance and hope. Sadly, on the palate the cavalry never quite gets there. 40%.

Glen Grant 170th Anniversary db (89) n23.5 t23.5 f20 b22. The odd mildly sulphured cask has slipped through the net here to reduce what was shaping to be something magnificent. Still enjoyable, though. 46%

Glen Grant Five Decades bott 2013 db (92) n24 the kind of aroma which leaves you transfixed: the trademark crisp, juicy barley is there in force, but the darker, deeper tones rumble with a spiced orange lead: sublimely complex; t23.5 the delivery is full of the usual malty zest for life. There is a unique clarity to the barley of Glen Grant and here, on delivery and for a few a few moments after, this goes into overdrive. The mid ground is more muddled with tannin and burnt raisin making their presence felt; f21.5 tangy marmalade; b23 a nose and delivery of astonishing complexity. Hardly surprising the fade cannot keep up the pace. 46%

Glen Grant The Major's Reserve bott Mar 10 db (85.5) n21.5 t23 f20 b21. Forget about the so-so nose and finish. This is one of those drams that demands you melt into your chair on delivery, such is the fresh beauty of the malt and stunning honeycomb threads which tie themselves around every taste bud. Pity about the ultra dry, caramel-rich finish, but apparently nearly all the sherry butts have now been used up at the distillery. Thank gawd for that. 40%

⬦ **Cadenhead's Authentic Collection Glen Grant 31 Year Old** sherry casks, dist 1985 (94) n22.5 feels like an oak tree has been felled and planted in your glass: sawdust as well as tannin. But enough maple syrup and molasses to balance things out; nutty, salty and sharp malt; t24 excellent depth on delivery. At first the malt and some raisin get an early showing... but in comes the oak by the forest load. The burnt fruitcake has enough sultanas to kept it alive and well and now we are back to walnut cake with some malty cream...and raisins..; f23.5 stunning coffee fade...with a little cream and garibaldi biscuit; b24 defies the odds to deliver a really marvellous old malt. 44.8%. sc.

The Classic Cask Glen Grant 21 Year Old European oak hogshead, cask no. 139, dist 1993, bott 2015 (91) n23.5 t23.5 f22 b22 Not quite classic, but the nose and delivery are superb. 46% (92 proof). sc. 328 bottles.

Endangered Drams Glen Grant 20 Year Old dist 1992, bott 2013 (86.5) n22 t23 f20 b21.5. Something of the newly baled straw about this. An outstanding pick up on delivery with a rich oiliness to the grist. But bitters slightly too alarmingly later. 55%. sc.

⬦ **The First Editions Glen Grant Aged 25 Years 1992** refill hogshead, cask no. 13358, bott 2017 (92) n23 the story here is about the varying malt tones, ranging from grassy to dried hay; t23.5 the house elegance on delivery with ear perfect weight to the body and malty sugars; f22.5 dries slightly as the expected oak finally arrives. Spices up considerably also before a late tang destroys; b23 just an astonishing exhibition of flavoursome malt tones. 48.2%. nc ncf sc. 180 bottles.

The Golden Cask Glen Grant 12 Years Old cask no. CM 218, dist 2002, bott 2015 (91) n24 t23.5 f23 b23.5 From the sweet, sexy nose to the pulsing delivery, this malt exudes natural, naked beauty... 58.9%. sc. 213 bottles.

Gordon & MacPhail Distillery Label Glen Grant 2005 (82) n20 t22 f20 b20. Considering that Glen Grant and Gordon and MacPhail are almost inseparable, unusual to find they haven't quite got the balance right on this bottling. Too tangy by half. *43%*

◈ **Gordon & MacPhail Distillery Label Glen Grant 2008** bott 7 Dec 16 (84.5) n22 t22 f20 b20.5 For a Glen Grant this is remarkably short in stature but long in caramel. The toffee notes close just as the fresh barley grapples free of the early vanillas. A late bitterness also drags down the complexity. Easy drinking but none of the usual Glen Grant sparkle. *43%*.

Gordon & MacPhail Glen Grant 65 Years Old 1950 cask no. 2747 (90) n22.5 t22 f23 b22.5 By 'eck! This is an oldie: it's got grey whiskers, this has! Forests of intimidating oak greet you on the nose, warning you of the tannin attack to come on the palate. Timber...!!! It arrives with no holds barred but, thankfully, a legion of sugars and spices step up to the plate to try and calm matters. Ulmo honey begins the task, but proves inadequate. Treacle and spices are brought in as emergency and do a job. But it is containment, rather than balancing. So it gets a score of 85 (21-21-22-21). Then time in the glass works its magic and hey presto! Sugars and grasses galore to entertain and balance things out. Oh and a small matter of peat, as well... *63.5%. sc.*

Gordon & MacPhail Rare Vintage Glen Grant 50 Year Old (89.5) n23 t22 f22 b22.5 Shows a frightening degree of age. Yet, against the odds, hangs together as a delicious unit. *43%.*

Gordon & MacPhail Rare Vintage Glen Grant 1948 (96) n24.5 t23.5 f24 b24 So, I bring down the curtain on another Jim Murray's Whisky Bible: this is the last of the 1,241 new whiskies I have analysed for the 2017 edition. When it began, where I wrote this was a part of Europe. Now it is destined to no longer be. But in the course of the maturing life of this malt the world has changed and changed again; in so many ways beyond recognition. The people who made this still had ration books following World War Two and are, most likely, no longer with us now. In the year this was distilled, filled into barrel and rolled into warehouse my parents were married. In the week I tasted this I placed my 95-year-old mother in an old people's home for the very first time. A poignant whisky, indeed. And I admit, without shame, that I write this with a tear in the eye. This is, indeed, the perfect whisky to reflect what this spirit represents so vividly and like no any other: the passing of time... *40%.*

◈ **Gordon & MacPhail Rare Vintage Glen Grant 1949** (94) n23.5 the tannins, which benevolently control the show lock stock and barrel, express themselves in a series of fruity tones, the majority of them orange-related and through a number of species of varying citrus intensity, as well as muscovado sugars helping to radiate a more non-specific fruitiness. A light fruit and nut depth does just hint, with a bit of imagination, at something malty; t24 ah... malt! It is a fleeting moment of erudition but it soon vanishes for the citrus to return and then countless layers of ever-intensifying oak; the mid-ground softens and spices up and the dark sugars build tentatively; f23 just enough mocha and molasses to keep the more extreme of the tannins at bay...but this tastes and feels all of its near 70 years... b23.5 true brinkmanship. True brilliance. A malt seemingly on the edge but steps back from the brink to give one final, magnificent performance. You can still see the special, indelible wow factor which clings to it like the natural beauty on an aged film star... *40%.*

Gordon & MacPhail Rare Vintage Glen Grant 1952 (96.5) n24 t24 f24 b24.5 the 1952 vintage Glen Grant has always been one of the finest post war bottlings they have consistently bottled. I had expected the quality to dip. It hasn't. I can honestly tell you that there is very little that is better than tasting a 1952 vintage: it gets my vote every time... *40%*

Gordon & MacPhail Rare Vintage Glen Grant 1953 (87.5) n20.5 t21.5 f23.5 b22. For a while, the oak is in total control and allowing little but forests of tannin to make their play. But slowly the oaky sharpness throttles back and allows increasing amounts of vanilla-rich sugars to come through. Best of all, and the saviour of this malt, is the French-style praline which holds the mid ground before Manuka honey takes on the role of absorbing the oak. Some journey, this. *40%*

Gordon & MacPhail Rare Vintage Glen Grant 1954 (89) n23 t21.5 f22.5 b22 hangs on for dear life. But just about stays in the camp of excellence having nearly outstayed its welcome. *40%*

Gordon & MacPhail Rare Vintage Glen Grant 1956 (95.5) n23 t23.5 f24.5 b24.5 Just as it appears to have done in the cask, it just improves as it goes along on the palate... *40%*

◈ **Gordon & MacPhail Rare Vintage Glen Grant 1957** (97) n24 give it 20 minute in the glass and the exotic fruits are rolled out like the red carpet for whisky royalty. The oak has that little edge suggesting that it is past its allotted years, yet the barley remains intact and giving, as does the vanilla and ulmo honey. As it oxidizes further, some gooseberry jam begins to make a contribution and soften the oak's grip even further; further down the time line more honeys appear, none of them aggressive, but thin layers and caressing just like the most delicate of peat reeks which hides but without success; **t24.5** simply sits on the tongue singing...then melts away. The malt, even after 60 years, is intact and fresh enough to gently arouse, salivate and lay foundations where required. Upon these the lightest of oaks rest, and from here we pick up passing dry Lubek marzipan and sophisticated, weightless spices which drift on the current of complex, understated honey tones; **f23.5** soft, soft, and softer still....the malt, vanilla and honey simply drift away....; **b25** in November 2017 I reach a significant milestone in my life. So to bring up the 1,000th whisky tasted for Jim Murray's Whisky Bible 2017 it had to be a whisky from the year of my birth from a distillery which has won as many of my awards as any in Scotland. And this is the 15th edition of the Bible...which means I have been writing this book for exactly a quarter of my life....with almost 20,000 different whiskies tasted in that time it seems like longer....much longer... Right, back to this whisky. What an inspired choice that was...! Pour, but don't touch for about 20 minutes. Like a First Growth Bordeaux, let the whisky open and oxidize. And when you do finally taste – not with ice or water, but by the Murray Method, though go easy on the heat - watch carefully as each sniff and small mouthful gives a slightly different result...for the first hour for the better each time. A whisky to be worshipped... 40%.

◇ **Gordon & MacPhail Rare Vintage Glen Grant 1960** (96.5) **n24** more very old Demerara rum than whisky as the coffee and sugars combine wonderfully for a real dusky, fruity heavyweight aroma and as those rum notes die off, eucalyptus replace them; **t24** if the nose wasn't sonorous enough then this really takes you into some of the deepest recesses of your taste buds. Astonishing blend of treacle, Manuka honey, dates, muscovado sugar, high roast Java and toasty tannins both soothes and pounds the palate with a fragile bittersweet balance which one feels could be tipped over – one way or the other – at any given moment; **f24** a long, rummy slow glow of the same, once that the delicate spices are firmly established, though now the threat of dominance from either faction has gone; **b24.5** I think this how every whisky lover pictures an ancient malt...but dare not imagine they'd ever be lucky enough to find. Well done the good people who manned Glen Grant 57 years ago. Congratulations Gordon and MacPhail!! 40%.

◇ **Gordon & MacPhail Rare Vintage Glen Grant 1961** (95) **n24** adorable! The mocha has no shortage of cream and muscovado sugars are emptied into it by the spoon full. Complexity levels shoot through the roof as the Blue Mountain coffee lays gentle fingers over the whole; **t24** the dark, toasty sugars form the dais on which all the fruit and tannins proudly stand; **f23** long, toasty to its final breath yet never bitter and so full of crisp sugars; **b24** defies its years without breaking sweat. A remarkable whisky in countless ways... 40%.

◇ **Gordon & MacPhail Rare Vintage Glen Grant 1963** (89.5) **n23** heavy duty coffee and fruit cake; **t22.5** full on tannin at first, despite the gorgeously silky molten butterscotch texture. The sugars, of a mixed muscovado and molasses style, battle manfully to keep the balance; **f21.5** toasted butterscotch and lightly spiced sherry trifle; **b22.5** a malt so hard trying to keep the tannins at bay that the narrative is sometimes lost. Some stunning moments, nonetheless. 40%.

Gordon & MacPhail Rare Vintage Glen Grant 1965 (94) **n23 t23.5 f24 b23.5** The casks in use here have sorely tested the resolve of this obviously high quality distillate. It nearly buckles under, but not quite... 40%

◇ **Gordon & MacPhail Rare Vintage Glen Grant 1966** (93.5) **n22.5** it takes a good 15 minutes to breathe in the glass before the first sugars begin to make inroads into the tannin. These are citrusy with a modicum of pear juice. Eventually, as the oak turns more into a nuttiness, it becomes an attractive proposition and a surprisingly gristy one at that...; **t23.5** it takes even longer for the palate to open...but it is worth the wait. Pear juice again, now thinning the ulmo honey. This in turn thins the vanilla which, originally, had boasted a taut tannin structure. Now the malt is softened...and, indeed there is a distinctive maltiness to, this, too; **f24** at first, almost impenetrable tannin. Half an hour in and you really could not ask for a more relaxed and elegant finale; **b23.5** tired, yes. Asleep, by no means... 40%.

◇ **Kingsbury Gold Glen Grant 20 Year Old** hogshead, cask no. 110775, dist 1996 (92.5) **n23** a complex, teasing and understated array of light barley notes offer the usual varying degrees of sweetness and intensity...; **t23.5** how can something so seemingly light offer such power on delivery? Like a thoroughbred horse, this is sleek and the muscular barley ripples under the outer sheen; **f22.5** a little bitterness from the barrel. But the malt remains unfazed; **b23.5** you can hardly go wrong with Glen Grant in a decent bourbon cask. And Kingsbury haven't. Charming. 53.8%. 263 bottles. sc.

Le Gus't Selection III Glen Grant 1992 hogshead, cask no. 55415, bott 2014 **(93)** n23.5 t24 f22 b23.5 as though the distillery has been moved to sit beside the sea....52.6%. sc.

⬦ **Liquid Treasures Glen Grant 20 Year Old** bourbon cask, dist 1996, bott 2016 **(88.5)** n21.5 the old barrel at play which ensures a slight sharp note to where the usual gentle malty note should be; t23 beautiful impact on delivery with the distillery's outstanding barley richness on full display; f21.5 that vague tanginess returns; b22.5 a workaday Glen Grant which would offer a malty lustre to any blend. 54.4%. Fairy Tales Edition.

⬦ **Old Particular Glen Grant 21 Years Old** refill barrel, cask no. 11332, dist Jun 95, bott Sept 16 **(94)** n23.5 the strands of barley stretch out like leaves on summer fern. Clearly defined, seemingly basic, but closer examination reveals so much more. The oak is a proud accompaniment, with a Lincoln biscuit and vanilla gentleness; t23.5 just eye-watering fresh and alive: the sugars dissolve first, some like icing sugar, then the more intense and low to fade light honey tones. All around the barley pulses; f23 the oak is slightly more pronounced now, though the sugars remain though now in lightly molassed form; b24 just from this single cask you can find traces of the DNA of whisky greatness. This is wonderfully sophisticated stuff. 51.5%. nc ncf sc. 206 bottles.

⬦ **Scotch Malt Whisky Society Cask 9.112 20 Year Old** refill ex-bourbon hogshead, dist 23 Apr 96 **(89)** n22.5 the light spice nip stirs up an otherwise docile aroma: the creamed vanillins overshadow the malt, though a little muscovado sugar helps infuse a delicate fruitiness; t23 the silkiest of deliveries, with the cream toffee acting the pillow. Barley does build, successfully and with it a salivating juiciness. The mid-ground is already tangy as the cask gives way a little; f21.5 just a little too bitter for its own good; b22 here's a great example of putting outstanding spirit into a less worthy cask. 61%.

GLENGYLE
Campbeltown, 2004. J&A Mitchell & Co. Working.

Kilkerran 12 Year Old db **(90.5)** n22.5 very polite phenols offer a surprisingly fresh mintiness to the countenance. Wafer light body, and a wafer light caramel has been extracted from the genteel oak; t23 despite the dozen years in cask, this still retains a degree of youth about it. But the malts are confident and take advantage of the overall lack of body to spread out and blossom; f22.5 light, with a chocolate chip mint finale; b22.5 a malt far more comfortable at this age than some of the previous, younger, bottlings from a few years back. Has a fragile feel to it and the air of a malt which must be treated gently and with respect. 46%

GLEN KEITH
Speyside, 1957. Chivas Brothers. Working (re-opened 14th June 2013).

Glen Keith 10 Years Old db **(80)** n22 t21 f18 b19. A malty if thin dram that finishes with a whimper after an impressively refreshing, grassy start. 43%

Eiling Lim Glen Keith 21 Years Old 1992 bott 2014 **(95.5)** n24 t24 f23.5 b24 Gen Keith was used for a time by Chivas as a distillery to make their peated malt. There is peat on this, albeit in delicate amounts. But this bottling certainly underlines that on its day, it really was capable of making high grade spirit, something which at the time was in dispute. A distillery gem. 48.2%. nc ncf sc. 48 bottles. 5th Release.

⬦ **The Cooper's Choice Glen Keith 22 Year Old** Madeira finish, dist 1993, bott 2015 **(92.5)** n23 the Madeira is clearly at work here with a dominant gooseberry jelly sheen and spiced resonance to the nose; t22.5 again, the fruit is all over the malt on delivery, giving a similar sheen to the delivery as found on the nose; moves into chocolate mousse territory; f23.5 a superb spiced chocolate finish, though the vanillas rally at the very end; b23.5 good, clean fruit gives a clipped feel to this highly attractive malt. 46%. nc ncf sc. The Vintage Malt Whisky Co.

⬦ **The First Editions Glen Keith Aged 21 Years 1995** refill hogshead, cask no. 13122, bott 2016 **(90)** n22.5 singularly malty. A light squeeze of lemon freshens it further; t23 eye-wateringly juicy and the green barley overcomes all else; f22.5 a very slight touch of digestive biscuit dries and thickens the persistent malt; b22 a straight down the line, no-nonsense Speysider. Love it! 53.8%. nc ncf sc. 119 bottles.

⬦ **Hunter Laing's Distiller's Art Glen Keith Aged 20 Years** refill hogshead, dist Mar 96, bott 2016 **(86)** n22 t22.5 f20 b21.5 Straight as a dye malt for the most part where the natural caramels make an early impact amid the intense, barley and muscovado sugars. But a tang from the oak gives the spicy finish a slight edge. 48%. nc ncf sc. 351 bottles.

⬦ **Kingsbury Gold Glen Keith 23 Year Old** hogshead, cask no. 82796, dist 1993 **(91.5)** n23 even after nearly quarter of a century the grist sparkles; quite salty, too; t23.5 briliant delivery:

three dimensional barley, again intensified by the saltiness, sharpened further by salivating grst; **f22** a little bitterness on the fade but the spices now come into play; **b23** Glen Keith in absolutely top form. So satisfying! *53.7%. 205 bottles. sc.*

Maltmountains Glen Keith 20 Years Old hogshead, dist 1995, bott 2015 (84.5) **n21.5 t21 f21 b21.** Crisp, fragile and malty. A clean dram with few pretentions above being standard blending fodder. *48.8%*

Master of Malt Single Cask Glen Keith 19 Year Old dist 8 Nov 95, bott 30 Mar 15 (82) **n21 t21 f20 b20.** More tangy second hand and second class cask spoiling the show. The barley tries to sparkle, but the battle is unequal. *56.6%. sc. 192 bottles.*

⬙ **Old Malt Cask Glen Keith Aged 20 Years** refill butt, cask no. 13359, dist 96, bott Feb 17 (86.5) **n21.5 t22.5 f21 b21.5** No problems regarding the butt, which is always a relief. Yet despite the good age, the malt displays a freshness and concentrated gristy character of a malt probably little more than half its age. Ridiculously easy drinking. *50%. nc ncf sc. 726 bottles.*

⬙ **Old Malt Cask Glen Keith Aged 21 Years** refill hogshead, cask no. 13125, dist Nov 95, bott Nov 16 (87) **n22 t22.5 f21 b21.5** A very similar feller to the First Editions bottling. Except here we see what happens when the cask is just a little less relaxed and doesn't give a leg up to the malt in the right places. *50%. nc ncf sc. 181 bottles.*

The Single Cask Glen Keith 20 Year Old cask no. 171225, dist 08 Nov 95, bott 22 Feb 16 (88) **n22** butterscotch tart with the emphasis on the pastry. A green maltiness pervades throughout; **t22** zingy, tangy, sharp barley: a light distillate meeting a tiring cask; spices briefly perform; **f22** slightly bitter oils, some leaning towards cocoa, but still the barley has the last word; **b22** a single minded single malt. And the fixation is barley... *45.8%. nc ncf sc.*

Spirits Shop Selection & Sansibar Whisky Glen Keith 1995 bourbon cask, bott 2015 (87) **n22 t21.5 f22 b21.5.** A simplistic though fully enjoyable Speysider. The excellent vanilla and spice on the finish lifts it above the average. *51.4%. 210 bottles.*

⬙ **The Whisky Agency Glen Keith 1993 (92.5) n22.5** just beginning to tire. But the malt retains control – just! – helped along the way by a marmalade and molten sugar boost; **t24** that is one sublime delivery: an amazing array of sugars, all of them delicate. There's the obvious gristy barley which melts first, then muscovado and weak heather honey. The oils are nearly perfect in density, allowing every barley note to be heard clearly; **f23** a drier version of the palate, though with the sugars now on half power and the tannins upped in strength; **b23** amazing to find a Glen Keith handling this kind of age without breaking sweat. Delicious. *48.6%.*

Whisky-Fässle Glen Keith 1996 barrel, bott 2015 (84.5) **n21.5 t21.5 f20.5 b21.** Thin, with a heated debate between the gristy, sweet malt and taciturn oak. The emphasis is on the heated. *52.3%*

⬙ **World of Orchids Glen Keith 19 Year Old** bourbon cask, dist 1995 (89.5) **n22.5** big malt. Tannins more than make up the numbers, but the spice it offers is gentle and slightly herbal; **t23.5** highly attractive, big malt and male syrup delivery with a pleasing ginger-hinted follow through; **f21** back to more standard concentrated malt, but the oak now becomes a little too excited, bitter and out of sorts; **b22.5** the intensely passionate moments are truly outstanding. *53.5%.*

GLENKINCHIE

Lowlands, 1837. Diageo. Working.

Glenkinchie 12 Years Old db (85) **n19 t22.5 f21.5 b22.** The last 'Kinchie 12 I encountered was beyond woeful. This is anything but. Still not firing on all cylinders and can definitely do better. But there is a fabulous vibrancy to this which nearly all the bottlings I have tasted in the last few years have sadly lacked. Impressive. *43%*

Glenkinchie Aged 15 Years The Distillers Edition Amontillado finished, dist 1992, bott 2007 db (94) **n23.5 t24 f23 b23.5.** Now this is absolutely top class wine cask finishing. One of my last whiskies of the night, and one to take home with me. Sophisticated, intelligent and classy. *46%*

Glenkinchie 20 Years Old db (85.5) **n21 t22 f21.5 b21.** When I sampled this, I thought: "hang on, haven't I tasted this one before?" When I checked with my tasting notes for one or two independents who bottled around this age a year or two ago, I found they were nigh identical to what I was going to say here. Well, you can't say its not a consistent dram. The battle of the citrus-barley against the welling oak is a rich and entertaining one. *58.4%*

⬙ **Glenkinchie Aged 24 Years** dist 1991 db (95) **n24** citrus and green banana melt gently together to form richer aspect to the clear barley. The sugars appear to be from an even harvest of the oak and the grain, so allow the light spices from the tannins safe, unmolested passage; **t24** the biggest Lowland delivery in the marketplace today: huge barley and tannin on a wonderful oil wave crashes home, with crisp sugary splinters flying in all directions; **f23** age is catching up by the minute as hefty vanilla and tannin make their toasty mark; spiced ulmo honey weaves a magic healing spell; **b24** the old managers at Glenkinchie a generation ago felt their malt didn't quite have the body to become a big aged malt. At the time – roughly about the time this was made – you could see why from the evidence of the fragile 12-years-old. This, though, reveals the distillery in a new light and I'd love to see those responsible for making this aware of joyous fruits of their labours. *57.2%. 5,928 bottles. Diageo Special Releases 2016.*

Glenkinchie 1992 The Manager's Choice db **(78) n19 t22 f18 b19.** Has a lot going for it on delivery with a barley explosion which rocks you back in your chair and has you salivating like a rabies victim. But the rest of it is just too off key. *58.1%. Diageo.*

Cadenhead's Small Batch Glenkinchie 28 Year Old bourbon hogshead, dist 1987, bott Apr 16 **(93.5) n23.5 t24 f22.5 b23.5** Really defies belief that a 'Kinchie can eat up this number of years. Yet it does so with aplomb: goes down a treat! *53.3%. sc. 240 bottles.*

THE GLENLIVET
Speyside, 1824. Chivas Brothers. Working.

The Glenlivet Aged 12 Years db **(79.5) n22 t21 f18 b18.5.** Wonderful nose and very early development but then flattens out towards the kind of caramel finish you just wouldn't traditionally associate with this malt, and further weakened by a bitter, furry finale. *40%*

The Glenlivet Aged 12 Years Old First Fill Matured db **(91) n22.5 t22.5 f23 b23.** A quite wonderful whisky, far truer to The Glenlivet than the standard 12 and one which every malt whisky lover should try once in their journey through the amber stuff. Forget the tasting notes on the bottle, which bear little relation to what is inside. A gem of a dram. *40%*

The Glenlivet Excellence 12 Year Old db **(87) n22 t21.5 f22 b21.5.** Low key but very clean. The emphasis is on delicate. *40%. Visitor Centre and Asian exclusive.*

The Glenlivet 15 Years of Age db **(80) n19 t21 f20 b20.** Undeniable charm to the countless waves of malt and oak. But don't expect much in the way of complexity or charisma. *40%*

The Glenlivet Aged 18 Years bott Feb 10 db **(91) n22** attractive mixture of honeycombed bourbon and fruitcake; **t23.5** oh...just didn't expect that...!! Fabulous, honey-sweet and slightly sharp edge to the barley: excellent weight and mouthfeel with the honeycomb on the nose making slow but decisive incursions; **f23** a very slight technical flaw drops it half a point, but there is no taking away from the improbable length of the dissolving honey and barley...some gentle chewing is required, especially with the late juices and vanilla arriving; **b23** a hugely improved bottling seriously worth discovering in this form. Appears to have thrown off its old shackles and offers up an intensity that leaves you giving a little groan of pleasure. *43%*

⟩⟩ **The Glenlivet 18 Years of Age** bott code: 2017/02/02 LKPL0386 db **(83.5) n22 t22 f19 b20.5** This is a rather flat version of a usually rich malt. Has the odd honey-charmed moment and the spices aren't hiding, either. But way too much caramel has turned the usual undulations on the palate to something of pancake proportions. A little furry at the death, also. *43%.*

The Glenlivet Alpha db **(92) n23.5 t24 f21.5 b23.** You get the feeling some people have worked very hard at creating a multi-toned, complex creature celebrating the distillery's position at the centre of Speyside. They have succeeded. Just a cask selection or two away from a potential major Bible award. Maybe for the next bottling.... *50%*

The Glenlivet Archive 21 Years of Age batch no. 0513M db **(95.5) n24 t24 f23.5 b24** Less archive and more achieve. For getting so many honey tones to work together without it getting overly sweet or syrupy really is a major achievement. *43%*

The Glenlivet Cipher db **(96.5) n24.5 t24 f23.5 b24.5** It has taken over half an hour to distil these tasting notes into something that will fit the book: we have more new entries than normal and I'm running out of room. Few whiskies I taste this year, however, will compare to this. *48%*

The Glenlivet Conglass 14 db **(92.5) n22 t23 f23.5 b24** A joyous barley and high quality oak interplay: probably what this distillery does best of all. *59.8% WB16/043*

The Glenlivet Founder's Reserve db **(78.5) n20 t21.5 f18 b19.** Really can't believe what a shy and passionless whisky this is (not to mention flawed). The strength gives the game away slightly as to where the malt is positioned. But I had hoped for a little more than malty tokenism. *40%*

⟩⟩ **The Glenlivet Founder's Reserve** bott code: 2017/04/04 LCPL 0591 db **(88.5) n23** charmingly layered malt with a mid-range Digestive biscuit saltiness but also offering grassy barley and spice, also...; **t22** a huge malt delivery but a degree of caramel rushes in quickly; **f21.5** light butterscotch and spice; **b22** anyone who can remember the less than impressive start to this brand will be pretty amazed at just how deliciously approachable it is now. *40%.*

The Glenlivet French Oak Reserve 15 Years of Age Limousin oak casks db (**91**) n22.5 t23 f22.5 b23. I have to say that after tasting nearly 800 cask strength whiskies, to come across something at the ancient 40% is a shock to the system. My taste buds say merci... And, what is more, a bottle of this shall remain in my dining room for guests. Having, a lifetime ago, lived with a wonderful French girl for three years I suspect I know how her country folk will regard that... Oh, and forgive a personal message to a literary friend: Bobby-Ann...keep a bottle of this beside the Ancient Age... 40%

⬩ **The Glenlivet 15 Years of Age French Oak Reserve** bott code: 2016/12/19 LCPK 2465 db (**93**) n23.5 the attractive sharpness to the citrus is perfectly countered by the firmness and quiet intensity of the tannins; t23 a far more uplifting volley of juicy barley than has ever been the case before on FOR15 with a seriously sharp edge to the malt. The liquorice-led tannin starts slowly but builds up a head of steam; f23 a toffee apple finale with still that juicy barley flickering about; the spice arrives late but warms fast...; b23.5 many years ago when this first came out it wasn't very good, to be honest. Then it was re-shaped, upped a gear and became a very enjoyable dram, indeed. Now, having apparently been steered on a slightly different course again, it is just excellent...An expression that has evolved slowly but quite beautifully. 40%.

The Glenlivet The Guardians' Chapter db (**81.5**) n20 t21 f20 b20.5. Read the chapter – but can make neither head nor tail of it. A brief moment of honeyed enjoyment. But nothing else really adds up. Just doesn't gel. 48.7%. WB15/120

The Glenlivet Master Distiller's Reserve db (**86.5**) n22.5 t22 f20.5 b21.5. I chose this as my 800th whisky to taste for the 2012 Bible against the Founder's Reserve on the strength of the nose over the first 30 seconds. Oh, well. Shows you the pricelessness of time when evaluating a whisky... 40%

⬩ **The Glenlivet The Master Distiller's Reserve** bott code: 2016/10/04 LCPK 1866 db (**86.5**) n22.5 t22 f20.5 b21 It is a shame the malty sparkle on the nose and delivery isn't matched by what follows. A pleasant, safe dram. But too toffee-rich and doesn't develop as this great distillery should. 40%.

The Glenlivet The Master Distiller's Reserve Small Batch batch no. 9378/003 db (**82**) n19 t22 f20 b21. Succulent mouth feel. But just a little dull and off key in one or two vital areas. 40%

⬩ **The Glenlivet The Master Distiller's Reserve Small Batch** batch no. 9378/006 db (**93**) n23.5 superb weight: spices are busy and not without purpose as they add another layer to a fruity aroma where moist date and black cherry are prominent; t24 one of the best mouth feels of any of The Glenlivet range. Both succulent and offering just the right degree of oil to allow the malt to escape its grapey clutches to give a real barley juiciness to it all. A light golden syrup adds welcome sweetness as the spice returns and this time with a tannin touch; f22.5 not quite the perfect sherry influence but the furriness is so minor it only registers late on and to little effect. The malt and muscovado sugars work well with the spice and vanilla for the long tail...; b23.5 by far the best Master Distillers Reserve in Glenlivet's armoury. 40%

The Glenlivet The Master Distiller's Reserve Solera Vatted bott date: 2015/11/30 db (**91**) n23 t23.5 f21.5 b23 Although Solera vatted, no trace here of the dreaded 'S' word...or even grape dominance. 40%

⬩ **The Glenlivet The Master Distiller's Reserve Solera Vatted** bott code: 2017/03/01 LCPL 0371 db (**89.5**) n22.5 t23 f22 b22 Pretty much in line with the 2015 bottling above, except there is slightly more caramel here shaving the top off the higher notes. 40%.

The Glenlivet Nàdurra First Fill Selection batch no. FF0714, first fill American white oak casks, bott 07/14 db (**95.5**) n23.5 mmmm! A naughtily spicy cove: a real nose tingle. No question the oak leads the way with a dry flourish; the sweeter barley is left in its wake...; t24.5 a sumptuously rich delivery. And though the oils are healthy, never is there a threat to the complexity. The spices on the nose arrive just after the malt has made a sweet opening. But then we hit a massive crescendo as the dry tannins thud home almost with a degree of aggression: all this in the first half dozen beats. Red liquorice and treacle pudding fills the mid ground; walnut oil subtly adds a further oaky presence; f23.5 a long interweaving between the oak and barley, although it is the malt which fades faster...; b24 now that is what I call a whisky... 63.1%. ncf.

⬩ **The Glenlivet Nàdurra First Fill Selection Batch No. FF0117** first fill American white oak casks, bott Jan 17 db (**91**) n22.5 the genteel quality of the malt means there is no firm opposition to the slow spreading of Kentucky-like notes, especially the red liquorice and billowing spice; t23.5 explosive arrival on the palate – like a pin ball zooming in for a perfect strike. Going with the first fill territory comes spice...and this is probably the spiciest Speysider on the market this year. It takes a few flavour waves to retreat before the white heat of those blistering spices arrive...and then subside. This, chiefly, exercises the brain and taste buds. But away from that other things are happening, also, like shards of honey and concentrated malt being found among the tannins; **f22.5** just a little bitter on the finish, though the sugars do at last get a longer hearing; **b22.5** for those who adore their Speysides honeyed and spiced, Mind, what I'd give for them to bring out a Nadura from 100% second fill bourbon cask – then what fun time could be had creating a perfect vatting of the two...and what a whisky would result! *59.1%. ncf.*

◇ **The Glenlivet Nàdurra Oloroso Matured Batch No. OI0317** first fill Oloroso sherry casks, bott Mar 17 db (83) n21 t21 f19 b20 Spicy, honey and succulent. But a slight fault: three guesses... *60.3%. ncf.*

The Glenlivet Nàdurra Peated Cask Finish batch no. PW0715, bott Jul 15 db (90) n22.5 t22.5 f23 b22.5 The fact that this is simply the effect of peat cask finishing, the ultra-delicate nature of Glenlivet's malt, is clearly underlined. *61.5%. ncf.*

◇ **The Glenlivet Nàdurra Peated Whisky Cask Finish Batch No. PW0715** heavily peated whisky casks, bott Jul 15 db (95.5) n23.5 soft, lightly smoked chocolate mint; t24 sheer quality! The gentle delivery defies the bottling strength and rolls out a salivating, intensely malty introduction with peppered cocoa sweetened by heather honey and sprig of mint; f24 long, with the vanillas arriving in force but only to give an ice cream effect to the mint chocolate which has been the main theme throughout; b24 an indubitably beautiful whisky, and one which might even win over a few non-peated devotees... *61.5%. ncf.*

The Glenlivet XXV Twenty Five Years of Age batch no. 0115B, finished in first fill Oloroso sherry casks db (88) n24.5 t22 f20 b21.5 What a shame this is not at 46% or even 50% to allow the oils to keep slightly tighter control. The nose, though: wow! *43%*

◇ **Gordon & MacPhail Distillery Label Glenlivet 2002** bott 1 Mar 17 (91.5) n23 grassy and flighty: clean, cut glass...; t23 salivating, bubbling barley at first, then chalky vanilla; f22.5 a light cocoa sign off; b23 delicious, but annoyingly under powered. *43%.*

Gordon & MacPhail Rare Vintage Glenlivet 1974 (94.5) n23 t24 f23.5 b24 These are the types of whisky I hope above hope at seeing a few times each year. A malt well punctuated with oak to confirm great age, but the balance not even threatened, let alone lost. *43%*

◇ **Simon Brown Glenlivet Distillery 1995** ex-bourbon cask, cask no. HE112013-01, dist Sept 95, bott Nov 13 (90) n23.5 delicate in the extreme: crème brule and rice pudding. Hints also of physalis and vague coriander amid the vanilla; t23 the sugars strike early, mainly of a Demerara disposition. Red liquorice and juicy barley...before the oak comes in with a startlingly dry, almost custard powdery, signature...; f21 the custard powder dominates...; b22.5 suffers a little from being bottled at too weak a strength: the oils are fractured allowing the oak far too chalky a say, though the nose may have benefitted slightly. Lovely complex stuff, all the same.... *43%. nc ncf sc.*

GLENLOCHY
Highlands (Western), 1898–1983. Diageo. Closed.
Gordon & MacPhail Rare Old Glenlochy 1979 (95) n23.5 t24 f23.5 b24 it has been many years since a bottle from this long lost distillery turned up and that was such a classic, I can remember every nuance of it even now. This shows far greater age, but the way with which the malt takes it in its stride will become the stuff of legend. I held back on tasting this until today, August 2nd 2013, because my lad David this afternoon moved into the first home he has bought, with new wife Rachael and little Abi. It is near Fort William, the remote west coast Highland town in which this whisky was made, and where David will be teaching next year. His first job after moving in, though, will be to continue editing this book, for he worked on the Whisky Bible for a number of editions as researcher and editor over the years. So I can think of no better way of wishing David a happy life in his new home than by toasting him with what turned out to be a stunningly beautiful malt from one of the rarest of all the lost distilleries which, by strange coincidence, was first put up for sale exactly 100 years ago. So, to David, Rachael & little Abigail... your new home! And this time I swallowed.. *46%. ncf.*

GLENLOSSIE
Speyside, 1876. Diageo. Working.
Eiling Lim Glenlossie 23 Years Old 1992 bott 2015 (94.5) n23.5 t23.5 f23.5 b24 Beautiful integrity to the barley, this positively radiates charm having spent 23 profitable years in a very good cask. *51.1%. nc ncf sc. 100 bottles. 10th Release.*

Gordon & MacPhail Connoisseurs Choice Glenlossie dist 1995, bott 2013 (96) n24 t24 f24 b24 getting harder and harder to find a dud Lossie these days: glad people are getting a chance to be in on one of the best kept secrets in Scotland... This one is truly glorious: absolutely exceptional even by the distillery' very high standards. *46%. nc ncf. WB15/149*

Gordon & MacPhail Connoisseurs Choice Glenlossie 2004 (87) n21.5 t23.5 f21.5 b21. Such a pleasant malt. Boasts a little saltiness on both the nose and delivery and the first five or six waves after delivery are fizzing as a Lossie should. Especially with malt. But then goes all caramel rich and a little dull. Like buying a Ferrari, revving up the engine getting to 0-60 in four seconds...and then running out of gas and cruising to a standstill. 46%

Old Malt Cask Glenlossie Aged 17 Years refill hogshead, cask no. 11564, dist Nov 97, bott Jun 15 (87.5) n22 t22 f21.5 b22. A glossy Lossie with all the emphasis on the juicy, gleaming barley. Unashamedly simplistic but with late vanilla involvement. 50%. nc ncf sc. 328 bottles.

Old Particular Speyside Glenlossie 17 Years Old refill hogshead, cask no. 10861, dist Jan 04, bott Aug 15 (91.5) n24 t23 f22 b22.5 Gorgeous stuff, but worth getting for the nose alone. 48.4%. nc ncf sc. 294 bottles.

⟡ **Scotch Malt Whisky Society Cask 46.45 23 Year Old** refill ex-bourbon hogshead, dist 17 Nov 92 (89.5) n22.5 a fascinating spiciness builds between the mountain of grapefruit-laden grist on one side and liquorice-tinged oaky hills on the other; t22.5 a lovely sheen to the barley: for a moment covered in crispy sugars, then a salivating explosion of citrusy grist; f22 a little grapefruit tang persists; b22.5 what a glossy Lossie....! 52.7%.

Spirits Shop Selection & Sansibar Whisky Glenlossie 1992 bourbon cask, bott 2015 (95) n23.5 t24 f23.5 b24 So effortlessly beautiful: a genuine star whisky 51.7%. 317 bottles.

⟡ **WoodWinters Drochaid 10 Year Old** (92.5) n23 a three dimensional maltiness, mixing gristy, grassy and bready notes in about equal measures; t23.5 salty and salivating sharpness to the barley; a little tannin squeezes its way in; f23 demerara sugar and a lightly spiced liquorice note closes the show...eventually...; b23 given the right cask and 'Lossie can be as lively as they come. And this is the right cask...! 60.7%. sc. 345 bottles.

GLEN MHOR
Highlands (Northern), 1892–1983. Diageo. Demolished.

Glen Mhor 1976 Rare Malt db (92.5) n23 t24 f22 b23.5. You just dream of truly great whisky sitting in your glass from time to time. But you don't expect it, especially from such an old cask. This was the best example from this distillery I've tasted in 30 years...until the Glenkeir version was unleashed! If you ever want to see a scotch that has stretched the use of oak as far it will go without detriment, here it is. What a pity the distillery has gone because the Mhor the merrier... 52.2%

GLENMORANGIE
Highlands (Northern), 1843. Glenmorangie Plc. Working.

Glenmorangie 10 Years Old db (94) n24 perhaps the most enigmatic aroma of them all: delicate yet assertive, sweet yet dry, young yet oaky: a malty tone poem; t22 flaky oakiness throughout but there is an impossibly complex toastiness to the barley which seems to suggest the lightest hint of smoke; f24 amazingly long for such a light dram, drying from the initial sweetness but with flaked almonds amid the oakier, rich cocoa notes; you might find the occasional "orange variant", where the extra degree of oak, usually from a few too many first-fill casks, has flattened out the more extreme peaks and toughs of complexity (scores about 89). But these are pretty rare – almost a collector's item – and overall this remains one of the great single malts: a whisky of uncompromising aesthetic beauty from the first enigmatic whiff to the last teasing and tantalising gulp. Complexity at its most complex. 40%

Glenmorangie 15 Years Old db (90.5) n23 chunky and fruity: something distinctly sugar candy about this one; the barley's no slouch, either; and, just to raise the eyebrows, just the faintest waft of something smoky...; t23 silky, a tad sultry, and serious interplay between oak and barley; a real, satisfying juiciness to this one; f22 dries towards the oaky side of things, but just a faint squeeze of liquorice adds extra weight; b22.5 exudes quality. 43%

Glenmorangie 15 Years Old Sauternes Wood Finish db (68) n16 t18 f17 b17. I had hoped – and expected – an improvement on the sulphured version I came across last time. Oh, whisky! Why are you such a cruel mistress...? 46%

Glenmorangie 18 Years Old db (91) n22 pleasant if unconvincing spotted dick; t23 sharp, eye-watering mix of fruit and mainly honeyed barley; nutty and, with the confident vanillas, forming a breakfast cereal completeness; f23 Cocoa Krispies; b23 having thrown off some previous gremlins, now a perfect start to the day whisky... 43%

⟡ **Glenmorangie 19 Year Old** db (94) n24 light fruit ensures an ethereal feel totally making a mockery of nearly two decades in the cask: fresh, subtle and sophisticated; t23.5 the most brittle and vulnerable malt I have experienced from this distillery. Every note is gossamer thin, the grist can fracture any moment; the delicate fruit shatter into millions of pieces if you chew too hard...bitters...? **f22.5** yes, a slight bitter notes creeps in briefly. But it creeps out again as the light gooseberry and lighter barley notes play their game of peek-a-boo...; **b24** fruity or malty...? I can't decide...but then I don't think for a moment that you're supposed to be able to... 43%.

Glenmorangie 25 Years Old db (95.5) **n24** it's strap yourself in time: this is a massive nose with more layers, twists and turns than you can shake a thief at. Soft, mildly lush Lubec marzipan is sandwiched between fruit bonbons and myriad barley tones. Worth taking half an hour over this one, and no kidding... **t24** the clarity on the nose is matched here. Every single wave of flavour is there in crystal form, starting, naturally, with the barley but this is soon paired with various unidentified fruits. The result is salivation. Towards the middle the oak shows form and does so in various cocoa-tinged ways; every nuance is delicately carved, almost fragile, but the overall picture is one of strength; **f23.5** medium length with the cocoa heading towards medium roast Java **b24** every bit as statesmanlike and elegant as a whisky of this age from such a blinding distillery should be. Ticks every single box for a 25-year-old and is Morangie's most improved malt by the distance of Tain to Wellingborough. There is a hint of genius with each unfolding wave of flavours with this one: a whisky that will go in 99/100 whisky lover's top 50 malts of all time. And that includes the Peatheads. 43%

Glenmorangie 30 Years Old db (72) **n17 t18 f19 b18.** From the evidence in the glass the jury is out on whether it has been spruced up a little in a poor sherry cask – and spruce is the operative word: lots of pine on this wrinkly. 44.1%

Glenmorangie Vintage 1975 db (89) **n23 t23 f21 b22.** A charming, fruity and beautifully spiced oldie. 43%

Glenmorangie Artisan Casks db (93) **n23 t23.5 f23 b23.5.** If whisky could be sexed, this would be a woman. Every time I encounter Morangie Artisan, it pops up with a new look, a different perfume. And mood. It appears not to be able to make up its mind. But does it know how to pout, seduce and win your heart...? Oh yes. 46%

⟨⟩ **Glenmorangie Astar** db (93) **n24** not sure you'll find a more demure 'Morangie than this nose-wise: it is as if every every individual grain of malt has stood up to be counted for one of the cleanest semi-gristy noses in recent times from this distillery. A little less first fill bourbon cask apparent, so the oak has to settle for a very half-heated vanilla tone. A light saltiness for a moment moves us towards a Digestive biscuit aroma; **t23.5** a silky caress of intense barley, coated in Demerara sugars – for a moment we are in German caramelised biscuit territory; **f22** a light bitterness from some older casks filters through; the spices now begin to build; **b23.5** Astar has moved a long way from the first bottling which left me scratching my head. This is one of the maltiest of all their range, though the lightness of touch means that any bitterness can be too easily detected. 52.5%.

Glenmorangie Bacalta db (87) **n22 t22.5 f21 b21.5.** Unusually for a Glenmorangie the narrative is muffled and indistinct. Has some lovely moments, but a bit sharp and lacking in places. 46%

Glenmorangie Burgundy Wood Finish db (72) **n17.5 t19.5 f18 b18.** Sulphured whisky de table. 43%

⟨⟩ **Glenmorangie Cadboll** db (86.5) **n21 t23.5 f20.5 b21.5** Every year a challenging new breed of Glenmorangie appears to be thrown into the mix, as though to fully test the taste buds. This is this year's offering: different again, with neither the nose nor finish quite up to par with the outstanding delivery – indeed, the finale is pretty bitter, indeed. But the texture and intensity of the barley on arrival is borderline brilliant, as is the most wonderful caramel which frames it with a buttery sweetness. 43.1%.

Glenmorangie Cellar 13 Ten Years Old db (88.5) **n22 t22.5 f22 b22** Oh, if only I could lose weight as efficiently as this appears to have done... oh, I have! My love and thanks to Nancy, Nigel and Ann Marie. 43%

Glenmorangie Companta Clos de Tart & Rasteau casks, dist 27 Jan 99, bott 14 Nov 13 db (74) **n17 t20 f18 b19**. "I don't think you'll be a fan of this one, Jim" said the Glenmorangie blender to me, letting me know the sample was on its way. How right he was. Have to say there is some breath-taking fruit to be had before the sulphur does its worst. 46%. ncf.

Glenmorangie Dornoch db (94) **n23.5** light and sea breezy: grist on a coastal wing. The gristiness extends to the sugars which stick to a simple but effective path. The secret to its charm, though, is the clarity and layering... **t23** even on delivery the malt arrives on all levels and in different hues, ranging from sweet and fresh to a duller, oak-dried digestive biscuit – but quite tightly bound; **f23.5** a beautiful unravelling: those tighter notes relax offering a procession of further biscuity, malty themes – not without a light sprinkling of salt – and then a denser malt extract feel; **b24** a rare Glenmorangie which this time does not put the emphasis on fruit or oak influence. But this appears to concentrate on the malt itself, taking it through a routine which reveals as many angles and facets as it can possibly conjure. Even if the casks are from a central warehouse, at times a seascape has been created by a light salty influence – so befitting the whisky's name. A real treat. *43%*

Glenmorangie Ealanta 1993 Vintage db (**97.5**) n24 t24 f24.5 b25 When is a bourbon not a bourbon? When it is a Scotch single malt...And here we have potentially the World Whisky of the Year. Free from the embarrassing nonsense which passes for today's sherry butt, and undamaged by less than careful after use care of second-hand bourbon casks, we see what happens when the more telling aspects of oak, the business end which gives bourbon that extra edge, blends with the some of the very finest malt made in Scotland. Something approaching one of the best whiskies of my lifetime is the result... *46%*

Glenmorangie Elegance db (**92**) n22 quite herbal and soothing; t24 the thinnest layer of icing sugar coats the silk-soft malt; every bit as gentle as the nose suggests; f22 medium to short with some attractive rolling vanilla; b24 a surprise package that is not entirely dissimilar to the Golden Rum, only a tad sweeter. *43%*

Glemorangie Finealta db (**84.5**) n21 t22 f20.5 b21. Plump and thick, one of the creamiest malts around. For what it lacks in fine detail it makes up for in effect, especially the perky oaky spices. *46%*

⬥ **Glenmorangie Grand Vintage Malt 1989** db (**94**) n23.5 elaborate layering of crunchy barley and crunchier brown sugars...plus a stratum of under-ripe gooseberry; t23.5 the nose shouts "salivating"...and the moment it hits the palate...it certainly is! Lovely chocolate fruit, but also something of an exotic Indian sweet about this also; f23 love the long gristy fade and very well controlled spice; for a strange moment or two there appears to be a hint of smoke, but it could also be heftier, chocolate mousse tannin....or maybe a bit of both; b24 a stunning, silky blend of a single malt where the flavour profile – and even texture - has obviously been sculpted. As much a work of art as a dram. *43.1%*

Glenmorangie Grand Vintage Malt 1990 db (**94**) n24 t24 f22.5 b23.5 Grand by name, grand by nature...almost. For a malt this outstandingly good, it really should have been at 46% minimum... *43%*

Glenmorangie Lasanta sherry casks db (**68.5**) n16 t19 f16 b17.5. The sherry problem has increased dramatically rather than being solved. *46%*

Glenmorangie Lasanta Aged 12 Years sherry cask finish db (**93**) n23.5 t24 f22 b23.5 A delightful surprise: every bottling of Lasanta I'd ever tasted had been sulphur ruined. But this new 12-y-o incarnation has got off to a flying start. Although a little bit of a niggle on the finish, I can live with that in the present climate. Here's to a faultless second bottling... *43%*

Glenmorangie Legends The Duthac db (**91.5**) n23.5 t23.5 f21.5 b23 Not spoken to their blender, Bill Lumsden, about this one. But he's been busy on this, though not so busy as to get rid of the unwelcome you-know-what from the wine casks. Educated guess: some kind of finish involving virgin oak, or at least first fill bourbon, and sherry, probably PX on account of the intensity of the crisp sugar. *43%. ncf.*

Glenmorangie Madeira Wood Finish db (**78**) n19.5 t20.5 f19 b19. One of the real problems with wine finishes is getting the point of balance right when the fruit, barley and oak are in harmony. Here it is on a par with me singing in the shower, though frankly my aroma would be a notch or two up. *43%*

Glenmorangie Margaux Cask Finish db (**88**) n22 t22 f22 b22. Even taking every whisky with an open mind, I admit this was better than my subconscious might have considered. Certainly better than the near undrinkable Ch. Margaux '57 I used to bring out for my birthday each year some 20-odd years ago... *46%*

Glenmorangie Milsean db (**94**) n23 t23.5 f23.5 b24 A quite beautiful malt which goes out of its way to put the orangey in 'Morangie... *46%*

Glenmorangie Nectar D'or Sauternes Finish db (**94**) n23 t24 f23 b24 Great to see French casks that actually complement a whisky – so rare! This has replaced the Madeira finish. But there are some similar sweet-fruit characteristics. An exercise in outrageously good sweet-dry balancing. *46%*

⬥ **Glenmorangie Private Edition 9 Spios** db (**95.5**) n23 roasty and seductively attractive: healthy spice fits beautifully with the light mocha notes; t24.5 mmmmm!! What a delivery! The malt is in supercharged form, sensationally intense yet the trick is the layering: this is not a wall of barley but a slow build up, one line above the next. The sweetness is provided by deft and tactile ulmo honey which mingles with the grist, then a more lightweight orange blossom honey...all the while bowing lower than the malt which reigns supreme; **f23.5** superb spices tangle and pulse, but never outflank the malt. Even the oak is happy to provide only the lightest of vanilla flourishes; **b24.5** Glenmorangie displaying countless layers of brilliance. Breathtakingly beautiful. *46%.*

Glenmorangie Quinta Ruban Port Finish db **(92) n24 t23 f22 b23** This replacement of the original Port finish shows a genuine understanding of the importance of grape-oak balance. Both are portrayed with clarity and confidence. This is a form of cask finishing that has progressed from experimentation to certainty. *46%*

Glenmorangie Sherry Wood Finish db **(84) n23 t21 f20 b20**. Stupendous clean sherry nose, then disappoints with a somewhat bland display on the palate. *43%*

Glenmorangie Signet db **(80.5) n20 t21.5 f19 b20**. A great whisky holed below the waterline by oak of unsatisfactory quality. Tragic. *46%. Travel Retail Exclusive.*

Glenmorangie Sonnalta PX db **(96.5) n24 t24 f24.5b24** Remains a giant among the tall stills. A mesmeric whisky... *46%*

Glenmorangie Taghta db **(92) n23 t23 f23 b23** A curious Glenmorangie which, unusually, appears not to be trying to make a statement or force a point. This is an old Sunday afternoon film of a dram: an old-fashioned black and whitie, (home grown and not an Ealing, or Bogie or Edward G Robinson) where, whether we have seen it before or not, we know pretty much what is going to happen, in a reassuring kind of a way... *46%*

Glenmorangie Tarlogan db **(95) n24 t24 f22.5 b23.5** Interesting. I have just tasted three new Dalmore. Identical colour and some very similar toffeed characteristics. I allowed a whisky-loving visitor to taste them, without telling him what they were. He could barely tell them apart. Here, I have three new Glenmorangies. All of a different hue. I may not like them all; we will see. But at least I know there will be remarkable differences between them. This fabulous malt radiates the countryside in a way few drams have done before. As refreshing as an early morning dip in a Scottish pond... *43%*

Glenmorangie Traditional db **(90.5) n22** orange blossom, barley sugar and chalk dust; **t23** delicate delivery revelling in gentle complexity: really playful young-ish malt makes for a clean start and middle; **f22.5** soft mocha notes play out a quiet finish; **b23** an improved dram with much more to say, but does so quietly. *57.1%*

Glenmorangie Tayne db **(87.5) n21 t22.5 f22 b22**. Tangy back story. But also a curious early combination between butterscotch and Werther's Original candy. The malt – topped with a splash of double cream - in the centre ground, though, is the star showing. *43%. Travel Retail Exclusive.*

Glenmorangie Tùsail Private Edition db **(92) n24.5** if you sniff this too hard, you might break the whisky into a thousand pieces... just so gentle, wafer-thin shards of barley, butterscotch, boiled pear, vanilla, marzipan...and all watched over by brittle spices; **t23** the delivery mirrors the nose: the first six or seven waves are simply sketches of most of the things you find in the aroma, yet with no weight or substance at all...the mid-ground becomes little more simple and vanilla-driven, though with a delicate ulmo honey thread; **f21.5** lightweight vanilla and barley; only the spices make a noise; bitters very slightly at death; **b23** doesn't quite live up to the nose. But that would have been a big ask! From the Understated School of Glenmorangie. *46%. ncf.*

GLEN MORAY
Speyside, 1897. La Martiniquaise. Working.

Glen Moray Classic 8 Years Old db **(86) n20 t22 f21 b23.** A vast improvement on previous bottlings with the sluggish fatness replaced by a thinner, barley-rich, slightly sweeter and more precise mouthfeel. *40%*

Glen Moray 10 Years Old Chardonnay Matured db **(73.5) n18.5 t19 f18 b18.** Tighter than a wine cork. *40%*

Glen Moray 12 Years Old db **(90) n22.5 t22 f23 b22.5** I have always regarded this as the measuring stick by which all other malty and clean Speysiders should be tried and tested. It is still a fabulous whisky, full of malty intricacies. Something has fallen off the edge, perhaps, but minutely so. Still think a trick or two is being missed by bottling this at 40%: the natural timbre of this malt demands 46% and no less.... *40%*

Glen Moray 16 Years Old db **(74) n19 t19 f18 b19.** A serious dip in form. Drab. *40%*

Glen Moray 20 Years Old db **(80) n22 t22 f18 b18.** With so much natural cream toffee, it is hard to believe that this has so many years on it. After a quick, refreshing start it pans out, if anything, a little dull. *40%*

Glen Moray Aged 25 Years Port Cask Finish dist 1988 db **(88) n23 t22.5 f20.5 b22** Thought I'd celebrate Andy Murray's second Wimbledon victory, which he completed just a few minutes ago, by having another go at a Glen Moray 25-year-old (Moray is pronounced Murray). I remember last time being slightly disappointed with this expression. Well this later bottling is a little better, but nowhere near the brilliance Murray displayed in gaining revenge for Canada last year getting World Whisky of the Year. Curiously, if this is a 25-year-old and was distilled in 1988, then presumably it was bottled in 2013...the first time Murray won Wimbledon! *43%*

Glen Moray 25 Year Old Port Cask Finish batch 2 db (95) n23.5 t23.5 f24 b24 Some quite first rate port pipes are involved here. Absolutely clean as a whistle and without any form of off-note. A distillery I have a very soft spot for showing very unusual depth – and age. Brilliant. *43%. 3295 bottles.*

Glen Moray Aged 25 Years Portwood Finish Rare Vintage Limited Edition bott code. 3153, dist 1986 db (87.5) n22.5 t22 f21 b22. Just get the feeling that the Port pipe has not quite added what was desired. *43%*

◇◇ **Glen Moray Aged 25 Years Port Cask Finish** dist 1988, bott code L709759A 2017/04/07 db (94) n23 fat fruit, hefty in disposition but with a light spice and vanilla thread toning it down slightly; t23.5 salivating barley on delivery, invigorated further by a light maple syrup and black cherry sweetness; f23.5 long, though it refuses to budge far from the rich, increasingly spicy grape; b24 a lovely intense malt where the Port casks leave big fruity fingerprints at every turn. *43%.*

Glen Moray 30 Years Old db (92.5) n23.5 it's probably the deftness of the old-fashioned Speyside smoke in tandem with the structured fruits that makes this so special; t23.5 for a light Speysider, the degree of barley to oak is remarkable: soft, oil-gilde d barley is met by a wonderful, if brief, spice prickle; f22.5 deft layering of vanilla and cocoa; a sprinkle of muscovado sugar repels any darker oak notes; b23 for all its years, this is comfortable malt, untroubled by time. There is no mistaking quality. *43%*

Glen Moray 1984 db (83) n20 t22 f20 b21. Mouthwatering and incredibly refreshing malt for its age. *40%*

Glen Moray 1989 db (86) n23 t22 f20 b21. Doesn't quite live up to the fruit smoothie nose but I'm being a little picky here. *40%*

◇◇ **Glen Moray Bourbon Cask 1994** cask no. 42/0, bott code. 25/04/17 170635 db (93.5) n23.5 all kinds of honey and dark sugars lurk about...probably with intent to mug the chocolate; t23.5 huge, dynamic delivery: intense muscovado sugars and liquorice do well to capture the barley, itself of major proportions; mid-ground softens with liquid honey and barley; f23 long with a satisfying mocha and vanilla interplay. Light spice and red liquorice; b23.5 for most people in England Glen Moray is a highly productive goalscorer for Brighton. But it would be great is the world woke up to just what lovely whisky can come from this much under-rated distillery. *56.4%. sc.*

Glen Moray Classic db (86.5) n22 t21.5 f21.5 b21.5. The nose is the star with a wonderful, clean barley-fruit tandem, but what follows cannot quite match its sure-footed wit. *40%*

Glen Moray Classic Port Cask Finish db (89.5) n21 t21.5 f23.5 b23.5 A malt which has to somehow work its way to the exit...and finally does so with supreme confidence and a touch of class along the way... *40%*

Glen Moray Elgin Classic Chardonnay Cask Finish db (73) n19 t19 f17 b18. Juicy. But sulphur-dulled. *40%*

Glen Moray Elgin Classic Sherry Cask Finish db (85) n21 t22 f20.5 b21.5. Must be a cream sherry, because this is one exceptionally creamy malt. A bit of a late sulphur tang wipes off a few marks, but the delicious grapey positives outweigh the negatives. *40%*

Glen Moray Elgin Heritage Aged 15 Years db (74) n19 t20 f17 b18. Dulled by some poor, sulphur-laden sherry butts. Glen Moray is one of the maltiest drams on God's earth and at its most evocative in ex-bourbon. Who needs sherry? *40%*

Glen Moray Elgin Heritage Aged 18 Years db (94) n23.5 t24 f23 b23.5 Absolutely true to the Glen Moray style. Superb. *47%*

◇◇ **Glen Moray Mastery** db (89.5) n23.5 spiced sultana and salty malt: beautifully layered and weighted; t22.5 soft texture, a burst of spice, then malt...then flattens out with the grape; f21.5 vanilla, raisin and continued spice; b22 has an expensive feel to this, to be honest. But, though a huge GM fan, have to say that for all its very clean, attractive, unblemished fruit; for all its juiciness I'm afraid it's just a little bit too one-dimensional. No doubting its charm and elegance, however. *52.3%.*

◇◇ **Glen Moray Peated Cask 1994** cask no. 904/70, bott code. 25/04/17 170637 db (91) n22.5 the sweet smoke has as much mintiness about it as it does Arbroath Smokie; t23 delicate smoke has been absorbed into the slightly liquorice and fudge sweetness; soft mouth feel yet interestingly peppered with spice from an early point; **f22** lightly smoked butterscotch; **b23.5** a minor masterclass in smoky subtlety if ever there was one... 56.3%. sc.

Glen Moray Peated Classic db (87.5) **n21.5 t22.5 f21.5 b22**. Really never thought I'd see this distillery, once the quintessential Speyside unpeated dram, gone all smoky... A little bit of a work in progress. And a minor word to the wise to their blenders: by reducing to 40% you've broken up the oils a shade – but tellingly - too much, which can be crucial in peaty whiskies. Up to 46% next bottling and I think you'll find things fall into place – and not apart... Some minor erotic moments, though, especially on the fourth or fifth beats, when the sugars and smoked vanilla do work well together. Too fleeting, though. 40%

⬦ **Glen Moray Sherry Cask Finish 1994** cask no. 904/57, bott code. 25/04/17 170636 db (92) **n23.5** curious that the peppery spices here are every bit as important as the sugar-deprived fruit; the tannins offer a distinctly bourbon-style liquorice thread...but again without the usual honey accompaniment; **t23** big fruit on delivery – but of a style a few old timers in the industry will be nodding with quiet approval at: very big, concentrated grape skin, seemingly minus the juicy meat. Dry and powdery on the palate with a light cocoa sprinkling and a light, vanilla-sawdusty tone, also; **f22** just a little bit of lingering bitterness on the late finish, though have to say: not sure the exact cause; **b23.5** old-fashioned, traditional dry oloroso influence in its most resounding form. A must find malt for those looking to broaden their positive whisky experiences. 56.7%. sc.

Acla Selection Glen Moray 27 Years Old hogshead, dist 1988, bott 2015 (82.5) **n21.5 t21.5 f19.5 b20**. Not a malt that can always travel through the years without showing wear and tear. Here the oak takes its toll, biting deep into the game, grassier elements of the barley. But the tannin dominates in the end. 46.5%. nc ncf.

⬦ **Alos Sansibar Whisky Glen Moray 1988** bott 2016 (94) **n23.5** no doubting the age. But the integrity of the barley has easily withstood the tannin attack. Over-ripe pear offers a fruity diversion; **t24** the delivery may creak with age, but the extra injection of gristy barley does all it can to maintain a younger shape. Lovely cocoa tones, weighted with molasses and perked up by spice, begin to fill the mid-ground; **f23** that chocolate spice refuses to relinquish its post and lessens the light ...; **b23.5** imagine Glen Moray as a bar of chocolate... 45.1%.

Best Dram Glen Moray 17 Years Old (86.5) **n22 t21 f22 b21.5**. Just a little tang to the cask detracts from a very well made malt of the intensely barley-rich Glen Moray school. 55.4%

⬦ **Best Dram Glen Moray 18 Year Old** Lagavulin PX Octave finish, dist 1998, bott 2016 (87) **n22.5 t23 f21 b20.5** Glen Moray as, undoubtedly, you will never have seen it before: certainly I haven't! An intriguing if slightly confusing mish-mash of styles, though offering a creaminess alien to the distillery. Enjoyable, but the over enthusiastic sweetness often seems forced and unsteady while the tang at the end does few favours. Good spices and sulphur-free, though. 54.9%.

Big Market Sonderabfüllung Nr. 15 Glen Moray 1998 bott 2015 (91.5) **n22 t23.5 f22.5 b23.5** Lively and chirpy, this is a clean, upbeat malt offering a surprise smoky note so there's no shortage of depth, too. A lovely way to celebrate 50 years...! 57.3%. 50th Anniversary bottling.

Cadenhead's Wine Cask Glen Moray 23 Year Old Sauternes cask, dist 1992, bott Apr 16 (89.5) **n22 t24 f22 b21.5** A clean but curious malt which seems to have more dust-ups in ten minutes than the average volume of Kill Bill... 52%. sc. 252 bottles.

Chapter 7 Glen Moray 1990 25 Years Old (93.5) **n23.5 t23.5 f23 b23.5** Resplendent in the juiciest barley imaginable. Vague smoke drifts in and out teasingly. Unusually for a Glen Moray, shows no signs of wear and tear for its age. 57%

⬦ **Demijohn Glen Moray 9 Year Old** cask no. 5858, bott 20 Jan 17 (95) **n23.5** beautiful interplay with golden syrup and barley on one side and a prickly spice on the other: quite lovely...; **t24** the quintessential Moray delivery: an outpouring of intense barley quickly backed by lucid tannins yielding a top grape spiciness; the oils carry a slightly youthful cocoa element; **f23.5** long, still gently oiled with the barley sugar and spices lasting a very long time; **b24** a Glen Moray exactly how it should be considering cask type and age: wonderful! 60.2%. sc.

⬦ **Hepburn's Choice Glen Moray 9 Years Old** refill bourbon barrel, dist 2007, bott 2016 (87.5) **n22 t23 f21 b21.5** Massive caramel credentials. The nose and delivery is one huge malt and cream toffee fest, with Glen Moray in is most single style mode. Only a little oak bitterness at the death interfers with these simple delights. 46%. nc ncf sc. 370 bottles.

⬦ **Old Malt Cask Glen Moray Aged 21 Years** refill hogshead, cask no. 12819, dist Mar 95, bott Aug 16 (89.5) **n22** a little sandalwood adds backbone to the grassy freshness; the barley builds in single-minded intensity in the usual house style; **t23** massively satisfying delivery with a little extra fizz and spice on the concentrated malt – a textbook mouth feel; **f22** the oak not only gains a foothold but begins to make some mocha inroads; **b22.5** Moray at its most charming. 50%. nc ncf sc. 111 bottles.

Old Particular Speyside Glen Moray 20 Years Old refill hogshead, cask no. 10871, dist Mar 95, bott Aug 15 (**86.5**) **n21.5 t22.5 f20.5 b22**. Feverishly malty in that trademark Glen Moray style. Juicy and salty, too. Tangy finish. 51.5%. nc ncf sc. 264 bottles.

◈ **Provenance Glen Moray Aged 8 Years** refill hogshead, cask no. 11621, dist Jun 08, bott Feb 17 (**86**) **n21.5 t22.5 f21 b21** Just not really enough in the tank to raise this above being young, lively but undercooked – especially on the nose and finish. 46%. nc ncf sc. 367 bottles.

◈ **Provenance Glen Moray Aged 10 Years** refill hogshead, cask no. 11186, dist Jun 05, bott Mar 16 (**86**) **n21.5 t22 f21 b21.5** A beautifully made, salivating malt with the barley coming at you from all directions. But the antiquity of the cask means little meaningful is added oak-wise. 46%. nc ncf sc.

◈ **Provenance Glen Moray Aged 12 Years** refill hogshead, cask no. 11622, dist May 04, bott Feb 17 (**90.5**) **n21** just a shade too new makey and off key, especially for this age; **t23.5** oh...now there's a turn up for the book. Certainly, the earliest moments on the palate confirm youth. But the enormous intensity of the grassy grist sets the taste buds off into a salivating fervour. Lovely green apple, muscovado sugar and very late-middle heather honey ensures a stunning ride; **f23** slows as the spices and light tannins follow the path of the vanilla; **b23** the nose hints at a malt not yet ready for bottling. The delivery reveals something entirely different! Lovely. 46%. nc ncf sc. 379 bottles.

◈ **Sansibar Whisky Glen Moray 25 Year Old** dist 1991, bott 2016 (**96**) **n24** simply magnificent: myriad light fruit notes, almost a fruit cocktail, with cherries and diced apple in particular abundance. The custard is a little salty; **t24** big and bruising delivery. Both the intense barley and marginally bigger oak battle for supremacy from the off. Enough barley sugar and ulmo honey notes are on hand to get the measure of the peppery oak; **f24** fabulously undulating finish with the sweeter and spicier elements taking turns to dominate the very long, mocha-enriched tapering finish; **b24** a great distillery overcoming the years with extraordinary panache. One of the great Moray 25s... 50.9%.

Scotch Malt Whisky Society Cask 35.137 Aged 25 Years 1st fill barrel, dist 25 Aug 89, bott 22 Jun 15 (**94**) **n23.5 t24 f23 b23.5** Unlikely you will find a crisper and more sweet Speyside malt all year. Astonishing! 52.8%. nc ncf sc. 87 bottles.

◈ **Scotch Malt Whisky Society Cask 35.185 22 Year Old** first fill toasted oak hogshead, dist 17 Nov 94 (**95.5**) **n24** touches every person's inner bourbon with its rich kumquat and liquorice tannin which takes this nose deep into Kentucky. Brilliantly complex: any bourbon blender would be proud of this cask...; **t24** at least some barley on delivery! But the caramels leached from the oak soon smother the malt the best it can. The spices start peacefully but soon get a bit warlike while the citrus notes build steadily on the orange blossom honey; **f23** a little bitterness creeps in, most un-bourbon-like towards the finish. But still plenty of butterscotch and spice to be getting on with; **b24.5** some of these heavily toasted experimental casks have not quite hit the heights one hopes for. This one, by happy contrast, has far exceeded expectation... 57.5%.

◈ **Simon Brown Glen Moray** ex-bourbon & finished in ex-Pedro Ximénez cask, dist Aug 98, bott Nov 14 (**84.5**) **n22 t22 f19.5 b21** My word! It is like sticking your head in a tub of molasses: I am in Jamaica again. Maybe not quite so pungent, as a definite – or perhaps that should be defiant – malty theme strikes up. Certainly the body of the piece is as thick and muscular as any Glen Moray you are ever likely to encounter. But the bitter finish, I suspect in direct contrast to what had been planned, brings very limited joy, alas. 46%. nc ncf sc.

◈ **Spirits Shop Selection Glen Moray 1996** sherry butt, bott 2016 (**61**) **n14 t19 f14 b14** A must have for sulphur lovers. 49.2%. 310 bottles. A joint bottling with Sansibar Whisky.

Svenska Eldvatten Glen Moray 1991 ex-bourbon barrel, dist Feb 91 (**96.5**) **n24 t24 f24 b24.5** If you want to see why Glen Moray should always be bottled from ex-bourbon cask, then look no further than this. A classic example of a classic but tragically misunderstood and abused distillery. 57.5%. sc.

Whiskyjace 10th Anniversary Glen Moray 17 Years Old 1998 bourbon cask, bott 2015 (**89**) **n22 t23 f22 b22** "Glen Moray" goes through this like "Blackpool" is found in a stick of rock candy. A very decent cask which maximises the malty potential. 57.6%

◈ **Wilson & Morgan Barrel Selection Glen Moray 13 Year Old 2016** 1st fill bourbon barrel, dist 2007 (**92.5**) **n22.5** still a hint of something a little green but the freshness of the malt is invigorating; **t24** truly glorious delivery and early follow through; almost faultless, in fact. The mouth feel has just enough weight to give gravitas but there is lightness of touch to ensure the barley offers varying levels of sweetness and intensity; a thin band of heather honey frames the work; **f22** old enough to offer a little oaky tang to the uncomplicated finish; **b23** a distillery which feels so at home at this age in a decent bourbon barrel. 48%.

GLEN ORD
Highlands (Northern), 1838. Diageo. Working.
Glen Ord Aged 12 Years db **(81)** n20 t23 f18 b20. Just when you thought it safe to go back...for a while Diageo ditched the sherry-style Ord. It has returned. Better than some years ago, when it was an unhappy shadow of its once-great self, but without the sparkle of the vaguely-smoked bottling of a year or two back. Nothing wrong with the rich arrival, but the finish is a mess. I'll open the next bottling with trepidation... 43%

Glen Ord 25 Years Old dist 1978 db **(95)** n24 t24 f23 b24. Stupendous vatting here: cask selection at its very highest to display Ord in all its far too rarely seen magnificence. 58.3%

Glen Ord 28 Years Old db **(90)** n22 t23 f22 b23. This is mega whisky showing slight traces of sap, especially on the nose, but otherwise a concentrate of many of the qualities I remember from this distillery before it was bottled in a much ruined form. Blisteringly beautiful. 58.3%

Glen Ord 30 Years Old db **(87)** n22 t21 f23 b21. Creaking with oak, but such is the polish to the barley some serious class is on show. 58.8%

Singleton of Glen Ord 12 Years Old db **(89)** n22.5 t22.5 f22 b22 A fabulous improvement on the last bottling I encountered. Still possesses blood oranges to die for, but greatly enhanced by some sublime spices and a magnificent juiciness. 40%

Singleton of Glen Ord 32 Year Old db **(91)** n23.5 t23 f22 b22.5. Delicious. But if ever a malt has screamed out to be at 46%, this is it. 40%

Cadenhead's Authentic Collection Glen Ord 11 Year Old butt, dist 2004 **(95.5)** n23.5 t23.5 f24.5 b24 Exceptionally high quality malt from a very high quality – unspoiled! – butt...! 60.6%

⬧ **Cadenhead's Small Batch International Glen Ord 11 Year Old** dist 2005 **(87.5)** n21.5 t22.5 f22 b21.5 Glen Ord at its most intense and, in this case, most wild. This is a slow developer for an 11-year-old so a degree of fresh young malt has a say at every turn. The result is a salivating, biting wildcat of a dram which is magnificent fun but hardly one for the purists! 56.2%.

⬧ **Old Malt Cask Glen Ord Aged 12 Years** refill hogshead, cask no. 12812, dist Sept 04, bott Oct 16 **(88.5)** n22.5 a light pithy quality to this with the vanilla drying the uncluttered barley; **t22** salivating yet with a very simple malt message; the middle ground fills and thickens as some oils begin to congregate; **f22** attractive spiced biscuit; **b22** malty and quietly satisfying. 50%. nc ncf sc. 337 bottles.

⬧ **Provenance Glen Ord Aged 11 Years** refill hogshead, cask no. 11215, dist Sept 04, bott May 16 **(92)** n23 a wonderful barley complexation: sweet and gristy yet clean with refreshing citrus clarity. Holds its weight impressively; **t23** silky with a vaguely coppery sub-strata which ramps up the weight despite the oak mainly holding back; **f23** sublime spices dance amid the rich and persistent barley; **b23** it is a rare whisky which can leech so little from the cask yet be quite so full blooded... 46%. nc ncf sc.

GLENROTHES
Speyside, 1878. Edrington. Working.
Glenrothes 2001 dist 25 May 01, bott 13 db **(72)** n16 t21 f17 b18. The sulphur in Spain makes this whisky very plain. 43% WB15/297

The Glenrothes Alba Reserve db **(87.5)** n22 t22 f21.5 b22. You know that smartly groomed, polite but rather dull chap you invariable get at dinner parties? 40%

The Glenrothes Elders' Reserve db **(75.5)** n19 t20.5 f17.5 b18.5. Now when I was a young man, young man, Scotch single malt whisky tasted a lot better than this, you know. Well, could hardly have tasted worse, could it?! That nice young Mr Lloyd George wouldn't have put up with this rubbish, oh no. He would have sent in the troops and nationalised the industry, that's what he would have done. Hung anyone guilty of using sherry butts stinking of sulphur. Or shot 'em. Only fair. These young blenders... Blenders?!? Don't know they are born... In my day... 43% WB16/046

The Glenrothes Manse Reserve db **(74)** n18.5 t20 f17 b18.5. More like Mansfield Reserves... 43% WB16/045

The Glenrothes Minister's Reserve db (**91**) n22.5 trace sulphur, but by Genrothes standards this is pretty amazing: the grape really does come through with a spring in its juicy step; t23.5 absolutely top dollar sherry at work: a gorgeous sultana-laden sweetness but backed by the most luscious mouth feel, aided by a little liquorice from the oak; f22 a little manuka honey fights off successfully the late bitterness from the obligatory dodgy butt; b23 I think the Minister had a little word with someone upstairs... 43% WB16/047

The Glenrothes Sherry Cask Reserve db (**68**) n16 t19 f16 b17. Inevitable, I suppose... The tragedy is that before some bloke stuffed lighted sulphur candles into these sherry butts, thereby ruining them and the whisky which would later mature in them, they were obviously the dog's...; and had they been left unmolested we would have been nosing and tasting something of intense brilliance. Exasperating doesn't even begin to cover it. 40% WB16/044

◈ **Cadenhead's Small Batch International Glenrothes 27 Year Old** bourbon & rum casks, dist 1989 (**93.5**) n22.5 the sugars from a rum cask often tighten the nose and restrict full development: you get the feeling that this is probably a case in point. Very pleasant with its mysterious, fruity edge, but still restrained... Even so, on this evidence I'm expecting a lot on delivery... t24.5...and my god! I have not been disappointed! One of the arrivals of the year, without doubt. Certainly one of the most honey-laden with acacia honey couched in a gorgeous soft, malty oil. Spices poke and prod but both sugars and barley refuse to loosen their grip; f23 a large portion of butterscotch tart, though with a late bitterness; b23.5 I think only Cadenhead's could have come up with this minor classic. 53.7%.

◈ **Eiling Lim Glenrothes 19 Year Old** PX cask, dist 1997, bott 2016 (**71.5**) n18 t19.5 f15 b18 Sulphur riddled. 50.2%. 201 bottles.

The First Editions Glenrothes Aged 19 Years 1996 refill hogshead, cask no. 12125, bott 2015 (**84.5**) n20.5 t23 f20 b21. For those turned on by the aroma of sweaty armpits, this could be a very exciting whisky for you. After an eye-watering, salty and sexily honeyed delivery, it does tail off towards a tired tanginess towards the end. Still, lacking in character it most certainly isn't...! 56.2%. nc ncf sc. 242 bottles.

◈ **The First Editions Glenrothes Aged 20 Years 1996** refill hogshead, cask no. 12125, bott 2016 (**88**) n22.5 there's a nose from the past: egg nog but here with a squeeze of lime; t22 the barley is on full volume, though this can't entirely drown out the nagging, lively oak; f21.5 dries a little overenthusiastically; b22 not short on character! 53.5%. nc ncf sc. 171 bottles.

◈ **Liquid Treasures Glenrothes 19 Year Old** refill butt, dist 1997, bott 2017 (**89**) n22 salty, citrusy barley; t22.5 salivating, salty, citrusy barley; f22 now spicy, citrusy barley – with a simple dry oak finale; b22.5 makes no attempt at great complexity, but does the malt thing rather well. 59.4%. Faces of Angkor Edition.

Old Malt Cask Glenrothes Aged 18 Years red wine finished barrel, cask no. 12122, dist Sept 97, bott Nov 15 (**89**) n22.5 t21.5 f23.5 b21.5 A good example of a cask bottled when the fruit and malt hadn't quite gelled. But there is enough quality abounding for it to work out okay in the end. 47.8%. nc ncf sc. 256 bottles.

◈ **Old Malt Cask Glenrothes Aged 20 Years** refill hogshead, cask no. 13093, dist Jul 96, bott Nov 16 (**92.5**) n22.5 citrus and putty: oddly attractive; t23.5 intense, clean, salivating barley. So much to chew on and the early spices raise the stakes further; f23 a superb fade. A little salt is rubbed into the gathering tannin but it is the layering of the barley that stars; b23.5 a beautiful Speysider just dripping in personality. 50%. nc ncf sc. 180 bottles.

◈ **Old Particular Glenrothes 12 Years Old** sherry butt, cask no. 11170, dist May 04, bott Jun 16 (**79.5**) n20 t21.5 f18 b20 Despite the obvious sulphur at play, some of the richer oloroso tones carry enough Demerara sugar to help with damage limitation. 48.4%. nc ncf sc. 490 bottles.

◈ **Old Particular Glenrothes 12 Years Old** sherry butt, cask no. 11601, dist Feb 05, bott Mar 17 (**71**) n17 t19 f17 b18 One guess... The perfect gift for Mrs Merkel... 48.4%. nc ncf sc. 402 bottles.

◈ **Scotch Malt Whisky Society Cask 30.92 24 Year Old** refill ex-bourbon barrel, dist 21 Feb 92 (**95.5**) n24 a 20 minute nose, minimum. Despite the age, diced apple and pear figures healthily while the barley skips between grassy and biscuity in equal measure. Spices are light yet help accentuate the oak; t24 lands on the palate like a butterfly on a flower. Fresh malt, seemingly...then a far more deep salted caramel tart. Somehow the malt revives and takes control once more; f23 malty still, but with an intense creamy vanilla fade; b24.5 pure malty magic! For the distillery and age, just about perfection... 46.7%.

◈ **The Single Cask Glenrothes Aged 19 Years** cask no. L1097, dist 8 Oct 97, bott 13 Jan 17 (**79**) n18 t22 f19 b20 Dripping in fruit and coffee but, sadly, that is not all....and I don't mean the spices. One strictly for the German and central European market where this type of s-affected cask might be appreciated. *58.5%. nc ncf sc. 85 bottles.*

⬧ **The Single Cask Glenrothes Aged 19 Years** cask no. T497, dist 28 Apr 97, bott 13 Jan 17 **(90.5) n22** from the outrageously over-the-top grape school of sherry...; **t23** whoosh...!! The palate is flooded with over-ripe plums and raisins, all in a sherry trifle gooeyness. The spices are profound and quite wonderful...; **f23.5** over-moistened, over-raisined and over cooked fruit cake is mixed in with chocolate pudding. The spices continue to burrow into the taste buds...; **b22** about as subtle as a sherry pie in the face. Almost a self-lampooning of a sherry-matured Speysider, but at least swamped with fruit rather than sulphur. So amen to that...!!! *58%. nc ncf sc. 86 bottles.*

That Boutique-y Whisky Company Glenrothes 10 Year Old batch 2 **(68) n16 t18 f17 b17.** Clunking caramels and even clunkier you-know-what...*45.8%. 294 bottles.*

⬧ **The Whisky Barrel Burns Malt Glenrothes 19 Year Old 1997** sherry butt, cask no. 7157 **(88) n23** anyone who remembers opening a packet of Payne's chocolate raisin sweets will recognise this rich and alluring aroma immediately...; **t23.5** yes it drips in oloroso to an almost vulgar degree, but the sub plot of Jamaican Blue Mountain coffee and molasses casts a wonderfully complex and delicate spell...; **f20** it takes time for the sulphur treatment to get through, but when it does the dryness is oppressive; **b21.5** tragically close to a potential award-winning malt. Sherry butts rarely come along this beautifully structured. But those very late furry notes cannot be ignored (though those unable to detect sulphur might just have found one of their whiskies of the year). Still, what a pity... *53.5%. sc.*

⬧ **The Whisky Chamber Glenrothes 20 Year Old** ex-bourbon cask, dist 1996 **(87) n21.5 t22 f21.5 b22** A pleasant malt, but one of remarkably little character. Often simple barley is the only embellishment to the vanilla. Attractive cream toffee, also. But a little bitterness, too. *53.1%.*

⬧ **Whisky-Fässle Glenrothes 18 Year Old** sherry butt, dist 1997, bott 2016 **(79) n22 t21 f17 b19** Back in my Fleet Street days of the 1980s we used to pile into El Vinos and, through the blinding blue haze of tobacco smoke and the deafening din of larger-than-life, extrovert journos, portly barristers and haggard police chiefs each trying to outdo the other with stories to stretch belief to breaking; while the barman would supply a Speyside malt, like this, the colour of teak and displaying more oloroso traits than your average bottle of sherry. This is identical in colour, though the sulphury just-struck match aroma then emanated from the regulars, not the whisky. *51.8%.*

⬧ **Wilson & Morgan Barrel Selection Glenrothes 18 Year Old 2016** Oloroso sherry finish, cask no. 8734/35/36, dist 1997 **(71) n18 t20.5 f15 b17.5** A classic for the sulphur lovers. *57.6%.*

⬧ **World of Orchids Glenrothes 20 Year Old** bourbon cask, dist 1996 **(89.5) n23** a hint of apple pie on the still vaguely gristy barley. The usual spices at work; **t22.5** outstandingly well distilled and a kind cask: the malt in intense and quite weighty but shows just the right degree of sweetness; **f21.5** maybe the cask isn't so kind after all: a little very late bitterness creeps in to compete with the vanilla-malt mix; **b22.5** n medals for complexity. But a really gorgeous slug of intense malt... *49.1%.*

GLEN SCOTIA
Campbeltown, 1832. Loch Lomond Distillers. Working

Glen Scotia Aged 10 Years bourbon cask, bott Dec 12 db **(90.5) n22.5 t23.5 f22 b22.5.** Fabulous to see Scotia back in this excellent nick again. *46%. nc ncf.*

Glen Scotia 12 Years Old db **(73.5) n18 t19 f18 b18.5.** Ooops! I once said you could write a book about this called "Murder by Caramel." Now it would be a short story called "Murder by Flavours Unknown." What is happening here? Well, a dozen years ago Glen Scotia was not quite the place to be for consistent whisky, unlike now. Here, the caramel is the only constant as the constituent parts disintegrate. *40%*

Glen Scotia Aged 12 Years bourbon cask, bott Dec 12 db **(89) n22 t22 f23 b22.** Simplistic but delicious. *46%. nc ncf.*

Glen Scotia 14 Year Old Peated bourbon cask db **(87) n21.5 t22 f21.5 b22.** A very straight bat played by this one: a malty up and downer with few frills others than a slow though ineffective build up of smoke. *50%. nc ncf.*

Glen Scotia Aged 15 Years American oak barrels db **(91.5) n22.5** a serious buzz of lively, working tannin to this. All dark sugars and spice, it suggests a malt which means business; **t23** mouth-filling deep, roasty, slightly fat, vaguely salty, massively chewy. A kind of molasses feel with the sweetness reduced; **f23** long, with a lovely, buttery oiliness giving a sheen to the late liquorice; the spices really do come into their own; **b23** great to see this rather special little distillery produce something quite so confident and complete. *46%. ncf.*

Glen Scotia Aged 16 Years bourbon cask, bott Dec 12 db (87) **n22 t22 f21 b22**. Signs of a less than brilliant distillate which has been ironed out to some good effect in the cask. *46%. nc ncf.*

Glen Scotia Aged 18 Years bourbon cask, bott Dec 12 db (77) **n20 t21 f17 b19**. Malty but hot as Hades: a reminder of a less than glorious period in the distillery's history. *46%. nc ncf.*

Glen Scotia Aged 21 Years bourbon cask, bott Dec 12 db (86.5) **n21.5 t22.5 f21 b21.5**. Appears nothing like its age: the very vaguely smoked malt is entirely on top and offers little deviation. A playful spice reminds you oak is involved somewhere. *46%. nc ncf.*

Glen Scotia Double Cask finished in American oak & Pedro Ximenez sherry casks db (85.5) **n22 t22 f20.5 b21**. When blending, I do not like to get too involved with PX casks, unless I know for certain I can shape the effect to further or enrich the storyline on the palate. The reason is that PX means the complexity of a malt can easily come to a sticky end. That has happened here with both the malt and grape cancelling each other out. Soft and easy drinking with an excellent early delivery spike of intensity. But a dull middle and finish. And dull has never been a word I have associated with this distillery. Ever. *46%. ncf.*

Glen Scotia Single Cask Distillery Edition 001 cask no. 196, dist Dec 02, bott May 15 db (94) **n23 t24 f23.5 b23.5** A delicious malt which makes the most of what is available. Love it! *56.1%. sc.*

Glen Scotia Single Cask Distillery Edition No. 002 cask no. 332/543-1, dist Jun 03, bott Aug 15 db (94.5) **n23 t24 f23.5 b24** So busy and alive with internecine battling for control. No overall winners, other than the lucky person tasting this. *56.4%. ncf sc.*

Glen Scotia Single Cask Distillery Edition No. 003 cask no. 536, dist Dec 06, bott Apr 16 db (85) **n20 t21.5 f22 b21.5**. Malty, juicy and all that. And good light molasses, too. But someone was in a big hurry to get home for Christmas by the look of this thin offering: appears as though the stills were run like the clappers...or do I mean sleigh bells.... *56.9%. ncf sc.*

Glen Scotia Victoriana db (89.5) **n23 t23 f21.5 b22** An unusual malt for a cask strength. Beyond the nose there is limited layering, instead concentrating on the malt-toffee intertwangling. *51.5%*

Cadenhead's Sherry Cask Glen Scotia 15 Year Old dist 2000, bott Apr 16 (95.5) **n24 t24 f23.5 b24** A clean, rich sherry butt. A malt spirit brimming with character. What's not to like...? Again, Cadenhead come up with something just a little special... *50.5%. sc. 252 bottles.*

Maltbarn Glen Scotia 1992 ex-bourbon cask, bott 2016 (88.5) **n22 t22.5 f22 b22** What it lacks in finesse, it makes up for in personality. *53.3%. sc. 144 bottles.*

GLEN SPEY
Speyside, 1885. Diageo. Working.

Glen Spey Aged 12 Years db (90) **n23** the kind of firm, busy malt you expect from this distillery plus some lovely spice; **t22** mouthwatering and fresh, a layer of honey makes for an easy three or four minutes; **f22** drier vanilla, but the pulsing oak is controlled and stylish; **b23** very similar to the first Glen Spey I can remember in this range, the one before the over-toffeed effort of two years ago. Great to see it back to its more natural, stunningly beautiful self. *43%*

◈ **The First Editions Glen Spey Aged 25 Years 1990** refill hogshead, cask no. 12824, bott 2016 (89) **n21.5** a tangy saltiness suggests a tiring of the oak; **t23.5** that's more like it! The barley appears to be inches thick, ensuring a wonderful chewiness to the salivating sharpness. Eye-watering in part, but that salty oak is never far from the scene; **f22** excellent oils stick to their task; **b22** some serious signs of great age here. But the malt stands just firm enough to give an illusion of effortless control...though I suspect it was very hard work! *53.9%. nc ncf sc. 78 bottles.*

◈ **The First Editions Glen Spey Aged 25 Years 1991** refill hogshead, cask no. 13307, bott 2017 (93) **n22.5** such a soft touch: the barley is clean and with just enough age apparent to make the most of the natural caramel to remind you of freshly bitten toffee apple; **t23.5** disarmingly delicate: Speyside malt acting like Speyside malt by allowing the barley by far the greater say with the vanilla and spices a respectful distance behind; sharp, though never too much so...and just-so sweetness...; **f22.5** just more of the same...; **b23** a blueprint showing how an old Speyside whisky, even one as fragile as Glen Spey, can still be delicate and wonderfully layered. *50.7%. nc ncf sc. 132 bottles.*

◈ **Liquid Sun Glen Spey 26 Years Old** dist 1988 (87) **n23 t21.5 f21 b21.5** The nose star bills with a fabulous lemon curd tart and crème brule double header. Sadly, there is not enough weight and structure to the malt to be able to comfortably hold the weight of the oak which dominates and crushes. Still some orange blossom honey does its best at damage limitation. 41.1%.

◇◇◇ **Old Malt Cask Glen Spey Aged 18 Years** refill hogshead, cask no. 11239, dist Jan 97, bott Feb 15 (87.5) n21.5 t22 f22 b22 Lip-smackingly malty. But has none of the body that makes its sister cask with Old Particular such a success. Easy and pleasant, though. 50%. nc ncf sc. 249 bottles.

◇◇◇ **Old Malt Cask Glen Spey Aged 25 Years** refill hogshead, cask no. 12803, dist Oct 90, bott Aug 16 (95) n23.5 how do you get freshly cut grass on a 25-year-old...? As sweet and fresh and an early spring morning, but a light dabbing of citrus to counter any oaky intrusion; t24.5 the king of deliveries...or maybe I mean queen. For this is so delicate you feel it could perish on your palate at any given moment. Salivating despite the healthy oakiness, though its chalky outlines always play second fiddle to the lightly oiled, vaguely honeyed malt; f23 thins as that chalkiness makes inroads; b24 this was never designed to be a single malt of this great vintage. Rather, the top or luxurious and ample middle dressing for a number of old-aged blends. This is a wonderful example of why. Just groans with understated refinement. Magnificent balance and posture throughout: a class act. 50%. nc ncf sc. 95 bottles.

◇◇◇ **Old Malt Cask Glen Spey Aged 25 Years** refill hogshead, cask no. 13306, dist Dec 91, bott Feb 17 (89) n22 odd nose: those old enough to remember Germoline will be fascinated by this. Despite the soft antiseptic bite, there are no phenols. Instead light citrus tones accumulate; t23 excellent mouth feel: the oils offer just the right degree of lushness to give the barley a red carpet treatment; f22 back to a far more basic vanilla scheme; b22 an attractive and slightly quirky bottling. 50%. nc ncf sc. 182 bottles.

◇◇◇ **Old Particular Glen Spey 18 Years Old** refill hogshead, cask no. 11336, dist Dec 97, bott Sept 16 (90.5) n22 light with a few patchy signs of wear. Overtly dry but a little liquorice sweetens; t22 an attractive greenness clings despite the years as the malt bursts into juicy song; f23.5 much better balance between the oak and malt; makes the most of the oils for a long and tidy finish; b23 after a faltering, insecure start blossoms into a real charmer. 48.4%. nc ncf sc. 328 bottles.

GLENTAUCHERS
Speyside, 1898. Chivas Brothers. Working.

Cadenhead's Authentic Collection Glentauchers 38 Year Old bourbon hogshead, dist 1976, bott April 15 (95.5) n23.5 t23.5 f24.5 b24 Usually you'll find this whisky left another couple of years to find its way into a delicate, complex 40 year-old. Here, though, is a rare chance to see what one of the mainstays of great blending adds to the party. Elegance, sophistication and complexity....that's what! 50.8%. sc. 210 bottles.

Distilleries Collection Glentauchers Aged 18 Years 1996 bott 2014 (88.5) n22.5 t23 f21 b22 'Tauchers is always at its best when the spirit rather than the cask has the slightly louder voice. Here, the barrel pipes up above the malt, though still to highly attractive effect. 52.1%. Bottled for Scotch Malt Sales Ltd.

Five Lions Glentauchers Aged 13 Years 2nd fill American bourbon barrel, dist Jul 02, bott Nov 15 (92) n22 t23.5 f23 b23.5 What a beautifully honest dram! 55.6%. nc ncf.

◇◇◇ **Gordon & MacPhail Distillery Label Glentauchers 1997** bott 13 Dec 16 (82.5) n20 t22 f19 b21.5 An awkward and uncomfortable 'Tauchers well below par for the distillery. Muffled and muted throughout, the nose and finish struggle to find the right key and a little furry. Even the mid-ground, usually so full of convoluted malt, is flat and toffee dominant. 43%.

Grindlay's Selection Glentauchers 1996 (89) n22.5 t22.5 f22 b22 A very clean and solid Speysider with sugars at a premium. 54.5%. nc ncf. 210 bottles.

Hepburn's Choice Glentauchers 6 Years Old refill hogshead, dist 2009, bott 2016 (86) n21.5 t22 f21 b21.5. Was shaping up quite well, this youngster. Fulsome malt, as to be expected, ably assisted by a short buttery-vanilla charge and a slightly surprising degree of spice. 46%. nc ncf sc. 397 bottles.

◇◇◇ **Hepburn's Choice Glentauchers 7 Years Old** refill hogshead, dist 2009, bott 2016 (88.5) n22 suet pudding; t22.5 eye-wateringly tight and sparkling barley; f22 a collection of gristy sugars plus the vaguest outline of vanilla; b22 a simple, well-made malt. 46%. nc ncf sc. 320 bottles.

◇◇◇ **Hidden Spirits Glentauchers 20 Year Old** cask no. GT617, dist 1996, bott 2017 (90) n22 cream toffee, light citrus and a sprig of mint; t23 driving barley on delivery, delicate drier oak notes in its wake; remains salivating for a good while, some secondary Demerara sugars picking up the baton; chewy toffee throughout; f22.5 reverts to a drier, slightly creamier mocha and toasty fudge; b22.5 a very safe and conservative Tauchers allowing the natural caramels a free hand. 55.3%. sc.

Old Particular Speyside Glentauchers 18 Years Old refill barrel, cask no. 10779, dist Dec 96, bott May 15 (92.5) n23.5 t23.5 f22.5 b23 Another beautiful 'Tauchers, just revelling in the essence of Speyside. 48.4%. nc ncf sc. 186 bottles.

⟐ **Old Particular Glentauchers 20 Years Old** refill barrel, cask no. 11635, dist Dec 96, bott Mar 17 (95.5) n24 I could nose this charmer all night and into the early hours...there is a fruity dexterity to this upon which I could lecture for hours on end. We are talking the thinnest slivers here: kiwi fruit, psysallis, Chinese pear...exotic yet fresh and rich. The malt has a gristy quality emboldened by the lightest and most demur golden syrup...; t24 you really couldn't ask for a better delivery: so gentle as the malt lands like snowflakes, so complex as the spices meet the fuller red liquorice and crystalised ginger notes...; f23.5 a little bitterness creeps in, but the extension to the delivery fades as unhurried as a Scottish Highland summer sunset...; b24 have to admit: will be drinking a mouthful of this before bed tonight. This is the perfect Speyside experience! 51.5%. nc ncf sc. 223 bottles.

⟐ **Provenance Glentauchers Aged 7 Years** refill hogshead, cask no. 11330, dist Apr 09, bott Aug 16 (87) n22 t21 f22 b22 A less than taxing malt-fest which intriguingly seems to have something of the American "White Dog" about it.... 46%. nc ncf sc. 402 bottles.

Provenance Glentauchers Aged 9 Years bott Mar 16 (90) n21.5 t22.5 f23 b23 Unusually coastal for a 'Tauchers, but it still churns out delicious malt almost with its eyes closed. 46%. nc ncf sc.

⟐ **Scotch Malt Whisky Society Cask 63.36 26 Year Old** refill ex-bourbon barrel, dist 19 Dec 89 (92) n23.5 superb! Rich while intricate. Toasted mallows; vanilla infused with pear juice; a little freshness to the barley still – after all these years...; t23 and it is that grassy barley which displays first. The juiciness is thickened by lemon curd tart plus vague pineapple and cream; f22.5 happy to fade out to simplistic vanilla; b23 so consistent, this distillery: just makes it look all so easy... 51.8%.

The Single Cask Glentauchers 14 Year Old cask no. 15827, dist 26 Jan 02, bott 22 Feb 16 (96.5) n24 t24.5 f24 b24 Absolute bloody nectar. I remember – it must be well over 20 years ago now; maybe 25, sitting in the brewer's office at Glentauchers discussing my appreciation bordering on love of this malt. I even nearly bought the old distillery manager's house to turn into my Scottish HQ. He was a quiet, charming man, the brewer, surprised that anyone outside of the distillery had noticed just how good their whisky was: indeed, I was the first who had ever come to pay their respects...and learn. For it was hardly ever seen as a single malt. This cask, as quiet yet true to the distillery as the old brewer, will give you some insight as to why I have banged the gong so hard and for so long for this distillery which here presents nearly as perfect a single malt as it is a blending whisky. 45.8%. nc ncf sc.

⟐ **Single Cask Collection Glentauchers 17 Years Old 1996** bourbon hogshead (91) n22.5 excellent age-accentuating vanilla comfortably couched by brittle barley; t23 tingling, peppered sugars overcome by a giant wave of juicy barley; the oak is visible on the ebb tide...; f22.5 remains warming with a playful and busy oak-barley interplay; b23 shows this underrated distillery in bright mood. 55.2%. sc.

⟐ **Single Cask Collection Glentauchers 20 Year Old** bourbon barrel, cask no. 3620, dist 04 Apr 96, bott 06 Sept 16 (91.5) n23.5 Swiss Roll with a little lime amid the creamy filling. The oak suggests the vaguest hint of spice, but it is barely a whisper; t22.5 firm grain; the sugars have been equalled by the drier tannins. Vague spice flickers but always the barley stands firm; f22.5 almost a bread crust toastiness; an elegant, unhurried, mildly peppered fade; b23 much more like it: after tasting a few 'Tauchers which barely did this wonderful distillery justice, here is a bottling at last which encapsulates its splendidly subtle fare. Holds its age well. 49.1%. 170 bottles. sc.

That Boutique-y Whisky Company Glentauchers 17 Year Old batch 2 (91) n22.5 t23 f22.5 b23 This distillery is brilliant without even trying... 48.8%. 508 bottles.

⟐ **The Whisky Barrel Burns Malt Glentauchers 8 Year Old 2008** sherry butt, cask no. 900184 (77) n21 t21 f17 b18 Plenty of toffee apple. But the bitterness bites deep and hard. 50%. sc.

⟐ **Whisky Krüger Glentauchers 10 Years Old** bott 2016 (94.5) n24 supremely delicate fruitcake: sultanas rather than raisins, muscovado sugars over molasses; almonds taking the place of walnuts...; the hints of ginger and freshly budding mint takes this to another level...; t23.5 as you expect with a 'Tauchers, the weight is just about faultless. So, too, is the sweet/dry interplay and the pacing of the spices and sugars as they are slowly introduced;

f23 although at its weakest point, the vanillas easily stand up to scrutiny and even add ballast; **b24** one very substantial, high quality and truly sophisticated malt. *62.9%*.

GLENTURRET
Highlands (Perthshire), 1775. Edrington. Working.

Glenturret Aged 8 Years db **(88) n21 t22 f23 b22**. Technically no prizewinner. But the dexterity of the honey is charming, as this distillery has a tendency sometimes to be. *40%*

The Glenturret Aged 10 Years db **(76) n19 t18 f20 b19**. Lots of trademark honey but some less than impressive contributions from both cask and the stillman. *40%*

The Glenturret Aged 15 Years db **(87) n21 t22 f22 b22**. A beautifully clean, small-still style dram that would have benefitted from being bottled at a fuller strength. A discontinued bottling now: if you see it, it is worth the small investment. *40%*

The Glenturret Fly's 16 Masters Edition db **(96) n24.5 t24 f23.5 b24.5** When I first found Glenturret some 30 years so ago, their whisky was exceptionally rare – on account of their size and having been closed for a very long time – but the few bottlings they produced had a very distinctive, indeed unique, feel. Then it changed as they used more Highland Distillers sherry butts which were, frankly, the kiss of death. Here, though, we appear to have reverted back to exactly how it tasted half a lifetime ago. Rich, kissed with copper and stirred with honey. It is, as is fitting to old Fly, the dog's bollocks... *44%. 1,740 bottles.*

⬩ **Glenturret 30 Year Old** db **(94) n23** my word, this is a tired old malt: the oak has ganged up in its most funereal, sawdusty, chalky manner but has been thwarted in its attempt to bury its whisky thanks to some heroic honey and citrus notes which simply refuse to die. Better still, they rally for a copper-rich orange-blossom honey and lime juice hurrah...! **t24** the fabulous honey and maple syrup tones again combine with that coppery sheen to cock a snook at the oak which gathers like vultures just the other side of the lightly-smoked curtain; **f23** miraculously, a little malt enters the fray to add some unexpected lightness to the spicy gloom: once more the rabid oak is thwarted; **b24** the ultimate exhibition of brinkmanship, surely: hangs on to its integrity by a cat's whisker... *43.4%*.

⬩ **Glenturret Peated Drummond** db **(87) n21 t23.5 f21 b21.5** The wide cut from the small still means the odd feint creeps into this one; the peat is too much on the sparse side to paper over the cracks. However, the delivery is something that has to be experienced. A new make freshness can be found all over the show, but even that gives way as the golden syrup and smoke mingle for one of the briefest yet most beautiful star quality moments of the whisky year. *58.9%*.

The Glenturret Peated Edition db **(86) n20.5 t22 f21.5 b22**. Pleasant enough, for sure, even if the nose is a bit rough. But in the grand scheme of things, just another peated malt and one of no special distinction. Surely they should concentrate on being Glenturret: there is only one of those.... *43%*

The Glenturret Sherry Edition db **(78) n19 t21 f19 b19**. Not sure if this sherry lark is the best direction for this great distillery to take. *43%*

The Glenturret Triple Wood Edition db **(84) n20 t22.5 f20 b21.5**. Not the happiest of whiskies, but recovers from its obvious wounds by concentrating on the juicy grain, rather than the grape. *43%*

⬩ **The Cooper's Choice Glenturret 30 Year Old** dist 1986, bott 2017 **(93.5) n23** the aroma of when I used to rub linseed into my bat at the start of a cricket season, or before an important game where I was opening and wanted to get away from the chit-chat of the changing room and concentrate on my game by massaging in the oil...; diced apples and pears...; **t23.5** a rich, sumptuous delivery (from the whisky, not the fast bowler trying to knock my block off at 70mph...) where the barley reigns supreme despite the close attentions of the tannins. Gorgeous small still oils soften any oaky input while a gentle praline and strangely salty Demerara ensure the mid-ground remains beautifully preserved; **f23** spices develop so subtly you at first barely notice they are there. But they sing prettily as the gentle butterscotch unfurls; **b24** what a charming and evocative cask this is. *48.5%. nc ncf sc. The Vintage Malt Whisky Co.*

⬩ **The MacPhail's Collection Glenturret 2004 (84) n20.5 t22.5 f20 b21** A tad heavy on the cut here, which makes for a thick, enjoyable dram but one that doesn't entirely convince; nor, indeed does the late oak involvement. The usual honey notes are at a premium, though there is little shortage of malt and caramel. *43%*.

Old Particular Highland Glenturret 27 Years Old refill hogshead, dist Dec 88, bott Mar 16 **(90.5) n23.5 t22.5 f22 b22.5** Scores extra points for being an exemplary showing of what sets Glenturret apart. A must have for those looking to create a library of malts which perfectly represent their distillery style. *45.4%. nc ncf sc. 264 bottles.*

Old Particular Highland Glenturret 28 Years Old cask no. 11028, dist Nov 87 **(95.5) n24 t23.5 f24 b24** As near as damn it faultless so far as a single cask of Glenturret goes. 51.5%

◇◇◇ **Old Particular Glenturret 28 Years Old** refill hogshead, cask no. 11199, dist Nov 87, bott Jun 16 **(95.5) n24** you know when you are onto a decent Glenturret cask: the honey appears to come in surround sound. A stunning exhibition of heather honey in particular on display while the tannins and barley link majestically to add a subtle and faultless backbone; **t24** the delivery is at first barley concentrate, and with a thick mouth feel to match the flavour intensity. But the honey begins to feed in and make its presence felt...; **f23** such subtle spices amid the honey-soaked oak; **b24.5** simply delicious: the little distillery in very big form. The distillery style distilled, quite literary. 45.9%. nc ncf sc. 171 bottles.

◇◇◇ **That Boutique-y Whisky Company Glenturret 35 Year Old (96) n24.5** Glenturret at its most Perthshire honeyed! This is heather honey distilled, surely; a kind of Highland Park but in the most intense, concentrated form imaginable, complete with a light trail of smoke and geriatric oak prodding you like an impatient pensioner; **t24.5** not that far off perfection. The honey has thinned just enough for it to conquer every corner of the palate and, amazingly, there is even a malty edge to this, not unlike certain toasty malt breakfast cereals. That spices should arrive is an inevitability: the question is, how will they fit in? The answer is soon in coming: perfectly...; **f23** just a little of the jaded oak to the finale, which is understandable, though the gentle smoke and mocha compensates beautifully; **b24** thank heaven they've bottled just enough to keep any self-respecting whisky lover going for a year... 47.7%. 365 bottles.

◇◇◇ **Whisky Broker Glenturret 26 Year Old** Barolo wine barrique, cask no. 220, dist 11 May 94, bott 23 Feb 17 **(88.5) n22** hard as nails. The usual soft honey of this distillery has been brutally usurped by a flinty fruitiness which, while not unattractive, does not speak "Glenturret" to me. A light British Airways boiled tomato sub plot, too...; **t22** sharp delivery – and still with that really crisp fruit edge that gets more winey by the second; **f22.5** outstanding muscovado sugar and spice mix; the fade pulses with escaped barley...at last! **b22** the colour of rust – and there is a distinct steeliness to this one. 55.5%.

GLENUGIE

Highlands (Eastern). 1834–1983. Whitbread. Closed.

Deoch an Doras Glenugie 30 Years Old dist 1980, bott 2011 db **(87) n22 t23.5 f19.5 b22.** It is now 2017 and it has been six long years since this arrived in my tasting room - something I didn't expect to see again: a distillery bottling of Glenugie. Well, technically, anyway, as Glenugie was part of the Chivas group when it died in the 1980s. As far as I can remember they only brought it out once, either as a seven- or five-year-old. I think that went to Italy, so when I walked around the old site just after it closed, it was a Gordon and MacPhail bottling I drank from and it tasted nothing like this! Just a shame there is a very slight flaw in the sherry butt, but just great to see it in bottle again. 52.13%. nc ncf.

GLENURY ROYAL

Highlands (Eastern), 1868–1985. Diageo. Demolished.

Glenury Royal 36 Years Old db **(89) n21 t23 f22 b23.** An undulating dram, hitting highs and lows. The finish, in particular, is impressive: just when it looks on its last legs, it revives delightfully. The whole package, though far from perfect, is pretty astounding. 50.2%

Glenury Royal 40 Year Old Limited Edition dist 1970, bott 2011 db **(84) n20.5 t20 f22 b21.5.** Glenury is these days so rare I kept this back as a treat to savour as I neared the end of the book. The finale throws up a number of interesting citrus equations. But the oak, for the most part, is too rampant here and makes for a puckering experience. 59.4%. 1,500 bottles.

◇◇◇ **Gordon & MacPhail Rare Old Glenury Royal 1984 (95.5) n23** yes, some major tannins. But these are balanced by impeccable salty, malty tones lightly sweetened with heather honey as well as a drier diced coconut; a playful hint of smoke can still be detected even now...; **t24** the texture is truly stunning: the malt and honey have melted into a lightly viscous, confiding and friendly blanket, wrapping the cocoa-sprinkled tannins in an irresistible, balancing sweetness; a little spice seeps out through the middle; **f23.5** a long heather-honey and delicate smoke fade in the tradition of the very best distilleries...; **b25** in the rare instances of the early 1980s I tasted a young Glenury, it was never this good and hardly looked up for 30 years in the cask. But this incredibly rare bottling of the malt, the best I have ever encountered from Glenury and distilled in the final days of its 117 year existence, stands its ground proudly and performs, unforgettably, the Last Post with magical honeyed notes... 46%.

HAZELBURN (see Springbank)

HIGHLAND PARK
Highlands (Island–Orkney), 1795. Edrington. Working.

Highland Park 8 Years Old db (87) n22 t22 f22 b21. A journey back in time for some of us: this is the orginal distillery bottling of the 70s and 80s, bottles of which are still doing the rounds in obscure Japanese bars and specialist outlets such as the Whisky Exchange. 40%

Highland Park 10 Year Old Ambassador's Choice db (74) n17.5 t20 f17.5 b19. Some of the casks are so badly sulphured, I'm surprised there hasn't been a diplomatic incident... 46%

Highland Park Aged 12 Years db (78) n19 t21 f19 b19. Let's just hope that the choice of casks for this bottling was a freak. To be honest, this was one of my favourite whiskies of all time, one of my desert island drams, and I could weep. 40% WB16/048

Highland Park Aged 15 Years db (85) n21 t22 f21 b21. Had to re-taste this several times, surprised as I was by just how relatively flat this was. A hill of honey forms the early delivery, but then... 40%

Highland Park Earl Magnus Aged 15 Years 1st edition db (76.5) n20 t21 f17.5 b18. Tight and bitter. 52.6%. 5976 bottles.

Highland Park Loki Aged 15 Years db (96) n24 t24 f23.5 b24.5 the weirdness of the heather apart, a bit of a trip back in time. A higher smoke ratio than the bottlings of more recent years which new converts to the distillery will be unfamiliar with, but reverting to the levels regularly found in the 1970s and 80s, probably right through to about 1993/94. Which is a very good thing because the secret of the peat at HP was that, as puffed out as it could be in the old days, it never interfered with the overall complexity, other than adding to it. Which is exactly the case here. Beyond excellent! 48.7%. Edrington.

Highland Park 16 Years Old db (88) n23 t23 f20 b22. I tasted this the day it first came out at one of the Heathrow whisky shops. I thought it a bit flat and uninspiring. This sample, maybe from another bottling, is more impressive and showing true Highland Park colours, the finish apart. 40%. Exclusively available in Duty Free/Travel Retail.

Highland Park Thor Aged 16 Years db (87.5) n22.5 t23.5 f19 b22.5. Now, from what I remember of my Norse gods, Thor was the God of Thunder. Which is a bit spooky seeing as hailstones are crashing down outside as I write this and lightning is striking overhead. Certainly a whisky built on power. Even taking into account the glitch in one or two of the casks, a dram to be savoured on delivery. 52.1%. 23,000 bottles.

Highland Park Ice Edition Aged 17 Years db (87) n22 t23 f21 b21. The smoke drifts around unti it finds some spices. Frustrating: you expect it to kick on but it stubbornly refuses to. Caramel and vanilla up front, then bitters out. 53.9%.

Highland Park Aged 18 Years db (95.5) n23.5 t24 f24 b24 If familiarity breeds contempt, then it has yet to happen between myself and HP 18. This is a must-have dram. I show it to ladies the world over to win their hearts, minds and tastebuds when it comes to whisky. And the more time I spend with it, the more I become aware and appreciative of its extraordinary consistency. The very latest bottlings have been astonishing, possibly because colouring has now been dropped, and wisely so. Why in any way reduce what is one of the world's great whisky experiences? Such has been the staggering consistency of this dram I have thought of late of promoting the distillery into the world's top three: only Ardbeg and Buffalo Trace have been bottling whisk(e)y of such quality over a wide range of ages in such metronomic fashion. Anyway, enough: a glass of something honeyed and dazzling calls... 43%

Highland Park Aged 21 Years db (82.5) n20.5 t22 f19 b21. Good news and bad news. The good news is that they appear to have done away with the insane notion of reducing this to 40% abv. The bad news: a sulphured sherry butt has found its way into this bottling. 47.5%

Highland Park Aged 25 Years db (96) n24 t24 f24 b24 I am a relieved man: the finest HP 25 for a number of years which displays the distillery's unmistakable fingerprints with a pride bordering on arrogance. One of the most improved bottlings of the year: an emperor of a dram. 48.1%

Highland Park Aged 30 Years db (90) n22 t22.5 f23 b22.5 A very dramatic shift from the last bottling I tasted; this has taken a fruitier route. Sheer quality, though. 48.1%

Highland Park 40 Years Old db (90.5) n20.5 t22.5 f24 b23.5 Picking splinters from my nose with this one. Some of the casks used here have obviously choked on oak, and I feared the worst. But such is the brilliance of the resilience by being on the money with the honey, you can say only that it has pulled off an amazing feat with the peat. Sheer poetry... 48.3%

Highland Park 50 Years Old dist Jan 60 db (96.5) n24.5 t24 f24 b24 Old whiskies tend to react to unchartered territory as far as time in the oak is concerned in quite different ways.

This grey beard has certainly given us a new slant. Nothing unique about the nose. But when one is usually confronted with those characteristics on the nose, what follows on the palate moves towards a reasonably predictable path. Not here. Truly unique – as it should be after all this time. 44.8%. sc. 275 bottles.

Highland Park Dark Origins db (80) n19 t23 f18 b20. Part of that Dark Origin must be cocoa, as there is an abundance of delicious high grade chocolate here. But the other part is not so much dark as yellow, as sulphur is around on the nose and finish in particular - and does plenty of damage. Genuinely disappointing to see one of the world's greatest distilleries refusing to play to its strengths and putting so much of its weight on its Achilles heel. 46.8%. ncf

Highland Park Earl Haakon db (92) n22.5 t24 f22.5 b23. A fabulous malt offering some of the best individual moments of the year. But appears to run out of steam about two thirds in. 54.9%. 3,300 bottles.

Highland Park Einar db (90.5) n23 soft, warmingly smoky, toffee apple; t23 fresh, salivating delivery but bordered by tannin and imbued with spice; vague heather honey; f22 dry with the tannins and spices buzzing to the end; b22.5 a curious style of HP which shows most of its usual traits but possesses an extra sharpness. 40% WB15/328

Highland Park Freya 1st fill ex-bourbon casks db (88.5) n22 t23 f21.5 b22. The majestic honey on delivery makes up for some of the untidier moments. 52.10%.

Highland Park Harald db (74.5) n19 t20 f17 b18.5. Warrior Harald has been wounded by sulphur. Fatally. 40% WB15/337

Highland Park Hjärta db (79.5) n18.5 t22 f19 b20. In part, really does celebrate the honeycomb character of Highland Park to the full. But obviously a major blemish or two in there as well. 58.1%. 3924 bottles.

Highland Park King Christian db (83.5) n22 t22.5 f18.5 b20.5. A hefty malt with a massive fruit influence. But struggles for balance and to keep full control of the, ultimately, off-key grapey input. Despite the sub-standard finale, there is much to enjoy with the early malt-fruit battles on delivery that offer a weighty and buttery introduction to the diffused molasses and vanilla. But with the spice arrives the Achilles heel... 46.8%

Highland Park Leif Eriksson bourbon and American oak db (86) n22 t22 f21 b21. The usual distillery traits have gone AWOL while all kinds of caramel notes have usurped them. That said, this has to be one of the softest drams you'll find. 40%. Edrington.

Highland Park Ragnavald db (87.5) n21.5 t22 f22 b22. Thickset and muscular, this malt offers a slightly different type of earthiness to the usual HP. Even the malt has its moment in the sun. But the overall portrait hangs from the wall at a slight tilt... 45.05%

Highland Park Sigurd db (96) n23.5 t24.5 f23.5 b24.5 Breath-taking, star-studded and ridiculously complex reminder that this distillery is capable of serving up some of the best whisky the world can enjoy. 43%

Highland Park Svein db (87) n22 t22 f21.5 b21.5. A soft, friendly dram with good spice pick up. But rather too dependent on a tannin-toffee theme. 40% WB15/318

◈ **Cadenhead's Authentic Collection Highland Park 28 Year Old** port cask, dist 1988 (94) n23.5 a peppery fruitiness balances out with the salty malt very attractively; t24 imagine a brand new Jag slipping effortlessly through the gears as it builds up momentum. A silk glove on the steering wheel as the salty moist dates and molasses ride effortlessly over the busy spices; f23.5 only at the very death does the trademark light smokiness begin to filter through..; b24 not often you find a wine cask which works with HP, as this is such a complex whisky the fruit can prevent the most subtle notes being heard. But this is still a very busy and beautifully proportioned dram of the highest order... 49.6%. sc.

◈ **The Cooper's Choice Highland Park 21 Year Old** dist 1995, bott 2017 (89.5) n22 the last time I came across this degree of salt was when the bloke in the Fish 'n' Chip shop went a bit over the top with the seasoning. The most coastal if not maritime HP aroma of all time, surely...indeed, I'm sure I can nose Gannets, Arctic Skuas, Puffins...; t23 eye-wateringly sharp, again as though salt has been added. After calming down a little, heather honey (actually, yes it is...before I remembered this was HP!) makes a significant contribution before a salty vanilla thread re-emerges; f22 a slight tang from the oak offers bitterness, though not before the barley sugar and salted butter makes for an elegant exit; b22.5 not sure if this cask was stored just off the Atlantic...or in it... 49.5%. nc ncf sc. The Vintage Malt Whisky Co.

Edinburgh Whisky The Library Collection Highland Park 2000 first fill ex-bourbon, dist 24 Aug 00, bott 2015 (92) n23.5 t22 f23.5 b23 After the uncharacteristic scramble on delivery this becomes a classic HP for its age, as is the nose. Rather lovely. 46%. sc.

The First Editions Highland Park Aged 18 Years 1997 refill hogshead, cask no. 12099, bott 2015 (91.5) n22 t23 f23.5 b23 Just a little on the tight side at first. Needs persuasion to give up its secrets, but with some cajoling, it finally does...and then doesn't stop yapping... *56.7%. nc ncf sc. 231 bottles.*

Gordon & MacPhail Cask Strength Highland Park 2007 (91.5) n23 t23 f22.5 b23 Beautifully structured. *59.2%*

◇ **Gordon & MacPhail Cask Strength Highland Park 2007** bott 2 Nov 16 (88) n22 one of the lightest HP noses for its age for a very long while: the honey is there but fractured, not its usual, seamless self. The bittiness includes a half-cooked smokiness and unstructured vanilla; t22.5 much better delivery and in keeping with the distillery's style: the peat pops up early and in busy fashion; the honey remains light and non-commital; f21.5 just a slight bitterness further adds; b22 HP in insecure mode: how many will not have quite seen it before... *58.8%.*

◇ **Hunter Laing's Old & Rare Highland Park Aged 18 Years** refill hogshead, dist Sept 97, bott Apr 16 (95) n23.5 heather honey abounds, while a wisp of smoke can be encountered here and there...I kid you not...!! t24 in essence, it's the nose, but now with an extra twist of orange blossom honey; f23.5 dries on distillery lines with some stunning spices bringing up the rear; b24 really, this could come from only one distillery in the world...almost a parody of itself. Beautiful. *54.6%. nc ncf sc. 266 bottles.*

◇ **The MacPhail's Collection Highland Park 1989** (92) n23.5 pure, unambiguous HP: there really is heather honey as well as delicate peat....cliches, perhaps...but undeniably there...; saltier than some bottlings and with a boiled barley sugar candy crispness, too; t23 light on the normal oils but the malt intensifies sublimely. Moves towards a butterscotch middle, yet with the lightest smoke trail imaginable; f22.5 the vanillas push up the weight; a little citrus tang towards the very finish; b23 so many of the distillery's more recognisable traits on delicious display. *43%.*

Scotch Malt Whisky Society Cask 4.212 Aged 19 Years refill hogshead, dist 30 Nov 95, bott 27 Jul 15 (84) n21 t21.5 f20.5 b21. A frustrating dram. Marked down slightly because an HP of this age should be offering so much more, especially when it comes to balance. The fault lies with the cask, which is too obtrusive and injects a tang that subtracts from both the honey and smoke. Harsh words for a harsh whisky. *55.4%. nc ncf sc. 258 bottles.*

◇ **Spirits Shop Selection Highland Park 1992** bourbon cask, bott 2016 (93) n24 superb array of sugars and honeys all ploughed into a lightly oaked field. Chocolate malted milk biscuit aworks so well with the heather and orange blossom honeys; t23.5 slightly fatter than the average HP but the early mix of buttered toast and honey with the pinging spices is a delight; f22.5 bitters vaguely as the oak tires; b23 the nose and delivery are as close to the archetypal HP 25-year-old – well near 25! – as you are likely to find. *51.4%. 278 bottles. A joint bottling with Sansibar Whisky.*

◇ **WoodWinters Northern Star 21 Year Old** dist 1995 (96.5) n24 just a few more phenols than is normally found for a HP of this age and that extra smoke does no harm at all. It would be ridiculous and beyond a cliché to expect heather honey...but there she blows, that understated sweet note that just creeps in above the acidic, anthracite bite and below the soothing citrus which lightens the entire picture; t24 spot on delivery: the spices arrive early, but not before the tannin has already began knocking on the door. Dominant, though, is the gently salted malt which cushions all impacts with a velvet glove; f24 long, lightly smoked and with the gentlest fade of walnut cake accompanying Jamaican Blue Mountain coffee with the most apologetic inclusion of milk and a little dark liquorice on the side; b24.5 for me, 21 was always the optimum age for HP...and always, without exception, in an ex bourbon cask. Or, at least, non-sherry. With a stunning bottling like this, surely some kind of award winner this year, it is hard to argue... *60.7%. sc. 278 bottles.*

◇ **Xtra Old Particular Highland Park 18 Years Old** refill hogshead, cask no. 11364, dist Sept 97, bott Aug 16 (88) n22.5 tangy oak gives a seriously salty edge to the mushy smoke; t22 the honey arrives early but again is tagged by that salivating twang; f21.5 the spices rumble with a little bit of niggle; b22 eye-wateringly bold and penetrating. *54%. nc ncf sc. 285 bottles.*

IMPERIAL
Speyside, 1897. Chivas Brothers. Silent.

Imperial Aged 15 Years "Special Distillery Bottling" db (69) n17 t18 f17 b17. At least one very poor cask, hot spirit and overly sweet. Apart from that it's wonderful. *46%*

Gordon & MacPhail Imperial 1995 (87.5) n21.5 t23 f21 b22. Impressively sweet, with more grist than you might believe possible for a malt this old. Good spice involvement, too. Light, limited but delicious. *43%*

⬩ **Kingsbury Gold Imperial 21 Year Old** hogshead, cask no. 50408, dist 1995 **(84.5)** n20.5 t22.5 f20 b21.5 The nose alone would stop most blenders from making this a force in their creation. But the slow burn of the malt on the palate has many delightful and surprising qualities, especially the sleight of hand so far as the humble sugars are concerned. Light but attractive. *51.7%. 171 bottles. sc.*

Signatory Vintage Un-Chillfiltered Collection Imperial 20 Years Old hogshead, cask no. 50228, dist 18 Sept 95, bott 27 Oct 10 **(89)** n22 t23.5 f21.5 b22 An impressive and enjoyable rendition of a malt which often fails to sparkle. The glitter on delivery is sublime. *56.3%. nc ncf. Bottled for Alca da Fans.*

INCHGOWER
Speyside, 1872. Diageo. Working.

Inchgower 1993 The Manager's Choice db **(84.5)** n21 t21.5 f21 b21. Like your malts subtle, delicate, clean and sophisticated? Don't bother with this one if you do. This has all the feel of a malt that's been spray painted onto the taste buds: thick, chewy and resilient. Can't help but like that mix of hazelnut and Demerara, though. You can stand a spoon in it. *61.9%*

Best Dram Inchgower 35 Years Old (92) n22.5 t23.5 f23 b23 This is so wrong, it's right. They were making big pungent malt like this when I first went to the distillery, at a time when this cask still hadn't matured as far as being called whisky. And though there are no shortage of rough edges, the uncompromising enormity, almost brutality, is something to inspire awe. Outrageously delicious. *476%*

⬩ **Cadenhead's Authentic Collection Inchgower 27 Year Old** bourbon casks, dist 1989 **(89.5)** n22.5 wow...how busy is that...??? Diced orange peel, freshly laid tar for a road, green apple, and undercurrent of barley sugar. Doesn't come more eclectic than that...; t22 aggressive in a delicious kind of way: has the house dirtiness that has been there since it first ran from the still, but the spices and slushing barley juices more than compensate; f22 oily, spicy and some decent late ulmo honey; b23 the Inchgower spirit distilled back in about 1990 was a real roughhouse pretty much devoid of shape and meaning thanks to years of neglect of the overworked stills. As often as not, this type of spirit over good time becomes a genuinely fascinating and entertaining malt. Here is such a case: an excellent reflection of the distillery in its day. *53.2%.*

Gordon & MacPhail Connoisseurs Choice Inchgower 2005 (74) n18.5 t20 f17 b18.5. I have long been looking forward to the day when I get a sexy, clean, delicate Inchgower to wow me. Sadly, today certainly isn't that day... *46%*

⬩ **Hepburn's Choice Inchgower 7 Years Old** sherry hogshead, dist 2008, bott 2016 **(86.5)** n22.5 t21.5 f21 b21.5 Good old Inchgower! If you are looking for a good, earthy malt with a bit of attitude, this is so often your man! Some weak but recognisable oily grape stars in the mid-points. *46%. nc ncf sc. 380 bottles.*

Hepburn's Choice Inchgower 8 Years Old wine finished hogshead, dist 2008, bott 2016 **(81)** n21 t20 f20.5 b19.5. The threads of malt and grape rarely meet. *46%. nc ncf sc. 395 botts.*

⬩ **Hepburn's Choice Inchgower 9 Years Old** refill hogshead, dist 2008, bott 2017 **(84)** n20 t22 f21 b21 Chalk.... *46%. nc ncf sc. 365 bottles.*

⬩ **Hepburn's Choice Inchgower 9 Years Old** refill hogshead, dist 2008, bott 2017 **(91.5)** n22.5 t23 f22.5 b23.5 Cheese. Hard to believe that this and the other Hepburn's Inchgower 2017 bottling are related: they have so little in common. Where the other is dry overall and often grating and tangy, this version abounds in controlled malty sweetness. It possesses the lot: fresh grist, sugared lemon and well-weighted spices. And even some oak-shaved butterscotch to complete the balance. Superb. *46%. nc ncf sc. 278 bottles.*

Maltbarn Inchgower 1990 ex-bourbon cask, bott 2015 **(86.5)** n21.5 t22.5 f21 b21.5. Barely a malt for the squeamish, both the bite and the eye-watering oiliness could easily overcome the faint hearted. But there is also something deliciously uncouth and natural to this which appeals, not least the dominating chocolate fudge. *51.4%. sc. 135 bottles.*

⬩ **Old Malt Cask Inchgower Aged 20 Years** sherry butt, cask no. 12301, dist Sept 95, bott Feb 16 **(88.5)** n22 fights off the fruit to make the malty message loud and clear; t23 superb delivery with an intense, white wine and liquorice main theme; f21 dulls slightly but the damage is limited; some very late cocoa; b22.5 not a faultless cask. But the malt itself has the balls to take on any off-key messages and bang them back into line. *50%. nc ncf sc. 377 bottles.*

Old Masters Inchgower 28 Year Old cask no. 11506, bott 2016 **(87)** n21 t22.5 f21.5 b22. A serious rarity to find a near 30-year-old malt at this kind of strength. It is just as well, for the oils in this maintain the whisky's integrity – especially on the finish. The nose remains dirty in the house style of the time but the delivery and follow-through give much to chew over in a particularly Jack Daniel's kind of way. Indeed, JD lovers might quite enjoy this, though don't expect the same sugar content. 60.2%

Old Particular Speyside Inchgower 20 Years Old refill butt, cask no. 10880, dist May 95, bott Aug 15 (87.5) n21.5 t22 f22 b22. Even after so long a time in such excellent oak, the excesses of the still house cannot be fully corrected or the oils fully managed. But there is no little charm in the essence of must which permeates through this, the nose and delivery being particularly pippy. Lovely whisky, for all its pits and warts. 51.5%. nc ncf sc. 690 bottles.

Old Particular Speyside Inchgower 25 Years Old refill hogshead, cask no. 10879, dist Oct 89, bott Aug 15 (93.5) n24 t23.5 f22.5 b23.5 So rare to find a whisky from this distillery so yielding and complex. Big, but hides it well... 51.5%. nc ncf sc. 294 bottles.

◈ **Provenance Inchgower Aged 8 Years** refill hogshead, cask no. 11227, dist Mar 09, bott May 16 (90.5) n23.5 a typically rough and ready Inchgower nose, but the thickness and intensity of the barley really does hit extraordinary heights; t22.5 bites with confidence as the barley concentrate eats menacingly into the palate leaving some light, oaky tide marks; f22 the youthfulness seems accentuated here but spices add to the controlled mayhem; b22.5 forget the age: this is pure, unsophisticated enjoyment! 46%. nc ncf sc.

INVERLEVEN
Lowland, 1938–1991. Demolished.

Deoch an Doras Inverleven 36 Years Old dist 1973 (94.5) n24 t23.5 f23 b24 As light on the palate as a morning mist. This distillery just wasn't designed to make a malt of this antiquity, yet this is to the manor born. 48.85%. nc ncf. Chivas Brothers. 500 bottles.

ISLE OF ARRAN
Highlands (Island–Arran), 1995. Isle of Arran Distillers. Working.

Isle of Arran Machrie Moor 5th Edition bott 2014 db (91.5) n22.5 t24 f22 b23 A few tired old bourbon barrels have taken the score down slightly on last year. But the spirit itself is nothing short of brilliant. 46% WB16/049

The Arran Malt 10 Year Old db (87) n22.5 t22.5 f20 b22. It has been a while since I last officially tasted this. If they are wiling to accept some friendly advice, I think the blenders should tone down on raising any fruit profile and concentrate on the malt, which is amongst the best in the business. 46%. nc ncf.

The Arran Malt 12 Years Old db (85) n21.5 t22 f20.5 b21 Hmmmm. Surprise one, this. There must be more than one bottling already of this. The first I tasted was perhaps slightly on the oaky side but otherwise intact and salt-honeyed where need be. This one has a bit of a tang: very drinkable, but definitely a less than brilliant cask around. 46%

The Arran Malt Aged 14 Years db (89.5) n22 t23.5 f21.5 b22.5. A superb whisky, but the evidence that there has been a subtle shift in emphasis, with the oak now taking too keen an interest, is easily attained. 46%. ncf.

The Arran Malt Aged 17 Years db (91.5) n23.5 t23.5 f21.5 b23 "Matured in the finest ex-Sherry casks" trills the back label. And, by and large, they are right. Maybe a single less than finest imparts the light furriness to the finish. But by present day sherry butt standards, a pretty outstanding effort. 46%. nc ncf. 9000 bottles. WB15/152

The Arran Malt Fino Sherry Cask Finish db (82.5) n21 t20 f21 b20.5. Pretty tight with the bitterness not being properly compensated for. 50%

Acla Selection Arran 17 Years Old refill sherry cask, dist 1997, bott 2014 (89) n22.5 t23 f21.5 b22 A very old sherry butt, thankfully free from a sulphury curse. More of an intriguing than classy dram. 51.6%. nc ncf.

Acla Selection Arran 17 Years Old rum wood, dist 1997, bott 2014 (88.5) n21.5 t22 f22.5 b22.5 Rum casks have a tendency to give a malt a crisp, if tough, outer shell. This is no exception. 50.7%. nc ncf.

A.D. Rattray Arran 2011 cask no. 5 (80) n22 t21 f18 b19. An eye-watering tang grips this malt. The intensity of the malt almost defies both description and belief. But another tangy note makes for a slightly uncomfortable journey... 58.5%. sc.

BDRAM Isle of Arran 1996 17 Year Old hogshead, cask no. 1293, dist Sept 96, bott Jun 14 (92.5) n23 t23 f23 b23.5 Arran at its least extrovert and most malty and complex. That smoke thread is intriguing: perhaps an ex-Islay cask. Stunning without even breaking sweat. 54.7%. Bottled by Morrison & Mackay Ltd.

C & S Dram Collection Isle of Arran Aged 17 Years sherry puncheon, cask no. 670, dist 28 Apr 97, bott 23 Mar 15 (76) n19.5 t19 f18.5 b19. A tight dram which never relaxes and veers towards an uncomfortable bitterness, despite the odd bout of juiciness. 58.7%. sc. 603 bottles.

Cadenhead's Sherry Cask Arran 19 Year Old Fino sherry cask, dist 1996, bott 2016 (86) **n23 t23 f19 b21.** Mouthwatering and clean for the most part, a nagging bitterness arrives late on. The early moments are monumental, though... 54%. sc.

Chapter 7 Isle of Arran 1996 18 Years Old cask no. 879 (86) **n21.5 t22 f21 b21.5.** An outwardly attractive dram, though hampered by an imbalance between the oak and the malt. A slight tanginess on the finish and sharpness throughout suggests a cask that was not prepared for another 18 years, so best to concentrate on the very fine depth to the malt instead. 57.2%. sc. 262 bottles.

Gordon & MacPhail Connoisseurs Choice Arran 2006 (84) **n21 t22 f20 b21.** Dry, a little tight in places and fails to relax into its normal, complex stride. 46%

⟨⟩ **The Grey Wolf Isle of Arran 21 Year Old 1996** sherry hogshead, cask no. 82 (90.5) **n23.5** wonderful balance and interplay on the fruitcake: a little prickly with dried orange peel giving a tang to the dark sugars; a certain something from the sherry drops it half a point...; **t24** brilliant....just brilliant...! One of the best sherry influenced deliveries ever from Arran: the rich, moist fruitcake meets big, warming spice and surging but controlled tannin. Salivating with both rich, thick barley and juicy sultanas...multi-layered and wonderful! **f20** spicy at first, then slowly unravels with a familiar bitterness...; **b23** though obviously flawed, still not too bad a sherry cask with the dreaded "s" word on slow burn and arriving long after the party... Just live for that delivery... 50.7%. sc. 334 bottles.

Kingsbury Gold Isle of Arran 18 Year Old 1996 hogshead, cask no. 11451 (93.5) **n24 t23.5 f22.5 b23.5** Though Arran, to me, is still at its most interesting when around the dozen years mark with a mix of new and second fill ex-bourbon barrels, this at 18 really does fly the distillery's flag with great distinction. 52.9%. sc. 281 bottles.

Le Gus't Selection IV Isle of Arran 1996 puncheon, cask no. 1634, bott 2015 (68) **n17 t18 f16 b17.** Yes, there are attractive sugars to be had. But you pay a high price with the unforgiving, cask-induced dryness. Grim. 51.1%. sc.

Old Malt Cask Arran Aged 19 Years refill hogshead, cask no. 11885, dist Sept 96, bott Sept 15 (91) **n22 t23 f23 b23** A "new" distillery entering new territory age-wise. Nothing like as integrated at when around the 12-13 mark. But has enough good habits under its belt to comfortably cruise through this test. 50%. nc ncf sc. 288 bottles.

Old Particular Highland Arran 19 Years Old refill hogshead, cask no. 10864, dist Feb 97, bott Jul 15 (88.5) **n22 t22 f22.5 b22** Arran peaks a good half dozen years earlier than this bottling age. So this has done well to last the course – just - and provide attractive and chewable depth. 48.4%. nc ncf sc. 252 bottles.

⟨⟩ **Old Particular Arran 20 Years Old** refill hogshead, cask no. 11345, dist Aug 96, bott Sept 16 (96) **n24.5** a nose worth buying the bottle for alone: play spot the honey as ulmo, heather and Manuka all mix in with the richest of barley characters. Butterscotch abounds, too...; **t24** the oils, thickened further by the intense barley and vanilla, are enlivened by salt and a creamy bourbon vanilla/red liquorice richness; **f23** long. With the tannins being chased by a return of the ulmo honey; **b24.5** an energetic, vibrant yet sensual malt which is defying the years, especially to those who doubted it would stand up to this kind of ageing with such finesse...and that includes me...! This is quite brilliant whisky. 51.5%. nc ncf sc. 287 bottles.

⟨⟩ **Old Particular Arran 21 Years Old** refill hogshead, cask no. 11608, dist Jan 97, bott Mar 17 (92.5) **n23** salted dates melts into a gently spiced liquorice daze...; **t23** never come across a mouth feel from an Arran like this before: the oiliness appears higher than usual but absorbs the toast and orange blossom honey with ease. Like the nose, the fruitiness is no more than window dressing: the real power is held by the tannins; **f23** toasty, with the malt at last vocal but still a big wave of hickory-rich tannin has to be hurdled in the final, spicy waves; **b23.5** a cask beyond its sell by date...but here we're taking a distillery into previously unexplored territory. Truly amazing, historic dramming... 44.4%. nc ncf sc. 136 bottles.

⟨⟩ **Romantic Rhine Collection Isle of Arran 19 Year Old** sherry puncheon, cask no. 1306, dist 17 Sept 96, bott 12 Oct 15 (94) **n23.5 t23.5 f23 b24** Bravo! A sherry butt from this period not caked in sulphur! I remember testing many when the first couple of year's casks had been filled and the majority of sherry butts were sulphur stained. This is as clean as it is delicious: a substantial, unspoiled malt. 52.5%. sc. 120 bottles.

Scotch Malt Whisky Society Cask 121.82 Aged 15 Years refill hogshead, dist 2 Dec 99, bott 22 Jun 15 (94) **n23.5 t24 f23 b23.5** An excellent representation of the distillery: appears to have its character to a tee. 57.6%. nc ncf sc. 269 bottles.

⟨⟩ **Scotch Malt Whisky Society Cask 121.89 16 Year Old** refill ex-bourbon hogshead, dist 2 Dec 99 (92) **n23.5** lovely mix of kumquat and blood orange: the secondary malt phase is both salty and slightly peppery. The oak is uniquely represented by paper, as in a brand new opened book...; **t23** what a charming disposition: neither the faultless barley nor the citrus and pear fruitiness will dominate one over the other. So again the salt leeches in, upping the overall flavour intensity; **f22.5** just the vaguest hint of tired oak tang, but the malt and mocha copes well; **b23** by Arran standards, not the greatest bourbon oak. But the quality is undiminished. 54.1%.

◈ **Simon Brown Arran Distillery 1997** barrel, cask no. 97/1504, dist Aug 97, bott Feb 14 **(96.5) n24.5** not sure about nosing this all day...think I could have my snout in this all week...! The most complex nose so far this year ranging from green tomato to cherry brandy. Yet it is the honey that stars, mainly for the bewildering and glorious subtlety with which it has its say. The oak has a Fox's Party Rings cookie sweetness to it while the ulmo honey is thinned by cucumber and red liquorice...; **t24.5** one would be forgiven for expecting the delivery to be a come down from the nose, yet it is nothing of the sort. A salty gristiness melts into the palate setting up a highly salivating yet astonishingly spicy theme as the oak contributes without a shred of negativity; the honey appears to have been brought back to its flowery components but the sugars are subtle, even and soothing; **f23.5** long, still gently peppery but the vanilla trailing into the distance; **b24** Isle of Arran distillery when wisely kept away from sherry butts (which as often as not renders it malt ordinaire) often boasts all the attributes of a world superdistillery. This wonderful bottling shows exactly why. 46%. nc ncf sc.

◈ **That Boutique-y Whisky Company Arran 19 Year Old** batch 6 **(94) n23.5** as though the cask has been siting for the last 19 years in an orange grove: orange blossom honey dominates, though it appears to have been lightly salted; **t24** quite fantastic! The amazing liveliness to the intense barley and subtle fruits makes this an immediate star turn. Again plenty of salt appears to season and concentrate the flavour profile, though it softens as a light, oily mocha arrives; **f23** long with a marmalade/blood orange tang; somehow the malt can be detected at the very death; **b23.5** I was convinced Arran would struggle to reach this kind of age intact. This, and other recent bottlings of a similar vintage, have proved me quite wrong. 49.7%. 250 bottles.

Whiskybroker Isle of Arran 19 Year Old hogshead, cask no. 1381, dist 23 Sept 96, bott 30 Nov 15 **(88) n22.5 t22 f21.5 b22** Fascinating stuff, but showing distinct oak fatigue. 51.5%. sc.

Whisky Tales Arran 18 Years Old (89) n22.5 t22.5 f22 b22 Entirely enjoyable. But at no moment is this an easy ride. 49.8%

ISLE OF JURA
Highlands (Island–Jura), 1810. Whyte and Mackay. Working.

Isle Of Jura Aged 10 Years db **(79.5) n19 t22 f19 b19.5.** Perhaps a little livelier than before, but still miles short of where you might hope it to be. 40%

Isle Of Jura Aged 16 Years db **(90.5) n21.5 t23.5 f23 b23** A massive improvement, this time celebrating its salty, earthy heritage to good effect. The odd strange, less than harmonious note. But by far and away the most improved Jura for a long, long while. 40%

Isle of Jura 21 Years Old Cask Strength db **(92) n22 t24 f23 b23.** Every mouthful exudes class and quality. A must-have for Scottish Island collectors... or those who know how to appreciate a damn fine malt 58.1%

Isle of Jura 30 Years Old db **(89) n22.5 t22.5 f22 b22.** A relaxed dram with the caramel dousing the higher notes just as they started to get very interesting. If there is a way of bringing down these presumably natural caramels – it is a 30 years old, so who in their right mind would add colouring? – this would score very highly, indeed. 40%

Isle of Jura 40 Years Old finished in oloroso wood db **(90) n23** a different species of Jura from anything you are likely to have seen before: swamped in sherry, there is a vague, rather odd smokiness to this. Not to mention salty, sea-side rockpools. As a pairing (sherry and smoke), the odd couple... which works and doesn't work at the same time. Strange... **t22** syrupy sweet delivery with thick waves of fruit and then an apologetic 'ahem' from the smoke, which drifts in nervously. Again, everything is awkward... **f22** remains soft and velvety, though now strands of bitter, salty oak and molasses drift in and out; **b23** throw the Jura textbooks away. This is something very different. Completely out of sync in so many ways, but... 40%

Jura Elements "Air" db **(76) n19.5 t19 f18.5 b19.** Initially, I thought this was earth: there is something strangely dirty and flat about both nose and delivery. Plenty of fruits here and there but just doesn't get the pulse racing at all. 45%

Jura Elements "Earth" db **(89) n23.5 t22 f21.5 b22.** I haven't spoken to blender Richard Paterson about these whiskies yet. No doubt I'll be greeted with a knee on the nuts for declaring two as duds. My guess is that this is the youngest of the quartet by a distance and that is probably why it is the best. The peat profile is very different and challenging. I'd still love to see this in its natural plumage as the caramel really does put the brakes on the complexity and development. Otherwise we could have had an elementary classic. 45%

Jura Elements "Fire" db (86.5) n22.5 t21.5 f21 b21.5. Pleasant fare, the highlight coming with the vaguely Canadian-style nose thanks to a classic toffee-oak mix well known east of the Rockies. Some botanicals also there to be sniffed at while a few busy oaky notes pep up the barley-juiced delivery, too. Sadly, just a shade too toffee dependent. 45%

Jura Elements "Water" db (73.5) n18.5 t19 f18 b18. Oranges by the box-full trying to get out but the mouth is sent into puckering spasm by the same sulphur which spoils the nose. 50%

 Isle of Jura One For The Road Aged 22 Years Pinot Noir finish db (89) n23 fruit toffee fudge: raisins aplenty; t23 again, pleasant. But more of the same with a really attractive toffee fudge effect and a slow build of spice; f21 seems to hit a one dimensional dead end with a massive build-up of vanilla, though the limited spices continue; b22 enjoyable though ultimately a bit too straight and, just like the single road on Jura, goes nowhere... 47%. nc ncf.

Jura Prophecy profoundly peated db (90.5) n23.5 t23 f22 b22 Youthful, well made and I prophesy this will be one of Jura's top scorers in 2011... 46%

Jura Superstition db (73.5) n17 t19 f18 b18.5. I thought this could only improve. I was wrong. One to superstitiously avoid. 43%

Jura Tastival 2016 triple sherry finish db (67) n17 t18 f15 b17. Sulphur. In triplicate. 51%. ncf.

Jura Turas-Mara db (82.5) n20.5 t22 f19 b21. Some irresistible Jaffa Cake moments. But the oils are rather too severe and tangy. 42%. Travel Retail Exclusive.

Acla Selection Isle of Jura 24 Years Old ex-bourbon hogshead, dist 1988, bott 2013 (88) n21.5 t22.5 f22 b22 A superb recovery from a malt I initially thought had died from old age. No shortage of wrinkles. 47.5%. nc ncf.

The First Editions Jura Aged 24 Years 1991 refill hogshead, cask no. 11791, bott 2015 (88.5) n22 t23 f21.5 b22 Not always a distillery which hits the heights, but this is a sweet and charming bottling. 55%. nc ncf sc. 181 bottles.

 Hepburn's Choice Jura 8 Years Old refill hogshead, dist 2008, bott 2017 (87) n20 t23.5 f21.5 b22 A bipolar malt: after a truly average, off-key nose the delivery – full of voluptuous barley both gristy and even boasting sensual ulmo honey – makes for one of the surprise package whiskies this year. The finish, though, is not all it might be despite the vague spices. 46%. nc ncf sc. 332 bottles.

Kingsbury Silver Isle of Jura 21 Year Old 1992 hogshead, cask no. 10580 (88) n21 t23 f22 b22 Happy to project a bipolar personality. Enjoyable throughout. 46%. sc. 216 bottles.

Old Malt Cask Jura Aged 24 Years refill hogshead, cask no. 12288, dist Feb 92, bott Feb 16 (91.5) n22.5 t23 f23 b23 As enjoyable and relaxed a Jura as I can remember for a long while. 50%. nc ncf sc. 281 bottles.

 Old Malt Cask Jura Aged 25 Years refill hogshead, cask no. 13274, dist Feb 91, bott Feb 17 (81.5) n20.5 t22 f19 b20 Just not enough character or panache to see off the more tangy, faltering elements of the oak. Still, ride that tidal wave of malt when it arrives just after delivery... 50%. nc ncf sc. 168 bottles.

 Provenance Jura Aged 8 Years refill hogshead, cask no. 11628, dist Jul 08, bott Feb 17 (87) n22 t22 f21 b22 Nuttier than a squirrel's jockstrap. 46%. nc ncf sc. 380 bottles.

 Provenance Jura Aged 10 Years refill hogshead, cask no. 11353, dist Apr 06, bott Nov 16 (87.5) n22 t22 f22 b21.5 Great to see Jura at its classic age sans caramel. But it is also lacking on the oak front. Which means we have the malt in its most naked form and though still blushing in its new-make freshness, has body enough to maximise the barley and spices for a very enjoyable experience. Clean, salivating with some excellent muscovado sugars ensuring weight to the texture. 46%. nc ncf sc. 397 bottles.

Scotch Malt Whisky Society Cask 31.30 Aged 26 Years refill hogshead, dist 27 Sept 88, bott 31 Oct 15 (88) n21.5 t22.5 f21.5 b22.5 A curious malt showing its strengths and weaknesses equally. But the good bits are very good... 48.4%. nc ncf sc. 204 bottles.

Xtra Old Particular Highland Jura 25 Years Old refill hogshead, cask no. 11067, dist Feb 91, bott Feb 16 (86.5) n21.5 t22 f21.5 b21.5. Begins with a grudging thinness. Fattens for a short while as the barley beats its chest. But doesn't take long before it returns to its meagre tale. 50.2%. nc ncf sc. 269 bottles

KILCHOMAN

Islay, 2005. Kilchoman Distillery Co. Working.

Kilchoman 2 Isles Single Cask Guze Cask Finish cask no. 688/2010, dist 04 Nov 10, bott 7 Oct 15 db (95.5) n23.5 t24.5 f24 b24.5 My first ever Guze finish, as far as I can remember.

And with it keeping such a low profile, colour apart, hopefully not my last. *60.3%. nc ncf sc. 262 bottles. Bottled for Dominic & Prince.*

Kilchoman 2007 Vintage dist 2007, bott 2013 db **(95.5) n24.5 t24 f23 b24** Credit where credit is due. This malt has moved on in quality expedientially from one vintage to the next since its first unsteady, Bambiesque, feinty bottlings. Not hint of feints now. But excellence is writ large... *46%. WB15/116*

Kilchoman 100% Islay The 5th Edition db **(95.5) n23.5 t24 f24 b24** 100% stunning. *50%. nc ncf.*

❖ **Kilchoman 100% Islay 7th Edition** db **(88) n22.5** a mix of grist and mash room about this: a very flighty aroma with the peat levels low, thus exposing more of the barrel than usual. None of the usual arrogant youth about this, though the citrus style confirms no great age, either; **t22.5** a delicate delivery where the sugars have a bigger than healthy say on delivery. The phenols are flibbertigibbets of things, always there but not making any kind of serious or meaningful contributions; **f21.5** by Kilchoman standards a disappointingly dull finale with a low smoke presence and little more than the vanilla on display: never quite gels; **b21.5** at times a lovely experience, and one showing some older ages than normal. But ultimately unlikely to go down in the annals of Kilchoman as one of their great vintages... Looks like this was taken from the casks right in the middle of the flavours not quite harmonising – it is possible the previous month they had and another two months on they might well have again: an unfortunately timed bottling. *50%.*

Kilchoman Guze Cask Finish cask no. 678/2010, dist 4 Oct 10 db **(94) n23.5 t24 f23.5 b24** Different bottling and strength as the same whisky above. Curiously, the peat on this one is markedly more jagged and confident, although the overall balance and effect is only slightly altered, but enough to chip off the richer aspects of this malt. *59%. nc ncf sc. Bottled for The Wine Boutique Franks, Malta*

Kilchoman Loch Gorm sherry cask, dist 2010, bott 2015 db **(83) n20 t22 f20 b21.** Just not my kind of thing, this type of big peat and grape mix. I'm afraid I stand accused, rightly, of being Gormless... *50%. nc ncf.*

Kilchoman Machir Bay bott 2014 db **(92) n23 t24 f22 b23** Some 25 years ago, Machir Bay would be where my children and I tried to play blow football: it was us against the impossible, relentless winds which howled off the sea with a will and singularity of mind that could not be tamed. There was only ever one winner. So, interesting to see that they have created a malt to reflect those very rare days when you can explore the length of it untroubled by nature. As lovely as this whisky is, I think I would have enjoyed it more had it reflected the Bay in all its fury... *46%. ncf nc. WB15/27*

Kilchoman Machir Bay bott 2015 db **(94.5) n23 t24 f23.5 b24** A thudding, thumping dram hitting you like a Dave Mackay tackle. Big peat, perfectly representing a big malt. *50%. nc ncf.*

Kilchoman Sanaig bourbon & sherry casks, bott 2016 db **(89.5) n23** full on smoke, slightly rounded down by the fruit; **t22** a distinctly muzzled delivery: the peat clears its throat to make a statement when soft grape intervenes, so little is said until the middle ground is reached and an oily smokiness is announced; **f22** slightly thin, despite the oils, and a little light grape accompanying the gentle smoke; **b22.5** never quite seen a Kilchoman toe the line this way before... *46%. nc ncf.*

Kilchoman Single Cask Release bourbon, cask no.473/2008, dist 25 Sep 08, bott 16 Sep 13 db **(95.5) n23.5 t24 f24 b24** Most of the whiskies I have tasted from this distillery this year have been truly exceptional. Here is another one. *61%. ncf nc. Bottled in celebration of the 5th year of The Whisky Show. The Whisky Exchange. WB15/278*

KINCLAITH
Lowlands, 1957–1975. Closed. Dismantled.

Mo Òr Collection Kinclaith 1969 41 Years Old first fill bourbon hogshead, cask no. 301453A, dist 28 May 69, bott 29 Oct 10 **(85.5) n22 t22 f20.5 b21.** Hangs on gamely to the last vestiges of life, though the oak, without being overtly aggressive, is squeezing all the breath of out of it. *46%. nc ncf sc. Release No. 2. The Whisky Talker. 164 bottles.*

KINGSBARNS
Lowland, 2014. Wemyss. Working.

❖ **Kingsbarns Spirit Drink** bott code L 25 02 16 db **(95) n23.5 t24 f23.5 b24** This is the new make spirit from the fledgling Lowlander, Kingsbarns. And whatever their cuts points and running speeds were for this: take note and abide by them! An exceptionally high quality cut which obviously benefits from the added transient richness of a new still but enjoys a sublime sweetness to both the barley and the late cocoa. How promising... 63.5%.

KNOCKANDO

Speyside, 1898. Diageo. Working.

Knockando 1990 db (83) n21 t22 f20 b20. The most fruity Knockando I've come across with some attractive salty notes. Dry, but a little extra malty sweetness these days. 40%

KNOCKDHU

Speyside, 1894. Inver House Distillers. Working.

AnCnoc 12 Year Old db (94.5) n24 t23 f23.5 b24.5 A more complete or confident Speyside-style malt you are unlikely to find. Shimmers with everything that is great about Scotch whisky... always a reliable dram, but this is stupendous. 40%

AnCnoc 16 Years Old db (91.5) n22 sharp, pithy, salty, busy...; t23.5 those salts crash headlong into the taste buds and then give way to massive spice and barley; soft sugars and vanilla follow at a distance; f23 salted mocha and spice; b23 unquestionably the spiciest AnCnoc of all time. Has this distillery been moved to the coast..? 46%

AnCnoc 18 Years Old db (88.5) n22.5 a curious mix of prickly spice and buttered raisin shortcake; t23 the palate is swamped by malt and vanilla; malt sharp and two-toned, as though the third fill bourbon casks more than equal first. But the middle is a little dull, with fruit fudge the order of the day; f21 disappointingly short of charisma: monotone fruit, perhaps, but badly lacking in lengthening sugars; b22 cleaner sherry at work here. But again, the contours of the malt have been flattened out badly. 46%. nc ncf.

AnCnoc 22 Year Old db (87) n22 t21.5 f22 b21.5. Often a malt which blossoms before being a teenager, as does the fruits of Knockdhu; struggles to cope comfortably with the inevitable oakiness of old age. Here is such a case. 46%. Inverhouse Distillers.

AnCnoc 24 Years Old db (94) n23 t24.5 f22.5 b24 Big, broad-shouldered malt which carries a lot of weight but hardly veers away from the massively fruity path. For sherry loving whisky drinkers everywhere... 46%. nc ncf.

AnCnoc 26 Years Old Highland Selection db (89) n23 t22 f23 b21. There is a little flat moment between the middle and finish for which I have chipped off a point or two. That apart, superb. 48.2%

AnCnoc 30 Years Old db (85) n21 t23 f19 b22. Seat-of-the-pants whisky that is just on the turn. Still has a twinkle in the eye, though. 49%

AnCnoc 35 Years Old db (86) n21 t21 f22.5 b21.5. Tries to take the exotic fruit route to antiquity but headed off at the pass by a massive dollop of natural caramels. The slow burn on the spice is an unexpected extra treat, though. 43%

AnCnoc 35 Years Old bourbon and sherry casks db (88) n22.5 t22 f21.5 b22. The usual big barley sheen has dulled with time here. Some attractive cocoa notes do compensate. 44.3%. nc ncf.

AnCnoc 1975 bott 2014 db (90) n23.5 creaking, crumbling oak at every turn. Fortunately there's enough sugar at play – a blend of maple syrup and molasses – to see off any negative points. When some form of equality is established, the rich fruitcake comes out to play...; t23 all kinds of timber notes up front but the fruit gushes in quickly to form a lush cushion. Two year old Melton Hunt Cake with fully burned raisin; f21.5 just a little bit of awkward bitterness – and an odd furriness – joins the fruit; b22.5 if it showed any more signs of age, it'd need its own Zimmer frame. But the deep, fruity sugars are a superb restorative. 44.2%. nc ncf.

An Cnoc 1993 db (89) n22 t21 f24 b22. Quite an odd one this. I have tasted it a couple of times with different samples and there is a variance. This one takes an oakier path and then invites the barley to do its stuff. Delicious, but underscores the deft touch of the standard 12-year-old. 46%

AnCnoc 1994 db (88.5) n22.5 t22.5 f21.5 b22. Coasts through effortlessly, showing the odd flash of brilliance here and there. Just get the feeling that it never quite gets out of third gear... 46%. ncf.

AnCnoc 1995 db (84.5) n21 t22 f20.5 b21. Very plump for a Knockdhu with caramel notes on a par with the citrus and burgeoning bourbon. Some barley juice escapes on delivery but the finish is peculiarly dry for the distillery. 46%

AnCnoc 1999 db (95.5) n24 t24 f23.5 b24 I noticed as I was putting the bottle away that on their back label their description includes "Colour: soft, very aromatic with a hint of honey and lemon in the foreground" and "Nose: amber with a slight yellow hue." Which would make this malt pretty unique. But this is worth getting for far more than just the collectors' item typo: this is brilliant whisky – one of their best vintage malts for a very long time. In fact, one of their best ever bottlings...period. *46%. nc ncf. WB15/160*

AnCnoc 2000 bott Sept 14 db **(87)** n21.5 t23 f21.5 b21.5. Knockdhu whisky is at its best in a judicious mix of ex-bourbon barrels, as it is they which can fully exploit – and allow unrestricted access to show - the abnormal complexity of the malt. It appears sherry butts have been introduced here. And though there is no OTT sulphur, a flattening process – similar to that experienced when caramel is inserted – has occurred. Some lovely chocolate fruit and nut notes, and all round enjoyable stuff. But the higher complexity has been trimmed. *46%. nc ncf.*

AnCnoc 2001 bott Dec 15 db **(92)** n23.5 not sure I can get enough of those citrus notes..wow! t23.5 tell me, 'cos I can't decide: is it the malt or that citrus that is making me drown in my own saliva...? f22 at last the tannins get a word in, though still pretty muted as plenty of toffee makes for a chewy finish; b23 cruises effortlessly along like a 2001 Jag... *46%. nc ncf.*

⬧ **AnCnoc 2002** bott Mar 17, bott code: L17/089 R17/5104 IB db **(86)** n21.5 t23 f20.5 b21 Not a style that naturally suits anCnoc, which is perhaps in a league of its own when it comes to soaring, salivating high-end barley. This, by slightly disappointing contrast, tries to head towards a far more weighted style, which works in part – especially on delivery and for a few toffee-honey waves after – but not for the entire picture. Overall, it is enjoyable and well spiced, but a mushy, tangy, untidy finish shows up the failings of the odd cask used. This is a distillery whose spirit yearns for ex-bourbon so its stunning naked form can be worshipped, loved and salivated over. *46%.*

AnCnoc Barrow 13.5 ppm phenols db **(88)** n22 t21 f23 b22 A quite peculiar Knockdhu. The usual subtle richness of texture is curiously absent. As are friendly sugars. The strange angles of the phenols fascinate, however. *46%. nc ncf. Exclusive to travel retail.*

AnCnoc Blas db **(67)** n16 t18 f16 b17. Blast! Great chocolate. Shame about the sulphur.... *54%. nc ncf.*

AnCnoc Black Hill Reserve db **(81)** n20 t22 f19 b20. The furriness threatened on the nose and realised at the finish does this great distillery no favours at all. *46%. nc ncf. Exclusive to travel retail.*

AnCnoc Cutter 20.5 ppm phenols db **(96.5)** n24 t24 f24 b24.5 Brilliant! An adjective I am far more used to associating with anCnoc than some of the others I have had to use this year. The most Ardbeg-esque mainland malt I have ever encountered. *46%. nc ncf.*

AnCnoc Flaughter 14.8 ppm phenols db **(88.5)** n23 t22 f21.5 b22 interesting to compare the relative heavy handedness of this against the Rutter. A lovely whisky this may be, but has nothing like the poise or balance. *46%. ncf nc. WB15/345*

AnCnoc Peter Arkle Limited Edition db **(87.5)** n22.5 t22.5 f20.5 b22. A floral nose, with lavender and honeysuckle in abundance. Also offers dried orange peel. But the malt doesn't move on from there as one might hope, becoming just a little too sugary and caramel stodgy for the malt to do itself justice. All that said, a great dram to chew on for a few minutes! *46%. ncf nc. WB15/321*

⬧ **AnCnoc Rùdhan** bott code: L16/273 R16/5391 db **(94.5)** n24 a lovely mix of both peat and anthracite reek in hushed and murmured tones but loud enough to eclipse most else. The gristiness appears to also encompass a delicate citrus note and dank bluebell wood, earth and all...; t23.5 just glorious.... It is late Spring and outside my tasting lab I can see a fledgling goldfinch and green finch side-by-side taking their first, nervous, unsure steps to feed themselves. On a nearby tree a baby long-tailed tit is doing the exact same thing. Those tentative movements seem perfectly to reflect the delicate and vulnerable nature of the peat...seemingly moving into new areas of the palate without confidence, but once there soon finding its feet. The malt enjoys a silky sheen attached to the molasses while the spices start quietly but turns up the volume surreptitiously; f23.5 a slightly fuller oil than might be expected helps lengthen the beautifully delicate fade; b24 hard to imagine a mainland Scottish distillery producing a more complex, elegant and wholly ingratiating peated malt... What a gem this is! *46%.*

AnCnoc Rutter 11 ppm phenols db **(96.5)** n24.5 t24.5 f23.5 b24 I remember vividly, at this great distillery's Centenary party exactly 20 years ago this summer, mentioning to the then distillery manager that I thought that the style of the malt produced at Knockdhu was perfectly geared to make a lightly malted peat along the lines of its neighbour, Ardmore. Only for a few weeks of the year I ventured. I'm pretty certain this malt was not a result of that observation, but it is heartening to see that my instincts were right: it's a sensation! *46%. ncf nc. WB15/320*

Whiskyjace 10th Anniversary Knockdhu 7 Years Old 2008 bourbon cask, bott 2015 **(89)** n22 t23 f22 b22 Despite it being too young for its own good, the glass almost explodes with character....!! Just impossible not to love. *55.2%*

LADYBURN

Lowlands, 1966–2000. William Grant & Sons. Closed.

Mo Òr Collection Rare Ayrshire 1974 36 Years Old first fill bourbon barrel, cask no. 2608, dist 10 May 74, bott 1 Nov 11 **(89.5) n22 t23.5 f22 b22.5.** I had a feeling it'd be this distillery when I saw the title on the label... it couldn't be much else! Fascinating to think that I was in final countdown for my 'O' levels when this was made. It appears to have dealt with the passing years better than I have. Even so, I had not been prepared for this. For years during the very early 1990s Grant's blender David Stewart sent me samples of this stuff and it was, to put it mildly, not great. Some were the oakiest malt I ever tasted in my life. And, to compound matters further, the distillery's own bottling was truly awful. But this cask has re-written history. 46%. nc ncf sc. Release No. 4. The Whisky Talker. 261 bottles.

LAGAVULIN

Islay, 1816. Diageo. Working.

Lagavulin 12 Years Old 8th release, bott 2008 db **(94.5) n24 t24.5 f22.5 b23.5.** Sensational malt: simply by doing all the simple things rather brilliantly. 56.4%

Lagavulin 12 Years Old 10th release, bott 2010 db **(94.5) n23.5 t24 f23.5 b23.5.** Keeps on track with previous Releases. Though this is the first where the lowering of the ppms from 50 to 35 really do seem noticeable. Quite beautiful, nonetheless. 56.5%

Lagavulin 12 Year Old refill American oak casks db **(95.5) n23.5** beautifully salty. A squeeze of lime heralds in the phenols which grow to manageable levels; **t24** more explosive depth than a depth charger. The phenols are happy to tag along with a light molasses sweetness and vaguely liquorice drier tone; intriguingly, there is even a touch of underlying youth to this; **f24** at its most comfortable when it is steered a vaguely vanilla-enriched route into the sunset; **b24** at the age I cut my Lagavulin teeth on, long before the 16-year-old was even the twinkle in a blender's eye. Not as peaty as then, to be honest. But for subtlety, this doesn't compare unfavourably... 48.8%. Diageo Special Releases 2015.

◈ **Lagavulin 12 Years Old** db **(96) n24** the exceptional balance between the citrus and vanillas means the hefty peat appears much lighter than it actually is. There is also a slight over-ripe pear beside the passionfruit, and the orange-blossom honey is well tended by muscovado sugars. The peat billows rather than bellows and lands softly on the nose buds, caressing and confiding; **t24** there is a certain youthfulness in the delivery not apparent on the aroma, while the peat has a slightly more jagged edge. The sugars are also more crystalline; **f23.5** soft butterscotch melts into the smoky mass while the spices at last come into play...; **b24.5** just so beautifully made and matured and such a faultless exhibition of weight maximisation from a minimalist impact. Brilliant! 57.7%. Diageo Special Releases 2016.

Lagavulin 16 Years Old db **(95) n24 t24 f23 b24** Although i have enjoyed this whisky countless times socially, it is the first time for a while I have dragged it into the Tasting Room for professional analysis for the Bible. If anyone has noticed a slight change in Lagavulin, they would be right. The peat remains profound but much more delicate than before, while the oils appear to have receded. A different shape and weight dispersal for sure. But the sky-high quality remains just the same. 43%

◈ **Dramfool Avian Gull 8 Year Old** bourbon cask **(95.5) n24** restrained smoke, insofar that it takes its time to build. But as it wars and oxidises, the phenols begin to mount. Quite powerful, acidic, anthracite bite too. Some grapefruit can be found under the ashes...; **t23.5** an oily milk chocolate lead has, at first, as much weight as the smoke. But, as on the nose, it grows and goes; **f24** wonderfully long: the milk chocolate persists, molasses counters the first signs of oak while the density of the phenols lessens by not one iota...; **b24** if Diageo don't bring out an 8-year-old Lagavulin exclusive bourbon cask after this, they must be mad... 59.2%. sc. 202 bottles.

◈ **Gleann Mor Lagavulin** dist 08 May 06 **(95) n24** the stillman should take a bow: this is distillate cut to perfection. So astonishingly clean and precise that the phenols appear to be back to its old 50ppm days thanks to the smoke being uncluttered by over burdensome oils – as well as a used but decent cask which gives a very limited tannin imprint at this stage of development; **t24** simply gorgeous: rarely have I come across a Lagavulin which takes me back to my days of crawling about their warehouses before the distillery's owners lost their sense of fun and proportion. The ratio of peat to sugar appears to have been figured out and executed to the nth degree: a peaty whisky for those looking for a lot more than just peat...; **f23** a vague bitterness takes a point off the tally but the compensating and clever spice build restores half a mark; **b24** a near faultless bottling. If only we could see Lagavulin like this more often: Diageo are missing a trick... 58.6%.

That Boutique-y Whisky Company Lagavulin batch 1 **(94.5)** n23.5 t24 f23.5 b23.5 A very unusual chance to grab a Lagavulin with kindergarten characteristics: rare to find this malt with so little oak etched into it. A real last-thing-at-night malt, or after a meal of steak barely troubled by heat.... Beautifully made and a genuine treat of a dram. *54.5%. 101 bottles.*

That Boutique-y Whisky Company Lagavulin 10 Year Old batch 2 **(96.5)** n24.5 t24 f24 b24 A great whisky from a great distillery plucked at just the right age (indeed, being surprisingly youthful) and in all its naked beauty. Sublime. A bit like a Jim Murray Whisky Bible.... *53.7%. 239 bottles.*

LAPHROAIG

Islay, 1815. Beam Inc. Working.

Laphroaig 10 Years Old db **(90)** n24 t23 f20.5 b22.5 Has reverted back slightly towards a heavier style in more recent bottling, though I would like to see that old oomph at the very death. Even so, this is, indisputably, a classic whisky. The favourite of Prince Charles apparently: he will make a wise king... *40%*

Laphroaig 10 Years Old Original Cask Strength db **(92)** n22 a duller nose than usual: caramel reducing the normal iodine kick; t24 recovers supremely for the early delivery with some stunning black peppers exploding all over the palate leaving behind a trail of peat smoke; the controlled sweetness to the barley is sublime; f23 again there is a caramel edge to the finish, but this does not entirely prevent a fizzing finale; b23 caramel apart, this is much truer to form than one or two or more recent bottlings, aided by the fresh, gristy sweetness and explosive spices. Wonderful! *55.7%*

Laphroaig Aged 15 Years db **(79)** n20 t20 f19 b20. A hugely disappointing, lacklustre dram that is oily and woefully short on complexity. Not what one comes to expect either from this distillery or age. *43%*

Laphroaig 18 Years Old db **(94)** n24 t23.5 f23 b23.5 This is Laphroaig's replacement to the woefully inadequate and gutless 15-year-old. And talk about taking a giant step in the right direction. Absolutely brimming with character and panache, from the first molecules escaping the bottle as you pour to the very final ember dying on the middle of your tongue. *48%*

Laphroaig Aged 25 Years db **(94)** n23 t24 f23.5 b23.5 Like the 27-y-o, an Islay which doesn't suffer for sherry involvement. Very different from a standard, bourbon barrel-aged Laphroaig with much of the usually complexity reined in, though its development is first class. This one's all about effect - and it works a treat! *40%*

Laphroaig Aged 30 Years db **(94)** n24 t23 f23 b24. The best Laphroaig of all time? Nope, because the 40-y-o is perhaps better still... just. However, Laphroaig of this subtlety and charm gives even the very finest Ardbeg a run for its money. A sheer treat that should be bottled at greater strength. *43%*

Laphroaig Aged 40 Years db **(94)** n23 t24 f23 b24. Mind-blowing. A malt that defies all logic and theory to be in this kind of shape at such age. The Jane Fonda of Islay whisky. *43%*

◈ **Laphroaig The 1815 Legacy Edition** bott code: L7059VB1 2070 db **(92.5)** n24 almost Laphroaig in concentrated form. The peat somehow seems intensified and ultra-acidic, as though a different, deeper, darker type of turf has been employed. Then there is the saltiness also, which cries of a sea breeze in the same way as an oystercatcher. The fruit is toasty, but no more than a hint under the shadow of the commanding phenols; t24 soft and loquacious, this tells of grist yielding its sweet, smoky secrets; heather honey and rising spices. The saltiness has receded but is there enough to raise the flavour profiles when need be; f21 the main fruit constituent is a tell-tale furriness which dries the sugars while the smoke and spices continue to pulse; b23.5 a sherry butt away from one of the best new whiskies of the year. *48%. Travel Retail Exclusive.*

Laphroaig Au Cuan Mòr db **(95)** n24 t24 f23 b24 You don't need to squint at the back label to be told that first fill bourbon barrels are at work here: this is where Kentucky, Jerez and Islay merges with breath-taking ease and harmony. *48%. Travel retail exclusive.*

Laphroaig Cairdeas bourbon barrels and Amontillado seasoned traditional hogsheads, bott 2014 db **(92.5)** n22.5 t23 f23.5 b23.5 As dry as Laphroaig gets. Rather beautifully made and so delicate you feel it might simply crumble in your mouth. *51.4%.*

◈ **Laphroaig Four Oak** bott code: L6327VB1 2359 db **(88)** n22 a different style of Laphroaig aroma: thinner in weight with the phenols loitering around rather than ganging up...; t22.5 a thinner body, also, on delivery. Sugars arrive early and in force, mostly of the darker molasses and muscovado style; a degree of lushness develops, though the smoke watches on from a discreet distance; f21.5 just slightly bitter and furry at the death; b22 attractive, but the smoke seems a little in awe of the oak as it is unusually quiet. *40%. Travel Retail Exclusive.*

Laphroaig Lore db (94) n23.5 t24 f23 b23.5 Seeing how much I adore this distillery – and treasure my near 40 years of tasting its exceptional malt and visiting its astonishing home – I left to become my 750th new whisky for the 2016 Whisky Bible. "Our richest expression ever" the label promised. It isn't. Big, fat and chunky? Tick. Bounding with phenols? Yep. Enjoyable? Aye! Richest expression ever. Nah. Not quite. Still, a friendly beast worth cuddling up with. And, whatever they say on the label, this is a stunner! 48%. ncf.

Laphroaig PX Cask bourbon, quarter and Pedro Ximenez casks db (96) n23.5 t24.5 f24 b24. I get the feeling that this is a breathtaking success despite the inclusion of Pedro Ximenez casks. This ultra sweet wine is often paired with smoky malt, often with disastrous consequences. Here it has worked, but only because the PX has been controlled itself by absolutely outstanding oak. And the ability of the smoke to take on several roles and personas simultaneously. A quite beautiful whisky and unquestionably one of the great malts of the year...in spite of itself. 48%. Travel Retail exclusive.

Laphroaig Quarter Cask db (96) n23 t24 f24 b25 A great distillery back to its awesome, if a little sweet, self. Layer upon layer of sexed-up peatiness. The previous bottling just needed a little extra complexity on the nose for this to hit mega malt status. Now it has been achieved... 48%

Laphroaig Select db (89) n22 t22 f23 b22 Missed a trick by not being unchillfiltered at 46%. An apre-taste squint at the back label revealed some virgin oak casks had been used here, which explains much! 40%. WB15/117

Laphroaig Triple Wood ex-bourbon, quarter and European oak casks db (86) n21 t21.5 f21.5 b21. A pleasing and formidable dram. But one where the peat takes perhaps just too much of a back seat. Or, rather, is somewhat neutralised to the point of directional loss. The sugars, driven home by the heavy weight of oak, help give the whisky a gloss almost unrecognisable for this distillery. Even so, an attractive whisky in many ways. 48%. ncf.

⬩ **The First Editions Laphroaig Aged 15 Years 2001** refill hogshead, cask no. 12787, bott 2016 (77) n18 t20 f20 b19 Big peat. Bizarre fruit. Please reconstruct...Meet. Never. Twains. Shall. The. 56.2%. nc ncf sc. 270 bottles.

⬩ **The First Editions Laphroaig Aged 16 Years 2000** refill butt, cask no. 13277, bott 2017 (81) n21 t23 f18 b19 A very different animal to its sister cask 12276. Here a tightness on the nose suggests there may be some sherry cask interference further down the line, which duly occurs. But not after a sensational phenolic blast off involving Fishermen's Friends and liquorice. 58.1%. nc ncf sc. 306 bottles.

The First Editions Laphroaig Aged 19 Years 1996 refill hogshead, cask no. 11784, bott 2015 (95.5) n24 t23.5 f24 b24 The salty sootiness after even all these years suggests a whisky that started somewhere above the 35ppm phenols two decades ago. Uncompromising and confident enough to not worry about showing its age. Take your time to discover the levels of complexity here: you'll be pretty amazed. Love it! 56.5%. nc ncf sc. 188 bottles.

Hidden Spirits Laphroaig LPH.015 14 Years Old cask no. 111712, dist 2000, bott 2015 (92.5) n23 t23 f23 b23.5 A quite lovely bottling, showing the distillery in a rather starched and rigid pose. Yet the excellent oak at play ensures for the drinker that time spent equals complexity discovered. 48%. sc.

MacAlabur Laphroaig 16 Year Old bourbon barrel, cask no. 700288, dist 30 Jul 98, bott 25 Oct 14 (94.5) n23.5 t23.5 f23.5 b24 Refuses to depend on the peat, which it shows with restraint. Elegant and uses the light citrus present to great effect. Charming. 57.3%. sc. 230 bottles.

⬩ **Old Malt Cask Laphroaig Aged 12 Years** refill hogshead, cask no. 13433, dist Sept 04, bott Feb 17 (92) n23.5 something vaguely seminal about this: the peat is like a beacon – it is hard to concentrate on other aspects of the nose when the phenols are this mesmerising...; t24 few malts this year will boast such a splendid and varied array of sugars on delivery, ranging from icing sugar which just melts in the mouth to a more pugnacious and brooding molasses which sits tight and throbs beside the spices; all the time the smoke bellows forth; f21.5 a degree of marmalade bitterness enters the frays: the molassed smoke remains; b23 not perfect: enough faults to underline it was made by man. But seriously big! 50%. nc ncf sc. 324 bottles.

Old Malt Cask Laphroaig Aged 15 Years refill butt, cask no. 11642, dist Apr 00, bott Jun 15 (90) n22.5 t23 f22 b25.5 A moody and deep rendition which never veers off its hefty script. 50%. nc ncf sc. 479 bottles.

Old Malt Cask Laphroaig Aged 15 Years cask no. 11708, dist Apr 00, bott Jul 15 (84.5) n21 t21 f21.5 b21. The oak has given this one a youthful edge for its age. Excellent shape to the smoke, but,overall, feels somehow thin and incomplete. 50%. nc ncf sc. 156 bottles.

Old Malt Cask Laphroaig Aged 15 Years refill butt, cask no. 12537, dist Feb 01, bott Apr 16 (88) n23.5 t23 f19.5 b22 The brash, slightly bitter finale cannot take away from the earlier beauty. 50%. nc ncf sc. 357 bottles.

⟐ **Old Malt Cask Laphroaig Aged 15 Years** refill butt, cask no. 12774, dist Feb 01, bott Aug 16 (68) n17 t18 f16 b17 Even the peat can't hide the sulphur. Mind you, I can see them fighting over this in Germany. Oh well, with my taste buds hoisting the battered white flag that's the end of my working day... 50%. nc ncf sc. 377 bottles.

⟐ **Old Malt Cask Laphroaig Aged 16 Years** refill butt, cask no. 13276, dist Apr 00, bott Feb 17 (93) n23 big, powdery phenols reveal the sugars to be slightly adrift; t23.5 enormous delivery: staggering smoke with a fabulous cloves, mint and molasses; f23 long, with a salty praline finale to the molassed phenols; b23.5 a refill butt that's a clean as a whistle. Just as well, for this is superb! 50%. nc ncf sc. 359 bottles.

Old Particular Islay Laphroaig 14 Years Old refill butt, cask no. 10880, dist Feb 01, bott Aug 15 (95) n24 t23.5 f23.5 b24 Fabulously complex and busy. And always with plenty of feel-good qualities. A classic of its rather unusual type. 48.4%. nc ncf sc. 390 bottles.

Old Particular Islay Laphroaig 15 Years Old refill hogshead, cask no. 10791, dist Jun 00, bott Jun 15 (94) n23.5 t24 f23 b23.5 How can a whisky so big be so subtle? Fabulous pacing to this and an elegance to match its confidence. Beautiful! 48.4%. nc ncf sc. 234 bottles.

Old Particular Islay Laphroaig 15 Years Old refill hogshead, cask no. 10791, dist Jun 00, bott Dec 15 (95) n24 t23.5 f23.5 b24 Very sexy malt. Just purrs at you, sometimes showing its claws...Brilliant! 48.4%. nc ncf sc. 234 bottles.

⟐ **Provenance Laphroaig Aged 10 Years** refill hogshead, cask no. 11333, dist Nov 05, bott Aug 16 (87) n21.5 t22 f21.5 b22 Seriously sooty and just a little on the bitter side. Patchy, though not without some big smoky moments. 46%. nc ncf sc. 403 bottles.

⟐ **Provenance Laphroaig Aged 12 Years** refill hogshead, cask no. 11686, dist Sept 04, bott Feb 17 (87.5) n22 t22 f22 b21.5 Big and gristy. The spices can't make their mind up whether to attack or sit back. The cask offers little and the all-round picture seems blurred and out of focus. Still a treat of peataholics, though... 46%. nc ncf sc. 350 bottles.

Scotch Malt Whisky Society Cask 29.181 Aged 20 Years refill barrel, dist 04 Apr 95, bott 21 Mar 16 (94.5) n23 t24 f23.5 b24 Just love it when a big whisky like this just cruises through the gears, showing its power only as a reminder of its capabilities... 57.6%. nc ncf sc. 204 bottles.

⟐ **Scotch Malt Whisky Society Cask 29.191 16 Year Old** refill ex-bourbon barrel, dist 1 Jul 99 (96) n24.5 exemplary: not only ticks all the boxes, but finds a few extra ones to fill in. Its main storyline is one of peat ash in the hearth: dry with that intricate citrus note that every great Islay seems to possess. No bitterness (unusual for an old Allied cask), no oils, no superfluous sugars, though just the right amount of molasses seeps in. And no wild, over the top, oak - though the tannins bed down with the phenols with exceptional good grace; t24 many messages sent at once on delivery: the oak does hint at this kind of age...but the malt doesn't. The early juiciness celebrates a fresh gristiness which soon sinks into an oily sea. Ulmo honey is hinted at, as is treacle pudding and butterscotch entirely caked in peat; f23 the oils lengthen, the sugars balance.; b24.5 a 16-year-old Laphroaig – interesting to compare with a Lagavulin...! Though not many single casks will outpoint this true classic: indeed, it is nigh impossible to extract more from a single barrel. 59%. 234 bottles.

Svenska Eldvatten Laphroaig 2005 ex-bourbon barrel, dist Mar 05, bott Apr 15 (93.5) n23.5 t23 f23.5 b23.5 Never sets a foot wrong from nose to finale. Excellent! 56.9%. sc.

⟐ **That Boutique-y Whisky Company Laphroaig 12 Year Old batch 1** (72.5) n16 t21 f17.7 b18 Is the modern parlance "whisky fail"? 52.4%. 421 bottles.

Whiskyjace Laphroaig 16 Years Old 1998 bourbon barrel & refill sherry cask, bott 2014 (77) n19 t21 f19 b18. A malt which lurches around the palate like Frankenstein's monster after guzzling back a crate of local slivovitz! The sherry and the peat never find a single point of common ground from start to finish. Not even sulphur at play: seems pretty clean to me. Just a malt, engulfed in discordant wine and peat notes, that refuses to work, other than the neutral early sugars. The lovely people at Whiskyjace; I have a simple question: why? Why.....??? 51.2%

Whisky Tales Laphroaig 18 Years Old (82.5) n20.5 t22.5 f18.5 b21. Some way from a standard Laphroaig. The nose tells the story of a tired cask and gives away the ending: that it will interfere further down the line. And the finish is, indeed, untidy. Some major sugars on show, though, especially on the silky delivery. A buttery smokiness is not without merit. 52.9%

LINKWOOD

Speyside, 1820. Diageo. Working.

Linkwood 12 Years Old db (94.5) n23.5 t24 f23 b24 Possibly the most improved distillery bottling in recent times. Having gone through a period of dreadful casks, it appears to have come through to the other side very much on top and close to how some of us remember it a quarter of a century ago. Sublime malt: one of the most glittering gems in the Diageo crown. *43%*

⬦ **Linkwood Aged 37 Years** dist 1978 db (87.5) n23 t22 f21 b21.5 This is old whisky from a distillery rarely exposed to this kind of antiquity. Rather, this would normally end up giving succour to a high class blend. The lightness of the spirit means that some of its faults a little too clearly exposed here, especially the bitterness at the death. But there would have to be something wrong with you not to savour the blood orange and marmalade thread which ensures the oak doesn't get all its own way. *50.3%. 6,114 bottles. Diageo Special Releases 2016.*

Best Dram Linkwood 14 Years Old (94) n23.5 t23.5f23 b24 As I wrote these notes, a male blackcap jinked around in the bushes outside my window, and under the table in my garden. Yet its early Spring-warbled song was scarcely more lovely or in tune than this whisky... *55.9%*

Fadandel.dk Linkwood 21 Years Old cask no. 7127, dist 5 Jun 95, bott 6 Jun 16 (93) n23 t23.5 f23 b23.5 A quite studied, controlled and elegant dram. *47.5%. nc ncf sc. 237 bottles.*

The First Editions Linkwood Aged 18 Years 1997 refill hogshead, cask no. 11789, bott 2015 (83.5) n21 t21.5 f20 b21. Typically Linkwoodian, in that you are never quite sure what mood it will arrive in. Well, this one's chewing bubblegum −as the nose confirms − and is in a fiery frame of mind. The oak is relentlessly dry at the end. *59.5%. nc ncf sc. 148 bottles.*

⬦ **Gordon & MacPhail Distillery Label Linkwood 15 Year Old** (83) n20 t23 f19 b21 Lots of big, biscuity malt. But a bitterness on the nose and finish is out of keeping with the rich delivery. *43%.*

⬦ **Gordon & MacPhail Rare Vintage Linkwood 1954** (87) n22 t21 f22.5 b21.5 Still hangs on in there, a bit on its last legs....but alive and kicking. Oak − lashings of tannin − is there by the small copse load. Sawdust and pencil shaving for all. But the last pulses of grape offer enough fruit and succour − and succulence − to get the malt through to the end without being further scathed. Some good liquorice and Manuka honey further helps the cause. *40%.*

⬦ **Gordon & MacPhail Rare Vintage Linkwood 1972** (90.5) n22.5 huge vanilla presence: the dry strain of age is beginning to show; t22 eye-watering, puckering tannin delivery. Demerara sugars wok overtime to keep things in order, but it is a struggle; the mid-ground does settle as layers of malt form alongside the oak; f23 that's more like it: some truly classy phrases shape on the palate as the gentle spice and clever use of the late-developing honey ups the complexity; b23 a beautiful malt which takes its time to tame the big age statement but then does so with surprising ease... *43%.*

⬦ **Gordon & MacPhail Rare Vintage Linkwood 1973** (93) n23.5 beautifully manicured old oak radiates serious age with a sub-strata of hickory to ensure you get the message; the acacia honey is measured to perfection; t23 demerara sugar and molasses sweeten the rampant toastiness while some high roast Java coffee also stakes a claim; f23.5 less jostling for position now: relaxed sugars make way for muscovado as a non-specific fruitiness adds to the feeling of great vintage; the lovely Java offers a soothing continuum...; b23 don't know about late night dram: one for first thing in the morning instead of your coffee... *43%.*

⬦ **Hepburn's Choice Linkwood 10 Years Old** refill hogshead, dist 2006, bott 2017 (87.5) n21.5 t22.5 f21.5 b22 The very limited shaping from oak means this is another malt where the barley has an almost disproportionate say. Fortunately, the little oak present is for the good and just gives a slight vanilla and spiced aspect to the grist. Dries attractively. *46%. nc ncf sc. 382 bottles.*

Hidden Spirits Linkwood LKW.716 18 Years Old cask no. LK9716, dist 1997, bott 2016 (94.4) n23.5 t24 f23 b24 Here's a great example of why this makes such superb blending malt: imagine the malty surge this would offer! As it is, as a single malt, not half bad, either... *48%. sc.*

Hunter Laing's Distiller's Art Linkwood Aged 18 Years refill hogshead, dist 1997, bott 2016 (82) n21 t21 f20 b20. A very similar cove to the First Editions Linkwood. An almost identical puckering to the huge dry oak finish, but with less oil to maximise the sugars. *48%. nc ncf sc. 148 bottles.*

Maltbarn Linkwood 1998 ex-bourbon cask, bott 2015 (89.5) n22.5 classic school butterscotch tart; t23 a happy mix of light oak and lighter barley. The sugars have nowhere to hide, so briefly dazzle; f22 the thin finish dries towards spiced cocoa; b22.5 slightly anorexic. But still very pretty. *49.3%. sc. 205 bottles.*

Old Malt Cask Linkwood Aged 18 Years refill hogshead, cask no. 11565, dist Jun 97, bott Jul 15 (87) **n21.5 t22 f21.5 b22.** The accent is firmly on the oak from the first sniff to the last gurgle. At times, there is enough barley to offer a counter point, and a dusting of cocoa to emphasise the oaky dominance. *50%. nc ncf sc. 257 bottles.*

Old Malt Cask Linkwood Aged 18 Years refill hogshead, cask no. 12106, dist Jun 97, bott Nov 15 (95) **n24 t24 f23 b24** A sophisticated dram for those who prefer their Martinis very dry and their whiskies stunning. All too easy to overlook the greatness of this bottling: truly glorious. *50%. nc ncf sc. 335 bottles.*

⬧ **Old Malt Cask Linkwood Aged 19 Years** refill hogshead, cask no. 13269, dist Jun 97, bott Jan 17 (91.5) **n22.5** vanilla appears to carry weight but the light lime touch balances beautifully; **t23.5** succulent delivery with sublime malt. Again the citrus busies itself with seeing off the oak; **f22.5** dries but the oily, milky mocha compensates and lengthens; **b23** the lovey citrus sub-plot enthralls. *50%. nc ncf sc. 303 bottles.*

⬧ **Old Particular Linkwood 21 Years Old** refill hogshead, cask no. 11357, dist May 95, bott Sept 16 (87.5) **n21.5 t22.5 f21.5 b22** Apart from the delivery, when a barley-rich passion appears to overcome it, this is an otherwise shy and quiet dram seemingly trying not to get noticed. Concentrate hard, though, and there are plenty of gooseberry and cocoa notes to also enjoy. *51.5%. nc ncf sc. 283 bottles.*

⬧ **Old Particular Linkwood 21 Years Old** refill hogshead, cask no. 11599, dist Jun 95, bott Mar 17 (92) **n22.5** generous pear drop contribution: beautifully distilled and benefitting from a sympathetic cask; **t23** busy and mouth-watering. The malt begins to intensify but the fruity vanilla offers a timely, creamy balance; **f23.5** now enters into a seriously complex mode with the addition of some measured molasses and spice; the late mocha works a treat; **b23** now that is how you want a 21-year-old Likwood to taste...!! *51.5%. nc ncf sc. 234 bottles.*

⬧ **Scyfion Linkwood Troyanda Zakapattya Wine Cask Finish 19 Years Old** (88.5) **n22.5** busy and spiced. The oaky sub-plot becomes more prevalent the longer you nose...; **t23** sharp and breath-catching delivery: absolutely alive with vivid flavours early on with the grape in the ascendancy. The sugars have a rye-like fruity crispness; **f21** just a little furry and tangy amid the brazen cocoa; **b22** fascinating: multi-layered, though doesn't work on all fronts. But enough major plusses to make for a pleasing experience. *46%.*

Scotch Malt Whisky Society Cask 39.112 Aged 25 Years refill hogshead, dist 16 Oct 89, bott 21 Sept 15 (89.5) **n23.5 t22.5 f22 b22** Enjoys the odd spectacular moment, especially on the nose. But plucked from the warehouse about three summers too late... *49%. nc ncf sc. 248 bottles.*

Scotch Malt Whisky Society Cask 39.117 Aged 24 Years refill hogshead, dist 29 Oct 90, bott 30 Nov 15 (85.5) **n23 t21 f21.5 b20** The texture of this malt is exceptionally soft. Which sits in contrast to the attack of malt and oak, making for the odd uncomfortable moment. A few years beyond its optimum age. *46.5%. nc ncf sc. 204 bottles.*

⬧ **Scotch Malt Whisky Society Cask 39.132 15 Year Old** virgin heavy toast medium char oak butt, dist 1 Jun 00 (87) **n21.5 t23 f21 b21.5** An up and down malt with a massive variance in the way in which it conducts itself. Many people will be bored by the single-minded aspect of the intense cream toffee which dominates the late middle and finish. But that is to overlook the aftermath of the delivery which peaks dramatically with an infusion of spice and salivating barley. Even then the toffee is well represented. *58.6%.*

The Single Cask Linkwood Aged 18 Years cask no. 7122, dist 05 Jun 95, bott 19 Jun 13 (93) **n23 t23.5 f23 b23.5** Beautifully made. Wonderfully matured. Absolute fun! *51.2%. nc ncf sc.*

That Boutique-y Whisky Company Linkwood batch 1 (91) **n22 t23.5 f22.5 b23** The nutty sugars are the star turn. A satisfying and complex malt. *51.2%. 92 bottles.*

That Boutique-y Whisky Company Linkwood batch 2 (85) **n21 t23 f21 b20.** Reminds me of something between central European oak and horse chestnut wood at play here. The chocolate mousse intensity is lovely on one hand. But the overall bigness of the wood really does annihilate any chance of overall balance to match the intriguing flavour profile. In the meantime, any traces of malt have vanished... Still, can't say I don't absolutely love that molassed sugar kick early on. Different. *54.7%. 135 bottles.*

⬧ **That Boutique-y Whisky Company Linkwood 26 Year Old** batch 3 (95.5) **n24** outwardly soft vanilla but sniff below the surface for an almost blackcurrant-sharp fruit note; notice, also, how the tannins have a little more clout than you first think...; **t24** oh, you beauty! This is explosive with a small "e" as though every flavour burst is controlled without being muzzled. Again, there is a degree of fruit to this, now more like a chewy candy, but like the nose it is the grip of the tannin which really pushes the buttons; superb spice throughout; **f23.5** the spices continue on slow burn, the tannins never letting you forget the great age of this untainted malt; **b24** old school Linkwood at its most intense and effervescent. Brilliant. *52.3%. 54 bottles.*

The Whisky Chamber Linkwood 10 Years Old ex-bourbon barrel, cask no. 99/2005, dist 20 Jul 05, bott 05 Jan 16 (88.5) n22 t22.5 f22 b22 A warming, vaguely aggressive dram which rarely steers away from the malty path. 59.3%. nc sc.

LITTLEMILL
Lowland, 1772. Loch Lomond Distillers. Demolished.

Littlemill 21 Year Old 2nd Release bourbon cask db (87) n22 t21.5 f21.5 b22. So thin you expect it to fragment into a zillion pieces on the palate. But the improvement on this as a new make almost defies belief. The sugars are crisp enough to shatter on your teeth, the malt is stone hard and fractured and, on the finish, does show some definite charm before showing its less attractive teeth....and its roots... Overall, though, more than enjoyable. 47%. nc ncf.

Littlemill 25 Year Old db (92.5) n22 t24 f23 b23.5 Another example of a malt which is practically undrinkable in its fiery, punkish youth but that is now a reformed, gentle character in older age. 52%

Littlemill 1964 db (82) n21 t20 f21 b20. A soft-natured, bourbony chap that shows little of the manic tendencies that made this one of Scotland's most-feared malts. Talk about mellowing with age... 40%

Eiling Lim Littlemill 24 Years Old 1990 bott 2014 (82) n21 t20 f21 b20. The anger of its youth has been reduced to the point of this now rocking back and forth in its oaky chair, absent-mindedly singing songs of vanilla and spicy battles of yore... 46.8%. nc ncf sc. 113 bottles. 8th Release.

◇ **Glen Fahrn Airline Nr. 16 Littlemill 23 Year Old** cask no. 16215, dist 1989 (95) n23.5 biting, as Littlemill should. But that doesn't detract from the complexity of the vaguely – and surprisingly – smoked malt which has the odd teaspoonful of golden syrup to soothe things...; t24.5 now that is lush with a capital L: Lush, in fact...; the bite and spices form an almost perfect foil to the syrupy, silky malt. This is like making love where your partner is caressing you sensually with one hand...and using the other to stick three inch nails into you...; f23.5 very milky mocha with insane degrees of malt; b24 another Littlemill that has not only passed the test of time but has a Masters degree... And a must have for those with a penchant for sado-erotic whisky... 52.9%. sc.

◇ **Gordon & MacPhail Rare Old Littlemill 1991** (87) n21 t22.5 f21.5 b22 This is a very odd whisky. Make no mistake: it has its fair share of deliciousness. But its make up means it is so hard to relax to as the pages and chapters of its story on the palate fly past. There is, for instance, a strange fruitiness to this of a style I can't quite pinpoint. Not from the sugars, for sure. A kind of washed out lime. Then there are the big malt notes, enormous and seriously delicious. But just as one is about mark highly, in comes a secondary flavour wave of bitter, unkempt tannin...and malt. But from where...? An enjoyable conundrum. 46%.

◇ **Hunter Laing's Old & Rare Littlemill Aged 27 Years** refill hogshead, dist Nov 88, bott Apr 16 (95) n23 little sign of the usual hostility the nostrils expect to encounter from a Littlemill. The sugars are almost angular in their firmness, crisp and offering both a barley and oaky edge. As intriguing as it is attractive...; t24 wow! Littlemill laying down a sugary red carpet for the tannins to make first an elegant and even entry, allowing the spices to gather in good time. Warming yet always courteous and full of crunchy Demerara quality. Once the brain has come to terms with this, you are fully aware that the barley has stacked in massive proportions; just enough bite and roughage to confirm this is the real thing...; f23.5 long, with the spices still tingling but the barley sugar still in total control...; b24.5 always intriguing to see how one of Scotland's most singular former late distilleries is faring as its stocks around the warehouses begin to thin. And it gladdens my heart to say that this cask is of rare good quality: indeed, it is absolutely delicious – not something that could be said of the spirit when the near uncontrollable stills remained in use a generation ago. Unquestionably one of the greatest Littlemills ever made available to the public: perhaps the surprise turn of the Whisky Bible 2018.. Only 93 bottles, eh? Better get one, then... 57.3%. nc ncf sc. 95 bottles.

LOCH LOMOND
Highlands (Southwestern), 1966. Loch Lomond Distillers. Working.

Loch Lomond Aged 12 Years db (93.5) n22.5 a triangular battle between spices, malt and an almost coppery-metallic fruitiness; t23.5 so succulent! Not sure if the distiller at the time was playing about with some high propane yeast which just explodes with fruit, but there is a richness to this malt which really does deserve applause; f23.5 good grief! I've been through some Loch Lomond casks over the years but not sure where they dug these up from. Never before seen spice quite like it, or such a sublime balance with the fruity malt. And when I say fruit, please don't think grape..; **b24** great to see they now have the stocks to allow this malt to really flex its muscles... 46%. ncf.

Loch Lomond 14 Year Old Peated bourbon cask db (83) **n21 t21.5 f20.5 b20**. Lomond can do a lot, lot better than this. Huge malts but entirely out of sync and never comfortable with the oils present. This isn't the Loch Lomond I know and love. 46% nc ncf.

Loch Lomond Aged 18 Years db (89.5) **n22** subtle, Ardmore-style peat tones sinking into lightly fruited morass; **t23** silky and slick, dark muscovado sugars merge with the more intense malts; **f22.5** a slow re-kindling of almost apologetic smoky embers; the sugars – and probably esters - keep the fruitiness alive; **b22.5** there is always something slightly irresistible when you come across a single malt where the peat beats a gentle rhythm rather than its own chest... 46%. ncf.

Loch Lomond 21 Years Old db (89.5) **n22.5 t23 f22 b22**. A little while since I last tasted this, and pretty close to exactly how I remember it. Seems to revel in its own enormity! 43%

Loch Lomond Organic 12 Year Old bourbon cask db (83.5) **n19 t20 f23 b21.5**. A malty beast. But in some respects has more in common with a German still than a traditional pot. Definite traces of feint. 48%. nc ncf.

Loch Lomond Original bourbon casks db (81.5) **n20 t21 f20 b20.5**. Hmmm. Surprisingly feinty, though the really wide cut does ensure a huge number of flavours. A distinctly German style to this. 40%

Glengarry 12 Year Old db (92.5) **n22.5 t23.5 f23 b23.5** Probably the most intense malt on the market today. Astonishing. And stunning. 46%. ncf.

Inchmurrin 12 Years Old db (86.5) **n21.5 t22 f21.5 b21.5**. A significantly improved dram which is a bit of a malt soup. Love the Demerara injection. 40%

Inchmurrin Aged 15 Years bourbon cask, bott Dec 12 db (86) **n22 t21.5 f21 b21.5**. Slightly tangy with an edge to the cask which interferes with the usual malty pleasure. 46%. nc ncf.

Inchmurrin Aged 18 Years bourbon cask, bott Dec 12 db (92.5) **n22.5 t23.5 f23.5 b23**. Loch Lomond distillery in its brightest colours. 46%. nc ncf. Glen Catrine Bonded Warehouse Ltd.

Inchmurrin Aged 21 Years bourbon cask, bott Dec 12 db (90) **n22 t23 f22.5 b22.5**. This has spent 21 years in a very exceptional cask. Not exactly breathtaking complexity, but what it does is completed with aplomb. 46%. nc ncf. Glen Catrine Bonded Warehouse Ltd.

Inchmurrin Loch Lomond Island Collection 12 Year Old db (87) **n21.5 t22 f21.5 b22**. A thick malty offering with a weighty grist and maple syrup infusion. Big and clumsy. 46%. ncf.

Inchmurrin Island Collection Aged 18 Years db (87) **n21 t22.5 f21.5 b22**. Wow! That is quite a tangle of flavours and messages. Not quite sure where the "summer grass' on the label comes from. But date and walnut cake...now that would have made sense. Big and rather beautiful in an ugly kind of way... 46%. ncf. Loch Lomond Whiskies

Inchmurrin Island Collection Madeira Wood Finish db (77) **n17 t23 f18 b19**. Alas, it wasn't only sherry butts which were sulphur damaged. Mind you, the explosion of golden sultana on delivery is worth the discomfort. 46%. ncf. Loch Lomond Whiskies

◈ **ePower Croftengea 10 Year Old** bourbon hogshead, dist 2006, bott 2016 (84.5) **n19 t23 f21 b21.5** No accolades for the cut, for there are feinty fingerprints all over this. But top marks for the recovery as the sweet, gristy maltiness and the spiced light phenols really are sublime. 51.6%.

◈ **The First Editions Inchmurrin Aged 32 Years 1984** refill hogshead, cask no. 13363, bott 2017 (88) **n21.5** typical Loch Lomond still lumpiness. At its best when a distinctive bourbon sweet resin note wanders through; **t23** what a mouth filler! The most dense malt of the day – and I am about to pack in after nearly ten hours' tasting – with an oily butterscotch and malted loaf middle clinging to the palate; some burnt fudge ambles around, also; **f21.5** a bitter marmalade finale; **b22** thick and satisfying. 46.5%. nc ncf sc. 101 bottles.

Old Malt Cask Inchmurrin Aged 31 Years refill barrel, cask no. 12255, dist Jun 84, bott Apr 16 (91.5) **n22.5 t23 f22.5 b23.5** Brilliant to see this malt in such fine fettle! A rare treat from this uniquely-styled malt. And carries its years effortlessly. 47.1%. nc ncf sc. 288 bottles.

◈ **Old Malt Cask Inchmurrin Aged 32 Years** refill hogshead, cask no. 13362, dist Jun 84, bott Feb 17 (87.5) **n21.5 t23 f21 b22** Some beautiful moments to this one, a malt so thick you feel you need to stir it with a spoon. Not for first time an Inchmurrin fortified with butterscotch and fudge which makes for a big chewy experience. Let down slightly only on the bittering finish. 46.5%. nc ncf sc. 101 bottles.

◈ **Scotch Malt Whisky Society Cask 112.15 16 Year Old** second fill ex-bourbon barrel, dist 25 Jul 00 (91) **n23.5** sublime complexity: layered citrus and spice overlapping. A secondary plane of liquorice-clad bourbon notes play a complex game; **t22.5** only some of the usual oils found on this whisky style but the ones in force ram home the enormity of the malt. Excellent butter and spice throughout; f22 duller vanillas and butterscotch; b23 more saline to this Inchmurrin than is the norm. 56%.

⬥ **Simon Brown Croftengea** ex-bourbon cask, dist Mar 06, bott Jul 16 (84.5) n19 t22.5 f21.5 b21.5 Nothing wrong with the cask. Just not the greatest cut ever taken from a run. A dirty nose flags there are problems and for all the smoky Peak Frean biscuits and dashing smoked maple syrup, it never quite finds its equilibrium. 43%. nc ncf sc.

⬥ **Single Cask Collection Croftengea Aged 10 Years** bourbon hogshead (92) n22.5 chunky, vaguely off beam, a dense smokiness mixed in with moss and tannin: unique! t23.5 sweet to the nth degree at first, the sugars seemingly carved from solidified molten molasses and maple syrup. Slowly, a smokiness emerges...; f23 back now to the oak and an array of subtle spices. A little cooling mint chocolate to finish...; b23 Loch Lomond stills at their most bruising, but this really is a fabulous dram full of weight and charisma. A rare treat! 53.8%. sc.

LOCHSIDE
Highlands (Eastern), 1957–1992. Chivas Brothers. Demolished.
The Cooper's Choice Lochside 1967 Aged 44 Years cask no. 807 (96.5) n24.5 t24.5 f23.5 b24 It is amazing that I had to travel 6,000 miles to find this in British Columbia. But, this is the kind of whisky you would travel four times that kind of distance to experience. Easily one of the top ten single casks I have tasted in the last five years. 41.5%. 354 bottles.

LONGMORN
Speyside, 1895. Chivas Brothers. Working.
Longmorn 15 Years Old db (93) n23 t24 f22 b24 These latest bottlings are the best yet: previous ones had shown just a little too much oak but this has hit a perfect compromise. An all-time Speyside great. 45%

Longmorn 16 Years Old db (84.5) n20.5 t22 f21 b21. This was one of the disappointments of the 2008 edition, thanks to the lacklustre nose and finish. This time we see a cautious nudge in the right direction: the colour has been dropped fractionally and the nose celebrates with a sharper barley kick with a peppery accompaniment. The non-existent (caramel apart) finale of yore now offers a distinct wave of butterscotch and thinned honey...and still some spice. Only the delivery has dropped a tad...but a price worth paying for the overall improvement. Still a way to go before the real Longmorn 16 shines in our glasses for all to see and fall deeply in love with. Come on lads in the Chivas lab: we know you can do it... 48%

⬥ **Longmorn 23 Year Old** db (93) n23 the natural caramels carry a slightly Canadian feel to this; thick vanilla but the layering of malt is stunning; a very slight earthy vegetable note gives weight; t24 dull ulmo honey weaves about the butterscotch and barley sugar like a bat around a tree, flitting here and dipping there; occasional juicy malty shews amazing clarity; f23 in comes the timber and spices, though both are on their best behaviour and offer the barley and butterscotch full respect; b23.5 I can just imagine how this would be such rich top dressing for the finest blend I could concoct: as a single malt it is no less a delight. 48%. ncf.

Longmorn The Distiller's Choice bott 2015/12/09 db (84.5) n21.5 t22 f20.5 b20.5. The steam train depicted on the label would have needed some fuel to get it to its destination. Not enough coal, and it would certainly break down somewhere en route. Likewise, this is underpowered at 40%, with the oils badly broken down, thus allowing the finish to become a little too chalky and one or two less well-balanced notes to have too great a say. Pleasant in its early toffeed maltiness, but a little too tangy for its own good...and just runs out of puff... 40%

Acla Selection Longmorn 21 Years Old bourbon hogshead, dist 1992, bott 2014 (89) n22.5 t22.5 f22 b22 Quite a creamy version. Ultra simplistic for its age, having taken on a fair chunk of natural caramel from the oak. 52.1%. nc ncf.

Gordon & MacPhail Distillery Label Longmorn 2002 (77) n19 t20 f19 b19. I have been marvelling at Longmorn, originally through G&M's astonishing old 12-year-old, longer than a great many readers of this book have been on this planet: certainly before they discovered whisky. And I have never known these great bottlers to get their cask selection for Longmorn this wrong. Despite the attractive marmalade and honey thread, this is disappointing, off-key and incoherent. A one-off, I am sure. 43%

⬥ **Gordon & MacPhail Rare Vintage Longmorn 1967** (87.5) n21.5 t21.5 f22.5 b22 The sheer force of the tannin on the nose warns of a malt which will be taking few prisoners, and so it proves. Many whiskies remind you of certain breakfast experiences, though the one here is burnt toast! It is not until about the fifth mouthful that the palate acclimatises sufficiently to see the sugars, a bit like making out figures in the dark. But as you get accustomed, those sugars turn into more attractive honey tones and no small degree of balance – as well as pleasure – is found. *43%*.

Hidden Spirits Longmorn LNG.315 11 Years Old cask no. 11198, dist 2003, bott 2015 (**96.5**) n24 t24 f24 b24.5 The name "Hidden Spirit" is hardly lost on this pure work of art. How many years – decades even – have I been saying that Longmorn should be bottled no more than 12 years and without added colouring? And here we have it. A single cask, maybe. But the previously hidden beauty of this distillery unmasked and naked for all to see. This has to be in line for a potential Single Cask of the Year... *48%. sc.*

Highlander Inn Longmorn Aged 23 Years cask no. 48514, dist 10 Jan 92, bott 22 Sept 15 (**94.5**) n23.5 t24 f23 b24 A profound malt which projects its impressive personality with gusto. At times closer to bourbon than barley... *48%. sc. 228 bottles.*

◈ **Hunter Laing's Old & Rare Longmorn Aged 30 Years** refill hogshead, dist Oct 85, bott May 16 (**95.5**) n24.5 toffee apple, though we not only have crisp, freshly bitten crunchy ones, but Pink Lady at work, too. Red liquorice also abounds, as do molten muscovado sugars; plenty of vanillas, but these always seem to fade into the apple...; t24 rich and fulfilling delivery with varying aspects of oak. A lovely mix of caramelised biscuit and spiced barley sugar means the vanilla is again restrained; f23 dries, but the fade is slow and elegant; b24 mesmerically beautiful: a rare bottling that does the distillery full justice. This is a work of art. *49.2%. nc ncf sc. 157 bottles.*

Kingsbury Gold Longmorn 18 Year Old 1996 hogshead, cask no. 11443 (**92**) n23 t23 f22.5 b23.5 Hugely satisfying whisky with never a dull moment. *53.9%. sc. 241 bottles.*

Old Particular Speyside Longmorn 18 Years Old new wood hogshead, cask no. 11070, dist Oct 98, bott Feb 16 (**84**) n22 t21 f20 b21. Two distinct strands to this malt. The positive one being the high quality, intense, sweet barley. Less desired is the classic Allied bitter bourbon cask syndrome. *48.4%. nc ncf sc. 328 bottles.*

◈ **Old Particular Longmorn 20 Years Old** refill hogshead, cask no. 11626, dist Oct 96, bott Mar 17 (**90**) n22.5 complex and beautifully weighted. Just a little salt on the lemon-drizzle malt; did I mention the malt....? t23 that salt on the nose certainly ramps up the flavours on delivery: this is mega-intense! One of the maltiest drams of the year by a country mile: Maltesers in concentrated concentrate. Add the salt to the spice and it is impossible not to salivate; f22 fizzles out slightly as the cask tires and bitters slightly; b22.5 Longmorn unplugged. Away from the awful caramel straightjacket in which it is normally found, you can see why blenders love to use this to make the malt in a blend talk very loudly. *51.5%. nc ncf sc. 263 bottles.*

◈ **Old Particular Longmorn 21 Years Old** refill hogshead, cask no. 11334, dist Dec 94, bott Sept 16 (**91**) n22 a curious mix of cucumber on a slightly meaty maltiness; t23.5 the sugars, so shy on the nose, arrive early on in gristy concentrate form. Salivating despite the vaguely bourbon-style liquorice and vanilla beginning to make a weighty statement; f22.5 excellent spice on the long fade; b23 always a treat to taste the distillery's fruits without it being under a toffee blanket. And also slightly younger than its years thanks to a polite though not too indulgent cask... *51.5%. nc ncf sc. 265 bottles.*

Scotch Malt Whisky Society Cask 7.127 Aged 30 Years refill hogshead, dist 24 Sept 95, bott 25 Jan 16 (**92.5**) n23 t23 f23 b23.5 A malt at its very age limit, but wears the wrinkles with panache. *53.1%. nc ncf sc. 24 bottles.*

Scotch Malt Whisky Society Cask 7.129 Aged 30 Years refill hogshead, dist 24 Sept 95, bott 22 Feb 16 (**95.5**) n24 t23.5 f24 b24 Longmorn at its very finest. *57.4%. nc ncf sc. 72 bottles.*

Single Cask Collection Longmorn Aged 23 Years bourbon hogshead (**96**) n24.5 t24 f23.5 b24 Almost impossible to find fault: perfectly distilled and matured in a cask shaped in heaven. A thing of profound beauty. *52.1%. sc.*

That Boutique-y Whisky Company Longmorn batch 1 (**86**) n21 t23.5 f20.5 b21. A lovely dram where the intensity of the malt hurtles through the roof. But from the very first nose, you sense not all is dunky-hory owing to the restrictions of the old bourbon cask. And this is accentuated towards the finale. *52%. 157 bottles.*

◈ **WoodWinters Fiadhaich 27 Year Old** (**95**) n24 take as long as you like: the toffee apple lead has a wonderful supporting cast of Manuka honey, black pepper, red liquorice, butterscotch, oak shavings and salty popcorn which can keep you enthralled for hours...; t24 exemplary weight on delivery: the malt swims in just enough oil to coat the palate separately from the spiced muscovado sugars which are on its heels; f23 the vanilla waves come at varied pace and intensity; the spices persist while the tannins begin to offer a degree of noticeable age; b24 superb! *54.6%. sc. 278 bottles.*

THE MACALLAN

Speyside, 1824. Edrington. Working.

The Macallan 7 Years Old db (89) n23 t23 f21 b22. An outstanding dram that underlines just how good young malts can be. Fun, fabulous and in recent bottlings has upped the clarity of the sherry intensity to profound new heights. 40%

The Macallan Fine Oak 8 Years Old db (82.5) n20.5 t22 f20 b20. A slight flaw has entered the mix here. Even so, the barley fights to create a distinctive sharpness. However, a rogue sherry butt has put paid to any hopes the honey and spice normally found in this brand. 40%

The Macallan 10 Years Old db (91) n23 t23 f21.5 b23.5 For a great many of us, it is with the Mac 10 our great Speyside odyssey began. It has to be said that in recent years it has been something of a shadow of its former great self. However, this is the best version I have come across for a while. Not perhaps in the same league as those bottlings in the 1970s which made us re-evaluate the possibilities of single malt. But fine enough to show just how great this whisky can be when the butts have not been tainted and, towards the end, the balance between barley and grape is a relatively equal one. 40%

The Macallan 10 Years Old Cask Strength db (85) n20 t22 f22 b21. Enjoyable and a would give chewing gum a run for its money. But over-egged the sherry here and not a patch on the previous bottling. 58.8%. Duty Free.

The Macallan Fine Oak 10 Years Old db (90) n23 t22.5 f21.5 b22 Much more on the ball than the last bottling of this I came across. Malts really come as understated or clever than this. 40%

The Macallan Sherry Oak 12 Years Old db (93) n24 t23.5 f22.5 b23 I have to say that some Macallan 12 I have tasted on the road has let me down in the last year or so. This is virtually faultless. Virtually a time machine back to another era... 40%

The Macallan 12 Years Old Sherry Oak Elegancia db (86) n23 t22 f20 b21. Promises, but delivers only to an extent. 40%

The Macallan Fine Oak 12 Years Old db (95.5) n24 faultless, intense sherry light enough to allow the fabulous apple and cinnamon to blend in with the greengage and grape; t24 a near perfect entry: firm, rummy sugars are thinned by a barley-grape double act; juicy yet enough vanilla to ensure structure and layering; f23.5 delicate spice keeps the finish going and refuses to let the muscovado-grape take control; b24 a whisky whose quality has hit the stratosphere since I last tasted it. I encountered a disappointing one early in the year. This has restored my faith to the point of being a disciple... 40%

Macallan Gran Reserva Aged 12 Years db (92) n23 massive cream sherry background with well matured fruit cake to the fore: big, clean, luxurious in a wonderfully old-fashioned way. Oh, and a sprinkling of crushed sultana just in case the grapey message didn't get across... t24 a startlingly unusual combination on delivery: dry yet juicy! The ultra fruity lushness is dappled with soft spices; oak arriving early-ish does little to alter the path of the sweetening fruit; just a hint of hickory reveals the oak's handiwork towards the middle; f22 dry, as oloroso does, with a vaguely sweeter edge sparked by notes of dried date; the delicate but busy spices battle through to the toffeed end; b23 well, you don't get many of these to the pound. A real throwback. The oloroso threatens to overwhelm but there is enough intrigue to make for a quite lovely dram which, as all good whiskies should, never quite tells the story the same way twice. Not entirely without blemish, but I'm being picky. A Macallan soaked in oloroso which traditionalists will swoon over. 45.6%

The Macallan Fine Oak 15 Years Old db (79.5) n19 t21.5 f19 b20. As the stock of the Fine oak 12 rises, so its 15-y-o brother, once one of my Favourite drams, falls. Plenty to enjoy, but a few sulphur stains remove the gloss. 43%

The Macallan Fine Oak 17 Years Old db (82) n19.5 t22 f19.5 b21. Where once it couldn't quite make up its mind on just where to sit, it has now gone across to the sherry benches. Sadly, there are a few dissenters. 43%

The Macallan Sherry Oak 18 Years Old db (87) n24 t22 f20 b21. Underpowered. The body doesn't even come close to matching the nose which builds up the expectancy to enormous levels and, by comparison to the Independents, this at 43% appears weak and unrepresentative. Why this isn't at 46% at the very least and unambiguously uncoloured, I have no idea. 43%

The Macallan Fine Oak 18 Years Old db (94.5) n23.5 t24 f23 b24 Is this the new Fine Oak 15 in terms of complexity? That original bottling thrived on the balance between casks types. This is much more accentuated on a cream sherry persona. But this sample is sulphur-free and quite fabulous. 43%

The Macallan Fine Oak 21 Years Old db (84) n21 t22 f20 b21. An improvement on the characterless dullard I last encountered. But the peaks aren't quite high enough to counter the sulphur notes and make this a great malt. 43%

The Macallan 25 Years Old db (84.5) n22 t21 f20.5 b21. Dry with an even drier oloroso residue; blood orange adds to the fruity mix. Something, though, is not entirely right about this and one fears from the bitter tang at the death that a rogue butt has gained entry to what should be the most hallowed of dumping troughs. 43%

The Macallan Fine Oak 25 Years Old db (90) n22 t23.5 f22 b22.5 The first time I tasted this brand a few years back I was knocked off my perch by the peat reek which wafted about with cheerful abandon. Here the smoke is tighter, more shy and of a distinctly more anthracitic quality. Even so, the sweet juiciness of the grape juxtaposes gamely with the obvious age to create a malt of obvious class. 43%

The Macallan Fine Oak 25 Years Old db (89) n23 t23 f21 b22. Very similar to the Fine Oak 18. However, the signature smoke has vanished, as I suppose over time it must. Not entirely clean sherry, but much remains to enjoy. 43%

The Macallan Fine Oak 30 Years Old db (81.5) n22 t22 f18 b19.5. For all its many riches on delivery, especially those moments of great bourbon-honey glory, it has been comprehensively bowled middle stump by the sherry. Gutted. 43%

The Macallan Millennium 50 Years Old (1949) db (90) n23 t22 f22 b23. Magnificent finesse and charm despite some big oak makes this another Macallan to die for. 40%

The Macallan Lalique III 57 Years Old db (95) n24.5 t23 f23.5 b24. I chose this as my 1,000th new whisky tasted for the 2012 Bible not just because of my long-standing deep love affair with this distillery, but also because I honestly felt it had perhaps the best chance to offer not just a glimpse at the past but also the possibility of a whisky experience that sets the hairs on the back of my neck on end. I really wasn't disappointed. It is almost scary to think that this was from a vintage that would have supplied the whiskies I tasted when getting to first discover their 21-year-old. Then, I remember, I thought the malt almost too comfortable for its age. I expected a bit more of a struggle in the glass. No less than 36 years on, the same thing crosses the mind: how does this whisky find it so easy to fit into such enormous shoes? No experience with this whisky under an hour pays sufficient tribute to what it is all about. Checking my watch, I am writing this just two minutes under two hours after first nosing this malt. The score started at 88.5. With time, warmth, oxidation and understanding that score has risen to 95. It has spent 57 years in the cask; it deserves two hours to be heard. It takes that time, at least, to not just hear what it has to say to interpret it, but to put it into context. And for certain notes, once locked away and forgotten, to be slowly released. The last Lalique was good. But simply not this good. 48.5%

The Macallan 1824 db (88) n24 t23.5 f19 b21.5. Absolutely magnificent whisky, in part. But there are times my job is depressing...and this is one of them.. 48%

The Macallan 1824 Estate Reserve db (90.5) n22 excellent clean grape with an intriguing dusting of mint; t23 almost a Jamaican pot still rum sheen and sweetness; beautiful weight and even some barley present; f22.5 satisfying, gorgeously clean with very good vanilla-grape balance; b23 don't know about Reserve: definitely good enough for the First Team. 45.7%

The Macallan 1824 Select Oak db (82) n19 t22 f20 b21. Soft, silky, sometimes sugary... and tangy. Not convinced every oak selected was quite the right one. 40%

The Macallan 1851 Inspiration db (77) n19.5 t19.5 f19 b19. Flat and uninspirational in 2008. 41%

Macallan Cask Strength db (94) n22 t24 f24 b24. One of those big sherry babies; it's like surfacing a massive wave of barley-sweetened sherry. Go for the ride. 58.6%. USA.

The Macallan Estate Reserve db (84) n22 t22 f20 b20. Doh! So much juice lurking about, but so much bitterness, too. ...grrrrr!!!! 45.7%

The Macallan Fine Oak Master's Edition db (91) n23 t23 f22 b23 Adorable. 42.8%

The Macallan Fine Oak Whisky Maker's Selection db (92) n22 t23 f23 b24. This is a dram of exquisite sophistication. Coy, mildly cocoaed dryness, set against just enough barley and fruit sweetness here and there to see off any hints of austerity. Some great work has gone on in the lab to make this happen: fabulous stuff! 42.8%. Duty Free.

The Macallan Gold sherry oak cask db (89.5) n22 t23.5 f21.5 b22.5. No Macallan I have tasted since my first in 1975 has been sculpted to show the distillery in such delicate form. 40%

The Macallan Oscuro db (95.5) n24.5 t24 f23 b24. Oh, if all sherried whiskies could be that kind - and taste bud-blowingly fabulous! 46.5%

The Macallan Ruby sherry oak cask db (92.5) n23 t24 f22 b23.5. Those longer in the tooth who remember the Macallan 10 of 30 years ago will nod approvingly at this chap. Perhaps one butt away from a gong! 43%.

The Macallan Sienna sherry cask db (94.5) n23 t24 f23.5 b24. The pre-bottling sample presented to me was much more vibrant than this early on, but lacked the overall easy charm and readily flowing general complexity of the finished article. A huge and pleasing improvement. 43%.

The Macallan Rare Cask Black db (83.5) n21.5 t22 f19 b21. Pretty rich and some intense, molasses, black cherry and liquorice notes to die for. But some pretty off-key ones, too. Overall, average fare. 48%

The Macallan Royal Marriage db (89) n23.5 t22.5 f21 b22. Some amazing moments to remember. 46.8%

The Macallan Select Oak db (83) n23 t21 f19 b20. Exceptionally dry and tight; and a little furry despite the early fruitiness. 40%

The Macallan Whisky Makers Edition db (76) n19 t20 f18 b19. Distorted and embittered by the horrific "S" element... 42.8%

The Macallan Woodlands Limited Edition Estate Bottling db (86) n21 t23 f21 b21. Toffee towards the finish brings a premature halt to a wonderfully mollased early delivery. 40%

⬦ **Gleann Mor Macallan 1985** dist 18 Jun 85 (94.5) n23.5 banana and custard, anyone? Some roasted almost with ulmo honey also offers a superb accompaniment to the barley; t24 spices erupt immediately on contact: the rich green barley notes try to douse the flames, but it is futile. The sweetness is demure, though has a hint of mallow and Demerara sugar; f23 the oak shows the odd limp, but the mocha compensates...; b24 one deliciously attractive and spicy Macallan. 53.8%.

Heiko Thieme's 1974 Macallan 65th Birthday Bottling cask no. 16807 dist 25 Nov 74 bott Jul 08 (94) n23 t23 f24 b24 This is not whisky because it is 38%abv. It is Scottish spirit. However, this is more of a whisky than a great many samples I have tasted this year. Ageism is outlawed. So is sexism. But alcoholism isn't....!! Try and become a friend of Herr Thieme and grab hold of something a little special. 38% 238 bottles.

Hunter Laing's Old & Rare Macallan Aged 25 Years refill hogshead, dist May 90, bott Jan 16 (93) n23.5 t24 f22.5 b23 I can remember the day when a Macallan 25-year-old represented the highest peak of Scotland's single malt whisky range. Things have moved on over the years, though this still celebrates a Speysider showing good grace outside its usual comfort zone... 50.3%. nc ncf sc. 212 bottles.

⬦ **Hunter Laing's Old & Rare Macallan Aged 25 Years** refill hogshead, dist Mar 91, bott Jan 17 (91) n23 possesses the little extra weight you expect from the small stills of Macallan and makes superb use of it to thicken the striated malt; t23 the kind of delivery that makes one purr. The oak gets in on the act – and forcefully so – a little too early but the thick, salty barley keeps its balance; f22 the malt marches on at the vanguard of the demure sugars. But the oak does show a little late clumsiness; b23 fabulous weight. 51.2%. nc ncf. 222 bottles.

That Boutique-y Whisky Company Macallan 25 Year Old batch 5 (97) n24.5 t24 f24 b24.5 See my notes for the Hunter Laing 25. Now, this I must say, is not a million miles away from how I remember ye olde Macallan from three decades back... So good I could weep... 48.8%. 126 bottles.

⬦ **That Boutique-y Whisky Company Macallan 29 Year Old** batch 6 (89) n22.5 some serious burnt raisin and molasses; t23.5 sensual and velvety toasty sugars with maybe maple syrup at play; the sugars outperform the plums and sultanas; big spice forms towards the middle; f21 someone forgot to take the fruitcake out of the oven...; b22 you get the feeling the optimum time for this cask may have been five or six years ago. Still, big and full of trademark Macallan richness and, thankfully, no sulphur present. 43.5%. 293 bottles.

⬦ **Xtra Old Particular Speyside Macallan 25 Years Old** refill butt, cask no. 11489, dist Mar 91, bott Nov 16 (94) n23.5 adroitly sweet: a little acacia honey melts into the Lubeck marzipan; such dignity with age...; t23.5 those honeys go into overdrive and bring into the fray a spiced maple syrup. All the time the barley radiates its richness; f23 a little drier as the vanilla drives home; b24 always melts the heart to find an unsullied Macallan showing such marvellously effortless timing and depth. Gorgeous. 51.1%. nc ncf sc. 231 bottles.

MACDUFF

Speyside, 1963. John Dewar & Sons. Working.

The Deveron 12 Year Old db (87.5) n22 t22 f21.5 b22. Buttery and pleasant. But feels like driving a Ferrari with a Fiat Uno engine. Woefully underpowered and slightly too flat in too many places where it should be soaring. The trademark honey notes cannot be entirely defied, however. 40%

The Deveron 18 Year Old db **(94) n24.5** oh well, this is a 20 minuter. Evolves as it warms and oxidises. Almost a sherbet lemon kick at times, with freshly diced apple and halved Chinese gooseberry. The malt is present, but happy for delicate exotic fruits to quietly dominate the show; **t23.5** silky, with much more malt at the helm. A vague bitter tannin note, too; **f22.5** spiced honey alongside that vaguely bitter tannin; **b23.5** each bottle should be stamped" Class: handle with care"... 40%

Endangered Drams Macduff 8 Year Old sherry butt, cask no. 900204, dist 05 Mar 07, bott 01 Sept 15 **(88.5) n22.5 t23 f21 b22** Oooh, so close to being a really excellent dram. 65.4%. sc.

The Golden Cask Macduff 33 Years Old cask no. CM 210, dist 1980, bott 2014 **(87.5) n22 t22.5 f21 b22**. A compact malt for its age, undone slightly by a bitter thread which begins on the nose and peaks on the finish. But being a Macduff, still plenty of honey tones to entertain, admire and celebrate, especially just after the initial delivery. Watch out for the Fisherman's Friend nose which underlines the age. 47.5%. sc. 125 bottles.

Hepburn's Choice Macduff 8 Year Old refill hogshead, dist 2008, bott 2016 **(85.5) n21 t22 f21 b21.5** A very bitty dram, though where it takes off on delivery, with a big fruit note lumping with a slightly salty barley, it soars very high, indeed! 46%. nc ncf sc. 405 bottles.

Old Malt Cask Macduff Aged 18 Years refill hogshead, cask no. 11785, dist Apr 97, bott Aug 15 **(94) n23 t24 f23 b24** Macduff has it within its capabilities of being a truly great distillery. Here we get a good look at the intense, delicious complexity it has to offer. A marvellous malt. 50%. nc ncf sc. 296 bottles.

Old Particular Macduff 25 Years Old refill hogshead, cask no. 11358, dist Dec 90, bott Sept 16 **(88.5) n22.5** a lovely mix of heather honey and marmalade. The oak is just a little off colour; **t22.5** wow! A delivery that has you grabbing the arms of your seat. The intensity of the barley conquers all while the sugars momentarily dazzle. Then comes that oak bite...; **f21.5** the late bitterness is, like the nose, reminiscent of marmalade; **b22** this is a curious soul: the honey is truly resplendent. But there is a little tired oak tang which just chips away at the finer points of what would have been a stunning malt. 49.1%. nc ncf sc. 136 bottles.

The Single Cask Macduff Aged 19 Years cask no. 5278, dist 1991 **(88.5) n22** malty, but offers a distinct nip, too; a vague citrus thread lightens the mood; **t23** much more relaxed on delivery where the barley and caramels merge before the spices arrive; **f21.5** remains malty, with a little extra butterscotch. The tannins bitter; **b22** one of the most simplistic MacDuffs I've encountered in years. The overall malt thrust, though, is excellent. 53.5%. nc ncf sc.

That Boutique-y Whisky Company Macduff batch 2 **(70) n18 t19 f16 b17**. Just...duff... 49.6%. 101 bottles.

That Boutique-y Whisky Company Macduff 11 Year Old (93) n23 orange blossom honey mixes with a blend of vanilla and grist; **t23.5** classy start: the barley is not just lush but also in near concentrated form. The vanilla offers strands of over-ripe banana and spice; **f23** long, with a very distant puff of phenol on the lingering spice; attractive praline on the fade, also; **b23.5** a lilting, pleasantly oiled dram which makes the best from its sugary contours. The most vague hint of smoke pops up randomly. 49.1%. 164 bottles.

That Boutique-y Whisky Company Macduff 18 Year Old batch 3 **(88.5) n22** sharp, angular and green despite its age. Spice and spirit nip are very closely related; **t23** much better: the malt stands its ground with a huge display of intense barley muscling out all-comers. A little saltiness finds a gap, as does a rich biscuit depth, plus a faint milk chocolate inflection; **f21.5** a little lazy and vanilla dominant; **b22** a delicious dram which never seems to settle into a comfortable rhythm but finds the right tune. 48.6%. 372 bottles.

The Warehouse Collection Macduff Aged 18 Years bourbon hogshead, cask no. 5252, dist 09 Sept 97, bott 20 Jan 16 **(95.5) n24 t24 f23.5 b24** A sound, complete whisky where the malt offers a firm texture. A classic of its type. 55.9%. nc ncf. 211 bottles.

The Whisky Barrel Macduff 1990 Burns Malt 25 Years Old cask no. 1271 **(91) n22.5 t23.5 f22 b23** As whisky barrels go, this is a big 'un! And the fruit fair hangs off the oaky branches. 55.4%. sc.

Xtra Old Particular Highland Macduff 25 Years Old sherry butt, dist Feb 90, bott Nov 15 **(74.5) n19 t19.5 f17 b19**. A discordant whisky which never quite finds the right key, as hard as it tries. 54.1%. nc ncf sc. 287 bottles.

MANNOCHMORE
Speyside, 1971. Diageo. Working.

Mannochmore Aged 12 Years db **(84) n22 t21 f20 b21**. As usual the mouth arrival fails to live up to the great nose. Quite a greasy dram with sweet malt and bitter oak. 43%.

⟡ **Mannochmore Aged 25 Years** dist 1990 db **(90)** n22 serious oaky nip and bite. Just when it seems the tannins are becoming a little too much crushed sugared almonds and sweet chestnut drinks in to save the day; t23.5 far more sugars on the delivery than found on the nose; the tannins are almost running amok from the first moment but maple syrup soothes...just; the early spices morph into a more creamy mocha middle; f22 remains dry and borderline OTT with the oak; the sugars go up a gear in dark intensity in order to keep them in check; in the end both are neutered and dull caramel reigns supreme; b23 less a whisky and more a battle, starting on your nose and spreading over onto your palate (a little ironic, seeing as this is whisky number 633 for the year). Will the evil tannins destroy all before them, or can enough sugars be conjured up to keep them at bay? Some may feel the evil forces prevailed, others that it was a victory for the goodies. You decide... 53.4%. 3,954 bottles. Diageo Special Releases 2016.

⟡ **Alos Sansibar Whisky Mannochmore 1988** bott 2016 **(88.5)** n22.5 something of old lumber about this; an old cupboard that has been unopened for a few years. A little tight, but the malt does make the right noises; t22 like the nose, the tart malt, mutedly salivating, feels it is operating in a restricted space; the sugars have just enough attractive edge to carry it; f22 an entirely different phase as a lovely toasty fudge effect wins through; b22 not sure what that was all about. But overall, pretty lovely I must say... 47.9%.

Cadenhead Single Cask Mannochmore 37 Year Old bourbon hogshead, dist 1977 **(95.5)** n23 t24 f24 b24.5 The nose tells of a decade too many summers and out of control tannin. The experience on the palate could not be more different: if you don't have a free half hour to explore this whisky, don't even think about starting on it. Truly fantastic stuff! 49.4%. sc. 210 bottles.

Gordon & MacPhail Connoisseurs Choice Mannochmore 1994 **(95.5)** n24 t24 f23.5 b24 Full of vitality, charm and class. Quite irresistible. 46%.

⟡ **The Whisky Agency Mannochmore 28 Years Old** dist 1988 **(93.5)** n23.5 playfully complex: the sugars have a fruity muscovado lilt and there is still a gristy feel and a touch of peardrop... even after nearly 30 years! Amazing! A little shaved walnut both rounds it off and adds weight; t23.5 just skims the palate with those gentle fruits before heading off onto a more pronounced malty theme; f23 you want the vanilla to go lightly and disturb the buttery malt only enough to quietly remind you of its age: it does exactly that...; b23.5 quite superb. 46%. Bottled for La Maison du Whisky.

⟡ **Whisky-Fässle Mannochmore 10 Year Old** hogshead, dist 1988, bott 2016 **(92)** n23.5 a little liquorice on the heather honey: beautifully weighted and consistent; t23.5 the honey on the nose doesn't disappoint and offers surprising extra weight to the salivating, intense barley; f22 the oak makes a surprising late bitter surge considering the age; b23 impressively confident and solid. A real malty-plus treat. 46%.

MILLBURN

Highlands (Northern), 1807–1985. Diageo. Demolished.

Millburn 1969 Rare Malt db **(77)** n19 t21 f18 b19. Some lovely bourbon-honey touches but sadly over the hill and declining fast. Nothing like as interesting or entertaining as the massage parlour that was firebombed a few yards from my office twenty minutes ago. Or as smoky... 51.3%

MILTONDUFF

Speyside, 1824. Chivas Brothers. Working.

Miltonduff Aged 15 Years bott code L00/123 db **(86)** n23 t22 f20 b21. Some casks beyond their years have crept in and unsettled this one. But some real big salty moments to savour, too. 46%

⟡ **Cadenhead's Authentic Collection Miltonduff 38 Year Old** bourbon casks, dist 1978 **(93)** n23.5 just slightly beyond the point of comfortable exotic fruit: the tannins have a bit of attitude now. But the mix of orange blossom honey and faintest outline of heather honey makes for superb nosing; t23.5 that little bit of spite in the tannins is always evident but, just like the nose, there are so many positives, too. Best is the mouth feel, which is as silky as it gets, and that chocolate orange which lingers with the malt; f23 the bite has gone: just a soft orangey journey home; b23 a great distillery and a great bottling once it comes to terms with its advanced old age... 46.5%.

Cadenhead's Wine Cask Miltonduff 21 Year Old Chateau Lafitte cask, dist 1994, bott Apr 16 **(94)** n23 t23.5 f24 b23.5 Almost arrogantly satisfying. 51.5%. sc. 228 bottles.

⟡ **Gordon & MacPhail Cask Strength Miltonduff 1994** bott 29 Sept 16 **(93.5)** n24 about as clean and voluptuous a fruit involvement as you could dare wish for: the spices and sugars perform at roughly equal volume – which is pretty loud – while a liquorice and honeycomb sub plot gives a rich Kentucky-style involvement, also; **t23.5** wonderfully sweet yet not a cloying moment: lashings of maple syrup and a crisper muscovado and sultana background mixes sublimely with the spice; **f22.5** a blood orange bitterness creeps into the long finish: beware the distant sulphur echo; **b23.5** a stunning, enveloping malt. *60.4%*.

⁜ **Hepburn's Choice Miltonduff 7 Years Old** sherry hogshead, dist 2009, bott 2016 **(73) n17 t21 f17 b18** Very malty and the sugars try manfully to thrive. But, alas, the sherry puts the "duff" in the Miltonduff... *46%. nc ncf sc. 429 bottles.*

⁜ **Hunter Laing's Distiller's Art Miltonduff Aged 22 Years** refill hogshead, dist Apr 94, bott 2016 **(91) n22** diluted manuka honey and vanilla; **t23** mouth-filling delivery with the spices arriving early. Light muscovado sugars and liquorice meet these spices head on while the barley and vanilla battle, albeit rather limply, for the middle ground; **f23** some red liquorice lingers but the barley, still no less salivating, remains the star turn. Just a very slight hint of something distantly smoky to the intriguing finish; **b23** a liquorice chew... *48%. nc ncf sc. 287 bottles.*

⁜ **Hunter Laing's Old & Rare Miltonduff Aged 34 Years** refill hogshead, dist Jun 82, bott Jun 16 **(93) n23.5** massive oak, bordering OTT. Such is the complexity of the vanilla ice cream and lime topping as it mingles with a bourbon-style red liquorice and physalis that the excesses are soon ignored and forgotten; **t23.5** mmmm!!! Just let that concentrated barley melt onto the palate. And, yes, that stubborn old oak is soon in hot pursuit, but again the spices mingling with the muscovado sugars make for a gorgeous experience; **f23** as the sugars slowly fade the oak becomes that little bit louder. But there is still enough barley and friendly vanilla to see this dram home...; **b23** just enough tannin has made a mark here to leave no doubt about the geriatric quality of this malt. Indeed, in lesser whiskies it might have been regarded as too much. But such is the overall high quality, the occasional pulses of big oak can be seen as a proud war wound... *50.8%. nc ncf sc. 196 bottles.*

⁜ **Liquid Sun Miltonduff 20 Years Old** dist 1995 **(92) n23** nose this carefully: it is a blueprint of exactly how this distillery should be at this age. Medium weight with a lovely apple pie and ice cream sweet/sharpness...; **t23.5** ridiculously refreshing for a malt this old: the integrity of the barley is undiminished, the pace of the released sweetness classic; **f22.5** remains juicy well into the fade; a little butterscotch and spice join the malt rather than overtake it; **b23** true Miltonduff in both essence and esprit. *51.1%.*

Maltbarn Miltonduff 1989 ex-bourbon cask, bott 2015 **(76.5) n18.5 t21.5 f18.5 b18.** An almost classic bitter "Allied cask" element to this which sends warning signals to the nose of the bumpy ride ahead. Some cocoa notes try to intervene, as do the Demerara sugars which briefly make for a lovely (if off-key!) delivery. Disappointing. Well, it's Friday 13th, what should I have expected...?. *51.2%. sc. 156 bottles.*

⁜ **Old Malt Cask Miltonduff Aged 21 Years** refill hogshead, cask no. 13271, dist Apr 95, bott Feb 17 **(85) n22.5 t21.5 f20 b21** More than a hint of Cream Soda. Despite some average oak influence the malt comes through mainly unscathed. Disjointed and tangy, though. *50%. nc ncf sc. 269 bottles.*

Old Particular Speyside Miltonduff 15 Years Old refill hogshead, dist Jun 00, bott Aug 15 **(94.5) n23 t24 f23.5 b24** A great distillery going effortlessly through its paces. The span and scope of the barley is truly awesome. Hardly surprising that this malt is key to some of Scotland's very top blends. *48.4%. nc ncf sc. 294 bottles.*

⁜ **Old Particular Miltonduff 21 Years Old** refill barrel, cask no. 11537, dist Feb 95, bott Nov 16 **(88.5) n22** the light sprinkling of vanilla-themed oak is soon overpowered by the wrinkleless barley; **t23** salivating. The body is weak but the malt is deliciously willing; **f21.5** an ultra light fade with again the barley ruling the roost; **b22** a malt which is such ambrosia to a good blender needs just a little more tannin than this to do itself justice when fully exposed. An understated delight, all the same. *51.5%. nc ncf sc. 244 bottles.*

⁜ **Provenance Miltonduff Aged 7 Years** refill hogshead, cask no. 11532, dist Jul 09, bott Nov 16 **(84) n21.5 t21.5 f20 b21** The odd line of marshmallow to be found in the malty text. But so young the writing is barely joined up. *46%. nc ncf sc. 399 bottles.*

The Single Cask Miltonduff 21 Year Old cask no. 2594, dist 07 Feb 02, bott 22 Feb 16 **(90.5) n23 t23 f22.5 b22.5** Simply must be a first fill cask forgotten or inaccessible at the top of a warehouse: it has the feel of a beautiful woman who had spent too many years bathing naked on sun-drenched beaches. *45.8%. nc ncf sc.*

The Warehouse Collection Miltonduff Aged 20 Years bourbon barrel, cask no. 12392, dist 08 Feb 95, bott 30 Oct 15 **(81.5) n20 t21.5 f20 b20.** A particular sharpness to the nose – and again after the raging delivery subsides - would have the men and women in white lab coats marking a little cross next to this one: green, malty and stark. *59.1%. nc ncf. 157 bottles.*

The Whisky Chamber Miltonduff 9 Years Old ex-sherry hogshead, cask no. 900873, dist 28 Jun 06, bott 26 Jan 16 **(88) n22 t22.5 f21.5 b22** Big and spicy. And clean! But not really as balanced as it might have been given a few more years, as the youth is always apparent and argumentative. *59.6%. nc sc.*

◈ **The Whisky Chamber Miltonduff 10 Year Old** 1st fill sherry hogshead, dist 2006 **(84) n22 t23 f19 b20** That this is a first fill sherry cask there is no doubt, delivery has much more in common with Spain than Scotland. The intensity of the grape as it hits the palate is extraordinary – certainly a throwback. But soon a gruff, throaty furriness reveals a degree of weakness that grows. The malt, apart from the odd strata to be found on the nose, has been eviscerated. *59.4%.*

MORTLACH
Speyside, 1824. Diageo. Working.

Mortlach Aged 16 Years db **(87) n20 t23 f22 b22.** Once it gets past the bold if very mildly sulphured nose, the rest of the journey is superb. Earlier Mortlachs in this range had a slightly unclean feel to them and the nose here doesn't inspire confidence. But from arrival on the palate onwards, it's sure-footed, fruity and even refreshing... and always delicious. *43%*

Mortlach 18 Year Old db **(75) n19 t19 f18 b19.** When I first tasted Mortlach, probably over 30 years ago now, it really wasn't even close to this. Something went very wrong in the late '80s, I can tell you...*43.4%. Diageo.*

Mortlach 25 Year Old db **(91.5) n23** just love the lemon grass alongside the liquorice and hickory; **t23.5** thick and palate-encompassing. The sugars are pretty toasty with a light mocha element in play; **f22.5** crisp finale with a return of the citrus, sitting confidently with the late spice; **b22.5** much more like it. The sugars may be pretty full on, but there is enough depth and complexity for a narrative to be told. Very much a better Mortlach on so many levels. *43.4%.*

Mortlach Rare Old db **(79) n20 t21 f19 b19.** Not rare enough... *43.4%. Diageo.*

Mortlach Special Strength db **(79.5) n20 t21.5 f19 b19.** Does whisky come any more cloyingly sweet than Mortlach...? Not in my experience.... *49%. Diageo.*

Cadenhead's Authentic Collection Mortlach 26 Year Old butt, dist 1988 **(76.5) n19 t20 f18 b18.5.** The better grape notes do possess a certain charm. But, sadly, very much a Mortlach of its time. *56.1%. sc.*

Gordon & MacPhail Exclusive Single Malt Mortlach 1994 1st fill sherry butt, cask no. 8180, dist 31 Aug 94, bott Feb 15 **(92) n22.5 t23 f23.5 b23** So good to encounter a pretty unsullied sherry butt: well done G&M. *46%. nc ncf sc. 623 bottles. Bottled for the Swedish Whisky Federation.*

Gordon & MacPhail Rare Vintage Mortlach 1954 (93) n22 t23 f24 b24 Has defied the years to put up a very idiosyncratic performance...Wonderful! *43%*

Hepburn's Choice Mortlach 7 Years Old refill barrel, dist 2007, bott 2015 **(92) n23 t23 b23** Lovers of the original Glenfiddich brand (from just up the road) before it became a dour 12-year-old will fully appreciate this lively offering – as well as be jolted back a fair few years – and, indeed, ponder a much-missed dram. Just so beautiful.... *46%. nc ncf sc. 248 bottles.*

Hepburn's Choice Mortlach 7 Years Old refill hogshead, dist 2008, bott 2015 **(88) n22.5 t22 f21.5 b22** A pleasant if doughy dram missing some of the joie de vivre of Hepburn's 2007 distillation. *46%. nc ncf sc. 427 bottles.*

◈ **Hepburn's Choice Mortlach 7 Years Old** refill hogshead, dist 2010, bott 2017 **(85) n21.5 t22.5 f21 b20** The oak has made a no show, allowing the gristy barley the entire run of the glass. Barely any colour or complexity, it is just as well the spirit is of decent Speyside standard. *46%. nc ncf sc. 404 bottles.*

◈ **Hepburn's Choice Mortlach 8 Years Old** bourbon barrel, dist 2007, bott 2016 **(90.5) n22.5** oily, richly bodied and even some echoes of the lightest phenols drifting on the gristy wind; **t23** stunning texture – and no less stunning sugar-spice interplay. Fattened further by that beautifully delicate smoke element, perhaps from an old Islay cask; **f22.5** long, drying with measured aplomb as the oils fade; **b22.5** great to see this distillery returning to its old excellent self after two decades of grimness. *46%. nc ncf sc. 298 bottles.*

Old Malt Cask Mortlach Aged 11 Years refill hogshead, cask no. 12150, dist Nov 04, bott Nov 15 **(87.5) n21.5 t21.5 f22.5 b22.** Some remnants of the old Mortlach syrupy style here. Heavy duty malt, not without some charm as the muscovado sugar and manuka honey combine, and even offer some attractive liquorice, too. But, at times, it is an undignified grapple, though never less than tasty and always chewy. Oh, those who like the brown Liquorice Allsorts are in for a minor treat here... *50%. nc ncf sc. 435 bottles.*

◈ **Old Malt Cask Mortlach Aged 12 Years** refill hogshead, cask no. 13298, dist Jan 05, bott Feb 17 **(89) n22** intense malt with a dollop of vanilla; **t22** intense malt with two dollops of vanilla; **f23** intense malt with three dollops of vanilla and a squirt of spice; **b22** ok: a bit of a one trick pony, I agree. But some trick! *50%. nc ncf sc. 315 bottles.*

Old Particular Speyside Mortlach 11 Years Old refill hogshead, dist Jan 04, bott Dec 15 **(88.5) n22 t23 f21.5 b22** There is no doubting that after many lean years due to its truly terrible cask portfolio, Mortlach is on the mend. A very presentable, if marginally youthful, dram. *48.4%. nc ncf sc. 381 bottles.*

◇ **Old Particular Mortlach 12 Years Old** refill hogshead, cask no. 11595, dist Mar 05, bott Apr 17 **(90) n22** classic sugared almonds; **t23** vanilla ice cream of the extra creamy variety; big gristy-sweet barley with an eye-watering grassiness, also; **f22.5** wonderful slow infusion of tannins introduces the age with classy nonchalance; **b22.5** one very fat Speysider...! *48.4%. nc ncf sc. 329 bottles.*

Scotch Malt Whisky Society Cask 76.122 Aged 27 Years refill hogshead, dist 22 Sept 87, bott 23 Mar 15 **(85.5) n22 t22.5 f20 b21.** The finish suggests this was an early treated cask, when the distillery owners put a sherry-like concoction into the barrel to give it a Spanish butt effect. Sadly, most had a sulphur edge. Here the sulphur is quite light, so it may have escaped the worst of the treatment. Enough juicy sweet grape to still impress. *53.6%. nc ncf sc. 211 bottles.*

◇ **Scotch Malt Whisky Society Cask 76.131 15 Year Old** first fill French oak hogshead, dist 30 Sept 01 **(86.5) n22.5 t21.5 f21 b21.5** You can use the best oak on the planet...it will take you so far: probably in this case from about 81 points to nearly 87. This is indifferent distillate and only the boldness yet restrained elegance of the tannin saves the day. Excellent chocolate nut. *57.8%.*

Scyfion Mortlach 1996 Odesskoe Chernoe cask finish, bott 2015 **(96.5) n23.5 t24.5 f24 b24.5** The first time in over 15,000 whiskies tasted for the Bible I have encountered a Odesskoe Chernoe finish. I sincerely hope it shall not be the last: an absolutely inspired choice. Make no mistake: this is a masterpiece. *46%. nc ncf sc. 330 bottles.*

That Boutique-y Whisky Company Mortlach batch 1 **(84) n20.5 t21.5 f21 b21.** A tetchy, impatient whisky, harrying the taste buds with its sharp, vaguely off key maltiness. Got to admire its eye-watering qualities, for all its limitations. *49.6%. 89 bottles.*

◇ **That Boutique-y Whisky Company Mortlach 18 Year Old** batch 3 **(85.5) n21 t22 f21 b21.5** Not quite this distillery's finest vintage. Heavy and sticky on the palate having been cumbersome on the nose. Furry on the finish. Love the mucky molasses, though! *48.9%. 363 bottles.*

◇ **That Boutique-y Whisky Company Mortlach 22 Year Old** batch 4 **(87.5) n21 t23 f21.5 b22** Unusually malty and intense for a Mortlach of this period with some massive barley sugar notes. Some of the gluey untidiness that is the distillery's signature but the big malt wins! *52.6%. 200 bottles.*

MOSSTOWIE
Speyside, 1964–1981. Chivas Brothers. Closed.

Rare Old Mosstowie 1979 (84.5) n21.5 t21 f21 b21. Edging inextricably well beyond its sell by date. But there is a lovely walnut cream cake (topped off with brown sugar and spices) to this which warms the cockles. Bless... *43%. Gordon & MacPhail.*

NORTH PORT
Highlands (Eastern), 1820–1983. Diageo. Demolished.

Brechin 1977 db **(78) n19 t21 f18 b20.** Fire and brimstone was never an unknown quantity with the whisky from this doomed distillery. Some soothing oils are poured on this troubled – and sometimes attractively honeyed – water of life. *54.2%*

OBAN
Highlands (Western), 1794. Diageo. Working.

Oban 14 Years Old db **(79) n19 t22 f18 b20.** Absolutely all over the place. The cask selection sits very uncomfortably with the malt. I look forward to the resumption of normality to this great but ill-served distillery. *43%*

Oban The Distillers Edition special release OD 162.FX, dist 1998, bott 2013 db **(87.5) n22.5 t22.5 f21 b21.5.** Some attractive kumquat and blood orange makes for a fruity and rich malt, though just a little furry towards the finish. Decent Demerara early on, too. *43%*

Oban Little Bay db **(87.5) n21 t23 f21.5 b22.** A pleasant, refreshing simple dram. Clean and juicy in part and some wonderful oak-laden spice to stir things up a little. Just a little too much chewy toffee near the end, though. *43%*

PITTYVAICH

Speyside, 1975–1993. Diageo. Demolished.

Pittyvaich Aged 12 Years db (64) n16 t18 f15 b15. It was hard to imagine this whisky getting worse. But somehow it has achieved it. From fire-water to cloying undrinkability. What amazes me is not that this is such bad whisky: we have long known that Pittyvaich can be as grim as it gets. It's the fact they bother bottling it and inflicting it on the public. Vat this with malt from Fettercairn and neighbouring Dufftown and you'll have the perfect dram for masochists. Or those who have entirely lost the will to live. Jesus... 43%. Flora and Fauna.

Pittyvaich 25 Year Old refill American oak hogsheads & first fill ex-bourbon barrels, dist 1989 db (80) n21 t20 f19 b20. No matter what collar you put on it, once a Rottweiler, always a Rottweiler... 499%. 5,922 bottles. Diageo Special Releases 2015.

PORT ELLEN

Islay, 1825–1983. Diageo. Closed.

Port Ellen 1979 db (93) n22 t23 f24 b24 Takes so long to get out of the traps, you wonder if anything is going to happen. But when it does, my word...it's glorious! 57.5%

Port Ellen 32 Year Old refill European oak butts, dist 1983 db (97) n24.5 t24.5 f24 b24 That was as different as it was unexpected: with all that fresh fruit, Port Ellen as you may never have seen it before (if you have ever seen it at all...!) Usually I shy away from smoke and grape. Here, though, it works like an old, priceless charm. When I was in the grounds of the old distillery this Spring, a Blackcap sang for a mate with exquisite beauty. It did not, though, match the heart-rendering song of this tragically lost distillery. 50.4%. 2,964 bottles. Diageo Special Releases 2015.

⬩ **Port Ellen Aged 37 Years** dist 1978 db (91) n24.5 a mesmerising spice and phenol mix: backed by liquorice, hickory and dry molasses, even the malt gets an airing. But the tannins are about as powerful as they could possibly be without quite breaking the spell...; t22.5 gristy, salivating start, with the phenols further back from the stage than you might expect. Solid gristy sugars before the damn bursts and the tannins rush in, though the spices act as a diversion; f22 dry and tannic, with just enough natural caramel to see us through to the end; b22 the bark is far better than the bite: one of the great noses of the year cannot be backed up on the palate as the oak is simply too demanding. An historical experience, but ensure you spend as much time nosing as you do tasting... 55.2%. 2,940 bottles. Diageo Special Releases 2016.

⬩ **Gordon & MacPhail Rare Old Port Ellen 1979** (90.5) n22 scant smoke as the spices bite and send tannic and tired messages...; a defiant citrus note rekindles some life...; t23 beautiful vanilla and lightly smoked butterscotch fill the palate alongside the dominant gristy maltiness on which the vaguest peat can still be detected. Light and flour-led, the dryness is added to by the exhausted oak; f22.5 dry but still a charming though weak peat-grist pulse...; b23 really not helped by being reduced to 46%, the oils have been broken up to allow the oak a much drier more sawdusty personality. Somehow pulls itself together to present a pretty, if dishevelled, figure... 46%.

PULTENEY

Highlands (Northern), 1826. Inver House Distillers. Working.

Old Pulteney Aged 12 Years db (90.5) n22 t23 f22.5 b23 A cleaner, zestier more joyous composition than the old 43%, though that has less to do with strength than overall construction. A dramatic whisky which, with further care, could get even closer to the truth of this distillery. 40%

⬩ **Old Pulteney Aged 12 Years** bott code L15/030 R15/5046 IB db (91) n22.5 t23 f22.5 b23 Remarkably consistent from the bottling above. The salt continues to ensure lustre, though this bottling has a little extra – and welcome – barley gristiness. 40%. ncf.

Old Pulteney Aged 12 Years db (85) n22 t23 f19 b21. There are few malts whose finish dies as spectacularly as this. The nose and delivery are spot on with a real buzz and panache. The delivery in particular just bowls you over with its sharp barley integrity: real pulse-racing stuff! Then... toffee...!!! Grrrr!!! If it is caramel causing this, then it can be easily remedied. And in the process we'd have a malt absolutely basking in the low 90s...! 43%

Old Pulteney Aged 15 Years db (91) n21 t24 f23 b23 Only on about the fourth or fifth mouthful do you start getting the picture here: enormously complex with a genuine coastal edge to this. The complexity is awesome. 54.9%

Old Pulteney Aged 17 Years db (95) n22 t25 f24 b24 The nose confirms that some of the casks at work here are not A1. Even so, the whisky performs to the kind of levels some distillers could only dream of. 46%

⬦ **Old Pulteney Aged 17 Years** bott code: L15/329 R15/5530 IB db **(82) n20.5 t22.5 f19 b20** This is usually one of the greatest whiskies bottled anywhere in the world. But not even something of Pulteney 17's usually unfathomable excellence and charisma can withstand this degree of sulphur. Much greater care has to be taken in the bottling hall to preserve the integrity of what should be one of Scotland's most beautiful offerings to the world. *46%. ncf.*

Old Pulteney Aged 21 Years db **(97.5) n25** if you had the formula to perfectly transform salt, citrus, the most delicate smoke imaginable, sharp barley, more gristy barley, light vanilla, toasty vanilla, roasted hazelnut, thinned manuka honey, lavender honey, arbutus blossom and cherry blossom, light hickory, liquorice, and the softest demerera sugar into the aroma of a whisky, you still wouldn't quite be able to recreate this perfection...; **t24** the sugars arrive: first gristy and malt-laden, then Demerara. This is followed by a salty, nerve-tingling journey of barley at varying intensity and then a slow but magnificently complete delivery of spice...; **f24** those spices continue to buzz, the vanillas dovetail with the malt and the fruit displaying a puckering, lively intensity. Ridiculously long fade for a malt so seemingly light, the salts and spices kiss the taste buds goodnight...; **b24.5** by far and away one of the great whiskies of 2012, absolutely exploding from the glass with vitality, charisma and class. One of Scotland's great undiscovered distilleries about to become discovered, I think... and rightly so! *46%*

Old Pulteney 30 Years Old db **(92) n23.5** fabulous mix of Jaffa cake and bourbon, seasoned by a pinch of salt; **t23.5** an early, unexpected, wave of light smoke and silkier oak gives immediate depth. But stunning, ultra-juicy citrus and barley ensures this doesn't get all big and brooding; **f22** thinner and oakier with a playful oak-spice tingle; plenty of vanilla controls the drier aspects; **b23** I had to laugh when I tasted this: indeed, it had me scrambling for a copy of the 2009 Bible to check for sure what I had written. And there it was: after bemoaning the over oaking I conjectured, "As Pulteney has the fascinating tendency to radically shift style over not too long a period, I can't wait for the next instalment." And barely a year on, here it is. Pretty far removed from last year's offering and an absolute peach of a dram that laughs in the face of its 30 years... *45%*

Old Pulteney 35 Year Old db **(89) n23** the dry ginger doesn't do anything to make this feel younger than its 35 years; a meeting place of various forms of tannin, some sweeter than others. But it is those delicate muscovado sugars alongside the manuka honey, alongside the ginger, which are key; **t21.5** much harder to keep it together on the palate:th attractive mouth feel is undermined by the drier oa elements, some of which are very dry; **f22.5** some lovely mint chocolate does offer great charm; **b22** a malt on the perimeter of its comfort zone. But there are enough gold nuggets included to make this work. Just. *46%. Inverhouse Distilleries.*

Old Pulteney Aged 40 Years db **(95) n23.5** gosh! That's pretty aged stuff with the exotic fruit hanging on by a fingernail. Some major bourbon notes now evident – and lip-smacking; **t23.5** massive delivery, again with tannins coming from every angle. But a mix of liquorice, dates, burnt raisin and honey cope well while spices tingle; **f24** settles for a long essay of happy old bourbon-style led whisky; **b24** this malt still flies as close to the sun as possible. But some extra fruit, honey and spice now grasps the tannins by the throat to ensure a whisky of enormous magnitude and complexity *51.3%*

Old Pulteney 1990 Vintage American oak ex bourbon & Spanish oak ex sherry butts. db **(85) n21 t23 f21 b20.** As you know, anything which mentions sherry butts gets me nervous – and for good reason. Even with a World Great distillery like Pulteney. Oddly enough, this bottling is, as near a dammit, free of sulphur. Yee-hah! The bad news, though, is that it is also untroubled by complexity as well. It reminded me of some heavily sherried peaty jobs...and then I learned that that ex Islay casks were involved. That may or may not be it. But have to say, beyond the first big, salivating, lightly spiced moments on delivery you wait for the story to unfurl...and it all turns out to be dull rumours. *46%. Inverhouse Distilleries.*

Old Pulteney Duncansby Head Lighthouse bourbon and sherry casks db **(90.5) n23 t23 f22 b22.5** Beginning to wonder if Pulteney is into making whisky or cakes. And malt straight from the oven. *46% WB15/329*

Old Pulteney Dunnet Head Lighthouse bourbon & sherry casks db **(90.5) n22 t23.5 f22 b23** Loads to chew over with this heavyweight. *46%. nc ncf. Exclusive to travel retail.*

Old Pulteney Navigator bourbon & sherry casks db **(80) n19 t23 f18 b20.** Sherry butts have clearly been added to this. Not sure why, as the sulphur only detracts from the early honey riches. The compass is working when the honey and cocoa notes briefly harmonise in beautiful tandem. But otherwise, badly off course. *46%. nc ncf.*

⬦ **Old Pulteney Navigator** bourbon & sherry casks, bott code: L15/207 R15/5318 IB db **(78) n19 t22 f18 b19** Even further lost in sulphurous territory than before... *46%. ncf.*

Old Pulteney Noss Head Lighthouse bourbon casks db (84) n22.5 t22 f19 b20.5. If Noss Head was as light as this dram, it'd have gone half way through its first half decent storm. An apparent slight overuse of third and less sturdy second fill casks means the finale bitters out considerably. A shame, as the nose and delivery is about as fine a display of citrus maltiness as you'll find. 46%. Travel retail exclusive. WB15/327

Old Pulteney Pentland Skerries Lighthouse db (85) n21 t22 f20.5 b21.5. A chewy dram with an emphasis on the fruit. Sound, evens enjoys the odd chocolate-toffee moment. But a little sulphur, apparent on the nose, creeps in to take the gloss off. 46%. WB15/323

◈ **Cadenhead's Authentic Collection Old Pulteney 11 Year Old** bourbon hogshead, dist 2006 (87) n22.5 crushed grape pips.....??? Bourbon cask...? Definitely pithy...; t23 youthful, gristy, oily, varying degrees of light fruit notes – pear especially – and volcanic spices; f23 long, malty with those spices burning a hole in the taste buds still...; the gentle oils offer a welcome calm and balm...; b22.5 never quite encountered a Pulteney like this! Certainly the most spiced at this age I have seen in some 30 years and though from bourbon there is a profound fruitiness and pithy quality. A very strange but truly delicious experience. But I wouldn't have recognised this as a Pulteney in 50 years... 56.1%. sc.

Cadenhead's Authentic Collection Pulteney 25 Year Old bourbon hogshead, dist 1990, bott 2016 (89.5) n23 t23.5 f21 b22 Forget the finish. The nose and delivery have your senses on full alert! 50.5%. sc.

Gordon & MacPhail MacPhail's Collection Pulteney 1982 (92.5) n23.5 t23 f23 b23 One of the few distilleries which takes the passing of time in its stride. Big tannin presence for sure – no problem! 43%

Gordon & MacPhail MacPhail's Collection Pulteney 2005 (91.5) n22.5 t23 f23 b23 Classy! 43%

ROSEBANK

Lowlands, 1840–1993. Diageo. Closed. (But if there is a God will surely one day re-open)

Rosebank Aged 12 Years db (95) n24 t24 f23 b24. Infinitely better than the last bottling, this is quite legendary stuff, even better than the old 8-y-o version, though probably a point or two down regarding complexity. The kind of whisky that brings a tear to the eye... for many a reason... 43%. Flora and Fauna.

Rosebank 21 Year Old refill American oak casks, dist 1992 db (95.5) n23.5 a textbook of complexity: nutty biscuits – Maryland Cookie is about the closest – meets spiced, diced runner beans as a sweet earthiness nestles into the malt and delicate honey; t24 a surprising coastal kick of sugars and salt mixing in with the vanilla and butterscotch clad malt; f24 long, with the light oils being used to the full to draw out the ulmo honey...and a further dusting of salt...; b24 Rosebank is at its very best at eight-years-old. Well, that won't happen again, so great to see it has proven successful at 21... 55.3%. 4,530 bottles. Diageo Special Releases 2014.

Rosebank 21 Years Old Special Release db (94) n24 t23.5 f23 b23.5 Can any Lowland be compared to a fully blossomed Rosebank? This is whisky to both savour and worship for this is nectar in a Rose... 53.8%. nc ncf.

Rosebank 25 Years Old db (96) n24.5 t23.5 f24 b24. I had to sit back, take a deep breath and get my head around this. It was like Highland Park but with a huge injection of sweetened chocolate on the finale and weight – and even smoke – from a Rosebank I had never quite seen before. And believe me, as this distillery's greatest champion, I've tasted a few hundred, possibly thousands, of casks of this stuff over the last 25 years. Is this the greatest of all time? I am beginning to wonder. Is it the most extraordinary since the single malt revolution took off? Certainly. Do I endorse it? My god, yes! 61.4%

ROYAL BRACKLA

Speyside, 1812. John Dewar & Sons. Working.

Royal Brackla Aged 10 Years db (73) n18 t20 f17 b18. A distinct lowering of the colours since I last tasted this. What on earth is going on? 40%

Royal Brackla 12 Year Old db (82.5) n21.5 t21 f20 b20. Just one of those bottlings which is pleasant enough if you are just looking for something to drink without too much thought, but there is a frustrating lack of harmony and purpose in this for those of us looking to be entertained. 40%

Royal Brackla 21 Year Old db (91) n23.5 wonderful dried lychee kick sets the tone for the sweetness of the malt; t23 silky malt, with a shade of coastal salt ensuring the full flavours are wrung out; f22 creamy chocolate ice cream before the spices arrive; b22.5 now that's much more like it! 40%

Cadenhead's Wine Cask Royal Brackla 23 Year Old claret wine barrel, dist 1992 **(93)** n23.5 t23 f23.5 b23 Wow! This has come from a truly exceptional cask. Stunningly clean. *52.9%. sc.*

◈◈ **Old Malt Cask Royal Brackla Aged 18 Years** refill barrel, cask no. 13429, dist May 98, bott Feb 17 **(92.5)** n23 an intriguing smokiness surprises and offers the perfect ballast to the more esoteric malts on display; citrus adds just the right freshness; t22.5 a half-hearted delivery with no faction willing to take the lead. Eventually a united front of intense, concentrated malt and no less rich vanilla make their mark. Watered ulmo honey and red liquorice underline the depth and sweetness; f23.5 now in its element as the sugars, spices and malt meet the oils with alacrity. The smoke spotted on the nose makes a very late return, with a toasty molassed biscuit note bringing up the rear alongside the grape juice; b23.5 an excellent cask has ensured harmony. Superb! *50%. nc ncf sc. 244 bottles.*

ROYAL LOCHNAGAR
Highlands (Eastern), 1826. Diageo. Working.

Royal Lochnagar Aged 12 Years db **(84)** n21 t22 f20 b21. More care has been taken with this than some other bottlings from this wonderful distillery. But I still can't understand why it never quite manages to get out of third gear...or is the caramel on the finish the giveaway...? *40%*

ST. MAGDALENE
Lowlands, 1798–1983. Diageo. Demolished.

Linlithgow 30 Years Old dist 1973 db **(70)** n18 t18 f16 b18. A brave but ultimately futile effort from a malt that is way past its sell-by date. *59.6%*

SCAPA
Highlands (Island–Orkney), 1885. Chivas Brothers. Working.

Scapa 12 Years Old db **(88)** n23 t22 f21 b22. Always a joy. *40%*

Scapa 14 Years Old db **(88)** n22 t22.5 f21.5 b22. Enormous variation from bottling to bottling. In Canada I have tasted one that I gave 94 to: but don't have notes or sample here. This one is a bit of dis-service due to the over-the-top caramel added which appears to douse the usual honeyed balance. Usually, this is one of the truly great malts of the Chivas empire and a classic islander. *40%*

Scapa 16 Years Old db **(81)** n21 t20.5 f19.5 b20. For it to be so tamed and toothless is a crime against a truly great whisky which, handled correctly, would be easily among the finest the world has to offer. *40%*

Scapa Skiren db **(89.5)** n22.5 tangy, salted orange and deep vanilla; t22.5 major malt which steps on the salivation pedal almost immediately; the tannins are layered, offering some ice cream, including cone; f22 the sugars tail off leaving this a little lightweight; b22.5 chaps who created this: lovely, you really have to power this one up a bit... *40%*

SPEYBURN
Speyside, 1897. Inver House Distillers. Working.

◈◈ **Speyburn Aged 10 Years** bott code: L16/303 R165434 IB db **(84.5)** n21 t21.5 f21 b21 Appears to celebrate and even emphasises its remarkable thinness of body. As usual, juicy with a dominant toffee character. *40%*.

Speyside 12 Years Old db **(85)** n22 t22 f20.5 b21.5 Copious honey and malt on delivery. Simplistic, effective but a tad bitter on finish. *40%*

Speyburn Aged 25 Years db **(92)** n22 t24 f23 b23. Either they have re-bottled very quickly or I got the diagnosis dreadfully wrong first time round. Previously I wasn't overly impressed; now I'm taken aback by its beauty. Some change. *46%*

◈◈ **Speyburn Arranta Casks** first fill ex-bourbon casks bott code: L16/097 R16/5130 IB db **(90)** n22 if the malt were any lighter it would vanish: much weightier caramel and spice dominates; t23 that is a lovely delivery! The malt just about gathers sufficient depth to make a charming, salivating, impact, though it is quickly outpaced by a light heather honey sweetness, then liquorice and ever-increasing and warming spice; f22 remains layered and relatively complex, the lightly sweetened tannins have a long, spicy fade perhaps closer in keeping with Kentucky than the Spey valley...; b23 Speyburn at its most vocal and interesting: rather beautifully constructed. *46%*.

◈◈ **Speyburn Bradon Orach** bott code: L17/039 R17/5048 IB db **(75)** n19 t19 f18.5 b18.5 Remains one of the most curious distillery bottlings on Speyside and one still unable to find either its balance or a coherent dialogue. *40%*.

◇ **Gordon & MacPhail Cask Strength Speyburn 2006** bott 27 Oct 16 **(91.5) n22** very slender body with little meat but just enough barley, vanilla and thin golden syrup garnered to make for an attractive nose; **t23.5** one of the most intense and clean barley deliveries from a Speyburn to be found in bottle for a very long time: subtle spices and sugars add beautifully to the structure; the mid-ground is a wonderful mix of ulmo and heather honey with a slight coconut sub-plot; **f22.5** returns to a more lazy, non-committal personality but enough molasses and spice stays on track; **b23.5** comfortably out performs the distillery's own 10-year-old bottling...truly magnificent cask use. *59.2%.*

◇ **Hepburn's Choice Speyburn 5 Years Old** refill butt, dist 2007, bott 2017 **(87)** n22 t22 f21.5 b21.5 Like taking a sample from my blending room shelf: a great opportunity to see how this ticks as a staple malt in so many brands. Citrus fresh, gristy-sweet and clean despite the cask type. And very oily. 46%. nc ncf sc. 795 bottles.

Hepburn's Choice Speyburn 10 Years Old sherry butt, dist 2004, bott 2015 **(82)** n20.5 t21 f20.5 b20. As stark and austere a Speysider as you'll find. Clean but thin and I'd say it never quite gets out of second gear – but not entirely sure it has one...! 46%. nc ncf sc. 444 bottles.

Hidden Spirits Speyburn 8 Years Old cask no. SP715, dist 2007, bott 2015 **(84.5) n21 t22 f20.5 b21.** Entirely competent though non-complex malt with a lemon sherbet kick. Light bodied even though a decent cask is at play. 48%. sc.

◇ **Provenance Speyburn Aged 10 Years** refill hogshead, cask no. 11641, dist Jan 07, bott Feb 17 **(88) n21.5** suet pudding and grist; **t22.5** lovely, ever-intensifying barley with a dull spice on the gentle vanilla; **f22** thins quickly but retains its integrity; **b22** Speyburn rarely win prizes for complexity – and this doesn't. But for sheer malty riches, this is one enjoyable bottling. 46%. nc ncf sc. 359 bottles.

◇ **Provenance Speyburn Aged 12 Years** sherry butt, cask no. 11654, dist Feb 05, bott Feb 17 **(87.5) n21.5 t22.5 f21.5 b22** A sherry butt and no sulphur! True to distillery form, this is a bottling which offers only limited scope and depth. That said, the thin malt and eye-watering, fruity muscovado sugars form a decent pairing with the barley. Simple and very pleasant. 46%. nc ncf sc. 806 bottles.

◇ **The Whisky Chamber Speyburn 11 Year Old** ex-brandy cask, dist 2005 **(89.5) n21.5** a grating fruitiness replaces the malt with a touch of impatient belligerence; **t23** much better! The sugars form a guard of honour on delivery allowing a short phase of maltiness to develop before the muscovado sugars cook up their fruity theme; **f22.5** highly attractive spice and vanilla; **b22.5** Speyburn is a such a fragile, threadbare soul at the best of times that I wondered how it would fare against the persistent, almost hostile, fruitiness of a brandy cask. No surprises, the brandy won. Or to be more precise, the malt extracted the best out the brandy, especially the sugars, to bolster its its own meagre personality. *60.4%.*

THE SPEYSIDE DISTILLERY

Speyside, 1990. Speyside Distillers. Working.

Spey 12 Years Old limited edition, finished in new oak casks db **(85.5) n21.5 t23 f19.5 b21.5.** One of the hardest whiskies I have had to define this year: it is a curious mixture of niggling faults and charming positives which come together to create a truly unique scotch. The crescendo is reached early after the delivery with an amalgamation of acacia honey, barley sugar and butter notes interlocking with something bordering classicism. However, the nose and finish, despite the chalky oak, reveals that something was lacking in the original distillate or, to be more precise, was rather more than it should have been. Still, some hard work has obviously gone into maximising the strengths of a distillery that had hitherto failed to raise the pulse and impresses for that alone. 40%. nc. 8,000 bottles.

Spey 18 Years Old ltd edition, fresh sherry casks db **(82.5) n19 t23.5 f19 b21.** What a shame this malt has been brushed with sulphur. Apparent on nose and finish, it still can't diminish from the joy of the juicy grape on delivery and the excellent weight as the liquorice and treacle add their gentle treasures and pleasures. So close to a true classic. 46%. nc.

Spey Chairman's Choice db **(77) n19 t21 f18 b19.** Their Chairman's Choice, maybe. But not mine... 40%

◇ **Spey Fumare** db **(90.5) n22** minty phenols. Delicate with a light touch of grated milk chocolate; **t23.5** salivating, for a moment heads towards an oily richness then has second thoughts. Checks back to a more citrusy juiciness with the phenols taking their time to regain their intensity; **f22** a little sparse in part with the peat and sugars thinning out noticeably; **b23** a very different type of peaty malt with some surprising twists and turns. As fascinating as it is quietly delicious. I am looking at Speyside distillery in a new light... 46%. nc ncf.

Spey Royal Choice db (87) n21 t23 f21 b22. "I'll have the slightly feinty one, Fortescue." "Of course, Your Highness. Would that be the slightly feinty one which has a surprising softness on the palate, a bit like a moist date and walnut cake? But with a touch too much oil on the finish?" "That's the blighter! No ice, Fortescue!" "Perish the thought, Sir." Or water, Forters. One must drink according to the Murray Method, don't you know!" "Very wise, Sir." 46%

Spey Tenné finished in Tawny Port casks db (90) n22.5 t23 f22 b22.5 Upon pouring, the handsome pink blush tells you one of three things: i) someone has swiped the whisky and filled the bottle with Matheus Rose instead; ii) I have just located where I put the pink paraffin or iii) this whisky has been matured in brand spanking new port casks. Far from a technical paragon of virtue so far as distilling is concerned. But those Tawny Port casks have brought something rather magical to the table. And glass. 46%. nc. 18,000 bottles.

⟡ **Spey Trutina** bourbon casks db (90) n22.5 a fragile aroma where you just daren't sniff too hard....as clean, fresh, grassy barley as you'll find...; t23 pristine, mildly concentrated young barley benefiting from the gentlest prodding of a citrus and icing sugar mix; f22 the extraordinary lightness of the spirit allows the tannins, as meagre as they are, to make a bigger contribution than would first appear possible; b22.5 the best Speyside Distillery bottling I have encountered for a very long time. Entirely feint free and beautifully made. 46%. nc ncf.

Beinn Dubh db (82) n20 t21 f21 b20. Mountains. Dogs. Who can tell the difference...? I suppose to a degree I can, as this has for more rummy undertones and is slightly less inclined to layering than the old Danish version. 43%

C&S Dram Collection Speyside Aged 22 Years sherry puncheon, cask no. 942, dist 11 Nov 91, bott 17 Mar 14 (94) n23.5 t24 f23 b23.5 The aroma of clean, untainted sherry is so rare it took me a few moments to recognise here. Superb malt... 62%. sc. 514 bottles.

The Golden Cask Speyside 23 Years Old cask no. CM 223, dist 1992, bott 2015 (85.5) n22 t21.5 f21 b21. Certainly some treacle at play here, as well as some decent malt. But there is an aggressive edge, too, which cannot be accounted for simply by its strength alone. 61.7%. sc. 434 bottles.

Old Malt Cask Speyside Aged 21 Years sherry butt, cask no. 12162, dist Dec 93, bott Nov 15 (71.5) n17.5 t19 f17 b18. Even the lashings of honey the barley has conjured up cannot entirely dampen the excesses of the sulphur. 50%. nc ncf. 390 bottles.

⟡ **Old Particular Speyside 15 Years Old** refill hogshead, cask no. 11483, dist Dec 00, bott Nov 16 (83.5) n20 t22 f20 b21.5 Certainly no shortage of barley as the malt grips, sometimes with sharp fingernails digging into the palate. Hot and a spirit which patently wasn't too well cared for at birth. The oils and light vanilla caress are attractively redeeming features. 48.4%. nc ncf sc. 333 bottles.

Romantic Rhine Collection Speyside 23 Year Old sherry puncheon, cask no. 943, dist 11 Nov 91, bott 09 Oct 15 (94) n23.5 t24 f23 b23.5 Wow! Absolutely nothing wrong with this sherry cask. Monumental stuff! 60.8%. sc. 68 bottles.

Simon Brown The Speyside Distillery bourbon casks until May 12, Nicaragun Rum cask until Jun 14, dist Feb 99, bott Jun 14 (94.5) n24 t23.5 f23 b24 As someone who has probably monitored this whisky more closely than any other independent whisky expert, I can put my hand on my heart and say I have never tasted better from this distillery. Indeed, I had no idea it could be this good. Well done to all concerned! 43%. nc ncf.

Whiskybroker Speyside 15 Year Old hogshead, cask no. 2380, dist 26 Oct 00, bott 09 Sept 15 (94.5) n24 t23.5 f23 b24 An entirely atypical malt from this distillery. The malt is loud, proud and rather wonderfully made. Nothing like I have ever seen from the Speyside distillery... 50.3%. sc.

Whiskyjace 10th Anniversary The Speyside Distillery 21 Years Old 1995 bourbon cask, bott 2016 (90.5) n23 t22.5 f22 b23 The malt from this distillery at this time was varied. This is way up in the upper echelons.... 54.1%

SPRINGBANK

Campbeltown, 1828. J&A Mitchell & Co. Working.

Springbank Aged 10 Years db (89.5) n22 t23 f22 b22.5. Although the inherent youthfulness of the 10-y-o has not changed, the depth of body around it has. Keeps the taste buds on full alert. 46%

Springbank Aged 10 Years (100 Proof) db (86) n21.5 t22 f21 b21.5. Trying to map a Springbank demands all the skills required of a young 18th century British naval officer attempting to record the exact form and shape of a newly discovered land just after his sextant had fallen into the sea. There is no exact point on which you can fix...and so it is here. A shifting dram that never quite tastes the same twice, but one constant, sadly, is the bitterness towards the finale. Elsewhere, it's one hell of a journey...! 57%

Springbank Aged 15 Years db (88.5) n22.5 t22 f22 b22. Last time I had one of these, sulphur spoiled the party. Not this time. But the combination of oil and caramel does detract from the complexity a little. 46%

Springbank Aged 18 Years db (90.5) n23 busy in the wonderful Springbank way; delicate greengage and date; nippy; t23 yummy, mouthwatering barley and green banana. Fresh with excellent light acacia honey; f21.5 fabulous oak layering, including chocolate. A little off-key furriness from a sherry butt late on; b23 just one so-so butt away from bliss... 46%

Springbank Aged 21 Years db (90) n22 t23 f22.5 b22.5 A few years ago I was at Springbank when they were bottling a very dark, old-fashioned style 21-year-old. I asked if I could take a 10cl sample with me for inclusion in the Bible; they said they would send it on, though I tasted a glass there and then just for enjoyment's sake. They never did send it, which was a shame. For had they, they most probably would have carried off World Whisky of the Year. This, though very good, is not quite in the same class. But just to mark how special this brand has always been to me, I have made this the 500th new single malt scotch and 700th new whisky in all of the 2015 Whisky Bible. 46%. WB15/096

Hazelburn Aged 8 Years bourbon cask, bott 2011 db (94.5) n23 t24 f23.5 b24 A very curious coppery sheen adds extra lustre and does no harm to a very well made spirit filled into top grade oak. For an eight year old malt, something extra special. 46%

Longrow Aged 10 Years db (78) n19 t20 f19 b20. This has completely bemused me: bereft not only of the usual to-die-for smoke, its warts are exposed badly, as this is way too young. Sweet and malty, perhaps, and technically better than the marks I'm giving it – but this is Longrow, dammit! I am astonished. 46%

Longrow Aged 10 Years 100 Proof db (86) n20 t23 f22 b21. Still bizarrely smokeless – well, maybe a flicker of smoke as you may find the involuntary twitching of a leg of a dying fly – but the mouthfeel is much better here and although a bit too oily and dense for complexity to get going, a genuinely decent ride heading towards Hazelburn-esque barley intensity. Love it, because this oozes class. But where's the ruddy peat...?! 57%

Longrow 14 Years Old refill bourbon and sherry casks db (89) n24 t23.5 f19 b22.5. Again, a sherry butt proves the Achilles heel. 46%

Longrow Aged 18 Years (94.5) n25 t23 f23 b23.5 If you gently peat a blend of ulmo, manuka and heather honey you might end up with something as breathtakingly stunning as this. But you probably won't... 46%. WB15/103

Classic Whisky & Lifestyle Springbank 15 Year Old 2000 rum cask (80.5) n21 t21.5 f19 b19. In the early '90s, Springbank became the first distillery to commercially bottle rum cask whisky. I know, because it was I who found the puncheons sitting forgotten in their warehouse. And hence their famous "Green" whisky was born. This, though, is not a patch on those casks of a quarter of a century ago. The sugars are slapdash, the oak input is undisciplined and the overall effect is bewildering. Only the wonderful spices make sense. 471%. 247 bottles.

Dà Mhile Organic Springbank Director's Cut 23 Years Old cask no. 233 (91) n22.5 t23 f22.5 b23 The first Da Mhile where the oak is in the driving seat. The complexity levels remain magnificently high and the road it takes is a panoramic one. 50%

ePower Springbank 15 Year Old sherry cask, dist 1999, bott 2015 (88) n22.5 t23 f20.5 b22 Heavy duty malt offering a very unusual, frankly fascinating, sherry aspect. 43%. Selected by Best Dram.

Hunter Laing's Old & Rare Springbank Aged 22 Years refill hogshead, dist Dec 93, bott Jan 16 (93) n23 t23 f23.5 b23.5 Not a malt for those looking for a bland brand. 53.9%. nc ncf sc. 212 bottles.

Old Particular Campbeltown Springbank 18 Years Old refill hogshead, cask no. 10737, dist Oct 96, bott Feb 15 (88) n22.5 t22 f22b21.5 A clunky, oily malt which still hasn't quite woken up yet. 48.4%. nc ncf sc. 360 bottles.

Sansibar Whisky Springbank Aged 22 Years 1993 bott 2015 (79) n19 t22 f19 b19. Neither fish nor fowl. Springbanks aren't meant to be smoky (that's Longrow's prerogative) but this one is. Half-heartedly. Throw in a cask kicking out way too great a lactose imprint, having, presumably, been around the block once too often. And you have an unusually unsatisfactory Springbank. 51.8%. sc. 150 bottles.

⬧ **Xtra Old Particular Campbeltown Springbank 21 Years Old** refill butt, cask no. 11366, dist Jun 95, bott Aug 16 (91) n23 a lot older in character than its 21 given years: a semi-eucalyptus note reinforces the oak and gives a biting, spiced answer to the low key fruit; t23 the fruit, slightly shy on the nose, shows no such timidity on delivery and goes on all out juicy, grapey attack. Attractively silky and armed with delicate Manuka honey, it still has no option but to give way to the mounting tannins; f22 dries to a burnt toast degree; caramel and butterscotch equal things slightly b23 don't worry: it may be a refill butt, but all is safe. As you'd expect from a Springbank, complex, demanding and intriguing in equal measure. *54.8%. nc ncf sc. 131 bottles.*

STRATHISLA
Speyside, 1786. Chivas Brothers. Working.

Strathisla 12 Years Old db (85.5) n21.5 t22 f21 b21. A slight reduction in strength from the old bottling and a significant ramping up of toffee notes means this is a malt which will do little to exert your taste buds. Only a profusion of spice is able to cut through the monotonous style. Always sad to see such a lovely distillery so comprehensively gagged. *40%.*

Strathisla Distillery Edition 15 Years Old db (94) n23 t23 f24 b24 What a belter! The distillery is beautiful enough to visit: to take away a bottle of this as well would just be too good to be true! *53.7%*

Cadenhead's Authentic Collection Strathisla 25 Year Old bourbon hogshead, dist 1989, bott July 15 (94) n24 t23.5 f23 b23.5 Everything that can be asked of a 25-year-old Speysider, and from this distillery in particular. *42.7%. sc. 150 bottles.*

Gordon & MacPhail Rare Vintage Strathisla 1965 (84.5) n21.5 t22 f19.5 b21.5. There is a type of old Speysider which appears to have drowned in a vat of ancient Oloroso. This is one such example. The degree of oak is borderline scary, but all the splinters vanish in this gloopy – if, at times, curiously delicious – mix of tinned tomato and sherry: the tomato being tinned, not the sherry. Anyway, the tiredness of the oak is underlined by the most ungracious of bitter of finishes. *43%*

⬥ **Gordon & MacPhail Rare Vintage Strathisla 1960** (96) n23.5 a half-hour's worth of anyone time: outrageously fruity but has acted like a collector of tannins, so the raisins are seriously toasted – a bit like a fruit cake where every bit is the outside; that means molasses should abound...and it does! t24 the tannins have been brought forward to have the first say. But before they can speak clearly, in whooshes the fruit and takes its breath away – and probably yours', too; f24.5 one of those where the finish is so long, you are not sure quite where it starts: dried dates, old Flore plums, mocha as well as praline, liquorice, very thin eucalyptus, hickory and dried out molasses and Manuka honey...it rambles forever onwards...; b24 this was a sherry cask style that 20 years ago I would have criticised for being far too heavy and over the top. In the two decades which have now passed such, has become the appalling state of Scottish sherry butt stock, that I now fling my arms around this style of whisky with love, glee and reverence. Yes, of course it is still over the top. But the enormity and lusciousness of the grape has protected the cask for the best part of 60 years now, allowing the tannins to go so far and no further. And, of course, there is not an atom of sulphur to be detected: the blenders of that day simply would never have allowed it. Worth raiding your piggy bank and exploring this now lost style. *43%.*

⬥ **Scotch Malt Whisky Society Cask 58.19 10 Year Old** virgin heavy toast medium char oak hogshead, dist 30 Mar 06 (79.5) n20 t20.5 f19 b20 Tangy, off beam and, though the malt flashes wildly here and there, awfully disappointing - especially considering the distillery. *57.7%.*

STRATHMILL
Speyside, 1891. Diageo. Working.

Strathmill 25 Year Old refill American oak casks, dist 1988 db (89) n23 t22 f22 b22 A blending malt which reveals the kind of big malty deal it offers older brands. *52.4%. 2,700 bottles. Diageo Special Releases 2014.*

Cadenhead's Wine Cask Strathmill 19 Year Old Chateau Lafitte barrel, dist 1995 (72) n18 t19 f17 b18. Sulphur afoot with the Laffite *55.1%*

TALISKER
Highlands (Island–Skye), 1832. Diageo. Working.

Talisker Aged 10 Years db (93) n23 t23 f24 b23 The deadening caramel that had crept into recent bottlings of the 10-y-o has retreated, and although that extraordinary, that wholly unique finale has still to be re-found in its unblemished, explosive entirety, this is much, much closer to the mark and a quite stupendous malt to be enjoyed at any time. But at night especially. *45.8%*

Talisker 12 Years Old Friends of the Classic Malts db (86) n22 t21.5 f21 b21.5. Decent, sweet, lightly smoked...but the explosion which made this distillery unique - the old kerpow! - appears kaput. 45.8%

Talisker Aged 14 Years The Distillers Edition Jerez Amoroso cask, dist 1993, bott 2007 db (90.5) n23 t23 f22 b22.5. Certainly on the nose, one of the more old-fashioned peppery Taliskers I've come across for a while. Still I mourn the loss of the nuclear effect it once had, but the sheer quality of this compensates. 45.8%

Talisker Aged 20 Years db (95) n24 t24 f23 b24. I have been tasting Talisker for 28 years. This is the best bottling ever. Miss this and your life will be incomplete. 62%

Talisker 25 Years Old db (88) n22.5 t22 f21.5 b22. Pretty taken aback by this one: it has taken a fancy to being a bit of a Bowmore, complete with a bountiful supply of Fisherman's Friends. 45.8%

Talisker 30 Years Old db (93.5) n23 complex and slightly bitty, lemon-lightened phenols, sitting comfortably atop a pile of buttery egg custard tart. A lot sexier than it sounds...! t24 the citrus leads the way here, too. It helps intensify the juiciness of the barley, though a countering liquorice and crunchy Demerara sugar sweetness amplifies the age. The smoke is restrained though not beyond offering a spice throb; f23 just a few shuddering oaky passes, but the smoke, sugar, spice and even a little salted butter ensure the fade is long and satisfying; b23.5 much fresher and more infinitely entertaining than the 25 year old...!!! 45.8%

Talisker 30 Years Old db (84.5) n21 t21.5 f21 b21. Toffee-rich and pretty one dimensional. Did I ever expect to say that about a Talisker at 30...? 53.1%

Talisker 57 Degrees North db (95) n24 t24.5 f23 b23.5 A glowing tribute, I hope, for a glowing whisky... 57%

Talisker Dark Storm charred oak db (92) n22 t23.5 f23 b23.5 Much more like it! Unlike the Storm, which appeared to labour under some indifferent American oak, this is just brimming with vitality and purpose. 45.8%

Talisker Port Ruighe db (88) n22 t22 f22 b22. Sails into port without changing course 45.8%.

Talisker Skye (85) n21 t22 f21 b21. The sweetest, most docile Talisker I can ever remember with the spices working hard in the background but weirdly shackled. More Toffee Sky than Vanilla... 45.8% WB16/051

Talisker Storm db (85.5) n20 t23 f21 b21.5 The nose didn't exactly go down a storm in my tasting room. There are some deft seashore touches, but the odd poor cask –evident on the finish, also - has undone the good. But it does recover on the palate early on with an even, undemanding and attractively sweet display showing malt to a higher degree than I have seen any Talisker before. 45.8%.

Hepburn's Choice Talisker 5 Years Old refill hogshead, dist 2009, bott 2015 (88) n21.5 t22.5 f22 b22 Must be about 30 years since I first came face-to-face with a Talisker of this age in a blending lab. Much more peppery then, with less oil and the smoke, I remember, standing out with an almost three-dimensional clarity against all else. It has changed in the three passing decades. Not for the better, alas, with a much more Caol Ila-esque quality. Judged as a whisky alone, though, still decent, if not outstanding. 46%. nc ncf sc. 216 bottles.

⟩ **Hepburn's Choice Talisker 5 Years Old** refill hogshead, dist 2011, bott 2017 (86.5) n21.5 t22.5 f21 b21.5 Thought this would be a fascinating malt to mark the 200th new whisky tasted for Bible 2018. Just trace outlines of cask involvement and at times of peat also which takes a back seat to the rigid metallic backbone (actually,just discovered I described a similar Talisker bottling metallic over a week ago...beginning to see a theme here). Just nothing like the samples of Talisker 5 I tasted 20 years ago, but enough gristy sweetness to enjoy. 46%. nc ncf sc. 406 bottles.

⟩ **Hepburn's Choice Talisker 6 Years Old** refill hogshead, dist 2010, bott 2016 (84.5) n21 t22.5 f20 b21 Very little is getting in the way of the peat here in a bottling which shows Talisker at its most phenolic. Struggles, though, for a satisfactory balance as the nose and finish are stark and metallic. 46%. nc ncf sc. 368 bottles.

⟩ **Old Malt Cask Talisker Aged 7 Years** refill hogshead, cask no. 13273, dist Nov 09, bott Feb 17 (88.5) n21.5 thin, copper-lacking nose. Decent spices but all just a little too laid back and bland; t23 that's more like it. Spices, certainly. But these are well mannered gentlemen quite happy to take their turn with the vaguely smoked vanilla and citrus sharpened barley; that lack of copper still makes a mark; f22 medium length with more gentle smoke and dark sugars and a slow gathering of oak and spice; b22 enjoyable. But still can't help wondering: what the hell has happened to the fire, that spiced inferno, of torturous pleasure which once made this distillery truly unique....? 50%. nc ncf sc. 393 bottles.

⬧⬧⬧ **Old Malt Cask Talisker Aged 8 Years** refill hogshead, cask no. 12657, dist Apr 08, bott Jun 16 (86) n21.5 t22.5 f21 b21 A curious bottling, this. At various times we are treated to light smoke, butterscotch tart, Demerara sugar and mocha. Yet all a little tangy and it all never quite adds up. *50%. nc ncf sc. 151 bottles.*

⬧⬧⬧ **Provenance Talisker Aged 7 Years** refill hogshead, cask no. 11525, dist Nov 09, bott Nov 16 (88.5) n22 something of the plastic raincoat about this one...; t22.5 brilliant grist delivery ensures the most salivating romp; the peat is marked; f22 just enough vanilla to ensure some welcome complexity; b22 none of the old Talisker spice bite, but the smoky, youthful charm is very pleasing. *46%. nc ncf sc. 421 bottles.*

⬧⬧⬧ **Provenance Talisker Aged 8 Years** refill hogshead, cask no. 11178, dist Apr 08, bott May 16 (88.5) n22 a gentle mix of custard powder and delicate smoke; t22.5 juicy yet with a profoundly metallic edge. Enough oils, phenols and barley to entertain; f22 smoked custard cream biscuits; b22 not a Talisker 8 as those of us old enough will remember it from a lifetime ago. But rewardingly eccentric nonetheless. *46%. nc ncf sc.*

TAMDHU
Speyside, 1897. Ian Macleod Distillers. Working (re-opened 3rd March 2013).

Tamdhu db (84.5) n20 t22.5 f21 b21. So-so nose, but there is no disputing the fabulous, stylistic honey on delivery. The silkiest Speyside delivery of them all. *40%*

Tamdhu Aged 10 Years oak sherry cask db (69.5) n17 t18.5 f17 b17. A much better malt when they stick exclusively to ex-bourbon casks, as used to be the case. *40%*

Tamdhu Aged 18 Years bott code L0602G L12 20/08 db (74.5) n19 t19 f18 b18.5. Bitterly disappointing. Literally. *43%.*

Tamdhu 25 Years Old db (88) n22 t22 f21 b23. Radiates quality. *43%*

Tamdhu Batch Strength db (80) n19.5 t21.5 f19 b20. A chunky bruiser of a dram. What it misses in sophistication, it makes up for with a brooding sugary, spicy oomph... *58.8%*

Hepburn's Choice Tamdhu 9 Years Old refill hogshead, dist 2006, bott 2016 (92.5) n22.5 some youthful malty fizz; t23.5 melt-in-the-mouth grist. Rather beautifully weighted sugars to encase the clear barley; f22.5 beautifully polite oak ensures a lovely milky mocha flourish; b24 beautifully made malt matured in a superb cask and plucked when still in full bloom. A gem of a Tamdhu. *46%. nc ncf sc. 405 bottles.*

⬧⬧⬧ **The First Editions Tamdhu Aged 18 Years 1998** refill hogshead, cask no. 12826, bott 2016 (86.5) n21.5 t22 f21.5 b21.5 Something of the Grappa about this, though here on malty steroids. Almost brutal in part, this is where a seemingly gentle Speysider takes you down a quiet alleyway and roughs you up a bit... *52.2%. nc ncf sc. 126 bottles.*

⬧⬧⬧ **Hepburn's Choice Tamdhu 9 Years Old** refill hogshead, dist 2007, bott 2017 (84.5) n21.5 t22 f20 b21 Those of you living in the country and chewing straw from time to time will recognise the main properties of this malt. *46%. nc ncf sc. 354 bottles.*

⬧⬧⬧ **Hunter Laing's Distiller's Art Tamdhu Aged 18 Years** refill hogshead, dist Aug 98, bott 2016 (88.5) n22 the big malt challenges the oak to try and take control: the oak backs off as the marzipan-style sugars mount; t22.5 crisp and crystal clear barley. Firm to the point of clattering about the palate as though trying to chip your teeth. Strangely satisfying despite the obvious edge; f22 some late oils help keep the maltiness to the fore...; b22 no frills but plenty of malty thrills. *48%. nc ncf sc. 130 bottles.*

Old Malt Cask Tamdhu Aged 27 Years refill hogshead, cask no. 12004, dist Jun 88, bott Oct 15 (87.5) n22 t21.5 f22 b22. Eye-wateringly tart, but given an unexpected boost by a gentle fillip of peat. Rather too thin for greatness, but the phenols extract the most out of the juicy barley. *45.9%. nc ncf sc. 164 bottles.*

Old Particular Speyside Tamdhu 14 Years Old refill hogshead, dist Oct 01, bott Dec 15 (87) n22 t22 f21.5 b21.5. Clean, juicy, exceptionally malty. But, for its age, pretty undercooked. *48.4%. nc ncf sc. 328 bottles.*

Old Particular Speyside Tamdhu 17 Years Old refill hogshead, cask no. 10768, dist Mar 98, bott May 15 (85.5) n21.5 t21.5 f21 b21.5. Sizzles on the palate somewhat. Neither the barley or the limited tannin can forge enough personality to overcome the bite. *48.4%. nc ncf sc. 234 bottles.*

⬧⬧⬧ **Old Particular Tamdhu 18 Years Old** refill hogshead, cask no. 11472, dist May 98, bott Nov 16 (86) n21 t22.5 f21 b21.5 Sharp, sweet, malty, well-oiled and revels in its bubble gum chewiness – and taste. *48.4%. nc ncf sc. 248 bottles.*

⬧⬧⬧ **Provenance Tamdhu Aged 9 Years** refill hogshead, cask no. 11217, dist Nov 06, bott May 16 (83.5) n20.5 t21 f21 b21 Pleasant, malty, clean but stark. Rather overplays the limitations of a limited distillery. *46%. nc ncf sc.*

⋙ **Provenance Tamdhu Aged 10 Years** refill hogshead, cask no. 11636, dist Nov 06, bott Feb 17 **(87.5) n21.5 t22.5 f21.5 b22** A beautifully sticky malt. Not the most well-endowed in the complexity stakes, but carries its youthful and exuberant malt with an impressive degree of confidence. 46%. nc ncf sc. 445 bottles.

⋙ **Provenance Tamdhu Aged 12 Years** refill butt, cask no. 11337, dist Mar 04, bott Aug 16 **(79) n20 t20 f19 b20** The malt works impressively to overcome the dulling effect of the sherry butt. A gentle, pleasing ride for those immune to sherry cask's little spells... 46%. nc ncf sc. 346 bottles.

Simon Brown Tamdhu bourbon casks, dist Sept 89, bott Jun 05 **(90) n23 t22.5 f22 b22.5** Not renowned for true excellence, the distillery does come up with the odd elegant little charmer like this now and again. 46%. nc ncf.

TAMNAVULIN
Speyside. 1966. Whyte and Mackay. Working.

Tamnavulin 1966 Aged 35 Years cream sherry butt db **(91) n24 t22 f23 b22**. For those who love great old sherry, this is an absolute. Perhaps too much sherry to ever make it a true great, but there is no denying such quality. 52.6%

⋙ **Tamnavulin Double Cask** batch no. 0308 db **(87.5) n22.5 t22.5 f21 b21.5** A bottling which deserves – and perhaps needs – to be at 46% at least. Reduced down to this strength it is levelled to a much chalkier, drier plane than it requires to fully project the oils, sugars and obvious intricacies. Entirely pleasant as it is, with an attractive clean maltiness to the thinned golden syrup as well as well-mannered spicing. But, overall, refuses to open out and develop as you might hope or expect. A 92-plus whisky just waiting to happen... 40%

⋙ **C & S Dram Collection Tamnavulin 7 Years Old** hogshead, cask no. 2391, dist 15 Apr 09, bott 26 Sept 16 **(88) n22** green and tangy; **t23** strap yourself in for one of the purest, least tarnished malty assaults of your life. The odd hint of cocoa, but...that barley...!! **f21.5** a little discordant between the simplistic malt and unflattering oak; **b21.5** a substantial malt all the more intense due to its tender years. 57.1%. sc. 310 bottles.

TEANINICH
Highlands (Northern), 1817. Diageo. Working.

Gordon & MacPhail Connoisseurs Choice Teaninich 2006 (86.5) n22 t22 f21 b21.5. Sugary and unsophisticated, has all the bells and whistles required for a very decent blending malt, though one from a decent cask. Lots of spice and busyness, though thins out a little too quickly. 46%.

Gordon & MacPhail Connoisseurs Choice Teaninich 2008 (82) n19 t21.5 f21.5 b21. Disappointing malt, the nose showing that it would take an astonishing spirit to overcome the faults evident. It does recover to a degree, employing an attractive chewiness seemingly fashioned by big malt and bigger caramels. Even salivating at times. 46%

⋙ **Scotch Malt Whisky Society Cask 59.54 32 Year Old** refill ex-bourbon hogshead, dist 8 Nov 83 **(87.5) n21 t23.5 f21 b22** An old malt with a short fuse. Positively bristles on delivery with the most explosive spices arriving early. The barley offers several degrees of change in a well layered malt presentation, but the intensity of the spice deflects attention from an otherwise lovely show. The natural caramels are huge and chewy, as are the tannins as it over enthusiastically shows its years. 46%.

TOBERMORY
Highlands (Island–Mull), 1795. Burn Stewart Distillers. Working.

Tobermory 10 Years Old db **(73.5) n17.5 t19 f18 b19.** The last time I tasted an official Tobermory 10 for the Bible, I was aghast with what I found. So I prodded this sample I had before me of the new 46.3% version with all the confidence Wile E Coyote might have with a failed stick of Acme dynamite. No explosions in the glass or on my palate to report. And though this is still a long way short, and I'm talking light years here, of the technical excellence of the old days, the uncomplicated sweet maltiness has a very basic charm. The nose and finish, though, are still very hard going. 46.3%

Tobermory Aged 15 Years db **(93) n23.5 t23.5 f23 b23** A tang to the oils on both nose and finish suggests an over widened middle. But such is the quality of the sherry butts and the intensity of the salt-stained malt, all is forgiven. 46.3%. nc ncf.

Tobermory Aged 15 Years Limited Edition db **(72.5) n17 t18 f19 b18.5.** Another poorly made whisky: the nose and delivery tells you all you need to know. 46.3%

Tobermory 42 Year Old db (94.5) n23.5 t23.5 f23.5 b24 A real journey back in time. Wonderful. 47.7%

Ledaig Aged 10 Years db (85.5) n20 t22.5 f21.5 b21.5. Almost a Bowmore in disguise, such are its distinctive cough sweet qualities. Massive peat: easily one of the highest phenol Ledaigs of all time. But, as usual, a slight hiccup on the technical front. Hard work not to enjoy it, though. 46.3%. nc ncf.

Ledaig Aged 10 Years db (63) n14 t17 f15 b17. What the hell is going on? Butyric and peat in a ghoulish harmony on nose and palate that is not for the squeamish. 43%

Ledaig Aged 12 Years db (90) n23 t23.5 f21.5 b22 It has ever been known that there is the finest of lines between genius and madness. A side-by-side comparison of the Ledaig 10 and 12 will probably be one of whisky's best examples of this of all time... 43%

Ledaig 18 Year Old batch 2 db (71) n16 t20 f17 b18. There are many ways to describe this whisky. Well made, alas, is not one of them. The nose sets off many alarms, especially on the feinty front. And though some exceptional oak repairs some of the damage, it cannot quite do enough. Sugary, too – and occasionally cloyingly so. 46.3%. nc ncf.

⧫ **Ledaig 19 Year Old Marsala Finish** db (92) n23.5 this is profound smoke, even more robust and concentrated than when Tobermory first begun distilling their peaty spirit a long, long time ago. There is also a raw element to it also: this is not soothed or couched in oils: the phenols are base and feral, the fruit barely has a chance to get a word in edgeways. It is hard not to become hooked to this unsophisticatedly acrid, sooty attack...; t23 oddly enough, where the fruit barely registers on the nose, it is the first on the palate's roll call. Also, there is softness here for the first time, though by the time the phenols arrive we are back to a rough battle with little finesse; f22.5 settles for a smoky, slightly spikey spice buzz, all the while the phenols rumbling in the background; b23 hardly textbook malt but a real gung-ho adventure story on the palate. 51%.

⧫ **Ledaig 42 Year Old** db (93) n23.5 if the oak were a person, it'd have got a telegram from the Queen a long time ago...huge age yet the big peat acts like a sticking plaster – complete with Germolene. Under the smoky haze sweet spearmint and eucalyptus mark the passing years...; t24 bravo! There are muscovado sugars and untainted phenols enough to see off whatever oaky inroads might be made. Actually, the tannins take their time allowing the most salivating sugars and even barley to make a mockery of the passage of four decades; f22 begins to tighten as the toasty oak begin to march into town, dries and aggressively bitters by the moment; a little light spice brazens it out; b23.5 only on the nose and very finish do we encounter excessive age which is borderline OTT but somehow stays within levels of toleration. For the most part this is a triumph of smoky elegance over advancing years. 46.7%.

Ledaig Dùsgadh 42 Aged 42 Years db (96) n25 t24.5 f22.5 b24 It has to be about 30 years ago I tasted my first-ever Ledaig – as a 12 year old peated malt. This must be from the same stocks, only this has been housed in exceptional casks. Who would have thought, three decades on, that it would turn into some of the best malt bottled in a very long time. A smoky experience unlikely to be forgotten. 46.3%

Ledaig 1996 db (88) n21 some annoying barrels in there have seen better days and the tang distracts from what would have been a playful smokiness; t23.5 grip your seat, fling your head back, close your eyes and chew...we are in business. Absolutely sublime mouth feel: dense yet passable, lush yet never boggy. The dark sugars and barley intertwangle quite deliciously with the underplayed smoke...; f21 long, smoky bacon and still that lovely oil trace. Thins out towards a pasty austerity just when it starts getting really interesting.... damn it...!! b22.5 a malt you feel is at times reaching for the stars. But has to settle for an, ultimately, barren planet. 46.3%

Acla Selection Ledaig 8 Years Old ex-bourbon hogshead, dist 2005, bott 2014 db (89) n22 t22.5 f22 b22.5 A deft whisky which errs on the understated. 51.4%. nc ncf.

⧫ **Best Dram Ledaig 8 Year Old** bourbon barrel, dist 2008, bott 2016 (94) n23 a lovely mix of anthracite and peat just lightened slightly by sweet potato being cooked over a blackthorn fire; t23.5 huge oils really do ramp up the smoke. The honey is a sublime mix of ulmo and Manuka with a light liquorice glaze; f23.5 long, drying though the sugars are now more molassed; b24 Ledaig back to its adorable best. 57%.

Big Market Sonderabfüllung Nr. 13 Tobermory 1995 bott 2014 (93) n23 t23.5 f23 b23.5 You may find a maltier island whisky than this. But not many. Just love it 54.3%

C & S Dram Collection Ledaig Aged 17 Years hogshead, cask no. 640378, dist 01 Oct 97, bott 23 Mar 15 (81.5) n19 t21.5 f21 b20. A clumsy, massively oiled, sugar-laden dram which has matured in a very decent cask. Which is just as well, as the nose confirms that this was not particularly well made. If it's just the smoke you are after, then it might just do the job. 50.9%. sc. 295 bottles.

⬥ **Cadenhead's Authentic Collection Ledaig 11 Year Old** bourbon casks, dist 2005 **(94.5)** n24 a dry, spicy peatiness bordered by apple crumble and clove; fresh, briny and substantial; t23.5 salivating from kick off. The malt is shovelled around the palate with magnificent muscovado sugars engulfed in peatiness; f23.5 long, and not only well distilled but now benefitting from an excellent cask: not a hint of bitterness as the light buttery phenols merge with the vanilla and late arriving citrus; b23.5 much more like it: those who remember the first-ever bottlings of Ledaig will seriously appreciate this! 61.8%.

⬥ **Dramfool Tobermory 21 Year Old** bourbon cask, cask no. 127/1996 **(86.5)** n22 t21.5 f21.5 b21.5 Originally distilled at high speed off the still, the thinness and burn is pretty much there to be seen. As is the malt which stretched and sugary, but at least lasts the entire distance. Some excellent oak has helped repair the damage and add some welcome backbone and soothing buttery notes. 56.7%. sc. 247 bottles.

Endangered Drams Tobermory 9 Year Old cask no. 900095, dist Sept 05, bott Dec 14 **(86.5)** n21.5 t22 f21.5 b21.5. A curious creature. This is a Ledaig version of the distillery's output. Incredibly weighty though, apart from a massive explosion of peat on delivery, never feels comfortable. Particularly rough and jarring in part, which is some achievement considering the lubricating oils on show. 46%. sc.

⬥ **Fadandel.dk Ledaig 15 Year Old** cask no. 71, dist Sept 00, bott Jun 16 **(89.5)** n23 a briny, kippery launch on the nose, liberally salted and with the phenols coming at the nose with hob-nailed boots; t22.5 a rousing delivery, the taste buds under siege from the eye-watering grist. Well oiled, but only a light smattering of Demerara counters the barley. The caramels take time to arrive, but do so in force; f21.5 a little bitter and dry; distant spice warms; b22.5 a sharp malt with its eyes on effect rather than complexity. 57%. nc ncf sc. 300 bottles.

The First Editions Tobermory Aged 21 Years 1994 refill hogshead, cask no. 11833, bott 2015 **(85.5)** n21 t22.5 f21 b21. Big malt, and a twiddle of salt. But steadfastly refuses to go anywhere or further the narrative. 'Tis all about the interaction between pretty simple barley and clean but flaky oak. 58.6%. nc ncf sc. 125 bottles.

The Golden Cask Ledaig 9 Years Old cask no. CM 212, dist 2005, bott 2015 **(91.5)** n22.5 t23 f22.5 b23.5 A thin body, perhaps. But some smoky meat on it, too. 61.3%. sc. 312 bottles.

Gordon & MacPhail Connoisseurs Choice Ledaig 2000 **(88.5)** n22 t22.5 f22 b22 Ledaig at its very oiliest, though by no means smokiest. 46%

⬥ **Le Gus't Selection V Ledaig 2008** first fill bourbon, cask no. 700751, bott 2016 **(95.5)** n23.5 t24.5 f23.5 b24 My outstanding Chief Researcher, Vinny, had, with a very rare aberration, marked this down as a Tobermory: a mistake which, before the truth dawned, had me reaching for my smelling salts! This is as big and phenolic Ledaig I have encountered in 30 years. Something went wrong when they were sorting out the phenols levels here. And what was wrong, was so very right... 60.3%. sc.

Hepburn's Choice Tobermory Smoky & Peaty 8 Years Old refill hogshead, dist 2008, bott 2016 **(94)** n23.5 t24 f23 b23.5 Though marked as "Tobermory" the smokiness reveals this as a full-blown Ledaig. Fresh, quite beautifully made and very satisfying malt. 46%. nc ncf sc. 401 bottles.

⬥ **Kingsbury Gold Ledaig 19 Year Old** hogshead, cask no. 800106, dist 1997 **(79.5)** n19 t21 f20.5 b19 Not exactly a vintage time in this distillery's history. And although there is no denying the peaty impact, the overall disharmony and discontent amid the ranks is all too clear to see. 53.1%. 288 bottles. sc.

Maltmountains Tobermory 20 Years Old hogshead, dist 1995, bott 2015 **(86)** n21.5 t22 f21.5 b21. An intriguing, collectors' malt. Although a Tobermory, it was probably bottled after a Ledaig run – or it is a cask which once held peated malt – because the phenols play a vital role here. Like so much Tobermory, the actual distillation quality is not of Premiership quality: the oily nuttiness underlines the score there. But the phenols do help to up the mocha content to acceptable degrees. 48.4%. 48 bottles.

⬥ **Old Malt Cask Tobermory Aged 20 Years** refill hogshead, cask no. 13190, dist Jul 96, bott Jan 17 **(89)** n23 sprightly and defying its years. All kinds of fresh citrus notes reminds one of sweet shop, or some bakers, on a hot summer's day; t22.5 a perfect translation from nose to delivery, though those higher, mouth-watering barley tones fade surprisingly quickly as the oak makes its mark; f21.5 drier despite the slight tang; b22 such a wonderful nose and delivery! 50%. nc ncf sc. 242 bottles.

Old Malt Cask Tobermory Aged 21 Years sherry butt, cask no. 11891, dist Jul 94, bott Sept 15 **(73)** n18 t19 f18 b18. Don't blame the sherry butt. That is fine – indeed, it has been wasted!

It is all down to the bloody awful distillate made at the distillery. Almost worth rubber-necking for... 50%. nc ncf sc. 645 bottles.

Old Particular Highland Ledaig 10 Years Old (86) n22 t21 f22 b21. Lazily smoked and nutty, overall a bit of a disappointment as the stills appear to have been run ragged here. The malt barely sticks to the palate, while the smoke arrives in a gristy sweetness. 65.4%. Bottled for Big Market Berlin. 50th Anniversary bottling.

Old Particular Highland Ledaig 10 Years Old refill hogshead, dist Sept 05, bott Dec 15 (83) n20 t22 f20 b21. The pleasing peatiness does its best to mask a less than brilliant piece of distilling. Fails, though not without a fight. 48.4%. nc ncf sc. 349 bottles.

⬧ **Old Particular Ledaig 15 Years Old** refill hogshead, cask no. 11605, dist May 01, bott Mar 17 (85.5) n22.5 t21.5 f20 b21.5 The star turn has to be the nose, which is startlingly reminiscent of the air breathed in an island distillery warehouse on a dank December morn. However, despite the prompting of the modest peat, the dram never quite takes off and suffers from an unhelpful tangy residue. 48.4%. nc ncf sc. 355 bottles.

⬧ **Old Particular Ledaig 18 Years Old** refill butt, cask no. 11211, dist Apr 98, bott Jun 16 (83) n23 t23 f17 b20 Chunky, rip-roaring peat meets its match with a Melton Hunt Cake fruit onslaught: the marriage is turbulent, passionate and spellbindingly sexy...the divorce is messy and sulphur-laden.... 48.4%. nc ncf sc. 252 bottles.

Old Particular Highland Tobermory 20 Years Old refill hogshead, cask no. 10813, dist Jul 95, bott Jul 15 (91) n22 t23 f23 b23 Effortlessly beautiful. Charming and elegant throughout. 51.5%. nc ncf sc. 288 bottles.

⬧ **Old Particular Tobermory 21 Years Old** refill hogshead, cask no. 10950, dist Jul 94, bott Dec 15 (88) n21.5 sharp in part, the oak tries to disrupt the subtler tones of citrus-lined smoke; t23 recovers quickly on the palate as the delivery melds the juicier barley into the relaxed peat; f21.5 a slight wobble on the finale as the oak tires noticeably; b22 a little tangy in part, the soft smoke hides the majority of the cracks. 51.5%. nc ncf sc. 306 bottles.

Provenance Ledaig Aged 7 Years bott Mar 16 (88) n22.5 t22.5 f21 b22 A game little blighter for its age. What it lacks in complexity it makes up for with simple, smoky charm... 46%. nc ncf sc.

⬧ **Provenance Ledaig Aged 8 Years** refill hogshead, cask no. 11327, dist Feb 08, bott Aug 16 (90.5) n23 dry, sooty and, for all its youthful limitations, strangely satisfying in its depth...; t23 oily and gristy, as though a liberally sugared blend of Port Ellen when it was this age and Caol Ila; f22.5 the oils maintain their course, though the oak offers a surprisingly bitter turn which the intense sugars and smoke handle comfortably; b22 a high phenol level appears to be at play here, which makes this a must for peatophiles. 46%. nc ncf sc. 459 bottles.

Scotch Malt Whisky Society Cask 42.18 Aged 9 Years refill barrel, dist 05 Oct 06, bott 25 Jan 16 (85) n21 t21.5 f21 b21.5. Just from the cream soda nose – with a little smoked vanilla ice cream mixed in – you know you are in for an oily experience. While that comes true, the slight aggression to the middle, depicting a slightly hurried distillation, does come as a surprise. The light, unobtrusive smoke tries, along with the full-on sugars, to soothe. 59.3%. nc ncf sc. 234 bottles.

Simon Brown Tobermory American oak casks, dist Apr 94, bott Mar 06 (71.5) n18 t19.5 f16.5 b17.5. There are times you have to hold your hands up and say: sorry, this isn't very well made whisky. And this is one of them. Malty, for sure. But far too many crosses in the boxes. 46%. nc ncf.

⬧ **The Single Cask Tobermory Aged 22 Years** cask no. A394, dist 29 Mar 94, bott 13 Jan 17 (94) n24 over two decades of very good oak influence has resulted in a highly complex aroma needing a good 20 minutes to fully understand and explore. The malt is still intact and visible, but forms the gentler tones to soften the busy babblings of the tannin. These are peppery and pointed, a tad herbal as well as earthy in a dank bluebell wood kind of way; the sugars are discreet but, if you can spot them, of vaguely molassed disposition; there is also a grapefruit-style citrus note just to help the malt lighten matters; t23.5 brilliant! Just as busy as the nose, except now the malt is totally up front and in command, while the spices, like most of the tannin-related flavours take the hindmost; f22.5 just a little bitterness creeps into the light, malty fade; b24 what a fabulous example of the distillery at its most complex! 59.1%. nc ncf sc. 86 bottles.

Whic Tobermory 20 Years Old bourbon hogshead, cask no 1241, dist 18 Jul 95, bott 17 Aug 15 (90.5) n22 t23 f22.5 b23 Teeming with personality. The honey and sugars do a sound job between them. 54.8%. sc. 132 bottles.

The Whisky Cask Company Ledaig 17 Years Old bourbon hogshead, dist 1999 (93.5) n23 t23.5 f23.5 b23.5 A bit of a collector's item: a moderately oily and beautifully made malt from the turn of the century Tobermory. 51.5%

✧✧ **World of Orchids Tobermory 20 Year Old** bourbon cask, dist 1994 **(88)** n22 malty and mellifluous; t23 those honey notes take little time to present themselves, again alongside some sturdy barley. Spices begin to warm the mid-ground; f21 just a little jumbled, tangy oak amid the persistent barley; b22 take the off-beam finish out of the equation and this is a delightful malt. 47.9%.

TOMATIN
Speyside, 1897. Takara, Shuzo and Okura & Co. Working.

✧✧ **Tomatin 8 Years Old** bourbon & sherry casks db **(89)** n22 polite, though youthful exuberance is easy to spot. So is the fruitiness which displays a distant tang; t23 fabulous delivery of wet-behind-the-ears barley and under-ripe greengages: salivating and a lovely lead into the massive toffee; f21.5 just a little furriness to the latte coffee; b22.5 a malt very proud of its youth. 40%. Travel Retail Exclusive.

Tomatin 10 Year Old MacAlabur 10th Anniversary first fill ex-bourbon cask, cask no. 1874, dist 7 May 03, bott 28 Apr 14 db **(92.5)** n23 t24 f22.5 b23 That must have been one underused bourbon cask in Kentucky, because the tannins never release their grip. 58.4%. sc. 228 bottles. Bottled for the MacAlabur Barrel Society.

Tomatin 12 Years Old db **(85.5)** n21 t21.5 f22 b21. Reverted back to a delicately sherried style, or at least shows signs of a touch of fruit, as opposed to the single-minded maltfest it had recently been. So, nudge or two closer to the 18-y-o as a style and shows nothing other than good grace and no shortage of barley, either. 40%

Tomatin 12 Year Old finished in Spanish sherry casks db **(91.5)** n23 t23.5 f21.5 b23.5 For a great many years, Tomatin operated under severe financial restrictions. This meant that some of the wood brought to the distillery during this period was hardly of top-notch quality. This has made life difficult for those charged with moulding the stocks into workable expressions. I take my hat off to the creator of this: some great work is evident, despite the finish. 43%

Tomatin 14 Year Old Port Finish db **(92.5)** n23 under-ripe greengage shows some nip and spice; t24 salivating, as a Tomatin delivery so often is. But here we get all juiced up by succulent fruit, helped along by glazed muscvado; f22.5 the fruit tails off allowing the vanilla and spice an easy ride; b23 allows the top notch port a clear road. 46%. ncf.

✧✧ **Tomatin 15 Years Old** American oak casks db **(89.5)** n22.5 grass and hay mixed together; malted breakfast cereal with a sprinkling of muscovado sugar; t22.5 concentrated malt delivery. Salivating, with a profound ulmo honey and vanilla mix; f22 remains steadfastly malty, though the oak shows just a little sign of wear and tear as a degree of bitterness emerges; the spices rise to the challenge; b22.5 a delicious exhibition of malt. 46%. Travel Retail Exclusive.

Tomatin Aged 15 Years ex bourbon cask, bott 2010 db **(86)** n21 t22 f21.5 b21.5. One of the most malty drams on the market today. Perhaps suffers a little from the 43% strength as some of the lesser oak notes get a slightly disruptive foothold. But the intense, juicy barley trademark remains clear and delicious. 43% Tomatin Distillery

Tomatin 15 Years Old bourbon barrels and Spanish Tempranillo wine casks db **(88.5)** n22 t23 f21 b22.5. Not free from the odd problem with the Spanish wine casks but gets away with it as the overall complexity and enjoyment levels are high. 52%

Tomatin 15 Year Old Cadenhead's Anniversary bourbon barrel, Pedro Ximenez first fill cask finish, cask 34876 dist 30 Nov 01, bott 11 Apr 16 db **(93)** n23.5 t23.5 f23 b23 I actually began nosing this in the dark, before I was aware of the distillery. But I certainly knew the cask type: the PX drips all over this malt like a murderer's fingers drip blood over a knife. Guys, you are meant to dump the PX before putting the whisky in, right...? Oh, no sulphur by the way..yippee...!! 56.1%. ncf sc. Bottled for Cadenhead's Switzerland.

Tomatin Aged 18 Years db **(85)** n22 t21 f21 b21. I have always held a torch for this distillery and it is good to see some of the official older stuff being released. This one has some serious zing to it, leaving your tastebuds to pucker up - especially as the oak hits. 40%

Tomatin 18 Years Old db **(88)** n22.5 t22 f21.5 b22. What a well-mannered malt. As though it grew up in a loving, caring family and behaves itself impeccably from first nose to last whimpering finale; 43%

Tomatin 25 Years Old db **(89)** n22 t23 f21.5 b22.5. Not a nasty bone in its body: understated but significant. 43%

Tomatin 30 Years Old db **(91)** n22 t23 f23.5 b22.5 Malts of this age rarely maintain such a level of viscosity. Soft oils can often be damaging to a whisky, because they often refuse to allow character to flourish. Yet here we have a whisky that has come to terms with its age with great grace. And no little class. 49.3%

Tomatin 30 Year Old European & American oak casks db (85.5) n21 t21 f22.5 b21. Unusually for an ancient malt, the whisky becomes more comfortable as it wears its aged shoes. The delivery is just a bit too enthusiastic on the oaky front, but the natural caramels soften the journey rather delightfully. 46%. ncf.

Tomatin 36 Year Old American & European oak db (96.5) n24 t24.5 f23.5 b24.5 The difference between old oak and the newer stuff is brilliantly displayed here. Make no mistake: this is a masterpiece of a malt. 46%

Tomatin 40 Years Old db (89.5) n21.5 t22 f23 b23. Not quite sure how it's done it, but somehow it has made it through all those oaky scares to make for one very impressive 40-y-o!! Often it shows the character of a bourbon on a Zimmer. 42.9%

◇ **Tomatin 40 Years Old** Oloroso sherry casks db (87.5) n21.5 t23 f21 b22 One of those malts which offers a graceful peep at the past, when sherry butts were clean and offered nothing to fear. But no matter how good the cask time takes its toll and the intense chalkiness reveals tannins that have got slightly the better of the barley. Thankfully the grape is still intact and brings us a beautiful raisin and date depth before the chalk returns a little more determined than before. 43%. Travel Retail Exclusive.

◇ **Tomatin 1995 Olorosso Sherry** db (82) n21 t22 f19 b20 You can peel the grape off the malt. But one of the sherry butts wasn't quite as spotless as one might hope for. The inevitable tang arrives towards the finish. 46%.

Tomatin 2002 Whisky L Beijing - Shanghai 2015 American oak hogshead, cask no. 33196, dist 25 Jan 02, bott 10 Jun 15 db (95) n23.5 t24 f23.5 b24 Spectacularly serious whisky! Takes the oak element to the max without tipping over the edge, thanks to an absolutely top quality bourbon cask. About as enormous as this distillery gets. 57.8%. sc. 288 bottles.

Tomatin Highland 1988 Vintage db (86.5) n22 t22 f21 b21.5. Few whiskies in the world shows off its malty muscle like Tomatin and here, briefly, it goes into overdrive. For the most part, a happy meeting of slightly salty malt and oak. 46%. ncf.

◇ **Tomatin Cabernet Sauvignon 2002 Edition** db (82) n21 t22 f18 b21 Surprising degree of weight to this one. The fruit is not quite flawless with a little bit of a buzz on the nose and finish especially. But the rich mouthfeel and a pleasant, lush Garibaldi biscuit effect does ensure some very satisfying phases. 46%.

◇ **Tomatin Caribbean Rum 2007 Edition** db (89.5) n22 the spice prickle is little more than a tease, the sugars a murmur that let you know they are there, the malt seemingly bound tight within the oils; t23 fascinating delivery at one you have crisp, brittle sugars as well as thick, lush oils – about as polarised a start as you could make. The sugars play the more important role as they appear to release both the barley and the spices. But it is all very low key...; f22 and lower key as the vanillas at last arrive on the quiet fade; b22.5 beautifully clean malt though, as is their wont, the rum casks keep everything tight. 46%.

Tomatin Contrast Bourbon Casks from 1973, 1977, 1988, 2002, 2006 db (94.5) n24 t24 f22.5 b24 This is exceptionally fine malt whisky boasting an advanced degree of structure and complexity. If you don't have half an hour to spare to do it justice, don't even open the bottle... 46%. Packaged with sherry edition.

Tomatin Contrast Sherry Casks from 1973, 1977, 1988, 2002, 2006 db (87) n21 t22 f22 b22. Certainly a contrast with the bourbon, not least on the complexity front. No damaging off notes, even if the nose is a little tight. But though the grape makes itself heard, it never spreads its wings and flies in this curiously muted offering. 46%. Packaged with bourbon edition.

◇ **Tomatin Five Virtues Series Earth Peated Malt** refill hogshead oak casks db (88) n22 a hard and metallic nose with a half-hearted peat attachment; a hint of citrus helps balance things; t22.5 much better delivery. This really is a firm malt, though couched in a softer smoke this time. But soon hardens though at the middle; f21.5 really pretty thin with only the spices to hang on to; b22 can honestly say I have never seen Tomatin in this kind of shape before: enjoyable once you acclimatise... 46%.

◇ **Tomatin Five Virtues Series Fire Heavily Charred Oak** de-charred/re-charred oak fired casks db (94) n23.5 adorable Demerara sugars and red liquorice light up the clean barley; t24 so fresh and clean, this is a beautifully crisp delivery. Rich malted barley abounds, but always in a land of sugared tannin and spice; f23 medium length with the spices picking up wonderfully; b23.5 high class malt with a sweet bourbon drizzle. 46%.

◇ **Tomatin Five Virtues Series Metal Bourbon Barrels** first fill bourbon barrels db (95) n24 one of my favourite combinations on the planet: Tomatin and bourbon cask. The interplay between the red liquorice, orange blossom honey and tannin is fabulous. Yet at no time is the trademark intense barley ever diluted or lost...; t24 the gloss on the oils here take some study. Malt appears to stick to the plate and with it ulmo honey and maple syrup. The spices arrive later but, initially, with little gusto; **f23** bigger spice now and a gentle vanilla fade; **b24** there's metal enough in the "Earth" bottling. Was wondering where the metal comes into things here. As these are first fill bourbon casks, wonder if it was the type of warehouse they came from in Kentucky... Anyway, talking metal: this is pure gold... 46%.

◈ **Tomatin Five Virtues Series Water Winter Distillation** sherry butts & bourbon barrels db **(72) n18 t20 f16 b18** A small degree of molassed chocolate escapes the grim sulphured tightness of the sherry. 46%.

◈ **Tomatin Five Virtues Series Wood Selected Oak Casks** French, American & Hungarian oak casks db **(90) n22.5** Demerara sugars from each and every way: tannins add an extra degree of sharpness and spice; vaguely chaotic, but works attractively; **t23** for all the shenanigans on the nose, it is the malt which bursts through unsullied and to maximum salivating effect. The tannins are on its tail, but the sugars re-emerge with a spicy accompaniment and make for youthful but busy dramming; **f21.5** a little hint of cocoa, but also a shade of furriness from, presumably, the Tokay; **b23** a Franco-Hungarian truce means the malt and bourbon casks can work their magic...Some truly brilliant and unique phrases here. 46%.

◈ **Tomatin Highland Grand Select** db **(92.5) n23** the style with which this distillery is most comfortable: healthy fresh barley and solid, though not too emphatic, oak. Pleasing light citrus, too; **t23** excellent delivery: the two major players share equal billing but the muscovado sugars add a vague fruity piquancy; **f23.5** some fabulous chocolate nut on the finish; **b23** measured and elegant. 43%.

◈ **Tomatin Highland Legacy** db **(88) n22** simplistic, untaxing malt and vanilla **t22.5** best bit of the experience: the big malt and marzipan surge and interweaving of sharp tannins; **f21.5** a light, malty buzz; **b22** clean, nutty malt but beyond that unremarkable. 43%.

Tomatin Warehouse 6 Collection 1971 db **(87) n22 t22 f21.5 b21.5.** Just one of those terribly frustrating malts where you just have to say: sorry, chaps, but you allowed this one to wallow in the warehouse a summer or two too long. Some superb vanilla and butterscotch, but the tannins have just a little bit too much of a scowl to their faces...That said, still plenty to savour and a fair bit of spice to show there's still life in the old dog... 45.8%

◈ **Cù Bòcan 2005** db **(91) n22.5** the youngest nose from a distillery bottling in Scotland this year: a real new make freshness at work here, though it is set against an injection of rabid tannin, a bizarre unidentified phenol note and muscovado....phew! **t23.5** have some hankies ready: eye-watering enough to be a tear-jerker. The young barley notes offer malt in pure concentrated form while the spices run riot through the sugars; **f22** just a little bitterness towards the end; **b23** one of the most intriguing whiskies out there today: you never know quite what is going to land on your lap. Here the battle between a very young malt personality and spice is worth the entrance fee alone... Love it! 50%.

Cù Bòcan 1988 db **(89.5) n23** quite a dry smokiness; no shortage of herbal notes, too....; **t22.5** soft oils encourage the vanillas as much as the light smoke; **f21.5** reverts to its naturally dry stance; a few spices liven things up while some late mocha does offer a sweeter edge; **b22.5** continually smoulders... 51.5%. nc ncf. 2,200 bottles.

Cù Bòcan The Bourbon Edition fully matured in bourbon casks db **(84) n21.5 t22 f20 b20.5.** The malt battles hard to overcome the poor cask bitterness. But fails. 46%

Cù Bòcan Highland Single Malt virgin oak, bourbon & sherry casks db **(85.5) n21 t21 f22 b21.5.** An old fashioned dram: the type Pitt the Younger, or Pitt the Embryo might remember... and appreciate. Appears to be nearer new make than fully matured Scotch: the big player is the oak which, almost, bourbon-like, shovels cart loads of caramel and muscovado into the mix. Green...and engrossing. 46%

Cù Bòcan Highland Single Malt 1989 Vintage db **(95.5) n23 t24 f24.5 b24** the last Cu Bocan I got my nose around, I likened to Pitt the Younger. Well, the only pit here would be a peat one... This is not only absolutely superb whisky, but a bit of a shock, too...Indeed, I am stunned! 53.2%. ncf.

Cù Bòcan The Sherry Edition fully matured in sherry casks db **(83) n20 t22 f20 b21.** For several magic seconds, the delivery and first four or five flavour waves after offer delicious malt polished by high grade grape. But it is all far too short-lived as off-key notes abound on the nose and finish. 46%

Cù Bòcan The Virgin Oak Edition fully matured in virgin oak casks db **(94.5) n23.5 t23.5 f23.5 b24** Don't expect a quiet little whisky to nuzzle into. This chap has attitude, and no little complexity. Magnificent use of differing honey styles: overall a delightful box of tricks. 46%

BDRAM Tomatin 1994 19 Year Old hogshead, cask no. 12351, dist 2 Nov 94, bott 6 Nov 13 **(89.5) n21.5 t23 f22.5 b22.5** A slightly over-aged malt still very true to the character of the distillery: delicious! 55.5%. Bottled by Morrison & Mackay Ltd.

◈ **The Cyprus Whisky Association Tomatin 2006** first fill bourbon barrel, cask no. 4191, dist 05 Oct 06, bott 18 Apr 16 (93) **n23** if you want to study malt in all its forms and weights, simply stick your nose above a glass of this...phenomenal...! **t23.5** typical surge of Tomatin-style malt, though accompanied by a very un-Tomatin display of rampant spices. The sugars – plus a little ulmo honey – perform a delicate balancing act; **f23** really lovely fade with the oak lightly tapping on the malty window asking to come in; **b23.5** a very impressive choice of cask by the Cyprus Whisky Association: this is as much a pre-prandial loosener as it is a late night puzzler. Gorgeous. 58.9%. sc. 222 bottles.

◈ **The First Editions Tomatin Aged 22 Years 1994** refill hogshead, cask no. 13275, bott 2017 (92.5) **n22.5** some fruit at work: crushed grape pips, over-aged, dry apple dominate the landscape; oak casts a threatening shadow...; **t24** melt-in-the-mouth barley but the oak is knocking loudly and impatiently on the door. A real fracas on the palate as the malt tries to play down the oaky impact but the stunning silkiness – helped by a gentle praline chocolate and molasses subplot – ensures all works out for the best; **f22.5** dry, a little tangy and tiring; **b23.5** feeling its age but hangs in there impressively. 47.4%. nc ncf sc. 274 bottles.

The Golden Cask Tomatin 20 Years Old cask no. CM 221, dist 1994, bott 2015 (86.5) **n21 t23 f21.5 b21**. No shortage of merit in this big, oak-infested dram. But the tannins play too fierce a role and, once the brown sugars have been washed away, what remains is just a little too splintery for its own good. 53.9%. sc. 257 bottles.

Gordon & MacPhail Cask Strength Tomatin 2004 (92.5) **n23.5 t23 f23 b23** A model malt. Fabulously structured and shows all its barley-rich clarity. 61.2%

Gordon & MacPhail Connoisseurs Choice Tomatin 2002 (89) **n22.5** malt; **t22** malt; **f22** malt; **b22.5** so simplistically, yet deliciously, malty! Laid back and entertains without even trying. 46%

◈ **Old Malt Cask Tomatin Aged 21 Years** refill hogshead, cask no. 13268, dist Dec 95, bott Feb 17 (86) **n22 t22 f20.5 b21.5** Atypical of a Tomatin with the malt playing a very silent second fiddle to the must-style fruit pips. Thin, pleasant but, by Tomatin standards, unconvincing. 50%. nc ncf sc. 309 bottles.

◈ **Scotch Malt Whisky Society Cask 11.32 8 Year Old** first fill ex-bourbon barrel, dist 6 Jun 08 (95.5) **n23.5** what an impressive mix of firm oak, rich malt and deft Demerara sugars: not a wobble or off note to be found **t24** splendid malt-lashed delivery. Tomatin is one of the maltiest of all distilleries and here the barley appears in bread and buttery form. You could sink a well into the oils but the spice-sugar mix is unfathomable; **f24** more and more chewy malt and Worther's Originals...; **b24** give me a bottle of youthful, beautifully confident malt like this over an over-aged one any day...Brilliant...! 61.6%.

The Warehouse Collection Tomatin Aged 20 Years bourbon barrel, cask no. 2798, dist 02 Nov 94, bott 30 Oct 15 (94) **n23 t24 f23.5 b23.5** This cask puts me in mind of a blender who a good dozen years ago now had major problems with a new brand he was working on. His budget would not allow his malt content to go much above about 30%, and try as hard as he might, he just could not impart the lingering malty layering as he wanted. At his wits' end, he rang me for help and told me the malts he had put together. "So you are not using Tomatin, then?" I observed. He confirmed he wasn't. "Can you get any?" I asked. He thought he could. A week later he rang me. Bingo! He had cracked it, thanks to the Tomatin. Taste this and you'll see exactly why... 58.7%. nc ncf. 103 bottles.

Whiskybroker Tomatin 21 Year Old refill hogshead, cask no. 2323011258, dist 14 Oct 94, bott 12 Feb 16 (82.5) **n19 t22.5 f20.5 b20.5**. A creamy, malty whisky. But a few too many summers have seen the cask give up a few of its more milky elements. The late delivery does offer a pleasant chocolate lime moment or two, though. 53.4%. sc.

TOMINTOUL

Speyside, 1965. Angus Dundee. Working.

Tomintoul Aged 10 Years db (83.5) **n21 t20 f21.5 b21**. Has bucked up recently to offer a juicy, salivating barley thrust. Yet still a little on the thin side, despite some late oak. 40%

◈ **Tomintoul Aged 10 Years** bott code: L16 02149 CB2 db (84.5) **n20.5 t22 f21 b21** A very consistent dram but far too much emphasis of the chocolate toffee rather than the big malt you feel is bursting to break free. 40%

Tomintoul Aged 12 Years Oloroso Sherry Cask Finish db (73.5) **n18.5 t19 f18 b18**. Tomintoul, with good reason, styles itself as "The Gentle Dram" and you'll hear no argument from me about that one. However, the sherry influence here offers a rough ride. 40%

Tomintoul Aged 14 Years db (91) **n23.5 t23 f21.5**. This guy has shortened its breath somewhat: with the distinct thinness to the barley and oak arriving a little flustered and half-hearted rather than with a confident stride; b23 remains a beautiful whisky full of vitality and displaying the malt in its most naked and vulnerable state. But I get the feeling that perhaps a few too many third fills, or under-performing seconds, has resulted in the intensity and hair-raising harmony of the truly great previous bottlings just being slightly undercooked. That said, still a worthy and delicious dram! 46%. nc ncf.

Tomintoul Aged 15 Years Portwood Finish db (94) n23 both the malt and grape drip from the glass – in about equal measure; t23.5 salivating yet weighty. The spices check in early, the only luggage being some excellent vanilla notes, as the oak reminds us of the decent age. The fruit pootles along without a care in the world; f23.5 superb, understated finish: plenty of evidence still of a plummy fruit...and still the barley carries through; b24 so rare to find a wine finish which maximises the fruit to the full without allowing it to dominate. Charming. And so clean. Probably a brilliant whisky to help repair my damaged palate after tasting yet another s******ed sherry butt. I'll keep this one handy...46%. nc ncf. 5,820 bottles.

Tomintoul Aged 16 Years db (94.5) n24.5 t23.5 f23 b23.5 Confirms Tomintoul's ability to dice with greatness. 40%

Tomintoul Aged 21 Years db (94) n24 t24 f22.5 b23.5 Just how good this whisky would have been at cask strength or even at 46 absolutely terrifies me. 40%.

Tomintoul Aged 25 Years db (95) n25 t24 f23 b23.5 A quiet masterpiece from one of Scotland's criminally underappreciated great distilleries. 43%

Tomintoul Aged 40 Years db (86) n22 t21 f21.5 b21.5. Groans every single one of its 40 years. Some lovely malty moments still, as well as butterscotch. But the oak has just jogged on past the sign that said 'Greatness' and carried straight on into the woods... 43.1%. nc ncf. 500 bottles.

Tomintoul 1976 Vintage bott 2013 db (94.5) n25 t22 f23.5 b24 When you get that amount of exotic fruit on the nose, you know there is going to be a massive oaky kickback somewhere. However, this copes brilliantly and even has something fruitier up its sleeve further down the line. This can be taken as one of your five fruits a day... 40%

Tomintoul Five Decades bott Jul 15 db (94.5) n23.5 t24 f23 b24 Writing this Bible, and the inordinate amount of time it takes, day and night, night and day, week in, month out, means that I have to turn down most invites to attend the opening of distilleries and the celebration of anniversaries. Just can't fit it in. So glad the 50th anniversary of Tomintoul came to me in the shape of this luxurious dram. Another whisky that leaves you scratching your head to wonder why Whyte and Mackay sold this brilliant distillery: as though the manager wanted to get rid of the star player to harmonise the dressing room. Anyway, happy 50th birthday, Tomintoul distillery: you are in loving hands now and able to fulfil your enormous potential. 50%. nc ncf. 5,230 bottles.

Tomintoul With A Peaty Tang db (94) n23 t24 f23 b24. A bit more than a tang, believe me! Faultlessly clean distillate that revels in its unaccustomed peaty role. The age is confusing and appears mixed, with both young and older traits being evident. 40%

Old Ballantruan db (89.5) n23.5 t23 f21 b22 Profound young malt which could easily be taken for an Islay. 50%. ncf.

Old Ballantruan Aged 10 Years bott code 1706.15 db (94.5) n23.5 oily now, in a Caol Ila style: the phenols cling to the nose. Clean, with vanilla unhindered despite the smoke; t23.5 not sure I have ever come across a smoked whisky which is so oily yet so juicy: very odd! Just like the nose, the vanilla and peat are the two main characters, but a light smattering of maple syrup does no harm; f23.5 long. Spices at last arrive and oils recede as it dries; b24 can't say this is a spectacular peated malt. But everything is brilliantly in proportion and so sublimely balanced. 50%. ncf.

◈ **Hepburn's Choice Tomintoul 10 Years Old** refill butt, dist 2006, bott 2016 (81.5) n21.5 t21 f19 b20 Silky and malty. But never quite takes off or sits comfortably on the palate. A little furry and spiked on the finish. 46%. nc ncf sc. 654 bottles.

◈ **Kingsbury Gold Tomintoul 16 Year Old** butt, cask no. 9525, dist 1999 (95) n23 Cadbury's Fruit and Nut chocolate – with the emphasis on the fruit and with a few fat, freshly squashed sultanas added for good measure; t24 salivating, though here for the unusual reason of intense fruit and spice. The barley arrives late and with an apology; f24 oh, those spices...and back we go to fruit and nut chocolate – though with a bit of Old Jamaica spice...; b24 suspect this sherry butt has done the rounds: no sulphur off notes whatsoever and enough fruit to make significant and enjoyable contribution. What a wonderful surprise this is! Technically faultless. 59%. 560 bottles. sc.

◈ **The Single Cask Tomintoul Aged 22 Years** cask no. 2156, dist 1995 (93) n22.5 a pleasing mix of mint, bluebells and thinned clove; spiced, of course and soft heather-honey to man-mark it; **t23** the salivating malts gather early then radiate a light citrusy Demerara sugar; spices fill the mid-ground alongside liquorice and marzipan; **f23.5** some oils form now to change the shape and keep the show on the road: all the flavours found in the mid-ground of the palate extend their lives with a little mocha being added at the very death; **b24** one of those rare malts which just gets better as it goes along. Superb! *53.2%. nc ncf sc.*

That Boutique-y Whisky Company Tomintoul batch 2 **(88)** n22 t23 f21.5 b21.5 Malts rarely come much cleaner. An odd distinctive fruitiness more akin to brandy. *54.1%. 71 bottles.*

TORMORE
Speyside, 1960. Chivas Brothers. Working.

Tormore 12 Years Old db **(75)** n19 t19 f19 b18. For those who like whisky in their caramel. *40%*

Tormore Aged 14 Years batch no. A1308, bott 2013 db **(83.5)** n21 t21.5 f20.5 b20.5. Toffeed, flat and inoffensive. Good dram to have last thing at night: chances are you'll be asleep before you finish the glass... *43% WB15/326*

Tormore Aged 15 Years "Special Distillery Bottling" db **(71)** n17 t18 f19 b17. Even a supposed pick of choice casks can't save this from its fiery fate. *46%*

Tormore Aged 16 Years batch no. B1309, bott 09 2013 db **(95)** n23.5 t24 f23.5 b24 Tormore as I have never seen it before. The label talks about the "long and dry" finish. It does the bottling such a disservice: this is magnificently complex with cocoa notes a thing of sheer beauty. A landmark bottling for Tormore. *48%*

Alos Sansibar Whisky Tormore 1988 bott 2016 **(86)** n21.5 t23 f20 b21.5 If you do try this try not to concentrate too much on the tangy finish supplied by an unhappy oak note. Instead concentrate on the delivery which boasts a fabulous boiled fruit and barley sugar candy mix. *50.4%.*

Chapter 7 Tormore 1995 19 Year Old bourbon hogshead, cask no. 20159 **(94.5)** n23.5 t24 f23 b24 For a Tormore, this is right up there. No: despite its usual rough and ready antics, this is beyond all possible expectation. But just dig that delivery! Groovy, baby! *55.7%. sc. 209 bottles.*

The Cooper's Choice Tormore Sweet & Smoky Islay cask, port cask finish, bott 2017 **(96)** n23.5 most smoke cask matured whiskies give only a gentle reminder of its origin: this one is positively bursting with phenols in a way you'd expect a peaty whisky to behave: extraordinary...; **t24.5** and here we go again on delivery: substantial phenols, certainly enough to dominate the early exchanges. But slowly the juicy fruitiness begins to make inroads, until we have a Cadbury's Dairy Fruit middle with a medium and elegant smoke guard of honour; **f23.5** vanillas begin to leak into the mix, but it is an elegant fade with no bitterness or aggression of any sort...; **b24.5** not a style of Tormore you really expect to see. Someone has done a very good job on this to produce probably the best Tormore I have ever encountered. A big surprise and genuine treat of a dram. And certainly one of my left field favourites of the year... *56.5%. nc ncf sc. The Vintage Malt Whisky Co.*

The First Editions Tormore Aged 25 Years 1992 refill butt, cask no. 13311, bott 2017 **(93)** n23 you might swear there is the phantom of something smoky lurking on the gentle fruit; grape must has a pithy streak; **t23.5** brilliant! Tormore as its most expansive: the outstanding oak gives a lustre to the muscovado sugars and vanilla. The spice is three dimensional, especially against the silky countenance; **f23** long with a light pepper attached to the dry pear. Still a little salivating at the very end...and that hint of smoke returns, too; **b23.5** not too bad a butt at all. Outstanding, in fact, and not an atom of sulphur to be seen. *55.9%. nc ncf sc. 434 bottles.*

Gordon & MacPhail Connoisseurs Choice Tormore 1998 (87) n21.5 t22.5 f21.5 b21.5. A sober and, at times, suave malt. Silky soft, it is comfortable in its malty skin but rarely ventures away from the barley theme. Limited in scope, but delicious in what it does. *46%*

Gordon & MacPhail Cask Strength Tormore 2004 (85.5) n21 t22 f21 b21.5. An above standard Tormore which really blasts out its malty credentials at full volume. The sugars threaten to overdo things slightly and the heat is not all to do with the alcohol. But all this more than make up for the wallpaper paste, nutty aroma. *61.2%*

Old Malt Cask Tormore Aged 27 Years refill butt, cask no. 12239, dist Nov 88, bott Apr 16 **(84.5)** n20.5 t22.5 f20.5 b21. From the marking, you can see it has a flaw. Yet the nuttiness, richness of the unsullied grape impresses. *50%. nc ncf sc. 268 bottles.*

Old Malt Cask Tormore Aged 28 Years sherry butt, cask no. 13189, dist Nov 88, bott Jan 17 **(77)** n17 t21 f19 b20 Full credit here to Tormore which, though not being one of Scotland's more gifted distilleries, has put up a brave fight and offered some massively juicy barley to see off the worst excesses of the off-tune sherry butt. *50%. nc ncf sc. 403 bottles.*

Single Cask Collection Tormore Aged 20 Years bourbon hogshead (77.5) n19.5 t21 f19 b18. Thinly structured malt. Sweet, momentarily citrusy. But never forms a sensible combination of flavours. 53.1%. sc.

◈ **Spirits Shop Selection Tormore 1988** bourbon cask, bott 2016 (87) n21.5 t23.5 f20.5 b21.5 For a bourbon cask, this is one very confusing dram. Certainly Tormore is not a malt you normally align with complexity. But here there is so much going on with a fruity, muscovado, fresh date theme that it takes a little while for the cask's origins to make their mark. The finish is of the usual hard, unyielding house style. But the delivery, when peaking, is magnificent. 51.6%. 228 bottles. A joint bottling with Sansibar Whisky.

Whisky Live Tel Aviv Tormore 19 Years Old hogshead, cask no. 20315, dist 1995, bott 2015 (85.5) n19 t22.5 f22 b22. The nose may not be up to much. But there is no denying the attractiveness of the malty, milk-chocolate theme. Like a distilled night-time cup of cocoa. 49.1%. sc. 289 bottles.

TULLIBARDINE
Highlands (Perthshire), 1949. Tullibardine Ltd. Working.

Tullibardine Aged 20 Years db (92.5) n22.5 busy and can't decide which weight to adopt; ethereal hazelnut and citrus rise above the languid tannins; t24 no doubting the richness of body and the exceptional weight: first it is scorched yet juicy barley by the cartload, then thudding oak with just enough ulmo honey to oil the wheels. And then rampaging spice; f22.5 settles for more prosaic butterscotch but the spices continue to bristle; b23.5 while there are whiskies like this in the world, there is a point to this book... 43%

Tullibardine Aged 25 Years db (86.5) n22 t22 f21 b21.5. There can be too much of a good thing. And although the intricacies of the honey makes you sigh inwardly with pleasure, the overall rigidity and fundamentalism of the oak goes a little too far. 43%

◈ **Tullibardine 1970** db (96.5) n25 ancient oak but the caress on the nose of the most profound exotic fruit – and the distinguished style with which it is effortlessly delivered makes this something extra special. There is a hint of pineapple and passion fruit but the acidity is kept in check by mango and the most genteel hint of smoke you are ever likely to encounter. Frankly, I could nose this all day long, like hours of foreplay without carrying out the act...; t24.5 the malt and fruit dissolves on the palate without you having to do anything. The tannins possess the most subtle of spices which shape the mid-ground and offer unexpected life and activity. But before we reach that point we have already encountered the malts, thick in constitution and radiating as gently as possible a Manuka and ulmo honey blend of sweetness, tempered by a chalk dry but entirely delightful vanilla; from somewhere a little mocha can be found, too...; f23 the chalkiness continues, with a little citrus joining the vanilla now...; b24s I am a professional wordsmith with a very long time in whisky. Yet words, any words, can barely do justice... 40.5%.

Tullibardine 225 sauternes cask finish db (85) n20 t22.5 f21 b21.5. Hits the heights early on in the delivery when the honey and Lubeck marzipan are at full throttle. 43%

Tullibardine 228 Burgundy cask finish db (82) n21 t22 f18 b21. No shortage of bitter chocolate. Flawed but a wow for those looking for mega dry malt. 43%

Tullibardine 500 sherry cask finish db (79.5) n19 t21 f19 b20.5. The usual problems from Jerez, but the grape ensures maximum chewability. 43%

◈ **Tullibardine The Murray** dist 2004, bott 2016 db (94.5) n23.5 the most beautiful barley, still gristy and sugar-bound combine with the greenest greengages. Yet the fruit appears to be only an extension of the muscovado sugars which slowly yields to the ever-intensifying spice...wow! t24 it had to be clean and salivating....and it is. Lovers of Glen Moray, Cardhu and Tomatin will recognise this barley style, as though sugars and vanillas are falling from the ever-expanding malt; f23 the spices have to deal with a minor bitterness but the creamy butterscotch joins forces to see it off; b24 beautiful, fulsome whisky which just pulses with personality. Still, I think my lawyers are twitching at this one: for the avoidance of doubt, this whisky has absolutely nothing to do with me and I make no money from any sales. 56.1%. The Marquess Collection.

Tullibardine Sovereign bourbon barrel db (89.5) n22.5 a kind of 'what's what' of bourbon aromas: an entire regiment of delicate oaky tones from the standard butterscotch through to polished oak floors. But all tinged with a green-ish barley note. Always light and a little chalky; t23 the nose is transferred almost in identical form to the delivery: more light sugars at play here and a little nutty, too; f21.5 a slight tang to the fading milky Sugar Puffs; b22.5 beautifully salivating despite the intricate oak notes. 43%

◈ **Hunter Laing's Old & Rare Tullibardine Aged 25 Years** refill hogshead, dist Sept 90, bott Apr 16 (84) n23 t21.5 f19.5 b21 Sadly, the event doesn't live up to the hype on the nose. Where the aroma is a tone-poem in which orange blossom honey has a leading role, the oak-dominant, flat delivery and bitter finish is nothing like. *479%. nc ncf sc. 174 bottles.*

Old Malt Cask Tullibardine Aged 21 Years sherry butt, cask no. 12143, dist May 94, bott Nov 15 (85.5) **n21 t22 f21 b21.5**. Absolutely no sulphur on the cask; indeed, hard to see where the sherry makes its mark at all. Instead, we have a very basic, malt-charged offering which is never less than pleasant, though limited, in scope. *50%. nc ncf sc. 302 bottles.*

Scotch Malt Whisky Society Cask 28.30 Aged 25 Years 2nd fill Sauternes hogshead, dist 25 Jun 90, bott 31 Oct 15 (89) **n22 t22.5 f22 b22.5** Impressively understated. *53.3%. nc ncf sc. 228 bottles.*

That Boutique-y Whisky Company Tullibardine batch 1 (89) **n21 t23 f22.5 b22.5** Lovely, untaxing whisky with enough going on to keep the taste buds on full alert. *50.1%. 159 bottles.*

WOLFBURN

⬧ **Wolfburn Aurora** sherry oak casks db (91.5) **n22.5** several layers at play: a kind of an egg-nog, custardy tone which combines with the grape to create a sherry trifle effect; as well as an oilier, prickly spiced heavier tone to the barley which is clearly from the distillation; **t24** brilliant...absolutely brilliant. Both the young gristy malt and the most delicate apricot and green gooseberry note to combine for as sensual a delivery you are likely to find. The mid-ground thickens quickly and quite huskily too. First with coarser barley and then some searing spice; **f22** bitters out as the slightly wide cut from the still takes effect; **b23** early days at a distillery and still finding their feet with the still. The cut on this was wider than on the previous bottling I sampled, but there is no faulting the use of the 100% sulphur-free sherry butt. There is the odd aspect of genius attached to this dram, for sure. For the record: just vatted this with some OTT oak-hit sherry-cask 1954 malt in need of the kiss of life, or like a vampire in need of a virgin's blood: I suspect the first time a Wolfburn has been mixed with a 60-year-old Speysider. Result? One of the most complex and complete experiences of the last couple of months – a would-be award winner, were it commercially available! Stunning! *46%. nc ncf.*

⬧ **Wolfburn Single Malt Scotch Whisky** db (91.5) **n23** the tannins have just taken enough shine off the new make to ensure this has all the right whisky vibes. Still very youthful, with the grist retaining citrus-imbued fizz, but an elegant smokiness drifts around ensuring weight and substance; **t23** mmm! Superb delivery! Yes, this may be a youngster, but the weight of the barley-enriched oil is wonderful, especially seeing as there is not a single note of feintiness to be had. With this oil, the smoke, so apparent on the nose, plays a lesser part, though it still hangs around to give a lightly peated accent to the gentle cocoa; **f22.5** the finish always undoes the young-uns, though here just enough oak is involved to ensure the lingering malt doesn't fade alone; **b23** this is a very young malt showing an intriguing wispy smokiness, its evenness more in line with having been matured in ex-Islay casks than using low phenol barley. Still, it might have been, and, if so, perhaps reveals a style that would not have been entirely unknown to the people of Thurso when they last drank this during Victorian times. It is probably 30 years ago I was shown to a spot in the town where I was told the original distillery had been. Now it is back, and eclipses Pulteney as the producers of the most northerly mainland Scottish whisky. For all its youth, its excellence of quality glimmers from the glass: a malt as beautifully flighted as a cricket ball delivered by the most crafted of spinners. And offers a delightful turn on the palate, too. The building of a new distillery, no matter how romantic its location or story, does not guarantee good whisky. So I am delighted for those involved in a project as exhausting as this that a very good whisky is exactly what they have on their hands. *46%. nc ncf.*

UNSPECIFIED SINGLE MALTS (CAMPBELTOWN)

Cadenhead's Campbeltown Malt (92) **n22 t24 f23 b23**. On their home turf you'd expect them to get it right... and, my word, so they do!! *59.5%*

UNSPECIFIED SINGLE MALTS (HIGHLAND)

Alexander Murray & Co Bon Accord Highland Single Malt (82.5) **n21 t21.5 f20 b20.** Fudge whisky. Pleasant, but way too simple. *40%*

Alexander Murray & Co Highland Single Malt 1964 49 Years Old (88) **n22 t23 f21.5 b21.5**. For a malt bottled on the cusp of its 50th anniversary of being distilled, beyond the delivery it is hard to find a narrative here. Often malts of this age are simply too oaky and lopsided to be of any significance on the greatness front. This certainly has its fair share of tannin, and even a hint of bourbon on the nose. But it is the reticence of the malt to give much of a clue to what's been happening all these years which is perplexing: I cannot remember a bottled whisky of this age which is so comprehensively gagged on the mid-ground and finish. At times you can almost chew the golden syrup-dripping sawdust. And the spices at the death are superb. No doubting it has some genuinely lovely moments, and if you are looking for a very old malt which simply exudes soft, aged, occasionally charming benevolence, then this could be for you. But, overall, it is all so frustratingly fuddled and fudged. *40%*

Alexander Murray & Co Highland Single Malt 1995 19 Years Old (85) n21 t22 f21 b21. Agreeably spiced toffee. *40%*

⬧ **Glenwill RV** rum cask finish (80) n21 t21 f19 b19 Mainly toffeed, characterless and just zzzzzzzzzz.... *40%. Quality Spirits International.*

⬧ **Glenwill S = 1** sherry butt finish (73) n19 t21.5 f16 b17.5 S = Sulphur. *40%. Quality Spirits International.*

⬧ **Grangestone Master's Selection Highland Single Malt** bourbon cask finish (87) n22.5 t22 f21 b21.5 An attractive interplay between tannin and toffee, though the complexity is limited – especially on the simplistic finish. Good, though brief, molasses lift off on delivery. *40%. Quality Spirits International.*

⬧ **Hepburn's Choice Nice 'N Peaty 10 Years Old** refill hogshead, dist 2006, bott 2016 (87) n21.5 t22 f21.5 b22 Well, that was nice 'n' peaty...! *46%. nc ncf sc. 355 bottles.*

⬧ **Hepburn's Choice Nice 'N Peaty 10 Years Old** red wine finished barrique, dist 2006, bott 2016 (89) n22 curiously, the smoke is more pronounced amid the fruit than it is in their standard cask...; t22 juicy volley of grist and boiled fruit sweets; f22.5 best part so far with a real dovetailing of grape and phenol; some late spice with mocha; b22.5 well, that was nice 'n' fruity...! *46%. nc ncf sc. 352 bottles.*

⬧ **Master of Malt Highland Single Malt** (86.5) n21.5 t22 f21.5 b21.5 Pleasant, absolutely middle of the road malt with a juicy, nutty and toffee-rich character. *40%.*

⬧ **Muirhead's Silver Seal Aged 12 Years Highland Single Malt** (87.5) n22 t22 f21 b21.5 Satisfyingly salivating. The vanillas arrive with a lemon escort from the first moment, ensuring a semi-ethereal element to this. Lightly oiled and a little nutty, just a tad too much caramel at the times you want the malt to begin to fly. *40%. Tullibardine Ltd.*

⬧ **Muirhead's Silver Seal Aged 16 Years Highland Single Malt** (86) n21 t23 f20.5 b21.5 A hefty malt with a battling, earthy aroma. Hits its zenith about four or five flavour waves after delivery when it strikes up a stunning spicy walnut cake and date middle. Flags towards the finish, even becoming a little flat and furry, save for the wonderful spices.... *40%. Tullibardine Ltd.*

⬧ **Muirhead's Silver Seal Maturity Highland Single Malt** (84) n19.5 t22 f21 b21.5 Though called "Maturity" the malt displays a youthful gristiness from time to time. Not technically the greatest nose, the malt recovers brightly on the palate with a volley of varied sugars and spice, including a light smothering of heather honey. *40%. Tullibardine Ltd.*

⬧ **Scotch Universe Kepler-186f 187° U.71' 1775.1"** first fill Port pipe, dist 2001, bott 2016 (89.5) n23 antique shops packed to the gunnels with ancient brown furniture; salted nuts; t22.5 thick and salivating, the fruit, mostly dry and angular, drips from every corner of the palate; f21.5 bitter cocoa and blood orange; b22.5 that Port pipe must have been very fresh, indeed... *59%.*

⬧ **Tesco Finest Aged 12 Years Highland Single Malt** bott code L63353 (80.5) n20 t21 f19 b20.5 Quite possibly one of the most boring single malts of all time: not recommended as a night cap as you'll doze off by the time you reach the third step on your stairs, and it won't be the effect of the alcohol. Bland barely covers it. With the amount of cream toffee found on the nose and palate not sure if this should be stocked in the Spirits or Sweets aisles. Do I like it? No. Do I dislike it? No. But if I am putting 12-year-old malt into my body, I'd like it to have some semblance of character. I suppose it was designed to offend nobody: a mute hardly can. Trouble is, it is hardly likely to get new drinkers wanting to come back and discover more about single malt, either. Oh well, I suppose that buggers up any chance of getting The Bible stocked and sold by Tesco this year. But I'm afraid they need to hear the truth. *40%.*

Trader Joe's Highland Single Malt 1996 17 Years Old (86.5) n21.5 t22 f21.5 b21.5. Some serious juiciness and spice on the delivery. The spices last the course. *40%.*

UNSPECIFIED SINGLE MALTS (ISLAND)

Master Of Malt Island Single Malt (91.5) n22.5 t23 f22.5 b23.5. Don't know about Lord of the Isles. More like Lord of the Flies...Fruit flies, that is...! They would be hard pressed to find even an over-ripe mango any juicier than this gorgeous malt... *40%*

UNSPECIFIED SINGLE MALTS (ISLAY)

Ben Bracken Islay Single Malt 22 Years Old dist 1993 (96) n24.5 a rare, absolutely spot on marriage between grand old oak, but beautifully manicured and controlled peat reek;

with the vaguest citrus peeping from just around the corner, this is just glorious...; t24 a beautifully soft delivery, smoky, velvet fingers caressing the taste buds. The oak is tinged with a bourbony signature; f23.5 soft spices play out, at first with a delicate sweetness, then dries powerfully as the oak and soot take hold. Would not like to have seen this go another summer: this has somehow kept its integrity; b24 a real old timer showing its oaky scars with pride. A serious late night dram. And with an unspoiled palate, for this will be one of your smoky treats of the year... 40%

Cask Islay (91.5) n22.5 ashy and dry. Oh, and smoky; t23 soft oils dissolve to be replaced by lively spice, citrus and polite Demerara sugar. Oh, and some smoke...; f22.5 good length thanks to the remaining oil with a light smattering of vanilla. The sugars also linger...as does the smoke; b23 does what it says on the tin. 46%. A.D. Rattray

Eilan Gillan Islay Single Malt bourbon refill casks, dist 2010, bott 2015 **(91.5)** n23 vibrant peat, not overly troubled by oak. Clean, textbook malt with just the first traces of something attractively coastal. Just a few strands of citrus lightens the load; t23 there are times I adore that blend-style bite, even with a single malt. And this is perfect. The youth of the spirit gouges into the palate, but then offers an oily, smoky kiss to apologise; f22.5 dry, despite the first strains of vanilla coming though. The peat throbs, dries and intensifies to the last sooty moment; b23 it's Leap Year's Day and a charming way to officially kick off tasting for the 2017 Bible! No doubting the youth and I especially chose a youngster hoping it would have enough bite and attitude to slap my taste buds back into action. It has not disappointed me in any way. A little belter! Ignore the descriptor on the label, though. It is nothing like...Oh well, one down, another 999 (at least!) to go... 43%. nc ncf.

◈ **Eiling Lim Bessie's Dram (88)** n22.5 a real acidic and salty bite to the peat. Substantial phenols, around the 35ppm mark which ensures a dry edge; t22.5 classic Islay: a little muscovado sugar makes for a gentle start but the peat hammers home hard and with spiced intent; f21 the cask plays up slightly to bring a degree of bitterness into play. But the sugars and spice do their job, as do the continued phenols; b22 a distinctly Laphroaigian type dram complete with Allied style bitter cask (oh, I have just spotted that this is Laphroaig...!!!), s plenty to enjoy. 51.3%.

Elements of Islay AR4 (93.5) n23.5 t23.5 f23 b23.5. Massive oak infusion: the slow burn of smoke leaves no doubt to distillery. Clever oily-dry interplay plus hickory and cocoa-orange. 58.1% WB15/341

Elements of Islay Ar5 (76) n19 t20 f18 b19. One element too many in this fruity and off-key version. 57.8% WB16/017

Elements of Islay Bn5 (82.5) n19.5 t22 f20 b21. Peat a'plenty, but perhaps a few too many tangy moments than are desirable. 54.9% WB16/014

Elements of Islay BN6 (80) n20 t22 f19 b19. Simply too sweet and cloying for its own good. Zero complexity as the molasses, golden syrup and manuka honey go ballistic. Off key finale. 56.9% WB15/346

Elements of Islay BR5 (96) n24 t24.5 f23.5 b24. An unpeated masterpiece of the Laddie old school. Possibly the most complete and harmonious alloy of honeys bottled this year. Genius. 53.8% WB15/296

Elements of Islay BW3 (90.5) n22.5 t23.5 f22 b22.5. A playful Bowmore showing a copper sharpness amid the more languid smoke. Fabulous delivery: acacia and ulmo honey starring. 51.6% WB15/289

Elements of Islay Bw4 (87) n22 t22.5 f20.5 b22. Low peated and highly sugared; the spices are more than welcome. 51.6% WB16/016

Elements of Islay Cl7 (91) n22 t23.5 f22.5 b23. At times thick enough to be like dementedly peated clotted cream...with vanilla and Demerara sugar stirred in. 58.5% WB16/015

Elements of Islay CL6 (94) n23 t24 f23 b24. Less oil means more balance for this stunning Caol IIa. The major citrus element cuts through the peat; light sugar and malt salivates. 61.2% WB15/290

Elements of Islay LG4 (87.5) n22 t23 f21 b21.5. Typical huge Lagavulin but untypical sharpness on delivery & sweet finish. The phenols are of a smoked mackerel variety. 55.7% WB15/287

Elements of Islay LP4 (89) n22.5 t22.5 f22 b22. Profound peat at its earthiest. A tangy delivery but then soothing, as muscovado sugars & vanillas arrive. A gentle giant. 54.8% WB15/286

Elements of Islay LP5 (92) n23.5 t22.5 f22 b22. Elements is right for this Laphroaig: what we are getting here is the malt at its gristiest with the sugars releasing the smoke beautifully. 52.4% WB15/288

ePower Islay Malt bourbon cask, dist 2009, bott 2015 **(93)** n23.5 t23.5 f22.5 b23.5 Some stunning moments for a malt so young. 52.3%

ePower Islay Malt Port cask, dist 2009, bott 2015 (88.5) n22 t22.5 f22 b22 Some really lovely moments, but the youthful discord has nowhere to hide. 52.7%

◇ **Liquid Treasures Islay Malt 8 Year Old** bourbon cask, dist 2008, bott 2016 (92.5) n23 moderately young and lively phenol boasts a highly acidic edge; good oils present, also: very clean...; t23.5 lush delivery with both a young, gristy sweetness and excellent acacia honey build, also; so much to chew on including the mid-ground butterscotch tart; f23 the oils stick around and lengthen the smoke and growing – and glowing – spice; b23 high ranking malt and very good cask makes for an excellent if simplistic 8-year-old. 58.5%. Fairy Tales Edition.

◇ **Master of Malt Islay Single Malt** (90.5) n22 fabulous grist effect, allow the substantial phenol content to disappear sweetly on the wind...; t23 considering the strength, a surprising degree of oil to this ensuring the big smoke is painted as broadly around the palate as possible. The gristy sugars are still working well; f22.5 drier, but spicier, too; b23 a smoky, gristy must for peat heads. 40%.

◇ **Master of Malt Single Cask Williamson 6 Year Old** dist 2009 (94.5) n24 the kind of phenols which knock you a foot further back into your chair... Dry, sooty and becomes more concentrated as time progresses. A little bit of the farmyard about this (which, living in the remote country, as I do, I simply adore!) with the sugars limited to some pretty dry molasses; t23.5 a different hue to the delivery than nose. Far more sugars present, working exceptionally hard alongside a leathery spiciness. The richness of the liquorice and delicate praline is softened only by the gristiness of the smoky barley; f23 the butterscotch is punctuated with countless layers of smoke; b24 is the 62.5 the strength or phenol level? Probably both. Williamson is a very smoky boy. And a very beautiful one, too. 62.2%. sc.

Port Askaig 100 Proof (96.5) n24 can't ask for much more: the clarity matches the purity of the pale yellow colour, and that tint helps explain the nose. Deft vanillas can be heard here, alongside gristy malt; confident, yet never arrogant or boastful peat. Astonishing...; t24 the sugars melt in the moth on impact. Just a light oiliness coats the mouth sufficiently for the citrus phenols to ensure there are two distinct weights on display. Yet, somehow, they seem equally poised...; f24 what perfect oak must have been deployed here. No off notes or buzz. Just the insistent and steadying hand of vanilla/butterscotch to add a gentle counter to the spice and smoke; b24.5 just exemplary, high quality Islay: a must experience malt. If you find a more beautifully paced, weighted and elegant Islay this year, I'd really like to hear about it... 57.1%

◇ **Scotch Universe Callisto I 110° R1.2′ 1846.4″** American bourbon hogshead, dist 2007, bott 2016 (92) n23 mainly dry with the accent on a peaty sootiness; t23.5 yes, we have lift off! This is a massive take off with the phenols immediately exploding across the palate though muscovado sugar is there in almost the same abundance as the peat; oily, with growing vanillas; f22 the sugars keep going but bitters out at the death; b23.5 the delivery is out of this world. 57.3%.

Smokey Joe Islay Malt (94.5) n23 high level phenols are broadcast on an oily, salty, coastal wind...; t24 the delivery, snug in its peaty overcoat, is good...the following waves of smoke are truly exceptional. A just-so degree of dark sugar and liquorice embrace the phenols...; f23.5 a vague bitterness, but caught in its tracks by the gradual ascent of delicious cocoa notes; b24 a high quality Islay ticking all the required boxes. 46%

Spirits Shop Selection & Sansibar Whisky Islay Malt 2007 bourbon cask, bott 2015 (92.5) n24 adorable balance on the sweet-dry front; the salt lifts the many understated segments; the grapefruit adds a beguiling lightness of touch; t23 just like on the nose, the smoke borders on the belligerent but thinks better of it. Some youthful notes counter the punchy peat; f22.5 light vanilla with gentle phenolic layering; b23 very satisfying. 51.6%. 323 bottles.

◇ **That Boutique-y Whisky Company Williamson 6 Year Old** batch 1 (86.5) n22.5 t22 f20.5 b21.5 Smoky, pleasant, easy going, friendly. But also, I'm afraid to say, a little boring, too. 50.2%. 595 bottles.

The Whisky Agency Acla Selection South of Islay Aged 7 Years bourbon hogshead, dist 2007, bott 2015 (86) n21.5 t22 f21.5 b21. A smoky, new-makey rough diamond that is still to be cut. Some enjoyable individual traits, especially from the marauding smoke, but at that juncture in its life where the harmonisation is yet to kick in. But for sheer fun... ten out of ten!! 53.6%. nc ncf. 120 bottles.

◇ **The Whisky Chamber Buair An Diabhail Vol. XII** (92.5) n23 slightly pugnacious and threatening: some spice squaring up early on. A sooty, drier undertone; t23.5 the first couple of beats are soft, vaguely silky and sugar laden. But then it is hard not to cough as the spices and spirit bit deep and with rolling eyes. Immediately dry after the maple and Manuka honey start....and dries further; **f23** the spice buzzes and pounds like an old wound; no shortage of cocoa attached to the soot; **b23.5** after the initial immense bite – something of Great White Shark proportions – eventually settles down into a much more docile and delicious beast. *58.1%. sc.*

Whisky-Fässle Southshore Islay Malt 2007 hogshead, bott 2015 **(91) n23 t23 f22 b23** No great age, but certainly some excellent interplay. Superb use of honey tones to offset yet compliment the peat. *55.7%*

Whisky-Fässle Southshore Islay Malt 2009 hogshead, bott 2015 **(87) n22 t22.5 f21 b21.5.** A curiously flat sample from a distillery where I would expect better balance, even at this age. Certainly has some excellent early moments but, just a tad too young for the composition to have hit a point of equilibrium. *52.3%*

William Cadenhead Islay 7 Year Old claret wine barrel, dist 1992 **(94) n23.5 t24 f23 b23.5** A rather lovely offering from Chateau Phenol. For a 7-year-old malt, truly brilliant! *59.1%. sc.*

UNSPECIFIED SINGLE MALTS (LOWLAND)

Tweeddale Single Lowland Malt Scotch Whisky 14 Years db **(89) n21.5 t23.5 f22 b22** busy, bustling, elegant and old-fashioned...like a small borders town. *62%. nc ncf sc. Stonedean Ltd.*

UNSPECIFIED SINGLE MALTS (SPEYSIDE)

Acla Special Edition No.1 Somewhere in Speyside 38 Years Old refill sherry wood, dist 1977, bott 2015 **(82.5) n20 t21.5 f20 b21.** Some lovely cocoa moments. But elsewhere, too bitter and out of sorts. *46.8%. nc ncf.*

⬦ **Alos Sansibar Whisky Speyside Region 1975** bott 2016 **(96.5) n24.5** exotic fruit at its most erotic. The layering of sugars, even the variation of the muscovado, makes for the most glorious half hour of discovery. No less complex are the degrees of citrus which, like the sugars seem to shift like Sahara sands into ever-changing shapes and depths; **t24** there we go: exemplary degrees of oil settling gently on the palate and cushioning the arrival of the nutty tannins and more rigid and probing spices. The sugars, like the nose, enjoy a fruity essence, slightly less exotic now; **f24** remains sticky and lightly spiced. The vanillas have now gone up an extra notch and moved more towards butterscotch, though coffee walnut whip lingers at the death; **b24** great malt plus magnificent cask multiplied by time equals an unforgettable whisky experience. Exquisite. *46.9%.*

Ben Bracken Speyside Single Malt Aged 8 Years American white oak bourbon barrels **(85.5) n21.5 t22.5 f20 b21.5.** Juicy and pleasant, with an attractive honey and molasses middle. But the caramel wipes out any meaningful complexity. *40%*

Ben Bracken Speyside Single Malt 28 Years Old dist 1987 **(84.5) n22 t21 f21.5 b20.** The early promise on delivery – where the malt powers through with spice on its coattails – isn't backed up quite as one may wish. Goes through a number of tangy turns, where even after 28 years the tannin appears to be uneasy with the malt, or perhaps the other way round, before it settles down for a light vanilla finish, tinged with the lightest coating of ulmo honey. *40%*

Eilan Gillan Speyside Single Malt 2009 sherry casks, bott 2015 **(73) n18.5 t19 f17.5 b18.** Some sugar and spice wades in to try and save the day. But never gets going and a very average finish is attacked by light sulphur. *43%. nc ncf.*

ePower Speyside Malt 19 Years Old refill sherry hogshead, dist 1996, bott 2015 **(91.5) n23 t24 f21.5 b23** A sherry cask from the 90s which is just about sulphur-free: ePower to the person responsible for this bottling...! *49.6%*

⬦ **Glenbrynth Aged 21 Years** bott code L8W6323 2103 **(86.5) n22.5 t22 f21 b21** What starts off as a super-sexy nose with apple tart aplenty, tails off into a more prosaic fudge fest as the caramels get a constrictor-like grip: a bit of a bore at the end... *43%. OTI Africa.*

⬦ **Glen Castle Aged 20 Years Sherry Cask Finish** dist 1996 **(94) n23.5** busy, with diced apple and pear liberally sprinkled with spice; vanilla blancmange and crushed Maryland cookie can all be located in a beautifully balanced aroma; **t23.5** superb weight of light oils and muscovado sugars mingle with the gristy malt and increasingly toasted raisin; **f23** long, with slightly overcooked Melton Hunt fruitcake; the spices continue their busy career; **b24** lucky Japanese! A really satisfying, high quality single malt. *54.1%. ncf. Quality Spirits International*

⬦ **Glen Castle Aged 28 Years** sherry cask, dist 1996 **(96.5) n24.5** faultless casks: this is taking us right through the entire check list for great aged sherry cask whisky and ticking every box. Possibly the best balance between prickly spice and concentrated date and walnut

16.

cake I have encountered this year. Anything less than 15 minutes study of this would be doing it an injustice: not that far off perfection... **t24** how many layers of fruit does this delivery boast? Each one of a slightly different hue; a slight saline feel ramps up the flavour intensity even further while the spices, slow to begin with not only catch up but buzz like demented bees. Here and there a distinctive burst of tannin arrives on the scene like puffs of smoke from ack-ack flack; **f24** long, ridiculously long and at last, inevitably, we head into weighty Melton Mowbray Hunt Cake phase, much later than normal in this kind of whisky. The oloroso soaks into the burnt raisins and molasses while the toastiness suggests the cake has just been slightly overcooked...; **b24** a quality spirit from Quality Spirits: sherry butts from before the sulphur plague. Just look how magnificent this is...! Surely an award winner this year of some type... 59%. ncf. *Quality Spirits International.*

James King Aged 12 Years bott code L6Y 7422 2810 **(84.5) n21 t22 f21 b20.5** "From one of the most revered distilleries in Scotland," crows the label. Glen Toffee, presumably. Chaps, please turn the caramel down – it is obvious that some stupendous notes are trying to get out and speak: give them – and the drinker - a chance. 43%. *Quality Spirits International.*

Master of Malt 60 Year Old Speyside (85) n24.5 t21 f19 b20.5 Such a brave try. The delivery for a moment keeps you hoping there is still enough malt at play to see off the pencil-shaving tannins...but it is not to be. That doesn't mean that you can't spend a good half hour to an hour simply worshipping the nose: name a fruit and it appears to be there. And as it oxidises, it is there – then gone to be replaced with another fruit. A carousel of citrus and mushy conference pear, a fleeting moment of cherry cake, then fruitcake; molasses comes and goes, as does the liquorice and hickory. Sadly, the taste doesn't have the same life force beyond the first few seconds. But that nose.... Just amazing... 42.2%.

Master of Malt Speyside Single Malt (88.5) n22 light and gristy with a delicate caramel thread; **t22.5** clean delivery, salivating with the oak slowly becoming a match for the malt; **f22** a relaxed, undemanding spiced toffee finale; **b22** not the most exciting malt you'll find but certainly one of the most relaxed and comfortable. 40%.

Scotch Universe Mercury I 106° U.1.1' 1897.2" first fill American bourbon barrel, dist 2007, bott 2016 **(95) n23.5** an ulmo honey extravaganza: the barley adds a degree of crispness and this appears in both grassy and malty form; **t24** stunning delivery. It sees the honey on the nose and raises it a sublime liquorice-spice sub strata: almost immediately. The big barley finally arrives in the late middle ground; a rich, sure-footed texture is strengthened further by the lights tannins....uh, oh! That honey...!! **f23.5** the spices and ulmo honey mix persist and slowly move towards a toffee-cocoa fade; **b24** for those who prefer a little whisky in their honey. stunning! 52.9%.

Scotch Universe Pollux I 97° U.2.2' 1967.2" Oloroso sherry butt, dist 2008, bott 2016 **(72) n17 t20 f18 b17** Oh dear... OK if you like burnt raisin, but otherwise...oh, dear; oh dear.... 59%.

Spey River Aged 12 Years bourbon oak **(88.5) n22.5** golden syrup weighed down with intense malt and toffee; **t22.5** silky texture with toffee to the fore, a quick release of spice, but a slow intertwangling of caramel and vanilla; **f21.5** butterscotch and light spice; **b22** attractive. But you get the feeling the toffee notes are holding back a top-rate malt. 40%. *Quality Spirits International.*

Spey River Double Cask American oak casks, bourbon cask finish **(76) n19 t21 f18 b18.** I was fascinated to see how this unusual maturation technique panned out: but I was not expecting this, or anything like. Not dissimilar to some American micro distillery malts with a tobacco character attached to the sweet sugars. Seriously odd. 40%. *Quality Spirits International.*

Spirits Shop Selection Speyside Malt 1973 sherry cask, bott 2016 **(92) n21.5** borderline: the oak is beginning to make some major oaky and salty inroads here to the detriment of the balancing sugars. On the good side, a bourbon outline rises, despite this being ex-sherry. Tiring by the second...; **t24** ahhh...what a relief. The early pounding of oak doesn't materialise (though it is expected further along the track) and instead we get a stunning Danish marzipan and orange jelly mix, complete with light, milky chocolate; it is the texture, though, that stars as the softness is a genuine shock; **f22.5** still the big oak surge fails to materialise, though tannin levels rise with the spices; **b24** a whisky that needs a good half hour in the glass to open and show its full potential. On the nose it appears close to extinction; the performance on the palate suggests otherwise. 52%. 240 bottles. A joint bottling with Sansibar Whisky.

Spirits Shop Selection & Sansibar Whisky Speyside Malt 1975 sherry butt, bott 2015 **(93.5) n24 t24 f22 b23.5** If you want to see what a sherry butt tasted like the first time I went to a Scottish distillery – way back in 1975 – give this a sniff and swirl around the chops. Absolutely clean and faultless... Make no mistake: this is absolutely top quality, Premier League whisky. *51.3%. 425 bottles.*

Spirits Shop Selection & Sansibar Whisky Speyside Malt 1977 sherry butt, bott 2015 **(95) n24 t24 f23.5 b24** An OAP malt that is past its best, for sure. But still has enough depth and pride and utter beauty to seduce and then entirely enrapture. Superb! *46.1%*

Spirits Shop Selection & Sansibar Whisky Speyside Malt 1980 sherry butt, bott 2015 **(85) n21 t22.5 f20 b21.5**. Exceptionally salty for a Speysider, with an eye-watering tang to the fruit also. Not a malt which stands on ceremony or on the fence. Bitter finale, but only after some attractive vanilla. *47.3%. 387 bottles.*

◈ **Spirits Shop Selection Speyside Very Old Selection** sherry butt, bott 2016 **(90.5) n23** the grape is grappling still: moist fruitcake with dark cherries and raisins; **t23.5** silk. Absolute silk. It is as though the sugars have melted to form a pool for the light spices to dive into and the fruits to bob around in...; **f21.5** perhaps a little bitter and flat by comparison; **b22.5** this little sweetie is not about complexity, but effect. And it certainly has a good effect upon me... *46.3%. 322 bottles. A joint bottling with Sansibar Whisky.*

◈ **The Whisky Agency Speyside Region Single Malt 1973 (95.5) n24** exotic fruit with knobs on: low sugar gooseberry tart adds a more prosaic compliment, as does the salted lime sharpness...; big old age tannin...but expertly handled by the fruit; **t24.5** hard to remember this is actually a spirit – a whisky! – when it kisses the palate so tenderly on delivery: soft barley covers it. Gentle caramels regally coat the mouth, muscovado sugar walking two steps behind; **f23.5** the spices are slow to get going, but now make up for lost time..; **b24** those into the exotic fruit school of ye olde Speysiders will be pretty delighted with this: ticks every box....with a quilled flourish. *46.9%.*

Whisky-Fässle Speyside Region 1975 Fino butt, bott 2016 **(96) n24 t24 f24 b24** From a butt pre-dating the sulphur disaster. Truly the stuff of legend – and a pointer to whisky lovers of what real sherry-matured whisky should be. *47.4%*

Whisky-Fässle Speyside Region 1977 sherry butt, bott 2015 **(89.5) n22** nutty and rich; **t23** some unsubtle but enjoyable molasses and dates; **f22** a little bitter, but retains the nutty thread; **b22.5** effectively delicious, though a little slapdash. *46.2%*

UNSPECIFIED SINGLE MALTS (GENERAL)

Abbey Whisky Anon The Rare Casks Batch One Aged 13 Years oloroso sherry cask finish, dist 2001, bott 2015 **(89.5) n23.5 t24 f20 b22** A little sulphur hangs around at the finish, but better than most. No need for this brand to be Anon whatsoever. *51.5% sc. 90 bottles.*

The Classic Cask 40 Year Old batch no. SW.107, dist 1972, bott 2012 **(94.5) n24 t24 f23 b23.5** Defies the years with a compelling and erudite display. *43% (86 proof)*

The Corriemhor Cigar Reserve sherry & bourbon casks **(84.5) n21 t22 f20.5 b21.5**. You must forgive me if I judge this as a whisky alone. I have never smoked a cigar in my life; not even taken as much as an unlit cigarette to my lips. Not once. Ever. Some doctors and medical specialists in the field reckon it is why my nose and taste buds are so synchronised and alert. So if this is brilliant with a cigar, Cuban or otherwise, I will take your word for it. As a single malt in its own right, it is nutty, lush and pleasant. But rather lacking in complexity, scope or excitement. Dull, in fact. *46%*

Hepburn's Choice Nice & Peaty 9 Years Old refill hogshead, dist 2006, bott 2016 **(88) n22 t22.5 f22 b21.5** Very easy to find when searching on my computer for this entry: I have never used the word "nice" for any whisky since the first Bible tasting note was written way back in 2003...Anyway, this is a modest little dram which is, indeed, nice and peaty....Doh! *46%. nc ncf sc. 404 bottles.*

◈ **Glen Castle Rum Cask Finish (81.5) n20 t21.5 f21 b19** It must have been over 25 years ago now that I brought to the world the first ever rum cask matured whisky, which I discovered in a long-forgotten corner of a Campbeltown warehouse. It deservedly gained great notoriety and thereafter I went out of my way to taste as many rum cask matured or finished malts as were out there. This one is unique, but for all the wrong reasons. As the sugars which normally define the crispness of the whisky appear to have been underdone by other sugars in toffee form, thus neutralising the effect. Pleasant enough. But so dull. *40%. Quality Spirits International.*

◈ **Glen Castle Sherry Cask Finish (80) n21 t21 f19 b19** Clean sherry at work here, it appears, though so intense is the toffee the fruit (like anything else) can barely be heard. A malt neutered by caramel. *40%. Quality Spirits International.*

◈ **Lotus Lord 20 Year Old 1996** sherry cask finish **(91.5) n23.5** hugely enticing, come hither date and walnut tart, as well as a big lump bitten out of a crunchy toffee apple; a fabulous spiced molasses and maple syrup sub plot, softened by butterscotch; **t23.5** the body is much lighter on delivery than expected, allowing those spices a quicker path on goal than normal. The vanillas are huge, then a slow laying down of toasty raisin and light liquorice; **f21.5** just strays a little into a furry path, though the spices remain in top form; **b23** the sherry butts do impart a degree of late sulphur, but by then your heart will have been won. *53.3%. ncf. 12,200 bottles. Quality Spirits International.*

◈ **Lotus Lord 24 Year Old** (95) **n24** lychee to the fore, helped along by stewed apple: superb; the vanillas are beautifully weighted; **t24** textbook body, offering just enough oils to coat every inch of palate, but light enough for every nuance to come through unmolested. The malt is still evident despite the obvious fruit and oak influence; the toast and spices build slowly and politely into something substantial; the background butterscotch is never far from the surface, in either taste, sweetness or texture; **f23** liquorice, mocha and muscovado sugars. The very vaguest of furry notes, but entirely forgivable; **b24** what a delightful and classy malt. *53.3%. ncf. 6,200 bottles. Quality Spirits International.*

◈ **Lotus Lord 28 Year Old 1988** sherry casks (96) **n24.5** even the drips are drips with oloroso. Probably the most outrageously high church sherry and tannin you will find this year – and maybe for a few more. Totally over the top in the massiveness of the toasty grape…but it is a sniff for a sore nose…; **t24** tastes identical to the nose or, rather, how the nose projects itself and defines the degree of expectation; we are talking Melton Hunt cake wallowing in a bowl of oloroso with burnt molasses sprinkled on top for good measure; the spice attack is short and surprisingly gentle; **f23.5** difficult to get this hardcore toastiness without a feel of scorched oak and raisin, which the bitterness confirms; some extra high roast Java coffee sees out the finale; **b24** some 20 years ago I might have given this malt a bit of a ticking off for being far too sherry dominant. But, my! How times have changed. I am so relieved to find absolutely no sulphur at work here, I am smothering with kisses what seems like a long-lost son… *58.4%. ncf. 5,000 bottles. Quality Spirits International.*

◈ **Master of Malt New-Make Malt Spirit** (93) **n22.5 t23.5 f23 b23.5** The light body on the nose gives the lie to the splendour of the thickening malt on delivery. Pretty decent, mouth-filling new make. *63.5%.*

Peat's Beast (88.5) **n22 t22.5 f22 b22** "To tame the beast we recommend a dash of water." I don't. Recommend, instead, you use the Murray Method to warm up to body temp; otherwise you fracture the delicate oils and the sugars which hold this together vanish way too soon. *46%. ncf.*

Raasay While We Wait finished in Tuscan red wine casks (77) **n18 t21.5 f18.5 b19**. I have always maintained that it is a dangerous tactic to link the name of a planned distillery with a malt which doesn't actually come from it. When in professional advisor mode, I always warn against it. I sincerely hope the distillery is built on Raasay one day by R&B, but to say that certain whiskies from other distilleries will taste like what theirs, not yet even constructed, one day might, is fraught with dangers: the truth is, you never know exactly what you'll get –with as much meticulous planning as you like - until you get it. However their whisky one day turns out, they must ensure they don't ruin it by putting it into wine casks as poor as these. *46%. nc ncf. R&B Distillers.*

Saar Whisky Gruwehewwel 2nd Edition bourbon cask, dist 2007, bott 2015 (91) **n23 t23 f22.5 b22.5** An oily Islay if ever there was one… *55.2%. nc ncf sc.*

◈ **SaarWhisky Gruwehewwel Edition 3** dist 2007 bott 2015 (96) **n24.5** stunning, classic Islay. As salty as it is phenolic you could close your eyes and hear the Hebridean waves crashing and the gulls calling…; any dryness picked up also has an unashamedly peaty slant; **t24** a controlled lushness, so the oils don't dominate but voluptuously encourage. Sweet from both the peaty grist and the delicate Demerara sugars; a balancing dryness from the peaty ashes is sublime; **f23** long, almost lazy in the way to just allows the previous riches just trail off into the distance with nothing added or taken away.. **b24.5** no problem giving this truly great whisky the high score and award it deserves. But, as a lifelong Millwall supporter, I just wish they'd drop the West Ham Utd motif… *50.3%.*

Saar Whisky Hüttengold bourbon cask, dist 2007, bott 2015 (85.5) **n22.5 t22 f20 b21**. A little tart, but high quality distillate saves the day. The nose is the star of the show, with its sooty dryness. *52.3%. nc ncf sc.*

Saar Whisky Schwenker 2nd Edition bourbon cask, dist 2008, bott 2015 (89) **n23 t22.5 f21 b22.5** If "schwenker" means salty, then they've called it! *53.5%. nc ncf sc.*

◈ **That Boutique-y Whisky Company Secret Distillery No. 1 9 Year Old** batch 2 (79) **n22 t22 f16 b19** Interesting case, this. High quality malt in partially top quality oak. But this is a malt, as a single malt rather than blend, that needs a good few years to bed down – more than given here. For a blend (I mean a real blend with grain whisky, not a vatted malt) you can work with this to utilise its meatier aspects. But as a single malt you have to ensure that all the big notes don't smother the underdeveloped smaller ones. And this, alas, is what has happened here. It helps if the dreaded S word isn't present, either... *51.7%. 1,220 bottles.*

◇ **That Boutique-y Whisky Company Secret Distillery 2 21 Year Old** (95) n24 shimmering barley augmented by a mix of dry coconut, shrill lime and blistering spice: exceptionally well balanced; **t23.5** the sugars are shrouded in fresh, powdery grist, making a mockery of its 21 years. The result is a salivating, beautifully light delivery that sets the tongue buzzing; **f23.5** returns to a more sombre and prosaic maltiness mixed with weightier caramels and timber. The spices, though, hit just the right pitch of agitation; **b24** there is no secret to this malt's sparkling beauty. *49.7%. 420 bottles.*

Scottish Vatted Malts
(also Pure Malts/Blended Malt Scotch)

100 Pipers Aged 8 Years Blended Malt (74) n19 t20 f17 b18. A better nose, perhaps, and some spice on arrival. But when you consider the Speysiders at their disposal, all those mouth-wateringly grassy possibilities, it is such a shame to find something as bland as this. *40%*

Abrachan Triple Oak Matured (77) n19 t21 f18 b19. Some superb sugars on delivery, but a fuzzy, furry bitterness sadly gives the game away. *42%*

Acla Selection Burnside 23 Years Old bourbon hogshead, dist 1992, bott 2015 (93) n23.5 t23 f23 b23.5 What a magnificent piece of oak this was given the chance to grow up in. As I taste this in my remote garden, a song thrush is celebrating the setting of the sun in spectacular triple-whistled fashion: between the whisky and the bird, nature's harmony cannot be better represented. *50.4%. nc ncf.*

Angels' Nectar (81) n21 t21 f19 b20. This angel has a bitter tooth... *40%*

Angel's Nectar Blended Malt Rich Peat Edition (90.5) n22.5 t23 f22.5 b22.5 Excellently-made malt: sticks unerringly to the script. *46%*

Ballantine's Pure Malt Aged 12 Years bott code. LKAC1538 (88.5) n22.5 t23 f21 b22. No sign of the peat being reintroduced to major effect, although the orange is a welcome addition. Remains a charmer. *40%. Chivas.*

Bell's Signature Blend Limited Edition (83.5) n19 t22 f21 b21.5. The front label makes large that this vatted malt has Blair Athol and Inchgower at the heart of it as they are "two fine malts selected for their exceptionally rich character". Kind of like saying you have invited the Kray twins to your knees up as they might liven it up a bit. Well those two distilleries were both part of the original Bell's empire, so fair dos. But to call them both fine malts is perhaps stretching the imagination somewhat. A robust vatting to say the least. And, to be honest, once you get past the nose, good back-slapping fun. *40%. 90,000 bottles.*

Ben Bracken Blended Malt Aged 12 Years (85.5) n22.5 t21 f21 b21. Quite a tight malt with a predominantly toffee theme. *40%*

Big Peat Batch 31 (90.5) n23 love it: superb mix of allotment bonfire and peat reek. Some young spirit offering great energy; **t22** gristy sweet delivery pounded by spicy attitude; a blast of hickory and cocoa; **f22.5** the smoke rumbles along, but there is no letting up in intensity of peat or spice; **b23** good to see it has maintained its cheery high standard. Youthful, boisterous and challenging throughout. *46%. nc ncf. Douglas Laing & Co.*

Big Peat Bärlin Edition (91.5) n22.5 t22.5 f23 b23 I imagine the Peat Heads of Berlin are, rightly, very happy fellows... *50%. ncf. Bottled for Big Market Berlin, 50th Anniversary bottling.*

Black Face 8 Years Old (78.5) n18.5 t22 f19 b19. A huge malt explosion in the kisser on delivery, but otherwise not that pretty to behold. *46%. The Vintage Malt Whisky Co Ltd.*

◇ **Blairmhor Aged 8 Years** bott code L15/058 R15/5083 (86) n22.5 t22 f20.5 b21 Probably a dram never drunk by people of a certain political persuasion who would have been more impressed had it been called Blairless... An attractive malt which suffers from a surfeit of caramel and a cramped finale, though there is a big juicy, ripe pear and malt surge through the middle. *40%. International Beverage Holdings Ltd.*

Burns Nectar (89.5) n22 t22 f23 b22.5. A delight of a dram and with all that honey around, "Nectar" is about right. *40%*

Carme 10 Years Old (79) n21.5 t20 f18.5 b19. On paper Ardmore and Clynelish should work well together. But vatting is not done on paper and here you have two malts cancelling each other out and some less than great wood sticking its oar in. *43%*

Castle Rock Aged 12 Years Blended Malt (87) n22.5 t23 f19.5 b22. Stupendously refreshing: the finish apart, I just love this style of malt. *40%*

Cearban (79.5) n18 t21.5 f20 b19. The label shows a shark. It should be a whale: this is massive. Sweet with the malts not quite on the same wavelength. 40%. Robert Graham Ltd.

Chapter 7 Peatside 2009 Barrique cask, Port finish, cask no. 5511 (94.5) n23.5 t23.5 f24 b23.5 There is a touch of genius to this... 46%. sc.

◇ **Chivas Regal Ultis** bott code LPNK1759 2016/09/16 (89.5) n22.5 hefty aroma: thick with caramel and honey nut candy; t23 the high point: magnificent mouth feel with an outstanding mix of heather honey, light liquorice, a malty pulse and molasses. Plus, of course, the caramel...; f21.5 thins surprisingly, considering the earlier depth, but the caramels play a part here; b22.5 this vatted malt is the legacy of Chivas' five master blenders. But to pay real respect to them, just remove the caramel from the bottling hall. The whisky will be light coloured, for sure, but I suspect the flavour profile will blow us all away... 40%. Chivas Brothers Ltd.

Clan Campbell 8 Years Old Pure Malt (82) n20 t22 f20 b20. Enjoyable, extremely safe whisky that tries to offend nobody. The star quality is all on the complex delivery, then it's toffee. 40%. Chivas Brothers.

Clan Denny (Bowmore, Bunnahabhain, Caol Ila and Laphroaig) (94) n24 t23 f23 b24. A very different take on Islay with heavy peats somehow having a floating quality. 40%

Clan Denny Islay (86.5) n21.5 t23 f21 b21. A curiously bipolar malt with the sweetness and bitterness at times going to extremes. Some niggardly oak has taken the edge of what might have been a sublime malt as the peat and spices at times positively glistens with honey. 46.5%. nc ncf sc. Douglas Laing & Co.

Clan Denny Speyside (87) n22 t22 f21 b22. A Tamdhu-esque oiliness pervades here and slightly detracts from the complexity. That said, the early freshness is rather lovely. 46%

◇ **Compass Box 3 Year Old Deluxe** bott Aug 16 (96) n24 myriad tannins showing significant oak interest; the malt (as in barley) is there but only as an onlooker as major fruit note – both citrus and exotic – make their oaky mark; the most gentle smoky breeze drifts through...; t24 no 3-year-old malt – vatted or otherwise - will come close to this on the delivery front. Massive age with the fruits now firmly down the ancient exotic path. Best, though, is the eye-watering sharp sugars and low level smoke dovetailing to full, incongruous effect; f24 long, with a lovely spice burn as praline and marzipan engulf the ancient vanillas; b24 quite possibly the oldest three-year-old I have ever tasted. Being Compass Box, I have no doubt the flavour of irony is as powerful as any other here: surely this has to be a bunch of ancient malts with a tiny flash of something three years old, making up just a fraction of the composition. If so (and I strongly suspect it is), then it does much – as I am sure it has been designed – to both flag and up undermine the utterly idiotic rules/laws set out by the appalling Scotch Whisky Association, that does not allow blenders to show what actually makes up their whisky - only the age of the youngest constituent no matter how large or, in this case, miniscule its contribution may have been. The SWA: perhaps the only trade body that has been able to get government backing to confuse the public and ensure they have no idea what they are paying for. So, a brilliant whisky on all counts. 46%. nc ncf. 3,282 bottles.

Compass Box Eleuthera Marriage married for nine months in an American oak Hogshead (86) n22 t22 f20 b22. I'm not sure if it's the name that gets me on edge here, but as big and robust as it is I still can't help feeling that the oak has bitten too deep. Any chance of a Compass Box Divorce...? 49.2%. Compass Box for La Maison du Whisky.

Compass Box Enlightenment bott Apr 16 (94.5) n24.5 t24 f22.5 b23.5 After the run of disappointing vatted malts I have tasted today, trust Compass Box to come to the rescue. This is not a whisky to have when in a hurry: the nose alone is worth a good 15 minutes... 46%. nc ncf. 5,922 bottles.

Compass Box Flaming Heart Fifteenth Anniversary bott Jul 15 (96.5) n24 my very old friend at Compass Box appears to have mellowed with age. Once, this would have been a test to see how many splinters my nose could withstand. Now it is simply teased, then kissed. And there is nothing flaming at all; rather, a sigh of malty memories and the most gentle nod towards a smoky peace in life...; t24.5 I should have known better. He lulled me into a false sense of security. The delivery is a peach (actually, there does appear to be something peach-like in there, or is it melon..?) The dexterity of the smoke, now in total harmony with the mocha is something that warms not just the palate but the heart. It is not aflame, just glowing pleasantly...; f23.5 the vanillas make their excuses and stay, the smoke fades with aplomb while the muscovado inspired fruit hangs around to give balance; b24.5 Really, John? Fifteen years? I mean: 15 years....??? Fucking hell! Oh, by the way, mate. It's a bloody masterpiece... 48.9%. nc ncf. 12,060 bottles.

Compass Box The Lost Blend (95.5) n23 there are gristy, vanila notes....but these cower as the peat begins to grasp hold of the situation and ushers in the spice; t23.5 sensuously soft, sweet and oily: a little gristiness returns but the spices are proinent; a thin layer of ulmo honey breaks free of the smoke; **f24.5** an elegant finish allowing all parties an even say. Vanilla and caramel naturally complete the tale, though not before high class marzipan makes its welcome mark. The smoke lingers contentedly and without threat; **b24.5** I may be wrong, but I have a feeling that when the nose and flavour profile was being constructed, a little extra smoke than first planned was added. Seems that way by the manner in which the phenols just pipe up a little louder than it first seems... 46%

Compass Box The Peat Monster Cask Strength (89) n23.5 fascinating arm wrestle between the drier, ashy notes and a more expansive peatiness, rich in dark sugars; some delicate citrus furthers the complexity; **t23** superb weight: just the right amount of oils help maximise the heather honey; the smoke is happy to hint rather than holler; **f20.5** just a little bit of oak bitterness but countered by the persistent sweetness; the smoke now blends with the spices; **b22** plenty of peat between your teeth but deserving of some better oak. 5/3%

Compass Box The Peat Monster Reserve (92) n23 t23.5 f22.5 b23. At times a bit of a Sweet Monster...beautiful stuff! 48.9%

⟐ **Compass Box The Peat Monster Swedish Whisky Federation** (91) n23 thumping peat in both dry ash and oily format. A little citrus tries to balance things; **t23** big oils bring a tidal wave of Demerara sugars....all engulfed in phenols, of course; the spices have been patient but kick in now...; **f22** a little oak bitterness seeps through but the smoke remains substantial; **b23** what can you say? Its peaty. And it's a monster...! 46%. 2,000 bottles.

Compass Box The Peat Monster Tenth Anniversary Release bott Sept 13 (95) n24 t24 f23 b24 here we appear to see a mix, or compromise, between the sweeter bottling of two years ago and last year's searing dryness. And, unlike most compromises, this one works... 48.9%. 5,700 bottles.

Compass Box The Spice Tree first-fill and refill American oak. Secondary maturation: heavily toasted new French oak (95.5) n24.5 t24.5 f23 b23.5. Having initially been chopped down by the SWA, who were indignant that extra staves had been inserted into the casks, The Spice Tree is not only back but in full bloom. Indeed, the blossom on this, created by the use of fresh oak barrel heads, is more intoxicating than its predecessor – mainly because there is a more even and less dramatic personality to this. Not just a great malt, but a serious contender for Jim Murray Whisky Bible 2011 World Whisky of the Year. 46%

⟐ **Compass Box Spice Tree Extravaganza** bott Aug 16 (94.5) n24 there is a barely discernible oiliness to this which makes a huge difference to the shape of the nose: the acacia honey hangs as though in suspended animation, the diced lime peel dips in and out of consciousness, the aged tannins (no minor force) nip here and kiss there...; **t23.5** a soft red carpet is laid out for the sugars and spices which arrive at a slow, measured pace, elegantly and hand-in-hand. First the lush malts lead the way and then move to one side to allow the star turn. Thinned golden syrup and a peppery, tannin-tinged double act in effortless harmony; **f23** the oils have been reduced taking the sugars. The spices prevail and age becomes a factor once more...; **b24** perhaps the most important factor to this whisky, which will be overlooked probably by about 99% of those who taste this, is not so much the taste itself but the mouth feel and balance. In other words, it is not always the words that are said which are most important, but the way they are delivered. That is the secret to this complex beauty. 46%. nc ncf. 12,240 bottles.

Cutty Sark Blended Malt (92.5) n22 t24 f23 b23.5. Sheer quality: as if two styles have been placed in the bottle and told to fight it out between them. What a treat! 40%.

Deerstalker Blended Malt Highland Edition (94) n23.5 t23.5 f23 b24 A quite beautiful whisky by any standards. 43%

⟐ **Deerstalker Blended Malt Peated Edition** (84.5) n22.5 t22 f19 b21 A slightly strange mixture: on one hand creamy, sweet and friendly, on the other somewhat metallic and harsh. Struggles to find either balance or a comfortable course. The finish is way off key and vaguely furry. 43%.

⟐ **Demijohn Islay Blended Malt 6 Year Old** cask no. 5512, bott 10 Sept 15 (91) n23 punchy soot: acrid smoke with a fruity softener; **t23** firm, borderline brittle. Much more grape and malt on show early on before the smoke makes a significant mark; **f22** the smoke has nailed itself to the cause and is joined by spices; **b23** a very jolly kind of malt, the delicate fruit offering a chirpiness to the chipper young peats. Thoroughly enjoyable. 42.5%.

Eiling Lim Older Than Old Blended Malt Whisky (87.5) n21.5 t22 f22 b22. Charming malt. Entirely non-taxing with a light Arbroath Smoky element as the main thread and genteel vanilla notes filling most of the gaps. 46.5%

Elements of Islay Peat (91.5) n23 is it possible to have too much peat? Not for some I know and for serious peat heads the uncompromising enormity and acidic bite of this will get them very excited, indeed...; **t24** even I had to take a few moments to get my bearing and senses back together after this delivery. As though copious barrels of concentrated peat juice has been added to maple syrup. Eye-watering....; **f22** fades surprisingly quickly as vanilla begins to build and a slight bitterness creeps in; **b22.5** this is rather more than elementary Islay, trust me.... 46%

⬧ **ePower Extra Old Blended Malt Whisky** (93) **n23** no shortage of oak for those needing to put a log on the fire...a smoky one...; **t23.5** salivating delivery, which is a surprise after the nose! Really juicy, intense malt first with a starburst of succulent, gristy sugars then with a light heather honey sparkle. The phenols are wonderfully poised, the spices on best behaviour; **f23** dries in a chalky fashion but the spiced honey is always on guard; **b23.5** this is beautifully constructed vatted malt and suggests some pretty good age, also. 45.2%.

ePower Westport 14 Years Old bourbon hogshead, dist 1999, bott 2014 (93) **n23** a complex malt bordering on a bourbon personality: the light liquorice, borderline hickory and molasses harmonise beautifully with the crisp barley; **t23.5** brilliantly agile delivery: even a light smattering of Love Heart candy on this with an effervescent fizz to the barley; **f23** long, clean and determined barley; faultless vanilla; **b23.5** a cask which just knew how to make the most of the malt it contained. 52.1%

The Famous Grouse 10 Years Old Malt (77) **n19 t20 f19 b19.** The nose and finish headed south in the last Winter and landed in the sulphur marshes of Jerez. 40%. Edrington Group.

The Famous Grouse 15 Years Old Malt (86) **n21 t22 f21.5 b21.5.** Salty and smoky with a real sharp twang. 43%. Edrington Group.

The Famous Grouse 15 Years Old Malt (86) **n19 t24 f22 b21.** There had been a hint of the "s" word on the nose, but it got away with it. Now it has crossed that fine – and fatal – line where the petulance of the sulphur has thrown all else slightly out of kilter. All, that is, apart from the delivery which is a pure symphony of fruit and spice deserving a far better introduction and final movement. Some moving, beautiful moments. Flawed genius or what...? 40%

The Famous Grouse 18 Years Old Malt (82) **n19 t21.5 f21 b20.5.** Some highly attractive honey outweighs the odd uncomfortable moment. 43%. Edrington Group.

The Famous Grouse Malt 21 Years Old (91) **n22 t24 f22 b23.** A very dangerous dram: the sort where the third or fourth would slip down without noticing. Wonderful scotch! 43%.

The Famous Grouse 30 Years Old Malt (94) **n23.5 t24 f23 b23.5.** Whisky of this sky-high quality is exactly what vatted malt should be all about. Outrageously good. 43%

 Five Lions Burnside 22 Years Old 2nd fill Oloroso sherry hogshead, dist May 93, bott Nov 15 (93) **n23** classical cream sherry nose; **t23.5** gorgeous bite to the crisp Demerara sugars before a gentle sultana and sponge cake softness arrives; **f23** dries with the grape; **b23.5** an unimpeachable sherry butt - amazing! 55.5%. nc ncf.

Five Lions Westport 18 Years Old 1st fill sherry butt, dist Oct 97, bott Nov 15 (95) **n23.5** quite dazzling display of spiced dates and nuts; **t24** a top-ranking sherry butt working in great harmony with top ranking Glenmorangie. Oh, sorry it isn't is it... Anyway, Melton Hunt Cake to the fore; **f23.5** long, rich deep fruit continues, the spices rumbling still and tannins just getting a little weighty; **b24** brilliant! 59.7%. nc ncf.

⬧ **Glenalmond Highland Blended Malt** (84) **n21 t22 f20.5 b20.5** Chugs along in safe, non-demanding caramel-rich fashion. 40%. The Vintage Malt Whisky Co.

Glenn (89.5) **n22** no shortage of nip and nibble on the grassy nose: **t23** clean, salivating and fresh. Gets even more malty as it progresses on the palate, the oak making a low-key, vaguely honeyed entrance about half way in; **f22** the oak takes a tangy twist; **b22.5** a forceful malt. Seems as though at least two strands of the thread are trying to outdo each other. Enjoyable, but erratic towards the end. 50%. Svenska Eldvatten.

Glenalmond 2001 Vintage (82.5) **n22 t21.5 f19 b20.** Glenkumquat, more like: the most citrusy malt I have tasted in a very long time. 40%. The Vintage Malt Whisky Co Ltd.

Glenalmond "Everyday" (89.5) **n21.5 t23.5 f22 b22.5.** They are not joking; this really is an everyday whisky. Glorious malt which is so dangerously easy to drink. 40%

Glen Brynth Aged 12 Years Blended Malt (87) **n22.5 t23 f19.5 b22.** Deja vu...! Thought I was going mad: identical to the Castle Rock I tasted this morning, right down to the (very) bitter end ..!!! 40%. Quality Spirits International.

Glenbrynth Blended Malt 12 Years (87.5) **n22.5 t22.5 f21 b21.5.** Heavyweight malt which gets off to a rip-roaring start on the delivery but falls away somewhat from the mid ground onwards. 43%. OTI Africa.

Glenbrynth Ruby 40 Year Old Limited Edition (94) **n23.5 t24 f23 b23.5.** Has all the hallmarks of a completely OTT, far too old sherry butt being brought back to life with the aid of a livelier barrel. A magnificent experience, full of fun and evidence of some top quality vatting at work, too. 43%. OTI Africa.

Glenbrynth Ruby 40 Year Old bott code L8V 7439 04/11/11 **(95)** n24 such enormous age on this: the tannins, showing the odd wrinkle here and there, make no secret of the fact. Yet the infusion of light orange blossom honey, softly spiced bread pudding and livened with a squeeze of lime ensure complexity levels are on max; **t23.5** melt-on-delivery malts make the mouthfeel wonderfully inclusive, despite the tannins creaking a bit. Shortly in, muscovado and barley sugars double underline the malt's richness while on other levels the weightier oak has ditched its stoop to ensure a firm spine and busy spice; **f23.5** almost a rum-like ester adds a sheen to the sugars. The tannins are now vanilla rich and, miraculously, free from ageing symptoms; **b24** you cannot ask much more from a 40-year-old vatted malt than this. Amazing what a lack of colouring (and sulphured sherry casks) can do – like let the whisky speak for itself and allow you to follow its myriad paths, its highways and byways, without the route being blocked by toffee or a rabid bitterness. Each and every cask included in this great whisky should be applauded, as should the blender. 43%. OTI Africa.

Glendower 8 Years Old (84) n21.5 t21 f20.5 b21 Nutty and spicy. 43%

The Glenfohry Aged 8 Years Special Reserve (73) n19 t19 f17 b18. Some of the malt used here appears to have come from a still where the safe has not so much been broken into, but just broken! Oily and feinty, to say the least. Normally I would glower at anyone who even thought of putting a coke into their malt. Here, I think it might be for the best.. 40%

Glen Talloch Blended Malt Aged 8 Years (85.5) n21 t23 f20.5 b21. An invigorating and engulfing vatting, full of intrinsic barley tones on delivery. But the caramel is too strident for further complexity. 40%

Glen Turner Heritage Double Wood Bourbon & Madeira casks, bott code. L311657A **(85.5)** n21.5 t22 f21 b21. A very curious amalgamation of flavours. The oak appears to be in shock with the way the fruit is coming on to it and offers a bitter backlash. No faulting the crisp delivery with busy sugar and spice for a few moments brightening the palate. 40%.

Glen Turner Pure Malt Aged 8 Years L525956A **(84)** n20 t22 f22 b20. A lush and lively vatting annoyingly over dependent on thick toffee but simply brimming with fabulously mouth-watering barley and over-ripe blood oranges. To those who bottle this, I say: let me into your lab. I can help you bring out something sublime!! 40%

Gleann Mór Vatted Whisky Over 40 Years Old (92.5) n23.5 deep tannins escape from every pore: marmalade on slightly overdone toast; **t23.5** magnificent landing! Cruises in with a velvety concoction of intense malt and vanilla, sweetened gently by a little ulmo honey and mildly overbaked caramelised biscuit; **f22.5** a few serious tannins make themselves heard, as do the politer spices; **b23** an oldie and a goodie...Mor, please...!!! 47%

Glen Orchy (80.5) n19.5 t21.5 f19.5 b20. Not exactly the most subtle of vatted malts though when the juicy barley briefly pours through on delivery, enjoyable. 40%. Lidl.

Glen Orchy 5 Year Old Blended Malt Scotch Whisky (88.5) n22 t22.5 f22 b22. Excellent malt plus very decent casks equals light-bodied fun. 40%. Lidl.

Glen Orrin (68) n16.5 t17.5 f17 b17. In its favour, it doesn't appear to be troubled by caramel. Which means the nose and palate are exposed to the full force of this quite dreadful whisky. 40%.

Glen Orrin Six Year Old (88) n22 t23 f21 b22. A vatting that has improved in the short time it has been around, now displaying some lovely orangey notes on the nose and a genuinely lushness to the body and spice on the finish. You can almost forgive the caramel, this being such a well balanced, full-bodied ride. A quality show for the price. 40%

Grand Macnish Six Cask Edition bott code L14/8867 **(85.7)** n21 t23 f19.5 b22 A late night chewathon: this is big, ballsy with little time for prisoners. Not exactly free from the odd flaw. But the delivery and middle have wonderful molten walnut and orange cake quality and a lush mouth feel to match. 40%. MacDuff International Ltd.

Hedges and Butler Special Pure Malt (83) n20 t21 f22 b21. Just so laid back: nosed and tasted blind I'd swear this was a blend (you know, a real blend with grains and stuff) because of the biting lightness and youth. Just love the citrus theme and, err...graininess...!! 40%

Highland Harvest Organic Blended Malt 7 Casks batch 002 **(86.5)** n21.5 t22.5 f21 b21.5 Not even remotely complex. But pleasant enough. 40% WB15/371

Highland Journey Blended Malt (94.5) n23.5 t23.5 f23.5 b24 I have been on some memorable Highland journeys in my life, but few have been quite as comfortable as this one. 46.2%. Hunter Laing & Co.

J & B Exception Aged 12 Years (80) n20 t23 f18 b19. Very pleasant in so many ways. A charming sweetness develops quickly, with excellent soft honeycomb. But the nose and finish are just so...so...dull...!! For the last 30 years J&B has meant, to me, (and probably within that old company) exceptionally clean, fresh Speysiders offering a crisp, mouth-watering treat. I feel this is off target. 40%. Diageo/Justerini & Brooks.

J & B Nox (89) n23 t23 f21 b22. A teasing, pleasing little number that is unmistakably from the J&B stable. 40%. Diageo.

John Black 8 Years Old Honey (88) n21 t22.5 f22.5 b22. A charming vatting. 40%

John Black 10 Years Old Peaty (91) n23 salty and peaty; t23 soft and peaty; f22 delicate and peaty; b23 classy and er...peaty. 40%. Tullibardine Distillery.

Johnnie Walker Green Label 15 Years Old (95) n24 t23.5 f23.5 b24. God, I love this stuff...this is exactly how a vatted malt should be and one of the best samples I've come across since its launch. 43%. Diageo.

Jon, Mark and Robbo's The Rich Spicy One (89) n22 t23 f22 b22. So much better without the dodgy casks: a real late night dram of distinction though the spices perhaps a little on the subtle side... 40%. Edrington.

Jon, Mark and Robbo's The Smoky Peaty One (92) n23 t22 f23 b24. Genuinely high-class whisky where the peat is full-on yet allows impressive complexity and malt development. A malt for those who appreciate the better, more elegant things in life. 40%. Edrington.

The Loch Fyne The Living Cask 1745 (94.5) n23.5 an intriguing two-toned nose which, if you concentrate on one side, offers firm smokiness giving further edge to the unyielding malts; and from the other angle is a complete softie...! t23.5 the delivery takes the path of the second option with an immediate eiderdown softness on delivery but doesn't duck out of juicy and, at times, forceful barleysugar then Fisherman Friend notes...all very sweet shop; f23.5 remains silky; now with a few spices joining the rolling smoke; b24 one of the best whiskies ever created at quarter to six in the evening....and one quite impossbie not to love. 46.3%

The Loch Fyne The Living Cask Batch One (92) n22 the harsh smoke generates little more than a wispy buzz; the banana, ulmo honey, gristy malt and growing spice is the perfect foil; t23.5 a volley of intense sugars, further enlivened by prickly spice makes for a memorable kick off. The smoke continues to drift and offer anchor; unusually, the texture actually becomes silkier as the flavours develop; f23 a series of liquorice, fudge and crisp sugar notes, all on top of a blend of genteel and tangy phenols, makes for an easy exit; b23.5 absolutely charming. 46.3%

The Loch Fyne The Living Cask Batch Two (78) n18 t21 f19 b20. A charming coincidence today: the first time I visited the Loch Fyne whisky shop, about 30 years ago, I spotted my first ever Spotted Flycatcher at Inveraray Castle. Just a few minutes before tasting this, a spotted flycatcher visited my garden for the first time this summer – and it is now late July. It must have known... Thirty years ago, though, the sherry-influenced bottlings available were so much better than today... 43.6%

The Loch Fyne The Living Cask Batch Four (88) n21 an intriguing mix of Lincoln biscuits and oily vanilla...; t22.5 a real malt fest for the delivery: light castor sugar sprinkled on the tame vanilla; f22 the oily texture on delivery lasts the course, but reduces enough for the spice to make a meaningful entrance; b22.5 oh well, batch 3 gave us the slip but we caught up with Batch 4 which is a vast improvement on 2. A genuinely oily cove; and astonishingly malty, too... 43.6%

The Lost Distillery Company Stratheden batch no. 2/II (86) n22 t21.5 f21 b21.5. A dry malt boasting sporadic muscovado fruity sweetness and the vaguest of underlying phenols. Pleasant, though by no means perfect. I wish the company well, but have to say that putting today's casks together to recreate a malt last distilled in 1926 (and which no-one living has probably ever tasted) is fanciful, to put it mildly. In those days bourbon casks weren't available so not in use, sherry ones were then of a significantly higher standard and the peat, almost certainly, would have been a little more punchy than here. 46%. nc ncf.

Mackinlay's Rare Old Highland Malt (89) n22 t22 f22 b23. Possibly the most delicate malt whisky I can remember coming from the labs of Whyte and Mackay. Thought it still, on the palate, must rank as heavy medium. This is designed as an approximation of the whisky found at Shackleton's camp in the Antarctic. And as a life-long Mackinlay drinker myself, it is great to find a whisky bearing its name that, on the nose only, briefly reminds me of the defter touches which won my heart over 30 years ago. That was with a blend: this is a vatted malt. And a delicious one. In case you wondered: I did resist the temptation to use ice. 47.3%

Master of Malt Reference Series I (82) n19.5 t23 f19 b20.5. Not quite the happiest of bunnies at times, as it occasionally struggles to find a balance in the face of big, not entirely desired, oils. That said, nothing to stop you embracing the enormity of the date & sugar-drizzled barley soon after delivery & during the period it has escaped a certain feintiness. 47.5% WB15/349

Master of Malt Reference Series I.1 (87.5) n21 t23 f21.5 b22. No enormous age – or at least oak involvement - as confirmed by the nose. But some wonderful moments as the juicy, clean barley hits the palate running. 47.5%

Master of Malt Reference Series I.2 (93) n23 the delicate smokiness is accentuated by the crispness of the barley sub strata; t23 the barley is first to hit, juicy and clean; delicate sugars dissolve merrily; f23.5 the phenols slowly reassert themselves, but never at the cost of the delicate barley tones; b23.5 a charming marriage between Fisherman's Friend phenols and balletic barley. 47.4%

Master of Malt Reference Series I.3 (91) n22 dry, oak-steered with a nod towards mocha; t22.5 a deft, peaceful delivery with no drama but loads of development; f23.5 lightly sweetened cocoa powder makes for a fabulous ending: reminiscent of Merlin lollies of yesteryear; b23 it's all about the chocolate... 47.1%

Master of Malt Reference Series II (84.5) n20 t22 f21.5 b21. The oils have been toned down for this one, though the sugars have reached shrieking point. Malty, but perhaps a tad too cloying for its own good. 47.5% WB15/350

Master of Malt Reference Series II.1 (88) n21 nothing wrong with it: just dull and uninspiring; t23 a rich seam of malt appears to be of an oily disposition; f22 again, technically sound. Plenty of rich malt and all that plus a hint of spice; b22 an oily cove... 47.5%

Master of Malt Reference Series II.2 (87) n22 t22.5 f21 b21.5. Soft lemon drizzle on chunky malt plus an enjoyable volley of sugary grist early on. 47.4%

Master of Malt Reference Series II.3 (89) n21.5 floral – a dank bluebell wood; t22.5 mouth-filling malt. Playful oils and a steady ramping up of the malt intensity; f22.5 something of a malt cereal about the finale; a little butterscotch tart thickens the effect; b22.5 reminiscent of a Kentucky maltshake. 47.2%

Master of Malt Reference Series III (88) n22 t23 f21 b22 Still one for the sweet toothed, but you don't need a diagram at the back to tell you some decent age has been added to this vatting. The odd blemish, but great fun. 47.5% WB15/351

Master of Malt Reference Series III.1 (89.5) n22.5 a squeeze of blood orange and grapefruit set the malt off beautifully; t23 thrusts malt at the taste buds like a politician rams his party line down your earholes; f21.5 a little vanilla and spice, though the malt lingers; a tad bitter late on; b22.5 if you like your malt malty, vote for this. 47.7%

Master of Malt Reference Series III.2 (92.5) n22.5 earthy, yet enticingly malty. And thick...; t23 superb Malteser style delivery: massive malt with an attractive milk chocolate element; f24 good grief!! That malt just doesn't know when to call it a day. A little ulmo honey has joined in to intensify the sweetness slightly; even some late spice adds to the ultra late complexity; b23 similar to III.1, except without the bitter bits. 47.5%

Master of Malt Reference Series III.3 (78) n19.5 t21.5 f18 b19. Fruity, fat, sweet. A tad furry. And somewhat one-dimensional. 47.5%

➤ **Master of Malt Single Cask Peatside 5 Year Old** dist 2011 (85) n21.5 t23 f20 b20.5 What an odd cove this is. Starts like a train, an express at that, then hits the buffers soon into its journey. The delivery makes a lie of the unkempt nose with an explosion of muscovado sugars, liquorice and thick malt and peat. The confounded thing then vanishes into a morass of toffee. So bloody annoying! 61.8%. sc.

➤ **Master of Malt Single Cask Wardhead 19 Year Old** dist 1997 (94) n22.5 light, airy but a tad tired. A little bit of cocoa and liquorice has strayed into the delicate malt; t24 salivating with concentrated malt: this is beautifully distilled and the cask is a winner, too. A dried peach moment but it is the thick vanilla and barley concentrate which stars; f23.5 now we have the fabulous vanilla moving in with astonishingly well-mannered vanilla; a lightly spiced butterscotch is still outgunned by the barley; b24 so easy to mistake this for a Glenfiddich, which happens to peak around this age....the quality of the oak is just about perfection. 52%. sc.

Matisse 12 Year Old Blended Malt (93) n23.5 t23 f22.5 b23. Succulent, clean-as-a-whistle mixture of malts with zero bitterness and not even a whisper of an off note: easily the best form I have ever seen this brand in. Superb. 40%. Matisse Spirits Co Ltd.

Matisse Aged 12 Years (79) n17 t21 f20 b21. Not sure if some finishing or re-casking has been going on here to liven it up. Has some genuine buzz on the palate, but intriguing weirdness, too. Don't bother nosing this one. 40%. The Matisse Spirits Co Ltd.

Milroy's of Soho Finest Blended Malt (76) n18 t19 f20 b19. Full flavoured, nutty, malty but hardly textbook. 40%. Milroy's of Soho.

Mo'land (82) n21 t22 f19 b20. Extra malty but lumbering and on the bitter side. 40%.

Monkey Shoulder batch 27 (79.5) n21 t21.5 f18 b19. Been a while since I lasted tasted this one. Though its claims to be Batch 27, I assume all bottlings are Batch 27 seeing as they are from 27 casks. This one, whichever it is, has a distinctive fault found especially at the finale, which is disappointing. Even before hitting that point a big toffeed personality makes for a pleasant if limited experience. 40%. *William Grant & Sons.*

New Town Blends The Advocate's Batch (87.5) n21.5 t22.5 f21.5 b22. Attractive, pleasant and, though a vatting, simplistic. A youthful catch on the nose suggests development might be limited, but it makes amends by the sheer charm of the light, clean, earnest malt. A lovely dram before lunch, I suggest. 43%. *Edinburgh Whisky Ltd.*

"No Age Declared" The Unique Pure Malt Very Limited Edition 16-49 Years (85) n22.5 t19.5 f22 b21. Very drinkable. But this is odd stuff: as the ages are as they are, and as it tastes as it does, I can surmise only that the casks were added together as a matter of necessity rather than any great blending thought or planning. Certainly the malt never finds a rhythm but maybe it's the eclectic style on the finish that finally wins through. 45%. *Samaroli.*

Old St Andrews Fireside (88.5) n22 t22.5 f21.5 b22.5. Beautifully driven... 40%.

Old St Andrews Nightcap (89) n21.5 t24 f21 b22.5. Some delightful weight and mass but perhaps a bit too much toffee takes its toll. 40%. *Old St Andrews Ltd.*

Old St Andrews Twilight (94.5) n24 t23.5 f23 b24. Less Twilight as Sunrise as this is full of invigorating freshness which fills the heart with hope and joy: Lip-smacking Scotch malt whisky as it should be. Anyone who thinks the vatted malt served up for golf lovers in these novelty bottles are a load of old balls are a fair way off target... 40%. *Old St Andrews Ltd.*

The Pearls of Scotland Burnside 1992 20 Year Old cask no. 7350, dist Dec 92, bott Nov 13 (85) n22 t22 f20 b21. You can tell this is 99% Balvenie: it just has real problems handling the oak at this age. Nothing too much wrong with the nose for those into over-ripe banana. And the delivery boasts excellent mouth feel and early sugars until the merciless tannin bites deep. 55.8%.

Poit Dhubh 8 Bliadhna (90) n22.5 t23.5 f21.5 b22.5. Though the smoke which marked this vatting has vanished, it has more than compensated with a complex beefing up of the core barley tones. Cracking whisky. 43%. ncf. *Pràban na Linne.*

Poit Dhubh 12 Bliadhna (77) n20 t20 f18 b19. Toffee-apples. Without the apples. 43%. ncf. *Pràban na Linne.*

Poit Dhubh 21 Bliadhna (86) n22 t22.5 f21 b20.5. Over generous toffee has robbed us of what would have been a very classy malt. 43%. ncf. *Pràban na Linne.*

The Pot Still Scotch Vatted Malt Over 8 Years Old (90) n22 t24 f22 b22. Such sophistication: the Charlotte Rampling of Scotch. 43.5%. ncf. *Celtic Whisky Compagnie, France.*

Prime Blue Pure Malt (83) n21 t21 f21 b20. Steady, with a real chewy toffee middle. Friendly stuff. 40%

Prime Blue 12 Years Old Pure Malt (78) n20 t20 f19 b19. A touch of fruit but tart. 40%

Prime Blue 17 Years Old Pure Malt (88) n23 t21 f22 b22. Lovely, lively vatting: something to get your teeth into! 40%

Prime Blue 21 Years Old Pure Malt (77) n21 t20 f18 b18. After the teasing, bourbony nose the remainder disappoints with a caramel-rich flatness. The reprise of a style of whisky I thought had vanished about four or five years ago 40%

Queens & Kings Mary, Queen of Scots (91.5) n22.5 attractive mix of green apple and light smoke; t23 inspired delivery: the sugars arrive in droves, mainly Demerara, though the later smoke and spice tangle is a delight; f23 a beautiful vanilla and butterscotch fade; the delicate smoke ensures a gentle base note; the spices ensure a degree of late liveliness...; b23 a very comfortable assembling of malt. Impressed. 55.6%. *Mr. Whisky.*

Queens & Kings Robert The Bruce (88) n21 the light smoke seems to be neutered by toffee; t23.5 the brilliant delivery lifts the malt out of the doldrums. Smoked manuka honey to the fore; much, much better! f21.5 some dull cocoa and spice, but oak bitterness, too; b22 a bit of a wobbly vatting, where the part of the peat and its effects have not been thoroughly thought through. 54%. *Mr Whisky.*

Rattray's Selection Blended Malt 19 Years Old Batch 1 Benrinnes sherry hogsheads (89.5) n22 t23.5 f21.5 b22.5. Absolutely love it! Offers just the right degree of mouth-watering complexity. not a malt for those looking for the sit-on-the-fence wishy-washy type. 55.8%. *Auchentoshan, Bowmore, Balblair & BenRiach. A.D. Rattray Ltd.*

Sansibar Whisky Very Old Vatted (74.5) n19 t19 f18 b18.5. Pretty smoky for a Speyside. But bitter and off key. 45.6%

◈ **Scotch Universe Voyager I 231° U.4.4'F 1886.2"TS** first fill Côte de Beaune wine barrique, dist 1997, bott 2016 (78) n20 t21 f18 b19 Voyager...that's me! A voyager through the universe of whisky having travelled on for what seems now like lightyears. And despite all the malty planets I have explored, I still don't like whiskies which are either sulphured or over fruity. Or both. *52.9%*.

Scottish Collie (86.5) n22 t23 f20.5 b21. A really young pup of a vatting. Full of life and fun but muzzled by toffee at the death. *40%. Quality Spirits International.*

Scottish Collie 5 Years Old (90.5) n22.5 t23 f22 b23. Fabulous mixing here showing just what malt whisky can do at this brilliant and under-rated age. Lively and complex with the malts wonderfully herded and penned. Without colouring and at 50% abv I bet this would have been given a right wolf-whistle. Perfect for one man and his grog. *40%.*

Scottish Collie 8 Years Old (85.5) n22 t21.5 f21 b21. A good boy. But just wants to sleep rather than play. *40%. Quality Spirits International.*

Scottish Collie 12 Years Old (82) n20 t22 f20 b20. For a malt that's aged 84 in Collie years, it understandably smells a bit funny and refuses to do many tricks. If you want some fun you'll need a younger version. *40%. Quality Spirits International.*

Scottish Leader Imperial Blended Malt (77) n20 t20 f18 b19. Now don't be confused here: this isn't Imperial malt from Speyside. And although it says Blended, it is 100% malt. What is clear, though, is that this is pretty average stuff. *40%. Burn Stewart.*

Scottish Leader Aged 14 Years (80) n21 t21 f19 b19. A cleaner, less peaty version than the no-age statement vatting, but still fails to entirely ignite the tastebuds *40%. Burn Stewart.*

Scott's Selection Burnside 1994 (93) n23.5 t24 f22.5 b23.5. I may well be wrong. But I think this is the first time I have seen a Burnside, which is a cask of Balvenie spoiled as a single malt by having a spoonful of same age Glenfiddich added to it, in a commercial bottling rather than as a sample in my blending lab! Believe me: it was well worth waiting for...! *56.7%.*

Sheep Dip (84) n19 t22 f22 b21. Young and sprightly like a new-born lamb, this enjoys a fresh, mouthwatering grassy style wth a touch of spice. Maligned by some, but to me a clever, accomplished vatting of alluring complexity. *40%*

Sheep Dip 'Old Hebridean' 1990 dist in or before 1990 (94) n23 t24 f23.5 b23.5. You honey!! Now, that's what I call a whisky...!! *40%. The Spencerfield Spirit Co.*

⬦ **Shetland Reel Batch No. 1** (72) n18 t22 f15 b17 I am just glad that the sulphur comes from dodgy casks used in this vatting of other distillery's malts and not their own. If this isn't a great lesson for the Shetland lads not to touch sherry butts with a pole that can stretch from Lerwick to Norway, I don't know what is. *47%. 1,800 bottles.*

⬦ **Shetland Reel Batch No. 2** (90) n23.5 now that is one magnificent aroma...! The smoke offers both a base note and, in its higher form, a lead. Fruity elements of Melton Mowbray Hunt Cake combine with light liquorice and heather honey. A hint of a weakness docks it half a mark, but it is well masked by the peat...; t23 gloriously silk and soft, allowing both the honey and smoke to go freestyle. Burnt raisin and spices abound; f21 good oils for the fault spotted on the nose returns...; b22.5 a rogue sherry butt cannot entirely undo the many excellent qualities of this vatting. *47%. 1,800 bottles.*

Simon Brown The Captain's Pure Scotch Malt Islay bourbon casks, dist 2010, bott 2015 (91) n22.5 a dense aroma, like oily smoke; t23 silky oils hold in the golden syrup and spices with ease; f22.5 a touch of grist is a late reminder of the youth; a lovely powdery peat fade; b23 a young malt delighted to display its sugary side. Exceptionally easy going. *43%. nc ncf.*

Simon Brown The Captain's Pure Scotch Malt Speyside Highlands sherry casks, dist 2009, bott 2015 (80) n18.5 t21.5 f20 b20. As present day sherry butts go, not too bad. It bounces back from a poor nose with some impressive honey on delivery – and this manages to keep going long into when the less attractive notes of the sherry return. *43%. nc ncf.*

S'Mokey (88) n22.5 t22 f21.5 b22. Delicate, sweet and more lightly smoked than the nose advertises. *40%.*

Smokey Joe Islay Malt (87) n21.5 t22 f21.5 b22. A soft, soporific version of a smoky Islay. No thumping of waves here: the tide is out. *46%. ncf. Angus Dundee Distillers.*

Spirit of Caledonia Flaitheanas 18 Years Old (94) n23.5 oak shavings and tannin-based spices quietly and attractively dominate: so elegant.; t24 superb arrival of both spice and ulmo honey, then a slow malty infusion; f23 long, with butterscotch in the driving seat; b23.5 now that is a proper vatted malt...!!! *578%. Mr Whisky.*

Svenska Eldvatten Blended Malt 1994 ex-sherry butt, dist Aug 94 (71) n18 t18 f17 b18. There is nothing I need to say... *54.5%. sc.*

Tambowie (84.5) n21.5 t21.5 f20.5 b21. A decent improvement on the nondescript bottling of yore. I have re-included this to both celebrate its newly acquired lightly fruited attractiveness...and to celebrate the 125th anniversary of the long departed

Tambowie Distillery whose whisky, I am sure, tasted nothing like this. *40%. The Vintage Malt Whisky Co Ltd.*

⬦ **That Boutique-y Whisky Company Islay Blended Malt No 1 23 Year Old** batch 1 (94.5) n24 impressive. Distinct layering of the peats here with the sharper, more acidic style a little louder than the throat lozenge phenol; t23.5 if you do have a sore throat the attack on delivery will do it no harm at all and should see off all known germs; the honey is crystalline, the grist salivating; some lemon and vague ginger enters the fray - I suppose they had to seeing as this is about medicinal as it comes...; f23 a little milky mocha to go with the Fisherman's Friend; b24 probably the most delicious cure for anything and everything... *46.3%. 419 bottles.*

⬦ **That Boutique-y Whisky Company Blended Malt Whisky No. 1 23 Year Old** batch 2 (88.5) n21.5 the ancient tannins are a bit too grumpy for comfort; t23 didn't expect that! Massive surge of concentrated malt, the barley dipping into some fudge to see it through. Lovely texture...; f22 having tasted them, I can assure you there is a roast acorn nuttiness at play toward the end; b22 pretty tired but hangs in there gamely and even shows some astonishing malty liveliness! *48.8%. 409 bottles.*

That Boutique-y Whisky Company Blended Malt No. 2 batch 1 (72) n17.5 t19 f17.5 b18. Unmolested , the grape would have been spectacular, especially with the big cocoa finish. But the cask has done its damage. *48.3%. 370 bottles.*

That Boutique-y Whisky Company Blended Malt No. 2 batch 2 (84.5) n21.5 t21 f21.5 b20.5. The sugars are a bit too flash and uncouth. Elsewhere, just a tad too tart and struggles to find a balance. *43.1%. 415 bottles.*

That Boutique-y Whisky Company Islay Blended Malt No. 2 27 Year Old batch 1 (84.5) n20 t21.5 f21.5 b21.5. That unique and vivid Fisherman's Friend character, alongside Love Hearts candy, suggests Bowmore is at the heart of this one. *473%. 88 bottles.*

Treasurer 1874 Reserve Cask (90.5) n23 t23 f22.5 b22. Some judicious adding has been carried out here in the Robert Graham shop. Amazing for a living cask that I detect no major sulphur faultlines. Excellent! *51%. Live casks available in all Robert Graham shops.*

Triple Wood Blended Malt Scotch Whisky (77) n17.5 t22 f18.5 b19. At least one wood too many. Tangy...for all the wrong reasons. *42%. Lidl.*

⬦ **Usquaebach Cask Strength 2016 Release** (86) n21.5 t23.5 f20 b21 A curate's egg of a dram. The fruitiness is hit and miss: more miss than hit. But there is also a hugely attractive, shimmering sharpness, also, with the barley sparkling on the palate in fabulous fashion. Sadly, the caramels and then dull tanginess is hardly the progression hoped for. *571%. ncf.*

Vintner's Choice Speyside 10 Years Old (84) n21.5 t22 f20 b20.5. Pleasant. But with the quality of the Speysiders Grants have to play with, the dullness is a bit hard to fathom. *40%.*

Waitrose Pure Highland Malt (86.5) n22 t22 f20.5 b22. Blood orange by the cartload: amazingly tangy and fresh; bitters out at the finish. This is one highly improved malt and great to see a supermarket bottling showing some serious attitude...as well as taste!! Fun, refreshing and enjoyable. *40%*

The Warehouse Dram Braon Peat batch 4, bott 11 Dec 15 (81.5) n21.5 t22 f18 b20. An unusual nose: for some reason reminds me of washing on the line – soapy, perhaps? Strange! Actually, also the smell outside the kitchen of my old school mate Phil Rush's house when his mum had been doing the washing, back in the early '70s. A pattern is forming here... *57%*

⬦ **Wemyss Malts The Hive** (87) n21.5 t22 f22 b21.5 A lush, easy-drinking dram but one with a surprising lack of high spots: it is as though someone has made the common but fatal mistake of putting together styles that have cancelled each other out – certainly at this strength - rather than bringing the best out of and enhancing the other. No lack of honey and spice, for sure, but also toffee aplenty. *46%. ncf.*

⬦ **Wemyss Malts The Hive Batch Strength** batch 001 (90.5) n22 lazy hints of heather honey, as well a cream toffee; t23.5 ahhh...! That's more like it! The delivery, at times a little tart and fruity (as opposed to fruit tarty..) rams home those honey notes with abandon and there is no surprise when the spices arrive in force; the star turn is the rich, lightly oiled mouth feel which keeps the golden syrup and treacle running as long as possible; f22 returns back to sleepy mode with fudge and spice seeing out the last moments; b23 a lovely malt which is heavily dependent on the honey and spice. And there is nothing wrong with that! *54.5%. ncf. 6,000 bottles.*

⬦ **Wemyss Malts Kiln Embers** (94.5) n23.5 ashy, dry and acidic on one level; citrusy, muscovado-sweet and lightly oiled on another...charming; t23.5 the oils arrive first – and in greater intensity than the nose suggests. The nose is spot on though with the sweet-dry interplay, which here bounces around the palate until the sugar, all toasty and deep, finally win; **f23.5** a manicured finale with the silky oily hanging on to the smoky embers...; **b24** quite quite beautiful. 46%. ncf.

⟜ **Wemyss Malts Peat Chimney (84.5) n21.5 t21.5 f21 b20.5** A sharp, muddled malt whose unbalanced kippery nose is a peaty indication of what is to follow. Each avenue explored appears to narrow into a dead end: a tight, restricted, frustrating experience. 46%. ncf.

⟜ **Wemyss Malts Peat Chimney Batch Strength** batch 001 **(87.5) n22 t23 f21 b21.5** Much more comfortable and happy with itself than the 46% version, mainly thanks to the extra oils allowing the molasses to integrate to greater effect with the smoke. But the tinny, off kilter finale shows that some elements here simply refuse to bond. 57%. ncf. 6,000 bottles.

⟜ **Wemyss Malts Spice King (90) n23.5** brilliant display of rich tannins: hickory, muscovado sugar and a nibbling, gently smoked spice link to excellent effect; **t22.5** salivating and sweet delivery; a little grist thickens the mix; **f22** classic vanilla and butterscotch fade; a very late and light sprinkling of spice...; **b22** a lovely malt, but beyond the nose the spices of note are conspicuous by their absence and not a patch on those found on The Hive... 46%. ncf.

⟜ **Wemyss Malts Spice King Batch Strength Batch 001 (95.5) n23.5** fruity muscovado, delicate smoke and confident, tingling spice do what they say on the label...; **t24.5** magnificent delivery! Huge tannin thuds into the taste buds taking no prisoners. Enough sugars are present to prevent splinters and instead we get a huge spice blast with a gorgeous treacle and ulmo honey middle to sooth the battered nerve endings, the smoke arrives to minimise the storm **f23.5** red liquorice, vanilla and now light orange blossom honey counter the tingling spices; **b24** notably different in character and storyline to the 46% version...and here spices are in no shortage whatsoever...! Stunningly gorgeous. 56%. ncf. 6,000 bottles.

⟜ **Whisky-Fässle Blended Malt Whisky** very old sherry butt, bott 2016 **(87.5) n23 t23 f20 b21.5** Unquestionably some fruity - and fruit cakey - appeal on the nose with the grape showing both a catholic and zesty personality, and this is matched somewhat in the early moments of the rich delivery. But dulls and bitters out within a short period leaving a lopsided tale being told, all the interesting bits being in the opening chapters. 45.2%.

⟜ **Whisky-Fässle Blended Malt Whisky** very old sherry butt, bott 2016 **(94) n24** hefty nose with thoroughbred tannins poking out of the dense grape with rigid determination; **t23.5** beautifully crafted fruit, two-toned and juicy. The sugars boast a molassed richness which matches the plummy fruitiness perfectly; soft vanillas and spices begin to fill the middle ground; **f22.5** a vague bitterness from tired oak (nothing as sinister or insidious as sulphur, as this is not present) just makes a presence, but the vanilla and spice still rule; **b24** a much better balance to this with the oak having a welcome equal say in matters and giving the whisky an air of antiquity. 45.4%.

Whyte & Mackay Blended Malt Scotch Whisky (78) n19 t22 f18 b19. You know when the engine to your car is sort of misfiring and feels a bit sluggish and rough...? 40%. Waitrose.

Wild Scotsman Scotch Malt Whisky (Black Label) batch no. CBV001 **(91) n23.5 t23.5 f21 b23.** The type of dram you drink from a dirty glass. Formidable and entertaining. 47%

Wild Scotsman Aged 15 Years Vatted Malt (95) n23 t24 f24 b24. If anyone wants an object lesson as to why you don't screw your whisky with caramel, here it is. Jeff Topping can feel a justifiable sense of pride in his new whisky: for its age, it is an unreconstituted masterpiece... 46% (92 proof). nc ncf. USA.

William Grant & Sons Rare Cask Reserves 25 Years Old Blended Malt Scotch Whisky (82) n21 t22 f19 b20. Mouth-filling, chewy and mildly fruity, doesn't quite grow into the decent start offered and finishes untidily. 47%. Exclusive to The Whisky Shop.

Wilson & Morgan Barrel Selection Speybridge sherry wood, dist 2001, bott 2015 **(94) n23.5 t24 f23 b23.5** Almost spot on sherry butts at work here. No sulphur involvement to speak of, so you can simply concentrate on the embracing beauty of the sugars. And so rare to encounter a sherried malt with no bitterness on the finish whatsoever. 45.9%

Wilson & Morgan Barrel Selection Westport sherry wood, dist 1997, bott 2014 **(93.5) n23.5 t24 f22.5 b23.5** Oh...!!! The charm of virtually clean sherry butts!! Almost no sulphur here....just magnificent whisky! 48%

Mystery Malts

Chieftain's Limited Edition Aged 40 Years hogshead **(78) n22 t22 f16 b18.** Oak-ravaged and predictably bitter on the death (those of you who enjoy Continental bitters might go for this..!). But the lead up does offer a short, though sublime and intense honey kick. The finish, though... 48.5%. Ian Macleod.

Scottish Grain

It's a bit weird, really. Many whisky lovers stay clear of blended Scotch, preferring instead single malts. The reason, I am often told, is that the grain included in a blend makes it rough and ready. Yet I wish I had a twenty pound note for each time I have been told in recent years how much someone enjoys a single grain. The ones that the connoisseurs die for are the older versions, usually special independent bottlings displaying great age and more often than not brandishing a lavish Canadian or bourbon style.

Like single malts, grain distilleries produce whisky bearing their own style and signature. And, also, some display characteristics and a richness that can surprise and delight. Most of the grains available in (usually specialist) whisky outlets are pretty elderly. Being made from maize and wheat helps give them either that Canadian or, depending on the freshness of the cask, an unmistakable bourbony style. So older grains display far greater body than is commonly anticipated.

During the last year the grain whisky lover has been spoiled for choice. Especially those with deep pockets seeking the rarest of the grains, those which were seldom available to blenders even when those now lost distilleries were in full production. Top of the tree comes Garnheath, one of the lighter grains in its youth though now offering a unique charm whenever it surfaces. Two new casks yielded just 300 bottles between them - each of them nectar.

The Last Drop, as is their speciality, somehow unearthed a 44-year-old Lochside; there were some fine Carsebridges to be had from both Hunter and Douglas Laing, each company bringing out 50-year-olds; and four new bottlings of Caledonian passed through my tasting room, the Whiskybroker's 28-year-old racking up no less than 95 points to top them all, including one from the distillery's former owners, Diageo.

But it was that more prosaic, and still breathing, distillery of Invergordon which eclipsed them all, the independent bottlers Whiskyjace honouring us with a stunning 24-year-old.

Jim Murray's Whisky Bible Scotch Grain of the Year Winners	
2004-07	N/A
2008	Duncan Taylor Port Dundas 1973
2009	The Clan Denny Dumbarton Aged 43 Years
2010	Duncan Taylor North British 1978
2011	The Clan Denny Dumbarton Aged 40 Years
2012	The Clan Denny Cambus 47 Years Old
2013	SMWS G5.3 Aged 18 Years (Invergordon)
2014	The Clan Denny Dumbarton 48 Years Old
2015	The Sovereign Single Cask Port Dundas 1978
2016	The Clan Deny Cambus 25 Years Old
2017	Whiskyjace Invergordon 24 Year Old
2018	Cambus Aged 40 Years

Single Grain Scotch
CALEDONIAN

The Cally 40 Year Old refill American oak hogsheads, dist 1974 db **(88.5) n23.5** the vanilla merges with the ulmo honey, in total control; **t23** sharper than a butcher's knife: eye-watering explosion of what seems like unmalted barley and sugar-laden corn; **f20** bitters out as the oak begins to disintegrate; **b22** this poor old sod is tiring before your nose and taste buds. But it hangs on grimly to give the best show it can. Quite touching, really...we are witnessing first hand the slow death of a once great distillery. *53.3%. 5,060 bottles. Diageo Special Releases 2015.*

The Sovereign Caledonian 41 Years Old refill hogshead, cask no. 11836, dist Mar 74, bott Sept 15 **(88) n22.5 t23 f20.5 b22** A long way from a perfect old grain. But enough character and flavour to see it through. *50.2%. nc ncf sc. 200 bottles.*

Spirit of Caledonia Invergordon 24 Years Old (84.5) n23 t22 f20.5 b21. Soft and yielding, as an Invergordon should be. And spicy in part, too. But a little tobacco on the nose and overbearing bitterness on the finish. *56%. Mr. Whisky.*

◇ **That Boutique-y Whisky Company Caledonian 29 Year Old** batch 2 **(96) n24** a nose with so much promise! An underground spiciness suggests personality; over-ripe bananas and peaches and cream...this is going to be yummy; **t24.5** what a to-die-for delivery. Soft but by no means cloying; sweet but controlled and in tune to contrast the drier vanillas. It is a grain that feels exactly right on the palate before we really get into the nitty gritty of the flavour profile. A little ulmo honey links with melted praline while a jam roly-poly and butterscotch middle still stints slightly on the sugars; **f23.5** a heavenly fade of slow dissolving and gentle amplification of spices...; **b24** the best Caledonian I have tasted in a very long time. A true classic! *47.7%. 310 bottles.*

Whiskybroker Caledonian 28 Year Old refill hogshead, cask no. 23882, dist 20 Apr 87, bott 29 Jan 16 **(95) n23.5 t24 f23.5 b24** Very unusually, I can't tell for sure if wheat or corn is at play here. The spice prickle suggests the former, as does the limitations of the oils. But the depth to the sugar and vanilla, especially towards the end is of a corn style. Probably wheat, but whichever – a stunner. *54.6%. sc.*

CAMBUS

◇ **Cambus Aged 40 Years** dist 1975 db **(97) n24.5** not, perhaps the most wide-ranging of noses as far as different aroma traits are concerned. But it does what it sets out to do with something akin to perfection. Caramels simply don't come this intense yet pitch-perfect. The corn, oak, toasty sugars and all else to be found all seems wrapped one way or another in caramelised form with varying levels of honey and roast at work. So the feeling of age, great age. Yet as though preserved in caramel...extraordinary and beyond beautiful; **t24** no surprises then that the delivery is firm to the point of crunchiness. And, again, it is concentrated caramel sweetened with honey, Manuka and ulmo, ensuring that the age doesn't take a turn for the sinister. It needs spices to balance the mouth experience away from deliciously sweet...and it arrives on schedule and with purpose; **f23.5** long unravelling of the many elements and personalities which make up the caramel, especially the corn, with some late burnt toast and marmalade at the very death; **b25** I chose this as my 600th whisky for Bible 2018: a tragically lost distillery capable of making the finest whisky you might expect to find at 40 years of age. And my hunch was correct: this is flawless. *52.7%. 1,812 bottles. Diageo Special Releases 2016.*

◇ **Best Dram Cambus 25 Year Old** sherry hogshead, dist 1991, bott 2017 **(86) n21 t22.5 f21 b21.5** A bitter-sweet experience...literally! Quite a tangy finish. *55%.*

◇ **The Cooper's Choice Cambus 25 Year Old** sherry wood, dist 1991, bott 2017 **(94) n23.5** thumping clean oloroso, complete with spice and the extra weight of age; **t23.5** big, chewy, salivating....then the fruit rams itself home with a big sultana crescendo; the tannins ensure a darker, more bitter side evens things out; **f23** the finish confirms we have a sherry influence free from sulphur. Even late on the grape is visible and still succulent; **b24** another of the parcel of Cambus 1991 to have hit the market this year...and of the sherry-matured this is by far the best. *51.5%. nc ncf sc. The Vintage Malt Whisky Co.*

◇ **Liquid Treasures Cambus 25 Year Old** sherry butt, dist 1991, bott 2017 **(88) n22.5** really odd: the combination of tight, peppery spices on the intense, sweet wine, plus a certain dusty note, means I have sneezed every time I have tried to nose this over the last half hour. That, for me, can also detect hidden sulphur....we'll see...; **t22.5** the Cambus comes through only as the body shape: all else is the magnificently lush, slightly puckering grape; **f21** the barely noticeable sulphur is on slow burn and arrives maybe three or four minutes after tasting. Detracts, though not by much...; **b22** a whisky not to be sneezed at.. *52.7%. Faces of Angkor Edition.*

⟪⟫ **MacAlabur Cambus 25 Years Old** bourbon hogshead, cask no. 79900, dist 24 Sept 91, bott 10 Oct 16 **(95.5) n24** unlikely you will encounter a Cambus which so beguilingly encapsulates the aroma of this great, tragically lost, distillery: a hint of rice pudding with a little golden syrup to sweeten; over-ripe conference pear and corn oil heads you towards something vaguely Canadian...; **t24** soft and salivating on delivery, as the best Cambus tends to be, then the trademark controlled spice explosion directly matching the ulmo honey and drying Danish marzipan and accompanying dark chocolate; **f23.5** the long oils and spices continue to harmonise with the sugars; **b24** should be in a frame and found in the Tate Modern... 62%. nc ncf sc. 221 bottles.

⟪⟫ **Old Particular Cambus 24 Years Old** refill hogshead, cask no. 11172, dist Sept 91, bott Apr 16 **(87) n22 t22.5 f21 b21.5** Begins to display some tangy wear and tear as a little tightness from the oak takes the edge off an otherwise delightful show. 51.5%. nc ncf sc. 249 bottles.

⟪⟫ **Old Particular Cambus 25 Years Old** refill hogshead, cask no. 11353, dist Sept 91, bott Sept 16 **(89) n23** gentle kumquats and vanilla curd tart; the age is always very apparent; **t22** the oak hits you between the eyes but mix of light muscovado sugars just keep the vanilla in check; **f22** vanilla rules; some lazy late spice and cocoa; **b22** quite a muted grain which seems to be working so extra hard to keep the oak under control that it forgets to expand its character. Always a joy, though. 55.4%. nc ncf sc. 282 bottles.

Old Particular Cambus 27 Years Old refill hogshead, cask no. 10940, dist Sept 88, bott Sept 15 **(91) n23 t23 b23** Even as this whisky nears its third decade, it acts slightly differently than most grain but keeping to its style and character rather than giving way to the march of the oak. Quite lovely. 51.5%. nc ncf sc. 270 bottles.

⟪⟫ **Old Particular Cambus 28 Years Old** refill hogshead, cask no. 11607, dist Sept 88, bott Mar 17 **(89.5) n22** a little sharpness from the cask cuts through the soothing oily vanilla; **t23.5** much more like it as the sugars mount a serious early attack on the taste buds - offering about as much punch as a two-year-old nipper. Very buttery.; **f21.5** a vague bitterness creeps into the fading oils; **b22.5** a gentle Cambus where just a little mischief from the cask makes a disproportionate impact on the delicate grain. 50.1%. nc ncf sc. 280 bottles.

⟪⟫ **Scotch Malt Whisky Society Cask G8.8 26 Year Old** refill ex-bourbon hogshead, dist 18 Jun 90 **(20) n23.5** Walnut Whip candy, with special emphasis on the fondant. Even a vague milk chocolate note to be had...before the spices begin to louden; **t23.5** and just like a fondant the delivery is soft, oily and sweet. Light traces of ulmo honey stretch that sweetness. The vanilla becomes more dominant as the spices evolve; **f22** a little bitterness creeps in from the oak; **b23** a slightly naughty cask tries to take the gloss off a brilliant grain: it fails. 56.7%.

⟪⟫ **The Sovereign Cambus 25 Years Old** refill hogshead, cask no. 13051, dist Sept 91, bott Nov 16 **(95) n24** the perfect nose for rum lovers...; some really serious age on this; **t24** you could stand your spoon in this...well, until it dissolved. Massive rum – errr, sorry I mean grain, with the sugars in rich molten state and the tannin battling every hint of flavour for supremacy. But so true if the golden syrup and ulmo honey the balance is never breeched; **f23.5** outstanding late spice and bunt fudge; **b24** substantial whisky: just packed to the last atom with character. Delicious! 55.5%. nc ncf sc. 271 bottles.

That Boutique-y Whisky Company Cambus batch 1 **(94) n23 t23.5 f23.5 b24** A brilliant bottling very much of the top quality Canadian school. Leaves you in no doubt of the magnitude of our loss with this ex-distillery. 45.1%. 41 bottles.

⟪⟫ **The Whisky Agency Cambus 1988 (92) n23** a singular weightiness leans heavily on the Lubek marzipan; **t24** brilliant delivery: not just molten marzipan but walnuts and light ulmo honey mixed in with a raspberry and cream Swiss Roll. The vanilla starts to delve into the sweetness; **f22** bitters out just a little too enthusiastically; **b23** some of the moments on this are pure 24 carat Grain gold. 47.4%.

⟪⟫ **Whisky Broker Cambus 25 Year Old** sherry butt, cask no. 62929, dist 08 Aug 91, bott 08 Mar 17 **(88.5) n22** spiced walnut cake...at the top of a sherry trifle...; **t23.5** wow, those spices really have an agenda! Seriously warming, but leave enough space for the bitter-sweet battle to carry on unhindered, with the oak having a slightly tightening grip over the muscovado and vanilla; **f21** dries and furs up slightly; **b22** so many positives here, but the slight sulphur taint does have a late effect. 56.9%.

⟪⟫ **The Whisky Chamber Cambus 25 Year Old** refill sherry cask, dist 1991 **(83) n22 t22 f19 b20** There appears to have been a run Cambus bottled this year thick with corn-oiled promise, but then crashing into small sulphured rocks. Not enough to sink the grain, but at least hole it... 53.1%.

⟪⟫ **Xtra Old Particular Cambus 40 Years Old** refill hogshead, cask no. 11572, dist Sept 76, bott Nov 16 **(97) n24.5** for those of us who can delve back to a childhood when sweet shops sold Blackjacks and Fruit Salad from the jar at a farthing a go, mysterious pouches of pipe tobacco radiated myriad aromas. For small non-smokers there was a "tobacco" made from strands of coconut dipped in treacle...and here is that aroma, moist and framed in old oak, like the floorboards of my little corner sweetshop in its Surrey village; this is salty, also, and the vanilla appears to have a slight overcooked feel to it, though nothing ruinous...; **t24.5** the corn oil appears to be a taster for various types of honey: as usual ulmo is at the forefront, then a more salivating acacia and heather mix, the latter also appropriately, putting down some roots. The maple syrup is little more than a light covering but the spices also stir up the taste buds, though, like everything else here, in a proportionate and gentle manner; **f23.5** long, if a little quiet now, with the most vague hint of burnt toast; **b24.5** when Cambus was still alive its output at standard blending ages was, for me, the finest of all the grains with Dumbarton following closely behind. As the grain matured towards middle and old age it lost the edge it had over the others...until now. For this bottling shines like a beacon and reveals in extraordinary detail just how truly great Cambus distillery was. *53.1%. nc ncf sc. 108 bottles.*

CAMERONBRIDGE

Cadenhead's Small Batch Cameronbridge Aged 24 Years bourbon hogsheads, dist 1989, bott 2013 **(92) n21.5 t23.5 f23 b23.5** A pleasing grain with idea above its supposedly lowly station. Kicks the crap out of a great many single malts it is supposed to kow-tow to. *46%. 618 bottles. WB15/167*

◇ **Old Particular Cameronbridge 24 Years Old** refill hogshead, cask no. 11225, dist Oct 91, bott Apr 16 **(95) n24** soft and alluring with a hint of something rock-hard through the middle: top notch grain. Wonderful vanilla aspect to this, with a caramelised sweetness that softens into acacia honey; the oak notes tend to hint of the other side of the Atlantic...; **t24** rich mouth feel which would bamboozle anyone tasting this blind! The oils are well up for this and fully support the light sugars as they massage the vanillins; **f23** dries and spices up rather sexily; **b24** very hard to ask any more of a grain whisky than that: beautiful. *51.5%. nc ncf sc. 461 bottles.*

Old Particular Cameronbridge 25 Years Old refill butt, cask no. 10806, dist Jun 90, bott Jun 15 **(91.5) n22.5 t23.5 f22.5 b23** A blistering grain which, at this strength, shows you an old grain warts and all. As fabulous as it is fascinating. *60.6%. nc ncf sc. 282 bottles.*

◇ **Old Particular Cameronbridge 25 Years Old** refill hogshead, cask no. 11316, dist Oct 91, bott Oct 16 **(94) n23.5** a confident march of Demerara sugars...even slightly rum-like for a while before a sweeter bourbon note saunters in; **t23** fat with a thick cornmeal chewiness; some brown sugars reappear; **f23.5** really impressed with the way the sugars begin to take charge rather than the drier oak: forms a lovely counter to the buzzing spice; **b24** if anyone says grain whisky is light and neutral, please put them in the direction of this. *54.5%. nc ncf sc. 276 bottles.*

◇ **That Boutique-y Whisky Company Cameronbridge 24 Year Old** batch 1 **(93.5) n23.5** goes slightly easier on the sugars than others of this age from C'Bridge. Pays more attention to the vanillins and even a certain grassiness; **t23** soft, though not as soft as some. The sugars are of the bleached variety and melt in the mouth. Becomes a little busier, drier and spicier as it proceeds; **f24** some thicker oils help with an ice cream fade, complete with wafer and chocolate sauce; **b23** takes its time to enter the super league – but gets there... *49.6%. 211 bottles.*

◇ **Xtra Old Particular Cameronbridge 32 Years Old** refill hogshead, cask no. 11342, dist Mar 84, bott Aug 16 **(96.5) n24.5** where does one start? So complex, it is hard to try. Think bourbon meets Canadian meets Coffey still Guyanese rum. So many layers of sugar, perhaps even more layers of tannin; **t24** unusually for grain, the spices arrive first, practically queuing at the taste buds to have their say. Fortunately, the limp oils and myriad sugar tones act as the perfect sponge to absorb the spicy blows with a vanilla softness calming matters further; **f23.5** long with sublime oak layering and higher peaks of the brown sugars still showing; **b24.5** quite indisputably magnificent. A contender for Scotch Grain of the Year. *56.2%. nc ncf sc. 254 bottles.*

CARSEBRIDGE

◇ **Dramfool Carsebridge 52 Year Old** cask nos. 89153, 89154, 89155 & 89157, dist 1964 **(95) n23.5** butterscotch wrapped in cream toffee... as soft and sensual as you can expect any 50-year-old whisky to be...; **t24** silky, again with that big cream toffee – Toffo – landing, though now we begin to see the tannins unravel slowly and with grace. Spices are light at first but build into something significant while a mix of creamy liquorice and maple syrup ensures a charming balance; **f23.5** the spices circle like a kite on a thermal; the tannins and caramels embrace warmly; **b24** I doubt if you'll find a softer and more gentle whisky anywhere in the world this year... *40.8%. 50 bottles.*

⟩ **Old Particular Carsebridge 33 Years Old** refill hogshead, cask no. 11339, dist Dec 82, bott Sept 16 (94.5) n23 far closer to wooden still Demerara rum than a Scottish grain: , sweet, honeyed fingerprints all over the deft tannin; t24.5 OK, I really have just tapped into an old barrel in Guyana, right: if I look outside there will be hummingbirds feeing off crimson plants and the sun will be beating relentlessly down....nope, a few apologetic snowflakes are drifting from the leaden early Spring skies and blackbirds are hopping about in mixed confusion and agitation...; even here my palate is coated with the most fabulously decadent honey and controlled butterscotch tannin (not unlike the ancient old casks of Demerara) kiss my taste buds with rare tenderness; f23.5 more of the same, though a little bitterness from the cask does surface; b23.5 as grain whiskies go, what a stunning old rum this is...! 44.9%. nc ncf sc. 253 bottles.

⟩ **The Sovereign Carsebridge 42 Years Old** refill hogshead, cask no. 11848, dist Jan 73, bott Sept 15 (88.5) n22.5 t22 f21.5 b22.5 Had no idea it was possible to cram so much natural caramel into one bottle! 48.9%. nc ncf sc. 221 bottles.

⟩ **The Sovereign Carsebridge 42 Years Old** refill hogshead, cask no. 12366, dist May 73, bott Apr 16 (77) n18 t22 f18 b19 Very similar in style to old whiskies rounded off in sherry to take out the oaky claws with the nose and finish great disappointments. But I'm sure they wouldn't be that suicidal..! 53.1%. nc ncf sc. 167 bottles.

⟩ **The Sovereign Carsebridge 43 Years Old** refill butt, cask no. 12653, dist May 73, bott Jun 16 (86.5) n21 t22 f21.5 b22 Despite being matured in an old sherry cask, this has much more rich caramel sloshing about the palate than fruit, complete with a tiring bitterness. It is if the two Sovereign Carsebridge samples I have been sent are in reverse... 54.3%. nc ncf sc. 345 bottles.

⟩ **The Sovereign Carsebridge 50 Years Old** refill hogshead, cask no. 11847, dist Oct 65, bott Oct 15 (95) n24 t24 f23 b24 Cannot ask for much more with a grain of this age. How can oak and sugars be in near perfect sync after half a century –amazing! 41.5%. nc ncf sc. 267 bottles.

⟩ **That Boutique-y Whisky Company Carsebridge 52 Year Old** batch 1 (95) n23.5 t24 f23.5 b24 Apart from the most minute extra tannin on the nose, an identical whisky to the Dramfool Carsebridge 52 above. 40.5%. 252 bottles.

⟩ **Xtra Old Particular Carsebridge 40 Years Old** refill hogshead, cask no. 11529, dist Oct 76, bott Nov 16 (93) n23 lime marmalade on lightly buttered toast; vaguely acidic; t23.5 silky delivery with an immediate controlled explosion of Canadian- bordering bourbon notes, the corn always at the fore, the sugars growing weightier and more dark by the moment; f23 long with a tapering corn and ulmo honey finale; b23.5 a surprisingly simplistic whisky considering its age, but what it does do is achieved with rare panache. 53.7%. nc ncf sc. 230 bottles.

Xtra Old Particular Carsebridge 50 Years Old refill hogshead, dist Oct 65, bott Nov 15 (91.5) n23 t22.5 f23 b23 As delicious as it is fascinating. 40.1%. nc ncf sc. 101 bottles.

DUMBARTON

⟩ **Fadandel.dk Dumbarton 30 Year Old** bourbon cask, cask no. 25241, dist 18 Mar 87, bott 27 Mar 17 (89.5) n22.5 much saltier than usual with a dry caramel wafer thread. Despite the salt, the tune seems to be one more usually hummed in Canada than Kentucky...; t23 silky and sweet delivery. A little corn oil fattens the continued buttery notes further; f22 substantial caramel and spice; a little late cask bitterness; b22 Lovely whisky, but Dumbarton in its most simplistic form. 57.2%. nc ncf sc. 168 bottles.

⟩ **The Last Drop Dumbarton 54 Year Old** 2nd fill bourbon barrel, dist 19 Jan 61 (96) n24.5 t24.5 f23 b24 Dumbarton here displays, with an ease almost bordering arrogance, why it is the doyen of grain whiskies. It is no coincidence that the greatest ancient blended whiskies I have tasted include liberal amounts of Dumbarton. As you can see here, it has the ability to be firm enough for backbone to form, yet soft enough to ensure a yielding countenance, too. A grain, glorying in its 55th year... 43.5%. sc. 34 bottles.

⟩ **The Sovereign Dumbarton 29 Years Old** refill barrel, cask no. 13049, dist Mar 87, bott Nov 16 (96.5) n25 it is one of those: a half hour nose which can be indulged in for twice that time without ever getting bored or seemingly finding the same sequence of characters twice. The outline is distinctly bourbonesque. But of the busier small grain variety. Making tiny, random cameo appearances in no particular order aew marshmallow, vanilla pods, rice pudding, spearmint, Manuka honey, red liquorice, physalis, and various teasing spices... Just... wow!!! t24.5 mouth-watering, tingling delivery made all the more stunning by not just the depth and intensity of the oil but its near perfect proportion. Busy spices simmer, though tagged by a mix of maple syrup and molasses....; f23 those spices continue to warm, the sugars continue to sooth and counter in wonderful unison; the oak just begins to creak towards the very end, but understandably so...; **b24** a mercurial, beautifully paced grain of the very highest order. Truly classic! *54.7%. nc ncf sc. 235 bottles.*

⟐ **The Whisky Barrel Dumbarton 30 Year Old** barrel, cask no. 13436, dist 1987 **(96.5) n24** there is more of a shimmer than a sheen to this: a fascinating mix of fresher, greener note and those vaguely salty and dry; the vanilla, like the grain is firm and shows no sign of weakness; **t24.5** light oils create the perfect environment for the rich honey to be fully maximised, all the more surprising as there is no hint of this to come on the nose! Salivating heather honey and maple syrup combine for something very special indeed; **f24** balances out with butterscotch and a soothing corn and vanilla fade; **b24** Dumbarton at anything from 21to 30 is about as good as grain whisky gets (hence why Ballantine's can be sensational), providing it has lived in the right cask. And this is the right cask... *56.7%. sc. 197 bottles.*

GARNHEATH

⟐ **The Cooper's Choice Garnheath 28 Year Old** dist 1986, bott 2015 **(94.5) n23.5** what a stunning intertwangling of vaguely spicy vanilla notes and the fruity grain...; **t24** top dog mouth feel: soft and oily yet never unctuous. What looks like corn oil absorbs the oak with ease and has more than enough ulmo honey to spare; **f23** long, still soft and subtle and not a single bitter note of despair from the oak; **b24** Garnheath at this relatively young age is tragically rare. And I'll be surprised if you'll see much more of this I the forthcoming years. High quality whisky at he peak of its range, rare or not... *55%. nc ncf sc. The Vintage Malt Whisky Co.*

⟐ **The Cooper's Choice Garnheath 37 Year Old** dist 1978, bott 2015 **(91) n22** sharp and green, a citrus note massages the dominating vanilla; **t23.5** beautiful delivery with myriad sugar tones striking early, some of which are very sweet indeed: for a moment the sweetest Scotch tasted this year. The oils are big, but subside enough to let in the tannins; **f22.5** after such a sugar exhibition, any bitterness from the oak appears to be accentuated; **b23** really shows none of its age. Surprisingly sweet and pliant for a grain so old. *46%. nc ncf sc. The Vintage Malt Whisky Co.*

⟐ **The Cooper's Choice Garnheath 48 Year Old** dist 1967, bott 2016 **(96) n24** big, deep manuka honey and molasses. The spices revolve around the big tannins; **t24** astonishingly rich. delivery: sticky thick corn oil sucks into its midst a liquorice and heather honey intensity, but keeps the lid of the threatening spice; **f24** so much vanilla...the honey lasts the pace without breaking sweat. The spices now come out to play...; **b24** it is an honour to experience a whisky both so rare and gorgeous. Perhaps not the most complex, but what it does do is carried out close to perfection. A must find grain. *41.5%. nc ncf sc. The Vintage Malt Whisky Co.*

⟐ **That Boutique-y Whisky Company Garnheath 42 Year Old** batch 1 **(90) n22.5** butterscotch tart...of the Canadian school; **t22.5** sweet corn oil is pleasant but somewhat one dimensional; a little ulmo honey helps; **f22.5** a real old Canadian whisky style to this finish with light red liquorice thickening the vanilla-rich corn oil further; **b22.5** attractive, but labours slightly under the weight of oils and oak. *44.3%. 120 bottles.*

Xtra Old Particular Garnheath 41 Years Old refill barrel, dist Feb 74, bott Dec 15 **(94) n24 t24 f22.5 b23.5** The rarest of the rare grains and - as though aware of its unique place in the lexicon of vanishing scotch - doesn't disappoint for a moment. *48.9%. nc ncf sc. 141 bottles.*

Xtra Old Particular Garnheath 42 Years Old refill barrel, dist Feb 74, bott Feb 16 **(93) n23 t23 f23.5 b23.5** Sticks firmly to a caramel and vanilla script. *48.2%. nc ncf sc. 162 bottles.*

⟐ **Xtra Old Particular Garnheath 42 Years Old** refill butt, cask no. 11209, dist Feb 74, bott Jun 16 **(89.5) n22.5** lots of butterscotch but the tannins hold a Demerara crispness; **t23** silky delivery with ulmo honey son in the loop. The corn oil shimmers for a short time before vanishing; **f21.5** lots of similarities to the Boutique-y bottling...then a slight bitterness creeps in; **b22.5** a kind of brighter version of the Boutique-y bottling, other thn the finish... *44.5%. nc ncf sc. 130 bottles.*

GIRVAN

The Girvan Patent Still Over 25 Years Old db **(84.5) n21.5 t21.5 f20.5 b21.** A pretty accurate representation of the character these stills were sometimes quietly known for at this time, complete with some trademark sulphury notes – presumably from the still, not cask, as I do pick up some balancing American white oak character. *42%. nc.*

The Girvan Patent Still No. 4 Apps db **(87) n21.5 t22 f21.5 b22.** A first look at probably the lightest of all Scotland grain whiskies. A little cream soda sweetens a soft, rather sweet, but spineless affair. The vanillas get a good, unmolested outing too. *42% WB15/369*

Old Particular Girvan 21 Years Old refill barrel, dist May 94, bott Nov 15 **(85) n21 t22.5 f20 b21.5.** Fat, monosyllabic and, after the initial juicy delivery, makes little attempt to move into complex lands. The finish has a number of oaky constraints. *51.5%. nc ncf sc. 215 bottles.*

Old Particular Girvan 25 Years Old refill barrel, cask no. 10805, dist Dec 89, bott Jun 15 **(91)** n22 t23.5 f22.5 b23 Clean and deeply satisfying. With so many warming spices at work, this would add possibly more to a blend than a blender might be happy with. *51.5%. nc ncf sc. 232 bottles.*

Old Particular Girvan 25 Years Old refill barrel, cask no. 10939, dist Mar 90, bott Sept 15 **(87.5)** n21.5 t22.5 f21.5 b22. Not quite such an accommodating barrel as cask 10805. But the juiciness and spices are there, though the tannins are a bit more argumentative. *51.3%. nc ncf sc. 162 bottles.*

Old Particular Girvan 27 Years Old refill barrel, dist Jun 88, bott Nov 15 **(94.5)** n23 t23.5 f24 b24 An any time of the day restorative... Truly beautiful. *62.6%. nc ncf sc. 192 bottles.*

◈ **The Sovereign Girvan 25 Years Old** bourbon barrel, cask no. 13285, dist Oct 91, bott Mar 17 **(91)** n22.5 lovely early spice links beautifully with liquorice; t23 sharp, semi-aggressive start – the grain is not to be trifled with. Nor the sugars which tumble onto the palate like a carbon-structured avalanche. Mainly of a Demerara style but fortified with butterscotch; f22.5 some citrus arrives from somewhere to up the juiciness levels again; b23 with this degree of spice at work, presumably distilled from wheat. *58.9%. nc ncf sc. 342 bottles.*

The Sovereign Girvan 36 Years Old refill hogshead, cask no. 12276, dist May 79, bott Feb 16 **(91.5)** n23 t23 f22.5 b23 Robust and rich. *51%. nc ncf sc. 322 bottles.*

That Boutique-y Whisky Company Girvan 52 Year Old batch 1 **(92.5)** n24 t23.5 f22.5 b22.5 Over 50 years old and still this strength! What's all that about??? There again, if a Scotch is going to be for all intents a bourbon, what do you expect...? *51.1%. 114 bottles.*

◈ **That Boutique-y Whisky Company Girvan 52 Year Old** batch 2 **(95.5)** n24 yikes...the spices!! It may be 52 years old, but the aroma has the energy of whisky a third that age, with the spices raging about the place with the sugars cowering (was this a very early wheat grain, I wonder...); t24 if you are looking for respite on deliver...tough! The spices attack from the first instant and at will...this is warming stuff. The sugars can now get a word in – just – and they tend to be of a muscovado style, salivating and satisfying and eking out what little juicy oil can be found; f23.5 calms, to a degree. More molasses now, but still with pulsing spice and a little chocolate fudge b24 Girvan is, of course, an anagram of raving... which is what this is from the moment you pour it into the glass. This has some very serious oomph.... even after half a century! For its staggering age, one of the most amazing whisky forces of all time. *51.1%. 102 bottles.*

INVERGORDON

◈ **The Cooper's Choice Invergordon 30 Year Old** dist 1984, bott 2015 **(93)** n23 ulmo honey and spice for once not wrapped up in the distillery's big oils...; t24 magnificent delivery – absolutely spot on! This is a controlled explosion of flavours, a bewildering intensity which, once it dies down, allows a clearer view of the complexity; big spice – perhaps wheat induced - and cocoa meld with the fudgy, Manuka honey. Thick vanilla pours in soon after, to give something like a spiced milkshake effect; f22.5 calms and quietens so the vanilla and intertwangles with the still crisp sugars; just the vaguest hint of very late bitterness; b23.5 Invergordon benefitting from some exceptional oak these last three decades... *57%. nc ncf sc. The Vintage Malt Whisky Co.*

◈ **ePower Invergordon 43 Year Old** bourbon hogshead, dist 1972, bott 2016 **(87)** n21.5 t23 f21.5 b21.5 Absolutely no escaping the attitude to this. A slightly off-key cask has endowed a perceptible and unflattering tang which slightly undoes some of the good work carried out by the rampaging honey... *49%.*

Maltbarn Invergordon ex-bourbon cask, bott 2015 **(87.5)** n21.5 t22.5 f21.5 b22. Pure blending fodder: a fat floozy which would go with anything. The slight tang to the cask does little damage, but lacks complexity. Knows how to give a brief but fun time. *51.3%. sc. 132 bottles.*

◈ **Old Particular Invergordon 18 Years Old** refill barrel, cask no. 11197, dist May 97, bott May 16 **(86.5)** n22 t22.5 f20.5 b21.5 Sweet, a tad sappy, fat and a little one-dimensional. Bitterness at the death, though spices compensate slightly. *48.4%. nc ncf sc. 236 bottles.*

Old Particular Invergordon 21 Years Old refill barrel, dist Oct 94, bott Nov 15 **(73)** n18 t19 f18 b18. A bad day or two at the fermenters still hasn't been corrected after over 20 years... *50.7%. nc ncf sc. 206 bottles.*

◈ **Old Particular Invergordon 21 Years Old** refill barrel, cask no. 11091, dist Oct 94, bott Feb 16 **(94)** n23.5 slightly overcooked toast with lightly salted butter and lime jelly spread all over it...; t24 the caress of the mildly honeyed oils could hardly be softer: orange blossom honey and butterscotch dictate the agenda, but could hardly do so in a more apologetic way; f23 just a vague bitterness but more than matched by a buzzing, understated (of course!) spice); b23.5 a near faultless cask allows this Invergordon to confirm that few grain whiskies on the planet are anything like as yielding. *52.8%. nc ncf sc. 204 bottles.*

Old Particular Invergordon 28 Years Old refill butt, dist Aug 87, bott Nov 15 **(87.5) n20.5 t23.5 f22 b22.** A sugary procession. Though oily, the tannins do get through alongside some considerable spices. Juicy and delightfully nippy at times, though deprived of greatness by a dullard nose and a slightly nagging tanginess. *56.5%. nc ncf sc. 490 bottles.*

⬩ **Saar Whisky Invergordon 1972** dist Dec 72, bott Sept 16 **(94.5) n23.5** Canadian style in so many ways. Light spices make a measured impact on the caramel...; **t24** magnificent delivery. Salivating from the first moment with a green freshness mixing comfortably with the light oils and elegant spice. The caramel from the nose can be picked up quickly here, but orange blossom honey thins and sweetens; **f23** clearly back to a Canadian style on the fade which is long and accentuates the natural toffees; **b24** a beautiful grain showing a style of whisky that will be lost to Scotland within the next decade. *49.1%. nc ncf sc.*

⬩ **Sansibar Whisky Invergordon 1973** bott 2016 **(95) n24** marzipan off a fruitcake, as a molassed spiciness appears to be attached; **t24** not just molasses on delivery, but Manuka honey, peppers and a dose of high propane vanilla concentrate; the sub plot, as though undisturbed by the light volcanic actions elsewhere, is a steady stream of toffee; **f23** after running rich on the sugars for so long, the finish rapidly declines in intensity and thins out to leave the lightest of toffee, vanilla and spice fades; **b24** one for those with a sweet tooth. And probably no less a delight for those who haven't... *51.8%.*

The Single Cask Invergordon Aged 27 Years cask no. 8118, dist 1 Feb 88, bott 1 Feb 16 **(94) n23 t24.5 f22.5 b24** With the smoke in situ, it is as if a smoky blend is at play here. Highly unusual for a single grain. But one I think most people will ask for a second glass of. Superb! *45.8%. nc ncf sc.*

The Sovereign Invergordon 27 Years Old refill hogshead, cask no. 11853, dist Feb 88, bott Sept 15 **(83) n21 t22 f20 b20.** A few vegetable notes are briefly outshone by the sugars. But never quite finds a happy balance. *51.1%. nc ncf sc. 299 bottles.*

⬩ **The Sovereign Invergordon 40 Years Old** refill hogshead, cask no. 13278, dist Jan 77, bott Feb 17 **(92.5) n23.5** forthright on the oaky front with all the spices and general busyness sponsored by the tannins. A plethora of mixed spice notes have the ability to either burn or tickle, as the intensity dictates. The sugars have a sombre molassed edge, also apparently moulded by the cask; **t23** typical Invergordon oiliness, though not quite sweet enough to be on the syrupy side. Cream toffee caramel fills the palate, interrupted only by light spice; **f23** more of the same; **b23** elegant, technically faultless and a grain which sticks to its theme. *47.8%. nc ncf sc. 390 bottles.*

⬩ **The Sovereign Invergordon 50 Years Old** refill hogshead, cask no. 12235, dist Mar 66, bott Apr 16 **(87) n21.5 t23 f21 b21.5** When a grain cask has been through the good times and is now beginning to add only a tightening note, it is time to blend. Here we see an old grain shovelling out caramel and butterscotch as though it is going out of fashion and bravely trying to see off the tinkering intrusions off the tannin. Still an enjoyable whisky in its own right, if you are prepared to forgive the scars of passing time. *50%. nc ncf sc. 261 bottles.*

Spirits Shop Selection & Sansibar Whisky Invergordon 1973 bourbon cask, bott 2015 **(94.5) n23.5 t23.5 f23.5 b24** A cracking grain with more buzz than a bee on performance-enhancing drugs... *52.2%. 2016. 240 bottles.*

Svenska Eldvatten Invergordon 1972 ex-bourbon barrel, dist Dec 72, bott Mar 16 **(91.5) n23.5 t23 f23 b22** An oily cove absolutely bursting at the seams with sugars. *48.9%. sc.*

That Boutique-y Whisky Company Invergordon 43 Year Old batch 5 **(88.5) n23 t22 f21 b22.5** The oils are perhaps a little too consuming here. *47.7%. 528 bottles.*

⬩ **That Boutique-y Whisky Company Invergordon 43 Year Old** batch 11 **(86.5) n21.5 t23 f21 b21** Mixed feelings: part of me loves the fact the public gets a chance to see a single cask at this age. Putting my blender's hat on, what I could have done with this in a blend: accentuating its positives and disappearing its negatives. A poor barrel means there are a few too many negatives, but at least the delivery and first five or six waves of the follow through allow you to enjoy a brief glimpse of a corn oil and muscovado heaven. *48.2%. 186 bottles.*

⬩ **The Whisky Agency Invergordon 44 Years Old** dist 1972 **(94.5) n23.5** the spice, though little more than an afterthought, both balances out and adds the vaguest welcome zip to the unrelenting toffee caramel...; **t24** so succulent and sugary: as salivating as grain gets thanks to a light orange blossom honey on the Toffo; **f23** a late busy caramel flavour profile which was once common in maturing casks just off the Great Lakes; **b24** Invergordan at its most unremittingly old Canadian... *49%. Bottled for La Maison du Whisky.*

Whiskybroker Invergordon 43 Year Old bourbon barrel, cask no. 1300000003, dist 13 Dec 72, bott 14 Dec 15 **(91.5) n23 t23.5 f22 b23** Canadian whisky lovers will fight over a grain like this one.. *49.9%. sc.*

Whiskyjace Invergordon 24 Years Old 1991 bourbon hogshead, bott 2015 (96) n24 t24 f23.5 b24.5 A truly exceptional example of this distillery at this age at its absolute richest. Great Scotch, grain or not. A lot of money has been spent securing this distillery over the last two decades: too much, really. Taste a whisky like this, and maybe you can find a reason.. 55.8%

⁂ **Wilson & Morgan Barrel Selection Invergordon 42 Year Old 2016** cask no. 13000000042, dist 1973 (87) n22 t23.5 f20 b21.5 Compared to some other Invergordons of a similar vintage released in the last year this one is handicapped by a far less happy and intricate cask, thus allowing the nose and finish to wander off piste towards a tangy bitterness. Has its great moments, though, especially when the spice engages and the ulmo honey and toffee first strike the palate in concentrated form. 52%. sc.

⁂ **World of Orchids Invergordon 43 Year Old** bourbon cask, dist 1973 (89) n22 corn rich, honeyed but rather ponderous; t23 typically fat but a highly attractive honeycomb personality begins to spread with some willing and warming spices not far behind; f21.5 bitters out in a way one might suspect from the nose; b22.5 no great pretensions to greatness: an out and out blending grain which would have added to the desired honey-enriching effect. 46.7%.

LOCH LOMOND

Loch Lomond Single Grain db (93) n23 crisp sugars are willing to absorb the vanilla; t23.5 indeed, the sugars on the nose are indicative of a sweet grain, for the delivery centres around the maple syrup lead. The oak is something like most anchors at work: barely visible to invisible; f23 the oaks do have a say, though you have to wait a while on the long finale. A little spice arrives, too; b23.5 elegant grain; keeps the sweetness controlled. 46%

⁂ **Old Particular Loch Lomond 19 Years Old** refill hogshead, cask no. 11184, dist Dec 96, bott May 16 (88) n22 fat, with an unchallenging vanilla theme; t22 cream toffee; f22 cream toffee and vanilla; b22 one of the most simplistic, untaxing, spiceless, yet strangely faultless grains on the market. 51.5%. nc ncf sc. 341 bottles.

That Boutique-y Whisky Company Loch Lomond batch 2 (89) n22 t23 f22 b22 One of the softest grains ever produced in Scotland and here it shows all its accommodating sugars to the full... 47.8%. 91 bottles.

⁂ **That Boutique-y Whisky Company Loch Lomond 19 Year Old** batch 3 (88.5) n22 simple spiced vanillins, but hints of bitterness which may really come to life later... t23 very attractive delivery with a medium intensity fatness, then a massive surge of juicy sugars f21.5 ah, bitters out from the not such great oak as expected; b22 a simplistic, lightly spiced, slightly flawed grain which ticks just enough boxes to make you want to explore at length. 49.7%. 267 bottles.

LOCHSIDE

⁂ **The Cooper's Choice Lochside 44 Year Old** dist 1964, bott 2015 (92.5) n23.5 not unlike a bourbon-Canadian blend (yes, I have encountered such a thing) where a muscular coconut-honey candy theme dominates the subservient vanilla; t24 salivating and soft, corn oils drift among the obliging sugars without a care in the world; you can hear the tannins knocking, but only the spices gain entry; f22 back to a coconut toffee thread; bitters late on; b23 it's hangs on in there, giving in to its age only in the final moments... 41.2%. nc ncf sc. The Vintage Malt Whisky Co.

NORTH BRITISH

Friends Over A Couple of Casks Port Sgioba 4 25 Years Old bourbon barrel, cask no. 3227, dist 22 Jan 91, bott 26 Jan 16 (92) n23 t23.5 f22.5 b23 As a 15-year-old, would tick every box for a blender. Sweet, lush, impeccably constructed and offering just the right amount of honey. 54.8%. nc ncf sc. 229 bottles.

Old Particular North British 21 Years Old refill hogshead, cask no. 10797 (91) n22 t23 f23 b23 Superbly made and makes the most of an untroubled cask to show just how rich the corn can be. A very shapely frame for a blend. 50.9%. nc ncf sc. 294 bottles.

⁂ **Old Particular North British 21 Years Old** refill barrel, cask no. 10996,, dist Oct 94, bott Nov 15 (91) n22 slightly untidy at times with its banana and butterscotch nose; t23.5 brilliant delivery! Almost bipolar in that it is at once soft and soothing and on a different plane takes off with the most salivating volley of light sugars you'll find in any grain; f23 backs up the delivery with a rabid spiciness b23 you expect plenty of oomph on delivery...and my word, you get it!! 48.1%. nc ncf sc. 212 bottles.

Old Particular North British 24 Years Old refill hogshead, dist Oct 91, bott Nov 15 (94) n23 t24 f23.5 b23.5 A smoky grain! Wonder which distillery on Islay this cask is from! A hundred barrels of this in a blend would give the unsuspecting poor old blender a heart attack! Understatedly delicious. 49.4%. nc ncf sc. 256 bottles.

Old Particular North British 27 Years Old refill barrel, cask no. 10938, dist Jul 88, bott Sept 15 (93.5) n23.5 t24 f22.5 b23.5 If anyone tells you grain is neutral, then shove a glass of this in their hand! 50.2%. nc ncf sc. 168 bottles.

⟫ **The Sovereign North British 55 Years Old** refill butt, cask no. 13328, dist Dec 61, bott Feb 17 (85) n21 t23 f19 b21 Not sure if this has been "freshened up" as they call it these days in a newer sherry butt, as there is a more contemporary style of grape at play here... and a finish to match... When at its peak, is as succulent and sexy as they come... 55.1%. nc ncf sc. 144 bottles.

That Boutique-y Whisky Company North British batch 2 (87) n22 t22.5 f21 b21.5. Hard to imagine a grain being more sweet and lush than this one on delivery, helped on the complexity front by a squeeze of citrus. As is so often the case with sweet whiskies, severe bitterness follows later. An enormous degree of Canadian character to this, especially on the nose, 49.3%.

NORTH OF SCOTLAND
The Pearls of Scotland North of Scotland 1971 dist Dec 71, bott Apr 15 (95.5) n25 t23.5 f23 b24 What a beautifully elegant old lady...and one with virtually no wrinkles... 43.6%

PORT DUNDAS
Port Dundas 20 Years Old Special Release 2011 db (90) n21.5 t22 f23.5 b23. Can a whisky be a little too silky. This one tries, especially on the non-committal nose and over friendly delivery. But once the spices rise, things get very interesting... 57.4%. nc ncf sc.

⟫ **Old Particular Port Dundas 12 Years Old** refill barrel, cask no. 11340, dist Jun 04, bott Sept 16 (84.5) n22 t22 f20 b20.5 Grain ordinaire. Plenty of sugary if one dimensional flavour on delivery but the finish is a bit clumsy and bitter. 48.4%. nc ncf sc. 247 bottles.

Old Particular Port Dundas 25 Years Old refill hogshead, cask no. 10941, dist Feb 90, bott Sept 15 (87) n22 t22 f21.5 b21.5. Displays that attractive creamy fruitiness that makes for the filling of a Jammy Dodger. Pity, then, the tangy barrel is just a tad dodgy... 51.5%. nc ncf sc. 258 bottles.

Old Particular Port Dundas 27 Years Old refill hogshead, cask no. 10941, dist Oct 88, bott Nov 15 (92.5) n23.5 t23 f23 b23 Makes as little fuss as possible, but still gives the palate a busy workout. Elegant stuff. 54.8%. nc ncf sc. 218 bottles.

⟫ **Old Particular Port Dundas 27 Years Old** refill hogshead, cask no. 11333, dist Feb 91, bott Sept 16 (92) n23.5 some attractive fruitiness to this, nectarines almost. Gorgeous weight with the vanilla melting into the simmering pie...; t23.5 spot on mouth feel: lush, lightly oiled – presumably from corn oil – with the sugars again morphing into something vaguely fruity; f22 bitters out slightly as light oaky spices arrive; b23 at its best, as soft, sweet and slightly furry as a ripening peach. 51.5%. nc ncf sc. 206 bottles.

The Sovereign Port Dundas 27 Years Old refill hogshead, cask no. 12135, dist Oct 88, bott Oct 15 (95.5) n23.5 t23.5 f24 b24.5 Compact and deliciously intense. Just so right in so many aspects. 56.7%. nc ncf sc. 221 bottles.

⟫ **The Sovereign Port Dundas 27 Years Old** refill hogshead, cask no. 12635, dist Oct 88, bott Jun 16 (93) n23 for a cask strength grain, noses rarely come this soft and delicate: the sugars and vanilla are in an oily thrall. The result is a gentle and sweet caress; t24 the kind of delivery you dream of from a grain whisky: so intense at times that the flavour profile is almost opaque before finally you make sense of the corn oil and maple syrup which drift apart with the pace of tectonic plates; the spices fizz with effect; f22.5 the oak tires just enough to offer a glimpse of bitterness amid the prevailing sugars; b23.5 curious one this: all the lush sweetness of corn oil but the bold spices of wheat. After 27 years, hard to detect exactly which is which, though I'll plump for corn. Whichever, superb! 56.1%. nc ncf sc. 191 bottles.

⟫ **The Sovereign Port Dundas 28 Years Old** refill hogshead, cask no. 13046, dist Oct 88, bott Nov 16 (94.5) n24.5 there is a pomp and splendour about this nose which borders on the arrogant. The blend of Manuka and ulmo honey is refined, the allowing of just-so vanillins to underline the age apparently carried out with a debonair wave. Sublime...; t24 of course the sugars have to arrive in double-quick time, chiming in superbly with the spices. The oil is mid-viscosity at first, then thins; the spices regroup for a major burst; f22.5 just bitters out slightly as the vanillas build; b23.5 another lost distillery showing magnificently and why blended whisky is not going to improve anytime soon... 55.1%. nc ncf sc. 253 bottles.

⟨⟩ **That Boutique-y Whisky Company Port Dundas 25 Year Old** batch 1 **(95)** n24 it's not just the golden syrup and spice; it's not just the soft oils that hang in the air and keep everything together; it's not just the near perfect weight...it's just...everything! t24 that golden syrup and spice in liquid form: even the vanilla has a honeyed shell...; f23 long, thanks to those oils. And a glorious fade down with not a single off note from the old cask; b24.5 a little bit special... *48.2%. 115 bottles.*

⟨⟩ **World of Orchids Port Dundas 24 Year Old** bourbon cask, dist 1989 **(92)** n22 quite ordinary: light with just some quietly grazing vanillas; t24 ah...extraordinary! Rich with a stupendously well-choreographed sugar-spice arrival, completely in tandem and with nether outflanking the other. The sweetness is of the icing sugar, melt-in-the-mouth variety one normally associated with grist; f23 retreats to a quieter, more vanilla-led life...; b23 don't expect great complexity...just a whole lot of technically faultless deliciousness. *56.1%.*

STRATHCLYDE

⟨⟩ **Old Particular Strathclyde 11 Years Old** sherry butt, cask no. 11484, dist Nov 05, bott Jan 17 **(92.5)** n23.5 not only clean grape but even a hint of age on the sherry not unlike a superior late bottle vintage; t23.5 teeming spices from the off...the ulmo honey and treacle is relentless; f22.5 a little bit of oak bitterness gatecrashes at the end; b23 well who'd've thought it: a near flawless sherry butt! Trouble is, it slightly subdues the original spirit, though still a superb experience. *55.5%. nc ncf sc. 306 bottles.*

⟨⟩ **Old Particular Strathclyde 20 Years Old** refill barrel, cask no. 11128, dist Apr 96, bott May 16 **(86)** n21 t22.5 f20.5 b22 Sweet, chewy but has something of the Gorbals' roughhouse about it. *50.6%. nc ncf sc. 187 bottles.*

⟨⟩ **Old Particular Strathclyde 25 Years Old** refill barrel, cask no. 11335, dist Aug 90, bott Sept 16 **(87)** n21.5 t22 f21.5 b22 A tangy beast with a metallic feel that subdues the sweetness which had gathered after delivery. Plenty of nip and bite, which is fun, but refuses to settle. *51.5%. nc ncf sc. 116 bottles.*

The Sovereign Strathclyde 25 Years Old refill barrel, cask no. 12281, dist Aug 90, bott Feb 16 **(88)** n21.5 t23 f21.5 b22 Many of the characteristics found in the OP of the same vintage (see above) but a far less accommodating cask. *51.7%. nc ncf sc. 176 bottles.*

⟨⟩ **The Sovereign Strathclyde 26 Years Old** refill barrel, cask no. 13045, dist Aug 90, bott Nov 16 **(77)** n19 t21 f18 b19 The pugnacious, lightly off-key nose offers fair warning of the Brillo pad delivery which scratches some unforgiving sugars onto the palate. The finish, though, suffers from a mixture of poor original distillate and a cask without the means to compensate. *54.5%. nc ncf sc. 241 bottles.*

⟨⟩ **That Boutique-y Whisky Company Strathclyde 30 Year Old** batch 1 **(87.5)** n22 t22.5 f21 b22 A grain that gives you a right punch in the throat on delivery. The sugars are profound but without structure and of very limited complexity. *53.1%. 228 bottles.*

UNSPECIFIED SINGLE GRAIN

Borders finished in Oloroso sherry casks **(66)** n15 t18 f15 b18. Finished being the operative word. Has no-one else been listening regarding the total mess sherry butts are in. I wonder why I bother sometimes. Jeez... *51.7%. nc ncf. R&B Distillers.*

Haig Club toasted oak casks **(89)** n21.5 t23 f22.5 b22 When I first saw this, I wasn't quite sure whether to laugh or cry. Because 25 years ago bottles of single grain whisky were the unique domain of the flat cap brigade, the miners and other working class in the Kirkcaldy area of Scotland. Their grain, Cameron Brig, would be drunk with a splash, mixed with Coke or ginger, even occasionally with Irn Bru, or straight and unmolested as a chaser to the ubiquitous kegged heavy, McEwan's lager or a bottle of Sweetheart stout. When I suggested to the hierarchy at United Distillers, the forerunners of Diageo, that in their finer grains they had a product which could conquer the world, the looks I got ranged from sympathy for my lack of understanding in matters whisky to downright concern about my mental wellbeing. I had suggested the exquisite Cambus, now lost to us like so many other grain distilleries in those passing years, should be brought out as a high class singleton. It was pointed out to me that single grain was, always had been and always will be, the preferred choice of the less sophisticated; those not wishing to pay too much for their dram. Fast forward a quarter of a century and here sits a gorgeously expensive bottle in a deep cobalt blue normally associated with Ballantine's and a very classy, heavyweight stopper. In it is a grain which, if the advertising is to be believed, is the preferred choice not of the back street bar room idlers carefully counting their pennies but of its major ambassador David Beckham: it is the drop to be savoured by the moneyed, jet-set sophisticates. My, oh my. Let's not call this hype. Let's just say it has taken some genius exec in a suit half a lifetime – and probably most of his or hers - to come around to my way of thinking and convince those in the offices on the floor above to go for it. Wonder if I qualify for 10 percent of their profit for suggesting it all those years back...or, preferably, five percent of their advertising budget. Meanwhile, I look forward to watching David pouring this into some of his Clynelish and Talisker. After all, no-one can Blend it like Beckham... 40%. WB15/408

Svenska Eldvatten Grain 1964 ex-bourbon barrel, dist Dec 72, bott Mar 16 (95) n23.5 t24 f23.5 b24 I remember a couple of years back someone publicly poured scorn on me for saying blends now are vastly different to yesteryear because of the grain. Well, look at the way corn has shaped this baby: far closer to Canadian or even bourbon (or US Corn Whiskey to be more precise) than today's Scotch because of the extraordinary effect of the maize... 52.1%. sc.

◈ **Whisky-Fässle Lowland Single Grain 52 Year Old** barrel, dist 1964, bott 2016 (90.5) n23 huge caramel...with a little squashed sultana for company; t23 soft and sensuous as a great grain should be. Salivating, too, after the initial caramel and vanilla surge has quietened. Some very serious chocolate through the middle section; f21.5 the caramel continues, then takes a slightly fruitier pose – before constricting slightly; b23 although from a barrel, the mystery fruitiness is there in all its strengths and weaknesses... 47.7%.

◈ **WoodWinters The Five Distinguished and Rare Aged 39 Years** (93) n22.5 heavy duty oily corn whisky sexed up with a honeycomb, lime and spice complexity; t24 now it enters a different league: the amalgamation of molasses and spice hits the palate with as much elegance as it does power – which is considerable. The corn fills the palate in the same way smoke envelopes a peated malt. But this is light enough for the acacia honey to embrace the meringue pie and red liquorice; f23 dry vanilla but good, pulsing spice; outstanding oak leaves not a trace of tiredness; b23.5 a grain of marvellous pedigree and integrity, at least equal to the vast majority of single malts whiskies you will find... 51%. sc. 330 bottles.

Vatted Grain

◈ **Angus Dundee Distillers Blended Grain 50 Year Old** (91.5) n23 as old and creaking as a soon to retire Chelsea centre-half. Has given great service, but definitely a few cracks where there had been none a few years before. That said, the very light eucalyptus and heather honey work together charmingly; t23.5 as silky as an Antonio Conte title winning side. Soaks up layers of tannins and counter attacks quickly with thrusting vanilla and ulmo honey; f22 good spice helps deflect from the tiring oak; b23 just champion...! 40.1%.

Compass Box Hedonism first fill American oak cask, bott 20 Feb 13 (84) n22 t22 f19 b20. Just too fat, too sweet and too bitter at the finale to work to great effect. Some decent oak on both nose and delivery, though. 43%. nc ncf. Compass Box Whisky Company.

Compass Box Hedonism Maximus (93.5) n25 t22.5 f23 b23. Bourbon Maximus... 46%

Compass Box Hedonism Quindecimus (88.5) n22.5 a drizzle of lemon on custard; t22 simple sugars and a little oil; f22 even late on, a hint of juiciness; b22 sweet and refreshingly ordinary grain. Well made and unspectacularly delicious. 46%

◈ **The Cooper's Choice Golden Grain 51 Year Old** dist 1964, bott 2016 (87.5) n22 t23.5 f20 b22 A lovely vatted grain with as many spoonfulls of honey as you like. Sadly, some tired oak radiates some significant bitterness at the death. 51%. nc ncf sc. The Vintage Malt Whisky Co.

◈ **The Sovereign Blended Grain 28 Years Old** bourbon barrel, cask no. 13327, dist Dec 64, bott Mar 17 (96) n24.5 huge age on the nose; kumquats drying out in the bowl, liquorice both red and black with a little ground black pepper. More profound bourbon notes as each minute passes and as the air gets in. Praline and butterscotch, too...; t24 soft, soft, soft... every element, be it the lightest sugar, the most fragile vanilla, thin walnut oil simply melts on the palate after landing with all the impact of a snowflake: no whisky on the planet can be more delicate; f23.5 drier now as the light Demerara sugar gives way to the half-hearted vanilla; b24 may be completely wrong, but a theory. There is a dryness here which suggests big age, maybe so big that the strength of a barrel fell below 40%abv... so had to be added to another to restore it back to whisky again. As I say: just a theory. But it'd fit the structure of this beautifully fragile old grain perfectly. 47.9%. nc ncf sc. 221 bottles.

William Grant & Sons Rare Cask Reserves 25 Years Old Blended Grain Scotch Whisky (92.5) n23 t23.5 f23 b23. A really interesting one, this. In the old days, blenders always spent as much time vatting the grains together as they did the malts, for if they did not work well as a unit it was unlikely harmony would be found in their blend. A long time ago I was taught to, whenever possible, use a soft grain to counter a firmer one, and vice versa. Today, there are far fewer blends to choose from, though 25 years ago the choice was wider. So interesting to see that this grain is soft-dominated with very little backbone at all. Delicious. But screams for some backbone. 47%. Exclusive to The Whisky Shop.

Scottish Blends

If any whisky is suffering an identity crisis just now, it must be the good old Scottish blend.

Once the staple, the absolute mainstay, of the Scotch whisky industry it has seen its market share increasingly buried under the inexorable, incoming tide that is single malt. But worse, the present-day blender has his hands tied in a way no previous generation of blenders have had before.

Now stocks must be monitored with a third eye, one that can judge the demand on their single malt casks and at increasingly varied ages. Worse, the blender cannot now, as was once the case, create blends with subtly shifting textures - the result of carefully using different types of grain. So many grain distilleries have closed in the last quarter of a century that now most blends seem remarkably similar to others. And there is, of course, the problem of sherry butts which has been fully documented over the years in the Whisky Bible.

For Jim Murray's Whisky Bible 2018 I tasted or re-tasted 128 blends in total, a quite significant number. And there is no doubt that the lack of choice of grain for blenders is beginning to pose a problem for the industry. What was particularly noticeable was the number of blends which now lack a crisp backbone and have softened their stance, making them chewy and pliable on the palate but often lacking the crispness which can maximise the complexity of the malts on display. By the time you add in the caramel, the results can sometimes be just a little too cloying.

Naturally, it was the bigger blenders - those possessing by far the largest stocks - who best escaped this narrowing down of style among the younger blends in particular, as the always impressive Ballantine's Finest displayed with its usual structured enormity displayed with aplomb to once more pick up an award.

Yet after three successive years of very old blends being named Blend of the Year thanks to The Last Drop, this year the title went to something very different. It was the irrepressable Compass Box taking the top accolade with their remarkable Double Single: one malt and one grain.

It was further, delicious, proof that blending is about feel and balance, the understanding of how to maximise the flavours and not complicate things too much which so often leads to the sparkle being dulled. It was, quite literally, the clear winner....

Jim Murray's Whisky Bible Scottish Blend of the Year Winners	
2004	William Grant's 21 Year Old
2005	William Grant's 21 Year Old
2006	William Lawson Aged 18 Years
2007	Old Parr Superior 18 Years Old
2008	Old Parr Superior 18 Years Old
2009	The Last Drop
2010	Ballantine's 17 Years Old
2011	Ballantine's 17 Years Old
2012	Ballantine's 17 Years Old
2013	Ballantine's 17 Years Old
2014	Ballantine's 17 Years Old
2015	The Last Drop 1965
2016	The Last Drop 50 Years Old
2017	The Last Drop 1971
2018	Compass Box The Double Single

Scottish Blends

100 Pipers **(74)** n18.5 t18 f19 b18.5. An improved blend, even with a touch of spice to the finish. I get the feeling the grains are a bit less aggressive than they for so long were. I'd let you know for sure, if only I could get through the caramel. 40%. Chivas.

⬩ **100 Pipers** bott code LKVK2677 2016/07/01 **(74)** n18 t19 f19 b18 These 100 Pipers deserve an award. How can they have played for so many years and still be so off key and out of tune? It is an art form, I swear. I feel like giving the blend a special gong for so many years of consistent awfulness. 40%. Chivas Brothers Ltd.

⬩ **The Antiquary** bott code L 02 08 16 **(86)** n20 t22 f22 b21 Appears to be going along the present day trend of spongy, super soft grain which doesn't always do the best of favours to the obviously high quality malt in here. Pleasantly sweet and chewy with an attractive base note. 40%. Tomatin Distillery.

Antiquary 12 Years Old **(92)** n23.5 t23.5 f22 b23 A staggering about turn for a blend which, for a very long time, has flown the Speyside flag. 40%. Tomatin Distillery.

⬩ **The Antiquary Aged 12 Years** bott code L 17 12 15 **(87.5)** n21.5 t22 f22 b22 The smoke I so well remember from previous bottlings appears to have dispersed. Instead we have an ultra-lush blend dependent on molasses and spice to punch through the major toffee. 40%. Tomatin Distillery.

Antiquary 21 Years Old **(93)** n23.5 t23.5 f23 b23 A huge blend, scoring a magnificent 93 points. But I have tasted better, and another sample, direct from the blending lab, came with even greater complexity and less apparent caramel. A top-notch blend of rare distinction. 43%

⬩ **The Antiquary Aged 21 Years** bott code 2016/02/29 LK30215 **(92.5)** n23 some very confident weight on the nose here: gentle, though slightly earthy, smoke mingles with the orange blossom honey; t23.5 excellent delivery: caramel and dates hold the fort until an oily smokiness turns up. Never less than succulent; f23 a beautiful lime note is the perfect match for the gently smoked mocha and spice; a very slight tang at the death; b23 if you are not sure what I mean by a beautifully paced whisky, try this and find out. 43%. Tomatin Distillery.

⬩ **The Antiquary Aged 35 Years** bott code L 24 08 15 **(96.5)** n24 absolutely classic Speyside-style exotic fruit on the top dressing malt, the sharpness amplified by the crisper, clean grain which shows no sign of tiring; t24 classic delivery: immediate spice but kept under control by the more sugary elements of the grain. The malt is pristine and sensationally three dimensional, really ramping up the light fruitiness and well as a distinctive sugar barley candy; f24 long and so relaxed you can only purr. The sugars remain of the boiled sweet/fruit candy type, though the malts and butterscotch intermingling at the end, and then dovetailing with the spices is a rare exhibition of how a great fade should really be...; b24.5 enjoy some of the grains involved in this beauty: their type and ability to add to the complexity is, tragically, a dying breed: the hardest whisky I have found so far to spit out...and I'm on dram number 530....! Antiquary's late, great blender, Jim Milne, would shed a tear of joy for this creation of unreconstructed beauty and brilliance, as this was just out of his school of elegance. 46%. Tomatin Distillery.

Ballaglass Blended Scotch Whisky **(85)** n21 t22 f21 b21. Perfectly enjoyable, chewy – but clean – blend full of toffee and fudge. Very good weight and impressive, oily body. 40%.

Ballantine's Aged 12 Years **(84.5)** n21.5 t22 f19 b21. Attractive but odd fellow, this, with a touch of juniper to the nose and furry bitter marmalade on the finish. But some excellent barley-cocoa moments, too. 43%. Chivas.

Ballantine's 12 Years Old **(87)** n21 t22 f21 b23. The kind of old-fashioned, mildly moody blend Colonel Farquharson-Smythe (retired) might have recognised when relaxing at the 19th hole back in the early '50s. Too good for a squirt of soda, mind. 40%. Chivas Bros.

Ballantine's 17 Years Old **(97.5)** n24.5 t24 f24 b25 Now only slightly less weighty than of old. After a change of style it has comfortably reverted back to its sophisticated, mildly erotic old self. One of the most beautiful, complex and stunningly structured whiskies ever created. Truly the epitome of great Scotch. 43%.

Ballantine's Aged 21 Years **(94)** n23.5 t24 f23.5 b24 Even though the strength has been reduced, presumably to eek out rare stocks, the beauty of this blend hasn't. 40%.

Ballantine's Aged 30 Years **(95.5)** n24.5 t24 f23 b24 A fascinating malt, slightly underpowered perhaps, which I have had to put to one side and keep coming back to see what it will say and do next... 40%.

⬩ **Ballantine's Aged 30 Years** bott code LKRK1934 2016/05/16 **(96)** n24.5 t24 f22.5 b24 Practically a replay of the bottle I tasted last year, right down to that very late, barely perceptible furriness. Simply one of the world's most sensual drams... 40%. Chivas Brothers Ltd.

Ballantine's Finest **(96)** n24 t24 f23.5 b24.5 As a standard blend this is coming through as a major work of art. Each time I taste this the weight has gone up a notch or two more and the sweetness has increased to balance out with the drier grain elements. Take a mouthful of this and experience the work of a blender very much at the top of his game. 40%. *Chivas Bros.*

◇ **Ballantine's Finest** bott code LKEK4068 2016/10/04 (96) n23.5 t24 f24 b24.5 The consistency and enormity of this blend fair staggers me. It is often my go to blend when travelling the world as I pretty much know what I'll get, within its normal parameters. This bottling has a little extra sweetness on the smoke but exceeds expectation on the finish with a slightly more clever use of the spices and Demerara sugars as they merge with the peat. Just such a big and satisfying experience. 40%. *Chivas Brothers Ltd*

Ballantine's Hard Fired (86.5) n22 t22 f21 b21.5. Despite the smoky and toasty elements to this, you're left waiting for it to take off....or even go somewhere. Perhaps just a little too soft, friendly and grain indulgent. Decent, enjoyable blend, of course, but a little out of the Ballantine's usual circle of high class friends. 40%

◇ **Ballantine's Limited release no. A27380** (96) n24 t24.5 f23.5 b24 Each Limited release has a slightly different stance and this one holds its posture with more debonair, lighter-on-foot poise. The vague furry note of recent bottlings is missing here or, rather, is of the least consequence. The fruit, also, is more of a sheen than a statement more room for the malt and vanilla to play and the spices to impart age. It may be soft on both nose and palate – especially the delivery – as the grains have obviously been vatted to create minimum traction, but it is a blend of quiet substance. Another Ballantine's brand this year hitting the 96 or more mark. Astonishing, absolutely astonishing...more a case of Ballantine's Unlimited... 40%. *Chivas Brothers Ltd.*

Ballantine's Limited Release no. L40055 (96.5) n24 t25 f23 b24.5 A vaguely weightier incarnation than the last bottling I came across, and here the oils have a much more emboldening role. Indeed, this is a more embracing and confiding version, increasing even more the slightly austere part of its character, and, in doing so, just slightly upping the degree of sophistication. Even though this is only by fractions, it is enough to make it not only a world class whisky, but one of the great whiskies of 2015. And without that late, lightly furry finish, that audible whisper of a taint, almost certainly World Whisky of the Year. 40%

Ballantine's Limited Release No. L88960 (94.5) n24 t24 f23 b23.5. This goes over much of the same ground as L40055, so in the interests of conserving space I'll keep this brief. Whenever you taste a Ballantine's Limited, you get the feeling of an old genius at work: that brilliant blend of bite and genteel sophistication. The main difference I feel here is a slight change in the grain structure, so when the vague weakness from the odd less-than-perfect sherry butt arrives, there isn't quite the sweet body to see it off. Still magnificent, though. And a cocoa shading is sublime. 40%

Ballantine's Master's (82) n21 t22 f19 b20. Excellent lively grain and chewy malt, but the always suspect, grain-drizzled finish has become even more nondescript in recent bottlings. 40%

◇ **Ballantine's Master's** bott code LKAK1001 2016/03/09 (85) n21 t22 f21 b21 The label promises a "fresh take" on this blend. And I admit, it is far more agreeable than before with a little coconut oil and apple help to give it a lift and the sugars herded into attractive use. But still far too dependent of caramel input, which may round the whisky but flattens it all rather too well. 40%. *Chivas Brothers Ltd.*

Ballantine's Rare Limited (89.5) n23.5 t22.5 f21.5 b22 A heavier, more mouth watering blend than the "Bluebottle" version. 43%. *ncf. Chivas.*

Bell's Original (91) n23 t22.5 f22.5 b23 Your whisky sleuth came across the new version for the first time in the bar of a London theatre back in December 2009 during the interval of "The 39 Steps". To say I was impressed and pleasantly surprised is putting it mildly. And with the whisky, too, which is a massive improvement on the relatively stagnant 8-year-old especially with the subtle extra smoky weight. If the blender asks me: "Did I get it right, Sir?" then the answer has to be a resounding "yes". 40%

Bells 8 Years Old (85) n21.5 t22.5 f20 b21. Some mixed messages here: on one hand it is telling me that it has been faithful to some of the old Bells distilleries – hence a slight dirty note, especially on the finish. On the other, there are some sublime specks of complexity and weight. Quite literally the rough and the smooth. 40%. *Diageo.*

Black & White (91) n22 t23 f22.5 b23.5 This one hasn't gone to the dogs: quite the opposite. I always go a bit misty-eyed when I taste something this traditional: the crisp grains work to maximum effect in reflecting the malts. A classic of its type. 40%. *Diageo.*

Black Bottle (74.5) n18 t20.5 f17 b18. Barely a shadow of its once masterful, great self. 40%.

◇ **Black Bottle** bott code 2038310 L3 16165 (94.5) n23.5 complex: yes, there is a little earthy cabbage note in there. But the mix of hickory, Fisherman's Friend cough sweet, light smoke, molasses and even leather make for something attractively different; t23.5 wow! How succulent is that! The grains maybe of the stereotypically fluffy variety we find today, but the way it is moulded into a far richer and beautifully balanced mouth-filler is stunning. Maple syrup and liquorice work hard for maximum effect while the spices have a little edge to them; **f23.5** long, lightly oiled and a slow evaporation of the sugars; no shortage of spiced butterscotch to complete the tale; **b24** not the byword for macho complexity it was 15 years ago but after a lull in its fortunes it is back to something that can rightfully boast excellence. Brilliant. *40%.*

Black Bottle 10 Years Old (89) **n22 t23 f22 b23** A stupendous blend of weight and poise, but possessing little of the all-round steaming, rampaging sexuality of the younger version... but like the younger version showing a degree less peat: here perhaps even two. Not, I hope, the start of a new trend under the new owners. *40%*

Black Dog 12 Years Old (92) **n21 t23 f24 b24.** Offering genuine sophistication and élan. This minor classic will probably require two or three glass-fulls before you take the bait... *42.8%*

Black Dog Century (89) **n21 t23 f23 b22.** I adore this style of no-nonsense, full bodied bruising blend which amid the muscle offers exemplary dexterity and finesse. What entertainment in every glass!! *42.8%. McDowell & Co Ltd. Blended in Scotland/Bottled in India.*

Black Grouse (94) **n23 t24 f23 b24.** A superb return to a peaty blend for Edrington for the first time since they sold Black Bottle. Not entirely different from that brand, either, from the Highland Distillers days with the smokiness being superbly couched by sweet malts. *40%*

The Black Grouse Alpha Edition (72.5) **n17 t19.5 f17 b18.** Dreadfully sulphured. *40%*

⬥ **Black Hound** (83) **n21 t21.5 f21 b20.5** Here's to Max! Max grain in this but no complaints here as the relatively limited caramel doesn't spoil the enjoyment of what feels like (though obviously isn't) a single distillery output. Crisp at first, then succulent, chewy cream toffee. *40%. Quality Spirits International.*

Black Ram Aged 12 Years (85) **n21 t23 f21 b20.** An upfront blend that gives its all in the chewy delivery. Some major oak in there but it's all ultra soft toffee and molasses towards the finish. *40%. Vinprom Peshtera, Bulgaria.*

⬥ **Black Stripe** (77) **n19 t20 f19 b19** Untidy without being characterful. *40%. Quality Spirits International.*

Blend No. 888 (86.5) **n20 t21.5 f23 b22.** A good old-fashioned, rip-roaring, nippy blend with a fudge-honey style many of a certain age will fondly remember from the 60s and 70s. Love it! *40%. The House of MacDuff.*

Boxes Blend (90) **n22.5 t23.5 f21 b23.** A box which gets plenty of ticks. *40.9%. ncf.*

Buchanan's De Luxe 12 Years Old (82) **n18 t21 f22 b21.** The nose shows more than just a single fault and the character simply refuses to get out of second gear. Certainly pleasant, and some of the chocolate notes towards the end are gorgeous. But just not the normal brilliant show-stopper! *40%. Diageo.*

Buchanan's Red Seal (90) **n22 t23 f22 b23** Exceptional, no-frills blend whose apparent simplicity paradoxically celebrates its complexity. *40%. Diageo.*

Cadenhead's Putachieside Aged 12 Years (91) **n23** no shortage of citrus and vanilla: fresh, and the flaky, puff-pastry topping is fitting; **t23** the sugars and oils make an early assault. A little bitterness from the oak creeps in; **f22** malty-lemon sawdust; **b23** not tasted for a while and delighted to re-discover this understated little gem. Also, has to be one of the best labels of any scotch going... *40% WB15/357*

Campbeltown Loch (94) **n23 t24 f23.5 b23.5** Over 30 years ago, this blend was one of my preferred drams at home. Not seen it for a while, so disappeared from The Bible. Found again and though it has changed a little in structure, its overall excellence takes me back to when I was a young man. *40% WB15/355*

Campbeltown Loch Aged 15 Years (88) **n22.5 t22.5 f21 b22** Well weighted with the age in no hurry to arrive. *40%. Springbank Distillers.*

Cambletown Loch 21 Years Old db (83) **n21 t23 f19 b20** Neither the nose or finish are much to write home about, the latter being a little tangy and bitter. But the delivery is rich and comforting: like a Digestive biscuit dunked in coffee. A seemingly decent malt content and a bit of toffee before the furry finale. *46%. WB15/102*

Castle Rock (81) **n20 t20.5 f20 b20.5.** Clean and juicy entertainment. *40%*

Catto's Aged 25 Years (85.5) **n22 t22.5 f19.5 b21.5.** A hugely enjoyable yet immensely frustrating dram. The higher fruit and spice notes are a delight, but it all appears to be played out in a padded cell of cream caramel. One assumes the natural oak caramels have gone into overdrive. Had they not, we would have had a supreme blend scoring well into the 90s. Elsewhere the increased furriness on the finale has not improved matters. *40%*

⬥ **Catto's Aged 25 Years** bott code RV9499 (94.5) **n23** the accent, as one might hope, is on varying degrees of honey: here ulmo and orange blossom have joint star billing in this very soft and friendly performance; **t24** excellent grains are at the vanguard of a glorious charm offensive: maple syrup, Lubek marzipan and barley sugar dissolves slowly into the vanillas; **f23** even as the sugars fade enough light spices rises to meet the demands of the oak; **b24.5** a far better experience than the last time I officially tasted a Catto's 25 seven or eight years ago. Both malts and grains are of the charming style once associated with Catto's Rare : so jaw-droppingly elegant... 40%. International Beverage Holdings Ltd.

Catto's Deluxe 12 Years Old (79.5) **n20** **t21.5** **f18** **b20**. Refreshing and spicy in part, but still a note in there which doesn't quite work. 40%. Inverhouse Distillers.

Catto's Deluxe 12 Years Old bott code L 18 03 16 (86.5) **n21.5** **t22** **f21.5** **b21.5** A safe, sweet and sumptuous blend which places major emphasis to the molasses. Won't win any beauty contests but there is a weighty earthiness, also. 40%. International Beverage Holdings Ltd.

Catto's Rare Old Scottish (92) **n23.5** **t23.5** **f22** **b23** Currently one of my regular blends to drink at home. Astonishingly old-fashioned with a perfect accent on clean Speyside and crisp grain. In the last year or so it has taken on a sublime sparkle on the nose and palate. An absolutely masterful whisky which both refreshes and relaxes. 40%. James Catto & Co.

Catto's Rare Old Scottish bott code L 25 01 16 (83) **n20.5** **t21** **f20.5** **b21** Once fresh as dew on morning grass, this has changed in recent years with a different grain profile which no longer magnifies the malt. Adopted a rougher, more toffeed approach from its once clean cut personality: not even a close approximation of the minor classic it once was. 40%. International Beverage Holdings Ltd.

Chequers Deluxe (78.5) **n19.5** **t20** **f19** **b20**. Charm, elegance, sophistication...not a single sign of any of them. Still if you want a bit of rough and tumble, just the job. 40%. Diageo.

The Chivas 18 Ultimate Cask Collection First Fill American Oak (95.5) **n24** another blend that has taken about 20 minutes to get the picture, such is the complexity. Some delightful saltiness to this heightens the sharpness of the grassier, Speyside malts – which is unusual. The sugars are low key, of the lighter more muted muscovado type, while the deft vanilla reminds you of the age rather than tells you it...; **t23.5** majestic delivery: at once salivating and sharp...yet dense! Again, an unusual combination, making full use of the grain; **f24** just brilliant...brilliant!!! Lasts forever with ridiculously clever use of both grain and oilier malts. The vanillas stay entirely in balance with the spices and lingering, slightly citric, malt; **b24** immeasurably superior to any Chivas 18 I have tasted before. A true whisky lover's whisky... 48%. ncf.

Chivas Regal Aged 12 Years (83.5) **n20.5** **t22.5** **f20** **b20.5**. Chewy fruit toffee. Silky grain mouth-feel with a toasty, oaky presence. 40%. Chivas.

Chivas Regal Aged 12 Years bott code 2017/01/31 LPAL 0162 (93) **n23** a distinctive but relatively low level smoke gives a surprising weight to this beyond the caramel. Spices nip and fizz but in controlled and friendly manner: there is actual layering and structure to this...; **t23.5** silk soft, tick. But instead of just heading off in its normal chewy direction, it now offers even more layers than on the nose. The luxuriant date and walnut toffee is the main theme, but I wasn't expecting the juicy, salivating qualities which pinpoint the Speyside maltiness which flickers over the palate, as does that understated smoke; a sensuous praline note makes itself increasingly heard while the molasses do a great job; **f22.5** back to toffee and spice...and the praline; **b24** last year I was in a British Airways Business Lounge somewhere in the world and spotted at the bar two different Chivas Regal 12s: the labels had differing designs. I asked for a glass of each and tried them side by side. The first one, from the older label, was the pleasant but forgettable blend I expected and knew so well. The newer version wasn't: had it not been time to get my flight I would have ordered a second glass of it....and I can't remember the last time I did that. What I have here is something very much like that surprise Chivas I discovered. This is, unquestionably, the best Chivas 12 I've encountered for a very long time (and I'm talking at least 20 years): pretty impressive use of the understated smoke, especially on the nose, which works well with that date and walnut toffee. I really could enjoy a second glass of this, though still a very different, delicate animal to the one I grew up with in the mid-70s. Actually, I just have had a second glass of this: delicious....! 40%. Chivas Brothers Ltd.

Chivas Regal Aged 18 Years (73.5) **n17.5** **t20** **f17.5** **b18.5**. The nose is dulled by a whiff of sulphur and confirmation that all is not well comes with the disagreeably dry, bitter finish. Early on in the delivery some apples and spices show promise but it is an unequal battle against the caramel and off notes. 40%

Chivas Regal Aged 18 Years bott code LKRL0346 2017/01/30 (86) **n22** **t22** **f21** **b21** A great improvement on the last bottling I encountered with a pleasing chewiness and understated spiciness. But this remains far too dependent on a big caramel surge for both taste and structure. 40%. Chivas Brothers Ltd.

Chivas Regal 25 Years Old (95) n23 t23.5 f24 b24.5. Unadulterated class where the grain-malt balance is exemplary and the deft intertwangling of well-mannered oak and elegant barley leaves you demanding another glass. Brilliant! *40%*

◈◈◈ **Chivas Regal Aged 25 Years** bott code 2017/03/01 LPML0373 (95.5) n24.5 all day and all night nose commanding your time: dense with dates and heather honey, but there are lighter aspects, too, which require and deserve attention. Probably a perfection of spices at play, as they both shape yet assist while a rich thread of malt can be found with ease. Hard to imagine a blend with better weight...; t24.5 ridiculously succulent: sultanas and burnt raisin are at the vanguard of a rich yet controlled delivery and follow through, while the chocolate backbone also offers nuts and more dates, slightly drier now than on the nose, also. The mouth feel, steered by the outstanding grains, is truly perfect and the pace of development a lesson in the true blender's almost lost art; f22.5 long, with a wonderfully fruity swirl to the ulmo and heather honeys. Just a slight tang of the sherry butt furs things up slightly...; b24 this is quite brilliant whisky. Maybe just one sherry butt away from what would almost certainly have been among the top three whiskies of the year... *40%. Chivas Brothers Ltd.*

Chivas Regal Extra (86) n20 t24 f20.5 b21.5. Chivas, but seemingly from the Whyte and MacKay school of thick, impenetrable blends. The nose may have the odd undesirable element and the finish reflects those same trace failings. But if chewy date and walnuts in a sea of creamy toffee is your thing, then this malt is for you. This, though, does show genuine complexity, so I have to admit to adoring the lush delivery and early middle section: the mouth-feel is truly magnificent. Good spice, too. Flawed genius comes to mind. *40%*

◈◈◈ **Chivas Regal The Chivas Brother's Blend Aged 12 Years** bott code 2016/04/12 LPEK0613 (81.5) n21 t21.5 f19 b20 Oh, brother! Fabulous texture but a furry finish... *40%. Chivas Brothers Ltd.*

Clan Campbell (86.5) n21.5 t22.5 f21 b21.5. I'll wager that if I could taste this whisky before the colouring is added it would be scoring into the 90s. Not a single off note; a sublime early array of Speysidey freshness but dulls at the end. *40%. Chivas.*

◈◈◈ **Clan Campbell** bott code LR3 1047 13/09/05 (89) n21.5 attractive sweet young grain, but a little Speyside grassiness grows on top; t23 succulent delivery: a mouth-watering mix of light icing sugars, something vaguely gristier and a wonderful clean grain velvetiness. The mid ground is soft, slightly chalky with developing butterscotch; f22 a gentle spiciness breezes in; b22.5 amazing what happens when you reduce the colouring Last time I tasted this I could barely find the whisky for all the toffee. Now it positively shines in the glass. Love it! *40%. Chivas Brothers Ltd.*

◈◈◈ **Clan Campbell Dark** rum barrel finish, bott code 2017/03/29 LPHL 0570 (89.5) n22 full bodied with a light toastiness to the base sugars. The grain is fat and friendly; t23 brilliant delivery: the grain is in total sync with the maple syrup and light, pulsing spice. Salivating for a while and you fancy onto the odd malt note pops up, though not too many...; f22 rumbling spice and fudge; b22.5 putting my rum blender's hat on here, can't think which barrels they used to get this degree of colour and sweetness. Still, I'm not arguing; it's a really lovely, accommodating dram. *40%. Chivas Brothers Ltd.*

Clan Gold 3 Year Old (95) n23.5 t24 f23.5 b24. A blend-drinkers blend which will also slay the hearts of Speyside single malt lovers. For me, this is love at first sip... *40%*

Clan Gold Blended 15 Years Old (91) n21.5 t23 f23.5 b23 An unusual blend for the 21st century, which steadfastly refuses to blast you away with over the top flavour and/or aroma profiles and instead depends on subtlety and poise despite the obvious richness of flavour. The grains make an impact but only by creating the frame in which the more complex notes can be admired. *40%*

Clan Gold Blended 18 Years Old (94.5) n23 t24 f23.5 b24. Almost the ultimate prepandrial whisky with its at once robust yet delicate working over of the taste buds by the carefully muzzled juiciness of the malt. This is the real deal: a truly classy act which at first appears to wallow in a sea of simplicity but then bursts out into something very much more complex and alluring. About as clean and charming an 18-year-old blend as you are likely to find. *40%*

◈◈◈ **Clan Gold 18 Years of Age** bott code L6X 7616 0611 (95) n24 the layering on the nose stops you in your tracks: Eskimos have hundreds of different words for snow, apparently: I wonder how many there are for vanilla... For this is an exhibition of subtlety and variation. And also age profiles as some of the tannins carry their age proudly, others hide it behind a honeyed mask; despite the majoring sweet notes, there are no less subtle spices to complete the picture...; t24 so soft it seems to melt and disappear virtually the moment it lands...a bit like a snowflake. The sugars, like on the nose, appear to be at the tiller but the course it steers cannot avoid those vanillas once more and now quite confident spices which have more to say by the second...and much louder; **f23** a little mocha arrives late on – it is not unexpected. The butterscotch is warmed with lingering spice and even now the mouth feel remains soft and warmly embracing; **b24** nothing like as juicy and cleverly fruity as it once was, yet marriage between malt and grain seldom comes more happy than this... *40%. Quality Spirits International.*

Clan Gold Finest bott code L10Z 6253 1902 **(83) n20 t21 f21 b21** Sweet, silky, soft and caramel heavy. Decent late spice. *40%. Quality Spirits International.*

Clan MacGregor (92) n22 t24 f23 b23 Just gets better and better. Now a true classic and getting up there with Grant's. *43%*

Clan Murray bott code L9X 7694 1411 **(86) n20 t22.5 f21.5 b22** For the avoidance of doubt: no, this not my blend. No, I am not the blender. No, I do not get a royalty from sales. If I could have had a tenner for each time I've had to answer that over the last decade or so I could have bought my own island somewhere, or Millwall FC... Anyway, back to the whisky. Far better nose than it has shown in the past and the delivery has an eye-watering bite, the finish a roguish spice. Rough-ish but very ready... *40%. The BenRiach Distillery Co. Ltd.*

Clansman (80.5) n20.5 t21 f19 b20. Sweet, grainy and soft. *40%. Loch Lomond.*

Clansman bott code L3/170/15 **(84) n21 t22 f20 b21** More to it than of old, though still very soft, the dark sugars and spice have a very pleasant input. *40%. Loch Lomond Group.*

The Claymore (85) n19 t22 f22 b22. These days you are run through by spices. The blend is pure Paterson in style with guts etc, which is not something you always like to associate with a Claymore; some delightful muscovado sugar at the death. Get the nose sorted and a very decent and complex whisky is there to be had. *40%. Whyte & Mackay Distillers Ltd.*

The Classic Cask 23 Year Old Caribbean Rum Barrels Finish European oak butt, batch no. #SW.110, dist 1992, bott 2016 **(92) n23.5** attractive, juicy wine gum aroma, lie pastels especially. Light spices flutter past; delicate vanilla; **t23** much softer delivery than the normal rum finish, the sugars refusing to take the hard-edged route. Exceptionally salivating with muscovado rather than Demerara sugars at work! **f22.5** long, at first vanilla dominant, then spices out; **b23** a beautifully crafted, satisfying blend. *43% (86 proof). 760 bottles.*

The Classic Cask 23 Year Old Oloroso Sherry Butt European oak butt, batch no. #SW.109, dist 1992, bott 2016 **(78.5) n18.5 t23 f18 b19** Damn and blast the mild sulphur on this – the sixth such tainted bottling I have tasted today and my taste buds are hoisting the white flag: that's me done for this session. The nose warns of what is to come, though the juicy, fruity vibrancy on delivery is sublime. The finish, though... *43% (86 proof). 771 bottles.*

The Classic Cask 23 Year Old Original Cask European oak butt, batch no. #SW.108, dist 1992, bott 2016 **(88.5) n22** blood oranges; a tad furry; **t23.5** exemplary mouth feel: brilliant marriage of semi-firm grains and yielding Demerara sugars; the fruit is happy to play second fiddle, though slowly a lovely grape, lychee and pear mix begins to take shape; **f21** just an outline of a furriness begins to unsettle the taste buds **b22** yes, there is a small amount of sulphur here. Nothing fatal, though enough to knock what would have been an outstanding blend in a direction you'd prefer it didn't go. Curses! *43% (86 proof). 782 bottles.*

The Classic Cask 23 Year Old Port Pipe Finish European oak butt, batch no. #SW.111, dist 1992, bott 2016 **(90.5) n23.5** a heady aroma with even a light phenolic touch to add extra weight to the big fruit signature. A degree of Saxby's Christmas Pudding, the slight salty nuttiness countering the delicate molasses; **t23** such a soft grain at work here, but t is the deft fruit which keeps the taste buds pricked and alive to the subtle changes. Again, a degree of saltiness sharpens the fruit, though the red liquorice and barley sugar stir things up, also; **f21.5** a little mocha but a slight tanginess, also; **b22.5** forget the slight blemish towards the end. Worth exploring as this complex blend takes you down countless avenues... *43% (86 proof). 769 bottles.*

Compass Box Asyla 1st fill American oak ex-bourbon, bott May 10 **(93) n24 t24 f22.5 b23.5** If you can hear a purring noise, it is me tasting this... *40%. nc ncf.*

Compass Box Asyla Marriage nine months in an American oak barrel **(88) n22 t23 f21 b22** A lovely blend, but can't help feeling that this was one marriage that lasted too long. *43.6%. Compass Box Whisky for La Maison du Whisky in commemoration of their 50th Anniversary.*

Compass Box Delilah's Limited Release American oak, bott Jul 13 **(89.5) n23 t22 f22 b22.5.** A clean and satisfying blend which ramps up the sugars when need be. I'll be surprised if you get to the point where you couldn't take any more... *40%. 6400 bottles.*

Compass Box Delilah's Limited Release Small Batch American oak **(92.5) n23 t23.5 f23 b23** blends rarely come more honeyed, or even sweeter, than this with every last sugary element seemingly extracted from the oak. My only sorrow for this whisky, given its American theme, was that it wasn't bottled as a 101 (ie 50.5% abv) instead of the rather underpowered 80 proof – because you have the feeling this would have become pretty three dimensional and leapt from the glass. And then down your throat with serious effect. *40%. nc ncf. WB15/171*

⬦ **Compass Box The Double Single** bott Mar 17 (97) n24.5 one of those noses so delicate you daren't breath in too hard for fear of shattering it into a million pieces. The citrus, a kind of orange blossom honey thinned with the juices of Jaffa, is of the cleanest style imaginable; likewise the barley is fresh and gristy. One of the most ethereal and elegant noses of all time....; t25 perfection. This is faultless. This is exactly how whisky should be. A delivery you hope to encounter – or create – but suspect you probably never will. And here it is: in all its understated, genteel, feminine, seductive majesty. It is the nose all over again, but this time in liquid form, a physicality which curls against our taste buds and caresses them with the most erotic, arousing finger-tip touch...; f23.5 nothing can quite follow the delivery and follow through, but it tries. Though the oaks can now be heard, a little bitterly by comparison, while the spices up the tingling factor; b24 by no means the first time I have encountered a single malt and grain in the same bottle. But I am hard pressed to remember one that was even close to being this wonderful...This is Compass Box's finest moment... 46%. nc ncf. 5,838 bottles.

Compass Box The Entertainer Limited Edition bott Aug 12 (88.5) n21.5 t22.5 f22 b22. A pleasant blend, though the tanginess is perhaps a little too sharp. 46%. Compass Box Whisky Company. 1000 bottles. Commissioned by Selfridges.

Compass Box Great King St. Artist's Blend (93) n24 t23 f22.5 b23.5. The nose of this uncoloured and non-chill filtered whisky is not dissimilar to some better known blends before they have colouring added to do its worst. A beautiful young thing this blend: nubile, naked and dangerously come hither. Compass Box's founder John Glaser has done some memorable work in recent years, though one has always had the feeling that he has still been learning his trade, sometimes forcing the issue a little too enthusiastically. Here, there is absolutely no doubting that he has come of age as a blender. 43%. nc ncf.

Compass Box Great King Street Experimental Batch #00-V4 bott Sep 13 (93) n22.5 t24 f23 b23.5. A blend combining astonishing vibrancy with oaky Russian roulette. Not a dram to do things by halves... 43%. 3,439 bottles.

Compass Box Great King Street Experimental Batch #TR-06 bott Sep 13 (92) n22 the most dense of all the GKS I have yet tasted. All, including batch 00-V4 have shewn signs of younger malts offering a bright outlet. This, though, is a distant rumble, like highway traffic a mile off, of tannin, toast and smoke; t23.5 unlike on the nose, the first to display a sweet, buttery maltiness, mixed with the gentle elements of the grain. And there is sweet smoke, too which holds the middle until the tannins return; f23 long, oily, with a smoked Demerara theme. The oak, though, rumbles and grumbles on; b23.5 I think this one's been rumbled... 43%.

Compass Box Great King Street Glasgow Blend (88.5) n22 playful phenols delight, but a strange wrong un of a note detracts and distracts; t23.5 some clever interplay on delivery: the smoke appears to have its own way early on, but the grain clears a path of clarity, along which brighter, more honeyed notes occasionally travel; f21 soft oils ensure a gentle landing, but those odd discordant notes detected on the nose bob up again, especially at the death; b22 just the odd note seems out of place here and there: delicious but not the usual Compass Box precision. 43%

Compass Box The Circus bott Mar 16 (93) n23 roll up, roll up and nose a fascinating juxtapositioning of the Fisherman's Friend-style smokiness with a sharp citric malt/grain mix...; t23.5 eye-wateringly tart start: a strange mix of undercooked and overcooked jam tarts, with a smoked liquorice middle; f23 remains, thick, dark and brooding: no high wires here – these are all base notes; b23.5 Scotland's very own Clown Royal... 49%. nc ncf. 2,490 bottles.

Compass Box This Is Not A Luxury Whisky bott Aug 15 (81) n20 t21.5 f19.5 b20. Correct. 53.1%. nc ncf. 4,992 bottles.

Consulate (87) n21.5 t22 f22 b21.5 I assume this weighty and pleasant dram was designed to accompany Passport (whose chewiness it now resembles) in the drinks cabinet. I suggest, if buying them, use Visa. 40%. Quality Spirits International. ⊙ ⊙

Crawford's (83.5) n19 t21 f22 b21.5. A lovely spice display helps overcome the caramel. 40%.

Cutty Black (83) n20 t23 f19 b21. Both nose and finish are dwarfed and flung into the realms of ordinariness by the magnificently substantial delivery. Whilst there is a taint to the nose, its richness augers well for what is to follow; and you won't be disappointed. At times it behaves like a Highland Park with a toffeed spine, such is the richness and depth of the honey and dates and complexity of the grain-vanilla background. But those warning notes on the nose are there for good reason and the finish tells you why. Would not be surprised to see this score into the 90s on a different bottling day. 40%. Edrington.

Cutty Sark (78) n19 t21 f19 b19. Crisp and juicy. But a nipping furriness, too. 40%

⬦ **Cutty Sark** bott code L60355 L7 (84.5) n21 t22 f20 b21.5 To some extent an improvement on a couple of years back when this blend was vanishing in character. But could still do with some urgent extra restorative work. For as long I can remember the grain on this was crisp and brought the sharpest, juiciest notes imaginable from the Speyside malts: indeed, that was its trademark character. Now, like so many standard blends, it is bubble gum soft and spreads the sugars evenly with the malts fighting to be heard. Only very mild sulphur tones to the crippling ones I had previously found. But it really does need to re-work the grain...if it can find it. 40%. Edrington.

Cutty Sark Aged 12 Years (92) n22 t24 f23 b23 At last! Cutty 12 at full sail...and blended whisky rarely looks any more beautiful! 40%. Edrington.

Cutty Sark Aged 15 Years (82) n19 t22 f20 b21. Attempts to take the honey route. But seriously dulled by toffee and the odd sulphured cask. 40%. Edrington.

Cutty Sark Aged 18 Years (88) n22 t22 f22 b22 Lost the subtle fruitiness which worked so well. Easy-going and attractive. 43%

Cutty Sark Aged 25 Years (91) n21 t23.5 f22.5 b23 Magnificent, though not quite flawless, this whisky is as elegant and effortlessly powerful as the ship after which the brand was named... 45.7%. Berry Bros & Rudd.

◈ **Cutty Sark Prohibition Edition** American oak, bott code L0401W L4 11/18 (91) n21.5 right: let's just ignore the traces of the dreaded S word here and concentrate on the other aspects: the grain has a rare firmness for these days, and doesn't appear to be of the super-sweet cloying style. As a result, the malts and their intricacies are actually visible, like stars in a clear sky...; t25 let me judge the first 30 seconds from the moment it passes the lips. This is a rare case of perfection: you can shake my Whisky Bible and very few if any, will drop out. But the weight and the mouth feel really is perfection. As are the slow sugar releases, build-up of tannins and arrival of warming spices: faultless. The grain has a slightly skiddy feel against the tongue; the malts are very carefully crafted displaying a mainly Speyside malt biscuit-richness but then, cunningly, a series of weightier, chewier waves. So annoyed I really have to spit this out from a professional perspective. Borderline genius and of a very old, almost lost style...; f20 dammit. The S word reappears, not massively but it stays...; b24.5 probably the best label and presentation of any whisky in the world this year: sheer class. On the back label they use the word authentic. Which is a very interesting concept. Except authentic whisky sent to the USA back in the 1920s wouldn't have that annoying and debilitating rumble of sulphur, detectable on both nose and finish. And I suspect the malt content would have been higher – and the grain used showing far more of a corn-oily character. That all said, I doubt the blender of the day would have achieved better delivery or balance: indeed, this delivery has to be one of the highlights of the whisky year. You will not be surprised to discover my resolve cracked, and I swallowed a full mouthful of this special blend. And, gee: it was swell, bud... 50%. Edrington.

Cutty Sark Storm (81.5) n18 t23.5 f19.5 b20.5. When the wind is set fair, which is mainly on delivery and for the first six or seven flavour waves which follow, we really do have an astonishingly beautiful blend, seemingly high in malt content and really putting the accent on ulmo honey and marzipan: a breath-taking combination. This is assisted by a gorgeous weight to the silky body and a light raspberry jam moment to the late arriving Ecuadorian cocoa. All magnificent. However, the blend, as Cutty sadly tends to, sails into sulphurous seas. 40%. Edrington.

Demijohn Finest Blended Scotch Whisky (88) n21 strange, out of shape, but soft; t22 salivating delivery with an enveloping softness to the grain; the malts eventually mould into the style; f23 remains tangy to the end, even with a touch of marmalade thrown in; b22 OK, now that's spooky. You really don't expect tasting notes written ten years ago to exactly fit the bill today. But that is exactly what happens here: well maybe not quite exactly. Ten years ago I wrote of the "wonderful firmness of the grain" where today, like 90% of all blends, it is much more yielding and soft than before. Thankfully, it hasn't detracted from the enjoyment. 40%. ⊙⊙

Dew of Ben Nevis Blue Label (82) n19 t22 f20 b21. The odd off-key note is handsomely outnumbered by deliciously complex mocha and demerara tones. Ditch the caramel and you'd have a sizzler! 40%. Ben Nevis Distillery. Replacement for Dew of Ben Nevis Millennium Blend.

Dew of Ben Nevis Special Reserve (85) n19 t21 f23 b22. A much juicier blend than of old, still sporting some bruising and rough patches. But that kind of makes this all the more attractive, with the caramel mixing with some fuller malts to provide a date and nuts effect which makes for a grand finale. 40%. Ben Nevis Distillery.

Dew of Ben Nevis Supreme Selection (77) n18 t20 f20 b19. Some lovely raspberry jam swiss roll moments here. But the grain could be friendlier, especially on the nose. 40%

Dewar's Special Reserve 12 Years Old (84) n20 t23 f19 b22. Some s... you know what... has crept onboard here and duffed up the nose and finish. A shame because elements of the delivery and background balance shows some serious blending went on here. 40%

Dewar's 18 Years Old (93) n23 t24 f22.5 b23.5 Here is a classic case of where great blends are not all about the malt. The grain plays in many ways the most significant role here, as it is the perfect backdrop to see the complexity of the malt at its clearest. Simply magnificent blending with the use of flawless whisky. 43%. John Dewar & Sons.

Dewar's 18 Year Old Founders Reserve (86.5) n22.5 t22 f20.5 b21.5. A big, blustering dram which doesn't stint on the fruit. A lovely, thin seam of golden syrup runs through the piece, but the dull, aching finale is somewhat out of character. 40%. John Dewar & Sons.

Dewar's Signature (93) n24 t23.5 f22 b23.5. A slight departure in style, with the fruit becoming just a little sharper and juicier. Top range blending and if the odd butt could be weeded out, this'd be an award winner for sure. 43%

Dewar's White Label (78.5) n19 t21.5 f19 b19. When on song, one of my preferred daily blends. But not when like this, with its accentuated bitter-sweet polarisation. 40%

Dhoon Glen (86) n21 t22 f21.5 b21.5 Full of big flavours, broad grainy strokes and copious amounts of dark sugars including chocolate fudge and now a little extra spice, too. Goes dhoon a treat... 40%. Lombard Scotch Whisky Ltd. ☉☉

Dimple 12 Years Old (86.5) n22 t22 f21.5 b21. Lots of sultana; the spice adds aggression. 40%.

Dimple 15 Years Old (87.5) n20 t21 f24 b22.5. Only on the late middle and finish does this particular flower unfurl and to magnificently complex effect. The texture of the grains in particular delight while the strands of barley entwine. A type of treat for the more technically minded of the serious blend drinkers among you. 40%. Diageo.

The Famous Grouse (89) n22 t23 f21.5 b22.5 It almost seems that Grouse is, by degrees, moving from its traditional position of a light blend to something much closer to Grant's as a middle-weighted dram. Again the colouring has been raised a fraction and now the body and depth have been adjusted to follow suit. Have to say that this is one very complex whisky these days: I had spotted slight changes when drinking it socially, but this was the first time I had a chance to sit down and professionally analyse what was happening in the glass. A fascinating and tasty bird, indeed. 40%. Edrington Group.

⬦ **The Famous Grouse** bott code L4812TL1 25/08 (88.5) n22.5 a chicken coop straw aroma reveals that the higher levels of smoke have been maintained. Muscovado sugars paint a light fruity note which compliments well; t23 the grain has become just a little softer and enveloping these days, thus accentuating the friendlier heather-honey tones. The smoke forms a pleasant background noise and adds a degree of extra weight; f21 a slight tang these days, though the earlier sugars now sweeten the lightly minted mocha; b22 changed its stance a few years back from light blend to a middle-weighted one and has worked hard to keep that position with thoughtful use of the phenols. Unlike many other brands it has not gone colouring mad and the little toffee apparent does nothing to spoil the narrative and complexity: I doff my hat. 40%.

The Famous Grouse Gold Reserve (90) n23.5 t23 f21.5 b22 Great to know the value of the Gold Reserve is going up...as should the strength of this blend. The old-fashioned 40% just ain't enough carats. 40%. Edrington Group.

The Famous Grouse Married Strength (82.5) n19 t22 f20 b21.5. The nose is nutty and toffeed. But despite the delightful, silky sweetness and gentle Speyside-style maltiness which forms the main markers for this soft blend, the nose, like the finish, also shows a little bitter furriness has, sadly, entered into the mix. Not a patch on the standard Grouse of a decade ago. 45.9% WB16/019

The Famous Grouse Mellow Gold sherry & bourbon casks (85) n20 t23.5 f20 b21.5. While the nose and finish tell us a little too much about the state of the sherry butts used, there is no harm tuning into the delivery and follow though which are, unquestionably, beautiful. The texture is silk normally found on the most expensive lingerie, and as sexy as who you might find inside it; while the honey is a fabulous mix of ulmo and orange blossom. 40%

The Famous Grouse Smoky Black (87) n22 t22 f21 b22. Black Grouse by any other name. Flawed in the usual tangy, furry Grouse fashion. But have to say there is a certain roughness and randomness about the sugars that I find very appealing. A smoky style that Bowmore lovers might enjoy. A genuinely beautiful, smoky, ugly, black duckling. Sorry, I mean Grouse. 40%

⬦ **Firean** blend no. 005, bottling line. 003, bott code. L17066 (91.5) n23 a generous smokiness which, though soft and embracing, leaves enough room for the delicate citrus to thrive; t23.5 such an impressive delivery. The peat makes itself known immediately but then has the good grace to dissolve away with the molasses, leaving the sweet, sot grains to take up the middle ground; f22 a grainy vanilla with the slenderest peaty thread; b23 does the heart good encounter to encounter a blend so happy to embrace its smokier self. Deliciously impressive. 40%. Burlington Drinks.

Fort Glen The Blender's Reserve Aged 12 Years (88.5) n21.5 t23 f21.5 b22.5 An entirely enjoyable blend which is clean and boasting decent complexity and weight. *40%*

Fort Glen The Distiller's Reserve (78) n18 t22 f19 b19. Juicy, salivating delivery as it storms the ramparts. Draws down the portcullis elsewhere. *40%. The Fort Glen Whisky Company.*

Fraser MacDonald (85) n21 t21.5 f21 b21.5. Some fudge towards the middle and end but the journey there is an enjoyable one. *40%. Loch Lomond Distillers.*

Gairloch (79) n19 t20 f20 b20. For those who like their butterscotch at 40% abv. *40%*

Gleann Mór Blended Whisky 18 Year Old (87) n21.5 t23 f20.5 b22. A few passages in this are outstanding, especially when the delicate honey appears to collide with the softest smoke. A slight bitterness does jar somewhat, though the softness of the grain is quite seriously seductive 43.9%

⬩ **Gleann Mór 40 Year Old Blend** (94) n23 a mini oak forest at work here but there are enough sugars on the barley to easily cope; t23.5 salivating even before the silky grain gets to work. The layering of vanilla is deft and puts the tannins in their place for the time being. Soft textured, the malt also become visible, as does a gentle liquorice and molasses involvement; f23.5 back comes the tannins when those sweeter elements are spent, but in such a civilised fashion, one can only sigh...; b24 some 52-year-old Carsebridge makes up about a fifth of this blend, but I suspect the big oak comes from one of the malts. A supreme old whisky which cherishes its age. 44.6%.

Glenalba Aged 22 Years Sherry Cask Finish batch no. JS/322, lot no. 0745C, dist 1993 (90) n22 hard to get past the clean grape. No bite. No layering, as such. Just very pleasant fruit..., perhaps with chocolate shavings; t23.5 silky delivery: about as soft and caressing as whisky comes. The grains must be at work here, for the grape has a rounded, airy feel that is not at all common. Hard to distinguish the malt and the course it is trying to take; f23.5 a rather superb mix of chocolate and sherry...rather like an expensive Belgian liqueur...; b21 a pristine sherry effect. No off notes whatsoever. If there is a downside, it is the fact that the sherry evens out the complexity of the blend. I mean, surely...that has to be the purpose of a blend: complexity and balance, right....? That said, for the experience alone...all rather lovely and deserving of further exploration...! *40%*

Glenalba Aged 25 Years Sherry Cask Finish batch no. SE/425, lot no. 0274J, dist 1990 (89) n22 salty, seaweedy but the sherry is almost glutinous...; t23.5 wow! What's not to love about this? Intense grape, like the 22-year-old old slowly giving way to high percentage cocoa – and that liqueur effect is in full swing; f22.5 the drying experience gets even drier; b21.5 a lovely whisky, though again the unreconstructed sherry effect does few favours to the overall layering and balance. Maybe the vaguest hint of something with the 'S' word, though very low key... *40%*

Glenalba Aged 34 Years Sherry Cask Finish batch no. JM/012, lot no. 0862B, dist 1981 (95.5) n24 now that is one hell of a sherry-infested nose: exceptionally clean, high quality butts only deployed here. And this one allows the layering and structure demanded of a high-class blend: it is not all about the grape. A few telling tannin notes filter through, but it is the malt, clearly recognisable under a slightly salty skin, which really ramps up the complexity; t24 magnificent! Gosh, where does one begin?! A beautiful liquid Jaffa Cake effect, with the fruit converting into tangy citrus, under a crisp cocoa shell; something akin to smoke makes a meandering appearance. But the spices are so busy yet beautifully balanced against the softness of the grape; f23.5 long and perfectly assisted by the light oils which coat the palate with the high class sherry. The spices buzz with contentment, while a late interplay of tannin and malt underlines lingering complexity; b24 a beautifully dry, sophisticated blend. Benefits from the use of what is about as good a sherry butt as I have encountered: not even the hint of a hint of an off-note. Where the 22 and 25 year editions are rather overcome by the magnitude of the grape, this one has enough in reserve to take the sherry in its stride and use it to excellent effect. Truly superb Scotch. *40%*

Glen Brynth (70.5) n18 t19 f16 b17.5. Bitter and awkward. *43%*

⬩ **Glenbrynth Premium Three Year Old** (82) n19 t21 f21 b21 An enormously improved, salivating, toasty blend making full use of the rich muscovado sugars on display. Good late spice, too. *43%. OTI Africa.*

Glenbrynth 8 Year Old (88) n21.5 t22 f22.5 b22. An impressive blend which improves second by second on the palate. *40%. OTI Africa.*

Glenbrynth Pearl 30 Year Old Limited Edition (90.5) n22.5 t23.5 f21.5 b23 Attractive, beautifully weighted, no off notes...though perhaps quietened by toffee. Still a treat of a blend. *43%. OTI Africa.*

⟡ **Glenbrynth Pearl 30 Year Old** bott code L8V 7410 28/11/11 (88) n22.5 huge age, the oak exceeding the 30 year statement, creaking with tannins barely able to push their Zimmer frames about. Beyond this exhibition of decrepitude comes a series of friendlier notes, coconut in maple syrup amongst the youngest of them...; t22.5 a spongy delivery, alive at first with intense caramel and muscovado sugar. Then its tiring sugars to the fore, collapsing under the weight of drier vanillas. Burnt toast with ulmo honey coming to the rescue; f21 a bit of tingling buzz here....; b22 a genuinely strange blend. Not sure how this whisky was mapped out in the creator's mind. A hit and miss hotchpotch but when it is good, it is very good.. 43%. OTI Africa.

⟡ **The Glengarry** bott code L3/301/15 (80) n19 t21 f20 b20 A brand that would once make me wince has upped its game beyond recognition. Even has the nerve to now possess an attractively satisfying as well as silky disposition. 40%. Loch Lomond Group.

Glen Lyon (85) n19 t22.5 f22 b21.5. Works a lot better than the nose suggests: seriously chewy with a rabid spice attack and lots of juices. For those who have just retired as dynamite testers. Unpretentious fun. 43%. Diageo.

Glen Talloch Choice Rare & Old (85.5) n20.5 t22.5 f21 b21.5. A very pleasing sharpness to the delivery reveals the barley in all its Speyside-style finery, The grain itself is soothing, especially when the caramel notes kick in. 40%. ncf.

Glen Talloch Gold Aged 12 Years (85) n21 t22 f21 b21. Impressive grain at work insuring a deft, velvety caress to the palate. Mainly caramel speaking, despite the age, though there is an attractive spice buzz towards the thin-ish finish. 40%

⟡ **Glen Talloch Peated** (77) n18 t20 f20 b19 The awful tobacco nose needs some serious work on it. The taste is overly sweet, mushy and shapeless, like far too many blends these days. Requires a complete refit. 40%. Boomsma Distillery.

Glory Leading Aged 32 Years (88.5) n22.5 just get a load of those beautifully spiced apples and pears...; t22.5 an alloy of some of the softest grains in the market means the malt has a problem establishing a foothold. The early imbalance stabilises as the spices begin their assault, the malt following in timidly behind; f21.5 much better balance now: outstanding spice radiation plus some beguiling soft malt. A strange tobacco note at the death; b22 at times a little heavy handed and out of sync. But the overall experience is one of stunningly spiced enjoyment. 43%

Glory Leading Blended Scotch Whisky 30 Years Old American oak casks (93) n22.5 t23 f23.5 b24 a big, clever, satisfying blend which just gets better and better... though not too sure about the Crystal Palace style eagle on the label. Even so, love it! 43%

Golden Piper (86.5) n22 t21 f22 b21.5. A firm, clean blend with a steady flush through of diverse sugars. The grain does all the steering and therefore complexity is limited. But the overall freshness is a delight. 43%. Whisky Shack.

The Gordon Highlanders (86) n21 t22 f21 b22. Lush and juicy, there is a distinctive Speysidey feel to this one with the grains doing their best to accentuate the developing spice. Plenty of feel good factor here. 40%. William Grant & Sons.

Grand Macnish (79) n19 t21 f19 b20. Welcome back to an old friend...but the years have caught up with it. Still on the feral side, but has exchanged its robust good looks for an unwashed and unkempt appearance on the palate. Will do a great job to bring some life back to you, though. 43%. MacDuff International Ltd.

⟡ **Grand Macnish** bott code L16/8404 (85.5) n21.5 t22 f21 b21 Never a blend for the lily-livered this brand has always been a byword for a whisky with big character. It can still claim that, except now we have a much more absorbing grain at play which undermines the blend's former maltiness. 40%. MacDuff International Ltd.

Grand Macnish 12 Years Old (86) n21 t22 f21.5 b21.5. A grander Grand Macnich than of old with the wonderful feather pillow delivery maintained and a greater harmonisation of the malt, especially those which contain a honey-copper sheen. 40%. MacDuff.

⟡ **Grand Macnish Black Edition** charred Bourbon casks, bott code L15 8863 (94.5) n24 brilliant! Supremely clever use of the phenols: not so light to tease you, not so heavy as to overpower the other complex characters at work. Gorgeous spices and just the right amount of muscovado sugars; t23.5 outstanding delivery in which maple syrup and tannins work as counterweights; caramel and smoke slowly gangs up while the spices buzz; the grains have a welcome brittleness and allow the malts a free hand; f23 for all the obvious toffee, the smoke and spice still keep on giving; b24 a blended whisky classic. 40%. MacDuff International Ltd.

⟡ **Grant's Aged 12 Years** bott code: L6X 6682 1305 (96) n24 hugely enticing aroma: a non-specific fruitiness appears to bounce off some crisper grain while a vague rumbling smoke offers a deeper, third dimension; t24 brilliant delivery in terms of both flavour and mouth feel. Both lush and firm (as you always hope a blend will be but sadly these days is all too rarely), the sugars are not so much refined as restrained, but enough Demerara is present to perk up the vanillas and praline; the texture really is incredibly sexy...; **f23.5** slightly salty and dry in part, there is a slight malty echo before the tannins move towards a mocha finale; as any great whisky should, the finish never quite seems to end...; **b24.5** there is no doubting that their 12-year-old has improved dramatically in recent years. Doubtless better grain than their standard blend, but also a slightly braver use of phenols has paid handsome dividends. Sits proudly alongside Johnny Walker Black as one of the world's must have 12-year-old blends. For me, the perfect daily dram. 40%.

Grant's Cask Editions No. 1 Ale Cask Finish bott code: L1X 7354 1809 **(91)** n22.5 attractive Demerara firmness and even a malty swirl; the green, youthful freshness charms; **t23** juicy delivery and firmer than the Family Reserve with much more sharpness and clarity; big sugars build; **f22.5** a pleasing spiced mocha fade; **b23** a much cleaner, more precise blend than when this was first launched, with less noticeable beer character: impressive. 40%.

Grant's Cask Editions No. 2 Sherry Cask Finish bott code: L3Z 7760 0211 **(84.5)** n21.5 **t22 f20 b21** A lovely fresh, fruity and salivating edge to this even boasting an early honeyed sheen. Complexity has been sacrificed for effect, however. 40%.

Grant's The Family Reserve bott code: L3A 8017 1711 **(85)** n21 t22 f21 b21 What was once the very finest, most complex nose in the entire Scotch whisky lexicon is now, on this evidence, a mushy shadow of its former self. Where once there was a judicious mix of softer and firmer grain to ensure the malts could make the most eloquent of speeches, now there is just a spongy sweetness which shouts loud enough to silence the poetry. If you like your blend fat, sweet, chewy, softer than quicksand and boasting a bitter, vaguely off-key finale here you go. But for those of us who once revered Grant's as the greatest of all standard blends, a whisky whose artistry once gilt-framed the very finest Scotland had to offer, this will not be a glass of cheer. I cannot blame the blender: he can work only with what he has available. And today, after a succession of nonsensical grain distillery closures (nonsensical to anyone who understands whisky, but not the soul-less bean counters who haven't the first clue) the choice in his lab is limited. It would be like blaming the manager of Bradford City for being a third tier football club because they won the FA Cup in 1910. Times change. And not, sadly, always for the better... 40%.

Grant's Signature bott code: L1Z 7468 1609 **(79)** n19 t22 f18 b20 Smudged. 40%.

The Great Macaulay **(86.5)** n22 t21.5 f21.5 b21.5 The character is one mainly of trudging, attractive caramel bolstered by busy, warming spice. The nose shows some degree of complexity. By no means unpleasant. 40%. Quality Spirits International.

Green Plaid 12 Years Old **(89)** n22 t23 f22 b22 Beautifully constructed; juicy. 40%.

Guneagal Aged 12 Years **(85.5)** n21 t22.5 f20.5 b21.5. The salty, sweaty armpit nose gives way to an even saltier delivery, helped along by sweet glycerine and a boiled candy fruity sweetness. The finish is a little roughhouse by comparison. 40%. William Grant & Sons.

Haddington House **(81)** n20 t21 f20 b20 Good grief! This has changed since I last tasted it over a decade ago. Gone is its light, bright juicy character and in its place a singularly sweet, cloying blend due, I suspect, to a very different grain input. 40%. Quality Spirits International.

Haig Gold Label **(88)** n21 t23 f22 b22 What had before been pretty standard stuff has upped the complexity by an impressive distance. 40%. Diageo.

Hankey Bannister **(84.5)** n20.5 t22 f21 b21. Lots of early life and even a malt kick early on. Toffee later. 40%. Inverhouse Distillers.

Hankey Bannister 12 Years Old **(86.5)** n22 t21.5 f21 b22. A much improved blend with a nose and early delivery which makes full play of the blending company's Speyside malts. Plenty of toffee on the finish. 40%. Inverhouse Distillers.

Hankey Bannister 21 Years Old **(95)** n23.5 a fruity ensemble, clean, vibrant and loath to show its age **t24** as juicy as the nose suggests, except for the odd rumble of distant smoke; a firm, barley-sugar hardness as the grains keep control; **f23.5** the arrival of the oak adds further weight and for the first time begins to behave like a 21-y-o; long, now with decent spice and with some crusty dryness at the very death; **b24** with top dressing like this and some obviously complex secondary malts, too, how can it fail? 43%.

Hankey Bannister 25 Years Old **(91)** n22.5 t24 f21.5 b23 Follows on in style and quality to 21-year-old. Gorgeous. 40%

Hankey Bannister 40 Years Old **(89)** n22 t23 f22 b22. This blend has been put together to mark the 250th anniversary of the forging of the business relations between Messrs. Hankey and Bannister. And although the oak creaks like a ship of its day, there is enough verve and viscosity to ensure a rather delicious toast to the gentlemen. Love it! 44%. Inverhouse.

Hankey Bannister 40 Year Old **(94)** n23.5 t23.5 f23 b24. Pure quality. The attention to detail is sublime. 44.3%. Inverhouse Distillers.

Hankey Bannister Heritage Blend (92) n23 despite the evidence of sherry the spiced chocolate fudge keeps you spellbound; t24 at moments like this, one's taste buds are purely in love. They are being caressed, serenaded and kisses by the most glorious of old grains, encrusted with a Speyside-syle maltiness which makes you purr with pleasure; f22 the weakness on the nose returns, though sparingly. Outstanding late Malteser candy style confirms a very decent malt depth; b23 just so soft and sensual... 46%. Inverhouse Distillers.

Harveys Lewes Blend Eight Year Old batch 4 (93) n23.5 t23 f23 b23.5 First tasted this in the front parlour of legendary Harvey's brewer Miles Jenner's home just after Christmas. It tasted quite different from their previous bottlings – and quite superb. Nosed and tasted now several months on in the cold analytical light of a tasting room...helped along with that deft addition of subtle peat, it still does. Superb! 40%

Hazelwood 18 Year Old (88) n23.5 top-notch dispersal of subtle notes: walnut cream cake with a pinch of vanilla. The malt is low key but distinctly Speyside-style in its clarity, despite the odd wisp of something a little heavier; t22.5 creamy-textured. Soft ulmo honey gives way to the thickening vanilla and toffee; f20.5 bitters slightly at the turned-up ending; b22 until the final furry moments, a genuine little, understated, charmer. 40%. William Grant & Sons.

Hazelwood 21 Year Old (74) n19 t20 f17 b18. Some decent acacia honey tries to battle against the bitter imbalance. 40%. William Grant & Sons.

Hazelwood 25 Year Old (89.5) n22 full on fruit underscored by the muscular tannins: simple, but satisfying; t23 wonderful delivery: a momentous mix of muscovado and maple syrup but with the toasty tannins offering an even more roasty depth; f22 a slight, non-spiced buzz to the finish. But that roastiness – akin to burnt fudge – gives much to chew over; b22.5 distinctly chunky. 40%. William Grant & Sons.

High Commissioner (88.5) n22.5 t22.5 f20.5 b22.5 Now I admit I had a hand in cleaning this brand up a couple of years back, giving it a good polish and much needed balance complexity. But I don't remember leaving it in quite this good a shape. Just a bitter semi-off note on the finish, otherwise this guy would have been in the 90s. What a great fun, three-course dram this is... 40%. Loch Lomond Distillers.

⟳ **High Commissioner** bott code L2/305/16 (87.5) n21.5 t22.5 f21.5 b22 Boasts an unusually well balanced disposition for a young blend, not at all cowered into being a one trick caramelled pony. Instead, we are treated to a fulsome array of huskier and duskier notes, especially the molasses mixing with a hint of phenol. Delicious. 40%. Loch Lomond Group.

Highland Baron (85.5) n21 t22 f21 b21.5. A very clean, sweet and competent young blend showing admirable weight and depth. 40%. Loch Lomond Distillers.

Highland Baron (88.5) n22 trace smoke works beautifully with the sweet and lithe grain; t22.5 outstanding mouth feel: chewy and sweet but always within the realms of balance and god taste. A little chocolate and honey arrives with that hint of smoke; f22 silky, lightly spiced, vaguely smoked, molassed mocha; b22 has seriously upped the smoke and honey ratio in recent years. Deserves its Baronetcy. 40%. Lombard Scotch Whisky Ltd. ⊙ ⊙

Highland Bird (77) n19 t19 f19 b20. I've has a few of these over the years, I admit. But I can't remember one quite as rough and ready as this... 40%. Quality Spirits International.

⟳ **Highland Bird** bott code L9Z 6253 2302 (83.5) n21 t21 f20.5 b21 I've had a few of these over the years, I can tell you. Glasses of this whisky, as well. As for the blend, this is by far and away the cleanest, enjoyable and most well-balanced yet: a dram on the up. 40%. Quality Spirits International.

Highland Harvest Organic Scotch Whisky (76) n18 t21 f19 b18. A very interesting blend. Great try, but a little bit of a lost opportunity here as I don't think the balance is quite right. But at least I now know what organic caramel tastes like... 40%

Highland Mist (88.5) n20.5 t23 f22.5 b22.5 Fabulously fun whisky bursting from the bottle with character and mischief. Had to admit, broke all my own rules and just had to have a glass of this after doing the notes... 40%. Loch Lomond Distillers.

Highland Piper (79) n20 t20 f19 b20. Good quaffing blend – if sweet - of sticky toffee and dates. Some gin on the nose – and finish. 40%

Highland Pride (86) n21 t22 f21.5 b21.5. A beefy, weighty thick dram with plenty to chew on. The developing sweetness is a joy. 40%. Whyte & Mackay Distillers Ltd.

Highland Queen Blended Scotch Whisky (86.5) n22 t21 f21.5 b22. Lots of grains at play here. But what grains?! Clean and crisp with a superb bite which balances the softening mouth feel attractively. Old fashioned and delicious. 40%

⟳ **Highland Queen** bott code L12 356 (87) n22.5 t22.5 f20.5 b21.5 If the caramels on this could be reduced slightly what a brilliant blend we'd have on our hands here. As it is, the nose is a hotbed of complex intrigue with earthier and lighter honeyed notes combining sublimely while the delivery allows the sugars, vanillas and spices room to make their cases. Bar the spices, just all dies off a little too soon. 40%. Tullibardine Ltd.

⟐ **Highland Queen Aged 8 Years** bott code L15 071 **(89.5) n23** beautifully rich and rounded in its time-honoured way, though less fruit now (though some boiled apples remain) and more honeyed; **t22.5** gloriously succulent with its chewability going off the scale; muscovado sugars and spices force the agenda in the mid ground; **f21.5** despite a caramel onslaught the spices win by a distance; **b22.5** a classy blend showing great character and entertainment value. 40%. Tullibardine Ltd.

Highland Queen Aged 12 Years Blended Scotch Whisky (87) n22 t22 f21 b22. A polite, slightly more sophisticated version of the 8-year-old...but without the passion and drama! 40%

⟐ **Highland Queen Aged 12 Years** bott code L15 071 **(90) n23** delicious gooseberry tart with an earthy, tannin undertone; **t22.5** golden syrup majors on delivery, then a slow spreading of a vaguely phenolic but distinctly spicy vanilla theme; **f22** caramel and spice: simple but wonderfully effective; **b22.5** a much weightier blend than it used to be, displaying excellent pace of flavour development on the palate. Decent stuff! 40%. Tullibardine Ltd.

⟐ **Highland Queen Sherry Cask Finish** bott code L16 201 **(81.5) n19 t22 f19 b21.5** The sherry isn't exactly free from sin, and the grape easily overpowers the nuances of the blend itself. So, attractive to a degree, but... 40%. Tullibardine Ltd.

⟐ **Highland Queen 1561** bott code L16/80 28.01.16 **(94) n23.5** just so elegant and demur: the malt is grassy, clean and crisp enough to crack is sniffed too hard. The vanillas reveal a very respectful degree of tannin from the oak, encapsulated by muscovado sugars and marzipan; other notes are salty, green, young and flighty...; **t23.5** salivating delivery but, like the nose, in a measured non-forceful way. Again the maltiness is apparent even with a gristy flourish – but the vanillas are not too far behind; **f23** soft, sensual with a controlled, slightly citrussy sweetness; **b24**. As it happens, I have a home where on a living room wall is an old oil painting of Fotheringhay, where the life of Mary Queen of Scots, the Highland Queen, ended on an executioners' block in 1561. Indeed, the house is quite close by and sits near the River Nene which passes through Fotheringhay. The village itself is quiet, particularly fragrant during Spring and Summer and with an unmistakable feel of history and elegance. Not at all unlike this excellent and most distinguished blend. 40%. Tullibardine Ltd.

⟐ **Highland Queen 1561 30 Years Old** bott code LF13017261 261 **(88.5) n23.5** the trick of an ancient blend is that you want it to show its age as a Victorian beauty might show her ankle: in a subtle, teasing and arousing way... The nose has pulled it off brilliantly, even if there is a hint of the dreaded S word to be caught on the fruit...; **t23.5** perfect weight and sugary sheen to the delivery; the caramels and fruits are just about neck and neck in influence; the muscovado sugars are bright and crunchy; **f19.5** becomes just a little too furry and tangy...; **b22** shame about the finish. Until then we had one of the sweetest yet gentle blends of the year. 40%. Tullibardine Ltd.

⟐ **Highland Queen Majesty Classic** bott code L14/8634 09.08.14 **(92) n24** just love it! Toffee apple and freshly baked apple tart shews the central character in no small way; delicate, balancing smoke plays peek and boo...; **t23** usual silky delivery: clean and earthy malt can both be detected within a moment of hitting the palate; salivating, sharp at times but a fat caramel note begins to take hold; **f22** a lightly spiced, even delicately smoked, toffee chew; **b23** the brilliant nose isn't quite matched by the pragmatism of the overall taste experience but a blend to savour nonetheless. 40%. Tullibardine Ltd.

⟐ **Highland Queen Majesty Aged 12 Years** bott code L15/8538 19/08/15 **(86.5) n22 t22 f21 b21.5** A pleasant but lazy blend considering its age. Lots of explosive malt on delivery, some with a lemon sherbet fizz. But a heavy dependence on caramel quietens the party, though a late spice surge gate-crashes to welcome effect. 40%. Tullibardine Ltd.

⟐ **Highland Queen Majesty Aged 16 Years** bott code L15/8265 06 07 15 **(88) n22.5** the house style of lemon sherbet is in full fizz...; **t22.5** salivating, malty delivery with oaky reinforcements soon arriving; **f21.5** caramel wafers and vanilla ice cream make for a simplistic finale; **b22** enjoyable, yet leaves you with a feeling that it could have offered a little bit more. 40%. Tullibardine Ltd.

Highland Reserve (80) n19 t21.5 f19.5 b20 See tasting notes for 43% below. 40%. Quality Spirits International. ☺ ☺

⟐ **Highland Reserve** bott code B154 **(80) n19 t21.5 f19.5 b20** An easy quaffing, silky and profoundly grained, toffee-enriched blend. 43%. Quality Spirits International.

Highland Warriors (82) n20 t21 f20.5 b20.5 This warrior must be wanting to raid a few grain stores... 40%. Quality Spirits International. ☺ ☺

The Highland Way (82.5) n20 t21 f21 b20.5 Grainy, with a big sweet toffee middle which makes for a slightly juicy dram of a class barely distinguishable from so many other standard blends. 40%. Quality Spirits International. ⊙ ⊙

⟫ **The Highland Way** bott code B445 (83.5) n20 t21.5 f21 b21 More Milky Way than Highland Way... Very similar to the 40% version, except some extra milk chocolate at the finish. 43%. Quality Spirits International.

⟫ **Islay Mist Aged 8 Years Amontillado Napoleon Cask Finish** bott code L16/8826 (76) n19 t20 f18 b19 For those of you not carrying the sulphur recognition gene, I suspect this will be a delight. For those of us that do, well sorry: but not tonight, Napoleon. And this sulphur is a bit of a carry on, MacDuff... 43%. MacDuff International Ltd.

⟫ **Islay Mist Aged 8 Years Manzanilla La Gitana Cask Finish** bott code L15/8293 (85) n21.5 t22 f20 b21.5 Lots of phenolic cough sweet properties but the fruit and smoke form a tight, enclosed union with little room for scope. The finish is a rather too bitter. 40%. MacDuff International Ltd.

⟫ **Islay Mist Aged 12 Years** bott code L16/8089 (86) n22.5 t22 f20.5 b21 Slightly on the disappointing side by Islay Mist's high standards. The nose, with its smoked toffee apple, promises a playful complexity. But an overdose of dull caramel snuffs out any chance of that. 40%. MacDuff International Ltd.

⟫ **Islay Mist Aged 17 Years** bott code L15/8826 (96) n24 floral and fruity, there is a delicate peaty earthiness in which both characteristics can flourish. Salty liquorice, sawdust and a dozy nuttiness helps complete one of the most relaxed noses on the market; t24 sumptuous mouth feel with both ulmo and orange blossom honey sharing the driving seat before, almost imperceptibly, the smoke begins leeching out from the juicy barley and spicier vanillas; f23.5 long, with the return to a muscovado sugar sweetness taking place in almost slow motion. The phenols have now gathered enough ammunition to pulse out a wonderful spice tatto...; b24.5 a truly brilliant blend that should have no water added and be spared as much time as you can afford. 40%. MacDuff International Ltd.

⟫ **Islay Mist Deluxe** bott code L16/8283 (87) n22 t22 f21.5 b21.5 A charmingly brazen blend, offering young peat to you with far less reserve than it once did. More an Islay Fog than Mist... 40%. MacDuff International Ltd.

⟫ **Islay Mist Peated Reserve** bott code L15 9:67 (92.5) n23.5 that there is a substantial peat presence there is no doubt. The fact you have to work to find it makes for an intriguing introduction. A hint of toffee raisin ensures good weight even before the phenols begin to seep through with their salt buttered kipper depth; t23 excellent grain use: just enough silkiness to give the smoke extra roundness but not enough in which it can get lost. Molasses and liquorice offer a slight bourbon feel for a moment or two before the salty peat is restored; f22.5 long, quiet, clean and still the smoke gently keeping everything grounded; b23.5 the accent is on subtlety and balance: a very classy piece of whisky engineering. 40%. MacDuff International Ltd.

Isle of Skye 8 Years Old (94) n23 t24 f23.5 b23.5. Where once peat ruled and with its grain ally formed a smoky iron fist, now honey and subtlety reigns. A change of character and pace which may disappoint gung-ho peat freaks but will intrigue and delight those looking for a more sophisticated dram. 40%. Ian Macleod.

Isle of Skye 21 years Old (91) n21 t23.5 f23 b23.5 What an absolute charmer! The malt content appears pretty high, but the overall balance is wonderful. 40%. Ian Macleod.

Isle of Skye 50 Years Old (82.5) n21.5 t21 f20 b20. Drier incarnation than the 50% version. But still the age has yet to be balanced out, towards the end in particular. Early on some distinguished moments involving something vaguely smoked and a sweetened spice. 41.6%

The Jacobite (78.5) n18 t18.5 f22 b20. Neither the nose or delivery are of the cleanest style. But comes into its own towards the finish when the thick soup of a whisky thins to allow an attractive degree of complexity. Not for those with catholic tastes. 40%. Booker.

James Alexander (85.5) n21 t21.5 f21.5 b21.5. Some lovely spices link the grassier Speysiders to the earthier elements. 40%. Quality Spirits International.

James King (81) n20 t19.5 f21 b20.5 A slightly more well balanced and equally weighted blend than it once was with better use of spice and cocoa. 43%. Quality Spirits International. ⊙ ⊙

James King Aged 5 Years (84) n19.5 t21 f21.5 b21.5 While the nose never quite gets going, things are quite different on the palate. And if you find a more agreeable chocolate fudge blend this year, please let me know. 43%. Quality Spirits International. ⊙ ⊙

James King Aged 8 Years (86) n21 t21 f22 b22 A far better constructed blend than of old, with the grains far more able to deal with the demands of the caramel. Fresh and salivating early on, despite the lushness, one can even fancy spotting the odd malt note before the spiced fudge takes command. 43%. Quality Spirits International. ⊙ ⊙

James King 12 Years Old (81) n19 t23 f19 b20. Caramel dulls the nose and finish. But for some time a quite beautiful blend soars about the taste buds offering exemplary complexity and weight. 40%. *Quality Spirits International.*

⊰⊱ **James King Aged 12 Years** bott code B289 (84.5) n21 t22 f20.5 b21 The malt has a far grander say than the 40% version, chipping in with an elementary Speyside note on both nose and delivery. It doesn't take long for the fudge-rich grain to take command, though. Easy, un-taxing whisky. 43%. *Quality Spirits International.*

J&B Jet (79.5) n19 t20 f20.5 b20. Never quite gets off the ground due to carrying too heavy a load. Unrecognisable to its pomp in the old J&B days: this one is far too weighty and never properly finds either balance or thrust. 40%. *Diageo.*

J&B Reserve Aged 15 Years (78) n23 t19 f18 b18. What a crying shame. The sophisticated and demure nose is just so wonderfully seductive but what follows is an open-eyed, passionless embrace. Coarsely grain-dominant and unbalanced, this is frustrating beyond words and not worthy to be mentioned in the same breath as the old, original J&B 15 which, by vivid contrast, was a malty, salivating fruit-fest and minor classic. 40%. *Diageo.*

J&B Rare (88.5) n21.5 t22.5 f22 b22.5 I have been drinking a lot of J&B from a previous time of late, due to the death of their former blender Jim Milne. I think he would have been pretty taken aback by the youthful zip offered here: whether it is down to a decrease in age or the use of slightly more tired casks – or both – is hard to say. 40%. *Diageo.*

Johnnie Walker Black Label 12 Years Old (95.5) n23.5 pretty sharp grain: hard and buffeting the nose; a buffer of yielding smoke, apple pie and delicate spice cushions the encounter; t24.5 if there is a silkier delivery on the market today, I have not seen it: this is sublime stuff with the grains singing the sweetest hymns as they go down, taking with them a near perfection of weighty smoke lightened by brilliantly balanced barley which leans towards both soft apple and crème broulee; f23.5 those reassuringly rigid grains re-emerge and with them the most juicy Speysidey malts imaginable; the lovely sheen to the finish underlines the good age of the whiskies used; b24 here it is: one of the world's most masterful whiskies back in all its complex glory. A bottle like this is like being visited by an old lover. It just warms the heart and excites. 40%. *Diageo.*

⊰⊱ **Johnnie Walker Blenders' Batch Bourbon Cask & Rye Finish** bott code L7219CA002 00034598 (89.5) n21.5 untaxing and even with emphasis on the caramel; t23 now comes alive on the palate with a sharp flourish of lively oak and vaguest of spice; this has hefty weight both from the caramels and the stodgy malt which balance well with the silky grains. Subtle orange blossom honey before much heftier chocolate fudge; f22.5 long, with the spices upped slightly; dry vanilla on the fade; b22.5 great to see someone have the good sense to try to make the most of rye. If they can tame the caramels the results will be better still. 40%. *Diageo.*

Johnnie Walker Blue Label (88) n21 t24 f21 b22 What a frustrating blend! Just so close to brilliance but the nose and finish are slightly out of kilter. Worth the experience of the mouth arrival alone. 43%. *Diageo.*

Johnnie Walker Blue Label The Casks Edition (97) n24.5 t24.5 f23.5 b24.5. This is a triumph of scotch whisky blending. With not as much as a hint of a single off note to be traced from the tip of the nose to tail, this shameless exhibition of complexity and brilliance is the star turn in the Diageo portfolio right now. Indeed, it is the type of blend that every person who genuinely adores whisky must experience for the good of their soul....if only once in their life. 55.8%.

Johnnie Walker Double Black (94.5) n23 t23.5 f24 b24. Double tops! Rolling along the taste buds like distant thunder, this is a welcome and impressive addition to the Johnnie Walker stable. Perhaps not as complete and rounded as the original Johnnie Walker Black...but, then, what is? 40%.

Johnnie Walker Explorers' Club Collection The Gold Route (89) n23.5 t24 f19.5 b22. Much of this blend is truly the stuff of golden dreams. Like its Explorer's Club stable mate, some attention has to be paid to the disappointing finish. Worth sending out an expedition, though, just for the beautiful nose and delivery... 40%. *Diageo.*

Johnnie Walker Explorer's Club Collection 'The Royal Route' (93) n24.5 t24 f21.5 b23 A fabulous journey, travelling first Class most of the way. But to have discovered more, could have been bottled at 46% for a much more panoramic view of the great whiskies on show. 40%. *Diageo*

Johnnie Walker Explorers' Club Collection The Spice Road (84.5) n22 t23.5 f18 b21. Sublime delivery of exceptionally intense juiciness: in fact, probably the juiciest blend released this year. But the bitter, fuzzy finish reveals certain casks haven't helped. 40%.

Johnnie Walker Gold Label Reserve (91.5) n23 t24 f22 b23. Moments of true star quality here, but the finish could do with a polish. 40%. *Diageo.*

Johnnie Walker King George V db (88) n23 t22 f21 b22 One assumes that King George V is no relation to George IV. This has genuine style and breeding, if a tad too much caramel. 43%

Johnnie Walker Platinum Label Aged 18 Years (88) n22 t23 f21 b22. This blend might sound like some kind of Airmiles card. Which wouldn't be too inappropriate, though this is more Business than First... 40%. Diageo.

Johnnie Walker Red Label (87.5) n22 t22 f21.5 b22. The ongoing move through the scales quality-wise appears to suggest we have a work still in progress here. This sample has skimped on the smoke, though not quality. Yet a few months back when I was in the BA Business Lounge at Heathrow's new Terminal Five, I nearly keeled from almost being overcome by peat in the earliest JW Red I had tasted in decades. I found another bottle and I'm still not sure which represents the real Striding Man. 40%. Diageo.

Johnnie Walker Select Casks Aged 10 Years Rye Cask Finish (90) n22.5 t23 f21.5 b23 With the use of first fill bourbon casks and ex-rye barrels for finishing, hardly surprising this is the Johnnie Walker with the most Kentuckian feel of them all. Yet it's even more Canadian, still. 46% (92 Proof)

Johnnie Walker X.R Aged 21 Years (94) n23.5 t24 f23 b23.5. How weird: I nosed this blind before seeing what the brand was. My first thought was: "mmm, same structure of Crown Royal XR. Canadian??? No, there's smoke!" Then looked at what was before me and spotted it was its sister whisky from the Johnnie Walker stable. A coincidence? I don't think so... 40%.

John Walker & Sons Private Collection 2014 Edition (90) n23.5 t23.5 f21 b22 Delicious and frustrating in equal measure. 46.8%

John Walker & Sons Private Collection 2015 Edition (95.5) n24 t24 f23.5 b24 Possibly one less than perfect cask away from World Whisky of the Year... 46.8%

Kenmore Special Reserve Aged 5 Years bott code L07285 (75) n18 t20 f19 b18. Recovers to a degree from the poor nose. A must-have for those who prefer their Scotch big-flavoured and gawky. 40%

⬦ **King Charles** (82) n21 t21 f20 b20 From the salty, sweaty armpit nose (which I know some people absolutely love in a whisky!) to the OTT sugar attack before the bitter finish, this isn't quite one for the purists. Hard to imagine a grain any more soft and enveloping. 40%. Quality Spirits International.

King Glenorsen (81) n20 t21 f20 b20. Pleasant and easy drinking enough. But the young grains dominate completely. Designed, I think, to be neutralised by ice. 40%

King Robert II (77) n19 t19 f20 b19. A bustier, more bruising batch than the last 40 per cent version. Handles the OTT caramel much better. Agreeably weighty slugging whisky. 43%.

⬦ **Label 5 Aged 12 Years** bott code L515467C (90) n23 a lively nose, full of kumquat, raspberry cream Swiss Roll and deft smoke; clean for a blend these days and with the precision of an Exocet; t22.5 the vanillas wallow in the icing sugar for a while before the vanillas at last appear; f22 just a little tang, but still soft and sweet; the smoke arrives, thin and apologetically at the very end, though the late spice is much bolder; b22.5 one of the easiest drams you'll find this year with just enough complexity to lift it into the higher echelons. 40%. La Martiniquaise.

⬦ **Label 5 Extra Rare Aged 18 Years** bott code L5301576 (87.5) n21.5 t22.5 f22 b21.5 You have to say this is pleasant. But from an 18-year-old blend you should be saying so much more. Salivating and at times fresh and juicy, other than the late spice little gets the pulses racing in the vanilla and sugar morass. A tad too much toffee, alas. 40%. La Martiniquaise.

⬦ **Label 5 Classic Black** bott code L403055D (87) n22 t22 f21 b22 A malt famed for its indifferent nose now boasts an aroma boasting complexity, layering and spice. The mix of spice and muscovado sugars elsewhere is no less appealing, though the mouth feel is a little too fat and yielding. But what an improvement! 40%. La Martiniquaise.

Label 5 Gold Heritage (92) n22.5 t23.5 f22 b24 A very classy blend very skilfully constructed. A stunningly lovely texture, one of the very best I have encountered for a while, and no shortage of complexity ensures this is a rather special blend. I'll even forgive the dulling by caramel and light milkiness from the tired bourbon barrel. The overall excellence outweighs the odd blemish. 40%

Lang's Supreme Aged 5 Years (93.5) n23.5 t23.5 f23 b23.5. Every time I taste this the shape and structure has altered slightly. Here there is a fraction more smoke, installing a deeper confidence all round. This is blended whisky as it should be: Supreme in its ability to create shape and harmony. 40%. Ian Macleod Distillers Ltd.

The Last Drop 1965 American Standard Barrel (96.5) n24 t24.5 f23.5 b24.5 Almost impossible to imagine a blended whisky to be better balanced than this. If there is a cleverer use of honey or less intrusive oak in any blended whisky bottled in the last year, I have yet to taste it. An award winner if ever I tasted one. Magnificent doesn't quite cover it... 48.6%. Morrison Bowmore. The Last Drop Distillers Ltd.

The Last Drop 1971 Blended Scotch Whisky 45 Years Old (97) n24.5 t24 f24 b24.5 Even though I now know many of the people involved in the Last Drop, I am still not entirely sure how they keep doing it. Just how do they continue to unearth whiskies which are truly staggering; absolute marvels of their type? This one is astonishing because the grain used is just about faultless. And the peating levels can be found around about the perfect mark on the dial. Like an old Ballentine's which has sat and waited in a cask over four decades to be discovered and tell its wonderful, spellbinding and never-ending tale. Just mesmerically beautiful. 47%.

The Last Drop 50 Year Old Sherry Wood (97) n24 t24.5 f24 b24.5 You'd expect, after half a century in the cask, that this would be a quiet dram, just enjoying its final years with its feet up and arms behind its head. Instead we have a fairly aggressive blend determined to drive the abundant fruitiness it still possesses to the very hilt. It is backed up all the way by a surprising degree of warming, busy spice. There is a hell of a lot of life in this beautiful ol' dog... 51.2%

Lauder's (74) n18 t21 f17 b18. Well, it's consistent: you can say that for it! As usual, fabulous delivery, but as for the rest...oh dear. 40%. MacDuff International Ltd.

◈ **Lauder's** bott code L 08 10 14 4 BB (78.5) n19 t20 f19.5 b20 For those who like whisky with their cream toffee. Decent spice fizz, though. 40%. MacDuff International Ltd.

◈ **Lauder's Aged 15 Years** bott code L16/8189 (93) n23 hints of grape and sharper pear drop sink into a soft, grainy morass; t23.5 beautifully salivating delivery: thick, with structured fruit rather than the overbearing grape I was expecting; the mid-ground celebrates a wonderfully marriage between over-ripe pear and light spice; molasses and toasty fudge; f22.5 date, walnut, more fudge and molasses then, finally, a spiced butterscotch fade...; b24 not the big fat sherry influence of a decade ago...thank heavens...!! This is a gorgeous blend for dark, stormy nights. Well, any night really... 40%. MacDuff International Ltd.

◈ **Lauder's Oloroso Cask** bott code L 25 01 16 4 BB (86.5) n21.5 t24 f19 b22 A magnificent blend for those unable to nose or taste sulphur. For those who can, a nearly whisky as this is borderline brilliant. Yes, both nose and finish especially have their weakness, but the narrative of the delivery, not to mention the brilliance of the mouth feel and overall weight and pace of the dram is sublime. Before the sulphur hits we are treated to a truly glorious Jaffa cake mix of controlled fruity sweetness as good as any blend I have tasted this year. 40%. MacDuff International Ltd.

◈ **Lauder's Ruby Cask** bott code L 21 05 15 4 BB (94) n23 excellent spice prickle and oak layering; the clean fruit gives everything a polish; t24 mmmm! That is one outstanding mouth feel on the delivery: there is a sheen to the sharp Port-generated fruit plus a generous – though not too generous – sprinkling of muscovado sugar; a little ulmo honey thickens the middle. The trade-off between the crisp, crunchy fruit and sugars and the softer grains is sublime; f23 the spices are on slow burn but when they arrive they complement the oak perfectly; b24 a sophisticated little gem. 40%. MacDuff International Ltd.

◈ **Lauder's Queen Mary** bott code L 04 11 14 4 BB (86.5) n22.5 t21.5 f21 b21.5 The sweet oily aroma of Angel Cake and even some roast chestnut: the nose is certainly highly attractive. This almost translates through the body of blend when the caramel allows, the grains showing an oily strain and a slightly malty kick here and there. 40%. MacDuff International Ltd.

The Loch Fyne (89.5) n22 t23 f21.5 b23. This is an adorable old-style blend....a bit of a throwback. But no ruinous sherry notes...just clean and delicious. Well, mainly... 40%

Loch Lomond Blended Scotch (89) n22 t22.5 f22 b22.5 A fabulously improved blend: clean and precise and though malt is seemingly at a premium, a fine interplay. 40%

Loch Lomond Reserve db (86.5) n21.5 t22 f21.5 b21.5. A spongy, sweet, chewy, pleasant blend which is more of a take as you find statement than a layering of flavours. 40%

◈ **Loch Lomond Signature** bott code L3/306/15 (86) n22 t21.5 f21 b21.5 Not quite the malty force it can be, though the sugar almonds are a treat. Succulent and gently spiced though the caramel has just a little too much force towards the end. 40%. Loch Lomond Group.

Lochranza (83.5) n21 t21.5 f21 b20. Pleasant, clean, but, thanks to the caramel, goes easy on the complexity. 40%. Isle of Arran.

Logan (78.5) n19 t19 f20 b19.5. Entirely drinkable but a bit heavy-handed with the grains and caramel. 40%. Diageo.

Lombard Gold Label (88) n22 t22 f22 b22 after evaluating this I read the tasting notes on the back of the label and for about the first time this year thought: "actually, the bottlers have the description pretty spot on. So tasted it again, this time while reading the notes and found myself agreeing with every word: a first. Then I discovered why: they are my tasting notes from the 2007 Whisky Bible, though neither my name or book have been credited... A gold label, indeed... 40%. *Lombard Scotch Whisky Ltd.* ⊙

Lord Elcho (83.5) n20 t22 f21 b20.5 Such a vast improvement on the last bottling I encountered: this has lush grain at the front, middle and rear that entertains throughout, if a little one dimensionally. A little bit of a tweak and could be a high class blend. 40%. *Wemyss Malts.* ⊙ ⊙

Lord Elcho Aged 15 Years (89.5) n23.5 quite beautiful: toffee apple and a dusting of citrus and pineapple; t22.5 salivating and clean with the malts having an early gristy say before a little toffee moves into the equation; f21.5 spices up late on, but an otherwise disappointingly dull finale considering the brilliant start; b22 three or four years ago this was a 15-year-old version of the Lord Elcho standard blend today. So, small mercies, this has moved on somewhat and now offers up a genuinely charming and complex nose and delivery. One is therefore surprised to be disappointed by the denouement, taking into account the blend's history. Some more clever and attentive work on the middle and finish would have moved this into seriously high quality blend territory. But so much to enjoy as it is. 40%. *Wemyss Malts.* ⊙ ⊙

Lord Scot (77.5) n18.5 t20 f19.5 b19.5. A touch cloying but the mocha fudge ensures a friendly enough ride. 40%. *Loch Lomond Distillers.*

Lord Scot (86.5) n20 t22 f22.5 b22. A gorgeously lush honey and liquorice middle. 43%

The Lost Distilleries batch 2 (94) n22.5 t24 f23.5 b24. Whoever lost it better find it again: this is how you dream every whisky should be. 53.2%.

The Lost Distilleries Blend Batch 6 (91) n23.5 t23 f22 b22.5 The Lost Malt as well: completely grain dominant – but wonderfully lush and tasty. 49.3%

◇ **The Lost Distilleries Blend** batch 9 (91) n23 simplistic, gentle schmoozing of light citrus tones with more upfront vanilla; the grain has the bigger say; t23.5 big sugar blast on delivery – eyewateringly intense. Soft mocha and maltesers amble through the middle; f22.5 recedes back to a simple vanilla tale, though there is a a little tang, too; b23 the distilleries may be lost to us, but on the palate they are especially at home. 52.1%. 476 bottles.

Mac Na Mara (83) n20 t22.5 f20 b20.5. Absolutely brimming with salty, fruity character. But just a little more toffee and furriness than it needs. Enjoyable, though. 40%

◇ **Mac Na Mara** bott code L 25 08 14 2 07 48 BB (84) n21.5 t22 f19.5 b21 As usual, a glass of tricks as the flavours come tumbling at you from every direction. Few blends come saltier and the dry vanilla forges a fascinating balance with the rampant caramel. A fraction furry at the death. 40%. *Pràban na Linne Ltd.*

Mac Na Mara Rum Finish (93) n22 t24 f23 b24 High quality blending, and the usage of the rum appears to have retained the old Mac Na Mara style. 40%. *Praban na Linne.*

◇ **Mac Na Mara Rum Cask Finish** bott code L 23 05 16 3 BB (86) n22.5 t22 f21 b21.5 Lost a degree of the sugary crispness normally associated with this brand and after the initial rum embrace resorts far too quickly to a caramel-rich game-plan. 40%. *ncf. Pràban na Linne Ltd.*

◇ **MacArthur's** bott code L16/L31 R16/5192 IB 1735 (87.5) n21.5 t22 f21.5 b22.5 Not quite the tricky and cleverly smoked blend of a few years back. But still a weightier chap than a decade ago, not least because of the softer grain type. The malts do come through with just enough meaning to make for a well-balanced and thoroughly enjoyable offering. 40%. *International Beverage Holdings Ltd.*

MacQueens (89) n21.5 t22.5 f22.5 b22.5. I am long enough in the tooth now to remember blends like this found in quiet country hotels in the furthest-flung reaches of the Highlands beyond a generation ago. A wonderfully old-fashioned, traditional one might say, blend of a type that is getting harder and harder to find. 40%. *Quality Spirits International.*

◇ **MacQueens of Scotland Aged 3 Years** (86) n20.5 t22 f21.5 b22 Rare to find a blend revealing its age at 3 years, though of course many are that.... and a day. Enjoyable, with attractive weight and even an ulmo honey note to partner the spices which, combined, makes it distinctively a cut above for its type. 40%. *Quality Spirits International.*

◇ **MacQueens of Scotland Aged 8 Years** (78.5) n18 t21.5 f19 b20 A little furry and off key. 40%. *Quality Spirits International.*

◇ **MacQueens of Scotland Aged 12 Years** (89.5) n23 certain exotic fruit notes suggest a usage of malts older than 12. Lots of marzipan and vanilla abound as well as a light kumquat note; t22.5 silky delivery with a slow procession of drier vanillas bolstered by muscovado sugars and spice; the spices grow in confidence and effect; f21.5 soft, though the caramel has too great a say; b22.5 some outstanding malts have gone into this charming blend. 40%. *Quality Spirits International.*

Master of Malt Blended 10 Years Old 1st Edition (84.5) n21.5 t22.5 f20 b20.5. A pleasant enough, though hardly complex, blend benefitting from the lovely malty, then silky pick-up from delivery and a brief juicy barley sharpness. But unsettled elsewhere due, mainly, to using the wrong fit of grain: too firm when a little give was needed. 47.5%. ncf. WB15/353

◈ **Master of Malt 30 Year Old Blended Scotch Whisky** (86) n21.5 t23 f20 b21.5 Typical of Master of Malt blends it is the delivery which hits fever pitch in which myriad juicy notes make a mockery of the great age. Sadly, on this occasion both the nose and finish are undone by some ungainly oak interference and, latterly quite a tang. 47.5%.

◈ **Master of Malt 40 Year Old Blended Scotch Whisky** batch 1 (93.5) n24 magnificent! The subtlest hint of kiwi fruit gives extra life to something so ancient: the oaky notes have a threat of spice about them but butterscotch rues; t23.5 adorable barley sugars and grist on delivery with the usual salivating effect that bring. The lower oily grain and tannin notes rumble in as an afterthought and then take command; f22.5 those spices just keep on pulsing; b23.5 some outstanding oak at play here. For a blend the grains and malts appear a little isolated from the other, but the overall effect is still wonderful. 47.5%.

◈ **Master of Malt 50 Year Old Blended Scotch Whisky** (92.5) n24 the lightness of touch here is staggering. Malt and lightly spiced vanilla and ulmo honey appear to be polished by a lychee fruitiness; the very vaguest of smoke, too; t23.5 silk, melting in the mouth along with the sweet malty grist. A succession of boiled fruit sweet, especially pear and pineapple give way slightly as a little bitterness and sawdusty dryness seeps in from the oak; f22 a bitter-sweet fade; b23 hard to keep all the casks of over 50 years in line. But so much else is sublime. 47.5%.

Master Of Malt St Isidore (84) n21 t22 f20 b21. Sweet, lightly smoked but really struggles to put together a coherent story. Something, somewhere, is not quite right. 41.4%

Matisse 12 Years Old (90.5) n23 t23 f22 b22.5 Moved up yet another notch as this brand continues its development. Much more clean-malt oriented with a Speyside-style to the fore. Majestic and charming. 40%. Matisse Spirits Co Ltd.

Matisse 21 Years Old (86) n23 t22 f20 b21. Begins breathtakingly on the nose, with a full array of exotic fruit showing the older bourbon casks up to max effect. Nothing wrong with the early delivery, which offers a touch of honeycomb on the grain. But the caramel effect on the finish stops everything in its tracks. Soft and alluring, all the same. 40%

Matisse Old (85.5) n20 t23 f21 b21.5. Appears to improve each time I come across it. The nose is a bit on the grimy side and the finish disappears under a sea of caramel. But the delivery works deliciously, with a chewy weight which highlights the sweeter malts. 40%

Matisse Royal (81) n19 t22 f20 b20. Pleasant, if a little clumsy. Extra caramel appears to have scuppered the spice. 40%. Matisse Spirits Co Ltd.

McArthurs (89.5) n22 t22.5 f22 b23 One of the most improved blends on the market. The clever use of the peat is exceptional. 40%. Inverhouse Distillers.

Monarch of the Glen (81) n20 t21 f20 b20 A youthful grainfest wallowing in its fat and sweet personality. 40%. Quality Spirits International. ☺☺

Monarch of the Glen Aged 8 Years (82.5) n19 t20.5 f21.5 b21.5 The initially harsh grain takes time to settle but eventually finds a decent fudge and spiced mocha theme. 40%. Quality Spirits International. ☺☺

Monarch of the Glen Aged 12 Years (88.5) n22 a lovely fudge note goes well with the mocha; t22.5 has kept its glorious silk texture, though the fruits have vanished. Demerara sugar and chocolate hazelnut; f22 long, soft, slow raising of spice and vanilla; b22 I always enjoyed this for its unusual fruity nature. Well, the fruit has gone and been replaced by chocolate. A fair swap: it's still delicious! 40%. Quality Spirits International. ☺

Montrose (74.5) n18 t20 f18 b18.5. A battling performance but bitter defeat in the end. 40%.

◈ **Muirhead's Blue Seal** bott code L15 138 780 21 (84.5) n21.5 t21 f21 b21 A clean, uncluttered and attractive blend with heavy emphasis on grain and no shortage of caramel and spice. A distinct wisp of malt can be located from time to time. 40%. Tullibardine Ltd.

The Naked Grouse (76.5) n19 t21 f17.5 b19. Sweet. But reveals too many ugly sulphur tattoos. 40%.

Northern Scot (68) n16 t18 f17 b17. Heading South bigtime. 40%. Bruce and Co. for Tesco.

Oishii Wisukii Aged 36 Years (96) n24.5 t23.5 f24 b24 Normally, I'd suggest popping into the Highlander for a pint of beer. But if they happen to have any of this stuff there...break his bloody arm off: it's magnificent! 46.2%. The Highlander Inn, Craigellachie.

◈ **Old Masters G** (93) n24 as this was formerly "Freemason's Whisky" the perfect nose to experience blindfolded: as the depth of the fruity muscovado sugar and grain – and their happy intermingling - is charming. Under-ripe gooseberries sits with the citrus; t23 light, graceful with a fleeting caress of delicate and salivating Speyside malt before the silkier grain and spicier oak kicks in: superbly layered; f23 long, succulent, beautifully spiced with the growing cocoa and vanilla ensuring balance; late, elegant malt clings to the finale; b23 a high quality blend with enough clarity and complexity to suggest they have not stinted on the malt. The nose, in particular, is sublime. Thankfully they have gone easy on the colouring here, as it this is so delicate it could have ruined the artistry. *40%. Lombard Scotch Whisky Ltd.*

Old McDonald (83.5) n20 t22 f20.5 b21. Attractively tart and bracing where it needs to be with lovely grain bite. Lots of toffee, though. *43.%. The Last Drop Distillers. For India.*

Old Parr 12 Years Old (91.5) n21.5 t23.5 f23 b23.5 Perhaps on about the fourth of fifth mouthful, the penny drops that this is not just exceptionally good whisky: it is blending Parr excellence... *40%. Diageo.*

Old Parr Aged 15 Years (84) n19 t22 f21 b22. Absolutely massive sherry input here. Some of it is of the highest order. The nose, reveals, however, that some isn't... *43%*

Old Parr Classic 18 Years Old (84.5) n21 t21.5 f21 b21. A real jumbled, mixed bag with fruit and barley falling over each other and the grains offering little sympathy. Enough to enjoy, but with Old Parr, one expects a little more... *46%. Diageo.*

Old Parr Superior 18 Years Old batch no. L5171 (97) n25 t25 f23 b24. Year in, year out, this blend just gets better and better. This bottling struck me as a possible Whisky of the Year, but perhaps only an outsider. Familiarity, though, bred anything but contempt and over the passing months I have tried to get to the bottom of this truly great whisky. Blended whisky has long needed a champion. This grand old man looks just the chap. This is a worthy, if unexpected (even to me), Jim Murray' Whisky Bible 2007 World Whisky of the Year. *43%.*

Old Smuggler (85.5) n21 t22 f21 b21.5. A much sharper act than its Allied days with a new honeyed-maple syrup thread which is rather delightful. Could still do with toning down the caramel, though, to brighten the picture further. *40%. Campari, France.*

Old St Andrews Clubhouse (82) n18 t22 f21 b21. Not quite the clean, bright young thing it was many years back. But great to see back in my nosing glass after such a long while and though the nose hits the rough, the delivery is as sweetly struck as you might hope for. *40%*

Passport (83) n22 t19 f21 b21. It looks as though Chivas have decided to take the blend away from its original sophisticated, Business Class J&B/Cutty Sark, style for good now, as they have continued this decently quaffable but steerage quality blend with its big caramel kick and chewy, rather than lithe, body. *40%. Chivas.*

⬧ **Passport** bott code LKBL0720 2017/02/24 (81.5) n20 t21 f20 b20.5 Still can't get used to the brash golden colour of the whisky that shines back at me. This was once the Passport to whisky sophistication: pale and glistening on the palate rather than from the bottle with its cut glass, precision flavour-profile – First Class in every way. Now it is fat, flat, chewy, and fudged in every sense of the word. *40%. Chivas Brothers Ltd.*

Parkers (78) n17 t22 f20 b19. The nose has regressed, disappearing into ever more caramel, yet the mouth-watering lushness on the palate remains and the finish now holds greater complexity and interest. *40%. Angus Dundee.*

Queen Margot (85.5) n21.5 t22 f21 b21. A clean, silky-textured, sweet and caramel-rich blend of disarming simplicity. *40%*

Queen Margot (86) n21 t22 f21.5 b21.5. A lovely blend which makes no effort to skimp on a spicy depth. Plenty of cocoa from the grain late on but no shortage of good whiskies put to work. *40%. Wallace and Young for Lidl.*

Queen Margot Aged 5 Years (89) n22 t22.5 f22 b22.5 A vey attractive blend with a most agreeable level of chewability. The chocolate orange which bolsters the yielding grain appears to suggest some good, clean sherry influence along the way. *40%*

Queen Margot Aged 8 Years (85) n21 t22 f21 b21. Pleasant, untaxing, with a hint of oaky vanilla after the sugary crescendo. *40%*

Reliance PL (76) n18 t20 f19 b19. Some of the old spiciness evident. But has flattened out noticeably. *43%. Diageo.*

Robert Burns (85) n20 t22.5 f21 b21.5. Skeletal and juicy: very little fat and gets to the mouthwatering point pretty quickly. Genuine fun. *40%. Isle of Arran.*

The Royal & Ancient (80.5) n20 t21.5 f19 b20. Has thinned out dramatically in the last year or so. Now clean, untaxing, briefly mouth-watering and radiating young grain throughout. *40%*

Royal Park (87.5) n22 t22 f22 b21.5 A significantly improved blend which though still showing toffee appears to have cut down the amount, to the advantage of the busy vanilla, Demerara sugar and increased spices. Wholly enjoyable. Incidentally, the label helpfully informs us: "Distilled and Matured in Oak Casks." Who needs stills, eh...? *40%. Quality Spirits International.* ⊙ ⊙

Royal Salute 21 Years Old (92.5) n23 t23.5 f23 b23.5 If you are looking for the velvety character of yore, forget it. This one comes with some real character and is much the better for it. The grain, in particular, excels. *40%. Chivas.*

◈ **Royal Salute 21 Years Old** bott code LKSK2858 2016/07/13 **(96) n24** a lovely, glinting degree of citrus which just seems to sparkle off the roundest grain imaginable. A little malt can, with care, be detected, adding a Speyside-style barley-biscuity spin; **t23.5** succulent, though this time the malt is detectable earlier and more easily. The silky vanillas make for a soothing backdrop, though the spices are too half-hearted to be true; a mix of gristy sugars and muscovado makes for a light sweetness; **f24** a very quiet finale with the grains again clearly leading the way. Vague spicing as the butterscotch slowly builds while the praline cannot be ignored; **b24.5** elegant, sensual and the epitome of great blending. What else would you expect...? 40%. Chivas Brothers Ltd.

◈ **Royal Salute 21 Years Old The Polo Collection** bott code 2017/04/25 LPNL0722 **(95) n23.5** wow! A very different nose to the standard RS21: much earthier, warmer and bolder with a significant degree of tannin further adding weight; **t23.5** an oilier texture than the norm helps embed the light smoke and tannins without them causing too much of a storm. The grain is slightly firmer and more prickly (actually, for anyone interested in this kind of thing this appears to have a slightly different grain structure to the standard RS21). Exceptionally chewy, again with an earthiness displayed on the nose and a bigger spice surge than usual; **f24** long, with a wonderfully clever mix of Manuka honey with rich vanilla. That telling earthiness and spice continues its journey uninterrupted...; **b24** a significantly different RS21 to the last standard bottling I came across, this being very much meatier – which is rather apt seeing that horses are involved. Mixes suave sophistication with a certain ruggedness: not unlike polo, I suppose. Not a dram to chukker away under any circumstances... 40%. Chivas Brothers Ltd.

◈ **Royal Salute 32 Years Old Union of the Crowns** bott code 2017/01/17 LPNL0102 **(96.5) n24** a glossy nose in part, a lively, slightly sharp and fruity aroma in another: beautifully weighted and intriguing; some of the lilting oak and grain notes appear significantly above the 32 years stated...; **t24.5** magnificent...just so elegant. Allow it to sit on the palate, swirl it around gently and then just swoon as it melts in the mouth, leaving the most gorgeous deposits to be savoured. The honey is a blend in itself, with ulmo and heather at the forefront then a little orange blossom arriving towards the midway mark; the spices take their time to arrive, survey what they find and slowly begin to build in intensity, but only to a point. The texture is silk, helped along by a butteryness, the cream toffee...; **f24** so long and remains elegant, eschewing the bitterness which often marks blends of this age. The spices still keep at their same pace and intensity; **b24** I trust Nicola Sturgeon has given The Union of Crowns, this truly outstanding and worthy Scotch blend to celebrate the joining the kingdoms of England, Scotland and Ireland, her seal of approval and she will help promote it fervently as a great Scottish export... 40%. Chivas Brothers Ltd.

◈ **Royal Salute 38 Years Old Stone of Destiny** bott code 2016/12/20 LPNK2479 **(93.5) n24** oozes classic, understated ancient whisky notes, the grain in particular. Two toned in being seemingly soft but look closer and you'll find a much firmer crust beneath. The vast majority the aromas are oak-led, though this has been carefully and cleverly camouflaged by the lightest layering of ulmo honey which represents the malt with distinction but light enough to allow the more delicate kumquats and barely audible spices to underscore the great age; **t23.5** there you go: the mouth feel as anticipated! So soft and delicate, the gentle sugars melting before making any great statement; this is a blend based on whispers and rumours, rather than bold speeches. Salivating thanks to both a trickle of malt and honey. The grain does all in its power not to be noticed, yet accommodate all...; **f22.5** didn't see the light bitterness coming at the death, or such late arrival of spice; **b23.5** knowing the blender and having a pretty educated guess at the range of stocks he would have to work from, I tried to picture in my mind's eye how this whisky would nose and taste even before I opened the bottle. In particular, I tried to pre-guess the mouth feel, a character vital especially in older blends but often overlooked by those who eventually taste it, though it actually plays a significant role without the drinker realising it. Well, both the nose and mouth feel were just as I had imagined, though some aspects of the finish were slightly different. An engrossing and elegant dram. 40%. Chivas Brothers Ltd.

Royal Salute 62 Gun Salute (95.5) n24.5 t24 f23 b24 How do you get a bunch of varying whiskies in style, but each obviously growing a grey beard and probably cantankerous to boot, to settle in and harmonise with the others? A kind of Old People's Home for whisky, if you like. Well, here's how...43%. Chivas.

Royal Salute The Diamond Tribute (91) n23.5 t23 f21.5 b23. Ironic that a diamond is probably the hardest natural creation, yet this whisky is one of man's softest... 40%. Chivas.

Royal Salute The Eternal Reserve (89.5) n23 t23.5 f21 b22 One of those strange whiskies where so much happens on the nose and delivery, but much less when we head to the finish 40%

Royal Silk Reserve (93) n22 t24 f24 b23 I named this the best newcomer of 2001 and it hasn't let me down. A session blend for any time of the day, this just proves that you don't need piles of peat to create a blend of genuine stature. A must have. *40%*

⚜ **Royal Silk Reserve Aged 5 Years** (92.5) n23 the rarest of blends these days in that you can feel the grain and malts working together to create a delicate mosaic of a dram, most of the parts being white background but delicate colours forming the citrus and thin maple syrup...; t23 from the nose the delivery had to be salivating...and it doesn't disappoint. The grain dominates, not with exactly the same crunchy clarity as in its earliest days, but certainly with poise enough to maximise the delicate, Speyside style malts which are grassy, fresh and disciplined in their role; f23 more vanilla and a beautifully intricate spiciness; b23.5 I was lucky enough to be the first person outside the tasting lab to sample this whisky when it was launched at the turn of this century. It was quite wonderful then, it still is so today though the grains aren't quite as brittle and translucent as they were back then. Still, I admire beyond words the fact that the current blenders have eschewed the craze for obscuration by ladelling in the colouring as though lives depended on it. What we can nose and taste here in this heart-gladdeningly light (both in colour and personality) blend is whisky. As an aside, very unusual for a blend to hide its age away on the back label. *40%*

Royal Warrior (86) n21 t22 f21.5 b21.5. An entirely pleasant grain-rich, young, old fashioned blend which masters the prevalent sugars well when they appear to be getting out of hand. Extremely clean and beautifully rounded. *40%*

Sandy Mac (76) n18 t20 f19 b19. Basic, decent blend that's chunky and raw. *40%. Diageo.*

Scots Earl (76.5) n18 t20 f19 b19.5. Its name is Earl. And it must have upset someone in a previous life. Always thrived on its engaging disharmony. But just a tad too syrupy now. *40%*.

Scottish Collie (78) n18 t20 f20 b20 I thought I heard you saying it was a pity: pity I never had any good whiskies. But you're wrong. I have. Thousands of them. Thousands of them. And all drams.... *40%. Quality Spirits International.* ☺ ☺

⚜ **Scottish Collie** (80) n20 t21 f19 b20 A greatly improved bend with a far more vivacious delivery full of surprising juiciness and attractively controlled sweetness. Not as much toffee influence as had once been the case, so the spices cancels out the harsh finish. *43%. Quality Spirits International.*

⚜ **Scottish Leader Aged 12 Years** bott code P037533 L3 09.18 16082 (89.5) n22 a blend showing some tannin early on – that's a rare treat! Gently spiced, yet soft and with an ever growing heather honey character; t23 lush but, thankfully, not cloying. As on the nose, the main theme is a fascinating, warming interplay between the honey and spices – once more the tannins are on hand to age pedigree; f22 remains silky with a more spiced butterscotch tart personality; b22.5 a vast improvement on the last Leader 12 I encountered, this really finding a relaxed yet intriguing style. *40%.*

⚜ **Scottish Leader Original** bott code P03 555 L 08.35 16342 (83) n19 t22 f21 b21 Had this been the "original" Scottish leader I tasted 20 or so years ago we'd have a lighter coloured, less caramel heavy, more malt sparkling whisky. As it is, overcomes a cramped nose to offer some excellent complexity on delivery. *40%.*

⚜ **Scottish Leader Signature** bott code P038914 L316256 (90.5) n22 unashamedly smoky aroma automatically giving a subtle weight to balance the flightier grains and gentle honeys; t23.5 the delivery is stunning! The smoke and heather- and ulmo honeys wrapped in the beautiful mid-soft grain alongside the spices to massage the taste buds with controlled firmness, just loses its spell as the caramels build up; f22 a little residual smoke on the caramel and butterscotch; b23 thoroughly enjoyable and beautifully constructed blend in which thought has clearly gone into both weight, texture and flavour profiling: not a given for blends these days. The nose and delivery are waxy with a vague honey richness; the delivery uses that honey to full effect by offering a growing firmness and then busy interplay between light oak, spices and weightier malts. Had they gone a little easier on the dumbing-down toffee, this might have bagged an award. *40%.*

⚜ **Scottish Leader Supreme** bott code P039255 L3 14.21 16278 (77) n18.5 t20 f19 b19.5 Sticky, sweet and overly simple. *40%.*

Scottish Piper (80) n20 t20 f20 b20. A light, mildly- raw, sweet blend with lovely late vanilla intonation. *40%*

⚜ **Scottish Piper** bott code L17033 (82) n20 t20 f21.5 b20.5 Continues its traditional toffee drone, though with a spicier finale than before. *40%. Burlington Drinks.*

Scottish Prince (83.5) n21 t22 f20 b20.5. Muscular, but agreeably juicy. *40%*

Sia Blended Scotch Whisky (87) n21 t22.5 f21.5 b22. Rare to find a blend that's so up front with its smoke. Doesn't scrimp on the salivation stakes or sheer chewiness, either. *43%* .

Something Special (85) n21.5 t22 f20.5 b21. Mollycoddled by toffee, any murderous tendencies seem to have been fudged away, leaving just the odd moment of attractive complexity. You suspect there is a hit man in there somewhere trying to get out. *40%. Chivas.*

⬧ **Something Special** bott code LPFK 1116 2016/06/30 (90) n22 lifted dramatically by a gentle citrus note adding to the cream toffee: a very clean but soft nose...; t22.5 gorgeously lush without going down the cloyingly sweet route so many blends do, this enjoys a deliciously spiced honey middle and even the odd shaft of malt clearly bursting through; f23 the light tannins arrive with some toffee, but still that honey and spice continues; b22.5 one of the few blends that has actually improved in recent years. Always been an attractive, interesting if non-spectacular blend which I have enjoyed when meeting it at various bars with friends around the world. Now there is personality enough to punch through the toffee and leave you wanting more. *40%. Chivas Brothers Ltd.*

Something Special Legacy (92) n23 t22.5 f23 b23.5 Good, solid blender is David Boyd. And here he has married substance with subtlety. Lovely stuff. *40%*

Something Special Premium Aged 15 Years (89) n22 t23 f21 b23 Fabulous malt thread and some curious raisiny/sultana fruitiness, too. A blend-lover's blend. *40%.*

⬧ **Stag Hunter** (79) n19 t20 f20 b20 Hard to get past the gin-type nose. Not sure if this is a bottling nail issue, or if we have a blend that celebrates a botanical-style personality. *40%. Burlington Drinks.*

Stag's Head Blended Scotch Whisky (85.5) n21.5 t21.5 f21 b21.5. A thick, hefty nose and body, lush grain and lashings of caramel. Pleasant, sweet, nutty standard stuff. *40% (80 proof)*

Stewart's Old Blended (93) n22.5 t24 f23 b23.5 Really lovely whisky for those who like to close their eyes, contemplate and have a damned good chew. *40%*

Storm (94) n23 t23.5 f24 b23.5. A little gem of a blend that will take you by storm. *43%.*

Talisman 5 Years Old (85.5) n22 t22 f20.5 b21. Unquestionably an earthier, weightier version of what was once a Speyside romp. Soft peats also add extra sweetness. *40%*

Teacher's Aged 25 Years batch 1 (96.5) n24 t24.5 f23.5 b24.5 Only 1300 bottles means they will be hard pushed to create this exact style again. Worth a go, chaps: considering this is India bound, it is the Karma Sutra of blended scotch. *46%. Beam Inc. 1300 bottles. India & Far East Travel Retail exclusive.*

Teacher's Highland Cream (90) n23 t23 f22 b22 Not yet back to its best but a massive improvement on the 2005 bottlings. Harder grains to accentuate the malt will bring it closer to the classic of old. *40%*

Teacher's Origin (92) n23 t23 f23 b23 Almost brings a tear to the eye to taste a Scotch blend that really is a blend. With a better grain input (Dumbarton, say), this perhaps would have been one of the contenders of World Whisky of the Year. Superb! *40%*

⬧ **Teacher's Origin** (88.5) n22 t23.5 f21 b22 A fascinating blend among the softest on the market today. That is aided and abetted by the exceptionally high malt content, 65%, which makes this something of an inverted blend, as that, for most established brands, is the average grain content. What appears to be a high level of caramel also makes for a rounding of the edges, as well as evidence of sherry butts. The bad news is that that has resulted in a duller finish than perhaps might have been intended, which is even more pronounced given the impressive speech made on delivery. Lovely whisky, yes. But something, I feel, of a work in progress. Bringing the caramel down by the percentage points of the malt would be a very positive start... *42.8%. ncf.*

Té Bheag (86) n22 t21 f21.5 b21.5. Classic style of rich caramels and bite. *40%. ncf.*

⬧ **Té Bheag** bott code L 06 12 16 3 (83) n19 t22 f21 b21 Reverted to its mucky nose of yore but though caramel has the loudest voice it has retained its brilliant spice bite. *40%. ncf. Pràban na Linne Ltd.*

⬧ **Tesco Special Reserve Minimum 3 Years Old** bott code L6335 16/04171 (83.5) n19 t22 f21.5 b21 Improved of late. Now unashamedly in the date and walnut school of blends, where before it had only dabbled; thick, uncompromisingly sweet and cloying but with enough spice and salivation to make for pleasant and characterful bit of fun. *40%.*

⬧ **That Boutique-y Whisky Company Blended Whisky No. 1 50 Year Old** (96) n23.5 a blended whisky of box of chocolate liqueurs....? t25 as soft as a loving coo. Fruit then light, creamy fudgy caramels alight on the palate and then seems to magically transform into the milkiest chocolate mousse as a little Manuka and ulmo honey slowly dissolves into the mix: possibly the best delivery of any blend this year...; f23.5 just thins a little as the vanillas take up a more prominent position; b24 some of the moments encountered in this blend are the exact reason why no spirit on this planet comes close to whisky at its very finest. *46.6%. 2,000 bottles.*

⟫ **That Boutique-y Whisky Company Blended Whisky No. 2 18 Year Old** (86.5) n20 t22.5 f22 b22 The caramels from the oak are quite startling. The off-key nose is best ignored but lovers of fruity fudge will have a field day. 46.7%. 1,132 bottles.

⟫ **That Boutique-y Whisky Company Blended Whisky No. 3 23 Year Old** (91) n21 the trouble with blending in such small batches is that sometimes you can't get the nose to quite find harmony...; t23.5 ...though no such problem on delivery which revels in the enormous deployment of muscovado sugar and softer ulmo honey; a secondary taste structure is built by a crisper, fresher malt-based juiciness; f23 soft tannin and praline; b23.5 from the stuttering start on the nose this turns into rich, well-layered blend with no age scars whatsoever. 48.2%. 463 bottles.

The Tweeddale Blend Aged 10 Years (89.5) n22 t23.5 f21.5 b22.5 The first bottling of this blend since World War 2, it has been well worth waiting for. 46%. ncf. 50% malt. Stonedean.

The Tweeddale Blended Scotch Whisky Aged 14 Years batch 5 (92) n22.5 t23.5 f23 b23 I was salivating just at the prospect of this one, as I remember what a fresh article Batch 4 was. Well, this is even sharper in some places...yet curiously far more laid back and docile in others. 46%. nc ncf.

Ushers Green Stripe (85) n19 t22.5 f21.5 b22. Upped a notch or two in all-round quality. The juicy theme and clever weight is highly impressive and enjoyable. 43%. Diageo.

VAT 69 (84.5) n20 t22 f21 b21.5. Has thickened up in style: weightier, more macho, much more to say and a long way off that old lightweight. A little cleaning up wouldn't go amiss. 40%

Walton Royal Blend Deluxe Reserve (91.5) n22.5 t22 f23 b23 It's amazing what a dose of good quality peaty whisky can do to a blend. Certainly ensures it stands out as a deliciously chewy – and smoky – experience. 43%

White Horse (90.5) n22 t23 f22.5 b23 A malt which has subtly changed shape. Not just the smoke which gives it weight, but you get the feeling that some of Diageo's less delicate malts have been sent in to pack a punch. As long as they are kept in line, as is the case here – just – we can all enjoy a very big blend. 40%. Diageo.

White Horse Aged 12 Years (86) n21 t23 f21 b21. Enjoyable, complex if not always entirely harmonious. For instance, the apples and grapes on the nose appear on a limb from the grain and caramel and nothing like the thoroughbred of old. Lighter, more flaccid and caramel dominated. 40%. Diageo.

⟫ **Whyte & Mackay Aged 13 Years** bott code L6334 14/04116 (89.5) n22 attractive, tangy spiced kumquat; caramel....; t23.5 a toffee fruit bar with muscovado sugars lightening the load; still big and mouth-filling and even juicy; a little liquorice links with the date and walnut signature; f22 toffee and butterscotch, though with a late furry fade; b22 like the standard Whyte and Mackay...but thirteen years old and a little lighter... 40%.

⟫ **Whyte & Mackay Triple Matured** bott code 16/04120 L6329 (86.5) n21 t23.5 f20.5 b21.5 The kind of blend you can not only stand your spoon up in but your knife - table or carving - and fork – table or pitch - as well. The nose suggests something furry is in the offing which, sadly, the finale confirms. But the delivery really is such wonderful fun! Thick with intense toffee, which shapes both its flavour and mouth feel, and concentrated date and walnut cake. Roasty yet sweet thanks to the molasses this is about the chewiest blend on the market today. 40%.

William Lawson's Finest (85) n18.5 t22.5 f22 b22. Not only has the label become more colourful, but so, too, has the whisky. However that has not interfered with the joyous old-fashioned grainy bite. A complex and busy blend from the old charm school. 40%

William Lawson's Scottish Gold Aged 12 Years (89) n22 t23 f22 b22. For years Lawson's 12 was the best example of the combined wizardry of clean grain, unpeated barley and good bourbon cask that you could find anywhere in the world: a last-request dram before the firing squad. Today it is still excellent, but just another sherried blend. What's that saying about if it's not being broke...? 40%

Windsor 12 Years Old (81) n20 t21 f20 b20. Thick, walloped-on blend that you can stand a spoon in. Hard at times to get past the caramel. 40%. Diageo.

Windsor Aged 17 Years Super Premium (89) n23 t22 f22 b22. Still on the safe side for all its charm and quality. An extra dose of complexity would lift this onto another level. 40%

Windsor 21 Years Old (90) n20 t23 f24 b23. Recovers fabulously from the broken nose and envelopes the palate with a silky-sweet style unique to the Windsor scotch brand. Excellent. 40%. Diageo.

Ye Monks (86) n20 t23 f21.5 b21.5. Just hope they are praying for less caramel to maximize the complexity. Still, a decent spicy chew and outstanding bite which is great fun and worth finding when in South America. 40%. Diageo.

Irish Whiskey

Of all the whiskies in the world, it is Irish which probably causes most confusion amongst both established whisk(e)y lovers and the novices.

Ask anyone to define what is unique to Irish whiskey - apart from it being made in Ireland and the water likewise coming from that isle - and the answer, if the audiences around the world at my tastings are anything to go by, are in this order: i) it is triple distilled; ii) it is never, ever, made using peat; iii) they exclusively use sherry casks; iv) it comes from the oldest distillery in the world; v) it is made from a mixture of malted and unmalted barley.

Only one of these answers is true: the fifth. This is usually the final answer extracted from the audience when the last hand raised sticks to his guns after the previous four responses have been shot down.

And it is this type of whiskey, known as Irish Pot Still, which has again been named as Irish Whiskey of the Year. In 2016 it was the Midleton Dair Ghaelach, in 2014 and 2013 it was the Redbreast 12-years-old and in 2012 Power's John's Lane. This year it was, just like last year and previously in 2015, the Jameson Redbreast 21-years-old. Considering that 25 years ago Irish Distillers had decided to end the bottling of Pure Pot Still, not bad. Just shows what a little campaigning can do. Today Redbreast 21, when sulphur free, ranks among the world's elite. Remarkable as it may seem, after the best part of a century of contraction within the industry, much of it as painful as it was brutal, there were only four distilleries operating on the entire island of Ireland when John Lane's Pot Still was named Irish Whiskey of the Year in the autumn of 2011. Now there are 16.

How many of the new generation distillers have already or are planning to produce Pot Still is currently unclear. But if, seeking inspiration, they should pop over to England to see what's being made at St. George: young Pot Still at its most sublime. And not a sherry butt in sight.

Jim Murray's Whisky Bible Irish Whiskey of the Year Winners

	Irish Whiskey	Irish Pot Still Whiskey	Irish Single Malt	Irish Blend	Irish Single Cask
2004	Jameson	N/A	N/A	N/A	N/A
2005	Jameson	N/A	N/A	N/A	N/A
2006	Bushmills Rare 21	N/A	N/A	N/A	N/A
2007	Redbreast 15 Year Old	N/A	N/A	N/A	N/A
2008	Tyrconnel 10 Madeira Fin	N/A	N/A	N/A	N/A
2009	Jameson 2007 Vintage Reserve	N/A	N/A	N/A	N/A
2010	Redbreast 12 Year Old	N/A	N/A	N/A	N/A
2011	Sainsbury's Dun Leire 8	N/A	N/A	N/A	N/A
2012	Powers John's Lane Release 12	N/A	Sainsbury's Dun Leire 8	N/A	Jameson Rarest 07 Vintage Reserve
2013	Redbreast 12 Year Old	Redbreast 12 Cask Strength	Bushmills Aged 21	Jameson	Tyrconnell S C 11 Year Old
2014	Redbreast 12 Cask Strength	Redbreast 12 Cask Strength	Bushmills Aged 21	Jameson	N/A
2015	Redbreast Aged 21	Redbreast Aged 21	Bushmills Aged 21	Jameson	N/A
2016	Midleton Dair Ghaelach	Midleton Dair Ghaelach	SMWS 118.3 (Cooley) 1991	Powers Gold Label	N/A
2017	Redbreast Aged 21	Redbreast Aged 21	Bushmills 21 Year Old	Jameson	Teeling S C 2004
2018	Redbreast Aged 21	Redbreast Aged 21	Bushmills Aged 16	Bushmills Black Bush	Dunville's VR First Edition

Pure Pot Still
MIDLETON (old distillery)

Midleton 25 Years Old Pot Still db (92) n24 t24 f21 b23. A really enormous whiskey that is in the truest classic Irish style. The un-malted barley really does make the tastebuds hum and the oak has added fabulous depth. Interesting when tasted against an American rye – the closeness of the character is there to be experienced, but also the differences. A subtle mature whiskey of unquestionable quality. Superb. 43%

Midleton 30 Years Old Pot Still db (85) n19 t22 f22 b22. A typically brittle, crunchy Irish pot still where the un-malted grains have a telling say. The oak has travelled as far as it can without having an adverse effect. A chewy whiskey which revels in its bitter-sweet balance. An impressively tasty and fascinating insight into yesteryear. 45%

Midleton 1973 Pure Pot Still db (95) n24 t24 f23 b24. The enormous character of true Irish pot still whiskey (a mixture of malted and unmalted barley) appears to absorb age better than most other grain spirits. This one is in its element. But drink at full strength and at body temp (it is pretty closed when cool) for the most startling – and memorable effects. I have no idea how much this costs. But if you can find one and afford it... then buy it!! 56%

MIDLETON (new distillery)

Green Spot db (94.5) n23.5 t24 f23.5 b23.5. This honeyed state has remained a few years, and its sharpness has now been regained. Complex throughout. Unquestionably one of the world's greatest branded whiskies. 40%. Irish Distillers for Mitchell & Son, Dublin.

⬧ **Green Spot** bott code L622831252 db (95) n23.5 beautifully complex, though lighter than some previous Green Spots, where the pot still would sometimes form a rock-hard guard of honour. For this bottling, much more emphasis on the soft, over-ripe fruit - greengages especially – and soothing ulmo honey to soften the vanilla; t23.5 soft and salivating delivery – certainly unlike Green Spot of yesteryear – with the golden syrup and eucalyptus having the measure of each other; a little quince adds to the general fruity tone; f24 the more compact nature of the Pot Still at last makes its mark; this is a firm finish true to style but with the sugars and tannins working in tandem with it classic bitter-sweet (though mainly sweet!) fade; b24 a slightly different weight, pace and sugar emphasis to this bottling. But remains a true classic. 40%.

Green Spot Château Léoville Barton finished in Bordeaux Wine Casks db **(83.5)** n21.5 t22.5 f19 b20.5. Have a kind of proprietarily, fatherly feel about Green Spot, as it was an unknown whiskey outside Ireland until revealed to the world 21 years ago in my Irish Whiskey Almanac. And fitting this is finished in Ch. Leoville Barton as I have a fair bit of that from the 70s and 80s in my cellar – and the creators of Green Spot was Dublin's oldest wine shop. However, after all that, have to say that this is a disappointment. There are warning signs on the nose and confirmation on the finish that the wine barrel did not escape the dastardly sulphur treatment. Which means it is dull where it should be bright, though the delivery does reach out for complexity and there are some excellent light cocoa moments. But the sulphur wins. *46%*

⬦ **Green Spot Château Léoville Barton** finished in Bordeaux wine casks, bott code L622331248 db **(79)** n20 t22 f18 b19 I'd so desperately like to see this work. But, once again, far too tight and bitter for its own good. The damaging sulphur note is worthy of neither the great Green Spot or Leoville Barton names... *46%.*

Master Distiller's Selection Single Pot db **(94)** n23.5 t23.5 f23 b24 At the sweeter end of the Pot Still spectrum. The use of fruit as a background noise, rather than a lead, is a masterstroke. *46%. 500 bottles. ncf*

⬦ **Method and Madness Single Pot Still Irish Whiskey** sherry & American barrels, finished in French chestnut casks db **(88)** n22 the grape maintains a fruitcake richness despite the woody interference; t23 probably the softest Irish Pot Still landing I've ever encountered, the fruit and tannins combining to strip away the usual brittleness of the grain. Subdued spices, less so sugars...; f21 a degree of bitterness fights it out with the ulmo honey: not the sherry to blame, this time...; b22.5 ah...memories of the late 1970s or perhaps very early '80s. Walking in the lonely autumnal forests surrounding the tiny French village of Evecquemont, taking my girlfriend's family's soppy Alsatian for long walks, during which I would hoover up wild sweet chestnuts by the score. Never then figured it playing a part in whisky, especially Irish. Not sure it is the perfect marriage, but certainly adds to the whiskey lexicon. *46%.*

Midleton Barry Crockett Legacy db **(94)** n23.5 t24.5 f22.5 b23.5. Another fabulous Pot Still, very unusual for its clever use of the varied ages of the oak to form strata of intensity. One very sophisticated whiskey. *46%. ncf.*

⬦ **Midleton Barry Crockett Legacy American** bourbon barrels, bott code L623631258 db **(95)** n23.5 firm and beautifully spiced, there is a secondary strata of toffee and dates. But it is all about that beguiling spice; t24 sensual delivery, soft and opens in slow motion. The sugars begin with a light brushing of muscovado, though this deepens to a fudgy Manuka honey. All the time the spices, which begin as a distant pulse gathers in intent into something profound; f23.5 a long spiced coffee (as opposed to Coffey) fade, indicating too much caramel, but still with that firm line of unmistakable Pot Still radiating spices and warmth; b24 thank God for my dear old friend Barry Crockett. One of the top three most knowledgeable whiskey/whisky people I have known in my lifetime, you can at least be relieved that his name is synonymous with a truly great spirit. Fittingly, his whiskey is free of sherry butts, so I can just sit back and enjoy and not be on tenterhooks waiting for the first signs of a disastrous sulphur note to take hold. Indeed, the only thing that takes hold of you here is the Pot Still's stunning beauty... *46%. ncf.*

Midleton Dair Ghaelach db **(97)** n23.5 a plethora of bourbon-style liquorice and honey – though, here, closer to heather honey. Polished oak floors, melt-on-the-nose grain...and so it goes on...and on...and on... An odd hybrid of Kentucky and Irish...but a thoroughbred, of course...; t25 that is probably one of the great deliveries of the year. Absolutely abounds in pot still character, both being hard as nails and soft as a virgin's kiss. But the way it interacts with the ulmo honey/red liquorice/heather-honey-vanilla/embracing grain is something of a once in a lifetime experience. And, what's more, barely a hint of spice throughout...; f24 just long, gorgeously silky and soft and a delicious furtherance of the spellbinding flavour compounds of before...; b24.5 for heaven's sake. This is just too ridiculously beautiful...and so unmistakably Irish for all the virgin oak. Truly world class. *58.1%*

⬦ **Midleton Dair Ghaelach Grinsell's Wood Ballaghtobin Estate** American bourbon barrels, finished in Irish oak hogsheads, batch no. 1, tree no. 7, bott code L504031020 db **(97.5)** n24 the blarney is from the Irish oak: it is talking loudest and fastest, throwing at us tannins at a bewildering lick. Miraculously, these heavier oak notes are kept in check by deep, dark sugars of the roasty variety. Spices, usually the domain of the Pot Still, this time rise clearly from the oak, fiery and engulfed in blazing tannins. There is a fruity edge, too. Concentrated blood orange leads the way with a lighter sub-strata of lime and barley sugar...a nose like no other....; t25 this is ridiculously beautiful: no whiskey has the right to be as extraordinarily dramatic as those first five or six flavour waves which hit the palate. At first you think succulent praline spread, then molasses and finally you are moved into a third direction as the Pot Still not so much arrives but stands astride the story so far, surveying all before it with degree of contempt. Rock hard, pulsing barley rips the taste buds asunder, so the juiciness levels rise dramatically. The sugars arrive in oak-enslaved waves...; f24 the most sensual, chocolate-soaked, spiced finish of any whisk(e)y this year...let alone Irish....; b24.5 what we have here, if I'm not very much mistaken, is a potential World Whisky of the Year. Rarely these days am I given an entirely new flavour profile to chew on. Not only do I have that, but I am struggling to find any faults at all. Ireland is not known for its mountains: well, it certainly has one now. 57.9%. ncf.

Paddy Centenary Edition db (93) n22 t23.5 f24 b23.5. This 7-year-old Pure Pot Still whiskey really is a throwback. All Paddy's original whiskey from this era would have been from the old Midleton distillery which sits, in aspic, beside the one opened in 1975. Even with the likelihood of oats being in the mash in those days, still can't believe the original would have been quite as sweet on the palate – and soul – as this. 43%

Powers Aged 12 Years John's Lane Release db (96.5) n24 t25 f23.5 b24 This is a style of Irish Pot Still I have rarely seen outside the blending lab. I had many times thought of trying to find some of this and bottling it myself. No need now. I think I have just tasted Irish Whiskey of the Year, and certainly one of the top five world whiskies of the year. 46%

◇ **Powers Aged 12 Years John's Lane Release** bott code L623731261 (96) n23.5 slightly dusty at first: fudge and vanilla on one hand, on the other a fruitier firmer signature. Give it time and the sugars will begin to rise; t24.5 ah...Pot Still..!! Huge delivery with the firmness of the Pot Still working beautifully with the immediate sweetness of the maple syrup and ulmo honey: the texture of the mouth feel simply cannot be bettered. Spices spring early and, as is usually the case with top Pot Still, grow in intensity until they positively glow... Not a sipping whiskey: take a full mouthful and let the Pot Still work its unique, honeyed magic...; f23.5 lots of fudge at play but the spices still radiate and the sugars now have an almost metallic sheen and hardness; b24.5 a slightly different slant on the toffee and fudge – and now has a degree of rye-recipe bourbon about it - but firmly remains the go to Pot Still of quite staggering beauty. 46%. ncf.

Powers Signature Release db (92.5) n23 t24 f22 b23 I have lately become a little nervous of Irish matured in sherry. At the turn of this century there was plenty in the warehouse and sulphur was not a problem. Something has changed, for now it is. Here, there is not much, but just enough to it take the edge off what had been, until then, a wonderful experience. Hopefully in future bottlings this can be more carefully monitored and the oak profile adjusted. If so, greatness awaits... 46%. ncf.

◇ **Powers Signature Release** bott code L433231240 (87.5) n21 t23 f21.5 b22 A much lazier version of this excellent Pot Still than I have become used to. Far too much fudge at play here, undermining the layering and complexity. Sexy and chewy for sure and a must for those into dried dates. But the usual Pot Still character is a little masked and the usual slightly off key sherry butt turns up at the very last moment. 46%. ncf.

◇ **Powers Three Swallow Release** bott code L617031171 (83.5) n21 t21 f21.5 b20 Pleasant. No off notes. But vanishes into a sea of toffee. The fact it is pure Pot Still, apparently, is actually impossible to determine, In the last six months I have seen three swallows: a barn swallow, a Pacific and aa Wire-tailed. Wherever I saw them in the world, India, The Philippines, my back garden, they all swooped and darted in joyous abandon. This Three Swallow by Powers has, by vivid contrast, had its wings clipped. 40%. ncf.

◇ **Redbreast Aged 12 Years** bott code L634031413 db (88.5) n22.5 a bag of boiled cherry sweets. Fruit, fruit, fruit all the way, silky and soft... But where's the Pot still character...? A little hefty spice edges in to remind us it is there somewhere; t23 the nose re-visited. Silky fruit...and caramel, now...; f21 fruity, short and not bothering too much about complexity...; a very slight furriness grows...; b22 by far the flattest Redbreast I have tasted since...well, ever. Far too much reliance on obviously first-fill sherry, which had flattened out and virtually buried the unique personality of the Pot Still itself. Enjoyable, for sure. Beautiful, even, in its own way. But it should be so much better than this... 40%.

Redbreast Aged 12 Years Cask Strength batch B1/11 db (96) n24.5 t24.5 f23 b24 This is Irish pot still on steroids. And sporting an Irish brogue as thick as my great great grandfather John Murray's. To think, had I not included Redbreast in Jim Murray's Irish Whiskey Almanac back in 1994, after it had already been unceremoniously scrapped and discontinued, while championing the then entirely unknown Irish Pot Still cause this brand would no longer have been with us. If I get run over by a bus tomorrow, at least I have that as a tick when St Peter is totting up the plusses and minuses... And with the cask strength, he might even give me two... 57.7%. ncf. Irish Distillers.

Redbreast Aged 12 Years Cask Strength batch no. B1/13 db (95.5) n24 t24 f23.5 b24 Oh, for that bitterness. A potential World Whisky of the Year otherwise? Perhaps... 59.9%. ncf.

⟨⟨⟨ **Redbreast Aged 12 Years Cask Strength Edition** batch no. B1/16 db **(86.5) n22.5 t23 f20 b21** Again, far, far too much sherry on this has completely skewed the character. The Pot Still does fight through for some beautiful and massive moments early on, but it simply can't win the battle against the overwhelming fresh grape. Sulphur builds up at the end to put the tin hat on it... 57.2%. ncf.

Redbreast 15 Years Old db **(94) n23 t24 f23 b24.** For years I have been pleading for Irish Distillers to launch a pot still at 46%, natural colour and unchillfiltered. Well, I've got two out of three wishes. And what we have here is a truly great Irish whiskey and my pulse races in the certain knowledge it can get better still... 46%. ncf. France.

⟨⟨⟨ **Redbreast Aged 15 Years** bott code L624931266 db **(84) n21 t22 f20 b21** When you have this much sherry influence on a whiskey, it is likely that one day you will fall foul of the odd furry butt, as is the case here. 46%. ncf.

Redbreast Aged 21 Years db **(96) n24 t25 f23 b24** I have tasted no shortage of 21-year-old pot still before in my career, but that was some time back when the whiskey in question was usually from the original Jameson distillery in Dublin, or Power's. I also managed to get my hands on some old stuff from the original Midleton as well as Tullamore Dew and few others. That old spirit had been made at a time when those distilleries were in the process of being closed down and the quality was nothing like it once was. This, I admit, is the first I can remember from Midleton's rebuilt distillery and it knocks the spots of the Jameson and Power's. Those did not have the balance or the insouciance so far as the honey involvement was concerned or the all-round world-class star quality which positively radiates from the glass. Hopefully this gentle giant amongst the world's truly great whiskies and near blue print for the perfect pot still Irish is here to stay. Only for the next bottling absolutely no need for the pointless caramel and the damaging sherry, both which contribute in tarnishing the dazzling sheen. There are times when less is so significantly more. 46%. ncf. WB15/417

⟨⟨⟨ **Redbreast Aged 21 Years** bott code L612731109 db **(97) n24.5** just one of the most wonderful noses on this planet – and truly unique. The Pot Still weaves its unmistakable and unforgeable magic with that Mona Lisa-esque, imperceptible smile of sweetness just slightly off-setting the deeper non-malted depths...; a gentle hint of apricot and passion fruit does all that is required on the fruit front to guarantee balance; **t24** the sherry butts make an early statement on delivery. But the speech is light, undemanding and by no means pompous, so the other, myriad, qualities are quickly apparent and able to shape the experience. Indeed, the fruit is more of an exotic fruit pastel while the grain alternates between firmness and enveloping gentleness; **f24** so wonderfully long thanks to a build-up of oils which were not at first apparent. A cocoa-rich quality broadens across the palate while the busiest spices babbles away contentedly. And, just for good measure not a single sulphur note makes itself heard...; **b24.5** the mercifully restrained fruit and absolute total 100% absence of sulphur allows the Pot Still to display its not inconsiderable beauty unmolested and to the fullest extent. One of the world's most beautiful and iconic whisk(e)ys without doubt. The fact that so many facets of this whiskey are allowed to say their piece, yet never over-run their time and that the tenets are equally divided makes this one of the truly great whiskeys of the year. 46%. ncf.

⟨⟨⟨ **Redbreast All Sherry Single Cask** db **(73.5) n17 t23.5 f15 b18.** I mean: seriously guys....??? A single cask pure pot still whiskey and you bottle one with sulphur fingerprints all over it? I don't have the number of what cask this is from, so I hope yours will have come from clean sherry. If you have, you are in for a treat, because the sheer brilliance and magnitude of this whiskey was able to blot out the sulphur for a good seven or eight seconds as it reached heights of near perfection. A bowl of raspberries now and a 20 minute break to help cleanse my palate and relieve my tongue which is still seriously furred up. So frustrating, as I could see a clean butt of this getting Single Cask Whisky of the Year ... 59.9%. sc.

Redbreast Mano a Lámh db **(85) n22.5 t22.5 f19 b21** Curious that on an all sherry butt bottling, the most enjoyable flavour profile is a spiced chocolate one which begins about four or five beats after the original big, soppy, lush delivery. No prizes for guessing why the score goes down towards the finish. By the way: love the robin on the label – a kind of weird cross between an immature and adult robin with the face of a white wagtail thrown in. Like the whiskey type: unique! 46%. ncf.

⟨⟨⟨ **Redbreast Lustau Edition** sherry finish, bott code L622131242 db **(89.5) n22.5** hefty grape – a little flat but with a welcome salted orange blossom honey nip; **t23.5** unquestionably the softest and most well-rounded Pot Still whiskey I have ever encountered. A kind of fruit toffee structure, then a brief explosion of busy, warming Pot Still which makes this whiskey for sure; **f22** a slow pulse of spice offers life to the otherwise inert toffee-fruit; just enough sugar to see off the oaky bitterness which moves in; **b21.5** I somehow would have thought that, considering recent younger bottlings, going to the trouble of making a special sherry finish for a Redbreast is on a par with giving a gift of a barrel of sand to the Tuaregs... This bottling is attractive enough, with the fruit at its best on delivery when the whiskey goes through a spectacularly delicious phase. But this soon wears out, leaving a bitterness and slightly lopsided feel, especially at the death, as the balance struggles to be maintained. For those of you I know who refuse to touch anything sherry, this is entirely sulphur free I'm delighted to report. 46%. ncf.

Yellow Spot Aged 12 Years bourbon, sherry and Malaga casks db (88.5) n23.5 t22.5 f20 b22.5. If anything, just a shade too many wine casks used which somewhat drowns out the unique IP character. Reminds me of when Barry Walsh was working on the triple maturation theme of the Bushmills 16, probably about 15 years ago. Not until the very last days did all the components click. Just before then, it went through a phase like this (though obviously with malt, not IPS). Knowing current blender Billy Leighton as I do, I can see this whiskey improving in future batches as lessons are learned. not that there isn't already much to enjoy... 46%.

⬧ **Yellow Spot Aged 12 Years** bourbon barrels, sherry butts & Malaga casks, bott code L622431250 db (87) n22 t22 f21 b22 My previous comments stand for this, too. Except here we have a persistent bitterness towards the finish which reveals a weakness with one of the butts. An exceptionally bitty whiskey that does have its moments of soaring high, especially when the varying citrus note correlate. 46%. ncf.

OLD COMBER

Old Comber 30 Years Old Pure Pot Still (88) n23 t24 f20 b21. A classic example of a whiskey spending a few Summers too many in wood: increasing age doesn't equal excellence. That said, always very drinkable and early on positively sparkles with a stunning mouthfeel. Out of respect for the old I have made the markings for taste cover the first seven or eight seconds... 40%

Single Malt
COOLEY

Connemara bott code L9042 db (88) n23 t22.5 t20.5 b22. One of the softest smoked whiskies in the world which though quite lovely gives the impression it can't make its mind up about what it wants to be. 40%

Connemara Aged 8 Years db (85) n22.5 t21.5 f20 b21. Another Connemara lacking teeth. The peat charms, especially on the nose, but the complexity needs working on. 46%

Connemara Aged 12 Years bott code L9024 db (85.5) n23 t21.5 f20 b21. The nose, with its beautiful orange, fruity lilt, puts the shy smoke in the shade. 40%

Connemara Cask Strength bott code L9041 db (90) n21.5 t23 f22 b22.5. A juicy negative of the standard bottling: does its talking on the palate rather than nose. Maybe an absence of caramel notes might have something to do with that. 57.9%

Connemara Distillers Edition db (86) n22 t22.5 f20 b21.5. When I give whisk(e)y tastings around the world, I love to include Connemara. Firstly, people don't expect peated Irish. Secondly, their smoked whisky stock is eclectic and you never quite know what is going to come out of the bottle. This is a particularly tight, sharp style. No prisoners survived... 43%

Inish Turk Beg Maiden Voyage db (91.5) n22 t23.5 f22.5 b22.5 Brooding and quite delicious. 44%

Tullamore Dew Single Malt 10 Years Old db (91.5) n23 t23 f22.5 b23. The best whiskey I have ever encountered with a Tullamore label. Furtively complex and daringly delicate. If only they could find a way to minimise the toffee... 40%. William Grant & Sons.

The Tyrconnell Aged 10 Years Madeira Finish bott code L8136 db (91) n23 t23 f22 b23. Not quite the award-winning effort of a few years back, as those lilting high notes which so complemented the baser fruit tones haven't turned up here. But remains in the top echelon and still much here to delight the palate. 46%

The Tyrconnell Single Cask 11 Year Old db (95.5) n23.5 t25 f23 b24. Well, if there weren't enough reasons to go to Dublin, you now have this... 46%. sc. Exclusive to the Celtic Whiskey Shop.

Clonmel Peated Aged 8 Years (86) n22 t23 f20 b21. Take the toffee away and you would have one hell of an Irish. Claims to be "Pure Pot Still". It isn't (in Irish terms): it's malt. 40%

Craoi na Mona Irish Malt Whiskey (68) n16 t18 f17 b17. I'm afraid my Gaelic is slipping these days: I assume Craoi na Mona means "Feinty, badly made smoky malt"... (that's the end of my tasting for the day...) 40%

Glendalough Single Malt Irish Whiskey Aged 7 Years bourbon casks (79) n18 t22 f20 b19. Disappointing on so many levels. Malt at Cooley at 7-year-old, should, if the casks are picked assiduously, be vibrant and brimming with barley and vitality. That only happens for the odd moment or two on delivery. The nose reveals some pretty poor barrels at work while two much toffee flattens the experience. Love the spice, though. *46%. ncf.*

Glendalough Single Malt Irish Whiskey Aged 13 Years bourbon casks **(90) n22.5 t23 f21.5 b23** A rather beautiful whiskey, spilling over with spices. A few tired casks evident, though. *46%. ncf.*

Glen Dimplex (88) n23 t22 f21 b22. Overall, clean and classically Cooley. *40%*

Liquid Sun Cooley 1999 bott 2012 **(87) n22 t22 f21.5 b21.5** Awash with natural caramels and enjoyable in a horrible way...without the horrible. *53.2%. nc ncf sc. The Whisky Agency.*

Magilligan Cooley Pure Pot Still Single Malt (91) n22 t22 f24 b23. A touch of honey for good measure ...or maybe not..!! *43%. Ian MacLeod Distillers.*

Magilligan Irish Whiskey Peated Malt 8 Years Old (89) n21 t23 f22 b23. Such a different animal from the docile creature that formally passed as Magilligan peated. Quite lovely...and very classy. *43%. Ian Macleod Distillers.*

Merry's Single Malt (83) n20 t22 f20 b21. Ultra-clean barley rich nose is found on the early palate. The finish is flat, though. *40%*

Shannahan's (92) n23 t22 f24 b23. Cooley natural and unplugged: quite adorable. *40%*

Slieve Foy Single Malt Aged 8 Years bott code L9108 **(88) n23 t22.5 f21 b21.5.** Never deviates from its delicate touch. *40%. Cooley for Marks & Spencer.*

Tyrconnell 16 Year Old Single Malt (92) n22.5 t24 f22.5 b23 If anyone on here is old enough to remember Zoom lollies – and miss them as much as I after a gap of nearly half a century – then here's your chance to wallow down Memory Lane. So different. And so delicious! *46%*

Vom Fass Cooley Irish Single Malt 8 Years Old (88) n22 t22.5 f21.5 b22. A very decent, if undemonstrative, example of the distillery at an age which well suits. *40%*

The Wild Geese Single Malt (85.5) n21.5 t21 f22 b21. "A Rare Blend of Pure Aged Irish Malt Whiskies" says the front label. Yet it is a single malt. Confusing. And very unhelpful to a whisky public already being totally bamboozled by the bizarre and misguided antics of the Scotch Whisky Association. It is not a blend. It is a mixing of Cooley malt whiskey, as I understand it. The back label's "Smoother Because We Distil it Longer" is also a bit of a blarney. It's made in a pot still and whilst it is true that if you distil faster (by higher temperatures) you could well end up with "hot" whiskey, I am not aware of this being distilled at a significantly slower rate than at either Bushmills or Midleton. Or do they mean the cut of the run from the spirit still is longer, which would impart more oils – not all of them great? Just ignore the Wild Goose chase the labels send you on and enjoy the malt, with all its failings, for what it is (and this is pretty enjoyable in an agreeably rough and ready manner, though not exactly the stuff of Irish whiskey purists): which in this case for all its malt, toffee and delicate smoke, also appears to have more than a slight touch of feints - so maybe they were right all along...!!! *43%. Cooley for Avalon.*

⌁ **The Whisky Barrel Irish Single Malt 13 Year Old** sherry hogshead, cask no. 200501, dist 2003 **(82.5) n19 t21.5 f21 b21** Good grief....!!! This is my 1,151st whisk(e)y for the 2018 Bible...and I can safely say I have not encountered anything like this before...and very few in the near 20,000 samples for all the previous editions. It seems as though there is a strange unification or pact between some kind of skewed smoke and a sherry note the like of which I cannot even begin to describe. This is a gargoyle of a malt, strangely beautiful in its very ugliness. *52.7%. sc. 180 bottles.*

MIDLETON

⌁ **Method and Madness Single Malt Irish Whiskey** bourbon barrels, finished in French Limousin oak casks db **(92) n22** both the malt and bourbon barrel side of things are taking a back seat to the big European oak injection...taking the back seat in a limousine, to be precise...; **t23.5** big oils and golden syrup on delivery. Slowly, and not particularly subtly, the oak mounts and mounts in intensity; **f23** still a sheen, right through to the finish. Spices pitch up but it is the lightly salted mocha which has the most satisfying input. The complex flavours and continuing sugars keep the oak the right side of honest; **b23.5** a very different Irish which is quietly uncompromising and seriously tasty... *46%.*

OLD KILBEGGAN

The Spirit of Kilbeggan 1 Month (90.5) n22 t23 f23 b22.5. Wow!! They are really getting to grips with the apparatus. Full bodied and lush small still feel to this but radiating complexity, depth, barley and cocoa in equal measures. The development of the oils really does give this excellent length. Impressed! *65.5%*

The Spirit of Kilbeggan 1 Year (85) n20.5 t21 f22 b21.5. A veritable Bambi of a spirit: a typical one year old malt which, as hard as it tries, just can't locate its centre of gravity. Even so, the richness is impressive and some highly sugared chocolate mousse near the end is a treat. *62.7%*

The Spirit of Kilbeggan 2 Years (84) n20 t21 f22 b21. A tad raw and a little thin. There is some decent balance between oak and malt, but the overall feeling is that the still has not yet been quite mastered. *60.3%*

OLD BUSHMILLS

Bushmills Aged 10 Years matured in two woods db (92.5) n23 t23 f23 b23.5. Absolutely superb whiskey showing great balance and the usual Antrim 19th century pace with its favour development. The odd bottle of this I have come across over the last couple of years has been spoiled by the sherry involvement. But, this, as is usually the case, is absolutely spot on. *40%*

Bushmills Select Casks Aged 12 Years married with Caribbean rum cask db (95) n23 unusual moist rum and raisin cake effect: effective and just enough spice to deliver extra complexity. Just the very slightest hint of bourbon, too; t24 adorable malt richness; biscuity and stupendously seasoned yet always remains fresh and mouthwatering. The sweetness is very cleverly controlled; f24 there are just so many layers to this: the oak is a growing force, but restricts itself to a vanilla topping; b24 one of the most complex Bushmills in living memory, and probably since it was established in 1784. *40%*

Bushmills Aged 16 Years db (71) n18 t21 f15 b17. In my days as a consultant Irish whiskey blender, going through the Bushmills warehouses I found only one or two sulphur-treated butts. Alas, there are many more than that at play here. *40%*

Bushmills Aged 21 Years db (95.5) n24.5 t24 f23.5 b24 An Irish journey as beautiful as the dramatic landscape which borders the distillery. Magnificent. *40%*

Bushmills Sherry Cask Reserve Single Malt Whiskey first-fill Oloroso sherry butts db (80) n20.5 t22 f18 b19.5. Although I am always 100% impartial, I would be lying if I didn't say I wanted this whiskey to be not just a high scorer, but a potential Bible world champion. Because in my tasting room stands a fine and very large - oil portrait of the Bushmills Distillery, and it is a place I have enjoyed special moments at - and love the people there dearly. And, also, in a few moments Northern Ireland's miracle-making football team are about to take on Wales in the last 16 of the Euros. But, sadly, the news, from here at least, is not good. Among the sherry butts selected has been one - and I am sure it is only one - that has been lightly sulphur treated. It means that the fruit, rather than taking off and going into complexity overdrive, crumples slightly as the vague bitterness and tightness spreads around the palate. There are some lovely fruit moments, so there are. But Bushmills should be so much better than this. As an Irish whiskey blender of old, I have been lucky enough to work with Bushmills sherry butts in pristine condition...and they can be among the best whiskeys you'll ever find on this planet. Sadly this is not fully representative. I just hope the boys in green rise to greater heights than this bottling and don't fall to an own goal like the one scored here.... *40%*

Clontarf Single Malt (90.5) n23 t23 f22 b22.5. Beautiful in its simplicity, this has eschewed complexity for delicious minimalism; *40%. Clontarf Irish Whiskey Co.*

Connemara Original Peated Single Malt db (81.5) n21 t21.5 f19 b20.A bit of a while since the first thing I got off the nose and last thing on the finish was caramel. Not the Connemara I witnessed being launched in a blaze of defiant glory those decades back. This rather meek, pleasant, safe, lightly smoked version appears to have been sanitised. Today's Connemara it may sadly be. Original Connemara it is most certainly NOT...! *40%*

The Irishman Single Malt bottle no. E2496 (83) n20 t21 f21 b21. Highly pleasant malt but the coffee and toffee on the finish underline a caramel-style whiskey which may, potentially, offer so much more. *40%. Hot Irishman Ltd.*

Knappogue Castle Aged 12 Years bourbon cask matured (90) n23.5 t23 f21 b22.5. The massive toffee influence deflects from the huge character elsewhere which springs a few surprises. *40%. Castle Brands Group.*

The Whisky Cask Company Cù Chulainn 27 Years Old rum cask, dist 1988 (89) n22.5 t22.5 f22 b22.5 Apparently this is from Bushmills, so the whiskey I decided to taste before Northern Ireland's game against Poland, their first in international Finals since 1986. And the first time a player from my beloved Millwall, Shane Ferguson, has taken part since Tony Cascarino represented the Republic of Ireland in 1988. *45.7%*

UNSPECIFIED SINGLE MALTS

Barr an Uisce 1803 Irish Single Malt Aged 10 Years bourbon barrel (92) n22.5 t23.5 f23 b23 Not sure if I have ever come across an Irish whiskey with such a pathetically weak phenolic signature. Even so, a delicious offering...! Unspecified, but Cooley for sure. *46%. ncf.*

Chapter 7 Irish Single Malt 2001 13 Years Old sherry butt, cask no. 10836 (67.5) n17.5 t18 f15 b18. Sorry Chaps. Sweet as a nut it may be. But you have been seriously sulphured. 59.5%. sc. 293 bottles.

Chapter 7 Irish Single Malt 1999 16 Years Old rum cask, cask no. 5409 (94) n23 t23.5 f23.5 b24 Genuinely impressive. 573%. sc.

Dublin in the Rare Ould Times Single Malt Irish Whiskey Aged 10 Years bourbon barrel (81.5) n21 t21 f19 b20.5. It was a rare old time when they made single malt whiskey like this in Dublin, for they hardly ever did. The city was the centre of Pot Still Irish and though single malt was not unknown there, it was a scarce order at the bar. When it did come along, it is hard to believe it would have been this kind of age. And, indeed, this malt would have been happier had it been a couple of years younger: the bourbon barrel at work here has allowed little malty punch to get through, while the toffee middle and finish is disappointingly dull. 40%. Bottled by Glendalough Distillery for Pete St John.

◇ **The Dublin Liberties Copper Alley 10 Year Old** (88.5) n23 attractively fresh: diced banana sandwich, a sprinkling of muscovado, barley sugar, the laziest spice and a little fudge; t22 mid weight on the silky delivery: major amounts of toffee begin to form and clog up the development, other than the salivating spices; f21.5 just a little too quiet for comfort; b22 about an easy drinking a malt as you'll find with no shortage of sugars. The caramels are a bit ham-fisted, though. 46%. ncf.

◇ **Dunville's Aged 10 Years Single Malt** finished in ex-Pedro Ximénez sherry casks (78.5) n20 t21.5 f18 b19 Well, didn't quite see that coming. They may have launched a whisky with the best label of this and many years – a re-run of the old Classic Dunville's VR – but not quite the best whiskey with which to fill the bottle. The nose has a peculiar botanical note, juniper in particular, and this becomes a strange experience all round when the same note is picked upon the palate and then stretched and smothered – with everything else - by the furry PX. Lots of early flavours...but balance is at a serious premium. 46%. ncf.

◇ **Dunville's VR First Edition Aged 15 Years Single Malt** Port Morant rum cask finish, cask no. 193 (96.5) n24 wonderful, controlled, playful nip and bite, but I most adore the subtle layering of molasses over the magnificently clean barley; t24.5 just about perfect texture: PM casks have in them caramel entered into the wood before the rum is filled, giving the Demerara a rich-textured, coffee flavoured effect. That texture is apparent here, as is the light, milky coffee – a kind of Blue Mountain latte – then a breath-taking intertwangling of molasses and malt; all that said, look out, also, for the stunning juiciness on delivery...; f23.5 just bitters slightly as some of the oak tires. But the remnants of the dark sugars and rich, buttery barley and praline goes on seemingly forever...; b24.5 makes me wonder: it must have been about 15 years ago or so I was blending a high quality Pot Still rum and used some outstanding Port Morant for my creation. Some of the casks, I know, went on to be filled with Irish from Cooley (for some Irish I was blending at the same time)... Surely not... 57%. ncf sc.

Eiling Lim Irish Single Malt 22 Years Old 1991 bott 2014 (95.5) n23.5 t24 f24 b24 After 22 years, this must have been one of the most highly smoked whiskeys ever produced at Cooley. A genuine landmark malt in Irish whiskey history. 48.6%. nc ncf sc. 116 bottles. 6th Release.

◇ **Glendalough 7 Year Old Irish Single Malt Black Pitts Porter Finish** (81) n19 t21 f20 b21 Wearing my Panama Hattie, just got to say it's just Too Darn Hop! Would love to say You Do Something To Me and You're Sensational. But you don't and you aren't. Night and Day I hoped you'd Begin the Beguine...but there is no rhythm at all. I know in these whisky days Anything Goes but Make it Another Old-Fashioned, Please....That's enough Cole Porter references, thank you - Ed. 59%.

◇ **Glendalough 13 Year Old Irish Single Malt Mizunara Finish** (96) n23.5 the spiciest Irish nose this year. A slight cream soda sweetness where you might expect the malt to be; t24 gosh! Cream soda, indeed! Incredibly thick mouth feel bringing together the malt in ultra-concentrated form and a slightly tart gooseberry note which calms once the intense chocolate mousse becomes embroiled; f24 probably the most sensuous chocolate finish in the history of Irish whiskey... b24.5 different and adorable. 56%.

◇ **Glendalough 24 Year Old Irish Single Malt Madeira Finish** (86.5) n22.5 t22.5 f20.5 b20 OK, I know. The owners of this brand will be pretty pissed off with me. They have bought a 24-year-old malt. And what appears to be first use Madeira casks of the highest quality. Then put them together. Is there a sulphur fault with the wine cask? Not at all: it is perfect. So why the relatively low score compared to their Mizunara and Port Morant offerings? Well, if I can put my blender's hat on for a moment, allow me to explain. After 24 years, the malt will have a lot to say and deserves listening to. Some of the narrative will be cracked and in need of editing. So, yes, a finish of some sort might help. However, this Madeira cask is too fresh and pugnacious. It dominates bombastically and defines. Yes, it is delicious. But where is the 24-year-old malt? A few whispers can be heard...but it is me, me, me Madeira. Make no mistake: this whiskey enjoys some astonishing phrases of succulent beauty. But as a 24-year-old...it simply does not feel quite right or reverential enough... *54%.*

⬧ **Glendalough 24 Year Old Irish Single Malt Port Finish** (89.5) n22.5 firm and fruity, a little more spice than anticipated leaks from the glass....; t23.5 a sound a lip-smacking delivery in which both intense malt and an eye-wateringly juicy fruitiness play a big part. A little orange blossom honey ensured the required sweetness for an oldie like this and there are slightly salty moist dates, too; f21 heads at first in a mocha direction, then bitters in off-key somewhat as the spices invade; b22.5 if there were any cracks to this old whiskey, then the vivid Port certainly shored them up. *53%.*

⬧ **Glendalough 24 Year Old Irish Single Malt Sherry Finish** (94.5) n24 the richest of rich, toasted raisiny fruitcake with plenty of date and walnut on a side plate....; t24 oloroso on steroids: the grape begins life in concentrated form with dates and plums of the juiciest kind and spices to pucker things further; a slow transformation in mid-stream allows some malt to form a delicious raft on which the midweight tannins and vanillas are carried; f22.5 long, not quite perfect but the dryness also accentuates the burnt raisin and molasses; b24 a sherry cask with only the odd, but forgivable, atom of renegade sulphur. Lovely people of Glendalough: allow me to shake your hands and kiss your foreheads... a very old fashioned (and now horrendously and tragically rare) style indeed: more like a lifetime top quality sherry held, rather than finished. *53%.*

⬧ **Hyde No.1 President's Cask Aged 10 Years Single Malt** sherry cask finish (85.5) n23 t22 f20 b20.5 Pleased to report the sherry butt(s) used here offer no sulphur, so a clean malt with an outstanding fruity aroma. But it does quite literally fall flat because after the initial juicy, malty entry things go a bit quiet – especially towards the middle and finish where a dull vaguely fruity but big toffee note clings like a limpet. A wasted opportunity, one feels. *46%. ncf.*

⬧ **The Irishman Single Malt 17 Year Old** 1st fill Oloroso sherry casks (94) n23 the malt has vanished under the salty oloroso...but, my word, what sherry this is! t24 the enormity of the grape, the uncompromising cream sherry character, will hold erect any spoon you might like to stand in this. Like the nose, the malt side of things has been obliterated. And, also like the nose, there is a salty edge to this which ramps up the piquancy. The mid ground starts moving towards the toastier side of things; f23.5 a lovely fade of muscovado sugars in vanilla, spices and, at last, evidence of oak arousal...; b23.5 the sherry is far too dominant for this to be a well-balanced whiskey: it is all about effect. But this is a rare, as near as damn-it sulphur-free sherry influence and that ups the value and enjoyment of this malt greatly. *56%. ncf sc.*

Jack Ryan Single Malt Irish Whisky Aged 12 Years bourbon cask (92.5) n23.5 t23 f22.5 b23.5 Deft, very clean malt whisky where decent bourbon wood adds all kinds of beautifully paced complexity. Not even a hint of an off note. Impressive. *46%*

⬧ **Liquid Sun Irish Single Malt XO** (94) n23.5 such a gloriously understated and gentle blend of heather honey with a light sprinkling of Nice biscuit for good measure; t24 faultless, salivating delivery with a gristy maltiness. The sugars dissolve on the palate, though the weightier elements of acacia honey do stick around, as does the light oak-induced spices: absolutely top drawer stuff...; f23 dries towards a powdery vanilla finale, as this style of malt so often does; b23.5 This morning a daughter of Ireland and friend of mine died. Had you seen Delores Meredith walking purposefully with shopping bags in hand you would not have given her a second look: from the other side of the street she appeared just an ordinary lady who had strayed, wearily, into late middle age like so many of us. But in those bags would, most likely, be the shopping of others too infirm to leave their chair or bed and Del, without a second thought, would round up those vital little bits and bobs which made the lives of others a little easier to bear, always in her own time and often by foot. I had first met Del at a time I was tasting the final whiskies of the 2017 Whisky Bible and it was she, a carer, who greeted my mother at the Care Home she had just entered, nervously, on her very first day. Delores with her bright Irish eyes, thick Irish midland brogue and bottomless wells of warmth and saintly patience tenderly tried to ease my mum into her new life. Stroking her hand, or gently brushing her hair, she would tell my mum not to worry for she would be there to look after her, which she did with a love and devotion which came as naturally to her as breathing does to you and me My mother, though admonishing her for minor perceived offences, demonstrably adored her and it was obvious my mum, her sharp wits still fully about her and at war with the world, meant much to Del. So often what started in tears of frustration for my mum would end as tears of laughter for them both. And every day, unfailingly, Delores would give me a detailed run down of how things were progressing, or not as the case may be, and try and spend as much time with her as she could; or head off to find her various things from the chemist that could give extra strength to a very fragile old lady. Then, a few months in, Delores was diagnosed with cancer. Not one of those where you fight and have a hope but one of the insidious variety which has crept up on you and, when you find it, it is most probably too late. As, indeed, it proved to be. So today, Easter Sunday, Delores who had so much to live for and give passed away, while my mother heads on towards a 96th birthday she does not wish to see. Life can be cruel and ironic. But it can be wonderful, also. Because it gave me the chance to meet Delores Meredith, one of the most beautiful people I ever knew. And here, with this gorgeous Irish whiskey, I toast your memory, Del, and say thank you for being one of those special people who restores or reinforces one's faith in human nature with every meeting thanks to your myriad kindnesses and bountiful love. *50.3%*.

⬪ **Liquid Treasures Irish Malt** bourbon barrel, bott 2016 **(91)** n22.5 clean, non-fussy malt with minimal tannin at the vanguard, the steering being done by the fresh barley; light, salivating gristy sugars have a hay-making autumnal feel; **t23** sublime barley: the sugars could not be more perfectly weighted with just a vague heather-honey tone; **f22.5** the barley and vanilla vie for pole position while the spice first looks on then makes a stand; **b23** "very old" it may be, but the "aged" oak involvement, other than some drying chalky moments, is negligible. Even so, unquestionably delicious. *49.6%. Summer Dram Edition.*

Maltbarn Irish Malt 2001 bourbon cask, bott 2016 **(85)** n21 t23 f20 b21. A curious cask. Not happy either on nose or finish, where a degree of tightness restricts complexity. But the delivery is as beautiful as it is profound with a big Malteser signature. *48.3%. sc. 167 bottles.*

⬪ **Master of Malt Irish Single Malt 14 Year Old** dist 2001 **(72)** n18 t20 f16 b18 Bejabers! A massive noble rot onslaught...followed by a sulphur winter. *56.4%. sc.*

⬪ **The Quiet Man 8 Year Old** bourbon cask, Oloroso sherry finish **(84.5)** n23.5 t21.5 f19 b20.5 Pretty decent, though still heavily sulphured sherry butt been at play here. It is the nose which takes the plaudits, with its audacious lassoing of the bigger bourbon notes, fully-fledged tannins an' all, and then tying them to the orange blossom honey of the wine cask. The marriage on the nose is nowhere near matched on the bitty, untidy palate. *46%. ncf sc. 950 bottles.*

The Quiet Man 8 Year Old Single Malt Irish Whiskey bourbon casks **(89)** n22 t23 f21.5 b22.5 Had the finish not dulled quite so quickly this would have scored a lot higher. Nothing less than pleasant throughout. *40%*

⬪ **The Quiet Man 12 Year Old** Kentucky bourbon casks **(93)** n23 soft heather-honey and malty caramels mingle contentedly...and quietly...; **t23.5** a lush and luscious delivery with a more ulmo honey feel to things now. Salivating as the grassier elements of the barley still have a say, then delightful layering of vanillas; **f23** spices up in a quiet kind of way...; **b23.5** odd, isn't it? The owner of this brand named this whisky The Quiet Man in memory of his father, John Mulgrew, who was known by that epithet. Yet, coincidentally, it was Maurice Walsh, the grandfather of one of the greatest Irish whiskey blenders of all time, Barry Walsh, who wrote the novel The Quiet Man from which the film was made. I feel another movie coming on: The Silence of the Drams. But sssshhhh: don't tell anyone... *46%. ncf.*

Saar Whisky No. 7 Irish Single Malt bourbon cask, dist 2002, bott 2015 **(87.5)** n21.5 t23 f21 b22. Pleasingly malty. A few scars from the tiring cask but the overall experience is bright and one to savour. *48.7%. nc ncf sc.*

⬪ **Single Cask Collection Old Dunluce 14 Year Old** sherry hogshead, cask no. 10823, dist 18 Sept 01, bott 22 Jun 16 **(93)** n23.5 blood orange and burning spice...not to mention a bourbon style hickory subplot..; **t24** salivating despite the almost gungy thickness of the grape. Spices arrive early and with intent while the oak carried a vaguely bitter coffee banner; **f22.5** the light bitterness continues but the viscous nature of the sherry doesn't remotely lessen; **b23** profound grape of the most luscious variety. *56.9%. 319 bottles. sc.*

⬪ **Teeling Whiskey Brabazon Bottling Single Malt Series 01** sherry casks, bott Mar 17 **(92)** n23.5 an unusual but wholly delicious combination of sherry trifle and butterscotch tart; **t23.5** fat and chewy, the sugars, after their initial burst, keep a low profile. Unsweetened gooseberries and even rhubarb leads the fruit, with a little apricot and physalis adding a deft extra sharpness; during the late middle period a little praline briefly sweeps in; **f22** there is the most vague furriness; **b23** oooh, so close to a stupendous sherry influence. *49.5%. ncf.*

Teeling Whiskey Single Cask 2002 bourbon cask no. 7920, filled May 02, bott Jan 16 **(93)** n23 t23.5 f23 b23.5 One of the most deliciously citrus-laden Irish whiskeys you'll find for a while. A superb early evening glass filler. *59.9%. ncf sc.*

Teeling Whiskey Single Cask 2004 white burgundy cask, cask no. 1404, filled Oct 04, bott Sept 15 **(96.5)** n24 t24.5 f23.5 b24.5 One of the best single cask malts I have tasted from anywhere in the world for a long time. No sulphur, so don't worry about that. This is unadulterated, unreconstructed magnificence...! Faultless whisky. *58.8%. ncf sc.*

⟐ **Teeling Whiskey Single Cask** port cask no. 12628, dist 9 Nov 07, bott 21 Feb 17 **(94)** n23 busy and fruity: a real old fashioned sweet shop aroma here (complete with oak floorboards), especially when the boiled candy jars have been opened...; t24 fabulous delivery. The malt has kept its shape and character here and abounds with grassy freshness; the fruit enters on another level, closer to the spices, and adds a different form of juiciness together...; f23.5 rare to find port without a spicy storm, and it takes little urging...; plenty of late vanilla, but the jammy fruit sticks around – literally...; b23.5 the gentlest of fruity giants. 60%. nc ncf sc.

Teeling Whiskey Single Malt bott 07/2015 **(87.5)** n21.5 t23.5 f21 b21.5. Charming and, at times, intense malt impact with a lovely light fruit side-line. But a late bitterness confirms a degree of negativity from a tiring cask. The delivery, though, is pretty special. 46%. ncf.

⟐ **Teeling Whiskey Single Malt** bott Mar 17 **(89)** n22 soft, sleepy and barley-sugar sweet; t22 about the most simplistic juicy barley in all Ireland; f23 a slow butterscotch and spice arrival adds an elegant and beautifully paced touch; the malts retain lush and green to the end; b22 ostensibly, a slightly over-simplified malt. But the subtlety of the finish is worth waiting for. 46%. nc ncf.

⟐ **Teeling Whiskey Single Malt Aged 24 Years** Sauterne & bourbon casks, bott Aug 16 **(95.5)** n24 good grief...smoke!!! At 24 years.... Originally destined for Connemara, presumably, the light phenols have met their match with the bourbonesque oak intensity. A distinctive Liquorice Allsorts effect, though enhanced by the most delicate smoke and a semi-firm fruitiness...; t24.5 much lighter on delivery than on the nose; here the grape is at its very juiciest. The mid-ground enjoys a stunning smoked praline and sultana effect; ulmo honey melds into the middle; f23 the smoked sugar almonds and spices are superb...; delicate spices hum contentedly; b24 well done, Jack Teeling: you caught me off guard there! Done me up like a kipper - literally. Wasn't expecting a smoky malt of this great antiquity (by Irish standards) and its marriage to a Sauterne influence makes it a complete one-off. Love to be sent the wrong way sometimes. Has all the craggy charm of an Irish character actor. 46%. ncf.

⟐ **Teeling Whiskey Single Malt Aged 26 Years** rum cask, cask no. 16231, bott 21 Feb 17 **(96)** n24 now this is serious malt: it is fathomable – just. But really you have to be on full concentration to work out the subtleties of this thick nose...and subtle it is! Curiously, the prevailing note is that of bourbon, as there is a wonderful red liquorice and molasses theme throughout. Probe further to find the muscovado ensuring a wonderful, clean fruit tone, which even appears to include dates and over-ripe greengages. Elsewhere a little sawdust adds a buffering dryness and, inevitably, spices prickle...; t24 soft, salivating and beyond sumptuous. Just as on the nose, the sugars play up just as would be expected from a rum cask. Yet this stewed fruitiness is a real surprise package; f24 such elegance and complexity...wow! A long as a tale in an Irish pub with the slow – and I mean funereal – paced fade which makes a point of allowing in the drier notes while upping the spices and delicate mocha; slightly nutty as at last we see a very belated glimpse of the malt itself; b24 scratching my head, but this is probably the oldest Irish whiskey I have ever tasted from a distillery still working. All others of this antiquity – and beyond – have come from those which had closed many years before. Yes, the oldest – and one of the best... 57.9%. ncf sc.

⟐ **Teeling Whiskey Single Malt Vol III Revival Aged 14 Years** bourbon casks, finished in Pineau des Charentes barrels **(76.5)** n20.5 t21 f17 b18 'Tis a risky business, this cask finishing. Especially in French fortified wine, as well as sherry... 46%. nc ncf.

⟐ **Teeling Whiskey Single Malt Vol IV Revival Aged 14 Years** finished in ex-muscat barrels **(95)** n23.5 the grape certainly makes a big noise early on to show who is boss: the spices also noticeable are more likely from the wine than the cask, as they appear to have a closer association and are of a "love heart" candy nature; t23.5 such a soft landing with the salivating barley playing a bigger part here than at any phase on the nose; the fruit and spices slowly take control...; f24 what a stunning finish. Not a single off note from the cask or barley which remains ridiculously clean despite its 14 years in the cask. The spices are now of a more uniform rumble but slot in perfectly with the happy unison of malt and now creamy grape; b24 ...though this muscat appears to be bang on the money... indeed, this is a stunner! 46%. nc ncf.

Teeling Whiskey Vintage Reserve Silver Bottling 23 Years Old cask no. 6894 **(94.5)** n23 t24 f23.5 b24 Big, substantial with a big fruity essence, though it is the oak which always holds power. And what power....! Beautiful! 54%. sc. 187 bottles. Bottled for Shinanoya Tokyo.

Teeling Whiskey Vintage Reserve Silver Bottling 23 Years Old cask no. 10680 **(88.5)** n22.5 t22 f22 b22 A cask caught right on the edge of its age-range. 48.2%. sc. 192 bottles.

The Whisky Agency Acla Selection Irish Single Malt North of Ireland Aged 24 Years bourbon barrel, dist 1991, bott 2015 **(92.5)** n23.5 t23 f22.5 b23.5 A beautiful cask which has held off the years with aplomb and uses its deft smokiness to the most delicate of effects. Beautiful, so it is. *51.8%. nc ncf. 218 bottles.*

◇ **The Whisky Agency Irish Single Malt 27 Year Old** dist 1989, bott 2016 **(88.5) n22** husky and dry, the malty is grappling with the tannins just enough to feel there is slight strain in the air...; **t22.5** intense early barley, then a slow build-up of spiced sugars; rounded and glassy feel to this the malt appears condensed and unable to stretch; **f21.5** sticks to that restricted malty theme with the vanillas never quite finding the right rhythm; **b22.5** a malt on its way down. Rare to find an Irish this old, but I suspect this was a much more relaxed and complex dram a dozen years ago... Still highly enjoyable, though always a bit sad when you can see the cracks appearing... *45%. 177 bottles. A joint bottling with Eiling Lim.*

◇ **The Whisky Agency Irish Single Malt 1990 (92.5) n23** apologetic fruit has crept into the equation here, a kind of pastel candy style, half-hearted and mindful of sugar; **t23.5** salivating, malty and so soft; the mid-ground is a mass of caramel; **f23** the spices tune up pleasantly but the oils are drenched in vanilla; **b23** one of the most gentle and juicy malts of the year – from any country! *48.1%.*

◇ **Whisky-Fässle Irish Single Malt** extra old barrel, bott 2016 **(88) n22** there is a message coming from the oak that all is not well...; **t24** both weight and accompanying sugars rarely come better than this on delivery. Big caramel but the ulmo honey is the star.; **f20** slightly over eggs the natural caramel; bitters out somewhat; **b22** a very uneven malt which has been let down by the oak. *50.6%.*

Whisky-Fässle Irish Single Malt 1989 barrel, bott 2015 **(95.5) n24 t24 f23.5 b24** I may be wrong about this. But I doubt it so much and would bet a hundred smackers, minimum. Distilled originally as a smoky whisky by Cooley, it has been matured by them or was sold to Irish Distillers (who bought a lot more than they are happy to let on). Either way, it has found its way back into private hands as one of the oldest smoky Irish whiskeys of all time. And a sacred masterpiece from the green isle...An important whiskey of great historical significance. *47.2%.*

◇ **Writers' Tears Red Head Oloroso** sherry casks **(82.5) n21 t23 f18.5 b20** Always a dangerous game to play with sherry butts and this writer's tears are reserved for the light furry sulphur tones which, as will always be the case, stifle the enjoyment of the rich fruity delivery. *46%. ncf.*

Single Grain
COOLEY

Greenore 6 Year Old bott code L9015 db **(89) n23.5 t22.5 f21 b22.** Very enjoyable whiskey. But two points: cut the caramel and really see the baby sing. And secondly, as a "Small Batch" bottling, how about putting a batch number on the label...? *40%. Cooley.*

Greenore 8 Year Old bott code L8190 db **(86.5) n20 t22 f23 b21.5.** The vague hint of butyric on the nose is more than amply compensated by the gradual build up to something rather larger on the palate than you might have expected (and don't be surprised if the two events are linked). The corn oil is almost a meal in itself and the degree of accompanying sugar and corn flour is a treat. *40%. Cooley.*

Greenore 15 Years Old bott code L8044 db **(90) n23 t22.5 f22 b22.5.** The advent of the Kilbeggan 15 reminded us that there must be some grain of that age around, and here to prove it is a superb bottling of the stuff which, weirdly, is a lot better than the blend. Beautiful. *43%*

Greenore 18 Years Old db **(91) n22.5 t22.5 f23 b23.** This continuous still at Cooley should be marked by the State as an Irish national treasure. One of the most complex grains you'll ever find, even when heading into uncharted territory like this one. *46%. ncf. 4000 bottles.*

◇ **Hyde 1916 No.3 Áras Cask Aged 6 Years Single Grain** bott Feb 16 **(87) n22 t23 f20.5 b21.5** Cooley grain probably ranks as the best being made right now, with the loss of Dumbarton and Port Dundas in Scotland. Sadly, as deliciously rich as this is, far too much toffee on the finish rather detracts from its normal excellence. Highly enjoyable, but the flag flies nowhere near full mast. By the way: the 1916 on the label doesn't represent year of distillation or bottling. Or is there to celebrate the year of my dad's birth. No, it is something a little more political than that. *46%. ncf. 5,000 bottles.*

GLENDALOUGH

◇ **Glendalough 3 Year Old Irish Single Grain** sherry & Madeira butts db **(91) n22** dense grape but a sweet edge; **t23.5** the usual succulent mouth feel but now chewier with the spices alighting upon a gorgeous chocolate fruit and nut theme; **f22.5** a late, toasty bitterness while the spices rumble on; **b23** a much richer and more confident grain than their first, sherry-finished version. Excellent. *43%*.

Glendalough Double Barrel Irish Whiskey first aged in American bourbon casks, then Spanish oloroso casks **(88.5) n22.5** vague fruit, mainly of pears; **t23** succulent mouth feel with a juicy surge of barley and spice; **f21** dulls out but remains silky, though dry; **b22** a very pleasant malt but rather vague and at times a little dull. *42%*

MIDLETON

⬧ **Method and Madness Single Grain Irish Whiskey** bourbon barrels, finished in virgin Spanish oak casks db **(89.5) n22** huge tannin – pencil shavings: you can have too much of a good thing...; thankfully all kinds of sugar notes are lurking in the wings...; **t22.5** ah, much softer....and the sweetness!!! Unquestionably the sweetest Irish whiskey of all time as the sugars leeched from the oak gather to form a maple syrup, then ulmo honey guard of honour – and in apparently concentrated form. The hardest grain made in the British Isles has been reduced to a sugar-laden softie...; **f22** there had to be spices coming into play with such a big oak statement...and they turn up on cue...; **b23** if you've never tasted a sweet Spanish virgin before, here's your chance... *46%*.

TEELING

Teeling Single Grain Irish Whiskey (94) n23.5 t23.5 f23 b24 Presumably Cooley 'grain – as good as anything of its ilk on this planet. And showing it has enough about it to combine to stunning effect with some high quality wine casks. I've just had that Teeling feeling.... wonderful! *46%. ncf.*

Teeling Whiskey Single Grain wine cask finish, bott Aug 2015 **(89) n22 t23 f22 b22** Exceptionally soft and satisfying. *46%. ncf.*

⬧ **Teeling Whiskey Single Grain Wine Casks Finish** bott Jun 16 **(87) n21.5 t22 f21.5 b22** Silky, friendly with an attractive wine gum simplicity. *46%. ncf.*

Blends

Barr an Uisce Wicklow Rare Blended Irish Whiskey bourbon barrel, sherry cask finish **(87.5) n22.5 t22 f21 b22.** Busy whiskey with a creamy nose and sugar-gorged middle. However, the finish turns a tad bitter. *43%. ncf.*

Bushmills 12 Years Old Distillery Reserve db **(86) n22.5 t22.5 f20 b21.** This version has gone straight for the ultra lush feel. For those who want to take home some 40% abv fruit fudge from the distillery. *40%*

Bushmills 1608 400th Anniversary (83) n21 t21.5 f20 b20.5. Thin-bodied, hard as nails and sports a peculiarly Canadian feel. *46%. Diageo.*

Bushmills 1608 db **(87) n22 t23 f20 b22.** A blend which, through accident, evolution or design, has moved a long way in style from when first launched. More accent on fruit though, predictably, the casks aren't quite what they once were. Ignoring the furriness on the finish, there is much to enjoy on the grape-must nose and how the fruit bounces off the rigid grain on delivery. *46%*

Bushmills Black Bush (91) n23 t23 f21.5 b23.5. This famous old blend may be under new management and even blender. But still the high quality, top-notch complexity rolls around the glass and your palate. As beautiful as ever. *40%*

⬧ **Bushmills Black Bush** bott code L6140IB001 **(95) n23.5** a beautifully angular nose: the profound sherry influence is all grapey, soft and yielding while the grain is ramrod stiff and heads in single lines only. The result is unusual, enticing and surprisingly complex; **t24** a soft, mellifluous delivery with the malt standing up to be counted first and foremost, both offering a profound barley front and then a growing fruity tone. The hardy grain gives welcome backbone, though it's the malt again which chips in with a more delicate heather-honey tone; the texture may not be quite as heavy and thick as it once was but it has weight enough and enjoys a sticky succulence to make the most of the muscovado...; **f23.5** long with the grape caressing softly and the spices now making an excellent counter mark. The grain still offers a firm guiding light which the malt and very delicate tannins follow elegantly; **b24** of all the famous old blends in the British Isles, this has probably bucked the trend by being an improvement on its already excellent self. The warehouses of Bushmills distillery boast the highest quantity of quality, unsulphured sherry butts I have encountered in the last 20 years, and this is borne out by a blend which has significantly upped the wine influence in the recipe but has not paid a price for it, as has been the usual case in Scotland. Indeed, it has actually benefitted. This is a belter, even by its normal own high standards. Truly classic and should be far easier to find than is normally the case today. *40%.*

Bushmills Original (80) n19 t21 f20 b20. Remains one of the hardest whiskeys on the circuit with the Midleton grain at its most unflinching. There is a sweeter, faintly maltier edge to this now while the toffee and biscuits qualities remain. 40%

Cassidy's Distiller's Reserve bott code L8067 (84.5) n21.5 t22 f20 b21. Some salivating malt on flavour-exploding delivery, but all else tame and gentle. 40%. Cooley.

⬦ **Dunville's Three Crowns** (80) n19 t22 f19 b20 Three casks and Three Crowns. So three cheers for the return of one of the great names in Irish whiskey! Somewhere in my warehouse I have a few original bottles of this stuff I picked up in Ireland over the years and at auction. None I opened tasted quite like this. Have to say that, despite the rich-lip-smacking delivery, certain aspects of the tangy nose and finish don't quite gel and are a little off key. The coronation remains on hold... 43.5%.

⬦ **Dunville's Three Crowns Peated** (94.5) n23 don't expect puffing smoke or the embers of a peat fire. The lightest imaginable phenol drifts over the nose like glider over the Antrim coast: quiet and barely noticeable unless you look for it, but what it surveys is rather beautiful...; t24 stunning texture: a mix of light ulmo honey and mocha makes for the friendliest and most beautiful deliveries and follow through. The deft smoke drifts about without portfolio...; f23.5 long, slightly fruity now in an over-ripe gooseberry manner. Still the mocha and smoke make their quiet entreaties for attention; b24 even people purporting not to like peaty whisk(e)y will have a problem finding fault with this. This is a rare treat of an Irish. 43.5%.

Feckin Irish Whiskey (81) n20 t21 f20 b20. Tastes just about exactly the feckin same as the Feckin Strangford Gold... 40%. The Feckin Drinks Co.

⬦ **Flannigans Blended Irish Whiskey** (87.5) n21.5 t22.5 f21.5 b22 About as mouth-watering and easy going as blended Irish as I'll hope to find. Excellent sugars and velvety body ensure the most pleasant, if simple, of rides. Even a little spice peps up the flagging finish. 40%. Quality Spirits International.

⬦ **The Irishman Cask Strength 2016** 1st fill bourbon casks (90) n21.5 surprisingly non-committal and conservative for a whiskey this strength: just a squeeze of lemon on the vanilla; t23 that's much more like it!! The malt crashes against the palate to offer a puckering, grassy freshness; sharp, lemon sherbet and several waves of intense vanilla; f22.5 sweetened milky mocha...and a little spice; b23 doesn't try to overload the taste buds with too many flavour profiles: this one is all about shape, intensity and effect. 54%. ncf. 1,800 bottles.

Jameson (95) n24.5 Swoon...bizarrely shows even more Pot Still character than the Redbreast I tasted yesterday. Flinty to the point of cracking. The sherry is there but on reduced terms, allowing the firm grain to amplify the unmalted barley: truly brilliant; t24 mouth-watering delivery then wave upon wave of diamond-hard barley and grain; the odd eclectic layer of something sweetish and honeyed, but this is eye-watering stuff; f22.5 an annoying touch of caramel creeps in, costing points, but even beyond that you still cannot other than be charmed by the layering of cocoa, barley and light grape; b24 I thought I had detected in bottlings I had found around the world a very slight reduction in the Pot Still character that defines this truly classic whiskey. So I sat down with a fresh bottle in more controlled conditions...and was blown away as usual. The sharpness of the PS is vivid and unique; the supporting grain of the required crispness. Fear not: this very special whiskey remains in stunning, truly wondrous form. 40%

⬦ **Jameson** bott code L701012030 (87) n22 t22.5 f21 b21.5 Now, isn't that the way it always happens! Having tasted crisp, characterful true-to-form Jamesons around the globe for the last year or so, the one I get here for a re-taste is the "other" version. Suddenly the sexiest Irish on the market has become a dullard. Where it should be soaring with Pot Still it is laden with toffee. And a little sulphur nagging on the finish doesn't help, either. Does tick the other boxes, though. But hardly representative. 40%.

⬦ **Jameson 18 Years Old** bott code L629231345 (91) n22 grain dominant and soft. Was expecting a much richer input from the barrels but we have a more marmalade-fruity incursion, instead; t23 excellent two tone mouth feel with both backbone and blubber. A definite fruit pastel sweetness – and juiciness - with the spices showing early...and fading a little; f23 the softer elements keep the game going; the fruits remain sharp and the spices re-form; b23 definitely a change in direction from the last Jameson 18 I analysed. Much more grain focussed and paying less heed to the oak. 40%.

Jameson Black Barrel (91.5) n23 t23 f22.5 b23. Here's the problem faced by any Jameson blender: the column still grain from Midleton is the hardest on the palate made anywhere in the world. So how do you get it to mould into what you want? Usually you can't, so you have to make the whiskeys around it reflect and deflect for maximum effect. And that's what's going on here: a brittle whisky where the pot still element is magnified very cleverly indeed. Lovely stuff: New Yorkers are a lucky bunch! 40%. NY exclusive.

⬧ **Jameson Black Barrel** bott code L700431433 **(93)** n23 grain doesn't come more solid in character than this: a kind of White Bush on steroids. But, slowly, layers of sugars begin to become exposed, some as crisp as the grain, others soft and molten; t23.5 one of the most salivating deliveries of any Irish blend: little evidence of malt being at work here, again more the sugars and friendly, vaguely bourbon tannins producing the goods especially with the vivid, warming spices. Indeed, the spices become bolder by the second; the uncompromising hardness of the grain never goes away; f23 spiced vanilla on a light oil; the spices stretch the whiskey further than had first seemed possible b23.5 an improved, more sugar-laden and spicy whiskey. 40%.

Jameson The Blender's Dog **(92)** n23 t23.5 f22 b23.5 A clever blend, as this is just as much about mouth feel as it is flavour construction. You have made this dog do some entertaining tricks, Billy Leighton, my dear old friend... 43%. ncf. The Whisky Makers Series.

⬧ **Jameson The Blender's Dog** bott code L608231059 **(91.5)** n22.5 t23 f23 b23 A very slight variance on the previous sample (above) with the grain whiskey a little more dominant here despite the softer mouth feel. All the usual tricks and intrigues though a little less orange blossom honey a tad more maple syrup, which helps lengthen the finale. 43%. The Whiskey Makers Series.

Jameson Bold **(92)** n24 t23.5 f21.5 b23 Delicious stuff. But not to be confused with the excellent Indian malt, Bold, from Paul John, which is a lot Bolder than this... That said, a blender's blend with the nose making one purr with delight and appreciation. 40%. The Deconstructed Series.

⬧ **Jameson Bold** bott code L617431172 **(93)** n24 t23.5 f22.5 b23 Absolutely spot on with the tasting notes above. Only changes are slightly more fudge through the centre ground and a degree less bitterness on the finish, though still here. Crucially, however, the honey has a bigger late say. 40%. The Deconstructed Series.

Jameson Caskmates **(91.5)** n23.5 t23 f22 b23 Some serious elements of Jameson Gold involved in this, especially the acacia honey thread. Delightful. 40%

⬧ **Jameson Caskmates Stout Edition** bott code L629315085 **(93)** n22 a little dull and lacklustre and you have to hunt hard for the stout; t23.5 immediately there is a silkiness on delivery unlike any Jameson before: almost frothy at first, then slowly hard-edged sugars begin to appear – and grain also. Here we begin to start chewing hard, especially when the spices emerge; f24 a muffled hint of mocha near the delivery becomes much clearer now. How the mouth feel can become softer seems impossible...yet it does! A little milk and ulmo honey help douse any over enthusiasm of the spices; b23.5 a very different experience to the Teeling equivalent. Here, the beer is far less prevalent on nose and taste, but makes a significant – and highly positive - contribution to the mouth feel. A super lush experience. 40%.

Jameson The Cooper's Croze **(95)** n24 t23.5 f23.5 b24 This is one of the most softly spoken great orations on Irish whiskey in recent years. An understated masterpiece. 43%. ncf. The Whisky Makers Series.

⬧ **Jameson The Cooper's Croze** bott code L608231057 **(94.5)** n23.5 t24 f22.5 b24 Huh! Near enough same final score as last time, though a gentle change in emphasis and shape means the scoring itself was slightly different. Remains the most astonishingly lush and richly-flavoured of whiskeys, except on this bottling there is a bigger toffee surge, especially towards the finish and a gentle bitter tail off which has cost a half mark. Just remember: whatever anyone ever tells you, no two bottlings are identical: it is impossible. 43%. The Whiskey Makers Series.

Jameson Crested **(90)** n23 t24 f20.5 b22.5 When first introduced back in the early 1960s as Jameson's first-ever bottled whiskey, this was known as Crested 10. Now probably ditched the number so not to confuse with age. 40%

⬧ **Jameson Crested** bott code L635731441 **(91)** n23 t23.5 f22 b22.5 That's curious. A slight upping of the caramels here has slightly reduced the overall complexity, and the depth of the fruit. However, the bitter, off-key finish from my last sample is missing here making, when all is said and done, a slightly more satisfying all round experience. Swings and roundabouts... 40%.

Jameson The Distiller's Safe **(95)** n23.5 t24 f23.5 b24 Not sure if head distiller Brian Nation is any relation to former comedy scriptwriter Terry Nation, creator of The Daleks. Either way, this is Dalektable stuff and as beautifully timed as the funniest skits ever written. 43%. ncf. The Whisky Makers Series.

⬧ **Jameson The Distiller's Safe** bott code L60331023 **(93)** n24 t24 f22 b23 This brand's safe, too...at least for another bottling! As near as damn it a re-run of the last bottle I tasted, though here the butteryness kicks in sooner and there is a vague bitterness on the now chocolate-flaked finale. Still a stunner. 43%. The Whiskey Makers Series.

Jameson Gold Reserve **(88)** n22 t23 f20 b22. Enjoyable, but so very different: an absolute re-working with all the lighter, more definitively sweeter elements shaved mercilessly while the thicker oak is on a roll. Some distance from the masterpiece it once was. 40%

Jameson Lively (84.5) n21 t21.5 f21 b21. The belligerent grain of Midleton appears to be coming at you at full throttle and from all direction. The nose appears to be all grain, though a little toffee apple does creep in. The delivery is uncompromising: as hard as nails. 40%. *The Deconstructed Series.*

◇◇ **Jameson Lively bott code L617431174 (85.5) n21 t22 f21.5 b21** Well you have to applaud them for keeping to the script. A couple of thumbs up from the last bottling: the impact appears to have been softened very slightly (though, sadly, via toffee) and spices at the finish do no harm at all. 40%. *The Deconstructed Series.*

◇◇ **Jameson Round bott code L625831239 (93.5) n22.5** the Midleton grain is there to more than make up the number sand forms the most rigid of backbones. A series of meagre- no-frills sugars furnish those grains with the bare essentials of sweetness; **t24** ah...so that is where the roundness comes in! The delivery is like a sponge, revealing the softest molasses and maple syrup imaginable, even managing to remove the firmness from the grain; the mid-ground is a comfortable mix of half-hearted spice, coconut doused in golden syrup and an underlying vanilla...; **f23.5** long, with the oak now taking a keener interest. The vanilla dries slightly, becoming almost sawdusty towards the finale. Just a hint of lime is attached to late spice resurgence; **b23.5** just such a sensual whiskey... 40%. *The Deconstructed Series.*

◇◇ **Jameson Signature bott code L617531177 (93) n24** what a stunning aroma: lime Swiss Roll, aided and abetted by orange blossom honey and a very curious, an almost inexplicable, anthracite phenol buzz; **t23.5** soft as a the feather of quill, a light marmalade sharpness/ sweetness diluted by what seems like a maltiness, though the gathering fudge makes it difficult to pick out exactly; a little mocha and spice fill the middle ground; **f22.5** just a shade too much toffee on the still busy and spicy finish; **b23** no longer Signature Reserve, though every bit as good. This, though, like some other Jamesons of late appears to have an extra dose of caramel. Bring the colouring down and whiskey – and the scores here - will really fly! 40%.

Jameson Signature Reserve (93) n23.5 t23.5 f22.5 b23.5. Be assured that Signature, with its clever structuring of delicate and inter-weaving flavours, says far more about the blender, Billy Leighton, than it does John Jameson. 40%. *Irish Distillers.*

Kellan American oak cask **(84) n21 t22 f20 b21.** Safe whisky which is clean, sweet and showing many toffeed attributes. Decent spices, too. 40% (80 Proof). *Cooley.*

Kilbeggan bott code L7091 db (86) n21 t22 f21.5 b21.5. A much more confident blend by comparison with that faltering one of the last few years. Here, the malts make a significant drive towards increasing the overall complexity and gentle citrus style. 40%. *Cooley.*

Kilbeggan 15 Years Old bott code L7048 db (85.5) n21.5 t22 f21 b21. My word! 15 years, eh? How time flies! And on the subject of flying, surely I have winged my way back to Canada and am tasting a native blend. No, this is Irish albeit in sweet, deliciously rounded form. However, one cannot help feeling that the dark arts have been performed, as in an injection of caramel, which, as well as giving that Canadian feel has also probably shaved off some of the more complex notes to middle and finish. Even so, a sweet, silky experience. 40%. *Cooley.*

Kilbeggan 18 Year Old db (89) n23 t21.5 f22.5 b22. Although the impressive bottle lavishly claims "From the World's Oldest Distillery" I think one can take this as so much Blarney. It certainly had my researcher going, who lined this up for me under the Old Kilbeggan distillery, a forgivable mistake and one I think he will not be alone in making. This, so it appears on the palate, is a blend. From the quite excellent Cooley distillery, and it could be that whiskey used in this matured at Kilbeggan... which is another thing entirely. As for the whiskey: apart from some heavy handedness on the toffee, it really is quite a beautiful and delicate thing. 40%

Kilgeary bott code L8063 (79) n20 t20 f19 b20. There has always, and still proudly is, something strange about this blend. Cold tea on the nose and a bitter bite to the finish, sandwiches a brief flirtation with something sweet. 40%. *Cooley.*

Locke's bott code L8056 (85.5) n21 t22 f21.5 b21. Now, there you go!! Since I last really got round to analysing this one it has grown from a half-hearted kind of a waif to something altogether more gutsy and muscular. Sweeter, too, as the malts and grains combine harmoniously. A clean and pleasant experience with some decent malt fingerprints. 40%

Michael Collins A Blend (77) n19 t20 f19 b19. Michael Collins was known as the "big fellow". This pleasant, impressively spiced dram, might have enjoyed the same epithet had it not surrendered to and then been strangled by caramel on the finish. 40% (80 proof). *Cooley.*

Midleton Distillery Reserve (85) n22 t22 f20 b21. A whiskey which, for all its muscovado sweetness offers some memorable barley moments. 40%. *Irish Distillers Midleton Distillery only. Changes character slightly with each new vatting. This one is some departure.*

Midleton Very Rare 30th Anniversary Pearl Edition db (91) n23.5 t24 f21 b22.5 The nose and delivery will go down in Irish whiskey folklore... 53.1%

Midleton Very Rare 1984 (70) n19 t18 f17 b16. Disappointing with little backbone or balance. *40%. Irish Distillers.*

Midleton Very Rare 1985 (77) n20 t20 f18 b19. Medium-bodied and oily, this is a big improvement on the initial vintage. *40%. Irish Distillers.*

Midleton Very Rare 1986 (79) n21 t20 f18 b20. A very malty Midleton richer in character than previous vintages. *40%. Irish Distillers.*

Midleton Very Rare 1987 (77) n20 t19 f19 b19. Quite oaky at first until a late surge of excellent pot still. *40%. Irish Distillers.*

Midleton Very Rare 1988 (86) n23 t21 f21 b21. A landmark MVR as it is the first vintage to celebrate the Irish pot-still style. *40%. Irish Distillers.*

Midleton Very Rare 1989 (87) n22 t22 f22 b21. A real mouthful but has lost balance to achieve the effect. *40%. Irish Distillers.*

Midleton Very Rare 1990 (93) n23 t23 f24 b23. Astounding whiskey: one of the vintages every true Irish whiskey lover should hunt for. *40%. Irish Distillers.*

Midleton Very Rare 1991 (76) n19 t20 f19 b18. After the Lord Mayor's Show, relatively dull and uninspiring. *40%. Irish Distillers.*

Midleton Very Rare 1992 (84) n20 t20 f23 b21. Superb finish with outstanding use of feisty grain. *40%. Irish Distillers.*

Midleton Very Rare 1993 (88) n21 t22 f23 b22. big, brash and beautiful – the perfect way to celebrate the 10th-ever bottling of MVR. *40%. Irish Distillers.*

Midleton Very Rare 1994 (87) n22 t22 f21 b22. Another different style of MVR, one of amazing lushness. *40%. Irish Distillers.*

Midleton Very Rare 1995 (90) n23 t24 b21 b22. They don't come much bigger than this. Prepare a knife and fork to battle through this one. Fabulous. *40%. Irish Distillers.*

Midleton Very Rare 1996 (82) n21 t22 f19 b20. The grains lead a soft course, hardened by subtle pot still. Just missing a beat on the finish, though. *40%. Irish Distillers.*

Midleton Very Rare 1997 (83) n22 t21 f19 b21. The piercing pot still fruitiness of the nose is met by a countering grain of rare softness on the palate. Just dies on the finish when you want it to make a little speech. Very drinkable. *40%. Irish Distillers.*

Midleton Very Rare 1999 (89) n21 t23 f22 b23. One of the maltiest Midletons of all time: a superb blend. *40%. Irish Distillers.*

Midleton Very Rare 2000 (85) n22 t21 f21 b21. An extraordinary departure even by Midleton's eclectic standards. The pot still is like a distant church spire in an hypnotic Fen landscape. *40%. Irish Distillers.*

Midleton Very Rare 2001 (79) n21 t20 f18 b20. Extremely light but the finish is slightly on the bitter side. *40%. Irish Distillers.*

Midleton Very Rare 2002 (79) n20 t22 f18 b19. The nose is rather subdued and the finish is likewise toffee-quiet and shy. There are some fabulous middle moments, some of flashing genius, when the pot still and grain combine for a spicy kick, but the finish really is lacklustre and disappointing. *40%. Irish Distillers.*

Midleton Very Rare 2003 (84) n22 t22 f19 b21. Beautifully fruity on both nose and palate (even some orange blossom on aroma). But the delicious spicy richness that is in mid launch on the tastebuds is cut short by caramel on the middle and finish. A crying shame, but the best Midleton for a year or two. *40%. Irish Distillers.*

Midleton Very Rare 2004 (82) n21 t21 f19 b21. Yet again caramel is the dominant feature, though some quite wonderful citrus and spice escape the toffeed blitz. *40%.*

Midleton Very Rare 2005 (92) n23 t24 f22 b23. OK, you can take this one only as a rough translation. The sample I have worked from here is from the Irish Distillers blending lab, reduced to 40% in mine but without caramel added. And, as Midleton Very Rares always are at this stage, it's an absolute treat. Never has such a great blend suffered so in the hands of colouring and here the chirpiness of the pot still and élan of the honey (very Jameson Gold Label in part) show just what could be on offer given half the chance. Has wonderful natural colour and surely it is a matter of time before we see this great whiskey in its natural state. *40%*

Midleton Very Rare 2006 (92) n22 t24 f23 b23. As raw as a Dublin rough-house and for once not overly swamped with caramel. An uncut diamond. *40%*

Midleton Very Rare 2007 (83) n20 t22 f20 b21. Annoyingly buffeted from nose to finish by powering caramel. Some sweeter wisps do escape but the aroma suggests Canadian and insufficient Pot Still gets through to make this a Midleton of distinction. *40%. Irish Distillers*

Midleton Very Rare 2008 (88.5) n22 t23 f21.5 b22. A dense bottling which offers considerably more than the 2007 Vintage. Attractive, very drinkable and without the caramel it might really have hit the heights. *40%. Irish Distillers.*

Midleton Very Rare 2009 (95) n24 t24 f23 b24. I've been waiting a few years for one like this to come along. One of the most complex, cleanest and least caramel-spoiled bottlings for a good few years and one which makes the pot still character its centre piece. A genuine celebration of all things Midleton and Barry Crockett's excellence as a distiller in particular. *40%. Irish Distillers.*

Midleton Very Rare 2010 (84) n21 t22 f20 b21. A case of after the Lord Mayor's Show. Chewy and some decent sugars. But hard to make out detail through the fog of caramel. *40%*

Midleton Very Rare 2011 (81.5) n22.5 t20 f19 b20 Another disappointing version where the colour of its personality has been compromised for the sake of the colour in the bottle. A dullard of a whiskey, especially after the promising nose. *40%. Irish Distillers.*

Midleton Very Rare Irish Whisky 2012 db (89.5) n22 t23 f22 b22.5. Much more like it! After a couple of dud vintages, here we have a bottling worthy of its great name & heritage. *40%.*

Midleton Very Rare Irish Whisky 2014 db (78.5) n20.5 t22 f17 b19. Must say how odd it looks to see Brian Nation's signature scrawled across the label and not Barry Crockett's. Also, I was a bit worried by this one when I saw the depth of orange hue to this whiskey. Sadly, my fears were pretty well founded. Toffee creaks from every corner making for a mainly flat encounter with what should be an uplifting Irish. Some lift at about the midway point when something, probably pot still, throws off the shackles of its jailer and emerges briefly with spice. But all rather too little, especially in the face of a dull, disappointingly flawed, fuzzy finale. Midleton Very Rare should be, as the name implies, a lot, lot better than this safe but flabby, personality bypassed offering. The most frutrating aspect of this is that twice I have tasted MVR in lab form just prior to bottling. And both were quite stunning whiskeys. That was until the colouring was added in the bottling hall. *40% WB15/416*

Midleton Very Rare 2016 (87.5) n22 t22.5 f21.5 b21.5 The grain, not exactly the most yielding, has the clearest mandate to show its uncompromising personality A huge caramel presence softens the impact and leads to a big show of coffee towards the finish. But between these two OTT beasts the Pot Still is lost completely soon after its initial delicious impact on delivery. *40%.*

Paddy (74) n18.5 t20 f17.5 b18. Cleaned its act up a little. Even a touch of attractive citrus on the nose and delivery. But where does that cloying sweetness come from? As bland as an Irish peat bog but, sadly, nothing like so potentially tasty. *40%. Irish Distillers.*

Powers (91) n23 t24 f22 b22. Is it any coincidence that in this bottling the influence of the caramel has been significantly reduced and the whiskey is getting back to its old, brilliant self? I think not. Classic stuff. *40%. Irish Distillers.*

Powers Gold Label (87) n22 t22 f21 b22. The solid pot still, the very DNA of what made Powers, well, Powers is vanishing in front of our very noses. Yes, still some pot still around, but nothing like so pronounced in the way that made this, for decades, a truly one-off Irish and one of the world greats. Still delightful and with many charms but the rock hard pot still effect is sadly missed. What is going on here? *40%. Irish Distillers.*

Powers Gold Label (96) n23 t24.5 f24 b24.5 A slightly dfferent breed. This is not all about minute difference in strength...this is also about weight distribution and flavour pace. It is a subtly different blend...and all the better for it...Make no mistake: this is a truly classic Irish. *43.2%*

The Quiet Man Traditional Irish Whiskey bourbon casks (88.5) n22 t22 f22.5 b22 A gentle and genteel whiskey without an unfriendly voice. And with it I toast the memory of John Mulgrew. *40%*

Teeling Small Batch Irish Whiskey (87.5) n21 t23 f21.5 b22. Pleasant enough, and again showing high class grain. But a sharper liquorice/phenol note is out of kilter here and disrupts the natural flow of things, especially on the finish. *46%. ncf.*

Teeling Whiskey Small Batch rum casks, bott Feb 17 (89) n22 soft and with a sheen, as though burnished with sugar. A little spice juts out; t23 intensely sweet delivery. The mouth feel is massively sumptuous and yielding; f22 more sugars and spice on the vanilla; very slight bitter fade; b22 you have to be a little wary with rum casks as they can easily over-ride complexity, as is the case here. This, then, is all about effect and for that it can't be faulted. *46%. ncf.*

Teeling Whiskey Stout Cask Small Batch 200 Fathoms Imperial Stout finish, bott Mar 17 (92.5) n22.5 certainly a unique nose among the world's whiskies: this has a peculiar empty Guinness glass effect, one that has been left out on the garden table in the sun for a few hours. Leather and Demerara sugar each play a role in balancing the roastiness...; t23.5 silky sugars land lightly, a little ulmo honey, too. But elsewhere there are much duskier tones, semi-toasty but incredibly soft; f23 the feeling that you had a mouthful of stout – oat stout especially – about two or three minutes ago, as this is without any lingering bitterness...; b23.5 whiskey and chaser in one go... The extra roastiness imparts a distinctive extra weight which works exceptionally well. *46%. ncf.*

Tullamore Dew (85) n22 t21.5 f20.5 b21. The days of the throat being savaged by this one appear to be over. Much more pot still character from nose to finish and the rough edges remain, attractively, just that. 40%. *Campbell & Cochrane Group.*

Tullamore Dew 10 Years Old (81.5) n21 t21.5 f19 b20. A bright start from this new kid on the Tullamore block. Soft fruit and harder pot still make some kind of complexity, but peters out at the death. 40%. *Campbell & Cochrane Group.*

Tullamore Dew 12 Years Old (84.5) n21.5 t21.5 f20 b21.5. Silky thanks to some excellent Midleton grain: there are mouthwatering qualities here that make the most of the soft spices and gentle fruit. An improved whiskey, if still somewhat meek and shy. 40%. *Campbell & Cochrane Group.*

Tullamore Dew Black 43 (85) n19 t22 f22.5 b21.5. "Black". Now there's an original name for a new whiskey. Don't think it'll catch on, personally: after all, who has ever heard of a whisky being called "This or That" Black...?? But the whiskey might. Once you get past the usual Tullamore granite-like nose, here even more unyielding than usual, some rather engaging and complex (and especially spicy) things happen, though the caramel does its best to neuter them. 43%. *William Grant & Sons.*

Tullamore D.E.W Cider Cask Finished bott code. L2 65TD, bott 05/05/2015 (85.5) n21.5 t22 f21 b21. Experienced Whisky Bible readers will know that over the years I have tasted whisky matured either in cider casks or, more usually, in an environment where cider brandy is also maturing. That has always been with a single malt, though, and without exception the apple shines through. Here, though, the apple has to work overtime to get any change out of the hardest, least yielding grain on the planet. The result is an, at times, attractive blend, but also one which has its more unforgiving moments... 40%

Tullamore Dew Heritage (78) n20 t21 f18 b19. Tedious going with the caramel finish a real turn off. 40.0%. *Campbell & Cochrane Group.*

Uisce Beatha Real Irish Whiskey ex-Bourbon cask (81) n21 t20.5 f19.5 b20. The label blurb claims this is soft and subtle. That is, about as soft and subtle as if distilled from granite. Hard as nails with dominant grains; takes no prisoners at the death. 40%

Walker & Scott Irish Whiskey (85) n21 t22 f21 b21. Oddly, sharper grain has helped give his some extra edge through the toffee. A very decent blend. 40%

The Wild Geese Classic Blend (80.5) n20 t21 f19.5 b19. Easy going, pretty neutral and conservative. If you are looking for zip, zest and charisma you've picked the wrong goose (see below). 40%. *Cooley for Avalon.*

The Wild Geese Rare Irish (89.5) n22 t23 f22 b22.5. Just love this. The Cooley grain is working sublimely and dovetails with the malt in the same effortless way wild geese fly in perfect formation. A treat. 43%. *Cooley for Avalon.*

Writers Tears (93) n23.5 t24 f22 b23.5. Now that really was different. The first mix of pure Pot Still and single malt I have knowingly come across in a commercial bottling, but only because I wasn't aware of the make up of last year's Irishman Blend. The malt, like the Pot Still is, I understand from proprietor Bernard Walsh, from Midleton, but the two styles mixed shows a remarkably similar character to when I carried out an identical experiment with pure pot still and Bushmills the best part of a decade ago. A success and hopefully not a one off. Which is more than I can say for the label, a whiskey collectors – sorry, collector's – item in its own right. There is a wonderfully Irish irony that a whiskey dedicated to Ireland's extraordinary literary heritage should be represented by a label, even a brand name, so punctually inept; it's almost brilliant. The reason for the Writers (sic) Tears, if from the spirits of James Joyce, Samuel Beckett, George Bernard Shaw, Oscar Wilde and perhaps even Maurice Walsh, author of The Quiet Man whose even quieter grandson, Barry, became a legendary blender at Irish Distillers, will be open to debate: we will never know whether they laughed or cried. As far as the actual whiskey is concerned, though, I am sure they, to a man, would have no hesitation but to pen the most luminous and positive critiques possible. 40%. *Writers Tears Whiskey Co.*

◇ **Writers' Tears Vintage Cask 2016** ex-bourbon barrels, bott Sept 2016 (89) n22 t23 f22 b22 A pleasant, but mildly muted version of Irishman Cask Strength 2016, though here the spices arrive later. 2016. 53%. ncf. 2,640 bottles.

Poitin

◇ **Spirit of Dublin Irish Poitin** batch. 02 db (88.5) n22 t23 f21.5 b22 A whole lot cleaner than some – if not all - of the Irish poitin I've tasted from jam jars, lemonade bottles and recycled bottles of Power's over the last 40 years or so. Has the obvious "new make" aroma of unmatured malt, except perhaps a little less discernible copper. Peaks with a big gristy sugar surge about four or five flavour beats after the delivery, but thins a little quickly thereafter. 52.5%.

American Whiskey

I t is now eleven years since a bourbon won the coveted title of Jim Murray's Whisky Bible World Whisky of the Year. And you might think that with Kentucky going a record-equalling three years without the top award the greatest days may be in the past. Wrong.

For the consistency of the great bourbon and rye means that year on year it is found in the top three world whisky spots - sometimes occupying all positions. And it's probably for that reason on my tours around the globe I am asked by whisky shop owners and distributors if I know any good Kentucky and Tennessee brands, or contacts in their marketing departments, so they might bring a great American onboard. Because at last, after years of being in the shadows of Scotch whisky, bourbon and rye are being rightly recognised for their greatness, diversity and, increasingly often, enormity. Certainly, their consistency is the very thing which is winning over so many friends. Not that Kentucky and Tennessee is having it all its own way at the moment. Yes, the quality continues to improve there - providing you ignore the nonsense and lemming-like move towards cask finishes which despoils the unsullied name of bourbon. But for the second year running a distillery in Texas really does show that great bourbon can be made on both sides of the North American continent: last time out it Garrison Brothers in Hye, this time Balcone's of Waco, 125 miles away.

But the most romantic story by some distance is the naming of Colonel Taylor's 4 Grain Bourbon as not just American whiskey of the year but the Bible's number one Whisky in the World for 2018. For months earlier workers making alterations at Buffalo Trace accidentally broke through into an unknown chamber housing the remains of an old distillery. It did not take long to recognise this as the original E H Taylor plant. And with its discovery came the ending of a search I had begun well over 20 years ago, as for me the architecture didn't add up. Pouring over some vague old maps I had found in downtown Frankfort and enlisting the puzzled help of manager Joe Darmond and legendary distiller Elmer T Lee, I had narrowed its likely resting place either within the distillery but now demolished, or on some land just the other side of the Kentucky River. Now at last we know....and what a time to find out!

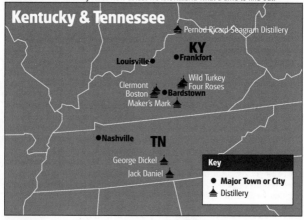

Kentucky & Tennessee

Pernod Ricard Seagram Distillery

KY

Louisville ● ●Frankfort

Wild Turkey
Clermont Four Roses
Boston ▲ ●Bardstown
Maker's Mark ▲

●Nashville **TN**

George Dickel ▲
Jack Daniel ▲

Key

● **Major Town or City**
▲ **Distillery**

Bardstown	Woodford Reserve
Heaven Hill	**Louisville**
Tom Moore	Early Times
Frankfort	Bernheim
Buffalo Trace	Stitzel Weller

Bourbon Distilleries

Bourbon confuses people. Often they don't even realise it is a whiskey, a situation not helped by leading British pub chains, such as Wetherspoon, whose bar menus list "whiskey" and "bourbon" in separate sections. And if I see the liqueur Southern Comfort listed as a bourbon one more time I may not be responsible for my actions.

Bourbon is a whiskey. It is made from grain and matured in oak, so really it can't be much else. To be legally called bourbon it must have been made with a minimum of 51% corn and matured in virgin oak casks for at least two years. Oh, and no colouring can be added other than that which comes naturally from the barrel.

Where it does differ, from, say Scotch, is that the straight whiskey from the distillery may be called by something other than that distillery name. Indeed, the distillery may change its name which has happened to two this year already and two others in the last three or four. So, to make things easy and reference as quick as possible, I shall list the Kentucky-based distilleries first and then their products in alphabetical order along with their owners and operational status.

BUFFALO TRACE Leestown, Frankfort. Sazerac. Operating.

BROWN-FORMAN Shively, Louisville. Brown-Forman. Operating.

FOUR ROSES Lawrenceburg. Kirin. Operating

HEAVEN HILL BERNHEIM DISTILLERY Louisville. Heaven Hill. Operating.

JIM BEAM Boston and Clermont. Fortune Brands. Operating.

MAKER'S MARK Loretto. Fortune Brands. Operating.

TOM MOORE Bardstown. Sazerac. Operating.

WILD TURKEY Lawrenceburg. Campari Group. Operating.

WOODFORD RESERVE Near Millville. Brown-Forman. Operating.

Jim Murray's Whisky Bible American Whiskey Award Winners

	Overall Winner	Bourbon	Rye	Microdistilleries
2004	George T. Stagg	George T. Stagg	Sazerac Rye 18 Years Old	McCarthy's Oregan Single Malt 3
2005	George T. Stagg	George T. Stagg	Sazerac Rye 18 Years Old	McCarthy's Oregan Single Malt
2006	George T. Stagg	George T. Stagg	Sazerac Rye 18 Years Old	McCarthy's Oregan Single Malt
2007	Buffalo Trace Experimental	Buffalo Trace Experimental	Rittenhouse Rye 21 Barrel No.28	McCarthy's Oregan Single Malt
2008	George T. Stagg 70.3%	George T. Stagg 70.3%	Old Potrero Hotaling's 11 Essay MCMVI-MMVII	Old Potrero Hotaling's 11 Essay MCMVI-MMVII
2009	George T. Stagg (144.8 Proof)	George T. Stagg (144.8 Proof)	Rittenhouse Rye 23 Barrel No.8	Stranahan's Colorado 5 Batch 11
2010	Sazerac Rye 18 (Fall 2008)	George T. Stagg (144.8 Proof)	Sazerac Rye 18 (Fall 2008)	N/A
2011	Thomas H. Handy Rye (129 Proof)	William Larue Weller (134.8 Proof)	Thomas H. Handy Rye (129 Proof)	N/A
2012	George T. Stagg (143 Proof)	George T. Stagg (143 Proof)	Thomas H. Handy Rye (126.9 Proof)	N/A
2013	Thomas H. Handy Rye (128.6 Proof)	William Larue Weller (133.5 Proof)	Thomas H. Handy Rye (128.6 Proof)	Balcones Brimstone
2014	William Larue Weller (123.4 Prof)	William Larue Weller (123.4 Proof)	Thomas H. Handy Rye (132.4 Proof)	Cowboy Bourbon Whiskey 3
2015	William Larue Weller	William Larue Weller	Sazerac Rye 18 (Fall 2013)	Arkansas Single Barrel Reserve #190
2016	Pikesville Straight Rye (110 Proof)	William Larue Weller	Pikesville Straight Rye (110 Proof)	Notch 12 Year Old
2017	Booker's Rye 13 Years 1 Mo 12 Days	William Larue Weller (134.6 Proof)	Booker's Rye 13 Years 1 Mo 12 Day	Garrison Brothers Cowboy 2009
2018	Colonel E.H. Taylor Four Grain 12	Colonel E.H. Taylor Four Grain 12	Thomas H. Handy Rye (126.2 Proof)	Balcone's Texas Blue Corn

Bourbon

1792 Full Proof Kentucky Straight Bourbon db (96) n24 t23.5 f24 b24.5 If all the 1,000 plus whiskies and whiskeys I taste for the Bible were of this standard, not only would the world be one bloody fantastic place but, at 40 minutes a go – the time it has taken to unravel this beast – this book would never get finished. But then you'd have no need for it... *62.5% (125 proof)*

◇ **1792 High Rye Kentucky Straight Bourbon** db (96) n23.5 a little French toast at first, then a very gradual build-up of roasty sugars, especially muscovado which impart a distinct fruitiness – perhaps reflecting the influence of the rye; t24.5 you don't actually realise it at first as the weight is so beautifully even, the flavours so cleverly distributed...but this is huge! The silky corn oil undercurrent doesn't represent the much firmer layering of rye which appears to give this bourbon its backbone. The sweetness and related fruit roams from black cherry jelly to treacle tart; f23.5 now butterscotch appears to take over, again taking the varying sugars and tannins in its stride; b24.5 my word! What an exhibition of controlled and sometimes disguised big flavours...! Stupendous! 47.15% (94.3 proof).

1792 Single Barrel Kentucky Straight Bourbon bott no K16 015 db (94.5) n23.5 t23.5 f24 b23.5 Surely it can be only a matter of time before this distillery pulls off a very major Whisky Bible award...Effortlessly brilliant. *49.3% (98.6 proof). sc.*

1792 Sweet Wheat Kentucky Straight Bourbon db (94.5) n23.5 t24 f23 b24 Barton had long been one of the wasted distilleries of the world, its product once bottled and sold way before its intricate, busy bourbon was able to sing to its fullest potential. Under the new management of Sazerac, we are now consistently seeing the greatness from this distillery that for decades was found only in its 6-year-old. This is a wheated, honeyed stunner. *45.6% (91.2 proof)*

Abraham Bowman Pioneer Spirit High Rye Bourbon Release No 12 dist 9/28/07, bott 7/24/15 db (92) n22 t23.5 f23 b23.5 Takes a little time to open up. But when it does it flowers better than a White Cornel... *50% (100 proof)*

Ancient Age Bonded (92) n23 t24 f23 b23. Unmistakably Buffalo Trace... with balls. *50%*

Ancient Ancient Age 10 Star (94.5) n23 t24 f23.5 b24. A bourbon which has slipped effortlessly through the gears over the last decade. It is now cruising and offers so many nuggets of pure joy this is now a must have for the serious bourbon devotee. Now a truly great bourbon which positively revels in its newfound complexity: a new 10 Star is born... *45%*

Ancient Ancient Age 10 Years Old (96) n23.5 t24 f24 b24.5. This whiskey is like shifting sands: same score as last time out, but the shape is quite different again. Somehow underlines the genius of the distillery that a world class whiskey can reach the same point of greatness, but by taking two different routes...However, in this case the bourbon actually finds something a little extra to move it on to a point very few whiskeys very rarely reach... *43%*

Baker's Aged 7 Years Kentucky Straight Bourbon Whiskey batch no. B-90-001 (95) n24 t23.5 f23.5 b24 One of those uncompromisingly delicious bourbons which makes spitting, as I have to do with each sample tasted, a very unnatural act... *53.5% (107 proof)*

Basil Hayden's Kentucky Straight Bourbon Whiskey bott code L5222 (87) n22.5 t22 f21 b21.5. Bigs up the bitter marmalade but a relatively thin bourbon with not enough depth to entirely manage the flattening and slightly unflattering vanilla. The usual rye-based backbone has gone missing. *40% (80 proof)*

Big Bottom Straight Bourbon 91 (95) n23 tight, in that small grain dominates over the corn, while making the most of its oils, and the oak is chunky, salty and chocolaty; t24 again, a big salty tang to this, but this then serves to bring out the enormity of the grains, in which the corn has fought back pole position; the middle is full of honey, liquorice and burgeoning spices; f24 and now the small grains are back behind the wheel for a tantalisingly complex finale; b24 stupendous bourbon. *45.5% (91 proof) ncf.*

Big Bottom Straight Bourbon 111 (85.5) n21.5 t20.5 f22.5 b21. An aggressive bourbon and that has nothing to do with the strength. The delivery is tart and lopsided. The sharpness recedes towards the middle and, finally, the lights shine as the praline and mocha enter the fray on the spicy finish. *55.5% (111 proof) ncf.*

Blade & Bow batch SW-B1 (84) n21.5 t21.5 f20 b21. A simple, if at times massively sweet, offering which minimises on complexity. *45.5%*

Blade and Bow 22 Year Old (95.5) n24 t24 f23.5 b24 This may not be the oldest bourbon brand on the market, but it creeks along as though it is. Every aspect says "Old Timer". But like many an old 'un, has a good story to tell... in this case, exceptional. *46% (92 proof)*

Blade & Bow DeLuxe batch WLCFSS-2 (88.5) n22.5 major liquorice contribution; t22.5 manuka honey and molasses counter the big toasty notes; f21 as the sugars fade, the toast burns...; b22.5 a steady ship which, initially, is heavy on the honey. *46%*

Blanton's (92) n21.5 t24 f23 b23.5. If it were not for the sluggish nose this would be a Whisky Bible Liquid Gold award winner for sure. On the palate it shows just why little can touch Buffalo Trace for quality at the moment... 40%

Blanton's Gold Original Single Barrel (96.5) n24 t24.5 f24 b24. It is improbable that a whiskey this enormous and with so many star turns can glide so effortlessly over the palate. One of the best Blanton's in years, this is true Gold standard... 46.5% (93 Proof)

Blanton's Takara (91.5) n24.5 t23 f22 b22. Not quite how many people might envisage a bourbon: certainly not butch enough to keep the wild west gunslingers happy. No this is a bourbon which searches for your feminine side. And being so light, leaves itself open for any off-key bitter notes which might just happen along the way. 49% (98 proof)

Blanton's Uncut/Unfiltered (96.5) n25 t24 f23.5 b24. Uncut. Unfiltered. Unbelievable. 65.9%

Booker's Bourbon 6 Years, 11 Months, 0 Days batch no. 2016-01 db (92.5) n24 t23.5 f22 b23 An usually fast tail off barely detracts from another beguiling bourbon. 63.95% (1279 proof)

Booker's 7 Years 2 Months 28 Days batch no. 2015-03 db (92.5) n23 t23.5 f22.5 b23.5 One very gentle giant. 63.6% (127.2 Proof)

Booker's 7 Years 5 Months batch no. C2014-05 db (95) n24 t24 f23 b24 Not for the simpering or squeamish. There's an oaky ambush to deal with. And if you ain't man (or woman) enough, then best to mosey on over to the sarsaparilla counter... 63.95%

Booker's Big Man, Small Batch 7 Years 2 Months 16 Days batch no. 2015-01 db (89.5) n22 t23 f22 b22.5 The driest Booker's I've happened across for a good while: probably ever. Matured for seven years in a warehouse located somewhere near the centre of the sun, one assumes... 64.35% (128.7 Proof)

Bowman Brother's Virginia Straight Bourbon (90) n21 t23 f23 b23. Quietly confident and complex: a bit of a gem waiting to be discovered. 45% (90 proof)

Buffalo Trace (92.5) n23 t24 f23.5 b23. Easily one of the lightest BTs I have tasted in a very long while. The rye has not just taken a back seat, but has fallen off the bus. 45%

⟡ **Buffalo Trace Experimental Collection Organic 6 Grain Whiskey 7 Years, 1 Month** dist 3-3-2010, bott 4-6-17, warehouse/floor H/3, rick/row/slot 4/2/4-11, sour mash type db (96) n23.5 well, that's busy! All kind of intricate grain notes, some recognisable, others not, make for a mosaic aroma. Bits and pieces everywhere, some green and sharp, others more earthy, fruity and compact. These tessellations appear to be held in place by a heather-honey glue; t24.5 that sharpness on the nose is slightly exaggerated on delivery, resulting in an improbably salivating delivery. A backdrop of spiced coffee plays second fiddle to the busyness of the grains, some of which are so light they drift around the palate, as opposed to the earthier tendencies of others plus the chunky oak which adds molasses, liquorice and Manuka honey into the mix; f24 one of the longest, most complex finishes of any bourbon I have found this year with spice buzz and squabbling grains rumbling far into the distance; b24 always great to start the working day off with an entirely new experience. And with this containing corn, buckwheat, brown rice, sorghum, wheat and rye it was certainly that: indeed, I had nosed and tasted the bourbon blind of the label or even the title entry above, for the sheer fun of trying to work out what this particular experiment was up to. I figured, easily, that it was a new grain recipe but I'd be lying if I said I recognised the constituent parts. Probably because while I have tasted whiskies and whiskeys containing all these individual grains, it was the first time I had encountered one where they had all been thrown together. I hope it won't be the last time that they do, because those who love their bourbons weighty and impossibly busy will be clamouring for more of this. 45% (90 proof).

Buffalo Trace Single Oak Project Barrel #132 (r1yKA1 *see key below*) db (95) n24 t23.5 f23.5 b24. This sample struck me for possessing, among the first batch of bottlings, the classic Buffalo Trace personality. Afterwards they revealed that it was of a profile which perhaps most closely matches their standard 8-year-old BT. Therefore it is this one I shall use as the tasting template. 45% (90 Proof)

Key to Buffalo Trace Single Oak Project Codes

Mash bill type: r = rye; w = wheat
Tree grain: 1 = course; 2 = average; 3 = tight
Tree cut: x = top half; y = bottom half
Warehouse type: K = rick; L = concrete
Entry strength: A = 125; B = 105
Seasoning: 1 = 6 Months; 2 = 12 Months
Char: All #4 except * = #3

Buffalo Trace Single Oak Project Barrel #1 (r3xKA1*) db (90.5) n22 t23 f23 b22.5. Soft corn oil aroma, buttery, big sugars building, silky texture, long. 45% (90 Proof)

Buffalo Trace Single Oak Project Barrel #2 (r3yKA1*) db (91.5) n23 t23 f22.5 b23. Bright rye on nose and delivery. Juicy red liquorice and soft corn oil to chew on... 45%

Buffalo Trace Single Oak Project Barrel #3 (r2xKA1) db (90.5) n22.5 t23 f22.5 b22.5. Nutty, dry aroma; apple fruitiness and brown sugars. 45% (90 Proof)

Buffalo Trace Single Oak Project Barrel #4 (r2yKA1) db (92) n23 t23 f23 b23. Exceptionally crisp; sharp rye, honeycomb, big liquorice. 45% (90 Proof)

Buffalo Trace Single Oak Project Barrel #5 (r2xLA1*) db (89) n23 t22.5 f21.5 b22. Dullish after a rye-intense and busy nose. Early muscovado followed by vanilla and spice. 45%

Buffalo Trace Single Oak Project Barrel #6 (r3yLA1*) db (90) n22.5 t22 f23 b22.5. Toast with salted butter and maple syrup. Prickly, mildly aggressive spice throughout. 45%

Buffalo Trace Single Oak Project Barrel #7 (r3xLA1) db (90.5) n23 t22.5 f22.5 b22.5. Prominent rye on nose and delivery; tannin rich, toasty with big liquorice fade. 45%

Buffalo Trace Single Oak Project Barrel #8 (r3yLA1) db (92.5) n23 t23 f23.5 b23. Crisp rye aroma. Fruity, firm, salivating. Spiced toffee and muscovado; toasty. 45% (90 Proof)

Buffalo Trace Single Oak Project Barrel #9 (r3xKA2*) db (90) n22 t22.5 f23 b22.5. Marmalade on singed toast. Soft oils: slow release of natural caramels and mocha. 45%

Buffalo Trace Single Oak Project Barrel #10 (r3yKA2*) db (93) n23.5 t23.5 f22.5 b23.5. Rich, delicate rye. Complex, busy body; rye oils, tannins; slow sugar build. Bitters. 45%

Buffalo Trace Single Oak Project Barrel #11 (r3xKA2) db (94.5) n23 t24 f23.5 b24. Pronounced accent on rye, especially on delivery. Oak nose upfront; good muscovado fade. 45%.

Buffalo Trace Single Oak Project Barrel #12 (r3yKA2) db (92) n24 t23 f22.5 b22.5. The floral, supremely balanced nose isn't matched on the palate in weight or complexity. 45%

Buffalo Trace Single Oak Project Barrel #13 (r3xLA2*) db (89.5) n22 t23 f22 b22.5. Soft, yielding tactile. Early juicy, rye stance, slow build of duller light vanilla. Late spice. 45%.

Buffalo Trace Single Oak Project Barrel #14 (r3yLA2*) db (95) n24 t24 f23 b24. Chocolate rye nose and body; silky texture; brown sugar and vanilla; rye-rich sweet finish. 45%

Buffalo Trace Single Oak Project Barrel #15 (r3xLA2) db (90.5) n22.5 t23 f22 b23. Mouth feel concentrates on sugars and spices, which grow well. Fruity on nose and finish. 45%.

Buffalo Trace Single Oak Project Barrel #16 (r3yLA2) db (91.5) n22.5 t23.5 f22.5 b23. Explosive delivery: big spices, juicy, firm rye. Silky middle butterscotch & ulmo honey finish. 45%.

Buffalo Trace Single Oak Project Barrel #17 (r3xKB1*) db (88.5) n21.5 t22.5 f22.5 b22. Liquorice nose; oily body sweetens; big vanilla, caramel; dull spice. 45% (90 Proof)

Buffalo Trace Single Oak Project Barrel #18 (r3yKB1*) db (92.5) n23 t23 f23.5 b23. Full bodied from nose to finish. Cocoa mingles with rye and rich corn oil. Deep, intense, even. 45%

Buffalo Trace Single Oak Project Barrel #19 (r3xKB1) db (93) n23 t23.5 f23 b23.5. Solid, crisp rye hallmark on nose, delivery. Sugars firm and fractured. Precise whiskey. Salivating. 45%

Buffalo Trace Single Oak Project Barrel #20 (r3yKB1) db (95) n23.5 t24 f23 b23.5. Buttery nose; profound rye kick on delivery; ulmo honey body; complex toasty fade. 45%

Buffalo Trace Single Oak Project Barrel #21 (r3xLB1*) db (92) n23 t23 f23 b23. Estery, clipped rye nose; salivating delivery, dark sugars, moderate spice. 45%

Buffalo Trace Single Oak Project Barrel #22 (r3yLB1*) db (91) n22 t23.5 f22.5 b23. Corn/rye mix nose with manuka honey; silky corn oil throughout. Sweet, soft. 45%.

Buffalo Trace Single Oak Project Barrel #23 (r3xLB1) db (89) n21 t22.5 f22.5 b23. Massive spices throughout; juicy, rye-dominated middle. Soft corn oil and rounded. 45%.

Buffalo Trace Single Oak Project Barrel #24 (r3xLB1) db (90) n22 t23 f22.5 b22.5. Big liquorice nose and delivery; toffee raisin; big corn oil; medium spice; even ulmo honey. 45%

Buffalo Trace Single Oak Project Barrel #25 (r3xKB2*) db (90.5) n22.5 t23 f22.5 b22.5. Much more accent on the rye and a slow revealing of rich caramels and Demerara. 45%

Buffalo Trace Single Oak Project Barrel #26 (r3yKB2*) db (89.5) n22 t23.5 f22 b22. A sugary volley follows a shy nose. Quietens quickly; small grains add complexity. 45%

Buffalo Trace Single Oak Project Barrel #27 (r3xKB2) db (95.5) n23 t24 f24.5 b24. Bold timber on nose and delivery; hickory and liquorice evident; a big spiced honey finale. 45%

Buffalo Trace Single Oak Project Barrel #28 (r3yKB2) db (94.5) n23 t24 f23.5 b24. Sublime balance between sugars and grains on body. Controlled spice; layered cocoa. 45%

Buffalo Trace Single Oak Project Barrel #29 (r3xLB2*) db (91) n23 t22.5 f23 b22.5. Crisp rye nose; more precise grain. Excellent spices. 45% (90 Proof)

Buffalo Trace Single Oak Project Barrel #30 (r3yLB2*) db (95.5) n23.5 t24 f24 b24. One of the most delicate yet: crisp rye and sugars, minty forthright oak. Clean yet deep. 45%

Buffalo Trace Single Oak Project Barrel #31 (r3xLB2) db (87.5) n22 t22 f21.5 b22. Dull, rumbling and herbal; oily caramel and sugars. Soft. 45% (90 Proof)

Buffalo Trace Single Oak Project Barrel #32 (r3yLB2) db (90.5) n23.5 t23 f21.5 b22.5. Soft corn oils dominate. Buttery, molten muscovado. Late hickory. Bitterish finish. 45%

Buffalo Trace Single Oak Project Barrel #33 (w3xKA1*) db **(94.5)** n24 t23.5 f23 b24. Huge, busy baking spiced cake; muscovado sugar delivery; remains sweet, silky and spicy; *45%*

Buffalo Trace Single Oak Project Barrel #34 (w3yKA1*) db **(90)** n21.5 t23.5 f22.5 b22.5. Lazy nose but big succulent spiced molasses on delivery, with a mint cocoa finale. *45%*

Buffalo Trace Single Oak Project Barrel #35 (w3xKA1) db **(89.5)** n22 t22 f23 b22.5. Soft mint, yeasty; soft toffee delivery, builds in spice. *45% (90 Proof)*

Buffalo Trace Single Oak Project Barrel #36 (w3yKA1) db **(91.5)** n23 t23 f22.5 b23. Vague rum and toffee; bold, salivating, slow spice. *45% (90 Proof)*

Buffalo Trace Single Oak Project Barrel #37 (w3xLA1*) db **(90)** n21 t23 f22 b22. Typical big spice beast. Complex, doughy middle with accent on butterscotch and citrus. *45% (90 Proof)*

Buffalo Trace Single Oak Project Barrel #38 (w3yLA1*) db **(87.5)** n22 t23.5 f20.5 b21.5. Fizzy, busy nose matched by massive spice attack on delivery. Bitter, thin finish. *45% (90 Proof)*

Buffalo Trace Single Oak Project Barrel #39 (w3xLA1) db **(87)** n21.5 t22 f21.5 b22. Oak dominated: a degree of bitterness runs from nose to finish. Spices build slowly. *45%*

Buffalo Trace Single Oak Project Barrel #40 (w3xLA1) db **(93)** n23 t23 f23.5 b23.5. Soft, spiced cake, big citrus; silky, oily, bananas and golden syrup; late spice, balancing bitters. *45%*

Buffalo Trace Single Oak Project Barrel #41 (w3xKA2*) db **(92.5)** n22 t23 f23.5 b24. Less spice than expected. Docile start, builds in intensity. Buttery, big sugars. Balanced. *45%*

Buffalo Trace Single Oak Project Barrel #42 (w3yKA2*) db **(85.5)** n22 t21.5 f21 b21. Tight nose opens slowly; sultana pudding with maple syrup. Sweet, late bitterness. *45%*

Buffalo Trace Single Oak Project Barrel #43 (w3xKA2) db **(89)** n22 t23 f22 b22. Dates & plum nose; succulent fruit with broad maple syrup & molasses flourish. Big late spice. *45%.*

Buffalo Trace Single Oak Project Barrel #44 (w3yKA2) db **(89)** n23 t23 f21 b22. Spice rack nose; superb warm liquorice eruption on palate but dull finale. *45%*

Buffalo Trace Single Oak Project Barrel #45 (w3xLA2*) db **(87)** n23 t22 f21 b21. Ginger and allspice nose; body thick corn oil and toffee. Short finish. *45%*

Buffalo Trace Single Oak Project Barrel #46 (w3yLA2*) db **(88)** n21.5 t22 f22.5 b22 Doughy aroma. Big corn oils and sugars. Late spice growth. Big vanilla. Quietly complex. *45%*

Buffalo Trace Single Oak Project Barrel #47 (w3xLA2) db **(88.5)** n22.5 t22 f22 b22. Floral, waxy aroma; sugars dominate on palate with vanilla-butterscotch-ulmo theme. *45%.*

Buffalo Trace Single Oak Project Barrel #48 (w3yLA2) db **(90.5)** n22 t23 f22.5 b23. Sound, rounded from first to last. Greater accent on sugar intensity and vanilla inclusion. *45%*

Buffalo Trace Single Oak Project Barrel #49 (w3xKB1) db **(93)** n24 t23 f23 b23. Chocolate spice, apples, oaky aroma; treacle pudding, soft oils; banana and custard; bitters. *45%*

Buffalo Trace Single Oak Project Barrel #50 (w3yKB1*) db **(88)** n21.5 t23 f23.5 b22. Flat nose. Muscovado delivery. Slow spices. Late liquorice. Even. Limited depth. *45% (90 Proof)*

Buffalo Trace Single Oak Project Barrel #51 (w3xKB1) db **(89.5)** n23 t23 f21.5 b22. Firm and well spiced from start. Oils play bigger role as sugar develops. *45%.*

Buffalo Trace Single Oak Project Barrel #52 (w3yKB1) db **(87.5)** n21.5 t22 f22 b22. Yeasty nose; blend of molasses and toffee on delivery then slow spice increase. *45%*

Buffalo Trace Single Oak Project Barrel #53 (w3xLB1*) db **(91)** n22 t23 f23 b23. Full bodied on nose and palate. Toasty, big liquorice and molasses. Even and elegant. *45%*

Buffalo Trace Single Oak Project Barrel #54 (w3yLB1*) db **(89)** n22 t23 f22.5 b22.5. Crisp sugars and coconut nose; big molassed delivery, nutty and gentle oil. Late vanilla. *45%*

Buffalo Trace Single Oak Project Barrel #55 (w3xLB1) db **(89)** n22 t22 f23 b22. Mocha nose with sturdy tannin and vanilla early on delivery. Red liquorice and vanilla late on. *45%.*

Buffalo Trace Single Oak Project Barrel #56 (w3yLB1) db **(91)** n24 t22.5 f22 b22.5. Chocolate vanilla and tannins; soft, slow build up of spice, oily; bitters. *45% (90 Proof)*

Buffalo Trace Single Oak Project Barrel #57 (w3xKB2*) db **(94)** n23 t23.5 f23.5 b24. Immediate spice kick on nose and delivery. Caramels and marmalade. Busy, balanced. *45%*

Buffalo Trace Single Oak Project Barrel #58 (w3yKB2*) db **(90.5)** n22.5 t23 f22.5 b22.5. Liquorice and Fisherman's Friend nose; molassed middle and big spice finish. *45%*

Buffalo Trace Single Oak Project Barrel #59 (w3xKB2) db **(92)** n22 t23.5 f23 b23.5. Lighter Fisherman's Friend; roasted fudge; busy small grains attack. Mega complex. *45%*

Buffalo Trace Single Oak Project Barrel #60 (w3yKB2) db **(87.5)** n22.5 t22.5 f21 b21.5. Aggression to spice nose; tame delivery and body. Soft corn oil and muscovado. *46%*

Buffalo Trace Single Oak Project Barrel #61 (w3xLB2*) db **(94.5)** n24 t23 f23.5 b24. Classic spiced wheat; Demerara sugars and spices abound. Big. *45% (90 Proof)*

Buffalo Trace Single Oak Project Barrel #62 (w3yLB2*) db **(88)** n22 t22.5 f21.5 b22. Caramel is leading theme; soft, big wheated spice. Oily. *45% (90 Proof)*

Buffalo Trace Single Oak Project Barrel #63 (w3xLB2) db **(95.5)** n24 t23 f24 b24.5. Subtle dates, spice, cocoa; gentle, oily, perfect spice build. Ultra complex. *45% (90 Proof)*

Buffalo Trace Single Oak Project Barrel #64 (w3yLB2) db (**91**) n22.5 t23.5 f22.5 b23. Citrus nose. Big oak and spice delivery; treacle tart and liquorice. Softens into caramel. *45%*

Buffalo Trace Single Oak Project Barrel #65 (r2xKA1) db (**91**) n23.5 t22 f23 b22.5. Small grain nose; crunchy muscovado, corn oil; liquorice, vanilla; late spice. Complex. *45%*

Buffalo Trace Single Oak Project Barrel #66 (r2yKA1*) db (88.5) n22.5 t22.5 f21.5 b22. Dry tannin dominates on nose and palate; good spice kick and treacle. Short finish. *45%*

Buffalo Trace Single Oak Project Barrel #67 (r2xKA1) db (89.5) n22 t23 f22 b22.5. Blandish nose; tart, tight, sharp, some toffee raisin. *45% (90 Proof)*

Buffalo Trace Single Oak Project Barrel #68 (r2yKA1) db (**92**) n22.5 t23 f23.5 b23. Rye depth; deeper, warmer spices, liquorice and light molasses. *45% (90 Proof)*

Buffalo Trace Single Oak Project Barrel #69 (r2xLA1*) db (94.5) n22.5 t24 f23.5 b24. Crisp, sharp rye on nose and delivery. Jagged muscovado and spice. Goes down a treat... *45%*

Buffalo Trace Single Oak Project Barrel #70 (r2yLA1*) db (91.5) n22.5 t23 f23 b23. Yielding caramel and vanilla. Rye and hot spice breaks up the sleepy theme. *45% (90 Proof)*

Buffalo Trace Single Oak Project Barrel #71 (r2xLA1) db (**92**) n22.5 t23 f23.5 b23. Busy, small grain and citrus nose; rye backbone then darker sugars and tannin. *45%*

Buffalo Trace Single Oak Project Barrel #72 (r2yLA1) db (89) n22.5 t23 f21.5 b22. Floral nose; juicy, tangy, citrus. Liquorice, sugary vanilla. Bitter marmalade finish. *45%*

Buffalo Trace Single Oak Project Barrel #73 (r2xKA2*) db (87.5) n21.5 t22 f22 b22. Tight, unyielding nose. Initially crisp rye then thick vanilla and baked apple blanket. *45%*

Buffalo Trace Single Oak Project Barrel #74 (r2yKA2*) db (88) n22 t22 f22 b22. Corny nose; more corn oil early on; syrup, huge rye sure on finish; bitters slightly. *45% (90 Proof)*

Buffalo Trace Single Oak Project Barrel #75 (r2xKA2) db (91.5) n23 t22.5 f23 b23. Clean with accent firmly on grain throughout. Spiced minty mocha middle and fade. *45%.*

Buffalo Trace Single Oak Project Barrel #76 (r2yKA2) db (89) n22.5 t22.5 f22 b22. Bristling rye on nose and delivery; fruity edge then dullish spiced fudge and mocha. *45%*

Buffalo Trace Single Oak Project Barrel #77 (r2xLA2*) db (88) n22 t23 f21 b22. Busy, bitty nose; sugary blast on delivery; spice follow through then vanilla overload. *45%.*

Buffalo Trace Single Oak Project Barrel #78 (r2yLA2*) db (89) n22.5 t22 f22.5 b22. Small grain busy nose; light spice to oils; light rye, late sugars; chewy caramels. *45% (90 Proof)*

Buffalo Trace Single Oak Project Barrel #79 (r2xLA2) db (90) n23 t23.5 f23 b23.5. Juicy crisp sugars. Toasty with slow liquorice burn. Creamed spiced hickory fade. Complex. *45%.*

Buffalo Trace Single Oak Project Barrel #80 (r2yLA2) db (91.5) n23 t22.5 f23 b23. Broad oily strokes on nose, delivery. Simple vanilla tannins and ulmo honey. *45%.*

Buffalo Trace Single Oak Project Barrel #81 (r2yKB1*) db (**94**) n23 t23 f24 b24. Candy shop fruitiness; delicate oils and flavour development; big yet subdued brown sugars. *45%*

Buffalo Trace Single Oak Project Barrel #82 (r2yKB1*) db (91.5) n23 t23.5 f22.5 b23. Liquoice, manuka honey; lurid rye bite and lychee fruitiness; mocha and Demerara. *45%*

Buffalo Trace Single Oak Project Barrel #83 (r2xKB1) db (**92**) n22.5 t23 f23.5 b23. Sharp, angular grain, rye dominant. Softer salty praline fade. *45%.*

Buffalo Trace Single Oak Project Barrel #84 (r2yKB1) db (**94**) n23.5 t24 f23 b23.5. Hefty nose mixing tannin, rye and hickory. Huge sugar and corn oil theme. *45%.*

Buffalo Trace Single Oak Project Barrel #85 (r2xLB1*) db (88.5) n21.5 t22.5 f22 b22.5. Shy nose of soft vanilla; firm body with more vanilla and butterscotch; low level sugar. *45%*

Buffalo Trace Single Oak Project Barrel #86 (r2yLB1*) db (90) n22.5 t22 f23 b22.5. Salty, sweaty nose; sharp delivery with rye, red liquorice dominant; spiced mocha finish. *45%*

Buffalo Trace Single Oak Project Barrel #87 (r2xLB1) db (93.5) n22.5 t23.5 f23.5 b24. Citrus-led nose; slow, corn oil start then explosive grain; rye, liquorice & honey to the fore. *45%.*

Buffalo Trace Single Oak Project Barrel #88 (r2yLB1) db (89) n23.5 t22 f21.5 b22. Hickory, rye nose; liquorice delivery big caramel surge; bitters on finish. *45% (90 Proof)*

Buffalo Trace Single Oak Project Barrel #89 (r2xKB2*) db (89.5) n22 t22.5 f22 b22.5. Rye radiates on nose and delivery. Big spice surge to the middle. Late mocha, liquorice. *45%*

Buffalo Trace Single Oak Project Barrel #90 (r2yKB2*) db (**94**) n23.5 t24 f23 b23.5. Big tannin, cocoa and caramel throughout. Major peppery spice. Complex. *45% (90 Proof)*

Buffalo Trace Single Oak Project Barrel #91 (r2xKB2) db (86.5) n21.5 t22 f21.5 b21.5. Half-cooked: dull caramel throughout. Short spice peak. Sweet, oily, lacking complexity. *45%*

Buffalo Trace Single Oak Project Barrel #92 (r2yKB2) db (**91**) n22 t23 f23 b23. Silky texture. Big corn oil but intense tannin thinned by beech honey. Hickory and maple syrup. *45%*

Buffalo Trace Single Oak Project Barrel #93 (r2xLB2*) db (89) n22.5 t22 f22 b22.5. Soft rye and sugars; juicy grain, tangy citrus, muscovado. *45% (90 Proof)*

Buffalo Trace Single Oak Project Barrel #94 (r2yLB2*) db (92.5) n22.5 t24 f23 b23. Rich, hefty. Slightly salty, crisp rye. Light caramel, hint of Guyanese rum. Delicate spice. *45%*

Buffalo Trace Single Oak Project Barrel #95 (r2xLB2) db **(94)** n23 t23.5 f23.5 b24. Citrus, banana; soft vanilla, profound rye sharpness, spices. Big. *45% (90 Proof)*

Buffalo Trace Single Oak Project Barrel #96 (r2yLB2) db **(89)** n22 t23.5 f21.5 b22. Bright, grainy delivery in contrast to oily nose and finish. Heavy, dry molasses at the death. *45%*

Buffalo Trace Single Oak Project Barrel #97 (w2xKA1*) db **(87)** n22.5 t22 f21.5 b21.5. Toffee apple nose; heavy corn oil, light muscovado sugar, bitters out; *45% (90 Proof)*

Buffalo Trace Single Oak Project Barrel #98 (w2yKA1*) db **(93)** n23 t23.5 f23 b23.5. Peppers on at full blast on nose and delivery; big oily liquorice and treacle counter. *45%*

Buffalo Trace Single Oak Project Barrel #99 (w2xKA1) db **(86.5)** n22 t22 f21 b21.5. Malty, vanilla; thin maple syrup, caramel. Dull. *45% (90 Proof)*

Buffalo Trace Single Oak Project Barrel #100 (w2xLA1) db **(94)** n23 t23.5 f23.5 b24. Busy, green, fresh; big juicy, vanilla, muscovado, spices. *45% (90 Proof)*

Buffalo Trace Single Oak Project Barrel #101 (w2xLA1) db **(96)** n23.5 t24 f23.5 b25. Unerring chocolate and mint aided by even muscovado, vanilla and spice. Hugely complex. *45%*

Buffalo Trace Single Oak Project Barrel #102 (w2xLA1*) db **(88.5)** n22 t22 f22.5 b22. Insane tannin on nose; overcooked caramel. Massive sugar-spice mix. *45% (90 Proof)*

Buffalo Trace Single Oak Project Barrel #103 (w2xLA1) db **(89)** n22.5 t22 f22 b22.5. Early spice on nose; prominent brown sugars on deliver; corn oil follow through. *45%*

Buffalo Trace Single Oak Project Barrel #104 (w2xLA1) db **(91)** n23 t23 f22.5 b22.5. Apple, cinnamon; light spice; corn oil; vanilla and ulmo honey; spices, bitters out. *45%*

Buffalo Trace Single Oak Project Barrel #105 (w2xKA2*) db **(89)** n22.5 t22 f22.5 b22. Spiced, lively nose; hot cross buns; oils and sugars build slowly; spices intensify at end. *45%*

Buffalo Trace Single Oak Project Barrel #106 (w2yKA2*) db **(92.5)** n24 t23 f23 b23.5. Mega complex nose: busy sugars and spices; silky texture; nougat, caramel. *45%*

Buffalo Trace Single Oak Project Barrel #107 (w2xKA2) db **(93.5)** n23.5 t23 f23 b24. Bold, rich nose; pepper bite; thick body: maple syrup, molasses, cocoa. Classic wheat recipe. 45%.

Buffalo Trace Single Oak Project Barrel #108 (w2yKA2) db **(94)** n22.5 t24 f23.5 b24. Soft, delicate. Ulmo honey leads the sugars; corn oil but complex liquorice and lavender. *45%*

Buffalo Trace Single Oak Project Barrel #109 (w2xLA2*) db **(87.5)** n21.5 t23.5 f21 b21.5. Dull nose and finish. Delivery lush, souped-up spiced caramel-toffee fudge. 45%.

Buffalo Trace Single Oak Project Barrel #110 (w2yLA2*) db **(89)** n22 t22.5 f22.5 b23. Intense caramel; liquorice and toffee middle, citrus and salt; caramel finish. *45% (90 Proof)*

Buffalo Trace Single Oak Project Barrel #111 (w2xLA2) db **(89)** n22.5 t22.5 f22 b22. Intriguing sugar operatic. Vary from castor to muscovado. Countering spices make it work. 45%.

Buffalo Trace Single Oak Project Barrel #112 (w2yLA2) db **(90)** n21.5 t23 f22.5 b23. Caramel fudge lead. Usual whited spice before heavier, liquorice development. *45%*

Buffalo Trace Single Oak Project Barrel #113 (w2xKB1*) db **(88)** n22.5 t22 f22 b21.5. Big vanilla nose; minor spice, oily, buttery vanilla. Simple. *45% (90 Proof)*

Buffalo Trace Single Oak Project Barrel #114 (w2yKB1*) db **(90)** n22 t23 f22 b23. Elements of citrus. Oily corn. Controlled spice. Earthy and sweet. *45% (90 Proof)*

Buffalo Trace Single Oak Project Barrel #115 (w2xKB1) db **(88.5)** n22 t22.5 f22 b22. An even mix of corn oil and persistant light sugars. Low level spice until finish. A tad dull. 45%.

Buffalo Trace Single Oak Project Barrel #116 (w2yKB1) db **(90.5)** n22 t22 f23.5 b23. Caramelised biscuit nose; polite, corny start; finish rich with hickory, manuka honey. 45%

Buffalo Trace Single Oak Project Barrel #117 (w2xLB1*) db **(82.5)** n20 t20.5 f22 b20. Weird pineapple nose; fruity delivery with spices trying to escape. Entirely different. *45%*

Buffalo Trace Single Oak Project Barrel #118 (w2yLB1*) db **(86)** n20.5 t21.5 f22 b22. Fruity (less than 117); big toffee body, busy spice, developing ulmo honey. Soft. *45%*

Buffalo Trace Single Oak Project Barrel #119 (w2xLB1) db **(93.5)** n22.5 t24 f23.5 b23.5. Spices from nose to fade, accompanied by chewy burnt fudge. French toast finale. Big. 45%.

Buffalo Trace Single Oak Project Barrel #120 (w2xLB1) db **(89.5)** n23 t22 f22.5 b22. Controlled oak throughout. Intermittent dry vanilla. Delicate sugars. *45% (90 Proof)*

Buffalo Trace Single Oak Project Barrel #121 (w2xKB2*) db **(89)** n22.5 t23 f21.5 b22. Citrusy corn oil apparent and dominates. Sugars rampant, spices shy. Rather flat finale. *45%*

Buffalo Trace Single Oak Project Barrel #122 (w2xKB2) db **(93)** n22 t23.5 f23.5 b24. Serious wheat-spice with cocoa back up. Demerara sugars evenly spread. Complex. *45%*

Buffalo Trace Single Oak Project Barrel #123 (w2xKB2) db **(85.5)** n21 t22 f21 b21.5. One of the dullest yet: limited sparkle despite light spice. Big caramel. *45% (90 Proof)*

Buffalo Trace Single Oak Project Barrel #124 (w2yKB2) db **(90.5)** n22.5 t23 f22.5 b22.5. The startling, extra sugars over #123 impact hugely. Juicy; oak (liquorice) support. *45%*

Buffalo Trace Single Oak Project Barrel #125 (w2xLB2*) db **(93)** n24 t22 f22.5 b22.5. Heavy oak, spices; firm, juicy. Softer caramel fade. 45% (90 Proof)

Buffalo Trace Single Oak Project Barrel #126 (w2yLB2*) db (**90**) n22 t23 f22.5 b22.5. Floral nose (primroses); elaborate delivery of spice and creamed mocha plus molasses. *45%*

Buffalo Trace Single Oak Project Barrel #127 (w2xLB2) db (**85.5**) n21.5 t22 f21 b21. Off balance, citrus; juicy at first, bitters later. *45% (90 Proof)*

Buffalo Trace Single Oak Project Barrel #128 (w2yLB2) db (**89**) n21.5 t22 f22.5 b22.5. Conservative nose, OTT spice on delivery. Molassed dates and walnut. *45% (90 Proof)*

Buffalo Trace Single Oak Project Barrel #129 (r1xKA1*) db (**88**) n22.5 t22 f22 b22. Firm grainy, tannin nose; nougat, nutty, corn oil; clean but dim vanilla fade. *45% (90 Proof)*

Buffalo Trace Single Oak Project Barrel #130 (r1yKA1*) db (**92.5**) n22 t23.5 f23 b24. Macho: cloaked in oak. Kumquats on nose, oily, punchy tannins on sharp, silky delivery. *45%*

Buffalo Trace Single Oak Project Barrel #131 (r1xKA1) db (**92.5**) n23 t23 f23.5 b23. Relaxed vanilla, light tannin; corn oily, icing sugars, marzipan. *45% (90 Proof)*

Buffalo Trace Single Oak Project Barrel #132
See above.

Buffalo Trace Single Oak Project Barrel #133 (r1xLA1*) db (**89**) n22.5 t23 f21 b22.5. Small grain busyness does the business: rye leads the dark sugar procession. Bitters out. *45%*

Buffalo Trace Single Oak Project Barrel #134 (r1yLA1*) db (**91.5**) n22.5 t23 f23 b23. Velvet delivery: big spice cushioned by muscovado and butterscotch. Mixed honey finale. *45%*

Buffalo Trace Single Oak Project Barrel #135 (r1xLA1) db (**92.5**) n23 t23 f23.5 b23. Chocolatey theme, except on firm, grainy nose. Silky oils, intense flavours, rye rigidity. *45%*

Buffalo Trace Single Oak Project Barrel #136 (r1yLA1) db (**92**) n23.5 t22.5 f23 b23. Liquorice on nose and delivery. Spicy. Richer oils. Demerara. Spice. *45% (90 Proof)*

Buffalo Trace Single Oak Project Barrel #137 (r1xKA2*) db (**90.5**) n22 t23.5 f22 b23. Fruity opening with a hardening rye presence and emphasis on muscovado. Late cocoa. *45%*

Buffalo Trace Single Oak Project Barrel #138 (r1yKA2*) db (**87**) n22.5 t21.5 f21.5 b21.5. Marzipan, citrus nose; dull delivery, slow build of muscovado and vanilla. Soft. *45%*

Buffalo Trace Single Oak Project Barrel #139 (r1xKA2) db (**88**) n22.5 t22 f21.5 b22. More or less flatlines throughout. Big corn oil with limited spice and cocoa. *45%.*

Buffalo Trace Single Oak Project Barrel #140 (r1yKA2) db (**93**) n23 t24 f23 b23. Classic bourbon: citrus-rich nose, thumping spicy molassed liquorice-hickory delivery. *45%*

Buffalo Trace Single Oak Project Barrel #141 (r1xKA2*) db (**90**) n23.5 t22 f22.5 b22. Busy nose & finish. Corn dominates the mid ground. Sugar, spice growth. Complex finale. *45%.*

Buffalo Trace Single Oak Project Barrel #142 (r1yLA2*) db (**89.5**) n22.5 t22.5 f22 b22.5. Light tannin nose; oils, liquorice, spice bite. More corn oil. Sugars, spicy vanilla. *45%*

Buffalo Trace Single Oak Project Barrel #143 (r1xLA2) db (**88.5**) n22.5 t22.5 f21.5 b22. Hickory drifts in and out of narrative. Light rye & vanilla. Very soft – overly gentle. *45%.*

Buffalo Trace Single Oak Project Barrel #144 (r1yLA2) db (**91**) n23 t23 f22.5 b22.5. Tannin led. Bristling dark sugars. Oily with comforting vanilla. *45%.*

Buffalo Trace Single Oak Project Barrel #145 (r1xKB1*) db (**91**) n22.5 t22 f23.5 b23. Nougat, cocoa; busy small grains; oily corn; spiced chocolate. *45% (90 Proof)*

Buffalo Trace Single Oak Project Barrel #146 (r1yKB1*) db (**93**) n23 t24 f22 b24. Rye dominates with clarity and aplomb. Crystal clean nose and delivery: Dundee cake. *45%*

Buffalo Trace Single Oak Project Barrel #147 (r1xKB1) db (**93**) n23.5 t23 f23.5 b23. Macho rye & tannins. Toasty & dry delivery; liquorice, sugars, soft spice gain ascendency. *45%.*

Buffalo Trace Single Oak Project Barrel #148 (r1yKB1) db (**94**) n22.5 t24 f23.5 b24. Quiet aroma but intense delivery. Big sugar up front, liquorice and manuka honey fade. *45%*

Buffalo Trace Single Oak Project Barrel #149 (r1xLB1*) db (**92**) n22.5 t23.5 f23 b23. Massive tannin influence. Heavy nose; heavier body with toasty liquorice and cocoa. *45%*

Buffalo Trace Single Oak Project Barrel #150 (r1yLB1*) db (**93**) n23 t23.5 f23 b23.5. Huge tannin softened by big dark sugars, hickory, sharp rye notes. Long, chewy finish. *45%*

Buffalo Trace Single Oak Project Barrel #151 (r1xLB1) db (**91.5**) n22 t23 f23.5 b23. Diced citrus; light body with busy grains. Powerful dark sugars gain upper hand. *45%.*

Buffalo Trace Single Oak Project Barrel #152 (r1yLB1) db (**81.5**) n21 t20.5 f20 b20.5. Vaguely butyric; harsh, hot fat corn, light rye; bitters out. *45% (90 Proof)*

Buffalo Trace Single Oak Project Barrel #153 (r1xKB2*) db (**94**) n23.5 t23.5 f23 b24. Complex nose, delivery. Big spice with crisp, juicy rye. Praline, delicate oils. Big but elegant. *45%*

Buffalo Trace Single Oak Project Barrel #154 (r1yKB2*) db (**92**) n22.5 t23 f23 b23.5. Rye dominates. Hard on palate; yet burnt raisin, lychee and muscovado soften. *45% (90 Proof)*

Buffalo Trace Single Oak Project Barrel #155 (r1xKB2) db (**93**) n23 t24 f22.5 b23.5. Fierce spice. Dynamic rye shapes all directions. Hickory and manuka honey combine. *45%*

Buffalo Trace Single Oak Project Barrel #156 (r1yKB2) db (**85.5**) n22 t21 f21.5 b21. Doesn't work. Spices too hot. Caramels and oils negate development. *45% (90 Proof)*

Buffalo Trace Single Oak Project Barrel #157 (r1xLB2*) db (84.5) n21 t21.5 f20.5 b21. Vague butyric; sharp, juicy corn with slow rye build. Bitter. 45% (90 Proof)

Buffalo Trace Single Oak Project Barrel #158 (r1yLB2*) db (88) n22 t22 f22 b22. Another brawny, corn-oily, oaky effort. Excellent cocoa, citrus and spice development. 45%

Buffalo Trace Single Oak Project Barrel #159 (r1xLB2) db (88) n20.5 t22.5 f22 b22.5. Vague butyric; firm sugars then watery, confident spices, soft honey. Complex. 45% (90 Proof)

Buffalo Trace Single Oak Project Barrel #160 (r1yLB2) db (92.5) n23.5 t23 f22 b23. A salty style with fruity, crisp rye right behind. Steady and firm. 45% (90 Proof)

Buffalo Trace Single Oak Project Barrel #161 (w1xKA1*) db (87) n21 t22 f22 b22. Cream caramel candy; juicy corn, oily; more caramel, Light spice. 45% (90 Proof)

Buffalo Trace Single Oak Project Barrel #162 (w1yKA1*) db (88.5) n22 t22 f22.5 b22. Cream soda and minty fudge. Early treacle kick then settles for simple life. 45%

Buffalo Trace Single Oak Project Barrel #163 (w1xKA1) db (90) n23 t22.5 f22 b22.5. Citrus, bubble gum; spiced muscovado sugars at first, bitters. 45% (90 Proof)

Buffalo Trace Single Oak Project Barrel #164 (w1yKA1) db (94.5) n23.5 t23 f24 b24. Citrus and vanilla; massive spice, building. Demerara. Warm and complex. 45% (90 Proof)

Buffalo Trace Single Oak Project barrel #165 (w1xLA1*) db (91.5) n22.5 t23 f23 b23. Lively, spice dominated. Ulmo honey offers superb back up. 45% (90 Proof)

Buffalo Trace Single Oak Project Barrel #166 (w1yLA1*) db (91) n22 t23 f23 b23. Heady, leathery. Sublime spice middle; molasses and liquorice enrich the tail. 45% (90 Proof)

Buffalo Trace Single Oak Project Barrel #167 (w1yLB1) db (94) n23.5 t23.5 f23 b24. Demerara, rummy; intense liquorice, hickory; dark sugars and big spice. 45% (90 Proof)

Buffalo Trace Single Oak Project Barrel #168 (w1xLA1) db (89.5) n22 t23 f22 b22.5. Clean, spiced nose; juicy grains with toffee and raisin. Mocha and liquorice on finish. 45%

Buffalo Trace Single Oak Project Barrel #169 (w1xKA2*) db (94) n23.5 t23.5 f23 b24. Spice, lavender & leather on delivery; spicy nose. Honey & corn oil follow through. 45% (90 proof)

Buffalo Trace Single Oak Project Barrel #170 (w1yKA2*) db (92.5) n22.5 t23 f23.5 b23.5. Sweet, spiced nose; firm, spicy delivery; Demerara and ulmo honey. 45% (90 Proof)

Buffalo Trace Single Oak Project Barrel #171 (w1xKA2) db (88.5) n22 t23 f21.5 b22. Friendly corn oils dominate. Estery. Dry finish after sugar and spice crescendo. 45%.

Buffalo Trace Single Oak Project Barrel #172 (w1yKA2) db (90.5) n22.5 t23 f22.5 b22.5. Tannins prevalent on nose and spiced delivery. Good bite, esters and oils. Late mocha. 45%

Buffalo Trace Single Oak Project Barrel #173 (w1xLA2*) db (91) n23.5 t23 f22 b22.5. Bold nose & delivery: honeycomb, tannins. Liquorice & vanilla middle; good spice balance. 45%

Buffalo Trace Single Oak Project Barrel #174 (w1yLA2*) db (89) n22 t23 f23 b22. Delicate oak; juicy corn, liquorice, light spices, buttery corn. Bitter marmalade. 45% (90 Proof)

Buffalo Trace Single Oak Project Barrel #175 (w1xLA2) db (91.5) n21.5 t23 f24 b23. Lazy nose, juicy delivery. Big vanilla profile. Buttery caramel; light honey & spice. Long. 45%.

Buffalo Trace Single Oak Project Barrel #176 (w1yLA2) db (89) n21.5 t22.5 f22.5 b22.5. Light caramel aroma; sharp, juicy (rye-esque) delivery with mocha & butter toffee finale. 45%.

Buffalo Trace Single Oak Project Barrel #177 (w1xKB1*) db (87) n21.5 t22 f22 b21.5. Vaguely spiced corn oil; soft, nutty, marzipan sweetness, citrus. Late mocha. 45% (90 Proof)

Buffalo Trace Single Oak Project Barrel #178 (w1yKB1*) db (88.5) n22.5 t23 f21.5 b21.5. Complex marzipan and Demerara nose and delivery; runs out of things to say. 45%

Buffalo Trace Single Oak Project Barrel #179 (w1xKB1) db (88) n21 t22 f22.5 b22.5 Dull caramel nose. Toffee caramel continues on palate. Late fudge sweetness. Growing spice. 45%.

Buffalo Trace Single Oak Project Barrel #180 (w1yKB1) db (92) n22 t23.5 f23 b23.5. Molasses/cough sweet nose; scrambled grains and citrus; thickens with corn at end. 45%

Buffalo Trace Single Oak Project Barrel #181 (w1xLB1*) db (94.5) n22.5 t24.5 f23 b23.5. Silky chocolate fudge delivery with perfect spice. Nose more austere, finish intense. 45%

Buffalo Trace Single Oak Project Barrel #182 (w1yLB1*) db (86) n21.5 t21.5 f22 b21. Nose over fruity; profound sugars but tart, thin body. Vanilla and mocha on finish. 45%

Buffalo Trace Single Oak Project Barrel #183 (w1xLB1) db (95.5) n24 t24 f23.5 b24. Intense. Brilliant fudge/honey/molasses delivery; cocoa finish; perfect spices: mini Weller! 45%.

Buffalo Trace Single Oak Project Barrel #184 (w1yLA1) db (93) n23.5 t23 f23 b23.5. Tannins, walnut oil; nutty, corn oils. Light spice, firm Demerara. Late fruity spice. Complex. 45%

Buffalo Trace Single Oak Project Barrel #185 (w1xKB2*) db (92.5) n23 t23.5 f23 b23. Dry, riveting nose; liquorice dominates the palate. Cocoa, hickory enlivened by sugars. 45%

Buffalo Trace Single Oak Project Barrel #186 (w1yKB2*) db (89.5) n23 t22.5 f22 b22.5. Rampant spice from delivery onwards. Burnt fudge and toasted raisin. 45% (90 Proof)

Buffalo Trace Single Oak Project Barrel #187 (w1xKB2) db (88) n22 t22 f22 b22. Exceptionally even and caramel rich. Unbalanced tannin and lack of spice. 45% (90 Proof)

Buffalo Trace Single Oak Project Barrel #188 (w1yKB2) db (**90**) n21.5 t23.5 f22.5 b22.5. Lazy nose. Bright delivery; citrusy corn oil and muscovado. Late mocha and liquorice. 45%

Buffalo Trace Single Oak Project Barrel #189 (w1xLB2*) db (88.5) n24 t22 f21 b21.5. Complex citrus, delicate yet big; tart, sweet, fresh, strangely off balance. 45% (90 Proof)

Buffalo Trace Single Oak Project Barrel #190 (w1yLB2*) db (**94**) n23.5 t24 f23 b23.5. Ulmo/manuka honey mix on nose and delivery; silky corn oil; spiced mocha. Complex. 45%

Buffalo Trace Single Oak Project Barrel #191 (w1xLB2) db (94.5) n23 t23.5 f24 b24. Big, spicy, classic; firm wheaty spiciness, juicy, thick caramels. Complex. 45% (90 Proof)

Buffalo Trace Single Oak Project Barrel #192 (w1yLB2) db (94.5) n23 t24 f23.5 b24. Demerara rum nose; heavy, dry liquorice body; late spice; molassed butterscotch finish. 45%

Buffalo Trace Experiment #7 Heavy Char Barrel charred white oak, dist 21 Jan 97, bott Oct 12 db (**77**) n20 t21.5 f17 b18.5. The very nature of experiments means that, sometimes, they go wrong. Perhaps a bit harsh for this one which, to be more precise, has not gone right. The nose has an almost bizarre sherry feel to it, the fruitiness really striking home on the attractive delivery. From then on, it's downhill, leaving an unattractive tang at the death. 45%

Buffalo Trace Experimental Collection 15 Minute Infrared Light Wave Barrels dist 10/13/09, barrelled 10/14/09, bott 03/31/16, still proof: 140, entry proof: 125, warehouse/floor: I/5, rick/row/slot: 1/5/1-4, age at bottling: 6 Years, 5 Months, evaporation: 32% db (**92**) n24 t23 f22 b23 Astonishing that it is now some 25 years since I first discussed infrared cask treatment with a Scottish distiller (and was sent samples of maturing spirit in such treated barrels) but it is only now that I have seen it commercially available. Good ol' Buffalo Trace for keeping the public on its toes! 45% (90 proof)

Buffalo Trace Experimental Collection 30 Minute Infrared Light Wave Barrels dist 10/13/09, barrelled 10/14/09, bott 03/31/16, still proof: 140, entry proof: 125, warehouse/floor: I/5, rick/row/slot: 1/5/1-8, age at bottling: 6 Years, 5 Months, evaporation: 32% db (**91**) n23 t23 f22.5 b22.5 Has quite a different gait to the 15 minute version, being far more oak dependent as well as aggressive. 45% (90 proof)

Buffalo Trace Experimental Collection Old Fashioned Sour Mash Entry Proof 105 dist 05/01/02, barrelled 05/01/02, bott 08/20/15, still proof: 135, warehouse/floor: I/7, rick/row/slot: 22/2/1, age at bottling: 13 Years, 3 Months, evaporation: 66.2% db (**93**) n23.5 t23.5 f23.5 b23.5 Fascinating comparison to the 125 entry. Much more liquorice and tannin, much less acacia honey. Seems older and hairier, which I would not necessarily have expected. 45% (90 proof)

Buffalo Trace Experimental Collection Old Fashioned Sour Mash Entry Proof 125 dist 05/01/02, barrelled 05/01/02, bott 08/20/15, still proof: 135, warehouse/floor: I/7, rick/row/slot: 50/2/1, age at bottling: 13 Years, 3 Months, evaporation: 54.8% db (**95**) n24 t24 f23 b24 An experiment which should be turned into reality... 45% (90 proof)

Buffalo Trace Experimental Collection 12 Year Old Bourbon From Floor #1 dist 11/29/01, barreled 11/30/01, bott 3/12/14, still proof: 140, entry proof: 125, warehouse/floor: K/1, rick/row/slot:1/1/1-4, charred white oak, age at bottling, 12 years, 3 months, evaporation: 27% db (91.5) n23.5 t23 f22.5 b22.5 Delicate bourbon with limited fight. 45%.

Buffalo Trace Experimental Collection 12 Year Old Wheated Bourbon From Floor #1 dist 04/24/02, barrelled 04/26/02, bott 11/03/14, still proof: 130, entry proof: 125, warehouse/floor: K/1, rick/row/slot: 1/3/1-5, age at bottling: 12 Years, 6 Months, evaporation: (88.5) n22 t22 f22.5 b21.5 Pleasant, but feels as though it is lurching around; not entirely convincing. 42% db 45%

Buffalo Trace Experimental Collection 12 Year Old Wheated Bourbon From Floor #5 dist 04/24/02, barrelled 04/26/02, bott 11/03/14, still proof: 130, entry proof: 125, warehouse/floor: K/5, rick/row/slot: 51/1/1-5, age at bottling: 12 Years, 6 Months, evaporation: (**91**) n22 t23 f22.5 b23.5 A gorgeously weighted whiskey and the pace of development on the palate is sublime. 47% db 45%

Buffalo Trace Experimental Collection 12 Year Old Wheated Bourbon From Floor #9 dist 04/24/02, barrelled 04/26/02, bott 11/04/14, still proof: 130, entry proof: 125, warehouse/floor: K/9, rick/row/slot: 44/1/1-5, age at bottling: 12 Years, 6 Months, evaporation: (89) n23 t21.5 f22.5 b22 Technically very good, but a little overly simple and single paced. 51% db 45%

Buffalo Trace Experimental Collection 12 Year Old Bourbon From Floor #5 dist 11/29/01, barreled 11/30/01, bott 3/12/14, still proof: 140, entry proof: 125, warehouse/floor: K/5, rick/row/slot:51/1/21-24, charred white oak, age at bottling, 12 years, 3 months, evaporation: 25% db (**91**) n22 t23 f23 b23 Though heavier, lacks some of the grace and complexity of its lower-matured stablemate. 45%.

Buffalo Trace Experimental Collection 12 Year Old Bourbon From Floor #9 dist 11/29/01, barreled 11/30/01, bott 3/12/14, still proof: 140, entry proof: 125, warehouse/

floor: K/9, rick/row/slot:44/1/13-16, charred white oak, age at bottling, 12 years, 3 months, evaporation: 49% db (95.5) n24 t24 f23.5 b24 Floorless...and confirms about bourbon maturation what we already know. And this distillery in particular... 45%.

Bulleit Bourbon (87) n21.5 t22 f21.5 b22. Vanilla-fashioned on both nose and flavour development. If it was looking to be big and brash, it's missed the target. If it wanted to be genteel and understated with a slightly undercooked feel yet always friendly, then bullseye... 45% (90 proof)

Bulleit Bourbon 10 Year Old (90) n23 just the right chunkiness to balance the mint with the spiced honeycomb; t22.5 the house vanilla style returns, except now a little extra lightly fruity muscovado sugar moves in; the corn oil is much more confident and rich; f22 good length and some sound seasoning to the red liquorice and vanilla; b22.5 not remotely spectacular. But does the simple things deliciously. 45.6% (91.2 proof)

Bulleit Bourbon Barrel Strength (91.5) n22.5 lazy muscovado and light layering of orange blossom honey; t22.5 the tannins and sugars are neck and neck, with neither giving ground. Juicy, with a brief small grain effervescence; f23.5 such a satisfying finish: how many strands and variations of chocolate can one whiskey get through...?; the liquorice and molasses are a beautiful accompaniment...; b23 the extra oils at full strength make such a huge difference in seeing the fuller picture. 59.6% (119.2 proof)

Calhoun Bros Straight Bourbon (84.5) n20.5 t22 f21 b21. Very different! A much wider cut than the norm on straight bourbon whisky results in an oily fellow which you can chew until your jaws ache. Massively toasty, vanilla gorged and intense. 43% (86 proof)

Charter 101 (95.5) n23.5 t24.5 f23.5 b24. Now here is a whiskey which has changed tack dramatically. In many ways it's like the Charter 101 of a year back. But this bottling suggests they have turned a warehouse into a giant beehive. Because few whiskeys offer this degree of honey. You can imagine that after all these years, rarely does a whiskey genuinely surprise me: this one has. No wonder there is such a buzz in the bourbon industry right now... 50.5%

Clarke's Old Kentucky Straight Sour Mash Whisky Bourbon (88.5) n22.5 t22 f22 b22. Honest and hugely impressive bourbon. The rich colour – and remember straight bourbon cannot be falsely coloured – tells its own tale. 40%. Aldi.

Colonel E H Taylor Barrel Proof (91) n23.5 t23 f22 b22.5. A big boy which turns out to be a bit of a softy in the end... 67.25% (134.5 Proof). nc ncf.

Colonel E H Taylor Cured Oak (93.5) n24 t24 f23 b23.5 Not sure about the oak being cured: coming from Buffalo Trace, I doubt if there was anything wrong with it in the first place...In many ways a much quieter than normal and delicate bourbon with the tannins harnessed and led to a path quite different from the normal toasty/liquorice style. 50%. (100 Proof)

⇨ **Colonel E.H. Taylor Four Grain Bottled in Bond Aged 12 Years** db (97.5) n24.5 this nose is an unashamed tease. The sheer, naked beauty: were I an old Kentucky spinster from post-bellum Frankfort, during the time of Mr E H Taylor, I would be getting the vapours and swooning at the wanton lasciviousness of this bourbon, the way it slowly undoes its buttons to reveal more and more of itself as it slowly oxidizes and increases in temperature. Is that a kind of a chocolate roast malt? Are those muscovado sugars teaming up with with a flash of rye to suggest something fruity? Are those vanillas, or maybe butterscotch, freshly fondled by liquorice? I thought that was a flash of spice, but maybe attached to barely perceptible ulmo honey...; t24.5 oh, oh, oh...! If the nose was good....then this delivery...! Soft, succulent, kisses; soothing yet exciting fingers of corn oil and lightly crisped rye softly touching, the palate fully aroused by the most sensual tips, all of them dark but none of them burnt. Yes, that ulmo honey hinted on the nose but enough only to complement the deeper Manuka honey and liquorice notes which have themselves been dried just enough to allow the cocoa and hickory to warm with a quietly warming spice and slowly hardening texture...; f24 just a slow, lightly oiled, gently spiced chocolate fade which goes on...and on... and on...and on...; b24.5 unquestionably one of the greatest whiskeys bottled worldwide in the last 12 months, simply because of the unfathomable depths of its complexity. Every aspect of great whiskey making clears its respective hurdle with yards to spare: brewing, distilling, maturation...the nose and taste confirms that a team of people knew exactly what they were doing...and achieved with rare distinction what they set out to do. Forget about the sheer, undiluted beauty of this bourbon: for me, it is simply a true honour – and thrill - to taste. 50% (100 proof).

Colonel E. H. Taylor Old Fashioned Sour Mash (94) n24 t23.5 f23 b23.5. When they say "old fashioned" they really aren't joking. This is a style which takes me back to my first bourbon tasting days of the mid 1970s. And, at the moment, it is hard to name another bourbon offering this unique, technically brilliant style. Outstanding! 50% (100 Proof)

Colonel E.H. Taylor Seasoned Wood db (93.5) n25 t24 f21.5 b23 I am sitting in my garden in near darkness tasting and writing this, the near-thousand-year-old church just 75 yards or so behind me clanging out that it is ten of the clock. Although mid-July, it is the first day warm enough in this apology of a British summer where I have been able to work outside. Oddly, it reminded me when I used to write my books and chapters on bourbon in the grounds of Buffalo Trace in the 1990s, the sun also set and a warm breeze kissing my face. No possums here for company, although the bats are already circling me, kindly protecting me from midges. And as I can't read the label of the whiskey, it makes my senses all the more alive. A whiskey, though not perfect, for when the sun sets but your day is really about to begin... 50% (100 proof)

Colonel E.H. Taylor Small Batch (94.5) n23 t24 f23.5 b24 From first nose, to last, the exemplary high quality of this bourbon is not for a second in dispute. 50% (100 proof)

Cougar Bourbon Aged 5 Years (95) n25 t24 f23 b23. If Karl Kennedy of Neighbours really is the whisky buff he reckons he is, I want to see a bottle of this in his home next to Dahl. By the way: where is Dahl these days...? (And by the way, Karl, the guy who married you and Susan in London is a fan of mine. So you had better listen up...!) 37% (74 proof). Foster's Group, Australia.

Daniel Stewart 8 Years Old (92.5) n22 t23 f23.5 b24. Stellar sophistication. Real complexity here, and, as 8-year-olds go, probably among the most complex of them all. A deep notch up on the previous bottling I encountered. 45%

Eagle Rare Aged 10 Years Single Barrel (89) n21.5 t23 f22 b22.5. A surprising trip, this, with some dramatic changes en route. 45%

Eagle Rare 17 Years Old bott Spring 2013 db (94) n23 t24 f23 b24 A much more profound bottling than the 2012 edition with the accent firmly on the heavy, chocolatey sugars. Shows BT to enormous advantage and is, above all, great fun. 45%. Buffalo Trace Antique Collection.

Eagle Rare 17 Year Old bott Spring 2014 db (95) n23 t24 f23.5 b23.5 One of the most relaxed and confident Eagle Rares I've encountered for a while. More telling sugar around than usual and a little less weighty. 45%.

Eagle Rare 17 Years Old bott Spring 2015 db (94.5) n24 the bourbon with the famous chocolate fudge nose – now at its very chocolate fudgiest...; t23.5 a corny-copia of rich oils. A little extra treacle to this one, though the Manuka honey remains a constant. A slightly rough bite despite the lubrication; f23.5 continues in that slightly rough manner with a sprig of mint now on board as, is usually the case, the chocolate fudge returns with a vengeance; b23.5 one very consistent, big and serious bourbon... 45% (90 proof)

⁂ **Eagle Rare 17 Years Old** bott Spring 2016 db (95) n24 the usual thick chocolate fudge is present and correct, but with a few extra esters offering apricot and mint; t23 a soft, silky delivery with the vigorous tannins arriving a little earlier than expected. A wonderful blend of Manuka honey, chocolate mousse and molasses turn up in their own time to cut the timber down to size...; f24 a slightly early fade but the slow revealing of the maple syrup and cocoa mix is more than sexy...; b24 an eagle with a slightly different plumage, this one really determined to display its tannin – though never at the cost of compromising its excellent complexity. 45% (90 proof).

Elijah Craig 18 Years Old Single Barrel barrel no. 3328, dist 8/9/91 (94.5) n25 t23.5 f22.5 b23.5. Masterful. Don't even bother opening the bottle unless you have an hour to spend. 45%

Elijah Craig Single Barrel Aged 18 Years barrel no. 4090, barrelled 6/14/97 db (94) n24 t23.5 f23 b23.5 A substantial bourbon. Busy, intense, never quite staying in one spot long enough to settle down: sounds like we are back to the bees again... 45% (90 proof). sc.

Elijah Craig 21 Year Old Single Barrel barrelled 26/11/90, barrel no. 41 db (95.5) n23.5 t24 f23.5 b24.5 Even by bourbon's high standards, this is a thing of rare beauty and of a type. One of the most subtle and sophisticated bottlings you'll ever find at this age and one for those who prefer their Martinis and gins dry. And I mean very dry.... 45%.

Elijah Craig Aged 23 Years Single Barrel barrel no. 26, barrelled 2.26.90 db (87) n21 t23 f21 b22. The citrus on this old boy is working overtime to ensure a degree of freshness combats the encroaching years. But it is a somewhat unequal battle and, finally, as was inevitable, slips under the tide of ancient oak like a man pushing a boulder up an interminable hill finally falls, spent, to the ground for the great rock to run over him on its way back downhill. That said, plenty of magic moments to be getting on with here, especially on delivery when there's a greater evenness between the light muscovado sugars and the more dogged tannins. Of course, the tannins win out in the end as the nose has accurately forecast, with a bitter –ish fade. But there is no shortage of understated elegance and charm along the way. 45%

⁂ **Elijah Craig Barrel Proof Kentucky Straight Bourbon** batch no. A117 db (94.5) n23.5 classic bourbon notes with the emphasis on busy small grains and a background kumquat and chocolate softener; t23.5 eye-watering arrival thanks to those fired up small grains;

inevitably the spices are soon upwardly mobile and on the attack, also. A lovely toffee and golden syrup middle cools the flames; **f24** the more forceful notes are spent, leaving a calmer mix of light red liquorice, ulmo honey and mocha: superb! **b23.5** an old-fashioned bourbon full of joy. *63.5% (127 proof).*

⟨⟩ **Elijah Craig Barrel Proof Kentucky Straight Bourbon** batch no. B517 db **(91) n23.5** healthy caramel theme with at first light liquorice relief which seems to grow...; a background ulmo honey sweetness back up the caramel further; **t23** thumping liquorice delivery with accompanying spice and light muscovado that gets toastier and intensifies into molasses; the caramels chug on...; **f22** returns decisively to its safer soft caramel mode; **b22.5** not exactly the most complex EC, but really makes the most of the big liquorice intervention. *62.1% (124.2 proof).*

Elijah Craig Barrel Proof Bourbon 12 Years of Aging db **(95.5) n23.5 t24 f24 b24** Not sure when I saw a darker bourbon at 12 years commercially available. Remember that in straight bourbon colour represents interaction between spirit and barrel. So expect big oak presence and you will not be disappointed! A bourbon for bourbon lovers with very hairy chests – male or female.. *67.1% (134.2 proof) ncf.*

⟨⟩ **Elijah Craig Small Batch Kentucky Straight Bourbon** db **(89.5) n22.5** light with a big caramel theme. The higher citrus and toasty molasses on strike now and again; **t22.5** seriously soft with diluted ulmo honey and concentrated caramels; **f22** continues to extract every last jot of toffee from the oak; spices inject some very late oomph; **b22.5** about as quiet and understated as Elijah Craig ever gets. *47% (94 proof).*

Elmer T Lee Single Barrel (91) n22 t23.5 f(22.5) b23. A sturdy, dense bourbon with above average sweetness. So effortless, it is hard to immediately realise that greatness has entered your glass. *45%*

Elmer T. Lee Single Barrel Bourbon 1919 - 2013 db **(96.5) n24.5 t24 f24 b24** I left this as the 1,145th and final new whisk(e)y to be tasted for the 2015 Jim Murray's Whisky Bible. Elmer, once a neighbour of mine, loved his garden and more than once I helped him safely remove squirrels without them being hurt in any way. Which makes this whiskey, seemingly gentle but with a backbone of American steel - yet on the nose flowing with floral notes, a touching and entirely apposite marker to his memory. And it delights me to say that I know, with absolute certainty, he would have been blown away by this barrel of glorious complexity. Elmer: with a glass of this rare genius I salute your memory, my friend. *46.5%*

Evan Williams 23 Years Old (94) n22 t23.5 f24.5 b24. Struts his stuff, refusing to allow age to slow him or dim the shine from his glowing grains. Now oak has taken its toll. This seems older than its 23 years... Or so I first thought. Then a light shone in my soul and it occurred to me: hang on...I have wines going back to the last century. For the older ones, do I not allow them to breathe? So I let the whiskey breathe. And, behold, it rose from the dead. This Methuselah of a whiskey had come alive once more...and how!! *53.5%*

Evan Williams Single Barrel 2004 Edition barrel no. 1, dist 19/03/2004, bott 16/11/2013 db **(89.5) n22** relatively simplistic: ulmo honey and vanilla enlivened by a faint dash of tangerine peel; **t24** profound early sugars, mainly of an icing and syrupy variety. The spices are dull, though weighty and plod and prod rather than stimulate; **f21.5** thins and vanillas out with surprising abruptness; **b22** demure: wouldn't say boo to a goose. *43.3%. 19th in the series.*

Four Roses 125th Anniversary Small Batch Bourbon OBSV - 18 years, OBSK - 13years, OESK- 13 years db **(96.5) n24 t24.5 f24 b24** Nosing and tasting a whiskey like this and, after a morning of sulphur-ruined horrors, I am reminded why I still do this job. A celebration of bourbon; a triumph of blending. *51.6%. ncf. 12468 bottles. WB15/385*

Four Roses Limited Edition 2014 Small Batch (94) n23.5 t24 f23 b23.5 just a little youthful undercurrent means, as beautiful as this whiskey is, it doesn't quite hit the heights of the 2013 verion. Still a beauty, though...; *60% approx 11,200*

Four Roses 2014 Limited Edition Single Barrel Aged 11 Years Recipe OESF db **(88.5) n22 t23.5 f21 b22** A pretty quiet cask refusing to scale the highest peaks. *60%.*

George T. Stagg (97.5) n24 t25 f24 b24.5. Astonishing how so much oak can form and yet have such limited negative impact and so few unpleasant side effects. These tasting notes took nearly four hours to compile. Yet they are still in a simplified form to fit into this book... George T Stagg is once again... staggering. *71.5% (143 Proof). ncf.*

George T. Stagg (Barrel Proof) db **(95) n24 t24 f23 b24** Quite beautiful bourbon of the top order. But not quite so breathtakingly complex and brain-shatteringly vivid as Staggs of past times. *64.1%. Buffalo Trace Antique Collection.*

George T. Stagg (96.5) n24.5 t24 f24 b24 The alcohol by volume of one of the sexiest whiskeys on the planet is 69...and it goes down a treat. Much harder to spit than swallow...*69.05% Buffalo Trace Antique Collection.*

George T. S●gg Limited Edition (96.5) n24 t24.5 f24 b24 As spectacular as a sunset from the hilltop village of Coldharbour in my beloved Surrey *71.4% (142.8 proof). ncf.*

George T. Stagg db (96.5) n24 never found sticky toffee pudding on a Stagg before, but it appears to have turned up here. Alongside the dates, teasing spices and complex array of dark sugars which makes this whiskey so unmistakable. So dense you feel it would make the most delicious possible swamp in another world, one you wouldn't too much mind being sucked into...; t24 and those toasty sugars really make a big stand on delivery, swiftly joined by a concentrated blend of hickory and coffee and slowly moulded into shape by the ever-hardening and increasingly more crystalline rye which, at last, makes itself heard; f24 now the corn oils make their stand, gluing themselves to the palate for a very long finale as the liquorice really does make a loud speech. The drier hickory tones detach themselves from the coffee to show that the tannins really do mean business...; b24.5 it is impossible not to finish a mouthful of George T without letting out a long, contented, slightly awe-felt and entirely fulfilled sigh, just as one might make after listening to the final strains of Vaughan Williams' London Symphony or Strauss' Tod und Verklarung. Most of the usual traits to be had in abundance, plus one or two slight differences as the pot was stirred for another dip into one of world's whisky's deepest caverns.... *69.1% (138.2 proof)*

◈ **George T. Stagg** db (97) n24 the usual Stagg repertoire soon hits its rhythm with an uncompromising series crispy rye and Demerara sugar notes on at full throttle, with the dates and mocha offering a softer ride; a little extra hickory on this one, perhaps; t24.5 stunning, salivating delivery, then the textbook radiating of all the component notes which makes up the beautiful whole. Again, it is the rye which is first to melt then the hickory from the nose steps up to the plate and, as usual, soon dances hand-in-hand with the coffee on the palate...; f24 long, with all the above slowly fading with an almost apologetic build up of spice to seemingly underscore great age; b24.5 amazing consistency: this is the fourth year running it has been given a score of 96.5 or above - a Stagg-ering achievement. *72.05% (144.1 proof).*

Hancock's Reserve Single Barrel (92) n25 t23 f21.5 b22.5. A slightly quieter example of this consistently fine brand. The nose, though, is the stuff of wet whiskey dreams... *44.45%*

◈ **Hogs 3 Bourbon Aged Over 3 Years** (86.5) n22.5 t21.5 f21 b21.5 A bang on standard mid-towards upper warehouse Kentucky 3-year-old with plenty of juicy but ungainly vanilla, Demerara sugar and citrus.... and absolutely no frills. *40% (80 proof). Quality Spirits International.*

I.W. Harper Kentucky Straight Bourbon (87.5) n22 t22 f21.5 b22. The puckeringly dry delivery and finish forms the toast for the well spiced light sugar sandwich. *41% (82 Proof)*

I.W. Harper Kentucky Straight Bourbon 15 Year Old (94.5) n23.5 t23.5 f24 b23.5 Class in a glass. *43% (86 Proof)*

Jefferson's Reserve batch no. 84 (91) n23 t23.5 f22 b23. Once a 15-year-old, no age statement here. But this has seen off a few Summers, sweetening with each passing one. *45.1%.*

Jim Beam Black Double Age Aged 8 Years (93) n23 t24 f22.5 b23.5. Rather than the big, noisy, thrill-seeking JB Black, here it is in quiet, reflective, sophisticated mode. Quite a shift. But no less enjoyable. *43% (86 proof)*

Jim Beam Bonded 100 Proof db (92.5) n22.5 a little lazy at first, but by degree begins to reveal light layers of small grain and slightly larger oak...; t23.5 soft, vaguely sugared start... then the small grains go berserk. The mouth is peppered with shotgun blasts of rye-infused small grain and then complex sugars, wide-ranging in style; so beautifully busy; f23 now a sublime toastiness kicks in, making the most now of the molasses and chicory; b23.5 takes its time to get going. But when it does, it just won't shut up.... Complex and compelling, the toastiness takes time to make itself felt but does so with panache. *50%*

Jim Beam Signature Craft Aged 12 Years db (92.5) n23 gorgeous roasted coffee and liquorice. The rye pokes through gamely; t23.5 soft delivery with a wonderful toasted fudge quality. Takes time for the rye to arrive but it does as the spices mount; f23 softly spiced with plenty of creamy mocha; b23 classic Beam: big rye and massive fruit. Quite lovely. *43% WB15/386*

John B. Stetson Straight Bourbon Whiskey (92) n23.5 t23.5 f22 b23. Absolutely love it! Quality: I take my hat off to you...*42%*

Jim Beam Signature Craft Brown Rice 11 Year Old db 45% (78) n20.5 t21 f18 b18.5. A whiskey I nosed and tasted before looking to see what it was. And immediately alarm bells rang and I was reaching to inspect the bottle in a state of panic and shock. RICE!!! Well that explains the unsatisfying simplicity to the finish where, really, only oak can be heard....apart from the wallpaper paste, that is. And the fact the whiskey never quite gets off the ground despite an attractive cocoa thread. Or was that actually real cocoa...? Sorry, but in the great name of Jim Beam, this is one that should have just stayed in the lab. *(90 Proof)*

Jim Beam Signature Craft Soft Red Wheat 11 Year Old db (92) n22 buttery with touches of seasoned oak and lightly spiced liquorice; t23.5 mouth-filling delivery yet with a sugary crispness. The spices go to town almost immediately, offering an almost spiced fruit loaf feel; t23 happy to take its time to disappear and rolls out the sugars for a last, gently spiced hurrah...; b23.5 a beautifully weighted bourbon making a big deal of the sugar-spice interplay. Hugely enjoyable and at times fascinating. *45% (90 Proof)*

Jim Beam Signature Craft Small Batch Quarter Cask Finished 3rd Release db (92) n23.5 delicate for any type of quarter cask: emphasis on citrus and subtlety rather than thumping oak; t23.5 soft delivery with beautifully weighted molten sugar and oils forming a match for the early spicy attack; light hickory forms the backbone; f22 a touch grainy with a little rye bite on the semi-thin finale; b23 quarter casks are not normally associated with deftness and poise. This one certainly is. Elegant, if a little lightweight at the end. *43% (86 Proof)*

John E. Fitzgerald Larceny (94) n23 t23.5 f23.5 b24. If this doesn't win a few converts to wheated bourbon, nothing will. A high quality, stunningly adorable whiskey, pulsing with elegance and personality. Every drinks cabinet should have this wonderful new addition to the bourbon lexicon. *46%*

John E. Fitzgerald Very Special Reserve Aged 20 Years (93) n22.5 the tannins are at full stretch here but remain intact thanks to a slight citrus tone which rescues the treacle and eucalyptus intro...; t24 the nose may be about to go twangy. But the delivery is another matter: a stunning marriage of corn oils that soothe and tannins which just begin to make you pucker slightly. Such yin and yang...! f23 butterscotch and vanilla had a plate of molasses tipped over it...; b23.5 a bourbon lover's bourbon! *45% (90 proof)*

John J Bowman Virginia Straight Bourbon Single Barrel (94) n23 t24 f23 b24. One of the biggest yet most easily relaxed and beautifully balanced bourbons on the market. *50%*

Johnny Drum (Black Label) (89.5) n22 t23 f21.5 b23. How often does that happen? The same whiskey, different strength, virtually same quality (though this has a little more depth) but gets there by a slightly different route. *43%*

Johnny Drum (Green Label) (89) n22.5 t23 f21 b22.5. Much more honey these days. Worth making a bee-line for. *40%*

Johnny Drum Private Stock (90.5) n22.5 t22.5 f23 b22.5. One of those bourbons where a single glass is never quite enough. Great stuff! *50.5% (101 proof)*

Kentucky Owl Kentucky Straight Bourbon Whiskey batch no. 2 (91) n22.5 liquorice, toasted mallow and no little tannin; t23.5 a beautifully delivery: the corn and sugars are evenly matched, though the darker, toastier notes eventually come through louder. Quite tangy and eye-watering in part with a spicy attack to the tongue; f22.5 a vague marmalade fruitiness which had been lurking around the perimeters now enter the fray, though the corn dictates; b22.5 a big, corn-led bourbon but with some extra oaky depth. *58.6% (117.2 proof). 1,380 bottles.*

Kentucky Vintage batch 08-72 (94.5) n23.5 t24.5 f23 b23.5 Staggered! I really didn't quite expect that. Previous bottlings I have enjoyed of this have had hair attached to the muscle. This is a very different Vintage, one that reaches for the feminine side of a macho whiskey. If you want to spend an hour just getting to know how sensitive your taste buds can be, hunt down this batch... *45%*

Knob Creek 2001 Limited Edition Kentucky Straight Bourbon batch 1, bott 2016 (89.5) n22.5 t22.5 f22 b22 Lovely bourbon, but not of a style one automatically associates with a usually hefty bourbon. *50% (100 proof)*

Knob Creek Aged 9 Years bott code L6154 (95.5) n23.5 t24 f23.5 b24.5 Seems like more barrels have been included from the lower echelons of the warehouse. Lighter, sweeter and more feminine. One of the most complex Knob Creeks I have ever encountered: a true Kentucky belle! *50% (100 proof)*

Knob Creek Aged 9 Years (94.5) n23.5 t24 f23.5 b23.5 No whiskey in the world has a more macho name, and this is not for the faint-hearted. Big, hard in character and expansive, it drives home its point with gusto, celebrating its explosive finish. *50%*

Knob Creek Single Barrel Reserve Aged 9 Years bott no L6133 (95) n23 love the impact of the small grain which is never less than equal to the weighty, honeyed tannin; so much vivid citrus at play...; t24 just so busy and beautiful! Like on the nose, the small grains impact immediately sending the taste buds into spasms of juicy glee. Ribald and juicy, the rye ensures a fruity edge while the spices man up early and with gusto; f24 long, with more of a cocoa link to add to the established liquorice; b24 a macho bourbon of a wonderfully high standard. Just a degree juicier than you normally find with a Knob Creek. *60% (120 proof)*

Maker's 46 (95) n23.5 t24.5 f23 b24 Some people have a problem with oak staves. I don't: whisky, after all, is about the interaction of a grain spirit and oak. This guy is all about the nose and, especially, the delivery. With so much controlled honey on show, it cannot be anything other than a show-stopper. Frankly, magnificent. I think I've met my Maker's... 47% (94 proof)

Maker's Mark (Red Seal) (91) n22.5 t23.5 f22 b23. The big honey injection has done no harm whatsoever. This sample came from a litre bottle and the whiskey was darker than normal. What you seem to have is the usual steady Maker's with a helping hand of extra weight. In fact this reminds me of the old Maker's Gold wax. 45%

⬥ **Mayor Pingree Aged 9 Years Straight Bourbon Whiskey** batch no. 16-314 (96) n23.5 classic bourbon nose: the oak projects a lovely manuka honey and red liquorice mix while the busy small grains ramp up the complexity levels; t24 magnificent delivery: so rare to find a bourbon which holds together so perfectly on delivery...the corn oils and light sprinkling of rye dances with the now dark liquorice, hickory and manuka honey in perfect time; f24 probably one of the best finishes in the world this year. The spices are so immaculately paced and weighted and act as the perfect foil for the Blue Mountain Jamaican coffee sweetened by a glorious Manuka and ulmo honey blend: sensational...; b24.5 this is my second darling Valentine from Indiana... 58.6% (1172 proof). ncf.

⬥ **Mayor Pingree Aged 10 Years Straight Bourbon Whiskey Single Barrel** barrel no. 2-1 (89) n22.5 hefty with some assertive tannins just taking the shine off the glossier acacia honey tones. The bourbon pedigree is unsullied, however; t22.5 the sugars are up and at the taste buds before anything else moves. First they are of a watery, processed nature, then thicken with the oils to form a more honeyed tone. The tannins, though slow off the mark, catch up to offer a bitter marmalade effect; f22 remains a little bitter but now spicy, too; b22 compare this to the 9-years-old to see what happens when the oak and grains are just very slightly off beat... 52.7% (1054 proof). ncf. 159 bottles.

Michter's No. 1 Bourbon (87) n23 t22.5 f20 b21.5. This one is mainly a nose job: all kinds of heavy liquorice and diced kumquat. But there is also a brooding tannin menace lurking in the shadows, which reveal themselves more fully – and with a tad of bitterness - on delivery and finish. 45.7%

Noah's Mill batch 10-170 (93) n23.5 t23.5 f23 b23. This monster of a bourbon just rumbles along on the palate like one of the four thunderstorms I have encountered in Kentucky today... 57.15%

Noah's Mill batch 13-81 (93.5) n23 gorgeous glazed almonds; a little citrus & cold coffee; t23.5 oddly enough, doesn't taste like the nose: much more macho, with the full blooded hickory & Demerara; enormous weight & depth; assorted honey notes begin to form; f22.5 gentle finale, reverting back to the style of the aroma. Excellent vanilla on sugars & weightier liquorice; b23.5 a full bodied classic bourbon which undulates over the palate. 57.15% (114.3 proof)

Old Fitzgerald Very Special 12 Years Old (93) n24 t23.5 f22.5 b23. There is always something that makes the heart sing when you come across a whiskey which appears so relaxed in its excellence. At the moment my heart is in the shower merrily lathering itself... 45%

Old Grand-Dad (90.5) n22 t23 f23 b23.5. This one's all about the small grains. A busy, lively bourbon, this offers little to remind me of the original Old Grand-Dad whiskey made out at Frankfort. That said, this is a whisk(e)y-lover's whiskey: in other words the excellence of the structure and complexity outweighs any historical misgivings. Enormously improved and now very much at home with its own busy style. 43%

Old Grand-Dad Bonded 100 Proof (94.5) n22.5 t24 f23.5 b24.5 Obviously Old Grand-dad knows a thing or two about classy whiskey: this is a magnificent version, even by its own high standards. It was always a winner and one you could bet your shirt on for showing how the small grains can impact upon complexity. But this appears to go a stage further. The base line is a touch deeper, so there is more ground to cover on the palate. It has been a whiskey-lover's whiskey for a little while and after a few barren years, has been inching itself back to its great Frankfort days. The fact that Beam's quality has risen over the last decade has played no insignificant part in that. 50% (100 proof)

Old Rip Van Winkle 10 Years Old (93) n24 t23 f23 b23. A much sharper cookie than it once was. And possibly a Maryland Cookie, too, what with the nuts and chocolate evident. As graceful as it is entertaining. 45% (90 Proof). Buffalo Trace.

Old Weller Antique 107 (96) n24.5 t24 f23.5 b24 This almost blew me off my chair. Always thought this was pleasant, if a little underwhelming, in the past. However, this bottling has had a few thousands volts passed through it as it now comes alive on the palate with a glorious blending of freshness and debonair aging. One of the surprise packages of 2012. 53.5% (107 proof)

Orphan Barrel 'Barterhouse' 20 Years Old (91) n22.5 t22.5 f23 b23 To think: this was still white dog when I first visited Old Stitz! 45.1%.

Orphan Barrel Forged Oak (87) n22 t22 f21 b22. Decent bourbon, but a little stiff and mechanical in its development. The finish has a tad too much toast for its own good. Still, a good chewing bourbon. 45.25%

Orphan Barrel Lost Prophet batch tul-tr-1 (92) n22.5 hickory and butterscotch pair off beautifully; t23.5 and in steams the liquorice, the old fashioned way, with molasses as its sidekick; f23 comfortable as the spices rise; b23 markedly more relaxed than Forged Oak and understands the value of good sugar-spice interplay. 45.05%

Orphan Barrel 'Old Blowhard' 26 Years Old (95) n23.5 t24 f23.5 b24 I do get my hands on a few samples of very old bourbon, but this seems to have a style more recognisable in the 1980s and early to mid '90s than now. Time warp whisky in every sense. Wonderful! 45.35%. Bottled in Tullahoma, aged 26 years, "found in Stitzel Weller".

Orphan Barrel Rhetoric 21 Year Old batch 0109-67 (94.5) n23.5 fabulous intensity from the get go: toasty and honeyed in the classic way with the small grains taking over the show to fizz and simper; t24 gosh....this really is something a little special: the sugars stand tall and proud, despite being swamped by lush corns oils bathed in liquorice-coated tannins: the sweetness, as with all great bourbons, appears to be in league with the spices; f23 dries but without bitterness and in perfect pace with the growing vanilla; b24 a bourbon drinker's bourbon. How's that for rhetoric...? 45%

Orphan Barrel Rhetoric 22 Year Old batch no. L6063J3 (87) n20.5 t23.5 f21 b22. Certainly has a few proud war wounds to show for 22 searing hot Kentucky summers. Some outstanding tannins and roasty sugars at play on delivery, and a few grapefruit notes for good measure. But some bitterness, also, as the oak gives up a degree of its less impressive qualities. Very hard to call it right on whiskeys this age. This comes home just the right side of very good, but another summer might have done some fair damage. 45.2% (90.4 proof)

Pappy Van Winkle's Family Reserve 15 Years Old (96) n24.5 t23.5 f24 b24 At a book signing in Canada a Bible enthusiast asked me which well-aged, wheated bourbon he should look for. I told him Pappy 15. He looked at me quizzically and said: "Well, that's what I thought, but in the Bible you have it down as rye-recipe." I told him he was wrong...until I checked there and then. And discovered he was right. Of course, Pappy has always been wheated and the lushness on the palate and spices radiating from it has always confirmed this. I'll put it down to not spitting enough. Or perhaps the speed at which I type whilst tasting. Sometimes you mean one thing – then another word comes out. Like when a member of my staff asks for a pay rise. I mean no. But somehow say yes. So apologies to any other I fooled out there. For not only is this a wheated bourbon. With its improbable degree of deftness for something so big, it has edged up a notch or two into a truly world great whiskey...whatever the recipe. 53.5% (107 proof)

⟐ **Parker's Heritage Collection 24 Year Old Bottled in Bond Bourbon** dist Fall 90 (95.5) n24 never quite come across an aroma like this before: the tannins are profound, scarily so, but seemingly kept in check by a glass wall of crystallised sugar and ginger. This is obviously from the oak and gives a sweet edge to the bourbon the like I have never previously encountered: as attractive as it is fascinating; nothing, though, can keep the spice in check...; t24 those sugars are first on the scene on delivery, against crystalline and brittle. They immediately encounter a clove and eucalyptus delivery, initially softened by corn oil, which looks like it wants to take the oak far beyond where it should go or is comfortable, but is somehow dragged back from the edge; spices immediately howl and bite while the tannins are calmed and merge quite beautifully with the solidified maple syrup and Manuka honey; f23.5 amazingly, there is no tiredness to the oak and the vanilla and butterscotch are no relaxed, willing to say their piece without over-aged bitterness; b24 for my 999th whisky for the 2018 Bible, thought I'd take on the oldest commercially bottled Kentucky bourbon I can ever remember seeing. Had no idea how this one would go, as the heat of the Midwest means there is little room for the whiskey to manoeuvre. What we actually have is a bourbon in previously unchartered territory and clearly experiencing new, sometimes mildly bewildering, sensations, having proudly gone where no bourbon has gone before... 50%.

⟐ **Parker's Heritage Collection 24 Year Old Bottled in Bond Bourbon** dist Spring 91 (96) n24 much more of a classic old (or younger in this case!) bourbon with the hickory, liquorice, spice and maple syrup all blooming – and booming - in unison; t24 firm sugars, crisp and business like, and even a small grain ditty just to seriously up the complexity credentials; f24 long, with a more tannin turn now as it moves towards a toasted nuts, sugars and grains. Elegant yet weighty and...nothing like a bourbon of this antiquity should be...; b24 straight 24s all the way through for the 24-year-old: how fitting. Wears its crown a little easier than the Fall 1990 version. Superb! *50%.*

Parker's Heritage Collection "Promise of Hope" Single Barrel 10 Years db (95) n24 t24 f23 b24 In an age when masters Distillers assume that noble title after about ten minutes in the job and for marketing reasons alone, it is touching to find a whiskey bottled in honour of a genuine Master Distiller, a man who has probably forgotten more about whiskey than the majority of the recent intake have so far learned. It is no less touching that part of the money raised from the sale of this whiskey will go to ALS charities, a condition under which Parker Beam now labours. *48%.*

Parker's Heritage Collection Sixth Edition Master Distillery's Blend Of Mashbills Aged Since 2001 db (94.5) n24 t23.5 f23 b24 Shows plenty of muscle, but subtlety and sophistication in equal measures, too. *63.5% (127 proof). ncf.*

Parker's Heritage Collection Wheated Mash Bill Bourbon Aged 10 Years (97) n24 t24 f24.5 b24.5. Hard to find the words that can do justice. I know Parker will be immensely proud of this. And with every good reason: I am working exceptionally hard to find a fault with this either from a technical distillation viewpoint or a maturation one. Or just for its sheer whiskeyness...A potential World Whisky of the Year. *62.1% (124.2 Proof). ncf.*

Redemption High Rye Bourbon (74.5) n19 t20 f17.5 b18. Hugely disappointing bottling. Vaguely butyric, and its failure to reach any high point of quality is really driven home by the car-crash finish, complete with less than pleasant tang. Seriously needs to redeem itself next time round. *46%*

Ridgemont Reserve 1792 Aged 8 Years (94.5) n23.5 t24 f23.5 b23.5 Now here is a whiskey which appears to have come to terms with its own strengths and, as with all bourbons and malts, limitations. Rarely did whiskey from Barton reach this level of maturity, so harnessing its charms always involves a bit of a learning curve. Each time I taste this it appears a little better than the last...and this sample is no exception to the rule. Excellent. *46.85% (93.7 Proof)*

Russell's Reserve Single Barrel (94) n23.5 t24 f23 b23.5. Old-fashioned, thick as treacle bourbon. Delicious. *55%. ncf. Wild Turkey.*

Russell's Reserve Small Batch 10 Year Old (92.5) n24.5 t23 f22 b23. Had the quality and complexity on the palate followed on from the nose I may well have had the world's No 1 whisky for 2012 in my glass. Just slum it with something quite wonderful, instead. Still waiting for an official explanation as to why this is a miserly 90 proof, when Jimmy Russell's preferred strength is 101, by the way... *45%. Wild Turkey.*

Stagg Jn (91.5) n22.5 t24 f22.5 b22.5. A whiskey of staggering brinkmanship. Who will blink first? The massive oak or the taste buds. To be honest, this is the kind of bourbon that sorts out the men from the boys, the women from the girls. Doesn't have quite enough covering sweetness of varying type and intensity to match the complexity found in the original Stagg. One that needs a very long time to get to the bottom of. *67.2% (134.4 proof)*

That Boutique-y Whisky Company Heaven Hill batch 1 (94) n23 t23.5 f24 b23.5 Now that's what I call bourbon! Travel back 30 years and taste some Heaven Hill, and – though a different distillery - you wouldn't be too far off! This bottling does the HH name proud! *50%. 240 bottles.*

Trails End Bourbon 8 Year Old (87) n21.5 t22.5 f21.5 b21.5. A light bourbon, where the end of the trail begins early. The citrus outpoints the tannins all too easily. *45% (90 Proof). Hood River Distillers, Inc.*

Very Old Barton 6 Years Old (92) n23 t23 f23 b23. One of those seemingly gifted bourbons that, swan-like, appears to glide at the surface but on closer inspection has loads going on underneath. *43%*

Very Old Barton 90 Proof (94) n23 t24 f23.5 b23.5. One of the most dangerously drinkable whiskeys in the world... *45% (90 proof)*

Virgin Bourbon 7 Years Old (96.5) n24 t24.5 f24 b24 This takes me back nearly 40 years to when I first began my love affair with bourbon and was still a bit of a whisky virgin. This was the very style that blew me away: big, uncompromising, rugged...yet with a heart of honeyed gold. It is the type of huge, box-ticking, honest bourbon that makes you get on your hands and knees and kiss Kentucky soil. *50.5% (101 proof)*

Virgin Bourbon 15 Years Old (92.5) n23.5 t23 f23.5 b23. The kind of bourbon you want to be left in a room with. *50.5% (101 proof)*

Virginia Gentleman (90.5) n22 t23 f23 b23.5. A Gentleman in every sense: and a pretty sophisticated one at that. 40% (80 Proof)

Weller 12 Years Old (93) n24 t23.5 f22.5 b23. Sheer quality. And an enormous leap in complexity and grace from the 7-y-o. 45%

Western Gold 6 Year Old Bourbon Whiskey (91.5) n22 t23 f22.5 b23 Taken from barrels sitting high in the warehouse, that's for sure. You get a lot for your six years... 40%.

Whiskey Thief Straight Bourbon (87) n22 t22 f21.5 b21.5. Straight as a die, unwavering bourbon which sticks to an uncomplicated, intense vanilla theme. Very pleasant. 40%

Wild Turkey 101 (91) n22 t23.5 f22.5 b23. By far the best 101 I have tasted in a decade: you simply can't do anything but go weak at the knees with that spice attack. 55.5% (101 proof)

Wild Turkey American Spirit Aged 15 Years (92) n24 t22.5 f22.5 b23. A delightful Wild Turkey that appears under par for a 100 proofer but offers much when you search those nooks and crannies of your palate. 50.0% (100 proof)

Wild Turkey Rare Breed bott code L0049FH (94) n22.5 t24.5 f23 b24. It is hard to credit that this is the same brand I have been tasting at regular intervals for quite a long while. Certainly nothing like this style has been around for a decade and it is massively far removed from two years ago. The nose threatens a whiskey limited in direction. But the delivery is as profound as it is entertaining. Even on this bottling's singular though fabulous style, not perhaps quite overall the gargantuan whiskey of recent years. But, seeing as it's only the nose which pegs it back a point or two, still one that would leave a big hole in your whiskey experience if you don't get around to trying. 54.1%

Willett Pot Still Reserve barrel no. 2421 (95.5) n24.5 t23 f24 b24. Another fabulous whiskey from Willett. You can so often trust them to deliver and here they have given us a bourbon showing serious oak injection, yet a sweetness which counters perfectly. 47%.

William Larue Weller db (97) n24 there is a clever layer of kumquat here I didn't expect: when I finish tasting, I'll thumb through my back notes and see if I have ever mentioned this before; don't think so. But the real star is the interplay between sweet and dry: the tannins are working hard to dry this out with a series of ground coffee notes, backed up by a distinct herbal note that moves towards spice. Balancing this out is a gorgeous mollassed tone, roasty and delicate. The tannins, though, are taken to the very edge...; t24.5 talk about controlled explosions... The intensity is breath-taking, but most astonishing is the way all the myriad flavours, no matter their size, are controlled and seemingly measured so, again, no one factor dominates. The tannins, for some, might be a little too vigorous. But for old hand big bourbon lovers, the supreme confidence in the way the sugars temper the proceedings is a sign of brilliance; f24 Fisherman's Friend cough sweets on steroids. Just so long with the corn oils doing their job with astonishing panache, also adding to the most subtle sweetening imaginable; b24.5 probably the driest WLW I have yet encountered. Yet the way the barely perceptible sugars react is one of the whisky wonders of the world... 67.3% (134.6 proof)

William Larue Weller (97.5) n24 t24.5 f24 b25 For any whiskey with a proof of 123.4, the only way is up...! Last year's Whisky Bible World Whisky of the Year Runner-up is going for the full title big time, no holds barred. Again, this is absolutely supreme class. 61.7% (123.4 proof). ncf. Buffalo Trace Antique Collection.

William Larue Weller dist Spring 2001 db (97.5) n24.5 t24.5 f24 b24.5 I always save this as one of the last whiskeys I taste for each Bible. In life you always need something to look forward to... 68.1%.

William Larue Weller (97) n24 t24.5 f24 b24.5 Just one of those whiskeys which makes sense of life, of whiskey. A collection and collaboration of flavours and shapes on the palate which simply beguile... 70.1% (140.2 proof).

⟡ **William Larue Weller** db (96) n24 surprisingly quiet by Weller standards: not so much in volume but in how busy it normally is. The usual fruity notes are absent with the muscovado sugars having gone AWOL. Instead a more restrained Blue Mountain Coffee note surprisingly lacking in spice...; t24.5 much more like it! Salivating, as a cascade of complex sugar tones mixing in with the weightier oaks leaves the palate enriched, chewing every atom of the sweet and toasty theme. The spices, normally at max revs, pootle along as though on a Sunday afternoon leisure drive...; f23.5 a surprising amount of caramel and muzzled spice make for a genteel finale...not something you'd always expect from this particular whiskey; b24 the most relaxed and lightly spiced Weller since its first launch. May lack its inherent oomph, but the deft, complex notes are still one of life's great pleasures... 67.7% (135.4 proof).

Woodford Reserve Batch 183 (89) n21.5 slight, a little flaky and with a random scattering of citrus and nutty tones; t22 slightly oilier than usual, the corn planting its flag with determination; **f23** mocha and caramel work charmingly together; **b22.5** a bourbon which at times enters the glass as a pleasant though undercooked offering. This batch has just enough in Reserve (geddit?) to make for a satisfying rather than slightly frustrating experience. 43.2%

Woodford Reserve Distiller's Select batch 95 **(91)** **n23 t23** **f22 b23**. Few bourbons so beautifully pit sweet against dry to such excellent effect. 43.2%

Woodford Reserve Double Oaked **(95)** **n24.5 t23.5 f23 b24** The old Labrot and Graham Distillery has just entered a new phase of excellence since its reopening. Well done blender on creating a bourbon not just of beauty but of great significance. 43.2% WB16/052

Woodford Reserve Master's Collection Four Grain **(95)** **n24 t24 f23 b24.** Sod's law would have it that the moment we removed this from the 2006 Bible, having appeared in the previous two editions without it ever making the shelves, it should at last be belatedly released. But a whiskey worth waiting for, or what? The tasting notes are not a million miles from the original. But this is better bourbon, one that appears to have received a significant polish in the intervening years. Nothing short of magnificent. 46.2%

Yellowstone Select Kentucky Straight Bourbon **(87)** **n22 t22 f21 b22.** Now there's a name from the past! Fatter and much more chewy than the Yellowstone of yesteryear. No shortage of molasses. 46.5% (93 proof). Bottled by Limestone Branch Distillery.

Tennessee Whiskey

◇ **The Single Cask Tennessee Aged 5 Years** cask no. P311 **(88)** **n22** heavily oiled and clumsy. But decent corn-tannin mix; **t21.5** this has to be the heaviest, oiliest Tennessee I have ever encountered. There are some lovely Manuka honey moments and intense liquorice but they struggle to free themselves of their sticky shackles; **f23** the oils at last calm down allowing a genuinely attractive mocha and liquorice finale, with a few spices thrown in for good measure; **b21.5** for a Tennessee, more of a Louisiana swamp... 59.7%. nc ncf sc. 115 bottles.

◇ **The Whisky Agency Tennessee Bourbon 2003** **(89.5)** **n21** shy, non-committal; **t23** not so the delivery which is jam-packed with lusciously sweet liquorice tones, the usual molasses seemingly has a little maple syrup for company; **f22.5** the maple syrup continues towards the end, picking up a little vanilla and spice along the way; **b23** hardly the most spectacular or complex Tennessee. But when it finally wakes up, it puts on a very pretty show. 52.6%.

◇ **Whisky-Fässle Fine Tennessee Whiskey 5 Year Old** barrel, dist 2011, bott 2016 **(89.5)** **n23.5** pretty classic as the toasty vanillas let rip...; **t22** excellent oils, then a profound roastiness to the proceedings. A little Manuka honey tries to make an impact, with almost embarrassingly limited success; **f21.5** retains a nagging bitterness; **b22.5** a real Jekyll and Hyde character. 51.4%.

◇ **Whisky Krüger 2011 Straight Tennessee Whiskey 4 Years Old** bott 2016 **(88)** **n23.5** molasses and liquorice being stirred in a giant cauldron...; **t22** despite the lush corn oils, this is hard as hails as the muscovado crunches onto the palate; **f21** bitter and metallic; **b21.5** hardly true to the nose. Expect a bumpy journey. 59.1%.

BENJAMIN PRICHARD

Benjamin Prichard's Tennessee Whiskey **(83)** **n21.5 t21 f20 b20.5.** Majestic fruity rye notes trill from the glass. Curiously yeasty as well; bounding with all kinds of freshly crushed brown sugar crystals. Pleasant enough, but doesn't gel like Prichard's bourbon. 40%

GEORGE DICKEL

◇ **George Dickel Aged 17 Years** bott code: L6154K1001 db **(94)** **n24** wonderful marriage of crisp, spicy rye and even crunchier muscovado sugars allows the toastier tannins room to develop without causing damage, even though it has gravitated to a light but sweetened mint and clove edge; **t24** so firm, indeed rock hard, you fear your teeth may be chipped trying to chew it. The small grains are dominant and expound a complex development which first includes a salivating delivery before moving on to the main vanilla, fudge and molasses exchanges; **f22.5** loads of natural caramels and butterscotch; **b23.5** the oldest George Dickel I have ever encountered has held its own well over the years. A defiant crispness to the piece makes for memorable drinking, though it is the accommodating and comfortable nose that wins the greatest plaudits... 43.5% (87 proof).

George Dickel Barrel Select **(90.5)** **n21** a little shy, almost indifferent. Vanilla at its most basic; maybe a strand of rye making any kind of move; **t23** ah, much more like it! Crisp, firm sugars helped along by even firmer rye...; ridiculously juicy from the start; **f23.5** more emphasis on liquorice, hickory and Manuka honey. Beautifully controlled spice...and that rye stars crisp and true...; **b23** the limited nose makes the heart sink. What happens once it hits the palate is another story entirely. Wonderful! *43%*

George Dickel Distillery Reserve Collection 17 Year Old (91.5) **n23.5** complex: nutty with a soft doughy appeal. The subtle vanilla is laced with subtler citrus while powdery muscovado sugar further keeps any growing tannin at bay; **t23.5** silky, melt-in-the-mouth delivery with corn oil having an early say before juicy, vaguely brittle rye offers a degree of backbone. The tannins roll in arm in arm with the Manuka honey **f21.5** a late bitterness has crept in but the sugar and spice see off most of the threat; **b23** outside of a warehouse, I'm not sure I've encountered a Tennessee whiskey of this antiquity before. I remember one I tasted some while back, possibly about a year older or two older than this, was black and like tasting eucalyptus concentrate. This is the opposite, showing extraordinary restraint for its age, an almost feminine charm. *43.5%*

⬦ **George Dickel No. 12** bott code: L7034R60011402 db **(89) n21.5** that unique floury as opposed to flowery nose which I had seen in their No 12 recipe, but not for the last few years: and that doesn't mean gristy, either, which is sweeter. The dull caramels are attractive but help give the feeling of a half-cooked Tennessee...; **t23.5** restrained sweetness still, but enough maple syrup and liquorice to make for an attractive experience; complex, understated, teasing and rather lovely; **f22** as the honey dies off slightly the spice finds an easier path to attention; **b22** in a way, a classic GD where you feel there much more still in the tank... *45% (90 proof).*

George Dickel Rye (95.5) **n24** sharper than a barber's blade. The fruity notes sparkle like a crystal chandelier. The rye is as crisp as you like, and no less clean: beautiful! **t23.5** like molten amber, there is a sublime rock-like quality to this. The grain is hard-edged, the spices every bit as jagged as the solidified, non-specific fruit radiating form the rye; **f24** long, with an excellent degree of vanilla. The finale is lengthy, with an ever gathering amount of cocoa thickening the proceedings: stunningly complex...; **b24** dare I say it? On this evidence, they do rye probably a fraction better than they produce straight Tennessee. This is a belter! *45%*

George Dickel Superior No 12 Brand Whisky (90.5) **n22.5 t23 f22.5 b22.5.** A different story told by George from the last one I heard. But certainly no less fascinating. *45%*

⬦ **Eiling Lim Tennessee Whisky** (92.5) **n23.5** hard, tight, brittle and abounding in small grain busyness...; **t23.5** the nose comes to life on the palate: hard, tight, brittle and so ridiculously busy! The sugars have a profound depth which appears to pick up the butterscotch as it digs deeper and deeper; **f22.5** long with that butterscotch just enjoying a little spice in its life...; **b23** the full strength of the whiskey does this no harm whatsoever as some of the sugars take on extraordinary dimensions. Beautifully made Tennessee. *51.5%.*

JACK DANIEL

Jack Daniel's 120th Anniversary of the White Rabbit Saloon (91) **n22.5 t23.5 f22 b23** On its best-behaved form. After the delivery, the oils are down a little, so not the usual bombastic offering from JD. Nonetheless, this is pure class and the clever use of sugars simply make you drool... *43%. Brown-Forman.*

Jack Daniel's Old No.7 Brand (Black Label) (92) **n23 t23 f22.5 b23.5.** Actually taken aback by this guy. The heavier oils have been stripped and the points here are for complexity...that should shock a few old Hell's Angels I know. *40%*

Jack Daniel's No. 27 Gold Double Barrelled extra matured in maple barrels **(82) n21 t21.5 f19 b20.5.** Pleasant enough. But it appears the peculiar tannins from the maple barrels have just done slightly too good a job of flattening out the higher, more complex notes from the grains themselves. Slightly bitters towards the finish also. Tennessee Gold with precious little sparkle at all... *40%*

Jack Daniel's Master Distiller Series No 1 db **(90.5) n24** wonderful dose of extra tangy kumquat over the normal JD signature; something of the fruity cough sweet about this one; **t22** a massive, pleasantly oiled mix of molassed fudge and liquorice; **f22** drier, toastier hickory; **b22.5** no mistaking the JD pedigree. Just a few telling extra degrees of fruit. *43% WB15/387*

Jack Daniel's Rested Tennessee Rye batch 2 **(88.5) n22 t23 f21 b22.5** Possibly the most intriguing whiskey of the year: America's most flavour-enhancing stills take on the world's most flavoursome grain. The result is surprisingly well mannered, though the oils from both the stills and grain do help obliterate any meaningful complexity. Probably the only world whiskey type I have never tasted in a warehouse at full strength (though I now intend to correct that). Instinct tells me a trick has been missed by not making this a 101...Oh, and one important thing. Normally I suggest you take your whiskey at body temperature. This is one whiskey which needs to be tasted at normal room temperature to keep the oils to a minimum and allow the rye maximum airtime. 40% WB16/022

Jack Daniel's Single Barrel Proof Tennessee Whiskey barrel no. 16-2572, rick no. L-19, bott 14 Apr 16 db (**94.5**) n23.5 t23.5 f24 b23.5 Now that is what you call Tennessee whiskey... 66.25% (132.5 proof). sc.

Jack Daniel's Single Barrel Tennessee Rye Whiskey barrel no. 16-1340, rick no. L-3, bott 24 Feb 16 db (**86.5**) n21 t22 f21.5 b22. I remember tasting a JD Rye last year which didn't come at me the way I expected. This, too, is surprisingly flat and oily in the places you expect it to sing. Yes, the burnt honey notes are lovely and it does have some of that heavyweight JD swagger we all love. But somehow the finer points of the grain are lost amid it all and we end up with a pretty muted whiskey. 45%. sc.

Corn Whiskey

Dixie Dew (**95**) n22.5 t24 f24 b24.5 I have kept in my previous tasting notes for this whiskey as they serve a valuable purpose. The three matured corn whiskeys I have before me are made by the same distillers. But, this time round, they could not be more different. From Mellow Corn to Dixie we have three whiskeys with very differing hues. This, quite frankly, is the darkest corn whiskey I have ever seen and one of world class stature with characteristics I have never found before in any whiskey. Any true connoisseur of whisk(e)y will make deals with Lucifer to experience this freak whiskey. There is no age statement...but this one has gray hairs attached to the cob... 50%

Georgia Moon Corn Whiskey "Less Than 30 Days Old" (**83.5**) n21.5 t22 f20 b20. If anyone has seen corn whiskey made – either in Georgia or Kentucky – then the unique aroma will be instantly recognisable from the fermenters and still house. Enjoyable stuff which does exactly what it says on the jar. 50%

J. W. Corn (**92.5**) n23 t23.5 f23 b23. In another life this could be bourbon. The corn holds the power, for sure. But the complexity and levels are so far advanced that this – again! – qualifies as very high grade whiskey. Wonderful that the normal high standard is being maintained for what is considered by many, quite wrongly, as an inferior spirit. 50%

Mellow Corn (**83**) n19 t21 f22 b21. Dull and oily on the nose, though the palate compensates with a scintillating array of sweet and spicy notes. 50%

Single Malt Rye
ANCHOR DISTILLERY

Old Potrero Single Malt Straight Rye Whiskey Essay 10-SRW-ARM-E (**94**) n24 t23 f24 b23 The whiskey from this distillery never fails to amaze. With the distillery now under new management it will be fascinating to see what lands in my tasting lab. Even at 75% quality we will still be blessed with astonishing whiskeys. 45% (90 proof)

Straight Rye

◇ **Basil Hayden's Rye Whiskey 2017 Release** re-barreled in charred oak quarter casks, bott code: L7129CLA 153330822 (**88.5**) n23 none of the big, crisp, biting grain you'd expect from the producers of Booker's Rye. Instead, we are handsomely indulged in soft honey and floral tones, themselves rather lovely and alluring....; t22 silky rather than brittle, toffee rather than fruity: didn't expect that! Pleasant enough but not quite the complexity levels one might hope for, though there is nothing wrong with the early salivation; f21.5 pretty flat-lined caramel; b22 you can have too much of a good thing and it appears here the quarter casks have managed to over dose this rye with a surfeit of caramel. 40% (80 proof).

Benjamin Prichard's Tennessee Rye Whiskey (**86**) n20 t21.5 f23 b21.5. Bit of a scruffy nose, but polishes up pleasantly. The rye itself is not of the sharp variety and at times is hard to identify. But the ulmo honey and lush butterscotch offer the gloss at the finish. 43%

Booker's Rye 13 Years, 1 Month, 12 Days batch no. 2016-LE db (**97.5**) n25 for a big, well matured rye, it just doesn't come better than this. In fact, it probably can't. It's as though a bar of rye and chocolate has been created for the nose to inspect. There is nibble and bite to the dominating rye, yet it is not all about the spices and grain. Such varying weight and depth, as well as an almost random detection of vanilla and citrus makes for exhaustively brain-draining, mind-blowing but quite glorious nosing....; t24 salivating...oh, so salivating! The perfect weight of grain and sugars make for a delivery of astonishing presence. Almost immediately, the cocoa, which teases on the nose, makes its presence felt here with a series of intense waves, all the time crashing against the rye and Demerara sugar rocks which act as the backbone; f24 those oils I mentioned...this is where they come into their own: gathering up the amazing depth, like starlings in Autumn. Still the cocoa leaks out, but never far away is that breath-taking rye as its accomplice and commander. And it all leaks and leaches for a very long time...; **b24.5** this was a rye made in the last days of when Jim Beam's Yellow Label was at its very peak. Then, it was the best rye commercially available. Today, it is simply a staggering example of a magnificent rye showing exactly what genius in terms of whiskey actually means. If this is not World Whisky of the Year for 2017, it will be only fragments of molecules away... 68.1% (136.2 proof)

Bulleit 95 Rye (96) **n25 t24.5 f22.5 B23.5** This is a style of rye, indeed whiskey, which is unique. Buffalo Trace makes an ultra high-quality rye which lasts the course longer. But nothing compares in nose and delivery to this...in fact few whiskies in the world get even close... 45%. Straight 95% rye mash whiskey.

⟡ **Bulleit 95 Rye** bott code: L6344R60010848 (83) **n20.5 t22 f20 b20.5** In some 30 years of tasting rye from the great Lawrenceburg, Indiana, distillery, this has to be the weirdest batch I have yet encountered. The highly unusual and mildly disturbing tobacco note on the nose appears to be a theme throughout the tasting experience. A rye which rallies briefly on delivery but ultimately falls flat on its face. 45% (90 proof).

Colonel E.H. Taylor Straight Rye (97) **n24 t24.5 f24 b24.5** reminds me of the younger ryes when Sazerac Handy first hit the shelves, with the emphasis on the clarity of the grain and the fallout of oak and spice. Really, a bottle which should never be left on a liquor store shelf. 50%

Cougar Rye (95) **n25 t24 f23 b23.** The Lawrenceburg, Indiana Distillery makes the finest rye I have ever tasted - and that is saying something. Here is a magnificent example of their astonishing capabilities. Good luck hunting the Cougar. 37%. Foster's Group, Australia.

Crater Lake Rye Whiskey Batch no. JA 08 db (83.5) **n20 t22 f20.5 b21.** A distinctly warming, peppery whiskey with an obvious high rye content. Would do itself better justice as a 100 proof whiskey as here the oils are broken down a little too enthusiastically, allowing unhelpful freedom to a tobacco note. Good early use of dark sugars, though. One to keep an eye on. 40%.

Devil's Bit Seven-Year-Old Single Barrel (93.5) **n22.5 t24 f23 b24.** A must-find rye from one of the most impressive small distilleries in the world. 47.7%. Edgefield Distillery.

Governor's Reserve Taos Lightning Straight Rye Whiskey (94.5) **n24** classic: the grain is clean, brittle, fruity – especially in crisp green apple - and radiates its type like an unerring beacon. Brilliant! **t24** absolutely more of the same, except a surprising oiliness cushions the impact on delivery; **f23** bitters out as a little spiced mocha takes its turn; **b23.5** now this is rye, believe me!!! Those who love the Lawrenceburg, Indiana, type rye (and who doesn't?!?) will adore this... 45% (90 proof). sc. Bottled by KGB Spirits LLC.

High West 12 Years Old Rye (92.5) **n22 t24 f23 b23.5.** A very clever rye which will hit a chord of appreciation for those who savour this whiskey style. 46%

High West Whiskey Rendezvous Rye Batch 12431 db (94.5) **n23.5 t24 f23 b24** After a few disappointing batches, this one appears to have found that vital spark. It could be a whole new set of whiskeys, a change of one barrel, or even the same whiskey re-stirred before bottling. It doesn't matter: something has clicked. 46%. ncf. WB15/176

Jim Beam Pre-Prohibition Style Rye db (95) **n23** crisp muscovado and rye: clean, precise and slightly dazzling; **t24.5** brilliant delivery: the old-fashioned juicy crispness on the palate of a Jim Beam rye has been restored, despite a background fudgy smokiness which dovetails with amazing finesse; a little manuka honey goes a long, long way; **f23.5** long, with the spices now grabbing hold. Fabulous mocha makes the most of the lingering sugar and fading rye; **b24** very similar to how Jim Bean Yellow Label was over 20 years ago. In other words: simply superb! 45% (90 Proof)

John David Albert's Taos Lightning Straight Rye Whiskey batch no. A1 (96) **n24** some vanilla concentrated tannins have dulled the usual crispness of the rye and thrown in extra spice for good measure; **t24.5** again, the oak is upfront and gets in on the grain's act. But this liquorice and chocolate addition still cannot douse the magical juiciness of the rye, which still enjoys a solo performance before rejoining the group. The spices are pretty warming; **f23.5** a little praline with the vanilla. But the spice and rye carry on together for a good while yet; **b24** some decent age to this has really ensured enormous complexity. And astonishing beauty. 45% (90 proof). sc. Bottled by KGB Spirits LLC.

Knob Creek Straight Rye Whiskey (92.5) **n23.5 t23.5 f22.5 b23** a slightly more genteel rye than I expected, if you compare standard Knob Creek to their usual bourbon. 50% (100 proof).

Knob Creek Straight Rye Whiskey batch L5349CLA (92.5) **n23.5 t23.5 f22.5 b23** Curious: just checked I scored a batch from last year at 92.5 also. Can't say this isn't consistent quality...! 50%

Michter's 10 Years Old Single Barrel Straight Rye barrel no. 16A113 (88) n22.5 t23 f20.5 b22 Michter's and rye go together like all the great names of America and success: like David Beckham and football, Christopher Nolan and Hollywood directing , Hugh Laurie and Hollywood acting, my old Fleet Street colleague Piers Morgan and chat shows, my girlfriend's old chum Simon Cowell and talent shows. This, though, isn't quite in the same league as the bottle I tasted from them last year, which was in a Saville Row suit compared to the dowdy hand-me-down here. Enjoyable, but by Michter's high standards... 46.4% (92.8 proof).

Michter's No. 1 Straight Rye (95.5) n23.5 t24 f24 b24 Truly classic rye whiskey. The stuff which makes one write swoonerisms... 42.4%

Pappy Van Winkle's Family Reserve Rye 13 Years Old (94) n24 t23.5 f23 b23.5 Uncompromising rye that successfully tells two stories simultaneously. A great improvement on the Winkle rye of old. 47.8%

Pikesville Straight Rye Whiskey Aged at Least 6 Years (97.5) n24.5 textbook: the fruitiness of the rye shimmers on the nose; a light spice tingles in Demerara rum fashion. Carry on nosing and you will, if patient and able enough, find unusual depths to which few whiskies reach. The tantalising chocolate-liquorice at about three quarters depth is one of the aromas of the year; t24.5 after that nose, the delivery just had to be majestic. And it is. The rye grain fair rattles against the teeth, the sugars – crystalline, dark and tinged with both molasses and muscovado – help bring its salivating qualities to maximum. Then those spices...those wonderful, bustling, fizzing spices...; f24 a lovely mix between ulmo and Zambian forest honey keeps the sweetness lingering to the end. The rye, of course, continues to sparkle and spice its way to the last embers of the fade...which is a long way away...; b24.5 the most stunning of ryes and the best from Heaven Hill for some time. 55% (110 Proof)

Redemption Riverboat Rye (78) n19 t21 f19 b19. Dry, weirdly off key and oily – and holed below the water line. 40%

Redemption Rye (85.5) n22 t22.5 f20 b21. The tobacco nose is a bit of a poser: how did that get there? Or the spearmint, which helps as you try to chew things over in your mind. The big rye wave on delivery is supported by mixed dark sugars. But there is something ashy about the finish. 46%

Rittenhouse Very Rare Single Barrel 21 Years Old (91) n25 t23 f21 b22. I may be wrong, but I would wager quite a large amount that no-one living has tasted more rye from around the world than I. So trust me when I tell you this is different, a genuine one-off in style. By rights such telling oak involvement should have killed the whisky stone dead: this is like someone being struck by lightning and then walking off slightly singed and with a limp, but otherwise OK. The closest style of whisky to rye is Irish pot still, a unique type where unmalted barley is used. And the closest whiskey I have tasted to this has been 35 to 50-year-old pot still Irish. What they have in common is a massive fruit base, so big that it can absorb and adapt to the oak input over many years. This has not escaped unscathed. But it has to be said that the nose alone makes this worthy of discovery, as does the glory of the rye as it first melts into the tastebuds. The term flawed genius could have been coined for this whisky alone. Yet, for all its excellence, I can so easily imagine someone, somewhere, claiming to be an expert on whiskey, bleating about the price tag of $150 a bottle. If they do, ignore them. Because, frankly, rye has been sold far too cheaply for far too long and that very cheapness has sculpted a false perception in people's minds about the quality and standing of the spirit. Well, 21 years in Kentucky equates to about 40 years in Scotland. And you try and find a 40-year-old Scotch for £75. If anything, they are giving this stuff away. The quality of the whiskey does vary from barrel to barrel and therefore bottle to bottle. So below I have given a summary of each individual bottling (averaging (91.1). The two with the highest scores show the least oak interference...yet are quite different in style. That's great whiskey for you. 50% (100 proof). ncf.

Barrel no. 1 (91) n25 t23 f21 b22. As above. 50%
Barrel no. 2 (89) n24 t23 f20 b22. Dryer, oakier. 50%
Barrel no. 3 (91) n24 t23 f22 b22. Fruity, soft. 50%
Barrel no. 4 (90) n25 t22 f21 b22. Enormous. 50%
Barrel no. 5 (93) n25 t23 f22 b23. Early rye surge. 50%
Barrel no. 6 (87) n23 t22 f20 b22. Juicy, vanilla. 50%
Barrel no. 7 (90) n23 t23 f22 b22. Even, soft, honeyed. 50%
Barrel no. 8 (95) n25 t24 f23 b23. The works: massive rye. 50%
Barrel no. 9 (91) n24 t23 f22 b22. Sharp rye, salivating. 50%

Barrel no. 10 (93) n25 t24 f22 b22. Complex, sweet. *50%*
Barrel no. 11 (93) n24 t24 f22 b23. Rich, juicy, spicy. *50%*
Barrel no. 12 (91) n25 t23 f21 b22. Near identical to no.1. *50%*
Barrel no. 13 (91) n24 t24 f21 b22. Citrus and toasty. *50%*
Barrel no. 14 (94) n25 t24 f22 b23. Big rye and marzipan. *50%*
Barrel no. 15 (88) n23 t22 f21 b22. Major oak influence. *50%*
Barrel no. 16 (90) n24 t24 f21 b22. Spicy and toffeed. *50%*
Barrel no. 17 (90) n23 t23 f22 b22. Flinty, firm, late rye kick. *50%*
Barrel no. 18 (91) n24 t24 f21 b22. Big rye delivery. *50%*
Barrel no. 19 (87) n23 t22 f21 b21. Major coffee input. *50%*
Barrel no. 20 (91) n23 t24 f22 b22. Spicy sugar candy. *50%*
Barrel no. 21 (94) n24 t23 f24 b23. Subtle, fruity. *50%*
Barrel no. 22 (89) n23 t22 f22 b22. Mollased rye. *50%*
Barrel no. 23 (94) n24 t23 f24 b23. Soft fruit, massive rye. *50%*
Barrel no. 24 (88) n23 t22 f21 b22. Intense oak and caramel. *50%*
Barrel no. 25 (93) n25 t22 f23 b23. Heavy rye and spice. *50%*
Barrel no. 26 (92) n23 t23 f23 b23. Subtle, delicate rye. *50%*
Barrel no. 27 (94) n25 t23 f23 b23. Delicate rye throughout. *50%*
Barrel no. 28 (96) n25 t24 f23 b24. Salivating, roasty, major. *50%*
Barrel no. 29 (88) n23 t22 f21 b22. Hot, fruity. *50%*
Barrel no. 30 (91) n24 t23 f22 b22. Warming cough sweets. *50%*
Barrel no. 31 (90) n25 t22 f21 b22. Aggressive rye. *50%*

Rittenhouse Rye Single Barrel Aged 25 Years (93.5) n24.5 t24 f22 b23. This is principally about the nose: a thing of rare beauty even in the highest peaks of the whiskey world. The story on the palate is much more about damage limitation with the oak going a bit nuts. But remember this: in Scottish years due to the heat in Kentucky, this would be a malt well in excess of 50 years. But even with the signs of fatigue, so crisp is that rye, so beautifully defined are its intrinsic qualities that the quality is still there to be clearly seen. Just don't judge on the first, second or even third mouthful. Your taste buds need time to relax & adjust. Only then will they accommodate and allow you to fully appreciate and enjoy the creaky old ride. At this age, though, always worth remembering that the best nose doesn't always equal the best tasting experience... *50% (100proof).*

Barrel no. 1 (93.5) n24.5 t24 f22 b23. As above. *50%*
Barrel no. 2 (88) n22 t24 f20 b22. Intense. Crisp, juicy; a tad soapy, bitter. *50%*
Barrel no. 3 (89.5) n23 t23.5 f21.5 b21.5. Fabulously crisp. Fruity. Mollassed. *50%*
Barrel no. 4 (85) n21.5 t21.5 f21 b21. Subdued fruit. Massive oak. *50%*
Barrel no. 5 (90.5) n25 t22.5 f21.5 b21.5. Complex. Mega oaked but spiced, fruity. *50%*
Barrel no. 6 (91.5) n24.5 t22 f23 b22. Tangy. Honeyed and hot. Spiced marmalade. *50%*
Barrel no. 7 (83.5) n20 t22 f20.5 b21. Treacle toffee amid the burnt apple. *50%*
Barrel no. 8 (90) n23.5 t23.5 f21 b22. Flinty, teeth-cracking rye. Crème brulee. *50%*
Barrel no. 9 (91) n23.5 t23.5 f22 b22. Massive ryefest. Mocha coated. *50%*
Barrel no. 10 (86.5) n22 t23 f20 b21.5. Early zip and juice. Tires towards caramel. *50%*
Barrel no. 11 (89) n24 t22 f21 b22. Honeycomb. Hickory. Caramel. Oil. *50%*
Barrel no. 12 (84.5) n22.5 t21 f20 b21. Delicate. Vanilla and caramel. Light. *50%*
Barrel no. 13 (89.5) n22.5 t23 f22 b22. Succulent. Yet rye remains firm. *50%*
Barrel no. 14 (88) n22 t23 f21 b22. Very similar to 13 but with extra caramel. *50%*
Barrel no. 15 (86) n21 t23 f20.5 b21.5. Lazy grain. Warming but flat. Caramel. *50%*
Barrel no. 16 (92) n23 t23 f23 b23. Sculpted rye: sugared fruit; a twist of juniper. *50%*
Barrel no. 17 (86.5) n22.5 t21.5 f21 b21.5. Fizzy, fruity spice calmed by caramel. *50%*
Barrel no. 18 (91) n23.5 t23.5 f21.5 b22.5. Pristine rye. Spice. Juicy molasses. Crisp. *50%*
Barrel no. 19 (96) n24 t23.5 f24.5 b23.5. Concentrated honeycomb and chocolate. *50%*
Barrel no. 20 (89.5) n23 t22 f22.5 b22. Cream toffee. Fruit and spice. *50%*
Barrel no. 21 (85) n21 t20 f23 b21. Severe oak delivery. Recovers with mocha toffee. *50%*
Barrel no. 22 (81) n20 t20 f21 b20. Mild sap. Fruity. Oily. *50%*
Barrel no. 23 (94) n23.5 t24 f23.5 b23. Rich. Fruity. Juicy. Clean. Corn oil. Cocoa. *50%*
Barrel no. 24 (88.5) n22.5 t22 f21 b22. Huge vanilla. Slow spice. *50%*
Barrel no. 25 (88) n22.5 t21.5 f22 b22. Custard and sugared fruit. Sharpens. *50%*
Barrel no. 26 (90.5) n22 t23 f23 b22.5. Classic crisp rye. Big, manageable oak. *50%*
Barrel no. 27 (88) n23 t22 f21.5 b21.5. Huge, honeyed oak. Oily. Dries at end. *50%*
Barrel no. 28 (91) n22.5 t23.5 f22.5 b22.5. Exemplary honeycomb-rye delivery. Spices. *50%*
Barrel no. 29 (94) n23.5 t24 f23 b23.5. Juicy rye; crisp sugar-vanilla-hickory fade. *50%*

Barrel no. 30 (94.5) n23 t24 f24 b23.5. Thick rye. Cocoa. Spices. *50%*

Barrel no. 31 (79) n21 t20 f19 b19. Lethargic. Bitter. *50%*

Barrel no. 32 (88) n21.5 t22.5 f22 b22. Relaxed honeycomb. Hint of mint. *50%*

Barrel no. 33 (88.5) n22.5 t22 f22 b22. Powering oak-rye battle. *50%*

Barrel no. 34 (84) n23 t21 f20 b20. Thick oak throughout. Corn oil. *50%*

Barrel no. 35 (93.5) n22.5 t23.5 f24 b23.5. Big rye. Demerara-hickory. Complex. *50%*

Barrel no. 36 (77) n21 t19 f18 b19. Bitter oak. *50%*

Russell's Reserve Rye 6 Year Old Small Batch bott. code L0194FH) (93.5) n24 t23.5 f22.5 b23.5. Lost none of its wit and sharpness: in fact has improved a notch or two in recent times. *45%*

Sazerac Kentucky Straight Rye Whiskey 18 Years Old bott 2012 (95.5) n24 t23 f24 b24.5. Unquestionably showing a different side to its personality this time out, allowing the rye to show its fruity personality to the full. *45%*

Sazerac Rye 18 Year Old bott Fall 2013 db (97) n24.5 t24.5 f24 b24 Another stir of the pot and up comes Sazerac 18 polished and wallowing in its own enormity. Rye whiskey exactly how it should be. *45%.*

Sazerac Rye 18 Year Old bott Spring 2014 db (96.5) n24.5 t24.5 f23.5 b24 Always one of the great and most fascinating whiskeys on the planet - essentially the same stuff year after year - plays out with each roll of the bottling dice. Here someone has cut off much of the oil... with stunning results. Way better than than last year's offering and much closer to its old self. *45%. Buffalo Trace Antique Collection*

Sazerac 18 Years Old bott Spring 2015 db (97) n25 cut-glass rye: crystalline rye notes don't get any more...well...crystalline than this. Spices nibble, bite and nip with a beguiling mix of playfulness and attitude, but it is the perfect foil for the more serene, herbal notes. Not sure how a nose can be so soft, yet diamond hard at one and the same moment...; t24 there you go! As though the nose has arrived on the palate. Except here there are far more brassy sugars immediately at work, but with a squeeze of lime to slightly break up the intensity. Mocha and praline notes add an almost phenolic weightiness in the same way smoke does on a light Islay. All the time, though, the rye can traced on every outline sharp, rigid and delicious; f24 long, making the most of the modest and so subtle oils which have, literally, stuck around. The tannins are evident but refuse to dominate and, instead, concentrate only on adding a further degree of weight and gravitas to the unruffled rye; b24 it is as though all excess oils have been drained from this whiskey in the last year or two and we are seeing something stark, naked and even more desirable than before. Technically sublime. *45% (90 proof).*

Sazerac 18 Years Old bott Spring 2016 db (95.5) n24 spices graze contentedly all around the margins of the soft aroma: there is little or no aggression. The rye manifests itself in both crisp, sugary tones as well as in full, classic fruity form wonderfully easing and satisfying; t24 superb delivery. Again understated with the grain washing over the taste buds only at first then become more clipped and crisp in time-honoured style; f23.5 a lovely fruit buzz mingling with muscovado-sweetened butterscotch and mocha: the lightly spiced rye never for a moment loses traction or direction; b24 simply a classic, gilt-edged rye. *45% (90 proof).*

Smooth Ambler Old Scout Straight Rye Aged 7 Years batch 17, bott 9 Nov 13 (82) n21 t22 f19 b20. Now this is odd. What do you get when you combine the characteristics of rye and gin? Something, probably, like this. Never been to these guys in West Virginia, though I'll try and make a point of paying a visit when next in that stunning state. No idea if they are involved with gin. But something about the botanical feel to the nose and finish in particular suggests they might. Perhaps a bottling problem for this single batch? Intrigued. *49.5% WB15/373*

Sonoma County Rye pot distilled from grain db (83.5) n21 t21.5 f20 b21. Sweet nougat, heavy duty, wide-cut oily. Quite German in style. *48%. 1512 Spirits. WB15/384*

Thomas H. Handy Sazerac db (95.5) n23.5 a hefty nose, the natural fruitiness of the rye given enormous weight by a dull but intense orange peel note on top of a crushed leaf (hang on, rings a bell..... yep, just checked with last year's bottling "crushed green leaves" I noted: spooky!), slightly herbal tea effect; t24.5 the oils missing in the Sazerac 18 have turned up here. So oily at first it takes a little while for the rye to really battle though and make its mark. But when it does...oh, boy! But for its enormity, the boom of the explosion, there is no carnage or collateral damage. Just a mouth-watering, juicy spume of spiced rye and wave after wave hits the taste buds with controlled power, reducing in time elegance; f23.5 retires to a more deft, cocoa-enriched and sober fade, with oak-enriched caramels and ulmo honey softening the buzz of the spice; b24 with each bottling, the style of the Thomas Handy moves away from the Sazerac 18 in style *63.45% (126.9 proof).*

Thomas H. Handy Sazerac Straight Rye Whiskey (97.5) n24 t24.5 f24.5 b24.5 This was World Whisky of the Year last year and anyone buying this on the strength of that will not be disappointed. Huge whiskey with not even the glimmer of a hint of an off note. Magnificent: an honour to taste and rye smiles all round... 66.2%. ncf.

Thomas H. Handy Sazerac Straight Rye (95.5) n24 t24 f23.5 b24 Perhaps because this has become something of a softie, without all those usual jagged and crisp rye notes, it doesn't quite hit the spot with quite the same delicious drama. Still a beauty, though. 64.6%

◇ **Thomas H. Handy Sazerac** db (96.5) n24 the hardened grain stands slightly aloof from the softer caramel and tannin tones lapping below it, sending out a beam of fruit into all parts as though a lighthouse of rye on a crunchy, rocky outcrop of Demerara sugar; t25 brilliant, brilliant, brilliant...!! You can ask no more from a rye than this: intense and unflinching in its ability to generate the most intense grain imaginable, thus offering a rare crunchiness and non-specific fruitiness at once, thus making the mouth salivate alarmingly! Crispy and massively spiced in equal measure, it really is the perfect rye delivery and middle; f23.5 a little bitterness from the oak begin to creep in with the rye now having dropped from its earlier storm into a gentle breeze. The caramels now hold sway, though the spices keep the taste buds alert; b24 when Thomas Handy hits the very height of its powers, which for a significant period it does here, very few whiskeys can match its eloquence and sheer force of nature. A whiskey to be as much worshipped as savoured... 63.1% (126.2 proof).

Turley Mill Straight Rye Western Whiskey aged 6 years, batch no. 12 (94) n23.5 the spicy rye makes no secret of its presence; t24 absolutely brilliant delivery: the rye is bursting out from every molecule: salivating, warming, rich, crisp, deep, multi-layered and every single nuance is rye related, even those the tannins have got their teeth into; f23 some late oils develop alongside the hesitant ulmo honey; b23.5 so, with this from KGB Spirits, here's my Cold War: don't add ice to this superb rye under any circumstances...58% (118 proof). sc. Bottled by KGB Spirits LLC.

Whistlepig Aged 10 Years db (88) n21 t22 f23 b22. Having tasted this after the Sazarac beasts, this could have disappeared without trace. But had enough sharpness and rye freshness to make for a very pleasant and worthwhile experience. 50% (100 proof)

WhistlePig Old World 12 Year Old European casks (87) n23 t23.5 f20 b20.5. What a tragedy! The spirit itself is magnificent. The grain positively glistens on both nose and delivery and is on a par with Kentucky's finest. Sadly, a pretty rough finish thanks to the cask...which is always the danger when dealing with European wine barrels. 45% (90 Proof)

Willett Family Estate Bottled Single Barrel Rye 4 Years Old Barrel no 45 (94) n23.5 t24 f23 b23.5. Truly satisfying rye which has in style more than a passing resemblance to the old Jim Beam yellow label rye of about 15 years ago. 55%

Straight Wheat Whiskey

Bernheim Original (91.5) n22 t23 f23 b23.5. By far the driest of the Bernheims I have encountered showing greater age and perhaps substance. Unique and spellbinding. 45%

Parker's Heritage Collection Original Batch Kentucky Straight Wheat Whiskey Aged 13 Years db (95.5) n23.5 t24 f23.5 b24.5 Not sure if they get Bassett's Liquorice Allsorts in the US. But, if they did, they would immediately recognise the brown ones in this...though in an insanely beautiful mutated form. So, so delicious....! 63.7%. ncf.

American Microdistilleries
10TH MOUNTAIN WHISKEY & SPIRIT COMPANY Vail, Colorado

◇ **10th Mountain Rocky Mountain Bourbon Whiskey Aged 6 Months** db (92) n22 t23 f23.5 b23.5 The youth of the spirit is apparent on the nose where slightly more hostile tannins have not yet had a chance to say howdy to the corn. But once on the palate the entire story changes as the maple syrup and molasses – and, amazingly, even liquorice already – makes a far better attempt to find a happy medium with the grain. Beautifully made and a really sumptuous and spice-ridden offering. 46% (92 proof).

◇ **10th Mountain Rye Whiskey Aged 6 Months** batch 10, bott 11.28.16 db (94.5) n23.5 t24 f23.5 b23.5 You don't have to be a genius to know that whoever mans the still at 10th Mountain knows exactly what he (or she) is doing. And whoever selects the oak is on his game, also. It is not a common experience to find a rye spirit which has been so lovingly handled – and seemingly with rare understanding, also. The grain is crisp, allowing its friable, fruity personality to star from nose to finish. It also infiltrates the sexy and sultry oily sub-plot in which most of the ulmo honey stars. But what makes this a star turn is the roasty, cocoa aspect to this which works so well with the rye-laden crispness. What a treat this is... Now, good people of 10th Mountain, you are holding out on us: the barrel strength version, if you please... 43% (86 proof).

⟡ **Colorado Clear Mountain Moonshine 100% Corn Whiskey** db (92.5) n23 t23.5 f23 b23 Whenever I pick up a pickle jar full of clear corn moonshine, it is near impossible to wipe the smile off my face...yesiree! So many happy moments over the last 30 years in some wilderness spots of the US where the local hooch has been handed to me in near identical receptacles... and by so many wonderful people. At a mere 80 proof, this weighs in at about the friendliest of them all – and possible the cleanest and sweetest. But the corn comes through as it should and it is hard not to pour yourself a refill...even in a tasting lab 3,500 miles from where I should be. *40% (80 proof).*

ALASKA DISTILLERY Wasilla, Alaska.

Alaska Proof Bourbon db (86) n22 t22.5 f20 b21.5. It must be Alaska and the lack of pollution or something. But how do these guys make their whiskey quite so clean....? For a rugged, wild land, it appears to concentrate on producing a bourbon which is borderline ethereal and all about sugary subtlety. The downside is that such lightness allows any weakness in the wood or distillation to be flagged up, though with nobody saluting. *40% (80 proof)*

ALLTECH Lexington, Kentucky.

Pearse Lyons Reserve (85) n22 t21 f21 b21. A fruity, grainy, pleasant whisky with the higher notes citrus dominant. Never quite finds a place to land or quite tells its story. Attractive but incomplete. *40% (80 proof)*

Town Branch Kentucky Straight Bourbon (88.5) n22.5 t21.5 f23 b22 A delicious Kentucky bourbon of considerable depth and charm. I think they have found their niche: bourbon. In Kentucky. Go for it, guys! *40% (80 proof)*

AMERICAN CRAFT WHISKEY DISTILLERY Redwood Valley, California.

Low Gap Bavarian Hard Wheat Aged 2 Years dist 31 Dec 10, bott 23 Jan 13 (76.5) n18 t21 f18.5 b19. There appears to be butyric on the nose and the finish bitters uncompromisingly. Despite the odd juicy, spicy high spot, not this distillery's finest moment. *43.1%*

ARIZONA DISTILLING Tempe, Arizona

Desert Durum Wheat Whiskey Batch no. 2 db (87.5) n21.5 t23 f21.5 b21.5. Another hairy-chested gung-ho whiskey which pins you back in your chair. And my notes for the first edition fits this one equally as well. Except here it loses out slightly by having a slightly too wide cut, meaning the feints bite on the nose and finish. But still about as macho as a whiskey gets. And as chocolatey, too. *46%.*

AXE AND THE OAK Colorado Springs, Colorado

⟡ **Axe and the Oak Bourbon Whiskey** batch no. 20 db (86.5) n20.5 t22.5 f21.5 b22 Although this is batch number 20, you still get the feeling this is a work in progress. The nose at times displays some most unbourbon-like traits with far more of the still and/or fermentation room than opened cask. But the whiskey recovers with admirable calm: on the palate the corn oils establish themselves and the rye present kicks in with a firm sweetness while the tannins crank up the light liquorice and spice. The soft chocolate mousse on the finish works well with the molasses. Promising. *46% (92 proof).*

⟡ **Axe and the Oak Cask Strength Bourbon Whiskey** batch no. 1 db (87.5) n21 t23 f21.5 b22 Big, bustling, no-prisoners whiskey which reveals quite a wide cut. That adds extra weight for sure, but a tanginess interrupts the flow of the excellent liquorice and molasses tones which had made the delivery and immediate aftermath something genuinely to savour. Get the cut right on the run and this will be one hell of a bourbon. *64.4% (128.8 proof).*

BAINBRIDGE ORGANIC DISTILLERS Bainbridge Island, Washington

Battle Point Organic Washington Wheat Whiskey (88.5) n21 t23 f22 b23 Soft and satisfying. The spices demanded from wheat whiskey, though short-lived, hit all the right spots. Very well made and impressive. *43%*

BALCONES DISTILLERY Waco, Texas.

⟡ **Balcones Baby Blue Corn Whisky Aged At Least 6 Months in Oak** batch no. BB17-1, bott 3-7-17 db (87) n22.5 t23 f20.5 b21 Spill a drop of this on your foot and you'll end up with a few broken toes. This is heavy corn whisky, just feeling the effects of a slightly wider cut than is the norm for this great distillery. The result is a profound whisky with some serious sugars but a lack of the usual balance. *46% (92 proof). nc ncf.*

◈ **Balcones Brimstone Texas Scrub Oak Smoked Whisky Aged At Least 1 Day in Oak** batch no. BRM17-1, bott 1-19-17 db (**92.5**) **n23.5** aroma is the cheapest way to travel: here I have been transported 50 years back in time to a Surrey garden shed and my dad surrounded by tins of creosote: the pungency of it never leaves you. And there are lighter phenols here, too, sweater as in smoky bacon; **t23** soft, oily mouthfeel. The Demerara sugars have stacked up early like a beaver builds a dam and with good reason: the smoke is about to unleash itself in full spate; **f22.5** a more tranquil, the sugars, phenols and spices each holding about equal share in the flavour portfolio, though the spice is in serious buying mode; **b23.5** a truly unique flavour profile that will be too much of a challenge for some but like ultimate surfing for the peat head. Once you become acclimatised you soon realise the balance is very impressive. *53% (106 proof). nc ncf.*

◈ **Balcones True Blue Straight 100 Proof Corn Whisky Aged At Least 24 Months in Oak** batch no. TB-100 16-1, bott 8-4-16 db (**90.5**) **n23.5** irresistible mix of golden syrup and corn oil; **t22.5** a starchy delivery, but it grows into its enormous body with a balanced mix of vanilla, eye-watering corn, liquorice and Manuka honey; **f22** more of the same, with a bigger accent on the tannins and spices; **b22.5** big! *50% (100 proof). nc ncf.*

◈ **Balcones True Blue Cask Strength Straight Corn Whisky Aged At Least 24 Months** batch no. TB 16-1, bott 8-3-16 db (**95**) **n24** the oak has a big, big say here: toasty and outflanking the sugars which seems stuck in the glutinous corn oil. The spices are genuinely scary...; **t24** a corn whisky delivery of your dreams: high voltage oil and maple syrup with a huge explosion of spiced liquorice, hickory and tannin in the mid-ground, the whole picture being swamped in spice; **f23.5** long, despite the oils now appearing to have quickly lessened. We are back to the toastier notes, allowing only the driest molasses to speak up for the sweeter notes, until a light natural caramel forms; **b23.5** their True Blue 100 Proof is big. This is a whole lot bigger... *65.7% (131.4 proof). nc ncf.*

◈ **Balcones Texas Blue Corn Straight Bourbon Whisky Aged At Least 24 Months in Oak** batch no. BCB 16-1, bott 7-7-16 db (**96.5**) **n24** this is massive: a half-hour aroma....if you are in a hurry. The molasses and Manuka honey appear to have become welded together, the spices are borderline painful...and when not inflicting pain, it is pure pleasure. There is hickory in league with maple syrup; and liquorice, of course, with a minty oakiness; **t24.5** the most impressive power always seems to be displayed when it is obvious it comes from a position of peace. And here we have soft, friendly, honeycombed, silky corn oils kissing, caressing and cajoling. While elsewhere on the palate the liquorice explodes, taking few prisoners and sparking off a spicy, ultra-salivating chain-reaction...: this is great bourbon, concentrated; **f24** this is about the gentle oils and thin layer of ulmo honey which soothe taste buds after an exhaustive round of masochism...; **b24** whatever you do, don't add anything to this. Not a drop of branch water: the adding of ice deserves a custodial sentence. Hard labour, in fact. I'll give you on the rocks: you should spend time smashing them...! No, the only thing this needs is time: a good half hour, undisturbed. A clean glass, warmed. And the ability to sit and listen to a great Texan tale as it speaks to you with both force and eloquence. This is an alpha male of a bourbon and when it tells you to listen up, you listen up good... *64.9% (129.8 proof). nc ncf.*

◈ **Balcones Texas Single Malt Whisky Classic Edition Aged At Least 18 Months in Oak** batch no. SM17-3, bott 4-19-17 db (**93**) **n23** the barley enjoys a roastiness without the usual bitter side effects on the nose; the tannins are also full on yet controlled by a light dash of kumquat and diced apple, the latter note a secondary string from the barley; **t23.5** ridiculously huge! You could carve your initials in the delivery, it is that dense: the malt notes are confined to barley sugar while a far more intense bourbon-style liquorice and butterscotch lead carries the oak's great interest; **f23** sticky ulmo honey and red liquorice carry the bourbon banner further, but the final waves are from ridiculously delicate grassy barley notes; **b23.5** most of the micro distillers have a bit of a problem when it comes to producing a single malt; but not these boys! Superb. *53% (106 proof). nc ncf.*

BENJAMIN PRICHARD'S DISTILLERY Kelso, Tennessee.
Benjamin Prichard's Lincoln County Lightning Tennessee Corn Whiskey (**89**) **n24 t22.5 f21 b22.** Another white whiskey. This one is very well made and though surprisingly lacking oils and weight has more than enough charm and riches. *45%*

BERKSHIRE MOUNTAIN DISTILLERS Great Barrington, Massachusetts.
Berkshire Bourbon Whiskey (**91.5**) **n23 t23.5 f23 b23.** A bourbon bursting with character: I am hooked! Another micro-gem. *43%*

BLUE RIDGE DISTILLING CO. Golden Valley, North Carolina.

Defiant American Single Malt Whisky 100% malted barely db (80.5) n19 t21 f20.5 b20. A wide cut ensures a chewy, honey and nougat feel to this. Barley, though, does not have the same flavour compounds to compensate for the oils. Undeniably tasty, if a little flawed! 41% (82 proof)

Blue Ridge Rye Whisky db (87) n21.5 t22.5 f21 b21. I remember once, when giving a talk about rye whiskey maybe 20 years ago now, I was asked about what the first ryes of Pennsylvania would have tasted like. And I remember saying that they would have been heavy beasts of a liquor: the distillers would have made the cut pretty wide and the oils would have anchored the heavier rye traits. I also said that the ryes which were floated down the river to market would have been a lot sweeter than those consumed in its home market, on account of the sugars coming in off the fresh oak barrels, if that was what they used. And on nosing and tasting this, I was put in mind of that lecture I gave, for this would have been one that was sent out to market. This is heavy and feinty, though the intensity of the rye papers over the smaller to medium sized cracks. And the sugars are intense. This is big, imperfect rye with character spilling out of the glass. But great fun and more than a nod to America's distilling past. 46% (92 proof)

BRECKENRIDGE DISTILLERY Breckenridge, Colorado.

Breckenridge Colorado Bourbon Whiskey Aged 2 Years (86) n22.5 t22 f20.5 b21. Full of character, big-hearted, chewy, slightly rugged bourbon where honey and cocoa thrives; spices make a telling impact. How apposite that probably the one and only town in Colorado named after a Kentuckian should end up making bourbon. Being close on 10,000 feet above sea level you'd think ice would come naturally with this. But it does pretty well without it, believe me... 43%

BREUCKELEN DISTILLING Brooklyn, New York.

77 Whiskey Local Rye & Corn 483 Days Old, American oak barrels, db (95) n24 t24 f23 b24 An absolute gem of a whiskey just dripping with rye. 45%

◇ **77 Whiskey Local Rye & Corn 538 Days Old** American oak barrels db (92.5) n22.5 expecting big, crisp rye: instead get a more rotund sweetness, almost like a freshly baked puff pastry full of raisin and high sugar content marzipan; t23.5 enormous. Obviously a slightly wide cut at play here as the oils are profound but the sugars are going through the roof. Mainly of a muscovado style but a little molasses also; f23 a light bitterness from that generous cut is evident. But the marzipan on the nose now shows its nuttier side; b23.5 the 377th whisky tasted for my Bible 2018 just had to be this. I remember last year tasting a younger version of this which was quite astonishing. Here the rye, which was so prominent last time, has been overtaken by the corn which has clipped its brittle wings. Still an astounding experience, nonetheless... 45% (90 proof).

◇ **77 Whiskey New York Wheat 519 Days Old** American oak barrels db (89.5) n22 German spiced biscuit – surely the perfect whiskey for Christmas in Cologne... t23 less German than the nose with the vanillas freely on tap before those spices, aided by some blood orange, come calling; f22 the big sugars recede before spoiling the moment; f22 busy, warming, though not quite blistering spice. A little golden syrup and molasses head off a bitter infiltration with ease; b22.5 just looked up my tasting notes for this whiskey from last year: identical score and very similar description. This is one very consistent whiskey!! 45% (90 proof).

77 Whiskey New York Wheat 622 Days Old American oak barrels db (89.5) n22 t23 f22 b22.5 A very busy whiskey which never quite decides which direction it wishes to take. Still, there's something to say for a mystery tour... 45%

CADÉE DISTILLERY Clinton, Washington.

Cadée Distillery Cascadia Rye Whiskey finished in Port barrels db (87) n21.5 t23 f21 b21.5. Works quite well. A vaguely wide cut does ramp up the oils. But the rye has enough crystalline firmness to cut through the fruit. Think this pretty high quality rye actually deserves better than being masked by the Port which, though clean and juicy, has a flattening effect. 43.5% (87 proof)

Cadée Distillery Deceptivus Bourbon Whiskey finished in Port barrels db (87) n21 t22 f22.5 b22. The sweet corn and the fruit combine to form a formidable chewiness. Attractive with some lovely ulmo honey also. The spiced chocolate fruit and vague nougat really does ensure an entertaining finale. 42.5% (85 proof)

CATOCTIN CREEK DISTILLERY Loudoun County, Virginia.

Braddock Oak Single Barrel Rye Whisky batch B17K1 db **(90)** n22.5 some pretty classic crunchy rye notes, complete with Demerara sugar; t23 brilliant delivery of brittle rye and very warming spice. The sugars do all that is expected and demanded of a rye, showing a fruity muscovado crunchiness to top of the clear grain notes; f22 just a tad oily from the generous cut; b22.5 it is heart-warming to see a distillery dedicated to making rye. Still the odd technical off-note but I am sure this will be corrected with time and experience. Plenty here to savour. 46% sc.

Catoctin Creek Cask Proof Roundstone Rye Whisky batch B17A2, charred new oak barrels db **(88)** n21.5 strangely muted for a rye: none of the usual crisp, fluting fruity notes associated with the grain...even found on their Braddock oak; t22.5 the thick rye is matched equally by the oily feints and brooding spice. Chewy and profound; f22 more mocha and liquorice than rye; the bite underlines the wide cut; b22 so much flavour. But needs to get those cuts cleaner to maximise the rye profile. 57.8% (115.6 proof). ncf.

Catoctin Creek Roundstone Rye Single Barrel Whisky batch B1IE43Y, new white oak barrels db **(87)** n22 t22 f21 b22 The thing that has to be said about Catoctin is the amazing consistency (and close scoring) of their brands. Oddly enough, for a single barrel this perhaps does the distillery least justice as it is the work of the stills rather than complexity of the grain which is most noticeable. But, as with the others, no shortage of personality. 40% (80 proof). sc.

Catoctin Creek Roundstone Rye Whisky batch B17G1, charred new oak barrels db **(88)** n21.5 earthy and deep; rye present but also a slight boiled vegetable note; t23.5 best delivery I have tasted yet from Catoctin where the big rye presence has been nailed, with the fruity, muscovado sugar encased tendrils stretch out in all directions...and deliciously so; f21 some light feints attach to the milky mocha; b22 the brighter end of the distillery's narrow spectrum: the rye here really is deliciously on song! 46% (92 proof). ncf.

CEDAR RIDGE DISTILLERY Swisher, Iowa.

Twelve Five Rye recipe: rye, corn & malted barley, batch no. 131304-A db **(87.5)** n23 t22.5 f20.5 b21.5. Some seriously big rye at work here and the nose is something to enjoy if not marvel at. Once the distillers can just narrow the middle cut, this will be a rye of serious magnitude. As it is, the feints just take the edge off an otherwise impressive rye. 47.5%

CHAMBERS BAY DISTILLERY University Place, Washington.

Greenhorn Bourbon aged for a minimum of 1 year, batch 1, bott 13 Dec 15 db **(74.5)** n18.5 t21 f17 b18. A sharp, eye-watering experience where an interesting fermentation has given the distiller little room for manoeuvre. 44% (88 proof)

CHARBAY DISTILLERY Napa Valley, California.

Charbay Hop Flavoured Whiskey release II, barrels 3-7 **(91)** n22 t22 f23 b24. Being distilled from beer which includes hops, it can – and will - be argued that this is not beer at all. However, what cannot be disputed is that this is a rich, full-on spirit that has set out to make a statement and has delivered it. Loudspeaker and all. 55%

CLEAR CREEK DISTILLERY Portland, Oregon.

McCarthy's Oregon Single Malt Aged 3 Years batch W14-01 Bott Sept 8 2014 **(96)** n24 t24 f23.5 b24.5 Steve McCarthy's hands may not still be on the tiller. But they might as well as be: this plots the same course he charted a great many years back in American micro distilling's very earliest days. Still the guiding star by which all other micro distilleries must follow: a kind of World Whiskey mile and sign post.... 42.5%

McCarthy's Oregon Single Malt Aged 3 Years batch W16-01, bott 6 May 16 db **(88.5)** n22 not the normal smoky bacon style peat: dry and abrupt; t23 excellent texture and a sublime display of smoky, gristy sugars mixed in with no less smoky Demerara; f21.5 the finish is short, miserly spiced, and strangely lacking in its usual depth; b22 for the first time since I tasted their first bottlings – in the days when my beard was still black – this whiskey has changed. Appears to have far less copper in the system to give the normal all-round richness; this is quite apparent on the nose and finish in particular. But they appear to have upped the peat ratio to good effect. 42.5% (85 proof)

COLORADO GOLD DISTILLERY Cedaredge, Colorado.

Colorado Gold Rye charred oak barrel no. 23, bott 31 Oct 15 db **(80)** n20 t21 f19.5 b19.5. Insane sugars – Manuka honey concentrate – still can't fully overcome the tobacco bitterness. A certain dirtiness when a rye should sparkle. 45% (90 proof). sc.

Colorado Gold Straight Bourbon aged 3 years, new oak barrel no. 43, bott 1 Dec 15 db **(91)** n22.5 coconut strands dipped in treacle. Some major golden syrup and tannin at work, too...; t23 amazingly syrupy delivery: about as sweet as bourbon gets – yet always delicious. The only dry notes kick in as the tannin really takes hold. But those golden syrup tones dominate; f23 long, and now better-structured as light spices kick in; b22.5 if you have a sweet tooth, buy a case...!! 45% (90 proof). sc.

Colorado Gold Straight Bourbon Over Two Years Old Single Barrel bott 8 Oct 11 **(86.5)** n21 t23 f21 b21.5. A bit of a whippersnapper of a bourbon. The nose and finish may lack depth. But it is a whiskey bursting with personality and the delivery is an understated treat. A light mocha thread weaves in and out of the muscovado. Fun. 40%

COPPER FOX DISTILLERY Sperryville, Virginia.

⟡ **Copper Fox Rye Whisky Aged 21 Months** bott 18 Jan 17 db **(94.5)** n23.5 one of the most cultured and distinctive aromas yet served up by this distillery, there is a beguiling complexity between the fruity rye and sweeter, softer malt. All this is placed in a smoky envelope far less intrusive than one normally associates with Copper Fox; t24 while the rye shares equal billing on the nose, it profoundly states it will do no such thing on the palate. The contra message between the soft delivery and then the rock hard grain is something that fills you with awe; f23 smokier towards the finish and now impressively spicy, also; b24 had this bottle on my tasting lab table ready to explore when I decided I needed to break off, rest my palate for a while and get some exercise. So, I went for a walk, and just as I reached the highest point of the remote countryside around me, I espied a fox crossing a field heading straight for me. Darker than usual, like unburnished copper. It stopped and stared at me as I stared at it, just a few yards separating us. It slunk off downhill in no great hurry and stopped with only its head showing above a hollow: again we regarded each other eye to eye for a few precious minutes. If only I had had this fabulous bottle with me... 47.5% (95 proof).

⟡ **Wasmund's Single Malt Whisky 24 Months Old** batch no. 135 db **(89)** n22 new mown hay outpoints the usual smoked apple- and cherrywood; t22.5 so soft: the smokiness has a slight tobacco feel for a moment or two before the ulmo honey and caramels begin to kick in; f22 custard cream biscuits dunked in a mocha; some very late spice; b22.5 quite a different style from Rick Wasmund this time. 48% (96 proof). ncf.

COPPERWORKS Seattle, Washington

⟡ **Copperworks American Single Malt Whiskey Release No. 001 Aged 30 Months** new American oak casks db **(91)** n23 such a delicate nose: the tannins here are polite to the point of being apologetic. All kinds of subtle kumquat and dried date notes to mix in with the vanilla; t22.5 a deft but sweet delivery appears to mix a gristy maltiness with light apple juice and liquorice; f22.5 butterscotch and vanilla add the drier tones to the muscovado sugars; b23 congratulations! An impressive first bottling for a new distillery in Seattle. Going along the lines of Stranahan Distillery, they are maturing their single malt in virgin American oak. This is a lighter, far less in-your-face version. Instead elegance appears to be the goal. Well, it has been achieved. 52% (104 proof). 1,530 bottles.

⟡ **Copperworks American Single Malt Whiskey Release No. 002 Aged 30 Months** new American oak casks db **(95)** n24 a brilliant nose: the blood orange and liquorice leave no doubts about the type of barrel at play. But this is very clean, unfussy distillate also. So the grain has a clear run with its sugars intact, thinning the picture but also adding wonderfully to the complexity; t23.5 wow, wow, wow...!! Eye-watering delivery. The tannins are right up there, toasty and intense. But the house style of rich citrus and muscovado sugars digs deep, until a much friendlier red liquorice and Manuka honey carry the oak's weighty banner; f23 long, and for the first time oils are at play. The sugars fade slowly as the heavier vanillas take hold. The spices, rampant on delivery, are now a more gentle massage and here and there a malty echo can still be heard reverberating amid the crisper Demeraras; b24 a higher part of the warehouse? More summer months within the 30? Somehow Copperwork has raised the game considerably with much broader and enveloping malt which has flourished in the extra oak. A three course single malt if ever there was one...! 53% (106 proof). 1,753 bottles.

⟡ **Copperworks American Single Malt Whiskey Release No. 003 Aged 34 Months** new American oak casks db **(92.5)** n24 this really is making a statement! I'm pretty certain this is 100% malted barley yet there is a crisp, fruity tang to this not unlike a rye: incredibly fruity...; t23.5 ...and there is that faux-rye note again bang on delivery: fascinating. Big orange peel, orange-blossom honey and juicy malt combine in an oily mass but allow the tannins easy access; a little bitterness in the mid-ground underscores the tangy fruit; **f22** the bitterness persists as a spicy buzz kicks in; **b23** the closest style to a rye I have ever found a single malt barley. Phenomenal...! *52% (104 proof). 1,559 bottles.*

⬦ **Copperworks American Single Malt Whiskey Release No. 004 Aged 31 Months** cask no. 44, new American oak cask db **(88.5) n22** attractive, sweet, but distinctly botanical; **t22** and there's those busy gin-style notes again, bang on delivery. Love the juiciness of the malt as it filters through; **f22.5** at last the barley has enough stamina to go it alone, other than the excellent toffee-vanillas from the oak; **b22** a very gin-like feel to this which casts a heavy shadow over the whiskey character. May be wrong, but suspect some gin was bottled not long before this whiskey was using some of the same equipment. *61.75% (123.5 proof). 219 bottles.*

CORNELIUS PASS ROADHOUSE DISTILLERY Hillsboro, Oregon.

McMenamins C.P.R. White Owl Distillery (93) n23.5 t23 f23 b23.5. Top dollar White Dog. Huge amount of copper helps expose all the honey available, especially on the nose. Superbly distilled and surging with barley and spice. *49.3%*

CORSAIR ARTISAN DISTILLERY Nashville, Tennessee.

Corsair Rye Moon (85) n20 t22.5 f21 b21.5. A sweet, well-weighted white dog with surprisingly little bite. The odd intense, crystalline rye moment is a joy. *46% (92 proof)*

Corsair Aged Rye (73.5) n18 t18 f19 b18.5. Hot and anarchic, not as well made as the Rye Moon. But has enough playful character to keep you guessing what's coming next. *46%*

Corsair Triple Smoke (92.5) n24 t23 f22 b23.5. The odd technical flaw, to pick nits. But, overall, a lovely whiskey with a curiously polite smoke style which refuses to dominate. Teasingly delicate and subtle...and different. *40%*

DAD'S HAT RYE DISTILLERY Bristol, Pennsylvania

⬦ **Dad's Hat Pennsylvania Straight Rye Whiskey Aged Minimum 3 Years** db **(91.5) n23** no doubting the key grain constituent here (rye 80% malted barley 20%) as the solidity of the nose is beyond question or reproach. Its only challenger is the oaky liquorice, though a hop-like fruity bitterness also hangs in the air; **t23.5** so firm and rye laden! Typical muscovado sugars and molasses abound before a light mint and coffee softness moves in; **f22** that persistent vague bitterness does gather momentum towards the end; **b23** the truest rye I have seen from you yet: I take my hat off to you guys...quite literally...! *47.5% (95 proof).*

DARK CORNER DISTILLERY Greenville, South Carolina

Dark Corner Moonshine Corn Whiskey (77.5) n18.5 t22 f18 b19. Full blooded sweet corn on delivery. But could do with some extra copper elsewhere. *50%*

DARK HORSE DISTILLERY Lenexa, Kansas

Dark Horse Reserve Bourbon Less Than Four Years Old Batch 2 **(93) n23 t23.5 f23 b23.5** Even though they appear to have used oak chips to bolster the overall richness of this bourbon, there is no taking away that this is the closest any whiskey produced by a microdistiller comes to the true Kentucky style. But even there, there are few which display so much vanilla. *44.5% (89 proof)*

Dark Horse Reunion Rye Less Than Four Years Old Batch 2 **(89) n22 t23 f22 b22** Another enormous, and truly memorable, offering from Dark Horse which is unambiguous in its style. Here, though, the cut was perhaps a little over generous (costing a point or two) with the very sharpest notes sacrificed. That said: just so big and delicious! *44.5% (89 proof)*

Long Shot White Whiskey bourbon mash **(88.5) n22 t22.5 f22 b22.** Seriously good, honest white dog: well made and gives the corn a free hand to shine. Love it. *40% (80 proof)*

DEERHAMMER DISTILLING COMPANY Buena Vista, Colorado

⬦ **Deerhammer American Single Malt Whiskey** virgin oak barrel #2 char, batch no. 32 db **(87.5) n21.5 t23.5 f20.5 b22** This, like most Colorado whiskeys, is huge. Had the cut been a little less generous, the oils a little less gripping and tangy, this would have scored exceptionally highly. For there is no doubting the deliciousness of the big toasted malt, the kumquat citrus element, the moreishness of the heavyweight dark fudge and the magnificent Java coffee. All these make a delivery and follow through to remember. I look forward to the next bottling where hopefully the cut is a little more careful: a very significant score awaits as this is borderline brilliant... *46% (92 proof). 870 bottles.*

DELAWARE PHOENIX DISTILLERY Walton, New York.

Rye Dog Batch 11-1 (78.5) n19 t21.5 f18 b19. Sweet, distinctive rye tang but a little short on copper sheen. 50% (100 proof)

DISTILLERY 291 Colorado Springs, Colorado.

◇ **291 Bad Guy Colorado Bourbon Whiskey Aged 525 Days** distilled from a bourbon mash, American oak barrel, aspen stave finished, barrel no. 2 db (93) n23.5 thumping aroma: toasted raisin bitter-sweetness; molasses over slightly burnt toast...; t23.5 no prizes for guessing the delivery has a distinctly dark and toasty feel: the corn is sits weightily but has a parched feel; the sugars are moody and offer a slightly burnt fudge feel; the liquorice is in concentrated format; f23 at last a calmer honey effect begin to allow the corn, sugars and late vanillas an easier ride; b23 even though this Bad Guy socks you one right between the eyes, raise a glass of this and toast a massive and desirable whiskey: in fact, everything about this is toasted....!! 59.7% (1194 proof). sc. 644 bottles.

◇ **291 Barrel Proof Colorado Whiskey Aged Less Than 2 Years** distilled from a rye malt mash, American oak barrel, aspen stave finished, barrel no. 90 db (95) n23.5 a brilliant cut, clean with no off notes, which allows the rye all the room it requires to sparkle in its fruitiest manner...; t24...as well as on the palate where the grain hits an early, crisp crescendo seemingly backed by a platoon of crunchy demerara notes; salivating and crustal clear; f23.5 a little oak leeches in and fogs up the rye triumphantalism: it's now the spices arrive...; b24 That a distillery can produce a young rye malt whiskey of this standard and something as magnificent as their 333 days bottling shows that Distillery 291 are way up there among the elite of the US micro-distillery movement. 63.1% (126.3 proof). sc. 48 bottles.

◇ **291 E Colorado 100% Rye Malt Whiskey Aged 291 Days** American oak barrel, aspen stave finished, batch no. 3 db (95.5) n23.5 an earthiness gives even greater weight to the rye which itself possesses a lumbering gait. Myriad floral tones – not least dank bluebells - impressively perk up the picture; the sweetened eucalyptus represents the oak with distinction; t24 chewy from the off...and gets chewier still. The grain influence is substantial and builds layer by layer, thicker and thickens, intensifying by the second. The top rye notes are hard and shrill, the lighter ones fruitier with a mix Demerara and muscovado sugars adding the required sweetness. The spices are as upbeat as they need to be to keep pace, then actually shift up a gear to really put on the style. Again, eucalyptus – perhaps with a touch of clove – ensures the tannins retain a bold and proud voice; f23.5 calms somewhat, though the rye retains its powers, reduced and allowing the Manuka honey room to soften the liquorice; b24.5 what a treat for the taste buds! Substantial and as full flavoured as they come. 62.3% (124.6 proof). 368 bottles.

◇ **291 E Colorado Bourbon Whiskey Aged 333 Days** American oak barrel, aspen stave finished, batch no. 2 db (96) n24 one of the best bourbon noses outside Kentucky I have yet encountered: the star turn is the beautiful manner in which the crisp, fruity muscovado sugars melt in the more rugged, sappy tannins. A soft hickory note drones in the background while what appears to be a hint of rye is detected now and again diving in and out of the kumquat; t24 the sugars line up on parade from the very first moment. Vanilla and butterscotch enriched corn oil coats the palate gently and it is upon this the roasty tannins cling for the duration; molasses and Manuka honey is present but toned down by the countering oaks: the complexity and relaxed pace of the intertwangling is sublime...; f24 long and more of the same. As the main flavours begin to fade, so the spices become a little noisier; b24 exceptional, enthralling, eclectic, engrossing, engaging, edifying, enticing, entirely extraordinary...encore! The whiskey which puts the E into three threes.... (the author would like to assure the public that no thesaurus, electronic or otherwise, was used in the writing of these tasting notes....) 63.4% (126.8 proof). 191 bottles.

◇ **291 E Colorado Whiskey Aged 405 Days** American oak barrel, aspen stave finished, batch no. 1 db (90.5) n22.5 unexpected French toast tone: delicate with the emphasis on ulmo honey and salted butter; t23.5 a very different prospect to the massive 333 day version with the flavours here almost of a whisper, rather than a macho bellow. Melt-in-the-mouth sugars dominate, quietly, the ulmo honey a further back up...; f22 a little bitterness on the gentle corn-rich fade; b22.5 elegant. 62.9% (125.9 proof). 198 bottles. Barrel select for The Stanley.

291 M Colorado Whiskey Rye Malt Mash Aged Less Than 2 Years Aspen Stave Finished barrel no. 1, American oak barrel db (95.5) n24 t24 f23.5 b24 The nose promises something quite immense. And not for a second does it let you down. A whiskey which needs not just a knife and fork, but a carving set, too...Bravo Disitillery 291! 63% (126.1 proof)

291 M Colorado Whiskey Rye Malt Mash Aged Less Than 2 Years Aspen Stave Finished barrel no. 3, American oak barrel db (86) n21.5 t22 f21 b21.5. Quite dapper rye appears through the slight mustiness on both nose and delivery. A little murky by comparison to Barrel 1's outlandishly high standards. *63.1% (126.2 proof)*

291 M Colorado Whiskey Rye Malt Mash Aged Less Than 2 Years Aspen Stave Finished batch no. 1, American oak barrels db (92.5) n22 t24 f23 b23.5 A surprisingly subtle rye considering its undoubted intensity. *62.9% (125.9 proof). 190 bottles.*

291 M Colorado Whiskey Rye Malt Mash Aged Less Than 2 Years Aspen Stave Finished barrel no. 5, American oak barrels db (89.5) n22.5 t23 f21.5 b22.5 When they say there's a high rye content in the mash recipe, they just ain't kidding, nosiree! A slightly cleaner cut would have piled on the points... *50% (100 proof). 55 bottles*

⬧ **291 Single Barrel Colorado Bourbon Whiskey Aged Less Than 2 Years** distilled from a bourbon mash, American oak barrel, aspen stave finished, barrel no. 33 db (87.5) n22 t23 f20.5 b22 Lots of fruit jelly at play here, working well with the big spice kick and profound vanilla. Enjoyable and correct other than a nagging bitterness which just skews the overall message. *50% (100 proof). sc. 60 bottles.*

DOWNSLOPE DISTILLING Centennial, Colorado.

⬧ **Double Diamond Whiskey** cask no. WR-283 db (86) n21 t22 f21.5 b21.5 The aroma of new-baled hay suggests a whiskey a long way from stating its original intentions. Some lovely light and citrusy sugars at play, nonetheless. *40% (80 proof). sc.*

⬧ **Double Diamond Whiskey Aged 4 Years Cognac Finish** cask no. WR-290 db (93) n23 dates and walnuts in abundance: much richer and fruity than your standard Cognac finish; boasts a bourbony characteristic, also, with a hint of liquorice and cough sweet: complex; t23 thick with a black cherry depth to the fruit; oily but the molasses handles it beautifully; f23.5 superb walnut cake washed down with mocha; more of a golden syrup sweetness now; b23. An old British advert from the 1960s for a beer warbled: "A Double Diamond Works Wonders, Works Wonders. A Double Diamond Works Wonders. So drink some today..." It could equally apply to this hugely different whiskey! *41% (82 proof). sc.*

⬧ **Downslope Malt Whiskey Aged 2 Years Cognac Finish** cask no. WR-260 db (77.5) n19.5 t21 f18 b19 The Cognac cask makes little headway against the feints. *48.5% (97 proof). sc.*

⬧ **Downslope Malt Whiskey Aged 3 Years Sherry Finish** cask no. WR-184 db (87) n20 t21 f24 b22 Doesn't really gel until towards the finish when the most brilliant chocolate mousse kicks in. Then, out of nowhere, it suddenly becomes something rather special... *50% (100 proof). sc.*

⬧ **Downslope Rye Whiskey** cask no. WR-235 db (90.5) n23.5 no mistaking the grain, as the aroma cuts deliciously and with a steely blade into the nostrils; some gorgeous "love heart" candy; t22 salivating rye, juicy and thick; a little nougat creeps into the middle; f22.5 the complex sugars, now including marzipan, find an easier rhythm towards the finish; the spices slowly blossom; b22.5 OK, not quite technically on the money but the flavour profile is a delight. *46% (92 proof). sc.*

DRY FLY DISTILLING Spokane, Washington

Dry Fly Bourbon 101 (88) n21.5 t23 f21.5 b22. A well made bourbon which, with a bit of extra complexity, would stand above some of its Kentucky colleagues. *50.5%*

Dry Fly Cask Strength Straight Wheat Whiskey (94.5) n23 t24 f23.5 b24 Quite beautiful whiskey. One every whisky lover should experience to further their understanding of this multi-faceted spirit. *60%*

Dry Fly Port Finish Wheat Whiskey (89) n22 t23 f22 b22. If you mixed whiskey and jam you might end up with this little charmer. *50% (100 proof)*

Dry Fly Straight Triticale Rye Wheat Hybrid (86) n22 t22 f21 b21. Pleasant and easy going. But very surprising degree of natural caramels fill in the gaps and shaves off the higher notes expected from the rye. *44% (88 proof)*

Dry Fly Washington Wheat Whiskey (89) n22 t22 f22.5 b22.5. Hugely impressive, well weighted and balanced and a much better use of wheat than bread, for instance... *40%*

EASTSIDE DISTILLING Portland, Oregon

Burnside Bourbon 4 Year Barrel-Aged bott 2012 (92) n24 t23.5 f22 b22.5. "Put some sideburns on your face!" screams the back label. Well, a whiskey far too gracious to put hairs on your chest though it would be a close shave to choose this or a Kentucky 4-y-o as one of the best young bourbon noses of the year...Just bristles with charm. *48%*

EDGEFIELD DISTILLERY Troutdale, Oregon.

Edgefield Hogshead Whisky 100% malted barley, batch 12-B **(94) n23.5 t24 f23 b23.5** Been a little while since I lasted tasted Edgefield. At that time they were seriously getting their act together. Now they deserve star billing in any bar. This is sheer quality and even though the cut is very fractionally wide, the two years in new oak has ensured something bordering magnificence. 46%

FEW SPIRITS DISTILLERY Evanston, Illinois.

FEW Bourbon Whiskey batch 15-57 db **(86.5) n21.5 t22 f21.5 b21.5.** Despite the house style of clattering oils, there is a delicious tenacity to the bigger liquorice-rich tannins which is thoroughly appealing. Not perfect, but not too shoddy, either. 46.5% (93 proof)

FEW Rye Whiskey batch 15-30 db **(85.5) n20 t22.5 f21.5 b21.5.** The first three or four mouthfuls might leave you pretty dazed. Even if you know and understand this distillery, as I do, you will not be quite prepared for this. Well certainly not the slightly cabbagey nose. The delivery takes a little while to get to grips with. But, in time, you will begin to see how the bullet-hard rye notes come into play here. The finish returns to a slightly feinty structure. Definitely worth that ten minutes to see the rye in all its glory. 46.5% (93 proof)

FEW Single Malt Whiskey batch 6/14, barrel no. 11-17 db **(81.5) n20 t20.5 f20.5 b20.5.** Massive nougat at play here. Few's whisky is hefty and oily on quiet days. Here, it fully pitches its full weight behind the major sugar, though the malt can be heard occasionally. 46.5% (93 proof). sc.

⚜ **That Boutique-y Whisky Company FEW 2 Year Old** batch 2 **(94.5) n23.5** so Kentuckian I had to double check I had poured the right whiskey. Huge liquorice, dates and walnuts, all wrapped up in a spicy molasses shell; **t24** what feels like corn oil pours all over the palate. Ulmo honey has its fingers in every pie while the headier dark sugars also play a deeper and more subtle role; so sexy and soft...; **f23.5** now the spices enter the fray. So clever and delicate with all the earlier notes fading with style; **b23.5** by far and away the best thing I have ever seen from this distillery, sticking so close to a Kentucky style it is impossible to tell them apart. So easy to have a Few 2 many... 51.8%. 275 bottles.

FINGER LAKES DISTILLING Burdett, New York.

Glen Thunder Corn Whiskey **(92.5) n23.5 t23 f23 b23.** Beautifully distilled, copper rich, Formula 1 quality, absolutely classic corn white dog. 45% (90 proof)

FLORIDA FARM DISTILLERS Umatilla, Florida

Palm Ridge Reserve Handmade Micro Batch Florida Whiskey orange and oak wood Less the 1 Year Old batch 29 **(94.5) n23 t24 f23.5 b24** I can see why everyone heads to Florida in the winter: obviously to try and grab one of the meager 6,000 bottles of this on offer each year. This is beautifully crafted, truly adorable whiskey where fruit appears to constantly have its hand on the tiller. And rather than blast in like a Hurricane from the sea, it breezes gently around the glass and palate with an easy elegance. I have relatives in Florida: about time I gave them another visit... 45% (90 proof)

GARRISON BROTHERS Hye, Texas.

Garrison Brothers Cowboy Bourbon Aged Four Years corn harvest 2009, #1 panhandle yellow dent corn variety, dist 2009, bott 2015 **(96.5) n23.5 t24.5 f24 b24.5** I have recently returned from a tasting tour of China where a 23-year-old Kentucky bourbon was one of my staple props. But even that would have to bow before such elephantine oakiness as this. Four years in Texas evidently equate to 23 in Kentucky: there's a Geography lesson for you. Whiskeys from this distillery have absolutely delighted and astonished me in the past: this proves, indubitably, it was no fluke. If you didn't think Texas was on the world map of Great Whisky, it is now... 67.5% (135 proof)

⚜ **Garrison Brothers Cowboy Bourbon Barrel Proof Aged Four Years** #1 panhandle white corn, corn harvest 2011, dist 2012, bott 2017 db **(96) n24** if you like the nose of your bourbon to be huge – and I mean bloody massive! – full of gargantuan liquorice and molasses and can drink only whiskey that will put hairs all over your chest, whatever your sex, then I'm afraid this will be far too big for you...; **t24** now here's the deal: about as big a bourbon as you'll uncork this year...yet the delivery is deft, melt-in-the-mouth and as delicate as anything you'll encounter. A massive corn and tannin mix is crammed with the Manuka honey and molasses which trademarks this bourbon, yet it projects a silky countenance on delivery and one humble enough to yield and salivate to extract every last atom of sweetness;

f24 long, the tannins layered to extraordinary depth but those dark sugars and light hickory are always on hand to ensure the sweet balance is never compromised; b24 these guys have proved once again that they do a mighty mean four-year-old... another improbably spectacular bourbon from Garrison Brothers. 68.5% (137 poof).

⟐ **Garrison Brothers Single Barrel Texas Straight Bourbon Whiskey Aged Three Years** #1 panhandle white corn, corn harvest 2011, cask no. 3306, dist 2012 db (94.5) n23 the tannins from the oak play it straight with a vanilla theme but the grains are busy and tumble around in bitter-sweet fashion; t23.5 superbly sweetened corn oil fills the palate with elegant brush strokes of sugars and spice; f24.5 oh, my word! What a finale...! Seems at first to be going quietly, then flickers back into life with the most sublime Manuka honey and molasses crescendo, trailing off into softer ulmo honey: almost perfect...! b23.5 47% (94 poof). sc. 55 bottles.

⟐ **Garrison Brothers Texas Straight Bourbon Whiskey Aged Three Years** #1 panhandle white corn, corn harvest 2011, dist 2012, bott 2016 db (88.5) n22 a real catwalk of small grain and delicate vanillas. A generous cut from the still racks up some extra oils; t22.5 those extra oils arrive early and will probably mean a chocolate....yep, here it come, earlier than expected: a big cocoa surge to play alongside the liquorice and mountainous molasses; f22 gently sweetened marmalade; b22 this is the first time any whiskey by Garrison has shown the remotest hint of a wide cut. So not quite the usual brilliance, but still plenty to be getting on with... 47% (94 poof).

Garrison Brothers Texas Straight Bourbon Aged Three Years corn harvest 2011, #1 panhandle white corn variety, dist 2012, bott 2015 (91.5) n23.5 t23 f22 b23 A hushed whiskey leaving the youthfulness to be fully heard. 47% (94 proof)

Garrison Brothers Texas Straight Bourbon Single Barrel Aged Two Years barrel no. 3804, corn harvest 2010, #1 panhandle white corn variety, dist 2011 (94.5) n24 t24 f22.5 b24 Astonishing: you won't find another bourbon of this age showing such beauty, even in Kentucky. 47% (94 proof)

⟐ **Cadenhead's Garrison Brothers 4 Years Old** dist 2012, bott 2016 (94.5) n24 bourbony bliss...something of the antique shop with polished old wood, and the bakers also with a crusty mixed grain vaguely yeasty and doughy freshness. So mixed...and wonderful...; t23.5 I was thinking that the usual Manuka honey and sugars from Garrison were missing on the nose...but do they turn up in force on delivery! Soft, roasty big molasses, then a slightly more serene degree of Manuka honey. Spices kicking in as the oak really does make an impact; f23 long as it rides the corn oils with an elegant fade which allowing the spices a quiet say; b24 a great move by Cadenhead to bottle a whiskey from a distillery I have raved about for quite a long time. This cask does nothing to undermine the distillery's excellence. 47%. 60 bottles. Chosen by Peter Siegenthaler.

GOLDEN NORTHWEST DISTILLERY Bow, Washington.

Golden Artisan Spirits Single Barrel Cask Strength (88) n20.5 t22.5 f23 b22 Much more like it! Not exactly textbook but excellent body and some lovely honey touches. 62.3%

GRAND TRAVERSE DISTILLERY Traverse City, Michigan

Bourbon Whiskey (88.5) n21 t22 f23 b22.5 an absolute charmer which just gets better as it goes along. 46% (92 proof)

Ole George Straight Rye Whiskey (80) n19 t21 f20 b20. Hard to mark this one. As a rye, it marks relatively low. As a gin, it would be higher. Not sure why, but there seems to be all kinds of botanical aromas and flavours involved here. Pleasant as a spirit – and I love the mouth feel. But the flavour make up is skewed. 46.5% (93 proof)

GREAT LAKES DISTILLERY Milwaukee, Wisconsin.

KinnicKinnic A Blend of American Whiskies (87) n21.5 t22.5 f21 b22. The bitterness is replaced by an extra dollop of nougat and honey. 43% (86 proof)

HAMILTON DISTILLERS Tuscon, Arizona.

Whiskey Del Bac Classic Unsmoked Single Malt batch US15-16, bott 19 Aug 15 db (91) n23 t23 f22 b23 These guys know how to make mighty fine whiskey. Literally, a cut above... 42% (84 proof)

Whiskey Del Bac Clear Mesquite Smoked Single Malt batch MC15-4, bott 2 Dec 15 db (91) n21.5 t23 f23.5 b23. I was in Arizona recently, but sadly didn't make it to this distillery. Shame: I would have loved to have seen how the smoking is carried out for one of the sweetest and most surprisingly soft, idiosyncratic and attractive white dogs currently barking. 45% (90 proof)

Whiskey Del Bac Dorado Mesquite Smoked Single Malt batch MC16-1, bott 29 Feb 16 db (**94**) n23 t23.5 f24 b23.5 Dang! I'd sure like to see a bottle of this come sliding up to me next time I'm-a-drinkin' in the Crystal Palace Saloon Bar in Tombstone, yesiree! And I'd take my own dirty glass – one smoked with mesquite!! *45% (90 proof). ncf.*

HIGH WEST DISTILLERY Park City, Utah.

High West Silver Oat (**86**) n20 t22 f22 b22. A white whiskey which at times struggles to find all the copper it needs. But so delicious is that sweet oat – a style that has enjoyed similar success in Austria – that some of the technical aberrations are forgiven. Soft and friendly. *40%*

HILLROCK ESTATE DISTILLERY Hudson Valley, New York.

Hillrock Double Cask Rye Whiskey American oak barrels, barrel no. 62, aged under 4 years db (**85.5**) n21.5 t21.5 f21.5 b21. A slightly untidy rye which I'm sure will improve as the distiller, stills and grain get better acquainted. Here, there are a host of vegetable notes, though the rye does have its moments. That distiller, by the way: Dave Pickerell. He'll go far.... *45%*

Hillrock Double Cask Rye Whiskey American oak barrels, barrel no. Port-4, aged under 4 years db (**88**) n22.5 slightly fruity, but no doubting the grain type; t21.5 takes a while to find its feet. But the rye really does come out fighting; f22 excellent spice as a little tannin invades; b22 a rare case of a Port finish working amid bourbon or rye, mainly because it eliminates the more aggressive vegetable notes and allows the attractive rye a relatively free hand. *45%*

Hillrock Single Malt Whiskey American oak barrels, finished in sherry casks, barrel no. HS-1, aged under 4 years db (**95.5**) n23.5 a surprise, complimentary package of rich plummy fruit and acidic soot; t24 beautiful dark sugars line up to make for a soft entrance, all revealing a more fruity aspect as they lighten. And, as they do, smoke gathers in force; the pace and weight of the spices is truly exceptional; f24 a gorgeously creamy finale, with spices and smoky chocolate gathering; b24 smoke and fruit rarely make happy bedfellows from a balancing viewpoint. Here they do, doubtless helped by the fact that, for once, the sherry butt does not possess a sulphur-stained edge. You won't get it until about the fifth mouthful: then is all clicks. The classiest of class acts. *48.2%*

Hillrock Solera Aged Bourbon Whiskey American oak barrels, finished in sherry casks, barrel no. 48 db (**89**) n22.5 both fruit and spirit seem unusually compartmentalised; t23 I'm assuming this is a rye-recipe mash as that grain does manage to punch through the half-hearted fruit; f21.5 a little bit on the flat side, as fruit and grain cancel each other out. But the spices tumble about deliciously; b22 a rare case of the wine finish working with a bourbon, but probably because the grape remains subtle. *48.2%*

HOUSE SPIRITS DISTILLERY Portland, Oregon

Westward Oregon Straight Malt Whiskey 2 Years Old batch 1 (**92.5**) n23 t23.5 f23 b23.5 Two years old, perhaps. But absolute star quality with the barley pulsing at every turn: just so satisfyingly mouth-filling and palate teasing. Another great whiskey from Portland. *45%*

IRON SMOKE WHISKEY Fairport, New York.

Iron Smoke Apple Wood Smoked Whiskey batch no. 9, bott 4/2/16 db (**94.5**) n23.5 t23.5 f23.5 b24 An unconventional whiskey from Fairport. Though by no means the first apple wood smoked, it has less vigour than its Virginian forefather and no shortage of class...With it having a little more body than the skeletal 40%abv, handle with care as this would be too easy to get smashed out of your skull... Love it! *40% (80 proof)*

◇ **Iron Smoke Apple Wood Smoked Whiskey** batch no. 10, bott 7/8/16 db (**95.5**) n24 the tannins being both heavy and haughty, the apple wood smoke shows a remarkable nimbleness – so the phenol acts as the agent which lightens the show...close in unique..! t24 brilliant weight again, this times with the muscovado sugars containing the tannins; the wood smoke again adds a lighter touch; f23.5 more toasty here but never moves towards bitterness; a little light coffee on the finale; b24 this is extraordinary whiskey. Normally I'd advise that a distiller ups from 40 to 46% abv minimum in order to keep the oils intact. Yet this barely needs it and shows a heftier personality that their last, excellent bottling. Genuinely sublime. *40% (80 proof).*

◇ **Iron Smoke Apple Wood Smoked Whiskey** batch no. 11, bott 3/28/17 db (**93.5**) n23 quite a fascinating little battle between anthracite-style acidity on the phenol and the more ethereal, sweeter apple; t23 the lighter style on delivery I had previously associated with this distillery. The tannins are gentle and need time to build while the smoke is a constant and ups both complexity and keeps the texture fascinatingly delicate; f23.5 the spice now has greater room in which to operate and bigger tannins to draw upon. The sugars remain delicate and dedicated to balance; b24 quite a step down in terms of weight and intensity to their last batch, as though this is a little younger. But most rewarding to see two different styles, yet both of the highest standard. Congratulations to these guys for really taking care with their whiskey. *40% (80 proof).*

JOURNEYMAN DISTILLERY Three Oaks, Michigan.

⟫ **Journeyman Buggy Whip Wheat Whiskey** batch 38 db (94.5) n24 sensational! A wheated nose just how it should be with the spices underlining the grain but not at the expense of the profound butterscotch tart...; t23.5 soft and sensual delivery. The sticky sugars pick up plenty of vanilla before merging with the ulmo honey; f23 the busy spices do everything expected of them at the death; b24 I'll climb aboard this buggy any day. What a beautiful wheat whiskey this is...cracking, in fact...! *45% (90 proof).*

⟫ **Journeyman Featherbone Bourbon Whiskey** batch 72 db (84) n21 t21.5 f20 b21.5 The first mouthful of this flung me back 50 years to when I was a kid tucked up in bed and having to swallow a couple of spoons-worth of cherry-flavoured cough syrup. I can picture their salesmen getting people to gather round and peddling this as Dr Journeyman's Elixir for Coughs and Colds. In truth, though, a forceful corn-rich, oily, muscovado-sugared bag of tricks. *45% (90 proof).*

⟫ **Journeyman Last Feather Rye Whiskey** batch 72 db (91) n22.5 uncomplicated, oily but unmistakable rye with a beautifully fruity accent; t23.5 love it!! From the first moment it passes the lips, the rye is off on a massive campaign to conquer the palate which it does by allowing little else to thrive. A succulent sweet oil carries the escaping spice and vanilla towards the finish; f22 a little maple syrup now, though a little bitterness creeps in; b23 truly a unique rye whiskey profile and one, that despite the odd fault, literally carries you on a delicious journey. *45% (90 proof).*

⟫ **Journeyman Silver Cross Whiskey** batch 61 db (86) n22 t22 f20.5 b21.5 I am a fan of this fascinating distillery, that's for sure, and wondering what they are up to next. Not sure if this was designed to ward off vampires, but to be on the safe side I tasted this long after the sun set. A serious mish-mash of a whiskey which celebrated a rich ulmo-honey sweetness, but is ultimately undone by a bitterness which, sadly, no amount of sugar can keep fully under control and gets you in the neck in the end... *45% (90 proof).*

KINGS COUNTY DISTILLERY Brooklyn, New York.

⟫ **Kings County Distillery Barrel Strength Straight Bourbon Whiskey Aged Two Years or More** batch no. 6, dist Fall 2012, bott Fall 2016 db (84) n22.5 t22 20.5 21 Tannin and liquorice on steroids: the palate gets more splinters than a pole dancer straddling and spinning round a plank of tinder wood.... This is insane whiskey but a must for sap suckers... *63%.*

⟫ **Kings County Distillery Bottled-in-Bond Straight Bourbon Whiskey Four Years Old** batch no. 3 db (94) n24 ye-haaaar!!! A Brooklyn bourbon with the hallmarks of something way out west. Massive liquorice, golden syrup and molasses. Yet for all its darn tootin' bourbony might, the corn oils render this nose real hospitable...; t23 huge delivery, as might have been predicted. The sugars are supercharged, thick and generous. But the tannins counter with muscular depth; f23.5 it's a corny, mocha and butterscotch finale; b23.5 easy to mistake as a fine old Kentucky bourbon: there is no higher praise than that...!! *50%.*

Kings County Distillery Bourbon Whiskey aged one year or more, batch no. 128 db (85.5) n22 t21.5 f21 b21. Pleasant enough bourbon. But perhaps over-dependent on the brown sugars and tannin and does not yet have quite enough substance and complexity. Certainly has some spice, though! *45%*

Kings County Distillery Bourbon Whiskey wine barrel finish, aged one year or more, batch no. 128 db (87.5) n21 t23.5 f21 b22. Okay, so this isn't bourbon, even if they want to call it that. But they have selected some excellent wine barrels here...and the result is memorable. The nose is a bit stodgy and too tannin heavy. But the delivery is astonishing where the weight of oak, grain and fruit are in magnificent harmony. The midground is pure cappuccino – with a bite of accompanying fruitcake. Thins dramatically at the finish and loses balance. But, wow! Some fabulous moments! *45%*

Kings County Distillery Peated Bourbon Whiskey aged one year or more, batch no. p4 db (94) n23.5 dark muscovado sugars mixed with orange peel, liquorice...and peat reek...!!!

First time I came across something like this was in my own blending lab...probably about 25 years ago! **t24** adorable delivery: thick corn oil is awash with molten muscovado. The smoke keeps a respectful distance, but is there with the ever-thickening tannins; **f23** spices grow, the peat murmurs, the tannins throb quietly amid the residual sugars; **b23.5** no problem with this. You can use peat-smoked grain and still produce bourbon, which is how I assume this was produced. Just not a bourbon finished in a peated cask. That ain't bourbon. Whatever this is – and it appears to be the former – it is quite stunningly lovely. 45%

Kings County Distillery Single Malt American whiskey made from peated malt, aged two years or more, batch no. 1 db **(87) n21.5 t23 f21 b21.5.** A well made malt, apparently making full use of pre-used bourbon casks. Excellent structure with some toasted honeycomb running through the piece. The smoke is pretty well disguised, though may be evident in the gentle spice. Tires a little at the thin finish. 47%

Kings County Moonshine Corn Whisky (92) n23 t23 f23 b23. Absolutely spot on corn whiskey: sweet, clean, berry-fruity, very well made; does exactly what it says on the tin. 40%

KOVAL DISTILLERY Chicago, Illinois.

Koval Single Barrel Bourbon Whiskey barrel no. 1|1|M9 db **(92) n23 t23.5 f22.5 b23** A different style of bourbon to Kentucky, but this is not short on quality or complexity. Excellent. 47%

Koval Single Barrel Four Grain Whiskey barrel no. 2I0DM5 db **(96) n24.5 t24 f23 b24.5** one of the most intriguing whiskies on the circuit! Last year didn't quite technically hit the heights, but this time round combines decent distillation with the mesmerising complexity of the grain. A very serious contender for US micro distillery whisky of the year. 47%

Koval Single Barrel Rye Whiskey barrel no. 8|1PM5 db **(88) n21** an odd mix of feints and business-like rye; **t22** salivating, of course, and boisterous when it gets to accentuating the grain; the sugars are dark and intent; **f22.5** settles on its best period when all quietens slightly into a more harmonious whole...and still quite juicy even late on; **b22.5** an extravagant whiskey, depending perhaps a little too much on a wide cut but still showing many a rye smile. 40%

KOZUBA & SONS DISTILLERY INC. St. Petersburg, Florida.

Mr. Rye Straight Rye Malt Whisky virgin American oak barrels db **(91) n23** big, impressive, unmistakable rye character, intensified and thickened by it being malt, so a little less crisp. Technically not quite perfect but the spices clear the nose beautifully; **t23.5** fabulous delivery! No prisoners taken, no shelter offered. Just pounding rye which offers a massive degree of layering; so many layers, in fact, almost impossible to count. Just so thick and chewy; **f22** the oils from the wide cut begin to create a bit of a slick; the spices carry on regardless; **b22.5** Okay, the cut has been maximised, but forgivably so. The quality of the rye malt is very high. 45%. ncf.

LAS VEGAS DISTILLERY Las Vegas, Nevada.

Nevada 150 Bourbon Whiskey American white oak barrels, aged 2 years, 4 months db **(92) n24** the quietest, most subtle bourbon on the market. The small grains can be heard only if you listen keenly. And so devoid are we of the usual background noise, even the barley makes its tentative presence felt...intriguing and fabulously sophisticated; **t22.5** light muscovado sugars lead the way, red liquorice and what appears to be rye are not far behind... all so gentle and clean; **f22.5** and now some spice...just! Outstanding vanilla fade with the small grains in close attendance; **b23.5** who would have thought that the loudest, brashest city in the world could conjure the most delicate, intricate and shy bourbon for many a year? Don't let this whisky fool you: it has much to say...but all in whispers... 45% (90 proof). 2,014 bottles.

LAWS WHISKEY HOUSE Denver, Colorado.

A.D. Law Four Grain Straight Bourbon Aged No Less Than 3 Years batch no. 1 db **(92) n23.5 t23.5 f22 b23** If your taste buds are a bit bored, then introduce them to this: grains rarely come busier or more confident. A bit oily from the very slightly wide cut. But this is superb whiskey demanding respect and attention 47.5%

A.D. Law Four Grain Straight Bourbon Aged No Less Than 3 Years batch no. 2 db **(94.5) n23 t24 f23.5 b24.** A better balanced version than Batch 1, as the slightly cleaner cut allows both the grain and oaks a far greater say, especially on the finish – where the tannins are quite sublime. A huge yet complex bourbon, cutting back on the citrus here, and one that long term lovers of Tom Moore Distillery will appreciate more than most. Confirms that truly classic bourbon is being made in Colorado...! 47.5%

A.D. Law Four Grain Straight Bourbon Aged No Less Than 3 Years batch no. 3 db (85.5) n21 t22 f21 b21.5. A clunky bottling which overdoes the oils all round. Need to get it cleaner and tighter like on Batch 2. Some inevitable chocolate, though of the tell-tale nougat variety... 47.5%

A.D. Law Four Grain Straight Bourbon Aged No Less Than 3 Years batch no. 4 db (91.5) n21.5 t24 f23 b23. A fascinating journey away from the initial oaky constraints on the nose to something which, on the palate, transforms into a bourbon not totally dissimilar to batch 1. The oils are positive here and harness all the chocolate intensity it possesses to maximum effect. For the first time, we have a mix of molasses and Demerara sugars not just in play but, at times, grabbing the steering wheel. Yummy barely covers it! 47.5%

A.D. Law Four Grain Straight Bourbon Aged No Less Than 3 Years batch no. 5 db (93) n22.5 t24 f22.5 b24. Another with the full emphasis on the busy grain. Still a generous cut which ushers in some extra blood orange, but the interplay between crisp, salivating grain and the sugar-coated, cocoa-enriched tannins is a delight. If only those oils could be contained slightly. 47.5%

A.D. Law Four Grain Straight Bourbon Aged No Less Than 3 Years batch no. 6 db (86.5) n21 t22.5 f21 b22. Back to a Tom Moore type grain-fest. Busy, complex but ultimately weighed down by just a little too much oil from the generous cut. Some excellent golden syrup on the salivating bits, though. 47.5%

A.D. Law Four Grain Straight Bourbon Aged No Less Than 3 Years batch no. 7 db (81) n20 t22 f19 b20. A substantial bourbon which has gone a little heavy on the oil. Have to keep an eye on the cuts or, like here, the grains won't get a meaningful word in edgeways. A dose of ulmo honey does spring to the rescue. 47.5%

◈ **A.D. Law Four Grain Straight Bourbon Whiskey Aged No Less Than 3 Years** batch no. 10 db (87) n21 t22.5 f21.5 b22 So close to being a magnificent whiskey. It is all there: the marzipan, the maple syrup, the chocolate-liquorice. Acting like a ball and chain are gentle feints which - now you see it, now you don't – have crept stealthily into the mix. Still plenty to delight. 47.5% (95 proof).

◈ **A.D. Law Four Grain Straight Bourbon Whiskey Aged No Less Than 3 Years** batch no. 11 db (82) n20.5 t21 f20 b20.5 If Batch 10 is borderline with the cut, this one has strayed openly into feints territory, the dull bite and spice confirming the nose's hefty tones. 47.5% (95 proof).

◈ **A.D. Law Four Grain Straight Bourbon Whiskey Aged No Less Than 3 Years Cask Strength** barrel no. 316 db (94) n22 a fruity charge on the nose: black cherry and kumquat just below that liquorice lead; t24.5 wow...what a delivery! Substantial corn in there but that simply acts as a conduit for the most astonishing unleashing of flavours imaginable. All the time the spices hum and occasionally burn; yet as good as the delivery is, the mid-ground meeting of Manuka honey with thicker caramel and possibly rye – sharp in its muscovado – is even better and sets the hairs standing...; f23.5 the oils gather to an even greater degree as a walnut and dates fade takes effect; b24 how can you not slightly fall in love with this distillery's whiskey...? 56.7% (113.4 proof).

◈ **A.D. Law Four Grain Straight Bourbon Whiskey Aged 5.5 Years** barrel no. 1 db (92.5) n24 one of the best Kentucky noses I've encountered in the orbiting states: red and black liquorice softened by confident Manuka honey and mocha: classic! t23 immediate feint alert on delivery, but this soon makes way as molasses and ulmo honey pour all over the palate; the heavy duty oiliness returns in the mid-ground; f22.5 lots of vanilla and Demerara sugar-sweetened Venezuela cocoa. But the oils and grumbling spice buzz tells its own story; b23 the textbook nose is not a perfect match with the more cumbersome delivery and follow through. That said, what a fabulous experience...; 47.5% (95 proof).

A.D. Law Origins Four Grain Straight Bourbon Bottled in Bond barrel no. 1 db (95) n23.5 t24 f23.5 b24 Indubitably sublime bourbon. More ticks than there are boxes... 50%

◈ **A.D. Law Four Grain Straight Bourbon Whiskey Bottled in Bond Aged No Less Than 4 Years** batch no. 1 db (93) n23 medium weight on the oils but seriously busy on the grain; t24 two quick dry waves on delivery is followed by half a dozen massive honey explosions, a mix between acacia and heather. Big corn oil; f22.5 the corn oils and light tannins effect a surprisingly delicate fade; b23.5 only a fractionally wide cut means the corn oils don't become too stodgy while the honey gets a good hearing. 50% (100 proof).

◈ **A.D. Law Four Grain Straight Bourbon Whiskey Bottled in Bond Aged No Less Than 4 Years** batch no. A17 db (92) n23.5 beautifully weighted and paced, this is a bourbon nose for bourbon lovers. Both the grains and oak are in accord, which benefits both the honey...and the drinker...! **t23** both delivery and aftermath are drenched in corn oil. But this is thin enough to allow the grains the busiest of displays where sweet and dry are constantly to be compared; the honey remains on the darker, Manuka style with molasses for back up; **f22.5** there is always a hint of a little feint somewhere and the spices now reveal themselves more easily. Excellent vanillas, though; **b23** its minor sin can be easily forgiven after such a heavenly experience. 50% (100 proof).

◈ **A.D. Law Hordeum Straight Malt Whiskey Aged No Less Than 3 Years** batch no. 1 db **(79) n18 t20 f21 b20** Improves as it goes along – it has to. The nose is a shock to the system, the delivery, initially, a little odd. Has a few moments in the sun with malt and golden syrup to the fore. But never mind: there is always the bourbon and corn! 42.5% (85 proof).

A.D. Law Secale Cask Strength Straight Rye Whiskey Aged 3 Years db **(86) n21 t22 f21.5 b21.5**. A muscular, husky rye. The oils come thick and fast, though the gently fruity message of the grain is not entirely overshadowed: indeed, this has the crispest rye of their bottlings thus far. A few nougat touches to this, though the tingling late spice does carry some Demerara. 55%

A.D. Law Secale Straight Rye Whiskey Aged 3 Years batch no. 1 db **(87.5) n22 t22.5 f21.5 b21.5**. Rye tart? Or tart rye? No doubting the grain type: a brittle delivery on the palate which absolutely crash lands and shatters on the taste buds. The house style of chocolate mousse mashed into the heavy tannin and grain prevails, but the finish has a year or two's work perhaps to get those required sugars demanded by all great ryes into play. Takes a bit of time to tune into this, but worth twiddling the knobs. 50%

A.D. Law Secale Straight Rye Whiskey Aged 3 Years batch no. 2 db **(82) n19 t21 f21 b21.** A gently feinty, nougat style not uncommon in the ryes of Austria. Needs some chewing. 50%

A.D. Law Secale Straight Rye Whiskey Aged 3 Years batch no. 3 db **(84) n21 t22 f20 b21.** Good grief! The palate is absolutely coated in thick rye for an ungainly, rather unsettling experience. Make no mistake: this is huge whiskey where both the oils and rye refuse to take prisoners. Far from flawless, but the sheer concentrated oomph of the rye leaves you smacking your lips for quite some time. Some decent sugars on display in the middle period. 50%

◈ **A.D. Law Secale Straight Rye Whiskey Aged No Less Than 4 Years** batch no. A17 db **(87) n22 t21 f22.5 b21.5** A relatively lightweight rye considering the feints with a distinct tartness which I think I have encountered in Law's whiskey before. The chocolate is a late treat. 50% (100 proof).

◈ **A.D. Law Secale Straight Rye Whiskey Aged No Less Than 4 Years** batch no. B17 db **(89.5) n23.5** at first a thick heavyweight – ten minutes of warmth reveals the rye grain in its most intense mode; **t23.5** impossible to find rye any thicker. Yet some alchemy turns the oils into the richest molasses-softened rye imaginable, complete with a chocolate fruit middle; **f21** oily **b21.5** some ryes are crisp and blow you away with their mix of power and dazzling finesse. There are others which are chunky and too hefty to really allow the grain to fly and sing. This bottling is stuck about halfway between the two... Give it a few minutes for the feints to burn off slightly and the nose and delivery really are special. 50% (100 proof).

◈ **A.D. Law Straight Corn Whiskey Bottled in Bond Aged No Less Than 4 Years** batch no. 1 db **(94.5) n23.5** no mistakin' the grain here: the corn is ripe and rich yet offering muted sweetness and spices. The tannins are its running mate...; **t23.5** more sugar showing on the oily delivery, though it soon makes way for the mocha middle; **f23.5** chocolate ice cream all the way, other than the late, inevitable, spice; **b24** Just returned from a two mile walk in the country with the spring sun setting: it reminded me of many such walks in Kentucky. Oddly enough, so, too, does this excellent and magnificently distilled corn whiskey. I'm really impressed with this! 50% (100 proof).

◈ **A.D. Law Triticom Straight Wheat Whiskey Aged No Less Than 3 Years** batch no. 1A db **(91.5) n22** ye gods...the spices!!! **t23.5** a delivery of quicksand: positively gloopy. But the spices soon arrive with a vengeance and just when you think they can't get any more warming...they do! The thick liquorice, Manuka honey and molasses arrive like firemen putting out a blaze; **f22.5** back to a slightly more sane highly spiced butterscotch **b23.5** a sticky bread pudding of a whiskey where the sugars and spices enter a previously unknown universe...Unique..? I should say so... A must try once in a lifetime experience. 50% (100 proof).

◈ **A.D. Law Two Grain Straight Bourbon Whiskey Bottled in Bond Aged No Less Than 4 Years** batch no. 1A db **(92.5) n23** classic bourbon nose of the Kentucky school: slightly minty but the liquorice and molasses speak eloquently; **t24** oily and spicy from the off, though here those oils are from the grain, not an over-generous cut. A decent spiced butterscotch middle, though it plays second fiddle to the massive liquorice; f22.5 the house chocolate mousse style is very much at home; b23 beautifully distilled. *50% (100 proof).*

LOST SPIRITS DISTILLERY Monterey County, California.

⬩ **Abomination The Crying of the Puma Heavily Peated Malt** (93) n23.5 acrid smoke billows from the glass softened only by a hint of something molassed and an indefinable fruit edge; t24 what the.....??? Have I landed on Islay and am tasting young massively peated spirit coping with an orgy of tannins...? f22.5 the smoke returns to a more sooty mode with maple syrup, molasses and −once more − that unrecognisable, half-hearted fruit note; b23 an utterly baffling experience. This is, for all intents and purposes a Scotch whisky: at least in personality. If this was distilled in the US, then they have cracked it. The thing I particularly couldn't work out was an unrecognisable fruit edge. And after tasting I dug out the bottle and read the small print (so small, the detail was left off the heading by my researchers) that Riesling seasoned oak staves had been used. From the bizarre label and even brand name to the battle on your palate this is a bewildering and nonsensical whisky − if it is whisky at all, as the term is never used. But wholly delicious if raw...and boasting an impact that blows the taste buds' doors down... *54%. nc ncf.*

⬩ **Abomination The Sayers of the Law Heavily Peated Malt** (94) n23 t23.5 f24 b23.5 More of the same as The Crying of the Puma. Except, despite the identical strength, this has a softer all-round feel and a much more Caol Ila-style oiliness to sooth and maximise the length of the sugars and lighten the smoky load. The fruit here is negligible other than muscovado sugar mixing in with the liquorice and ulmo honey. Feels older than the Puma and the spices are far more accentuated yet controlled, especially towards the complex coffee-stained finale. *54%. nc ncf.*

MIDDLE WEST SPIRITS Columbus, Ohio

⬩ **OYO Dark Pumpernickel Rye Whiskey** db (77) n20 t21.5 f17.5 b18 Too many tangy, bitter notes to ever feel comfortable, though the intensity of the rye for a brief spell after delivery has much going for it. Very similar to a number of central European distilleries who have yet to completely master their stills. But it is that tangy bitterness on the finish that most urgently needs eradicating. *45% (90 proof).*

⬩ **OYO Michelone Reserve Bourbon Whiskey** db (86) n22.5 t22 f20 b21.5 A mainly attractive, restrained bourbon showing limited age and therefore depth. Lovely small grains to the busy nose and the sugars rise early before the buttery spices begin, but runs out of steam quite soon after. Not too happy with the tangy finish. *45% (90 proof).*

⬩ **OYO Oloroso Wheat Whiskey** db (88) n23.5 that is a rather lovely nose, allowing the spices to make an immediate statement. Brown toasted bread, a little molasses and some grape jam makes for a very breakfast aroma...; t22.5 rich, thick even, on delivery with the light ginger and honey giving way to an astonishingly salivating and fruity middle. The spices are slow out of the blocks but begin to catch up; f20 a few feinty faults on the spirit begin to make themselves heard; b22 as any good wheat whiskey should, this radiates spices with abandon. The fruit helps paper over some cracks in the distillate, especially towards the weak finish. *51% (102 proof).*

⬩ **OYO Sherry Finished Bourbon Whiskey** db (86.5) n22 t22 f21 b21.5 My experience with sherry-finished whisky over the last two decades meant it was a case of "oh, no!" when I saw this, rather than OYO. However, the wine cask here is entirely sulphur free and clean, and instead of dirtying the whiskey, as is tragically so often the case in Scotland, actually goes a long way to overcoming some contentious elements of the distillate. Good spice and even better sweet grape theme. *43.25% (86.5 proof).*

MISSISSIPPI RIVER DISTILLERY Le Claire, Indiana

Cody Road Rye 2013 Batch 4 (86.5) n23 t22.5 f20 b21. The clean, fruity unambiguous rye on the nose is stunning. There is nothing too shoddy about the crisp, juicy grain on delivery, either. Just bitters out a little too enthusiastically from the midpoint onwards. *40%*

MOYLAN'S DISTILLING COMPANY Petaluma, California.

Moylan's American Cask Strength Single Malt Whisky Aged 4 Years finished in orange brandy, stout & French oak chardonnay barrels db (80) n19 t23 f19 b19. Ladies and Gentlemen of Moylan. I cannot fault you for your kaleidoscopic delivery which enthrals and entertains with a wild and delicious a cross section of fruity riches as you are likely to find. But remember: it is about balance. So don't lose sight of what a wide cut and hops from the stout can do... *58.7% (117.4 proof)*

Moylan's American Single Malt Whisky Aged 4 Years finished in orange brandy, stout & French oak chardonnay barrels db **(75.5) n18 t21.5 f18 b18.** The vital oils – and attendant sugars - have been destroyed by the water, allowing the hops far too great a domination. 43% (86 proof)

NELSON'S GREEN BRIER DISTILLERY Nashville, Tennessee.

Belle Meade Aged 9 Years Bourbon Finished in Oloroso Sherry Casks, batch no. 2D **(83) n21 t22.5 f19.5 b20.** Remember: it ain't bourbon!! The sherry casks saw to that! And, sadly, they have dulled down the far richer – and spikier - elements of the bourbon. Lots of tannin and spice, but, ultimately, off the pace and lacking balance. 45.2% (90.4 proof). Bottled by Nelson's Green Brier Distillery.

⬩ **Belle Meade Aged 9 Years Sherry Bourbon** finished in Oloroso sherry casks, batch no. 3 **(87) n22 t22 f21 b22** A far better sherry bottling than I tasted before from these guys. The actual bourbon itself is able to poke through the smothering fruit with far greater energy. The fruit is clean and clear enough to offer a second dimension, though still not too keen on that soupy flavour profile. 45.2% (90.4 proof). Bottled by Nelson's Green Brier Distillery.

⬩ **Belle Meade Cognac Bourbon** finished in XO Cognac casks, batch no. 2 **(78.5) n21 t20 f18.5 b19** Very frustrating. This distillery makes a very high class bourbon which is a joy to experience, and here it is being muzzled by the restrictive limitations of a poor Cognac cask. Seriously and untidily bitter from the midpoint onwards. 45.2% (90.4 proof). Bottled by Nelson's Green Brier Distillery.

⬩ **Belle Meade Madeira Bourbon** finished in Malmsey Madeira casks, batch no. 6 **(89) n23** dry and peppery and with a little small grain peeping out through the fruit; **t22** like the nose, a relatively dry delivery, as though the usual bourbon high end sugars have been partially neutralised. But the light hickory and dried plum works well together; **f21.5** a good spice fade on the vanilla raisin; **b22.5** give me a straight bourbon over a cask finished job any day. But this works as well as they come and even offers a degree of sophistication. 45.2% (90.4 proof). Bottled by Nelson's Green Brier Distillery.

Belle Meade Straight Bourbon Whiskey (92) n23.5 t23 f22.5 b23 A crisp, bright, beautifully made bourbon. The rye aspect of the recipe is pretty profound. 45.2% (90.4 proof). Bottled by Nelson's Green Brier Distillery.

Nelson's Green Brier Tennessee White Whiskey distilled from Bourbon mash db **(94) n23 t23.5 f24 b23.5.** More green dog than white dog...! Beautifully distilled spirit using superbly judged cutting points. A wonderfully trained and friendly dog, be it white or green... Bravo, whoever is responsible for this: I'm genuinely impressed. 45.5% (91 proof)

NEW HOLLAND BREWING COMPANY Holland, Michigan.

⬩ **New Holland Beer Barrel Bourbon** American white oak db **(83) n21.5 t21.5 f20 b20** For those who aren't the greatest fans of lightly hopped whiskey, slightly more bearable than their rye bottling... 40% (80 proof).

⬩ **New Holland Beer Barrel Rye** American white oak db **(80) n21 t21 f19 b19** Were this from Speyside, I daresay it would be called hopscotch... The hoppiest whisk(e)y I have tasted anywhere in the world. Apart from a brief chocolate intervention, this is seriously not my kind of thing. I mean: I love whisky and I love beer. But just not together. Less befuddled by it than befuggled... 40% (80 proof).

⬩ **New Holland Zeppelin Bend Reserve American Single Malt** sherry cask finish db **(87) n22 t21.5 f22 b21.5** My Panama off to the chaps at Zep Bend for finding some outstanding sherry casks to help infuse the most wonderful, succulent grape note to this mouth-filling malt and slow-burning cocoa. Rich fruit cake at its most moist and spicy, though a slight, off-key hop note somewhat paddles against the style and grain. Otherwise, close to being a stunner. 45% (90 proof).

Pitchfork Wheat Michigan-Grown Wheat Whiskey aged 14 months, American oak barrels db **(93) n22.5 t23.5 f23.5 b23.5** So love it! Like a digestive biscuit you want to dunk in your coffee...By far and away the best thing I have ever seen from this distillery: this really is top drawer microdistillery whiskey just brimming with flavours and personality. Genuinely impressed. 45% (90 proof).

Zeppelin Bend Straight Malt Whiskey American oak barrels db **(84.5) n21 t21.5 f21 b21** The Zep is back!! Not seen it for a while and this is a new model. Actually, in some ways barely recognise it from the last one I saw about five years ago. Much more effervescent than before, though that curious hop note I remember not only persists but appears to have been upped slightly. 45% (90 proof).

PARLIAMENT DISTILLERY Sumner, Washington.

Ghost Owl Pacific Northwest Whisky db **(88.5) n21.5 t22.5 f22 b22.5** On the sugary side of matters. But keeps just enough heavier tannin in reserve to ensure balance. 45% (90 proof)

Ghost Owl Pacific Northwest Rye Whisky db **(94.5) n23 t23.5 f24 b24** Simply outstanding rye. Can't lose, really: my favourite grain (rye) being distilled in one of my favourite places on the planet (the Pacific north west of USA) and one of my favourite birds on the label (a barn owl). Actually, quite recently, I was doing some work in a lab at a distillery in India when I walked into a nearby wood to stretch my legs, rest my nose and enjoy 15 minutes of bird watching. There was suddenly a clattering above my head, strange shadows on the forest floor before me and then a crashing sound and soft thud. Astonishingly, a barn owl had fallen dead from the sky just three or four feet from where I stood. Spooky. And almost as dramatic as this stunning rye. 45% (90 proof)

PEACH STREET DISTILLERS Pallisade, Colorado.

Colorado Straight Bourbon Aged More Than Two Years batch 40 **(92.5) n22.5 t23.5 f23 b23.5** The last bottle I tasted was around the batch 20 mark and was an impressive intro to this distillery. Remarkably, this batch enjoys an almost identical thumb print. But now there is much more sharpness and definition. Superb! 46% (92 proof)

RANGER CREEK DISTILLING, San Antonio, Texas

Ranger Creek .36 Single Barrel Texas Straight Bourbon aged 4 years, 6 months, barrel no. 506, 2015 vintage db **(89.5) n23.5 t23.5 f20.5 b22** Rich and roasty, has many attributes that are prerequisite for fine bourbon. Finish flames out for reasons that are easier to spot in the white dog, but still give hefty clues here. Didn't get this on their bottlings of a few years back...though, still a bourbon to follow on the heels of a juicy rib-eye. 48% (96 proof). sc.

Ranger Creek .36 Texas Bourbon (93) n23 t23.5 f23 b23.5 I would so love to get back to Texas and have this wash down a plate-filling, half cooked ribeye. It's pretty obvious they have used small barrels to create a gentle giant like this – even before you find confirmation on the bottle. This comes under their Small Caliber series of whiskeys. Don't you believe it: this is a howitzer of a bourbon. 48% (96 proof)

Ranger Creek .36 Texas Bourbon batch no. 530, Summer 2013 season db **(90.5) n21.5 t23.5 f22.5 b23** Boasts an array of stunning flavours which could shake the most jaded palate back into life. Lone star quality...! 48% (96 proof). Small Caliber Series.

Ranger Creek .36 White db **(84) n21 t22 f20 b21** A white dawg whose tail doesn't always wag. A deliciously jaw-dropping, juicy array of grain on delivery. But needs to get the copper content up to ensure a better pedigree. 50% (100 proof)

Ranger Creek .44 Texas Rye aged 9 months, batch no. 10, Spring 2015 season db **(88) n21 t22.5 f22.5 b22** I hadn't read the label properly, so it was only on nosing and then delivery that the full impact of its relative youth became known. Holds up well, though. 47% (94 proof). Small Caliber Series.

Ranger Creek Rimfire Mesquite Smoked Texas Single Malt batch 1 **(85) n21.5 t22 f20.5 b21.** As I have never tasted anything smoked with mesquite before – especially whiskey – I will have to guess that it is the tree of the semi-desert which is imparting a strange, mildly bitter tang on the finish. Whether it is also responsible for the enormous degree of creamed toffee, I am also not sure. Enjoyable, fascinating even...but something the ol' taste buds need a bit of acclimatising to. 43% (86 proof)

Ranger Creek Rimfire Mesquite Smoked Texas Single Malt aged 12 months, batch no. 12, Fall 2014 season db **(86.5) n20 t23 f21.5 b22** Ah! Mesquite Smoked. The second time I've had a malt thus treated. And the first time was...yes, you guessed it: Ranger Creek! This is a better edition, where here they have gathered the sugars together, especially the toffees, in impressive fashion. 43% (86 proof). Small Caliber Series.

RANSOM SPIRITS Sheridan, Oregon.

Ransom The Emerald 1865 Straight American Whiskey Batch 002 malted barley, unmalted barley, malted rye, malted oats. **(87.5) n22 t22.5 f21 b22.** The mash bill screams: "Irish whiskey". The oils found screams: "Oi! Let those foreshots run another five minutes...!!!" If this was cleaned up a little we would have a whiskey everyone would be talking about. Because, taking the feints out of the equation, the interplay and weight of those complex grains really make for the most delicious experiences. Indeed, even with its faults, this provides one fabulous ride on the palate. On the cusp of being an American great. 43.8%

RESERVOIR DISTILLERY Richmond, Virginia.

Reservoir Distillery Bourbon Whiskey batch no. 1, bott 2017 db (93) n24 huge tannin dominance: restored antique furniture, complete with beeswax. The spices have the devil about them, the Demerara sugars are dipped in caramel: overall, just magnificent...; t23.5 a thumping caramel delivery: this time the sugars have a bigger say, though the growth of the oak is as measured as it is profound; buttery friendly despite the big weight; f22 just a little oak-induced bitterness battles with the liquorice; b23.5 big, buxom, bang on the money bourbon! 50% (100 proof).

Reservoir Distillery Bourbon Whiskey batch no. 2, bott 2017 db (92.5) n23 lighter tannins with plenty of moist date; t23 corn oil drenched in maple syrup. A little ulmo honey tones the sweetness down; soft caramels lighten things further; f23 much more relaxed finale than batch 1 with far less oak intrusion; b23.5 no shrinking violet. But nothing like so muscular as the last batch, making the most of the natural caramels. 50% (100 proof).

Reservoir Distillery Bourbon Whiskey batch 2, bott 2013 db (93.5) n23.5 t23.5 f23 b23.5 This is all about the small grains: not sure if wheat and rye are both included, but wouldn't surprise me if they were. Complex and bitty only half covers it! 50% (100 proof)

Reservoir Distillery Bourbon Whiskey Holland's Brew batch no. 1, bott 2017 db (83.5) n21 t22 f20 b20.5 A wider cut ramps up the sugars and oils. But loses some of the overall balance and excellence of their standard bourbon. 50% (100 proof).

Reservoir Distillery Rye Whiskey batch no. 1, bott 2017 db (91.5) n23.5 big, unreconstructed rye, hefty and thick in oil: a secondary, crisper level also there to ensure a more traditional sharpness; a third layer, this time; t23 a reversal of the programme now: the rye begins with a meaningful, muscovado crunchiness as the grain offers a brief crystalised feel. But this is soon submerged by those substantial oils; f22 those oils stay the course; an inevitable dull spiciness appears; b23 made a little bit of a rod for its own back last year by releasing one of the best rye whiskeys of the year. The 2017 bottling remains delicious but the extra oils from the distillate make it harder for the grain to make the same dashing performance. 50% (100 proof).

Reservoir Distillery Rye Whiskey batch 2, bott 2016 db (95.5) n24 t24 f23.5 b24 There must be something in the DNA of the average Virginian in knowing how to make rye whiskey. I adore Richmond and I no less adore very good rye: indeed, I will always be proud to be its first advocate. I have some of my happiest memories of all time travelling in Virginia (the first time way back in 1967, now 50 years ago), and once with someone who was, still is and forever will be, very, very special. A truly great bitter-sweet whiskey to rekindle some beautiful, bitter-sweet memories... 50% (100 proof)

Reservoir Distillery Wheat Whiskey batch no. 1, bott 2017 db (91) n23 spices are on the attack – nothing the molasses and caramel can do about it! t23 chewy yet soft with the oil thin enough to make the most of the muscovado, cream caramel and bread pudding; f22.5 excellent length and the caramels stretching a long way; b22.5 a beautiful, understated wheat whiskey and a clear step up from the previous bottling. 50% (100 proof).

Reservoir Distillery Wheat Whiskey batch 5, bott 2015 db (87.5) n21 t23 f21.5 b22. Recovers superbly from a clumsy nose. The cut is just a little too generous. But the impact of the wheat is immediate on delivery and the grain unmistakable, combining some excellent spices with hickory and treacle follow-through. The big oils are never far away. 50% (100 proof)

ROCK TOWN DISTILLERY Little Rock, Arkansas.

Rock Town 6th Anniversary Four Grain Sour Mash Bourbon Whiskey Aged 30 Months db (89) n22.5 t22.5 f22 b22. A superb flavour combination. Interestingly, at 30 months old, this shows just how far this distillery has travelled in the improvement of its distillation techniques. Underlying the big wheat presence – which easily out-jousts the rye – are a few feints. Which simply push up the oil presence. 50%

Rock Town Arkansas Bourbon Whiskey Aged 13 Months batch no. 36 db (88.5) n22.5 t22 f22 b22. For a bourbon, this makes for a very presentable Corn Whiskey, or would have done had it been kept in the new oak a bit longer. 46% (92 proof)

Rock Town Arkansas Bourbon Whiskey Flavour Grain Series Barley db (95) n23 t24 f24 b24. Wow! That had me scampering to look for the sample bottle – Irish whiskey meets bourbon, I thought. And, indeed, 30% Arkansas unmalted barley in the recipe....corn, twice that amount. Totally magnificent. You can stop all the other whiskeys you do now and just concentrate on perfecting this stunner. Well, except your rye perhaps... The bite, the extraordinary dispersal of crisp sugars, the mouth-watering qualities, the spices, the chocolate....fabulous! 46% (92 proof)

Rock Town Arkansas Bourbon Whiskey Flavour Grain Series Sorghum db **(89.5)** n21.5 t22.5 f22 b22.5. Thick as a pea soup. Although the sorghum offers its own unique character, it also appears to have an effect on the texture, as well as the way in which the tannins lord it above the sugars. Substantial. *46% (92 proof)*

Rock Town Arkansas Hickory Smoked Whiskey Aged 11 Months from wheat mash, used oak, batch no. 27 db **(84)** n20.5 t21 f21.5 b21. Almost a bubble-gum character to this. The sweetness is unchecked by the insufficient tannin available. *45% (90 proof)*

Rock Town Arkansas Rye Whiskey Aged 15 Months batch no. 14 db **(95.5)** n24 t24 f23.5 b24. The nose will give any rye lover a serious hard on, as the effect of the grain is entirely maxed out, leaving the sugars to fill in the cracks only. The delivery, likewise, is so full of that grain's unique fruity character, one can only swoon. Brilliant! *46% (92 proof)*

ROGUE SPIRITS Newport, Oregon

Rogue Chipotle Whiskey ocean aged in oak barrels at least 6 months db **(84.5)** n21.5 t22 f21 b20. Peppery. Which, considering it has apparently been distilled with peppers, is hardly surprising. Interesting, chaps (especially with the countering honey). And entertaining. But using a vegetable disqualifies it from being a whiskey....!!! Does anyone happen to have a spare tortilla....? *40% (80 proof)*

Rogue Dead Guy Whiskey ocean aged in oak barrels at least 1 year db **(86)** n22.5 t22 f20.5 b21. Ah, I remember this guy from a year or two back: I had a bone to pick with him about his finish. Well, not the preferred drink of the Grim Reaper now, and makes good use of its malty, peppery structure. The finish is still a bit tangy and salty. But a big improvement. *40% (80 proof)*

Rogue Farms Oregon Rye Whiskey ocean aged in new oak barrels at least 4 months db **(74)** n18 t21 f17 b18. Rogue? You ain't joking... *40% (80 proof)*

Rogue Farms Oregon Single Malt Whiskey ocean aged in oak barrels at least 3 months db **(81.5)** n22 t22 f18 b19.5. Malty, gristy and pleasant at first. But like many of their whiskeys, it feels as though the Pacific ocean has leaked into the cask. I'm not sure what "ocean-aged" means exactly, but whatever it is, I do wish they'd stop it... *40% (80 proof)*

ROUGHSTOCK DISTILLERY Bozeman, Montana.

Roughstock Black Label (92.5) n22.5 t23.5 f23 b23.5. A very beautiful malt whiskey very well made which underlines the happy marriage between barley and virgin oak. A stunner! *64%*

ST GEORGE SPIRITS Alameda, California.

St Georges Single Malt Lot 15 db **(89)** n22 t22.5 f22.5 b22 Hah! Even in the pitch dark, sitting in my garden on the first warm evening of the year with the church about to strike midnight, I know, St George, that this is your whiskey. Because, nobody – nobody, I tells yer!! - has this delicate fruity edge to the malt (I'm sure it is malt). So, although it is now too dark to even properly see the label in the dull glow of this computer, let alone read it, I am writing this in your pre-set space, just knowing it is you. Have to say, normally this distillery has a slightly more impressive tone: this is just a little too young and flaky – yet still great fun! *43%*

SAINT JAMES SPIRITS Irwindale, California.

Peregrine Rock (83.5) n21 t20.5 f21.5 b20.5. Fruity and friendly, the wine and smoke combo work well-ish enough but the thumping oak injection highlights that maybe there isn't quite enough body to take in the ageing. Perhaps less time in the barrel will reduce the bitter orange finale. *40%*

SANTA FE SPIRITS Santa Fe, New Mexico.

◇ **Colkegan Single Malt Whiskey** American white oak barrels, batch no. 8 db **(87)** n22 t23.5 f20 b21.5 Once you get used to Mesquite-smoked malt it can become mildly addictive. So I have to concentrate hard and put my analyst's and blender's hats on here. The problem is the finish: it is just too much and numbs the tongue. But before it reaches that point I cannot other than heap praise on this: it has that unmistakable smoked almond tang on both nose and delivery and the muscovado sugars are profound. But once the Mesquite hits, the barley is lost to us. The mouth feel, though, really is pretty impressive. *46% (90 proof).*

◇ **Colkegan Single Malt Whiskey** American white oak barrels, batch no. 9 db **(90)** n23 good grief! I just picked out some malt. That's a first! The mesquite is much quieter: present, but hiding in a corner. The malt, spice and muscovado sugar appear to have the biggest say; **t23.5** lush and sugar intense on delivery, then a staggeringly beautiful unfurling of the incredibly thick malt, vanilla and ulmo honey; **f21** the mesquite catches up again, though still seemingly in docile mood until it begins to speed up on the hot spice front; loses balance somewhat; **b22.5** they have learned to control the Mesquite...! Much better! *46% (90 proof).*

◈ **Colkegan Single Malt Whiskey** American white oak barrels, batch no. 10 db **(91)** **n23** genuinely impressive: the phenols don't dig and gauge like they once did. Much more tame, so allowing the sugars a light caress and hickory an avenue, too...; **t23.5** that is really charming. Fat thanks to some light oils, there is a Fisherman's Friend cough sweet thread which intrigues. It matches the lightly molassed sugars and further hickory and liquorice; the spices arrive about halfway through the essay and build...; **f22** sugar and hickory begin to see out the game deliciously, but that pesky Mesquite finds a back door to turn things a little weird...; **b22.5** yep! Toning down the smoke has been a good move, but that finish still needs some attention...That said...superb! *46% (90 proof).*

SONOMA COUNTY DISTILLING CO. Rohnert Park, California.

◈ **Sonoma County Cherrywood Rye Whiskey** batch 4, bott 12/07/2016 db **(81)** **n19** **t21.5 f20 b20.5** I so wanted to fall in love with this whiskey: a magnificent label; the makers using the right ingredients and cask. I could even have put on Vivaldi at his most romantic as the rye had been matured for a minimum of Four Seasons. But sadly the tobacco grip on this is simply too tight. The grain, though unmistakable, bursts out and sparkles spasmodically, but little more than that. *478% (95.6 proof).*

◈ **Sonoma County Rye Whiskey** batch 14, bott 10/06/2016 db **(88)** **n21.5** the tobacco is with us, but to a much shyer degree. The unusually dry rye is bold and firm; **t23** quick tobacco sting, then a fabulous rye development both on fruity and crisper, sugary lines until it becomes fabulously, almost impossibly, intense; **f21.5** long, oily with a cherry soda finale; bitters out as expected; **b22** technically splutters a bit. But some sensational rye moments. *48% (96 proof).*

◈ **Sonoma County West of Kentucky Bourbon Whiskey No.1** batch 7, bott 08/31/2016 db **(95)** **n23.5** there is a genuine bourbon stance to this: red liquorice and molasses stand proudly side by side. But a phenol content, also, which has an important say in the makeup – from cherry wood, apparently; **t24** silky delivery with the corn oils in tip-top form. The sugars are of the ulmo honey and maple syrup variety but the crunchiness of the muscovado against the liquorice is superb; **f23.5** long, with the smoke seemingly kicking up a spiced finale; **b24** Californian bourbon a la Sonoma County. And it really is worth experiencing. *478% (95.6 proof).*

◈ **Sonoma County West of Kentucky Bourbon Whiskey No.2** batch 4, bott 12/16/2016 db **(87)** **n21.5 t23.5 f20 b22** A big, bold bourbon benefitting from a reduced tobacco trespass...though it does mount up late on. The delivery and middle, though, concentrates on the oily, succulent maple syrup and molasses mix, the following butterscotch theme and spices which enthusiastically punctuate the sweet narrative. *475% (95 proof).*

◈ **Sonoma County West of Kentucky Bourbon Whiskey No.3** batch 2, bott 01/20/2017 db **(77.5)** **n21 t21.5 f17 b18** Can't really make head nor tail of this. There is a custardy sweetness filling up some of the mid ground. But, some molasses apart, the recognisable bourbon landmarks are few and far between. Certainly as hot as Hades, especially on the tongue-torchingly aggressive finale. *46.5% (93 proof).*

SPIRIT HOUND DISTILLERS Lyons, Colorado.

Spirit Hound Distillers Straight Malt Whisky 2 Years Old batch 2 db **(93)** **n22.5 t24 f23 b23.5** This particular spirit hound has already learned a few tricks when it comes to making very good whiskey. Well done, boy....!!! *62.05%*

STEIN DISTILLERY Joseph, Oregon.

Straight Rye Whiskey Aged 2 Years cask no. 7 **(88)** **n23 t22 f21 b22.** A whiskey which offers up the grains to the full spotlight. A little more care with the cut and we have something special on our hands. *40%*

STONE BARN BRANDYWORKS DISTILLERY Portland, Oregon.

Hard Eight Unoaked Rye Whiskey **(86.5)** **n22.5 t21.5 f21 b21.5.** The excellent fruity-rye nose does not quite show the width of the cut which creates a buzzing oiliness. Good brown sugar balance. *40%*

STRANAHAN DISTILLERY Denver, Colorado.

Stranahan's Colorado Whiskey Batch #110 (91.5) n22 t23 f23 b23.5 Lovely interplay between crispy grain and even crispier sugars. Two-toned . Juicy and gorgeously spiced. 47%

Stranahan's Snowflake Cab Franc (95.5) n24 t24.5 f23 b24. A celebration of great whiskey, and a profound statement of what the small distilleries of the USA are capable of. 47%. sc.

SQUARE ONE BREWERY & DISTILLERY St. Louis, Missouri

J J Neukomm Missouri Malt Whisky Single Barrel (88.5) n21 t23 f22 b22.5 it was like being transferred back to Sperryville, Virginia, where Copper Fox whiskey was made. The cherry wood smoked malt has a highly distinctive voice, and here it is again. Except this really does appear to have dark cherry notes at work on the palate. Annoyingly, although single barrel, there is no distinguishing reference number. 45% (90 proof)

TACONIC DISTILLERY Stanfordville, New York.

Taconic Dutchess Private Reserve Straight Bourbon Whiskey db (86) n21.5 t22 f21 b21.5. A pretty bourbon, with the sugars sitting in the right place, if sometimes over enthusiastically. Good spice balance, roastiness and generous oils. Also, some decent rye in that mash bill it seems. 45% (90 proof)

Taconic Founder's Rye Whiskey db (90.5) n22.5 t23.5 f22 b22.5 Well done, people of Taconic distillery. You sure know how to make a rye whiskey..! 45% (90 proof)

◇ **Taconic Straight Bourbon Whiskey** db (92.5) n23 serious depth to the tannin: red liquorice and molasses abound. Roasty and good small grain portfolio, too...; t23.5 good grief...! It is the nose in liquid form...; f23 the sugars not only stay the course but have something left over, also: enough to sweeten the late mocha. Excellent vanillas, too; b23 I well remember their bourbon from last year: this appears to have upped a gear...not only in strength but in far better usage of the sugars. 57.5% (115 proof).

◇ **Taconic Straight Rye Whiskey** db (91.5) n22.5 sawdust falls upon the crisp grains to leave no doubt of the either whiskey type or hefty oak influence; towards the background there is an old Christmas pudding soaking in brandy...; t23.5 eye-watering delivery: all the suspects rye, tannin and the mysterious fruity brandy persona line up to be identified as the leader of the intense delivery; f22.5 thins, though now we have the big liquorice and tannin ensuring a heavily toasted finish; b23 if memory serves, this is the same distillery which came up with a resounding rye last year. This, though, has a different feel with the oak enclosing in on the grain like a python gets all up close and personal to a lamb. 57.5% (115 proof).

TOM'S FOOLERY Chargin Falls, Ohio.

Tom's Foolery Ohio Straight Bourbon Whiskey aged 3 Years, batch 6, dist 2012 db (83) n19 t22 f21 b21. Not sure if Tom's fooling or feinted. Superb arrival on palate with some pretty smart spices, well backed up by maple syrup. But the cut needs to be narrowed considerably. 45% (90 proof)

Tom's Foolery Ohio Straight Rye Whiskey finished in an apple brandy barrel, aged 3 Years, batch 2, dist 2012 db (92.5) n22.5 t24 f22.5 b23.5 Does finishing it in an apple brandy barrel mean this is a straight rye...? Either way, the extra fruit on top of the rye's already fruity nature appears to work. A beautifully vivid and memorable rye...which isn't quite as straight as Tom thinks... 45% (90 proof)

TRIPLE EIGHT DISTILLERY Nantucket, Massachusetts.

The Notch Aged 12 Years cask no. 026-055 dist 2002, bott 2014 db (96.5) n24 t24.5 f23.5 b24.5 Interesting to see this great whisky cope, as we all must do, with the passing of time. The quiet understatement and elegance of the 10-y-o has given way to a more brash and assertive, oak-stained version. Not that that is a criticism, as it does it with the usual Triple Eight panache. On the 8th of August 2008 (just two days after I had completed the 2009 Whisky Bible) I gave a speech at the distillery predicting that, from the samples I had tasted in their warehouses, this new venture was on course to be one of the great malt whisky distilleries of the world. I am heartened that, for once in my life, I got something right... 48%

TUTHILLTOWN SPIRITS Gardiner, New York.

Hudson Baby Bourbon Year 13 Batch E1 (86) n21 t21.5 f22 b21.5. A big, heavy duty bourbon. Feinty, though nothing like as oily as some previous bottlings I've encountered from these guys over the years. Enough toasted honeycomb and liquorice for this to make a few lovely noises. 46%. WB15/174

VAN BRUNT STILLHOUSE Brooklyn, New York.

Van Brunt Stillhouse American Whiskey db (80) n19 t20 f20.5 b20.5. A hard one to categorise: it is whiskey and it is American. The main strand is attached to the vanilla and butterscotch tart, perhaps with a little liquorice squirted on for weight. 40%

Van Brunt Stillhouse Bourbon db (81.5) n19 t21 f21 b20.5. For a bourbon, this has a peculiarly malty kick to it. Distinct whiff of the hay ricks about this, before the fledgling liquorice becomes involved. 42%

Van Brunt Stillhouse Rye db (86) n20.5 t22 f22 b21.5. Technically wins few awards. But something, seemingly instinctually, seems to have dragged out the very best from this distillery with its rye. The oils are a bit of a problem, yet the grain rises above it enough to tap out a delightfully fruity and spicy message, and even confident enough to, late on, stray into mocha land.... 42%

VALENTINE DISTILLING CO. Ferndale, Michigan.

◈ **Mayor Pingree Small Batch Bourbon Whiskey** batch no. 39 db (89.5) n23.5 a lighter style of bourbon from Valentine, here making the most of the fruity muscovado sugars and delicate maple syrup; t22.5 a very light delivery and it takes several flavour waves before an oily charge big enough to fully carry the vanilla-caramel theme is created. Tangy, lightly spiced butterscotch fills the middle; f21.5 just slightly over bitter as the wider elements of the cut make their mark; b22 a very different animal, or mayor, and obviously distilled in different stills from their 9- and 10-year-old Mayor Pingree brands. A little confusing for the punter but a very attractive if under-stated micro-bourbon without doubt. 45% (90 proof).

VIRGINIA DISTILLERY CO. Lovinston, Virginia.

◈ **Virginia Highland Malt Whisky Port Finished** batch no. 03 (87) n22 t22.5 f21 b21.5 A vibrant malt, youthful and sharp in places. Exceptionally crisp and clean but sporting an unusually thin body also which means that there is a slight jarring on the grain-fruit transmission. Displays an attractive consistent sweetness until the death when a vague bitterness develops. 46% (92 proof).

WESTLAND DISTILLERY Seattle, Washington.

Westland American Single Malt Whiskey Peated bott Sept 15 db (91.5) n23 a dry, powdery peatiness is enlivened by a sprig of mint; t23 muscovado sugar melts on delivery, followed by lightly peated barley grist. After the dry nose, now attractively juicy; f22.5 gently smoked vanilla; b23 lightly peated, polite and safe.. The gristy sugars refuse to be thwarted. 46% (92 Proof). nc ncf.

Westland American Single Malt Garryana 1/1 bott 18 Apr 2016 db (91) n23 the most delicate smoky and nutty aroma bound in a light muscovado and oak wrapping; t23.5 light sugars on delivery, as crunchy as you like: Demerara making way for the muscovado. The vanilla which follows really is complex stuff; the delicate phenolic anchor has hardly stirred; f22 a little thin once the sugars have dissolved; b22.5 a brittle but always delicious malt. 56.2% (112.4 proof). nc ncf.

◈ **Westland American Single Malt Garryana 2/1** bott 2017 db (89.5) n23 vaguely phenolic tannin with a distinctly nutty edge; t22 chewy, nutty then a breakout of delicate grist and icing sugars; a little citrus on the non-specific smoke; f22 the standard shy finale with a crisp vanilla fade; b22 this second bottling proves Westland have created a universally unique whisky style, though the cut from the still is a little generous. 50% nc ncf.

◈ **Westland American Single Malt Peat Week** db (92) n23 seemingly tame smoke, but patience is rewarded with a gorgeous bluebell wood earthiness and a gristy sweetness; t23.5 wow...! That grist makes a beautiful impact on delivery full of a massagingly delicate smoke and young, citrusy sugars; salivating and spruce; f22.5 light smoke butterscotch, again with a squeeze of citrus; b23 a distillery which does understated smoky whiskey rather well... 50% nc ncf.

Westland American Single Malt Sherry Wood db (72) n18 t20 f16 b18. Bitter and furry, disappointingly. 42% (92 proof). nc ncf.

◈ **Westland American Single Malt Winter 2016** db (88) n22 spiced brown sugar and a biscuity maltiness; t22.5 intense, sweet barley; juicy in stages; f21.5 settles into a slightly toastier malty mode with delicate muscovado sugars; b22 a straight up and down maltfest. 50% nc ncf.

WILLIE HOWELL SPIRITS

WH32137 (73.5) n15 **t**21 **f**18.5 **b**19. As big and intense as you'd expect from any spirit with a cut as wide as this. Very sweet corn oil ensures an uplifting body. *42.5%*

WOODINVILLE WHISKEY CO. Woodinville, Washington

⋄ **Woodinville Straight 100% Rye Whiskey** db **(95) n**24 much more grain dominant than their bourbon offering, which relies heavily on the complexity of the oak. Here the rye takes firm control and refuses to relinquish its brittle grasp; the freshly ground black pepper adds a third dimension...; **t**23.5 profound and unmistakable rye influence on delivery: fruity yet firm, spicy yet sweet, crispy yet soft the complexity and contrast is all you could ask for Mid-range oils but enough to ensure weight and length; **f**23.5 long and somehow the complexity levels rise! The Manuka honey and pepper do quiet battle while the rue offers a Love Heart candy; **b**24 rye distilling and maturation to a very high standard, especially for a micro distillery. *45% (90 proof).*

⋄ **Woodinville Straight Bourbon Whiskey** db **(93) n**24 such a wonderfully toasty nose with both leading grains and sugars revealing their dark, weightier side. But not far below that crusty surface is a gentle and happy marriage of lemon drizzle and Madeira cake; **t**23.5 as silky as delivery as promised by the nose. Telling oils carry both citrus and Manuka honey, but it is the salivating delivery which really stars especially with the melting of the light molasses and muscovado; **f**22.5 just a little oily bitterness infiltrates. But the caramels and vanillas from the cask are of the highest quality; **b**23 a few years back I highlighted this then fledgling distillery as one to watch. This latest, magnificent bottling alongside its sister rye shows you exactly why. What a joy! *45% (90 proof).*

WOODSTONE CREEK DISTILLERY Cincinnati, Ohio.

Woodstone Creek 10 Year Old Peated Malt (92) 24 23 22 23. Just read the previous tasting notes. There is nothing I can either add nor subtract. Quite, quite wonderful... *46.25%*

WYOMING WHISKEY Kirby, Wyoming.

⋄ **Wyoming Whiskey Double Cask Straight Bourbon Whiskey** finished in sherry casks db **(87.5) n**23 **t**22 **f**21 **b**21.5 Kind of leaves me scratching my head, this. Yes, the grape infusion is clean and profound, suffering not an atom of the sulphur pollution which wrecks so much scotch. But this is bourbon – which needs unsullied virgin oak. And here we get virtually no meaningful bourbon contribution but masses of delicious grape. Yes, some glorious fruit notes, but this needs more balance so the bourbon has a telling say. *50% (100 proof).*

⋄ **Wyoming Whiskey Single Barrel** barrel no. 1840 db **(87) n**22 **t**22 **f**21 **b**22 If you like your whiskey to have a big cream caramel and ulmo honey charge, then this guy is for you. Doesn't quite gel towards the end, though. *44% (88 proof).*

⋄ **Wyoming Whiskey Small Batch** batch no. 42 db **(86.5) n**22 **t**22.5 **f**20.5 **b**21.5 Another Wyoming which has so much going for it but (annoyingly!) falters at the final step towards the finale. Here the accent is on the vanilla and a rich, spicy fruity suet pudding middle. Hard not to like. *44% (88 proof).*

⋄ **Wyoming Whiskey Outryder** db **(88.5) n**22.5 the pithy fruit forms the most comfortable pillow on which the apologetic vanillas lie; **t**22.5 immediately salivating with an oily and grainy disposition. The sugars are of the very runny maple syrup variety; the spices are relaxed and build gently too; **f**21.5 bitters out in the house style; **b**22 perhaps should be called Easy Rider, as this is as gentle as it gets... *50% (100 proof).*

YELLOW ROSE DISTILLING Houston, Texas.

Yellow Rose Outlaw Bourbon Whiskey Over 6 Months batch 24 db **(87) n**20 **t**22.5 **f**23.5 **b**21. The closest whiskey in style found to this anywhere in the world is European, where chestnut casks have been deployed for finishing (at least!). A tannin-dominated whiskey, where the normal liquorice and honey tones don't really apply, though close relatives may be found. Delicious when it settles down towards the end but, overall, little balance to be had. Very different...and like a yellow rose, grows on you. *46%*

Yellow Rose Straight Rye Whiskey batch 26 **(79.5) n**20 **t**21.2 **f**18 **b**20. A distinctly oily gathering, though the sharper tones of the rye and headier tannins cancel each other out. Undone by a slight butyric note which does the whiskey, and drinker, few favours. *45%*

YAHARA BAY DISTILLERY Madison, Wisconsin.

Sample No 1 (87) n22.5 **t**22 **f**20.5 **b**22. A disarmingly elegant whiskey. *40%*

American/Kentucky Whiskey Blends

Ancient Age Preferred (73) n16.5 t19 f19.5 b18. A marginal improvement thanks mainly to a re-worked ripe corn-sweet delivery and the cocoa-rich finish. But still preferred, one assumes, by those who probably don't care how good this distillery's whisky can be... 40%

Beam's Eight Star (69.5) n17 t18 f17 b17.5. If you don't expect too much it won't let you down. 40%

Bellows (67) n17 t17.5 f16 b16.5 Just too thin. 40%

Calvert's Extra (79) n19 t20 f20 b20. Sweet and mega-toffeed. Just creaking with caramel but extra marks for the late spice. 40%

Carstair's White Seal (72) n16.5 t18.5 f19.5 b17.5 Possibly the cleanest blend about even offering a cocoa tang on the finale. Pleasant. 40%

The Hilhaven Lodge (88) n21.5 slight bourbon; t23 an attractive walnut cake theme and a lovely honeyed-bourbon note which is in full salivation made; f21.5 much lighter with toffee and vanilla; b22 clean, juicy, easy drinking whiskey. 40% (80 proof)

Kentucky Dale (64) n16 t17 f15 b16. Thin and spineless, though soft and decently sweet on delivery. The grain spirit completely dominates. 40%

Kessler (84.5) n20 t21 f22 b21.5. "Smooth As Silk" claims the label. And the boast is supported by what is in the bottle: a real toffee-mocha charmer with a chewy, spicy depth. 40%

PM Deluxe (75) n18 t18 f19 b18. Pleasant moments as the toffee melts in the mouth. 40%

Sunny Brook (79.5) n20 t21 f19 b19.5. An entirely agreeable blend with toffee and lightly oiled nuts. Plus a sunny disposition... 40%

Straight Malt Whiskey

Parker's Heritage Collection Kentucky Straight Malt Whiskey Aged 8 Years db (93) n23 t23.5 f23 b23.5 From the distillery which brought you wheat whisky, now comes malt – Kentucky style. As delicious as it is fascinating. 54% (108 proof)

Whiskey Distilled From Bourbon Mash

Angels Envy Bourbon Finished in Port Barrels (84) n20 t22 f21 b21. Almost like a chocolate raisin candy and fruitcake. Silky textured and juicy. 43.3% (86.6 proof)

Whiskey Distilled From Malt Mash

Woodford Reserve Master's Collection Classic Malt distilled from a malt mash db (79.5) n20 t21 f19 b19.5. Ok. So let me get my head around this. If their label and neck blurb is to believed, a spirit distilled from malt in the US and placed into used casks is a "whiskey distilled from a malt mash" while, as written on another product, a bourbon transferred into used casks is a bourbon. That appears to be Woodford's stance. Sorry, guys. Don't buy that argument for a second. If anyone argued that there appears to be more politicising, tactical manoeuvring and precedential games being played here as there is careful fermentation, distilling and blending, it would be hard to disagree. Says it is malt. But doesn't help by saying malt what. Presumably barley, as the nose offers nothing other than freshly cut hay. Which in a Scotch or Irish might be regarded as a problem, often pointing an accusing finger at fermentation. Sadly, the drinking experience, as sweet as it is, doesn't get much better. 45.2% WB15/382

Whiskey Distilled From Rye Mash

Angels Envy Rye Finished in Caribbean Rum Casks (78) n18.5 t20.5 f20 b19. Frankly, I was hardly expecting to have any teeth left after this sample. The hardest, most crisp of all whiskeys is rye. And if you want to give any whisk(e)y an extra degree of exoskeleton, then just finish it in a rum cask. And here we have the two together : yikes! Some twenty years ago I gave then Jack Daniel's blender Lincoln Henderson his first-ever taste of peated whisky: a Laphroaig. He hated it! I think he's waited a long time to return the compliment by showing me a style I did not know could exist. Beyond fascinating. Weird, even - hence the full tasting notes. One for the ladies with this liqueur-style smoothie. 50%

Other American Whiskey

1792 Port Finish Kentucky Straight Bourbon db (74) n19 t20 f18 b17. What a waste of great bourbon. Flat and mind-bogglingly uninteresting. The great, aged whiskey of Barton is far too good for this kind of lemming-type nonsense. 44.45% (88.9 proof)

⬦ **Abraham Bowman Gingerbread Cocoa Finished Bourbon** dist 12-12-06, bott 9-6-16 (86) n21 t22.5 f21 b21.5 Busy and industrious on the palate with a quite fascinating and complex spread of flavours, some ginger-related the majority not. But the nose is off key and the overall feel just doesn't feel whiskeyish enough. *45% (90 proof). Release No. 15.*

◈ **Abraham Bowman Sequential Series 2nd Use Barrels** dist 11-17-04, bott 5-1-17 db **(92.5) n23** firm nose with early sugar thrust with some piercing spice poking through unopposed. Fresh and attractively herbal; **t23** really clean delivery with surprising lack of oils from the corn. Those that are present help keep grounded the vanillins holding a drier oak fingerprint than you would expect to find in the distillery's bourbon; **f23.5** much more integrated grain and oak here, with a synchronisation to the layering of the lightly sweeter elements and drier ones; creamier now with an elegant and sober light butterscotch fade; **b23** 's'funny, I though. Doesn't nose right for a bourbon. Wrong kind of tannin: too quick on the naked brown sugars and spice instead of heavier liquorice and caramel frame. So checked the header and spotted the 2nd use barrels bit. Just shows, doesn't it, how unique and delicate true bourbon actually is, despite its enormity of flavour. *50% (100 proof). Release No. 16.*

◈ **Abraham Bowman Sequential Series 4th Use Barrels** dist 11-17-04, bott 5-1-17 db **(86.5) n22 t22 f21 b21.5** An early hint of honey quickly vanishes and we are quickly thrust into a straight-laced, bittering narrative. A bit like dating an ex-girlfriend's twin sister and finding she just doesn't have the same depth of character. And is only half as passionate. *50% (100 proof). Release No. 16.*

Buffalo Trace Experimental Collection French Oak Barrel Head Aged dist 03/31/05, barreled 04/01/05, bott 04/22/15, still proof: 140, entry proof: 125, warehouse/floor: K/8, rick/row/slot: 1/3/4, age at bottling: 10 Years, 0 Months, evaporation: 46% db **(95.5) n24 t24 f23.5 b24** In so many ways, classic BT – especially of the rye recipe. *45% (90 proof)*

High West Son of Bourye blend of bourbon & rye **(95) n23 t24.5 f23.5 b24** This son, presumably called Ryebon, is a stunningly stylish chap which comprehensively eclipses its lackluster parent... *46%*

Jim Beam Double Oak db **(86) n22 t22.5 f20.5 b21.** Attractive, caramel-soaked whiskey with a little too much fade after a big spice and liquorice delivery. *43%*

Knob Creek Smoked Maple (35) n10 t10 f10 b5. How can this be called a " Kentucky straight bourbon"? What is straight about this? Am I missing something here? About 98% closer to maple syrup than bourbon, this would make a pleasant spread on your breakfast toast. It may be whiskey, Jim (Beam), but not as we know it. *45% (90 proof)*

Michter's No. 1 American Whiskey (84.5) n21 t21.5 f21 b21. Sugar-coated, oily and easy going. About as friendly as any whiskey you'll find this year *41.7%*

Michter's No. 1 Sour Mash (86) n22 t22 f21 b21. A pleasant, clean, light whiskey: perhaps too clean at times. Good mocha throughout, with the accent on the coffee. *43%*

◈ **Trail's End Batch No 002 Kentucky Bourbon finished in Oregon Oak (92) n23.5** no mistakin' the bourbon, that's for sure: honey and liquorice at every gentle turn, spices galore – though all kindly muted - and a mysterious minty toffee tone, too; **t23** silky with an early, rich delivery of molten Demerara sugars, a soft rye-style fruitiness and lashings of caramel and vanilla; **f22.5** soft, with a buttery creaminess to the light sugars and now slightly more intense spice: all rather understated and beautiful; **b23** so, here we are: at the Trail's End. This is my final official day of tasting, having spent the last few months working six days a week to bring you Jim Murray's Whisky Bible 2018 on time. The romantic in me meant that this had to be my last whisk(e)y: what else would fit the bill? Especially as both Kentucky and Oregon are my two adopted states in the US. For the record, it is the 1,199th new whisky for Bible 2018, though there had been a couple of dozen additional re-tastes. And as I write the front of the Bible and we edit and finally put this book to bed, the odd straggler will come in to take the total over 1,200. But for me this, officially, is it...the Trail's End for another year.... *45% (90 proof).*

WhistlePig Old World 12 Year Madeira Finish European casks **(88) n21.5 t23.5 f21 b22** Not sure how this can be called a straight rye. But as a whiskey experience, certainly has its merits. *45%. (90 Proof)*

WhistlePig Old World 12 Year Port Finish European casks **(74) n18 t20 f18 b18.** Oily, dense and bitter *45%. (90 Proof)*

WhistlePig Old World 12 Year Sauternes Finish European casks **(79.5) n21 t22.5 f18 b18.** Has its brief moments of fun, mainly on delivery, when the rock-hard rye tries to keep out the surrounding, swamping fruit. But a very poor finish and very little balance throughout. *45%. (90 Proof)*

Canadian Whisky

The vastness of Canada is legendary. As is the remoteness of much of its land. But anyone who has not yet visited a distillery which sits serenely on the shores of Lake Manitoba more or less bang in the middle of the country and, in early Spring, venture a few miles out into the wilderness has really missed a trick.

Because there, just a dozen miles from the remotest distillery of them all, Gimli, you can stand and listen to the ice crack with a clean, primeval crispness unlike any other thing you will have experienced; a sound once heard by the very first hunters who ventured into these uncharted wastes. And hear a distant loon call its lonely, undulating, haunting song, its notes scudding for miles along the ice and vanishing into the snow which surrounds you. Of all the places on the planet, it is the one where you will feel a sensation as close to nature - and insignificance - as you are likely to find.

It was also a place where I felt that, surely, great whisky should be made. But in the early days of the Gimli distillery there was a feeling of frustration by the blenders who used it. Because they were simply unable to recreate the depth and complexity of the legendary Crown Royal brand it had been built to produce in place of the old, now closed, distilleries to the east. When, in their lab, they tasted the new Crown Royal against the old there were furrowed brows, a slight shaking of heads and an unspoken but unmistakable feeling of hopeless resignation.

To understand why, we have to dispense with the nonsense which appears to have been trotted out by some supposed expert in Canadian whisky or other

Yukon

BRITISH
COLUMBIA

ALBERTA

MANITOBA

Shelter Point   Okanagan
●Vancouver

Alberta
Highwood
Calgary

Palliser

Gimli

Key
● **Major Town or City**
▲ **Distillery**

who has, I have been advised by quite a few people I meet at my tastings, been writing somewhere that Canada has no history of blending from different distilleries. Certainly that is now the perceived view of many in the country. And it is just plain wrong: only a maniac would write such garbage as fact and completely undersell the provenance of Canadian whisky. Crown Royal, when in its pomp, was a meticulous blending of a number of different whiskies from the Seagram empire and by far the most complex whisky Canada had to offer.

The creases in the furrowed brows deepened as the end of the last century aproached. Because the key distilleries of LaSalle, Beupre and Waterloo were yielding the very last of their stocks, especially top quality pure rye, and although the much lighter make of Gimli was of a high standard, they had not yet been able to recreate the all round complexity as when adding the fruits of so many great distilleries together. The amount of experimentation with yeasts and distilling speeds and cutting times was a wonder to behold. But the race was on: could they, before the final stocks ran dry, produce the diversity of flavours to match the old, classic distilleries which were now not just closed but in some cases demolished?

When I had sat in the LaSalle blending lab for several days in the 1990s and worked my way through the near extinct whiskies in stock I recognised in Beupre a distillery which, had it survived, probably might have been capable of producing something as good, if not better, than anything else on this planet. And it was clear just what a vital contribution it made to Crown Royal's all round magnificence.

So I have monitored the Crown Royal brand with interest, especially since Gimli and the brand was acquired by Diageo some 15 years ago. And anyone doubting that this really was a truly great whisky should have accompanied me when I visited the home of my dear and now sadly lost friend Mike Smith and worked our way through his astonishing Crown Royal collection which showed how the brand's taste profile had evolved through the ages.

And, at last, it appears all that hard work, all those early days of experimentation and fine tuning at Gimli have paid off. For while the standard Crown Royal brand doesn't yet quite live up to its starry past, they have unleashed upon us a whisky which dazzles, startles and engulfs you in its natural beauty like an early spring morning on Lake Manitoba. The whisky is called Crown Royal Northern Harvest Rye. It is not only the best Canadian to be found in the market, it was Jim Murray's World Whisky of the Year 2016: batch L5085 N3 had redefined a nation's whisky.

The fact it should have achieved this at a time when Canadian whisky is at a nadir, with far too many brands dependent on adding too many unacceptable things as accepted flavouring agents, is providential. It shows that keeping the grains at a maximum and allowing them to be the flavouring agents - like Alberta Premium - is not just keeping true to the old Canadian traditions, but the way to go to drag it back onto the world's stage and give it a leading role. Walter Jonke and the other old Canadian blenders I knew understood this. Let this be a lesson to the present generation. And so many so-callled whisky experts.

ONTARIO

QUEBEC

▲ Glenora

Caldera ▲ NOVA SCOTIA

● Quebec

Valleyfield ● Montreal

▲ Still Waters

Canada Mist ▲ ● Toronto
▲ Forty Creek
▲ Kittling Ridge
▲ Walkerville

Jim Murray's Whisky Bible Canadian Whisky of the Year Winners	
2004	Seagram's VO
2005	Seagram's VO
2006	Alberta Premium
2007	Alberta Premium 25 Years Old
2008	Alberta Premium 25 Years Old
2009	Alberta Premium
2010	Wiser's Red Letter
2011	Crown Royal Special Reserve
2012	Crown Royal Special Reserve
2013	Masterson's 10 Year Old Straight Rye
2014	Masterson's 10 Year Old Straight Rye
2015	Masterson's 10 Year Old Straight Rye
2016	Crown Royal Northern Harvest Rye
2017	Crown Royal Northern Harvest Rye
2018	Crown Royal Northern Harvest Rye

Canadian Single Malts

CENTRAL CITY BREWERS & DISTILLERS LTD.

◇ **Lohin McKinnon Single Malt Whisky** batch no. LOT 0001 db **(89.5) n23.5** (scores 22 when first nosed before warming!). After ten minutes warming, the bees start swarming: copious amounts of honey linking stunningly with the deft vanillas. A sub plot of light chocolate and lemon utterly charms; **t23** (22 when cooler) superb weight on the delivery as the most eye-closingly delicious and salivating orange blossom honey spreads all over the intense barley; thickens in the mid-ground with praline and toffee nougat; **f21** no shortage of thick mocha and butterscotch as those extra oils leave their mark; **b22** always one of the favourite – and most treasured - moments in the many facets of my job is to taste a brand new whisky. I am always a little nervous, as I really don't like breaking it to new whisky makers that they need to get back to the drawing board. No such problem here: this malt is a noble first release. The cuts need adjusting very slightly to lessen the feints (indeed, how it sweetens when you nose a glass after it has been warmed for a good ten minutes and the higher oils evaporate underlines that the excess feints are pretty minor) and I'd work with a cannier mix of first and second fill ex-bourbon barrels to help up the honey character which so perfectly suits this malt. But this is a highly drinkable whisky and they are not that far away from producing an excellent one. Hearty congrats. 43%.

DEVINE SPIRITS

◇ **Glen Saanich Single Malt** batch no. 1, bourbon barrels db **(94) n22.5** a pretty cleanly distilled whisky showing a touch of youth and grist but still an impressive malt thickness...well-balanced and weighted....promising...and certainly wants to make you go on to the next step...; **t24** no disappointments on delivery, either. In fact, this is breathtakingly beautiful! Gorgeously weighted oils appear to help yield the maximum degree of intense malt, with just a little molasses helping the sweetness along; **f23.5** deft butterscotch and vanilla plus some lovely oaked spice. Yet, even now, it is the barley which glows most of all...; **b24** as a first bottling, genuinely superb. What it may lack in out and out complexity it more than makes up for with the unfettered brilliance of the malt and the all-round joy of the intense experience. Hope they can keep this standard going. Congratulations to all at deVine! 45%.

GLENORA

Glen Breton Rare Aged 10 Years bott 10 db **(89.5) n22 t23 f22 b22.5.** An impressive whisky: one of the best bottlings of this age for some while and showing the malt at full throttle. 43%

HIGHWOOD DISTILLERS

Highwood Distillers Centennial Whisky db (84.5) n21.5 t22 f20 b21 Toffee and raisin. Tangy, though the finish dries significantly. 40%.

Highwood Distillers Ninety 5 Year Old Whisky db (86.5) n21.5 t22 f21.5 b21.5 A sweet, simplistic whisky which, despite its thin body and big toffee theme, ramps up some very attractive spices. 45%.

Highwood Distillers Ninety 20 Year Old Whisky db (90) n23.5 superb aroma which beautifully encapsulates the age – and country - without there being a single fading note to be heard: a stunning array gentle sugars augment the lightest of vanilla and butterscotch themes. Naturally, the spices are a low key as possible, but hints of wheat; t22.5 a fragile, skeletal frame; the muscovado sugar muscle is undeveloped and any fattiness carries that prominent vanilla; f22 more of the same, though quieter and a little spicier; b22 this is a grand old man of Canadian whisky yet sprightly and full of very simple Canadian tales... 45%.

Canadian Rockies 10 Year Old (84.5) n21.5 t22 f20.5 b20.5. Resplendent in all its chewy one-dimensional caramel. 40%. Taiwan Exclusive.

Canadian Rockies 21 Year Old (88) n22 so light, with a mix of apple crumble and vanilla ice cream; t22 soft and simple as you like: vanilla and docile spice; f22 more of the same...; b22 not sure you can find a straighter, simpler whisky... 40%. Taiwan Exclusive.

Canadian Rockies 21 Year Old (91.5) n22.5 t23.5 f22.5 b23 Surely it just can't be a matter of 6% abv. This has far more personality and joie de vivre. 46%. Canadian Exclusive.

Canadian Rockies 34 Year Old (92.5) n23 t23 f23.5 b23 The most fun I've had with a 34-year-old Canadian for quite a few years now...though that was a little hotter than this... 79.3%. Taiwan Exclusive.

OKANAGAN SPIRITS CRAFT DISTILLERY

Laird of Fintry Single Malt Whisky French & American oak. db (84) n21 t22 f20 b21. A tangy, aromatic whisky where the oak appears to have a disproportionate say. Interesting marmalade depth. 40%. First Batch. 264 bottles.

PEMBERTON DISTILLERY

Pemberton Organic Single Malt Whisky 2010 ex-bourbon cask, cask no. 1, dist Aug 10, bott May 17 db (89) n22 solid grist holds its place tight and sees off the hint of wide cut but polishing up the malt; t22 superb sugars popping and fizzing all over the palate, some with a light citrusy feel; f22.5 less feint noticeable here (which is unusual in a whisky) as the sugars and oaky vanilla form a happy union; b22.5 I think 2010 was a classic vintage for Pemberton: this is rather lovely! 44%. nc ncf sc.

Pemberton Organic Single Malt Whisky 2010 ex-bourbon cask, cask no. 3, dist Oct 10, bott May 16 db (88) n21.5 t22.5 f22 b22 Massively malty. And they really can claim their very own idiosyncratic style: deliciously different. 45.6%. nc ncf sc.

Pemberton Organic Single Malt Whisky 2012 ex-bourbon cask, cask no. 4, dist Sept 12, bott Apr 17 db (84.5) n20 t21.5 f22 b21 Ooh, dear..! Got some of the cut points wrong here, which means the gentle peats don't stand much of a chance to do their stuff with the feints being a little too muscular. On the positive side, those oils gathered from the still do help fatten out and lengthen the sweet, gristy, barley-rich finale. 44%. nc ncf sc.

Pemberton Organic Single Malt Whisky 2013 ex-bourbon cask, cask no. 1, dist 11 Apr 13, bott May 17 db (85.5) n21 t21.5 f22 b21 I was thinking: "peat and nougat...I've encountered this before". And checking the Bible, I see I have...from Pemberton, with their 2011 bottling! Lots of sweet charm from the grist, but this is a malt which struggles to go to the next step of integration. 44%. nc ncf sc.

Pemberton Organic Single Malt Whisky Lightly Peated 2011 ex-bourbon cask, cask no. 1, dist 2011, bott May 16 db (84.5) n20.5 t22 f21 b21. The mix of peat and nougat make slightly uncomfortable bedfellows. Apparently, the first ever peated malt from this distillery north of Whistler – a tough art to master. 45%. nc ncf sc.

Pemberton Organic Single Malt Whisky Medium Peated 2012 ex-bourbon cask, cask no. 3, dist Aug 12, bott May 16 db (87.5) n21 t22.5 f22 b22. This one is all about the delivery: colossal barley on show despite the smoke. Again, a very wide cut from the stills means the oils tighten the sugars and experience and make for a challenging, tangy dram. 45.3%. nc ncf sc.

POTTER DISTILLING CO.

Cadenhead's World Whiskies Canada Potter Distilling Co. Aged 24 Years Bourbon barrel, bott Feb 14 (94.5) n23 t24 f23.5 b24 a true classic of the Canadian rye style...though of course without any rye at all. As a whisky, a little bit of a mystery. When at Potter distillers in British Columbia about 17 years ago, I remember they then had no maturing stock of their own as they did not distil large enough quantities. But they did have casks of maturing Canadian whisky they had bought in from the nearby Okanagan Distillery which, for a while, had made Canadian Club for the west coast and Far East market. No guarantees, but chances are it could be that – and they did make very good whisky there, evidenced by the outstanding old Bush Pilot single cask brand. *56.5%. 126 bottles. WB15/178*

SHELTER POINT DISTILLERY

◈ **Shelter Point Distillery Artisanal Cask Strength Whisky** American oak, finished in French oak db **(91) n22.5** the European tannin makes a statement here and a point of turning the vaguely wide cut into a thick chocolate malt: fascinating and increasingly enticing... **t23.5** light delivery for about a third of second in which you can spot the sweet barley, then... crash..! Just a few minutes before tasting this whisky I was attacked at lightning speed by a sparrowhawk which came at me from nowhere talons fully extended. Well, the huge tannin here arrives at the same velocity and with the same murderous intent. Wrapped up in those oaky notes is a mix of spice, molasses and Nutella which roar onto the taste buds with extraordinary effect, capturing and conquering all before it; **f22** the slightly wide cut is faintly detectable but the malts come out to play; **b23** looks as though the law in Canada now says you even have to have the barrels from both English and French language... A beautifully complex and intense malt. *54.8%. 1,200 bottles.*

Shelter Point Single Malt Whisky db **(89.5) n22 t23 f22.5 b22** A charming and very promising malt made by lovely people at a gorgeous distillery – and best when served very much at body temperature. I have been watching progress at Shelter Point – a remote distillery on Victoria Island in stunning British Columbia – since before it was actually built. And having looked at many of the early casks as they matured, I can tell you even better is to come, especially when more sugars are absorbed from the oak and a wider collection of barrels can be vatted for even greater complexity. Like the distillery, this is a whisky – even at this tender age - which just oozes personality. Congratulations to all concerned. *46%*

STILLWATERS DISTILLERY

Stalk & Barrel Single Malt Whisky cask 11 db **(87.5) n21.5 t22 f22 b22.** Attractively intense barley has all the space it requires to flourish thanks to a well distilled spirit impressively cut. Only a lack of complexity fails to crank the score a little higher. But if it's a malt whisky you want, with the accent on the malt, here's your man. *62.3%. sc.*

Stalk & Barrel Single Malt Whisky cask 13 db **(77) n20 t21 f17 b19.** Not quite the delight that is cask 11. Not sure if that is because the weaker strength means the water has broken up the oils a little bit too much for their own good, exposing a few feints. Or if the cut wasn't quite as carefully made this time round. Still plenty of malt to get on with, though. *46%. sc.*

YUKON BREWING

Two Brewers Yukon Single Malt Release 01 Classic db **(86.5) n21 t21.5 f22.5 b21.5.** Not sure if I have come across a Canadian so steeped with rich cocoa from first moment to last. A pretty wide cut from the still can be thanked for this, as the thick finish on the tongue will testify. But I admit, I could easily enjoy this, especially the extraordinary and utterly delicious, top quality French praline on the finish. *46%*

Two Brewers Yukon Single Malt Release 02 Special Finishes db **(80.5) n19 t21.5 f20 b20.** Sorry, chaps. You have some serious butyric going on there... *46%*

◈ **Two Brewers Yukon Single Malt Release 03 Peated** db **(86) n22 t21.5 f21 b21.5** Not the kind of smoke to get the peat heads up all excited and battering down doors to find a bottle. But a friendly and attractive phenol input, especially on the nose, though the delivery and follow though is far more about the Demerara sugars, light cocoa powder and oils. *46%*

◈ **Two Brewers Yukon Single Malt Release 04 Special Finishes** db **(89) n22** salty with an attractive dryness to the vanilla; **t22.5** salty and puckering on delivery; takes a while for the sweetening malt to make its mark which it finally does with aplomb; **f22** a superb latte coffee finish; **b22.5** takes a little while to pick up what this malt is trying to do, but once you find its rhythm, it is joy. *43%*

◈ **Two Brewers Yukon Single Malt Release 05 Innovative** db **(94) n23.5** now that's complex. Intriguing interplay of pear and kumquat with a slightly salty, very muted bourbon-style liquorice and molasses: seriously good...; **t23.5** exceptionally malty delivery: clean barley and ulmo honey combine with a graceful swoop of the palate; a little orange blossom honey enters the fray as it all becomes a little more tannin-rich and salty; **f23** a long barley fade with a light butterscotch and lime farewell; **b24** what a classy, complex, truly brilliant whisky this is. Take a bow, good people of the Yukon... *43%*.

Canadian Blended Whisky

Alberta Premium (95.5) n24 t25 f22.5 b24 It has just gone 8am and the Vancouver Island sky is one of clear blue. My windows are open to allow in some chilly, early Spring air and, though only the first week of March, an American robin sits in the arbutus tree, resplendent in its now two-toned leaves, calling for a mate, as it has done since 5.15 this morning, his song blending with the lively trill of the house finches and the doleful, maritime anthem of the gull. It seems the natural environment of Alberta Premium, back here to its rye-studded best after a couple I tasted socially in Canada last year appeared comparatively dull and restrained. I am tasting this from Bottle Lott No L93300197 and it is classic, generating all I expect and now demand. A national treasure. *40%*

Alberta Premium 25 Years Old (95) n24 t23 f23 b25. Faultless. Absolutely nothing dominates. Yet every aspect has its moment of conquest and glory. It is neither bitter nor sweet, yet both. It is neither soft nor hard on the palate yet both elements are there. Because of the 100% rye used, this is an entirely new style of whisky to hit the market. No Canadian I know has ever had this uncompromising brilliance, this trueness to style and form. And, frightening to think, it could be improved further by bottling at least 46% and un-chillfiltered. For any whisky lover who ever thought Canadian was incapable of hitting the heights among the world's greats. *40%. Alberta Distillers.*

Alberta Premium 30 Years (88.5) n23 t23.5 f20 b22. It doesn't take much to tip the balance of a whisky this delicate on the nose and delivery. Five extra years in the cask has nudged the oak just a little too far. However, savour the nose and delivery which are to die for. *40%*

Alberta Premium Dark Horse (84) n18 t22 f22 b22. The blurb on the back says it is crafted for the "next generation of whisky connoisseur". Fine. But personally, I'd always shape a whisky for the true connoisseurs of today... I have not spoken to the blending team at Alberta to discuss this and, as the book has to be finished within a week or two, I won't get a chance. But this is the most extraordinary development in Canadian I have seen for a while. The nose is not great: it really does seem as though fruit cordial has been given the lead role. But the taste really does challenge, and I have to say there are many aspects I enjoy. It is as though some peated malt has been added to the mix as the finish does have distinctive smokiness. And the balance has been expertly worked to ensure the sugars don't dominate while the spices are persistent. But if it falls down anywhere, the over reliance on the fruit apart, is the fact that Alberta makes the best spirit in Canada by a very great distance....yet someone has forgotten to ensure that fact is made clear in the taste and the nose especially. *45%*

Alberta Rye Whisky Dark Batch Blended Rye (86) n19 t23 f22 b22. A veritable fruitcake of a whisky – and about as moist and sultana-laden as you'll ever find. Not sure about that bitter-tobacco most un-Canadian nose, though. 45% (90 Proof)

Alberta Springs Aged 10 Years (83) n21 t21 f20 b20. Really appears to have had a bit of a flavourectomy. Sweet but all traces of complexity have vanished. *40%*.

Barton's Canadian 36 Months Old (78) n19 t20 f19 b20. Sweet, toffeed, easy-going. *40%*

Bowman's Canadian Whisky (90.5) n22 t22 f23.5 b23. A delicious blend for chocoholics. *40%*

Black Velvet (78) n18 t20 f20 b20. A distinctly off-key nose is compensated for by a rich corn and vanilla kick on the palate. But that famous spice flourish is a distant memory. Another big caramel number. *40%*

Caldera Distilling Hurricane 5 Whisky batch no. 0001 (87.5) n21.5 t22 f22 b22. Silky, soft. But lashings of toffee and sugars. Decent spices balance things up a little. *40% (80 proof)*

Campbell & Cooper Aged a Minimum of 36 Months (84.5) n21.5 t22 f20 b21. Huge flavour profile. An orchard of oranges on the nose and profound vanilla on delivery. *40%*

Canadian Club 100 Proof (89) n21 t23 f22 b23. If you are expecting this to be a high-octane version of the standard CC Premium, you'll be in for a shock. This is a much fruitier dram with an oilier body to absorb the extra strength. An entertaining blend. *50%.*

Canadian Club 100% Rye (92) n23 unmistakable pure rye grain but of the muted variety, rather than the chipped crunchy, fruity style. Slightly exotic, with a slight coconut and pineapple slant to the aroma, though the weightier oak plus some caramels offer good balance; t23.5 initially salivating as the rye bites, the delivery soon turns an oilier corner. The sugars are molassed, the grain are firm and increasingly toasty; **f22.5** late liquorice and a little bitterness from both the tannins and caramels. Long and remains substantial; **b23** will be interesting to see how this brand develops over the years. Rye is not the easiest grain to get right when blending differing ages and casks with varied histories: it is an art which takes time to perfect. This is a very attractive early bottling, though my money is on it becoming sharper in future vattings as the ability to show the grain above all else becomes more easily understood. Just so wonderful to see another excellent addition to the Canadian whisky lexicon. 40% (80 proof)

Canadian Club Chairman's Select 100% Rye (81.5) **n21 t21.5 f20 b19**. A bemusing whisky. The label proudly announces that here we have a whisky made from 100% rye. Great news: a Canadian eagerly anticipated. But the colour – a deep orange – looks a bit suspicious. And those fears prove well founded when the taste buds, as well as the nose, go looking for the rye influence in vain. Instead we have a massive toffee effect, offset by some busy spice. Colouring has ruined many a great whisky...and here we have a painful example. What a waste of good rye... 40%

Canadian Club Premium (92) **n23 t22.5 f23 b23.5**. A greatly improved whisky which now finds the fruit fitting into the mix with far more panache than of old. Once a niggardly whisky, often seemingly hell-bent on refusing to enter into any form of complexity: but not now! Great spices in particular. I'm impressed. 40%

Canadian Club Aged 6 Years (88.5) **n21.5 t22 f22.5 b22.5**. Not at all bad for a Canadian some purists turn their nose up at as it's designed for the American market. Just brimming with mouth-watering enormity and style. Dangerously moreish. 40%

Canadian Club Reserve Aged 10 Years (86) **n20 t22 f21.5 b22**. Odd cove, this. The nose is less than welcoming and offers a hotchpotch of somewhat discordant notes giving a jumbled message and less than well defined statement of intent. Decent delivery, though, shifting through the gears with some impressive and sultry fruit tying in well with a rare grain onslaught found in Canadian these days. The finish, though, just can't steer away from the rocks of bitterness, alas. Again, as so often appears to be the case with CC, the spices star. 40%

Canadian Club Classic Aged 12 Years (91.5) **n22 t24 f21.5 b23.5**. A confident whisky which makes the most of a honeycomb theme. 40%

Canadian Club Aged 20 Years (92.5) **n24 t21 f23.5 b23**. In previous years, CC20 has ranked among the worst whiskies I have tasted, not just in Canada, but the world. Their current bottling, though, is not even a distant relation. Sure, it has a big sherry investment. But the sheer elan and clever use of spice make this truly magnificent. Possibly the most pleasant surprise in my latest trawl through all Canada's whiskies. 40%

Canadian Five Star Rye Whisky (83) **n21 t22 f20 b20**. An entirely tame, well behaved Canadian which celebrates the inherent sweetness of the species. That said, the immediate impact on the palate is pretty delicious with a quick, flash explosion of something spicy. But it is the deft, satin-soft mouthfeel which may impress most. 40%

Canadian Hunter (85.5) **n20.5 t21 f22 b22**. Remains truly Canadian in style. The toffee has diminished, allowing far more coffee and cocoa to ensure a delightful middle and finish. 40%

Canadian Mist (78) **n19 t20.5 f18.5 b20**. Much livelier than previous incarnations despite the inherent, lightly fruited softness. 40%

Canadian Pure Gold (82) **n21.5 t20.5 f20 b20**. Full-bodied and still a notably lush whisky. The pure gold may have more to do with the caramel than the years in cask but the meat of this whisky still gives you plenty to chew over. I especially enjoy the gradual building of spices. 40%

Canadian Spirit (78) **n20 t20 f19 b19**. A real toffee-fest with a touch of hard grain around the edges. 40%. Carrington Distillers (Alberta Distillers).

Caribou Crossing Single Barrel (84) **n20 t22.5 f20 b21.5**. While the nose offers an unholy battle between some apple-fruity rye notes and dry, dusty caramel, there is a real pulsating delivery with the sharper spices helped along the way by the silkiness of the body. Though the caramel offers a toffee-fudge backdrop, a countering dry date sweetness does more than enough to keep it at bay. However, the finish dulls out as the caramel gains the upper hand, though the twitching spices do ensure a light, throbbing beat. An enjoyable Canadian, undoubtedly, I am somewhat perplexed by it. There is no reference to the barrel number so you won't know if you are buying from different casks. Also, if it is single barrel what is the point of the caramel? If it is to make all the casks taste the same, or similar, then why not just blend them together. A badly missed opportunity. 40%. Sazerac.

Centennial 10 Year Limited Edition (88.5) **n21.5 t23 f22 b22**. Retains its usual honey-flavoured breakfast cereal style, but the complexity has increased. Busy and charming. 40%

Century Reserve 8 Years Old Premium (82) **n20 t21 f20 b21**. Clean vanilla caramel. 40%

Century Reserve Custom Blend 15 Years Plus (88.5) **n21.5 t22 f23 b22**. After two days of being ambushed in every direction, or completely steamrollered by Canadian caramel, my tastebuds are in total shock. Caramel kept to an absolute minimum so that it hardly registers at all. Charming and refined drinking. *40%*

Century Reserve 21 Years Old (91.5) n23.5 t23 f23 b22. Quite beautiful, but a spirit that is as likely to appeal to rum lovers as whisky ones. *40%*

Century Reserve Custom Blend lot no. 1525 **(87) n21.5 t22 f21.5 b22.** An enjoyable whisky which doesn't quite reach its full potential. *40%*

Corby's Canadian 36 Months Old (85) n20 t21 f22 b22. Attractive with fine bitter-sweet balance and I love the late spice kick-back. *40%. Barton. Interesting label: as a keen ornithologist, I had no idea there were parrots in Canada. Must be related to the Norwegian Blue.*

Crown Royal (86) n22 t23.5 f19.5 b21. The Crown has spoken and it has been decreed that this once ultra grainy old whisky is taking its massive move to a silky fruitiness as far as it can go. It was certainly looking that way last time out; on this re-taste (and a few I have unofficially tasted) there is now no room for doubt. If you like grape, especially the sweeter variety, you'll love this. The highpoint is the sublime delivery and starburst of spice. The low point? The buzzy, unhappy finale. The Grain Is Dead. Long Live The Grape! *40%*

◈ **Crown Royal** bott code: 318 B4 2111 **(87.5) n22 t23 f21 b21.5** Carries on in the same style as above. But at least the finish is a lot happier now with welcome ulmo honey extending further and the spices also working overtime. Still a little residual bitterness shows more work is required but, unquestionably, keep on this course and they'll soon be getting there. *40%*

Crown Royal Black (85) n22 t23 f18.5 b21.5. Not for the squeamish: a Canadian which goes for it with bold strokes from the off which makes it a whisky worth discovering. The finish needs a rethink, though. *45%*

Crown Royal Cornerstone Blend (85.5) n21 t22 f21 b21.5. Something of a mish-mash, where a bold spiciness appears to try to come to terms with an, at times, random fruity note. One of the most curious aspects of this quite different whisky is the way in which the weight of the body continues to change. Intriguing. *40.3% (80.6 proof)*

Crown Royal DeLuxe (91.5) n23.5 superbly crafted nose profile: crisp and flinty/soft and yielding in equal measures, weight and pace. A little light pepper also counters the friendly sugars; **t23** the delivery is all about cracking, rock hard grains and fruity muscovado sugars. Some ripe pears sweeten further, though there is an oaky-caramel bitterness creeping in after the midpoint; **f22.5** mainly about the spiced vanilla; **b22.5** some serious blending went into this. Complex. *40% (80 proof)*

Crown Royal Hand Selected Barrel (90) n22 quintessential Canadian: corn oil and vanilla; **t23** concentrated corn oil relieved by ulmo honey, spice and the inevitable toffee; **f22.5** corn oil... and toffee. Thankfully the spice carries on buzzing; **b22.5** more Canadian than a punch in the kisser from an ice hockey player. *51.5%*

Crown Royal Hand Selected Barrel (94.5) n23.5 beautifully made and bursting with really high octane tannins, mainly around a deep vanilla. Lively, clean, with a gorgeous ice cream and muscovado sugar mix; **t24** ohhhh...!! So sensual. Corn oils, presumably, enriched in maple syrup at first before moving to a more earthy heather honey as the weight becomes far more of a factor; **f23.5** spices out to just the right degree. **b23.5** if this is a single barrel, it boasts extraordinary layering and complexity *51.5% (103 proof)*

Crown Royal Limited Edition (87) n22 t22.5 f20.5 b22. A much happier and productive blend than before with an attractive degree of complexity but the more bitter elements of the finish have been accentuated. *40%*

◈ **Crown Royal Noble Collection Wine Barrel Finished** lot no. 0100-43-B1245 **(87) n21 t22.5 f21.5 b22** A friendly, juicy Canadian. Because Canada is allowed to add things into their whisky – and fruit has (sadly) been a popular choice for the last 20 years – it is hard to see how a wine barrel finish will make a notable difference to a blend. So, perhaps the little cleverly diffused spice apart, it is a major ask to tell the difference between this and standard practice. My guess is the spice. Unquestionably pleasant, though. Despite the late bitterness. *40.5%.*

Crown Royal Northern Harvest Rye bott code L5085 N3 **(97.5) n25 t24.5 f23.5 b24.5** This is the kind of whisky you dream of dropping into your tasting room. Rye, that most eloquent of grains, not just turning up to charm and enthral but to also take us through a routine which reaches new heights of beauty and complexity. To say this is a masterpiece is barely doing it justice. *45%*

Crown Royal Northern Harvest Rye bott code L5099 **(94) n23** caramel plays a surprisingly leading role in this rye-swept drama. The sharpness of the grain, which helped carry all before it last year, here is blunted, though when its does finally come through it does so with restrained power, and some complimentary herbal and apple notes for good measure; **t24** ah here we go! Much more like it as the stunning good looks of last year's World Whisky of the Year come into focus on delivery, with a stunning salivating note for company. Moves swiftly into mocha mode and then begins to ship in friendly caramels; **f23.5** long, though the spices are not what are expected, nor the expected contrast between the brittle rye and later oils and caramels; **b23.5** superb whisky but just missing the magic of its all-conquering sister bottling. 45%.

Crown Royal Northern Harvest Rye bott code L5134 **(97) n24** much more like it: assertive, yet somehow relaxed and entreating. But here the rye glistens in the house three-dimensional style, at once bristling and bullish, yet kissing and caressing. The spices seem to have extra weight; **t24.5** mouth-watering as the rye hits the palate with the same force as the Demerara sugars. A real backbone to the rye which is in its crunchiest form, though with a few extra sugars up its sleeve from last year's winner; **f24** the spices assert themselves but without any force. The crisp rye and Demerara sugars, like the vanillas which have slowly assembled, seem to simply melt always leaving a spicy outline of where they once were; **b24.5** a close relation to last year's whisky sensation: Jim Murray's Whisky Bible World Whisky of the Year 2016. Not quite as truly incredible, but the link can very obvious and much more than bottling L5099 and a few others I have subsequently tasted, though not in controlled conditions like this. And, having just this moment tasted last year's winner, I can can confirm that it is a close-ish miss. Absolutely brilliant and helps carry on the work of its sister bottling in waking up the world to how good the very top Canadian whiskies can be... 45%.

◈ **Crown Royal Northern Harvest Rye** bott code: L6022 N5 **(96) n24.5** playful and delicate: the rye offers clarity but only half its normal rigidity, so allowing the oaky vanillas in for unprecedented scope; **t23.5** caramels delivery first, then an immediate – though quick explosion of brittle rye. The caramels returns even more supercharged and with them a plethora of sweeter notes, especially maple syrup and ulmo honey; **f24** the sugars pick up a duskier molasses note but still the sweet vanillas roll on, the rye signature peaking and fading at irregular intervals while the spices, though present, keep a low profile **b24.5** Breathtakingly clean rye with not a single note out of place, or the odd bitter note where not required: indeed, this is the sweetest Northern Harvest Rye I have yet encountered. Beautifully weighted and paced, this bottling does lack the stunning grain intensity which won it worldwide acclaim two years ago. 40%

Crown Royal Special Reserve (96) n24 t24 f24 b24 Complex, well weighted and simply radiant: it is like looking at a perfectly shaped, gossamer clad Deb at a ball. The ryes work astonishingly well here (they appear to be of the malted, ultra-fruity variety) and perhaps to best effect after Alberta Premium, though now it is a hard call between the two. 40%

Crown Royal XR Extra Rare lot no. L7064 N4 **(93.5) n24 t23 f23 b23.5.** Just about identical to the previous bottle above. The only difference is on the finish where the rye, fortified with spice, decides to hang back and battle it out to the death; the toffee and vanilla make a controlled retreat. Either the same bottling with a slightly different stance after a few years in the bottle, or a different one of extraordinary high consistency. 40%

Crown Royal XO (87.5) n22 t21 f22.5 b22. With an XO, one might have hoped for something eXtraOrdinary or at least eXOtic. Instead, we have a Canadian which carried on a little further where their Cask No 16 left off. Always a polite, if rather sweet whisky, it falls into the trap of allowing the Cognac casks a little too much say. Only on the finish, as the spices begin to find channels to flow into, does the character which, for generations, set Crown Royal apart from all other Canadians begin to make itself heard: complexity. 40% WB15/398

Danfield's Limited Edition Aged 21 Years (95) n24 t24 f23.5 b23.5. A quite brilliant first-time whisky. The back label claims this to be small batch, but there is no batch number on the bottle, alas. Or even a visible bottling code. But this is a five star performer. 40%

Danfield's Private Reserve (84.5) n20 t21.5 f22 b21. A curious, non-committal whisky which improves on the palate as it goes along. An overdose of caramel (yawn!!) has done it no favours, but there is character enough for it to pulse out some pretty tasty spice. Seamless and silky, for all the toffee there underlying corn-rich clarity is a bit of a turn on. 40%

8 Seconds Small Batch (86) n20 t22 f22.5 b21.5. Fruity, juicy, luxurious. Perhaps one of the few whiskies on the market anywhere in the world today which could slake a thirst. 40%

Forty Creek Barrel Select (86.5) n21.5 t22 f21 b21.5. Thank goodness that the sulphur taint I had found on this in recent years has now vanished. A lush, enjoyable easy-goer, this juices up attractively at the start and ends with an almost sophisticated dry pithiness. 40%

Forty Creek Confederation Oak Reserve lot 1867-B **(94.5) n23.5 t24 f23.5 b23.5.** Those who tasted the first batch of this will be intrigued by this follow up. The shape and intensity profile has been re-carved and all now fits together like a jigsaw. 40%

Forty Creek Copper Pot Reserve (91.5) n23 t23.5 f22 b23. One of the beauties of John Hall's whiskies at Forty Creek is that they follow no set pattern in the whisky would: they offer flavour profiles really quite different from anything else. That is why they are worth that bit of extra time for your palate to acclimatise. Here you are exceptionally well rewarded... 43%

Forty Creek Double Barrel Reserve lot 247 (86) n21.5 t22.5 f20.5 b21.5. Juicy ride with plenty to savour early on. But something is slightly off balance about the finish. 40%

Forty Creek Port Wood Reserve lot 61 (95.5) n24.5 oh my word! Very highest quality Turkish Delight with some pretty top score chocolate; the fruit hangs off the frame full of juice and muscovado sugars. It demands spices...and gets them – with the right pizzazz! t24 the delivery is pure silk in texture and the most stunning fruit and spice on delivery. Hard to know whether to suck as it melts in the mouth, or chew as the background depth is outrageously nutty, with more cocoa to thicken. It is the astonishing spice that really mesmerises, as it is of almost perfect intensity; f23 dries into an attractive crushed grape pip dryness, again with the spices lingering; b24 John P Hall has got his ducks in a row. Magnificent! 45%

Forty Creek Three Grain (76) n19 t20 f18 b19. Not quite as well assembled as some Three grains I have come across over the last few years. There is a lopsidedness to this one: we know the fruit dominates (and I still haven't a clue why, when surely this of all whiskies, just has to be about the grains!) but the bitterness interferes throughout. If there have been sherry casks used here, I would really have a close look at them. 40%

Fremont Mischief Whiskey batch MPJ-0803, bott 11 (77) n19 t20 f19 b19. Though this was from the Mischief distillery in Seattle, USA, the whiskey was produced in Canada. Overly sweet, overly toffeed and bereft of complexity. Like Alberta Springs on a very bad day. 40%

Gibson's Finest Aged 12 Years (77) n18 t20 f19 b20. Unlike the Sterling, going backwards rather than forwards. This is way too syrupy, fruity and toffee impacted. Despite the very good spice, almost closer to a liqueur than a true whisky style. 40%

Gibson's Finest Rare Aged 18 Years (95.5) n24 t24.5 f23.5 b23.5 So far ahead of both Sterling and the 12, it is hard to believe they are from the same stable. But make no mistake; this is pure thoroughbred: truly world class. 40%

Gibson's Finest 100th Grey Cup Special Edition (87) n21 t23 f21 b22. When the label tells you there is a hint of maple, they aren't joking... 40%

Gibson's Finest Canadian Whisky Bourbon Cask Rare Reserve (89) n23 t21 f23 b22. A much better version than the first bottling, the depth this time being massively greater. 40%

Gibson's New Oak (88) n22 t21 f23 b22. Distinctly different from any other Canadian doing the rounds: the oak influence makes a wonderful and clever impact. 40%

Gooderham & Worts Four Grain blend no. A.A1129 (94) n23 complex. Four grains, indeed! Fruity, as so many Canadians today insist on being. But deeply complex tones abound, each understated and elegant. The rye just about shades it...; t24 superb! So salivating! Deep and forever interweaving, the sturdier grains flip between offering a crisp fruitiness and a starker spiciness, especially as the wheat strikes home; the muscovado sugars pulse their fruity rhythm; f23.5 now the wheat dominates as the spices begin to seriously warm up, radiating short, sharp pulses: love it! b23.5 four there's a jolly good whisky...worts and all...! 44.4%

⬥ **Gooderham & Worts Little Trinity Three Grain Blend** (94) n23.5 busy and toasty. A honeycomb sweetness with the subtlest lavender and sandalwood driving up the complexity; t24 succulent delivery: soft, with the myriad sugars dissolving on or soon after impact. A Manuka and ulmo honey mix, thinned by butterscotch but roused by spice; f23 long, vanilla dominated, but still allows the complex sugars to have their say; b23.5 beautifully complex but will still suit those with catholic tastes... 45%. Ultra-Rare Craft Series.

Hiram Walker Special Old (93) n22.5 t24 f23 b23.5. Even with the extra degree of all-round harmony, this remains the most solid, uncompromising Canadian of them all. And I love it! Not least because this is the way Special old has been for a very long time with obviously no intentions of joining the fruity bandwagon. Honest, first class Canadian. 40%

⬥ **Hiram Walker Special Old Rye Whisky** bott code L16123 (90.5) n22.5 where once the grain would bite back at you, we are now on softer ground, more date and walnut than big grain; t23 still juicy, but not in that resounding rock-hard rye-grainy way. We have moved into a chewier, then firmer molasses and spice fruitcake mode...the fruits, once missing from this blend, have arrived...; f22.5 wow! Adorable spices but still the mouth feel is lush even now with muscovado sugars and maple syrup countering the now sexy spice...; b22.5 once one of my daily drinking ryes when in Canada, this has changed course a little in recent years, going easier on the classic old rye itself and making up for it with a richer, sweeter, fatter mouth feel. Not the same magic, but still hard not to love... 40%.

J.P. Wiser's 18 Year Old db (94) n22.5 dusty, fruity, busy. Soft, fruity sawdust to the sugars; t24 excellent early bite, though the oils make their mark early. Salivating and silky despite the spice build and a little cocoa to accompany the fruit; f23.5 comfortable, with a pleasing acceleration of spice; b24 exceptionally creamy but maintains the required sharpness. 40%.

⟡ **J.P. Wiser's 18 Years Old** bott code 54SL24 L16341 (94) n23 t24 f23 b24 Some great blending here means this is a slight notch up on the bottling above, though the styles are almost identical. Main differences here concern the fruit aspect: more prolific and spicier on the nose and then added moist date on the delivery. Significantly, there is more honey on the longer finish, also. Remains a deliciously rounded and satisfying whisky. 40%.

⟡ **J. P. Wiser's 35 Year Old** (96) n23.5 spices abound and, thrillingly, at varying pitches and intensities. The softer tones are supplied by apple pie as well as rhubarb and custard, giving the most gentle fruitiness while a mix of black and red liquorice mixes comfortably with the molasses to underline the age; t24 that is rather wonderful: the landing is soft, but the grains are not lost in a sea of bland as could so easily happen. Instead, the palate is peppered with some of the spices so rampant on the nose but also layers of ulmo honey and muscovado sugars, ensuring a serious juiciness despite the years; f24 a slow burn of spice, something akin to rye in both crispness and fruitiness and vanilla; a little bitterness reveals some tiring oak; b24.5 many, many years ago I tasted Canadian older than this in the blending lab. But I have never seen it before at this age as an official bottling. What I had before me on the lab table could not have engineered this style, so this is as fascinating as it is enjoyable. 50%. Ultra-Rare Craft Series.

J.P. Wiser's De Luxe (86) n20 t22.5 f21.5 b22. Still nothing like the classic, ultra-charming and almost fragile-delicate Wiser's of old. But this present bottling has got its head partly out of the sand by injecting a decently oaked spiciness to the proceedings and one might even fancy detecting shards of fruity- rye brightness beaming through the toffeed clutter. Definitely an impressive turn for the better and the kind of Canadian with a dangerous propensity to grow on you. If they had the nerve to cut the caramel, this could be a cracker... 40%

⟡ **J. P. Wiser's Dissertation** (89) n22 good' rye theme to this, yet set with a slow burn of spice; t22 a caramel-wrapped dark horse. The intensity of the grain takes time to make its mark, but eventually does so in toasty style, with a sweetness which is more a smirk than a smile; f22 good toasty molasses and accompanying spice; b22.5 a distinctive and quite different style being handsome, a little rugged but always brooding. 46.1%.

J.P. Wiser's Double Still Rye (94) n23.5 the rye is gorgeously crisp, its natural fruity notes augmented by spearmint; t23.5 every bit as salivating and full-flavoured as the nose predicts. Not as crunchy, maybe, until the Demerara sugars ram themselves home. But the spices arrive in the first few moments and continue building until they become quite a force; f23.5 long, oily, with that spice still impacting positively; b23.5 big, superb rye: a genuine triumph from Wiser's. 43.4%

J.P. Wiser's Hopped Whisky (77) n18 t21 f19 b19. Sorry chaps: one has to draw the line somewhere. But, despite my deep love for great beer, as a whisky this really isn't my kind of thing. Oh, and by the way: been tasting this kind of thing from Germany for the last decade... 40%

J.P. Wiser's Last Barrels Aged 14 Years (94.5) n24.5 I think I could nose this until the end of time: so complex are the oak notes and the way they merge or interplay with the corn and other grains, it is like watching a dance - a ballet more like – being played out before the nose...; as for the notes you can pick out...more than I have room or time for here. But Turkish delight, green tea, rye and mint are those which perhaps have the most telling influence; t23.5 a two-toned delivery: sharp grain and sugar against a corn note of quicksand-ish qualities...; f23.5 long – the corn oils ensure that – with fabulous development of vanilla; b23.5 you don't need to be pulsing with rye to ensure a complex Canadian of distinction. 45%

J.P. Wiser's Legacy (95) n24 t24.5 f22.5 b22.5. When my researcher got this bottle for me to taste, she was told by the Wiser's guy that I would love it, as it had been specially designed along the lines of what I considered essential attributes to Canadian whisky. Whether Mr Wiser was serious or not, such a statement both honoured and rankled slightly and made me entirely determined to find every fault with it I could and knock such impertinence down a peg or two. Instead, I was seduced like a 16-year-old virgin schoolboy in the hands of a 30-year-old vixen. An entirely disarming Canadian which is almost a whisky equivalent to the finest of the great French wines in its rich, unfolding style. Complex beyond belief, spiced almost to supernatural perfection, this is one of the great newcomers to world whisky in the last year. It will take a glass of true magnificence to outdo this for Canadian Whisky of the Year. 45%

⟡ **J. P. Wiser's One Fifty** (86) n22 t21.5 f21.5 b21 The nose gives hope as heather honey and spices stir. But another Canadian too jammed packed with caramel to enjoy to the fullest, though there is an attractive, if slightly bland, golden syrup thread running through the piece. 43.4%. Commemorative Series.

J.P. Wiser's Red Letter 2015 Release Virgin oak finish **(90.5) n22.5 t22.5 f23 b22.5** Stubbornly refusing to return to its complex grain past, electing instead to stick to the silky route of more recent years. The sugars are kept in control – just. At times, a little touch and go: this style has been taken as safely as it can go... A backbone to this would be worth so many more points... *43.4%. ncf.*

J.P. Wiser's Reserve (75) n19 t20 f18 b18. The nose offers curious tobacco while the palate is uneven, with the bitterness out of tandem with the runaway early sweetness. In the confusion the fruit never quite knows which way to turn. A once mighty whisky has fallen. And I now understand it might be the end of the line with the excellent Wiser's Small Batch coming in to replace it. So if you are a reserve fan, buy them up now. *43%*

J.P. Wiser's Rye (84.5) n21 t22 f20.5 b21. Sweet, soft and easy going. The delivery is classic Canadian, with an enjoyable corn oil-vanilla oak mix which initially doesn't go easy on the sugars. The finish, though, is more brittle toffee. *40%*

◈ **J. P. Wiser's Rye 15 Year Old (89) n22** the nose owes much more to a rum style than rye: the golden syrup and molasses make their mark; **t22.5** chewy. Very chewy. More golden syrup and toffee with a late spice development; again a rum-type sheen; **f22.5** simple spice and toffee; **b22** doesn't do too much. But what it does do, it does big... *40%*

◈ **J. P. Wiser's Rye Triple Barrel** bott code L16331 54SL24 **(85.5) n22 t21.5 f21 b21** Three types of toffee barrel by the looks of it. Pleasant but lacking complexity. *45%.*

J.P. Wiser's Small Batch (90.5) n21.5 t24 f22 b23. A real oddity with the nose & taste on different planets. The fruity onslaught promised by the drab nose never materialises and instead we are treated to a rich, grainy explosion. It's the spices, though, that take the plaudits. *43.4%*

J.P. Wiser's Special Blend (78) n19 t20 f19 b19. A plodding, pleasant whisky with no great desire to offer much beyond caramel. *40%*

J.P. Wiser's Spiced Torched Toffee (35) n9 t9 f8 b9 Whisky by name and law. But an absurdly sweet liqueur indeed. As an adorer of true whisky all I can say is this is to Canadian what the Coen brothers' remake of The Ladykillers was to the 1955 Ealing original... *43%*

J.P. Wiser's Spiced Whisky Vanilla db **(51) n16 t12 f11 b12.** The policy of the Whisky Bible is to not accept any spiced distillate as, by definition, being whisky. Only Canadian can escape that ban, as they are allowed to put up to 9.09% of whatever into their spirit and still call it whisky. That does not mean to say I am going to like it, though. And, believe me when I tell you I really can't stand this cloyingly sweet liqueur-like offering. Indeed, it may have "whisky" on the label, but this is about as much that great spirit as I am the next Hollywood pin up. *43%*

J.P. Wiser's Triple Barrel (85.5) n22 t21.5 f21 b21. The barrels, whatever their number, appear to be no match for the big caramel theme. *40% (80 proof)*

James Foxe (77.5) n20 t19.5 f19 b19. James could do with putting some weight on... *40%*

◈ **Lot 40 Cask Strength (88.5) n23.5** some mixed messages here: stunning fruit rye of the top order comes at you from one angle while a vaguely discordant note clearly from the cask zeroes in from another; **t24** the delivery makes you purr with delight: the rye is bold and fruity giving you all you desire from pure rye whisky; the mid-ground becomes a little turbulent as the vanillas arrive; **f20** uncomfortable, clumsy and tangy. The tannins have not reacted too well to the rye as the oak mounts up; **b22** at last! Lot 40 at full strength! You will not read this anywhere (or anything to do with my many whisky creations over the last 25 years as journalists can sometimes be a pathetically narrow-minded and jealous bunch disinclined to tell the true story if it doesn't suit their own agenda) but when I first created the style for Lot 40 a great many years back the first thing I proposed was that it should be a rye at cask strength. The idea was liked in principle but regarded way too radical for its time and dropped. So I helped come up with a weaker but still excellent rye. This is a different style to what I had in mind as the oak gives a slant I would have avoided. But it gladdens my heart to see it nonetheless. *53%. Ultra-Rare Craft Series.*

◈ **Lot No. 40 Rye Whisky** bott code 54SL24 L16344 **(96) n24** simultaneously sweet and dry with the amalgamation of clove and spearmint heading the cast. The spices are subdued, but the dried orange peel isn't, nor the light molasses which give extra depth to the crisper muscovado sugars; only a hint of tobacco scratches off half a mark...; **t24** the last bottling brought forward the crisper rye elements for the entry. This does the exact opposite: the delivery is soft and semi-succulent, then perhaps the most powerful honey tones I have ever encountered on a whisky – you can almost pick out the pollen! – fills the mid-ground, before those brittle rye notes arrive with the spices; **f23.5** long, with a slow build of darker, weightier tannins to balance against the rye. The intense honey has calmed to a quieter, thinner ulmo honey caramelisation; **b24.5** now this is very close to the rye I had in mind when first involved in putting this whisky together the best part of a couple of decades ago. Much more complex and satisfying than the previous re-introduced bottling I encountered...which in itself was magnificent. Here, though, the honey I had originally tried to lasso has been brilliantly recaptured. Happy to admit: this is better than my early efforts. There really is a Lot going on... Classic! 43%.

Masterson's 10 Year Old Straight Rye batch 003 (96.5) n24 t24 f24 b24.5 A magnificent whisky without any shadow of doubt. Rye is my favourite whisky type and this displays the style to a degree of excellence which is truly memorable in terms of a commercial bottling. Someone has done an outstanding job in selecting these casks. Interesting, however, that they don't actually state on the bottle that this is Canadian and confuse things a little further by spelling it "whiskey". My understanding is that this is unmalted rye from the outstanding Alberta Distillery in Calgary. What is certain is that this is a true classic of its style. And not so much Masterson's but Masterful. 45%

◇ **Masterson's 10 Year Old Straight Rye Whiskey** barrel finished in American oak, batch no. P5A3 (94.5) n24 subdued rye, only now and again hitting the crisp, piercing, sugar-crunchy high notes. Instead, there is a lower-toned hum of the grain's fruitiness, heavy and happy to mix it with the spicier notes of the tannin. All rather slow-motion...but engrossing; t24 salivating from the very first moment: lots of orange peel and tart, fruity rye notes which head off into a more chocolatey lilt; the mix of vanillas and caramels running through the middle charms; f23 quietens much quicker than usual. Alberta rye with that vanilla thread becoming broader; the oak tires towards the end; b23.5 lovely, as always. But this batch of Alberta does not have three dimensional grain sharpness which can, on its day, set it apart. That said, just sit back and try and unravel the extraordinary complexity of this: a bit like peeling an onion. But any tears that form here will be ones of joy... 45% (90 proof).

◇ **Masterson's 10 Year Old Straight Rye Whiskey** barrel finished in French oak, batch no. P573 (92) n22.5 punchy tannin goes head-to-head with florid rye...some battle...; t24 well, that's different! At first the palate comes under a welter of blows from the chunky oak before the sugars step in en-masse to balance things out with the most vivid display of golden syrup and Demerara sugar; f23 the rye still tries to make a fight of it, but that tannin is determined to land the bigger blows; b23.5 just a question here about the terminology of straight rye here: matured in a pre-used bourbon barrels and finished in another oak entirely. Really? Something to ponder while enjoying this barn-storming, slightly over oaked rye. 45% (90 proof).

◇ **Masterson's 10 Year Old Straight Rye Whiskey** barrel finished in Hungarian oak, batch no. P5H3 (95.5) n23.5 sharp fruit – kumquat mainly – which stands out above the firm tannin; t24 hard and brittle delivery: the rye grain begins to wind itself up for the big one but finds itself cut short and muted by a butterscotch and high tannin surge; a secondary levels shows a consistent fruitiness helping to keep the salivation levels high; f24 thick chocolate and fluting rye; spices take their time to arrive but are warming and busy when they finally do; b24 a complex and truly delicious rye with a quick unique fingerprint. Spectacularly beautiful. 45% (90 proof).

Okanagan Spirits Rye (88.5) n23 t22.5 f21 b22. A crisp, quite beautiful whisky with a youthful strain. Sort the thin finish out and we'd have something to really remember! Not, by the way, a whisky distilled at their new distillery. 40%

Pendleton 1910 Aged 12 Years Rye (83) n21 t22 f20 b20. Pleasant enough. But if it wasn't for the small degree of spice pepping up this fruitfest, it would be all rather too predictable. 40%

◇ **Pendleton Director's Reserve 2017 Aged 20 Years** (90) n22.5 outwardly, soft fruit with a mildly spicy backbone. Look more carefully – giving it a good ten minutes of your time - and you'll find that it is soft fruit with a mildly spicy backbone...; t22 even softer on delivery than the nose – which barely seemed possible - with the fruit initially sweeter and seemingly free of the oak which generated the spice, and extra weight; the muscovado sugar and thick caramel detaches slightly and polishes the mid-ground; f22.5 dries and spices up to very attractive effect; b23 if you don't enjoy this super-soft blend I'll eat my Pendleton Fedora hat. But don't worry, I never have less than three or four of them at any one time... 40% (80 proof).

Pendleton Midnight (78) n20 t21 f18 b19. Soft and soothing. But far more rampant fruit than grain. In fact, hard to detect the grain at all... 45% (90 Proof).

Pike Creek (92) n22 t23.5 f23 b23.5 A whisky that is more effect over substance, for this really has to be the softest, silkiest world whisky of 2015. And if you happen to like your taste buds being pampered and chocolate is your thing, this Canadian has your name written all over it. 40%

Pike Creek 10 Years Old finished in port barrels (80) n21.5 t22.5 f17 b19. The delivery is the highlight of the show by far as the fruit takes off backed by delicate spices and spongy softness. The nose needs some persuading to get going but when fully warmed, gives a preview of the delivery. The furry finish is a big disappointment, though. 40%

◇ **Pike Creek 10 Year Old Rum Barrels Finish** bott code 54SL24 L16174 EW07:30 (86.5) n22 t22.5 f20 b22 A far happier fellow than the Port finish, for sure – even though the slight furriness on the finale is a bit of a bore. Before reaching that point, though, there is a velvet revolution involving much honey. *42%*.

⬦ **Pike Creek 21 Year Old Single Malt Cask Finish** (87.5) n21 t23.5 f21.5 b21.5 Pleasant and fruity. As silky as you like with a moist date and spiced theme. But, doubtless, through the cask finish, the age and accompanying complexities seems to have been lost in translation somewhere... *45%. Ultra-Rare Craft Series.*

Potter's Special Old a blend of 5 to 11 year old rye whisky (91) n23.5 t23 f22 b22.5. More Canadian than a hockey punch-up – and, for all the spice, somewhat more gentle, too. *40%*

Rich and Rare (79) n20 t20 f20 b19. Simplistic and soft. One for toffee lovers. *40%*

Rich and Rare Reserve (86.5) n19.5 t21 f23.5 b22.5. Actually does what it says on the tin, certainly as to regard the "Rich" bit. But takes off when the finish spices up and even offers some ginger cake on the finale. Lovely stuff. *40%*

Royal Canadian Small Batch (88) n22 t22.5 f21.5 b22. A big Canadian with a pleasing silk and steel pulse. *40%. Sazerac.*

Royal Reserve Gold (94.5) n24 t23.5 f23 b24. Retains its position as a classy, classy Canadian that is an essay on balance. Don't confuse this with the much duller standard bottling: this has been moulded in recent years into one of the finest – and among its country's consumers - generally most underrated Canadians on the market. *40%*

Sam Barton Aged 5 Years (83.5) n19 t21.5 f22 b21. Sweet session whisky with a lovely maple syrup glow; some complexity on the finish. Friendly, hospitable: impossible not to like. *40%*.

Schenley Golden Wedding (92) n22 t24 f22 b23. Like a rare, solid marriage, this has improved over time. Always consistent and pleasant, there now appears to be a touch of extra age and maturity which has sent the complexity levels up dramatically. Quite sublime. *40%*

Seagram's Canadian 83 (86.5) n21 t22 f21.5 b22. A vastly improved blend which has drastically cut the caramel to reveal a melt-in-the-mouth, slightly crisp grain. There are some citrusy edges but the buttery vanilla and pleasing bite all go to make for a chic little number. *40%*

Seagram's VO (91) n22 t23.5 f22.5 b23. With a heavy heart I have to announce the king of rye-enriched Canadian, VO, is dead. Long live the corn-dominant VO. Over the years I have seen the old traditional character ebb away: now I have let go and have no option other than to embrace this whisky for what it has become: infinitely better than a couple of years back; not in the same league as a decade ago. But just taking it on face value, credit where credit is due. This is an enjoyably playful affair, full of vanilla-led good intention, corn and complexity. There is even assertive spice when needed and the most delicately fruity edge...though not rye-style. Thoughtfully blended and with no little skill, I am impressed. And look forward to seeing how this develops in future years. A treat which needs time to discover. *40%*

⬦ **Union 52** (90.5) n23 never quite encountered Canadian with quite this profile: a little eucalyptus and mixed spice embeds into the vanilla and orange peel...; t23 succulent delivery: fat mouth feel which ramps up the sugars, first from a muscovado fruitiness to a heftier molasses. Hickory and cough sweet through the late middle as a tannin effect takes hold; f22.5 the spices which have built substantially through the middle carry on despite the dramatic reduction of sugars; b23 a very different type of Canadian which is as busy as it gets. *40%*.

Western Gold Canadian Whisky (91) n23 t23 f22.5 b22.5. Clean and absolutely classic Canadian: you can't ask for much more, really. *40%*

White Owl (77.5) n19 t19.5 f20 b19. White whisky: in others words, a whisky the same colour as water. To both nose and taste somewhat reminds me of the long gone Manx whisky which was casks of fully matured scotch re-distilled and bottled. Sweet and pleasant. But I doubt if connoisseurs will give two hoots... *40%*

Windsor (86) n20 t21 f23 b22. Pleasant but the majority of edges found on the Canadian edition blunted. Some outstanding, almost attritional, spice towards the middle and finale, though. Soft and desirable throughout: a kind of feminine version of the native bottling. *40%*.

WhistlePig 15 Year Old Straight Rye Whiskey finished in Vermont Estate oak (90) n22 t23.5 f22 b22.5 Distinctive and delicious. *46% (92 proof)*

Canadian Wheat Whisky

Masterson's 12 Year Old Straight Wheat Whiskey batch 001 (92) n23 t23 f22.5 b23.5 Chose this as my 1,000th new whisk(e)y for Jim Murray WB 2015 because a couple of years back I uncorked their Rye...and tasted everything a great Canadian should be: indeed, it was a contender for my World Whisky of that year. Here I have their new wheat bottling. Not the blockbuster the rye bottling was: rye when distilled and matured to its fullest possibilities probably cannot be touched by any other grain. But this is a soft, melodious whisky, perfect for ending any day on a quiet high... *50% WB15/380*

Japanese Whisky

How fitting that in the age when the sun never sets on where whisky is produced it is from the land of the Rising Sun that the finest can now be found.

Recently Japan, for the first time ever, won Jim Murray's World Whisky of the Year with its insanely deep and satisfying Yamazaki Sherry Cask(s) 2013, a result which caused predicted consternation among more than a few. And a degree of surprise in Japan itself. The industry followed that up last year by commanding 5th spot with a very different but truly majestic specimen of a malt showing a style unique to Japan. How impressive.

It reminded me of when, about 15 years ago, I took my old mate Michael Jackson and a smattering of non-friends on a tour of the Yoichi distillery on Hokkaido, pointing out to them that here was a place where a malt could be made to mount a serious challenge to the best being made anywhere in the world. While there, a local journalist asked me what Japanese distillers could learn from Scotland. I caused a bit of a sharp intake of breath – and a pathetically gutless but entirely characteristic denial of association by some whisky periodical executive or other who had a clear idea which side his bread was buttered – when I said it was the other way round: it was more what the Scots could learn from the Japanese.

The reason for that comment was simple: the extraordinary attention to detail and tradition that was paid by Japanese distillers, those at Yoichi in particular, and the touching refusal to cut costs and corners. It meant that it was the most expensive whisky in the world per unit of alcohol to produce. But the quality was astonishingly high – and that would, surely, eventually reap its rewards as the world learned to embrace malt whisky made away from the Highlands and islands of Scotland which, then, was still to happen. Ironically, it was the Japanese distillers' habit to ape most things Scottish – the reason why there is a near century-old whisky distilling heritage there in the first place - that has meant that Yoichi, or the magnificent Hakushu, has yet to pick up the Bible's World Whisky of the Year award I expected for them. Because, sadly, there have been too many bottlings over the last decade tainted by sherry butts brought from Spain after having been sulphur treated. So I was also pleasantly surprised when I first nosed – then nosed again in near disbelief – then tasted the Yamazaki 2013 sherry offering. There was not even the vaguest hint that a single one of the casks used in the bottling had been anywhere near a sulphur candle. The result: something as close to single malt perfection as you will have found in a good many years. A single malt which no Scotch can at the moment get anywhere near and, oddly, takes me back to the Macallans of 30 years ago.

A Japanese custom of refusing to trade with their rivals has not helped expand their export market. Therefore a Japanese whisky, if not made completely from home-distilled spirit, will instead contain a percentage of Scotch rather than whisky from fellow Japanese distillers. This, ultimately, is doing the industry no favours at all. The practice is partly down to the traditional work ethics of company loyalty and an inherent, and these days false, belief, that Scotch whisky is automatically better than Japanese. Back in the late 1990s I planted the first seeds in trying to get rival distillers to discuss with each other the possibility of exchanging whiskies to ensure that their distilleries worked more economically. So it can only be hoped

Yamazaki ▲

● Osaka

● Fukuoka

Key	
●	**Major Town or City**
▲	Distillery

Jim Murray's Whisky Bible Japanese Whisky of the Year Winners	
2004	Pure Malt Black
2005	Nikka Single Cask Coffey Grain Whisky 1991
2006	The Cask of Hakusha 1989
2007	Nikka Single Cask Coffey Grain Whisky 1992
2008	Hanyu King of Diamonds
2009	Nikka Single Cask Coffey Grain Whisky 1992
2010	TSMWS 116.4
2011	Karuizawa 1967 Vintage
2012	Hibiki Aged 21 Years
2013	Hanyu Final Vintage 2000
2014	SMWS Cask 116.17 (Yoichi) 25
2015	Yamazaki Single Malt Sherry 13
2016	Yamazaki Mizunara
2017	Yamazaki Single Malt Sherry 16
2018	Nikka Coffey Malt Whisky

that the deserved lifting of the 2015 Jim Murray's Whisky Bible World Whisky of the Year crown, and the hitherto unprecedented international press it received has helped put the spotlight back on the great whiskies coming from the east. Because unless you live in Japan, you are likely to see only a fraction of the fabulous whisky produced there. The Scotch Malt Whisky Society should have a special medal struck as they have helped in recent years with some memorable bottlings from Japan, single cask snapshots of the greatness that is still to be be fully explored and mapped. A two-pronged attack would be useful: one by whisky outlets to actively track down and stock the widest Japanese stock they can afford, though because of the clamour for all things Yamazaki this now at last appears to be happening. And the distillers themselves, always on the conservative side of marketing, probably through a misplaced lack of belief, show us what they have.

And I don't mean just with malts. Because, even better still would be if the outside world could have at last access to the higher class blends produced there. But the Japanese whisky industry have themselves been slow coming forward. Just perhaps, with Yamazaki atop the world's whisky very own Mount Fuji, there are the first signs that they are at last ready to unleash upon us those hidden, majestic whiskies of Japan.

Single Malts
CHICHIBU

Chichibu 'On The Way' dist 2010 bott 2013 db **(93) n**23.5 **t**24 **f**22.5 **b**23. A malt which has already travelled far... 58.50%.

Chichibu 'The Peated' 2013 dist 2010 bott 2013 db **(96.5) n**24.5 **t**24.5 **f**23 **b**24.5 Clean, elegant, does exactly what it says on the tin...and a lot, lot more besides... 53.5%.

Chichubu Port Pipe dist 2009 bott 2013 db **(66) n**17 **t**18 **f**15 **b**16. A port pipe in an awful, off-key storm. 54.5%. Number One Drinks Company.

ePower Chichibu Double Barrel Mizunara heads hogshead & hard charred new barrels, dist 2012, bott 2015 **(88) n**21.5 off key: the various tones cannot find their own pitch...; **t**23.5 so enormous is the delivery, it is hard to know where to start. Probably the explosion of oak, which then leads to a stupendous sigh of varying sugars, though mainly differing muscovado types; **f**21 the discord on the nose is mirrored on the finish as it bitters out; **b**22 were it not for the spices, the sugars might have proved a little too much. Though not always hitting quite the right notes, this is big, profound malt. 61.1%

Ichiro's Malt Chichibu Chibidaru dist 2010, bott 2014 db **(92) n**22.5 husky malt: thick set with a mix of leather, dates and barley; **t**23.5 serious sugars arrive in an initial wave of dark muscovado; major oils ensure a big chewy depth; **f**23 long, as a malt with this amount of oil and sugar just must be; back to a few dried dates now, too. Lovely stuff...perfect for a cold night or even, perhaps, if you have a cold...; **b**23 this distillery certainly understands the meaning of "intense"... 53.5%. Number One Drinks Company.

Ichiro's Malt Chichibu Floor Malted 2009 **(85.5) n**22 **t**22.5 **f**20 **b**21. Big, pre-pubescent malt and barley statement, but barely in unison. Bitterness on the finish is unchecked. 50.5%.

Ichiro's Chichibu Peated 2009 **(91.5) n**23 **t**23.5 **f**22 **b**23. You can stand your chopsticks up in this one...works so beautifully in so many department. 50.5%

Ichiro's Malt Chichibu Peated 2015 dist 2010, bott 2015 db **(95) n**23.5 so young and gristy! Yet meticulously clean and, with its light citrus touch, aligned in style to the south Islay malts; **t**24 or with this degree of oil, Caol Ila...wow! **f**23.5 long, with the gristy sugars working a long rhythmic magic. The smoke remains intense; **b**24 had I tasted this blind, I would have mistaken it for an Islay. Quite sublimely made malt. As astonishing as it is beautiful... 62.5%. Number One Drinks Company.

Number One Asama 1999/2000 (71) n17 **t**19 **f**16 **b**19. Sulphured. 46%

FUJI GOTEMBA 1973. Kirin Distillers.

The Fuji Gotemba 15 Years Old db **(92) n**21 **t**23 **f**24 **b**24. Quality malt of great poise. 43%. Kirin.

HAKUSHU 1973. Suntory.

Hakushu Single Malt Whisky Aged 12 Years db **(91.5) n**22.5 **t**23.5 **f**22.5 **b**23. About identical to the 43.3% bottling. Please see those tasting notes for this little beauty. 43.5%

Hakushu Single Malt Aged 12 Years db **(91) n**22 **t**23 **f**23 **b**23. An even more lightly-peated version of the 40%, with the distillery's fabulous depth on full show. 43.3%

The Hakushu Single Malt Whisky Aged 15 Years Cask Strength db **(95) n**24 **t**23 **f**24 **b**24. Last time round I lamented the disappointing nose. This time perhaps only a degree of over eagerness from the oak has robbed this as a serious Whisky of the Year contender. No matter how you look at it, though, brilliant!! 56%

The Hakushu Single Malt Whisky Aged 25 Years db **(93) n**23 **t**24 **f**23 **b**23. A malt which is impossible not to be blown away by. 43%

The Hakushu Single Malt Whisky Sherry Cask bott 2014 db **(96.5) n**24.5 there we have it: a masterclass in what clean, untainted sherry butts are all about. A thousand levels of fruit intensity without a single off note – or even peculiar but unmistakable background hint of an off note which points to a sulphur problem at the very end of a whisky - when nearly all the other flavours have vanished. It is not there. The only problem, being over picky, is that the character of the distillery itself is hard to locate: the concentrated dates, plums and raisins, topped, naturally, with warming spice, means the malt itself has vanished somewhat...; **t**24 there we go. Find a comfortable chair for this one...it is going to take a very long time. Wave upon wave of fruitiness, all of varying degrees of intensity, roll and then crash over the palate. In its quiet moments, that's the odd toasted honeycomb mingling with butterscotch and vanilla bits – something other than fruit are apparent...; **f**24 long, elegant, gorgeously clean...but even more late toasted raisin...; **b**24 theoretically, this should have been World Whisky of the Year.

After all, Yamazaki – a distillery I regard as very slightly eclipsed in quality by Hakushu – won it last year using, like this, strictly unsulphured sherry butts. This is magnificent. One of the great whiskies of the year, for sure. However, the intensity of the grape has just strayed over that invisible line by a few molecules between being a vital cog and a shade too dominant. It is the finest of lines between genius and exceptional brilliance. *48%. ncf.*

Suntory Pure Malt Hakushu Aged 20 Years db (94) n23 t24 f23 b24. A hard-to-find malt, but find it you must. Yet another huge nail in the coffin of those who purport Japanese whisky to be automatically inferior to Scotch. *56%*

Scotch Malt Whisky Society Cask 120.8 Aged 13 Years 2nd fill hogshead, dist 31 Dec 00 (85.5) n21 t23 f20 b21.5. Some typical Hakushu flourishes but done down by a disappointing cask which added too much tired tang than is appreciated. Unusually salty and sharp, this should have been destined for a blend. *63.1%. sc. 250 bottles.*

HANYU

Ichiro's Malt Aged 20 Years (95.5) n24 t24 f23.5 b24. No this finish; no that finish. Just the distillery allowed to speak in its very own voice. And nothing more eloquent has been heard from it this year. Please, all those owning casks of Hanyu: for heaven's sake take note... *57.5%*

Ichiro's Malt Aged 23 Years (92.5) n23 t23.5 f23 b23. A fabulous malt you take your time over. *58%*

KARUIZAWA 1955. Mercian.

Karuizawa Pure Malt Aged 17 Years db (90) n20 t24 f23 b23. Brilliant whisky beautifully made and majestically matured. Neither sweetness nor dryness dominates, always the mark of a quality dram. *40%*

The Spirit Of Asama sherry cask (71.5) n17 t19 f17 b18.5. Sulphur hit. *48%.*

The Spirit Of Asama sherry cask (75) n18 t20 f18 b19. Lots of sultanas. Sweet. Pleasant in part. But it isn't just Scotland suffering from poor sherry butts. *55%.*

Scotch Malt Whisky Society Cask 132.6 Aged 12 Years refill butt. diss 32 Dec 2000. (84.5) n21 t23 f19 b21.5. Fabulous delivery. Surprisingly youthful in some ways, with echoes of a new make maltiness, but there is a vividity to the barley which really deserves better than the nose appears a little perfunctory and dull and a finish which is disappointingly tangy. *63% nc ncf sc.*

KIRIN

Kirin 18 Years Old db (86.5) n22 t22 f21.5 b21. Unquestionably over-aged. Even so, still puts up a decent show with juicy citrus trying to add a lighter touch to the uncompromising, ultra dense oak. As entertaining as it is challenging. *43%. Suntory.*

KOMAGATAKE

Komagatake 1992 Single Cask American white oak cask, cask no. 1144, dist 1992, bott 2009 db (93.5) n24.5 t23 f22.5 b23.5. You know when you've had a glass of this: beautiful and no shrinking violet. *46%. Mars.*

MIYAGIKYO *(see Sendai)*

NIKKA *(Coffey Still)*

◇ **Nikka Coffey Malt Whisky** db (96) n23.5 well spiced and clearly structured oak ensures the more ethereal malt is well grounded. Demerara sugars balance the accounts; t25 this is where this Coffey still goes into overdrive: the delivery is liquid silk. I detect two different honeys at work – ulmo and acacia with a little maple syrup or god measure. This mingles breathtakingly well with the light Malteser candy style malt and milk chocolate, all these beautiful tones clinging to the palate as the spices gather and intensify; f23.5 just a little oak bitterness and tiredness on the finish proves this is not some kind of erotic dream. There is still enough of the main feature though to take this malt to a happy ending...; b24 not quite the genius of the 12-year-old. But still one of the most tactile and sensual whiskies on the world whisky stage today. *45%.*

Nikka Whisky Single Coffey Malt 12 Years db (97) n23.5 t25 f24 b24.5. The Scotch Whisky Association would say that this is not single malt whisky because it is made in a Coffey still. When they can get their members to make whisky this stunning on a regular basis via their own pots and casks, then perhaps they should pipe up as their argument might then have a single atom of weight. *55%*

◈ **Nikka Whisky Single Malt Miyagikyo** db **(91.5)** n22 vanilla blancmange; t23 excellent early malt thrust on delivery, then thickens and allows in all kinds of fudgy sugars; f22.5 light spice, tannin and fudge; b23 thick, clumsy but deliciously malty. *45%.*

SENDAI 1969. Nikka.

Scotch Malt Whisky Society Cask 124.4 Aged 17 Years 1st fill butt, dist 22 Aug 96 **(94)** n24 where do you start with the fruit, apart from prize Melton Hunt Cake? Certainly the dates are juicy and the sultanas a little burnt. I think there is some oak in there somewhere...; t24 brilliant delivery with sublime bitter-sweet toasty-roasty delivery. Yes, there is oak there, and it comes up as hickory straight after the burnt raisin on delivery; f23 still toasted – burnt toast, in fact. But with a plum jam (that's gone easy on the sugar) covering it thickly; b23 if there is a complaint to be made, it is that, at times, one might forget that this is a whisky at all, resembling instead a glass of highest quality oloroso. *60%. sc. 479 bottles.*

Scotch Malt Whisky Society Cask 124.5 Aged 23 Years 1st fill hogshead, dist 12 Dec 90 **(96)** n23.5 countless layers: the majority oak-based, but so many hues and tones, ranging from chalky to sub-bourbon; big dry dates to spicy fruitcake – without the fruit but with plenty of molasses; t24.5 hold on tight: molasses concentrate has been dipped in tannin juice. Somehow, while the spices pepper you and the oak makes you draw breath, barley pops up out of nowhere for a juicy interlude...; f24 time and time again you think it is going OTT with the oak, then those molasses notes, as well as dark chocolate, intervene...brinkmanship of the sexiest kind...; b24 this isn't just how to grow old gracefully, but with style while making one hell of a statement! *66.7%. sc. 142 bottles.*

SHINSHU MARS

Mars Whisky Single Malt Komagatake Sherry & American White Oak 2011 db **(79.5)** n19 t22 f18.5 b20. My heart bleeds, as the high class – and intensity – of the malt is outstanding. Sadly, the sherry butt does not match the excellence of the distillate and results in a Mars that is slightly out of orbit... *57%*

◈ **ePower Komagatake** American Puncheon, dist Mar 13, bott Sept 16 **(96)** n23.5 think Malteser candy, sans chocolate. Crush it in your hand, then double the malt aroma...there you go! Add to that a light liquorice/hickory mix, all spiced up. Now we are getting there...; t24 it isn't just the clarity of the malty intensity on delivery which blows you away, but the unbelievably well controlled oil which magnifies it even further...; then there are the sugars – a light ulmo and orange blossom honey mix that really get the juices flowing; f24 at last the light tannins from the oak are able to make a weighty contribution, the vanillas seemingly adding to the intensity; b24.5 just fabulous for Japan's most malty whisky to be able to show its most intense and unique form without it being wrecked by awful sherry butts. What a malty treat this is! You could not ask for more. Well, actually you could...another glass, that is... *56.9%.*

SHIRAKAWA

Shirakawa 32 Years Old Single Malt **(94)** n23 t24 f23 b24. Just how big can an unpeated malt whisky get? The kind of malt that leaves you in awe, even when you thought you had seen and tasted them all. *55%. Takara.*

WHITE OAK DISTILLERY

White Oak Akashi Single Malt Whisky Aged 8 Years bott 2007 db **(74.5)** n18.5 t19.5 f17.5 b19. Always fascinating to find a malt from one of the smaller distilleries in a country. And I look forward to tracking this one down and visiting, something I have yet to do. There is certainly something distinctly small still about this one, with butyric and feintiness causing damage to nose and finish. For all the early malty presence on delivery, some of the off notes are a little on the uncomfortable side. *40%*

YAMAZAKI 1923. Suntory.

The Yamazaki Single Malt Whisky Aged 12 Years bott 2011 db **(90)** n23 t22 f22.5 b22.5. A complex and satisfying malt. *43%*

The Yamazaki Single Malt Aged 18 Years db **(96)** n23 a sublime blend of Java and Sumatra coffees, enriched by vanilla and even toastier tannins. The sugars, a mix of treacle and maple syrup try not to steal the show, but nearly do...; t24.5 oh, oh, oh...!!!! Possibly the softest yet most compelling delivery this year: the grape is doused in busy, ever intensifying spice, the toasty vanillas in those subtle sugars spotted on the nose. Overripe plums, juicy dates, stewed prunes...and all the time the spice buzzes, the sugars salivate; f24 long, with just a slow wind down of the previously intense fruit notes. The juices just keep on gushing, but meet almost perfectly with toasty, slightly milky mocha notes; the final strands are praline wafer...with chocolate fruit and nut, too; **b24.5** for its strength, probably one of the best whiskies in the world. And one of the most brilliantly and sexily balanced, too... All told, one glass is equal to about 45 minutes of sulphur-free satisfaction... 43%

Suntory Pure Malt Yamazaki 25 Years Old db (**91**) **n23 t23 f22 b23**. Being matured in Japan, the 25 years doesn't have quite the same value as Scotland. So perhaps in some ways this can lay claim to be one of the most enormously aged, oak-laden whiskies that has somehow kept its grace and star quality. 43%

The Yamazaki Single Malt Whisky Mizunara Japanese oak cask, bott 2014 db (**97**) **n25** the unmistakable and one off aroma of Japanese oak: a form of slightly aggressive bourbon where the spices are as busy as the light liquorice and hickory. But the malt has a massive presence, though you have to look for it first. The sugars are typically crisp for this style of oak and there is something of the Malteser chocolate candy about this, too: absolutely unique; **t24** the sugars ram home first – a peculiar mix of crystallised heather and ulmo honey with molasses – but the sweetness immediately limited by the more toffeed and tannic qualities of the intense oak. Polite spices are not too far behind and they, too, have a vaguely American quality, only a little more prickly. A delicate oil ensures the sugars cover as much distance as possible; **f23.5** late on, the spices pulse a backdrop to the vaguely bittering oak; **b24.5** no other malt offers this flavour profile. And as there are now very few Japanese oak casks still in the industry it is a malt worthy of as long a time as you can afford it. A very special whisky of very high quality. 48%

The Yamazaki Single Malt Whisky Puncheon bott 2013 db (**87**) **n22 t22 f21 b22**. Not to be confused with former Millwall footballer Jason Puncheon who scored a hat-trick against Crystal Palace a couple of years back. Does not possess his guile, balance or explosive finish. Even so, a pleasant dram even if you'd like to see it do more than just offer a sugary glow offset by some half decent spices. 48%. ncf. WB15/179

The Yamazaki Single Malt Whisky Sherry Cask bott 2013 db (**97.5**) **n24.5** when they say sherry, they are not joking: huge oloroso signature, nutty, thick, dry as rounded as a snooker ball. A nose that was not uncommon in the warehouses of Scotland three decades ago, but now as rare as...well, an unsulphured sherry butt...; **t24.5** every bit as silky as the nose promises. The sugars, spices, plum walnut cake and moist Melton Hunt Cake combine for something rather special; **f24** long, juicy dates, more walnuts, sultanas as big as a small planet...a light, teasing spice; **b24.5** one of the first sherry casks I have seen from Japan not in any way, shape or form touched by sulphur for a very long time. It is as if the oloroso cask was still half filled with the stuff when they filled with Yamazaki spirit. If anyone wants to find out roughly what the first Macallan 10-year-old I had in 1975 tasted like, then grab a bottle of this... 48%. ncf. WB15/180

Yamazaki Single Malt Sherry Cask 2016 Edition db (**96.5**) **n24.5** I was thinking: "I could nose this all day"...about half an hour ago... The richest, cleanest, most intense sherry with just enough tannin to poke its way through and ensure a more solid, spicy platform around which the bounteous fruit can hang; **t24** dense, both from the rich, full-bodied distillate as well as the sherry concentrate. Imagine a fruitcake reduced and reduced again and then you have some idea what is going on here: there is not just intense grape at work but juicy dates, over-ripe figs and molasses enough to power a W C Fields sketch....; **f24** not sure where the middle ends and the finish begins. Certainly dries as the tannins gather further momentum but always fruit residue, withered and intense, is in close company; **b24** a work of art. The oils, though, are markedly younger in style than the imperious 2013 edition. 48%

The Yamazaki Single Malt Whisky db (**86**) **n22 t22 f21 b21** A tame, malty affair which, after the initial barley burst on delivery, plays safety first. 43%

YOICHI 1934. Nikka.

◇ **Nikka Whisky Single Malt Yoichi** db (**91**) **n24** the sharpness, the sheer chutzpah and three dimensional quality of the barley has to be nosed to be believed. Neither sweet nor dry it is both. Or somewhere in between...it is almost impossible to tell. Nose prickle and fruit: green, under-ripe gooseberry. And something else besides...? **t24** Oh, oh, oh...the salivation That malt...THE malt. Oh, my word....!!! The palate is cleaned in a way those old enough to remember (and appreciate) the original non-age statement Glenfiddich managed. Except this has so much extra depth it defies logic. The sugars are on the lighter, melt-in-the-mouth gristy cum icing sugar variety, but there are spices which rise early have a commanding presence; **f21** long slow fade of stunning malt seemingly unchallenged until that very, very late furry intervention...; **b22** When 20 years ago I declared this as one of the top five distilleries in the world, I was considered quite mad: it was not sitting in Scotland. Indeed, the fact I had named a Japanese whisky at all, irrelevant of it being Yoichi, made a lot of people question my sanity and professionalism. Until they tasted this then unheard of malt for the first time, that is. In the last decade Yoichi have helped neither me nor themselves by bringing out far too many bottlings which have betrayed a sulphur weakness from a sherry butt. This bottling may have a borderline flaw, also – even I am struggling to be sure. But what I know for a fact is that of all the single malts worldwide I have tasted for this Bible 2018, this was the first to make me yelp and then stretch with pleasure, glass in hand raised as I rode the ecstasy. Yes, there is the most minor blemish on the very end of the finale, and for that it will not be contending for World Whisky of the Year. But, it was a very close run thing... 45%.

Yoichi Key Malt Aged 12 Years "Peaty & Salty" db (95) n23 t25 f23 b24. Of all the peated whiskies of the world, only Ardbeg can stand shoulder to shoulder with Yoichi when it comes to sheer complexity. Here is an astonishing example of why I rate Yoichi in the best five whiskies in the world. Forget the odd sulphur-tarnished bottling. Get Yoichi in its natural state with perfect balance between oak and malt and it delivers something approaching perfection. And this is just such a bottling. 55%. Nikka.

Yoichi 15 Years Old batch 06I08B db (91.5) n22 t23.5 f23 b23. For an early moment or two possibly one of the most salivating whiskies you'll get your kisser around this year. Wonderfully entertaining yet you still suspect that this is another Yoichi reduced in effect somewhat by either caramel and/or sherry. When it hits its stride, though, becomes a really busy whisky that gets tastebuds in a right lather. But I'm being picky as I know that this is one of the world's top five distilleries and am aware as anyone on this planet of its extraordinary capabilities. Great fun; great whisky – could be better still, but so much better than its siblings... 45%

Yoichi 20 Years Old db (95) n23 t23 f25 b24. I don't know how much they charge for this stuff but either alone or with mates get some for one hell of an experience. What makes it all the more remarkable is that there is a slight sulphury note on the nose: once you taste the stuff that becomes of little consequence. 52%. Nikka.

Scotch Malt Whisky Society 116.18 Aged 18 Years refill butt, dist 2 Feb 94 (89) n23 t23 f21 b22. Not one of the truly great Yoichis in its traditional style but a salty, oaky beast of a malt. 64.4%. nc ncf sc. 410 bottles.

Scotch Malt Whisky Society Cask 116.19 Aged 20 Years virgin oak puncheon, dist 2 Feb 94 (92) n23 so much bourbon-style honey...the oak influence is majestic; t23.5 fizzing tannins scorch the palate. But those sublime sugars – the manuka honey in particular – kiss everything better; f22.5 bitters very slightly as those tannins take a stranglehold; b23 huh! Just shows what happens when you don't concentrate. Poured the whisky, half noticing the colour. Expected a big blast of sherry (or something adjacent and pretty unpleasant) and got this enormous kick of bourbon. Beautiful; suits the distillery style perfectly. 61.3%. sc.

Scotch Malt Whisky Society Cask 116.20 Aged 26 Years virgin oak puncheon, dist 7 Nov 87 (82.5) n20 t22 f20 b20.5. I'm sure some people will do cartwheels to celebrate this no holds barred malt. For me, simply too old: when you get this degree of eucalyptus on the nose and finish, it has gone way beyond its best before date. Decent sugars briefly on delivery and burnt ones at the death, plus the odd phenolic moment. But more like an over aged rum. 61.6%. sc.

Vatted Malts

All Malt (86) n22 t21 f21 b22. The best example by a mile of an almost unique style of vatted whisky: both malt and "grain" are distilled from entirely malted barley, identical to Kasauli malt whisky in India. Stupendous grace and balance. 40%. Nikka.

All Malt "Pure & Rich" (89) n22 t24 f21 b22. Not unlike some bottlings of Highland Park with its emphasis on honey. If they could tone down the caramel it'd really be up there. 40%. Nikka.

Hokuto Pure Malt Aged 12 Years (86) n20 t22 f22 b22. An oaky threat never materialises: excellent mixing. 40%. Suntory.

Ichiro's Malt Double Distilleries bott 2010 (86.5) n22.5 t22 f21 b21. Some imperious barley-rich honey reigns supreme until a bitter wood note bites hard. 46%. Venture Whisky Ltd.

Ichiro's Malt Mizunara Wood Reserve (76) n19 t21 f18 b19. I have my Reservations about the Wood, too... 46%. Venture Whisky Ltd.

Malt Club "Pure & Clear" (83) n21 t22 f20 b20. Another improved vatting, much heavier and older than before with bigger spice. 40%. Nikka.

Mars Maltage Pure Malt 8 Years Old (84) n20 t21 f21 b22. A very level, intense, clean malt with no peaks or troughs, just a steady variance in the degree of sweetness and oak input. Impossible not to have a second glass of. 43%. Mars.

Nikka Malt 100 The Anniversary Aged 12 Years (73) n18 t19 f18 b18. The depressing and deadly fingerprint of sulphur is all over this. Shame, as the spices excel. 40%

Nikka Pure Malt Aged 21 Years batch 08I18D db **(89)** n23 t22.5 f21.5 b22. By far the best of the set. 43%

Nikka Pure Malt Aged 17 Years batch 08I30B db **(83)** n21 t21 f20 b21. A very similar shape to the 12-years-old, but older - obviously. Certainly the sherry butts have a big say and don't always do great favours to the high quality spirit. 43%

Nikka Pure Malt Aged 12 Years batch 10I24C db **(84)** n21.5 t21 f20 b21.5. The nose may be molassed, sticky treacle pudding, but it spices up on the palate. The dull buzz on the finish also tells a tale. 40%

Pure Malt Black batch 02C58A **(95)** n24 t23 f23 b25. Well, if anyone can show me a better-balanced whisky than this you know where to get hold of me. You open a bottle of this at your peril: best to do so in the company of friends. Either way, it will be empty before the night is over. 43%. Nikka.

Pure Malt Black batch 06F54B **(92)** n24 t24 f21 b23. Not the finish of old, but everything else is present and correct for a cracker! 43%. Nikka.

Pure Malt Red batch 02C30B **(86)** n21 t21 f22 b22. A light malt that appears heavier than it actually is with an almost imperceptible oiliness. 43%. Nikka.

Pure Malt Red batch 06F54C **(84)** n21 t22 f20 b21. Oak is the pathfinder here, but the oily vanilla-clad barley is light and mouth-watering. 43%. Nikka.

Pure Malt White batch 02C30C **(92)** n23 t24 f22 b23. A big peaty number displaying the most subtle of hands. 43%. Nikka.

Pure Malt White batch 06J26 **(91)** n22 t23 f22 b24. A sweet malt, but one with such deft use of peat and oak that one never really notices. Real class. 43%

Pure Malt White batch 10F46C **(90)** n23 t23 f22 b22. There is a peculiarly Japanese feel to this delicately peated delight. 43%

Southern Alps Pure Malt (93) n24 t23 f22 b24. This is a bottle I have only to look at to start salivating. Sadly, though, I drink sparingly from it as it is a hard whisky to find, even in Japan. Fresh, clean and totally stunning, the term "pure malt" could not be more apposite. Fabulous whisky: a very personal favourite. 40%. Suntory.

Suntory Pure Malt Whisky Kiyosato Field Ballet 25th Anniversary (88) n23.5 gentle: over-ripe plums, green apple and red liquorice; t22.5 the malt surges on delivery for a very sharp introduction; soon calms down with a vague Indian candy sweetness and a more assertive bourbon style; goes tits up as the end approaches; f20 an annoying tang as the balance is compromised; b22 so frustrating: a whisky destined for greatness is side-tracked by some off-kilter casks. 48%

Super Nikka Vatted Pure Malt (76) n20 t19 f19 b18. Decent and chewy but something doesn't quite click with this one. 55.5%. Nikka.

Taketsuru Pure Malt 12 Years Old (80) n19 t22 f19 b20. For its age, heavier than a sumo wrestler. But perhaps a little more agile over the tastebuds. Lovely silkiness impresses, but lots of toffee. 40%. Nikka.

Taketsuru Pure Malt 17 Years Old (89) n21 t22 f23 b23 Not a whisky for the squeamish. This is big stuff – about as big as it gets without peat or rye. No bar shelf or whisky club should be without one. 43%. Nikka.

Taketsuru Pure Malt 21 Years Old (88) n22 t21 f22 b23. A much more civilised and gracious offering than the 17 year old: there is certainly nothing linear about the character development from Taketsuru 12 to 21 inclusive. Serious whisky for the serious whisky drinker. 43%. Nikka.

Zen (84) n19 t22 f22 b21. Sweet, gristy malt; light and clean. 40%. Suntory.

Japanese Single Grain
CHITA

Suntory Single Grain Chita Distillery db **(92.5)** n23.5 one of the typical characteristics of this distillery's nose, indeed its overall character, is its unusual ability to appear soft and yielding yet with a rod of iron at the very same time. It is this dual personality that can be both a blessing from heaven and a curse when blending. But as a single grain it works a treat as the complexity levels are upped immediately, allowing the vaguely bitter-sweet grain and oaks to perform their various tricks; maple syrup also lends a helping hand; t23 just like the nose, there is a bipolar feel to the shape of this grain, the delivery consumed by soft oils, yet a far more rigid note apparent, to which the oak appears to attach. The sugars – or light honey to be more precise – is in line with the silkier oils; **f22.5** soft oils persist but the oak turns a little bitter; **b23** now that's more like it! Far more down the track of the Chita I have tasted through the years than the SMWS bottling. Then again, this is the brand new official distillery version, so perhaps no surprises there... 43%. *Available only in Nagoya Prefecture, Japan.*

KAWASAKI

Kawasaki Single Grain sherry butt, dist 1982, bott 2011 db (95.5) **n23.5 t24 f24 b24** My usual reaction to seeing the words "sherry" and "whisky" when in the context of Japanese whisky, is to feel the heart sinking like the sun. Sulphur is a problem that is no stranger to their whiskies. This, however, is a near perfect sherry butt, clean and invigorating. Grain or malt, it makes no difference: excellent spirit plus excellent cask equals (as often as not) magnificence. 65.5%.

NIKKA

Nikka Coffey Grain Whisky db (94.5) **n23.5** molten muscovado sugar; **t24** soft oils carry the thinned golden syrup aloft. Almost a semi-liqueur, but with that indefinable whiskyness which sets it apart.; **f23** the slight bitterness of the cask jolts the serenity of the oily sugars; **b24** whisky, from any part of the globe, does not come more soft or silky than this... 45% ⊙⊙

Blends

Black Nikka Aged 8 Years (82) **n20 t21 f21 b20.** Beautifully bourbony, especially on the nose. Lush, silky and great fun. Love it! 40%. *Nikka.*

The Blend of Nikka (90) **n21 t23 f22 b24.** An adorable blend that makes you sit up and take notice of every enormous mouthful. Classy, complex, charismatic and brilliantly balanced. 45%

Evermore (90) **n22 t23 f22 b23.** Top-grade, well-aged blended whisky with fabulous depth and complexity that never loses its sweet edge despite the oak. 40%. *Kirin.*

Ginko (78.5) **n20.5 t20 f19 b19.** Soft – probably too soft as it could do with some shape and attitude to shrug off the caramel. 46%. *Number One Drinks Company.*

Golden Horse Busyuu Deluxe (93) **n22 t24 f23 b24.** Whoever blended this has a genuine feel for whisky: a classic in its own right and one of astonishing complexity and textbook balance. 43%. *Toa Shuzo. To celebrate the year 2000.*

Hibiki (82) **n20 t19 f23 b20.** The grains here are fresh, forceful and merciless, the malts bouncing off them meekly. Lovely cocoa finale. A blend that brings a tear to the eye. Hard stuff – perfect after a hard day! Love it! 43%. *Suntory.*

Hibiki 50.5 Non Chillfiltered 17 Years Old (84) **n22 t22 f20 b20.** Pleasant enough in its own right. But against what this particular expression so recently was, hugely disappointing. Last year I lamented the extra use of caramel. This year it has gone through the roof, taking with it all the fineness of complexity that made this blend exceptional. Time for the blending lab to start talking to the bottling hall and sort this out. I want one of the great whiskies back...!! 50.5%. *Suntory.*

Hibiki Aged 30 Years (88) **n21 t22 f22 b23.** Still remains a very different animal from most other whiskies you might find: the smoke may have vanished somewhat but the sweet oakiness continues to draw its own unique map. 43%

Hokuto (86) **n22 t24 f19 b21.** A bemusing blend. At its peak, this is quite superb, cleverly blended whisky. The finish, though, suggests a big caramel input. If the caramel is natural, it should be tempered. If it is added for colouring purposes, then I don't see the point of having the whisky non-chillfiltered in the first place. 50.5%. ncf. *Suntory.*

Imperial (81) **n20 t22 f19 b20.** Flinty, hard grain softened by malt and vanilla but toffee dulled. 43%. *Suntory.*

Kakubin (92) **n23 t23 f22 b24.** Absolutely brilliant blend of stunningly refreshing and complex character. One of the most improved brands in the world. 40%. *Suntory.*

Kakubin Kuro 43° (89) **n22 t23 f22 b22.** Big, chewy whisky with ample evidence of old age but such is the intrusion of caramel it's hard to be entirely sure. 43%. *Suntory.*

Kakubin New (90) **n21 t24 f21 b24.** Seriously divine blending: a refreshing dram of the top order. 40%.

Kirin Whisky Tarujuku 50° (93) **n22.5 t24 f23 b23.5.** A blend not afraid to make a statement and does so boldly. A sheer joy. 50%. *Kirin Distillery Co Ltd.*

Master's Blend Aged 10 Years (87) **n21 t23 f22 b21.** Chewy, big and satisfying. 40%.

New Kakubin Suntory (see *Kakubin New*)

Nikka Master Blend Blended Whisky 12 Years Old 70th Anniversary (94) n24 t23 f24 b23. An awesome blend swimming in top quality sherry. Perhaps a fraction too much sweetness on the arrival, but I am nit-picking. A blend for those who like their whiskies to have something to say. And this one just won't shut up. *58%. Nikka.*

⬦ **Nikka Whisky From The Barrel** db (91) n22.5 happy to coast on the caramels but allowing a sharper malt punctuation; t23 salivating, and masterfully intense... as usual. Excellent molasses sub theme, then that sublime layering of lighter malts; the spices and honey come into play about halfway through and dovetail sublimely; f22.5 long, with rich spiced toffee; b23 I have been drinking this for a very long time – and still can't remember a bottle that's ever let me down. *51.4%.*

Nikka Whisky Tsuru Aged 17 Years (94) n23 t24 f23 b24. Unmistakingly Tsuru in character, very much in line, profile-wise, with the original bottling and if the caramel was cut this could challenge as a world whisky of the year. *43%*

Robert Brown (91) n22.5 t23 f22.5 b23. Just love these clean but full-flavoured blends: a real touch of quality here. *43%. Kirin Brewery Company Ltd.*

Royal 12 Years Old (91) n23 t23 f22 b23. A splendidly blended whisky with complexity being the main theme. Beautiful stuff that appears recently to have, with the exception of the nose, traded smoke for grape. *43%*

Royal Aged 15 Years (95) n25 t24 f22 b24. Unquestionably one of the great blends of the world that can be improved only by a reduction of toffee input. Sensual blending that every true whisky lover must experience: a kind of Japanese Old Parr 18. *43%*

Shirokaku (79) n19 t21 f20 b19. Some over-zealous toffee puts a cap on complexity. Good spices, though. *40%. Suntory.*

Special Reserve 10 Years Old (94) n23 t24 f23 b24. A beguiling whisky of near faultless complexity. Blending at its peak. *43%. Suntory.*

Special Reserve Aged 12 Years (89) n21 t24 f21 b23. A tactile, voluptuous malt that wraps itself like a sated lover around the tastebuds, though the complexity is compromised very slightly by bigger caramel than the 10-y-o. *40%. Suntory.*

Suntory Old (87) n21 t24 f20 b22. A delicate and comfortable blend that just appears to have over-simplified itself on the finale. Delicious, but could be much better than this. *40%*

Suntory Old Mild and Smooth (84) n19 t22 f21 b22. Chirpy and lively around the palate, the grains soften the crisp malts wonderfully. *40%*

Suntory Old Rich and Mellow (91) n22 t23 f23 b23. A pretty malt-rich blend with the grains offering a fat base. Impressive blending. *43%*

Super Nikka (93) n23 t23 f23 b24. A very, very fine blend which makes no apology whatsoever for the peaty complexity of Yoichi malt. Now, with less caramel, it's pretty classy stuff. However, Nikka being Nikka you might find the occasional bottling that is entirely devoid of peat, more honeyed and lighter in style (21-22-23-23 Total 89 – no less a quality turn, obviously). Either way, an absolutely brilliant day-to-day, anytime, any place dram. One of the true 24-carat, super nova commonplace blends not just in Japan, but in the world. *43%. Nikka.*

Super Nikka Rare Old batch 02I18D (90.5) n22 t23 f22.5 b23. Beautiful whisky which just sings a lilting malty refrain. Strange, though, to find it peatless. *43%. Nikka.*

Torys (76) n18 t19 f20 b19. Lots of toffee in the middle and at the end of this one. The grain used is top class and chewy. *37%. Suntory.*

Torys Whisky Square (80) n19 t20 f21 b20. At first glance a very similar blend to Torys, but very close scrutiny reveals slightly more "new loaf" nose and a better, spicier and less toffeed finale. *37%.*

Tsuru (93) n23 t24 f22 b24. Gentle and beautifully structured, genuinely mouthwatering, more-ish and effortlessly noble. If they had the confidence to cut the caramel, this would be even higher up the charts as one of the great blends of the world. And with Japanese whisky becoming far more globally accepted and sought after, now would be a very good time to start. As it is, in my house we pass the ceramic Tsuru bottle as one does the ship's decanter. And it empties very quickly. *43%. Nikka.*

The Whisky (88) n22 t22 f21 b23. A rich, confident and well-balanced dram. *43%. Suntory.*

White (80) n19 t21 f20 b20. Boring nose but explodes on the palate for a fresh, mouth-watering classic blend bite. *40%. Suntory.*

Za (79) n19 t21 f19 b20. Some lively boisterous grain offers a suet-pudding chewiness. A little bitter on the finish. *40%. Suntory.*

European Whisky

The debate about what it means to be European was one that seemingly never ended. That was until June 23rd 2016 when the people of Britain firmly decided that it should and they weren't. By contrast, the discussion on how to define the character of a European whisky is only just beginning.

And as more and more distilleries open throughout mainland Europe, Scandinavia and the British Isles, the styles are becoming wider and wider.

Small distillers in mainland Europe, especially those in the Alpine area, share common ground with their US counterparts in often coming late into whisky. Their first love, interest and spirit had been with fruit brandies. It seemed that if something grew in a tree or had a stone when you bit into it, you could be pretty confident that someone in Austria or California was making a clear, eye-watering spirit from it somewhere.

So perhaps it is not surprising that the whiskies which each year seem now to get the highest and most consistent marks are those built purely with whisky in mind. Mackmyra in Sweden. Penderyn in Wales. The aged whiskies representing Gold Cock in the Czech Republic came from state-built distilleries when the land was still Czechoslovakia. But, above all, it is becoming clear now that it is the English Whisky Company which has risen to the top and challenging all others to match the excellence of their malts. Norfolk may be most famous for its Christmas-culled poultry, but the whisky of St George's Distillery is no turkey.

To ram home this point they have, for the fourth year running walked off with wth European Whisky of the Year (Multiple Casks) and this year held on to their overall European Whisky of the Year title. This time with their staggering Pot Still. There is a pattern now: the smaller distileries of Langatun in Switzerland, Belgian Owl (an owl which has been growing in size in recent years) and Kornog are the ones you just know will give the serious players like St George's, Penderyn, Mackmyra and the medium-sized Stauning in Denmark a run for their money.

And there are new players on the scene, like the Cotswold Distillery just a short distance from me and The Lakes. Both in England, producing European whisky. How exciting. How ironic!

Jim Murray's Whisky Bible European Whisky of the Year Winners

	European Whisky Multiple Casks	European Whisky Single Cask
2004	**Waldviester Hafer Whisky 2000**	N/A
2005	**Hessicher Whisky (German Bourbon-style Whisky)**	N/A
2006	**Swissky Exklusiv Abfullung**	N/A
2007	**Mackmyra Preludium 03 Svensk Single Malt Whisky**	N/A
2008	**Mackmyra Privus 03 Svensk Single Malt Whisky**	N/A
2009	**Old Buck 2nd Release (Finland)**	N/A
2010	Santis Malt Highlander Dreifaltigheit	**Penderyn Port Wood Single Cask**
2011	**Mackmyra Brukswhisky**	The Belgian Owl Aged 44 Months
2012	Mackmyra Moment "Urberg"	**Penderyn Bourbon Matured S C**
2013	**Penderyn Portwood Swansea City Special**	Hicks & Healey Cornish Whiskey 2004
2014	**Mackmyra "Glod" (Glow)**	Santis Malt Swiss Highlander
2015	**English Whisky Co. Chapter 14 Not Peated**	The Belgian Owl Single Malt '64 Months'
2016	English Whisky Co. Chapter 16	**Kornog Chwee'hved 14 BC**
2017	**English Whisky Co. Chapter 14**	Langatun 6YO Pinot Noir Cask
2018	Penderyn Bryn Terfel	**The Norfolk Parched**

AUSTRIA

ACHENSEE'R EDELBRENNEREI FRANZ KOSTENZER Maurach. Working.

Whisky Alpin Grain Whisky Hafer 3 Years Old bott code L1/2013 db **(86)** n21 t22.5 f21.5 b21. A distinctly bitter-sweet affair. Good body and molasses kick. 40%

Whisky Alpin Single Malt Double Wood 11 Years Old bott code L1/2005 db **(83)** n22.5 t23 f18 b21. Lime jelly with some of Lubek's top marzipan gets this off to a cracking start, but a sulphur flaw takes its toll. 40%

Whisky Alpin Single Malt Roggen 8 Years Old bott code L2/2008 db **(84)** n19 t23.5 f20.5 b21. The marked beauty on the later stages of the delivery makes up for slap-dash oils from far too wide a cut on distillation. But for a few brief seconds simply marvel at just how intense that rye becomes and the astonishing marriage it has with a blend of honeys. Ulmo and acacia lead the field. 45%

Whisky Alpin Single Malt Sherry Cask Finish 8 Years Old bott code L2/2008 db **(83.5)** n19 t22.5 f21.5 b21.5. Big on the nougat nose. But the grape and oils appear to flatten the remainder of this malt out. A brief juiciness which thoroughly, if briefly, entertains.... 40%

Whisky Alpin Single Malt Smoky Finish 5 Years Old bott code L2/2011 db **(88.5)** n20.5 t22.5 f23.5 b22 An altogether more rounded whisky from them. Still technically fraught, but it is as though they have made this from smoked chocolate malt, because the degree of cocoa on this borders the bewildering...and beautiful! 42%

ALPEN WHISKY DISTILLERIE Franstanz. Working.

Alpenwhisky Single Malt first fill rum casks, dist Aug 12, bott 22 Jan 16 db **(89.5)** n21 t23.5 f22 b23 If you are going to call yourself the Alps Distillery, then it is no bad idea to produce massive whisky. And they have done just that with no little panache and style. By no means technically perfect, and they can thank the sugars for keeping a tight hold of the feints, but the overall view is breath-taking... 55.4%

Alpenwhisky Single Malt first fill sherry casks, dist Mar 11, bott 06 Jun 15 db **(82.5)** n19 t21.5 f21 b21. Very curious. The wide cut causes a few problems on the nose and, naturally, the finish. But the sherry cask is untainted and very decent quality. Sadly, the fruit is just a little too gentle to control the feints adequately: a bit like a five foot nothing policeman trying to apprehend a 6 foot 6 inch thug. As the distillery over time learns to tighten the cut points, this will shape up into a very impressive whisky. 45.8%

⬥ **Alpenwhisky Single Malt Crocodile Toast** new barrel, dist May 13, bott 14 Feb 17 db **(88)** n21.5 feinty, but an ultimately attractive combination nougat, cream toffee and crushed Maltesers; t23 an unlikely degree of deliciousness to the intense liquorice and malt. Gorgeous oils and lovely controlled spice, too; f21.5 malty but the feints make their inevitable return; b22 yes, I know: technically it is far from perfect with a good smattering of feint, but there is something just irresistible about the richness of the malt and coffee... 55%

⬥ **Alpenwhisky Single Malt Double Wood** port cask, dist Feb 11, bott 06 Mar 17 db **(77)** n18 t20 f20 b19 Fruity, for sure. But only for the feint-hearted...46%

BRENNEREI GUGLHOF Hallein. Working.

Tauern Rogg Single Malt Whisky Sauternes cask no. 93, dist 2011 db **(88.5)** n21 t23 f22 b22.5 Soft, sweet and satisfying. 42%. sc.

BRENNEREI ROSSETTI Kolsassberg. Working.

Rossetti Young & Fine Pure Single Malt bott code L582 db **(89.5)** n22 t23 f22 b22.5 I remember well the previous Rossetti I tasted: a bit of a gaunt, pasty lad: youthful and undernourished. The boy has grown. Perhaps a slight buzz on the finish, but an altogether burlier and more rounded character altogether. 43.5%

BROGER PRIVATBRENNEREI Klaus. Working.

Broger Burn Out Single Malt Whisky bott code L BO-12 db **(95)** n23.5 t24 f23.5 b24 When I saw I was faced with six new samples of Broger, I strapped myself in. I remember from old, that this is a distillery of extremes, with wildly varying quality. So I went for this one first – taking the bull by the horns. Closed my eyes...took a mouthful...and lived! Actually, the label should be one of billowing smoke, as you want as little flame as possible when smoking malt. And perhaps one, also, of sugar cane. Because the Demerara on this is highly impressive. A very pleasant surprise. Oh, and didn't I mention it? This is a mini masterpiece... 42%

Broger Distiller's Edition Single Malt Whisky Madeira cask db **(66)** n16 t17 f16 b17. Oh dear... The S word in abundance. *60.7%. 165 bottles.*

Broger Medium Smoked Single Malt Whisky bott code L MS-09 db **(94)** n23.5 t23.5 f23 b24 There is no doubt that this distillery knows exactly how to make smoky whisky...because this is a very different, more subtle, style to their peated efforts. *42%*

Broger Riebelmais Whisky bott code L Wh-Bo09 db **(87.5)** n22 t22 f21.5 b22. An attractive whisky with some starchy elements. Good sugar balance and soft vanilla. Maybe needs to be a little less reduced to maximise the meagre oils. *42%*

Broger Riebelmais Whisky sherry cask, dist 2009, bott Dec 15 db **(91.5)** n23.5 t23 f22 b23 There you go. There was me saying their Riebelmais needed to be closer to cask strength for it to maintain its integrity...and next sample up: Riebelmais at cask strength. Immediately the unbroken oils make their mark for a far more complete whisky. First came across this rare type of distillate maybe a dozen years ago – always works better at a fuller strength. *58%. sc.*

Broger Triple Cask Single Malt Whisky bott code L Wh-Tr09 db **(86.5)** n21 t22 f21.5 b22. By no means bad whisky: it is obviously well made distillate. But you can have too much of a good thing and here the sugars are just a tad too much in your face. Enjoyable, for sure. But just borderline liqueur... *42%*

DACHSTEIN DESTILLERIE Radstadt. Working

Mandlberggut Rock Whisky 5 Years **(82)** n20 t21.5 f20 b20.5. Rock by name and nature. A massively crisp whisky, as though you are crunching on crystals of sugar and grains of barley. The slight tobacco note means it never quite gets into full song but if owners Bernhard and Doris perhaps slow the stills a tad and cut a little finer, they might have on their hands a rock of ages to come... db *40%.*

◈ **Mandlberggut Rock Whisky 5 Years** bott code LWh11 db **(87)** n21 t22.5 f21.5 b22 A distillery on the rise! Massive improvement since I last tasted them and here the malt positively shimmers on the palate. Still so delicate the oils have a slightly over-important say but the grassy-lemon effect is truly delicious. *40.3%.*

DESTILLERIE GEORG HIEBL Haag. Working.

George Hiebl Mais Whisky 2004 db **(93)** n23 t23.5 f23 b23.5. More bourbon in character than some American bourbons I know...!! Beautifully matured, brilliantly matured and European whisky of the very highest order, Ye..haahhhh!! *43%*

DESTILLERIE ROGNER Rappottenstein. Working.

Rogner Waldviertel Whisky 3/3 db **(86.5)** n20 t22 f22.5 b22. Plane sailing once you get past the tight nose. A beautiful display of crisp sugars and come-back-for more grainy juiciness. Lovable stuff, for all its gliches. *41.7%. ncf.*

DESTILLERIE WEIDENAUER Kottes. Working

Waldviertler Classic Haferwhisky bottle code L05 db **(88)** n21 t23.5 f21 b22.5. A busy oat whisky of no little distinction, despite the lightest degree of butyric. Still, they have been making from this grain for a long time... *42%*

Waldviertler Dinkelmalz Dinkelwhisky mit 2/3, bottle code L08 db **(83.5)** n20 t22.5 f20 b21. Big, boisterous and, at times, bruising. The spice is out in force, as you might expect. But despite the enormity of the character, the thicker-than-desired cut works against it – on the nose and finish especially. *42%*

Waldviertler Dinkelwhisky bottle code L09 db **(94)** n23 t23.5 f23.5 b24 A beautifully made and matured whisky. So, so subtle... *42%*

Waldviertler Hafermalz Haferwhisky mit 2/3 bottle code L09 db **(91)** n22 t23.5 f22.5 b23 Every last drop of flavour successfully extracted. Lovely! *42%*

Waldviertler Limited Edition Hafermalz bottle code L08 db **(94)** n22 t24.5 f23.5 b24 One of a type. Every whisky collector should hunt this down. Superb. *42%*

Waldviertler Maiswhisky 100% Maisbrand, bottle code L09 db **(88.5)** n21.5 t23 f22 b22. A busy whisky with reasonable pretentions towards a bourbon style. *42%*

Waldviertler Single Malt dunkel Hafer-Whisky bottle code L09 db **(81.5)** n20 t22 f19 b20.5. Massive flavours. But the over generous cut offers a metallic edge. *42%*

DESTILLERIE WEUTZ St. Nikolai im Sausal. Working.

Franziska bott code. L070206/02 db The 5% elderflower means this is 100% not whisky. But a fascinating and eye-opening way to create a spirit very much in the young Kentucky rye style, especially in the nose. They certainly can do delicious... For the record, the scoring for enjoyment alone: **(93) n23.5 t23 f23.5 b23.** *48%. Malt refined with 5% elderflower.*

DISTILLERY ZWEIGER Mooskirchen. Working.

Zweiger Single Malt Whiskey Aged 4 Years Styrian oak db **(89) n22** distinctly European wood effect: pungent tannins with a sharp citrus-saltiness; **t22.5** big delivery, again with the tannins right at the forefront. Shapes impressively as delicate maple syrup mixes with orange blossom honey to offer balance; **f22** some late red liquorice spices up; **b22.5** fascinating malt with the oak playing a far more entertaining part than the barley. *40%*

⬥ **Zweiger Single Malt Whyskey Sherryfasslager** bott code SH/L0601/17 db **(76.5) n18 t21 f18 b19.5** No sulphur, you'll be pleased to know. But this feinty malt lurches around the palate like a man around the desert with no map or compass, only some attractive gristy sugars to keep it going. Finally collapses entirely lost. *43%.*

⬥ **Zweiger Smoked Prisoner** bott code SH/L0601/17 db **(89) n22** recently captured Arbroath smokies...; **t22** guilty of slight feintiness; hickory and spices are sent down after the early phenol kick; **f22.5** the dark sugars and mocha serve an attractively long term; **b22.5** probably not the whisky of choice for officials of the European Court of Human Rights. *44%.*

LAVA BRÄU Feldbach. Working.

⬥ **Mehr Leben Brisky Single Malt Eiche** dist 2013, bott code H 02|13 db **(87) n22 t22.5 f21.5 b22** "Brisky". Thought this was the first whisky made in Britain after the people had decided to get the hell out of Europe. But apparently not... A very well made malt with some serious loganberry on the nose – not exactly the most usual of aromas. But eventually disappears under its own weight of caramel on the palate. *40.8%.*

Mehr Leben Brisky Single Malt Whisky dist 2006, bott codeH 03|06 db **(87.5) n22.5 t22 f21 b22.** Lovely, fascinating nose, at times salty and sweaty, occasionally citrusy. And charmingly delicate on the palate, also, with a major citrus theme. *40.2%*

Mehr Leben Brisky Single Malt Whisky dist 2009, bott code B 0509 db **(91.5) n23 t23 f22.5 b23** A bottle worth finding and savouring. Gorgeous! *40.8%*

⬥ **Mehr Leben Genesis Brisky Single Cask Rare Malt** dist 2010, bott code G 04|10 db **(88.5) n22** like sticking your head in a bucket of freshly trod grapes...; **t23** well no chance of sulphur here: this is the freshest fruit influence I have ever come across – a bit like an insanely well fortified wine; **f22.5** settles down with some attractive vanilla and spiced praline...or perhaps I mean fruit and nut...; **b21** a delicious must have (and I mean must in both senses of the word) for those who love a little whisky in their fruit... *48.7%. sc.*

LEBE & GENIESSE Lagenrohr. Working

Bodding Lokn cask no. 8, dist 2010, bott 2014 db **(88) n22 t22.5 f21.5 b22.** Tight and toasty. But very young. *42%.*

⬥ **Bodding Lokn Golden Wheat Single Malt Lagerung Double Cask** Franz Limousin Eiche & Oloroso sherry fass, fass nr. 1120 & 111, gebrannt 2008 db **(91.5) n22.5** no nose on the planet has this signature: a kind of chocolate Jaffa Cake on Digestive Biscuit rather than sponge...if that makes sense. Lots of lime jelly baby, also: yes, it is fruity and sweet; **t23** where did this silkiness come from? With the wheat I was expecting a spice surge. Instead we have plum jam with a little back honey and a slow spice burn...; **f23** for the first time oak is represented, here by understated vanilla; **b23** though perhaps a little too sweet for some, this is truly one of a kind. Almost too beautiful and demur to drink... *45%. ncf.*

⬥ **Bodding Lokn Single Malt Lagerung Double Cask Sherry Finish** Amerikan Weisseiche & Oloroso sherry fass, fass nr. 11,14 & 372, gebrannt 2010 db **(95) n24** weighty and punchy: the spices are fast out of their traps; excellent oak-muscovado/sweet-dry balance; **t24** after a comfortable butterscotch start, the spices arrive and rip remorselessly into the sweeter notes; liquorice and molasses lick their wounds; **f23** quietens and a little grape begins to filter through; **b24** a mildly aggressive, oak-biased malt but beautifully made and matured. The sulphur-free sherry plays second fiddle to the American oak from first to last. High class malt. *43.5%. ncf.*

⬥ **Bodding Lokn Single Malt Smoky Lagerung Single Cask** Amerikan Weisseiche fass, fass nr. 9, gebrannt 2011 db **(86) n22 t22.5 f20.5 b21** A malt awash in the early stages with natural caramels and sweet, nutty phrasing to the barley. Also, satisfyingly lush on delivery. But just a little rough and ready on the very uneven and sugar-derived finish. *51%. ncf.*

⬥ **Bodding Lokn White Bull Spirit Malt** gebrannt 2010 db **(85.5) n21 t22.5 f21 b21** Malty and gristily sweet. But also a little copper starved, leading to a degree of tanginess. *46%. ncf.*

MARILLENHOF DESTILLERIE KAUSL Mühldorf. Working.

Wachauer Whisky "G" Single Barrel Gerste (Barley) bott code L6WG db **(90.5)** n22 t23 f22.5 b23. Absolutely charming and well made malt. *40%*

Wachauer Whisky Kausl bott code L: 13 WE db **(92)** n22 t23.5 f23.5 b23 Kausl appear to specialise in taking the tannin to the edge: the character is deep rooted in oak - literally - yet somehow they manage to get the intricacies of the grain - or perhaps grains - across. Brave. And either very lucky, or exceptionally skilful... Oh, and I say grains as I took the liberty to blend their four grains together and came up with something not entirely unlike this in style, complexity and balance - except perhaps slightly better and something over the 94 mark.... (!!) An impressive distillery worthy of great praise, for sure. *40%*

Wachauer Whisky Kausl Single Pure G Barley bott code L: 6WG db **(88)** n21.5 t22 f22.5 b22 Barley may be behind the grain. But the oak leads in every direction. *40%*

Wachauer Whisky Kausl Single Pure H Oat bott code L: 1WH db **(89)** n22 t22 f22.5 b22.5 Starting the day with some oats is supposed to be good for you. Usually my oat intake is at lunchtime when I mash up half a dozen or more oatcakes into mackerel and sometimes lighten with diced tomato. But if anyone is to ask me where you will find the best oat whisky, the answer has to be Austria. The startling intensity of the wood has an overbearing effect on the oats but the unique character of the grain shines through at the end. *40%*

Wachauer Whisky Kausl Single Pure Rye bott code L: 9WR db **(90.5)** n22 t23 f23 b22.5 You may not be surprised that I left the rye as the last of their four grains. This is the hardest of them all to get right, and also offers the greatest reward if they can pull it off. In the end, it turned out they surpassed themselves: a full-flavoured, at times crisp and fruity success. *40%*

Wachauer Whisky Kausl Single Pure W Wheat bott code L: 2WW db **(80)** n19 t20 f21 b20. Wheat is a hard grain to pull off at the best of times. But what appears to be a slight butyric note doesn't help the narrative and although it doesn't misfire quite so badly on the palate, the various constituents don't seem to gel too happily, either. *40%*

MARKUS WIESER GMBH Woesendorf in der Wachau. Austria.

Wieser Wahouua Single Malt WIESky American Oak bott code L1115 db **(85.5)** n21 t22 f21 b21.5. Never a dull moment as the treacle and maple syrup mix join forces with a light spice to battle against some ungainly oils from the distillate. Always pleasant, but never convincing. *40%. nc.*

Wieser Wahouua Single Malt WIESky Pinot Noir bott code L1015 db **(87)** n21 t22 f22 b22. A curious malt. Always soft, always polite and at times positively charming. But the fruit never makes much of a stand while the toffee has no such reservations. *40%. nc.*

Wieser Wahouua Single Malt WIESky Sherry Wood bott code L1015 db **(82.5)** n19 t21.5 f21 b21. The sherry is absolutely clean and problem free. But the fruit has to work very hard to overcome the excesses of a wide cut. The result is predictably nutty and stilted. Soft throughout and not entirely unattractive once you are past the nose. *40%. nc.*

MICHELEHOF Vorarlberg. Working.

Micheles Single Malt 6 Years Old 100% barley, dist 2008, bott code L8121 db **(78.5)** n19 t21 f19 b19.5. An oily, nutty affair which struggles hard to get over the effect of the wide cut. A few attractive salivating fudgy moments at about the halfway point. *43%*

PETER AFFENZELLER Alberndorf in der Riedmark. Working.

Peter Affenzeller Blended Whisky 7 Years Old dist 2008, bott code: L-1015302 db **(86.5)** n21.5 t22 f21.5 b21.5. An exceptionally sweet blend, but spices emerge to tone down the threatening excess. Love the Lubek marzipan which surfaces on the nose especially. But overall, a surprising degree of youthfulness. *42%*

Peter Affenzeller Single Malt Whisky 7 Years Old dist 2008, bott code: L-0841201 db **(95.5)** n23.5 t24.5 f23.5 b24 I defy any malt whisky lover, wherever you are in the world, not to entirely fall head over heals for this stunning whisky. *42%*

Peter Affenzeller White Malzbrand bott code: L-0821011 db **(89)** n22 t22 f22.5 b22.5. Beautifully cut new make: clean, with a fabulous slow burn of intensity. I'd expect a late spiced cocoa character, which is exactly what we get. Very acceptable copper content, too. Impressed: far more together than the last sample! *42%*

PFANNER Vorarlberg. Working.

Pfanner Single Malt dist 2009, bott code L 212 db **(74)** n19 t20 f16.5 b18.5. Nutty and some hefty feints late on puts a Pfanner in the works... *43%*

REISETBAUER Axberg, Thening. Working.

Reisetbauer Single Malt 7 Years Old Chardonnay casks db (84.5) n19 t23 f21 b21.5. So weird!! On my final spit I thought: "I'm sure I've tasted this whisky before." And looking in last year's Bible, there it was. Though I gave bigger marks to the finale than the delivery. The 'G' Spot is the exact middle, when the fruit goes into delicious overdrive. Perhaps just three or four waves before where I noticed it last time. A varied dram, with a degree of brilliance - only too short in length. 43%

Reisetbauer Single Malt 12 Years Old db (86.5) n19 t23.5 f22 b22. Presumably from the early days of the distillery when they hadn't quite got to grips with their cuts on the still. Recovers from a below-average nose to offer a sometimes sensational middle full of toffee and tannin and even a little Manuka honey. The heavier oils reassemble on the finale. 48%

⬦ **Reisetbauer 15 Years Old Single Malt** db (80.5) n18.5 t22.5 f19 b20.5 Those feints are still there in force, even after 15 years, which is some achievement. But, not for the first time, their malt recovers from a dodgy start to present an attractive chocolate nougat middle before succumbing to the oils for a second time. 48%.

STBG BRAUEREI SCHLOSS STARKENBERG Tarrenz. Working.

STGB Tiroler Single Malt Whisky Aged 3 Years db (94.5) n23.5 t23.5 f23.5 b24 A charmingly relaxed single malt which has been beautifully crafted. You cannot really ask for more from a three-year-old single malt. 40%

WHISKY-DESTILLERIE J. HAIDER Roggenreith. Working.

Dark Single Malt J.H. Cask Strength bott code L DSM 11 db (94.5) n22.5 t24.5 f24 b23.5 When it comes to almost bewildering intensity to a malt, this wonderful distillery is in a league of its own. Taste using the Murray Method to maximise the beauty. 64%

⬦ **J.H. 13 Years Old Single Malt** bott code L SM 03 FS db (96) n24 Anyone who has dried maple syrup, then mixed it in with Manuka honey will recognise instantly this form of enclosed sweetness: it is that lighter note over the liquorice and clove: stunning! t23.5 the delivery is a cross between very old bourbon and younger, high ester pot still rum. The spices fizz, but never quite attack, the vanillas darken but never quite brood. The sugars and malt combine for the salivating to begin as the mid-point is reached...; f24 that rarest of phenomena: big oak, toasty input but not a trace of bitterness: the spices and treacle see us through to the very distant end...; b24.5 one of the beauties of feints in whisky, is that the longer the spirit hangs around the more chance there is that they'll be burnt off. And I suspect this has happened here because this astonishing malt, doubtless from a cask they have matured for one of their longest periods, has little interference from the dark side of distilling. Its colossal malt, this distillation of genius, is honeyed uplands all the way... 69%. ncf sc.

⬦ **J.H. Rare Selection Dark Rye Malt** bott code L DRR 09 SG db (89.5) n20 the intense house nougat here does have an additional mocha depth...and something else besides; t23 big and chewy, the oils are reservoir deep. Slowly, the grain makes itself loud and clear and by the middle even enjoys a crispy fruitiness; f23.5 long, the oils having now receded and we are left with a rye and molasses tide mark; b23 still utterly unique and true to itself. 46%. ncf sc.

⬦ **J.H. Rare Selection Original Rye Whisky** bott code L RR 12 MÜ db (94) n23.5 fewer oils than the norm, resulting in the rye flag flying higher, prouder and more correctly than usual; t23.5 and there we go again: the emboldened rye grain is crisp and muscovado sugar coated to a wonderfully salivating and attractive degree; f23 the light outline of vanilla doesn't interfere with the rye and coffee sign off; b24 one of the cleanest and most technically correct J.H. whiskies I have ever encountered. What a treat! 46%. ncf sc.

Original Rye Whisky J.H. Selection bott code L R 05 db (94) n23 t24 f23.5 b23.5 An assured and elegant rye of high quality. 46%

Rare Selection Dark Rye Malt J.H bott code L DRR 09 SG db (93) n22.5 t24 f23 b23.5 When this distillery gets its rye right, few distilleries in the world can match it for extracting every last nuance from the grain. Not a jot of elegance – just flavour power all the way. db 46%. sc.

DESTILLERIE WEIDENAUER Kottes. Working.

Waldviertler Hafer-Malz (2007 Gold Medaille label on neck) db (91) n22 t22.5 f23 b23.5. One of those whiskies that just gets better the longer it stays on the palate. Also, a master class in achieving near perfection in the degree of sweetness generated. 42%

BELGIUM
THE BELGIAN OWL Grâce-Hollogne. Working.

The Belgian Owl Single Malt 36 Months first fill bourbon cask, bott code LB036088 db **(85.5) n21 t22 f21 b21.5.** It seems only correct that, as the church clock strikes midnight and a tawny owl calls eerily to one of its young nearby, I should taste this. So it is obvious I give two hoots about a whisky which has always done exceptionally well in the Whisky Bible - and deservedly so. Not sure if this is distilled from their new (or do I mean old?) Caperdonich still. But it fails to grip and reveal the intensity of their older make, this emphasising the tender 36 months with its playful, citric and juicy maltiness, rather than the barley which, previously, was aflame with passion and desire to entertain. 46%. nc ncf.

◆ **Belgian Owl Single Malt Whisky Aged 36 Months** first fill bourbon casks, bott code LB036282 db **(89.5) n22.5** about as polite a malt and vanilla handshake as you'll ever encounter...; **t22** a remarkably thin, watery delivery. But the grist slowly ramps up the malty amps and the tannins hold just enough weight and extra sugars in store to ensure the middle fills with riches; **f23** a very sophisticated finish: an underlying dry tone is elegantly outflanked by maple syrup and the most genteel cocoa...; **b22** a strange, unconvincing start is more than compensated for by the moreish finish. 46%. ncf.

◆ **Belgian Owl Single Malt Whisky Aged 36 Months** first fill bourbon casks, bott code LC036341 db **(92.5) n23** a few Kentucky notes make an early mark: love the Jaffa Cake theme but also the small grain bourbon complexity; **t23** silky, intensely malty delivery. Then we move back into a more bourbon-style feel as a liquorice and toasted fudge effect begins to gain the upper hand; **f23.5** wonderfully toasty: hints of molasses and chocolate malt; **b23** what a hugely satisfying whisky and a distinct notch up from its sister bottling. 46%. ncf.

◆ **Belgian Owl Single Malt Whisky The Private Angels Aged 36 Months** first fill bourbon casks, cask no. 035/200 db **(88) n22** soft and floral; **t22.5** usual feeble, spineless delivery. But the muscle builds as the malt becomes active; **f22** a vanilla and butterscotch tang; curiously salty; attractive late spice; **b21.5** a pleasant though directionless malt which seems to make it up as it goes along. 46%. ncf sc.

◆ **Belgian Owl Single Malt Whisky The Private Angels Aged 36 Months** first fill bourbon casks, cask no. 036/200 db **(96) n24** oh, that natural oak caramel .stunning! Hits that stunning no-man's-land between malt and bourbon with both factors evident in equal measure; adore the treacle tart intensity; **t24.5** one of the deliveries of the year so far: stunning mix of ulmo and Manuka honeys on one hand, red liquorice, manic malt and demented vanilla on another: something akin to genius, especially as soon as those spices let rip...; **f23.5** long, lush, languid. The vanilla has an oily depth normally associated with the fade of exceptionally high grade Canadian...; **b24** a malt of outstanding weight and complexity that is much more well suited to these higher strengths. A Belgian Owl of the old school and which I can give far more than two hoots for... 70.3%. ncf sc.

◆ **Belgian Owl Flavours of Nature The Private Angels Aged 36 Months** first fill bourbon casks, cask no. 040/200 db **(87) n22** malty but with no great designs to move beyond its vanilla-clad limits; a genuine breakfast cereal feel to this...; **t22.5** again malt has a clear, unobstructed path on delivery. But a lovely honey-enriched nutty depth slowly adds on the weight it needs; **f22** butterscotch with a red liquorice fade. Spices nibble with a degree of apology...; **b22** another pleasant malt with all kinds of attractive if half-hearted themes. But absolutely refuses to show any degree of firmness or confidence... 46%. ncf sc.

DESTILLERIE RADERMACHER Raeren. Working.

Lambertus Single Grain Aged 10 Years db **(44) n12 t12 f10 b10.** This is whisky...? Really???!!!!???? Well, that's what it says on the label, and this is a distillery I haven't got round to seeing in action (nor am I now very likely to be invited...). Let's check the label again... Ten years old...blah, blah. Single grain... blah, blah. But, frankly, this tastes like a liqueur rather than a whisky: the fruit flavours do not seem even remotely naturally evolved: synthetic is being kind. But apparently, this is whisky: I have re-checked the label. No mention of additives, so it must be. I am stunned. 40%

IF GOULDYS FILLIERS DISTILLERY Deinze. Working.

Goldly's Belgian Double Still Whisky Aged 10 Years db **(88) n21.5 t23 f21.5 b22.** Having actually discovered this whisky before the distillers – I'll explain one day...!! – I know this could be a lot better. The caramel does great damage to the finish in particular, which should dazzle with its complexity. Even so, a lovely, high-class whisky which should be comfortably in the 90s but falls short. 40%

CZECH REPUBLIC
Single Malt
RUDOLF JELÍNEK DISTILLERY Vizovice. Working.

⬦ **Gold Cock Single Grain Whisky 2008** Czech oak barrels, dist Feb 08, bott Mar 17 db (87) n22.5 t22 f21 b21.5 Being one of only a handful of people to have visited the old distillery in Tesetice in its operational days some two decades ago I can gauge with some accuracy the differences between the output of its original and new stills. Usually, when new stills are deployed for the first year or so an extra degree of copper gives a sharp, metallic feel to a spirit; this dies down after time. Here, quite the opposite seems true: there is less copper than was found in the original stills, so this is a lighter whisky which by the end is struggling to cope with the unique richness of the Czech oak. The nose does offer an attractive citrus note that was also absent from Tesetice's old King Barley brand. The early maple syrup found on the delivery can spread only so far before the oak takes control. 49.2%. nc ncf sc.

⬦ **Gold Cock Single Malt Whisky 8 Years Old** Czech oak barrels db (93) n23 lovely French toast aroma, sweet and with the odd ray of acacia honey brightening things further; the distinctive mid European vanillas are kept in Czech, so to speak...; t23.5 superb mouth feel: soft oils impart a lingering sweetness, mainly a mix of golden syrup and ulmo honey; the spices buzz distantly; f23 such a subtle finale: a little mocha but it is that sweetened vanilla which holds the cards; b23.5 a delightful whisky making full use of the wheat content to ramp up the oils and spices while the sugars missing on the 8-year-old appear to have found their way here... 49.2%. nc ncf.

Gold Cock Single Malt Whisky Aged 24 Years 1992 Czech oak barrels, cask no. 505, dist 4/1992, bott 5/2016 db (95.5) n23.5 t24 f24 b24 There is perhaps a one in three chance I tasted this whisky in the mid 1990s when it was only a nipper. In my 1997 Jim Murray's Complete Book of Whisky I wrote fondly of this maturing whisky as I was genuinely impressed. I see now I had good reason to be: it has navigated the passing years without hitting the rocks and passes no opportunity to radiate great personality. A bit like the wonderful people I met who made it... 61.5%. nc ncf sc. 246 bottles. Bottled for Black Stuff Irish Pub Olomouc.

Gold Cock Single Malt Whisky 1992 Limited Release Whisky Festival.cz barrelled Jun 92, bott Apr 15 db (97) n23.5 t25 f24 b24.5 Absolutely one of the great single barrels of the year. And, unquestionably, THE most sensual dram... 61.6%. ncf sc. 198 bottles.

Gold Cock Single Malt Whisky 1992 Slivovitz Finish Czech oak barrels db (95) n24 t24 f23.5 b23.5 Czech malt whisky. Matured in Czech oak. And finished in the wood that contained the Czech national spirit, slivovitz. Can you think of anything more beautiful and nakedly Czech than that? Well, I can. And I look forward to drinking it with her next time we meet... Czech-mate... 59.5%. nc ncf sc.

⬦ **Gold Cock Single Malt Whisky 2008 Virgin Oak** Czech oak barrels, dist Feb 08, bott Mar 17 db (96) n24 no other aroma on the planet boasts a signature which celebrates the sweeter, fruitier elements of bourbon alongside the creamier, treacle tart tones of an obviously non-American oak: the must subtle sweetness to any whisky this year; t24 for the first few moments were are transported to Kentucky as wave upon wave of liquorice and molasses crashes into the palate. Next a sexy buttery note thins things out and allows a barley-sugar/butterscotch middle to take hold; f24 long with more Worther's original butter candy and a slow reverting to the toasty liquorice and molasses...as though going full circle: amazing! b24 not often you get gold cocks and virgins mentioned in the same sentence in a drinks guide. Or anywhere else, come to that. Equally few rampant cocks can crow so loudly; no virgin give so passionately. A consummate whisky consummated... 61.5%. nc ncf sc. 270 bottles.

STOCK PLZEN - BOZKOV S.R.O. Plzen. Working
Hammer Head 1989 db (88.5) n22 t22.5 f22 b22. Don't bother looking for complexity: this is one of Europe's maltiest drams...if not the maltiest... 40.7%

Blends
Gold Cock Aged 3 Years "Red Feathers" bott 22/06/09 (86) n22 t21 f21.5 b21.5. Sensual and soft, this is melt-in-the-mouth whisky with a big nod towards the sweet caramels. 40%.

Granette Premium (82) n21 t22 f19 b20. Lighter than the spark of any girl that you will meet in the Czech Republic. Big toffee thrust. 40%

Printer's Aged 6 Years (86.5) n21.5 t22.5 f21 b21.5. Blended whisky is something often done rather well in the Czech Republic and this brand has managed to maintain its clean, malty integrity and style. Dangerously quaffable. 40%

DENMARK
BRAENDERIET LIMFJORDEN Øster Assels. Working.

Island of Mors Single Malt Danish Whisky db (87) n21.5 t22 f22 b21.5. A most curious – and delicious – whisky from Denmark. Though a single malt, it has the bite, underlying firmness, slimness of body, and thick line of caramel which one normally associates with a blend. Some lovely spices at play, as well as malt, but just needs to complex out slightly. 46%. ncf. 462 bottles.

BRAUNSTEIN DISTILLERY Køge. Working.

Braunstein Danish Single Malt Cask Edition no. 2 db (94) n23.5 youthful, attractively smoked bacon; even, though sharp and salty; clean, barley accented, with the sweetness veering towards banana and custard; t23.5 beautifully textured and, despite its obvious lack of passing seasons, displays enough accomplished, intense gristy notes to make for one of the most impressively layered whiskies you'll find on mainland Europe. Initially supplemented by a light Demerara sweetness, then eventually heads deliciously towards a chocolate mint middle, but the peat is paying attention all the time; f23 betrays its youth slightly. But, equally, the elegance is never in question; b24 seriously high quality distillate that has been faithfully supported by good grade oak. Complex, satisfying, and for its obviously tender years, truly excellent malt. A welcome addition to the Scandinavian – and world! – whisky lexicon. 62.4%

Braunstein Danish Single Malt Cask Edition no. 3 db (93) n22.5 t24 f23 b23.5. A very different experience to Edition No 2, with this being anchored not by peat but almost outrageous tannin and the astonishing sugar concentrate which accompanies it. For three, maybe four, glorious flavour waves the palate is almost swamped by oak at its most accomplished, yet still with good manners enough for the fresh gristy barley to also make a telling contribution. 62.3%

Braunstein Danish Single Malt Cask Edition no. 5 db (89.5) n22 t22 f23 b22.5. Takes a little time to sort itself out and decide what it wants to say. A confusion of fruit and peat makes things a bit thick for a while: such is the over-exuberance of youth! Juicy and eventually less muggy and more impressively smoky. 60.8%

Braunstein Danish Single Malt Cask Edition no. 6 db (94.5) n23.5 t23.5 f23.5 b24. What a class act this is! Everything beautifully weighted and measured: like a film star of the 1950s fitting perfectly into her tastefully revealing dress. The smoke appears to have been tailored with an unerring eye to allow both the highly sugared oak and more deftly sweetened barley to show its curves. A sublime layering of oil, and just the most playful of spice tingles – all softened by the most dazzling fruity muscovado sugars - really sets this off gloriously and papers over the youthful cracks expertly. What magnificence! 61.4%

Braunstein Danish Single Malt Library Collection 10:2 db (89.5) n23 t23 f21.5 b22. Though initially an oily chap, perhaps not helped by the lower strength as the breakdown in its structure by the finale is pretty marked, as the powdery ending portrays. Even so, its youth does not deter the intense malt richness, nor the light smoke which offers useful weight. 43%

Braunstein Danish Single Malt Library Collection 10:3 db (92) n23 t23 f22.5 b23.5. A comparative dullard by Braunstein's high standards. Yet still reeks of quality and class, even though the sharper edges have been rendered safe and flat by the big fruit injection.... and high water reduction. Silky soft, with a watered-down dark muscovado leaning. This allows the spices to come into their own late on, joining the intensifying cocoa with aplomb. Charming. 43%

Braunstein Danish Single Malt Library Collection 11:2 db (87.5) n22 t22.5 f21 b22. A bit sharp and tangy in places, especially towards the end. Very youthful, but still excels in its big malt kick; though finds balance a little more elusive. 46%

Braunstein Danish Single Malt Library Collection 14:2 db (91.5) n22 t22.5 f23.5 b23.5. No problems harnessing the dark, weighty sugars which ensures this malt is in for the long haul. A fruity fusillade on the nose but the delivery is divine: good oil structure, playful smoke and lovely tingling spice. All the time the barley thickens and the light ulmo and Manuka honey blend aid the growing spices. Complex and satisfying. 46%

Braunstein Danish Single Malt Library Collection 15:1 db (91) n22.5 t23 f23.5 b22. Another Braunstein where a massive tannin injection offers the main theme throughout. Not sure how they do it, but for all the oak, the integrity of the barley remains undiminished. At times, the obvious youthfulness of the malt makes this seem like a marriage between teenager and pensioner. Lurches about the palate a bit with the vanilla and caramel-rich sugars always on hand to soothe any arguments. 46%

Braunstein Danish Single Malt Cask Edition no. D28 db **(94)** n23.5 t23.5 f23 b24. Another big game malt from Braunstein. Not dissimilar in style to one of their malt cask collection: no. 6, I think. The smoke and oak appear to be dancing to the same tune and very much in step. Intense, the sugars are perhaps just a shade more weighted by vanilla with this one. Not a dram for those looking for a quiet few minutes... *61.4%*

Braunstein Danish Single Malt Library Collection e:7 db **(89.5)** n21 t23 f23 b22.5. A seriously complex whisky: unusually for this distillery, they have chosen to bottle at a point where the nose really is a stranger to harmonisation. Light smoke and jagged tannin juxtapose with the pithy fruit: they don't mix merrily. So they must have selected for the delivery, for this is absolutely stunning! While the nose is at odds, the sugars are all for one and one for all: gorgeous maple syrup with a touch of treacle thrown in. And a big spice bite to ram the intensity home. Some vague, estery, rummy notes emphasise the sugary input. Young, a little confused...but has so much to say. *60.2%*

FARY LOCHAN DESTILLERI Give. Working.

Fary Lochan Danish Single Malt batch 2, cask nos. 2011-04,09,11,12 & 13, filled 5 Nov 11, bott 27 Jan 16 db **(84)** n21 t21 f21.5 b20.5. A hugely promising whisky undone slightly by the width of the cut, which allows in a few too many heavy oils. There is no doubting the integrity of the barley and at times one hums with delight as its intensity hits the bullseye. But much peripheral bitterness needs to be trimmed away. *48%*

   Fary Lochan Forår db **(90)** n22 the lightest layer of smoke helps quieten a minor technical aberration...; t23 dissolves on the palate immediately: gristy smoke with castor sugar and over-ripe banana; f22.5 late, intricate spice amid the healthy butterscotch; b22.5 Denmark's most delicate whisky...by a distance. Youthful but quite lovely. *47%*.

Fary Lochan Vinter batch 1 db **(86)** n21.5 t22 f21 b21.5. A more handsome malt here with the sugars happy to go hand-in-hand with the vivid barley and lively spice. Marked down, though, by a bitter shadow which has a vaguely hoppy edge to it. *54%*

SMALL BATCH DISTILLERS Holstebro. Working

   Small Batch Distillers Peat by Peat db **(86.5)** n21 t22.5 f21 b22 Angular and forceful. From the very green, sugary and lightly smoked nose, through the eye-wateringly sharp and puckering delivery to the postulating, tangy finish there is no peace for the senses. *62%*.

   Small Batch Distillers Peat by Peat 3rd Edition American white oak virgin barrels, db **(89)** n22.5 the odd feint can be detected amid the massive phenol. Reminds me of what my dad's clothes smelt like after he came home from work after travelling on an early diesel train...; t23 rich and very sweet. The sugars are piled on high, most of them of the gristy variety, those oils giving them further density. Tannins begin to form...; f21 those feints have a slightly untidy edge now, but the smoke remains all powerful; b22.5 it is probably this whisky's foibles that make this so attractive. *60%*.

   Small Batch Distillers Peated Mystery 2nd Edition French virgin oak barrels db **(88)** n21.5 slightly peated; a rice stickiness; molten muscovado sugar; t23 changes tack and the immediate ulmo honey and spiced butterscotch tart is far from unique, but the slow building of a salty smokiness hints of something a lot more Scottish than Danish...; f21 the spices and smoke hangs around; b22.5 again, drops a few points for a few technical weaknesses, on the nose and finish especially. But the over-all picture is very pretty. *56%*.

   Small Batch Distillers Peated Rye db **(90)** n23 an unparalleled aroma: the rye offers two forms, the most noticeable a soft fruity quality. But under the comfortable, snug and enveloping eiderdown comes the hard pea of the granular grain. Sandwiched between this is a butterscotch-soaked smokiness which also offers a train-set oiliness I have only ever found once before...on a bottle of Ardbeg...in Denmark...! t22 immediately young and new make rich in a way the nose never is. The grain and smoke are here much less willing to gel, but the flavour compounds remain startling; f22.5 settles down at length into a far more harmonious marriage of light muscovado sugars and smoked ulmo honey. A degree of tobacco kicks in late on, suggesting a generous cut from the still; b22.5 playing around my lab over the years I have experimented with amalgamating the intense aroma and flavour of rye with the depth of a smoky malt. I had come up with some interesting concoctions but none, to my memory, quite matched the unique shape of this remarkable whisky, especially on the nose. Memorable...and very beautiful. *58%*.

   Small Batch Distillers RugBy db **(91.5)** n22.5 rye radiates from all directions, with the odd sharp, brittle note underlining the sugars; gently spiced; t23.5 a brilliant rye grain lift off: monumentally sharp and salivating there is the odd Lawrenceburg, Indiana, moment attached to this; the middle stretch is a playground for tart, fruity rye notes and more spice; **f22.5** softens with the oils and vanilla; **b23** a profound rye which, if cleaned up a bit would represent the grain with a touch of classicism. 58%.

◈ **Small Batch Distillers RugBy Extend** French virgin oak barrels db **(86.5) n21.5 t23.5 f21 b20.5** No denying the impact of the rye, or its high class crisp fruitiness, which can be fully enjoyed on the astonishing delivery and for a short while beyond. But a combination of the wide cut off the still and the unforgiven tannin means the balance of the whisky is lost far too early and easily. 60%.

STAUNING WHISKEY Skjern. Working.

◈ **Stauning Bourbon Oak Virgin Oak** dist 2012, bott Feb 17 db **(80.5) n20 t22.5 f19 b19** Slightly too feinty. Definitely too oaky. Plenty of sugars and spice to suck on, especially on delivery, but creates scant harmony. 47.8%.

Stauning Danish Single Malt Virgin Oak 2010 bott Sept 15 db **(94) n22.5 t23.5 f24 b24** A malt which takes its time to find its feet. But once it has, it stands steadfast in its excellence. 49.5%

Stauning KAOS dist 2011-2013, bott Feb 16 db **(94.5) n23 t24.5 f23 b24** An altogether better blending than their first attempt: indeed, rather well too layered and structured for true chaos... 46.5%

◈ **Stauning Kiesp** dist 2011-2013, bott Nov 16 db **(91) n21.5** somewhat feinty but recovers with a blood orange and maple syrup readjustment; **t23** succulent, fat, malty, grassy and deliciously tart; **f24** takes time to settle but moves into a gorgeous walnut and date mode with a mocha swiss role cake background....and then topped by a first brooding then warming spice rumble: seriously yummy; **b22.5** wins few prizes – or points – for its technical prowess. But for sheer flavour explosivity, this is some whisky...! 47.4%.

Stauning Peated 6th Edition dist 2012, bott Jun 16 db **(95) n23.5 t23.5 f23.5 b24.5** My God! When they say "peated", they bloody well mean peated...!!! So beautifully distilled: just makes technocrats like me purr...If you were not quite sure if Stauning qualifies as a Premier League distillery, this will most likely confirm it.. 51.5%

Stauning Traditional 4th Edition 2010 Single Malt, bott Sept 15 db **(87.5) n21.5 t22 f22 b22.** It is perhaps hard to imagine a malt whisky with more barley escaping from every pore. Indeed, there is something of the old English barley wine beer to this, though without the hop. But the slightly annoying oils attached to this – evidence of stretching the cut a little too far – tarnishes what might have been a golden cup. Highly entertaining, though far from perfect. 46.3%

Stauning Young Rye 2012, bott Jun 15 db **(88.5) n22** sharp, punchy and spiced. The crisper rye notes reward some searching through the oils; **t23** thick, lush and a slow revelation of the dry, red-liquorice-tinged concentrated rye; **f21.5** just a shade too oily; **b22** a generous cut mean the heavier oils linger.... 51%

Stauning Young Rye dist 2011-2013, bott Nov 15 db **(88) n21.5 t23.5 f21 b22** Had the cut been a little less wide, this would have been a Stauning stunner. A fascinating mix of the brilliant and not so brilliant... 50%

Stauning Young Rye 2013, bott Mar 16 db **(95) n23.5 t24 f23.5 b24** So thick with rye, you have to floss your teeth afterwards... 50.1%

◈ **Stauning Young Rye 2013** bott Nov 16 db **(92) n22.5** initially, had I been told this was a heavy Irish pot still, I would not have been surprised! The rye takes its time to exert its presence; **t23.5** but no doubting the rye here! Arrives early and by the spade-load, intense, sharp and unforgiving; as well as the normal muscovado fruitiness there is a juicy date thick sweetness also and a gathering butterscotch intensity; **f23** long, slightly oily from the cut but with mocha and throbbing spices; **b23** a five course meal of a rye with the grain at its most intense. 52.3%.

◈ **Stauning Young Rye 2013** bott Feb 17 db **(87.5) n21 t23 f22 b21.5** You really need a tin hat and find yourself a bunker for this one! This is one huge battle between the big, belligerent rye and the slightly OTT cut from the still which has introduced a massive oil personality and a surprisingly different animal to the 2013 distillation I tasted last year, where the rye had a far wider reach. More feints than usually found on a Stauning, though the fractious rye and mocha finish has to be tasted to be believed...! 48.4%.

THY WHISKY Snedsted. Working.

Thy Whisky Single Malt Cask no. 2a Hawboen db **(88) n21.5 t22 f22.5 b22** Not the type of malt you come across every day – or are likely to forget. At first, you sit there in stunned silence. Then you go back to it and discover that the dots join and, once acclimatised, the palate can identify a very enjoyable and complex whisky. If a little brash. *48%. ncf sc.*

Thy Whisky Single Malt Cask no. 2b Fjordboen db **(86) n21 t22 f21.5 b21.5.** Distinctly malty. Again the muscled tannin sports tattoos. *48%. ncf sc.*

Thy Whisky Single Malt Cask no. 3 Kræn Kræmmer db **(93.5) n23.5 t23.5 f23 b23.5** Always great to happen across a non-sulphured sherry cask: well done people of Thy! This really is a beautiful malt. *57.7%. ncf sc.*

⬥ **Thy Whisky No. 4 Kræn Klemme Single Malt** ex-bourbon fass, dist 10 Dec 12, tappet 15 Jul 16 db **(86) n21 t22.5 f21 b21.5** What a strange creature this is! A nondescript citrus note infiltrates the nose and early stages of the exceptionally clammy and sweet delivery. Soft and friendly natured, the vanilla ice cream finish is a bit odd at first but grows on you, as do the very late spices. *52%. nc ncf sc. 95 bottles.*

⬥ **Thy Whisky No. 5 Kræn Kusk Single Malt** ex-bourbon, PX finish fass, dist 27 Aug 11, tappet 17 Oct 16 db **(92.5) n23** single malt noses rarely come with as much of noble rot as this: lightly spiced, exploding sultanas but a distinctive barley and vanilla background for good measure; **t23.5** chewy, fat fruit – then a violent spice explosion. Flaming muscovado sugars are flung to every corner of the palate with concentrated grape everywhere; **f22.5** not a sulphur note in site: the perfectly fresh grape allows a light vanilla growth, but the ultra-late bitterness is slightly out of sync; **b23.5** not often you find a whisky where PX is particularly at home. But it certainly is here... *60.7%. nc ncf sc. 82 bottles.*

⬥ **Thy Whisky No. 6 Kræn Kræmmer Single Malt** ex-Olorosso, PX finish fass, dist Oct 13 to Mar 14, tappet Mar 17 db **(86.5) n21 t22 f21.5 b22** Well done, chaps! You have sourced a clean, unspoiled oloroso cask. That means the grape adds a fruity edge to the incredibly dense, sometimes juicy malt. A wide cut here results in a little off-key tang but the sultanas work overtime to make amends. Attractive. *50.4%. nc ncf. 642 bottles.*

TROLDEN DISTILLERY Kolding. Working.

⬥ **Trolden Nimbus The Kolding Single Malt No 3** dist 2012, bott 2016 db **(94) n24.5** a quietly rich nose: biscuit (including the coconut you find in Nice) mingles with a thin mix of heather- and orange-blossom honey, all slightly sharpened by a pinch of salt; understated and alluring, like the contents of see-through nightie in a half-lit room...; easily one of the most complex, sophisticated and perfectly weighted noses I have encountered this year; **t23.5** the malt makes the early running, with a farm loaf flowery gristiness; the oak arrives early and adds far more than is easily apparent on the nose, the tannins imbuing a toastiness to counter the delicate, fruity sugars; **f22.5** a little oiliness stretches the thinning finale; **b23.5** Denmark offers grey skies like no other country I know, or to use the distiller's own confusing term when describing their whisky: "unlike no other". Yet the sun is shining on this wonderful new malt with serene benevolence. Impressed! *46%. nc ncf.*

ENGLAND

ADNAMS Saffron Walden. Working.

Adnams Southwold Triple Grain Whisky No 2 American oak, bott 2013 **(87) n22 t22 f21 b22.** For my 999th new whisky for Bible 2015 I wanted, as this book's custom dictates, to choose something a little unusual. And here we have the first-ever Suffolk whisky, made at one of my favourite breweries in the world, Adnams. Not sure what happened to the first bottling but I have the second. And beside me is Percy, my Meyers parrot born in Norfolk not far from the Suffolk border while this cask was maturing. The most remarkable thing to report is the nose. It is, and I really have to find out how, the closest whisky I have ever encountered on nose that matches a decent biryani in its subtle Asian spicy complexity. To taste it is a lot more straightforward: a tad feinty, but those oils conjure up the spices which sit well with the intense sugars. The finish, naturally enough, is a little bitter and foggy from the feints...but with no uncomfortable edges. For now I shall stick to their almost incomparable bitter beer. But I shall be keeping a close eye... *43%. ncf. WB15/407*

BIMBER DISTILLERY London. Working.

⬥ **Bimber Single Malt 1 Year Old** ex-bourbon 190 litre casks, cask no. 8, filled 06 Jun 16, bott 5 Jun 17 db **(84) n21.5 t21.5 f20 b21** As the distillers at Bimber will discover, the path of maturation of any whisky is not a perfect upward curve. Instead, early maturing spirit – and whisky - peaks and troughs, sometimes violently, while different forces come into play and there is insufficient time for a courtship, let alone a marriage to take place. Most spirits around a year old are right slap bang in the middle of that wobble and we can see it here to a degree, and I expect it to see it in the others they have bottled. Some barrels at this age may be riding the wave and carrying out all kinds of stunning tricks; others might be in a trough with the wave about to crash over them. Here, none of the sugars or barley notes appear too confident in their handling of their other flavour profiles. So a whisky to enjoy watching trying to walk and sometimes falling – a bit like a toddler taking its first steps. *62.9%. sc.*

⬦ **Bimber Single Malt 1 Year Old** ex-port 225 litre casks, cask no. 40, bott 5 Jun 17 db (72.5) n17.5 t19 f18 b18 Oh dear... *62.2%. sc.*

⬦ **Bimber Single Malt 1 Year Old** ex-PX. 250 litre casks, cask no. 31, filled 06 Jul 16, bott 5 Jun 17 db (85) n21 t22 f21 b21 A jumbled message of sticky fruit, big sugar, bigger barley... and tobacco... *62.8%. sc.*

⬦ **Bimber Single Malt 1 Year Old** Virgin American oak 190 litre casks, cask no. 7, filled 06 Jun 16, bott 5 Jun 17 db (89) n22.5 t23 f21.5 b22 Eye-wateringly sharp barley in part, but the extra caramels and molassed sugars provided by the virgin oak helps bulldoze some of the less pesky off-key peaks into submission. Mildly brutal but entirely delicious. *62.2%. sc.*

⬦ **Bimber Single Malt New-Make Test Batch Sample** batch no. 25, bott 17 Nov 16 db (95.5) n24 t24 f23.5 b24 Quite possibly the best new make from a fledging distillery I have ever encountered: off the top of my head I cannot recall its master. Gorgeously rich despite being entirely feints-free with an astonishing castor sugar melt on the tail of the ultra-intense grist. Stylish and simply brilliant. *63%.*

⬦ **Bimber Single Malt Test Batch Sample** ex-bourbon 190 litre casks, cask no. 8, filled 06 Jun 16, bott 17 Nov 16 db (86.5) n20 t23 f22.5 b21 It is becoming obvious that the house style is lush with a full fat cream effect. For here the oils carry the generous sugars to far flung corners of the palate yet are no so dense as to undermine the spices. The nose and overall balance are a little confused as the harmony between oak and malt is going through a Trump-Yeltsin moment. *63%. sc.*

⬦ **Bimber Single Malt Test Batch Sample** ex-port 225 litre casks, cask no. 39, filled 06 Aug 16, bott 17 Nov 16 db (89) n21.5 t22 f23.5 b22 Those of us who remember Pink Paraffin will not be surprised by the explosive element to this, going by colour alone. But considering this malt spirit is little more than a year old, one can only gasp at the degree of intensity and complexity already evolved. Certainly a rough ride on both nose and delivery as the fruit and barley lurch about with little control. But soon the spices kick in, the sugars begin to dig in their heels late in the day something rather delicious arrives. Can't wait to see this in true whisky form... *63%. sc.*

⬦ **Bimber Single Malt Test Batch Sample** ex-PX 250 litre casks, cask no. 31, filled 06 Jul 16, bott 17 Nov 16 db (90.5) n22 t23 f23 b22.5 By and large, experience has taught me to trust PX casks the same way a sapper might trust a bomb which has suddenly stopped ticking. Yet it would be churlish of me to punish this too much for the grimly tight and aggressive delivery, for where this cask normally fails – on the nose and finish – here it is a boon, offering sturdy sugars to the even sturdier barley. Possibly the thickest-bodied spirit I will taste this year. And overall? Not bad at all... *62.5%. sc.*

⬦ **Bimber Single Malt Test Batch Sample** Virgin American oak 190 litre casks, cask no. 7, filled 06 Jun 16, bott 17 Nov 16 db (94) n23.5 t24 f23 b23.5 This is distillery is impressing me big time, I must admit. The delivery on this – not to mention the first five or six huge flavour waves which follow – shows what happens when you put very high class spirit into top quality oak. And make no mistake: this really is high class distillate. The spices have to be experienced to be believed but the faux bourbon effect, with its labarynthine dark sugar effect, is no less astonishing. What a not-quite-whisky treat....! *62.2%. sc.*

COTSWOLDS DISTILLERY Shipton-on-Stour. Working.

Cotswolds Distillery 5 Months batch no. 04/2015, ex-oloroso sherry cask, bott 1 Sept 15 db (89.5) n21.5 t23.5 f22 b22.5. The fact that this is, thankfully, a clean sherry butt means we can spot some clues to the future style of this malt. It is clearly small still type, revelling in all its inherent intensity. But we can already see a confirmation of the new make: this a malt which likes to get off to a dramatic start, pitching all the elements of the flavour profile together in the first few moments before letting things unravel. At this age you let the odd jarring moment go, as all maturing spirit lacks a degree of couthness, with a degree of extra roughage from the extra copper. *63.5%. ncf.*

Cotswolds Distillery 10 Months cask no. 32, ex-red wine cask, bott 1 Sept 15 db (91) n22 t23.5 f22.5 b23. This one, showing some of the first will-be whisky made at the distillery, has already begun to settle into a flavour rhythm. The body of the spirit is able to hold the powering fresh fruit with ease and allows the malt to interact from an early stage. Some very decent spices abound, though they have to work hard to get through the weightiness of the malt's weight. Again, a little sharpness at the finish: with the stills being brand new, that is entirely expected. Exceptionally promising malt from my neighbours just the other side of Banbury. *63.5%. ncf sc.*

   ♦ **Cotswolds Distillery Single Malt 25 Months Peated Quarter Casks** cask no. 221, bott 4 Jun 17 db (93.5) n23.5 t23 f23.5 b23.5 A malt which has no right to boast this kind of depth, and even-ness at this age. No doubt the smaller casks have helped by injecting sufficient tannin to stabilise a malt's natural tendency at this age to buck around in the barrel. But the big smoke has assisted, also, as that has added further weight and enriched a rather lovely toasty and roasty chocolate element that would be recognisable in the wonderful Double Stout brewed just up at the road at arguably Britain's finest brewery, Hook Norton. *62.4%. sc.*

   Cotswolds Distillery New Make batch no. 08/2015, bott 1 Sept 15 db (94) n23.5 t24 f23 b23.5. High quality new make still glistening with a coppery sheen on both nose and taste. And it is on delivery where it really stars, showing a gorgeous weight and great confidence as it maximises the malt. All spices and gristy sugars present and correct. The only thing missing is the usual cocoa dryness present on the finish of most good quality new makes. Maybe hiding behind the new still copper sharpness. *63.5%. ncf.*

   Cotswolds Distillery New Make Spirit batch no. WC 22:2:2, dist 29 May 16, bott 11 Jul 16 db (89) n20 t23.5 f23 b22.5. Slightly different character to the last new make bottling I tasted from them. Here, they have allowed the cut to be just a little too wide, impacting on the nose. Though that can mean a massive personality on delivery, which is in evidence here. Loads of malt and chocolate notes later on, and astonishing sugars in between. Yummy doesn't quite cover it. Though with my blender's technical hat on, a few marks dropped. Anyway, thought I'd taste this English whisky – made just a short journey from my tasting room - on the very day our new Prime Minister, Theresa May, formed a brand new cabinet which includes the Whisky Bible's local MP as Environment Secretary: here's to you, Andrea! *63.5%*

   ♦ **Cotswolds Distillery New Make Spirit Plumage Archer** bott 6 Jun 17 db (95) n23.5 t24 f23.5 b24 Absolutely top-notch, ultra-salivating and characterful new make which enjoys a stunning fruity flair (and, of course, not a wine cask in sight) before it settles down to the more basic business of radiating quite beautiful malt. Gorgeously weighted and excellent residual cocoa and spice. By quite peculiar coincidence, the last time I tasted the Cotswold's new make for The Bible, it was on the very day Theresa May was announced as Prime Minister. This sample for the 2018 Bible arrived today: on the morning, slightly less than a year later, that a chastened and greatly weakened Theresa May was confirmed at Buckingham Palace as Prime Minister again after limply and loosely "winning" a snap election. As this New Make would in barrel discover, a year is not very long in the life of a whisky. However, it can be a lifetime in British politics... *63.5%.*

   ♦ **Cotswolds Distillery Single Malt Prototype 29 Months** bott 6 Jun 17 db (90.5) n21.5 t24 f22.5 b22.5 This remarkable malt is all to do with oak: cut the spirit and it'll have rings on it.... Tannins screech at you on both the nose and finish and were they any louder they might be problematic. However, such is the staggering intensity of the barley and sugar delivery it never gets to that point... and one is able to forgive anything. Again, the sweet notes have been plucked from the barrel, a kind of distilled maple syrup in richness. The red liquorice and drier chalkiness towards the finish is also an oaky giveaway. What an experience...! *62.4%.*

   Cotswolds Distillery Single Malt Spirit 20 Months Old bourbon cask, cask no. 47, bott 11 Jul 16 db (91) n21.5 still clings to its new makey aroma...; t23 after an initial burst of slight feint we are almost overpowered by a glorious avalanche of intense, almost concentrated malty grist. The sugars are caught on an oily tide and crash relentlessly in to the spices; f23.5 a stunning interplay between chocolate, vanilla and grist; b23 coming along rather beautifully... *61.8%*

   Cotswolds Distillery Single Malt Spirit 20 Months Old ex-red wine cask (shaved, toasted & recharred), cask no. 58, bott 11 Jul 16 db (94) n22.5 very tight tannin: something more akin to lively bourbon than a single malt; t24 oh, do I have to spit...? Really...? Damn it! This is so, so lovely. Salivating malt from the very first second. But the levels of tannin-enriched barley and the varying intensity of the sugars is mesmerising. A slick oiliness appears to attach itself to the more profound dark muscovado; f23.5 long, with a light citrus edging to the vanilla; a light hint of treacle towards the end just as the spices get serious; b24 if they don't put the brakes on this, it'll be too old by the time it reaches 36 months. At this moment, simply stunning! *62.7%*

   ♦ **Cotswolds Distillery Single Malt 30 Months Re-rack** cask no. 4, bott 4 Jun 17 db (89.5) n22 t23.5 f21.5 b22.5 A thick malt, creamy textured and brimming with muscovado sugars and eye-watering tannin. To taste, a happy, agreeable mix of cream soda and chocolate raisin with a slow, almost, apologetic spiciness and a light degree of bitterness on the finish. One of those malts which hasn't quite found its feet as a fair bit of tannic turbulence is encountered on both nose and in in the aftershocks of delivery. But overall...wow! *62.4%. sc.*

HEALEY'S CORNISH CYDER FARM Penhallow. Working.
Hicks & Healey Cornish Whiskey 2004 Cask #32 dist 13 Feb 04, bott Feb 12 db **(96)** n24 t24.5 f23.5 b24. I picked this one up absent-mindedly, nosed...and was carried to Cornwall. I knew what it was without even opening my eyes. Unmistakable. And just so stunningly beautiful... *60.2%. ncf.*

LAKES DISTILLERY Cumbria. Working.
The Lakes Malt Spirit db **(90)** n23 t22 f22.5 b22.5. I have chosen this as the 999th new "whisky" for the 2017 Bible as a tribute to my dear old friend Harold Currie who was recently lost to us. Harold was behind the building of the Isle of Arran Distillery and a close bond, based mainly on mutual respect and fondness for the simple things in life – like St Mirren and football in general – formed between us. Both his sons played a part in getting this distillery off the ground, so though not yet a whisky, it is a special moment for me to taste their new-ish make. With the very first sip I ever have of this ground-breaking malt, I shall toast a very special old fiend: Harold Currie.... A lovely developing malt with a very puritanical cut ensuring the citrus has a big part to play. Massively promising as this is clean and characterful. But, my dear old friends, you have to bottle this stuff at something closer to cask strength: you have broken up the oils so we cannot quite see its full potential. *40%*

ST. GEORGE'S Rowdham. Working.
The English Whisky Co. Chapter 6 Unpeated cask no. 248, 249, 250, 251, dist Oct 10, bott Nov 13 db **(89.5)** n22.5 t22.5 a light honey thread distracts from the slightly new-makey breeze; t22 outrageously juicy on delivery, but the malt is febrile and takes time to happily link with the oak; f23 the slow pulsing of the dry cocoa is sublime though, unusually, this is from the spirit rather than the oak. Just how good the original spirit was becomes clear as the maltiness makes its mark; b22 a very solid score, though anything under 90 seems like a failure for this particular distillery. A rare occurrence where the youth of the spirit and the influence of the oak have been detached. Still a thing of youthful beauty when all is said and done. *60.2%. WB15/183*

The English Whisky Co. Chapter 7 Rum Cask cask no. 765, 766, dist Oct 09, bott May 14 db **(92)** n22.5 confidently crisp rum influence from the kickoff: a light, sugary shell encrusts the beautifully defined barley; t23 mmmm...!! Such a glorious fanfare of intense barley on delivery, which intensifies even further with a chunky gristiness during the slow progression; f23.5 quite wonderful finish: the rum re-emerges somewhat with a light sugary sheen to the charming chalky oak and citrus gristy mix; b23 an essay in understated deliciousness. A near perfect use of delicate sugar. *46%. nc ncf. 550 bottles. WB15/188*

The English Whisky Co. Chapter 7 cask no. 0765, 0766, dist Oct 09, bott May 14 db **(94)** n23 t23.5 f24 b23.5. Of all the English Whisky bottlings to its sister version (above), this is the closest in style despite the alcohol leap. Everything here, though, is more polished, concentrated and vivid....as you might expect. Quite superb. *59.9%. 96 bottles. WB15/187*

The English Whisky Co. Chapter 7 Single Malt Rum Cask cask no. 0459 & 0461, dist May 09, bott Apr 15 db **(91.5)** n22.5 t24.5 f22 b22.5 There is quite a profound difference between the delivery and finish. *59.9%. nc ncf.*

The English Whisky Co. Chapter 7 Rum Casks, cask no. 057, 059, 487 & 488, dist May 09, bott Feb 16 db **(92.5)** n23t23 f23 b23.5 You'll be hard pressed to find a better whisky to kick start an evening a tune up the taste buds before dinner. *46%. ncf nc.*

⁘ **The English Whisky Co. Chapter 7 Rum Cask** cask nos.471 & 472 db **(92.5)** n23 excellent confidence to the oak, the vanilla tucking neatly into the youthful barley and budding honey tones; t23.5 textbook delivery: a light golden syrup paves the way for the spices and barley to flourish which they do despite the background feel of young, salivating malt; a light sugary, rum induced coating covers the palate; f23 the warming spices rumble on; b23 what an amazingly consistent malt this is: the Chapter 7 Rum Cask has become one of highlights of my tasting year, simply because you suspect what you going to get...and never end up disappointed. Slightly more youthful than before, but still another minor gem from St George. *46%. nc ncf.*

The English Whisky Co. Chapter 9 Peated cask no. 0201, 0202, 0203 & 0205, dist Apr 10, bott Jul 13 db **(94)** n22.5 t23.5 f24, b24 Not sure an English whisky has ever come across this chocolatey in the history of...well, English whisky. For those of you who have decided to give up sex, here's its replacement... 59.4%. ncf nc. 96 bottles.

The English Whisky Co. Chapter 9 Peated cask no. 354, 355, 356 & 577, dist Apr 13, bott May 16 db **(93)** n22.5 t23.5 f23.5 f23.5 It quite beggars belief that this is a 3-y-o whisky. Just so beautiful...this must be the mid cut of the very heart of the run... 46%. ncf nc.

The English Whisky Co. Chapter 11 Heavily Peated ASB casks, cask no. 0062, 0065, dist Apr 09, bott Jul 12 db **(81)** n19 t22 f21 b19. A rare blemish. This malt is very much less than the sum of its parts as not enough attention was made in balancing out the peats and the sugars. Brief harmony as the sugars and oils hit the palate, but on the nose and for long periods in the mouth this is a free for all: young malts are temperamental. And here the balance has not been found. 46%. nc ncf.

The English Whisky Co. Chapter 11 Heavily Peated ASB casks, cask no. 639, 640, 641 & 642, dist Mar 08, bott Nov 11 db **(91.5)** n22.5 t23 f23 b23. One of the sweetest English whiskies for the last century... 46%. nc ncf.

The English Whisky Co. Chapter 13 Dragon cask no.527, 528, 827, 830, dist 2008, bott 2013 db **(92.5)** n23.5 t23.5 f22 b23.5 Take your time with this: like all the best whiskies, this is a moving target never sitting still and with so many elements camouflaged before being spotted. 49%. ncf nc. WB15/397

The English Whisky Co. Chapter 13 London db **(91)** n22 t24 f22 b23 The nose suggests sherry butts at work here, as does the slightly furry finale. But this is a superficial wound and the overall composition is rather lovely. 45%. nc ncf. WB15/181

The English Whisky Co. Chapter 13 Letter Box db **(87)** n21.5 t22.5 f21 b22. How odd. Some of the characteristics found on their 2014 St George's day bottling can be found here, too. Except for this latest edition, those flatter notes are flatter still. No shortage of malt, mind. 45%. nc ncf.

The English Whisky Co. Chapter 14 ASB Casks, cask no. 057, 059, 487 & 488, dist Sept 09, bott Jul 15 db **(94.5)** n24 t23.5 f23 b24 Only six years old! Boasts the complexity of a malt three times that age. Beautiful malt: simple as! 46%. ncf nc.

◇◇◇ **The English Whisky Co. Chapter 14 ASB Casks 5 Year Old** cask nos. 290, 291, 292 & 293, dist Nov 11, bott Nov 16 db **(92)** n23 as usual, radiates the aromas often found in old English tea rooms of freshly baked apple and pear tart, muscovado sugar and, unusually, but fitting the bill perfectly, lightly milked mocha...; t23.5 the essence of fruit, so charming and delicate on the nose, plays a lesser role as it is the barley in full, salivating concentrated form which pulls the strings. A little ulmo honey towards the finish, as well as egg custard tart; f22.5 plenty of vanilla and spice to till get on with as the oak bitters things slightly; b23 an intense, satisfying malt that keeps you guessing in which direction it is heading next. 46%. nc ncf.

The English Whisky Co. Chapter 14 Not Peated cask no. 120, 121, 122 & 123, dist Apr 11, bott Jun 16 db **(96)** n24 t24 f24 b24 There are less than 200 bottles of this unambiguously world-class and faultless nectar, apparently. What a bugger...! 58.8%. ncf nc. 192 bottles.

The English Whisky Co. Chapter 14 Single Malt (unpeated) cask no. 205, 181, 182, 183, dist Apr 10, bott May 15 db **(92.5)** n23 the oak plays little toffeed patterns upon the malt: soft and belying its age. The vanilla confirms more oak than usually seen from this distillery; t23.5 a beautiful oily cushion offers a tapestry of intense malt and toffee apple; f23 vanilla and butterscotch before a little toasted fudge begins to softly clear its throat...; b23 how can a malt at nearly 60%abv be so silky soft and sexy? A ridiculously gentle and genteel whisky. 58.8%. nc ncf.

The English Whisky Co. Chapter 15 Single Malt Heavily Peated cask no. 041, 042, 043, 043, dist Jun 09, bott Sept 14 db **(94.5)** n23.5 t24 f23.5 b23.5 If all whiskies were like this, I'd never get this book finished: so easy to go off into another world as you explore the peaty complexity to its character. Just great stuff! 58.4%. nc ncf. 192 bottles.

The English Whisky Co. Chapter 15 English Single Malt (peated) db **(94.5)** n23.5 t24 f23 b24. If you could take that single flaw out of the equation, you'd have just about perfect whisky for a five-year-old. As it is, you'll just have to make do with bloody magnificent.... And make no mistake: this is no poor man's Islay. It stands up with the world's elite. 58.4%. nc ncf.

The English Whisky Co. Chapter 15 Heavily Peated ASB casks, cask no. 180, 214, 215 & 216, dist May 10, bott Jan 16 db **(89.5)** n22 t23 f22.5 b22 A rare whisky where the sum is less than the parts. Never finds a rhythm or narrative: it is like a series of disconnected stories are told on the palate. Yet many moments are superb. 46%. ncf nc.

The English Whisky Co. Chapter 15 Heavily Peated cask no. 145, 146, 147 & 148, dist Feb 10, bott Sept 15 db **(95.5)** n23.5 t24 f24 b24 Almost from the Lagavulian of vaguely fruity, pretty oily, intensely peaty school of malt whisky. Sublime. 58.4%. ncf nc. 192 bottles.

The English Whisky Co. Chapter 16 Single Malt Peated, Sherry Cask cask nos. 693 & 694, dist Nov 07, bott Sept 14 db **(95)** n23 t24.5 f23.5 b24 there are few occasions when sherry and peat travel comfortably together, hand-in-hand. But here is one, thanks to the softness (and general cleanness) of the grape and non-bombastic, embracing style of the peat. As gentle giants go, this is benign and enormous... 58.3%. nc ncf.

⬧ **The English Whisky Co. Chapter 16** peated sherry casks db (95) n23.5 there is a distinct acidic bite to the peat which compliments the simplistic fruit wonderfully; a lovely smoked hickory depth to the fruit and nut; t24 succulent with equal early emphasis on both fruit and smoke, though the big surprise is the Caol Isla-esque depth of oiliness which gives, as well as the softest imaginable deliveries, the sugars in particular a much longer shelf life; the barley can still be spotted all though this, clean and proud and boasting no great age at all; f23.5 serious spice peppers the lingering grape. The smoke is in no hurry to go anywhere soon; b24 quite superbly vatted: the marriage between smoke and grape is a rare success for the style and there is not a single atom of sulphur to be bought. Truly brilliant! 46%. nc ncf.

⬧ **The English Whisky Co. Chapter 17 Small Batch Release** batch no. 01/2017, dist Jun 12, bott Jun 17 db (87) n22 t23.5 f20 b21.5 A typical St George's malt explosion, the delivery being something of a grist convention. But there is a tang to this with the tannins never quite being on the same song sheet as the malt. That all said, worth finding just for the spiced barley-caramel extravaganza on delivery alone...! 46%. nc ncf. 1,641 bottles.

⬧ **The English Whisky Co. Founders Private Cellar 2010** bourbon & virgin cask, cask 365, dist Dec 10, bott Mar 16 db (94) n23 lots of apples at play: toffee apple and apple strudel, to start...and a little steamed apple into the bargain. But there are delicate sugary tones, also – a little hint of maple syrup and on the vanilla and ever growing spices to compliment; t24 just won-der-ful....!!! There is no great age to the barley, so it still has its sheen and integrity intact, so dispensing a ridiculous juiciness. But the grist also meets the oak-laden sugars head on, so there is a dramatic peak to the sweetness, a rush of intense muscovado sugars, heather honey and light molasses...all found in the maltiest sea...wow! f23 the oak notes increase the spice levels and dryness, though the big butterscotch and barley keep things even; b24. Whisky snobs will put this comment down as an insult to this distillery (which it most certainly isn't), but certain elements of this malt – especially on the nose - have remarkable similarities with the long discontinued no age-statement Glenfiddich which, in its day, offered one of the most thrilling and pugnacious malt signatures on the world stage. This is a slightly more honey rich and magnificent version. 59.7%. nc ncf sc. 285 bottles.

The English Whisky Co. Original bourbon cask db (89) n22.5 so light. The malt seems distracted by the gently encroaching vanillas and with the oils scuppered at this strength the daintier notes have a slight advantage; rarely does barley come much greener than this...; t22.5 clean, soft, silky, exceptionally malty and then a surge of salivating gristly sweetness. It is like being licked to death by a neighbour's slobbering pet Labrador...; f22 the vanilla and light citrus fade are entirely in keeping; b22 when I first tasted this an odd thing happened. For a moment I thought I was tasting an old Scottish blend still in lab form and pre-bottled from over 25 years ago. I certainly didn't recognise it as Norfolk's finest. Pleasant, hugely enjoyable and friendly. But by EWC standards, pretty basic, too. 43%.

The English Whisky Co. Smokey bourbon cask db (93.5) n23 quite a different type of phenol here, sharp and acrid and not dissimilar to that found inside a crisp packet...; t23 ridiculously soft delivery. Like their "Original" at 43% this has a curious and not unattractive feel of an old blend about it, the lightness of the body being in stark contrast to the weight of the peat. Sugars, of course, abound but in beautifully controlled form; f23.5 now we hit super complexity as the phenols calm sufficiently for the light tannins and liquorice to make brilliant contrast to the glittering array of dark, toasty sugars; b24 they could have also written "smoky bacon cask".... 43%.

⬧ **The English Single Malt Whisky Smokey** bourbon casks, batch no. L001 16 db (90.5) n23 smoky; t23 oily and smoky; f22 smoky and bittering; b22.5 smoky... 43%. nc ncf.

⬧ **English Single Malt Whisky Smokey The Original** bourbon casks, batch no. L002 16 db (91) n22.5 nutty with simple light maple syrup and thin strands of malt, the odd one still quite young; t23.5 some controlled, warming spice immediately on delivery, then there's that maple syrup again ensuring both sweetness and the lushest mouth feel; nutty caramel and then rich fudge with the hints of a green apple sharpness from the youthful malt; f22 dries with a little date fruitiness and significant sawdusty vanilla; b23 very much a simplified version the previous Original thanks to a significant upping on the oak-drained sugars... 43%. nc ncf.

HRH Princess Charlotte of Cambridge db (95) n23.5 t24 f23.5 b24 To pay tribute to the latest member of the British royal family, I saved this as the 1,028th new and very last whisky for the 2016 Bible. Knowing first-hand her grandfather's taste for fine whisky, I am sure he will, like me, enjoy raising a glass of this most intensely malty bottling, which showcases the distillery in elegant style. 46%

 The Norfolk Single Grain Farmers American oak, batch no. 01/2016, bott 1 Nov 16 db **(91)** n23 now there's a half hour nose if ever there was one: in bourbon, they'd call it small grain complexity. Neither sweet nor dry, yet vaguely both, there is also a distinct salted porridge note to this, too; t24 bewildering delivery: as busy as a whisky can get with tiny little flavour explosions pinging around the palate. Slightly more sweetness than on the nose, as a little heather honey finds its range early on and stays the course. The texture has that distinct oily softness unique to oat whisky and presumably wheat with a deep, highly warming spiciness; f21.5 ah...just bitters slightly, a light, salty tang perhaps upping the sharper tannic notes; b22.5 I know that St George's outstanding distiller, David Fitt, has a partiality to this particular multi-grain (yes, multi-grain: not single grain, as seven different grain types are in the recipe...don't ask!) creation. I can see why, as it is a grand departure from its norm. It is engaging and intriguing, but falls very slightly towards the end as the harmonisation between grain and oak hasn't quite peaked... 45%. nc ncf sc. 1,998 bottles.

 The Norfolk Single Grain Malt 'N' Rye American oak, batch no. 01/2017, bott 23 Jan 17 db **(88)** n22 hefty and oily, the usual sharp fruity rye note is silenced by both barley and vanilla; t22.5 chewy, salivating and increasingly firm in texture as it progresses. Big oils, a light buzz of spice and ever-increasing butterscotch through the middle; f21.5 a little sharp, though oily; b22 a strange beast, absolutely bursting with flavour yet never quite finds the rhythm it seeks. 45%. nc ncf sc. 1,962 bottles.

 The Norfolk Single Grain Parched db **(96.5)** n24.5 that unmistakable mix of soft malt and rock hard barley grain leaves little doubt of the grain coupling here, to be sure, though nothing is said on the label. In classic Pot Still style, beautifully enhanced by an almost pollen-complex dry honey note, unique to this style of whisk(e)y; t24 quite fabulous. Not just the astonishing heather-honey delivery but the seemingly lush texture which hardens by the second. Curiously salivating and dry at one and the same moment...; f23.5 there is always a threat early on of spice with Pot Still, but it usually breaks out at the end when the most vigorous sugars are exhausted. The tannins kiss gently but dryly, while those spices rise perceptibly...; b24.5 a classic Irish "mod pot" style Irish pot still whiskey...from Norfolk! Nosed this when it was just a few months old...and it has moved on magnificently; indeed, beyond hope and expectation. Only the cat's bowler on the label and a green bottle seems to give the faintest hint towards anything Irish... For the record, by far the best Pot Still I have ever encountered made outside Ireland's shores... 45%. nc ncf sc.

Master of Malt Single Cask English Whisky Co. 5 Year Old oloroso sherry cask, dist Apr 10, bott Feb 16 **(75)** n18 t20 f18 b19. God! If only those silly sods in Spain hadn't shoved a sulphur candle in this. Even through the murk, there are some sugars at work which astound. What a malt this might have been. Bollocks! 65.3%. sc.

Master of Malt Single Cask English Whisky Co. 5 Year Old Heavily Peated bourbon cask, dist Jul 10, bott Feb 16 **(94)** n23.5 t24 f23 b23.5 You know when they say "heavily peated"...? Well, this is heavily peated...and, frankly, almost peerlessly made... 67.4%. sc.

Master of Malt Single Cask English Whisky Co. 7 Year Old bourbon cask, cask no. B1/490, dist Aug 08, bott Feb 16 **(92.5)** n23 t23 f22.5 b23 Very similar to cask B1/491 except this appears slightly further down the road in terms of development. 67.2%. sc.

Master of Malt Single Cask English Whisky Co. 7 Year Old bourbon cask, cask no. B1/491, dist Aug 08, bott Feb 16 **(90.5)** n23 t22.5 f22 b22.5 Still something of a new make feel to this. In a way, it's a shame it was bottled: I would have set this aside for another eight years at least, after which I think it would have thrust itself upon greatness... 67.3%. sc.

That Boutique-y Whisky Company English Whisky Co. 5 Year Old batch 1 **(91)** n22 t23 f22.5 b23.5 How do you get a malt this young to perform so many adult tricks...? 49.5%. 964 bottles.

FINLAND
THE HELSINKI DISTILLING COMPANY Helsinki. Working.

The Helsinki Distilling Co Single Malt 2014 Prelude 1 Year Old batch 5, cask no. 13-21, dist 01 Sept 14, bott 17 Dec 15 db **(91.5)** n22 t23 f23.5 b23. Just over a year old, yet dosed up with more tannin than some scotch malts see over 20 years... Presumably, either very small, heavily charred and/or virgin oak at play here. Delightfully distilled, the clarity of the spirit allows the oak extra dominance. But those rather angular molassed sugars, as well as the mocha, liquorice and toffee concentrate, work very well in tandem with the inevitable spices. By age, not actually whisky. But close your eyes and you'll never know: Fins aren't what they seem to be... 58%

◈ **The Helsinki Distilling Co. Prelude 23 Months Single Malt** 190 litre American virgin oak, cask no. 105, dist 23 Jun 15, bott 19 May 17 db **(89)** **n21.5 t22.5 f23 b22** Fabulous experience for the most part with a concentrated malt component you have to use a pneumatic drill to get through. Again, the signs are that the cut times are slightly more generous than their earlier distillations which affords a degree of extra flavour but does nothing for the overall precision and quality of the malt. Once more a wonderful coffee character, but this also boasts rich molasses and Manuka honey for good measure. *61%.*

◈ **The Helsinki Distilling Co. Prelude 24 Months 100% Rye** 55 litre French virgin oak, cask no. 91, dist 15 May 15, bott 19 May 17 db **(77)** **n19 t20 f19 b19** Mon Dieu! Stick to bourbon barrels: the cabbage-laden tannins here are so powerful they render the rye practically silent. And that seriously takes some doing. *62.7%.*

◈ **The Helsinki Distilling Co. Prelude 26 Months Straight Rye** 190 litre American virgin oak, cask no. 83, dist 19 Mar 15, bott 19 May 17 db **(88.5)** **n21.5 t23 f22 b22** A significantly wider cut than their earlier distillations and they'll have to watch this. Predictably, it mingles with the huge sugars off the grain and cask to create a coffee effect. Don't want that to distract from the mind-exploding and palate-pulsating rye which gives its all in one of the most full blooded samples I have tasted this year. A cleaner version would score a very high mark, indeed. *59.5%.*

◈ **The Helsinki Distilling Co. Prelude 31 Months Straight Rye** 28 litre French virgin oak, cask no. 27, dist 20 Oct 14, bott 19 May 17 db **(81.5)** **n21 t18 f23.5 b19** You can have too much of a good thing, I'm not sure the French oak was a good thing to start with... Still, no denying the stunning deliciousness of the coffee on the finish. But it is a bloody battle to get there... *61.5%.*

The Helsinki Distilling Co Single Malt 2015 batch 6, cask no. 15-SM5, dist 29 Jan 15, bott 02 Feb 15 db **(78.5)** **n19 t21 f19 b19.5.** Sweet: tick. Malty: tick. But that isn't quite enough when the copper has gone AWOL. *60.5%*

The Helsinki Distilling Co White Dog 100% Rye batch 5, dist 21 Oct 15, bott 16 Dec 15 db **(92.5)** **n23 t23 f23.5 b23.** A crisp, intense rye spirit which appears to achieve the goal that has been targeted. As well as the desired fruit note and spice, a little ulmo honey meanders around to sweeten the dose. I look forward to seeing its sister distillate make its mark over the forthcoming years. Impressive. *60.5%*

The Helsinki Distilling Co White Dog Straight Rye batch 63, dist 15 Dec 15, bott 17 Dec 15 db **(88)** **n22 t22 f22 b22.** Seemingly, less copper contact here than with their batch 5 100% rye. Salivating and filled with burgeoning rye, a drier run with a bigger spice kick. Good powdered cocoa finale, as it should be. *60.5%*

PANIMORAVINTOLA KOULU Turku. Working.

Sgoil Bourbon Cask 6 Years Old db **(88)** **n22.5** sultana fruit cake, sprinkled in fruity light muscovado sugar, ginger and nutmeg; **t22** distinctly doughy with a spiced spotted dog pudding feel; **f21.5** spiced ulmo honey does its best to overcome a nagging bitterness; **b22** not sure if you are meant to drink this or bake it... *59%. sc.*

Sgoil Sherry Cask db **(90)** **n23** my parrot, Percy, would absolutely kill for these juicy, musky sapphire grapes; **t23.5** something of the Torqui about this delivery: fat, intense and purposeful, with a slow unravelling of herbs and spices as it dries in the same pace a striptease artist slowly reveals her hidden charms; **f21.5** annoyingly bitters at the death, despite all the fruity attention; **b22.5** sherry...and clean as a whistle! A sulphur-free dram from Finland. *59%. sc. 80 bottles.*

PANIMORAVINTOLA BEER HUNTER'S Pori. Working.

Old Buck cask no. 4, dist Mar 04, bott Apr 10 db **(95)** **n24 t23 f24 b24.** Just read the tasting notes to the second release because, a dose of what almost seems like corn oil and ancient Demerara rum combined apart, oh - and an extra dose of oak, there is barely any difference. I will never, ever forget how I got this sample: I was giving a tasting in Helsinki a few months back to a horseshoe-shaped audience and a chap who had been sitting to my right and joining in with all the fun introduced himself afterwards as I signed a book for him as non other than Mika Heikkinen, the owner and distiller of this glorious whisky. I had not been told he was going to be there. His actual, touchingly humble words were: "You might be disappointed: you may think it rubbish and give it a low score. It just means I have to do better next time." No, I am not disappointed: I am astonished. No, it isn't rubbish: it is, frankly, one of the great whiskies of the year. And if you can do better next time, then you are almost certainly in line for the Bible's World Whisky of the Year award. *70.6%*

TEERENPELI Tahti. Working.

Teerenpeli Single Malt 10 Year Old bourbon & sherry casks db **(80)** n20 t21 f19 b20. Very hard to see what an average sherry butt can add to a malt as good as Teerenpeli's. And, sad to say, this is very average sherry wood, indeed... 43%

Teerenpeli Single Malt Distiller's Choice Aura Porter-wood matured db **(88.5)** n22 t22.5 f22 b22 Before tasting this, I thought my researcher had accidentally added an "er " to Port Finish. Until I saw the colour...and discovered the lurking hops. As curious as it is tasty! 43%. sc. 426 bottles.

Teerenpeli Single Malt Distiller's Choice KARHI Madeira cask finish db **(92.5)** n23 t23.5 f23 b23 A delicious malt which, in the glass, has a habit of disappearing into Finnair... 43%. 1882 bottles. Duty Free Exclusive.

Teerenpeli Single Malt Distiller's Choice RASI Moscatel cask finish db **(93)** n23.5 t24 f22.5 b23 I see this distillery is giving up its reputation of offering some of the biggest whisky in the world for a more subtle approach... 43%. 2554 bottles. Duty Free Exclusive.

Teerenpeli Single Malt Distiller's Choice Tallink Silja Edition Portwood Finish bourbon cask, finished in Port cask db **(93)** n23.5 t23.5 f23 b23 Typically Teerenpeli in its depth but now with well balanced fruitiness. 43% 1174 bottles.

Teerenpeli Kaski Single Malt sherry cask db **(90.5)** n23 t23.5 f21.5 b22.5. A pristine sherry butt ensures massive fruit. Impressed. 43%

⟫ **Teerenpeli Suomi 100 Single Malt Whisky** bott 26 Aug 16 db **(95)** n23.5 well, that's not peaty... (for those not used to British humour....it actually is. Very.); t24 The Parma violet on the nose arrives in double quick time here: the smoke is ethereal rather than earthy and builds up with the liquorice and manuka honey; f23.5 oh, if only this was at 46%...! The oils fragment allowing the smoke an early exit path, though the chocolate chip mint on the finale sits gorgeously with the remaining phenols; b24 brilliant: a Megastar...! 43%.

⟫ **Teerenpeli Tallink Silva Megastar Single Malt Whisky** bott 13 Feb 17 db **(93.5)** n23.5 has the fresh malty clarity of a top rank Speysider. An intriguing mix of barley sugar, pear drop and lemon sherbet; t24 what amazing clarity to this malt: beautifully distilled – this must have been the heart of the heart. The barley melts in the mouth and might have even got full points had the oils not been broken apart by the watering down...; f23 into every little vanilla some spice must fall...; b23 underpowered at 43%. But technically sublime... 43%.

FRANCE
Single Malt
DISTILLERIE ARTISANALE LEHMANN Obernai. Working.

Elsass Whisky Single Malt Whisky Alsacien Gold db **(84.5)** n21.5 t22 f20 b21. The family of my old French girlfriend, Dominique, had an Alsacien. Dog, not whisky. And despite the breed's ferocious nature, I bonded with it more than any other dog before or since. For it was just a friendly as this caramel-rich offering. But had a lot more energy and personality. 40%. ncf.

Elsass Whisky Single Malt Whisky Alsacien Origine bott code. LF02 db **(83)** n19 t22 f21 b21. The soft feintiness on the nose warns of the riches of the oils to come. But before they reassemble on the finish, there is a lovely barley moment about two thirds of the way through the passage which does impress. 40%. ncf.

Elsass Whisky Single Malt Whisky Alsacien Premium db **(86)** n20.5 t21.5 f22 b22. This is about as close as you'll get to an abstract single malt. The early discordant notes of the distillate are thrown against the canvas of the malt, and then fruit is randomly hurled at it, making a juicy, then spicy, splash. The overall picture when you stand back is not at all bad. But getting there is a bit messy. 50%. ncf.

DISTILLERIE BERTRAND Uberach. Working.

Uberach db **(77)** n21 t19 f18 b19. Big, bitter, booming. Gives impression something's happening between smoke and grape... whatever it is, there are no prisoners taken. 42.2%

DISTILLERIE CASTAN Villeneuve-sur-Vère. Working.

⟫ **Vilanova Berbie** db **(80)** n20 t21 f19 b20 For what it boasts in intensity it lacks in grace and elegance. Uncomfortable on both nose and finish thanks to less than impressive oak, it just has too much of everything. Some will doubtless find the concentrated prunes and molasses very much to their liking. 44%. ncf.

⟫ **Vilanova Berbie Single Cask** batch no. 13 db **(89.5)** n22.5 a charming grape pip aroma mingling with the still fresh barley: lively and fruity; t22 drops into neutral for a moment or two while both the fruit and barley try to work out who is boss. Only towards the late middle does a little spice and vanilla reveal it is the oak in charge; **f22.5** clean with a dry cocoa fade; **b22.5** a classic and very enjoyable pre-prandial whisky which sharpens up the taste buds without overly exercising them themselves. *42%. ncf sc.*

◇ **Vilanova New Spirit Single Malt Classic** db **(90.5) n23 t23 f22.5 b22** A well-made, light bodied and clean new made showing distinct signs of gristy barley and, surprisingly, vanilla. *45.1%. ncf.*

◇ **Vilanova New Spirit Single Malt Terrocita** db **(91.5) n23.5 t23 f22 b23** The peat adds both weight and sweetness to this lean white dog. Plenty of gristy chewiness; the toasty smoked molasses lingers. *45.1%. ncf.*

◇ **Vilanova Terrocita** db **(91.5) n23** smoky for certain. But there are other aspects here I can't quite nail: cherry fruitcake for sure but something else vegetable – rather than animal or mineral – which hangs on the reek...; **t23.5** a very sweet, relatively fat delivery. The sugars are pretty rotund and up front, most of them molassed but all with a vanilla aspect; that cherry fruit cake – albeit well smoked and slightly burnt – continues to linger; **f22** much dryer with a big vanilla layering; **b23** have to admit that this is a nose and flavour profile I have never quite encountered before. What a shame it wasn't at about 55% ab .think we might have been heading off the planet from terra firma to terro cito... *43%. ncf.*

DISTILLERIE DE MONSIEUR BALTHAZAR Hérisson. Working.

Hedgehog Straight Whisky Bourbonnais bott code. L2.16 db **(85.5) n20 t22.5 f21.5 b21.5.** You'd expect this to be a prickly little beast. Yet it is anything but: it celebrates the oils and honeys generated by the ample cut to the full and with only a minimum degree of spice. Eye-watering at its height, an unmistakable rye tartness maximises the flavour profile and dominates deliciously to the end. Get that cut a little tighter and what a magnificent whisky we would have here. *45%. ncf.*

DOMAINE DES HAUTES GLACES Saint-John-d'Hérans. Working.

Domaine des Hautes Glaces Flavis Single Cask Organic Whisky db (84.5) **n21 t20 f22.5 b21.** Well, you can't say it doesn't have personality. Actually, the maltiness, which improves as it goes along, does hit impressive proportions. And the gathering cocoa also shows the oak plays an important part. But one or two verses of this are well out of tune. *46%. sc.*

Domaine des Hautes Glaces Moissons Single Malt Organic Whisky db (86.5) **n20.5 t22 f22 b22.** Warming this to body temperature is vital as, when cool, it is not the most attractive proposition and scores badly. But when it is opened by body heat, the most delicate phenols show a subtlety and weight which were not before apparent, as do the tannins which reveal a more generous and inclusive element. The sugars are decidedly of an oaky bent with a dark toastiness which melt towards the tannins. *42%*

DISTILLERIE DES MENHIRS Bretagne. Working.

Eddu Gold db **(93) n22 t23 f24 b24.** Rarely do whiskies turn up in the glass so rich in character to the point of idiosyncrasy. Some purists will recoil from the more assertive elements. I simply rejoice. This is so proud to be different. And exceptionally good, to boot!! *43%*

Eddu Grey Rock db **(87.5) n21.5 t22 f22 b22.** A docile whisky reliant on friendly muscovado sugars which match the vanilla-oak very attractively. *40%*

◇ **Eddu Grey Rock Affinage Porto** db (83) **n19 t21 f22 b21** Tasting whisky from this distillery is like taking part in a lucky dip: no idea if you'll pick a winner or the booby prize. This has the uncontrollable nose of a dud, but the fruit helps it pick up on the palate to an acceptable level. Good late spices, too. *40%.*

Eddu Grey Rock Brocéliande db (86.5) **n22 t22.5 f20.5 b21.5.** Dense whisky which enjoys an enjoyable molassed fruitcake theme. A bit thin and wonky towards the finish. *40%*

Eddu Silver db (81) **n20 t22 f19 b20.** A curiosity of a whisky, though not up to the distillery's normal high standards. The base spirit hasn't been cut to advantage, so the feints tend to damage both nose and finish. Some astonishing sugars on deliver, though. *40%.*

Eddu Silver Broceliande db **(92.5) n23 t23 f23 b23.5.** Pure silk. A beautiful and engaging experience. *40%.*

◇ **Eddu Grey Silver The Original** db (92.5) **n23** like lying in a field with the straw freshly mown but not yet gathered, complete with a fresher grassy, slightly leafy note...and just beyond the hedge sits the cliff plunging into the salty sea...; **t23** fuller bodied than the nose: the malt is a little earthier now; a milky-topped, almost cream-frothy, mocha allows the Demerara sugar to melt on top; **f23.5** more chocolate now, though the sugars are just as stunning; **b23** j'adore! *40%.*

◇ **Eddu Grey Silver Sherry Cask Finish** db (81.5) n20 t21 f21.5 b19 Sherbet cask finish, surely. Fizzes in a lemon sherbet kind of way. No sulphur: no off notes like that, all. And even a degree of mocha at the finish. But there is not a semblance of balance here. Attractively weird. 46%.

DISTILLERIE DU PÉRIGOLD Sarlat. Working.

Lascaw Aged 12 Years Blended Malt Whisky bott 2-12-15 db (87) n21 t22 f22 b22. A very pleasant blend, very much of a Scotch style. Super soft, safe though sometimes juicy, this is perhaps held back by a constant caramel theme which tames the expected high points. 40%

DISTILLERIE GILBERT HOLL Ribeauvillé. Working.

◇ **Lac'Holl 8 Year Old Single Malt Whisky** db (69) n19 t20 f14 b16 If memory serves, this is the youngest Lac'Hol I have tasted. But without doubt it is the most singular and disappointing. The profile of their whisky is usually far from conventional but attractive; this one is utterly bizarre and ugly. The peculiar scenting on the Swedish aquavit-style nose, which appears to include coconut sunscreen and orange liqueur, is matched only by the finish which reminds me, late on, of Milk of Magnesia. This has not been a good tasting day: it just got a whole lot worse... 42%.

Lac'Holl Vieil Or 10 Years Old Single Malt Whisky db (92.5) n22.5 a mixed spice aroma more commonly found in a mainland Europe bakers than in a whisky. That said...wonderful! t23.5 a fascinating delivery: both dry and sweet simultaneously! Seriously complex with those spices, the majority of them dry, really working overtime to keep in pace with the gristier malt; the mid-ground appears to be drifting off into orange blossom honey land...; f23 long, with the sugars now in command; b23.5 a malt which gives one's taste buds a real working over. Superb balance. 42%

Lac'Holl Junior 13 Years Old Single Malt Whisky db (89) n22 usually a kind of green barley/tobacco note like this spells trouble. But there's a lovely diced coconut dipped in maple syrup secondary story, too...; t22.5 ooh, so refreshing! The barley is being launched around the palate, again with a gorgeous maple syrup accompaniment; f22 spices join the merry throng, plus slightly more bitter vanilla notes from the oak; b22.5 wow!! Bursts from the glass with so much charisma and charm. Perhaps not technically the finest of all time, but so much fun! Delicious!! 43%

Lac'Holl 15 Years Old Single Malt Whisky db (90.5) n23.5 beautiful. Delicate citrus and freshly plucked and squeezed grass. Freshly baked apple tart, too; t22.5 superb clarity on delivery, just as the nose promised. Malty with a freshness which makes a mockery of the passing decade and a half, with a slow infusion of delicate vanilla; f22 medium length, but the barley is almost three dimensional; light enough for the more bitter oak notes to carry through; b22.5 such a rare display of barley and gristy sugars. Very impressive malt. And fabulously refreshing. 42%

DISTILLERIE GLANN AR MOR Larmor-Pleubian. Working.

Glan Ar Mor Maris Otter Barley 03/16 db (91.5) n22.5 t23 b23 Well done, chaps! One of the cleanest, barley-rich, malts I have ever tasted from the distillery: no feints...but plenty of faints...!! 46%

Glan Ar Mor Taol Esa 4ed Gwech 15 db (81) n19 t20 f21.5 b20.5. Definitely a step in the right direction for the weakest of their brands. Loads of toffee and barley sugar at work. Still a bit messy, though. 46%

Kornog 2013 For The Auld Alliance first fill bourbon barrel db (94.5) n23 t24 f23.5 b24 An extraordinary whisky worthy of seeking and enjoying. In a style of its own. And when I say style...I mean style.... Specially tasted on 6th June 2014 to mark the 70th anniversary of the New Alliance... 58.7%.

Kornog Oloroso Sherry Cask 15 db (68) n17 t18 f16 b17. Fails spectacularly on so many levels. 46%

Kornog Pedro Ximenez Cask 15 db (82.5) n20 t21.5 f20 b21. A steady malt, a bit sticky in places – which is hardly a surprise. Also, feinty in parts. The barley shows good survival instincts, though, and battles through to the end. 46%

Kornog Roc'h Hir db (95) n23 t24.5 f23.5 b24 It appears that the days of feinty whisky from this distillery are just about over. This is a sophisticated malt and delicate enough to highlight any flaw. Beautifully distilled, superbly matured. Congratulations: this is high class whisky. 46%

Kornog Saint Erwan 2014 first fill bourbon barrel db (88) n23 t23 f20.5 b21.5 A slightly simplistic malt. But entirely charming. 50%.

Kornog Saint Erwan 2015 db **(84.5) n21 t21.5 f21 b21.** Butter smeared on the delicately smoked malt. Lovely sensations, but doesn't quite fire right. *50%. Celtic Whisky Compagnie.*

Kornog Saint Erwan 2016 db **(89) n21.5 t23.5 f22 b22** A beast of a whisky. *50%*

Kornog Saint Ivy 2016 db **(93.5) n21.5 t24 f24 b24** Another enormous, yet very pretty whisky from a distillery which is reaching superstar status. *59.1%*

Kornog Taouarc'h Chwec'hved 14 BC db **(97) n24 t24 f24.5 b24.5** Delicately distilled, marvellously matured...a triumph! One of the very best whiskies I have since the 2015 Bible. And confirmation, along with Seizud 14, that this distillery has entered true World Class status. *58.2%*

Kornog Taouarc'h Seizued 14 BC db **(95) n23** wispy smoke: first it's here, then it's not...; strands of peek-a-boo coconut; nipping, fizzing spices...; **t23.5** a ridiculously beautiful delivery: gristy peat, where the sugars dissolve on your tongue like a lozenge. The house ulmo honey style remains as residue, as does the softest smoke imaginable; **f24** long, sophisticated and delicate to the point of being too scared to move...but that smoke just lingers on...; **b24.5** very rare that whiskies just get better and better on the palate. But here is one such case. A whisky of whispers and intrigue. *46%. Celtic Whisky Compagnie.*

Kornog Taouarc'h Kentan 16 BC db **(94.5) n24** I could almost mistake this for an Ardbeg: the peat is profound yet teasingly layered, the citrus weaves a thin but telling thread; light spices nip and nibble...astonishing...and not dissimilar to one of their bottlings of last year, if memory serves...; **t23.5** what beautiful weight: oily and with some early heftiness. But it lightens as the smoke stretches further around the palate with the lightest touch of ulmo honey and spice; **f23** buttery, with a mocha fade to the smoke; **b24** this is serious malt. Unquestionably an equal to some of the peated beauties of Islay. *46%*

DISTILLERIE GRALLET-DUPIC Rozelieures. Working.

G.Rozelieures Whisky De Lorraine Single Malt Whisky bott code: L446 db **(87) n21.5 t22.5 f21 b22.** Exceptionally nutty. The blossoming of the sugars on delivery is always attractive, as are the complex nougat/caramel/cocoa tones. Though the feints are always a threat, the genteel pace and softness of the malt makes it well worth a look. *46%*

G.Rozelieures Whisky De Lorraine Single Malt Whisky Fumé Collection bott code: L415 db **(91.5) n23** a very sensuous marriage of delicate smoke and moist fruitcake, complete with orange peel. Like whispers in the dark...; **t24** you almost want to applaud the mouth feel alone: starts with a salivating intent, but soon thickens slightly into something a lot more in keeping with those sensual notes on the nose; **f22** a slight flaw from a cask dries the malt rapidly; **b22.5** but for a lingering off note, this would have scored very highly indeed. A vague smokiness gives this a lovely weight. *46%*

G.Rozelieures Whisky De Lorraine Single Malt Whisky Rare Collection bott code: L446 db **(88.5) n19.5** feinty; vaguely copper-starved; **t23.5** an amazing mix of golden syrup, liquorice, molasses and succulent dates make for one very memorable experience, especially when you consider the excellent balance offered by the spice; **f22.5** dries, though there is a muscovado-date combination that ensures a comfortable finish; **b23** one of the sweetest and most lush malts this year, but always delicious. *40%*

G.Rozelieures Whisky De Lorraine Single Malt Whisky Tourbé Collection bott code: L416 db **(92) n22** the smokiest of their four bottlings on show here, though never dense; **t23.5** the usual lush house style with a bombardment of sugars and spice. The smoke again, is present but remarkably laid back; **f23** quite an oily fade with ulmo honey seeing off any late bitter incursions; **b23.5** there is a feinty flaw to this, and even perhaps a slight lack of copper in the system; but the overall picture is a very pretty one. *46%*

DISTILLERIE GUILLON Louvois. Working.

Guillon No. 1 Single Malt de la montagne de Reims db **(87) n22 t21 f22 b22.** Right. I'm impressed. Not exactly faultless, but enough life here really to keep the tastebuds on full alert; By and large well made and truly enjoyable. Well done, Les Chaps! *46%*

DISTILLERIE MEYER Hohwarth. Working.

Meyer's Le Whisky Alsacien Blend Superieur db **(90) n22.5** moist date and walnut cake; **t23** house style of yielding silk and then further fruit and nut tones, almost vaguely sherry trifle; **f22** more of the same, though just with the volume down slightly; **b22.5** not a whisky you can easily say no to...Really charming. *40%*

Meyer's Le Whisky Alsacien Blend Superieur Pinot Noir Finish db **(83.5) n21.5 t21.5 f20 b21.** Slightly sticky on the palate as the fruit tries to take charge. Though pleasant, imbalanced somewhat by the late feints and lack of give from the grape. *40%*

Meyer's Le Whisky Alsacien Pur Malt No. 05169 db **(92) n22** a lovely fruit and nut overture with a decent spice buzz...; attractively soft; **t23.5** silky delivery, the early malt and building sugars do no more than kiss and caress. Salivating and fruity...and ridiculously soft; **f23** welcome spice to move things onto another level. But top rate vanilla, too. And that vague nuttiness re-emerges along with some molasses; **b23.5** my old Budgie, Borat, used to help himself to whatever whisky was going if no-one was watching. Sadly, he is no more and is buried in the garden overlooked by my tasting room. By contrast, my parrot, Percy, has never had a single drop of whisky in all his four years. Though he might be interested in this one, because he is a pure Meyer's. He has a sweet tooth, has Percy. Or do I mean beak? Anyway, I am sure he would bob his head up and down in appreciation of the sugary gristiness which pervades throughout this impressive dram. Who's a pretty whisky, then....? *40%*

Meyer's Whisky Alsacien Blend Superieur db **(88.5) n22.5 t22.5 f21.5 b22.** Impressively clean, barley-thick and confident: a delight. *40%*

DISTILLERIE WARENGHEM Lannion. Working.

Armorik db **(91) n23 t22 f23 b23.** I admit it; I blanched, when I first nosed this, so vivid was the memory of the last bottling. This, though ,was the most pleasant of surprises. Fabulous stuff: one of the most improved malts in the world. *40%*

Armorik Double Maturation finished in oloroso casks db **(75) n18.5 t20 f18 b18.5.** Dull and decidedly out of sorts. *46%. ncf.*

Armorik Millésime Matured for 10 Years cask no. 3261 db **(92) n22.5 t23 f23 b23.** Never quite know what you are going to get from these messieurs. Didn't expect this bottle of delights, I must say. The sweetness is a bit OTT at one point, but just copes. *56.1%. sc.*

Armorik Sherry Finish db **(92) n22.5 t23.5 f23 b23.5.** The first sherry finish today which has not had a sulphur problem...and I'm in my eighth working hour...! Bravo guys! If their Classic was a note on sophistication, then this was an essay. *40%*

DOMAINE MAVELA Aléria. Woring.

◇ **P&M Corsican Single Malt Whisky Aged 7 Years** db **(89) n23** an aroma unique to P&M: a strangely tight cluster of tannin notes alongside a two-tone orangey contribution which appears to both lighten and intensify at the situation, depending on the given moment; **t22.5** the citrus note links to ulmo honey before a malty, nutty, tannin-led tang begins to get the salivation going; **f21.5** bitters slightly as the clumsy tannin bites; **b22** never entirely sure of what stance to take, or where to maximise the malt, but some of the flavour shaping is fascinating. *42%. 6,600 bottles.*

◇ **P&M Corsican Single Malt Whisky Aged 12 Years** db **(92) n22.5** a thinned citrus note, not unlike lemon drizzle cake; **t23.5** ah...that's rather beautiful. In particular the mouth feel is studied beauty: relaxed grist pulse with muscovado sugars and melt-on-sight barley flour. The tannins are pliable and almost absurdly friendly; **f23** elegant spice buzz, understated and in keeping with the continuing citrus and vanilla; the vanilla tang is quietly confident but never over bearing; **b23** a gentle, characterful malt relaxed in its unique flavour profile. *42%. 1,100 bottles.*

P&M Corsican Single Malt Whisky Aged 14 Years db **(92) n23.5** a kind of strange muscovado-laced tannin with a meaty duck l'orange...unique – and very attractive; **t23** an instant battle between the good sugars and evil oak. Both land telling wounds on the other and it is the molasses which retreat...; **f22.5** pretty bitter and dry as the tannins really squeeze hard, though at least offering some cocoa as compensation; also some oils from a once thick cut begin to accumulate...; **b23** as we are moving back to the earlier days of the distillery, you can pick out the odd technical flaw that appears to have been ironed out later down the line. But always entertaining and intriguing with its series of bold strokes from the chunky oak nose to the bittering finish. *42%*

KAERILIS Le Palais. Working.

Kaerilis Le Grand Dérangement 15 Ans db **(78) n18 t22 f19 b19.** A breakdown of the oils doesn't help reveal the weaknesses from the distillate. A must for fans de nougat. *43%. nc ncf sc.*

Kaerilis l'Aube du Grand Dérangement 15 Ans db **(83.5) n20 t22.5 f20 b21.** Misfires when the revs are up, but purrs for moment on two on delivery as the sugar and barley kicks in to delicious effect. An enigmatic fruitiness enriches. *57%. nc ncf sc.*

WAMBRECHIES DISTILLERY Wambrechies. Working.

Wambrechies Single Malt Aged 8 Years db (83) n20 t21 f21 b21. There's that aroma again, just like the 3-y-o. Except how it kind of takes me back 30 years to when I hitchhiked across the Sahara. Some of the food I ate with the local families in Morocco and Algeria was among the best I have ever tasted. And here is an aroma I recognize from that time, though I can't say specifically what it is (tomatoes, maybe?). Attractive and unique to whisky, that's for sure. I rather like this malt. There is nothing quite comparable to it. One I need to investigate a whole lot more. 40%

UNSPECIFIED

Vicomte Single Malt Whisky Aged 8 Years Cognac barrels (86) n22 t22 f21 b21. Just like so much Cognac, this whisky has a distinctive toffee theme which makes for a rather too easy going malt. Just not enough peaks and troughs to add "interesting" to "enjoyable" in the description of this caramel-laden malt. From the attractive silky texture, I would not be surprised to learn the Cognac barrels in which this whisky laid were hand made by Asterix. 40% (80 proof)

Blends

Moon Harbour Pier 1 Sauternes cask finish (86.5) n20 t22.5 f22 b22. A sticky toffee, chewy number with a beautiful flavour spike as the apricot on the Sauternes kicks in and lingers. Shame about the nose, though, which cannot disguise far from peerless malt. 45.8%. ncf.

Vatted Malts
KAERILIS

Kaerilis Ster Vraz No 9 4 Year Old db (80) n22 t21 f18 b19. Plenty of salt and no little citrus. But undone by an oaky bitterness. 45%. nc ncf.

Kaerilis Ster Vraz No 9 4 Year Old db (87) n21.5 t23.5 f20 b22. What the hell was that...??? Something different, for sure. At its best, quite stunning. At its worst – at the death – hmmm, not great. Get your bucket and spade out for this one. 61.8%. nc ncf.

GERMANY
BAULAND BRENNEREI ALT ENDERLE ROSENBURG. WORKING.

Alt Enderle Neccarus 8 Years Old Single Malt Whisky db (90.5) n22 t23 f23 b22.5 A gently complex, delightful malt. Had it been scotch, I would have thought it was a coastal dram. Odd...! 43%

Alt Enderle Neccarus 12 Years Old Single Malt Whisky db (94) n23.5 t23.5 f23 b24 Technically, among the best malt I have ever encountered from Germany. 43%

Alt Enderle Neccarus 15 Years Old Port Fass Single Malt Whisky db (92.5) n23 another salty Neccarus: dry grape skin comes over in waves; t23.5 eye-watering fruit and saline mix; the sugars are subdues and of a fudgy style before mocha begins to soften the moment; f23 a lovely chocolate and raisin fade; b23 a chocolate mousse is on the loose. 51%

Alt Enderle Neccarus 15 Years Old Sherry Fass Single Malt Whisky db (86.5) n21 t22 f21.5 b22. Clean sherry. But, after the mouth-watering delivery, relatively sweet and simple with just not enough gear changes. Pleasant, if not up to the standard of the other Neccarus. 49%

BIRGITTA RUST PIEKFEINE BRÄNDE Bremen. Working.

Van Loon Single Malt Whisky dist 2012, bott Jul 2015 db (84) n20 t22.5 f20 b21. Anyone who has had nougat filled to the brim with juicy raisins and diced nut will recognise this one. Messy beginning and end, but very decent middle. Like so many other European distilleries, must learn to be more ruthless with the cut. 48%. 1,200 bottles.

⬥ **Van Loon 5 Year Old Single Malt Whisky** batch 2012 db (87.5) n21.5 t22.5 f21.5 b22 Retains the house nougat style but this bottling benefits from possessing an extra degree of fruitiness – in this case moist, juicy date – to go with the walnut. Falls at the odd technical hurdle, but the flavour profile has the odd moment of stunning, honeyed beauty and even elegance. 42%.

⬥ **Van Loon 5 Year Old Single Malt Whisky** batch 2012 db (85) n21.5 t22 f20 b21.5 Usually, a little extra strength will greatly enhance a complex whisky - if give it time in the glass. The exception is when the cut is already a little too wide, resulting in a lumpy, ultimately bitter effort. Where this does benefit is in the richness of the fruit and the light mocha effect. 55%.

BRENNEREI DANNENMANN Owen. Working.

Danne's Single Malt Schwäbischer Whisky Vom Bellerhof dist 09, cask strength, bott code L 0017 db **(87)** n20 t23 f22 b22. A huge whisky which kicks a lot harder than its 55% abv. Works a lot better than its sister 43% bottling, making the most of the golden syrup and grist mix, and the spiced cocoa fade. Pretty enjoyable. *54.9%*

BRENNEREI FELLER Dietenheim-Regglisweiler. Working

Augutus Corado Single Grain Whisky Port Cask db **(83)** n21.5 t23 f19 b20. Unlike their Valerie Amorone cask, where the malt and grape are in perfect harmony, here we have a situation where the fruit influence has bullied the barley into submission. And, sadly, the port pipe appears to have been treated somewhere along the way, thus imparting a dull furriness to the finish in particular. *40%*

Augustus Single Grain Aged 5 Years bott code los 1001 db **(87.5)** n21.5 t22.5 f21 b22. Exceptionally clean yet a little creamy; the greatest emphasis is on the thin sugars. Very enjoyable and charming, especially when those gentle spices arrive. But maybe just a little too genteel. *40%*

Valerie Amarone Single Malt Whisky 4 Years Old db **(95.5)** n23 t24.5 f23.5 b24.5 I think I'm in love with Valerie. *48%*

Valerie Amarone Cask Single Malt bott code los 114 db **(95)** n23 t24 f23.5 b24.5 Amorone comes from the Italian meaning "The Great Bitter." There is nothing bitter about this. But plenty that is great. So beautifully made and matured! *46%*

◈ **Valerie Single Malt Amarone Cask Strength** bott code 114 db **(95.5)** n24 the usual fruit piled on thick, though here there is more of a bite than previous bottlings..possibly because of the strength. Still the sumptuous moist date and walnut is really intoxicating...in every sense...; **t24** the delivery is a mix of pain and pleasure: the bite is deep, the kisses of the fruit and sugar lingering and meaningful. Molasses guarantees a weighty semi-dry tone to the sweetness while the fruit builds slowly in both oils and intensity. Moves more towards a mix of muscovado and Manuka honey for a short spell before the sweetness quickly vanishes and burnt raisin and mocha immerge...; **f23.5** more towards a long – very long - coffee cake finish...; **b24** they don't come more voluptuous and buxom than Valerie... *59%*.

Valerie Sherry Cask Single Malt bott code los 115 db **(86.5)** n21 t22.5 f21 b22. No sulphur, it seems. Yet for some reason this just doesn't get far off the ground. The nose is a bit dull while the palate seems to be under attack from a constant stream of caramel. By no means unpleasant and the immediate aftermath after the delivery is unquestionably the high point. But despite the active spices, never quite sits entirely right after that with the oils a little too aggressive. *46%*

BRENNEREI FRANK RODER Aalen - Wasseralfingen. Working.

Frank's Suebisch Cask Strength 2008 db **(91)** n22 t23 f23 b23. Frank has really got the hang of how to make the most of his still...a little stunner! And his cleanest yet. *57%*

BRENNEREI HENRICH Kriftel, Hessia. Working.

Gilors Port Cask sherry, bott code L13033, dist 2010, bott 2013 db **(86)** n20 t22 f22.5 b21.5. Thoroughly enjoyable and full of depth and no little fruit and spice. But the wide cut, apparent in the sherry version, is not tamed in quite the same effortless way. *44%. sc.*

BRENNEREI HÖHLER Aarbergen, Kettenbach. Working.

Whesskey Hessischer Barley-Whisky bott code GW 01-15 db **(84)** n19 t22 f21.5 b21.5. Follows a similar path to the corn whisky, except this has a dried grass/hay edge and never quite reaches those same heights of chocolatey deliciousness. *44%*

Whesskey Hessischer Blend-Whisky bott code BW 01-15 db **(90.5)** n23 a wonderful nose, with a Milky Bar nougat and milk chocolate lead and outstanding secondary Demerara sugars; **t22** rich from the off, with sugars linking early with spice to make for a massively busy start; **f23** chewy to the death with a little more nougat now coming in with toffee; the spices ramp up the ante...; **b22.5** a typical Hohler slightly flawed stunner. *44%*

Whesskey Hessischer Corn-Whisky bott code MW 01-15 db **(87.5)** n20.5 t23 f22 b22. Though the nose leaves you in no doubt about the feints at work, the beauty of the chocolate wafer and Nutella is there to be savoured. *44%*

Whesskey Hessischer Rye-Malt-Whisky bott code MW 01-15 db **(84.5)** n19 t22 f21.5 b22. After the usual less than impressive nose, this is an earthy beast which grows on you. Hefty hardly touches it: the chunky sugars aids the clanking rye no end. *44%*

Whesskey Hessischer Single Malt Whisky bott code CA 01-15 db **(81) n18.5 t21 f21 b20.5**. Despite the fact it has all kinds of flavour permutations, it is hard to get beyond the butyric. 44%

Whesskey Hessischer Whisky au Dinkel bott code DW 01-14 db **(86) n21 t21.5 f22 b21.5**. Brimming with character, the oils ensure the flavours keep building to the sweet end. Gristy at times, then more spicy as the oils accumulate. Plenty of burnt fudge as it progresses. 40%

BRENNEREI MACK, Gütenbach. Working

Kilpen Single Malt Malt Whisky Single Barrel bott code L14092108 **(88) n21.5** the vague heaviness of the still is perfectly countered by toffee and dates; **t22.5** gorgeous spice and barley mix. The sugars are half Demerara and half molasses; **f22** more creamy toffee, but beautifully spiced up; **b22** attractively distilled and delightfully matured whisky. 40%

BRENNEREI ZIEGLER Freudenberg, North Württemberg. Working.

Aureum 1865 5 Year Old db **(87) n21.5 t22 f21.5 b22**. A tad feinty and nutty, but the huge barley makes this entertaining and sweet in all the right places. 43%

Aureum 1865 2008 Cask Strength db **(84.5) n21 t21.5 f21 b21**. A massive whisky, in no little part due to the very wide cut back in 2008. The usual nougat, hazelnut and cocoa gang up in the thick oils. 53.9%

Aureum 1865 Château Lafite Rothschild casks, dist 2008, bott 2015 db **(85) n20.5 t23 f20 b21.5**. Tight, hard, grapey, beautifully sweet on delivery but with some furriness. 47%

Aureum 1865 Grave Digger 6 Year Old db **(88) n22** salty and oily. Layers of molasses; **t22.5** a yielding delivery, soft with fertile malt. Mocha arrives early, a light feint buzz a little later; **f22** excellent spice; the mocha notes persist; **b22** this grave digger goes deep. 43%

DESTILLERIE HERMANN MÜHLHÄUSER Oberwälden. Working.

Mühlhäuser Oberwalder Single Grain bott code L0612 db **(86.5) n22 t22 f21 b21.5**. Enjoyable, showing sturdy and at times sophisticated oak and good early sugar structure. The grain is a bit on the shy side, though: may have had a better chance to shine at 46%. 40%

Mühlhäuser Schwäbischer Whisky aus Korn db **(90) n22.5 t23 f22 b22.5**. So different! If you are into this, it'll be pastoral perfection. 40%

DESTILLERIE & BRENNEREI MICHAEL HABBEL Sprockhövel. Working

Hillock 4 1/2-12 bott code L4512 db **(88.5) n23.5 t22 f21 b22** On the nose I thought: wow! They've come up with a peatiness as close to an Islay style as I've ever seen in mainland Europe – watch out Scotland! Later I discovered that the whisky had been matured in ex-Islay casks. Either way, all rather lovely. 45%

DESTILLERIE RALF HAUER Bad Dürkheim. Working.

◈ **Saillt Mór Pfälze Eiche Single Malt Whisky** ex-bourbon casks, fass-nr. 18 & 19, Jahrgang 2012, gefüllt m 11/16 db **(93) n23** heavy, praline-nutty, thick malt. Controlled sweetness, freer spices; **t24** just as intense on delivery: that magnificent mocha-praline malty milkshake middle blows you away...! the molasses are added to whipped cream; **f22.5** a little dry and marginally bitter by comparison as the oaks make a stand; **b23.5** this distillery certainly knows how to make an impact. Gorgeous! 59.3%.

◈ **Saillt Mór Pfälze Eiche Single Malt Whisky** fass-nr. 3 & 4, Jahrgang 2012, gefüllt m 1/16 db **(89.5) n21.5** an oily, wide cut but well bandaged by attractive and increasingly full blooded tangerine notes; **t23.5** much better! Indeed, a delivery from the heavens as the chewy malt displays both grist and muscovado-laden tannins to their fullest advantage. Soft, but deep and intense; **f22** some of the oils from the wider cut hang around, as do spices; **b22.5** not technically as well gifted as other malts I have encountered from this distillery. But enjoys a big, expansive personality. 46%.

◈ **Saillt Mór Pfälze Eiche Single Malt Whisky** fass-nr. 21 & 22, Jahrgang 2013, gefüllt m 05/17 db **(91.5) n22.5** big tannin impact with accompanying spices; **t23.5** excellent oils help ramp up the barley's value from the first flavour wave. Gets more malty by the mega-mouth-watering moment; intensity and depth upped by big Manuka honey surge...and some pretty big tannin; **f22.5** the oak takes on a sweetened pencil shaving stance; spice buzz, balancing molasses caress; **b23** a departure from the normal style with a massive oak injection here. Superb, though. 46%.

Saillt Mór Pfälzer Eiche Single Malt Whisky new Palatinate oak, dist 4-8 Sept 12, bott 2 Nov 2015 db **(94) n24 t23.5 f23 b23.5** One of the most Scottish of all European malts, having something of a Dalwhinnie/Clynelish/Highland Park constitution. Or maybe constitution is not a good term to use regarding anything European at the moment... 46%

DESTILLERIE THOMAS SIPPEL Weisenheim am Berg. Working.

Palatinatus Single Malt Whisky Port wood finish, dist 2011 db **(80) n19 t21 f20 b20.** A nougat bar dipped in Port...? Sometimes you just have to hold your hand up and say: well, I'm afraid that didn't quite work quite as we hoped. Here is one. Lovely bottle, though... 45%

Palatinatus Single Malt Whisky German oak cask, dist 2012 db **(85.5) n20 t22 f22 b21.5.** Well, that was different! The sharp pungency of, presumably, the German oak, certainly offers a unique nose. And this transfers on to the palate, though the intense sugars – again, from the oak? – restore a degree of balance and even complexity as the juicier barley tones emerge. A truly unique malt that has been impressively distilled but offers just too vivid a flavour profile at times. Love the lemon on the early finish, mind.... 45%

EDELBRÄENDE-SENFT Salem-Rickenbach. Working.

Senft Bodensee Whisky bott code L-SW41, dist 2012, bott 2016 db **(86.5) n20 t21 f23.5 b22.** You know with this distillery that feints and nougat are on the cards. Well, they don't disappoint but at least this bottling shows, after a so-so delivery, a fabulous finale where the high grade Venezuela cocoa is mixed beautifully with no lesser grade molasses. The spices sign the malt off with aplomb. 42%

◇◇◇ **Senft Whisky** bott code L-SW43, dist 2012, bott 2016 db **(83.5) n19 t21 f22 b21.5** You have to laugh when you absent-mindedly nose a whisky, having mechanically opened it and poured...and then thought: "Senft!" without knowing what it actually was. This distillery does possess a unique character, especially on the nose, though here there is a little extra cabbage over the nougat. Recovers really well on the palate as the sugars claw back the balance. 42%. nc.

◇◇◇ **Senft Whisky** bott code L-SW44, dist 2013, bott 2017 db **(88) n22** minimal nougat, maximum chocolate fudge; **t22** much more precision to the oils allowing a superb butterscotch and spice theme; **f22** attractive, if thin, dark sugar fade; **b22** boasts the usual Senft foibles, but light years ahead of their previous bottling. 42%. nc.

EDELBRENNEREI BISCHOF Wartmannsroth. Working.

Stark & Eigenwillig Rebell Der Whisky Single Grain Chestnut Barrel Finish db **(93) n23** a series of spices and sugars not normally associated with oak, especially the mix of praline and marzipan; **t23** seriously thick on the palate: again intense, vaguely nutty sugars moving towards a lighter Milky Way creaminess. The spices are precise, and also with a sweet edge; **f23.5** heavy tannin late on but this morphs into a series of rich, high quality cocoa notes, accompanied perfectly by molasses; **b23.5** I didn't need to be told chestnut maturation was involved here: just one sniff tells you all you need to know. 44%

EDELBRENNEREI DIRKER Mömbris. Working.

Dirker Blended Whisky Aged 3 Years bott code L L 15 db **(87.5) n21 t22.5 f22 b22.** Beautifully soft and viscous with a highly attractive fruit and nut theme. Even some rather excellent spices late on to keep the show going. Impressed. 45%

Dirker Whisky Aged 3 Years bourbon cask, bott code L E 15 db **(81.5) n18 t22 f20.5 b21.** After the boiled sprouts, unfriendly nose, recovers quickly and nimbly on the palate. The burst of sugars and gristy oils attractively repairs some of the damage. 53%

Dirker Whisky Aged 4 Years Sassicaia cask, bott code L A 16 db **(80.5) n18.5 t22.5 f19 b20.5.** A deeply frustrating whisky. This is one exceptionally beautiful cask at work here - in the mid ground - offers all kinds of toffee apple and muscovado-sweetened mocha. Sadly, the initial spirit wasn't up to the barrel's standard. This really needs some cleaning up. 53%

EIFEL DESTILLATE Koblenz. Working.

◇◇◇ **Eifel Whisky 746.9 Single Barley Malt** Port cask, dist 2007, bott 2017 db **(86.5) n22 t22 f21.5 b21** This carries some of the same intensely eye-watering properties as the Rye Malt. The shimmer of fruit off the Port cask is as salivating as it gets. But the malt itself has to work a little too hard to make its contribution. Never quite finds its balance, but entertains all the way. 50%. nc ncf.

Eifel Whisky 746.9. Single German Barley Malt Whisky 8 Years Old db **(73) n17 t19 f18 b19.** I now have a bald patch where I have been scratching my head trying to work this one out. Wrong in so many ways. Yet the undertone has a rather charming fruity structure. 50%. sc.

Eifel Whisky 746.9 Single Wheat Malt Bordeaux cask, dist 2012, bott 2017 db (89.5) n22 toffee fruit and nut; t23 beautiful delivery: an elegant understated fruitiness is soft and velvety on impact. Good spice thrust at the halfway point which warms impressively; f22 more cream toffee punctuated by that charming spice; b22.5 a highly attractive, well-proportioned, nutty dram. 58.2%. nc ncf.

Eifel Whisky Cask 99 Single German Barley Malt Whisky 5 Years Old db (62) n16 t16 f15 b15. Just...aaaargghh! 57.5%. sc.

Eifel Whisky Einzelfass Single Malt 2016 American oak, ex-Bordeaux & Madeira casks, dist 2010 db (89) n22 t22.5 f22 b22.5 A toast to your distillery! Or, to be more precise, a drink to your toasty oak... 50%. sc.

Eifel Whisky Einzelfass Single Rye 2015 American oak, new bourbon & Bordeaux casks, dist 2009 db (96) n23.5 t24.5 f24 b24 Quite brilliant! Magnificently distilled and beautifully matured. One of the European whiskies of the year with no doubt whatsoever. 50%. sc.

Eifel Whisky Einzelfass Tripel Malt 2015 1st fill bourbon casks, ruby Port cask finish, dist 2010 db (93.5) n22.5 t24 f23 b24 Hearty handshakes, chaps, for a complex job exceptionally well done. 50%. sc.

Eifel Whisky Einzelfass Malz & Rauch 2015 1st fill bourbon casks, PX sherry cask finish, dist 2010 db (89) n21.5 t23.5 f22 b22 Lurching, lumbering: the kind of whisky that Laurel and Hardy would love. Because, when you add in the cumbersome youthfulness, this is a fine mess....! What is it with pitting peat against PX? When will people learn that they simply never balance out? That all said, I am sure some will regard this one of their greatest ever whisky experiences. And were I not such a miserable old perfectionist, I might be one of them... 50%. sc.

Eifel Whisky The Peaty Nougat New Make 150L New Acacia cask, dist 2017 db (62.5) n12.5 t18 f16 b16 Now that IS different! Minty cool and sweet. Also, reminds me of Arbroath Smokies, though more of the fish, than the smoke... 60%. nc ncf.

Eifel Whisky Rye Malt Malaga cask, dist 2012, bott 2016 db (88) n22.5 good grief! Another smoked rye, surely. But the addition of a Malaga cask into the mix, turns this into something of an olfactory soup...; t22.5 things are no less cluttered on delivery. The wine influence appears to be calling the shots though the odd eye-watering grain distracts with a mildly hysterical scream. The smoke disappears from the scene when it thinks the coast is clear. Were this a play it'd be a highly entertaining farce...; f21.5 tart and little confused; b21.5 Rye. Smoke. Wine cask. Scary. 46%. nc ncf.

Eifel Whisky Single Barley Malt Madeira cask, dist 2011, bott 2017 db (85) n20 t21.5 f22.5 b21 It is hard work to get through the nose and delivery, both of which have a bit of an attitude and are none too welcoming. But things settle down halfway into the mouthful, with the fruit deciding to make peace. The finish itself is placid with a light grapey softness to the rich caramel and vanilla. 50%. nc ncf sc.

Eifel Whisky Single Peated Barley Malt Palo Cortado sherry cask, dist 2012, bott 2017 db (86) n22 t21.5 f21 b21.5 Huge smoke involvement, especially on the nose. But a little too much cabbage on delivery makes it hard work for the excellent recovering alt and molasses mix to make up ground. 50%. nc ncf sc.

Eifel Whisky Single Rye rum cask, dist 2012, bott 2017 db (93) n23 as though the grain and sugars have been turned to stone: no yield on the aroma whatsoever...: fabulous! t23.5 some early oils carry excellent muscovado sugars. These diminish as the grain takes a stand and chirpy spices go on the attack; f23 the spices not only stand their ground but up the dosage considerably. A little caramel mixes in with the rye; b23.5 there is probably only one thing that can make a whisky more brittle on the palate than distilling from rye. And that is to put it in a rum cask... What an inspired idea this is! Oh, and this is the 778th whisky I have tasted for my 2018 Bible...and the first to make me cough..! 50%. nc ncf sc.

Eifel Whisky Triple Malt cask no 91, dist 2011, bott 2017 db (84.5) n21.5 t22 f20 b21 Towering delivery (well, what do you expect from Eifel?) of eye-watering muscovado sugars and cream caramels. But a bit clumsy and slap-happy with the feints. 56.5%. nc ncf sc.

FEINDESTILLERIE BÜCHNER Langenbogen. Working

Büchner Single Malt db (89) n22.5 superb malt: clean and alive with gristy sugars. Refreshing and sexy; t22 light oils, but never enough to discourage the barley from showing to full effect; f22.5 those oils confirm the wider cut, but celebrate their extra body with a malty, spicy display of defiance; b22 a wonderfully characterful and enjoyable malt. 43%

FINCH WHISKYDESTILLERIE Nellingen, Alb-Donau. Working.

Finch Schwäbischer Highland Whisky Barrique R bott code LA0004 db **(91.5)** n23; t23.5 f23 b23.5 As beautifully in sync as Germany's midfield, 42%

◇ **Finch Schwäbischer Highland Whisky Dinkel** Port bott code LA0011 db (85) n20.5 t22.5 f21 b21 Finch, usually, offers a whisky which either flies pretty high or crash lands. This year we have two additions to their range which do neither, or both –depending how you look at it. This one gets off to a faltering start with far too much oil from the cut apparent on the nose. But the lush Port helps fills the cracks though those big oils return late on. 42%.

Finch Schwäbischer Highland Whisky Single Malt bott code 1444LA0003 db **(78.8)** n19 t21 f19 b19.5. As I taste this, the German national anthem is being sung in the distant background on my radio as Germany take on Slovakia in the European Championships: how fitting! Sadly, this Finch is not singing anything like so impressively for, despite some attractive fudge, the oils are just a little too clunky and chunky. 42%

◇ **Finch Schwäbischer Hockland Whisky Destillers Edition** bott code LA0013 db **(87)** n22 t22 f21 b22 Firm and busy, all kind of muscovado sugars and caramels fill the palate with lush good intent. The finish bitters quite abruptly, but the clever sugar-spice mix leading up to this is worth experiencing. 42%.

GUTSBRENNEREI JOH. B. GEUTING Bocholt. Working.

J.B.G Münsterländer Single Grain Whisky new American white oak cask no. JBG 20, dist 26 Apr 10, bott 18 Sept 15 db **(86)** n20 t22.5 f21.5 b22. A few gremlins in the distilling process can be heard on the nose. But the soft, yielding and wonderfully juicy delivery compensates to a major degree, as do the following cocoa notes which flourish before a clunkiness sets in. Some very good moments. 42%. sc.

◇ **J.B.G Münsterländer Single Grain Aged 6 Years** American white oak, cask nos. 26,27 & 28, dist 12 Nov 10, bott 20 Mar 17 db **(86)** n21 t22 f21.5 b21.5 The house nougat and chocolate style is out in force here: the wide cut does offer a verdant note but the delivery is massively juicy and chewy. 42%. 1,000 bottles.

J.B.G Münsterländer Single Malt Whisky American white oak casks, cask nos. 40, 49 & 50, dist 22 Dec 11, bott 14 Mar 16 db **(88)** n21 t23 f22; b22 Creaky at times, but the good bits are genuinely excellent. 43%

◇ **J.B.G Münsterländer Single Malt** American white oak, cask nos. 148, 149, 150 & 151, dist 12 Mar 13, bott 27 Apr 17 db **(87.5)** n22 t22 f21.5 b22 By the time they had got round to distilling malt for this, it is obvious that they had learned to control their cuts a bit better. So not so much nougat and chewy oils here. A lighter malt altogether with the barley far more vocal though the dry, spiced finale does offer something for the nougat fans to grip on to. 43%. 1,319 bottles.

J.B.G Münsterländer Single Malt Whisky bourbon barrels nos. 1, 23, 24, dist 5 Nov 10, bott 21 Mar 14 db **(86.5)** n22.5 t22 f20.5 b21.5. A very wide cut means that we have a bit of a heavyweight on our hands here. Thick in oils, though not short on either big bourbon richness nor, later, an intense mocha fade. A degree of dried molasses balances out the ultra dry notes trying to get a foothold. By no means technically perfect, but one you cannot help liking. 43%. 937 bottles.

J.B.G Münsterländer Single Malt Whisky bourbon barrels, sherry oloroso cask finish, cask nos. JBG 96, 97, dist 21 Dec 11, bott 17 Mar 15 db **(83)** n21 t21.5 f20 b20.5. What with the density of the distillate from the over generous cut, and the (clean!) oloroso on top, reminds me of a cough syrup I used to take as a kid. 43%. 813 bottles.

◇ **J.B.G Münsterländer Single Malt** sherry Oloroso & sherry Pedro Xienez, cask nos. 3 0 & 2 PX, dist 22 Jan 14, bott 13 Mar 17 db **(85)** n19 t23 f21 b22 This is a bit like a puppy which really wants you to like it. The delivery is playful and charming, the faultless grape making all the right noises; your palate is licked by lovable fruit notes and the spices are lovely. But none of this can make up for the feints which do few favours for the finish and even less for the nose. Excellent non-sulphured sherry casks, though. 43%. 1,692 bottles.

HAMMERSCHMIEDE Zorge. Working.

The Glen Els Wayfare The Cask Strength bott code. L1587 db **(93)** n22.5 t23 f24 b23.5. Some kind of oily, hallucinogenic, sugar, cocoa and spice concoction which is played out at maximum volume. The word "big" hardly does it justice... 57.9%. nc ncf.

HAUSBRAUEREI ALTSTADTHOF Nürnberg. Working.

Ayrer's Bourbon Barrel Aged Organic Single Malt db **(87)** n22 t22.5 f21 b21. A slightly wide cut here has undone some supreme work by the casks. And at 51% abv, close to a Kentucky 101, has just the right mouth feel for the light liquorice and ulmo honey on display. But when so little metal is apparent in the spirit, those cuts have to be as clean as a whistle. 51%

Ayrer's PX Sherry Cask Finished Organic Single Malt dist 2009 db **(90)** n22 t22.5 f23 b22.5 Always brave to use PX, as the intensity of the sugars can sometimes put the malt into the tightest of straight-jackets. However, this is fine, sulphur-free butt and is eventually relaxed enough for the malt to share equal billing once it finds its rhythm. 56%

Ayrer's Red Organic Single Malt db **(86)** n21.5 t22 f21 b21.5. Quite dry and niggardly in places, a degree of chalkiness on the nose and delivery slightly undoing the sugars as they attempt to soar. Pleasant enough, but never quite gets into stride. 43%

Ayrer's Red Organic Single Malt db **(90.5)** n22.5 t22.5 f22.5 b23 An impressive malt, probably benefitting from the full strength, as the unbroken oils play a leading role in length and balance. 58%

Ayrer's White Organic Single Malt db **(86)** n21.5 t22 f21 b21.5. An attractive enough new make with good cut points, particularly hitting the heights with a big sugar surge in the mid-ground. But in this naked form, reveals a slight shortage of copper in the system. 46%

HINRICUS NOYTE'S-BRAUHAUS AM LOHBERG Wismar. Working.

Baltach Wismarian Single Malt Whisky db **(83)** n20.5 t21 f20.5 b21. Needs a defter touch on the still to ensure those hefty oils don't get through. Some decent redeeming honey, though. Fascinating light curry on the nose! 43%

KAUZEN-BRÄU Ochsenfurt. Working.

Old Owl Single Malt Whisky dist Apr 12, bott Sept 15 db **(91)** n23.5 t23 f22 b22.5 beautifully made and well matured whisky bursting with character, and a pretty unique one! 43%

KINZIGBRENNEREI MARTIN BROSAMER Biberach. Working.

Badischer Whisky Blended db **(87.5)** n21 t22.5 f22 b22. A little of the distillery's old nougat style shows its ankles, but otherwise, much cleaner with progressive sugars working in tandem with the growing, faintly wide-cut spice. Very pleasant. 42%

Biberacher Whisky Single Malt bott code L:MWJ15 db **(85)** n20 t22.5 f21 b21.5. A forthright, competent and confident delivery maximises every last degree of sugars in the grist for a sumptuous maltfest. The usual over–enthusiastic oils diminish the effect slightly on both nose and finish. 42%

Kinzigtäler Whisky Single Malt Smoke db **(88.5)** n21.5 maybe not technically on the money, but the pip-squeakingly dry smokiness also helps introduce a degree of cocoa to the scene; t22.5 a little fat, as usual, but the sugars now have a third, more phenolic dimension and linger attractively; f22 a rather lovely mix of chocolate and ginger cake; b22.5 the phenols have much to say. 42%

Schwarzwälder Whisky Rye db **(81)** n19 t22 f20 b20. Few aromas are more scary in whisky than over-cut, feinty rye. Here it is in full, spoon-standing oiliness. Which means the flavours can also power through the roof. Not exactly for the purist. 42%

KLEINBRENNEREI FITZKE Herbolzheim-Broggingen. Working.

◈ **Derrina Dinkelmalz Schwarzwälder Single Malt Whisky** bott code L 5512 db **(87.5)** n21.5 t22.5 f21.5 b21.5 Lovely whisky of the salivating – indeed, eye-watering - kind, though struggles to find a way of completely controlling the distinctive spelt sharpness. 43%.

◈ **Derrina Gerstenmalz Schwarzwälder Single Malt Whisky** bott code L 5412 db **(74)** n18 t19 f18 b19 You know this distillery, for all its usual brilliance, is going to bottle you a fail at some stage...and this is it! 43%.

Derrina Grünkern Schwarzwälder Single Grain Whisky bott code L 11012 db **(88.5)** n22 t22 f22 b22.5 A carefully constructed, disciplined whisky. 43%

Derrina Hirse Schwarzwälder Single Grain Whisky bott code L 6512 db **(84)** n20 t21 f22 b21. Never quite finds its rhythm or style. From the horsebox hay nose to the unsynchronised sugars and wide-cut oils, the narrative is confused and of limited attractiveness. Still has the odd pleasant moment or two, though. 43%

◈ **Derrina Kamut Ur-Weizen Schwarzwälder Single Grain Whisky** bott code L 12112 db **(93.5)** n23.5 the tannins mean business and radiate superb spiced liquorice. The sugars have to be molasses to match – and are. There is a secondary spice feel, also – quite apart from the tannin: and this appears softer and from the grain; **t23.5** could just repeat that delivery again and again and again...! Brilliant sugars and tannin crash in bound together by a silky softness which contrasts brilliantly with those busy spices; **f23** beautiful tannin pulse with those sugars lingering; **b23.5** give this whisky time in the glass, let it breathe, apply a little heat and....wow! *43%.*

⬧ **Derrina Purpur Ur-Weizen Schwarzwälder Single Grain Whisky** bott code L 14012 db **(95.5) n23.5** the closest alcoholic equivalent to bread coming out of the oven, being cut into and breathing in the steam....; **t24** voluptuous. Satin softness, the oils yielding yet carrying a wonderful mix of maple syrup, ulmo honey and very spicy hot cross buns; **f24** long, elegant, rich....and that's before the complexity levels are raised by the interplay between the liquorice-led tannins and the remaining dark sugars; the spices rattle on... **b24** this distillery does wheat whisky a lot better than most... *43%.*

Derrina Roggenmalz Schwarzwälder Single Malt Whisky bott code L 5612 db **(95) n23 t24.5 f23.5 b24** This distillery should take a bow. They have produced a very high class rye whisky! *43%*

Derrina Triticale Schwarzwälder Single Grain Whisky bott code L 10412 db **(89.5) n22.5 t22 f22.5 b22.5** Grows on you as the flavours open like a spring flower. *43%*

⬧ **Derrina Waldstauden Ur-Roggen Schwarzwälder Single Grain Whisky** bott code L 13612 db **(85) n19 t21.5 f23 b21.5** The one thing I will say about the Derrina Rye, is that is not just an odd fellow, but a unique one for its type. The house green style does few favours to the nose. But at least this version opens out on the palate, though through a big oily wall. The Manuka honey and recognisable rye on the finish works beautifully well with the late spices. *43%.*

⬧ **Derrina Weizenmalz Schwarzwälder Single Malt Whisky** bott code L 5712 db **(89.5) n22.5** salty pistachios ground up with molasses: seriously attractive...; **t22** big oils take their time to settle before a massive malt surge makes its mind up for it; **f22.5** just a fabulous finish with the lightest of feints moving the flavours towards a gorgeous oily almost chocolate ice cream finale; **b22.5** what I adore about this distillery is that you never quite know what is coming out of the bottle – but with the incentive that when it is good it is truly magnificent. This is a slightly unusual mid-range for them – but veering towards brilliant. *43%.*

KYMSEE WHISKY Grabenstätt. Working.

Kymsee Der Chiemsee Single Malt Whisky cask no. 2, dist Dec 2012 db **(87.5) n21 t23 f22 b21.5**. A fascinating malt. When sweet, it is very sweet with the molasses piled on thick. When it is bitter, it is so in a way which undermines the sweetness, rather than balancing with it. And the spices are borderline aggressive. Pleasant, and impressively distilled. But still a bit of an odd ball. *42%. sc.*

⬧ **Kymsee Der Chiemsee-Whisky Single Malt Quarter Cask Finish** fass nr. 1, dest May 13 db **(88) n22** earthy and floral - like walking through woods that the sun can rarely penetrate; **t22.5** a gabbling sweetness – semi-lurid white sugar in a French-toasty kind of way...; **f22** an amazing degree of natural caramels before a little bitterness closes in...; **b21.5** Kymsee have a very unusual way of doing things in the bottle. The marks as much for fascination as effect... *42%.*

⬧ **Kymsee Der Chiemsee-Whisky Single Malt Sherry Cask Finish** fass nr. 1, dest May 13 db **(85) n20 t22 f21.5 b21.5** The sherry, though rich and profound in its sultana and sticky suet pudding intent, plays second fiddle to the generous oils from the cut. *42%.*

MARDER EDELBRÄNDE Albbruck-Unteralpfen. Working.

Marder Single Malt Whisky Aged 3 Years bott 2015 db **(92) n22.5** wow! Impressive! No off notes...no unacceptable feints, generally clean, yet bursting with a spiced maltiness and even a light smattering of marmalade...; **t23.5** gorgeous mouth feel: beautifully weighted and oiled with a controlled intensity to the barley which revels in the light muscovado sugars without ever getting too sweet; throughout, there is a lovely sub-strata of hazelnut puree; **f23** some heavier oils congregate, though the process is slow and a little mocha offsets the growing dryness; **b23** very attractive whisky with plenty of character and complexity. *43%*

MÄRKISCHE SPEZIALITÄTEN BRENNEREI Hagen. Working.

DeCavo Handcrafted Single Malt Höhlenwhisky Fass-Nr. L 3 db **(89) n22 t23.5 f21 b22.5** Certainly knows how to make an impact...! *43%. sc. 262 bottles.*

DeCavo Handcrafted Single Malt Fass-Nr. L 13 db **(87) n22 t22 f21 b22.** A tame malt. First gristy, then a more complex development of vanilla and lighter, friendly sugars. *46%. sc.*

DeCavo Handcrafted Single Malt Fass-Nr. L 13 db (91) n22 t23 f23 b23 An astonishingly lush malt with an almost three dimensional sugar attack. Wow! 55%. sc.

Edelstahl Moonshiner White Single Malt bott code. L1/2015 db (87) n20.5 t23 f21.5 b22. The nose reveals just a little less copper than is desired, but the cut is a sound one: feint free and teaming with delicious, viscous malt and light ulmo honey. Attractive. 50%. sc.

NORDPFALZ BRENNEREI Höning. Working.

◈ **Taranis Pfälzer Single Malt Whisky 3 Years Old** port cask finish, dist Aug 13 db (88.5) n21the big sultana helps iron out the squabbling malt elements; t22.5 ah...!! Much better! The delivery is tinged with orange blossom honey but the malt really does kick up a head of steam; f22.5 complex yet relaxed: as though sucking on both barley sugar and a fruit pastel...late spices slowly build...; b22.5 a deliciously rich and juicy malt benefitting from an outstanding port cask. 50.1%. 213 bottles.

Taranis Pfälzer 5.5 Years Old Single Malt Whisky oloroso sherry cask, dist Sept 09 db (85.5) n19.5 t22.5 f22 b21.5. A clean oloroso butt. But one I have never before seen inject so much spice into: as though distilled from white pepper. The nose undermines the project by projecting the feints. But the lightning bolt delivery certainly ups the interest and some decent grape meanders to the gentler and much more sane finish. 50.7%. ncf. 480 bottles.

NUMBER NINE SPIRITUOSENMANUFAKTUR
Leinefelde-Worbis, Working.

The Nine Springs Single Malt Whisky Aged 3 Years virgin oak cask, cask no. 2 db (88.5) n22 a few feints kicking around, plus the odd slightly mouldy tangerine; t22.5 beautiful arrival with the emphasis on Venezuelan cocoa. Clings to the roof of the mouth like a limpet...; f22 feinty Fox's Orange Cream biscuits...if they still do them...; b22 though the oak should be the driving force, the thick cut from the still means the distillate has its hands on the steering wheel. 45%. nc ncf sc.

The Nine Springs Single Malt Whisky Aged 3 Years batch no. 1 db (91) n22.5 a plethora of healthy bourbon tones with the orange blossom honey and liquorice in harmony; t23 voluptuous and chewy, the delivery skirts around the rising chocolate orange and then focusses on the ever-intensifying tannins; f22.5 a little drier and the orange is discarded as the cocoa homes in; b23 for those who like their malt whiskies to be in touch with their bourbon side... 45%. nc ncf sc.

SAUERLÄNDER EDELBRENNEREI Ruthen-Kallenhardt. Working.

Thousand Mountains Mc Raven Single Malt Whisky cask no. L1003 03.2012 db (74.5) n16 t21 f18.5 b19. A massively wide cut means this is a gluepot of a whisky. Best ignore the nose and concentrate on the delivery which has its magnificently sugared moments. But, as is to be expected, an oily, untamed beast. 46.2%

SCHLENKERLA Bamberg, Working.

Schlenkerla db (79.5) n21 t18.5 f21 b19. Very much more like German lebkuchen biscuit/cake than whisky. Soft, vaguely phenolic, gingery and friendly – and the finish is surprisingly lovely, especially after the chaotic and confusing opening. A challenging whisky to say the least. 40%

SEVERIN SIMON Alzenau-Michelbach, Aschaffenburg. Working.

Simon's Bavarian Pure Pott Still db (86) n21 t22 f21 b22 Always great to renew acquaintances with this idiosyncratic malt. I remember lots of pine last time out. Here the pine is remarkable for its almost lack of interest in this whisky after the nose. Which means this is a better bottling, with the malt – man marked by crisp sugars – having a much louder say than normal. Some soft, creamy toffee and nougat at play. But the spices and barley are most enjoyable. 40%

SLYRS Schliersee-Neuhaus. Working.

Slyrs Bavarian Single Malt Sherry Edition No. 1 finished in Oloroso, lot no. L00354, bott 2013 db (86) n20 t22 f22 b22. Anyone out there who loves cream toffee and spice? This malt has your name on it. 46%

◈ **That Boutique-y Whisky Company Slyrs 3 Year Old** (94.5) n24 beautifully clean, thumping, in-your-face barley; the light citrus background adds even more clarity; t23.5 good grief! I'm not sure I have ever seen Slyrs in more malt-dominating mode; a background of grist and lemon drops enlivens the palate further; **f23.5** the vanillas rise slightly, but it is all about the fading malt; **b23.5** from the ultra-intense school of whisky. A malt-lover's dream and the most Scottish style dram they have yet produced. *52.5%. 691 bottles.*

SPERBERS DESTILLERIE Rentweinsdorf. Working.

Sperbers Destillerie Malt Whisky Anno 2010 los-nr. 40 db (86.5) **n21.5 t22 f21.5 b21.5**. One gets the distinct feeling this was distilled to a pretty high strength before being put into cask. Hard to spot the malt, but plenty of tannins from the oak. Still, quite delicious! *59%*

SPREEWÄLD BRENNEREI Schlepzig. Working.

Spreewälder Sloupisti Single Malt Whisky dist Oct 11, bott Mar 16 (94) **n23 t23.5 f24 b23.5** Absolutely my best whisky of the day! And with its portrayal of a stork in a bow tie and top hat, probably the best label of the year! My kind of whisky; my kind of distillery...!! *68.5%*

ST. KILIAN DISTILLERS GMBH Rüdenau. Working.

St. Kilian Distillers Turf Dog los-nummer: 161115 db (91) **n23 t23 f22 b23** The smoke, naturally, dominates like a hill-topping Schloss looking benevolently down upon the cowering village below. But there appears to be something of an uprising as first a metallic then a cocoa and molasses intensity begin to look for parity. Entertaining new make. *499%. 499 bottles.*

St. Kilian Distillers White Dog los-nummer: 160630 db (91.5) **n23.5 t23 f22.5 b22.5** A very competently made malt spirit. Reducing the new make – the white dog – to 43%abv means that the oils are broken down and the metallic element is a little more naked, resulting in a slightly lumpy finish and the grain not quite so in tune. Even so, very good indeed! *43%.*

St. Kilian Distillers White Dog Cask Strength los-nummer: 160801 db (94.5) **n23.5 t24 f23.5 b23.5** At near natural strength the oils ensure a fabulous harmony between the barley and copper, ensuring a rich, chewy, salivating experience and uninterrupted, balancing, sugars. Whoever manned – or womaned – the still certainly knew exactly where the centre cut was. A real thoroughbred doggie! *63.5%.*

STEINHAUSER 1. BODENSEE-WHISKY-DESTILLERIE Kressbronn. Working.

Brigantia 3 Years Old bott L-12/12 db (79) **n19 t21 f19 b20** Huge malt statement, as is the distillery style. But it appears someone decided to try and extract as much spirit as possible, because the cut seems to be a little too wide for comfort here: the oils are unforgiving. *43%*

Brigantia Single Malt Whisky vom Bodensee 3 Years Old bott code. 10/15 db (75) **n19 t19 f18 b19**. Sweet in part. But this distillery badly needs to get more copper into their spirit. *43%*

WEINGUT MÖßLEIN Kolitzheim. Working.

M Mößlein Fränkischer Grain Whisky 5 Jahre fass nr. 4, bott code. L750 1 16 db (83) **n20 t21.5 f20.5 b21**. Soft and pleasant, though the odd gremlin comes through on the nose and finish. The generous cut ensures a vague nougat thread alongside the inevitable cocoa. *40.5%. sc.*

M Mößlein Fränkischer Single Malt Whisky 5 Jahre fass nr. 5, bott code. L730-1-15 db (85) **n21 t22 f21 b21**. More comfortable with the single malt than with the grain, though better cut point selection has helped. Even so, the oils are still big on this while the light liquorice works well with the buzzing spices. *41%. sc.*

WHISKY-DESTILLERIE DREXLER Arrach. Working.

Drexler Arrach No 1 Single Cask Malt Whisky sherry cask no. 76, dist Jan 12, bott Nov 15 db (83) **n21 t22 f19.5 b20.5**. Now there's a beast! The fact it starts off with a generous cut from the still, inclusive of some chunky oils, would normally be enough to keep the average palate quiet for a while. But when you then get a massive combination of bourbon-style oak and then lashings of fruit on top of even that, then it becomes challenging. Just a little too bitter towards the end, though. Not for the faint hearted. *46%. sc.*

WHISKY-DESTILLERIE GRUEL Owen/Teck. Working.

Tecker Single Malt Whisky Port Cask Matured db (82.5) **n19 t21.5 f21 b21**. A toffee-raisin whisky with a big degree of burnt sugar. *43%. ncf.*

Tecker Single Grain Whisky Aged 5 Years db (84) **n21.5 t22 f20 b20.5**. Somewhere in the five years between the ten and this five-year-old, someone appears to have made the cut a little wider. *40%. ncf.*

Tecker Single Grain Whisky Aged 10 Years Chardonnay casks db **(93)** n23.5 t23 f23 b23.5 Now, that is all rather beautiful... *53.2%. ncf.*

WHISKY DESTILLERIE LIEBL Bad Kötzting. Working.

Coillmór Bavarian Single Malt Bordeaux Cask cask no. 398, dist Oct 09 db **(87)** n21.5 t21.5 f22 b22. A stable bottling allowing the fruit to make the best use of the light nougat to offer a rich, rounded, lightly fruited malt. Well balanced, salivating and a joy to experience. *46%.*

Coillmór Bavarian Single Malt Port Cask 8 Years Old cask no. 351, dist 4 May 07 db **(79.5)** n21 t20 f19 b19.5. Even a Port cask has problems seeing off the excesses of the massively heavy nougat. Rough. *46%. 1080 bottles.*

Coillmór Bavarian Single Malt Alabanach Peat American oak, cask no. 47, dist 17 Jul 10 db **(81.5)** n20 t21 f20 b20.5. I'll give the peat from this distillery one thing: it really is idiosyncratic. No other smoked whisky is so jarring and a liquid antonym of "rounded". An absolute must for any serious collector or student of peated whisky. *46%. 392 bottles.*

Coillmór Bavarian Single Malt American Oak cask nos. 60,214,229,268339, dist May 10 db **(83)** n21 t20 f21 b21. A malt with a huge nougat input. Lots of toffee, but curiously little sweetness. *43%. 1895 bottles.*

Coillmór Bavarian Single Malt Distillers Edition Peated Oloroso Sherry Cask cask no. 81, dist 28 Aug 10 db **(80)** n20 t21 f19 b20. When you see peat and oloroso on the same whisky label, it tends to be a bottling you leave until the end of the day's work. If anything can hide sulphur until it is too late, it is peat. Too often have my taste buds been wrecked in this fashion. Well, my palate is still intact. Just. Though it was a close run thing: there is a buzz on the finish which might be the fault of the cask. But so clanking and grinding is the original coarse peat spirit, it is hard to tell. If you are simply a smoke head, then this really might just be a whisky right down your strasse. *46%. 895 bottles.*

WHISKY DESTILLERIE BLAUE MAUS Eggolsheim. Working.

Austrasier Single Cask Grain Whisky cask no. 2, dist May 08, bott Jun 15 db **(88.5)** n22 not dissimilar to a spice-seasoned cake baking; t23 the softest delivery, then a slow rising of spiced – or is that herbed? – barley; f21.5 just a little bitter towards the end as the spices and other tannins merge; b22 few European whiskies come as flavoursome as this. *40%. sc.*

Blaue Maus Single Cask Malt Whisky fass/los nr. 1, destilliert Feb 08, abgefüllt Apr 16 db **(86.5)** n21 t23 f21 b21.5. Perhaps a tad over-exuberant on the cut which impacts on both nose and finish. But the delivery and middle are a lush, honey-riddled treat. *40%. sc.*

Blaue Maus Single Cask Malt Whisky fass/los nr. 2, destilliert Mar 06, abgefüllt May 16 db **(87)** n20.5 t22 f22.5 b22. The scary nose is compensated by a charming slow burn of light muscovado sugars and ulmo honey. The feinty bitters are kept in check. *40%. sc.*

Blaue Maus Single Cask Malt Whisky Fassstärke fass/los nr. 1, destilliert Mar 00, abgefüllt May 16 db **(92)** n23 very similar to the salty symphony played out on the nose of one of Robert's Fasstärke's last year, unless my memory is really going. Here, a little more citrus has been squeezed in; t22 a light feinty kick early on, then a succession of richer notes, vaguely veering towards a barley-intense middle; f24 a really beautifully layered, relaxed finale with a playing out of Manuka honey and light mocha; b23 a demure whisky for all its inner riches. The lack of spices is a surprise. *51.2%. sc.*

Blaue Maus Single Cask Malt Whisky Fassstärke fass/los nr. 1, destilliert Feb 01, abgefüllt May 16 db **(94.5)** n23.5 t24 f23 b24 An exhibition of just how to control a sugar and honey-dominated whisky. *47.5%. sc.*

Blaue Maus Single Cask Malt Whisky Fassstärke fass/los nr. 1, destilliert May 01, abgefüllt May 16 db **(89)** n23 t23.5 f22.5 b23 A kind of rum meets chocolate Liquorice Allsort. Just so much delicious character! *53.7%. sc.*

Blaue Maus Single Cask Malt Whisky Fassstärke German oak casks, cask no. 1, dist Jun 98, bott May 15 db **(94)** n22.5 whisky...? Pot still rum? A distillate of hay? Cream toffee concentrate...? t24 though the feints are apparent early on, the oils drag with them a fascinating mix of copper and manuka honey. That is just the start. Next comes that mind-boggling, puzzling and mesmerising display of multi-layered, fizzing, buzzing biting spice...; f23.5 here comes that toffee again. Though armed to the teeth in spices and ulmo honey; b24 a sexy, subtle malt which seduces you from the moment the first sweet drop touches your lips... *57.5%. sc.*

Blaue Maus Single Cask Malt Whisky Fassstärke German oak casks, cask no. 2, dist Jun 92, bott Jun 15 db **(92.5)** n22 about as salty and coastal as a malt might get...in mainly land-locked Germany; **t24** the lush delivery defies the strength...though the peppery spices don't. The early exchanges are all about honey: on the fourth mouthful, I had counted five different styles at play: manuka and heather lead the way, though. Liquorice and hickory underline the vintage; **f23** dry, with the hickory taking control. A little maple syrup comes to the rescue; but those spices just nip and bite...; **b23.5** an exhausting whisky to taste: so much is happening, it is hard to know which bit to concentrate on... 48.7%. sc.

Mary Read Single Cask Malt Whisky fass/los nr. 3, destilliert May 08, abgefüllt Apr 16 db (86.5) **n18.5 t22.5 f23.5 b22.** Maybe just a touch more feinty than normal. But the delightful chocolate nut-led recovery, so soft and beautifully layered, is well worth the initial pain. 40%. sc.

Mary Read Single Cask Malt Whisky German oak casks, cask no. 3, dist May 07, bott Jun 15 db (87) **n20 t23 f22 b22.** The feinty, nutty nose never quite finds happiness. But the fizzing, spicy delivery is awash with dark honey. 40%. sc.

Old Fahr III dist Jul 02 db (89) **n22.5 t22 f22 b22.5.** A complex battle of a dram. 40%

Old Fahr Single Cask Malt Whisky fass/los nr. 2, destilliert Apr 08, abgefüllt May 16 db (88.5) **n22** a lovely mix of nougat, ginger and orange blossom honey; **t23** wow, that ginger really does come out in force: some superb oils at play; **f21.5** a light maltiness finally appears; while the nougat re-emerges; a tad too dry on the finish perhaps; **b22** a tangy, complexly spiced whisky. 40%. sc.

Otto's Uisge Beatha Single Cask Malt Whisky fass/los nr. 2, destilliert Oct 10, abgefüllt May 16 db (94.5) **n23.5 t24 f23.5 b23.5** Robert has entered new territory with this: he has gone all Islay. Absolutely no trace of his usual house style. 55.6%. sc.

Spinnaker Single Cask Malt Whisky Fassstärke fass/los nr. 1, destilliert Mar 01, abgefüllt May 16 db (85) **n21 t21 f21.5 b21.5.** Relatively disappointing. Last year's Spinnaker revelled in the rum-like house style. This is less composed and more sculpted by the feints, thus giving the late cocoa notes maximum voice. 48.1%. sc.

Sylter Watt Single Cask Malt Whisky Aged 7 Years fass/los nr. 1, destilliert 2007 db (83.5) **n20 t21 f21.5 b21.** Curiously powdery, dry and spicy. Pretty feint heavy at times, though the sugars grow at a disarming rate. 42%. nc ncf sc.

Sylter Watt Single Cask Malt Whisky Aged 7 Years fass/los nr. 2, destilliert 2007 db (86.5) **n19.5 t22.5 f22 b22.5.** A pretty slinky whisky when it hits the palate. The nose has a curious cabbage and cucumber timbre, but once on board settles into a far more relaxed mode with light ulmo honey and various spices making for a delicious experience. 40%. sc.

Sylter Tide Single Cask Malt Whisky fass/los nr. 1, destilliert Jul 11, abgefüllt Mar 16 db (92) **n22.5** if this nose was any busier, it would collapse from exhaustion. Principally, some old fashioned Spanish orange on display alongside a much thicker malt nightcap...dreamy...; **t23** it noses thickly and arrives on the palate even thicker. We are back to Ovaltine, only in concentrated form...; **f23.5** healthy oils confirm the longevity of the finish: indeed, does it end at all? Still the intense malt dominates, though some drier tannin arrives to add some thrust; **b23** says "Single Malt"; and this is malt singularly... 40%. sc.

Sylter Tide Single Cask Malt Whisky fass/los nr. 2, destilliert Jul 11, abgefüllt May 16 db (88) **n22** liquorice, tannin and an earthy, vaguely medicinal aspect...; **t22** a real cough mixture zeal to this one...plenty of sugars have been stirred in to help it go down easier; **f22** intensely malty, but still that strangely cough sweet heaviness persists; **b22** to be taken three times a day after meals... 40.7%. sc.

⬦ **Sylter Tide Whisky** dest 2011, bott 2017 db (90.5) **n22** a little nougat but it is comprehensively outflanked by the grassy, salty barley. A little mocha and crushed toasted hazelnut adds pleasantly; **t23** usual Blaue Mouse oily malt intensity on delivery, then a slow adding of salted heather honey and praline; **f22.5** highly unusual finish, even for this unique distillery! An almost numbing effect to this, or cooling maybe. The concentrated malt remains intact but a secondary note I really don't recognise nor can explain gives an altogether – loosely minty – final phase; **b23** ever heard of Crusted Port? Well, here's the world's first Crusted Whisky... Truly unique flavour profile. 40%.

Blends

Kahlgrund Whisky Blend (86.5) **n21.5 t22 f21 b22.** A well balanced, impressively weighted whisky full of enjoyable sugars. But definitely from the nougat school of German distilling. 46%

German Vatted Malt

⬦ **Germania 2016 Malt Whisky** bott code L01B03R17 (73) **n18 t19 f18 b18** Off key and off target. 40%.

ITALIAN
PUNI WHISKY DISTILLERY Glurns, Bozen. Working.

PUNI Alba 3 Year Old batch no. 01/2015, marsala casks, finished in Islay casks db (95) n23 t24 f23.5 b24.5 Funny how you think of Italy, and it is all about passion and fieriness – be it their football manager or volcanos. Yet here we have, for all this whisky's enormity, a tale played out in the cask of genteel elegance despite the high drama. You almost feel Italian whisky has come of age with an offering this complex and charming. 43%

LATVIA
LATVIJAS BALZAMS Riga. Working.

L B Lavijas Belzams db (83) n20 t22 f20 b21. Soft and yielding on the palate, this is said to be made from Latvian rye, though of all the world's rye whiskies this really does have to be the softest and least fruity. I'll be astonished if there isn't a fair degree of thinning grain in there, too. 40%

LIECHTENSTEIN
TELSER DISTILLERY Triesen. Working.

Telser Liechtenstein Single Malt Whisky IX - Pinot Noir Edition Aged 7 Years db (94.5) n23.5 one of the best wine cask noses I have encountered this year: crisp, firm and devoid of off notes. Neither sweet nor dry or, rather, both – equally. One of those ten minute noses which prevents you from moving on with the tasting...; t24 superb delivery with that same firm grape, initially firm, slightly tart and salivating but then softened massively by the texture of the intense malt; f23 a gentle spice fade respects both the fruit and malt camps; b24 the Burgundian edge to this is clean and almost fascinating: this distillery does Pinot Noir-matured malt probably better than any other in the world. A big treat from a small country. 42.5%. nc ncf.

LUXEMBOURG
DISTILLERIE DIEDENACKER Niederdonven. Working.

Diedenacker Number One Rye Malt 2008 Aged 5 Years db (86) n22 t22 f21 b21. Not quite hitting the heights of their first bottling, but the nut and nougat is balanced well by crystallised treacle. 42%. 450 bottles.

◈ **Diedenacker Number One Aged 5 Years Rye & Malt 2011** db (89.5) n22 soft chocolate nougat; a mild bourbon note, too; t22.5 voluptuous and teaming with delicate malt, though the rye offers the skeleton on which it can; f23 back to the chocolate –praline, this time – but without the nougat; b22 Luxembourg's single cask for 2011 – literally! – has come up trumps: similar to first bottling where the grains serve up a feast of flavours. 42%.

◈ **Diedenacker Number One Aged 5 Years Rye & Malt 2012** db (85.5) n21.5 t22 f21 b21 With flavour this complex, it is too easy to misfire slightly. The extra feints wipe out much of the complexity. 42%.

THE NETHERLANDS
ZUIDAM BAARLE Nassau. Working.

Millstone Aged 12 Years Sherry Cask dist 26 Feb 99, bott 22 Mar 13 db (95) n24 t23.5 f23.5 b24 After last year's disappointing sherry bottling, thought I'd need some Dutch courage to tackle this one. But, instead, an excellent cask at work here which ensures an overflow of character. Just underlines the difference between putting a good quality spirit into a less than impressive cask or filling into top quality oak So, so elegant... 46% WB15/399

SLOVAKIA
NESTVILLE DISTILLERY Hniezdne. Working.

Nestville Blended Whisky No. 1 db (86) n21 t22 f21.5 b21.5. Sweetens in the right places, dries when required. And is even salivating, too. A real lightweight, this. Though always easy, attractive and singing sweetly, the overall plumage is a little dull. 40%

Nestville Blended Whisky 6 Years Old db (91) n23 t23 f22 b23 Blended, Slovak...it makes no difference: this is a beautifully constructed whisky. A genuine surprise package. 40%

Nestville Single Barrel Whisky 2009 dist May 09, bott 15 Dec 15 db (92) n23 t23 f22.5 b23.5 A beautifully balanced whisky, not just in flavour but in the interplay between the soft and then hardening mouth feel. A winner all the way. Which, hopefully, Slovakia's football team against England won't be. And if they are – I'll toast their success with a glass of this excellence. 40%. sc.

SPAIN

DYC Aged 8 Years (90) n22 t23 f22.5 b22.5. I really am a sucker for clean, cleverly constructed blends like this. Just so enjoyable! 40%

DYC Selected Blended Whisky (85.5) n21.5 t22 f21 b21. One of the cleanest and perhaps creamiest whiskies in Europe. Some gooseberry, like the malt, occasionally drifts in, ramping up the flavour profile which is anything but taxing. 40%

DYC Single Malt Whisky Aged 10 Years (91) n22 t23 f23 b23 Far more complex than it first seems. Like Segovia, where the distillery is based, worth exploring... 40%

SWEDEN

BOX DESTILLERI Bjärtrå. Working.

⬦ **Box Single Malt The 2nd Step Collection 03** bott Oct 16 db (95) n23.5 adore the ever thickening layer of smoke which drifts, a little spicily and dryly, over the ulmo and Manuka honey mix: genuinely complex and elegant aroma with a gristiness not unlike the lost nose of a Port Ellen when it was five or six years old; t24 so soft...though the spirit appears young, enough fudge and caramel has been leeched from the oak and oils from the distillate to ensure the softest and friendliest of landings. The smoke, which starts almost apologetically, builds up into a spicy force; f23.5 the oils ensure a long finale with a touch of phenolic walnut cake; b24 in football terms, does my tasting this straight after their American New Oak Finish make me a Box to Box writer...? Whatever, this is a joyous offering much more subtle and worthy of study: superb! 51.3%. nc ncf.

BOX Early Days 001 0ppm db (91.5) n23 t23 t23 f22.5 b23 For those who like their whisky malty and very well made. Almost modern classical Speyside style. 51.2%

⬦ **Box Single Malt American Oak** new American oak finish db (88.5) n22 smoky – and a very herbal, green leaf, bonfire-like smoke at that – against a deep tannin. Hardly a perfect fit, but always entertaining; t22.5 oak-thickened sugars arrive early and in force: maple syrup and liquorice at first, but that fades slightly as the phenols fight back; f22 all kinds of oaky splinters here as the spices bite. Some late molasses just keeps everything ticketyboo; b22 hardly a malt for those with lily-livered palates. This is a near enough unique flavour profile in world whisky where smoke and tannin smash head-first into the other. Beware of the flying fragments... 50.8%. nc ncf.

BOX The Archipelago 2016 41ppm db (95) n23.5 t24 f23.5 b24 Another Box which ticks all the right complexity credentials. This is one bloody fantastic distillery. Boys, I'm checking BA flights to Stockholm now....and if I can fly to the standard of this whisky, it can only be First Class. 56.5%

⬦ **Box Single Malt Dálvve** batch no. 2 db (86.5) n22 t22.5 f21 b21 Nothing particularly wrong with this whisky...but there is something just not right. The nose has its attractively nutty moments and the delivery enjoys a gripping intensity. But though gentle sugars and spices are present, there is a thinness to the finish in particular which underlines whisky's inability to sew together and balance satisfactorily. 46%. nc ncf.

BOX The Festival 2014 35ppm db (92) n22 t23.5 f23.5 b23 Not sure whether to applaud loudly, wave a white flag or just go and lie down for a few minutes... 53.5%

BOX The Festival 2015 24ppm db (92) n22 t23 f23.5 b23.5 Complex malt, really quite wonderfully distilled and matured to the brink...Curiously, although the lowest of the peated malt, the smoke here plays the biggest overall role of the three. 54.5%

BOX The Messenger 3ppm db (87.5) n22 t21.5 f22 b22. Juicy, malty, very well distilled. But perhaps too many fingerprints of an average old cask at play. Like Early Days, would still pass for a Speysider in a blind tasting... 48.4%

⬦ **Box Single Malt PX** Pedro Ximénez sherry cask finish db (93) n23 no prisoners here: both the tannins and the sugars are in killer mode: a vague feintiness stands no chance...; t24 what a stunning delivery! The intensity of the date and grape fruit along with the concentrated tannin and spices is enough to rip into the throat...in the most delightful way. The busy sugar coating is a thrilling caress; f23 a slight over-heaviness to the spirit reappears but those rip-roaring fruity sugars again thickly paper over the cracks; b23 this bottling should be used as the industry standard to show exactly how to make perfect use of a non-sulphured PX cask...! 56.7%. nc ncf.

⬦ **Swedish Whisky Federation Box Distillery** (94) n23.5 delicate, almost playful peek-a-boo peat; a little salty, sweaty almost, with both malt and tannin keeping on an even keel; the sweetness is restricted to thin ulmo honey; t23 mildly aggressive delivery on account of its youth rather than strength: nearly five years in a small cask means that certain youngish attributes are still hanging around, and they strike with a vengeance here. But that soon burns off and we have a wonderful, intensely sweet gristy malt and caramel follow through with both light smoke and slightly weightier tannin – and the inevitable spice that conjures up – having a voice; **f23.5** now settles into the style sought for: the interplay and beautiful layering of the buttery barley, sensual smoke and teasing tannin is enough to move one into, with abandon, administering an almighty avalanche of alliteration...; **b24** Box's aim was to create an elegant, lightly peated, high class malt. Mission accomplished. *56.4%. 2,000 bottles.*

GUTE DESTILLERI Havdhem. Working.

Gute Single Malt Whisky db **(95.5)** n24.5 t24 f23 b24 This is really quite weird. Back in the late 1970s and early 1980s, I used to comb old village stores looking for 1960s bottlings by Gordon and MacPhail single malts of Speyside and Highland whiskies as they were distilled just after the Second World War and early 1950s. Then, those whiskies had a little more smoke than was being used in the later 1950s. This malt has just hurled me back nearly 40 years. A malt very much in tune with a lost style in Scotland from some 60 years ago: I am stunned...!! *40%*

MACKMYRA Gästrikland. Working.

Mackmyra Midvinter Single Malt Art No MC-001 db **(94.5)** n23.5 t24 f23 b24 How fitting: probably the most Swedish of all the Mackmyra whiskies yet: reminds me of light-challenged days in that country when, at night, you would retreat to a restaurant and finish the evening with an aquavit, spiced to the owner's liking. The seasoning and smoking here takes us very close to that uniquely Swedish style. The sophistication takes the breath away... *46.1%*

Mackmyra Reserve "Queen of Fucking Everything" recipe: Rök, Bourbon barrel, Cask no. 32, dist 24/03/2010, bott 04/09/2014 db **(94)** n24 t24 f22.5 b23.5 After over 40 years of tasting whisky – some 25 of them professionally – this is the first time I have ever encountered a brand which includes in its title the word "Everything"... *53.4%*

NORRTELJE BRENNERI Norrtälje. Working.

Roslags Whisky dist 2009, batch 001 db **(85.5)** n19 t22.5 f22 b22. I doubt if ever I have nosed anything so identical to the haystacks I used to manoeuvre when I worked on a farm in my school holidays. And even the flavour has that unique half-forgotten timbre of how the bread to my sandwiches tasted when I had been handling the bales all day. Not sure if this is an astonishing addition to the European whisky lexicon, or its agricultural policy... That all said, definitely has something about it, and is rather gorgeously chewy, generously honeyed and very well spiced. *46%*

SMÖGEN WHISKY Hunnebostrand. Working.

Smögen Primör Svensk Single Malt Whisky db **(84.5)** n21.5 t22 f20 b21 Not the greatest fan of grape and smoky grist. This has its merits, though, as the fruit is succulent and the decent smoke cowers somewhat in its shadow. That said, the inevitable bitter furriness – hidden for the most part - rears its unwanted head. *63.7%*

Smögen Primör Svensk Single Malt Whisky bott 15 Nov 13 db **(85.5)** n22.5 t21.5 f20.5 b21. Well, it is smoky, alright: have no fear about that. But it is also fierce whisky, a little on the thin and hot side – as though the distiller was just letting the heat get a little too much to the stills. Enjoyable, though, and more than promising. *58%. Bottled for The Tasting Room, Norway.*

Smögen Svensk Single Malt Whisky Sherry Project 1:1 db **(89.5)** n22.5 t22.5 f22 b22.5 Wow! A clean sherry butt! What a difference that makes to a malt. Not as well made as some of their other whiskies, but beautifully matured. *51.8%*

Smögen Svensk Single Malt Whisky Sherry Project 1:2 db **(94)** n23.5 t23.5 f23 b24 What a fantastically clever whisky: you want to learn about balance and counter balance? Spend half an hour with this chap. A malt which fully maximises all its positives and papers over the cracks quite brilliantly. *55.7%*

Smögen Svensk Single Malt Whisky Sherry Project 1:3 db **(88.5)** n23.5 t22 f21 b22 The grape has certainly taken some of the sting out of the distillate, which remains on the aggressive side. *53.7%*

Smögen Svensk Single Malt Whisky Sherry Project 1:4 db **(90)** n23 t23 f21.5 b22.5 The grape is overt and intent on issuing a fruity blanket. *57.2%*

SPIRIT OF HVEN DISTILLERY Sankt Ibb. Working.

Spirit of Hven Organic Single Malt 7 Stars No. 4 Megrez db **(94)** n23 t24 f23.5 b23.5 Hven sent! A malt which doesn't pull a single punch. *45%*

⟫ **Spirit of Hven Seven Stars No. 5 Alioth Single Malt** db **(94.5)** n23.5 thumping tannins which take only a sideways glance at the roasty sugars and plum jam; t24 a fabulous cut with just oils enough to ensure both the softest of landings and longest of experiences. No feints or off notes, just a magnificent date and walnut richness and a barley-infused middle to be proud of; the spices on delivery burn off quickly; f23.5 soft with vanillas and sultanas continue hugging for the most gentle of goodbyes; b23.5 another Russian roulette European distillery where you have no idea of the quality you are about to face. This, though, is Hven. *45%.*

SWITZERLAND
ANDREAS VON OW DISTILLERY Busingen. Working.
Munot Malt dist Aug 10, bott 19 Sep 13 db **(87.5)** n22 t22 f21.5 b22. Sturdy and steady. The nose appears to offer more as a bourbon than malt and there is plenty of oak to chew on the palate. But the youthfulness is hinted at by firm oils and the light cocoa finish. *46%. sc.*

BAUERNHOF BRENNEREI LÜTHY Muhen. Working.
Herr Lüthy Pure Swiss No. 10 cask no. 508, destilliert 2011, abgefüllt 2015 db **(89.5)** n22.5 t23 f21.5 b22.5 A firm, impressively made and matured whisky worth finding. *43%*

BRAUEREI FALKEN Schaffhausen. Working.
Munot Malt Single Cask Limited Edition 2015 red wine cask no. 1-111 db **(87)** n22 t21.5 f22 b21.5. Has the thin feel of a whisky distilled initially to pretty high strength. The oak has by far the biggest script to learn here and only slowly does a balancing fruitiness emerge, though it remains gentle. Clean but warming. *57.1%. sc.*

Munot Malt Single Cask red wine cask no. 1-288 db **(86)** n22 t22 f21 b21. Very similar to their Limited Edition with the trace barley showing upfront, even briefly in a salivating manner, only to vanish under the chalky vanilla and vague fruit. The strength reduction means the oils aren't around to lengthen the finale. Pleasant but seriously lightweight. *46%. sc.*

BRENNEREI HANS ERISMANN Bülach-Eschenmosen. Working.
Tsyri Zürcher Swiss Single Cask Malt Whisky Aged 5 Years db **(86)** n21.5 t21.5 f21 b22. Quite a sharp, clean malt with tangy tannin. Big caramels soften the impact. The molasses do a good balancing job. *40%. sc.*

BRENNEREI KOBELT Marbach. Working.
Glen Rhine Whiskey 2011/4J db **(85)** n21.5 t22 f20 b21.5. A welter of sugary, soft, toffee tones with a squeeze of citrus to the malt to lightly freshen the experience. A vague burn on the finish. Pleasant and as untaxing as a Monaco bank account. *40%. sc. 181 bottles.*

BRAUREREI LOCHER Appenzell. Working.
Säntis Malt Himmelberg Edition oak beer casks, finished in wine casks db **(88)** n22 malt from the spirit? Or malt from the beer barrel, I wonder...Either way it is the mega intense fruit which balances out more comfortably; t22.5 powering sugars on delivery from a dessert wine type grape with light spices and a vague hop undertone; f21.5 a few extra hops from the beer barrel appear to blast their way through; b22 make mine a pint...! *43%*

BRENNEREI SCHWAB Oberwil. Working.
Buechibärger Whisky Single Malt Fassstärke 2006 Chardonnas Fass Nr. 27 db **(94.5)** n23 t24 f23.5 b24 A whisky to cherish... *55%. sc.*

Buechibärger Whisky Single Malt Fassstärke 2009 Chardonnas Fass Nr. 34 db **(75.5)** n19 t19.5 f18 b19. The cask cannot entirely overcome the severe limitations of the distillate. *42%. sc.*

BRENNEREI STADELMANN Altbüron. Working.
Luzerner Hinterländer Whiskey Nr. 6 db **(89.5)** n22 t22 f23 b22.5 Unspectacular, but doesn't try to be a superstar. Just offers a lovely malty narrative without a cross word or hint of attitude. *40%*

Luzerner Hinterländer Whiskey Nr. 7 db **(91)** n21.5 t23.5 f23 b23 Very much along the same lines as their Nr. 6 in many respects. Except this is softer still and, despite the restrictions of the natural caramel, has an extra degree of complexity. *40%*

BRENNEREI-ZENTRUM BAUERNHO Zug. Working.

Swissky db (91) n23 t23 f22 b23. While retaining a distinct character, this is the cleanest, most refreshing malt yet to come from mainland Europe. Hats off to Edi Bieri for this work of art. Moving stuff. 42%

DESTILLERIE EGNACH Egnach. Silent.

Thursky db (93) n24 t23.5 f22.5 b23. Such a beautifully even whisky! I am such a sucker for that clean fruity-spice style. Brilliant! 40%

DISTILLERIE ETTER Zug. Working.

Johnett Single Cask Swiss Single Malt Whisky Rum Trinidad Finish cask no. 93, dist Aug 11, bott Jun 15 db (95) n23 t24 f23.5 b24.5 Rum cask finishes seldom work because the hardness and occasional tartness of the sugar sends a force-field around the whisky which prevents it from opening up. Here, the opposite appears true, where the weaknesses found in their 2009 vintage appear to be sealed in, leaving the more complex notes a much freer hand. 51.1%. 280 bottles.

Johnett Swiss Single Malt Whisky 2009 dist May 09, bott Sept 15 db (84) n20.5 t21.5 f21 b21. Nutty, soft and welcoming, this focuses on the malt side of things: brimming with barley and even a smidgeon of ulmo honey. 44%. ncf.

DESTILLERIE HAGEN-RÜHLI Hüttwilen. Working.

Hagen's Best Whisky No. 2 lot no. 00403/04-03-08.08 db (87) n19 t23.5 f22 b22.5. Much more Swiss, small still style than previous bottling and although the nose isn't quite the most enticing, the delivery and follow through are a delight. Lovely whisky. 42%

DESTILLERIE MACARDO Strohwilen. Working.

Macardo Distillers Selection 2016 Single Malt Double Cask sherry & European oak casks db (88) n21.5 t22.5 f22 b22 A clean sherry butt. But it does make for a one-paced malt. 42%. 425 bottles.

Macardo Swiss Single Malt Whisky bourbon cask, dist 2009 db (93.5) n23 t23.5 f23.5 b23.5 A beautifully made and matured whisky: a credit to the distillery. And plucked from the warehouse not a day too soon. 42%

Macardo Swiss Bourbon dist 2009 db (87.5) n22.5 t22.5 f21 b21.5. If the Swiss had a navy and this was one of their ships, then it would be the one set on a straight course, never veering. There appears to be a rye involvement which attracts some delightful heather-honey with it, which is noticeable on both the nose and delivery. But the oak is perhaps just a little too determined to have the final say. 42%

Macardo Seven Swiss Single Malt Whisky dist 2008 db (88) n21.5 t22.5 f22 b22 A testy, temperamental whisky with the oak stamping its feet. The honey doesn't let it get all its own way, thankfully. 47%

EDELBRENNEREI BRUNSCHWILER Oberuzwil. Working.

B3 Fürsterländer Single Malt Whisky Los Nr. 2015 db (88.5) n22 t22 f22 b22.5 Does a great job of elevating the malt to prominence and keeping it there. Understatedly lovely. 40%

FREIHOF BRAUEREI Gossau. Working.

Gossauer Single Malt Whisky sherry cask no. 6, dist 23 Feb 13, bott 18 Jun 16 db (92.5) n23.5 t23 f23 b23 Can't argue with that: a clean cask and a profusion of fruit. 43%. sc. 50 bottles.

HIGHGLEN WHISKY DISTILLERY Santa Maria Val Müstair. Working.

HighGlen Raetia Prima Single Malt Swiss Whisky db (92) n22.5 t23 f23.5 b23 Worth getting a spoon for this. Amazing! 54.9%. 25 bottles.

HighGlen Raetia Secunda Single Malt Swiss Whisky db (93) n23.5 t24 f22 b23.5 Magnificent whisky of Alpine beauty. 64.1%. 30 bottles.

HighGlen Raetia Terza Single Malt Swiss Whisky db (88) n22 t23 f21 b22 Another mainly sweet malt, but this time barley-based and less oak oriented. 58.5%. 64 bottles.

HUMBEL DISTILLERY Stetten Aargau. Working.

OURBEER Aged 36 Months Single Malt Whisky Tokaj Finish dist 2002 db (88.5) n22 t22 f22.5 b22 A friend of mine who lives just a few villages from me was one of the people who successfully got Tokaj wine back on the map and he was a little surprised when I told him that for the whisky lover that has been something of a mixed blessing: most Tokay-finished or matured casks have been wrecked beyond redemption by sulphur. Thankfully, not this offering. Though, like its distant cousin, PX, the improbable intensity of the sugars do restrict the overall development of the malt. *50%*

OURBEER Single Malt Whisky dist 10, bott 23 Jul 14 db **(82)** n20 t21.5 f20 b20.5. A pretty unique aroma and flavour profile, strongly scented with spiced citrus and with a late herbal tang to the standard toffee. *43%*

KOBELT Marbach, St. Gallen. Working.
Glen Rhine Whiskey db **(88)** n21 t22.5 f21.5 b22. Try and pick your way through this one...can't think of another whisky in the world with that kind of fingerprint. *40%*. Corn & barley.

LANGATUN DISTILLERY Langenthal, Kanton Bern. Working.
Langatun 10 Years Langatun Distillery Single Malt Whisky Châteauneuf-du-Pape cask, cask no. 5, dist Mar 08, bott Mar 15 db **(96.5)** n23.5 t24 f24.5 b24.5 Just a few miles from where this distillery, with its ancient walls and in the shadow of a mediaeval schloss, now sits is the old town of Langenthal. But it is ancient village of Aarwangen that provides the perfect setting now, with the distillery close to the river from which the community takes its name and where, if you are lucky like me, you might even spot a Hoopoe on its summer visit. And with outstanding cheese made there as well, it is some kind of whisky heaven which the gods have sprinkled a little magic on. 49.12%. nc. 499 bottles.

◈ **Langantun 400 Years Kornhaus Single Malt** db **(94.5)** n23 busy layering of barley and vanilla with polite citrus perking things up wthout causing a stir.; **t24** of all the distilleries on mainland Europe, I think I love Langatun's ability to extract the maximum layers of malt above them all...; a little buttery in part which helps the light sweetness hang around a bit longer and helps absorb a slightly haughtier oakiness than first seems apparent; **f23.5** long with a little extra sweetness now as low intensity ulmo honey beds down with the malt and oaky butterscotch; **b24** whisky is a derivation of the Gaelic meaning "water of life". Tasting this after their Hell Fire, the accent here appears very much on the water... And, no, this isn't 400-year-old whisky...thankfully. Though the stunningly beautiful building in which the distillery is housed is of that vintage. Oh, and did I mention stunningly beautiful? Perfectly describes this malt... 49.12%.

◈ **Langantun Hell Fire** cask nr. 666, sherry cask, dist Sept 10, Bott Okt 16 db **(93)** n22 a malt which appears to make no attempt to hide its youth: fresh barley with a little New Make pungency, though a milk chocolate and sultana layer does much to offer extra layering; **t24** a right punch in the kisser for those not used to this kind of thing. A sensual kiss – with tongues – for those of us able to cope. Salivating in New make fashion but then comes a truly magnificent parade of beauty, starting with intense malt but then moving on in a surprisingly similar manner to the nose. The intertwangling of warming caramel with mocha and sultry sultana is nothing short of breath-taking....in every sense...; **f23.5** the remarkable strength of the malt means that the finish is unusual in that it appears to evaporate off the palate rather than simply fade away. Even so, the high quality malt left behind can be savoured for quite a while...; **b23.5** use the Murray method of tasting and it becomes a mere pussycat (OK, one with a few sharp claws) – even with no water added. I was going to make this the 666th whisky tasted for the 2018 Bible...but I forgot. So it is the 1,111th. Oh, hell...!!!! *81%*. 444 bottles.

Langatun Jacob's Dream Single Malt Whisky pinot noir cask, cask no. 97, dist 23 Mar 09, bott 15 Jun 15 db **(92.5)** n23.5 t24 f22 b23 Quite astonishing how this malt has the presence to comfortably fit into the shoes of such big wine casks.

Langatun Old Bear Single Malt bott code L 0116 db **(88)** n21.5 t22.5 f22 b22 Langatun whisky is such a force of nature, it doesn't seem natural to taste it much below natural strength, let alone at 40%. *40%*

Langatun Old Deer Single Malt bott code L 0116 db **(87.5)** n21.5 t22.5 f21.5 b22. This is one of the great distilleries of Europe, make no mistake. But here the cut strays just onto the wide side of things, though it is still brimming with hay and marmalade notes. The sugars are of the heather-honey variety. But those feints, a rarity - a collectors' item - for Langatun, just stifle the overall complexity. *40%*

Langatun Old Deer Cask Strength Single Malt bott code L 0116 db **(95.5)** n24 t24 f23.5 b24 Now that is what I was expecting...not the character of the 40% bottling. This is, quite simply, brilliant. *62.1%*

Langatun Old Mustang Bourbon 4 Year Old recipe: 60% corn, 40% barley malt db **(95.5)** n23.5 t24 f24 b24 This is Switzerland's answer to bourbon whiskey. Soon there will be a new Canton of Kentucky...yessirree!! Or at least there deserves to be in honour of this great whisky. 62.1%

Langatun Single Malt Whisky 6 Year Old Pinot Noir cask, cask no. 98, dist 18 Sept 09, bott 11 Nov 15 db **(96.5)** n23.5 t25 f23.5 b24.5 When last at this distillery in Switzerland, I spotted, quite amazingly, the exceptionally rare and bizarre hoopoe, having flown in probably from the Arab lands. While tasting this, I have been serenaded by not one but two song thrush: no less amazing because in my third summer here until now, 49 different species had visited, but none a song thrush. Its sister mistle thrush, yes. As well as cousins redwing and blackbird. But never a song thrush. Until today, where now there are two competing with each other for the song most beautifully delivered. And here we have a whisky in stunning harmony just like those two magnificent birds...and a whole lot rarer. 62.3%. nc sc. 100 bottles.

Langatun Winter Wedding Single Malt Whisky Châteuaneuf-du-Pape, Chardonnay & sherry casks, batch no. L 0614, dist Oct 09, bott Jan 15 db **(94.5)** n23.5 t24 f23 b24 Oh, and by the way: not only is this a truly great malt, but this has to be the best and most ingenious clasp I have ever seen to open a bottle of whisky! 46%. nc.

RUGENBRAU AG Matten bei Interlaken. Working.

Interlaken Swiss Highland Single Malt "Classic" oloroso sherry butt db **(95)** n23.5 t24 f23 b24. Hugely impressive. I have long said that the finest whiskies made on mainland Europe are to be found in Switzerland. Game, set and match... 46%

SANTISBLICK DESTILLERIE Niederbüren. Working.

Single Malt Madeira cask, bott code 91 von 300 db **(34)** n1 t16 f8 b9. This, without question, offers the scariest nose I have ever encountered on a commercially bottled whisky. Appallingly aggressive, I'll make this the last whisky I'll taste today (at least) - for I know I will regret it and my senses will need time to recover. Nosed at a safe distance, if such a thing exists, it appears to have been matured in a petrol barrel, though closer, braver inspection suggests it is peat of some sort at work. The palate gives some lie to this terrifying aroma, as my teeth still seem to be intact. Some burnt fudge running alongside the "smoke" makes the delivery not only bearable but for a few moments quite acceptable. But the finish, by contrast, is dry and after a short while you feel your tongue aflame...and it takes a while to put out the blaze. The Swiss are known as a peaceful people with a history of neutrality. Hardly surprising: with stocks of this stuff at hand, it is unlikely anyone will ever dare invade. 48%

Santisblick Single Malt im Vieille Prune Fass ausgereift bott code 266 von 500 db **(90)** n22 t23.5 f22.5 b22 Wow! Generates flavour like a dynamo churns out electricity... As a fatalist, few things scare me. Heights. Electricity. Angela Merkel. Oh, and as an ornithologist, Australian and Indian snakes. That's about it. Except, probably the name "Santisblick." Some years ago I tried two of their whiskies and I still am receiving counselling to this day. They were memorably awful, but I remember them so vividly as they still reappear in my worst whisky nightmares. So you will not be surprised that I approached these two whiskies of theirs as a bomb disposal officer might when he's aware that the device before him has already stopped ticking. It crossed my mind to contact the nearest high contamination unit to see if I could handle these in a sealed container via attached rubber gloves. But then realised that might present a problem when it came to nosing. So, as I so often do for the readers of this annual publication, I put my self-interest and safety aside and poured the sample into my glass, unprotected, in my tasting room. And do you know what? In the intervening years, the people of Santisblick have learned how to make a decent whisky.... Well, almost.... 48%

Santisblick 3 Jahre alt, im Sherryass ausgereift bott code 447 von 600 db **(60)** n22.5 t22.5 f5 b10 The delivery has a fabulous density to the dark muscovado fruitiness and structured malt; some spices begin to take off. But the finish shows its fabled fiery harshness of before. My taste buds were burning from this one some 24 hours after tasting. 43%

Whisky 3 Years Old bourbon cask, bott code L-130001 db **(83.5)** n21 t22 f21.5 b19. An odd but attractive whisky where the maltiness has been ramped up to nuclear strength. Best of all, though, is the body and overall mouth feel which is highly satisfying. A peculiar experience, though. 43%

Whisky 3 Years Old sherry cask, bott code 83 von 300 db **(59)** n13 t18 f12 b15. Probably the weirdest sherry matured whisky I have ever encountered. Words fail me for the nose and finish, the former being unreal and the latter being only too real in its grimness. 43%

SPEZIALITÄTENBRENNEREI ZÜRCHER Port. Working.

Single Lakeland Malt Whisky Anniversary Edition 8 Years Old Oloroso sherry casks, dist July 06, bott Aug 14 db **(86) n21 t23 f21.5 b21.5.** Annoyingly, a vague bitterness off-balances the malt after a pretty impressive start. Cream sherry doesn't come any creamier than this, nor more interesting with the early spices. But the malt is entirely lost under the sea of grape. Decent mid-range sugars, though, before that bitter cask note kicks in. *45%*

Single Lakeland Malt Whisky 6 Years Old Oloroso sherry casks, dist Oct 09, bott Nov 15 db **(91) n22 t24 f22 b23** Oh, a virtually sulphur-free sherry butt or two can make such a wonderful difference... *42%*

Weidhöfler Single Malt Whisky sherry casks, dist 05 May 11 db **(87.5) n22 t22.5 f21 b22.** Some sharp, lively fruit – not unlike pastels – on the nose, the delivery is much fatter and flatter. There are a few wonderful moments where the grape offers up its head in a defiant, bright-eyed pose, before dull vanillas flatten it. *41%. 114 bottles.*

WEINGUT CLERC BAMERT Ruteli im Buobental. Working.

Weingut Clerc Bamert Whisky Finest Pure Malt 8 Years Old db **(87) n22 t22 f21 b22.** Splutters and misfires on the finish, though not as badly as the single engine plane that has just gone, worryingly, overhead. Elsewhere some lovely malt, black cherry and caramel makes for a soft landing. *40%. sc nc.*

WHISKY CASTLE Elfingen. Working.

Castle Hill Single Malt Doublewood cask no. 492, dist Feb 08 db **(86) n21 t22 f21.5 b21.5.** Double wood, but only half the normal fun. Soft and seemingly alluring on delivery. Yet curiously flat in part and full of caramel. And a slight bitter tone, too. *43%. sc.*

Whisky Castle Single Malt Edition Käser cask no. 468 db **(93) n22 t24 f23.5 b23.5** / immense, magisterial and a castle for which there is no breaching... *68%. sc.*

Whisky Castle Single Malt Family Reserve cask no. 17 db **(91) n22 t23 f22.5 b23.5** It is a great many years now since I met the lovely family who are behind the Family Reserve at Whisky Castle. I was highly impressed with their whisky then; I am impressed now: this is beautifully and very carefully distilled without a single trace of feints. So I selected this as the malt of choice prior to Switzerland playing France in the European Championships. I think it will score a lot higher than the boys in red. *43%. sc.*

Whisky Castle Single Malt Oloroso cask no. 494, dist Mar 08 db **(84.5) n21 t23 f19.5 b21.** When they say Oloroso, they really aren't joking. The fruit pours from this like water from a spring. Rich, intense and about as sherry trifle as you'll ever get, too. But, alas, a light but discordant note troubles the serenity of what would have been something a little bit special. Bugger...! *48%. sc.*

Whisky Castle Single Malt Smoke Barley cask no. 489, dist Jan 07 db **(85.5) n21.5 t21 f22 b21.** Is it the youth? The vague feints, maybe? Either way, something doesn't quite ring true. And for all the smoky bacon on steroids, and the delicious sugars which fall into place and make sense only in the final chapter, you still can't help thinking that it is hard to interpret the overall picture. *43%. sc.*

Unspecified Swiss

ORMA Swiss Whisky Single Malt Zernez Edition cask no. 12-2 **(80) n21 t22 f18 b19.** Well, this is a very game whisky not frightened to stamp its unique personality over the palate. Some softening fruit, but not enough to keep the more thuggish elements of the distillate at bay. *46%. sc. 188 bottles.*

Vatted Malts

The Swiss Malt (95.5) n23 t24 f24 b24.5. Sumptuous and the stuff for late night naval gazing. When Orson Welles, as Harry Lime in the immortal Third Man, made a disparaging summary of all Switzerland's achievements over the centuries as the invention of the cuckoo clock, it was obvious he had never tasted this. A whisky the Swiss distilling nation can be rightly proud of. *50.2%. From 20 Swiss Distillers. 175 miniatures.*

WALES
PENDERYN Penderyn. Working.

Penderyn 41 db **(91.5) n22 t23 f24 b22.5.** Don't think for one moment it's the reduction of strength that makes this work so well. Rather, it is the outstanding integration of the outlandishly good Madeira casks with the vanilla. At usual strength this would have scored perhaps another couple of points. Oh, the lucky French for whom this was designed... *41%*

Penderyn Celt bott code. 53003 db **(94.5) n23 t24 f23.5 b24** Another Penderyn which works so beautifully. Congratulations on another cracking brand! This will be my whisky of choice when watching Wales' next European Championship game – against England. Though I will also make a vatting of this and some St George's...believe me, even if the game disappoints, the whisky won't...! *41%. ncf.*

Penderyn Celt bott code. 60402 db **(91) n22 t23 f23 b23** Delicious, but a slightly subdued version of the previous bottling. *41%. ncf.*

⬦ **Penderyn Celt** bott code 70474 db **(95) n23.5** you are walking in the wilds, having been in search of choughs. And having at last feasted your eyes on their blood-red bills you battle back against the elements, tired and cold wondering when you might be finding your inn and the ham and egg dinner that awaits. Suddenly, your nostrils pick up the distant smell of peat reek and you know you are nearly home...; **t24** so, so soft. The malt is in pretty concentrated form for Penderyn, the gristiness full of sugars and juice. But the texture is a caress in silk and the lightest smoke a kiss...; **f23.5** much thinner now with the meagre oils all but exhausted. The smoke is a vague pulse, the sugars now in a lightly spiced butterscotch form; **b24** this is like a malt for peat addicts trying to wean themselves off the phenols, but needing a lighter fix to keep them going. I doubt if any smoked whisky bottled anywhere in the world is as delicate as this... *41%. ncf.*

⬦ **Penderyn Icons of Wales No 5/50 Bryn Terfel** bourbon casks db **(96.5) n24** the gentleness of the aroma is its power: no physicality, just the gentle running over the senses of elegant vanilla-led tannins, half-hearted icing sugars, liquorice and lime. Not even a whisper, more a mime...; **t24.5** how do you describe a shimmer, a rumour, a hint? The lightest oil covers first the tongue and then beyond, amplifying notes that would otherwise be beyond detection. So the grist, so sensual in its near silent barley throes, the sugar melting on contact revealing a tidemark of dried heather honey and a grain of salt, the spice energetic yet on tiptoe...it is choreographed genius in a glass...; **f23.5** just more of the same, though the fade seems never quite to begin...or end; **b24.5** having seen Bryn Terfel perform live – many years ago now, I admit – I can vouch for this man's power on stage; his rare, uncanny ability to resonate with the soul. See Bryn and you get your full tenor's worth... So, this must be his alto-ego, for this is the most delicate malt ever bottled by Penderyn: ethereal, closer to the angelic voices in the closing movement of Faure's Requiem than Bryn's bass-baritone. To get that you would have needed to have added a lot of peat – and we would have ended up with Bryn Terfel....and that would never do... *41%. ncf.*

Penderyn Legend bott code. 52951 db **(92.5) n23 t23 f23 b23.5** Tasting this after Wales' historic and merited 2-1 victory over Slovakia, perhaps this should be called the Gareth Bale Edition. As it happens, I was dining with the Southampton chairman the day Bale made his professional first team debut, which happened to be against my side Millwall. "Look out for our young, full back, Bale, Jim. We have very high hopes for him," he confided. Who would have thought....? *41%. ncf.*

Penderyn Legend bott code. 53097 db **(91) n22 t23 f23 b23** So, equally, we must call this the Robson-Kanu bottling. A lovely build up in parts, though a bit ragged and off the shin. But still finishes to great effect.... *41%. ncf.*

⬦ **Penderyn Legend** bott code 61375 db **(94.5) n24** the most apricot I have ever encountered in a Penderyn; feminine, delicate and criminally alluring...; **t23.5** such elegant sweetness with the shadow of varied fruit combining with humble grist to produce a malt with enormous presence, despite the fact it simply melts on the tongue; the thin grape juice also ensures a clarity to the palate rare in any whisky in the world; **f23** more subdued with the vanillas offering just a smudge of citrus...; **b24** the blender is a lady? You don't say.... *41%. ncf.*

⬦ **Penderyn Legend** bott code 62873 db **(92.5) n23** major spiced vanilla; **t23** salivating, with the fruit in mildly aggressive form, thought the middle has a fascinating sweet-dry intertwangle which heads more towards a peach and apricot middle; **f23** a fruity vanilla fade with some crunchy muscovado ensuring not a hint of bitterness encroaches; the late mocha and molasses is a bit of last minute masterstroke; **b23.5** a much plainer, crisper version with the emphasis on the sugars. *41%. ncf.*

⬦ **Penderyn Legend** bott code 63223 db **(87.5) n21.5 t22 f22 b22** An entirely pleasant boyo, though by the almost unbelievably high standards now set by Penderyn this bottling seems overly content to chug along on a simplistic fruit and vanilla theme buoyed (or is that buoyoed?) by knuckle-dusting spice. *41%. ncf.*

⬦ **Penderyn Legend** bott code 70057 db **(91) n22** peach, apricot and playful vanillas; **t23** salivating and so clean! The fruits are much grapier here: squashy sultanas and even that distinctive grape juice sweetness; **f22.5** a little tangy as the spices and tannins hit harder; a little golden syrup ensures a sweet finale; **b23.5** a delightful procession of fruit and subtle sugars. *41%. ncf.*

Penderyn Madeira Finish bott code. 53436 db **(94)** **n22.5 t23.5 f24 b24** Despite the sugars, more in tune with the drier house style than the previous two bottlings; *46%. ncf.*

◆◇ **Penderyn Madeira Finish** bott code 61734 db **(93.5)** **n23** one of those super-dry noses Penderyn throws into the mix from time to time: curiously fruity, yet the sugars have taken the day off...; **t23.5** yep, a dry one! That said, the sugars, in hiding on the nose, slowly reveal themselves here and are of a gristy, muscovoado variety; the mid-ground reverts to a drier vanilla with a threat of spice which takes time to arrive...; **f23** well, the spices are here now, as is a dry, chalky crushed pip tone; **b24** the most sophisticated thing to emerge from Wales since Shirley Bassey. *46%. ncf.*

◆◇ **Penderyn Madeira Finish** bott code 61851 db **(92.5)** **n22.5** beautifully two-toned: the buxom plums against the house chalkiness; **t23** the plums win on delivery: salivating with the fruit augmented by an ulmo honey and muscovado sugar mix; **f23.5** long and now getting into serious complexity territory. The spices are on low and slow burn; some Walnut Whip chocolate enters on fade; **b23.5** every trait of this whisky displays a friendly aspect. *46%. ncf.*

◆◇ **Penderyn Madeira Finish** bott code 63503 db **(96)** **n24** Penderyn nutshelled: from the pithy fruit, to the chalky undertones, the polite but firm spice to dried maple syrup...absolutely everything is quietly spoken, yet together makes one beautiful noise...; **t24** more honey than normal – a kind of halfway house between heather and ulmo – but kept in check by the disciplined, dry vanilla; **f24** what a wonderful finale: the cocoa and spices could not be in better proportions if the whole thing had been built to order...; **b24** a whisky which just flows, effortlessly, from nose to finish without any recognisable flaws or cracks. My old mate, Jim Swan, who created this unique flavour profile, would have been proud... *46%. ncf.*

◆◇ **Penderyn Madeira Finish** bott code 70395 db **(92)** **n23** a drier manifestation, though here the tannins really are a lot noisier than usual - even to boasting the vaguest bourbon note - showing greater oak involvement; **t23.5** the big oak is confirmed on the delivery and if the tannins don't spell it out for you, the very early spice arrival will. The fruit is a little more of a back seat driver here steering with fresher than normal grape and more militant muscovado sugars; **f23** the increasingly more frequent mocha and muscovado finish has some decent spices to cope with, as well; **b23.5** a fascinating yet still delicious shift in oaky emphasis. *46%. ncf.*

◆◇ **Penderyn Madeira Finish** bott code 71021 db **(87)** **n21 t22.5 f21.5 b21.5** Full of mouth-filling fruit, chalky tannins and spice. Plenty to chew on and enjoy, but just lacking that usual Penderyn harmony. *46%. ncf.*

Penderyn Myth bott code. 52853 db **(95)** **n23.5 t23.5 f24 b24** One of the most subtle and most beautifully balanced Penderyns of all time. Had it been at 46% with a longer finale, would have been one of the distillery's highest scorers ever. *41%. ncf.*

Penderyn Myth bott code. 53306 db **(93.5)** **n23 t23 f23.5 b24** Yeth, much more a hit than a myth... *41%. ncf.*

◆◇ **Penderyn Myth** bott code 70193 db **(93.5)** **n23** a serious bourbon kick to this with a liquorice, hickory and molasses blend taking centre stage; the light grape fruitiness is happy to stand in the wings; **t24** so ridiculously soft. A fabulously understated oiliness plays a far bigger role than you might think, allowing the vanilla cream biscuits and ulmo honey to stick to the palate; at first, the fruit is nowhere to be seen...; **f23** long, with the ripe greengage note at last arriving, then lingering and apparent even through the big bourbon-style spice build up; **b23.5** perplexing how a whisky at a lower strength can have more body than bottlings which are higher. But Penderyn is nothing if not different...! *41%. ncf.*

◆◇ **Penderyn Myth** bott code 70732 db **(91)** **n22** of a dry, pithy bent with a sharp prickle; **t22.5** fulsome oils arrive early and stay the course. Much more malty than nose, though those drier vanillas and pip-like qualities are quick off the mark; **f23.5** brilliantly shifts into bourbon gear with the tannins eking out every molasses and liquorice note it can find: the sign off is an amazing dry-sweet interface; **b23** a complex malt which just grows and grows... *41%. ncf.*

Penderyn Peated bott 1 Dec 14 db **(91)** **n22** outwardly dry, but a subplot of delicate sugars and phenols intrigue; **t23.5** one of the softest and most silky deliveries from Penderyn: a bed of oil allows the honey and lazy smoke to fall onto the palate without any shockwaves; **f22.5** long, drying, even with a tangy sharpness. The phenols, half-hearted at their liveliest, allow the spices to take over for the remainder of the flight; **b23** a gentle Penderyn with little more than a sprinkling of smoke... *46%. ncf.*

Penderyn Peated bott code. 53032 db **(94)** **n23 t24 f23 b24** As Wales are, within the next hour, kicking off their first competitive Finals since 1958, I thought I would show solidarity with them by today tasting Penderyn. Even though I have a fair chunk of Welsh blood – my father's mother's family originate from Pembroke Dock – that has not coloured my view that this is another absolutely beautiful, subtle whisky with the most sexy, teasing smokiness on the market. Just hope Wales perform half as well as this accomplished malt. Not that I have anything against the lovely people of Slovakia, especially those in the gorgeous city of Bratislava: the Taff versus the Danube. No contest... 46%. ncf.

Penderyn Portwood bott code 615121 db (**91**) n22.5 many of the Madeira wood characteristics, except the grape is more heavily slapped on here; t23 some early profound sugars soften into a light muscovado style; f22.5 unusual for any whisky to be quite so salivating towards the finish. The late spice and cocoa does no harm at all; b23 a striking Penderyn where the flavours sometimes come across more vividly than usual. 46%. ncf sc.

◇◇ **Penderyn Portwood** bott code 61522 db (**86.5**) n21.5 t22.5 f21 b21.5 Not sure if I have become spoilt by the brain-exploding brilliance of so many of Penderyn's whiskies this year. But, by comparison, this offering refuses to get me looking at the glass with unalloyed wonderment. Instead, I feel myself shouting at it, mentally, to start talking to me. Yes, I know about the fruit, the dates especially. And also the chocolate and molasses which develop with the enormous oils. But then it just stops in its tracks, like a mule refusing to take a further step. Technically, nothing wrong with either distillate or cask. And, yes, there are some great moments. But we are now getting to the stage of expecting more from this world-class distillery. 46%. ncf.

◇◇ **Penderyn Portwood** bott code 63185 db (**95**) n23.5 fabulously mixed bag of sweet and dry but the fruit looms above it all like some deity; t23.5 the delivery happily celebrates the richness of the toffee-raisin lead and the slow enveloping of the chocolate; healthy oils accentuate when need be, spices underline the already accentuated; f24 complexity kicks in here as the spices begin to actually shape the experience; Manuka honey and muscovado sugars are enriched further by molasses and dates, but the sugars are controlled by the drier, high grade tannins; b24 doubtless, some people will taste these two Portwood whiskies side by side and wonder why one scores an OK, the other very highly. Well, they may be similar in myriad ways, but they are different where it matters. Just look at the chemical composition of salt and sugar: not much in it, is there...? 46%. ncf.

Penderyn Portwood Single Cask PT165 db (**95**) n23.5 t24.5 f23 b24 This is the last of the bottlings sent to me from Penderyn. And I have to say that since the distillery first opened, this has been the best year so far with the most consistent and attractive whiskies I have yet encountered from them. Always one of the highlights of the year, Penderyn, and so pleased they have enhanced their reputation further. 46%. ncf sc.

Penderyn Rich Oak db (**93**) n23 t24 f23 b23 a curious, even unique, line-up of flavours makes for a massively enjoyable and occasionally head-scratching experience. 50%. ncf. 1,113 bottles.

◇◇ **Penderyn Sherrywood** bott code 70232 db (**81.5**) n20 t22.5 f19 b20 Big spice and magnificent creamy toffee raisin. But all rather tight and constricted. On nose and finish especially. 46%. ncf.

◇◇ **Penderyn Single Cask Portwood** cask no. PT255 db (**94**) n23.5 blindfolded and nosed in a room entirely devoid of light you would be able to recognise this as a port-matured whisky. Actually, you might first call it Port, but only on further nasal inspection will you detect the slowly unveiled shards of whisky notes. They grow in stature to slowly, finally equal in value the initially obscurantist fruit jelly. At first we are aware of black cherry, both glazed and natural, plus the low sugar grape jam. Slowly the tannins come into focus, as do the spices, strangely lifting and deepening the aroma at the same time. Further patience is rewarded with a secondary fruit note – juicy plums this time – as well as a light praline note and an apologetic molasses sweetness; t23.5 above the flavour, the first thing to grab your attention is the mouth feel itself. The landing is deft, with not even a hint of a jerkiness or application of the brakes. Just a cotton wool gentleness, a brief dash of brazen fruit then a sumptuous taxiing around the taste buds. The nose, had you been patient enough, had hinted at praline and here it arrives not only early but far more obviously than you'd expect. Fry's Turkish Delight in full chocolate surround; f23 long, thanks to the gentlest oils, still fresh and fruity and now spiced significantly; b24 the most ruby to claret-hued whisky I have ever encountered in bottled form: it like a Ch. Margaux. Only a whisky for after a fine meal, not during... 58.9%. ncf sc.

◇◇ **Penderyn Single Cask Rich Oak** cask no. D161 db (**91**) n22 dense, almost impenetrable. The sugars have a big toffee signature; t24 ah, that's better! The delivery is not just intense but able to allow the more complex elements a few moments to stretch themselves. That said, again we have a limited number to choose from – the natural caramels from the oak being the leader, but there is also a delicious but fascinating concentrated date and walnut thread, signed off by a vague botanical sub-plot; f22 walnuts and walnut oil lingering, along with the dullest spice ever recorded; **b23** a deliciously thick and intense whisky which is not too bothered about narrative or detail but knows how to create an effect. *59.8%. ncf sc. 289 bottles.*

Penderyn Single Cask PT9 LMDW Vintage 2003 db **(96) n24 t23.5 f24 b24.5** In the bottle, the whisky looks as though this could be attached to a transfusion unit. There again, this really is the blood of life... Amazing! *58%. ncf sc.*

Penderyn That Try bott code. 60403 db **(91.5) n22.5 t23.5 f22.5 b23.5** Delicate and, for the strength, this is surprisingly oily and fat. And now after THAT try, surely they are going to have to bring out THAT goal...will it be Bale's – the first in a Welsh finals game since Pele scored for Brazil in 1958? Or is it still to come after I tasted this...and maybe against England... *41%. ncf. 50 bottles.*

British Blends

The One British Blended Whisky (84.5) n22 t21.5 f20 b21. Although it doesn't say so on the bottle, I understand this is made from a blend of malts from England, Ireland, Scotland and Wales. It says "blend" which implies the use of grain, though this is probably not so...another example of the confusion caused by the brainless and arrogant change of terminology from "vatted" to denote a blend of malts insisted upon by the Scotch Whisky Association. Not yet checked, but would have thought that as not scotch, they still would have been entitled to call it a vatting. The mind boggles over what they will do with this whisky if Scotland votes for independence in a few weeks' times. Doubtless the SWA will make some kind of noise... Anyway, back to the action. The label does claim this is a whisky of "intriguing complexity". If true, the term will have to be redefined. The nose, sure enough, does offer just enough smoky and citrus twists and turns to wonder what will happen next. But the delivery on the palate is a disappointment, with any complexity desired submerged under a welter of dull caramels. Just too flat and soft for its own good: back to the drawing board....and possibly without scotch... *40% WB15/406*

European Blends

Black Mountain Excellence Whisky Selection No. 1 (85) n21.5 t22 f20.5 b21. Thin, delicate, clean, toffeed and with an early sweet peak. *42%*

Black Mountain Premium Whisky Sélection No. 2 (85.5) n21 t21.5 f22 b21. Just like the No 1 bottling, this is grain dominant and simplistic. Though less sweet and more vigorously spiced throughout. Not at all unpleasant. *40%*

MISCELLANEOUS

Michel Couvreur Blossoming 14 Year Old Single Malt Whisky sherry cask **(75) n18 t20 f18 b19.** The thing that blossoms most is a bitterness from the sherry cask. *45%*

Michel Couvreur Candid 8 Year Old Single Malt Whisky sherry cask **(90) n22 t22.5 f23 b22.5** The smoke wins the arm-wrestle with the grape. *49%*

Michel Couvreur Couvruer's Clearach 3 Year Old Single Malt Cereal Spirit sherry cask **(89) n22 t23 f22 b22** A seriously odd whisky, but hard not to enjoy. *43%*

Michel Couvreur Intravagan'za 3 Year Old Single Malt Cereal Spirit sherry cask **(84.5) n21 t22 f20.5 b21.** Another oddball experience. Again, the sherry dominates virtually all aspects and holds too tight a noose around the grain's neck. *50%*

Michel Couvreur Overaged 12 Year Old Blended Malt Whisky (87.5) n21.5 t22 f22 b22. Attractive, with no shortage of molasses. Heavy, chewy, hints of Fisherman's Friend and also possession a surprisingly delicate grassy maltiness. *43%*

Michel Couvreur Special Vatting 12 Year Old Blended Malt Whisky sherry cask **(77) n18 t20 f19 b19.** Not the kindest of sherry casks... *45%*

Michel Couvreur Spirale 26 Year Old Single Malt Whisky Jura Vin de Paille finish **(88) n22 t22 f22 b22** Pretty one-dimensional. But that dimension, luckily, happens to be pretty enjoyable. *47%*

Michel Couvreur Very Sherried 25 Year Old Single Malt Whisky sherry cask **(86.5) n22 t22 f21.5 b21.** No off-notes from the sherry here. But the strange thing about this malt is that the grape is so single-minded and bossing proceedings with such dominance, it is hard to recognise the quarter of a century of maturation. A whisky with such a lack of balance is always a bit unnerving, especially when the sugars – or date concentrate - are so cloying. *45%*

Nomad Outland Whisky (82) n21 t22 f20 b19. The entire shape of the whisky is lost under the tsunami of the PX casks. So first comes the scary sugars...followed by a very bitter finish with no happy midpoint. All-in-all, I have tasted whisky liqueurs less sweet than this... *41.3% WB16/006*

Deciphered and Distilled. The Bible's European Guide to Whisky Labels

English	German	French
Malt	Malz	Malt
Grain	Getreide	céréales
Wheat	Weizen	blé
Barley	Gerste	orge
Rye	Roggen	seigle
Spelt	Dinkel	épeautre
Corn	Mais	maïs
Oat	Hafer	avoine
Peated	getorft	tourbé
Smoked	geraucht	fumé
Organic	biologisch	biologique
Cask	Fass	fût
Matured in/Aged in	gereift in	vieilli en
Finish	Nachreifung	déverdissage
Double Maturation	Zweitreifung	deuxième maturation
Oak	Eiche	chêne
Toasted	wärmebehandelt	grillé
Charred	ausgeflammt, verkohlt	carbonisé
Years	Jahre	ans
Months	Monate	mois
Days	Tage	journées
Chill Filtration	Kühlfiltration	filtration à froid
Non Chill Filtered	nicht kühlgefiltert	non filtré à froid
No Colouring	nicht gefärbt	non coloré
Cask Strength	Fassstärke	brut du fût
Single Cask	Einzelfass	single cask
Cask No.	Fass-Nummer	numéro du fût
Batch	Charge	Lot/charge
Distillation Date	Destillations-Datum	date de distillation
Bottling Date	Abfüll-Datum	date de mise en bouteille
Alcohol by Volume/abv	Volumenprozente/% vol.	teneur en alcool/abv
Proof (American)	amerikanische Einheit für % vol.	unité américaine

Danish	Dutch	Swedish
Malt	Gerst	Malt
Korn	graan	säd
hvede	tarwe	vete
byg	gerst	korn
rug	rogge	råg
spelt	spelt	speltvete
majs	mais	majs
havre	haver	havre
tørv	geturfd	torvrökt
røget	gerookt	rökt
organisk	biologisch/organisch	ekologisk
fad	vat	fat
modning i	gerijpt in	mognad på/lagrad på
finish	narijping/finish	slutlagrat
dobbelt modning	dubbele rijping	dubbellagrat
egetræ	eik	ek
ristet	getoast	rostad
forkullet	gebrand	kolad
år	jaren	år
måned	maanden	månader
dage	dagen	dagar
kold filtrering	koude-filtratie	kylfiltrering
ikke kold filtreret	niet koud gefilterd	ej kylfiltrerad
ikke farvet	niet bijgekleurd	inga färgämnen
fadstyrke	vatsterkte	fatstyrka
enkelt fad	enkel vat	enkelfat
fad nr.	vat nummer	fatnummer
parti/batch	serie/batch	batch
destillations dato	distillatie datum	destilleringsdatum
aftapnings dato	bottel datum	buteljeringsdatum
volumenprocent	alcoholpercentage/% vol	volymprocent/% vol.
Proof	amerikaanse aanduiding voor % vol	Amerikanska proof

World Whiskies

I have long said that whisky can be made just about anywhere in the world; that it is not writ large in stone that it is the inalienable right for just Scotland, Ireland, Kentucky and Canada to have it all to themselves. And so, it seems, it is increasingly being proved. Perhaps only sandy deserts and fields of ironstone can prevent its make physically and Islam culturally, though even that has not been a barrier to malt whisky being distilled in both Pakistan and Turkey. Whilst not even the world's highest mountains or jungle can prevent the spread of barley and copper pot.

Outside of North America and Europe, whisky's traditional nesting sites, you can head in any direction and find it being made. Australia, in particular, has gained a deserved reputation for magnificent malt though, like its finest wines, can be hard to locate outside its own country. Limeburner's Distillery has been knocking on the door of greatness for a while and this year carried off the Bible's Southern Hemisphere title with the earthy Dark Winter.

World class whisky can be found in other surprising lush and tropical climes with Taiwan leading the way thanks to the wonderful Kavalan distillery, a serial Bible award winner.

Japan has long represented Asia with distinction and whisky-making there is in such an advanced state and at a high standard Jim Murray's Whisky Bible has given it its own section - and World Whisky of the Year for 2015!. But while neighbouring South Korea has ended its malt distilling venture, further east, and at a very unlikely altitude, Nepal has forged a small industry to team up, geographically, with fellow malt distillers India and Pakistan. The main malt whisky from this region making inroads in world markets is India's Amrut single malt.

Actually, inroads is hardly doing them justice. Full-bloodied trailblazing, more like. So good now is their whisky they were, with their fantastically complex brand, Fusion deservedly awarded Jim Murray's Whisky Bible 2010 Third Finest Whisky in the World. That represented a watershed not just for the distillery, but Indian whisky as a whole and in a broader sense the entire world whisky movement: it proved beyond doubt that excellent distilling and maturation wherever you are on this planet will be recognised and rewarded. Following hard on Amrut's tail is the ever-improving and high-flavoured malt from the Paul John distillery in Goa who this year pick up ther first award for Asian Whisky of the Year with their Kanya .

Jim Murray's Whisky Bible World Whiskies of the Year Winners

	Asian Whisky	Southern Hemisphere Whisky
2010	**Amrut Fusion**	N/A
2011	**Amrut Intermediate Sherry Matured**	N/A
2012	Amrut Two Continents 2nd Edition	**Kavalan Solist Fino Single Cask**
2013	N/A	**Sullivan's Cove Single Cask HH0509**
2014	Kavalan Podium Single Malt	**Timboon Single Malt Whisky**
2015	Kavalan Single Malt Whisky	**NZ Willowbank 1988 25 years Old**
2016	**Amrut Greedy Angels 46%**	Heartwood Port 71.3%
2017	**Kavalan Solist Moscatel**	Heartwood Any Port in a Storm
2018	Paul John Kanya	**Limeburner's Dark Winter**

ARGENTINA
Blends
Breeders Choice (84) n21 t22 f21 b20. A sweet blend using Scottish malt and, at the helm, an unusually lush Argentinian grain. *40%*

AUSTRALIA
BAKERY HILL North Bayswater, Victoria. Working.
Bakery Hill Classic Malt cask no. 1015 db **(91.5)** n23 t23 f22.5 b23. A beautiful malt for sure. Compared to its cask strength sister bottling, this has a far more sawdusty, dry feel though the cocoa finale is an extra bonus. *46%*

Bakery Hill Classic Malt cask no. 1015 db **(95)** n23.5 t24 f23.5 b24 Emphasis on a fruit character, but always stunningly subtle in its execution. But it pays off because it never falls out of sync or balance. *60%*

Bakery Hill Classic Malt cask no. 1415 db **(93.5)** n23 t23 f24 b23.5. As the 60% version below, except here there is far less emphasis on the light phenols and more, especially late on, on the bready sugars. *46%*

Bakery Hill Classic Malt cask no. 1415 db **(94.5)** n23.5 t24 f23.5 b23.5 This is the seventh Bakery Hill whisky I have tasted today. And in the many years I have been sampling this stuff, I cannot remember when I was faced with such a long line of outstanding whisky from this Melbourne distillery. This is truly stunning malt, the light smokiness doing it no harm whatsoever. *60%*

Bakery Hill Classic Malt cask no. 3115 db **(92)** n22.5 t23.4 f22.5 b23.5. Markedly more conservative than the sister bottling below with far less emphasis on the citrus and more on a gristy maltiness. The oils do stay remarkably intact and even aid the complexity of the delivery. *46%*

Bakery Hill Classic Malt cask no. 3115 db **(91.5)** n23 t23 f22.5 b23 Another malt which has no compunction about hitting hard. Bruising and delightful. *60%*

Bakery Hill Peated Malt cask no. 0315 db **(91)** n22.5 t23 f22.5 b23. As below, but without quite building the same intensity. Still a treat. *46%*

Bakery Hill Peated Malt cask no. 0315 db **(93)** n23.5 t23 f23 b23.5 Every last drop of oil is extracted for maximum complexity and effect. Lovely stuff! *60%*

Bakery Hill Peated Malt cask no. 0715 db **(90)** n22.5 t22 f23 b22.5 As below, except the lack of oils does rip away a degree of the sweetness and durability. *46%*

Bakery Hill Peated Malt cask no. 0715 db **(91.5)** n23 t22.5 f23 b23 Bakery Dave still knows how to treat us to a rip-roaring, snorting smoky one. What fun! And really does have a touch of the Teacher's about it – which even for malt is a serious compliment. *59%*

Bakery Hill Peated Malt cask no. 104 db **(90.5)** n22 t22.5 f23 b23 Give yourself a good 20 minutes with this one, using the Murray method. You will be rewarded... *52%*

Bakery Hill Double Wood cask no. 3159 db **(84.5)** n21 t21.5 f21 b21. Pleasant. Apart from a slight bum note on the nose, nothing particularly wrong with this. Just a bit dull and uninteresting I'm afraid, the whole experience being a little too flat. **46%**

Bakery Hill Double Wood cask no. 4477 db **(87.5)** n21.5 t22 f22 b22. Lightly smoked, possibly to the extent it may not have meant to be. Even more lightly fruity. But a little bit of cancelling out on both sides here – so often the case. Juicy enough it needs to be *46%*

Bakery Hill Double Wood cask no. 4905 db **(82)** n18.5 t22 f20.5 b21. About as subtle as a fruity custard pie in the face. For a few moments, the delivery is a grapey delight, but too much bubblegum at play. Compared to the brilliance of the other Bakery Hill whiskies, the Double Wood range doesn't quite measure up, alas. *52%*

BELGROVE DISTILLERY Tasmania. Working.
⬧ **Belgrove Distillery Oat Whisky** bott 19 Apr 17 db **(95)** n23.5 a beautiful halfway point between freshly baked bread and porridge: the sugars are of the delicate maple syrup variety and indulge the sharper tannin notes with god nature; t24 oats are notoriously difficult to make whisky from because of the mess it makes; it is rather more glutinous than other grains. The mushy mouthfeel tends to support this, but its very thickness – aided by the fact it is cask strength – means that every sugary nuance sticks around that much longer, as do the balancing spices. A beautiful, zesty lemon and lime citrus note also digs in alongside the orange blossom honey; f23.5 long, with the spices leading the way. The tannins are distant but the butterscotch particularly buttery...; b24 oats and whisky was long ago associated with the Irish. And many Irish ended up in Australia. So there was something inevitable about this whisky turning up in my tasting room one day. What could not be so easily predicted was the outstanding quality of

369

the product. This is top quality whisky and make no mistake: anyone wanting to get their oats every night will now be left with a very satisfied glow, indeed... *58%*.

⬦ **Belgrove Distillery Peated Rye Whisky** bott 17 Mar 17 db **(95) n23.5** the rye is of the brittle, sharp variety: as firm in grain as it is sugar; there is also a background earthiness... presumably the peat...; **t24.5** stunning clarity to the grain: this is from distillate of the highest order! The rye is hard and big enough to chisel the faces of Australian Premiers into and the softening smoke only appears to make the grain firmer still; gorgeous, lightly smoked mocha with crisp muscovado sugars fill up the mid-ground; **f23** though obviously from the very heart of the run, there are just enough oils present to stretch the finale and allow the spices and fruity grain an extended life; **b24** It is a well-known fact that Denmark and Australia have so much in common they are viewed as parallel, if not identical, countries. For instance, both nations cover almost the same number of square miles and are entirely surrounded by seas (except for a bridge to their neighbouring state, Belgium and Japan respectively) yet admit all-comers to live no matter from where they hail, no questions asked; both countries share an almost identical population and climate, are governed by blood-lusting, expansionist Emperors, while each country's national emblems are birds that bound around the place with eggs in their pockets and animals that cannot fly but sticks their head in the sand (Denmark being particularly noted for its deserts); the national language of both countries is New Zealandish, their currencies the Euro and national sports Darts. Both countries drive neither on the left nor right side of the road, but straight down the middle and, like Ireland, they are entirely free of venomous snakes. They also, amazingly, both make a peated rye whisky. Huh! I knew you wouldn't believe the last one, but it is true; I have them here in my lab side by side. But here the two countries part: Australia's version wins by a nose...not to mention taste, finish and balance.... *64.8%*.

Belgrove Distillery Rye Whisky 100% Rye Aged 3 Years ex-Overeem French oak Port cask, bott 22 Jun 15 db **(94.5) n23.5 t24.5 f23 b23.5** What a memorable rye. The grain leads on both nose and delivery in the same way Watson leads with his pads. *61%. ncf.*

Belgrove Distillery Rye Whisky 100% Rye Pinot Noir cask, bott 22 Feb 16 db **(94) n24 t23.5 f23 b23.5** Really excellent rye. Not sure I would have selected a Pinot cask, though, as the rye naturally offers fruitiness galore. Still, as a distiller, I doff my hat to you, Peter Bignell. Because, when all is said and done, it works rather brilliantly. *57%. ncf.*

⬦ **Belgrove Distillery Rye Whisky 100% Rye** bott 8 Mar 17 db **(82.5) n20 t22 f19.5 b21** By Belgrove's phenomenally high standards a little tart and off the mark. It is as though the cut was never quite sorted out on this one, leaving a massively flavoured whisky but one where the oils don't quite do their job correctly. *45%.*

DEVIL'S DISTILLERY Tasmania. working

⬦ **Tasmania Moonshine Company Tasmania Malt Spirit** batch 80001, bott 15 Mar 17 db **(84.5) n21 t22 f20.5 b21** Would probably benefit from being at full strength: there is a thinness to the spirit which reducing to 43% accentuates. A little copper-poor but sweet caramel rich. *43%.*

HEARTWOOD DISTILLERS Tasmania. Working.

The Good Convict Port cask, cask no. HH0543, dist Nov 00, bott Jun 15 db **(96) n24 t24 f24 b24** No problems with this cask. Has done its time, and has come away even and rounded. Massively impressive distilling and maturation: just beautiful! *71.3%. sc. 100 bottles.*

⬦ **Heartwood 3of/3** cask no. LD 643, vatted Jan 14, bott Jan 17 **(94) n24** if tannin and grape have ever been at such fever pitch and crashed into each other at such high velocity, then I've missed it. This has no right to be a brilliant nose, yet it is. The grape is juicy and pure, the bourbon notes at their most roasty. Yet, somehow the twains not only meet but kiss and wrap loving arms around the other...; **t23.5** the taste buds, salivating at full throttle, have nowhere to hide: the salty, punchy fruitiness covers ground quickly, aided by orange blossom honey. Now the tannins arrive, first with a chocolatey nonchalance... and then there is a jaded feel to them; **f23** Brazil nut and butterscotch try to dampen the over-aged oak; **b23.5** seemingly distilled by Zeus...this comes across as significantly older than Bill Lark's jokes...which until now hadn't seemed possible. *67.5%. sc. 125 bottles.*

⬦ **Heartwood @*$% · &*** 2nd fill Port cask, 2 x 1st fill sherry finish, cask no. TD0124, filled Aug 06, bott May 17 **(96) n23.5** &%%*+A!$ · &%$% ** · $+A fruit; **t24** fruit * · $((££A · $& %!* · *; **f24** $%&A)_ · spices · · A(£++* · ; **b24.5** just f*£%ing &%A*)+$ *62.5%. sc. 337 bottles.*

Heartwood Any Port in a Storm cask nos. HH 593 (95%) & LD 644 (5%), Summer batch, bott Dec 15 **(96) n24 t24 f24 b24** Another stunningly massive malt from Heartwood. One of the world's great single casks of the year for sure. *69.1%. 160 bottles.*

Heartwood The Beagle 3 Tasmania Vatted Malt Whisky nine Lark & Tasmania Distillery casks, bott May 15 (95.5) n23.5 t24 f24 b24 A more clotted version of Beagle 2. 68.4%. 220 bottles.

⬥ **Heartwood The Beagle 4** bott Feb 17 (94.5) n23.5 think of a bourbon with a kind of fuzzy smoky haze hanging around it, then topped off with over-ripe plums... There you go..! t23.5 think of over-ripe plums thrown head-first into a massive bourbon cauldron, tannins wherever you look, and all this wrapped in a fuzzy smoky haze...; f24 at last calms so all before comes to pass, yet there are extra molasses just to make life a little more subtle; b23.5 bloody hell...! 61%. 187 bottles.

Heartwood Convict Resurrection American oak Port, cask no. HH0239, dist Mar 00, bott Dec 14 (82.5) n22.5 t22 f19 b19. From the crème brûlée nose to the sherry (well, port!) trifle delivery, we know we are in for fruity beast. But, sadly, there is a mildly off-key dullness present which means a balance is never quite achieved. 72%.

Heartwood Devil in the Detail bourbon cask, cask no. HH0244, dist Apr 00, bott May 15 db (95.5) n23.5 t24 f24 b24 Probably did the enamel on my teeth few favours, but did my heart good. Magnificent malt! 73.5%. 152 bottles.

Heartwood Dregs Volume 1 Tasmanian Vatted Malt Whisky distilled at Lark and Tasmania Distillery, bott Jan 16 (89) n22 a suety, fruity mish-mash; t22.5 pretty sharp fruit brings a tear to the eye; a little biting, too; f22 a decent chocolate mousse fade; b22.5 pleasant and juicy but comes across as slightly less well-structured than it might. 66.1%. 110 bottles.

Heartwood Spiritual Journey sherry cask no. LD300, dist Apr 07, bott Mar 16 (94) n23.5 the peat bludgeons you; the fruit softens you to death; t24 I know some will adore this and talk lovingly of it until their tongues fall out. But I always have a slight problem with big grape and peat together as the wall of flavour can sometimes be a little too big to scale; still, the juiciness is almost unparalleled; even I, the biggest peat/sherry sceptic living, am arm-wrestled by the sheer enormity and seduced by the sexiest of shapes, into admitting that this is...bloody brilliant...; f22.5 seemingly tones down like a spent force, though, in reality, that finale still has more muscle than about 95% of all whiskies out there; oh, and then there is the late choc ice...; b24 when I read "sherry" on a Scotch, Irish and Japanese, my heart sinks and I bring the glass to my nose as might a man bring a gun to his head, with five loaded chambers and one empty. With Oz whisky, though, sulphur is never, thankfully, an issue. 67.9%. 100 bottles.

HELLYERS ROAD Tasmania. Working.

Hellyers Road 2002 1st fill bourbon barrels, dist 14 Nov 02, bott 24 Apr 15 db (87) n22 t22.5 f21 b22. A characterful malt which has come a long way since that first copper-starved distillate was made. Plenty of lime and light muscovado sugars have added a zappy mouth-watering quality to enjoy. Even some chocolate milkshake towards the finish. Impressive. 46.2%. nc ncf. 1,500 bottles. Bottled for the Swedish Whisky Federation.

⬥ **Hellyers Road Henry's Legacy Wey River** American oak casks, Pinot Noir finish db (88.5) n22.5 striking fruit, with a little vegetable lurking in the background: obviously one of your five a day...; t23 the fruit and spice form a deliciously mouth-puckering duo; the light cocoa towards the middle balances out well; f21 a little dry and strained; b22 Wey River...? Thought for a moment we had our first whisky from my native county of Surrey...! Mouth-watering and entirely presentable single malt enlivened and enriched by an exceptionally healthy wine cask which has imparted just the right degree of sharpness and weight. Good spices, also. 60.8%.

⬥ **Hellyers Road Port Cask Matured Aged 12 Years** French oak db (85.5) n22 t22.5 f20 b21 Certainly has the required chutzpah from the Australian port to carry a fruity strut, but let down slightly by the noticeable lack of copper depth. 48.9%.

Hellyers Road Single Malt Whisky 12 Year Old Original db (84.5) n19 t22 f21.5 b22. Forget the nose and get stuck into the massive malt. 46.2%.

Hellyers Road Single Malt Whisky Henry's Legacy 'The Gorge' db (83) n21.5 t21 f20 b20.5. Eye-wateringly sharp in places, its best bits hang on a vaguely smoky, molasses-sweetened coffee note. 46.2%.

Hellyers Road Single Malt Whisky Original db (84) n20.5 t22 f20.5 b21. Bolstered on last year's bottling thanks to a profound malt surge on delivery. Citrus fruity in part, but both nose and the tingle at the finish demands more copper. 46.2%.

Hellyers Road Single Malt Whisky Port Matured db (88) n22.5 spiced, juicy fruitcake; t23 superb delivery with the grape ripping home onto the throat with spice, then soothing and kissing better with its salivating freshness; f20.5 a tad off key but the spices are busy and biting; b22 without question the direction this distillery should take. Some wonderful moments. 46.2%.

Hellyers Road Single Malt Whisky Port Matured db **(89.5) n23 t23 f21 b22.5** An absolutely top dog wine cask has done a splendid job on this malt. Impressive. And, what's more, Australia haven't lost a wicket – and even scored 28 runs - in all the time it took me to taste this... 48.9%

Hellyers Road Single Malt Whisky Saint Valentine's Peak db **(85.5) n22.5 t22 f20 b21**. Regular readers of Jim Murray's Whisky Bible know that I traditionally taste the Australian whisky during the First Test of an Ashes series, if one is being played – which seems like every six months in recent years. So it is fitting I tasted St Valentine's on the day of a massacre – the Aussies are currently 128-6 in their second innings, still needing almost 300 more runs to win. This malt has done a lot better than Clarke's sorry mob. Still pretty rough towards the finish, the gorgeous fruit effect on the nose works well into the delivery. At least the last embers show some coffee cake attractiveness. Now, I'd better hurry up with the remaining Aussie whiskies before Broad and Co bring the game to an early close on just the 4th day... 60.1%

LARK DISTILLERY Tasmania. Working.

The Beagle Tasmanian Vatted Malt Whisky batch no. 2, bott Aug 14 db **(95) n23 t24 f23.5 b24.5** Another ridiculously fine whisky from Australia. 68.3%. 160 bottles.

⁂ **Heartwood Calm Before The Storm 2009** Oloroso sherry cask, cask no. LD588, filled Nov 09, bott Nov 16 **(96) n24** the sherry (real as opposed to Australian) has a big, spicy impact on this, even to the extent that it takes a quite few moments before I realise this malt has a peaty perspective. It can be seen here and there bobbing around on the oloroso, in the same way a Velvet Scoter might be sighted by telescope far out to sea and visible only when the swell brings it into view...; **t24.5** for a moment one is speechless. Such is the overload of grape that the lights dim, sounds vanishes and the only sensation is that of gargantuan grape, concentrated and dizzying in its scale. We are back to velvet again, for despite the fruity mass, the overall feel is soft and silky, with molasses furthering both depth and sweetness; **f23.5** long, with the smoke back into view and the spices now buoyant and crying loudly...; **b24** please do this as my 500th whisky for the Whisky Bible 2018 – part out of respect to Bill Lark and also, as there is Oloroso involvement, I like to live dangerously... 66.4%. sc. 292 bottles.

⁂ **Heartwood Dare To Be Different Oloroso** sherry cask, cask no. LD 542, filled Nov 08, bott Nov 16 **(94.5) n23.5** the grape is of the burnt raisin variety, the sugars molassed, thick, dry and overcooked; **t24** the kind of delivery which makes any self-respecting whisky lover swoon. Chewy, massively spiced and warming, fruit pastel sweet....; **f22.5** yes, there is the very vaguest sulphur edge to this (and it takes a little while to build up any kind of discernible presence) but so weak as to make no telling difference as the liquorice bites in hard; **b23.5** as you know, Bill Lark, when it comes to oloroso casks, I Dare Not To Be Diffident. But as I know you are one of the few whisky people who, like me , can spot sulphur from 100 paces, am completely confident this would be a first rate bottling...! 65.5%. sc. 330 bottles.

⁂ **Heartwood Mediocrity Be Damned** Oloroso sherry cask, cask no. LD 530, filled Sept 08, bott Aug 16 **(94) n24** huge nutty, toasty nose of the big, moist fruitcake variety – not entirely unlike some of the more traditional old Christmas puddings. The liquorice and molasses also have much to say; **t23.5** the palate is gilded with an intense toasted raisin and Manuka honey mix, thick and radiating sweetness, toastiness and spices in about equal measure...; f23 just dries with the vaguest of furry rumbles...; **b23.5** this bottling, the label tells us, is dedicated to Lyn Lark, an extraordinary woman who, like this whisky, is much loved, admired and appreciated by at least two middle aged beardies... 67.2%. sc. 280 bottles.

Lark Distillery Limited Release Heavily Peated cask no. LD670 db **(89.5) n22 t23.5 f22 b22** I think Bill's having a lark: as heavy peated whiskies go, this is pretty, well...not heavily peated... 46%. sc.

Lark Distillery Limited Release Heavily Peated cask no. LD690 db **(90.5) n23 t23 f22 b22.5** Fabulous, heavy duty whisky where, bizarrely, in the scheme of things, peat is at a premium... 61.6%. sc.

LIMEBURNERS Albany, Western Australia. Working.

⁂ **Limeburners Single Malt Whisky** American Oak refill American oak bourbon barrels db **(86) n22; t22 f20 b22** Just a hint of feint here and there – and especially at the finish - unsettles the generous sugars. Though, from the lemon curd tart nose to the acacia honey late middle, the good far outweighs the bad. 43%.

Limeburners Single Malt Whisky Barrel M91 ex-bourbon American oak barrique and finished in an old Australian sherry cask db **(80) n19 t21 f20 b20**. The stale tobacco on the nose and rumbling, off key finish says something about the feints involved. The delicious clarity of the fruit is a tick for the "sherry" cask. *43%. ncf. 355 bottles.*

⬩ **Limeburners Single Malt Whisky Darkest Winter** ex-bourbon American oak cask, barrel no. M348 db **(96.5) n24** my imagination, or is there peat at work here...? Yes, definitely smoke of some sort but nothing like the phenols one associates with Scotland. With some muscled tannins, this is a very different – and attractive – nose; **t24.5** the delivery, for a malt boasting 65%abv, is a bit of a pussycat. As soft and silky as you can imagine thanks to the most clever and delicate oils imaginable, the smoky, gristy sugars ensure an even friendlier entrance before a wonderful tidal wave of Demerara sugar and spices crash in on the party; **f24** relatively quiet, but the smoke and spice prickle lingers deliciously; some very late chocolate mousse adds to the pretty finish; **b24** whatever you do, DON'T add water: you'll absolutely wreck the intricate oils which sets this whisky apart and makes this fabulous malt tick, as well as ensuring a rougher ride. *65.1%. ncf sc.*

⬩ **Limeburners Single Malt Whisky Directors Cut** Australian port cask finish, barrel no. M230 db **(95) n23.5** a thick aroma: the grape for a moment forms an impenetrable barrier through which little else can pass, then, like eyes becoming accustomed to the dark, the nose picks out outlines of smoky phenols as well as liquorice and black cherry notes, as well as spices which begin, slowly, to pass through the fruity shield...; **t24** a fractionally lighter delivery, thankfully. So those spices mark an early impression and complement – even maximise – the effects of the muscovado sugars; slowly a light smokiness develops, so the weight never drops, but simply changes character; **f23.5** long, vaguely lush with the fruit beginning to again intensify; **b24** a little bit of Western Australian magic with not a single tang, off-note or any sense of disproportion. Magnificent! *59.5%. ncf sc. 202 bottles.*

⬩ **Limeburners Single Malt Whisky Heavy Peat** 200 litre ex-bourbon American oak, barrel no. M226 db **(94.5) n23.5** may be "heavily peated" but the phenols are very much in accord with the cocoa tones from the oak; **t24** just brilliant! The oils are again spot on and allow the muscovado sugars, hickory, praline and delicate phenols to merge into one delicious mass; **f23** spicy; just a little bitterness from the oak comes into play at the death; **b24** the third world-class malt I have tasted from Limeburners in a row. This distillery has single-handedly put Western Australia up there in the great whisky-making regions of the world. *61%. ncf sc. 212 bottles.*

⬩ **Limeburners Single Malt Whisky Port Cask** second fill bourbon barrels, port cask finish, barrel no. M283 db **(88) n22** massive clean grape augmented by much-needed spice; **t23** fat, rich, one-dimensional fruit on delivery: a mix of slightly sour plums and brain-scouring spices; **f21** here go the spices again. Trouble is, it is all quiet beyond the fruity front; **b22** 100% fruit, 0% subtlety. This insanely fortified wine (or so it seems!) is a must for grape lovers out there....literally! *61%. ncf sc. 244 bottles.*

⬩ **Limeburners Single Malt Whisky Sherry Cask** second fill bourbon barrels, sherry cask finish, barrel no. M269 db **(91.5) n22** a sultana fest...; **t23.5** the famous Limeburner oils make an immediate impact, coating the mouth and spreading more thinly the beautiful moist fruitcake effect; a little salty through the middle and massively salivating; here and there the malt can be located, occasionally in gristy mode; **f23** some lovely tannins form orderly layers; the spices busy, the fruit increasingly threadbare....; **b23** a fascinating and delicious structure and complexity the port cask finish is unable to match. *60.4%. ncf sc. 199 bottles.*

OLD HOBART DISTILLERY Tasmania. Working.

Overeem Single Malt Whisky Port Cask Matured cask no. OHD-096 db **(84) n21 t21.5 f20.5 b21.** Big, but doesn't have the excellence of the Port cask as in OHD-104 to get away with a few technical frailties. *43%. sc.*

Overeem Single Malt Whisky Port Cask Matured cask no. OHD-104 db **(91.5) n22.5 t23 f23 b23** Just dig that chocolate, digger...! *43%. sc.*

⬩ **Overeem Single Malt Whisky Sherry Cask Matured** cask no. OHD-097 db **(89) n22.5** grape...the meat, pips, skins...you name it, every part of the fruit appears to be in there; **t22.5** chewy, soft and good molasses inclusion in the fruitcake; **f22** a little bitter, though some very late praline chocolate wafer ends matters on a high; **b22** a curious bottling from Overeem which, on this occasion, battles to find the right rhythm. *43%. sc.*

⬩ **Overeem Single Malt Whisky Sherry Cask Matured** cask no. OHD-098 db **(95) n23** a clever oiliness appears to magnify the toasty fruit and tannin; **t23.5** indeed, there are oils abounding and the sharp, toasty raisins and accompanying spices make the most of it; **f24.5** what an amazing finale: from beast to jaw-dropping beauty. The fruits calm in intensity to release soft molasses and Manuka honey; then the mocha and fading praline is nothing short of sensational...; **b24** confirms this is a malt very much more at home at natural high strength. A late night dram of rare magnificence. *60%. sc.*

That Boutique-y Whisky Company Overeem batch 2 **(89.5) n22 t23 f22 b22.5** For those who think Oz whiskies tend to be full on, bruising buggers, cop a load of this... *52.9%. 75 bottles.*

REDLANDS ESTATE DISTILLERY Tasmania. Working.

Redlands Estate Single Malt Whisky Pinot cask, cask no. RD008#14, bott 18 Dec 15 **(89.5) n22.5** despite the obvious Pinot undercurrent, the main structure is centred around the tannins, which offer a red liquorice deftness; **t22.5** fat, chewy and rich with grape skin and spice; **f22** sensual and dry with a big vanilla contribution; **b22.5** a lovely bottling, but not often you see a whisky take more from the tannin than the freely available wine... *46%. sc.*

SHENE ESTATE DISTILLERY Tasmania. Working.

Mackey Tasmanian Single Malt First Release Aged 6 Years Port cask 001, bott 2015 db **(89) n22 t23 f21.5 b22.5** As a first release, the distillers can hold their heads very high... *49%. sc. 125 bottles.*

Mackey Tasmanian Single Malt Aged 6 Years Port cask 002, bott 2015 db **(94.5) n23 t24 f23.5 b24** Some seriously fast learning here because, for a second bottling, this is stunning. Uncharacteristically subtle for an Australian... *49%. sc. 151 bottles.*

SMALL CONCERN DISTILLERY Tasmania. Working.

Cadenhead's Authentic Collection Cradle Mountain Aged 18 Years (81) n20 t22 f20 b19. A nutty monster of a malt. A strange nougat-like note really is packed with hazelnuts. Sadly, the fruit and the grain have yet to find a way to achieve harmony. *52.9%*

Cradle Mountain Pure Tasmanian Malt db **(87) n21 t22 f21 b23.** A knock-out malt from a sadly now lost distillery in Tasmania. Faultlessly clean stuff with lots of new oak character but sufficient body to guarantee complexity. *43%*

SOUTHERN COAST DISTILLERS Adelaide, South Australia. Working.

Southern Coast Single Malt Batch 003 db **(79.5) n18 t19 f23 b19.5.** Third time unlucky. Lots of oils and berserk honey. But too feinty, though this went to some finishing school, believe me...! *46%. ncf.*

Southern Coast Single Malt Batch 004 db **(82.5) n20 t22 f20.5 b20.** An earthy, slightly musty dram with a pleasing essence of honey but struggles to find structure or balance. *46%*

Southern Coast Single Malt Batch 005 db **(83.5) n21.5 t22 f20 b20.** Starts off like a Jack Hobbs or Brian Lara or Alec Stewart taking the Aussie quick bowling apart. There is even an unusual, but mightily attractive, sweetened Vegemite hint to this (not as strange as it sounds, actually). But the middle stump is removed by the hefty finish: the cricketing equivalent of an ungainly, head-up hoick to cow corner.... *46%*

Southern Coast Single Malt Batch 006 db **(95) n24 t24 f23.5 b24.** When I saw these Southern Coast Whiskies before me, my eyes lit up. Here was my journey to Demerara. Much cheaper and less problem-riddled than any trip I normally make to Guyana..and with less chance of coming away with my normal stomach complaint. Batches 4 and 5 let me down. But Batch 6.... even the sun has come out for the first time in three days as I nose this... Georgetown, here I come... *46%*

TASMAN DISTILLERY Tasmania. Working.

Great Outback Rare Old Australian Single Malt db **(92) n24 t24 f21 b23.** What can you say? An Australian whisky distillery makes a malt to grace the world's stage. But you can't find it outside of Australia. This will have to be rectified. *40%*

TASMANIA DISTILLERY Tasmania. Working.

Sullivan's Cove 2000 American Oak Single Cask cask no. HH0332, dist 02 Jun 00, bott 28 Jan 16 **(90.5) n22.5** charming, uncomplicated but well-constructed malt; **t23** intense malt kick off then a barley sugar follow-through; **f22.5** vanilla and malt; **b22.5** well, that was malty! *47.5%. sc.*

Sullivan's Cove 2000 American Oak Single Cask cask no. HH0354, dist 13 Jun 00, bott 27 Jan 16 **(86) n21.5 t22 f21 b21.5.** Another big malty job. But a niggardly cask suppresses complexity. *47.5%. sc.*

Sullivan's Cove 2000 French Oak Single Cask cask no. HH00419, dist 04 Aug 00, bott 27 Nov 15 **(92) n23 t23.5 f22.5 b23** Just a series of very positive confident notes somehow finding a very pleasant tune. *47.5%. sc.*

Sullivan's Cove American Oak Single Cask cask no. HH0047, dist 9 Nov 99, bott 30 Apr 14 db (95.5) n24 t24 f23.5 b24 Exemplary malt whisky: absolutely beautiful. 47.5%

TIMBOON RAILWAY SHED DISTILLERY Victoria. Working.

Timboon Single Malt Whisky 2010 dist 05/09/10, bott 03/06/15 db (96) n24 t24 f24 b24 How can any critic fault a whisky this magnificent and mega...? A late night dram...but don't leave it too late to give it the full half hour treatment it deserves. 69%

◇◇◇ **Timboon Single Malt Whisky Christie's Cut** dist 29 Aug 12, bott 30 Mar 17 db (90.5) n22.5 chunky dates and no little vanilla; t23.5 something so Timboon about this: the intensity and sweetness come at you like an Exocet leaving behind it a fruity train. The sugars are heavily molassed and thick so a toasty effect prevails; the mouth feel is thick, chewy though not quite syrupy; f21.5 after so many sugars the fade is a touch bitty and uneven though the oils from the distillate have a say here; b23 Christie 1, Tom 0. 60%.

◇◇◇ **Timboon Single Malt Whisky Port Expression** dist 5 Sept 10, bott 25 Jul 16 db (96) n24 t24 f24 b24 Such a profound whisky I thought to myself: "I've tasted this before". And, indeed, looking through previous Whisky Bibles I see I have had the great fortune to come face-to-face with Timboon's distillate of 5th Sept 2010 on a previous occasion. And what do you know...? Just like this, it scored straight 24s... Even more remarkable (as I don't think this has ever happened before in the history of the Whisky Bible), despite two extra years in the cask, my tasting notes above fit this bottling to the slightest nuance. It is happening again.... 66.7%.

◇◇◇ **Timboon Single Malt Whisky Tom's Cut** dist 15 May 13, bott 25 Jul 16 db (84.5) n21.5 t22 f20 b21 Tim's cut, surely.... Just a little on the young and imbalanced side, where the massive components have yet to snugly find place and order in their whisky world... 58%.

TIN SHED DISTILLING COMPANY Adelaide, South Australia. Working.

◇◇◇ **Iniquity Gold Label Single Malt Batch 001** db (92.5) n23 clean, intense fruit: a hint of spice but the muscovado sugars help the balance no end; t23.5 the taste buds are smothered in the most gorgeously soft and tactile fruit notes, especially over-ripe plum and dates; a little oily but the molasses helps with that rich fruitcake experience; f23 remains chewy and as it fades the roastiness intensifies dramatically; b23 less a whisky, more of a journey... 60%. ncf.

◇◇◇ **Iniquity Gold Label Single Malt Batch 002** db (87.5) n22 t22.5 f21.5 b21.5 The nose is tannin rich and threatening but some diluted maple syrup keeps it safe and honest...while the delivery throws you back across the room with its explosive spices. But in the back of your mind you fear for the tannin intensity. And with justification for, despite the mocha element, the oak plays just too great and aggressive a part for greatness. That all said, my Blender's instincts kicked in automatically: buy both bottles and make a mix of about 75% Batch 1 and 25% Batch 2. The lush, ultra-complex and amazingly gentle chocolate fruit bar result scores a good 94-95 points... 60%. ncf.

Iniquity Single Malt Port casks Batch 001 db (94) n23 if I say the nose is huge, I am telling only half the story: we have dates, plums, walnuts, raisins...; t23.5 just as silky on the palate as the nose promises: an intense Cadbury's Fruit and Nut feel to this one; f23.5 a predictably long finish, with the spice joining in the rich, fruity fun...; b24 a gorgeous experience and quite a start for this new distillery: they will have to work overtime to keep this standard up. 46%. ncf.

Iniquity Single Malt Port casks Batch 002 db (87) n21 t23 f21 b22. A sharper, less inclusive bottling than Batch 1. Still profound, silky fruit: a truly lip-smacking start. But a metallic note creeps in later on. 46%. ncf.

Iniquity Single Malt Port casks Batch 003 rum cask finished db (85) n20 t22.5 f21.5 b21.5. Tin shed loads of personality once you get away from the confused nose. As time allows the glass to settle, the butyric decreases and a degree of South American-style rum begins to make a shout. But it's all a right hubbub and bloody confused. The finish is usually where you get confirmation of all not being quite right with the world and, sure enough, a slightly non-coppery tone emerges. All that said, the delivery is a celebration of all things sugar and entirely enjoyable. Get the feeling, though, that these stills would make better rum than whisky. 46%. ncf.

Iniquity Single Malt Batch 004 db (89) n22.5 t22 f22.5 b22 A distillery which has long fascinated me, and I am so frustrated I still haven't been able to find the time to visit. This is their maltiest offering so far...by a distance. 46%. ncf.

Iniquity Single Malt Batch 005 db (82.3) n20.5 t21 f20.5 b20.5. Malty, nutty but way too feinty, Not a patch on Batch 004. 46%. ncf.

⬦ **Iniquity Single Malt Batch 006** db (89.5) n21.5 a tad on the nougat side; t22 black cherries in chocolate...but only after a predictable nougat landing; f23.5 wow! That delicious black cherry travels a long way and fades alongside melt-in-the-mouth praline and vanilla wafer; b22.5 this whisky is a one stop candy store... 46%. ncf.

⬦ **Iniquity Single Malt Batch 007** db (89) n22 so many rich bourbon notes! A few oils, but these appear to help the honey and liquorice fuse; t23 an immediate tingle on delivery then a build of rich toffee and molasses; f22 well spiced and full of roasted fudge; b22 a better distilled malt, oddly, with this eschewing the staggering black cherry of Batch 6 to give this a more Kentuckian feel. 46%. ncf.

Vatted Malts

Heartwood 2 of /3 Tasmanian Malt Whisky distilled at Lark 8 & 6 Years and Tasmania Distillery 16 Years, Port, peated & sherry casks, bott Apr 16 (95.5) n23.5 t24 f24 b24 Make no mistake: the vatting of these casks from these two distilleries and over such wide ages really is a work of art: a study of fruit, as well. 68.1%. 189 bottles.

Tasmanian Double Malt Whisky Unpeated (87.5) n22 t22 f21.5 b22. Not a chance of getting bored with this guy. A sweet tooth would be useful. 43%. The Nant Distillery.

Unspecified Grain

3Souls Small Batch Australian Single Malt Whisky Batch 1 new American oak cask, cask no. SC30, dist Jul 08, bott Aug 15 (87.5) n21.5 t23 f21 b22. A sturdy malt displaying a degree of bitterness on both nose and finish. But the parade of sugars, some of them thick honey textured – is a treat on delivery. 46.7%. sc.

3Souls Small Batch Australian Single Malt Whisky Batch 2 Port cask, cask no. SC35, dist Oct 09, bott Aug 15 (90.5) n22 t23 f22.5 b23 Apparently, an unspecified Australian. If the finish was anything to go by, made in Victoria, I'd say.... 46.3%. sc.

3Souls Small Batch Australian Single Malt Whisky Batch 3 Pedro Ximenez cask, cask no. SC41, dist Dec 10, bott Aug 15 (79) n20 t21 f19 b19. Either too sweet or too bitter. Like many a PX whisky, comes to a sticky end... 52.1%. sc.

BRAZIL
HEUBLEIN DISTILLERY

Durfee Hall Malt Whisky db (81) n18 t22 f20 b21. Superbly made whisky; the intensity of the malt is beautifully layered without ever becoming too sweet. Very light bodied and immaculately clean. Good whisky by any standards. 43%

UNION DISTILLERY

Barrilete db (72) n18 t19 f18 b17. Nothing particularly wrong with it technically; it just lacks vitality. Thin but extremely malt intense. 39.1%

Blends

Cockland Gold Blended Whisky (73) n18 t18 f19 b18. Silky caramel. Traces of malt there, but never quite gets it up. 38%. Fante.

Gold Cup Special Reserve (84.5) n21 t22.5 f20 b21. Ultra soft, easily drinkable and, at times, highly impressive blend which is hampered by a dustiness bestowed upon it by the nagging caramels on both nose and finish. Some lovely early honey does help lift it, though, and there is also attractive Swiss roll jam towards the finish. Yet never quite gets out of third gear despite the most delicate hint of smoke. 39%. Campari, Brasil.

Gran Par (77) n19.5 t22 f17.5 b18. The delivery is eleven seconds of vaguely malty glory. The remainder is thin and caramelled with no age to live up to the name. And with Par in the title and bagpipes and kilt in the motif, how long before the SWA buys a case of it...? 39%

BHUTAN

K5 Premium Spirit Himalayan Whisky bott 2013 (88) n22 t23 f21 b22 Absolutely nothing wrong with the Bhutan grain but more judicious cask selection (i.e remove the odd one or two sub-standard Scotch barrels) and this really could be an irresistible little charmer. As a first attempt, really impressive. This whisky is a mix of Scotch malt and grain made in Bhutan. So it was fitting that seeing as parts of that mysterious, land-locked mountainous country rises to some 23,000 feet, I was just slightly above that height when I first learned of the whisky. While on board a flight to Asia I witnessed the brand's manager trying to talk an airline into carrying it. He then assured me I'd love it. Actually, clean that malt up a bit and I really could! 40%

INDIA
AMRUT DISTILLERY

Amrut Fusion batch no. 01, bott Mar 09 db **(97) n24 t24 f24 b25.** One of the most complex and intriguing new whiskies of 2010 that needs about two days and half a bottle to get even close to fathoming. Not exactly a textbook whisky, with a few edges grinding together like tectonic plates. And there is even odd note, like the fruit and a kind of furry, oaky buzz, which I have never seen before. But that is the point of whiskies like this: to be different, to offer a unique slant. But, ultimately, to entertain and delight. And here it ticks all boxes accordingly. To the extent that this has to be one of the great whiskies found anywhere in the world this year. And the fact it is Indian? Irrelevant: from distillation to maturation this is genius whisky, from whichever continent... *50%*

Amrut Fusion batch 10, bott Mar 11 db **(94.5) n24 t24 f22.5 b23.5.** Superb whisky, though to be plotted on a different map to the now legendary Whisky Bible award-winning Batch 1. This is a much more delicate affair: more hints and shadows rather than statements and substance. Still, though, a fabulous malt whisky in Amrut's best style. *50%. nc.*

Amrut Greedy Angels 10 Years Old batch no. 1, bott Sept 14 db **(96.5) n24.5 t24 f23.5 b24.5** when I visited my first Indian distillery, some 20 years ago, the last thing I thought I would ever experience would be a native malt reaching double figures in age. All those I tasted showed decline to the point of undrinkability at only half that age. However, cellared warehousing and far more judicial oak selection means that not only is there now an Indian malt whisky reaching double figures in age, it has reached a stage of magnificence on its maturation road. I first tasted this at the distillery itself in the Spring of 2015. But waited until August 2015, making this the second to last whisky sampled for the 2016 Bible, before officially reviewing it under neutral conditions in the UK. What is apparent is that wherever in the world you experience this, you are being royally entertained - bewitched and mesmerised, to be nearer the truth - by one of the most remarkable whiskies of all time. *46%. 284 bottles.*

Amrut Greedy Angels 10 Years Old batch no. 1, bott Sept 14 db **(96) n24 t24 f24 b24.** As above. Except at this strength it is all a little oilier; tighter in its delivery and demeanour, with a bit more shouting where there were once whispers. All the same flavours are present and correct, though they all rush through at a greater pace to get to the finale. Beautiful, salivating...and dazzlingly brilliant. *71%*

Amrut Greedy Angels dist 3 Oct 04, bott 15 Nov 12 db **(96) n25 t24 f23 b24.** So here we have it: an 8-year-old Indian whisky. Matured in a cellar, luckily, but still has the hallmarks often seen on certain Speysiders in their late 30s...a series of Caperdonichs from about five or six years ago spring to mind. Except their noses were never this good: in fact, few noses have ever been better – it is certainly unsurpassed this year...worldwide. A true whisky great of the last decade. *50%*

Amrut Naarangi batch no. 1, bott Dec 14 db **(94) n23 t23.5 f24 b23.5** The first sherry I know of worldwide which has had orange peel added to it in the butt to help infuse delicate citrus flavour to the maturing whisky which was to follow. Oddly enough, the whisky is in its element when the fruit levels have receded... *50%. 900 bottles.*

Amrut 100 Peated Single Malt ex-bourbon/virgin oak barrels db **(92) n23 t23 f23.5 b22.5.** Ironically, though one of the older whiskies to come from this distillery, the nose shows a little bit of youth. A quite different style from Amrut's other peated offerings and it was obviously intended. Further proof that this distillery has grown not only in stature but confidence. And with very good reason. *57.1%. nc ncf.*

JOHN DISTILLERIES

Paul John Brilliance db **(94.5) n23.5 t24 f23.5 b23.5** Yet another astonishing malt from India. *46%*

Paul John Brilliance batch no. 3, bott July 16 db **(94) n24** the burgeoning house style of orange blossom honey is brought out to the full here, giving an almost phenolic density to this – even though there is no peat. The light liquorice from the ex-bourbon casks joins the vanilla and sugars dealt out by the oak in equal measure; **t24** this was a malt designed to get the most out of the barley and here the juices arrive in force and early on. Much less copper than the first bottling, showing this relatively new distillery is moving on, but the spices and light mocha make a handsome contribution; **f22.5** perhaps short on sugars late on, but the gently oiled malt continues to pulse away with panache; **b23.5** it is impossible not to be impressed. Complexity is the key word here. And though it has moved on a little – mainly through tannin – from its earliest rendition, the layering and structure remains superb. The tail needs a little attention, but I am being ultra-strict: this is excellent whisky and make no mistake. *46%*

Paul John Edited db (96.5) n24.5 t24.5 f23.5 b24 A new Indian classic: a sublime malt from the subcontinent. To be more precise: a world classic! Think of Ardmore at its most alluring: one of Scotland's finest and most complex single malts, yet somehow possessing a saltiness and depth more befitting Islay. Then stir in a small degree of ulmo honey and bourbon-style hickory and liquorice. Plus subtle chocolate mint. And there you have it...the smoke drifting around stirring up spicy tales of the east. A world class whisky to be talked about with reverence without doubt... 52.9%

 Paul John Exceptional db (95) n23 the natural caramels of the oak are forming an impressive presence, though they never build up so much as to subtract from the intense malt and light liquorice; t24 an engagingly soft delivery which at first sets out the caramel and then moves into gorgeously salivating barley tones. Layered in weight and malty intensity...; f24 the oak has the final word, though it is a sophisticated rather than a loud one. Gentle spices and a little gristy citrus, even in the final throes; b24 the sheer elan of the controlled intensity is something to behold: Indian malt at its maltiest and most charmingly expressed. 47%. ncf.

Paul John Indian Single Malt Bold batch no. 01 db (95.5) n23.5 t24 f23.5 b24.5 One of the most weighty and chewable Indian whiskies of all time – yet it is not just about peat. So many elements to this, you expect a bottle to weigh the equivalent of a block of lead. This truly great whisky, so complex and absorbing, needs a good 20 minutes minimum of your time to adequately explore. 46%

 Paul John Kanya db (96) n23.5 deft acacia and heather-honey mingle contentedly with the heavier oaky notes to offer a subdued sweetness but one which compliments the intense malt perfectly; t24 ah...! Those honeys are unleashed early on, seemingly free of their oaky shackles and help drive the salivating qualities of the barley through the roof; excellent oils with a gentle liquorice and hickory. A little citrus darts around but very much hanging on to the coat-tails of the malt; f24 long, thanks to those never-ending oils. Even towards the finale there is still Manuka honey to be found with the sub-strata of soft caramel taking the sting out of the gathering spice; b24.5 when a distillery can find honey at the very end of the its flavour range and profile, you know they have cracked it. Superb! 50%. ncf.

Paul John Mars Orbiter db (95) n24 here's a fabulous example of how tannins can be used to maximum effect without the oak overwhelming the more subtle aspects of the vatting. So fabulously toasty where the smokiness and sweetness become blurred as the muscovado sugars move into something closer to dank orange blossom honey...; t23.5 beautifully lush delivery where the tannins are straining at the leash but kept at bay by several waves of intense maltiness; again the sugars and tannins appear to harmonise rather than, as Mars might prefer, go to war; f23.5 long, with myriad spices trailing the tannins like comet dust. All the while the toasty sugars hold their line and nerve...; b24 we have lift off!! Out of this world whisky! 578%

Paul John Olorosso Sherry Cask Finish db (94.5) n23.5 evidence of the grape arrives early: clean and well structured. As spices form around it, it opens out to become more rounded and confident, even allowing vanilla to play an important role: intriguing! t23.5 the delivery is soft and immediately salivating. Again, the fruit shows its hand quickly enough with an overly moist Melton Hunt Cake feel, as the raisins begin to feel a little more toasty and the molasses take up residence; f23.5 spiced orange peel melds into the growing mocha as the intensity fails to diminish; b24 oh, for the rare joy of a sulphur-free malt. And as complex a one as this, to boot. 574%. ncf.

Paul John Single Malt Cask No 161 Non Peated (94) n22.5 t24.5 f23 b24. A malt which has much to say but does so with a quiet intensity. This really is a class act... 57%

Paul John Single Malt Single Cask No 164 Non Peated (96) n24 t24 f24 b24. It is hardly believable that this is a three year old single malt: the unstinting high humidity of Goa and even higher temperature, perhaps helped along by three months of monsoons, appears to have given this whisky a degree of complexity which, even in Kentucky, it might have taken a dozen years to compile. This is single malt, but one with a hint of paradise...57%

Paul John Peated Single Malt db (89) n23 t22 f21.5 b22.5. A delicately peaty guy which gangs up on you slowly. The smoke-infused layering of sugars is the star turn, though. 55.5%

Paul John Single Malt Cask No 692 Peated db (95.5) n24 t23.5 f24 b24. Hard to believe a whisky apparently so young in years can offer such complexity. But that's Goa for you... 58.5%

Paul John Single Malt Cask No 777 Peated db (95) n23.5 t24 f23.5 b24. A Paul John which tries to offer as much delicate honey as the peat will allow. Something of rare, understated beauty. And though I often fly 777s, few take off as well as this and here there is no need for a seat belt... 59.7%

Paul John Single Malt Cask No 780 Peated db (96) n24 t24 f24 b24. Warning. If you are a bit of a dithering, wishy-washy whisky drinker, don't go anywhere near this stuff: this bottling is for serious whisky drinkers only... 57.3%

Paul John Single Malt Cask No 784 Peated db (95.5) n23.5 t23.5 f24.5 b24. The understated smoke ensures an elegant yet chewy experience. 59.2%

Paul John Single Malt Cask No 1444 Non Peated db (95.5) n23.5 t24 f24 b24 Among the most intensely malty Indian whiskies ever to have been bottled. Quite superb. 59.7%

Paul John Single Cask No 1833 db (95.5) n23.5 t24 f24 b24 Just....wow! A cask with more star quality than a Bollywood Blockbuster...and, for all its enormity, a whole lot more subtlety and finesse, also... 60.5%. sc.

Paul John Single Malt Cask No 1844 Non Peated db (94.5) n23 t24 f23.5 b24 Let someone taste this blind, tell them it is three years old...and see their reaction. A big malt showing elegance and good grace throughout. 60.5%

Paul John Single Malt Cask No 1846 Non Peated db (96) n23.5 t23 f25 b24.5 A very deep, complex whisky with many hills and canyons to explore. The finish orbits and often touches perfection. A profound malt. 60.8%

Paul John Single Malt-Classic (Un Peated) db (95) n23.5 t24 f23.5 b24 Further evidence that Indian whisky is on the rise. So charming...and irresistible. 55.2%

Paul John Select Cask Peated (96) n24 a sexy, sultry, sympathetic exhibition of smoke on varying levels...though all of them soft. A tantalising chocolate mint hangs of the embers, which glow both sweet and dry. Peated whisky from outside Islay rarely comes as complex and beautiful as this, or as deliciously gristy; t24 a massive delivery. Massive yet tender and subtle. How does that happen? Again, cocoa quickly fills the middle but there is more than enough molasses to counter. The weight and depth are spot on, as are the spices which get off to a delicate start but soon get into the swing of things; f24 long, fabulously oiled and just-so amounts of gristy sugars clinging to the smoke. As charming and impressionistic as an Indian kitchen fire wafting its smoke over a remote village in the nearby valleys; b24 a peated malt whisky which will make a few people sit up and take even further notice of Indian whisky. World class... 46%

PONDA DISTILLERY

Stillman's Dram Single Malt Whisky Limited Edition bourbon cask no. 11186-90 (94) n23 t23 f24 b24. Well, I thought I had tasted it all with the Amrut cask strength. And then this arrived at my lab...!! I predicted many years back that India would dish out some top grade malt before too long. But I'd be stretching the truth if I said I thought it would ever be this good... 42.8%. McDowell & Co Ltd, India.

RAMPUR DISTILLERY

⬥ **Rampur Vintage Select Indian Single Malt Whisky** batch no. 383, bott Jun 16 db (89) n22.5 a curiously scented malt, as though it has run from stills through the wardrobe of a millionaire and into the cask. Mainly malty, but the gentle fruits, mango in particular, are quite a sexy surprise...; t23 much more like it: this is more like the rich, well-weighted malt I discovered all those years back. Good cask management means the tannins harmonise with the malt effortlessly; f21 some serious spice builds, but there is that scented tang again...; b22.5 although I first went to this distillery over 20 years ago, it is the first time I have ever tasted it in my own lab back here in the UK. In those days, it was 100% designated for blended whisky: I argued it should be a single malt. On this evidence, you can see why... 43%. ncf.

Blends

Peter Scot Malt Whisky (84) n20 t21 f22 b21. Enjoyable balance between sweetness and oak and entertainingly enlivened by what appears to be some young, juicy malt. 42.8%.

Rendezvous (95.5) n24 t24 f23.5 b24.5. A new Indian classic. A sublime malt from the subcontinent. 46%

Royal Stag Barrel Select batch 212, bott 17 Feb 12 (75.5) n20.5 t19 f17 b18. Thin and sweet. But should be shot to put it out of its misery. 42.8% Mix of Scotch malt and India grain spirit.

Seagram's Blenders Pride Reserve Collection (77) n19 t20 f19 b19. Way too reliant on the grain and the malt submerged under the caramel. Soft, clean and painfully non-committal. 42.8%. Mix of Scotch malt and India grain spirit.

Signature (81.5) n22.5 t22 f17.5 b19.5. Excellent, rich nose & delivery helped along with a healthy display of peat reek. But more attention has to be paid to the brutally thin finish. 42.8%

NEW ZEALAND
THE NEW ZEALAND WHISKY COMPANY

High Wheeler 3070 Singlewood Aged New Zealand Whisky (88.5) n23 the feel of very old oak is always just under the surface and sometimes above. Makes an intriguing mix with the citrus top note; t22.5 silky grain thins the malt drastically. The sugars evolve with confidence, light and of maple syrup variety f21 for a blend with such a high malt content, the barley should be dominating by now beside the oak. Yet somehow it is those soft sugars and little spice which signs off; b22 this is 30% grain (which has a very different, much thinner feel to the grain found in Scotland, for instance) and 70% malt. As soft and friendly as you like. *43%.*

The New Zealand Whisky Collection 25 Years Old Single Malt dist in Dunedin, matured in Oamaru, Ex-Bourbon casks (94.5) n23 t24 f23.5 b24 Around the time this was made, some of the malt was very lightly peated. Though it doesn't mention so on the bottle, I strongly suspect that – after 25 years wear and tear in the cask – this is one of them. Seriously charming malt. And historic – and for me, at least, as one of the very few to see it in operation – touchingly memorable. *46%*

The New Zealand Whisky Collection 1987 Single Malt Aged 27 Years dist in Dunedin, American oak casks (89) n22.5 t22.5 f22 b22 By no means the most complicated malt but enjoys a series of pleasant moments. *43%*

The New Zealand Whisky Collection South Island Single Malt Aged 25 Years dist in Dunedin, American oak, ex-Bourbon casks (85.5) n21.5 t21.5 f21 b21.5. Wow! This malt has taken a surprising direction in the 25 years since it was made. When, back in 1994, I tasted samples from a vast cross section of the maturing casks at the distillery in the days it was still working (and looked somewhat different to the charming picture on the inside back label) it had a far more compact, malt intense nature. This has opened and thinned out with a big vanilla input while the oak has kept a discreet distance. *40%*

THE SOUTHERN DISTILLING CO LTD

The MacKenzie Blended Malt Whiskey (85) n20 t22 f21 b22. A vaguely spicier, chalkier, mildly less honeyed version of Coaster. Quite banana-laden nose. *40%*

THOMSON WILLOWBANK

Thomson Single Malt 21 Years Old (84) n21 t22.5 f20.5 b20. Bit of a bimbo whisky: looks pretty and outwardly attractive but has picked up very little in its 21 years... *46%. sc.*

WILSON DISTILLERY

Cadenhead's World Whiskies Lammerlaw Aged 10 Years bourbon, bott 07 (91.5) n22 t23.5 f23 b23. Stunning bottlings like this can only leave one mourning the loss of this distillery. *48.9%*

Blends

Kiwi Whisky (37) n2 t12 f11 b12. Strewth! I mean, what can you say? Perhaps the first whisky containing single malt offering virtually no nose at all and the flavour appears to be grain neutral spirit plus lashings of caramel and (so I am told) some Lammerlaw single malt. The word bland has been redefined. As has whisky. *40%.*

Wilson's Superior Blend (89) n22 t23 f21 b23. Apparently has a mixed reception in its native New Zealand but I fail to see why: this is unambiguously outstanding blended whisky. On the nose you expect a mouthwatering mouthful and it delivers with aplomb. Despite this being a lower priced blend it is, intriguingly, a marriage of 60% original bottled 10-y-o Lammerlaw and 40% old Wilson's blend, explaining the high malt apparent. Dangerous and delicious and would be better still at a fuller strength...and with less caramel. *37.5%.*

MISCELLANEOUS

The New Zealand Whisky Collection Doublewood Aged 16 Years (87.5) n22 t22 f22.5 b21 Light, silky, fruity and an all-round lovely experience. But as a whisky leaves one somewhat frustrated as it is a bit of a one trick pony with variation and complexity very much at a premium. *40%.*

SOUTH AFRICA
JAMES SEDGWICK DISTILLERY

Three Ships 10 Years Old db (83) n21 t21 f20 b21. Seems to have changed character, with more emphasis on sherry and natural toffee. *43%*

Three Ships Aged 10 Years Single Malt Limited Edition db **(91)** n22.5 t22.5 f23 b23.5. If you are looking for a soft, sophisticated malt whose delicate fingers can sooth your troubled brow, then don't bother with this one. On the other hand, if you are looking for a bit of rough, some entertaining slap and tickle: a slam-bam shag of a whisky - a useful port in a storm - then your boat may just have sailed in... Beware: an evening with this and you'll be secretly coming back for more... *43%*

Bain's Cape Mountain Single Grain Whisky db **(85.5)** n21 t22 f21 b21.5. A lively, attractively structured whisky with more attitude than you might expect. Some lovely nip and bite despite the toffee and surprising degree of soft oils. *43%*

Blends

Drayman's Solera (86) n19 t22 f23 b22. For a change, the label gets it spot on with its description of chocolate orange: it is there in abundance. If they can get this nose sorted they would be on for an all round impressive dram. As it is, luxuriate in the excellent mouthfeel and gentle interplay between malt and oak. Oh and those chocolate oranges... *43%.*

Harrier (78) n20 t20 f19 b19. Not sure what has happened to this one. Has bittered to a significant degree while the smoke has vanished. A strange, almost synthetic, feel to this now. *43%. South African/Scotch Whisky.*

Knights (83) n20.5 t21 f20 b20.5. While the Harrier has crashed, the Knights is now full of promise. Also shows the odd bitter touch but a better all-round richer body not only absorbs the impacts but radiates some malty charm. *43%. South African/Scotch Whisky.*

Knights Aged 3 Years (87) n22 t22 f22 b22. This now appears to be 100% South African whisky if I understand the label correctly: "Distilled Matured and Bottled in South Africa." A vast improvement on when it was Scotch malt and South African grain. Bursting with attitude and vitality. When next in South Africa, this will be my daily dram for sure. Love it. *43%.*

Three Ships Bourbon Cask Finish (90) n22 t23 f22.5 b22.5. A soft, even whisky which enjoys its finest moments on delivery. Clean with a pressing, toasty oakiness to the sweeter malt elements. Always a delight. *43%*

Three Ships Premium Select Aged 5 Years (93) n23 t23.5 f23 b23.5. What a fabulous whisky. The blender has shown a rare degree of craft to make so little smoke do so much. Bravo! *43%. James Sedgwick Distillery.*

Three Ships Select (81) n19 t21 f20 b21. Busy and sweet. But I get the feeling that whatever South African malt may be found in Knights does a better job than its Scotch counterpart here. *43%. James Sedgwick Distillery.*

TAIWAN
KAVALAN DISTILLERY

Kavalan Distillery Reserve peaty cask, dist 2007, bott 23 Jan 2015 db **(95)** n23.5 t24.5 f23 b24 What a crackerjack cask this malt spent seven worthwhile and highly active and productive years maturing in. Starts so quietly, then becomes pretty loud. *55%.*

⟐ **Kavalan Distillery Reserve Single Malt** rum cask, cask no. M111104073A db **(93)** n23 more fruit than the norm for a rum cask malt with soft hints of physallis, apricot, date and even banana all making delicate contributions. Traces of muscovado and molasses, also...; t24 this is where the malt comes into its own: a big delivery but always under control. The malt flies around the palate and thickens in intensity, spices are busy and at times startle slightly; f22.5 a little bitterness – note an unknown problem with ex-rum casks – just slightly downplays the tangy barley; b23.5 I have always regarded rum maturation at one of the most severe tests for any distillery: it is often a challenge for a malt to shows the depth of its personality in an environment which is perfectly set to clip its wings. Though this may not soar quite like some other Kavalans, it has still passed its test with flying colours... *57.1%. 448 bottles.*

⟐ **Kavalan Single Malt** bott code: 2016:03:14 **(92)** n23 intense, slightly salty maltiness. The caramels are active but there is no damping down the diced pears and peaches; t23.5 soft and sensuous, the delivery first grips, then caresses and slowly, the malt, radiates juicily across the palate. The caramels dig in deep for a while, then the mid-palate comes back to life with a succession of vague, non-specific fruit notes, mingling with the thickening oak; spices arrive early but no more than keep the muscovado sugars company; f22.5 chocolate fudge fruit and nut candy, with a malty sign off; b23 an elegant and succulent malt which would do even greater justice to this wonderful distillery if they could find a way to harness the caramel... *40%.*

Kavalan Single Malt Amontillado Sherry Cask cask no. S100623016A db **(97)** n24 t24.5 f24 b24.5 Given the right bottling, Amontillado is probably my favourite sherry style. How many times, though, have I discovered its delicate, complex, understated nature perfectly transferred onto a singe malt? In some 35 years, this must be only the fourth or fifth time, and I doubt any quite displayed such truth to its style, such panache. Forget the unique and intriguing bottle design (though it is hard!). This is a classic whisky on so many levels that it will stay indelibly stamped on both taste buds and memory. What a magnificent whisky experience this is...!!! 56.3%. sc. 744 bottles. Limited edition 2014_1402.

Kavalan Single Malt Manzanilla Sherry Cask cask no. S100716002A db (95.5) n23 t24 f24 b24.5 A mouth-watering jape from Kavalan. The nose appears a tad tight and introverted. But as it relaxes on the palate it certainly lets the malt the freedom to take on the grape. Or is it the other way round? A sublime surprise package.... 578%. sc. 744 bottles. Limited edition 2014_1402.

Kavalan Solist Fino Sherry Cask db cask no. S060814021 (97) n24.5 t24 f24 b24.5. It might be argued that the one and only thing that makes this exceptional is the quality of the cask, rather than the actual malt it contains. Well, let me set the record straight in this one. Earlier this week I made a very rare escape from my tasting room and visited the Royal Albert Hall for the 34th Prom of the 2011 season. The highlight of the evening was Camille Saint-Saens Symphony No 3 – "Organ". Now some critics, when they can find time to extract themselves from their own rear ends, dismiss this as a commoners' piece; something to amuse the plebeian. What they appear to not have is neither the wit nor humanity to understand that Saint-Saens sewed into this work a degree of such subtle shade and emotion, especially in the less dramatic second movement, that it can, when treated correctly, affect those capable of normal warmth and feeling. With so many nerve endings tingling and nowhere to go Saint-Saens seemingly recognised that he required something profound – in this case the organ – to create a backbone. And someone able to use it to maximum effect. And there we had it the other day: the Royal Albert Hall's awe-inspiring organ, and Thomas Trotter to make it come alive: The Solist. And this is what we have here: a perfect fino sherry selected by the maestro Dr Jim Swan. But able to display its full magnificence only because the host spirit is so beautifully composed. Good whisky is, without question, a work of art; great whisky is a tone poem. And here, I beg to insist, is proof. 58.4%. nc ncf sc. 513 bottles.

Other Brands Available In Taiwan
Eagle Leader Storage Whisky (81.5) n20 t21 f21 b20.5. Attractively smoky with a surprisingly long finish for a whisky which initially appears to lack body. By no means straightforward, but never less than pleasant. 40%

Golden Hill Single Malt (75) n18 t20 f19 b18. An unwieldy heavyweight. 40%

Good Deer (in Chinese Characters) see McAdams Rye Whisky

Sea Pirates (77) n18 t21 f19 b19. More Johnny Depp than Errol Flynn. Attractive smoke, though. 40%

URUGUAY
Dunbar Anejo 5 Anos (85.5) n20 t22.5 f21.5 b21.5. A clean, mouth-wateringly attractive mix where the grain nips playfully and the Speyside malts are on best salivating behaviour. Decently blended and boasting a fine spice prickle, too. 40%

Seagram's Blenders Pride (83) n20.5 t22 f20b20.5. The busy, relatively rich delivery contrasts with the theme of the silky grains and caramel. Easy drinking. 40%

MISCELLANEOUS
Precinct No. 6 Kentucky Sour Mash spirits distilled from 50% corn & 50% cane, batch no. 2 db (60) n12 t18 f14 b16. If you were to say, this seems like half whisky and half rum, you'd be right. Because it is both. And neither. Similar to so-called and self-styled "whiskies" of the Far East and some South American countries where either cane or molasses is used. Except this has much more oak involvement and spice. 478% (95.6 proof).

CROSS-COUNTRY VATTED WHISKIES
Diggers & Ditch Doublemalt Spirit of the Anzacs (82.5) n21 t21 f20 b20.5. Soft, fruity but never quite gets it together. Always too thin and shapeless. I'll give it a D. 45%. A blend of New Zealand & Australian whisky.

Jim Beam Kentucky Dram (89) n22.5 t22.5 f21.5 b22.5 There may be some of you reading this who will remember tastings I did 15 or 20 years ago where, for fun and to show balancing effects, I vatted bourbon with smoky Scotch. At last someone has done it commercially. I suspect this is more for the American palate as the peat has been used sparingly. 40% (80 Proof)

Slàinte

This is the point where I say thank you to all those who have helped me write the Whisky Bible, showing my appreciation to all those who have chipped in one way or another. But this year is slightly different: the very day after I completed the Introduction - traditionally the very last piece of the Bible to written by me - my greatest supporter of them all, my old mum, died on her 96th birthday. I had brought her here to the beautiful gardens surrounding my tasting room to celebrate the special day as it was her favourite place on this earth. Still with a sharp mind and powerful will at such a great age, she had made me promise the day before, and with my book completed, that I would bring her here. I kept my promise. And it was here in this rural idyll, in the shade of an apple tree on a perfect summer's day with the birds singing sweetly around her and the flowers in bloom and after pulling both my and Jane's hands towards her, that she decided to let go. It was the beautiful end to an amazing and beautiful life, one that had survived the blitz and was dedicated to her family. She was, without question, my greatest believer and followed with pride my many trips abroad to further the word of whisky. Thank you, mum. For 59 years of unquestioned support, sacrifice and love, thank you: I was a very lucky man.

Also, of course, my usual thanks to my team of Vincent Flint-Hill, Peter Mayne, Billy Jeffrey, Robin Pulford, David Rankin and Jane Garnett. As well as Julia Nourney, Paul and Denise Egerton, Linda Mayne, David Hartley and Julie Barrie. As always, a massive hug to Heiko Thieme. And, finally, thanks to those below who have provided assistance and samples for the 2013 Bible onwards. For all those who have assisted in the previous decade, we remain indebted.

Mitch Abate; Andrew Abela; Emma Alessandrini; Mary Allison; Mike Almy; Ally Alpine; Nicole Anastasi; Tommy Andersen; Wayne Anderson; Kristina Anerfält-Jansson; Jane & Martin Armstrong; Hannah Arnold; Teemu Artukka; Scott & Sam Ashforth; Paul Aston; Kevin Atchinson; Ryan Baird; David Bakery; Duncan Baldwin; Clare Banner; Lauren Barrett; Stefan Baumgart; Steve Beam; Lauren Beck; Stefan Beck; Jan Beckers; Kirsteen Beeston; Becky Bell; Annie Bellis; Sigurd Belsnes; Franz Benner; Alexander Berger; John Bernasconi; Barry Bernstein; Stuart Bertra; Jodi Best; Marilena Bidaine; Peter Bignell; Menno Bijmolt; Sonat Birknecker Hart; Franziska Bishof; Rich Blair; Olivier Blanc; Elisabeth Blum; René Bobrink; Andreas Boessow; Anna Boger; Hans Bol; Mark Boley; Yvonne Bonner; Etienne Bouillon; Borat, Birgit Bornemeier; Kev & Karen Bowler; Phil Brandon; Caroline Brel; Stephen Bremner; Rebecca Brennan; Franz Brenner; Stephanie Bridge; Chris Brown; James Brown; Sara Browne; Ralf Brzeske; Michael Brzozowski; Alexander Buchholz; Ryan Burchett; Amy Burgess; Euan Campbell; Nathan Campbell; Kimla Carsten; Lauren Casey-Haiko; Bert Cason; Stuart Cassells; Jim Caudill; Danilo Cembrero; Lisa Chandler; Yuseff Cherney; Julia Christian; Morten Christensen; Claire Clark; Nick Clark; Anne-Marie Clarke; Joseph Clarkson; Fredi Clerc; Dr Martin Collis; Shelagh Considine; Christina Conte; Gabriel Corcoran; Lynn Cross; Rosie Cunningham; Brian Cox; Jason Craig; David Croll; Molly Cullen; Nathan Currie; Larry Currier; Benjamin Curtis; Danni Cutten; Dave Cuttino; Larry Currier; Mike DaRe; Alan Davis; Bryan Davis; Stephen Davies; Alasdair Day; Dick & Marti; Scott Dickson; Martin Diekmann; Dixon Dedman; Conor Dempsey; Paul Dempsey; Lauren Devine; Marie-Luise Dietich; Rob Dietrich; Hugo Diez; Arno Josef Dirker; Caroline Docherty; Oscar Dodd; Korrie Dodge; Angela D'Orazio; Jean Donnay; Kellie Du; Tim Duckett; Camille Duhr-Merges; Mariette Duhr-Merges; Gemma Duncan; Shane Dunning; Christophe Dupic; Jens Drewitz; Jochen Druffel; Michael D'souza; Kellie Du; Jonas Ebensperger; Lenny Eckstein; Ray Edwards; Winston Edwards; Carsten Ehrlich; Ben Ellefsen; Rebecca Elliott-Smith; Lucie Ellis; Thimo Elz; Maximilian Engel; Camilla Ericsson; Beanie Espey; James Espey; Brad Estabrooke; Patrick Evans; Jennifer Eveleigh; Selim Evin; Thomas Ewers; Charlotte Falconer; Lauren Fallert; Bruce Farquhar; David Faverot; Joanna Fearnside; Angus Ferguson; Walter Fitzke; Roland Feller; Andrea Ferrari; Holly Forbes; Tricia Fox; Jean-Arnaud Frantzen; Sascha Frozza; Barry Gallagher; Hans-Gerhard Fink; Sarah Fisher; David Fitt; Kent Fleischman; Martyn Flynn; Holly Forbes; Danny Gandert; Arno Gänsmantel; Patrick Garcia; Dan Garrison; Ralph Gemmel; Stefanie Geuting; Carole Gibson; Jonathan Gibson; Daniel Giraldo; John Glaser; John Glass; Emily Glynn; Emma Golds; Rodney Goodchild; Chloe Gordon; Jonathon Gordan; Tomer Goren; Lawrence Graham; Kelly Greenawalt; Hannah Gregory; Andrew Grey; George Grindlay; Rebecca Groom; Jason Grossmiller; Jan Groth; Viele Grube; Immanuel Gruel; Barbara

Grundler; Katia Guidolin; Stefanie Geuting Josh Hafer; Jasmin Haider; Jamie Hakim; Georgina Hall; Georges Hannimann; Claire Harris; Scott E Harris; Alistair Hart; Andrew Hart; Donald Hart; Stuart Harvey; Ralf Hauer; Elizabeth Haw; Steve Hawley; Ailsa Hayes; Ross Hendry; Lianne Herbruck; Thomas Herbruck; Jennifer Higgins; Jason Himstedt; Brian Hinson; Roland Hinterreiter; Tom Holder; Julie Holl Rebsomen; Arlette Holmes; Bernhard Höning; Jason Horn; Mike Howlings; Emma Hurley; Alex Huskingson; Thomas B. Ide; Jill Inglis; Rachel Showalter Inman; Victoria Irvine; Hannah Irwin; Kai Ivalo; Emma Jackson; Caroline James; Richard Jansson; Amelia James; Ulrich Jakob; Andrew Jarrell; Don Jennings; Michael John; Celine Johns; Eamonn Jones; Robert Joule; Aista Jukneviciute; Emiko Kaji; Jeff Kanof; Raphael Käser; Alfred Kausl; Christina Kavanaugh; Serena Kaye; Colin Keegan; Joy Kelso; James Kiernan; Kai Kilpinen; Daniel Kissling; Sara Klingberg; Martina Krainer; Franz Kostenzer; Pavlos Koumparos; Matt Kozuba; Martina Krainer; Larry Krass; Armin Krister; Karen Kushner; Sophie Lambert-Russell; Ryan Lang; Oliver Lange; Jürgen Laskowski; Sebastian Lauinger; Alan Laws; Darren Leitch; Christelle Le Lay; Cédric Leprette; Eiling Lim; Bryan Lin; Lars Lindberger; Mark T Litter; Steven Ljubicic; Kelly Locker; Vincent Löhn; Alistair Longwell; Dorene Lorenz; Claire Lormier; Sarah Ludington; Valentin Lutikov; C. Mark McDavid; Jane Macduff; Myriam Mackenzie; Julia Mackillop; Damian & Madeleine Mackey; John Maclellan; Rosalyn MacLeod; Derek Mair; Dennis Malcolm; Jari Mämmi; Sarah Manning; Stefan Marder; Ole Mark; Amaury Markey; Tim Marwood; Jennifer Masson; Gregor Mathieson; Leanne Matthews; Josh Mayr; Roxane Mazeaude; Stephen R McCarthy; Mark McDavid; Christy McFarlane; Angela Mcilrath; Catherine McKay; Jonny McMillan; Douglas McIvor; Heinz Meistermann; Sarah Messenger; Uwe Meuren; Raphael Meuwly; Herman C. Mihalich; Maggie Miller; Tatsuya Minagawa; Euan Mitchell; Jacqueline Mitchell; Paul Mitchell; Jeroen Moernaut; Stephan Mohr; Henk Mol; Nick Morgan; Celine Moran; Katy Moore; Maggie Morri; Elyse Morris; Michael Morris; Brendan J. Moylan; Miroslav Motyčka; Fabien Mueller; Raphael Meuwly; Dennis Mulder; Mike Müller; Michael Myers; Simone Nagel; Arthur Nägele; Andrew Nelstrop; Sandra Neuner; Stuart Nickerson; Alex Nicol; Jane Nicol; Jennifer Nicol; Jens Nielsen; Thorsten Niesner; Sharon Nijkerk; Zack Nobinger; Soren Norgaard; Julia Nourney; Michael Nychyk; Nathan Nye; Tom O'Connor; Richard Oldfield; Jonas Östberg; Casey Overeem; Ted Pappas; Lauri Pappinen; Jason Parker; Richard Parker; Katie Partridge; Sanjay Paul; Pascal Penderak; Percy; Jörg Pfeiffer; Alexandra Piciu; Amy Preske; Phil Prichard; Andreas Poulsen; George Quiney; Rachel Quinn; George Racz; Robert Ransom; Nidal Ramini; Sarah Rawlingson; Julie Holl Rebsomen; Michael Reckhard; Guy Rehorst; Michel Reick; Lutz Reifferscheid; Marco Reiner; Drexler Reinhard; Carrie Revell; Frederic Revol; Kay Riddoch; Massimo Righi; Nicol von Rijbroek; Karen Ripley; Patrick Roberts; James Robertson; Dr. Torsten Römer; Mark Rosendal Steiniche; Casey Ross; Anton Rossetti; Fabio Rossi; David Roussier; Ronnie Routledge; Stephane Rouveyrol; Matthias Rosinski; Ken Rose; Michal Rusiňak; Jim Rutledge; Caroline Rylance; Simi Sagoo; Paloma Salmeron Planells; Kiran Samra; Jasmine Sangria; Carla Santoni; Colette Savage; John Savage-Onstwedder; Kirsty Saville; Manuela Savona; Ian Schmidt; Fred Heinz Schober; Lorien Schramm; Becky Schultz; Birgitta Schulze van Loon; John Scott; Chris Seale; Mick & Tammy Secor; Tanya Seibold; Marina Sepp; Paul Shand; Steven Shand; Mike Sharples; Lorien Schramm; Rubyna Sheikh; Caley Shoemaker; Lauren Shayne Mayer; Jamie Siefken; Peter Siegenthaler; Sam Simmons; Alastair Sinclair; Sukhinder Singh; Thomas Sippel; Thomas Smidt-Kjaerby; Aidan Smith; Barbara Smith; Gigha Smith; Phil Smith; Marianna Smyth; Gunter Sommer; Orlin Sorensen; Oliver Späth; Cat Spencer; Colin Spoelma; Alexander Springensguth; Jolanda Stadelmann; Stauning; Silvia Steck; Guido Stohler Jeremy Adam Spiegel; Silvia Steck; Marlene Steiner; Vicky Stevens; Karen Stewart; Jakob Stjernholm; Katy Stollery; Greg Storm; Jarret Stuart; Jason Stubbs; Nicki Sturzaker; Peter Summer; Michael Svendsen; Henning Svoldgaard; Tom Swift; Cameron Syme; Daniel Szor; Solene Tailland; Shoko Takagi; Cheryl Targos; Chip Tate; Marko Tayburn; Elizabeth Teape; Emily Tedder; Marcel Telser; Celine Tetu; Kevyn Termet; Sarah Thacker; Johanne Theveney; Ryan Thompson; Laura Thomson; Kelly Tighe; Brian Toft; Jarrett Tomal; Katy Took; Hamish Torrie; Louise Towers; Hope Trawick; Matthias Trum; Anne Ulrich; Jens Unterweger; Richard Urquhart; Stuart Urquhart; CJ Van Dijk; Rifino Valentine; Lisandru Venturini; Rhea Vernon; Adam Vincent; Mariah Veis; Aurelien Villefranche; Lorraine Waddell; Josh Walker; Grace Waller; Emma Ware; Katharina Warter; Micheal Wells; Katrin Werner; Arne Wesche; Zoe Wesseon; Anna Wilson; Nick White; Peter White; Robert Whitehead; Lucy Whitehall; Stephanie Whitworth; Daniel Widmer; Markus Wieser; Julien Williems; George Wills; James Wills; Rinaldo Willy; Georgia Wilson; Ken Winchester; Arthur Winning; Ellie Winters; Stephen Worrall; Kate Wright; Frank Wu; Tom Wyss; Junko Yaguchi; Laura Young; Kiyoyuki Yoshimura; Bettina Zannier; Jörg Zahorodnyj; Ruslan Zamoskovny; Ulrich Jakob Zeni; Rama Zuniga; Ernst Zweiger; Руслан Замосковный. And, as ever, in warm memory of Mike Smith.